M000094777

# THEOLOGY
# OF THE
# NEW TESTAMENT

# GEORG STRECKER

# THEOLOGY
# OF THE
# NEW TESTAMENT

German Edition edited and completed by
Friedrich Wilhelm Horn

Translated by M. Eugene Boring

WALTER DE GRUYTER
NEW YORK · BERLIN

WESTMINSTER JOHN KNOX PRESS
LOUISVILLE

# ABOUT THE AUTHOR

*Georg Strecker* was professor of New Testament at the University of Göttingen

Originally published under the title *Theologie des Neues Testaments*
Copyright © 1996 by Walter de Gruyter & Co., Berlin

Copyright © 2000 by Walter de Gruyter GmbH & Co. KG, Berlin and New York
First edition 2000 copublished by Walter de Gruyter GmbH & Co. KG, Berlin and New York, and Westminster John Knox Press, Louisville, Kentucky

All rights reserved. No part of this book may be reproduced or transmitted in any form or by any means, electronic or mechanical, including photocopy, recording or any information storage and retrieval system, without prior permission in writing from the publisher.

♾ Printed on acid-free paper which falls within the guidelines of the ANSI to ensure permanence and durability

**Library of Congress Cataloging-in-Publication Data**

Strecker, Georg
[Theologie des Neuen Testaments. English]
Theology of the New Testament / Georg Strecker ; German edition edited and completed by Friedrich Wilhelm Horn ; translated by M. Eugene Boring.
-- 1st. ed. p. cm.
Includes bibliographical references (p.) and index.
ISBN 3110156520 -- ISBN 0-664-22336-2 (pbk.)
1. Bible. N.T. -- Theology. I. Horn, Friedrich Wilhelm. II. Title.
BS2397.S8513 2000
230'.0415--dc21                                                00-043147

**Die Deutsche Bibliothek – CIP Einheitsaufnahme**

Strecker, Georg
Theology of the new testament / Georg Strecker. Transl. by M. Eugene Boring. – German ed. / ed. and completed by Friedrich Wilhelm Horn. – New York ; Berlin : de Gruyter; Louisville : Westminster John Knox Press, 2000
  Dt. Ausg. u.d.T. : Strecker, Georg: Theologie des Neuen Testaments
  ISBN 3-11-015652-0

Printed in Germany
Typesetting: Readymade, Berlin
Printing and Binding: WB-Druck, Rieden/Allgäu
Cover design: Rainer Engel, Berlin

# Foreword

From 1975 on, Georg Strecker had in view two large scholarly publications that he labored to complete by the time of his retirement from the university: "Ethics of the New Testament" and "Theology of the New Testament." A timely completion of these two books was delayed by a variety of obligations and projects, such as his commentaries on the Johannine Letters and the Sermon on the Mount, his publications on the Pseudo-Clementine literature and the compilation of a concordance on these documents he had already begun during his doctoral study. The basic ideas he intended to pursue in each book are found in the essays "Strukturen einer neutestamentlichen Ethik," *ZThK* 75 (1978) and "Das Problem der Theologie des Neuen Testaments," WdF 367 (1975).

A severe illness that led to his death prevented the author himself from completing either work. When Georg Strecker learned that the physicians had given him only a few weeks to live, he asked me to bring his "Theology of the New Testament" to completion. The preliminary work on his "Ethics of the New Testament" had not proceeded far enough that its publication would be possible in the foreseeable future.

At this point in time the main sections of the "Theology of the New Testament" were essentially complete in manuscript or dictation on cassettes. Only the sections E. IV, F. II-III had no preliminary work; for them I alone am responsible. The manuscripts were then thoroughly edited. Here the guiding principle was that those sections completed by Strecker would receive no essential changes in their content, including those places where I would set the accents differently or would argue in a different manner. To be sure, there was additional work to be done in the footnotes and the bibliographies of secondary literature. Moreover, all citations and references were checked, corrected where necessary, and supplemented. Many file folders filled with notes accumulated over the years were reviewed. For the selection of material from these and its insertion into the text I alone bear the responsibility. Much of this had already been mentioned in Strecker's *Literaturgeschichte des Neuen Testaments* (Göttingen: Vandenhoeck & Ruprecht, 1992); English translation, *History of New Testament Literature* (Harrisburg: Trinity Press International, 1997). The reader is thus explicitly referred to this work.

Georg Strecker reported on his proposed structure for the "Theology of the New Testament" at the meeting of the SNTS in Madrid, 28 July 1992.

The introductory sentences of that lecture may well be repeated here: "The structure I am presenting is based on the final form of the New Testament texts, and is thus intentionally a theology of the New Testament oriented to redaction criticism. This means that each New Testament writing is evaluated according to its particular theological conception, so that the term 'theology of the New Testament' more precisely means the complex of theologies in the New Testament. Characteristic for a theology of the New Testament in redaction-critical perspective is the relation of syn-chrony and diachrony. The theological distinctiveness of the New Testa-ment authors to be arranged synchronically stands against the background of an earlier tradition that is to be seen diachronically, which for its part is stamped by a number of different theological conceptions. The presen-tation of the theologies of the New Testament authors is thus to be done in such a way that takes account of their reception and interpretation of this earlier tradition."

The completion of this *Theology of the New Testament* would not have been possible without much help given in a generous and cooperative spirit. The administration of the United Theological Seminary in Göttin-gen provided personnel and organizational help. As representatives of the many students and graduates who provided help over the past years the following may be named: Heidi Abken, Martina Janßen, Frank Klein-schmidt, Christina Lange, Elke Rathert, and Manfred Sablewski. Jörg Sievert may claim for himself the Pauline περισσότερον αὐτῶν πάντων ἐκοπίασα. Gisela Strecker and retired pastor Klaus-Dietrich Fricke checked all the references and provided help in editing the language and style of the manuscript. Margret Lessner provided the final version for the press. During the long sickness preceding the death of Georg Strecker she worked unselfishly to complete the *Theology of the New Testament*, disregarding her own concerns, and thus like those named above deserves the readers' gratitude.

Since 1996, when this Theology of the New Testament first appeared, New Testament scholars have repeatedly asked for an English translation. I am grateful that Professor M. Eugene Boring, Fort Worth, has accepted this assignment. For twenty-two years he was friend and colleague of Georg Strecker, spending his sabbatical leaves and summer research visits in Göttingen. The many conversations during this extended time allowed him to become thoroughly acquainted with the theological work of Georg Strecker.

*Mainz, January 2000*                              *Friedrich Wilhelm Horn*

# Translator's Preface

First, a personal note: I first met Georg Strecker at the AAR/SBL meeting in Los Angeles in 1972, at which time he graciously facilitated my first sabbatical visit to Göttingen in 1973. Over the years we became close friends during my several visits to Göttingen. He celebrated his sixtieth birthday in our home in Fort Worth in 1989. I was among the small group that celebrated his sixty-fifth birthday in Göttingen in 1994, when he already knew it would be his last. I am glad to have translated this book not only because of its inherent importance for the discipline of New Testament studies and Christian theology, but as a final expression of the respect and affection in which I held Georg Strecker.

Citations from the Bible are taken from the New Revised Standard Version unless the context calls for a different translation to retain the nuance reflected in the author's discussion, in which case I have translated the German or made an independent translation of the Greek text. Other ancient sources are generally cited according to standard English translations. I have sometimes adjusted the citation references accordingly. I have occasionally inserted a translator's note to clarify the meaning when the standard English translation differs from the German text cited by Strecker. A few printer's errors and mistaken Scripture references in the original have been corrected without notes. Abbreviations follow the standard format of TRE and/or JBL.

The reader may be grateful to the following members of the academic community of Brite Divinity School and Texas Christian University who assisted in the enormous task of adjusting the bibliography to English titles and pagination, and editing, proofreading and indexing the whole: Lana N. Byrd, Edward J. McMahon, Monica S. Meyers, Teresa Palmer, Joseph A. Weaks, and Brenda J. Wilson. To Frau Gisela Strecker, who carefully read and annotated a substantial part of my translation, I extend my special thanks. It has been a pleasure to work with Dr. Hasko von Bassi, Dr. Volker Gebhardt and Herr Klaus Otterburig of Walter de Gruyter, as well as Herr Wolfram Burckhardt.

*Fort Worth, 3 March 2000*                                                *M. Eugene Boring*

# Contents

*"For we cannot do anything against the truth,
but only for the truth." (2 Cor 13:8)*

# Introduction

## 1. What is "Theology of the New Testament?"

Bultmann, R. *Theology of the New Testament*, New York: Charles Scribner's Sons, 1951, 1955. 2:237-251.

Kattenbusch, F. "Die Entstehung einer christlichen Theologie. Zur Geschichte der Ausdrücke Θεολογία, Θεολογεῖν, Θεολόγος," *ZThK* 11 (1930) 161-205; also in *Libelli* 69, Darmstadt: Wissenschaftliche Buchgesellschaft, 1962[2].

Strecker, G. "Das Problem der Theologie des Neuen Testaments," in G. Strecker, *Eschaton und Historie. Aufsätze*. Göttingen: Vandenhoeck & Ruprecht, 1979, 260-290; also in G. Strecker, *Das Problem der Theologie des Neuen Testaments*. WdF 367. Darmstadt: Wissenschaftliche Buchgesellschaft, 1975, 1-31.

Theology has been assigned the task of illuminating the meaning of the myth that expresses transcendent reality in the language of this world. This is the interpretation already given in the oldest example of the word "theology" (θεολογία) in Plato's Dialogue "The Republic," (Resp 379 A). Here Plato has his teacher Socrates inquire about the "characteristic features of teaching about God" (τύποι περὶ θεολογίας). Accordingly, theology has to do with myths; to it is assigned the task of bringing out the deeper meaning of the stories about the gods. Education in the fine arts can help us to perceive this meaning. Accordingly, theology has the goal of laying bare the structures on which the myth is based, and such a course of investigation—when it happens in the right educational context—has a political consequence. In both the Platonic and Aristotelian systems philosophy is the real science that deals with the world and human beings, so that they attribute to theology only a lesser, provisional rank in their systems. Stoicism, on the other hand, places theology in the last place in a series of philosophical disciplines (dialectic, rhetoric, ethics, politics, physics, theology);[1] on this basis theology can be considered the "crown" of the Stoic system. Since it follows immediately after "physics," it also stands for "metaphysics," which not only names its place in the series following physics, but can also affirm that the theological question addresses that which transcends physics. According to the Stoic understand-

---

[1] As in Cleanthes of Assos, the successor of Zeno, founder of the Stoic school (d. ca. 232 B. C. E.). Cf. F. Kattenbusch, *Entstehung* 9-10.

ing theology deals with those unavoidable issues that essentially concern
human being as such. Humans know that they are determined by the
universal law of the world, physis (nature), that is identical with the divine
reason (νοῦς). The individual human being must shape his or her life in
harmony with this divine cosmic reason. Theology speaks of such an
orientation to the world, understands human being as a constituent element in the order of the cosmos.

The term "theology" is not found in the New Testament. It occurs for
the first time in Christian literature in the writings of the Church Fathers:
in the second century in Justin (Dial 56.113), and then in Clement of
Alexandria and Eusebius. Here it has the general meaning "teaching about
God" and reflects a Hellenizing of Christian faith that in the post-apostolic
age was smoothing out the differences between early Christian and Greek-
Hellenistic thought. In contrast, in the New Testament there is not yet an
intentional rational adjustment to the thought of the ancient world. The
New Testament authors do not speak philosophically of God in a distancing manner, just as they are not concerned to present their faith systematically. It is rather the case that each document addresses a concrete
situation. This is what Paul does in his letters, rightly described as "occasional writings." In them he tailors the message entrusted to him, the
gospel, to his particular churches, and understands such mission as a
"power of God" (Rom 1:16). His goal is not an abstract reflection on the
Christian faith, but the dynamic proclamation of the gospel of Jesus
Christ.

However, the message declared in the New Testament is not presented
apart from a systematic structure. As the whole person is claimed by this
message, human feelings are included as an element of the reality of faith.
But Christian faith, according to New Testament understanding, is not
identified solely with a "feeling of dependence," but includes and opens up
the understanding. Since all expressions of religious experience imply
structures of believing comprehension, even if the authors of the New
Testament documents were not necessarily aware of this in particular
cases, such cognitive structures were also fundamental to the New Testament's witness of the act of God in Jesus Christ. Such structures are the
subject of the following inquiry. In this process it is to be noted that the
New Testament authors speak and write as those who have themselves
been grasped by this subject matter, and in their testimony want to bring
to speech something that is of ultimate concern both to them and their
fellow human beings.

It is also the case that the adopting of the customary designation for
this presentation does not mean that its goal is to delineate "the" theology
of the New Testament, since the theological unity of the New Testament
documents suggested by this term cannot be presupposed. It is rather the
case that in the writings of the New Testament we are met with a multi-

plicity of theological conceptions. These are to be investigated and presented according to their own structures of thought, in relation to their
own historical and literary contexts. Especially, the specific affirmations of
the New Testament authors, the "redactors" of the traditional materials,
are to be highlighted by a diachronic and synchronic correlation of the
textual tradition. Accordingly, the goal is not a history of early Christian
religion or of early Christian theology, as imagined by the liberal theology
of the late nineteenth century. This approach supposed it could draw a
historical line from Jesus through the earliest Palestinian church, then the
Hellenistic church, then to Paul and the later Christian authors, showing
that it was more interested in historical developments than in the theological affirmations of the New Testament tradition.[2] In contrast to this
approach, we intend here to investigate the theological conceptions advocated by the New Testament authors on the basis of the theological
(church) traditions they had received.

The New Testament canon is presupposed as a historically-conditioned construct that participates in all the relativities of history, including
the phenomena involved in the history of literature. In presenting a theology of the New Testament there are good grounds to consider going
beyond the canonical boundaries and, for example, to include reflection on
the theological expressions of the Apostolic Fathers or the early Christian
apologists. However, once this approach is adopted, it is difficult to limit
the number and amount of material included from extra-canonical documents contemporary with and later than the New Testament, so that a
relative limitation of our study to the canonical documents and their
theological presuppositions is to be preferred on practical grounds. The
New Testament, in its given extent, is the foundation of the history of
Christian dogma and theology. The acceptance of it as the oldest documents of the Christian faith is the presupposition of the Christian life in
theory and practice, especially in the church's worship. In this connection
the critical function of the New Testament should also become clear. That
the New Testament has something to say to our present is not the least
important dimension of its claim and demand. In listening to what is said
in Scripture, the church understands itself as an "ecclesia semper reformanda," assures itself afresh of its origin, and lets itself be critically asked
whether in the concrete form in which it presently appears it is in line with
this foundational claim and demand. A biblicistic interpretation cannot do
justice to this claim and demand, since it does not reflect the tension
between the past reference of the text and the present reality of the church.
It is absolutely indispensable that the church in its current form and

---

[2]    Cf. W. Wrede, *Über Aufgabe und Methode der sogenannten neutestamentlichen
       Theologie*, Göttingen 1897; reprinted in G. Strecker, ed. *Das Problem der Theologie*
       81-154.

contemporary Christian self-understanding must allow itself to be measured by this claim and demand and make its journey of faith in a thorough encounter with the New Testament text, a journey that leads from knowledge of the texts through acknowledging them and finally to confession [Erkennen/Anerkennen/Bekennen]. This is the basic intention of the New Testament writings themselves (cf. John 20:31).

## 2. The Problem of a "Biblical Theology"

Ebeling, G. "What is 'Biblical Theology'?" in G. Ebeling, *Word and Faith*. Philadelphia: Fortress, 1963.

Grässer, E. "Offene Fragen im Umkreis einer Biblischen Theologie," *ZThK* 77 (1980) 200-221.

Hübner, H. "Biblische Theologie und Theologie des Neuen Testaments. Eine programmatische Skizze," *KuD* 27 (1981) 2-19.

Hübner, H. *Biblische Theologie des Neuen Testaments*. Vol. 1. *Prolegomena*. Göttingen: Vandenhoeck & Ruprecht, 1990.

Merk, O. *Biblische Theologie des Neuen Testaments in ihrer Anfangszeit. Ihre methodischen Probleme bei Johann Philipp Gabler und Georg Lorenz Bauer und deren Nachwirkungen*. MThSt 9. Marburg: Elwert, 1972.

Merk. O. "Biblische Theologie II. Neues Testament," *TRE* 6 (1980) 455-477.

Merk. O. "Theologie des Neuen Testaments und Biblische Theologie," in *Bilanz und Perspektiven gegenwärtiger Auslegung des Neuen Testaments*, ed. F. W. Horn. BZNW 75. Berlin–New York: W. de Gruyter, 1995. 112-143.

Oeming, M. *Gesamtbiblische Theologien der Gegenwart. Das Verhältnis von AT und NT in der hermeneutischen Diskussion seit Gerhard von Rad*. Stuttgart: J. C. B. Mohr (Paul Siebeck), 1987[2].

Räisänen, H. *Beyond New Testament Theology. A Story and a Programme*. London-Philadelphia: Fortress, 1990.

Reventlow, H. Graf. *Hauptprobleme der Biblischen Theologie im 20. Jahrhundert*. EdF 203. Darmstadt: Wissenschaftliche Buchgesellschaft, 1983.

Strecker, G. "'Biblische Theologie?' Kritische Bemerkungen zu den Entwürfen von Hartmut Gese und Peter Stuhlmacher," in *Kirche* FS G. Bornkamm for his 75th Birthday, ed. D. Lührmann and G. Strecker. Tübingen: J. C. B. Mohr (Paul Siebeck), 1980, 425-445.

Stuhlmacher, P. *Biblische Theologie des Neuen Testaments*. Vol.1. Göttingen: Vandenhoeck & Ruprecht, 1992.

The term "Biblical Theology" was rarely used prior to the Enlightenment, but even then referred to a common idea, presupposing the unity of the Old and New Testaments. Thus in 1671 it designates the "collegium biblicum" of Sebastian Schmidt, a textbook of Christian doctrine harmonizing statements from the Old and New Testaments under the headings of the standard theological topics. This procedure presupposes the orthodox view of the inspiration not only of the biblical message as a whole, but every detail of Holy Scripture ("verbal inspiration"). The Bible is regarded as a unity, a book of divine revelation free of all contradiction. The biblical authors were guided by the Holy Spirit and produced documents that were a secure foundation for Christian dogmatic theology.

The construction of a "biblical theology" so understood proceeds on the basis of three fundamental presuppositions:

1. *The unity of the Old and New Testament.* In this view there is no material difference between the Old and New Testaments. Both Testaments contain the one revelation of God. Fundamental is the dogma of "non-contradiction:" the traditions found in the Old and New Testaments do not contradict each other. In those places where tensions and contradictions appear to be present, the task of the exegete is to show that they harmonize.

2. *The integrity of the biblical canon.* The canon of the Old and New Testament is presupposed to be a separate body of material complete in itself. It is only by considering the Bible in such isolation that it can be seen as a book of revelations that cannot be questioned. Interpretation proceeds without reflecting the connections between biblical documents and other Jewish literature of antiquity. This approach leaves out of consideration the writings that emerged in the church contemporary with the New Testament, the early Christian extra-canonical literature.

3. *The identity of biblical teaching and dogmatic theology.* No basic distinction was made between Scripture and dogmatics. This is the presupposition of the topics of Christian faith composed of materials from the Old and New Testaments, in material agreement with the position of theology prior to the Enlightenment.

The following history of the discipline "theology of the New Testament" is to be understood as the history of the criticism and dissolution of the previous idea of a "biblical theology."

On 1: The material unity of the Old and New Testaments was first subjected to critical review under the influence of Enlightenment theology by Johann Philipp Gabler. His lecture on March 30, 1787, at the University of Altdorf bore the title "De iusto discrimine theologiae biblicae et dogmaticae regundisque recte utriusque finibus" ("On the Proper Distinction between Biblical and Dogmatic Theology and the Proper Determination of the Goal of Each"). Even if Gabler did not abandon the idea of a biblical dogmatic, but derived the topics of dogmatic theology from a comparison of several biblical passages, he still attended to the historical distinctions and material differences among the individual authors. In distinction from orthodox doctrine, he no longer advocated the view of divine inspiration of the Scripture that guaranteed the material unity of the Old and New Testaments. This is opposed to the historical awareness that distinctions must be made between individual periods of the old and new religion. This opened the way for a developmental model that—instead of attempting to ground timeless dogmatic truths from the bible—brought out the importance of the temporally-conditioned, historical situation of the Old and New Testament conceptions.

On 2: The "integrity of the biblical canon" had already been placed in question in the reformation of Martin Luther by the application of the hermeneutical principle "that which promotes Christ" ("Was Christum treibet").[3] A critical study of the canon from the perspective of the history of literature had been initiated by J. Ph. Gabler in the course of presenting his "system of a biblical theology" that not only called attention to linguistic and material distinctions between individual biblical authors, but took the apocryphal writings into consideration. Such historical relativizing of the biblical canon was continued in the model of historical dialectic advocated by Ferdinand Christian Baur. With his assignment of individual New Testament writings to a corresponding developmental stage of the Christian religion, he thereby decided what in the New Testament testified to the authentic meaning of the gospel, and thus what was of canonical authority. The "history of religions school" then followed this path consistently to the end. For it, the explanation of a text meant "placing it in the context of its historical development."[4] From this point of view, both the concept and delimitation of a canon became a problem. Thus Gustav Krüger objected to "operating with the concept 'New Testament' in any form when one is making a historical study of a period that does not yet know a 'New Testament'."[5] W. Wrede draws the inference that historical interest requires that *everything be taken into consideration that historically belongs together* within the whole of early Christian literature." Accordingly, the boundary for the material the discipline deals with is only to be drawn where the literature itself indicates a real break.[6]

On 3: With regard to the identity of biblical and dogmatic theology, the Reformation principle of "sola scriptura" already distinguished between the authority of the Scripture and its exposition in dogmatic theology or church tradition, even if this had not been systematically thought through.[7] If Sebastian Schmidt could still use biblical texts as "dicta probantia" for his book of Christian doctrine while presupposing the unity of Scripture and dogmatics, in Pietism a process is already beginning in which the plain meaning of the biblical text competes with scholastic, dogmatic theology.[8] The historical thinking of the Enlightenment had already led

---

[3]  M. Luther, *Vorrede auf die Epistel S. Jacobi und Jude*, WA.DB 7, 385.
[4]  W. Wrede, "Das theologische Studium und die Religionsgeschichte," in *Vorträge und Studien* (Tübingen 1907) 75.
[5]  G. Krüger, *Das Dogma vom Neuen Testament*, (Giessen 1896) 10.
[6]  Wrede, "Über Aufgabe und Methode," 86.
[7]  Cf. M. Luther's debate with the four-fold meaning of Scripture of medieval church tradition (WA Tr 5,5285; WA 7,97,23f); also WA 39/I, 47,19f (along with numerous applications in the context of scriptural expositions).
[8]  Cf. e. g. A. F. Büsching, *Gedanken von der Beschaffenheit und dem Vorzuge der biblisch-dogmatischen Theologie vor der alten und neuen scholastischen*, (Lemgo 1758).

J. Ph. Gabler to a consistent distinction between a historical biblical theology and a dogmatic didactic theology. The former is oriented to human and temporally-conditioned doctrinal forms; the latter deals with "the Christian religion of all times." So also in his portrayal of scriptural teaching a distinction is made between general concepts with their abiding form, on the one hand, and, on the other hand, their limitation to a particular period or to particular form of teaching, a distinction between "that which was truly divine in the utterances of the apostles and that which was incidental and purely human." In this distinction an important task is assigned to the criterion of reasonableness.[9]

The "methods of doctrinal concepts," as practiced in New Testament theology at the close of the nineteenth century,[10] attempted to answer the question of what in the Bible is to be considered the lasting statements of faith and what is to be considered only incidental accompanying baggage. It had the task of reconstructing the doctrinal concepts of the individual New Testament authors as completely as possible, and the merit of thereby portraying the individuality of the New Testament authors. But it fell into the twin dangers—as W. Wrede rightly objected—of (1) overrating the minimal basis in the texts for such a project and (2) subjecting the New Testament texts to a homogenization that threatened to neglect not only their concrete situation and historical development, but also the "power of religious sentiment" of New Testament thought.[11] To be sure, Christian faith is not to be identified with religious sentiment, but contains an "understanding," the basic characteristics of which are to be discerned especially from its historical concretion, especially in literary-historical forms, not least as these are recognized in the contrast between elements of Christian tradition and their redactional reformulation. A consistent differentiation between biblical teaching and dogmatic theology, especially when directed by a "disinterested striving after knowledge,"[12] would have the result that the theological affirmations of the New Testament would appear only in the context of a "history of early Christian religion."[13] Such incorporation of New Testament theology into general history, which is thoroughly justified when viewed from outside, would neglect the distinctive message of the documents placed together in the New Testament canon and fail to take note of the believing self-understanding of their

---

[9] J. Ph. Gabler, "Über die rechte Unterscheidung zwischen biblischer und dogmatischer Theologie und die rechte Bestimmung ihrer beider Ziele," in G. Strecker (ed.), *Das Problem der Theologie* 41f.

[10] Examples: B. Weiss, *Lehrbuch der Biblischen Theologie des Neuen Testaments*, (Berlin 1868), 1895[6], § 2, pp. 6ff; H.J. Holtzmann, *Lehrbuch der Neutestamentlichen Theologie* I.II, Tübingen 1911[2], especially I, 20-26.

[11] Cf. W. Wrede, "Über Aufgabe und Methode," 91ff.

[12] *Ibid.* 84.

[13] *Ibid.* 153f.

authors. "Dialectical theology" was right in objecting to a narrowing of the
exegetical task in the direction of historicism and liberal theology. Thus
Karl Barth emphasized the claim of the New Testament authors to be
witnesses of the "Word of God,"[14] and Rudolf Bultmann attempted to
portray the theological thought reflected in the New Testament documents with the help of "existentialist interpretation."[15] This interpretation derives from the New Testament text a self-understanding that is not
to be identified with general human self-awareness, but rather can lead to
the opening of one's eyes to reality. The self-understanding of the believer
implies, with the question of the source and destiny of human existence,
both a turning to the world and a diastasis over against the world. This
self-understanding has received a variety of expressions in the New Testament documents, but is always oriented to the Christ-event.

The Christ-event to which the early Christian kerygma testifies is the
decisive point of orientation from which the theological conception of the
New Testament authors proceeds. The kerygma is not to be subordinated
to the schema of a "biblical theology." The kerygma breaches the material
unity of Old and New Testaments, since despite the continuity with Old
Testament tradition, from the point of view both of literary history and
theology the New Testament stands in a relation of discontinuity to the
Old Testament. The kerygma is not the guarantee of the integrity of the
biblical canon, since the material content it affirms not only stands in
diastasis to the Old Testament, but also in the New Testament is interpreted in different ways. And the kerygma is not the self-evident presupposition of the unity of biblical and dogmatic theology. Rather, the New
Testament kerygma assigns to dogmatic theology the task of investigating
and developing the unity of theology in the past and the church's present.
If, in the juxtaposition to the religious and profane literature of Hellenism,
as also in comparison with the writings of the Old Testament and Judaism,
the distinctive features of the New Testament's message of the Christ are
perceived, then this means that as a result of the consistent historicizing,
as developed by the liberal history-of-religions school, and at the same
time applying the results of dialectical theology, the assignment must
read: "Theology of the New Testament."

---

[14]   K. Barth, *Der Römerbrief*, München 1922².
[15]   R. Bultmann, "Das Problem der Hermeneutik: (1950), in *Glauben und Verstehen*
        II 211-235.

# A.
# Redemption and Liberation—
# The Theology of Paul

Baur, F. C. *Paul, the Apostle of Jesus Christ, His Life and Work, His Epistles and His Doctrine*. London: Williams and Norgate, 1876[2].

Becker, J. *Paul: Apostle to the Gentiles*. Louisville: Westminster John Knox, 1993.

Beker, J. Chr. *Paul the Apostle: The Triumph of God in Life and Thought*. Philadelphia: Fortress Press, 1984[2].

Betz, H. D. "Paul," *ABD* V, 186–201.

Bornkamm, G. "Paulus," *RGG*[3] V (1961) 166–190.

Bornkamm, G. *Paul*. New York: Harper & Row, 1971.

Breytenbach, C. *Versöhnung. Eine Studie zur paulinischen Soteriologie*. WMANT 60. Neukirchen-Vluyn: Neukirchener, 1989.

Bultmann, R. "Paulus," *RGG*[2] IV. 1930, 1019–1045.

Davies, W. D. *Paul and Rabbinic Judaism. Some Rabbinic Elements in Pauline Theology*. London: SPCK, 1965[3].

Deissmann, A. *Paul: A Study in Social and Religious History*. New York: Harper & Brothers, 1957.

Eichholz, G. *Die Theologie des Paulus im Umriss*. Neukirchen-Vluyn: Neukirchener, 1983[4].

Feine, P. *Der Apostel Paulus. Das Ringen um das geschichtliche Verständnis des Paulus*. BFChTh II/12. Gütersloh: Gerd Mohn, 1927.

Hofius, O. *Paulusstudien*. WUNT 51. Tübingen: J. C. B. Mohr (Paul Siebeck), 1989.

Horn, F. W. "Paulusforschung," in F. W. Horn, ed. *Bilanz und Perspektiven gegenwärtiger Auslegung des Neuen Testaments*. BZNW 75. Berlin-New York: de Gruyter, 1995, 30–59.

Horn, F. W. *Das Angeld des Geistes. Studien zur paulinischen Pneumatologie*. FRLANT 154. Göttingen 1992.

Hübner, H. Die "Paulusforschung seit 1945," Ein kritischer Literaturbericht," *ANRW* II 25.4. (1987) 2649–2840.

Hübner, H. *The Law in Paul's Thought*. Edinburgh: T. & T. Clark, 1984.

Käsemann, E. *Perspectives on Paul*. Philadelphia: Fortress, 1971.

Koch, D.-A. *Die Schrift als Zeuge des Evangeliums. Untersuchungen zur Verwendung und zum Verständnis der Schrift bei Paulus*. BHTh 69. Tübingen: J. C. B. Mohr (Paul Siebeck), 1986.

Kuss, O. Paulus. *Die Rolle des Apostels in der theologischen Entwicklung der Urkirche*. Regensburg: Pustet, 1976[2].

Lohmeyer, E. *Grundlagen der paulinischen Theologie*. BHTh 1. Tübingen: J. C. B. Mohr (Paul Siebeck), 1929.

Lüdemann, G. *Paul, Apostle to the Gentiles. Studies in Chronology*. Foreword by John Knox. Philadelphia: Fortress, 1984.

Lüdemann, G. *Opposition to Paul in Jewish Christianity*. Minneapolis: Fortress, 1989.

Luz, U. *Das Geschichtsverständnis des Paulus*. BEvTh 49. Munich: Kaiser, 1968.
Merk, O. "Paulus-Forschung 1936–1985," *ThR* 53 (1988) 1–81.
Pedersen, S. *Die Paulinische Literatur und Theologie*. Skandinavische Beiträge, Teologiske Studier 7. Göttingen:Vandenhoeck & Ruprecht, 1980.
Rengstorf K. H., ed. *Das Paulusbild in der neueren deutschen Forschung*. WdF 24. Darmstadt: Wissenschaftliche Buchgesellschaft, 1982³.
Sanders, E. P. *Paul and Palestinian Judaism. A Comparison of Patterns of Religion*. Philadelphia: Fortress, 1977.
Sanders, E. P. *Paul*. New York: Oxford University Press, 1991.
Sanders, E. P. *Paul, the Law, and the Jewish People*. Philadelphia: Fortress, 1983.
Schelkle, K. H.*Paulus. Leben-Briefe-Theologie*. EdF 152, Darmstadt: Wissenschaftliche Buchgesellschaft, 1981.
Schnelle, U. *Gerechtigkeit und Christusgegenwart. Vorpaulinische und paulinische Tauftheologie*. GTA 24. Göttingen: Vandenhoeck & Ruprecht, 1986².
Schnelle, U. *Wandlungen im paulinischen Denken*. SBS 137. Stuttgart: Katholisches Bibelwerk, 1989.
Schweitzer, A.*Paul and His Interpreters: A Critical History*. London: Adam and Charles Black, 1912.
Schweitzer, A. *The Mysticism of Paul the Apostle*. New York: H. Holt and Company, 1931.
Strecker, G. "Befreiung und Rechtfertigung. Zur Stellung der Rechtfertigungslehre in der Theologie des Paulus," G. Strecker,*Eschaton und Historie: Aufsätze*. Göttingen: Vandenhoeck & Ruprecht, 1979, 479–508.
Wrede, W. *Paul*. London: Phillip Green, 1907.

## a)   Preliminary Methodological Comments[1]

The theology of the New Testament can be outlined from chronological or systematic points of view. Considerations of both chronology and subject matter speak in favor of beginning with the writings of the apostle Paul.

*Chronological:* Although the New Testament Evangelists refer back to an earlier time, the life of Jesus, and make this the subject of their narratives, they themselves belong to the second and third Christian generations, so that their theological conceptions reflect the situation of a later time. In contrast, the letters of Paul are the oldest writings of the New Testament. If one understands the theology of the New Testament as a theology of the New Testament documents, then beginning with the Pauline letters immediately suggests itself. It should not thereby be overlooked that older traditions have been worked into the New Testament writings; these traditions were set forth in the literary contexts appropriate to their function, as explicated by "redaction criticism."[2]

---

[1]   Cf. E. Käsemann, "The Problem of a New Testament Theology," *NTS* 19 (1973) 235–245, 243; G. Strecker, "Das Problem der Theologie des Neuen Testaments," 29–31; H. Hübner, *Biblische Theologie* 32 note 73.

[2]   Cf. below under A. I.— With regard to understanding the unity of the New Testament it would doubtless be more beneficial to begin with the kerygma of earliest

*Subject matter:* Paul is the only New Testament author who not only implies a theological system in his writings but who also has to a considerable extent worked out his thought systematically. Even though Romans should not be described as a "christianae religionis compendium" (Melanchthon), since it by no means addresses the whole range of topics of traditional dogmatics, it is still by far the most systematically developed theological writing of the New Testament. If on this basis Paul is the outstanding Christian theologian of the New Testament, this means that a theology of the New Testament which does not intend to neglect the later effects (*Wirkungsgeschichte*) of the New Testament writings including their present significance must take account of this central position of Pauline theology. This suggests the apostle to the Gentiles as the beginning point of New Testament theology, especially in a setting within a reformist church.

## b) Sources

### 1. Secondary Sources

Among the texts important for understanding the presuppositions, foundations, and connections of Pauline theology, to be named in the first place is the *Acts of the Apostles*. In this document Luke depicts the course of Paul's life, his mission to the Gentiles up to his arrival in Rome (Acts 13:1–28:31). Individual comments prior to this already refer to Paul (Acts 7:58; 8:1, 3; 9:1ff; 11:25–30). The picture of Paul derived from these reports is not only embedded within the temporal framework of the Pauline missionary journeys but also contains basic theological statements. Thus in the "Areopagus speech" (Acts 17:22–31), a natural theology dependent on Stoic tradition is placed in the mouth of Paul (cf. 17:28: "For we too are his [God's] offspring."). Moreover, in Luke's portrayal Paul conducts his mission under the authority of the twelve Jerusalem apostles. The Apostolic Decree (15:23–29 and 21:25; contrast Gal 2:1–10) arranges for Paul to conduct his Gentile mission by subjecting his converts to a minimal

---

Christianity rather than with the New Testament documents themselves. However, the term "kerygma" (originally, the "herald's message") has no one clear definition (cf. H. Conzelmann, *Theology* 8: the proclamation of the "earliest church," though Conzelmann gives a different definition in his "Was glaubte die frühe Christenheit?," *Theologie als Schriftauslegung. Aufsätze zum Neuen Testament* (BEvTh 65) Munich: Kaiser, 1974) 106–119: "early Christian confessional formulae." Cf. also W. Thüsing, *Die neutestamentlichen Theologien und Jesus Christus, I. Kriterien* (Düsseldorf: Patmos, 1981) 47–52, according to whom the New Testament documents different "interpretations of the kerygma of Jesus Christ" and the individual writings of the New Testament represent "new interpretations of the kerygma." The concept of the kerygma itself, however, remains an abstraction.

program of Jewish Christian observance of the ceremonial law. Just as this is the precondition of the mission of Paul and Barnabas among the Gentiles, so also in the Acts portrayal Paul himself avoids giving the appearance that he neglects the Jewish law in carrying out his mission (Acts 16:3; 21:26). This is not the historical apostle, as we know him from the Pauline letters, but a Lucan Paul. His goal is to preserve the unity of the history of salvation between Judaism and Christianity, between Jewish Christians and Gentile Christians. He is committed to a fundamental harmony and attempts to practice his harmonizing approach in dealing with the Jerusalem church in matters of both organization and theology. He is willing to sacrifice his own life for the sake of this harmony. In contrast, the authentic Pauline letters show Paul in conflict with opponents who appear both within and outside his churches; likewise, his relationship to the Jerusalem church is not free from tensions (cf. Gal 2:11ff). The authentic Paul places the claim of truth over ecclesiastical and theological harmony, places freedom over the requirements of organization, the authority of the Spirit over unconditional obedience to ecclesiastical rules. He claims to possess the Spirit no less than his opponents (2 Cor 6:6; 11:4), and to be fundamentally no different from the Jerusalem apostles in having seen the Risen One (1 Cor 15:7–11).

The author of Acts is not to be given sole responsibility for the formation of this picture of Paul. He can hardly have been a companion of Paul but belongs to the second or third Christian generation. He was later identified with a companion of Paul whose name we know from Philemon 24 and who was known as "Luke the physician" according to Colossians 4:14. The accounts provided by the author of Acts obviously derive from secondary tradition, mediated by the pre-Lucan churches who had already reworked the picture of Paul. This can be recognized from the Acts accounts of Paul's conversion (Acts 9, 22, 26). Here the author has a legend he had found in the tradition that he has elaborated into three different versions and inserted at appropriate places in his work. In the process he also shortened it with each retelling, in order to avoid repetitions. This depiction goes back to a tradition that prior to its incorporation into Acts had been composed as a legend honoring Paul—an idealizing, edifying story of the transformation of the persecutor into an outstanding advocate of the faith, the apostle to the Gentile world. Its legendary character is clarified by a comparison with authentic Pauline statements (Gal 1:15–16), as it is by comparison with Hellenistic-Jewish traditions of the conversion of the persecutor (2 Macc 3; cf. also Acts 10:1–48; Joseph and Aseneth 1–21). Adjustment to the ideas of a later generation is also indicated by those elements of legendary Pauline tradition that Luke has worked into the Acts narrative (e. g. Acts 13:8–12; 19:11–12; 14–16; 22:3), not the least of which are the authentically Lucan touches in his portrayal of the Pauline missionary journeys.

It is likewise the case that the *Pastoral Letters* (1 Timothy, 2 Timothy, Titus) do not represent the authentic apostle. Despite apparently concrete details from the life of Paul (e. g. 2 Tim 4:13; Tit 3:12–13), these do not reflect the "historical Paul" but belong to a picture of Paul that originated about the end of the first century. The Paul of the Pastoral Letters is the church teacher who transmits right doctrine to his students. His acknowledged apostolic dignity serves to counteract the "false teachers" with an authoritative churchly claim. He supports the ecclesiastical officials, the bishops, presbyters, deacons, and widows, in this struggle, for he is the first link in an apostolic chain of tradition, the individual members of which have "certainty" by their connection with him. They have this confidence not only in opposing the attacks of heretics but also in dealing with questions of truth within the churches, in that they can appeal to his incontestable authority.

Likewise the *Second Letter to the Thessalonians* was written under the name of Paul. Presupposing the unity of this writing, the Paul of 2 Thessalonians stands close to the Paul of the Pastoral Letters. In both the Pastorals and 2 Thessalonians appeal is made to the authority of Paul in order to ward off false teaching. In 2 Thessalonians Paul's authority is used in order to tone down the Christian-prophetic announcement of the immediate arrival of the parousia and to curb the expectation of the imminent end (2 Thess 2:2). Thereby the author obviously intends to correct 1 Thessalonians, in which an unbroken, acute expectation of the parousia is found. In contrast, the Paul of 2 Thessalonians is like an apocalyptic visionary who provides instruction on the phases of the end times, who would like to calm down a disturbed church that has been upset by a view of the coming end of all things. This fits the situation of a church that had long before resolved for itself the problem of the delay of the parousia but has now been confronted with a newly awakened apocalyptic enthusiasm. Accordingly, 2 Thessalonians cannot have been written much earlier than the Pastoral Letters. Even though the authentic Pauline letters reflect different positions with regard to the question of the nearness of the parousia, which let us perceive some development in the theology of Paul,[3] the authentic apostle is still far removed from the apocalyptic views of 2 Thessalonians, which claims his authority in order to solve the problems of a later epoch.

The picture of Paul mediated by the letters of *Colossians* and *Ephesians* is just as different from that of the authentic Pauline letters as that found in the Pastorals and 2 Thessalonians. This is seen, for example, in the stereotypical appeal to the confession and to Paul's apostolic office. Reference back to this authority goes beyond that which the historical Paul

---

[3] See below A. V.

presupposed as a matter of course, with regard both to the confessional tradition and the apostolic authority he claimed for himself. In addition, the arena of theological reflection is expanded and refined at the same time. It is expanded to the extent that Colossians and Ephesians profess a cosmological function of the Christ. According to Colossians 1:15 Christ is the "firstborn" (πρωτότοκος) of creation and at the same time its mediator. He has already won the eschatological victory over the cosmic powers, for he is also the firstborn of the dead (Col 1:18). As the resurrection hope is grounded on this cosmic function of the Christ, this can be understood as an expansion of the understanding of the cosmological christological statements made by Paul.[4] Alongside this is found a more refined reflection in comparison with Pauline theology. While in the authentic Pauline letters it is often not easy to determine the boundary between the individual and the Christian community, for in them the individual church member is addressed at the same time as the church as a whole and conversely the address to the whole church also includes the individual, by contrast in Colossians and Ephesians a further distinction has been made so that the ecclesiological aspect steps into the foreground in regard both to linguistic usage and theology. Now it is primarily the church that is addressed. We may take Colossians 1:24 as an example: the body of Christ is identified with the *ecclesia*. The christological universalism leads to corresponding consequences in ecclesiology, i.e. to an ecclesiological universalism. The apostle himself is now placed in this frame of reference; he too has an assignment for the whole of creation. In this connection is to be seen the most important difference between Colossians and Ephesians on the one side and the authentic Pauline letters on the other side: Christ is understood as the "head" (κεφαλή) of the church, the church as the "body" (σῶμα) of Christ (Col 1:18; Eph 1:22–23; 4:15; 5:23). Such a distinction is not possible for the authentic Paul; it is rather the case that he identifies the church with the body of Christ, i.e. with Christ himself (Rom 12, 1 Cor 12). So also in Colossians and Ephesians the understanding of Paul's apostleship is determined by the distinction between the church as the body and Christ as the head. It signals a change in Pauline thinking when Paul is placed within the field of tension between the cosmic Christ and the universal *ecclesia*. His apostolic office has been ecclesiasticized. With this point of departure, it is but a step to judge that Colossians and Ephesians were not written by Paul himself. This conclusion is unavoidable for Ephesians, which has Colossians as a source. This conclusion is not to be ruled out for Colossians as well, although here other factors are to be named that stand closer to the authentic Pauline

---

4    Cf. 1 Corinthians 2:8; 8:6; 2 Corinthians 4:4; Galatians 4:3, 9; Philippians 2:10.

letters (e. g. the epistolary conclusion of Colossians 4:7–17, that manifests great similarity to Philemon 23–24).[5]

## 2. Authentic Pauline Letters

**1. *1 Thessalonians*.** The oldest document in the New Testament is the first letter of Paul to the Thessalonians, the literary integrity of which is to be presupposed. Here we find an expectation of the near end advocated (1 Thess 4:13ff; 5:1ff) that is not repeated in this manner in the later Pauline letters. Moreover, essential elements of Paul's thought in the later letters are not found (e. g. Paul's understanding of the law and of justification). The specific way in which the expectation of the parousia is expressed in 1 Thessalonians gives a first indication of an awareness of the delay of the parousia. This places 1 Thessalonians at the chronological and material beginning point not only of Pauline eschatology but of Paul's theology as such.

**2. *1 and 2 Corinthians*.** The two Corinthian letters are the remnants of a more extensive correspondence that Paul carried on with the Corinthian church. 1 Corinthians 5:9–11 refers to an older letter to the Corinthians that has been lost. Second Corinthians also points to the existence of a series of several letters, even though the results of detailed literary analysis remain disputed. The final section of 2 Corinthians (chaps. 10–13) contains the "painful letter" written after the visit of Paul to Corinth between 1 and 2 Corinthians. The "painful letter" was followed by the "letter of reconciliation," essentially preserved in 2 Corinthians 1–8 (9). The apostle who becomes visible in this correspondence defends his commission over against the disputing groups in the Corinthian church. In Corinth there was not only a Pauline party but a Petrine party and an Apollos party; it is less likely that there was a "Christ party" (1 Cor 1:12; 3:4). Paul directs his Corinthian correspondence especially against attacks that had been launched against him by pneumatic-enthusiastic circles within the church. Paul was concerned with the order of the church and its stance within the world. In debate with those who dispute a future resurrection of the dead (1 Cor 15) he affirms the eschatological horizon of the cross and resurrection of Jesus Christ. This kerygma grounds Christian hope and legitimizes the apostle's message of reconciliation, as he

---

5   Cf. the introductions to the New Testament. The assumption that Colossians represents a later development of Pauline thinking and style (e. g. A. Wikenhauser, *Einleitung in das Neue Testament*, Freiburg: Herder, 1961[4], 298–299) offers no persuasive arguments. On this cf. W. Bujard, *Stilanalytische Untersuchungen zum Kolosserbrief als Beitrag zur Methodik von Sprachvergleichen* (StUNT 11. Göttingen: Vandenhoeck & Ruprecht, 1973).

defends it in 2 Corinthians against wandering Christian missionaries of Hellenistic-Jewish origin.

3. *Galatians.* The so-called "Judaizing" hypothesis is relatively correct in its approach to interpreting Galatians. In none of Paul's other letters is the threat to the Pauline churches by Jewish Christian teachers of the law expressed more clearly. Here for the first time the message of justification in the Pauline sense is articulated. It affirms that the apostle proclaims the free grace of God that justifies human beings, i.e. makes them right before God, without any condition or accomplishment on their part. Freedom from the law and justification (*Gerechtmachung*, "rightwising") by faith are its indispensable structural elements. The justifying, saving act of Christ (indicative) is followed by the imperative never again to yield to slavery under the yoke of the law (Gal 5:1) but to serve one another in love (5:13).

4. *Romans.* Paul's letter to the Romans was written after the Corinthian and Galatian controversies and uniquely reflects the systematic structure of Paul's thought. The writing deals with concrete problems of the Roman church and presupposes the situation of a real letter, since it is intended to prepare for the apostle's visit to Rome and his trip to Spain (Rom 15:22ff). Even though it is not a comprehensive compendium of systematic theology, the theoretical intention is still dominant: the fundamental theme is "righteousness by faith" (1:17). The following section then elaborates human solidarity in unrighteousness in which not only the necessity (1:18–3:20) but also the possibility (3:21–4:25) and reality (chaps. 5–8) of the righteousness of God is presented (= righteousness from God), as it has been revealed in the Christ event. The problem of "Israel" in salvation history (chaps. 9–11), as also the parenetic section (12:1–15:13) draw consequences from, on the one side, Paul's connection with his own people, and, on the other side, from the series indicative–imperative (cf. 12:1). While the unity of the letter can be presupposed except for a few post-Pauline glosses, this does not apply to chapter 16, which differs from the rest of Romans and is essentially derived from a letter of recommendation for "sister Phoebe."

5. *Philippians.* The letter of Paul to the church at Philippi is numbered among the prison letters. It is thus—since the hypothesis of an imprisonment of the apostle in Ephesus remains undemonstrated—probably written near the end of Paul's ministry. While the literary unity of the letter also continues to be debated—exegetes frequently proceed on the supposition that Philippians is a combination of two or three letters—the thesis of the unity of the letter can also still be maintained. This thesis is supported by the overarching purpose of the whole letter in its present form: against the background of his situation of imprisonment, his suffering as an apostle, Paul presents the essence of Christian joy and attempts to

confirm the church in the joy he also sees to be in them. The content of this eschatological joy is determined by looking back to the Christ event of the past and by orienting oneself to the future day of Jesus Christ. The apostle exhorts the church to realize that its ethical conduct on its journey through time must correspond to this eschatological joy.

6. *Philemon*. This is the shortest and most personal of Paul's letters. It is concerned with the relation between the slave Onesimus and his master Philemon. Onesimus had run away from his master, had sought out Paul in his place of imprisonment, had been converted by him and is now being sent back to his owner. We thus have here the first Christian document that takes a position on the issue of slavery. Paul does not challenge the existing social order but places its problematic on a different level in that he provides a new foundation for interpersonal human relations. That Onesimus is to be taken back not as a slave but as a brother (v. 16) indicates the ethical purpose of this writing: Christian love within the family of God is to overcome social distinctions.

## c) Later Influences

The apostle's letters did not get written solely on the basis of individual initiative but owe their existence to the reality of a close-knit Pauline circle in which Paul's life was embedded. They reflect the teacher-disciple relation, the "Pauline school," in which the apostle played the dominant role in relation to his coworkers. In the broader sense, the Pauline school includes not only the authentic Pauline letters but also the later writings composed in his name. They document the later influences that go back partly to oral tradition, partly to written tradition. Thus the writings already mentioned (the Pastorals, Colossians, Ephesians, 2 Thessalonians, Acts) reflect in a variety of ways the influence of Paul's person and preaching, but other later New Testament writings also show the effects of the Pauline school. This is seen, for example, in the letter formulae (prescript, prooemium, letter conclusion) and from the specifically Pauline structure of their thought. First Peter is only one example in which these marks are clearly recognizable. It is possible that Hebrews, which is characterized by an independent, Hellenistic-Jewish theology, was later considered to be a Pauline letter, as suggested by the apparently secondary conclusion (Heb 13:18, 22–25). An essential element of the theme of the Letter of James dealing with "faith and works" cannot be understood apart from the influence of Pauline tradition. Not only the deutero-Pauline letters but also the Johannine literature originated in Asia Minor, i.e. in the original Pauline missionary territory. This explains the presence of influences of the Pauline way of thinking. That such influences could also take place in an opposing sense is indicated by the author of 2 Peter, who explains with reference to the letters of "our beloved brother Paul" that they contain things difficult to understand, things which the "ignorant and unstable twist to their own destruction" (2 Pet 3:15–16).

It is no accident, then, that the Pauline influences effective at the beginning and middle of the second century are relatively small. To be sure, the Roman bishop Clement documents that Paul was acknowledged in the Roman church and cites 1 Corinthians in his writing addressed to the Corinthian church (cf. 1 Clem 47:1–3). Similarly, Ignatius of Antioch acknowledges the authority of Paul, just as he does that of Peter (Ignatius, *Romans* 4.3); alongside 1 Corinthians, he also obviously knows other Pauline letters (Romans, Thessalonians). Especially Polycarp acknowledges the authority of the apostle; he appeals to Paul's letter to the Philippians in his (second) letter to the church at Philippi (Polycarp 11.3). So also the Letter of Diognetus manifests some points of contact with Paul, just as do the apologist Justin and the *Shepherd of Hermas*. On the other hand, several second century authors do not refer to Paul at all (2 Clement, Barnabas, Papias, Hegesippus, Aristides). And even if the Christian Gnosticism of this time, such as the Valentinian school, seek to document their basic concepts by reference to Pauline theology, or when in the third century Mani, the founder of Manichaeism, appeals to Paul, it is still the case that the apostle's thought does not play the role that is sometimes ascribed to it because of the alleged proximity of his theological system to Gnosticism.[6] In contrast, Jewish Christian writings inspired by Gnosticism such as the source document "Kerygmata Petrou" of the Pseudo-Clementines, like the sect of the Elkesaites, are oriented in an antipauline direction on the basis of the Jewish legal observance they advocate. Even Marcion, still described by Adolf von Harnack as an "ultra-Paulinist,"[7] whose canon included alongside the Gospel of Luke only the most important Pauline letters, with regard to his theological views is hardly touched by Pauline thought. For him the decisive thing is a specific understanding of revelation, the distinction between the two gods: on the one side the Old Testament creator and on the other side the good God, the Father of Jesus Christ. Here we see something that is characteristic of the period of the formation of the early catholic church in general: the authority of Paul is, to be sure, acknowledged in a formal way but Paul's fundamental view of justification is hardly to be found. As clarified by the ancient church's preference for 1 Corinthians, it was especially the ethical instructions of the apostle that gained a hearing. This circumstance thus corresponds to a church situation that had to be open to the Hellenistic world, had to

---

[6]   Cf. A. Lindemann, *Paulus im ältesten Christentum. Das Bild des Apostels und die Rezeption der paulinischen Theologie in der frühchristlichen Literatur bis Marcion* (BHTh 58) (Tübingen: J. C. B. Mohr [Paul Siebeck], 1979).

[7]   A. v. Harnack, *Marcion: the Gospel of the Alien God* (Durham, N. C.: Labyrinth Press, 1990) 142–145.

adapt to a widespread consciousness of itself and the world flavored by the ethics of Stoicism, and to debate about how this was to be realized in practice.

If one surveys the course of church history, it is only in exceptional cases in which the apostle actually attains the rank that appears to be assigned to him on the basis of the central position of his writings in the New Testament canon. At one of the few propitious moments, Augustine came by his study of the Pauline letters to a doctrine of grace that speaks of the radical fallenness of humanity under sin for which the grace of God is the only remedy.[8] The reformer Martin Luther owes his pioneering insight that the righteousness of God does not annihilate guilty human beings but makes them righteous, not only to the reading of Augustine's writings but above all to the theology of Paul (Rom 1:17).[9] The founder of Methodism, John Wesley, came to the decisive turning point in his life by reading the Preface to Luther's *Commentary on Romans*. And the foundation of "dialectical theology" was laid by Karl Barth's dispute with liberal thought represented by his commentary on Romans, which set forth Paul's message of the righteousness of God which is alone able to save.[10]

# I. History-of-Religion Presuppositions—
# Prepauline Elements in Pauline Theology

Hübner, H. Die "Paulusforschung seit 1945," ein kritischer Literaturbericht, *ANRW* II 25.4. (1987) 2649–2840.

Merk, O. "Paulus-Forschung 1936–1985," *ThR* 53 (1988) 1–81.

Schoeps, H. J. *Paul: The Theology of the Apostle in the Light of Jewish Religious History*. Philadelphia: Westminster, 1961.

Schweitzer, A. *Paul and His Interpreters: A Critical History*. London: Adam and Charles Black, 1912.

The history of scholarship is characterized by a great variety of interpretations of Paul and thus a large number of different pictures of the apostle himself. Sometimes Paul is a rabbi, at other times a Hellenist or a Hellenistic Jewish Christian. The terms "chiliast," "Gnostic," "mystic," or "initiate" in the mystery cults have all been applied to him. Such evaluations not only illustrate the disparity of contemporary scholarship but also all

---

[8] Augustinus, *Ad Simplicianum de diversis quastionibus* I 1.2, CCSLXLIV (Brepols 1970).

[9] Cf. M. Luther, *Vorrede zu Band 1 der Opera Latina* (1545) WA 54, 185.12–186.20.

[10] K. Barth, *The Epistle to the Romans*. (London, New York, Toronto: Oxford University Press, 1953).

have points of contact in the theology of Paul himself.[1] From the point of view of the study of the history of religions, the theology of Paul is a syncretistic phenomenon, like that of earliest Christianity in general. In him religious streams of differing origins collide with each other. Moreover, the lack of unity and evenness is augmented by the fact that Paul's letters are all conditioned by the local situation to which each is addressed (= "occasional letters"). All this makes it more difficult to respond to the question of what might constitute the unity of Pauline thought amidst all this variety, the issue of what is to be understood as the "center" of Pauline theology.[2] Such a question is also posed for a purely historical investigation. If, as W. Wrede said, "Explanation [means] ... to set in the context of a historical development,"[3] then it appears that historical interpretation—as this was recognized in the history of religions school that stood within the kind of historicism considered to be outlawed—does coincide with the demonstration of existential truth. This calls attention to the historically-conditioned aspect of every statement of the truth but still reflects an unfounded optimism in academic research, and presupposes that the awareness of truth can be objectively motivated and perceived by historical study.

Nevertheless, the history of religions school has done us an undeniable service by, for example, having made the historical context of early Christianity accessible. Herman Gunkel was a pioneer in this area for the study of the Old Testament and laid the essential foundation for the understanding of Pauline pneumatology. Albert Eichhorn, Johannes Weiss, Wilhelm Heitmüller, William Wrede and Wilhelm Bousset, among others, investigated the history-of-religions presuppositions of the New Testament from different perspectives and decisively contributed to the illumination of the methodology of interpreting the New Testament from the point of view of the history of religions. They originally had twin goals in view. In the first place, they sought to find analogies in the history of religion, i.e. they looked for ideas in the religious environment of early Christianity that were parallel to those in the New Testament. In the second place, they inquired as to the *genetic connection*, i.e. the direct influences, that were

---

[1]   Inadmissible is the alternative position characteristic of the position of liberal theology, in which the religious genius of Paul is played off against the theologians, the naive against the reflective, piety against scholasticism (cf. A. Deissmann, *Paul: A Study in Social and Religious History* (New York: Harper & Brothers, 1957) 5–7. Such contrasts live from romantic prejudices, for the theological thought of Paul does not stand in contrast to lived faith as though they were alternatives.

[2]   Cf. e. g. W. Thüsing, *Per Christum in Deum. Studien zum Verhältnis von Christozentrik und Theozentrik in den paulinischen Hauptbriefen* (NTA 1) (Münster: Aschendorff, 1965²) 264–270; on this problem cf. also G. Eichholz, *Die Theologie des Paulus im Umriss* (Neukirchen-Vluyn: Neukirchener, 1972) 8–9.

[3]   Cf. W. Wrede, *Aufgabe und Methode* 6 note 4.

determinative for the New Testament world of ideas. To the extent that this is possible, in the following we will reflect on such genetic connections. The genuine Pauline elements stand in contrast to the demonstrable religious ideas that were already present in Paul's world. Comparison with pre-Pauline statements facilitates the recognition not only of the agreements but also the distinctions that are important for understanding Pauline theology. So also the results of such a comparison remains within the horizon of the history-of-religions perspective. This is part of the distancing process that is inherent in the historical-critical method as such. This focuses attention on the mythological elements in Pauline thought, elements that the apostle has reworked into his independent conception and in the process significantly modified.

While in such analyses of history-of-religions presuppositions the problem of genetic connections stands in the foreground, at the same time a goal with regard to the history of traditions is delineated, since an investigation of Pauline theology requires that one ask about pre-Pauline traditions. The distinctively Pauline elements stand out as "redaction" in contrast to the material adopted from pre-Pauline tradition. In Paul's letters he not only adopted traditional elements of non-Christian origin but also took over and reworked Christian tradition. Accordingly, the question of the history-of-religions presuppositions of Pauline theology may be divided into the three categories of Judaism, the pagan Hellenistic environment, and pre-Pauline Christian tradition.

### a) Judaism

Hengel, M. and U. Heckel, eds., *Paulus und das antike Judentum*. WUNT 58. Tübingen: J. C. B. Mohr (Paul Siebeck), 1991.
Niebuhr, K.-W. *Heidenapostel aus Israel: Die jüdische Identität des Paulus nach ihrer Darstellung in seinen Briefen*. WUNT 62. Tübingen: J. C. B. Mohr (Paul Siebeck), 1992.
Oepke, A. "Probleme der vorchristlichen Zeit des Paulus, wiederabgedruckt," K.H. Rengstorf, ed., *Das Paulusbild in der neueren deutschen Forschung*. Darmstadt: Wissenschaftliche Buchgesellschaft, 1964, 410–446.
Sanders, E. P. *Paul and Palestinian Judaism. A Comparison of Patterns of Religion*. Philadelphia: Fortress, 1977.

The view is widespread that the continuity between Judaism and Pauline thought was of decisive significance for Pauline theology. Accordingly, Paul continued to be a Jew after he became a Christian. In contrast to this view, Paul is seen as the one who understood himself to be the apostle to the Gentiles, whose apostolic call was included as a part of his conversion, whose self-understanding included a fundamental break with Judaism (Gal 1:13ff; Phil 3:7). Of course, even after his conversion the apostle continued to live within the world of Jewish ideas and to make extensive use of it in both his preaching and in the development of his theological thought. The fundamental Jewish ideas found in the Pauline letters reach back into the time prior to Paul's conversion, since before his call to be apostle to the Gentiles Paul was indeed a Jew in his own self-understanding and in the way he lived his life, rooted in the national, religious, and intellectual existence of his people. Although the Pauline letters hardly report biographical details from the life of Paul, the brief notices about the apostle's conversion and call (Gal 1:13–16) show that in comparison with his contemporaries the pre-Christian Paul excelled in the "Jewish way of life" (Ἰουδαϊσμός), and that he championed the ancestral traditions to an extreme degree, including persecution of the Christian congregations.

According to Adolf Schlatter,[4] this statement is to be interpreted on the basis of Acts 26:10–11. Paul's persecuting activity authorized by the high priest would accordingly have included a judicial function. The function of a judge, however —so it is further inferred—could only have been exercised by an ordained rabbi. Thus Paul must have been an ordained rabbi. (J. Jeremias also comes to this conclusion, in "War Paulus Witwer?" ZNW 25 [1926] 310–312, and in "Nochmals: Was Paulus Witwer?" ZNW 28 [1929] 321–323). It is questionable, however, whether rabbinic ordination was practiced at the time of the apostle (cf. R. Riesner, *Jesus als Lehrer* [WUNT II 7. Tübingen J.C.B. Mohr (Paul Siebeck)] 1988³ 266–276). Acts 26:10–11 thus reflects a later legendary tradition from which historical inferences about the pre-Christian Paul cannot be derived. We know nothing about the details of the persecution carried on by the pre-Christian Paul's persecution of Christian congregations. In Galatians 1 Paul only confirms the fact itself; he interprets it in the sense that as a persecutor he was attempting to defend the ancestral traditions. This corresponds to his Pharisaic background, which he documents himself.

More precise information about the pre-Christian period of Paul's life is provided by the passage Philippians 3:5–6 ("circumcised on the eighth day, a member of the people of Israel, of the tribe of Benjamin, a Hebrew born of Hebrews; as to the law, a Pharisee; as to zeal, a persecutor of the church; as to righteousness under the law, blameless"). The context reflects a debate with Jewish Christian or (more probably) Jewish opponents. These boast of their achievements in Judaism, especially their possession of the Law, which confer a higher status on Jews in contrast to Gentiles. To this the apostle responds: as a Christian he considers all such privileges to be garbage (V.8: σκύβαλα), although in his pre-Christian period he was subject to the Jewish law. Since his birth ("circumcised on the eighth day") his life had been determined by this Jewish legal system, which means not only demand but privilege: "Israel" is a distinguished title for the Jewish

---

[4]    A. Schlatter, *Die Geschichte der ersten Christenheit* (Göttingen: Vandenhoeck & Ruprecht, 1983⁶ [reprint ed. by R. Riesner]) 112–129. Cf. A. Oepke, *Probleme* 412–413.

people that indicates their honored status as God's chosen people.[5] Belonging to the tribe of Benjamin points to a privileged segment of this people, since Benjamin as the youngest of Jacob's sons was born in the Jewish fatherland. So also "Hebrew" was a title of honor within the Jewish context,[6] in distinction from the term "Jew," the term mostly used by outsiders.[7] Paul's family lived intentionally within the Jewish tradition; they were in the situation of being able to trace their genealogy back to the tribe of Benjamin. This corresponds to Paul's designation of himself as a "Pharisee;" he belonged to an influential religious group that placed a high value on living a strict Jewish manner of life,[8] in distinction from the "Sadducees," who were satisfied to make compromises with the Roman occupation authorities and were open to pagan cultural influences.

From this data provided by Paul himself, the inference is made that Paul is to be regarded primarily as a Palestinian Jew whose religious presuppositions are to be sought in the Jewish fatherland, in Palestine. Primarily two arguments are presented for this view: (1) Paul describes himself as a Pharisee (Phil 3:5). Pharisaism is authentically Palestinian and limited to the Palestinian area. (2) Paul was a disciple of the Jewish Torah scholar Gamaliel I, who taught in Jerusalem ca. 25–50 C. E. (cf.

---

5   Cf. 2 Corinthians 3:7; 11:22; Romans 9:6, 31; 10:19; 11:1–2, 25–26, and elsewhere—Paul has transferred this title of honor to the Christian community (Gal 6:16).

6   Cf. 2 Corinthians 11:22. The term Ἑβραῖος occasionally refers to the Hebrew language, as apparently in Acts 6:1 (in contrast to the "Hellenists"). However, neither a Palestinian origin nor a knowledge of the Hebrew language is to be inferred from this word either for Paul or for his opponents. It is rather the case that "Hebrews" was in Hellenistic Judaism a designation of the Jewish people in ancient times, just as it was for the pagan Greek world, so that the expression has a certain archaizing coloring (W. Gutbrod, TDNT 3.372–375; J. Wanke, *EWNT* 1.892–894: Corresponding to Jewish-Hellenistic propaganda "it is probable that Paul here presents himself first and foremost as a "full-blooded Jew" [H. Lietzmann, *1/2 Korintherbriefe* HNT. 150], a Jew who has remained loyal to the customs and practices of the ancestors..."). So also the secondary superscription of the New Testament "Letter to the Hebrews" does not purport to be addressed to Palestinian or Hebrew-speaking Jews but to Christians, upon whom the ancient Jewish title of honor is conferred.

7   Ἰουδαῖοι is also used by Paul in a distancing sense. Thus in parallel to the "Gentiles" (ἔθνη): 1 Corinthians 1:23–24; 10:32; 2 Corinthians 11:24; Romans 1:16; 2:9–10; 3:9, and elsewhere.

8   In Josephus' portrayal (*Ant* 8, 15, 17, 18; *Wars* 1 and 2; *Life* 38) the Pharisees, in their life and teaching, represent the Jewish people in their best light. Characteristic of them is the combination of piety and political engagement. This would mean that the persecution activity of the pre-Christian Paul is not necessarily motivated primarily by dogmatic and theoretical concerns (such as their understanding of the Law), and also makes it difficult to reconstruct a continuing connection between the Pharisaism prior to 70 C. E. and the rabbinism after 70. Cf. P. Schäfer, "Der vorrabbinische Pharisäismus," in M. Hengel and U. Heckel, eds. *Paulus und das antike Judentum* 170.

Acts 5:34; 22:3). Neither argument, however, is sound. With regard to the first argument: It is true, of course, that documented evidence for the Pharisees is limited almost exclusively to Palestine but they were active far beyond the Palestinian boundaries in the Jewish Diaspora. The first Evangelist, who is not writing within a Palestinian context, presupposes this when he charges the Pharisees and scribes with going over land and sea to make one proselyte (Matt 23:15). It is thus quite conceivable that Paul united with Pharisaism within the context of the Jewish Diaspora. With regard to the second argument: The origin of the notice about Paul's connection to Gamaliel is unknown. It was possibly an element of the legendary Pauline tradition that Luke found in the process of gathering Pauline materials, if it did not originate with Luke himself. It does correspond to the tendency of the Lucan delineation in Acts of the course of the apostle "from Jerusalem to Rome," "from the Jews to the Gentiles," and "from Jewish Christianity to Gentile Christianity."[9] Moreover, it is quite doubtful whether Paul was ever in Jerusalem prior to his conversion. The authentic letters of Paul point in a different direction: the first visit to Jerusalem reported by Paul was three years after his conversion, in order to seek out Cephas (Gal 1:18). This first, precisely documented visit of Paul to Jerusalem is presumably also the first visit to Jerusalem in the life of Paul, since according to Galatians 1:22 Paul had been unknown to the Christian congregations in Judea. This first visit was so short that it did not lead to a closer familiarity with Christians within Jerusalem and its near environs. This also makes it probable that Paul had never lived in Jerusalem prior to this visit.[10]

Paul did not grow up in Jerusalem but in the Jewish Diaspora. Acts reports that he came from Tarsus in Cilicia (Acts 9:11; 21:39; 22:3) and was a Roman citizen (e. g. Acts 16:37–38; 22:25–26). This is the basis of the double name attributed to him in the tradition. While in his letters to his Gentile Christian churches he refers to himself as Παῦλος, in Acts he is called Σαῦλος (Hebr. שָׁאוּל) prior to his own Gentile mission (e. g. Acts 7:58; 8:1, 3; 9:1, 8; cf. 13:9). Obviously "Saul" was his original Jewish name, while "Paul" was the cognomen appropriate to the Roman and Greek context, and indicated that its bearer was a Jew of the Diaspora.

---

[9]   This agrees with other reports about Paul that probably derive from Luke: Acts 7:58; 8:1; 11:30.

[10]  Galatians 1:22–23 does not provide evidence for the view that Paul persecuted the Jewish congregations but merely reports what these had heard, namely that the erstwhile persecutor (of the Christians in the Jewish Diaspora; cf. Gal 1:13, 17) had now become a preacher of the faith he once opposed. The attempt of M. Hengel, in opposition to the negative results from the Pauline letters, to affirm that the pre-Christian Paul persecuted the Christians in Jerusalem, is inspired by the Lucan picture of Paul (M. Hengel, *The Pre-Christian Paul* [Philadelphia: Trinity Press International; London: SCM Press, 1991]).

The roots of the thinking of the pre-Christian Paul are accordingly to be sought in Diaspora Judaism, i.e. in the realm of Hellenistic Judaism. Tarsus, with its mixed population of Greeks, Jews, and Orientals was famous in antiquity because of its philosophical and other academic educational institutions. It is obvious that in this intellectual environment Paul did not become an outstanding exponent of Greek scholarship but it is still the case that the intellectual and theological formation of the pre-Christian Paul is to be distinguished from that of Palestinian Judaism. That which is often claimed to be Paul's rabbinic manner of thought is rather to be attributed to the influences of Diaspora Judaism, as Paul became acquainted with it in his home town through Jewish teachers. The knowledge of the Torah possessed by the pre-Christian Paul derives from the tradition of Hellenistic Judaism. This can be seen in Paul's use of Scripture.

## 1. The Use of the Old Testament

Dodd, C. H. *According to the Scriptures. The Sub-Structure of New Testament Theology.* London: Nisbet, 1952.

Ellis, E. E. *Paul's Use of the Old Testament.* Edinburgh: T. & T. Clark, 1957.

Ellis, E. E. *Prophecy and Hermeneutic in Early Christianity.* WUNT 18. Tübingen: J. C. B. Mohr (Paul Siebeck), 1978.

Hanson, A. T. *Studies in Paul's Technique and Theology.* London: SPCK, 1974.

Harris, J. R. *Testimonies I,II.* Cambridge: Cambridge University Press, 1916.

Hays, R. B. *Echoes of Scripture in the Letters of Paul.* New Haven-London: Yale University Press, 1989.

Hellholm, D. "Paulus von Tarsos—Zum Problem der hellenistischen Ausbildung," Manuskript 1992; Norwegian Version, "Paulus Fra Tarsos. Til spørsmålet om Paulus' hellenistiske utdannelse," T. Eide and T. Hägg, eds., *Dionysos og Apollon. Religion og samfunn i antikkens Hellas* (Skrifter utgitt av det norske institutt i Athen 1). Bergen, 1989, 259–282.

Hirsch, E. *Das Alte Testament und die Predigt des Evangeliums* Tübingen: J. C. B. Mohr (Paul Siebeck), 1936.

Koch, D.-A. *Die Schrift als Zeuge des Evangeliums.* BHTh 69. Tübingen: J. C. B. Mohr (Paul Siebeck), 1986.

Michel, O. *Paulus und seine Bibel.* Darmstadt: Wissenschaftliche Buchgesellschaft, 1972[2].

Vielhauer, Ph. "Paulus und das Alte Testament," *Oikodome, Aufsätze zum Neuen Testament.* TB 65, G. Klein, ed., Munich: Kaiser, 1979, 196–228.

The extent to which the theology of Paul is shaped by Hellenistic-Jewish presuppositions is demonstrated by the Old Testament texts used in the Pauline letters. The first thing to be established about Paul's use of the Scripture is that the apostle presupposes a collection of writings that would later be described as the Old Testament canon. The extent of authoritative Jewish writings had not yet been finally decided but the process was almost complete. The matter is seen differently by H. Gese ("Erwägungen zur Einheit der biblischen Theologie, *ZThK* 67 [1970] 417–436; also *Vom*

*Sinai zum Zion* [BEvTh 64] [Munich: Kaiser, 1974] 11–30), who argues that the New Testament tradition intervenes in the process while a still flexible tradition was being formed: ... "It is in fact the case that we have to do with the formation of a tradition of what constitutes the Bible; ... The Old Testament originated through the New Testament. The New Testament forms the conclusion of a process of tradition that is essentially a unity, a continuum" (*Ibid.*, p. 14). However, the postulation of a temporal (and material) priority of the New Testament to the Old Testament neglects the fact that Josephus documents the existence of an Old Testament "canon" already for the time in which the New Testament writings were still being written (Josephus, *Antiquities*, Prooemium 12–13; 1.27ff). In addition, the Jewish delimitation of the canon is to be understood less as a delimitation over against Christianity than as the result of a general (including inner-Jewish) situation in the first century C. E.

There is not the slightest doubt that Paul (and/or his coworkers, to the extent that these, as members of the "Pauline school" participated in the preparatory work and composition of the Pauline letters) used the Greek translation of the Old Testament. He even cites the Septuagint text where it manifests errors in contrast to the Massoretic text.[11] He also follows the Septuagint where the Massoretic text would already have provided an appropriate wording for his purposes.[12]

To the extent that deviations from the Septuagint text are present in the Pauline citations, they may be explained in different ways. In the first place is to be considered that Paul himself, even when he had a written text before him, may not have cited it word for word. It is rather the case that changes in the text could have been made, consciously or unconsciously, in order to bring out the intended meaning being read into the text.[13] Moreover, we must reckon with the possibility that Paul used early recensions of the Septuagint that are not always identical with the text handed on to us.

An instructive example is presented by 1 Corinthians 15:54. The quotation κατεπόθη ὁ θάνατος εἰς νῖκος deviates from the Massoretic text (Isa

---

[11] E. g. Galatians 3:17.

[12] E. g. 1 Corinthians 2:16: cited is Isaiah 40:13 LXX (νοῦς κυρίου); the Massoretic רוּחַ יְהוָה = πνεῦμα κυρίου would actually have fitted the context better.

[13] Cf. below on Romans 1:17 (Hab 2:4) and other passages. Cf. additional such abbreviations of the cited text in 2 Corinthians 3:16 (Exod 34:34); Galatians 3:13 (Deut 21:23c); Romans 10:15 (Isa 52:7). The omission in Galatians 3:12 (Lev 18:5; this passage is cited in full in Romans 10:5) is an accommodation to the neighboring citation. An addition is found in Romans 10:11 (Isa 28:16c); the same citation is found in its unmodified form in Romans 9:33. This means that the exact wording of the Isaiah quotation is known by Paul, and that the addition is conscious. Cf. also Romans 4:3; Galatians 3:6 (Gen 15:6).

25:8) but also from the Septuagint tradition (thus in the passive κατεπόθη and in the reading εἰς νῖκος for the Hebrew לָנֶצַח). By contrast, there are verbatim agreements with the Jewish translators Theodotian and Aquila, as well as parallels in Symmachus.[14] Whether the agreement with Theodotian is proof of Paul's dependence on an "Ur-Theodotian" is a disputed point,[15] just as is the question of whether we may infer from this phenomenon that Theodotian is older than previously thought.[16] In any case, we must proceed on the assumption that the Septuagint text used by Paul can not always be identified with our Septuagint text. It may thus be the case that in 1 Corinthians 15:54 a pre-Christian Jewish text was used by Paul that corrects the Hebrew text in a manner corresponding to the scroll containing the Twelve Prophets from Muraba'at (ca. 50 C. E.). Such early recensions apparently influenced the later translators Theodotian, Aquila and Symmachus.[17]

This can also explain the two texts in which Paul otherwise would have appealed to the Hebrew text:[18] Romans 11:35 (Job 41:3) and 1 Corinthians 3:19 (Job 5:12–13). Since despite indications of linguistic improvement there is no demonstrable Pauline translation style, also here we have basically a Greek translation of the Old Testament that is to be regarded as a reworking of the Septuagint text.[19] Thus when attention is given to the variations named above, the Septuagint as Paul's basic text remains solidly established, and it is excluded that Paul ever used the original Hebrew text. To this extent Paul's use of the Scripture is representative of Hellenistic Judaism.

---

[14] While the Septuagint text of Isaiah 25:8 reads κατέπιεν ὁ θάνατος ἰσχύσας, for Theodotian there existed two different translations that render לָנֶצַח with εἰς νῖκος. Aquila καταποντίσει τὸν θάνατον εἰς νῖκος and the somewhat later Symmachus καταποθῆναι ποιήσει τὸν θάνατον εἰς τέλος.

[15] Contra e. g. A. Rahlfs, "Über Theodotian-Lesarten bei Justin," *ZNW* 20(1921) 182–199.

[16] The possibility that Theodotian did not work around 180 C. E., as indicated by the reference in Epiphanius (de mensuris et ponderibus, PG XLIII 264–265) but that the note in Irenaeus (*Heretics* 3.24) is more credible, is assumed by S. P. Brock, "Bibelübersetzungen I.2," *TRE* 6.163–172. Accordingly Theodotian's translation would be dated in the middle of the first century C. E.—which, however, does not increase the probability that Paul was dependent on Theodotian.

[17] Cf. R. Hanhart, *Das Neue Testament und die griechische Überlieferung des Judentums* (TU 125) (Berlin: W. de Gruyter, 1981) 293–303; and "Septuaginta," in W.H. Schmidt and W. Thiel-R. Hanhart, *Altes Testament* (GKT 1) (Stuttgart: Kohlhammer, 1988) 176–196. Similarly D.-A. Koch, *Die Schrift als Zeuge*, who speaks of a Hebraizing reworking of the Septuagint that Paul had in partly written form (57–81).

[18] So E. E. Ellis, *Paul's Use* 144 note 3.

[19] Cf. D.-A. Koch, *Die Schrift als Zeuge* 78–79.

*Excursus: The Testimony Book Hypothesis*

According to J. Rendel Harris a collection of quotations ("testimonies") existed in early Christianity that functioned in anti-Jewish polemic. This oldest Christian document was used not only by New Testament authors but by the Church Fathers. One must reckon with the use of this book in the Pauline letters. A testimony book hypothesis actually deserves more attention in the present state of research than it received in its own time. Since a collection of quotations was found in Cave Four at Qumran (4QTest: Deut 5:28–29; 18:18–19; Num 24:15–17; Deut 33:8–11; Josh 6:26), the possibility that early Christianity also made use of such collections in its preaching and teaching can no longer be disputed.[20] It can be assumed that the reflection-citations in the Gospel of Matthew derive to a considerable extent from a collection of quotations that lay before the Evangelist Matthew.[21] So also in the second century Melito of Sardis wrote "six books with excerpts from the Law and the Prophets," i.e. a testimony book.[22] Nonetheless, Harris' comprehensive hypothesis cannot be accepted in the form in which he advocated it for two reasons:

1. Such a written collection is not documented in the history of early Christian literature; this makes it difficult to postulate its existence that presumably lasted into the late Patristic period.

2. The problem of the tradition of New Testament quotations of the Old Testament may not be considered only from the point of view of literary connections. Harris' hypothesis leaves the oral tradition out of consideration. The phenomenon of oral tradition is also to be presupposed in regard to the school traditions and how they influenced the formation of New Testament literature.

C. H. Dodd posed a different hypothesis as an alternative to Harris' suggestion, in which the element of oral tradition played a stronger role. According to Dodd's thesis, within the oral tradition there were blocks of material containing selected passages from the Old Testament.[23] These sections, also called "pericope," were used in early Christian instruction as proof texts. They would have contained expositions of the apocalyptic-eschatological world of ideas, the new Israel and the Servant of God. However, the arrangement of the "blocks of material" remained hypothetical. Many agreements within the quoted material are determined by the

---

[20]   Cf. on 4Qtest: J. M. Allegro, "Further Messianic References in Qumran Literature," *JBL* 75 (1956) 174–187; J. A. Fitzmyer, "'4QTestimonia' and the New Testament," in *Essays on the Semitic Background of the New Testament* (London: G. Chapman, 1971) 59–89.

[21]   Cf. G. Strecker, *Weg der Gerechtigkeit* 49–85.

[22]   Cf. Eusebius, HE 4.26.13–26.

[23]   C. H. Dodd, *Scriptures* 126–127.

subject matter, occasionally also through textual interdependence within the literary history. Therefore the agreements that can be confirmed within the cited material that occurs in the New Testament and related early Christian literature should not be evaluated too extensively in terms of literary connections. Dodd was right, however, to call attention to the influence of oral tradition: early Christian preaching and instruction used Old Testament texts in order to make the Christ-kerygma understandable or also thereby to legitimate it through the proof from fulfilled prophecy. Paul presupposes this in a layer of oral tradition, which means in Christian traditions that have Hellenistic Jewish characteristics. The Letter to the Hebrews, with numerous parallels to citations in the Pauline letters, can be introduced here as an example, for it is a New Testament document written under Hellenistic Jewish presuppositions. Such a layer of tradition, the extent and coherence of which has of course not yet been proved, is of Christian origin and was adopted by Paul after his call to be an apostle and/or worked out by Paul himself and his school.[24]

The Jewish presuppositions of Pauline theology are also seen in the manner in which Paul interprets the text of the Old Testament. Here we may name the methods that are partially documented in rabbinic Judaism but also were already known in the Greek-speaking Judaism of the first Christian century.[25]

1. The *inference a minori ad maius*, "from the smaller to the greater," is found often. This method is recognizable in the Greek formula for comparison πολλῷ μᾶλλον or πόσῳ μᾶλλον. It is found in the Adam/Christ typology (Rom 5:15, 17), in the portrayal of the meaning of the death of Christ as "for us" (Rom 5:9–10), in discussing the problem of the role of Israel in salvation history (Rom 11:12 / Ps 68:23 LXX in 11:9, also 11:24), further in the juxtaposition of ministry of Moses and ministry of the Spirit (2 Cor 3:7–9, 11/Exod 34:30). In the rabbinic literature this hermeneutical method is called קַל וָחֹמֶר, "light and heavy." The reverse method is also documented, namely the conclusion "from the greater to the smaller" (*a maiori ad minus*; cf. Rom 8:32; 1 Cor 6:2–3).

2. The *inference by analogy* (in rabbinic tradition, גְּזֵרָה שָׁוָה = "equal decision"). Here two biblical passages that use the same terms are interpreted with reference to each other so that the one explains the other (thus

---

[24] The existence of pre-Pauline Christian collections of Scripture quotations is vigorously disputed by D.-A. Koch. His thesis is "that Paul, in the course of his own reading of Scripture, collected excerpts from Scripture passages which he could then refer to in the composition of his letters" (*Die Schrift als Zeuge* 253). This thesis, not entirely without justification, reckons with the independence of Paul's work but neglects the consideration of the activity of the Pauline school.

[25] Cf. O. Michel, *Paulus und seine Bibel* 91ff; D.-A. Koch, *Die Schrift als Zeuge* 199ff; G. Mayer, "Exegese II," *RAC* 6.1197–1198; on the types and structures of Pauline argumentation, cf. D. Hellholm 15–19.

Rom 4:3–8: Gen 15:6 and Ps 31:1–2 LXX; in each case the verb λογίζομαι appears in a different sense. Paul connects both passages so that λογίζομαι means both "consider faith to be righteousness" and "not count sins against one").

The two hermeneutical methods just mentioned belong to the seven rules ("Middoth") of Rabbi Hillel, which were a "collation of the main types of arguments in use at that time."[26] This does not necessarily mean, however, that Paul knew these rules or that he was a Hillelite.[27] Hillel used still other methods of proof and those just named were not only typical of Jewish teaching but have parallels in Hellenistic rhetoric, so that we may assume that the rabbinic methods themselves were influenced by their Hellenistic environment.

3. *Argumentum e silentio.* This method draws the consequences of the fact that something is not said in a particular text. For example, in Romans 4:6–8 David is cited according to Psalm 31:1–2 LXX: "Blessed is the person to whom the Lord does not impute sin." Since this text does not say that people must demonstrate their own works if God is to grant them justification, Paul infers from this the conclusion that justification does not come from works but from faith.

4. Also to be mentioned is the *argumentum e contrario*, found in Romans 3:4 and 1 Corinthians 14:22; 15:44 as well as in rabbinic writings (Mekhilta on Exod 12:1).

5. *Etymology of names.* Hellenistic Jewish exegesis had already used the theological interpretation of Old Testament names (cf. Philo *All* 3.244; cf. also Ber 7b; San 19b). A common interpretation understands Galatians 4:25 in this way ("The word Hagar means Mount Sinai in Arabia"). Paul interprets this "figuratively:" Hagar, Abraham's slave woman and concubine, receives a special function in the ordering of law and gospel; she symbolizes the Law given on Mount Sinai.

Two other methods are of fundamental significance, whose importance extends beyond those already mentioned:

6. *Allegorical Interpretation.* An allegory is a narrative representation, which in essential parts has figurative significance such that within the traditional narrative there is a deeper sense that is the real meaning of the

---

[26] H. L. Strack-G. Stemberger, *Introduction to the Talmud and Midrash* (Edinburgh: T. & T. Clark, 1991.) 19.

[27] Differently J. Jeremias, "Paulus als Hillelit," E. E. Ellis and M. Wilcox, eds., *Neotestamentica et Semitica* (FS M. Black) (Edinburgh: T. & T. Clark, 1969) 88–94, which names further parallels to Hillel. It is supposed that three additional Hillelite rules can be discerned in Paul: The fifth rule (general and specific) lets comprehensive and special commands interpret each other. Paul supposedly used this rule in Romans 13:9; Galatians 5:14. The sixth rule (getting a more precise meaning from a passage with the help of a related passage) is supposedly used in Galatians 3:16, and the use of the seventh rule (inference from the context) is documented by Romans 4:10–11a and Galatians 3:17.

text. Old Testament narratives are often read by Paul under the presupposition that they are allegorical portrayals that are thus actually oriented to their real sense that is hidden within them. But even when the verb ἀλληγορέω appears in Galatians 4:24, whether the juxtaposition of Hagar and Sarah (Gal 4:21–31) is really an allegory, and not more correctly understood as an instance of typological exegesis, is still a disputed point.[28] In any case, we have an allegory in 1 Corinthians 9:9, when Deuteronomy 25:4 ("You shall not muzzle an ox when it is treading out the grain") is interpreted in the sense that allows the apostle to claim financial support from the church. So also Galatians 3:16 with its typical identification formula ὅς ἐστιν Χριστός ("this is Christ") must be considered an allegory. The comparison Christ = Passover lamb, with the juxtaposition of old and new leaven (1 Cor 5:6–8) also approaches the allegorical method. The Hellenistic Jewish presuppositions for this method are documented above all in the works of Philo of Alexandria.[29] In Christian interpretation of the Old Testament after Paul, the allegorical method was increasingly practiced, as the Letter of Barnabas documents as an important example of this approach in early Christian literature.

7. *Typological interpretation of Scripture.* This approach understands the Old Testament narratives of real persons or events as anticipatory portrayals of other future persons or events. The focus of the argumentation is on the latter. The point of departure of this paralleling of Old Testament and Christian persons and events is the conviction of the Christian community that its past, present, and future can be illuminated by the "types" portrayed in the Old Testament texts, and that Christian

---

[28] D.-A. Koch, *Die Schrift als Zeuge* 210–211, and H.-J. Klauck, *Allegorie und Allegorese in synoptischen Gleichnistexten* (NTA 13) (Münster: Aschendorff, 1986²) 116–122, decide that this is a juxtaposition of the διαθῆκαι represented by both Hagar and Sarah, and thus an "allegorization" of Genesis 21. Differently Ph. Vielhauer, *Paulus und das Alte Testament* 200, according to whom the text is an example of typological exegesis despite the allegorization of the name, since "the figures and events here mentioned are not figurative code words for timeless truths but unique historical phenomena and are thus models, anticipatory forms of present realities."
  That the word ἀλληγορέω in this passage was used mistakenly has been widely accepted since John Chrysostum (PG LXI, 662). Cf. A. Oepke, *Der Brief des Paulus an die Galater* (ThHK 9) (Berlin: Theologische Verlagsanstalt, 1979⁴) 148; O. Michel, *Paulus* 110; E. E. Ellis, *Paul's Use* 52–53; similarly R. Bultmann, "Ursprung und Sinn der Typologie als Hermeneutischer Methode," in *Exegetica* 369–380 (377: "The typology in the interpretation of the story of Sarah and Hagar is mixed with allegory [Gal 4:21–31]).

[29] Cf. Philo Jos 28 σχεδὸν γὰρ τὰ πάντα ἢ τὰ πλεῖστα τῆς νομοθεσίας ἀλληγορεῖται ("almost all, or most of the lawgiving [concretely: the given law] is allegorized"); also the Septuagint preceded Paul in the use of the allegorical method. Cf. R. Mayer, "Geschichtserfahrung und Schriftauslegung. Zur Hermeneutik des frühen Judentums," in O. Loretz-W. Strolz, eds., *Die hermeutische Frage in der Theologie* (Schriften zum Weltgespräch 3), published by the Arbeitsgemeinschaft Weltgespräch (Wien-Freiburg 1968, 328ff.

theological consciousness can be strengthened by this style of interpretation. The temporal factor, i.e. the distinction between "then" and "now"
is constitutive for this hermeneutical method. The Old Testament is
interpreted from the point of view of the New Testament. The Hagar
episode of Galatians 4:21ff can be understood in this sense. So also
Abraham's being pronounced righteous on the basis of his faith is perceived as a typological expression for the justification of the godless (Rom
4:1–25). Moreover, we may speak of typological exegesis when a type is
juxtaposed to an antitype. Thus 1 Corinthians 15:21–22, where Adam the
type as the author of death is set over against the antitype, Christ as the
bringer of life. This contrasting arrangement of Adam and Christ is also
found in 1 Corinthians 15:45–47 and Romans 5:12–21.[30] Moreover, the
"new declaration of God's will" that is received in the "ministry of the
Spirit in glory" is antitypically set over against the Sinai law, in which the
"ministry of death" is expressed (2 Cor 3:6–11). While the vocabulary and
concepts discussed here were already present in Paul's given religious
environment, and while Paul, possibly in connection with his school,
made use of traditional units that had already been formed, this is also true
of 1 Corinthians 10:1–13, where various Jewish and Hellenistic elements
are used to express the meaning of the Christian sacraments baptism and
the Lord's Supper by juxtaposing them to the saving sacramental reality
experienced by the wilderness generation of Israel, which also occasions
the presentation of positive typological lessons, namely the warning
against sin and apostasy.

   According to R. Bultmann,[31] typological interpretation of Scripture
presupposes a cyclical understanding of history. The historical process
requires the idea of the recurrence of events (cf. the concept of the trans-
migration of souls). Such an interpretation is to be constrained, however,
by the fact that in Paul's typology there is a constant linear futuristic-
eschatological factor. So also the cyclical schema, according to which the
endtime corresponds to the time of primeval beginnings (*"Urzeit wird
Endzeit"*),[32] can imply a teleological orientation, thus expressing a view of

---

[30]  Cf. below in section A. I. b. 3., "Gnosticism."

[31]  R. Bultmann, *Exegetica* 369–380.

[32]  Cf. G. v. Rad, "Typologische Auslegung des Alten Testaments," *EvTh* 12 (1952/53)
     17–33; accordingly the basic idea of typology is "to be seen less in the idea of
     'repetition' than in that of 'correspondence.'" The correspondence is here tempo-
     rally determined: the ancient event is a type of the eschatological event" (*Ibid* 19).
     A different type of correspondence is found for example in Zechariah 1:11 (between
     the earthly and the heavenly); cf. also Exod 25:9 (the booths for the feast of Tab-
     ernacles correspond to the heavenly model), Isaiah 11:1–2 (David as type of the
     Messiah), Isaiah 43:14–21 (Exodus narrative as pattern of divine action). A Moses-
     Messiah-typology is known by the rabbinic literature: "As the first redeemer (Mo-
     ses) so also the last redeemer (the Messiah);" cf. PesK 49b, PesR 15 (72b), NuR 11
     (162b), anon. MidrHld 2,9 (100a) (cf. Bill I 69).

the course of history directed to a final goal. Intentionality is also presented in the schema "prophecy and fulfillment." In distinction from this, typology does not deal with those Old Testament prophecies consciously intended as predictions (2 Cor 6:2; Isa 49:8). It is rather the case that the mysterious meaning of the Old Testament was first perceived in the texts in retrospect. Differently than is the case with allegory, typological thinking is oriented to history. However, it is still not simply to be equated with a concept of salvation history, since the latter view is interested in demonstrating God's act in history as a temporal action open to reasonable observation.[33]

Old Testament citations are found primarily in the longer letters, especially in Romans and 1 Corinthians, and in Galatians,[34] but not very often in the smaller letters (1 Thess, Phil, Phlm). The idea that Paul cites the Old Testament when he is debating with his opponents is probably not the reason for this difference but rather that it is theoretical reflections that call for biblical confirmation. This corresponds to the fact that it is not the position of the opponents but issues of faith and congregational discipline that are illuminated by citations from the Old Testament, as well as the fact that the Old Testament is called upon not so much as proof texts for the ethical imperative,[35] but above all for Christology and for the Pauline soteriology with which it is integrally connected.

To be sure, Paul does not undertake to establish Jesus' messiahship by scriptural proof but there is no doubt that he regards the *person and work of Christ* as demonstrated in the holy Scripture. Although he does not produce direct quotations, he indicates the lines of connection that testify to the biblical character of the *Christ event*: the proclamation of the gospel of the Son of God / Son of David through the Old Testament prophets (Rom 1:2–3), the death and resurrection of Jesus "according to the Scriptures" (1 Cor 15:3–4), and the lordship of the shoot of Jesse over the nations (Rom 15:12). The direct quotations that confirm Jesus Christ as the "seed" of Abraham and thereby as the representative of the promise made to Abraham (Gal 3:16) receive a special importance, as do those that ground Jesus' passion[36] or eschatological lordship[37] in the Scriptures.

A christological orientation is also found in Paul's *soteriology*, as this is expressed in the juxtaposition of the first, natural Adam and the second,

---

[33] Cf. the Markan δεῖ (see below).

[34] Romans contains 51 citations from the Old Testament; 1 Corinthians contains 18; there are an additional 11 in 2 Corinthians and 10 in Galatians.

[35] Cf., however, Romans 12:19–20 (Deut 32:35a; Prov 25:21–22); 13:8–10 (Lev 19:18b); 1 Corinthians 5:13 (Deut 17:7c) and Galatians 5:14 (Lev 19:18b).

[36] Romans 15:3: Ps 68:10 LXX; the crucifixion of Jesus as liberation from the curse of the law, "becoming a curse for us" (Gal 3:13), based on Deuteronomy 21:23 "anyone hung on a tree is under God's curse").

[37] 1 Cor 15:25, 27, a combination of Psalm 110:1 and Psalm 8:7 LXX.

spiritual Adam (1 Cor 15:45 / Gen 2:7), or in the understanding of the blessing of Abraham as the object of the promise to all the nations (Gal 3:8 / Gen 12:3). In the context of the Abraham / Christ typology, the promise of the righteousness that comes by faith is clarified on the basis of Genesis 15:6 in Romans 4:3 and Galatians 3:6. The locus classicus of the doctrine of justification, the revelation of the righteousness of God from faith to faith (Rom 1:17), which is at the same time the theme of Romans, is demonstrated by the quotation from Habakkuk 2:4 LXX ("the righteous live by my faithfulness"). Paul has adapted this text to his purpose by omitting the μου, by separating the text from its original theological orientation, thus making it into an anthropological statement, thereby giving it the connotation of opposing the idea of justification by works. The Hagar / Sarah typology draws inferences from Isaiah 54:1 and Genesis 21:10, 12 regarding the life of those who have been born according to the Spirit, their life free from the law as those who are justified by faith (Gal 4:21ff). Similarly, the "Moses midrash" of 2 Corinthians 3 is contrasted with Exodus 34 to show the freedom and glory of the new Israel. That the whole of humanity before and apart from Christ is guilty before God is shown by the list of quotations in Romans 3:10–18, and the election of the Gentiles is demonstrated by a series of Old Testament texts (Rom 15:9–12). So also the reflections in Romans 9–11 on the problem of Israel within the history of salvation are documented by a variety of scriptural references that reveal the intensive exegetical work of Paul and his school.

Just as the Old Testament in the Pauline perspective is essentially determined by God's promise, and does not contain the gospel but promise and law,[38] there can be no dispute about the fact that such an interpretation of the Bible cannot be correct in terms of either the original meaning of the Old Testament texts or the contemporary Jewish understanding. From the perspective of historical criticism as practiced in the biblical interpretation of the present day it is therefore not to be imitated. The contrast between the original meaning of the Old Testament texts, and the meaning given to them in Paul's exegesis, is all too clear, especially since it is not seldom the case that he changes the reading of the text in order to adapt it to his meaning. This makes it all the more important to be aware of the hermeneutical key that determines Paul's citation of the Old Testament. Here we are not concerned with Paul's use of the Old Testament in his ethical instruction but with his theological interpretation. When one asks about the "theological center" of the Old Testament, one may state with E. Hirsch *cum grano salis* that at the center of the theology of the Pentateuch as well as the preaching of the Old Testament prophets

---

[38] Rightly L. Goppelt, *Theology of the New Testament* 2:56–57. That the history of ancient Israel is located under the rubric "promise" (ἐπαγγελία) is seen especially in Romans 4:13ff, 9:4ff; Gal 3:14ff; 4:23, 28.

stands the conviction that the Israelite people have been chosen by Yahweh and that this consciousness of their election determines the whole range of forms in which the people of Israel structured itself. Then for Paul's interpretation, by contrast, the definitive idea is that it is not the Old Testament law concerning the people but the gracious act of God revealed through Jesus Christ, not the powerful work in history of the divine covenant of the Old Testament but the direct relation of human beings to God revealed through Christ that opens up the way to understanding the Old Testament tradition. Therefore the specific interpretation of the Law by Paul, including its relation to the holy Scriptures of the Jewish people, receives a fundamental significance, as documented by 2 Corinthians 3 and the doctrine of justification in the major Pauline letters. It was for this reason that Paul never undertook to outline a history of the divine election in which the Christian church would appear as the continuation or supplement to the history of the Jewish people. So also the theologoumenon of "the immutability of God" revealed through Christ does not remove the relation of discontinuity that characterizes Paul's interpretation of the Old Testament, although for Paul the Father of Jesus Christ is indeed at the same time the God of Israel who spoke with the ancestors and acted on their behalf. But the Old Testament concept of Yahweh, the God of the covenant, who had obligated his people to keep the whole, indivisible Torah and who had also executed his will with military force, is considerably different from Paul's picture of the God who has redeemed humanity in Christ and has justified the ungodly. While the concept of the *one* God was no point of controversy at all between the Old and New Testaments, their pictures of this God were quite different and did contribute to the discontinuity between the two Testaments. Nor is the idea of one continuous stream of history documented by the doctrine of creation and the one Creator God who rules all, however much it is presupposed in the Pauline writings (cf. Rom 1:18ff; 1 Cor 8:6.)[39] This doctrine of creation does not have an independent theological function but is rather illuminated by its various relations to the Christ kerygma.[40]

The Christ event is accordingly the decisive point of departure and orientation that shapes all Paul's interpretation of the Old Testament. It is connected just as little to an idea of universal history as to some mathematical point abstracted from this line. Nor is its temporal character characterized completely by referring to the one saving event of the cross and resurrection. Although Paul does not reflect on the *vita Jesu*, he does

---

[39] Cf. below A. I. a. 3.
[40] Cf. Romans 1:18ff: the necessity of the revelation of Christ follows from the guilty involvement of the natural, this-worldly human being, who should be able to recognize God by his works in creation. Romans 8:39: the love of God revealed in Jesus Christ conquers all worldly powers.

presuppose the earthly life of Jesus (cf. Gal 4:4; 1 Cor 11:23). The past history of Jesus Christ does not begin with the incarnation, however but is the past history of the preexistent one who was with God before the creation of the world (Phil 2:6). It is the reality of Christ that transcends and comprehends time that lets the Old Testament be understood as a Christian document, for it is not the Scripture in relation to the Christ event but the Christ event in relation to the Scripture which is the ultimate norm that determines Paul's interpretation of the Bible.[41]

The concept of the preexistence of Christ is more presupposed by Paul than explicitly developed. Alongside Philippians 2:6, especially to be named is the title "Son of God," which implies the pre-temporal existence of the Son in connection with the concept of his being sent into the world (cf. Gal 4:4 "But when the fullness of time had come, God sent his Son, born of a woman, born under the law,..."). So also the designation of Christ as the "image of God" (εἰκὼν τοῦ θεοῦ: 2 Cor 4:4), which suggests the idea of preexistence not only by its connection to Genesis 1:26 but

---

[41]   This approach was carried out consistently by Wilhelm Vischer when he finds Christ already manifest in the Old Testament and is willing to apply the designation "Christian" to the testimony of the church when it acknowledges this unity of the two Testaments; such unity then means the identification of Jesus Christ with the Messiah of Israel (W. Vischer. *The Witness of the Old Testament to Christ* [London: Lutterworth, 1949]). Nonetheless, from the historical perspective the Old Testament is a document of the Jewish faith, so that the differences between Old Testament-Jewish messianology and New Testament Christology cannot be smoothed out.

The matter is seen differently by Rudolf Bultmann, who, to be sure, would like to acknowledge the Old Testament explication of the law as an abiding moral demand, and states that the unconditionedness of its moral demand presupposes that the world is not at human disposal and that human existence is a temporal / historical being in relation to God and the neighbor, and that this is the point of agreement between Old Testament and New Testament faith in God. But he acknowledges no direct revelation of the Word of God in the Old Testament, so that the Old Testament's declarations of grace are bound irrevocably to the people of Israel. Since human existence in the Old Testament perspective is shattered by the collision between its relation to God by virtue of creation and its being bound to history, the Old Testament as a document of the failure of the history of Israel is as a whole no history of revelation. It is rather the case that in it the promise is concretized, the promise that is realized in the New Testament ("The significance of the Old Testament for the Christian Faith," *The Old Testament and Christian Faith*, B. W. Anderson, ed. [New York: Harper & Row, 1963] and "Prophecy and Fulfillment," Claus Westermann, ed., and James Luther Mays, Eng. trans. ed., *Essays on Old Testament Hermeneutics* [Richmond, VA: John Knox, 1963]).

In addition to the hermeneutical approaches named above, the interpretation of the Old Testament can open up possibilities of human self-understanding in connection with the encounter with God it presupposes, especially by analysis of the anthropological structures as they are presented in the Psalms, for example. In interpreting and applying the Old Testament to its own situation, Christian preaching may not disregard the Christ event which is its foundation.

especially through the corresponding ideas in the Philonic doctrine of the Logos (*Spec Leg* 1.81; *Conf* 97; *Her* 231). A significant parallel from the point of view of the history of religions is also found in the Jewish teaching about wisdom. In a manner similar to Christ (1 Cor 8:6), preexistence and the mediation of creation is also affirmed of Sophia.[42] To be sure, Paul is not concerned with the construction of an objective system of history within which the concept of preexistence could be incorporated but the "now" of proclamation and the acceptance of the grace of God fulfills the preexistent reality of the Son of God and actualizes "today" the eschatological reality of the preexistent one.[43]

## 2. The Sophia Tradition

Conzelmann, H. "Die Mutter der Weisheit," *Zeit und Geschichte* (FS, R. Bultmann) Tübingen: J. C. B. Mohr (Paul Siebeck), 1964, 225–234.

Dahl, N. A. "Formgeschichtliche Beobachtungen zur Christusverkündigung in der Gemeindepredigt," *Neutestamentliche Studien für R. Bultmann*, E. Dinkler, ed. BZNW 21. Berlin: W. de Gruyter, 1957², 3–9.

Gese, H. *Lehre und Wirklichkeit in der alten Weisheit: Studien zu den Sprüchen Salomos und zu dem Buche Hiob.* Tübingen: J. C. B. Mohr (Paul Siebeck), 1958.

Küchler, M. *Frühjüdische Weisheitstraditionen.* OBO 26. Freiburg-Göttingen: Vandenhoeck & Ruprecht, 1979

Lietzmann, H. *The Beginnings of the Christian Church.* London: Lutterworth, 1949².

Macrae, G. W. "The Jewish Background of the Gnostic Sophia Myth," *NT* 12 (1970) 86–101.

Rudolph, K. "Sophia und Gnosis," *Altes Testament-Frühjudentum-Gnosis.* K. W. Tröger, ed. Berlin: W. de Gruyter, 1980, 221–237.

Schweizer, E. "Zur Herkunft der Präexistenzvorstellung bei Paulus." *Neotestamentica: deutsche und englische Aufsätze 1951–1963.* Zürich: Zwingli, 1963, 105–109.

Sellin, G. *Der Streit um die Auferstehung der Toten.* FRLANT 138. Göttingen: Vandenhoeck & Ruprecht, 1986.

Stadelmann, H. *Ben Sira als Schriftgelehrter.* WUNT II/6. Tübingen: J. C. B. Mohr (Paul Siebeck), 1980.

von Lips, H. *Weisheitliche Traditionen im Neuen Testament.* WMANT 64. Neukirchen-Vluyn: Neukirchener, 1990.

von Rad, G. *Theology of the Old Testament,* I. New York: Harper & Row, 1962.

Wilckens, U. "σοφία," *TDNT* VII (1966) 465–476, 496–528.

Windisch, H. "Die göttliche Weisheit der Juden und die paulinische Christologie," *Neutestamentliche Studien.* (FS G. Heinrici) UNT 6. Leipzig: J. C. Heinrichs, 1914, 220–234.

The kind of poetic wisdom tradition that goes back to ancient Israelite and general Near Eastern roots also played a significant role in Hellenistic Judaism. Differently than was the case in the literary genre of apocalyp-

---

[42] See below A. I. a. 2. on the Sophia tradition.
[43] Cf. 2 Corinthians 5:16–17; 6:2; Romans 3:26; 5:9, 11; 8:1; 11:30–32; 13:11; Galatians 2:20; 4:9, 29.

tic,[44] the wisdom writings were not the expression of a dualistic orientation in which the inequities of history would be reconciled at the eschaton
but dealt with sayings and speeches that sought to understand the world
of human beings in terms of its orderliness and to mediate reasonable
instructions by which people could come to terms with the problems of
everyday life. Wisdom attempted to bridge the gap between the ideal and
the real and to give insight into the relation between one's deeds and the
way one gets along in the world. In this regard the wisdom literature of the
Old Testament and later times became a constituent element of Jewish
ethics that has influenced New Testament writings in a variety of ways.

A distinction can be made between an "experiential wisdom" devoted
to the basic structures of human social life, and a more didactically oriented wisdom teaching intended to bring people to a higher educational
level.[45] Both types presuppose a variety of given structures within the
Jewish social world.[46]

The theological significance of the wisdom tradition is found in the fact
that it places the ethical awareness of human beings under the claim of
God and measures human ethical conduct by the divine command. After
all is said and done, the beginning of wisdom is still the "fear of the Lord,"
(Prov 1:7; Ps 111:10; Job 28:28). Just as the person led by wisdom acknowledges God's command and turns away from sin (Sir 18:27; cf. Prov
16:17), so also ignorance of the way of the Lord leads to wrong and guilt
(Wis 5:7). The goal is to practice what is reasonable in relations with one's
fellow human beings, corresponding to the conviction that the good is
always the reasonable and practical (Prov 3:1–2; 10:9; 15:10).

The world order, the knowledge of which constitutes the foundation of
wisdom, is ultimately not at human disposal. Thus the rule of wisdom
states that the industrious become rich and the lazy become poor; the rich
receive their deserved happiness in contrast to the poor (Prov 10:4–5, 15;
11:16b; 12:11, 24, 27; 13:18; 14:20; 19:4). Nevertheless, the admonition
is given to be merciful to the poor (Prov 14:21, 31; 17:5; 19:17; 21:13).

---

[44]   E. g. Job, Ecclesiastes, Proverbs, Sirach, Wisdom of Solomon.

[45]   Experiential wisdom is directed to the task of uncovering the hidden order of the
world in order thereby to manage one's own life better. It is important to note in
this connection that such experiential wisdom does not make a claim to ultimate
and absolute truth and validity. This distinguishes wisdom from philosophy, since
a system based on wisdom is constantly open to new experiences of wisdom and
thus in theory can never be thought of as a closed system.

In the case of didactic wisdom one should think of that kind of instruction that
has as its goal to teach people how to overcome their emotions, to practice patience,
so that in self control and the fear of God one can shape one's life in such a way
that it remains constant in good times and in bad. The Joseph story of Genesis 37,
39–50, a story constructed as didactic wisdom, is an instructive example of this
intention. Cf. von Rad, *Theology* 1:431, 440, 454.

[46]   Cf. H. v. Lips, *Weisheitliche Traditionen.*

This would be pointless, if the connection between wealth and human achievement, or between poverty and guilt, were a matter of direct observation that could be calculated. If that were so, then human beings should not interfere with this order of the world that has been established once and for all. On the one hand, the order of the world established by God is not at human disposal; on the other hand, this is not perceived in a fatalistic manner but the examples of wisdom's instruction reflect human responsibility and independent capacity to act.

The theological importance of the wisdom tradition increased for the Jewish people during the postexilic period. This is seen in the caesura between the older preexilic tradition of the "Proverbs of Solomon" (Prov 10–29)[47] in which wisdom sayings are strung together in a series, and the postexilic stratum (Prov 1–9) characterized by the call of *personified wisdom* and her instruction for those who lack understanding (Prov 1:20ff; 8:1ff). Sophia is distinguished from God, since it/she was created by the Spirit of God;[48] it/she goes forth "from the mouth of the Most High" (Sir 24:3) but is presented as an independent figure who wanders through heaven and earth (Sir 24:5–6), looking for a dwelling place among human beings, without being able to find a place to dwell (Sir 24:7; 1 Enoch 42:2). Only in Jacob and in Israel her "inheritance" does she find a home (Sir 24:8b, 10–11). Like the Holy Spirit, she is herself a gift of God (Wis 8:21; 9:1ff; cf. 1 Kings 3:9ff; Job 28:23). She invites to her banquet (Prov 9:1–6). Her goal is the salvation of human beings (Wis 9:18) and the gift of everlasting life, an immortality that brings one near to God (Wis 6:19–20; 8:17).

It is characteristic of Jewish wisdom literature which has been influenced by Hellenism that—in contrast to the priestly writing of the Old Testament—it is not bound to the salvation history of the Jewish people by the creation story but conversely the law given by God to his people is understood in terms of creation.[49] The statements about *wisdom's preexistence* both materially limit and go beyond wisdom's being as one of God's creatures: that wisdom was created before the foundation of the

---

47    Although Solomon is explicitly mentioned as the author only in Proverbs 10:1–22:16 and 25:1–29:27, the whole of chapters 10–29 is probably preexilic.

48    It is certainly the case that the concept of the hypostatization of wisdom is met for the first time in Proverbs 8:22ff; the supposed example in Job 28 is uncertain. On this cf. also H. Lietzmann, *History* 1:99–100; differently M. Hengel, *Judaism and Hellenism* 275–318.

49    Cf. G. von Rad, *Theology* 1:450–451. As Genesis 1 shows, the author of the "Priestly Document" (P) opens up the dimensions of history and thereby of salvation history on the basis of the creation story. According to P, one cannot speak of Israel apart from the theological data concerning creation. Therefore salvation history begins with the act of God in creation. Wisdom theology sees this in a different light: it regards the created world as an object to be critically observed, and with the created world as its point of departure attempts to make a connection to salvation history.

world guarantees that it/she has an existence that transcends the world and that will remain eternally.[50] Although wisdom too is a creature of God, it is still the case that it/she was called into being prior to all the other creatures (Sir 1:4–9). Its/her essence is divine, for "she is a reflection of eternal light, a spotless mirror of the working of God" (Wis 7:26). Consequently she is designated as "God's beloved."[51] Moreover, she can be regarded as a *participant in the creation of the world* (cf. Prov 3:19: "The Lord by wisdom founded the earth; by understanding he established the heavens."), for "wisdom [is] the fashioner of all things" (Wis 7:22; cf. 9:9), and however mysterious her essential being may be, she is clearly associated with the divine creative power (Job 28:25–27). The function of preservation the cosmos is thus attributed to her (Wis 7:27 τὰ πάντα καινίζει). All this makes clear that the Jewish wisdom literature is more interested in the cosmological interpretation of the wisdom concept than in the historical. It is also noticeable that in this connection the Jewish cultus recedes in importance.

In those passages where wisdom is identified with the Torah, it is not the observance of the ceremonial law that is the point at issue but right ethical conduct. Thus the terms "law" and "wisdom" can be interchangeable (Sir 24:23–27; 2 Baruch 38:2; cf. 44:14), or wisdom can be placed over against the nonobservance of the way of the Torah, just as wisdom as the fear of the Lord can be equated with the insight of avoiding evil (Job 28:28), for the words of wisdom teach righteousness (Wis 8:7). This fundamentally means that wisdom teaches what pleases God (Wis 9:9).

The wisdom tradition was more widespread and more varied within Hellenistic Judaism than is apparent in the extant texts. In Aristobulus[52] Jewish thought is fused with the concepts of Greek Stoic cosmology and epistemology. In yet another manner Philo of Alexandria exegetes the wisdom concepts under the influence of syncretistic streams of Hellenistic culture. On the one hand, wisdom is the mediator of revelation, in accord with the Old Testament and Jewish tradition. On the other hand, wisdom is interpreted as a mythological figure, so that lines of connection between Philo and later Gnostic views can be drawn.[53]

---

[50]   Sirach 24:9; Aristobulos in Eusebius, *Preparation for the Gospel* 13.12.10–11.

[51]   Proverbs 8:30 אָמוֹן, which really means "a pampered child;" translated by Luther as "master worker," which presupposes the participation of wisdom in the creation of the world.

[52]   The extant fragments come from the middle of the second century B. C. E.; cf. N. Walter, "Aristobulos," in *Jüdische Schriften aus hellenistisch-römischer Zeit* III. 2 (Gütersloh: Gerd Mohn 1975) 262.

[53]   Cf. Philo *Fug* 105–112: the Old Testament high priest is identified with the λόγος, who has God for his father and Wisdom for his mother. Whether the influence of the mystery religions is relevant here is disputed; cf. U. Wilckens, *TDNT* 7:501 n. 233.

Although a systematic scheme of the Philonic concept of the hypostases cannot be reconstructed[54] and Philo once connects the Logos with a system of five Powers, while another time he describes the Logos as a unity of only two primeval Powers, it is still clear that Philo's speculation proceeds from a concept of God in which God as the absolute Being is completely beyond human knowledge. There is no way that there could be a direct connection between this God and matter, which is thought of as very far down the ontological scale. It is rather the case that God makes use of bodiless forces, thought of as ideas. These are united in a comprehensive world-of-ideas, that can also be thought of as an ideal unity and identified with the concept of the "Logos." The Logos is accordingly the creative instrument of God, who/which stands between God and the world and mediates between the two. It is characteristic of him to have an intercessory function as the advocate of human beings before God; he/she/it is also described with the term "Sophia."

It is in this context within the history of religions that Paul finds himself when he speaks of divine wisdom or adopts wisdom traditions. The hymnic doxology of Romans 11:33–36 is reminiscent of wisdom language and content, when it affirms, in antithesis to current wisdom concepts, the inability of human thought in view of the unsearchable decisions of God. This is related to the immediately preceding v. 32, which affirms that God has had mercy on all even though no one deserves it, since all human beings live in disobedience to God. This fact is not understandable to human thinking and must seem inconceivable to human beings (v. 33). That God saves his creatures without any human achievement evokes the Pauline response and the hymnic doxology. The subject is the riches of divine wisdom. What was said in the Hellenistic Jewish wisdom tradition is also true for Paul: the divine wisdom is the depth of knowledge originally belonging only to itself; it participated in the creation of the world as God's advisor and had a share in the rich treasures of God. Such a wealth of ability to perceive God's ways Paul cannot affirm for human beings, who must rather confess themselves to be sinners before God, and who must take refuge in the "deus absconditus," the One who is now revealed in Jesus Christ.

The doxology that concludes the first main section of the Letter to the Romans thus does not only refer to the mystery of Israel's salvation history (Rom 9–11) but—as made clear by the direct connection with 11:32—to the disobedience of all human beings to the God who shows mercy without any basis in human achievement. Thus the outcome of the first part of Romans is maintained, at the beginning of which stands the proof that no one, neither Gentile nor Jew, can be justified before God by works of

---

[54]  Cf. Lietzmann, *History* 1:95–97

law (1:18–3:20) but that rather human beings can stand before God only by means of a righteousness "through faith for faith" (1:17).

The myth of the preexistent Sophia who reveals herself in this earthly world, though not directly cited by Paul, is apparently presupposed by him in 1 Corinthians 2:6–16. For the wisdom of God, the subject of the apostolic preaching, may not be understood merely as a doctrine about Christ,[55] but appears as the teacher of people who are led by God. She is identified with the Spirit that searches the deep things of God (vv. 10–13). This is in harmony with the Jewish wisdom tradition according to which hypostatized Wisdom is identified with the Spirit of God (Wis 1:4–7) and as such pervades all things, rules and renews the universe, while at the same time instructing those who understand and making them friends of God (Wis 7:21–8:1).

The closeness of the Pauline interpretation of Christology to the Jewish wisdom tradition is not to be overlooked. Just as the ancient wisdom teaching was aware of the concept that wisdom participated in the creation of the world, so Paul seems to take up this idea in 1 Corinthians 8:6, when he says that alongside God Christ is "through all things and we through him." A similar idea probably also motivated 1 Corinthians 10:4. There Exodus 17:6 is referred to in order to show that the people of Israel in the time of its wandering through the wilderness was accompanied by a visible manifestation of Christ. Just as Deuteronomy 30:12ff explains that the commandment given by God is not in heaven or beyond the sea but is near to human beings, so Paul also refers to this passage in his exposition in Romans 10:6–13. The word that stands near to human beings is identified with Christ, in direct verbal dependence on the Deuteronomy passage.

The personal figure of Wisdom, hidden from human beings and identified with the Spirit of God, is a suitable figure to represent preexistence. This interpretation of wisdom bears soteriological traits (1 Cor 2:7, 9). This is seen especially in the way in which it is presupposed that the divine plan of salvation was hidden from the aeons. This means at the same time that, similarly to the Jewish myth of Sophia, the Pauline understanding of wisdom has a cosmic background. To be sure, it is striking that the advent of wisdom in this world is not recognized by all. Thus the "rulers of this world" who "crucified the Lord of glory" (1 Cor 2:8) have no access to it. Their inability to recognize wisdom or even to be blessed with it, is demonstrated in the paradoxical event that they resist the saving wisdom of God. By so doing, and without being aware of it, they carry out the divine act of salvation and contribute to the face that God's saving will comes to fulfillment in the crucifixion. The "archons" are subjected to the act of the

---

[55]  Cf. H. Conzelmann, *1 Corinthians* (Hermeneia. Philadelphia: Fortress, 1975) 88 n. 69.

divine wisdom, while in the same moment they think that they have disposed of it. The worldly powers hostile to the divine wisdom are obviously identical with the demonic cosmic powers that exercise their authority through this-worldly authorities. To their essential being there belongs not only their ignorance of the revelation of divine wisdom in the Christ event but associated with it is an anti-God activity that found its high point in the crucifixion of Jesus. Their actions presuppose an underestimation/misjudgment of the saving plan of God expressible in terms of wisdom and manifest in the Crucified One, and is an indication of an onticly-determined manner of thinking that finds expression in the dualistic juxtaposition of the heavenly and earthly world, of divine wisdom and the demonic world, a kind of thought found not only in apocalypticism but also in wisdom. Therefore the concept of *descensus*, the descent of divine wisdom into the earthly, anti-God world is also necessarily implied, although the consequences that would be drawn from this by the later dualistic system of Christian Gnosticism, have not yet been made (cf. John 1:5, 11).

It is disputed whether in 1 Corinthians 2:6ff Paul presupposes the scheme of revelation that can be reconstructed for the Pauline school, which was possibly an element of their oral instruction. This schema is presented by N. A. Dahl in two variants:[56] Variation 1: The mystery once hidden from the world has now been revealed (Col 1:26–27; Eph 3:4–7, 8–11; Rom 16:25–26); Variation 2: That which was present before the foundation of the world has now been revealed at the end of the times (2 Tim 1:9–11; Titus 1:2–3; 1 Pet 1:18–21 and elsewhere). Presupposed here as the background is the pre-Pauline (and thus not genuinely Pauline) antithesis of the hiddenness and the revelation of the mystery of God. It is still possible that the specific stamp given to this tradition in the deuteropauline letters was encouraged by Paul himself. To be sure, Paul, in distinction from the deuteropauline authors, binds the revelation of divine wisdom to the cross event (1 Cor 2:2, 8) but he also does distinguish between elementary knowledge and deeper wisdom (2:6, 14–15), and he does not (yet) bring the pregnant juxtaposition "once / now" into a context having to do with knowledge, but the relationship to the later revelatory schema is not to be disputed. It becomes visible in the emphatic temporal connection of the juxtaposition of the hiddenness and revelation of divine wisdom (cf. 2:7).

Traces of Hellenistic Jewish wisdom tradition are visible already at the beginning of Paul's debate with the Corinthian opponents, when 1 Corinthians 1:17–31 places the foolishness of the cross of Jesus Christ over against the wisdom speech of the Corinthian pneumatics who are characterized by their rhetorical skill (1:17; 2:4). The saving "power of God" (1:18) that has been manifested in the cross event is in Paul's view explicitly not expressed in the kind of wisdom speech cultivated in Corinth. The Pauline reading of the matter becomes understandable when it is perceived what the wisdom speech in the "original" sense was concerned to do.

---

[56] N. A. Dahl, "Formgeschichtliche Beobachtungen."

While the Corinthian wisdom speech was oriented to immanent reality subject to examination by human reason, what Paul was concerned with was not a matter of human understanding of given empirical reality but a matter of the mystery of the revelation of God that takes place in history. If this is something that can only be grasped by faith, then it is something that cannot be apprehended by the instrument of a human doctrine of wisdom (1 Cor 2:4–5). To be sure, Paul himself emphasizes over against the Corinthians that he speaks with wisdom but he fills this term with different content than do the Greeks. While their wisdom is "of this world", the apostle speaks in contrast of the wisdom of God (1 Cor 2:6–7). Ancient philosophy had the goal of pressing forward in thought until it attained the knowledge of God but in Paul's understanding its attempt to explicate the transcendent in terms of immanence has been completely shattered. The inability to perceive the wisdom of God that preceded, surrounds, and preserves the world (1 Cor 1:21) is seen in the fact that the powers of this world nailed the Lord of glory to the cross (1 Cor 2:8). After human wisdom had thus itself demonstrated its own poverty, the salvation of humanity by God is introduced not through the medium of human rational possibilities but through the proclamation of the crucified Christ that appears as foolishness (1 Cor 1:21, 23). This wisdom that had previously been hidden (1 Cor 2:7) is now revealed to those who have been predestined to accept it. The divine wisdom thus makes possible what is denied to human wisdom: the knowledge of God that brings salvation (1 Cor 2:10–11). In this is reflected the adoption of Old Testament understandings of wisdom, since the role of mediator is attributed to wisdom who makes known God's saving power to human beings.

It is thus here presupposed that on the one hand the world finds itself "in the wisdom of God,"[57] while on the other hand the realm of the divine wisdom stands over against the sphere of the cosmos as two exclusive territories. For it is characteristic of the cosmos understood in this way that it places its trust not in God but in itself and becomes guilty of evaluating itself too highly. For the revelation of the saving of act of Christ, in contrast, it is characteristic that it does not occur in accordance with the categories of wisdom already present but paradoxically in the destruction of Jesus on the cross. Thus the Crucified One becomes to the earthly world a scandal and foolishness to Jews and Gentiles without distinction, but to those who believe he is the power and wisdom of God (1:23–24). While the predominate aspect here may be a purely conceptual identification of Christ and the wisdom of God, and not the equating of Christ with

---

[57]  1 Corinthians 1:21: ἐν τῇ σοφίᾳ τοῦ θεοῦ has a local meaning; this is not to be completely excluded when the ἐν is taken adverbially as expressing the accompanying circumstance of the failure of the cosmos to recognize God's wisdom (so A. M. Wedderburn, "ἐν τῇ σοφίᾳ τοῦ θεοῦ—1 Kor 1,21" ZNW 64 (1973) 132–134.

hypostatized wisdom,[58] it is still the case that here Paul stands on the ground of a preexistence Christology. This is also indicated by other parallels to the personal figure of Wisdom found in Hellenistic Judaism, so that the Sophia tradition of Judaism is to be evaluated as a significant element of Pauline or prepauline Christology. Moreover, the parenesis of the Pauline letters is characterized by ethical features similar to those typical of Jewish wisdom tradition. These are indirectly related to the concept of personal wisdom, and in addition stand within the framework of the complex of the Hellenistic Jewish stream of tradition that had provided the basic building blocks of Paul's thought, as mentioned frequently in the preceding discussion.

## 3. The Jewish Ethic

Dodd, C. H. "The Ethics of the Pauline Epistles," E.H. Sneath, ed., *The Evolution of Ethics*. New Haven: Yale University Press, 1927, 293–326.
Lohse, E. *Theological Ethics of the New Testament*. Minneapolis: Fortress, 1991.
Merk, O. *Handeln aus Glauben: Die Motivierungen der paulinischen Ethik*. MThSt 5. Marburg: N. G. Elbert, 1968.
Niebuhr, K.-W. *Gesetz und Paränese*. WUNT II 28. Tübingen: J. C. B. Mohr (Paul Siebeck), 1987.
Reinmuth, E. *Geist und Gesetz*. ThA 44. Berlin: Evangelische Verlagsanstalt, 1985.
Schnackenburg, R. *Die sittliche Botschaft des Neuen Testaments*. HThK.S 1+2. Freiburg: Herder, 1986, 1988.
Schrage, W. *The Ethics of the New Testament*. Philadelphia: Fortress, 1988.
Schulz, S. *Neutestamentliche Ethik*. Zürich: Calver, 1987.
Strecker, G. "Autonome Sittlichkeit und das Proprium der christlichen Ethik bei Paulus," *ThLZ* 104 (1979) 865–872.
Strecker, G. "Strukturen einer neutestamentlichen Ethik," *ZThK* 75 (1978) 117–146.
Wendland, H. D. *Ethik des Neuen Testaments*. GNT 4. Göttingen: Vandenhoeck & Ruprecht, 1970.
Wibbing, S. *Die Tugend und Lasterkataloge im Neuen Testament*. BZNW 25. Berlin: W. de Gruyter, 1959.

Among the history-of-religions presuppositions of Paul's theology there belongs also the forms and contents of the ethic that occupies a considerable proportion of the Pauline letters. Thus the second major part of the Letter to the Romans is exclusively concerned with ethical-parenetical

---

[58] Questions of detail remain open. For example, in 1 Corinthians 1:24, 30 does Paul intend an identification of Christ with the personified wisdom of God? (Cf. H. Windisch, "Die göttliche Weisheit" 225). Is E. Schweizer, "Präexistenzvorstellung" 109, correct that Paul is dependent on the concept of preexistence in Jewish wisdom speculation and not on an older myth? It is to be noted that the concept of preexistence belongs to a broad stream of Hellenistic and Jewish thought. The hymn in Philippians as well as the Pauline ἐν Χριστῷ Christology also exhibit parallels to the Hellenistic Jewish wisdom tradition and cast further light on the texts discussed above. This applies no less, of course, in regard to the broader horizon of Hellenistic Jewish syncretism as illustrated by Philo and others.

matters (Rom 12:1–15:33). The same is true of the Letter to the Galatians (Gal 5:1–6:10). Since the other letters also go into concrete relationships in the churches, in them too the hortatory and monitory element is of considerable importance. For example, both 1 Corinthians and Philemon are entirely dedicated to parenetic themes. Likewise, parenesis takes up much of the space of Philippians (Phil 1:27–2:18; 3:2–4:9), and an example of the early form of the Pauline ethic is presented by the parenetic section of 1 Thessalonians (4:1–5:22).

Is the Pauline ethic a *Christian* ethic? In view of the theological and sociological context, this question is clearly to be answered in the affirmative. The ethical norms for the Christian life apply within the sphere of Christ; they are grounded in the Christ event, by the indicative that speaks of the redemptive act of Christ. This event is the basis of the imperative of the new life.[59] Paul's ethic is characterized by the announcement of salvation from which the imperative of the Christian life is derived. It is still necessary, however, to note that in terms of detailed parenesis there is not a great difference between Paul's teaching and that of his religious environment. To be sure, it is not possible to find an ancient parallel for each item in Paul's ethical instruction. But it is still true in general that there is extensive agreement between Paul and the ethics of the Hellenistic world in both general principles and particular instructions. Many of Paul's ethical statements could also have been made within the non-Christian Jewish or Hellenistic world.

With the Jewish tradition Paul shares the faith in the one God, the creator.[60] Even though an isolated *doctrine of creation* is not developed and statements of creation theology appear primarily in a Christological-soteriological context (Rom 4:17; 9:19ff; 2 Cor 4:6), it is still clearly the case that the apostle confesses his faith in the one God of the Old Testament as the creator of the world. Thus Jewish norms can be derived from their connection with creation. Since God's invisible being can be recognized from his works in creation, the pagan world must have intentionally avoided accepting this knowledge that can perceive God as the "prima causa" of the cosmos. Instead, the pagan world devoted itself to polytheism and immorality (Rom 1:18–21). Although the influence of Hellenistic Jewish apologetic is not to be overlooked in this regard,[61] such a "natural

---

[59]    Cf. Galatians 5:25; Romans 6:1ff.

[60]    It is to be noted, however, that the Old Testament-Jewish concept of God the creator overlaps Hellenistic-Stoic teaching; cf. Epictetus, *Dissertations* 1.9.7 (τὸν θεὸν ποιητὴν ἔχειν καὶ πατέρα).

[61]    On this cf. E. J. Goodspeed, *A History of Early Christian Literature* (Chicago: Univ. of Chicago Press, 1942) 129ff. It is to be noticed that Romans 1:21 (γνόντες) affirms not only the possibility but the reality, of the knowledge of God among the Gentiles. This corresponds to an interpretation widespread in ancient Judaism, e. g. Jos *Apion* 2.190ff; 1 Enoch 2–5; 2 Baruch 54:17–18; cf. E. Reinmuth, *Geist und Gesetz* 43ff.

theology" has no independent function but is subordinated in the context to Paul's line of argument in which the Gentiles have fallen under God's wrath and their guilty conduct means they cannot be justified on the basis of any human accomplishment. Thus Romans 2:12–16 develops the argument: both Gentiles and Jews stand under the wrath of God (Rom 2:5, 9–11), for the demand of the law has been known by them also. This is a reality given in nature itself (2:14: φύσει τὰ τοῦ νόμου ποιῶσιν), because "the work of the law is written in their hearts." This is the testimony of their consciences, as it is of their thoughts that both accuse and excuse them (2:15). It is thus clear that the universal cosmic rulership of God the creator (cf. also 1 Cor 10:26 / Ps 24:1) corresponds to the general obligation of all humanity to obey the law of God given on Sinai or in nature.

There can be no doubt that this grounding of ethical statements is shaped not only by the Hellenistic Jewish tradition that is presupposed but also by dependence on the Stoic ethic, especially by the folk morality practiced in daily life. This is indicated not only by the fundamental obligation derived from the cosmic foundation of the law which has a "natural theology" as its presupposition as expressed in Romans 1:18ff but also by the individual commands. As an example Paul sets forth the binding norm of the "natural" over against "unnatural" sexual relations (Rom 1:26, φύσις). So also Paul bases his teaching on proper hair length on the "teaching of nature" (1 Cor 11:14–15). In the motivation and derivation of the Pauline ethic, there is an interlocking of elements from the Old Testament-Jewish faith in God the creator of the world and the Stoic doctrine of the orderly working of the cosmos by natural law. This also implies that the line between authentic Christian and non-Christian ethical statements is not to be drawn too clearly.[62]

The all-encompassing presence of the creator God makes it possible that *individual ethical instructions* can be traced back to the Old Testament or derived from it. They are connected with direct quotations that contain an ethical directive, for example Romans 12:19 ("never avenge yourselves" is supported by citing Deut 32:35 "Vengeance is mine, and recompense"). The collection Paul is taking for the poor in Jerusalem is motivated in 2 Corinthians 8:15 by Exodus 16:18 (the mutual equalizing of the amount of manna collected), and the standard is applied which has

---

[62] One example: While it is true enough that the term "lowliness, humility" (ταπεινο-φροσύνη) in the secular literature of the first century, including Josephus, was basically used with a negative connotation (W. Schrage, *The Ethics of the New Testament*, [Edinburgh: T. & T. Clark, 1988] 201), it is also the case that "being subject to one another" can also be a basic principle of Gentile ethics (cf. PsCallisth 1.22.4; Plut *Mor* II 142 E), so that "subordination" as such is not specifically Christian, and despite Philippians 2:8 has not only christological foundations but also bases that were adapted from general sociological contexts.

been provided by the God who himself gives freely (Ps 112:9, "He has distributed freely, he has given to the poor." In particular, the wisdom tradition of Greek speaking Judaism offers extensive material that has found a place in the ethical admonitions of the apostle. This is elucidated in the parenetic section Romans 12:9–21.[63] This is where the so-called *catalogues of vices and virtues* belong,[64] that for the most part arrange lists of moral offenses or (less often) virtues; they by no means reflect primarily the personal experience of the apostle but presuppose a long background in the history of the tradition.[65] The substance of the obligations, which are primarily social rather than religious, go back to the tradition of Hellenistic Judaism (possibly via an intermediate Christian level). They are mostly untouched by Paul's own literary interventions. Characteristic for the influence of Jewish-apologetic tradition in such catalogues are "immorality" (πορνεία) and "idolatry" (εἰδωλολατρία), since in the current understanding pagan polytheism was typified by "whoredom" (Deut 31:16; Isa 1:21; Wis 14:12–31), and the worship of idols always coincided with immorality (Sib Or III 29:ff). Thus in the vice catalogues immorality and idolatry are sometimes listed side by side (1 Cor 6:9; cf. 5:11). Also "licentiousness" (ἀσέλγεια) is considered synonymous with pagan worship (2 Cor 12:21; Gal 5:19–20). Doubtless the high value placed on marriage has Jewish roots (cf. Matt 5:31–32par; 1 Cor 7:2ff; with reference to Gen 1:28; 2:24).

First Corinthians is a good example of the formative influence of Jewish ethics on Pauline parenesis. Without interpreting the Old Testament Torah in a static sense, the general command to keep the "commandments of God" (ἐντολαὶ θεοῦ; 1 Cor 7:9) points back to the law of Moses. The Decalogue of the Old Testament is cited as binding on Christians. Alongside the *Decalogue*, the *command to love the neighbor* is cited as "fulfilling the law" and its summary (Rom 13:9–10; cf. Lev 19:18). In other contexts too, the fundamental meaning of the command to love one's fellow human beings appears as a summary of God's demand (1 Cor 13:1–13). Differently than in the Synoptic tradition (Matt 22:37–40par), Paul does not here make the connection to the command to love God (Deut 6:5). But the Christian led by the Spirit lives by the experience of the love

---

[63] Cf. in particular Romans 12:15 / Sirach 7:39 (7:34 LXX); Romans 12:16 / Proverbs 3:7; Romans 12:17 / Proverbs 3:4; 12:19; Deuteronomy 32:35; Romans 12:20/ Proverbs 25:21–22.

[64] Romans 1:29–31; 13:13; 1 Corinthians 5:10–11, 6:9–10; Galatians 5:19–23; cf. also Colossians 3:5–8, 12–14par; Mark 7:21–22par; Revelation 9:21; 21:8; 22:15.

[65] The beginnings are found already in the Old Testament (Hos 4:1–2; Jer 7:9; Prov 6:17ff). Cf. Wisdom 8:7; 14:24–25; 4 Maccabees 1:18–30; Testament of Issachar 7:2–6; Testament of Asher 2:5ff; 5:1; so also in Philo (Sacr 22; 27; Op 73; All 1.86) and in the popular philosophy (Epictetus Diss II 16.5; III 2.3.14; III 22.13; Diss Frgm IV.XIV; Plut LibEduc 13 A; Dio Or LXVI 1; LXIX 6).

of God revealed in Christ (Rom 5:5), just as the community as a whole can be described as "beloved" by God (ἀγαπητός; ἠγαπημένοι in 1 Thess 1:4). The agape-event sets people free to love God (Rom 8:28). Here are found the closest points of contact to the first table of the Decalogue, which is not cited by Paul. The center of gravity of the Pauline ethic lies, however, in the "law of Christ" with the charge to bear the "burdens" of Christian brothers and sisters (Gal 6:2) and by such a realization of the command to love the neighbor to fulfill "the whole law" (Gal 5:14).

When according to the Pauline understanding the love commandment not only provides a modus operandi for the Christian life but—for example, by the willingness to sacrifice oneself and the renunciation of egoistic self-realization that it includes—a drive toward concrete expressions of this command, the preparation is thereby given for a *programmatic separation between the ceremonial and the moral law*. Not only in the later major Pauline letters in which Paul radicalizes and systematizes his critique of the Law in connection with his message of justification but from the beginning of his apostolate to the Gentiles the apostle no longer advocates the necessity of keeping the Old Testament-Jewish law for salvation, which of course had already implicitly been annulled as the means of salvation by the Christian confession of the earliest Christian community in Jerusalem. His apostolic ethical instruction has as its subject matter without exception the eschatological moral law interpreted as the demand of God. This had already been anticipated in Diaspora Judaism. Philo of Alexandria had already relativized the obligatory nature of the ceremonial law by his thoroughgoing allegorization of the Mosaic tradition (*Conf* 190; *Sobr* 33). So also the author of the Letter of Aristeas places the commands "that have to do with piety and righteousness" above the Old Testament-Jewish purity laws, which he regards as merely having the function of preserving the outstanding importance of Judaism in comparison with other religions.[66]

The nuanced position that Paul adopts to the problem of the Old Testament law (cf. Rom 7:1–25a), especially the fundamental significance of the love command, makes clear that the Old Testament is not the only basis for Paul's ethical orientation. The apostle falls back on the accepted norms of his social environment.[67] Not least, the confidence motivated by

---

[66] *Arist* 128ff, 131. D. J. Moo rightly emphasizes that with the term νόμος Paul mostly indicates the unity of the Torah and does not make any distinction between the moral law and the ceremonial law ("'Law,' 'Works of the Law,' and Legalism in Paul," *WThJ* 45 [1983] 73–100). On the other hand, it should not be disputed that Paul *de facto* does not present the ceremonial law of the Old Testament as binding on Christians, though it does seem clear that he does this with regard to the moral law (cf. Rom 13:8–10; Gal 5:13ff).

[67] Cf. 1 Corinthians 11:16, where "custom" appears as a binding ethical norm; cf. also the role of "conscience," in e. g. Romans 13:5 and 1 Corinthians 10:25ff.

the Spirit relativizes the traditional casuistic legal prescriptions—in this Paul and his Corinthian opponents are in agreement— and is an expression of apostolic authority and freedom. The independence from the Jewish legal tradition is seen, on the one hand, in the juxtaposition of the state of the circumcised and the uncircumcised and, on the other hand, in keeping the divine commands (1 Cor 7:19). The Christian community overcomes the barrier that separates Jews and Greeks (Gal 3:28); the christologically motivated consciousness of freedom is characterized by the conviction "that nothing is unclean in itself; but it is unclean for anyone who thinks it unclean" (Rom 14:14). Thus Paul can agree with the principle advocated by those causing the trouble in Corinth that "All things are lawful," but adds the qualification, "all things are not beneficial." (1Cor 10:23). Christian freedom limits itself by its awareness of responsibility for the neighbor and for society. By such self-limitation Christian freedom unmistakably renounces every form of early Christian "self realization."

## b) Gentile-Hellenistic Influences

Aune, D. *The New Testament in Its Literary Environment*. LEC 8. Philadelphia: Westminster, 1987.

Berger, K. "Apostelbrief und apostolische Rede. Zum Formular frühchristlicher Briefe," *ZNW* 65 (1974) 190–231.

Betz, H. D. *Der Apostel Paulus und die sokratische Tradition*. BHTh 45. Tübingen: J. C. B. Mohr (Paul Siebeck), 1972.

Betz, H. D. *Galatians*. Hermeneia. Philadelphia: Fortress, 1979.

Betz, H. D. *Paulinische Studien*. GAufs. III. Tübingen: J. C. B. Mohr (Paul Siebeck), 1994.

Bultmann, R. *Primitive Christianity in its Contemporary Setting*.London and New York: Thames and Hudson, 1956.

Bultmann, R. *Der Stil der paulinischen Predigt und die kynisch-stoische Diatribe*. FRLANT 13. Göttingen: Vandenhoeck & Ruprecht, 1910 (Reprinted with an introductory word by Hans Hübner, Göttingen: Vandenhoeck & Ruprecht, 1984).

Classen, C. J. "Paulus und die antike Rhetorik," *ZNW* 82 (1991) 1–33.

Hellholm, D. Paulus von Tarsos—Zum Problem der hellenistischen Ausbildung, Manuskript 1992; Norwegian Version, "Paulus Fra Tarsos. Til spørsmålet om Paulus' hellenistiske utdannelse," T. Eide and T.Hägg, eds., *Dionysos og Apollon. Religion og samfunn i antikkens Hellas* (Skrifter utgitt av det norske institutt i Athen 1). Bergen, 1989, 259–282.

Prümm, K. *Religionsgeschichtliches Handbuch für den Raum der altchristlichen Umwelt*. Rome: Päpstliches Bibelinstitut, 1954.

Schmeller, T. *Paulus und die "Diatribe." Eine vergleichende Stilinterpretation*. NTA NF 19. Münster: Aschendorff, 1987.

Schmidt, K. L. "Paulus und die antike Welt," K.H. Rengstorf, ed., *Das Paulusbild in der neueren deutschen Forschung*. WdF 24. Darmstadt: Wissenschaftliche Buchgesellschaft, 1982[3], 214–245.

Schoon-Janssen, J. *Umstrittene 'Apologien' in den Paulusbriefen*. GTA 45. Göttingen: Vandenhoeck & Ruprecht, 1991.

Stowers, St. K. *The Diatribe and Paul's Letter to the Romans.* SBL.DS 57. Chico (Cal.): Scholars Press, 1981.

If the pre-Christian Paul is to be located within the framework of Hellenistic Judaism, this means that a clear separation cannot be made between authentically-Jewish and authentically-Hellenistic elements of his theology. To be sure, in his youth Paul had received an education that included both Jewish-Pharisaic instruction and pagan Greek and Hellenistic literary instruction. The latter is indicated by the (only) text that the apostle cites from sophisticated Greek literature, 1 Corinthians 15:33, a verse from the Greek comedic poet Menander (4th century B. C. E.), from his comedy *Thais*:

Φθείρουσιν ἤθη χρηστὰ ὁμιλίαι κακαί: "Bad company ruins good morals."

This is an iambic trimeter, consisting of six iambs (˘-), in which each two form a meter.[68] The quotation stands within a context of Pauline parenesis; it illustrates that Christians must not be conformed to the world and warns in particular against associating with those who deny the resurrection. It documents that fact that Paul not only grew up in a Hellenistic, Greek-speaking context but also had some familiarity with Greek literature.

A different problem is presented by the question of the manner in which Paul's literary formation and theological world of ideas was influenced by his Hellenistic environment. So far as his style of argument in the Pauline letters is concerned, Rudolf Bultmann had already analyzed Pauline rhetoric in his licentiate thesis and had attempted to prove that in his letters Paul had adopted the speech forms of the Cynic-Stoic popular philosophy. Even though the details remain disputed, since the concept and content of the "diatribe" have by no means been established with certainty and there was no such thing as "the" diatribe, we may still assume as our point of departure that Paul's linguistic style was influenced by the didactic style of the pagan (wandering) philosophers. Among such stylistic elements are word plays, rhetorical questions, parallelisms, antitheses, metaphors, and the introduction of objections of fictive opponents that are rejected with the cry μὴ γένοιτο ("may that never be").[69]

With regard to the Letter to the Galatians is to be asked whether it can be understood in terms of the eighteenth type of the τύποι ἐπιστολικοί of

---

[68] An iamb consists of a short and a long syllable; six iambs make 3 meters, or 1 trimeter. Other citations from Greek poets in the New Testament (Acts 17:28 and Titus 1:12) are not to be attributed to Paul.

[69] A. J. Malherbe, "μη γενοιτο in the Diatribe and Paul," HThR 73 (1980) 231–240; see also his *Moral Exhortation: A Greco-Roman Sourcebook* LEC 4 (Philadelphia: Westminster, 1986). See also J. Schoon-Janssen, *Umstritten "Apologien"* 82ff.

Ps.-Demetrius as an "apologetic document,"[70] or whether it is the case that differing letter forms have had their influence. The attempt by means of rhetorical analysis and epistolographical comparison to classify the Pauline letters clearly within the framework of ancient letter types has not yet succeeded, since we are lacking an accepted theory of ancient letter writing for the time of Paul. So also the frequently-used term "friendship letter" is too general to designate the distinctiveness of the Pauline letters to churches. It is not to be disputed, however, that the letters of the apostle have been influenced by the form of ancient letters in general. And even if Paul follows the oriental-Jewish formula in his letter prescripts, Hellenistic influences are not to be overlooked, just as echoes of the Greek letter form are found in the conclusions of his letters.[71]

The influence of Hellenistic thought on the theology of Paul is to be inferred especially from three problem areas of the history of religions, areas that are important not only for the language but also for the thought of Paul, even if direct genetic lines of connection may not always be drawn.

## 1.  The Mystery Religions

Barrett C. K. *The New Testament Background: Selected Documents*. San Francisco: Harper and Row, 1989².

Boring, M. E., K. Berger and C. Colpe, eds. *Hellenistic Commentary to the New Testament*. Nashville: Abingdon, 1995

Burkert, W. *Ancient Mystery Cults*. Boston: Harvard University Press, 1987.

Cumont, F. *The Oriental Religions in Roman Paganism*. Chicago: Open Court, 1911.

Klauck, H. J. *Herrenmahl und hellenistischer Kult*. NTA NF 15. Münster: Aschendorff, 1982.

Nilsson, M. P. *The Dionysiac Mysteries of the Hellenistic and Roman Age*. New York: Arno, 1957.

Nock, A. D. *Christianisme et Hellénisme*. LD 77. Paris 1973.

Nock, A. D. *Hellenistic Mysteries and Christian Sacraments, Essays on Religion and the Ancient World II*. Oxford: Oxford University Press, 1972, 791–820.

Reitzenstein, R. *Hellenistic Mystery-Religions: Their Basic Ideas and Significance*. Pittsburgh: Pickwick, 1978.

Wagner, G. *Das religionsgeschichtliche Problem von Röm 6:1–11*. AThANT 39. Zürich-Stuttgart: Calwer, 1962.

Wedderburn, A. J. M. *Baptism and Resurrection. Studies in Pauline Theology against Its Graeco-Roman Background*. WUNT 44. Tübingen: J. C. B. Mohr (Paul Siebeck), 1987.

---

[70]  So H. D. Betz, *Apostel Paulus* 40. Ps.-Demetrius (2 cent. BCE—1 cent. CE). There is considerable variation in the dating of the person and work of Ps.-Demetrius. The similarity to other Byzantine letter writers permits the assumption that the anonymous author lived in the late imperial period (cf. F. Wehrli, ed., *Die Schule des Aristoteles. Texte und Kommentar*, Heft IV. *Demetrios von Phaleron* [Basel-Stuttgart: Schwab & Co. Verlag, 1968²] 88).

[71]  Cf. G. Strecker, *History of New Testament Literature* 50–56.

Richard Reitzenstein affirmed a direct dependence of Paul on the ancient
mystery cults and attempted to prove this especially for Paul's dualistic
anthropology. Thereby theses of the history of religions school were taken
up and elaborated according to which early Christianity was very dependent on the mystery religions and may itself in the ancient world have
represented a variety of mystery cult piety.

In the Greek world were found mystery cults of Eleusis, Samothrace,
and others, not least the cult of Dionysus. In the Hellenistic period they
were found in all areas of the Roman Empire. From Phrygia came the cult
of Cybele and Attis, who had originally been a Syrian deity; from Syria
came the cult of Adonis and Atargatis ("the Syrian Goddess"); from Egypt
came the cult of Isis and Osiris. In later times the Persian Mithras cult
became important, especially as the cult of Roman soldiers.

The gods and goddesses of the mystery cults are essentially vegetation
deities, personifications of the growth and decay that takes place in nature.
A mystery drama pictures the dying and rising of the deity. The cult makes
present the destiny of the god, which is replicated in the experience of the
candidate when he or she is initiated into the cult and then ascends
through the various levels of initiation to the highest degree, that of the
"perfect" (τέλειοι). The goal of the religious experience of one initiated into
the mystery cult is divinization (ὁμοίωσις θεῷ). This is facilitated by the
mystery sacraments. This is illustrated by the "Taurobolium," the pouring
of the blood of an ox over the initiates,[72] or the initiatory rites of the Attis
or Osiris cults, which manifest a series of parallels to Christian baptism.
The latter involve an anointing, and the priest calls out to the initiate:

> Rejoice, you initiates; the god is saved; so also salvation from trouble is granted
> to us.[73]

That the priest of the Osiris cult does not declare that salvation has
already occurred for the initiate is reminiscent of Romans 6:1ff: in Paul's
view the believer, like the initiate in the mystery cult, participates sacramentally in the death and resurrection of Christ. This by no means involves a magical incorporation into the deity. It is rather the case that the
mystery cults also know, in a way that corresponds to the Pauline eschatological reservation, a dialectic that determines the life of the initiate. In
this earthly life there is no absolute "perfection;" for the τέλειοι also, an
anthropological dualism plays the decisive role.

A further important parallel consists in the fact that sacred meals were
also celebrated in the mystery cults. This is what facilitates the deification

---

[72]   Cf. Prudentius, *Peristephanon* 10.
[73]   Cf. Firm Mat ErrProfRel 22.1.

of the initiates. After the sacred meal, the worshipper of Attis makes the confession:

> I have eaten from the drum, I have drunk from the cymbal, I have become an initiate of Attis.[74]

The parallel is found in 1 Corinthians 11:23ff: in each case it is a matter of food and drink, the initiate approaches the cultic deity by means of the meal, there follows an incorporation into the cultic community and the goal is "being taken out of the worldly sphere," the liberation from sin and mortality.

To be sure, the parallels of the Christian sacraments to the mystery cults should not be overestimated. Christian baptism was derived primarily from the baptism of John the Baptist; on this basis alone it is to be considered primarily an eschatological sacrament. And the Lord's Supper points back to the life of Jesus in which Jesus' last meal with his disciples is reflected. No analogous historical reference is known in the mystery cults. The mystery drama is an unhistorical myth, even if it portrays the epic narrative of the destiny of the cultic hero. In contrast, for the celebration of the early Christian sacraments the reference to the Christ event that happened in the world of space and time is constitutive. Like the kerygma, so also the Christian sacraments are anchored in history. Such a "historical reservation" keeps early Christian piety prior to and alongside of Paul from being identified with a mystery piety. On the other hand, the mystery cults are very important for understanding Pauline theology. While from the point of view of the history of religions they cannot be considered the origin of Pauline ideas, they are still significant as analogies to Pauline theology. They are thus helpful for understanding particular theological vocabulary,[75] as well as providing basic elements in the structure of Pauline anthropology, for instance as it is expressed in the relation of the believer to Christ by dying and rising with him as well as in the dialectic of Christian existence. The gift of salvation that comes to the participant in the mystery religions has a strongly sacramental-substantial character. This should be included in reflections on the analogies between the mystery cults and Paul's own views.[76]

---

[74] Cf. Firm Mat ErrProfRel 18.1 (cf. Clement of Alexandria Prot II 15).

[75] E. g. for τέλειος: cf. 1 Corinthians 2:6 and Philippians 3:15; for σωτηρία, Romans 1:16; for πνευματικός, cf. e. g. 1 Corinthians 2:13.

[76] Cf. the ontological reflections that Paul articulates in 1 Corinthians 15:44 regarding the "spiritual body" (σῶμα πνευματικόν). It is disputed whether the contrast between πνεῦμα and ψυχή in 1 Corinthians 15 goes back to "Hellenistic ideas of rebirth in the mystery religions" and has a particular point of contact in the initiatory prayer of the Mithras liturgy, as supposed by R. Reitzenstein, *Mysterienreligion* 70–77. For a critique of this view, cf. F. W. Horn, *Das Angeld des Geistes* 192–194.

## 2. Stoicism

Bonhoeffer, A. *Epictet und die Stoa: Untersuchungen zur stoischen Philosophie*. Stuttgart: F. Enke, 1890 (Stuttgart-Bad Cannstatt 1968).
Bonhoeffer, A. *Epiktet und das Neue Testament*. RVV 10. Giessen: Frommann, 1911.
Braun, H. "Die Indifferenz der Welt bei Paulus und Epiktet," Braun, H., *Gesammelte Studien zum Neuen Testament und seiner Umwelt*. Tübingen: J. C. B. Mohr (Paul Siebeck), 1971³, 159–167.
Erskine, A. *The Hellenistic Stoa: Political Thought and Action*. Ithaca: Cornell, 1990.
Pohlenz, M. *Die Stoa: Geschichte einer geistigen Bewegung I-II*. Göttingen: Vandenhoeck & Ruprecht, 1984⁶, 1980⁵.
Pohlenz, M. *Grundfragen der stoischen Philosophie*. AGG III 26. Göttingen: Vandenhoeck & Ruprecht, 1940.
Texts:
Barrett, C. K. and C. J. Thornton, *The New Testament Background: Selected Documents*, San Francisco: Harper & Row, 1989, 80–94.
Leipoldt, J. und Grundmann, W. *Umwelt des Urchristentums II*. Berlin: Evangelische Verlagsanstalt, 1965, 315–333.

The Stoic philosophy that was founded by Zenon about 310 B.C.E. in Athens and whose chief advocates in the New Testament period were Epictetus and Seneca is based on a specific interpretation of nature (φύσις), namely of the cosmos enlivened by πνεῦμα. The world-logos is revealed in the physical world as the deity that determines the order of the world, and does this to such a degree that the two can almost be identified: the deity is the cosmos, the cosmos is the deity! It is the task of human beings to adjust to this given order of the world, for the world-logos is providence (πρόνοια); by establishing the law of nature, it subjects everything that happens to inevitable destiny (ἀνάγκη or εἱμαρμένη). The Stoic's goal is to harmonize his or her life with these necessities (κατὰ φύσιν ζῆν).[77] The Stoic philosophical system is based on cosmology. While it corresponds to some extent to the Gnostic system, it still does not know the decisive dualism of Gnosticism but is construed according to a basic monistic principle, and is thus basically optimistic and characterized by faith in reason. It is consistent with this that Stoicism then reinterpreted the old Greek religions traditions in a rationalistic manner in which the myths of the gods were demythologized and understood as cosmic processes.

The Stoic anthropology corresponds to its cosmology: the world-logos corresponds to human reason (λόγος or νοῦς).[78] Such a correlation has as its content that human beings have the possibility of willing what is good and divine, and the ability to do it. Whoever knows and understands the divine order of the world will also order his or her life by it. Wrongdoing is thus based on an error of which the person is guilty himself or herself,

---

[77] Chrysippus fr 16, in *Stoicorum Veterum Fragmenta collegit Ioannes ab Arnim*, Vol. III, Leipzig-Berlin 1923).
[78] Cf. Epictetus *Diss* I 9 (Leipoldt-Grundmann II 322.9–16); II 8.1 (325.3–5).

because thereby the claim of the world-logos is missed, the logos which is the essence of human being and the basis of human life. The freedom that belongs to the Stoic consists in the fact that human beings are in the situation of being able to do that which corresponds to nature ("freedom for"). At the same time, it affirms that human beings have a "freedom from" all that withstands the subjection of human beings to the world-logos (emotions, passions). Therefore the Stoic is basically a dehistoricized human being who can be touched neither by suffering nor joy. So also death holds no terrors for the Stoic, since death realizes a necessity of nature (ἀνάγκη). The knowledge of such a natural necessity makes the wise human being a victor over death.

The Pauline position differentiates itself from the ideal of the Stoic wise man precisely in those places in the Pauline letter corpus where Stoic influences have been supposed:

α) *Romans 1:18–32* stands at the beginning of the Letter to the Romans and marks the beginning of the first major section (1:18–3:20, "The Necessity of the Righteousness of God for Gentiles and Jews"). Paul wants to present the proof that neither Gentiles nor Jews already possess righteousness that all are dependent on grace, on the righteousness of God that comes through faith. The subsection 1:18–32 thematizes the problem in relation to the Gentiles. The point of departure is the affirmation that God has revealed himself to the Gentiles, i.e. that God's invisible being has been known since the creation of the world by his works, i.e. by the creation itself. This statement contains an originally Stoic view, for it is the Stoic in particular who can conclude on the basis of observing the cosmos itself that there is a world-logos that permeates the cosmos. For Paul it is not a matter of introducing a proof for the existence of God, not the theoretical question of the knowability of God that could result in reflections about the being and essence of God, but—and this is the second idea that has a parallel in Stoicism—Paul presupposes that knowledge of God means a knowledge of a law that lies at the basis of everything. His view thus corresponds to the Stoic view that the world-logos includes a binding law and demands unconditional obedience. From this there follows a third Stoic idea: closing oneself off from this natural knowledge of God means a life in unrighteousness (ἀδικία) which is at the same time a betrayal of one's own true being.

Paul uses this idea as a point of contact for his own theological exposition. Pauline theology thus accepts a natural, general knowledge of God, without thereby having a christological presupposition. Paul thus likewise adopts the Stoic conception according to which compelling evidence for the existence of God "*e consensu gentium*" can be presented: all peoples possess a knowledge of God independently of the preaching of the gospel. But such an adoption of Stoic ideas takes place only in the sense of a "point of contact;" for that God is recognizable by his works means for the

Gentiles that "they have no excuse" (1:20). Human beings stand under the wrath of God and find themselves in a situation in which there is no way out, a situation in which they cannot free themselves by their own power. In making use of this point of contact Paul does not therefore adopt the Stoic system in a positive way, nor is it a matter of a cosmically grounded optimism but a revelation of the haughtiness and conceit of human life prior to and apart from faith. The *"consensus gentium"* can thus not serve to assure oneself of a comprehensive harmony with a divine essence that is pervaded by the eternal laws of the cosmos, under whose guidance human beings may feel themselves to be secure, but rather has the task of making the chasm visible that separates God and humanity from one another in order to make human beings aware of the guilt that holds them captive. For Paul this makes the revelation of God in the Christ event necessary, a revelation that brings new possibilities to light through the righteousness of God, a revelation that means the end of the power of sin and the law.

Stoic ways of thinking are thus undoubtedly presupposed by Paul. They were widespread in the Hellenistic period and had also already been adopted by Hellenistic Judaism, as seen for example in Philo *Op* 3–12 or Wisdom of Solomon 12:1.

β) *1 Corinthians 7:29–31.* This text stands in the context of the problems of marriage and is the response to a question from the Corinthian church: what is the Christian position on the issue of the institution of marriage? Should a Christian consider it better to be married or to be single? Paul responds that, in view of the imminent eschatological catastrophe, it is good to remain unmarried; this corresponds to his own personal decision. Nonetheless, he here displays a nuanced attitude: while it is still better to remain unmarried, it is not forbidden to get married. The decisive thing is not a particular marital state but conduct that takes up both possibilities into itself: the attitude of "distance." This attitude is described by Paul with the expression "as if not" (ὡς μή):

> I mean, brothers and sisters, the appointed time has grown short; from now on, let even those who have wives be as though they had none, and those who mourn as though they were not mourning, and those who rejoice as though they were not rejoicing, and those who buy as though they had no possessions, and those who deal with the world as though they had no dealings with it. For the present form of this world is passing away. (1Cor 7:29–31).

Here the supreme commandment is not to be bound, to regard the things of the world with a certain distance, and to conduct oneself indifferently over against the world.

Such an attitude was also commended by the Stoic philosopher Epictetus, who lived until 138 C. E., in Greece. One should not bind oneself to this passing world; one should conduct oneself with regard to those human beings one loves as though they were fragile vessels, not allowing oneself to be governed by drives and passions that obscure clear judgment; one should not allow oneself to be shaken by anything but rather live without deep feelings (ἀταραξία). The attitude of "as if not" is expressed in distancing oneself from transitory things. It is grounded by the unity of human beings with the world-logos. This unity with the world order is the Archimedean point from which what happens in nature and human history can be regarded from a distance.

For Paul, the "as if not" is not motivated by a supposed unity with the world-logos but has a double basis: (1) by the orientation of life to the coming eschaton (1 Cor 7:29 "the appointed time has grown short;" 7:31, "the present form of the world is passing away"); the nearness of the parousia provides the basis for an attitude that deprives the things of this world of their claim to absolute power; and (2) the indicative of the Christ event determines the attitude "as if not." Thus 1 Corinthians 6:11 indicates: "But you were washed [through baptism], you were sanctified, you were justified in the name of the Lord Jesus Christ and in the Spirit of our God." By baptism the believer is united with Christ and taken out of the world, so that the world no longer exercises its power over him or her.

With this different point of view, the question of whether in 1 Corinthians 7 Paul is dependent on material from the Stoic thought world is also decided. The common denominator consists in the formally negative fact that the "as if not" presupposes in each case an attitude that is not oriented to the things of the world. However, the basis for this similar attitude is very different in each case. When in Romans 12:15 Paul commands "Rejoice with those who rejoice, weep with those who weep," this contradicts the ataraxias called for by the Stoics that commands one to keep oneself free from all feelings. For Paul, the demand of love is foundational. The command to turn to the neighbor and to human society in love stands in tension with the Stoic ideal oriented to the individual, the ideal of self control and self-realization which the wise man is able to achieve.

### 3.   Gnosis (the Adam Myth)

Bousset, W. *Hauptprobleme der Gnosis*, FRLANT 10. Göttingen: Vandenhoeck & Ruprecht, 1907; Reprint 1973.
Büchli, J. *"Der Poimandres," Ein paganisiertes Evangelium*. WUNT II/27. Tübingen: J. C. B. Mohr (Paul Siebeck), 1987.
Holzhausen, J. *"Der 'Mythos vom Menschen' im hellenistischen Ägypten," Eine Studie zum 'Poimandres' (= CH I), zu Valentin und dem gnostischen Mythos, athenäums monografien Theophaneia*. Beiträge zur Religions und Kirchengeschichte des Altertums 33. Bodenheim: Athenaeum Hain Hanstein, 1994.
Jonas, H. *Gnosis und spätantiker Geist I, II*. Göttingen: Vandenhoeck & Ruprecht, 1988[4], 1993.
Rudolph, K. *Gnosis: The Nature and History of Gnosticism*. San Francisco: Harper & Row, 1987.

Schmithals, W. *Gnosticism in Corinth*. Nashville: Abingdon, 1972.

Schmithals, W. *Neues Testament und Gnosis*. EdF 208. Darmstadt: Wissenschaftliche Buchgesellschaft, 1984.

Schmithals, W. *Paul and the Gnostics*. Nashville: Abingdon, 1972.

Schottroff, L. *Der Glaubende und die feindliche Welt*. WMANT 37. Neukirchen-Vluyn: Neukirchener, 1970.

Strecker, G. *Das Judenchristentum in den Pseudoklementinen*. TU 70. Berlin: Akademie Verlag, 1981².

Tröger, K.-W. ed., *Altes Testament-Frühjudentum-Gnosis*. Gütersloh: Gerd Mohn, 1980.

Tröger, K.-W., ed., *Gnosis und Neues Testament*. Gütersloh: Gerd Mohn, 1973.

Wilson, R. Mcl. *Gnosis and the New Testament*. Oxford: Blackwell, 1968.

That Paul lives in a complex network of religious ideas can be seen from the Adam / Christ typology presented in 1 Corinthians 15:20–22, 45–53 and Romans 5:12–21. The context in 1 Corinthians 15 deals with a written inquiry from the Corinthian church regarding the denial of the resurrection as advocated by some Corinthian Christians (15:12: "how can some of you say there is no resurrection of the dead?"). Although it is here not a dispute about the resurrection of Jesus but concerning the general resurrection, Paul begins with the kerygma of the atoning death and resurrection of Jesus and documents the latter by a series of witnesses who have seen the risen Lord, among whom he includes himself—albeit as the last.[79] This modulates into a statement that faith in the resurrection is constitutive of Christian faith itself (15:12–19), then to an "order of the resurrection" that lists the series of events to happen at the resurrection (15:20–28). Paul's defense of the resurrection faith appeals to the Adam / Christ parallel. Adam as the "first man" (ὁ πρῶτος ἄνθρωπος) is juxtaposed to Christ as the "second man" (ὁ δεύτερος ἄνθρωπος).[80] They are related to one another as type and antitype: Adam as the author and representative of death, Christ as the author and representative of life. This contrast has a fundamental anthropological significance. The first Adam has a natural body, the last Adam, in contrast, has a spiritual body. The first comes from the earth, the last from heaven. They stand over against each other as temporary and eternal, as mortal and immortal. Such a juxtaposition determines the possibility and reality of the being of human individuals: with the first Adam they are fallen into death but as believers they have the possibility of life in Christ (15:21–22).

The contrast between the earthly and the heavenly *anthropos* is not only to be traced back to the views of the Corinthian opponents of Paul, for the apostle presupposes that the church in general is familiar with this idea. He does not utilize the concept as though it were limited to his

---

[79]  1 Corinthians 15:1–11.

[80]  1 Corinthians 15:45, 47. Cf. the rabbinic paralleling of the "first redeemer" (Moses) and the "final redeemer" (the Messiah)

opponents in Corinth. On the contrary, in Romans 5:12–21 also he makes use of it independently of the situation in Corinth. The new aspect here is that the first man is not only the author of death but also of sin (Rom 5:12). This is incorporated in the overarching course of the argument, according to which the righteousness of God is not only a human possibility but is a reality, namely a reality manifest in Christ, who is the representative of life and righteousness. Thereby the contrasting idea is presupposed that the real situation for human beings without Christ is constituted by death and sin.

To answer the question of the origin of this view, less reference should be made to Paul's opponents. There are essentially three possibilities presented in the history of tradition for the derivation of this concept: (1) Paul himself is the creator of this view.[81] (2) Paul adopts a prepauline Christian Adam / Christ typology. In favor of this view is the fact that in 1 Corinthians 15:27 a Christian tradition of Old Testament citation can be introduced, a tradition that recurs in Hebrews 2:8 and perhaps stands in the background of 1 Corinthians 15:45. (3) The Adam / Christ typology has pre-Christian, prepauline, Jewish roots. This is suggested by the term "Adam" and the reference to the Old Testament creation story. Philo distinguishes two types of human beings: (a) the heavenly, spiritual man (the image and model), and (b) the earthly man formed from the earth.[82] Of course, differently than in Paul, for Philo the heavenly man is the first, and the earthly man the second, and Philo draws no comparison between the heavenly man and Adam.

Can this mythological view, according to which the two ἄνθρωποι are representatives of two mutually-exclusive powers (the power of death and the power of life), be directly derived from Genesis 1–3? Are we to assume that with the Adam / Christ typology Paul intends nothing more than an exegesis of Genesis 1:26–27 and 2:7? The decisive consideration is that in the Old Testament creation story, while Adam is, to be sure, partly responsible for the fate of death in which all humanity is now involved, he is still only the first member of a chain that goes back to him. In contrast, the (pre)Pauline Adam / Christ typology understands Adam as the representative of humanity; in him all have sinned, in him the fate of death happens to all. Here there is a physical unity between *the* human being and human *beings*, even if Paul himself does not take over this myth intact (cf. Rom 5:12). Obviously the view stands in the background that human beings as such are "incorporated" in the first *anthropos*, that they are ἐν τῷ Ἀδάμ (1 Cor 15:22; cf. Rom 5:15) and for precisely this reason they share

---

[81] So for example W. D. Davies, *Paul and Rabbinic Judaism: Some Rabbinic Elements in Pauline Theology* (London: SPCK, 1965³) 41–44.
[82] Cf. Philo *All* 1.31–32; *Op* 134.

the fate of Adam. This makes it impossible to trace the Pauline or prepauline Adam typology directly back to the Genesis story.

If Paul himself is not the creator of the Adam / Christ juxtaposition, then one can only relatively differentiate between the prepauline Christian structure and the prechristian structure on which it itself is based. In any case, a tradition is presupposed in which Adam has a significance that goes beyond that of the Old Testament creation story. Where in the religious environment of Paul was there the idea that Adam as the "original image" of humanity in which all human beings are physically incorporated had a universal function? Genuine Judaism has no such deterministic concept in which humanity in general is determined by sin and death by the act of the first human being. The corresponding dualistic idea in which Adam stands on the side of a vain world subjected to mortality and corruption is also foreign to authentic Judaism. In contrast, there are Jewish and Gnostic traditions with the tendency to modify the Genesis story of the fall so that it was not Adam who sinned but only his wife Eve, who is then guilty of all the problems to which this world is heir.[83] While for authentic Judaism the concept of God the creator is constitutive, the creator whose works praise him and who stands in fundamental harmony with the cosmos, the dualism that comes to light in the above examples belongs more to a Judaism of a heretical character, or, more precisely, a Hellenistic Judaism that has gone its own independent way.[84]

For a better understanding of this issue—not in the sense of its source in early Christianity but as a matter of analogy—we must mention the system that was formulated in the Christian Gnosticism of the second century. There is some evidence to support the view that while of course the Gnostic system as such was not of prechristian origin, its essential structural elements were already present in prechristian times. Constitu-

---

[83] Cf. Pseudo-Clementine Homilies 3.23–25; Life of Adam and Eve 3.18. 2 Enoch 31:6; Exc ex Theod 21:2; Gospel of Philip 71; Gospel of Bartholomew 4; Letter of Peter to Philip 139.28–140.1 (W. Schneemelcher, *New Testament Apocrypha* (rev. ed. 1991) 1:351.

[84] The reflections of H. J. Schoeps, according to whom "Gnosticism ... is never anything else but pagan Gnosticism," who argues that we must bid farewell to the idea of a Jewish or Christian Gnosticism (*Urgemeinde, Judenchristentum, Gnosis* [Tübingen: J. C. B. Mohr (Paul Siebeck), 1956] 39) are worthy of reflection, since they clearly designate the hiatus between mythological Gnosticism of a radically dualistic pattern and the thought world of Judaism or Christianity that is characterized by faith in the creator God and a historical redeemer figure. However, a pure form of pagan Gnosticism is also unavailable. Seen in a global perspective, it is a matter of Jewish or Hellenistic syncretism expressed in different manifestations. Within the framework of New Testament research, the Christian Gnostic systems of the second century C. E. that have a relatively transparent structure should be the point of departure for defining the term "Gnosticism." On this and the following, cf. G. Strecker, "Judenchristentum und Gnosis," in K.-W. Tröger, ed. *Altes Testament— Frühjudentum—Gnosis* 265ff.

tive for the Gnostic systems is a dualistic manner of thought: the qualitative distinction between God and the world, the great chasm between the
divine world (πλήρωμα) and matter (ὕλη). This is what made it necessary
to develop a doctrine of how the world came into being. Some elements of
the divine world became separated from the πλήρωμα. They sink like
sparks of light through the world of the aeons, until they come to the
material world in which they are held prisoner. The world came into being
by the uniting of ὕλη and the divine substance. In this way "Adam" was
not only the first human being but he represents humanity as such as a
part of the cosmos, captured within the world of matter, subject to mortality, enslaved by the powers of death, oriented toward a freedom that
could only come from beyond. The redemptive drama corresponds to this
cosmology: the heavenly redeemer descends from the divine pleroma into
the cosmos, brings gnosis to fallen humanity, thereby liberating the light
sparks held captive in matter, and leads them through the hostile aeons
(archons) back to the heavenly world.

The parallelism between these fundamentals of the system of the
mythological Christian Gnosticism and Paul's christological and anthropological concepts becomes even more clear when related ideas used by
Paul are taken into consideration and compared.[85] No doubt there is an
analogy between the Pauline "first man" and the Gnostic *Urmensch* who
by his fall from the heavenly world became imprisoned in matter and who
embraces human destiny in himself and his own destiny. The fate to
which the *Urmensch* was subjected is that which hangs over ever individual human being. This is thought of in Gnosticism in natural-ontologi-
cal terms; it expresses an ontological contemporaneity. On the other hand
the heavenly redeemer of Gnosticism (the "second man") embraces in
himself the redeemed human beings, he "incorporates" the light sparks
sunk in matter in his own body, redeems them through his own ascent to
heaven, and frees them by the impartation of knowledge from the powers
that have enslaved them. To be sure, the Pauline Adam / Christ typology
is not to be derived directly from the Gnostic myth. An essential difference
consists in the fact that the Gnostic system is constructed on a doctrine
of how the world came into being. Although there are echoes of cosmological ideas in the passage Romans 8:19ff (the created world hopes for the

---

[85]   Cf. the application of the εἰκών concept to Christ in 2 Corinthians 4:4 (see also
Philo Conf 96–97), as well as Romans 8:29; 1 Corinthians 15:49; Colossians 1:15.
Πνεῦμα (with a different valence): 2 Corinthians 3:17–18; 11:4; 1 Corinthians 2:14–
15; 7:40; Romans 8:5ff. Σῶμα: 2 Corinthians 5:6, 10; 1 Corinthians 12:12ff. On
this cf. W. Schmithals, "Die gnostische Elemente im Neuen Testament als herme-
neutisches Problem," in K. W. Tröger, ed. *Gnosis und Neues Testament* 359–381;
*Gnosticism in Corinth. An Investigation of the Letters to the Corinthians* (Nashville & New York: Abingdon, 1971) 235ff.

future revelation; it is in need of redemption!), the Pauline teaching about Adam is not oriented in a cosmological direction but an anthropological direction. Here too we find a parallel to the Gnostic thought world: in each case it is a matter of a dualistic anthropology, and a distinction is made between the man subject to mortality and enslaved to the powers of death on the one side, and on the other side the pneumatic self of the person who waits for redemption. This dualism is basically of a physical-ontological sort. "Being in Adam" is a "being subject to the world." While the Pauline idea of the first Adam and its anthropological significance corresponds to a certain extent to the Gnostic picture of human existence, this must be qualified by saying that Paul can speak not only of the physical enslavement of human beings in the world but also of the voluntary act of human beings that leads to death.[86] Points of correspondence are also visible in the soteriological concepts: salvation consists of liberation from the enslaving world powers; the redemptive event is also an ontological event. Pauline anthropological dualism stands closer to the Gnostic systems than it does to authentic Judaism.

There is an additional difference between Pauline theology and the analogous ideas in genuine Gnosticism. A characteristic feature of Christian Gnosticism is the soteriological conviction that the heavenly redeemer brings the perfect "salvation" (σωτηρία); for he mediates "knowledge" (γνῶσις) and thereby the possibility of leaving the world behind in the here and now. This is the basis on which Gnostics can advocate the understanding that they are absolutely separate from the world. This is also the point of departure for the variety of ethical lifestyles advocated in Gnosticism. Both responses are possible: a radical asceticism that attempts to hold itself unstained from every contamination by the world, and on the other hand a thoroughgoing libertinism for which everything is permitted, since Gnostics know themselves to have been set free from slavery to the world (although this latter is rarely attested in Gnosticism).

Paul's theology is unacquainted with such an extreme contemporizing of σωτηρία, in which salvation is entirely a present reality. Romans 5:17 speaks of death's "exercising dominion through the one (Adam),"(a given state of affairs that cannot be undone) but that those who have received grace and righteousness through Christ "*will* reign in life" (ἐν ζωῇ βασιλεύσουσιν).[87] Paul thus does not speak in the same way of the presence of life as he does of the natural, given presence of death. In this his "eschatological reservation" comes to expression. The consummation is still in the future; it is still to happen, and will happen in the eschatological future. This is a reflection of his apocalyptic thought. While Paul is not to

---

[86] Cf. Romans 5:12 and below under A. III. a. e.

[87] Cf. similarly 1 Corinthians 15:49: "Just as we have borne the image of the man of dust, we *will* also bear the image of the man of heaven."

be labeled an apocalyptist in the narrow literary sense, it is still the case that his theology is oriented to the eschatological future. At the same time, it must be said that his theology includes a series of factors that express the presence of salvation in the here and now. The central importance of his characteristic "in Christ" is indicative of this.[88] In opposition to an over emphasis on the apocalyptic elements in the theology of Paul, one must note the importance of the concept of the exalted Christ who leads his community in the present (a *mythological reservation*). Moreover, the Pauline soteriology not only has an orientation to the present and future but has a fundamental reference to the past, for it is rooted in the event of the cross and resurrection, as is made clear by the Christ kerygma taken over by Paul (*historical reservation*).[89]

## c)  Prepauline Christian Traditions

Bauer, W. *Der Wortgottesdienst der ältesten Christen.* SGV 148. Tübingen: J. C. B. Mohr (Paul Siebeck), 1930; also in G. Strecker, ed., *Aufsätze und Kleine Schriften.* Tübingen: J. C. B. Mohr (Paul Siebeck), 1967, 155–209.
Conzelmann, H. "Was glaubte die frühe Christenheit?," H. Conzelmann, *Theologie als Schriftauslegung: Aufsätze zum Neuen Testament.* BEvTh 65. Munich: Kaiser, 1974, 106–119.
Deichgräber, R. *Gotteshymnus und Christushymnus in der frühen Christenheit.* StUNT 5. Göttingen: Vandenhoeck & Ruprecht, 1967.
Schnelle, U. *Gerechtigkeit und Christusgegenwart. Vorpaulinische und paulinische Tauftheologie.* GTA 24. Göttingen: Vandenhoeck & Ruprecht, 1986².
Strecker, G. *History of New Testament Literature.* Harrisburg: Trinity Press International, 1997, 68–76.
von Lips, H. "Paulus und die Tradition," VF 36 (1991) 27–49.
Wengst, K. *Christologische Formeln und Lieder des Urchristentums.* StNT 7. Gütersloh: Gerd Mohn, 1972.

In the Letter to the Galatians Paul speaks of his call to be an apostle and in this context says that after his conversion near Damascus when he received the commission to be apostle to the Gentiles he did not consult with anyone, did not go up to Jerusalem but that he went immediately to Arabia, and did it for the purpose of carrying out his missionary work (Gal 1:16–17). This appears to indicate that Paul attributed his message entirely to the divine commission without reference to any human intermediaries. The Pauline account in Galatians 1 intends to affirm the apostle's independence from all human authorities, in particular the representatives of the earliest Jerusalem church. This of course does not mean that after his transformation from persecutor to preacher Paul did not receive any Christian instruction. On the contrary, it is to be presupposed that

[88]  Cf. below A. III. a. 1.
[89]  Cf. below on A. II. c. and A. III. c. 2.

the new convert made contact with other Christians. As reported in Acts 9:10–18, Paul was baptized in Damascus. In a way that corresponds to this, Paul's letters discuss both baptism and the instruction that accompanied it (1 Cor 12:13; Rom 6:3). Thus immediately after his call Paul was in contact with a stream of Christian tradition. From this tradition he took over the essential building blocks from which he constructed his own theology.

Since Paul became a member of a community with institutionalized worship practices, the traditions he received are primarily those associated with the cultic practices of the church. On the occasion of the sacramental celebration of the Lord's Supper the prepauline unit of tradition found in 1 Corinthians 11:23–25 is recited. To the worship of the church prior to Paul belongs the Aramaic acclamation "Maranatha" (1 Cor 16:22, "Our Lord, come!"); it expresses the eschatological expectation of the prepauline Christian community. Another cultic cry is represented by the κύριος Ἰησοῦς of 1 Corinthians 12:3. Brief kerygmatic formulae were used in the confession of faith made in the worship service, as well as in the general proclamation of the church.[90] The confessional affirmation of Jesus as the resurrected one is found in Romans 10:9 (cf. 1 Thess 4:14). Romans 1:3–4 and Philippians 2:6–11 are based on complex christological concepts. So also the use of christological titles (Son of God, Christ, Lord, and others) presuppose a level of prepauline reflection independent of fixed formulae. The parenetic materials in Paul's letters derive in part from church tradition, especially in the citation of "words of the Lord" that possess a normative character (cf. 1 Cor 7:10–11, 12, 25). That the Adam / Christ typology is of prepauline origin and that Paul might possibly have taken it over from Christian tradition has been discussed above. This is also a possibility for the testimonies (collections of Scripture texts) that are used in the Pauline letters (cf. the Excursus after A. I. a. 1.) So also Paul is dependent on church tradition for some of his apocalyptic material, as indicated by 1 Thessalonians 4:13ff and 5:2.

We will take three passages as examples of the kinds of Christian tradition that Paul received and made use of: Romans 1:3–4, Philippians 2:6–11, and 1 Corinthians 15:3ff. These passages that represent very different types of units with regard to form, content, and their points of origin within the history of the tradition are considered to belong to the kerygmatic forms characterized by a stylized language: poetic and formal

---

[90] E. g. Romans 3:25; 4:25; also 1 Thessalonians 1:9–10, a formula that could be used in evangelistic preaching to Gentiles, since it contains two of the affirmations fundamental to Christian faith: (a) worship of the true God and (b) the expectation of the return of Jesus the Son of God, who had been raised from the dead. Further documentation of prepauline acclamations, doxologies, and the like are found in K. Wengst, *Christologische Formeln* and G. Strecker, *History of New Testament Literature* 68–76.

in their rhythm, strophic structure and/or relative clauses and participles. "Kerygma" originally denoted the cry of the herald, a proclamation that announced a new state of affairs. Although in New Testament usage κήρυγμα has the general meaning of "preaching" (1 Cor 1:21; 2:4), the original sense (announcement, call to decision) is still discernable. The kerygma implies a call to repentance and is at the same time determined by a particular content. It is bound to history, for it does not mediate a timeless truth but is bound to its own time in a threefold sense:

(a) The language of the Kerygma is the language of the New Testament period.

(b) The predication it makes has to do with a particular history, since the kerygma is directed to specific hearers in an obligatory manner that challenges them to hear and decide. It is a call to decision launched into a specific historical situation.

(c) The content of the kerygma refers back to the Christ event, i.e. to an event that lies in the past from the point of view of the post-Easter Christian community. It is not the "historical Jesus," as represented by the period 1–30 C. E., that is the subject matter of the New Testament kerygma but Jesus as seen from the point of view of its Easter faith. The New Testament kerygma originated within the faith of the post-Easter Christian community and is at the same time the testimony to this faith.

## 1.   Romans 1:3b-4a

Hahn, F. *The Titles of Jesus in Christology; Their History in Early Christianity*. London: Lutterworth, 1969, 251ff.

Linnemann, E. "Tradition und Interpretation in Röm 1:3f," *EvTh* 31 (1971) 264–276.

Schweizer, E. "Röm 1:3f. und der Gegensatz von Fleisch und Geist vor und bei Paulus," *EvTh* 15 (1955) 563–571; also in E. Schweizer. *Neotestamentica: deutsche und englische Aufsätze 1951–1963*. Zürich-Stuttgart: Zwingli, 1963, 180–189.

Stuhlmacher, P. "Theologische Probleme des Römerbriefpräskripts," *EvTh* 27 (1967) 374–389.

Theobald M. "Dem Juden zuerst und auch dem Heiden," F. Mussner, P.-G. Müller and W. Stenger, eds., *Kontinuität und Einheit*, (FS F. Mussner). Freiburg: Herder, 1981. 376–392.

|  |  |  |
|---|---|---|
|  |  | [Jesus Christ] |
| (3b) | τοῦ γενομένου | who was descended |
|  | ἐκ σπέρματος Δαυὶδ κατὰ σάρκα | from David according to the flesh |
| (4a) | τοῦ ὁρισθέντος | and was declared to be |
|  | υἱοῦ θεοῦ | Son of God |
|  | ἐν δυνάμει κατὰ πνεῦμα ἁγιωσύνης | with power according to the spirit of holiness |
|  | ἐξ ἀναστάσεως νεκρῶν | by resurrection from the dead |

In the three-part prescript of Paul's Letter to the Romans (Rom 1:1–7) the designation of the sender has been greatly expanded by a kerygmatic formula; then follows the designation of the addressees and the greeting. To the church at Rome with which Paul is not personally acquainted, Paul presents himself as an apostle. The formula expresses the essential content of the gospel that Paul is commissioned to proclaim.

The unpauline language and style of 1:3b-4a indicates a traditional formula. The designation ἐκ σπέρματος Δαυίδ is found only here in Paul (also in the nonpauline 2 Tim 2:8). So also ὁρίζειν is a hapax legomenon within the Pauline corpus. The participial style (γενομένου, ὁρισθέντος) and the two-membered parallelism are characteristic for liturgical language. The formula was presumably preceded by a Ἰησοῦς Χριστός (as in 2 Tim 2:8) or a simple ὁ Ἰησοῦς to which the participles were connected.

According to E. Schweizer and F. Hahn, κατὰ σάρκα and κατὰ πνεῦμα ἁγιωσύνης were part of the original formula. Schweizer points to the unpauline πνεῦμα ἁγιωσύνης, which can be seen to be an expression of old Jewish tradition on the basis of Psalm 50:13 LXX, Isaiah 63:10–11, and Testament of Levi 18:11. From this perspective the σάρξ–πνεῦμα contrast represents the contrast between the earthly and heavenly sphere in the same schema as 1 Timothy 3:16, 1 Peter 3:18 and 4:6, while Paul himself uses the σάρξ–πνεῦμα contrast to express the opposition between sinful humanity and the holy God. To this it can be objected that the LXX form of the passages referred to, differently from the Testament of Levi, do not in fact have πνεῦμα ἁγιωσύνης but τὸ πνεῦμα τὸ ἅγιόν σου (Ps 50:13; similarly Isa 63:11) and τὸ πνεῦμα τὸ ἅγιον αὐτοῦ (Isa 63:10)'. We cannot speak of a broad Jewish base for this interpretation. At least two objections may be raised against the cited references for a nonpauline flesh / Spirit contrast that thinks in terms of two spheres: (1) the differing grammatical structures (1 Pet 3:18 and 4:6 have the dative, 1 Tim 3:16 the dative with ἐν) and (2) completely different meanings are expressed by "flesh and Spirit' in the purported parallels. In 1 Timothy 3:16 the contextual meaning implied by the four additional parallels is to be noted. To translate flesh and Spirit with the meaning "in the sphere of..." is impossible. In 1 Peter 4:6 the qualifications flesh / Spirit are referred to Christians, not to Christ. In contrast, by κατὰ σάρκα Paul means not only a paraphrase for sinful being but also a description of the earthly sphere of existence (cf. Rom 9:3; 1 Cor 10:18). If κατὰ σάρκα and κατὰ πνεῦμα are interpreted as Pauline insertions, then the question of the origin of the term ἁγιωσύνη is posed afresh. E. Linnemann has suggested that ἐν δυνάμει πνεύματος ἁγιωσύνης is to be presupposed as the form in the tradition. The problem with this is the linguistic difficulty then posed by the two unconnected genitives. Also, then Paul would have had to have changed the genitive πνεύματος to κατὰ πνεῦμα. Since Paul can qualify πνεῦμα by a genitive of apposition (e. g. Rom 8:2, πνεῦμα τῆς ζωῆς), and since the word ἁγιωσύνη in the New Testament is found exclusively in the Pauline letters (also in 2 Cor 7:1 and 1 Thess 3:13), we should assume that κατὰ σάρκα and κατὰ πνεῦμα ἁγιωσύνης are Pauline interpretative additions that in accord with the Pauline σάρξ/πνεῦμα scheme were inserted secondarily by Paul into the traditional unit.

The prepauline unit can thus be reconstructed as a formula of two lines that follows the initial naming of Christ with the same three-accent meter:

Ἰησοῦς (Χριστός)
γενόμενος ἐκ σπέρματος Δαυὶδ
ὁρισθεὶς υἱὸς θεοῦ ἐν δυνάμει ἐξ ἀναστάσεως νεκρῶν

This reconstructed form includes a reflection on both the earthly reality of Jesus and his heavenly existence. It does not deal with the synchronic

presence of Jesus' two natures (human and divine) but expresses a historical event: Jesus, the descendent of David, has been enthroned as God's
Son. The two forms of existence are arranged chronologically and are
separated from each other; ἐξ ἀναστάσεως νεκρῶν does not state the grounds
on which Jesus becomes Son of God but refers to the time of his exaltation.
This can also be described as "adoption" (cf. Mark 1:11); the second level
transcends the first; the Son of God is more than the son of David, for
Sonship to God includes the conquest of death.

> The titles "Son of God" and "son of David" are used numerous times in the New
> Testament but usually in isolation from each other. Except for Romans 1:3–4, only
> Acts 13:33ff directly combines the two. The Old Testament background is formed by
> texts such as Psalms 2:7, 89:1ff, and the prophecy of Nathan in 2 Samuel 7. They all
> echo the ritual of the inthronization of the Jewish king. In Nathan's prophecy Yahweh
> promises a unique relation to God to the royal line of David: "I will be his Father, and
> he will be my son" (2 Sam 7:14a). This declaration was part of the Jewish royal
> enthronement ritual in which the descendent of David was adopted and/or legiti-
> mated and installed in his royal power. Sonship to David and Sonship to God were
> originally not mutually exclusive but the meaning of each was conditioned by the
> other. The Davidic election is the presupposition of the status as Son of God and is
> not replaced by it. That 'son of David' is subordinate to 'Son of God' is illuminated
> by Hebrews 1:1–4: the inherited name "Son" is unique and higher than the angels,
> who are thought of as heavenly attendants in the inthronization scene in the throne
> room of God. That Jesus the descendent of David was adopted as Son of God at the
> time of his resurrection from the dead, as represented in the old inthronization ritual,
> is restricted in Romans 1:3–4 to the one descendent of David Jesus Christ: the
> promise of the Father / Son relationship applies to him alone.

The Greek prepauline traditional unit apparently derives from Hellenistic Jewish Christianity; the Jewish savior figure is identified with the seed
of David.[91] The formula does not refer to Jesus' passion and does not
reflect the atoning power of his death. In contrast, the concept of inthronization is central, which is temporally connected with the resurrection of
Jesus from the dead. The apocalyptic Jewish expectation of the general
resurrection of the dead has been combined with that of Jesus' own resurrection without any indication that Jesus is expected to return again at the
parousia. It is not the imminent advent arrival of Jesus as the Son of man
but his being installed as the powerful Son of God is the material content
of this kerygmatic formula. Possibly we have here the aggrandizement of
an originally particularistic Jewish Christian hope of salvation: the "Son
of God" breaks through the particularistic limitation; he is endowed with
δύναμις and as the Lord of the community is the victor over death.

Paul has indicated by the context how he wants the formula to be
understood. As in other passages he makes the preexistence of Jesus

---

[91]    Cf. the messianic expectation of the Son of David in the Psalms of Solomon 17:21
        (1 cent. B. C. E.).

Christ his point of departure (e. g. Phil 2:6), so here too he directs all the attention to the pairing of the fleshly and heavenly modes of existence of the son of David / Son of God contained in the formula by preceding it with the prophetic announcement of v. 2. The Pauline κατὰ σάρκα underscores the earthly realm of the flesh in which Jesus' sonship to David is located.[92] Perhaps thereby a negative qualification of the historical existence of Jesus is made,[93] and/or a connection with the realistic Jewish messianic expectation. In any case, his earthly mode of being is left behind and transcended by that of the Risen One, whose resurrection signifies his inthronization as Son of God. Even if the two-membered nature of the formula does not let it be located exactly in the history of the Pauline mission, it still points in a direction that is recognizable in the conception of the Letter to the Romans itself: "to the Jews first, then to the Gentiles" (Rom 1:16).

On the one hand, the expression κατὰ πνεῦμα ἁγιωσύνης as likewise a Pauline insertion manifests the sphere of sovereignty of the Risen One. This realm has a pneumatic quality so that those who belong to it also are incorporated into the sphere of the Spirit. On the other hand, ἁγιωσύνη also means "sanctification," "making holy," i.e. a manner of life that is flawless from the ethical point of view (so also in 2 Cor 7:1 and 1 Thess 3:13). Where the spiritual reality of the Risen One is present, there "holiness" must be practiced. Paul will clarify what he means by this in the course of the Letter to the Romans (cf. already in 1:18ff, and especially in chapters 12–15).

## 2.  Philippians 2:6–11

Barth, K. *The Epistle to the Philippians*.Richmond: John Knox, 1962.
Deissmann, A. *Light from the Ancient Near East; the New Testament Illustrated by Recently Discovered Texts of the Graeco-Roman World*. New York: Harper & Brothers, 1927[4].
Georgi, D. "Der vorpaulinische Hymnus Phil 2,6–11," *Zeit und Geschichte* (FS R. Bultmann), E. Dinkler, ed., Tübingen: Vandenhoeck & Ruprecht, 1964. 263–293
Hofius, O. *Der Christushymnus Phil 2,6–11*. WUNT 17. Tübingen: J. C. B. Mohr (Paul Siebeck), 1991[2].
Jeremias, J. "Zur Gedankenführung in den paulinischen Briefen," *Studia paulina* (FS J. de Zwaan). Haarlem: Erven F. Bohn, 1953. 146–162; also in J. Jeremias. *Abba. Studien zur neutestamentlichen Theologie und Zeitgeschichte*. Göttingen: Vandenhoeck & Ruprecht, 1966. 269–276.
Käsemann, E. "A Critical Analysis of Philippians 2:5–11,*God and Christ. Journal for Theology and Church* 5. R. W. Funk, ed. New York: Harper and Row, 1968, 45–88.

---

[92]  Cf. Romans 4:1: Abraham is our father "according to the flesh."
[93]  Possibly Paul's opponents in Corinth appealed to this (cf. D. Georgi, *The Opponents of Paul in Second Corinthians* [Philadelphia: Fortress Press, 1986] 276, "glorification of the earthly Jesus"); the connection here is not so much the issue of 2 Cor 5:16 as the opponents' appeal to Jerusalem in general.

Lohmeyer, E. *Kyrios Jesus. Eine Untersuchung zu Phil 2,5–11*. SHAW.PH 4. Heidelberg 1927, 1928. (= Darmstadt: Wissenschaftliche Buchgesellschaft, 1961²)

Martin, R. P. *Carmen Christi. Philippians II: 5–11 in Recent Interpretation and in the Setting of Early Christian Worship*. MSSNTS 4. Cambridge: Cambridge University Press, 1983².

Michel, O. "Zur Exegese von Phil 2,5–11," O. Michel. *Dienst am Wort. Gesammelte Aufsätze*. Ed. K. Haacker. Neukirchen-Vluyn: Neukirchener, 1986. 123–134.

Müller, U. B. "Der Christushymnus Phil 2,6–11," *ZNW* 79 (1988) 17–44.

Müller, U. B. *Die Menschwerdung des Gottessohnes*. SBS 140. Stuttgart: Katholisches Bibelwerk, 1990.

Strecker, G. "Redaktion und Tradition im Christushymnus Phil 2,6–11," *ZNW* 55 (1964) 63–78. Also in G. Strecker. *Eschaton und Historie. Aufsätze*. Göttingen: Vandenhoeck & Ruprecht, 1979. 142–157.

The kerygmatic formulations are related to history. Thus the distinction between the material that came to Paul in the tradition and the Pauline redaction of a text can be made clear. This is confirmed in yet another way by the prepauline hymn to Christ in Philippians 2:6–11.

|  |  |  |
|---|---|---|
|  |  | [Jesus Christ] |
| I. 6. | (α) ὃς ἐν μορφῇ θεοῦ ὑπάρχων | who, though he was in the form of God, |
|  | (β) οὐχ ἁρπαγμὸν ἡγήσατο | did not regard equality with God |
|  | τὸ εἶναι ἴσα θεῷ, | as something to be exploited |
| 7a | (α) ἀλλὰ ἑαυτὸν ἐκένωσεν | but emptied himself, |
|  | (β) μορφὴν δούλου λαβών, | taking the form of a slave, |
| 7b | (α) ἐν ὁμοιώματι ἀνθρώπων γενόμενος | being born in human likeness. |
|  | (β) καὶ σχήματι εὑρεθεὶς ὡς ἄνθρωπος | And being found in human form |
| 8 | ἐταπείνωσεν ἑαυτὸν | he humbled himself |
|  | γενόμενος ὑπήκοος μέχρι θανάτου, | and became obedient to the point of death |
|  | θανάτου δὲ σταυροῦ | — even death on a cross |
| II. 9. | (α) διὸ καὶ ὁ θεὸς αὐτὸν ὑπερύψωσεν | Therefore God also highly exalted him |
|  | (β) καὶ ἐχαρίσατο αὐτῷ τὸ ὄνομα | and gave him the name |
|  | τὸ ὑπὲρ πᾶν ὄνομα, | that is above every name, |
| 10 | (α) ἵνα ἐν τῷ ὀνόματι Ἰησοῦ | so that at the name of Jesus |
|  | πᾶν γόνυ κάμψῃ | every knee should bend, |
|  | (β) ἐπουρανίων καὶ ἐπιγείων | in heaven and on earth |
|  | καὶ καταχθονίων | and under the earth, |
| 11 | (α) καὶ πᾶσα γλῶσσα ἐξομολογήσηται | and every tongue should confess |
|  | (β) ὅτι κύριος Ἰησοῦς Χριστὸς | that Jesus Christ is Lord, |
|  | εἰς δόξαν θεοῦ πατρός. | to the glory of God the Father. |

Without going into the partition hypotheses that have been proposed for Paul's Letter to the Philippians,[94] we may state that this unit of tradition stands in a coherent context. In the major section 1:1–3:1 Paul portrays the nature of the eschatological joy (χαρά) and the way in which it is to be preserved in the responsible life of the community. It is within this context that the heavenly praise of the Kyrios Jesus Christ is set. The

---

[94] Cf. W. G. Kümmel, *Introduction* 332–335; Ph. Vielhauer, *Geschichte* 159–162.

christological affirmations of the hymn stand in a formal discrepancy to the parenetic context. The stylistic use of participles and relative pronouns reflects liturgical language, and the terminology is essentially unpauline. These observations favor the view that Paul has here inserted a prepauline traditional unit. Moreover, the passage can be divided into strophes: the song originally had six double lines, the whole consisting of two parts, with the beginning of the second part marked by the διό of 2:9.[95] If one proceeds on the basis that the hymn is structured in terms of a series of parallel couplets, then the whole of 2:8 is to be separated as a Pauline interpretation inserted into the traditional song, all the more so since it is characterized by Pauline vocabulary and contacts to the Pauline context.

## On the History of Research

*Karl Barth's* interpretation, which was dependent on a conservative orthodox exegetical tradition (J. Chr. K. v. Hofmann, J. Koegel,)[96] has been particularly influential on the history of exegesis, in that he rejected any "reference to the example of Christ." For Paul it was not a matter of Jesus as an ethical model to be imitated but a call into the reality of the grace that has been revealed in Christ. This determines the details of the Christ-psalm, which bears witness to the event of the incarnation.

A different exegetical tradition is represented by *O. Michel*, who attempts to understand the hymn within the context of the Aramaic language and the thought world it represents. The hymn accordingly originated in the earliest Palestinian church and is a witness to the oldest Christology of the original church, a Christology that was based on Isaiah 53 ("Zur Exegesis" 124, 129–130). But this exegetical basis is to be disputed: clear citations of Isaiah 53 or from the Servant of Yahweh songs in Deutero-Isaiah are found only in the late strata of the New Testament. The only relatively clear allusion to Isaiah 53 that can be detected in the Christ hymn is found in 2:10–11 (= Isa 45:23). It reflects the Greek text of the Old Testament (LXX!), not the Aramaic, and is not from one of the Servant of Yahweh songs but is originally an Old Testament self-predication of Yahweh, and so does not suggest an identification of Jesus with the Suffering Servant.

To be sure, *J. Jeremias* understands the ἑαυτὸν ἐκένωσεν (2:7) as a translation of the Hebrew text of Isaiah 53:12 ("he poured out himself to death")[97] But such a translation would be incomplete and does not take into consideration that 2:7 speaks of the preexistent Christ, who by no means can be identified with the earthly Servant of Yahweh.

---

[95] E. Lohmeyer, *Kurios Jesus* 4–7, divides the song into six strophes of two lines each, which is not consistent with the syntax. He also divides the whole into two parts, and considers 2:8c (θανάτου δὲ σταυροῦ) to be a Pauline interpretative addition.

[96] J. Chr. K. v. Hofmann. *Die heilige Schrift des neuen Testaments zusammenhängend untersucht* IV/3. *Der Brief Pauli an die Philipper* (Nördlingen, C. H. Beck, 1871); J. Koegel, *Christus der Herr. Erläuterungen zu Phil 2,5–11* (BFChTh 12,2) (Gütersloh: Gerd Mohn, 1908).

[97] J. Jeremias, *TDNT* 5:706; "Zu Phil 2,7: ἑαυτὸν ἐκένωσεν" in *Abba: Studien zur neutestamentlichen Theologie und Zeitgeschichte* (Göttingen: Vandenhoeck & Ruprecht, 1966) 308–313. This view is opposed by O. Michel, "Zur Exegese" and by G. Bornkamm, "Zum Verständnis des Christus-Hymnus Phil 2,6–11" in *Studien zu Antike und Urchristentum* II (BEvTh 28) Munich: Kaiser, 1963[2]) 177–187.

It is to the credit of *A. Deissmann* that he has provided new exegetical possibilities for understanding the New Testament by opening up the world of the Greek papyri. So also *W. Bauer* has in his lexicon provided a large number of parallels to the language of the New Testament from the Greek world. In the early period the early Christian gospel was fundamentally open to the "world." Thus the composer of the Christ hymn used the language and concepts of his own intellectual world to interpret the meaning of the Christ event, which was not the world of Palestinian but the world of Hellenistic thought.

The prepauline composition of the hymn contained two parts, the first dealing with the descent, the second with the exaltation of the Preexistent One. The first part stands near the world of Hellenistic thought, as indicated for example by the word μορφή; the second part betrays the influence of Jewish tradition by the allusion to Isaiah 45:23 in 2:10–11. The hymn obviously originated in a prepauline Hellenistic Jewish Christian context.

This Jewish Christianity had come to confess its faith in Christ by adopting the traditional scheme of the descent and ascent of a heavenly being, in such wise that the Christ had given up his divine being, his equality with God, in order to enter fully into the human sphere of being. The grammatical subject is "Christ Jesus" (2:5). Even in his lowliness Christ remains identical with himself. As incarnate he is still the heavenly being; he is not God *and* man but as a divine being he became man. The decisive fact in the drama of redemption is the humiliation of this heavenly being, his coming into the human world as a human being. This is the basis of his inthronization (διό in 2:9 referred originally to 2:7). The descent is the occasion and ground for the exaltation. Thereby the Christ becomes more than he had ever been previously; while as the Preexistent One he had been essentially "equal to God," he now receives a surpassing position of authority and power. The meaning of the inthronization is his installation as Cosmocrator. The community confesses its faith in the name of Christ as the Kyrios, the sovereign of the cosmos (2:9b). To be distinguished from this is the confession of the cosmic powers (2:10–11), which is grammatically marked off from the present situation of the community by the ἵνα-clause. The all-embracing worship of Christ as the Lord by the whole created world will not happen until the eschatological future. The orientation of the hymn as a whole is toward this apocalyptic future. While it may be that Christ's lordship over the world at present is hidden and is realized and made present only in the believing confession of the community, the community lives in the expectation of the eschatological future that will reveal that Jesus Christ is Lord of all.

The question of the soteriology of the prepauline hymn is to be answered in terms of the hymn's Christology and its apocalyptic orientation, for while it may be possible in principle to conceive of a soteriology without christological presuppositions, every Christology implies a soteriology. The connection between the Soter (Savior) and those who are saved by him consists in the fact that the redeemer has already preceded the redeemed in the way they still must travel. The victory over bodily reality, i.e. the earthly empirical world, as it has happened by the exaltation of Jesus Christ to be Lord, means for the community the grounding of its eschatological hope. Just as the Christ participated in the sphere of earthly bodily reality and then was taken out of it, so it will also happen to the believers—at the latest when all the cosmic powers offer their worship to the Kyrios as the Cosmocrator. The intent expressed in this apocalyptic orientation has a close parallel in Philippians 3:20–21, which presumably belongs to the same layer of tradition as the hymn of 2:6–11 ("... our citizenship is in heaven, and it is from there that we are expecting a Savior, the Lord Jesus Christ").

By the addition of 2:8 and the incorporation of this unit of tradition into its present context, Paul made a specific interpretation of the originally christological-soteriological affirmation of the hymn. It is not longer primarily a matter of expressing the apocalyptic expectation but of declaring that the Christ event has an ethical-normative significance. The low point of the descent of Christ is not the incarnation itself but his obedience that caused him to endure suffering and death. In this the one who had descended was obedient to the will of God, as this is made concrete in the drama of redemption. The obedience of Christ that was realized on the cross is the motive of his inthronization. This means for the community that the one who became human became a model for the community by his obedience.[98] This presupposes the Pauline indicative and points to a close connection between indicative and imperative. Just as the community knows itself to be determined by the indicative of the redemptive event and that it is incorporated into the sphere of Christ ("in Christ") so also the way the Kyrios conducted himself becomes a pattern that functions as an ethical norm. This meaning of the Pauline interpretation is indicated by the bracketing of 2:8 (ἐταπείνωσεν, "he humbled himself") with 2:3, the command to practice humility (ταπεινοφροσύνη), and by the connection of ὑπήκοος (2:8) with ὑπηκούσατε of 2:12. A similar ethical interpretation of the personal being of Christ is also found in Romans 15:3ff. It is not the ethical example of the historical Jesus but the humiliation and exaltation of the preexistent Kyrios that have such an ethical-normative significance for the community. The question, whether an

---

98  In accordance with this, the elliptic introductory sentence τοῦτο φρονεῖτε ἐν ὑμῖν ὃ καὶ ἐν Χριστῷ Ἰησοῦ (2:5) is not to be interpreted unambiguously in either a christological or ecclesiological sense. The lack of a verb in 2:5b leaves both possibilities open: the reminder of the community that it is founded on the Christ event of the past ("which also was in Christ Jesus") but also the reflection on the manner of conduct that is normative for the ethical life of the community ("which also should happen in Christ Jesus"). The actuality of being incorporated into the Christ-reality ("in Christ") means for the community both gift and assignment (*Gabe* and *Aufgabe*).

alternative is to be seen between the understanding of the humiliated Preexistent One as prototype (*Urbild*) or example (*Vorbild*),[99] as suggested in the older exegesis with various results, cannot be answered in the affirmative. The hymn includes both indicative and imperative elements. This is also to be confirmed over against more recent interpretations.[100]

## 3.   1 Corinthians 15:3a-5a

Conzelmann, H. "On the Analysis of the Confessional Formula in 1 Corinthians 15:3–5," *Interpretation* Vol. XX No. 1 (January, 1966) 15–25

Grass, H. *Ostergeschehen und Osterberichte.* Göttingen: Vandenhoeck & Ruprecht, 1970⁴.

Hoffmann, P., ed., *Zur neutestamentlichen Überlieferung von der Auferstehung Jesu.* WdF 522. Darmstadt: Wissenschaftliche Buchgesellschaft, 1988.

Lehmann, K. *Auferweckung am dritten Tag nach der Schrift. Früheste Christologie, Bekenntnisbildung und Schriftauslegung im Lichte von 1 Kor 15,3–5, QD 38.* Freiburg: Herder, 1968.

Lüdemann, G. *The Resurrection of Jesus: History, Experience, Theology.* Minneapolis: Fortress, 1994.

Mussner, F. "Zur stilistischen und semantischen Struktur der Formel 1 Kor 15,3–5," *Die Kirche des Anfangs.* FS H. Schürmann. Freiburg: Herder, 1978. 405–416.

von Campenhausen, H. *Der Ablauf der Osterereignisse und das leere Grab.* SHAW.PH. Heidelberg: C. Winter, 1977⁴.

von Campenhausen, H. *Der Ablauf der Osterereignisse und das leere Grab.* SHAW.PH. Heidelberg 1977⁴.

| 3a | (παρέδωκα γὰρ ὑμῖν ἐν πρώτοις, ὃ καὶ παρέλαβον,) | (For I handed on to you as of first importance what I in turn had received:) |
|---|---|---|
| 3b I | ὅτι Χριστὸς ἀπέθανεν | that Christ died |
| | ὑπὲρ τῶν ἁμαρτιῶν ἡμῶν | for our sins |
| | κατὰ τὰς γραφάς | in accordance with the scriptures, |
| 4 II | καὶ ὅτι ἐτάφη | and that he was buried, |
| III | καὶ ὅτι ἐγήγερται | and that he was raised |
| | τῇ ἡμέρᾳ τῇ τρίτῃ | on the third day |
| | κατὰ τὰς γραφάς | in accordance with the scriptures |
| 5a IV | καὶ ὅτι ὤφθη Κηφᾷ | and that he appeared to Cephas |

The beginning of the traditional unit is clearly marked by the insertion of ὅτι Χριστός. The end of the unit is more difficult to recognize, since the enumeration of the witnesses of the resurrection extends to the naming of

---

⁹⁹ Cf. E. Käsemann, "A Critical Analysis of Philippians 2:5–11," *Journal for Theology and the Church*, ed. R. W. Funk in association with G. Ebeling (*God and Christ: Existence and Province.* New York: Harper and Row, Inc., 1968) 45–88.

¹⁰⁰ U. B. Müller, *Der Brief des Paulus an die Philipper* (ThHK 11/1. Berlin: Theologische Verlagsanstalte, 1993) 111–113, presents Matthew 23:12par as parallels for the parenetic scheme of humiliation and exaltation and wants to show a proximity to the wisdom tradition (Prov 29:23; Sir 2:3–4, and elsewhere). The hymn (without 2:8c and 11c) accordingly calls for imitation of Christ, praises his voluntary humiliation, and shows that with Christ God has demonstrated the validity of the ancient connection between deed and result.

Paul himself (15:8), which obviously cannot have been included in the prepauline unit. The list named in vv. 6–7 cannot have originally been a unit. The consistently symmetrical way in which the first part of the list is enumerated is determined by the construction with καὶ ὅτι; this suggests 15:5a as the original conclusion of the traditional unit. In favor of this is not only the appearance formula of Luke 24:34 that is limited to Simon Peter alone but also the Pauline connecting particle ἔπειτα with which the enumeration is continued in 5b.

The insight that a piece of earlier tradition is found in this passage is first found in J. W. Straatmann.[101] According to A. Seeberg,[102] Paul cites a traditional formula in 1 Corinthians 15:3–5. A. v. Harnack[103] reconstructs two competing traditions that were present in the tradition: (1) 15:3b-5: a double appearance of the Risen One to Peter and to the Twelve, and (2) in 15:7 a double appearance to James and all the apostles. This double tradition reflects the tensions in the earliest Jerusalem church, in which the claims of Peter and James stood over against each other. Against this hypothesis is to be objected, however, that the two formulae are not equivalent, since the second merely lists names and can hardly ever have existed independently. It must rather have been the case that such a list was originally connected with a kerygmatic declaration. It is thus more likely that Paul himself secondarily expanded the traditional formula (15:3b-5a) by adding additional names from the oral tradition.

The prepauline formula contains four lines of differing weight. The emphasis falls on lines I and III; here the essential content of the kerygma is presented: the death and resurrection of Jesus. The second line (II) functions to confirm the death of Jesus; the burial demonstrates the factual reality of Jesus death. This line accordingly has no independent importance, and is not some sort of anticipatory testimony of the factual reality of the empty tomb. So also line IV refers back to the preceding line III; it underscores the statement that Jesus was raised: the appearance to Cephas demonstrates the fact of the preceding resurrection of Jesus.

The formula is not interested in the fact of the death and resurrection as events in and of themselves, however, but interprets them: the death happened "for our sins according to the Scriptures;" the death of Jesus is understood as an "atoning death." It thus corresponds to the testimony of the Scripture and thereby to the will of God as this is presented in the Old Testament.[104] What is intended is the general affirmation: the atoning

---

[101] J. W. Straatmann, *De realiteit van's Heeren opstanding uit de dooden en hare verdedigers* (Gronigen 1862).

[102] A. Seeberg, *Der Katechismus der Urchristenheit* (Leipzig: Quelle & Meyer, 1903) (= TB 26, Munich: Kaiser, 1966) 50ff.

[103] A. v. Harnack, *Die Verklärungsgeschichte Jesu, der Bericht des Paulus 1 Kor 15,3ff und die beiden Christusvisionen des Petrus* (SPAW.PH. Berlin: W. de Gruyter, 1922) 62–80.

[104] The assumption that Isaiah 53:8–9 ("...he was cut off from the land of the living, stricken for the transgression of my people. They made his grave with the wicked

death of Jesus is according to the Scripture; there is no need to think that a particular passage of Scripture is presupposed (cf. Mark 14:49).

So also line III is amplified by a reference to Scripture, which is joined directly to the expression "raised on the third day."[105] Again, it is questionable whether a particular passage is in mind (for instance Hos 6:2, "on the third day he will raise us up, that we may live before him"). Here too the general affirmation could stand in the background that the resurrection on the third day is in principle according to the Scripture. At the same time, it can remain an open question whether in this passage "on the third day" the first appearances of the Risen One occurred on the third day or whether this datum was derived solely from Hosea 6:2.[106]

The reference to the witnesses of the appearances provides an indication of the basis on which the formula originated. Cephas is the Aramaic name for Simon Peter. Since he occupied the leading position in the circle of the Twelve and for a while was leader of the earliest Jerusalem church, one could suppose that the formula comes from Jerusalem. The arguments for a retranslation into Aramaic are not convincing.[107] The expression κατὰ τὰς γραφάς is not Semitic. The same is true of the anarthrous Χριστός. The formula thus originated in the Greek linguistic sphere. This does not necessarily exclude that it goes back to Palestinian soil. It then probably points not to Jerusalem[108] but to Galilee, for the first resurrection appearances took place in Galilee. The composers of the formula were

---

and his tomb with the rich") is the basis cannot be convincingly demonstrated (contra J. Jeremias *The Eucharistic Words of Jesus* [New York: Charles Scribner's Sons, 1966] 103). The German edition of 1967 contains further arguments by Jeremias.

[105] B. M. Metzger's claim that "according to the Scriptures" applies only to "he was raised" is off target ("Ein Vorschlag zur Bedeutung von 1 Kor 15,4b," in P. Hoffmann, ed. *Zur neutestamentlichen Überlieferung von der Auferstehung Jesu* [WdF 522. Darmstadt: Wissenschaftliche Buchgesellschaft, 1988] 126–132.) Similarly J. Roloff, *Neues Testament* (Neukirchen-Vluyn: Neukirchener, 1985⁴) 197: "The death and resurrection are here considered the two decisive saving events. Each of them is accompanied by two interpretative glosses: the statement about Jesus' death by 'for our sins' and 'according to the Scriptures;' the statement about Jesus' resurrection by 'on the third day' and again 'according to the Scriptures' ... the concord with the Scriptures is not said of his death for our sins, and analogously not of his resurrection on the third day but of his death and resurrection in general." But the grammatical structure of this verse speaks against this hypothesis.

[106] Less probably Matthew 12:40 (Jonah 2:1); cf. the listing of other but even less convincing explanatory attempts by H. Grass, *Ostergeschehen* 127ff.

[107] Differently J. Jeremias *Eucharistic Words*; cf. also the critique of H. Conzelmann, "On the Analysis of the Confessional Formula in I Corinthians 15:3–5," *Interpretation* 20/1 (January 1966) 15–25, esp. 18.

[108] Contra H. Conzelmann, "Confessional Formula" 22, who argues that the formula or the tradition on which it rests could possibly have originated in Jerusalem that this is not probable. The tradition of the appearances soon made its way to Jerusalem where the circle of the Twelve was located.

possibly Hellenistic Jewish Christian missionaries. There is no indication that the formula derived specifically from Antioch. Theoretically all areas come into consideration in which Hellenistic Jewish Christianity was present prior to Paul.

The formula affirms the saving significance of the fact of Jesus' death as declared in preaching and instruction, just as it does the fact of Jesus' resurrection as documented by the witnesses of the appearances. As the reality of the death of Jesus was demonstrated by his being placed in the tomb, so also the resurrection of Jesus is not a reality in and of itself but only to the extent that it is a verifiable fact as it is experienced in the appearances. The resurrection of Jesus is not "proven" by the empty tomb but experienced in the visions of the witnesses. The Christ kerygma is then essentially the kerygma of the witnesses. The Jesus event as the content of the kerygma is not separable from the role of the witnesses. This of course does not mean that Jesus rose exclusively into the kerygma and evaporated into a mere idea but rather that the kerygma includes reference to the historical event as a constitutive element.

Paul expanded the traditional formula by naming additional witnesses of the appearances after "Cephas" (15:6–7): the Twelve, the leading circle of the earliest Jerusalem church, to which Peter belonged as leader; then the appearance to the five hundred brothers and sisters, an event that is not to be identified with Pentecost[109] but reflects an otherwise unknown appearance episode. That the majority of the five hundred are still alive as Paul writes breaks the purely narrative framework and indicates the Pauline intention; it affirms: these claims can be checked.

James is the brother of the Lord; "all the apostles" means a circle of missionaries that bear the title of apostle; it is not identical with the Twelve. Paul includes himself in this category of "apostles," as the last one. By this means his own testimony is authorized, just as is the case for the other witnesses. As the final witness to the appearances he stands at the endpoint of a historical series, which legitimizes his claim to be an apostle. This is the way he expresses it in his confrontation with the Corinthian pneumatics. These spiritualize the resurrection event and in their spirit-enthusiasm locate themselves as already beyond death. In contrast to this the Pauline line of argument has the intention of bringing to expression the historical reservation: the resurrection of Jesus is not to be restricted to an inner event but is a "historical" reality. Therefore the

---

[109] This thesis was advocated by C. H. Weisse, *Die evangelische Geschichte kritisch und philosophisch bearbeitet* (Leipzig 1838) 416–420, later by E. v. Dobschütz and A. v. Harnack; cf. S. MacL. Gilmour, "Die Christophanie vor mehr als fünfhundert Brüdern," P. Hoffmann, ed. *Zur neutestamentlichen Überlieferung* 133–138. Additional publications of Gilmour are listed in G. Luedemann, *Resurrection* 225 n. 403.

future resurrection will also "really" happen. With this argumentation Paul here emphasizes the historical foundation of his proclamation as he does nowhere else. He was compelled to do this by the debate with his opponents. The original kerygma is expanded in the direction history, with the result that the resurrection of Jesus receives the appearance of a miraculous event certified by evidence.[110]

# II. The Person of Jesus Christ

Paul traces his conversion and call to be an apostle to a "revelation of the Son of God," i.e. to a knowledge of Christ that laid the foundation for a new existence (Gal 1:16). The theology of Paul therefore has a christological point of departure. At its beginning stands neither a doctrine of God nor a doctrine of creation, nor does he begin with a distinctively Pauline understanding of the law or justification. If Christ is God's gracious turning to humanity and promise to them, as well as representing the divine claim on humanity, then this means that in the Pauline interpretation the understanding of God is incorporated into the Pauline interpretation of the Christ event. On this basis, the person of Christ should be the place to begin. The liberation that comes through Christ will be dealt with only in second place. This corresponds to the classical distinction between the person and work of Jesus Christ. The work of Christ is not to be recognized apart from the object of this work, human beings. The liberation that comes through Christ can not be portrayed without speaking of the liberated human beings. Therefore the third section will articulate the anthropological elements of Pauline theology.

Just as in the Pauline understanding Christians are people who have been freed by the Christ event, so the church is the community of the free (Part IV). This means that Paul can understand the eschatological reality of salvation as a present reality. But it also has a future reality: the church is the community of those who are saved "in hope" (Rom 8:24). Accord-

---

[110] Something like this is expressed in Acts 17:31. R. Bultmann sees a contradiction between the Pauline line of argument in 1 Corinthians 15:1ff and the authentic content of the preaching of the apostle; he states in his argument with Karl Barth that "this is a dangerous procedure" (literally "how fatal this line of argument is;" "New Testament and Mythology" in *Kerygma and Myth: A Theological Debate*, ed. H.-W. Bartsch [New York: Harper, 1961] 1–44; 39). In fact Paul's argumentation is in tension with his presupposition that his conviction of the truth of the Christian faith is not derivable from general principles, as it is in tension with his understanding expressed elsewhere of the cross and resurrection event as part of the eschatological saving act of God, a faith that is withdrawn from the realm of rational argument that can in its authentic sense only be experienced as faith itself.

ingly, the final section will develop Paul's eschatological concepts *in extensio* (Part V: The Future of the Free). Paul's eschatology does not define a *"locus de novissimis,"* is thus not a doctrinal topic that is handled as the final item in a list of Pauline doctrines in a systematic theology but eschatology is included in all his theological affirmations.

### a) The Names of the Christ

Berger, K. "Zum traditionsgeschichtlichen Hintergrund christologischer Hoheitstitel," *NTS* 17 (1970/71) 391–425.
Braun, H. "The Meaning of New Testament Christology," *God and Christ. Journal for Theology and Church* 5. R. W. Funk, ed. New York: Harper & Row, 1968, 89–127.
Dunn, J. D. G. *Christology in the Making.* Philadelphia: Westminster, 1980.
Fuller, R. H. *The Foundation of New Testament Christology.* New York: Scribner, 1965.
Hahn, F. *The Titles of Jesus in Christology; Their History in Early Christianity.* London: Lutterworth, 1969.
Kim, S. *The Origin of Paul's Gospel.* WUNT II/4. Tübingen: J. C. B. Mohr (Paul Siebeck), 1984[2].

H. Braun has pointed out the disparity of New Testament Christologies, how they for example come to expression in the difference between the Christology of John and Paul on the one hand and that of the Synoptics on the other, and has drawn the following conclusion from this phenomenon: anthropology is the constant, Christology is the variable. It must be objected against this that the anthropological statements of the New Testament writers are not to be isolated from their christological statements. Since they stand in a close connection with Christology, the disparity of Christologies must also result in a disparity of anthropologies. This can be illustrated by the different christological titles found in Paul: without exception the prepauline titles of Christ represent originally different theological conceptions.

### 1. Son of David

Burger, C. *Jesus als Davidssohn.* FRLANT 98. Göttingen: Vandenhoeck & Ruprecht, 1970.
Hahn, F. "υἱός," *EWNT* III (1983) 912–937.
Karrer, M. *Der Gesalbte. Die Grundlagen des Christustitels.* FRLANT 151. Göttingen: Vandenhoeck & Ruprecht, 1991.
Lohse, E. "υἱὸς Δαυίδ," *TDNT* VIII (1969) 482–488.
Wrede, W. "Jesus als Davidssohn," W. Wrede. *Vorträge und Studien.* Tübingen: J. C. B. Mohr (Paul Siebeck), 1907. 147–177.

The title υἱὸς Δαυίδ is not found in Paul but is presupposed by the pre-Pauline confessional formula in Romans 1:3. "Son of David" is a Jewish messianic designation, though it is not found in precisely this form until

after the Old Testament period.[1] It takes up the Old Testament promise
of a Davidic kingship that would never pass away (2 Sam 7:12–16) and the
expectation of a "branch of David" (Jer 23:5; 33:15; Zech 3:8; 6:12) and
points not only to the descendents of the Jewish king David but the expectation of salvation associated with the Davidic line. In ancient Judaism
the "ben David" is the expected Messiah, the salvific figure who will bring
the future of the Jewish people to a magnificent conclusion. Such a Messiah is a messianic military commander. The salvation he brings is political salvation. The expectation of his coming has apocalyptic features.[2]

Earliest Christianity took over this title and applied it to Jesus. The
genealogies of Jesus (Matt 1:1ff; Luke 3:23ff) want to show that Joseph, the
father of Jesus, is a descendent of David. The two genealogies in Matthew
and Luke differ considerably from each other. We are obviously dealing
with secondary constructions that presuppose the theologoumenon of the
Davidic sonship. It thus appears that the Hellenistic concept of the virgin
birth was worked in only later (Matt 1:16), since the genealogies originally
refer to Joseph as the natural father of Jesus. In this connection the note
of Eusebius that appeals to the report of Hegesippus deserves attention
(Eusebius HE 3.19–20). According to Eusebius, the emperor Domitian
summoned two descendents of Jude the brother of the Lord to appear
before his court, because they belonged to the Davidic family and it was
obviously feared that they might become the focus of political unrest. If
this note is accurate, at the end of the first century Christian relatives of
the Lord traced their genealogy back to David. This does not mean, however, that the genealogies of Jesus in the New Testament are authentic. It
is possible that the consciousness of being descendents of David was
generated in Jesus' family as the effect of the theologoumenon of Jesus as
the Messianic Son of David.

The pericope about the issue of Davidic sonship (Mark 12:35–37par;
cf. Acts 2:34), by contrasting "Son of David" and "Lord," is clearly critical
of the Son of David Christology. It is difficult to understand the passage
as a scribal disputation about the relation of these two titles to each other,[3]
nor does it attempt to resolve the given problem in the sense of a two stage
Christology on the lines of Romans 1:3–4.[4] The pericope allows us to
perceive that the application of the title "Son of David" to Jesus was a
disputed issue in early Christian tradition.

---

[1]    Psalms of Solomon 17:21; cf. Isaiah 11:1–9; Ezekiel 34:23; 37:24; Psalm 89:21; cf.
       also Amos 9:11–15; Micah 5:1–5; Zechariah 4:1–14.
[2]    Cf. 1 Enoch 45:3ff; 46; 4 Ezra 7:28ff; 12:32; Psalms of Solomon 17:21; 4QIsa 11;
       4QPatr 3–5; 4QFlor 10–13.
[3]    So E. Lohse, *TDNT* 8:488.
[4]    Cf. J. Gnilka, *Das Evangelium nach Markus* (EKK II 21) (Neukirchen-Vluyn: Neu-
       kirchener, 1979) 171.

The Son of David Christology apparently originated in that Jewish Christianity that venerated Jesus as the savior sent to the Jewish people, the fulfiller of the promises given to the ancestors. It thus originally belonged to a national, particularistic religiosity. The Christology of Gentile Christianity had distanced itself from this understanding. The term "Son of David" had been depoliticized; neither is the term associated in the early Christian documents with apocalypticism.[5] This title was able to survive as an element of kerygmatic formulae ("seed of David": in addition to Rom 1:3 especially 2 Tim 2:8) or the biographical tradition (Luke 1:27; 2:11) and especially in the context of healing pericopes that are set in the context of the life of Jesus, and thus have the nationalistic Jewish background as their narrative, literary presupposition.[6] They serve the narrator's edifying intention. But even in the confessional formulae there is no outstanding significance, since the meaning of the term is subordinated to other christological designations.

## 2. Son of God

Delling, G. "Die Bezeichnung 'Söhne Gottes' in der jüdischen Literatur der hellenistisch-römischen Zeit," J. Jervell and W. A. Meeks, eds., *God's Christ and his People*. Oslo: Universitetsforl., 1977. 18–28.

Hengel, M. *The Son of God: The Origin of Christology and the History of Jewish-Hellenistic Religion*. Philadelphia: Fortress, 1976.

Kramer, W. *Christ, Lord, Son of God*. Naperville: A. R. Allenson, 1966.

Lohse, E. "υἱός," *TDNT* VIII (1969) 357–362.

Merklein, H. "Zur Entstehung der Aussagen vom präexistenten Sohn Gottes," G. Dautzenberg-H. Merklein-K. Müller, eds., *Zur Geschichte des Urchristentums*. QD 87. Freiburg-Basel-Wien: Herder, 1979. 33–62.

Norden, E. *Die Geburt des Kindes, Geschichte einer religiösen Idee*. SBW 3. Leipzig-Berlin 1931²; Darmstadt: Wissenschaftliche Buchgesellschaft, 1958.

Pokorný, P. *Der Gottessohn. Literarische Übersicht und Fragestellung*. ThSt 109. Zürich: Zwingli, 1971.

Talbert, C. H. *What is a Gospel? The Genre of the Canonical Gospel*. Philadelphia: Fortress, 1977.

Vielhauer, Ph. "Erwägungen zur Christologie des Markusevangeliums," Ph. Vielhauer. *Aufsätze zum Neuen Testament*. TB 31. Munich: Kaiser, 1965. 199–214.

Wetter, G. P. *Der Sohn Gottes*. FRLANT 26. Göttingen: Vandenhoeck & Ruprecht, 1916.

Windisch, H. *Paulus und Christus. Ein biblisch-religionsgeschichtlicher Vergleich*. UNT 24. Leipzig: J. C. Hindrichs, 1934.

The title υἱὸς (τοῦ) θεοῦ points first to that stream of Judaism in which the king of Israel could be indirectly described as "Son of God." Psalm 2:7

---

5   Differently F. Hahn, *The Titles of Jesus in Christology* 240–246, according to whom the oldest tradition of the Son of David Christology was apocalyptic (his evidence: Luke 1:68–75 and Rev 5:5).

6   Mark 10:47fpar; Matthew 9:27; 12:23; 15:22; cf. 21:9,15.

presents an example that speaks of a royal inthronization in which Yahweh acknowledges the king of Israel as his son, i.e. that God adopts or legitimizes the Judean king.[7] So also the prophecy of Nathan to king David in 2 Samuel 7:11–12, 14 can be understood in the sense of a royal messianic theology.[8] Adoption, installation into office, and conferral of authority to rule are the characteristic features of the Israelite / Jewish Messiah understood as Son of God.[9] From this point of departure there is no direct access to the Pauline Christology of Jesus as Son of God. The Israelite king as Son of Yahweh obviously had national and political functions. When Jesus is called "Son of God" in the Gospels this is not in order to designate him as a political ruler,[10] but he is placed in the category of the divine men who are endowed with supernatural power and who are acknowledged in the Greek and Hellenistic world to be "sons of God." A θεῖος ἀνήρ is a son of God who, like Hercules or other ancient heroes, strides across the earth doing wonderful deeds of power. Thus Jesus performs healing miracles, exorcisms, and powerful deeds that show him to be a supernatural, more-

---

[7]   Cf. also Ps 89:4–5, 20–38.
[8]   Cf. 2 Samuel 7:14a ("I will be his father, and he will be my son."). A messianic interpretation of the passage is found in 4Qflor 1.11–13; cf. also 1Qsa 2.11.
[9]   E. Lohse, TDNT 8:361–363, shows that postbiblical Judaism spoke of the "Son of God" only in with reference to passages understood to refer the promised Messiah (Ps 2:7; 2 Sam 7:14a) but otherwise avoided this term as a designation of the Messiah. Thus in 4Qflor 1.11–13, while 2 Samuel 7:14 is cited, the term "Son of God" is not used. In 1 Enoch 105:2 "my Son" is secondary; in 4 Ezra 7:28, 13:32, 37, 52; 14:9, the term παῖς is presupposed for the Greek. F. Hahn's supposition that "in Old Testament and Jewish tradition not only the concept of the Messiah as God's Son was found but the title 'Son of God' was used" (EWNT 3.916) has so far not been documented in the texts themselves. Because of the strictly monotheistic understanding of God in Judaism and the physical component suggested by the title "Son of God" such a messianic use of the term is improbable. That does not exclude that in ancient Judaism the Israelites could be called "sons of God" (Deut 14:1; WisSol 9:7; 12:19, 21) or that the people of Israel could be called "Son of God" (Exod 4:22; WisSol 18:13), or that pious individual Israelites could be so designated (Wis Sol 2:18; Joseph and Aseneth 21:4).
[10]  To be sure, it is relatively seldom the case that the title "Son of God" is applied to the Hellenistic rulers (but cf. A. Deissmann, *Light from the Ancient East* 346–347). As a rule the royal dynasty is connected to the god of the state. In the Greek world there was the idea that heroes such as Hercules had Zeus as their father and a human being as their mother (Homer II 19.98ff). It was said of famous philosophers such as Plato or Aristotle that Apollo had begotten them (Plut QuaestConv VIII 1,2; Orig Cels I 37; Diog Laert 3,2; 5,1; Apul De Platone I). In Stoic popular philosophy the old idea that Zeus was the father of the gods and of particular human beings had become the doctrine that Zeus was the father of human beings in general (Epic Diss I 3.1). So also in the Greek world it was said of Hercules the Son of God that he had gone to Olympus and had been invested with divine functions (Apollodorus II 7.7), just as also of θεῖοι ἀνδρές such as Apollonius of Tyana (Philostratus, *Life of Appolonius* 8.30) or Peregrinus Proteus (Lucian, *Death of Peregrinus* 36, 39). Cf. W. v. Martiz, *TDNT* 8:336, and below B III c 3.

than-human being. Hellenistic Judaism had already applied the "divine man" concept to Old Testament figures.[11] In the Hellenistic thought world this term was understood in a physical sense. The supernatural nature of this heavenly being comes to expression in his deeds but also in his physiological makeup. Such a physical understanding of "son of God" is presupposed in the New Testament when Jesus is understood as born of a virgin. Here Hellenistic Jewish Christianity has accommodated its understanding of the Christ of faith to the Hellenistic milieu (Matt 1:18ff; Luke 1:26ff). In contrast, the understanding of Jesus as having been adopted as Son of God at his baptism is closer to the Old Testament / Jewish royal messianic Theology, which has possibly been influenced by an ancient Egyptian inthronization ritual[12]—as also may be the case in the transfiguration story (Mark 9:2) in which Jesus is proclaimed as Son of God.

In Paul the title υἱὸς θεοῦ is applied primarily not to the earthly Jesus but to the exalted Christ. It is found in prepauline formulae as well as in Pauline expressions.[13] For the prepauline tradition in which Jesus appears as Son of God, a distinction is to be made between:

(1) *Adoption*[14] as Son of God and

(2) The *sending* (ἐξαποστέλλειν) of the Son of God. A sending formula is found in Galatians 4:4–5 ("But when the fullness of time had come, God sent his Son, born of a woman, born under the law, in order to redeem those who were under the law, so that we might receive adoption as children [lit. 'sons'].")[15] The sending of the Son is the basis for the believer's "sonship" to God. Paul interprets this by identifying "sonship" with the gift of the Spirit and becoming an heir (Gal 4:6–7).

(3) The *"giving over"* of the Son is affirmed in Romans 8:32 ("He who did not withhold his own Son but gave him up for all of us, will he not with him also give us everything else?") and in Galatians 2:20 ("the life I now live in the flesh I live by faith in the Son of God, who loved me and gave himself for me"). The "giving over" (παραδίδωμι) can be identified with the assumption of earthly existence (as in Phil 2:7, λαβών) but the Pauline understanding is primarily oriented to the passion. God is the acting

---

11  On the whole subject, see also H. Windisch, *Paul und Christus;* C. H. Holladay, *THEIOS ANER in Hellenistic Judaism: A Critique of the Use of This Category in New Testament Christology* (SBLDS 40. Missoula: Scholars Press, 1977). Cf. Philo Gig 60ff (Abraham); Sacr 9 (Moses); Plant 29 (David); Imm 138–139 (Elijah); also Josephus Ant III 180, 318 (Moses) X 35 (Isaiah). On the basis of Deuteronomy 33:1, Philo calls Moses a "divine man" (Mut 25, 125); cf. also Joseph and Aseneth 21:4 (Joseph as "son of the Most High").

12  Cf. E. Norden, *Geburt des Kindes* 166ff; Ph. Vielhauer, *Erwägungen zur Christologie* 212–213.

13  Paul uses the title in his own formulations: Romans 1:3, 9; 5:10; 8:29; 1 Corinthians 1:9; 15:28; 2 Corinthians 1:19; Galatians 1:16; 4:6.

14  Cf. Romans 1:4.

15  Cf. also Romans 8:3 (πέμψας)

subject: the Son is delivered over to suffering and death by the divine decision. The Son gives himself over to the Father's will that calls him to accept the fate of the cross. For believers, this means: their existence is grounded in the "extra nos," in the death of the Son of God Jesus Christ on the cross as the death of the Revealer. The significance of this saving act is underscored by the fact that Paul understands Christ as the pre-existent Son of God (cf. Phil 2:6). This is the sense in which Paul also interprets the sending-formulae and the giving-over-formulae.

A special position with the Son of God Christology is occupied by 1 Thessalonians 1:9b-10, a prepauline formula that apparently comes from the mission carried on by Hellenistic Jewish Christians.[16] The formula has two members, pointing to the believers' worship of God and their awaiting God's Son from heaven.[17] The addressees are presupposed to be Gentiles; the monotheistic faith is a given for Jews. The concept of God is found here in connection with the expectation of the parousia. Just as the Son of God is regarded as the "savior" from the future wrath, so he is also the guarantor of the believers' security in the future judgment. Such a decided apocalyptic trait in the framework of the Son of God Christology is unique.

The last example, in comparison with the other passages, shows the disparate nature of the New Testament Son of God Christology. The fact that it was influenced at its origins by different streams of influence from the thought worlds of Judaism and the Hellenistic world shows that this predicate could be used in different christological contexts. There were essentially two elements that already had substantial connections with this title prior to Paul: (1) the concept of adoption corresponding to the Old Testament and Jewish and/or ancient Egyptian royal ideology, and (2) the physical component, especially as connected with the theologoumenon of the virgin birth, which stands nearer to the Hellenistic / Gentile world of thought. The details of the concept υἱὸς τοῦ θεοῦ could be adapted in different senses. This is the reason the term is never restricted by Paul to specific theological topics. In Pauline theology the term became a general designation for the bearer of the eschatological event of salvation.

## 3. Kyrios

Bousset, W. Jesus der Herr. Nachträge und Auseinandersetzungen zu Kyrios Christos. FRLANT 25. Göttingen: Vandenhoeck & Ruprecht, 1916.
Bousset, W. Kyrios Christos. A History of the Belief in Christ from the Beginnings of Christianity to Irenaeus. FRLANT 21. Göttingen: Vandenhoeck & Ruprecht, 1921[6].
Fauth, W. "Kyrios, Kyria," KP III 413–417.

---

[16]  Cf. differently T. Holtz, Der erste Brief an die Thessalonicher (EKK VIII) (Neu-kirchen-Vluyn: Neukirchener, 1986) 60ff, and the discussion of Holtz above.

[17]  E. Schweizer, υἱός TDNT 8:372, supposes that there was an original statement about the Son of Man that Paul has reinterpreted by inserting the Son of God title.

Fitzmyer, J. A. "κύριος," *EWNT* II (1981) 811–820.
Fitzmyer, J. A. "The Semitic Background of the New Testament *Kyrios* Title," *A Wandering Aramean*. Missoula: Scholars Press, 1979, 115–117.
Foerster, W. "κύριος," *TDNT* III (1938) 1038–1056.1081–1095.
Hanhart, R. *Drei Studien zum Judentum*. TEH 140. Munich: Kaiser, 1967. 57–62.
Schulz, S. "Maranatha und Kyrios Jesus," *ZNW* 53 (1962) 125–144.
Vielhauer, Ph. *Ein Weg zur neutestamentlichen Christologie? ders., Aufsätze zum Neuen Testament*. TB 31. Munich: Kaiser, 1965. 141–198.

The Kyrios title occupies a central position within Pauline theology. Bousset posed the influential thesis that κύριος is a Hellenistic-oriental title that originally had been applied to pagan cultic deities and was applied to Jesus in Hellenistic Christianity. In this way Jesus as the bringer of salvation from the perspective of Christian faith is supposed to have been distinguished from the deities of the Hellenistic cults. It appears at first to speak against this thesis that according to the picture in the Synoptic Gospels Jesus was addressed with the title *Kyrios*; but it must be asked whether this title actually goes back to the time of Jesus,[18] since it is to be noted that the portraits of Jesus in the Synoptics represent a later repainting in which the earlier pictures were painted over. To the extent that a cultic usage of the term can be perceived there, it originates within the church tradition. At the most it might be supposed that the historical Jesus was addressed with the Aramaic *"Mare"* (מָרֵא), which was then translated into Greek as κύριε.[19] Of course, we cannot be certain of even this, and in any case it is not possible from such a usage to derive any inference about the christological status attributed to Jesus.

Weighty considerations speak against Bousset's thesis: Thus the early Christian acclamation "Maranatha" in 1 Corinthians 15:22 (מָרָנָא תָא, "Our Lord, come").[20] The Aramaic formula could come from the earliest Palestinian church and then have been taken over without translation in the worship of the Pauline Hellenistic churches. Jesus here receives the Aramaic predication *"Mare"* in combination with the first person plural suffix. The earliest church could thereby have adopted the designation for God, as it lay before them in the book of Daniel.[21] Aramaic inscriptions also show that Oriental deities were addressed as *"Mare."*[22] The Qumran

[18] So F. Hahn, *The Titles of Jesus in Christology* 73ff.
[19] S. F. Hahn, *The Titles of Jesus in Christology* 79–81, according to whom the original form with the first person suffix מָר was in circulation along with an alternate form רַבִּי.
[20] Another possibility is to read "Maran atha" (מָרַן אֲתָא = "Our Lord has come.") On the basis of Revelation 22:20 however, the imperative interpretation is to be preferred.
[21] מָרֵא of course stands here only in the construct relation: Daniel 2:47 וּמָרֵא מַלְכִין (the Lord of kings) and Daniel 5:23 מָרֵא שְׁמַיָּא (the Lord of heaven).
[22] Cf. the documentation in H. Donner-W. Rölling KAI 1–3, Wiesbaden 1962–1964; 1973³ (Volume 2: Commentary No. 201, 246–248, 251, 256).

literature has three examples of the use of the absolute (מָרֵא); or the *status emphaticus* (מָרָא) as a designation for God.[23] To be sure, the complete equation Yahweh-מָרִיא-κύριος is not thereby given.[24] Neither is it the case that such religious use of the term was very widespread. All the same, a Christian Aramaic language realm can be perceived within which it would have been possible with the suffixed form "Maranatha" to express a specific rank and office to Jesus that stands within the apocalyptic thought world. This corresponds to the concept of the Son of Man, which is also apocalyptic: just as the "day of the Son of Man" is expected at the Endtime,[25] so in the acclamation Maranatha the conviction is expressed that at the parousia Jesus will appear as the Mar-Kyrios.[26]

The invocation of Jesus as "our Lord" or as "my Lord" cannot be identified with the absolute ὁ κύριος or the vocative κύριε that emerged in the Greek speaking stream of earliest Christianity.[27] This usage is to be traced back to Gentile Christian churches. Here the Hellenistic-cultic understanding of the Kyrios has been influential—as Bousset correctly recognized. It is characteristic of this piety that Jesus is understood to be the cult hero who is present in the worship.[28] While Paul does presuppose such a way of thinking,[29] alongside this he also has the combination that includes the possessive pronoun, which corresponds to Palestinian usage.[30]

The hymn in Philippians 2:6–11 documents the transition in the history of the tradition from the apocalyptic *Mare-Kyrios* address of the earliest Palestinian church to the Hellenistic Christian predication of the present *Kyrios*. The two strophes point to a chronological distinction: 2:9

---

23   11QTgJob 34.12 (24.6); 1QGenApoc 20.12–13, 15; 4Qen^b 1. IV 5 = 1 Enoch 10.9; cf. K. Beyer, *Die aramäischen Texte vom Toten Meer samt den Inschriften aus Palästina, des Testaments Levi aus der Kairoer Genisa, der Fastenrolle und den alten talmudischen Zitaten* (Göttingen: Vandenhoeck & Ruprecht, 1984) 175, 238, 292.

24   Correctly: J. A. Fitzmyer, *Semitic Background* 131.

25   Daniel 7:13–14; 1 Enoch 45:3; 62:1; 61:5 (the day of the elect); 4 Ezra 13:3; 13:52 (the day of the servant); Luke 17:22–30 (the days of the Son of Man).

26   R. Bultmann, *Theology* 1:51–52 avoids this conclusion by postulating that מָרֵא in this formula originally referred not to Jesus but to God. This is hardly probable, since in Judaism God was rarely addressed with מָר, and since the Greek translation of this invocation clearly is directed to Jesus (Rev 22:20; Did 10:6).

27   Cf. Luke 6:46 κύριε κύριε; Revelation 22:20: ἔρχου κύριε Ἰησοῦ. Differently J. A. Fitzmyer, "The Semitic Background of the New Testament *Kyrios* Title," *A Wandering Aramean*. Missoula: Scholars Press, 1979, 115–117.

28   In the same way pagan cultic deities such as Asclepius were thought of as present in their cultic rituals; cf. also the designation of the mystery goddess Isis as Kyria; W. Foerster, *TDNT* 3:1046–1058.

29   For the absolute ὁ κύριος cf. e. g. Philippians 2:11; 1 Corinthians 8:6; Philemon 5.

30   E. g. 1 Thessalonians 1:3, "hope in our Lord Jesus Christ;" Romans 1:4; 1 Corinthians 1:7–8; 9:1; Galatians 6:14.

contains the confession of the community to its Lord, whose name is "now" praised. In contrast, the following verses 10–11 point to the eschatological future; only then will the apocalyptic honoring of Jesus by the cosmic powers take place. Here the apocalyptic-Palestinian *Mare-Kyrios* Christology is used.[31] The Philippian Christ-hymn unites the Jewish-Christian Palestinian with the Gentile-Christian Hellenistic Christology.

Thus while Paul's apocalyptic Marana tha acclamation presupposes an Aramaic-Palestinian background in the congregational liturgy, his absolute usage of the term goes back to the Hellenistic tradition.[32] This might suggest that the influence of the LXX on the formation of the Kyrios titles should not be overestimated. This would harmonize with the fact that in the Septuagint texts that were written by Jews for Jews and presumably were intended for use in worship, the Tetragrammaton יהוה was not translated but reproduced in the Hebrew letters.[33] Accordingly, the translation of the Tetragrammaton with "Kyrios" cannot be presupposed as a general practice for the Pauline period. However, Paul does cite LXX texts in which the Tetragrammaton is rendered with *Kyrios*.[34] It is hardly a matter of an exclusively Pauline or Christian coinage,[35] but Paul is making use of a translation made by Jews in order to communicate with Greeks. The influence of oral tradition may also need to be taken into consideration.[36] In individual cases this works out as follows: in the texts Paul cites the title is used predominately of Yahweh but Paul himself can apply it to either God or to Christ.

It is probably the case that in the prepauline Christian tradition the title Kyrios in the Greek Old Testament had already been applied to

---

[31]   In addition to the allusion to the allusion to Isaiah 45:23 LXX, cf. also Isaiah 45:25 LXX (ἀπὸ κυρίου).

[32]   Cf. 1 Corinthians 8:5,"Indeed, even though there may be so-called gods in heaven or on earth—as in fact there are many gods and many lords—"; κύριοι here is a designation for the cultic deities.

[33]   It is disputed whether this represents an old form of the text, or whether it is not rather the case that the instances of יהוה has been inserted secondarily in later texts to replace an original κύριος. A. Pietersma makes a persuasive argument for this latter view in "Kyrios or Tetragram: A Renewed Quest for the Original LXX," *De Septuaginta* (Festschrift for J. W. Wevers) (Missisauga, Ont., 1984) 85–101.

[34]   Cf. 1 Corinthians 3:20; Romans 9:28–29; 10:16; 11:3, 34 and elsewhere; cf. also 1 Thessalonians 4:6.

[35]   Contra Ph. Vielhauer, "Ein Weg zur neutestamentlichen Christologie;" cf. correctly R. Hanhart, *Drei Studien zum Judaism* 59–60.

[36]   So D.-A. Koch, *Die Schrift als Zeuge* 86–87: at the time of Paul it was generally assumed that the Tetragrammaton was to be orally translated with κύριος. Thus Paul's written use of κύριος was not particularly innovative. This corresponds to the practice of ancient Hellenistic Judaism; cf. Philo Somn 1.163; Abr 121; All 96; Plant 86; Mut 15, 19, 24; WisSol 3:10; 4:18; 2 Maccabees 2:8; 3:33, and elsewhere. (Contra Conzelmann, *Theology* 83.)

Christ. The verbatim citation of Joel 2:23 (LXX 3:5) in Romans 10:13 is connected by Paul not to God but to Christ.[37] In accord with this, the Corinthian church is described by Paul as a community of people who "call upon the name of our Lord Jesus Christ."[38] In this prepauline designation of the Christian community the Kyrios title of the LXX had already been applied to Jesus.[39] The circumstance of the application to Jesus of the Septuagint's designation for God stands alongside the other factors that give meaning to the Kyrios title but is especially significant for Paul's understanding of the title. Jesus Christ can be thought of in the same terms used for the creator God of the Old Testament. Thus in 1 Corinthians 10:26 the universal (creator) power of Yahweh is, on the basis of Psalm 24:1 (23:1 LXX), conferred on Christ: "The earth is the Lord's and all that is in it, the world, and those who live in it." Similarly, the Christ-hymn of Philippians the cosmic worship of Yahweh is now applied to the Kyrios Jesus Christ.[40]

Kyrios designates the cosmic Lord of the community. Thus it is said in the prepauline formula 1 Corinthians 8:6:

... yet for us there is one God, the Father, from whom are all things and for whom we exist, and one Lord, Jesus Christ, through whom are all things and through whom we exist.

Here the concepts of preexistence and creation are associated with the Kyrios title. This connection will have been made in Hellenistic Jewish Christianity within the sphere of influence of Stoic thought. The "lordship" of Christ is manifest in the presently-effective cosmic dimension of his activity. This sometimes comes to expression in the concluding greetings of Pauline letters,[41] just as it does in their introductions.[42] Alongside the creator God of the Old Testament–Jewish tradition and the Hellenistic tradition, stands the Kyrios Jesus, who—differently that the "many Lords" of the pagan cults—participates in the all-encompassing sovereignty of his Father.

---

[37]    Romans 10:13: Πᾶς γὰρ ὃς ἂν ἐπικαλέσηται τὸ ὄνομα κυρίου σωθήσεται.
[38]    1 Corinthians 1:2; cf. Acts 2:21; 9:14, 21; 22:16.
[39]    Cf. Deuteronomy 4:7; Psalm 98:6 LXX; 1 Chronicles 13:6.
[40]    Philippians 2:10–11.
[41]    1 Thessalonians 5:28, "The grace of our Lord Jesus Christ be with you." The genitive τοῦ κυρίου is a genitive of source (grace is given by the Lord Jesus) and only secondarily an objective genitive: the grace that the Lord Jesus grants is he himself. Cf. Romans 16:20; 1 Corinthians 16:23; Galatians 6:18; Philippians 4:23; 2 Corinthians 13:13.
[42]    1 Corinthians 1:3, "Grace to you and peace from God our Father and the Lord Jesus Christ." In this salutation Hellenistic and Jewish elements are combined: χάρις appears to reflect the greeting χαίρειν typical of Greek letters, while εἰρήνη corresponds to the customary oriental greeting. Cf. 2 Corinthians 1:2; Galatians 1:3; Philippians 1:2; 1 Thessalonians 1:1; Romans 1:7, and elsewhere.

Kyrios is originally an appellative, a designation that needs to be supplemented by a personal name. Thus the community originally invoked not κύριε but the κύριος Ἰησοῦς (1 Cor 12:3; 10:9), and the eschatological confession of the cosmic powers sounds forth as κύριος Ἰησοῦς Χριστός (Phil 2:11). That such an expectation has already been realized in the present experience of the community and the Kyrios title bound up with the present exercise of sovereignty by the Kyrios Jesus, is indicated by the connection with the "name" (ὄνομα): the gathering of the community for worship is united in the name of the Lord Jesus in order to turn the sinner over to Satan (1 Cor 5:4–5). The name Ἰησοῦς is more than a mere appellation; it has an almost magical power and indicates not only the existence of a sphere of power, for the actual fact of the matter is that by naming the name of Jesus the sphere of power of the Lord Jesus is established. Where the name of Jesus is spoken, there the power of the Lord Jesus is effective.

The essential nature of the apostolic preaching can also be understood in this perspective. According to 2 Corinthians 4:5 the extension of the realm of Christ's lordship happens by means of preaching, for through the word of the apostle is grounded the community of those who call on the name of the Lord Jesus and are incorporated within the sphere of Jesus' power. Apart from that, the naming of the name of the Kyrios Jesus has a constitutive significance for the worship life of the community: in the baptismal ceremony, in connection with the act of baptism the name of the Lord Jesus is spoken and the baptismal candidate is thereby brought under the power of the Lord Jesus. First Corinthians 6:11 reflects the influence of the baptismal liturgy:

... you were washed [in the waters of baptism], you were sanctified, you were justified in the name of the Lord Jesus Christ and in the Spirit of our God.

The Spirit is the gift given in baptism; it incorporates the one being baptized into the eschatological reality of salvation. The same happens when the name of the Lord Jesus Christ is invoked. It is not only the water that in connection with the Spirit possesses an eschatological quality the invocation of the name of Jesus brings a new state of affairs into being; it means the conferral of the eschatological gift of salvation by the incorporation of the baptized into the realm of sovereignty of the Kyrios Jesus.

The eucharist is called by Paul the "Lord's Supper" (1 Cor 11:20, κυριακὸν δεῖπνον) because it is practiced under the command and promise of the Kyrios. It mediates communion with the exalted Lord, which also corresponds to the designation "the Lord's Table" (1 Cor 10:21, τράπεζα κυρίου).

Through word and sacrament believers become subjects in the realm of the Lord's sovereignty. The whole life of the believer receives its norm for action from the Kyrios. The Christian's assignment is "to serve the

Lord" (Rom 12:11 τῷ κυρίῳ δουλεύειν) or "to please the Lord" (1 Cor 7:32 ἀρέσκειν τῷ κυρίῳ). The believer's concrete experience and act is not separable from the Kyrios but happens "in the Lord" (ἐν τῷ κυρίῳ).[43] The Kyrios is the authority who is present in the community, who comprehends all the expressions of the believers' life.[44]

Kyrios means essentially the exalted, present Lord of the community; so also in 2 Corinthians 3:17, where the way in which the Lord is present is explained: "The Lord is the Spirit" (ὁ κύριος τὸ πνεῦμά ἐστιν).[45] W. Bousset considers this passage to be the central statement of Pauline Christology. Faith in Christ is then essentially faith in the Spirit. One may not take this text out of its context—it deals with Paul's exegetical explanation of the preceding citation from the Old Testament (Exod 34:34), in which the contrast letter / spirit is addressed—but it is still true: whoever belongs to the Lord no longer belongs to the old order of the letter but is incorporated in the new order of the Spirit (2 Cor 3:6). The copula ἐστίν therefore not only has an explicative function, according to which Kyrios merely "means" πνεῦμα. It is rather the case that 3:18 suggests that a pneumatic mode of being is the appropriate form of existence of the exalted Lord of the community. Paul here intends not only an interpretation of the term "Kyrios" by means of the pneuma concept but comes close to identifying them: those who live in communion with the Kyrios find themselves in the sphere of the Spirit. Of course Paul knows of no mystical unity of Christ or Christians and the Spirit but rather distinguishes between the "Spirit of Christ" and the believers (Phil 1:19), and he differentiates the Spirit from the believers when he speaks of the divine sending of the Spirit of Christ (Gal 4:6). On the other hand, a statement about the "Spirit of God" can be continued by referring to the "Spirit of Christ" (Rom 8:9), and the distinction that has been made is also bridged when Paul declares that the "communion of the Holy Spirit" is at the same time communion with the "grace of the Lord Jesus Christ" and the "love of God" (2 Cor 13:13).

Paul not only refers to the present Lord but also the past, earthly life of Jesus as the Kyrios. This is the one who instituted the Lord's Supper on

---

[43] So especially in parenetic contexts: Romans 14:14; 1 Corinthians 4:17; 7:22, 39; 9:1–2; 11:11; 15:58; Galatians 5:10; Philippians 3:1; 4:1; 1 Thessalonians 3:8.

[44] This is the basis for F. Neugebauer's argument that in Paul's writings "Christ" is a personified indicative, while "Kyrios" is a personified imperative ("Das Paulinische 'In Christo'," NTS 4 (1957/58) 124–138; 128; and In Christus. Eine Untersuchung zum paulinischen Glaubensverständnis [Göttingen: Vandenhoeck & Ruprecht, 1961]). While this exegesis may be one-sided, as will be pointed out in the following section on the title "Christ," it is still correctly emphasized that the title "Kyrios" has an important function in parenetic contexts.

[45] Cf. F. W. Horn, Angeld des Geistes 324–345.

the night in which he was betrayed (1 Cor 11:23). The saving event of the past is an event in the life of the Kyrios Jesus: he was killed by the Jews (1 Thess 2:15), died on the cross (Gal 6:14), and was raised from the dead (Rom 4:24).

As is the case with the past, so also the future is determined by the "lordship" (κυριότης) of Jesus. The concrete goal of the hope of the community is the parousia of the Kyrios Jesus (1 Thess 2:19). The focus of the future expectation is the "day of the Kyrios Jesus" (1 Cor 1:8; 2 Cor 1:14). In the future the Kyrios will appear as the "Savior" (σωτήρ, Phil 3:20). This future expectation corresponds to the acclamation "Maranatha" in its apocalyptic meaning and reflects the Palestinian-Jewish roots of the Kyrios title.

Kyrios is the central christological predicate of Pauline theology. It is Paul's own preferred title when he formulates his statements without dependence on the tradition. This is the reason that the essential structures of Pauline thought can be discerned by the use of this title in the apostle's letters.

## 4.   Christ

de Jonge, M. "The Earliest Christian Use of Christos. Some Suggestions," *NTS* 32 (1986) 321–343.

Grundmann, W. "χρίω etc.," *TDNT* IX (1973) 540–566.

Hengel, M. Erwägungen zum Sprachgebrauch von Χριστός bei Paulus und in der 'vorpaulinischen Überlieferung', M.D. Hooker-S. G. Wilson, eds., *Paul and Paulinism. Essays in honour of C. K. Barrett*. London: Lutterworth, 1982. 135–159.

Karrer, M. *Der Gesalbte. Die Grundlagen des Christustitels*. FRLANT 151. Göttingen: Vandenhoeck & Ruprecht, 1991.

The title ὁ Χριστός ("the anointed one") was originally the translation of the Old Testament-Hebrew מָשִׁיחַ, a title that in ancient Israel referred primarily to the political ruler. An "anointing" is also associated in the tradition with prophets[46] and priests.[47] As the "anointed of Yahweh" (מְשִׁיחַ יְהוָה)[48] the Israelite king had a supernatural authority that raised him above his ordinary contemporaries. The "Messiah" first became a designation for the eschatological bringer of salvation when it was referred to the future. The term did not yet possess this function in the pre-exilic prophecies of salvation of Isaiah, in which, to be sure, the royal figure of an anointed bringer of salvation was expected in the future but the title "Messiah" is not used in this connection. In post-exilic prophecy (Haggai

---

[46]   1 Kings 19:15–16; cf. Isaiah 61:1.
[47]   Numbers 4:3, 5, 16; 6:15.
[48]   1 Samuel 24:7ff; 2 Samuel 1:14ff; cf. Psalm 2:2; in the Davidic psalms 18:51; 20:7; 28:8.

and Zechariah) there are expressed hopes for a king and a high priest who will be savior figures; in Zechariah 4:14 these are named "anointed ones" (בְּנֵי הַיִּצְהָר, "sons of oil) by applying the picture of two olive trees to them, to be sure only within the context of an expectation of the near eschatological consummation that was soon extinguished. It is not until the apocalyptic literature of postbiblical Judaism that "Messiah" designates the eschatological bringer of salvation.[49] In the time of Jesus there was an extraordinary variety of messianic ideas in contemporary Judaism. At Qumran there was an expectation of two messianic figures who would appear at the Endtime, a priestly Messiah from Aaron and a political, royal Messiah from Israel.[50]

Jesus probably did not present himself as the Messiah.[51] If Jesus had believed that he was the Messiah and had so presented himself to the public, one would have to expect that the Synoptic tradition would have transmitted a clear dispute with the Jewish messianic ideas of Jesus' time. That is not the case; the so-called title on the cross (Mark 15:26par; ὁ βασιλεὺς τῶν Ἰουδαίων) cannot be presented as evidence for this thesis. The appearance of the historical Jesus before the public is comparable to that of John the Baptist. Accordingly, Jesus did not claim to be the national Messiah of the Jewish people but rather a prophet of the last days. The title "Christ" was first given to Jesus after Easter, corresponding to other christological titles used to interpret the significance of the Risen One. Possibly Acts 2:36 can be cited as documenting this:

> Therefore let the entire house of Israel know with certainty that God has made him both Lord and Messiah, this Jesus whom you crucified.

The context, of course, is to be attributed to Luke but the brief formula reflects the fact that the community's confession of Jesus as the Χριστός began with and was based on its faith in Jesus' resurrection.

The use of the term in early Christianity alternated between titular usage and understanding Χριστός as a personal name. The titular use, often recognized by the preceding article, is found especially frequently in the context of discussions with the Jews (John 7:26–27, 41; 11:27), as well as in such passages as Peter's confession at Caesarea Philippi (Mark 8:29parr, "You are the Christ") and apparently in an archaizing sense in

---

[49] Psalms of Solomon 18:5, 8; cf. also 17:32 (possibly a Christian interpolation); 1 Enoch 48:10; 52:4; "my Messiah," 2 Baruch 39:7; 40:1; 72:2.

[50] וּמְשִׁיחֵי אַהֲרֹן וְיִשְׂרָאֵל (the Messiahs of Aaron and Israel): 1QS 9.11; CD 12.23; 13.1; 14.19; 19.10–11; 20.1.

[51] W. Wrede had already arrived at these results, in The Messianic Secret (Cambridge & London: James Clarke & Co. Ltd., 1971; first German edition 1901), though one may have second thoughts about the details of his argument.

Acts 2:31 and 3:18. The tendency of the tradition was for the titular usage to recede in favor of the personal name.

In the Pauline letters it cannot always be clearly determined whether ὁ Χριστός is understood as a title or a proper name. The predominate usage is Χριστός as a proper name. The article is often added only for formal reasons, such as when the genitive is used. The use as a proper name is clear in the combination Ἰησοῦς Χριστός (e.g. Gal 3:1; Phil 1:11). The definite article is also frequently used anaphorically before Χριστός; it refers Χριστός back to something previously mentioned (e.g. 1 Corinthians 15:15, the Christ just named). Here it is not so much the title as the proper name that is presupposed. On the other hand the titular usage shines through in several passages: Romans 9:3, 5; 1 Corinthians 10:4; 12:12. In many passages, of course, there is no reason for any alternative interpretation. When Paul speaks of "the Christ," he always thinks of Jesus Christ; thus even the titular usage has overtones of the proper name, so that at the most it is a matter of different emphases.

It is characteristic of Pauline usage of Χριστός that the word is used in connection with statements about the atoning death of Jesus (e.g. Rom 5:8) and that Christ is the one whom God raised from the dead (Rom 8:11, Gal 1:1; 1 Cor 15:3ff, 12, 20). It thus derives from formulae in the prepauline tradition, presumably from Greek-speaking Jewish Christianity, and was elaborated by Paul himself: "Christ" is closely related to the saving event of the death and resurrection of Jesus.[52]

The term Χριστός is also preferred in the context of ecclesiological statements, as in the fundamental affirmations of the church as the "body of Christ" (σῶμα Χριστοῦ) but also with reference to individual congregations or local churches as "assemblies of Christ" or "congregations of Christ" (Rom 16:16 ἐκκλησίαι Χριστοῦ). Especially the expression "in Christ" (ἐν Χριστῷ) has primarily an ecclesiological sense (1 Thess 2:14; Gal 1:22);[53] it is thus found in the Pauline and deuteropauline letters as well as in the Johannine literature and was possibly first formulated by Paul himself.[54] Here belong also parenetic statements, e.g. Romans 15:7 ("Welcome one another, therefore, just as Christ has welcomed you, for the glory of God") and Romans 15:2–3. These instructions are oriented to the Christ event as the saving act of God but are directed to the church that lives its life "in Christ."

---

[52] Cf. Galatians 3:1; 6:14 (crucifixion).
[53] Cf. on the other hand "with Christ" (σὺν Χριστῷ): Romans 6:8; Philippians 1:23, and analogously "with Jesus" (σὺν Ἰησοῦ): 2 Corinthians 4:14 and elsewhere.
[54] H. H. Schade, *Apokalyptische Christologie bei Paulus. Studien zum Zusammenhang von Christologie und Eschatologie in den Paulusbriefen* (GTA 18) (Göttingen: Vandenhoeck & Ruprecht, 1984²) 146.

Finally, Χριστός is used in the context of preaching. "Christ" is the subject of the Christian message[55] and is named in connection with εὐαγγέλιον or with the missionary commission of the apostle (ἀπόστολος τοῦ Χριστοῦ). Relatively late, and mostly in isolated cases, Χριστός is connected to statements about the parousia (e.g. the "day of Christ," Phil 1:6, 10; 2:16); it thus appears in the Philippian letter in place of the corresponding apocalyptic use of the Kyrios title. It is striking that the letter to the Philippians manifests a preference for the designation Χριστός. Differently than is the case with the Kyrios title, with Χριστός the emphasis falls without doubt on the two events of the death and resurrection of Jesus understood as the saving act of God but otherwise the same elements are found that are associated with "Kyrios:" the Christ is not only a figure of past history but is also the exalted and future Messiah. This is the reason that the two christological designations can be used interchangeably.[56] For Paul, Χριστός has lost its original sense of a national Messiah; Paul is here obviously dependent on the usage of Hellenistic Jewish Christians,[57] to whom the name "Christians" (Χριστιανοί) was first applied (Acts 11:26).

## 5. Jesus

Foerster, "Ἰησοῦς," *TDNT* III (1938) 284–293.

In Paul neither Ἰησοῦς nor ὁ Ἰησοῦς is a christological title but a proper name. In contrast to Matthew 1:21, it is obvious that Paul does not reflect on the original Hebrew meaning of the word, "Yahweh helps." In later Christian Gnosticism a distinction was made between the earthly Jesus and the heavenly Christ, in docetic Gnosticism to the detriment of the earthly Jesus. Paul does not know such a distinction himself and does not presuppose it in those to whom he writes.[58] Just as Χριστός is not to be restricted to the Christ of the past or the exalted Christ, so also for the name of Jesus. Jesus is the name of the eschatological bringer of salvation who reveals and mediates salvation to the community in the past, present, and future. This name goes back to the tradition from the historical Jesus but Paul does not restrict it to this. The acclamation κύριος Ἰησοῦς as expressed in early Christian worship (1 Cor 12:3) is not directed to the earthly Jesus but includes a confession of the exalted Lord of the community. The parallel ἀνάθεμα Ἰησοῦς ("Jesus is accursed") is a reaction, a

---

55    As the object of κηρύσσειν: 1 Corinthians 15:1ff; Philippians 1:15ff.
56    Romans 6:23; 16:18; 2 Corinthians 4:4–5; Philemon 20.
57    Cf. the non-titular usage in the prepauline traditional material (Rom 6:3–4).
58    This includes his opponents at Corinth, in contrast to the view of W. Schmithals, *Gnosticism in Corinth. An Investigation of the Letters to the Corinthians* (Nashville & New York: Abingdon, 1971) 113–116 and L. Schottroff, *Der Glaubende und die feindliche Welt* (WMANT 37) (Neukirchen-Vluyn: Neukirchener, 1970) 166–167.

counter formation that is apparently a Pauline rhetorical supplement that need not necessarily lead one to suppose that Paul's opponents had actually cursed Jesus in the worship services.

The usage of the name Ἰησοῦς is thus to a large extent parallel to Χριστός; this is due to the fact that for Paul in both cases it is primarily the name of the eschatological bringer of salvation.

### b) Jesus and Paul

Bultmann, R. *Das Verhältnis der urchristlichen Christusbotschaft zum historischen Jesus.* SHA 1962³; also in R. Bultmann. *Exegetica.* Tübingen: J. C. B. Mohr (Paul Siebeck), 1967. 445–469.
Bultmann, R. "The Significance of the Historical Jesus for the Theology of Paul," in *Faith and Understanding* I. New York: Harper & Row, 1969.
Fuchs, E. "The Quest of the Historical Jesus," *Studies of the Historical Jesus.* Naperville: Alec R. Allenson, 1964, 11–31.
Jüngel, E. *Paulus und Jesus. Eine Untersuchung zur Präzisierung der Frage nach dem Ursprung der Christologie.* HUTh 2. Tübingen: J. C. B. Mohr (Paul Siebeck), 1986⁶.
Käsemann, E. "Blind Alleys in the 'Jesus of History' Controversy," *New Testament Questions of Today.* Philadelphia: Fortress, 1969, 23–65.
Kümmel, W. G. "Jesus und Paulus," W. G. Kümmel. *Heilsgeschehen und Geschichte, GAufs. 1933–1964.* MThSt 3. Marburg: N. G. Elwert, 1965. 81–106.
Schelkle, K. H. *Paulus.* EdF 152. Darmstadt:Wissenschaftliche Buchgesellschaft, 1988².
Weiss, J. *Jesus' Proclamation of the Kingdom of God.* Philadelphia: Fortress, 1971 (= 1892).
Wrede, W. *Paulus.* RV 1. Halle 1904 (=1907²); also in K.H. Rengstorf, ed., *Das Paulusbild in der neueren deutschen Forschung.* WdF 24. Darmstadt: Wissenschaftliche Buchgesellschaft, 1982³. 1–97.

How are Jesus and Paul related? W. G. Kümmel points to the problem of determining their relationship: "For if Paul ... manifests a tendency to preach a different message than Jesus, then his claim to be an apostle of Christ is erroneous; and if Jesus' message did not lay the foundation for the proclamation of the earliest church including Paul, then in fact Jesus was not the founder of Christianity."[59] This thesis assumes what is to be proved, namely that Paul, when he names himself an "apostle of Christ," in fact sees himself in fundamental continuity with the historical Jesus. However: since Paul bases his call to be apostle to the Gentiles on a revelation of the Son of God (Gal 1:15–16), his apostleship is determined primarily by his relation to the exalted Son of God (Gal 1:16, τὸν υἱὸν αὐτοῦ). Nonetheless, the question of Paul's relation to the historical Jesus has an important function, even if it approaches the task of delineating Pauline Christology from a different conception of what Christology is than Paul's own.

---

[59] W. G. Kümmel, *Jesus und Paulus* 83.

## 1.   History of Research

*W. Wrede* wrote his book on Paul under the influence of the history of religions school and its way of asking the question, and thereby arrived at the famous conclusion that Paul was the "second founder of Christianity"[60] and that Pauline theology constitutes a breach in the history of Christian tradition. According to this view, the relation of Paul to Jesus would be only a matter of discontinuity.

W. Wrede attained his results on the basis of two sets of ideas that are foundational for the theology of Paul: (a) Paul's doctrine of redemption based on the mythological schema of the descending and exalted redeemer and thus could not be derived from the impression made by the personality of the historical Jesus, and (b) Paul's doctrine of justification, which W. Wrede understood as Paul's "battle doctrine" over against Judaism and Jewish Christianity, which likewise is not to be found in the teaching of the historical Jesus.[61] This results in an absolute difference between Jesus and Paul. There is no question about which side of this issue Wrede chose for himself, which fits the picture of the historical Jesus as the proclaimer of true morality drawn by Protestant liberalism. In contrast to this, conservative scholars held fast to the Christian tradition that the Jesus event was rightly interpreted by the kerygma of the cross and resurrection of Jesus Christ and thus also rightly understood by the apostle Paul.[62]

W. Wrede's standpoint is thus characterized by a specific understanding of Jesus, namely the picture of Jesus prevalent in Protestant liberalism. Through the scholarly work of the same "academic stream" to which Wrede belonged, the history-of-religions school, this picture was shattered at almost the same time. J. Weiss' discovery that the historical Jesus is to be placed in the apocalyptic thought world of his time had as its result that the distancing process that had already affected Wrede's picture of Paul now begin to work on his picture of Jesus.[63]

*R. Bultmann* took up this thesis of his teacher J. Weiss and developed it further in a positive direction. On the question of the material relation between Jesus and Paul, he achieved the result that while there was no historical continuity between Jesus and Paul, there was a material agree-

60   W. Wrede, *Paul* (London: Philip Greene, 1907) 179.
61   W. Wrede, *Paul* 130–131.
62   Cf. the Foreword in the volume of collected essays edited by K. H. Rengstorf, *Das Paulusbild in der neueren deutschen Forschung* (WdF 24) (Darmstadt: Wissenschaftliche Buchgesellschaft, 1982³) vii–xv.
63   In J. Weiss this stands in contrast to the understanding of the kingdom of God in A. Ritschl, who understood the kingdom of God as an immanent moral force of the human community. Over against this Weiss interpreted the kingdom of God as an apocalyptic phenomenon (cf. J. Weiss, *Jesus' Proclamation of the Kingdom of God* (Lives of Jesus Series. Philadelphia: Fortress Press, 1971). Cf. B. Lannert, *Die Wiederentdeckung der neutestamentlichen Eschatologie durch Johannes Weiss* (TANZ 2. Tübingen: Francke, 1989).

ment between them that came to expression in their understanding of the Law: both Jesus and Paul made the distinction between human law and the original will of God, even though they interpreted and expressed this in two different forms. They had in common the conviction that human beings could not justify themselves before God by their own power but, as expressed in the parable of the Prodigal Son, human beings are totally dependent on God's grace. Their common denominator thus consists in their understanding of human existence, in the manner in which humans understanding their own existence before God.

In contrast, however, Jesus and Paul differ in their eschatological conceptions. Jesus looks ahead to a future that has not yet arrived, and announces the coming of the kingdom of God. Paul, however, declares that the turn of the aeons has already taken place: by Jesus' advent, cross, and resurrection the situation of the world has been definitively changed, and people live in the dialectic of the "already" and "not yet" of the presence of the eschaton.

R. Bultmann's conception of the relation between Jesus and Paul contributed significantly to understanding the unity of the New Testament message but did not mean that a historical continuity between Jesus and Paul had been established. The issue of how important the historical Jesus was for Paul was answered by saying that the "that" of the historical fact of Jesus' existence was important for Paul but the "what" of Jesus' message was barely touched upon.

E. *Fuchs* attempted to bridge the "ugly ditch" between the historical Jesus and the kerygmatic Christ by going back to Jesus' conduct: Jesus dared to act in God's place, by drawing sinners into his presence and accepting them. Jesus' parables are nothing other than a demonstration of this conduct, for Jesus speaks the language of love, which is the language of God's reality. The saving event is a word event in that it is the event of love. From this point of departure, the question of the relation of Jesus and Paul is to be answered in terms of fundamental agreement, for in Jesus' life the language of love became an event, and Paul can not go beyond that. At the most the theology could only say in another way the same thing that had already come into language through Jesus but this still means that under these presuppositions the historical Jesus could be identified with the kerygmatic Christ.

E. *Jüngel* drew the following conclusions regarding the Jesus-Paul problem. For him the doctrine of justification as the center of Pauline theology is juxtaposed to the preaching of Jesus as it is essentially expressed in the parables. Both the Pauline doctrine of justification and in the preaching of Jesus essentially deal with an "authentically eschatological model..., in which the eschaton itself is expressed in different ways."[64] In Paul it is the

---

[64]  E. Jüngel, *Paulus und Jesus* 266.

righteousness of God, which determines his theology, while in Jesus it is the kingdom of God, which is the theme of his parables and in any case must be understood as an eschatological phenomenon. Thus in both Jesus and Paul the eschaton comes into language: in the announcement of the eschatological kingdom of God by Jesus and in the announcement of the eschatological righteousness of God by Paul God's eschatological "yes" to human beings makes available a new being, and in both Paul and Jesus God's eschatological "yes" is the word of love.

Of course, Bultmann's insight that Jesus and Paul conceived the eschaton differently must not be neglected. Paul looks back on the eschatological event inasmuch as the eschaton has already come to speech in the past through Christ. In contrast, Jesus' own eschatology is clearly and non-dialectically [einlinig] oriented to the future in which the eschaton eo ipso will occur. But in Jüngel's view this difference between Jesus and Paul is not significant, since in Jesus' preaching God is near, independently of how the nearness of the eschaton is understood. The problem of the nearness of the end first emerged as a problem as the result of Jesus' preaching, so that the original future orientation faded away in favor of Jesus' announcement of salvation in the present. Thus in his view the difference between Jesus and Paul is only a linguistic difference. In both cases it is a matter of the eschatological "yes" of God that is the basis of both language events. Prior to all historical continuity lies the eschatological continuity.[65]

Here it must be asked wither the Jesus who comes into language in this way is really the historical Jesus or is a mere abstraction stripped of every concrete reality. It appears that behind the concept of an eschatological continuity that is prior to a historical-sociological continuity lies a Greek understanding of God in which God is a timeless, eternal phenomenon constantly identical with himself, so that the different ways of understanding the faith are only reflections of this God who is always and only identical with himself and can be unified in him. In the documents of the New Testament, however, the phenomenon "God" is not an abstraction but One who can only be spoken of as one speaks of human beings who are related to God. God only comes into language as he is reflected in human ways of believing. These are extraordinarily different, and it must be asked whether and how they can be brought into congruence with each other. Thus "the relation of Jesus and Paul" remains a problem that can only be dealt with in connection with its historical concretions, in a manner that attributes an appropriate importance to history itself.[66]

---

[65] Cf. E. Jüngel, ibid.
[66] Similar to E. Jüngel is H. Weder, Das Kreuz Jesu bei Paulus (FRLANT 125) (Göttingen: Vandenhoeck & Ruprecht, 1981). There appears to be here a mixture of historical and historic thinking (historisch and geschichtlich) when it is said with

## 2. The Witness of the Historical Jesus

The apostle Paul never knew the historical Jesus. The possibility that Paul had a personal knowledge of Jesus cannot be inferred even if one considers Luke's account in Acts 7:58–8:3 as historical, according to which Saul was present in Jerusalem at the stoning of Stephen, for it does not deal with a witness of the life of Jesus but with an event that belongs in the early history of the Jerusalem church. It is probably the case that the basis of this report was not an authentic memory but a secondary legend, perhaps created by Luke himself. As stated above, one should think a long time before accepting the tradition that Paul was a pupil of Rabbi Gamaliel, and it is problematic to assume that Paul had ever been in Jerusalem prior to the first visit he mentions in Galatians 1:18–19, when he went up to Jerusalem to visit Cephas.[67] Whatever information about Jesus' life Paul had could have come from his meeting with Cephas / Peter. On the other hand, Paul also received some knowledge of Jesus from the tradition of the Hellenistic Jewish Christian church to which he had access after his conversion.

A limited quantity of tradition about Jesus can be recognized in the Pauline letters, such as the tradition of the cross (e.g. 1 Cor 1:18ff) or of Jesus' passion (2 Cor 1:5; Phil 3:10), alongside which are also found traces of the tradition of the sayings of the Lord. In 1 Corinthians 7:25 Paul emphasizes that he has no command of the Kyrios with regard to the question of virgins, which presupposes that a collection of Jesus' sayings was available to the apostle. This collection is presumably cited in 1 Corinthians 7:10–11: "To the married I give this command—not I but the Lord—that the wife should not separate from her husband (but if she does separate, let her remain unmarried or else be reconciled to her husband), and that the husband should not divorce his wife."[68] Another quote is found in the same context (1 Cor 9:14): "In the same way, the Lord commanded that those who proclaim the gospel should get their living by the gospel."[69] In addition, the saying about the Lord's parousia may derive from this collection (1 Thess 4:15–16),[70] as well as—though more likely from independent liturgical tradition—the words of institution of the

---

reference to Paul that much speaks for the fact "that the origin of his theology of the cross and thus the center of his theological thought is indebted to the repeated revelation of the crucified one to Paul as the Son of God" (229). However, Paul generally does not speak of the cross of Jesus in isolation but in connection with the kerygma he had received of the cross *and* resurrection of Jesus Christ. The center of Pauline theology is the (differentiated) exposition of this one saving event announced in the kerygma.

[67] See above A. I. a.
[68] Cf. Mark 10:12par.
[69] Cf. Matthew 10:10par
[70] Cf. Mark 13:26–27par.

Lord's Supper (1 Cor 11:23ff).[71] One may also mention echoes of Synoptic sayings of the Lord, although it is not clear that they are derived from a collection (Rom 12:14; 14:14; 1 Thess 5:2).[72]

Paul thus knows traditions of the sayings of the Lord. From case to case it is of course questionable whether it is a matter of authentic words of Jesus or formations of the Christian communities, in which charismatic prophets delivered instructions from the risen Lord. It is striking that the stock of traditions in Paul's letters that go back to the life of Jesus is very small. From the historical point of view, Paul hardly betrays knowledge of more than the fact that Jesus lived, of his death, and of a few of his sayings. Presumably Paul stood in a stream of Christian tradition that contained only a few elements of Jesus tradition. It is clear that Paul had no interest in a historical inquiry about the life of Jesus.

It must still be explained why Paul is interested in the "that" (*das Dass*) of Jesus' existence but not in the "what"(*das Was*) of his life and teaching. By way of anticipation, we should say at this point that the verse often cited in this connection, 2 Corinthians 5:16, must be bracketed out of this discussion ("From now on, therefore, we regard no one from a human point of view [lit. 'according to the flesh']; even though we once knew Christ from a human point of view [lit. 'according to the flesh'], we know him no longer in that way"). While this verse is not to be struck from this passage as a gloss,[73] it is also no evidence for the view that Paul knew the historical Jesus. Χριστός is here as elsewhere the Christ of faith, i.e. the cosmic Kyrios of the church. In antithesis to the Corinthian pneumatics, Paul declares: knowing Christ in a human way is of no value. To be sure, one can know Christ in a human (i.e. "fleshly") way, such as in an ecstatic vision, as Paul even claims for himself (2 Cor 12:1ff) but this only means that one has left everything up to a human way of knowing. In the Christ event the power of the flesh has been broken, the believer is "a new creation" (2 Cor 5:17). This means that knowledge of Christ too is no longer a matter of knowing by human means but must be realized by radical obedience. Thus this passage has nothing to do with the earthly Jesus but deals with how the cosmic Christ is known.

There is accordingly a hopeless task to attempt to draw a line of continuity that shows detailed agreement between the historical Jesus and the theology of Paul. Such attempts must realize that every historical movement includes an element of discontinuity. Pauline theology can be traced back to the historical Jesus only via the intermediate stages of the Palestinian and Hellenistic church. In comparison to the elements of continuity that can be shown, the discontinuity between the theology of Paul and the

---

[71]   Cf. Mark 14:22par, and A. III. C. 3. above.

[72]   Romans 12:14: "Bless those who persecute you" (cf. Matt 5:44); Romans 14:14, "nothing is unclean in itself" (cf. Matt 15:11); 1 Thess 5:2, "the day of the Lord will come like a thief in the night (cf. Matt 24:43).

[73]   Contra W. Schmithals, "Zwei gnostische Glossen im Zweiten Korintherbrief," *EvTh* 18 (1958) 552–573.

proclamation of the historical Jesus is more significant. Moreover, the attempt to establish such a continuity is problematic in itself. W. Pannenberg[74] has argued that the Christian message has no foundation and would simply become an illusion if it loses its connection with the historical Jesus. But if he means by this that faith can assure itself by appeal to the historical Jesus, one must ask whether the destiny of faith is not precisely to lose its foundation by such an appeal. In reality this procedure simply postpones the date on which one must decide whether Christian faith is grounded in truth or is an illusion. The alternative "faith or illusion" belongs to the nature of faith in every time and situation. It cannot be eliminated by calling on the historical Jesus as the guarantor of faith.[75]

## 3. *Jesus in the Kerygma of Paul*

Within the framework of Pauline theology the center of gravity of the "Jesus and Paul" issue does not lie on the question of the historical (*historisch*) Jesus but on the question of Jesus in the kerygma, which means on the historic (*geschichtlich*) Christ as proclaimed by Paul. This in turn raises the question, "What is the significance of the past, earthly Jesus in Pauline theology?"[76] The kerygmatic Christ is at one and the same time the fact and interpretation of the personal Christ event of the past. In this sense R. Bultmann's thesis is correct: "in the preaching of Paul the historic (*geschichtlich*) person Jesus becomes gospel."[77] So understood, the human being Jesus is constitutive for the Pauline kerygma; he is the expression of the *historical reservation* of Pauline theology. Of course it is a matter of an interpreted Jesus, who receives his reality, his

---

[74] W. Pannenberg, *Grundzüge der Christologie* (Gütersloh: Gerd Mohn, 1990[7]) 20; "Die Auferstehung Jesu und die Zukunft des Menschen," KuD 24 (1978) 104–117.

[75] Cf. G. Strecker, "Die historische und theologische Problematik der Jesusfrage," *EvTh* 29 (1969) 453–476, also in *Eschaton und Historie* 159–182. On the issue of "implied Christology" in R. Bultmann, *Theology* 1:43: to affirm this for the ministry of the historical Jesus contradicts Bultmann's own account at the beginning of this *Theology of the New Testament*, according to which Jesus belongs to Judaism, and was thus presented as belonging to the category of the Old Testament prophets—even though an outstanding one—who announced the coming time of salvation but was not himself identical with the bringer of salvation. Bultmann's statement is to be modified: Jesus' call to decision does not imply a Christology but rather a soteriology, since Jesus' call was a call to salvation (not to himself).

[76] When we speak of the Christ of past history, we presuppose that the affirmation of the Christ kerygma includes a reference to the historical past but we renounce any interpretation that goes beyond the historical "that" of Jesus' existence and attempts to fill in the details of the historical "what" of Jesus' life and teaching. This does not dispute the view, however, that the "that" of the historical Jesus in the Pauline sense is connected with a particular idea of its content.

[77] R. Bultmann, *Glauben und Verstehen* 1:202.

status, and his eschatological quality through the event of the cross and resurrection. According to Paul's interpretation the proclaimed Kyrios is not an idea, nor is he only a mythical heavenly being but the self-manifestation of God in human history. Thereby the docetic understanding is excluded in which Jesus' humanity plays no essential role in Christology.

The Christ of past history is even less to be grasped by historical method, in purely human categories, for he is no rabbi or philosopher who delivers timeless truths. To the extent that Paul understands the Kyrios as authoritative teacher, it is primarily a matter of the exalted Lord. Nor does Paul honor Jesus as a human personality marked out by outstanding human qualities, a figure who would be available for psychological interpretation, for the Christ of past history even in his humanity continues to be the Kyrios who is spoken of in mythological terms. Here the *mythological reservation* stands against the Ebionite understanding, in which Jesus was only a human being.

The question of the Jesus of past history in the Pauline kerygma is the question of the supporting foundation of Pauline Christology:

(α) *The Jesus of past history in the Pauline kerygma is the preexistent, incarnate, and exalted Christ.*

Paul's Jesus is not to be bracketed out of the realm of myth. He is firmly enclosed within the mythological scheme of humiliation and exaltation. This is the way Paul received it from the prepauline Christian community (cf. Phil 2:6ff). Thus Jesus can be named the "image of God" (2 Cor 4:4, εἰκὼν τοῦ θεοῦ). Such a gnosticizing manner of speaking points to the pretemporal being of Christ, his preexistence, which is also the presupposition of the giving-over and sending formulae and for the Adam-Christ typology. As a heavenly being, the Jesus of past history is for Paul an exponent of the Spirit and belongs to the sphere of the Spirit (cf. 1 Cor 15:45, Christ as πνεῦμα ζῳοποιοῦν, "life giving Spirit"). The Spirit stands in contrast to the world, sin, and law. In the Jesus of past history the apparently impossible occurs: the Spirit Christ is subjected to the law (Gal 4:4). The Preexistent One was sent in the form of sinful flesh (Rom 8:3; cf. 2 Cor 8:9). The paradox inherent in the Pauline understanding of Jesus is seen in the uniting of things that cannot be united, the unity of Spirit and flesh, of God and the world. This christological dualism is the point of departure for Pauline soteriology and implies a paradoxical anthropology.

The inthronization of Jesus to be Kyrios and Cosmocrator has as its goal the elimination of the christological paradox (cf. Phil 2:9–11). Since this belongs to the realm of myth, not the realm of logos, it follows that the kerygmatic Jesus in Paul's theology cannot be separated from the person of the mythic Christ. The Christ event cannot be united with objective history (*Historie*) in such wise that it becomes the object of rational thought. Its real essence is not accessible to rational knowledge but to the understanding that rests on faith, since it is faith that is articulated in Paul's christological affirmations and is at the same time the goal of Pauline proclamation. In the Pauline kerygma the Jesus of past history can only be perceived by faith. He is not an independent witness and basis for faith apart from faith itself. From the human point of view there is no other ground of faith than faith itself. Believers know, however, that the basis of their faith and life is not accessible to reason.

(β) *The Jesus of past history in the Pauline kerygma is the norm for ethical conduct.*
When Paul speaks of the Jesus event of the past, he distinguishes the incarnation of Christ from the preceding form of existence of the Pre-existent One and the following form of existence of the lordship of the Kyrios. The fact that the being of the incarnate Christ is the ethical norm for the church is not a minimal factor in the way the being of the incarnate Christ is pictured. That Paul can interpret the mythological scheme of the humiliation and exaltation of Christ in this sense is seen in the Pauline verse Philippians 2:8 ("... he humbled himself and became obedient to the point of death—even death on a cross"). The incarnation of the Preexistent One is understood as an expression of the obedience of Jesus; it is only for this reason that the hymn is inserted into this context of Pauline church parenesis.[78]

In the parenetic statement of 2 Corinthians 10:1 ("I myself, Paul, appeal to you by the meekness and gentleness of Christ—I who am humble when face to face with you but bold toward you when I am away!—" (2Cor 10:1), Paul refers to the "meekness" (πραΰτης) and "gentleness" (ἐπιείκεια) of Christ. Both are manifest in the weakness of the apostle. When he is "humble" (ταπεινός), he is in the same situation as the incarnate Christ. The goal of this parenesis is that the community likewise acknowledge that it lives in this situation of humility and realizes it in their own lives. The way in which the Jesus of past history lived his life as the incarnate Christ, in humility, obedience, and self-giving, has an exemplary significance for the church: not in the sense of a moral example that could be read off the surface of the life of the historical Jesus but as an expression of the incarnation of the Son of God. This life was the manifestation of obedience and self-giving that the community is encouraged to follow, and which it can follow, because it is preceded by the ethical demand inherent in the event of the incarnation.

---

[78] Cf. the detailed evidence in G. Strecker, "Redaktion und Tradition im Christus-hymnus Phil 2,6–11," *ZNW* 55 (1964) 63–78 (reprinted in *Eschaton und Historie* 142–147).

It is consistent with this when the members of the church at Thessalonica are called to "imitate" Paul and the Kyrios, and when the apostle challenges the Corinthians to imitate his own example (1 Cor 11:1). That Christ is to be acknowledged as an ethical example is seen also in Romans 15:3: the admonition to live in a way that is considerate of the weak and not merely to please ourselves is based on the example of Christ: "For Christ did not please himself; but, as it is written, 'The insults of those who insult you have fallen on me'," for the purpose of his incarnation was to be a servant to others. Thus Christ appeared in history as "servant" (διάκονος), who "has welcomed you,"; this is the basis of the command to welcome one another.[79]

(γ) *The Jesus of past history of the Pauline kerygma is the Christ who was crucified and raised from the dead.*
As indicated above,[80] in his dispute with the Corinthians Paul had attempted to legitimate the resurrection of Jesus by historical evidence. On the one hand, this contradicts the kind of argumentation Paul uses elsewhere, where Paul does in fact confirm the crucifixion and resurrection of Jesus especially in connection with traditional formulaic material but is not concerned to present a list of evidences. On the other hand, here the apostle does come into fundamental contradiction with one of the central theses of his theology, according to which eschatological salvation is not a matter of evidence presented in a human court of opinion but is promised only to those who unconditionally believe, to those who renounce their own achievements including that of rational proof. As proclaimed saving events, the cross and resurrection of Jesus demand faith from the hearer, not rational investigation. As events in space and time they appear to be available to the historian's investigation but it is only as interpreted by faith that they are appropriated as saving events and as constitutive of the believer's self-understanding. The cross and resurrection have to do with the historical Jesus, inasmuch as these are confessed as the incarnate preexistent Christ. The cross and resurrection of Jesus, like the other events related to the historical Jesus, as the saving events that constitute the basis of faith are embedded in the Christ myth of the humiliated and exalted Kyrios.

---

[79] W. G. Kümmel, *Jesus und Paulus* 87 is of the opinion that he can infer on the basis of the data mentioned above that it was not only the existence of the incarnate Jesus that was important for Paul but that the character of the concrete figure of Jesus was significant for his theology. This is basically correct but for Paul it was not Jesus as a historical figure but Jesus as the incarnate mythical Christ that was important. This kind of concretization is not open to the methods of the historian. The encounter with the historic Christ cannot negate the kerygma, which is accomplished in faith.

[80] See above I. C. 3. on 1 Corinthians 15:3b-5a.

## c)   The Cross and Resurrection of Jesus Christ[81]

Barth, G. *Der Tod Jesu Christi im Verständnis des Neuen Testaments.* Neukirchen-Vluyn: Neukirchener, 1992.
Breytenbach, C. *Versöhnung. Eine Studie zur paulinischen Soteriologie.* WMANT 60. Neukirchen-Vluyn: Neukirchener, 1989.
Friedrich, G. *Die Verkündigung des Todes Jesu im Neuen Testament.* BThSt 6. Neukirchen-Vluyn: Neukirchener, 1982.
Grass, H. *Ostergeschehen und Osterberichte.* Göttingen: Vandenhoeck & Ruprecht, 1970⁴.
Hengel, M. "Der stellvertretende Sühnetod Jesu," IKaZ 9. 1980. 1–25.135–147.
Herrmann, J. and F. Büchsel, "ἱλαστήριον," *TDNT* III (1938) 319–323.
Käsemann, E. "The Saving Significance of the Death of Jesus in Paul," in E. Käsemann, *Pauline Perspectives.* Philadelphia: Fortress, 1971, 32–59.
Kraus, W. *Der Tod Jesu als Heiligtumsweihe.* WMANT 66. Neukirchen-Vluyn d: Neukirchener, 1991.
Merklein, H. "Der Tod Jesu als stellvertretender Sühnetod. Entwicklung und Gehalt einer zentralen neutestamentlichen Aussage," H. Merklein. *Studien zu Jesus und Paulus.* Tübingen: J. C. B. Mohr (Paul Siebeck), 1987. 181–191.
Pokorný, P. *The Genesis of Christology: Foundations for a Theology of the New Testament.* Edinburgh: T. & T. Clark, 1987.
von Campenhausen, H. Frhr. "The Event of Easter and the Empty Tomb," *Tradition and Life in the Church.* Philadelphia: Fortress, 1968, 42–89.

If the historian seeks for usable historical information in the theology of Paul, he or she cannot fail to notice the fact of Jesus' death on the cross. Paul is not concerned, however, with Jesus' death as a historical fact but with the interpretation of the meaning of this death. The prepauline tradition already knows differing interpretations, and this complexity continues to be reflected in the Pauline letters. To be distinguished are:

---

[81]   When Paul speaks of the death of Jesus, he uses the terms for "dying" customary for his time: ἀποθνήσκω (1 Thess 4:14; 5:10; Gal 2:21; Rom 5:8; 8:34 [1 Cor 15:3]); ἀποκτείνω ("kill"): 1 Thess 2:15; θάνατος: Rom 5:10; 1 Cor 11:26; Phil 2:8 and elsewhere; in addition the concrete σταυρός: 1 Cor 1:17–18; Gal 5:11; 6:12, 14; σταυρόω: 1 Cor 1:23; 2:2, 8; Gal 3:1 and elsewhere. The expression παθήματα τοῦ Χριστοῦ (2 Cor 1:5; Phil 3:10) refers to the suffering of Jesus death; in addition, Paul knew some elements of the passion tradition (cf. 1 Cor 11:23).
With regard to the terms for the rising or resurrection of Jesus, the New Testament uses the substantive ἀνάστασις (e.g. Rom 1:4), ἐξανάστασις (Phil 3:11), or ἔγερσις (Matt 27:53) only in the sense of a general resurrection. The verbs used are ἀνίστημι (1 Thess 4:14, "rise") or ἐγείρω ("raise," "resurrect"). In the latter case it is disputed whether the relatively frequent passive usage (Rom 4:25; 6:4, 9; 7:4; 8:34 and elsewhere) is to be understood as a *passivum divinum* ("divine passive," with God as the understood actor). The passive can also have the meaning of the middle voice ("arise," "raise oneself") and thus be used as a synonym of ἀνίστημι (cf. J. Kremer, EWNT I 906). On the other hand the active is often construed with "God" as the subject (1 Thess 1:10; 1 Cor 6:14; 15:15; Gal 1:1; Rom 4:24; 8:11; 10:9), so that it is not unusual for the passive forms to be understood as a divine passive.

1. In connection with the concept of forgiveness of sins, the death of Jesus is understood as a *sin offering*. This is the case where the "blood" of Jesus is spoken of; cf. 1 Cor 11:25, 27 (in connection with the establishment of the καινὴ διαθήκη = the new declaration of the will of God; Exodus 24:8: covenant sacrifice); 1 Corinthians 15:3–4 (the death of Jesus ὑπὲρ ἁμαρτιῶν); also 2 Corinthians 5:14 (εἷς ὑπὲρ πάντων ἀπέθανεν) or Romans 5:6, 8 (ὑπὲρ ἡμῶν). The presupposition is the cultic concept that blood is a means of atonement; thereby God appears as a judge who pronounces acquittal; cf. Romans 5:9 ("we have been justified by his blood"); Romans 3:25 ("whom God put forward as a sacrifice of atonement [ἱλαστήριον] by his blood." In this passage ἱλαστήριον is to be understood not so much as representing the LXX translation of כַּפֹּרֶת (= "mercy seat": Exod 25:17–22; Lev 16:13–15) but rather in the sense of Hellenistic Jewish usage (= "means of atonement").[82]

2. Moreover, the death of Jesus is interpreted as *substitutionary*. Here the ideas associated with criminal law may play a role; thus in Romans 8:3 "God ... by sending his own Son ... condemned sin in the flesh") and Galatians 3:13 ("Christ redeemed us from the curse of the law by becoming a curse for us [= in our place]; similarly 2 Corinthians 5:14 ("one died for all") and 2 Corinthians 5:21 ("For our sake he [God] made him [Christ] to be sin who knew no sin, so that in him we might become the righteousness of God").[83]

3. Finally, the death of Jesus can be understood as a *ransom*. According to Galatians 3:13aα Christ has "redeemed us from the curse of the law;" he has paid the price by which slaves are freed. The freedom that comes to people by being ransomed is freedom from the punishment to which they were subject because of their violations of the law. In Paul's understand-

---

[82]   As in 4 Maccabees 17:21–22; cf. O. Michel, *Der Brief an die Römer* (KEK 4) (Göttingen: Vandenhoeck & Ruprecht, 1978¹⁴) 151–152; E. Käsemann, *Commentary on Romans* (Grand Rapids: Wm. B. Eerdmans Publishing Co., 1980) 97. Differently F. Büchsel, TDNT 3:320–323. B. Janowski has attempted to show that in the Old Testament "atonement" does not mean appeasement or reconciliation of God but the means established by God for overcoming the fatal effects of sin within the cause/effect framework in which one's deeds necessarily lead to certain effects. Cf. B. Janowski, *Studien zur Sühnetheologie der Priesterschrift und zur Wurzel KPR im Alten Orient und im Alten Testament* (WMANT 55. Neukirchen-Vluyn: Neukirchener, 1982); cf. also H. Merklein, *Der Tod Jesu als stellvertretender Sühnetod* 182–183.

[83]   The concepts of sin offering and substitution both often presuppose that God as the acting subject. This is seen especially in the expression "giving up / over" (παραδίδωμι), for example in the prepauline formula of Romans 4:25 (presumably influenced by Isa 53:6, 12; cf. 1 Clem 16.7, 14); similarly Romans 8:32. On the other hand, it may be that sometimes the sovereign decision of the Christ who gave himself up for his own is emphasized, as in Galatians 2:20, which can also be expressed with the simple δίδωμι (Gal 1:4; cf. Mark 10:45).

ing, it goes beyond that to freedom from the powers of sin and death that enslave human existence. In such statements it cannot be asked to whom the purchase price is paid (the devil?); it is rather the case that the idea of being "ransomed" through the death of Jesus is used metaphorically (cf. Gal 4:5 with "sonship" as the intent of the metaphor).

The resurrection is named in close connection with statements about Jesus' death. The prepauline kerygma can be distilled into the confessional formula "Christ died and was raised." This resonates as the core component of the confessional statement of 1 Corinthians 15:3ff, and especially in the formulae that speak of Christ's self-giving, such as Romans 4:25: "... who was handed over to death for our trespasses and was raised for our justification." The passive ἠγέρθη can be interpreted as the act of God, who is portrayed as the active subject: it is God who raised the Lord Jesus from the dead. Parallel to this, ἀνέστη is found in such statements as 1 Thessalonians 4:14, "For since we believe that Jesus died and rose again...".

The cross and resurrection / rising of Jesus are events of the past. Although they are referred to the Jesus of past history, they are not to be identified merely as historical facts. While the death of Jesus is a fact of history, this cannot be said in the same way of the resurrection of Jesus. The resurrection event itself is not pictured in the Easter traditions. All that is available to the historian is the vision of the Risen One as reported by witnesses of the resurrection. The visionary appearance of the Risen One cannot document the historicity of a bodily resurrection of Jesus but only the datum of the beginning of the resurrection faith.

The question of the historicity of the resurrection of Jesus is often connected to the tradition of the "empty tomb." However, we are not dealing here with an idea from the earliest period, for the motif expressed in this tradition only gradually took shape.

The Evangelist Mark relates that the women stood at the tomb and heard the voice of the angel, "He is risen; he is not here" (16:6). Matthew knows a story about a conspiracy among the Jewish leaders to persuade those who had guarded the tomb to spread the rumor that the body of Jesus had been stolen from the tomb at night. This was supposed to be the basis of the fact that "this story is still told among the Jews to this day" (Matt 28:15). The motif of the empty tomb was thus shaped in the dispute with (Jewish) opponents. This motif is developed especially in the Gospel of John: the linen cloths in which the corpse of Jesus had been wrapped are carefully folded up (20:6–7), and Mary Magdalene experienced an appearance of the risen Lord at the empty tomb (20:11ff). It may be that the tradition of the Johannine school has here been influenced by anti-docetic influences.

Paul has no interest in the empty tomb. As has been indicated above, it cannot be inferred from 1 Corinthians 15:4a (ἐτάφη) that the confessional statement about the resurrection of Jesus necessarily includes the idea of the empty tomb. It is rather the case that in this context the reference to the burial is intended only to document the reality of Jesus' death. The witnesses of the resurrection in 1 Corinthians 15 are not witnesses of the empty tomb but of the appearances of the Risen One.

From Paul's apocalyptic thought world, the expectation of the future resurrection of the dead, motifs can be inferred that are also informative of
his understanding of the resurrection of Jesus. On the basis of his concept
of the bodiliness of the future resurrection of Christian believers, Paul
draws conclusions about the bodily resurrection of Christ. Does therefore
the future bodily resurrection presuppose a raising of the earthly body and
thus presuppose an empty tomb?

*1 Thessalonians 4:13–18* deals with the future destiny of fellow Christians who
have died, as well as what will happen to believers who are still alive at the parousia.
At the coming of the Lord, both living and dead believers will stand before him. The
continuing identity of personhood is presupposed, i.e. that the resurrected person is
the same as the one who had lived an earthly life. This does not necessarily mean,
however, that the earthly body is raised.

*1 Corinthians 15:35–49*: Here too the identity of the earthly with the resurrected
person is presupposed. The new bodily form, however, is completely different from
the old. The resurrected person is clothed with a spiritual body (σῶμα πνευματικόν),
and the old body (σῶμα ψυχικόν) is laid aside. Thereby the idea is excluded that for
the future existence of the one who is resurrected it is necessary that the earthly body
be revived, and thus that the tomb would be empty.

*2 Corinthians 5:1–10* declares that for the believer an eternal house stands ready
in heaven, and that the earthly tent will be taken down. However one decides the
question of whether Paul thought that immediately after death one receives the new
body or whether an intermediate state is presupposed, in any case it is clear that the
earthly tent (= the earthly body) is taken down and disposed of at death. This text
affirms that the earthly body will not be transformed, in contrast to the conception
of 1 Corinthians 15 but rather that it will be replaced by a new body, the "heavenly
dwelling." The new body existence comes from God. It is characteristic that here there
is much less resonance with the Jewish apocalyptic hope of the resurrection, and more
of a Hellenistic-syncretistic ("gnostic") concept at work. This excludes the tendency
to interpret the resurrection event in terms of an earthly body, as this appears to be
presupposed in the apocalyptic tradition.

In *Philippians 3:20–21* Paul uses a piece of apocalyptic tradition. This text too
affirms the transformation that is to occur at the parousia: the earthly person who is
subject to mortality (τὸ σῶμα τῆς ταπεινώσεως) will be changed into "the body of his
glory" (σῶμα τῆς δόξης). The resurrection body is distinguished from the earthly body
analogous to the way the glorious world to come (δόξα) is distinguished from the
present earthly world.

*Romans 8:23* points to the sighing of the creation in a kind of bodily existence that
belongs to the temporal world. This means that the kind of reality in the world of the
resurrection that human redemption as it is to happen at the eschaton is not only the
redemption of the body but also redemption from the earthly body.[84]

The Pauline resurrection faith does not include the idea that the earthly
bodily existence is continued after death or is later taken up again. It is
only personal existence (σῶμα) that is continued.[85] The personal existence

---

[84]    Contra F. Büchsel, *TDNT* 4:352.
[85]    To whatever extent Paul can also understand the term σῶμα in the sense of the
human body (e.g. 1 Cor 5:3; 6:18; Rom 1:24; 8:10, 13; 1 Thess 5:23), and to

of human beings is not bound to the earthly, material body. Pauline resurrection faith does not mean that the graves will become empty but believers whose hope is in Christ are given confidence of entrance into the heavenly δόξα.

From this point of departure, conclusions can be drawn with regard to the Pauline understanding of the resurrection of Jesus. The affirmation of Jesus' resurrection found in the prepauline tradition does not say that the tomb was empty. The report of the empty tomb is open to the possibility of misunderstanding and unbelief, as seen in the example of the deception perpetrated by the Jewish leaders (Matt 28:11–15). Talk of the empty tomb can also be misunderstood in the sense that the resurrection could be thought of as another of Jesus' miracles. In the Pauline understanding, however, the resurrection of Jesus is not a demonstrable "miracle" but the saving event itself. This means: Jesus lives! Regarded historically, this means that the resurrection of Jesus—quite apart from the visionary experiences of the witnesses to the resurrection—is not a matter of proof but for Paul it is nonetheless an "event;" it belongs to the pneumatic sphere, the realm of the πνεῦμα θεοῦ. It can be perceived and appropriated by those who are moved by the Spirit, by believers, who confess their faith in this event as the saving act of God.

The historian, however, may come to the conclusion that the event of the resurrection is not historically authenticated; it cannot be verified in the realm of time and space. To this corresponds the thesis of R. Bultmann adopted by W. Marxsen, that the resurrection is merely the interpretation of the death of Jesus.[86] This exegesis and hermeneutic appears to be consistent with the historical-critical method. But for Paul, the resurrection of Jesus was not only an interpretation of the death of Jesus but a saving event incorporated into the realm of the pneumatic Christ, who by the resurrection was exalted from being the *"Christus incarnatus"* to be-

---

whatever extent the formal aspect ("gestalt") plays a role (1 Cor 15:35, 37–38, 40), it is still indisputable that the word σῶμα can also have the generic meaning of "person" ("I;" cf. Rom 12:1; Phil 1:20). Thus it can be said, "man does not *have* a σῶμα; he *is* σῶμα" (R. Bultmann, *Theology* 1:194). A human being is σῶμα inasmuch as one has a relation to oneself. In this connection the Pauline understanding of the resurrection makes a double statement: (a) the overcoming of the earthly mode of existence by the gift of a heavenly mode of existence, which includes a radical transformation of the givenness of the earthly conditions of existence, and (b) the identity of the personal existence before and after death (cf. 1 Thess 4:17; Phil 1:23).

[86] R. Bultmann, "The Significance of the Historical Jesus for the Theology of Paul," *Faith and Understanding* I:220–246; W. Marxsen, "The Resurrection of Jesus as a Historical and Theological Problem," C. F. D. Moule, ed., *The Significance of the Message of the Resurrection for Faith in Jesus Christ* (SBT 2/8) (London: SCM Press, 1968); *The Resurrection of Jesus of Nazareth* (Philadelphia: Fortress Press, 1970) 138–148.

come the *"Christus praesens"* of the Christian community. Corresponding to the Pauline witness to the resurrection, salvation is irrevocably bound to the person of Jesus Christ. The church knows itself to be determined by the Christ event of past history and at the same time grounds its hope for the future in this past event. The person of the Jesus of past history is identical with the resurrected Christ, just as in Paul's view the personhood of the believer will be identical with the resurrected person at the future general resurrection. The resurrected and exalted Kyrios stands in continuity with the earthly Jesus. The unity of the exalted and the earthly Jesus is motivated by the mythological scheme of humiliation and exaltation of the Preexistent One. Such a "mythological identity" is indicated by both the saving events that in reality represent the *one* saving act of God: the death and resurrection of Jesus in which the eschatological "Yes" of God is spoken to humanity. Such a divine affirmation cannot be pictured in clear concepts; but it is experienced by faith in the word that comes through preaching and sacrament. Here it is seen that Jesus Christ is living and active in the word, i.e. in the community called into being by this word. Not least, he is present in the sacrament, for in baptism believers participate in the death of Jesus, so that they may live with the risen Christ (Rom 6:1ff).

### d)   God and Christ

Althaus, P. "Das Bild Gottes bei Paulus," ThBL 20 (1941) 81–92.

Bornkamm, G. "The Revelation of God's Wrath (Romans 1–3)," G. Bornkamm. *Early Christian Experience*. London: SCM Press, 1969, 47–70.

Cullmann, O. *The Christology of the New Testament*. Philadelphia: Westminster, 1959, 234–237.

Delling, G. "ΜΟΝΟΣ ΘΕΟΣ," G. Delling. *Studien zum Neuen Testament und zum hellenistischen Judentum. GAufs. 1950–1968.* Göttingen: Vandenhoeck & Ruprecht, 1970, 391–400.

Delling, G. "Zusammengesetzte Gottes- und Christusbezeichnungen in den Paulusbriefen," G. Delling. *Studien zum Neuen Testament und zum hellenistischen Judentum. Gaufs. 1950–1968.* Göttingen: Vandenhoeck & Ruprecht, 1970, 417–424.

Grässer, E. "'Ein einziger ist Gott' (Röm 3,30). Zum christologischen Gottesverständnis bei Paulus," *Ich will euer Gott werden.* SBS 100. Stuttgart: Katholisches Bibelwerk, 1981. 177–205.

Holtz, T. "Theologie und Christologie bei Paulus," *Glaube und Eschatologie.* FS W. G. Kümmel, hg. v. E. Grässer and O. Merk. Göttingen: Vandenhoeck & Ruprecht, 1975. 105–121.

Klumbies, P. G. *Die Rede von Gott bei Paulus in ihrem zeitgeschichtlichen Kontext.* FRLANT 155. Göttingen: Vandenhoeck & Ruprecht, 1992.

Kreitzer, L. J. *Jesus and God in Paul's Eschatology.* JSNT 19. Sheffield: Sheffield University Press, 1987.

Lindemann, A. "Die Rede von Gott in der paulinischen Theologie," ThGl 69 (1979) 357–376.

Peterson, E. Εἷς θεός. *Epigraphische, formgeschichtliche und religionsgeschichtliche Untersuchungen.* FRLANT 41. Göttingen: Vandenhoeck & Ruprecht, 1926.

Schrage, W. "Theologie und Christologie bei Paulus und Jesus auf dem Hintergrund der modernen Gottesfrage," *EvTh* 36 (1976) 121–154.

Whiteley, D. E. H. *The Theology of St. Paul.* Oxford: Blackwell, 1964. 118–123.

Whittaker, J. "Neopythagoreanism and Negative Theology," J. Whittaker. *Studies in Platonism and Patristic Thought.* London: Variorum Reprints, 1984.

The issue of the relation of "God" and "Christ" is not to be understood as though it were posed as the problem of the internal relations among the members of the Trinity but is a matter of how two persons are to be related.

1. *The background from the perspective of the history of religion.* As has been the case with previous issues, so also with regard to the question of the relation of God and Christ in Pauline theology: the twin roots of Paul's theology come into play. First, there is the Old Testament-Jewish doctrine of God, for Paul's faith is monotheistic, oriented to the one God, the Creator. In addition to this, the Hellenistic-oriental reverence for the Kyrios is presupposed and is applied in some passages to Jesus. Over against the Kyrioi, Jesus is the one Lord; as the Risen One, he is the Cosmocrator. This would seem to suggest that Paul advocates a ditheistic concept. Such a deduction from history-of-religion premises is to be qualified. The concept of the Old Testament-Jewish Creator God can also accommodate the idea of a "Messiah" who stands especially close to God and who is often of a non-human origin.[87] On the other hand, the Hellenistic Kyrios cult does not exclude the Olympian world of he gods and thus does not exclude the concept of a God superior to other divine beings,[88] so that the coordination or subordination of the Kyrios in relation to the one deity is not necessarily an impossible idea in Hellenistic thought.

2. *The functional relation.* The relation "God / Christ" is expressed in liturgical formulae, e.g. Romans 15:6, "... so that together you may with one voice glorify the God and Father of our Lord Jesus Christ" (δοξάζητε τὸν θεὸν καὶ πατέρα τοῦ κυρίου ἡμῶν Ἰησοῦ Χριστοῦ.) The same liturgical formula is found in the deuteropauline letter 2 Thessalonians 1:12. Since Paul is hardly encouraging the church to worship two gods, the καί is to be understood epexegetically. What Paul means is: God, who is the father

---

[87] Cf. the concept of the Son of Man (Dan 7:13).
[88] Cf. Cleanthes hymn to Zeus, on which see S. Lauer, "Der Zeushymnus des Kleanthes," in M. Brocke et al, eds., *Das Vaterunser* (Freiburg: Herder, 1974) 156–162. Cf. also M. Pohlenz, *Die Stoa* 1:108–110. For details, see G. Delling, ΜΟΝΟΣ ΘΕΟΣ 391–395. On the whole subject see also the worship of the magical goddess Selene (*The Greek Magical Papyri in Translation*, ed. H. D. Betz. Chicago: University of Chicago Press, 1986) 86–92; also the encomium of Aristeidus on Zeus (E. Norden, *Agnostos Theos* 164).

of the Lord Jesus Christ (καί = "namely"). God is God in such wise that he reveals his fatherhood in relation to Jesus Christ as the Lord and Son of God. The relation between God and Christ is defined by the father/son relationship. This corresponds to Philippians 4:20, "To God, namely our Father, be glory..." (cf. also 1 Thess 3:11). Here God is the Father of human beings. The hymnic formula in 1 Corinthians 8:6 is to be understood in the same way, "yet for us there is one God, the Father, from whom are all things and for whom we exist and one Lord, Jesus Christ, through whom are all things and through whom we exist." To be sure, the Lord Jesus is the Son of the Father in a special way but his relation to God is defined in terms of subordination. Pauline Christology is essentially subordinationist. This corresponds to the fact that Paul thinks in a thoroughly theocentric manner, as illustrated by the christological formulae in which Christ is "sent" and "given over."[89]

Just as the relation between God and Christ is to be interpreted in terms of subordination, the series in 1 Corinthians 11:3 is characteristic: ... Christ is the head of every man, and the husband is the head of his wife, and God is the head of Christ." Here is a clear progression from below to above, from woman to man, from man to Christ, from Christ to God. The subordination of Christ is also seen in 1 Corinthians 3:23 ("... you belong to Christ, and Christ belongs to God," and in 1 Corinthians 15:28, speaking of the eschatological events: "When all things are subjected to him, then the Son himself will also be subjected to the one who put all things in subjection under him, so that God may be all in all," as well as in Philippians 2:8–9 (the obedience to Christ to the will of God leads to exaltation and installation of the Christ to become Kyrios).

The subordination of the Son to the Father need not be interpreted in a scholastic manner. Paul develops no ontology or metaphysical conception. Paul has primarily a functional understanding of the God/Christ relationship. Paul is less concerned to describe the nature of divine being than to portray the concrete act of God in and through Christ. God accomplishes his liberating act through the obedience of the Son. Since Paul does not work out the God / Christ relationship in ontological terms, we may well understand that the portrayal of this relationship is by no means carried out consistently. While in 2 Corinthians 5:19 ("... in Christ God was reconciling the world to himself, ...") comes near to identifying God and Christ, here too such a statement is meant functionally: it is God who is met in Christ. The act of Christ is the saving act of God (cf. Phil 2:6). This is said in an even more exclusive way in Romans 9:5 ("... to them belong the patriarchs, and from them, according to the flesh, comes the Messiah, who is over all, God blessed forever"). Here Christ is described

---

[89]    Cf. above A. II. A. 2.

as θεός;[90] this has parallels in the Johannine writings (John 1:18; 20:28; 1 John 5:20) and in the letter of Pliny, according to whom the Christians meet in the morning and sing a hymn to Christ "as to a god."[91]

It is often the case that Paul does not distinguish between God and Christ. Just as prayers are directed to God, so prayers can be addressed to Christ the Lord. Christians are those who "call on the name of the Kyrios" (1 Cor 1:2, ἐπικαλεῖσθαι τὸ ὄνομα τοῦ κυρίου). Paul himself turns in personal prayer to the Kyrios, praying for the removal of the "thorn in the flesh" (presumably a chronic ailment),[92] and he prays to the Kyrios for the salvation of the community, that they may be filled with *agape* (1 Thess 3:12). The apostle thus anticipates what will happen at the end of history when the whole cosmos will worship the Kyrios as the Cosmocrator.[93]

That in the Pauline Christology Christ is assigned a subordinate rank to God is not meant in an absolute sense is seen in the paralleling of God and Christ, as reflected in the prepauline formula of 1 Corinthians 8:6 already mentioned. It is also found in the salutation of the epistolary prescripts (e.g. 2 Cor 1:2; Phil 1:2: "Grace to you and peace from God our Father and the Lord Jesus Christ"). Here the Kyrios is the one acknowledged to have the power of the eschatological gifts at his disposal in the same manner as does God, and to be able to grant them to others.

The variety in the way the relation of Christ to God is expressed does not need to be understood in such a way that Christ becomes only a cipher for the saving event. For Paul it is not the manifestation of an idea but the encounter with a Thou. Like the relation between God and Christ, the Christ event itself is structured in personal terms. One may doubtless ask with R. Bultmann whether speaking of the act of God is to be identified as mythological language.[94] And one will have to answer this question in the affirmative, if one interprets "myth" in an appropriately broad sense. In any case, this is the way H. Braun understood it when he attempted to demythologize God-language so that "God" would be "a certain kind of human relationship."[95]

---

90  This is, of course, not undisputed; if the division of clauses is understood differently, ὁ ὤν can be understood to begin a new sentence: "from them, according to the flesh, comes the Messiah. God who is over all be blessed forever." However, the text printed above is to be preferred as the *lectio difficilior*.

91  Cf. Pliny Letter 10.96. A more extensive identification is found in the letters of Ignatius, where Father and Son are both designated as "God." Cf. IgnEph 1.1, ἐν αἵματι θεοῦ; esp. 7.2 and 18.2 (θεὸς ἡμῶν); IgnTrall 7.1; IgnRom prescript, 3.3; IgnSm 1.1.

92  2 Corinthians 12:8. The word κύριος refers not to God but to Christ, going back to the previous verse in which the "power of Christ" (ἡ δύναμις τοῦ Χριστοῦ) is manifest in the weakness of the apostle (2 Cor 12:9).

93  Cf. Phil 2:10–11; also "Marana tha" (1 Cor 16:22), on which see above A. II. A. 3.

94  R. Bultmann, "New Testament and Mythology," in Hans-Werner Bartsch, ed. *Kerygma and Myth. A Theological Debate, Volume II.* (London: SPCK, 1962) 43.

95  H. Braun, "Die Problematik einer Theologie des Neuen Testaments," in *Gesammelte Studien zum Neuen Testament und seiner Umwelt* (Tübingen, 1962 [=1971³]) 325–341; 341.

However, this interpretation would at the same time eliminate a characteristic feature of Pauline thought: the "extra nos" of salvation. That the saving event is not identified with an internal event in human existence but is grounded in something that happens external to human existence, is no longer expressed by such a definition. By way of contrast, speaking of God and Christ as persons preserves the "extra nos" dimension and lets God and Christ be perceived as our opposite numbers, so to speak—as subjects in their own right who encounter us as other persons do. This personal conceptuality, this speaking of God as the Father or of the preexistent Christ as the Son is an element of mythological thinking and brings to light the inadequacy of speaking about God in human language at all. That such language cannot make appropriate and adequate statements about God's being was recognized by the Middle Platonists and the later advocates of Neoplatonic thought, who were willing to speak of God only by means of the "via negativa."[96] This perspective has influenced Pauline language when God is designated the "invisible" (ἀόρατος, Rom 1:20) or the "immortal" (ἄφθαρτος, Rom 1:23) One. Thus the category of personality also stands in need of interpretation; it must be supplemented by the knowledge that in speaking of God every concept and every description is inadequate; once again it is precisely this that points to the "extra nos" that is constitutive for both Paul's Christology and his doctrine of God.[97]

How little this personal concept is to be absolutized is seen in the liturgical formula of 2 Corinthians 13:13 ("The grace of the Lord Jesus Christ, the love of God, and the communion of the Holy Spirit be with all of you"). This triadic formula was later understood in the sense of a Trinitarian statement. While it is true that from time to time Paul can personify the term πνεῦμα, it is not appropriate in passages such as this.[98] For Paul the Spirit is primarily an "it," a substance or power that is thought of in spatial terms.

3. *The content of the Pauline doctrine of God* corresponds to the background presupposed from the point of view of the history of religions. The Pauline understanding of God is Old Testament–Jewish. Although the analogues in the Greek–Hellenistic doctrines of God may not be ignored, it is the Old Testament–Jewish context that must be considered primary: God is the creator of the world, the one who calls forth light from darkness (2 Cor 4:6; cf. Gen 1:3), the one who created human beings (1 Cor 11:8ff), the one to whom the whole earth belongs (1 Cor 10:26). Such creative activity means that God possesses an all-comprehending power (Rom

---

[96] According to J. Whittaker, *Neopythagoreanism* 169ff, the manner of expression of the negative theology does not primarily indicate the denying of a connection but rather that the designated quality has been exceeded or transcended. The quality ἀόρατος would then mean not primarily "invisible," so that the deity could be apprehended only in a mystical sense. In any case, Paul too is concerned with the transcendent divine being that exceeds the human horizon of perception and expression.

[97] Cf. also Romans 11:33–36: both Jewish and Stoic traits can be recognized in the hymnic expression of praise, and the confession of the "unsearchable ways of God" also manifests an Old Testament background (cf. Isa 40:13; Job 41:3; in addition, cf. Apocalypse of Baruch 14:8ff). E. Norden, *Agnostos Theos* 242ff; E. Käsemann, *Commentary on Romans*, 314–315.

[98] Cf. Romans 8:16, 26; 15:30; 1 Corinthians 2:10, 12.

11:36; 1 Cor 8:6). The omnipotence of God comes to expression especially in the concept of the world judgment: God is the one who judges the
whole world (1 Thess 1:10; Rom 3:5 = the day of wrath; Rom 2:5). Here
too Paul does not really distinguish between God and Christ, for Christ
too is portrayed as judge of the world, who will exercise his judgment at
the parousia (1 Thess 2:19; 1 Cor 4:5); correspondingly, the location from
which this judgment is pronounced can be called the "judgment seat of
God" in one place (Rom 14:10) and the "judgment seat of Christ" in
another (2 Cor 5:10).

The last judgment means the final revelation and execution of the
"wrath of God," the ὀργὴ θεοῦ (Rom 5:9; 1 Thess 1:10). This too is part of
the Jewish-apocalyptic thought world. The Pauline doctrine of God is
oriented to the future. The ὀργὴ θεοῦ is essentially an apocalyptic item. But
it is already manifest in the present. When it is said in 1 Thessalonians
2:16, ἔφθασεν δὲ ἐπ᾽ αὐτοὺς [Ἰουδαίους] ἡ ὀργὴ εἰς τέλος, the phrase εἰς τέλος
means "for ever," "always," (i.e., that from now on the Jews stand under
the eternal wrath of God),[99] or "to the extreme," "finally," according to
which the whole history of Israel is understood as an expression of disobedience and turning away from God's will. In each case the "wrath of
God" is understood to be a reality at work in the present. For Paul this is
based on the fact that the Jews are persecuting their Christian compatriots
(2:15). According to Romans 9, that the promises to Israel have not been
fulfilled and the preaching of the gospel has been rejected by the Jews has
its basis in the wrath of God, so that the Jews can be described as "vessels
of wrath" (9:22). God has the authority and power to deal with them
according to his unlimited will, just as a potter does with the objects he
or she has made (9:21). Election and rejection take place according to the
sovereign decision of God (cf. Rom 9:13, "As it is written, 'I have loved
Jacob but I have hated Esau'"). Human beings stand under the divine
"predestination." While the ὀργὴ θεοῦ can be perceived in the rejection of
the gospel by human beings, it is not to be grounded in a one-sided
manner. God's way of dealing is finally a hidden matter. It is the "deus
absconditus" who appears as the God of ὀργή.

The wrath of God is directed not only against Jews but in the same way
against Gentiles: they recognized God in the works of creation but did not
honor him as God (Rom 1:18ff). That is why the wrath of God is already
manifest in the present, for because they refuse to acknowledge God's
power and will, they fall prey to godlessness and unrighteousness.[100] This
is the point of departure for the Pauline message of the righteousness of
God that has happened in the Christ event: the Christ event brings about

---

[99] Cf. below A. IV. c.
[100] Cf. P. Feine, *Theologie des Neuen Testaments* 195 ("God's punishment for sin is
to let people sin").

reconciliation with God, namely salvation from the wrath of God (Rom 5:9–10). Only the letter to the Romans speaks of the wrath of God and its being overcome. It is thus a constitutive element of the Pauline concept of justification. The apostle does not reflect abstractly about the existence or essence of God but in mythological language of God's act the being of God comes to expression, as it has been disclosed to humanity in the Christ event.

# III. The Liberation through Christ

In the following we will pursue the question of the "work of Christ" not in the sense of an objectively ascertainable salvific act as though the results of the Christ event could be portrayed as "objective acts of salvation;" for the work of Christ cannot be spoken of in any other way than at the same time speaking of the person for whom it is done. As the object of the saving act that can be spoken of in christological terms, the human being is not a being with no will of its own but an engaged personal being who can respond in faith to the divine gift. The saving act of Christ to which human beings respond in faith, is in the first place:

## a) Liberation from the Powers of the Flesh, Sin and Death

Foerster, W. "σῴζω etc.," TDNT VII (1964) 966–969.980–1012.1015–1024.
Heckel, U. Kraft in Schwachheit. Untersuchungen zu 2 Kor 10–13. WUNT II 56. Tübingen: Vandenhoeck & Ruprecht, 1993.
Jones, F. S. "Freiheit" in den Briefen des Apostels Paulus. GTA 34. Göttingen: Vandenhoeck & Ruprecht, 1987.
Niederwimmer, K. "ἐλεύθερος etc.," EWNT I (1980) 1052–1058.
Niederwimmer, K. Der Begriff der Freiheit im Neuen Testament. TBT 11. Berlin: Töpelmann, 1966.
Schelkle, K. H. "σωτήρ etc.," EWNT III (1983) 781–788.
Schweitzer, A. The Mysticism of Paul the Apostle. New York: H. Holt and Company, 1931.
Strecker, G. "Befreiung und Rechtfertigung," Rechtfertigung. (FS E. Käsemann). Tübingen: J. C. B. Mohr (Paul Siebeck), 1976. 479–508; also in G. Strecker. Eschaton und Historie. Aufsätze. Göttingen: Vandenhoeck & Ruprecht, 1979. 229–259.
Thüsing, W. Per Christum in Deum. NTA NF 1. Münster: Aschendorff, 1969[2].
Vollenweider, S. Freiheit als neue Schöpfung. Eine Untersuchung zur Eleutheria bei Paulus und in seiner Umwelt. FRLANT 147. Göttingen: Vandenhoeck & Ruprecht, 1989.
Wrede, W. Paulus. RV 1. Halle 1904 (= 1907[2]), also in K.H. Rengstorf, ed., Das Paulusbild in der neueren deutschen Forschung. WdF 24. Darmstadt: Wissenschaftliche Buchgesellschaft, 1982[3]. 1–97.

William Wrede distinguished two series of ideas in Pauline theology: the doctrine of redemption and the doctrine of justification. One can also place the whole theology of Paul under the rubric "redemption," if this concept is understood in a comprehensive sense. The same is true of the theme "liberation," which likewise can embrace the whole of Pauline theology. It is important for understanding the following that the concept of liberation be understood primarily as liberation from the powers of the flesh, sin, and death, and be distinguished on both formal and material grounds from the Pauline doctrine of justification. Such delimitation is suggested by the awareness that Paul's understanding of justification is constructed on the basis of the Old Testament–Jewish thought world and characterized by a juridical terminology, while the concept of redemption, or of liberation in the narrower sense, has Hellenistic-syncretistic features alongside its Jewish characteristics, and possesses a fundamental ontological structure (that is then only secondarily applied to the conception of justification).

## 1. The Formula "In Christ"

Büchsel, F. "'In Christus' bei Paulus," *ZNW* 42 (1949) 141–158.
Deissmann, A. *Die neutestamentliche Formel "In Christo Jesu."* Marburg-Tübingen: N. G. Elwert, 1892.
Neugebauer, F. "Das paulinische 'in Christo,'" *NTS* 4 (1957/58) 124–138.
Neugebauer, F. *In Christus. Eine Untersuchung zum paulinischen Glaubensverständnis.* Göttingen: Vandenhoeck & Ruprecht, 1961.
Schnelle, U. *Gerechtigkeit und Christusgegenwart. Vorpaulinische und paulinische Tauftheologie.* GTA 24. Göttingen: Vandenhoeck & Ruprecht, 1986[2].
Wedderburn, A. J. M. "Some Observations on Paul's Use of the phrases 'in Christ' and 'with Christ,'" *JSNT* 25 (1985) 83–97.

From the point of view of the study of the history of religions, the question of the origin of the formula ἐν Χριστῷ is still disputed. It is not seldom the case that the influence of (pre-Christian) Gnosticism is suggested, as is that of Old Testament–Jewish tradition. In each case the relation of both the individual and the community as a whole to Christ as the mediator of eschatological salvation is expressed by this formula.

In his foundational study *Adolf Deissmann* posited the thesis that ἐν Χριστῷ is to be understood in a local/spatial sense. Christ is understood as the realm, the sphere, into which the Christian is incorporated. The apostle's supposed "Christ mysticism" has often been mentioned in this connection. Subsequent study was considerably influenced by Deissmann's view. It has been found especially attractive where scholars have attempted to explain Paul's theology in relation to Gnosticism. The concept "mysticism" also seemed to be helpful in solving the problem of how Paul's thought could be translated into the present.[1] But one should not

---

[1]    Cf. A. Schweitzer, *Mysticism of Paul* 378.

speak of a Pauline Christ mysticism, since it is characteristic of mystics that they are absorbed into the Other and become identical with God or Christ ("I am you"), but Paul understands the relation of human beings to Christ in the sense of personal encounter in which the two persons remain distinct; the person of Christ is not dissolved.

*Friedrich Büchsel* energetically opposed Deissmann's thesis. According to Büchsel, the ἐν of the formula is not essentially local/spatial ("in Christ") but is to be understood mostly in an instrumental ("through Christ," Gal 2:17, "by means of Christ"), modal ("like Christ," Col 2:6) or causal ("in the Lord" Phil 4:4 and elsewhere) sense. In his view the spatial sense is only rarely present, and there in a figurative, transferred sense.[2] This means that the Pauline ἐν Χριστῷ is to be interpreted primarily in view of an Old Testament–Jewish background, and that especially the instrumental and causal meanings allow overtones of the Old Testament sacrificial conceptuality (ἐν = בְּ) to be recognized as essential elements of this formula. However correct it may be to point out the complex connections of the "in Christ" formula and to attend to its pointing "to the whole revelatory act of God," it would still be misguided to exclude the spatial meaning almost without exception. Paul could use ἐν Χριστῷ εἶναι as a stereotypical expression for "to be a Christian," for whoever is "in Christ" is a Christian. Thus according to Romans 16:7 Andronicus and Junia(s) are those "who were in Christ before me," i.e. who were Christians before I was. In accord with the pneumatic background ("Spirit-Christ"), this usage points to a context of interpretation in which the expression was understood in a spatial sense.[3]

*Fritz Neugebauer* has made the suggestion that ἐν Χριστῷ εἶναι be understood as meaning "determined by the Christ event," since the dative Χριστῷ refers to the saving event that is to be interpreted christologically. While the Christ event is here seen as a past event and rightly emphasizes the "Christus incarnatus," this must not be done in such a way that the "Christus praesens" is not included in the meaning. The ἐν Χριστῷ εἶναι points not only to the Christ of the past but at the same time to the present Lord of the church.

Thus the formula should be paraphrased with *incorporated in the Christ-reality*, which includes not only a christological affirmation but also an ecclesiological statement. This formula is concerned to express something about not only the saving acts of the past but also the present

---

[2] E.g. Colossians 1:19; 2:3, 9; but cf. Büchsel, "In Christus" 148 ("These passages speak of the significance of Christ for believers that he has by virtue of his predominant position in the whole revelatory activity of God.")

[3] Cf. also 1 Thessalonians 2:14; 4:16; Galatians 1:22. "This underlying spatial concept gives us the clue to the true significance of the formula ἐν Χριστῷ Ἰησοῦ and its parallels. Yet here too, there is both a local and an instrumental element." A. Oepke, ἐν *TDNT* 2:542.

lordship of the Kyrios[4] implemented by divine power. This means at the same time that an ecclesial element is included: whoever is "in Christ" belongs to the church, for he or she is a member of the body of Christ (cf. 1 Cor 12:12ff).

Since the Christian has been incorporated into the Christ reality, he or she is determined by the indicative of the saving event. This is mediated through baptism[5] and implies the separation from a world that is subject to flesh, sin, and death, and on the positive side means to have a new being (cf. 2 Cor 5:17). This new being is not dependent on contemplation and is not to be identified with a mystic being but is independent of feelings and contemplation; it is a reality that determines one's human life as a whole. Thus alongside the frequently used formula "in Christ," Paul can also place the statement, "Christ lives in me" (Gal 2:20; Rom 8:10). Those who are in Christ no longer belong to themselves but to the Kyrios. They have died with Christ in order to be raised with Christ.[6] They have been incorporated into the sphere of the Spirit, the Spirit that has taken possession of them and teaches them to call out ἀββά, πατήρ; for the Spirit is the guarantee and pledge of sonship (Rom 8:14ff).

Accordingly, ἐν Χριστῷ εἶναι is a comprehensive expression for the Pauline understanding of being a Christian and is mostly identical to the indicative parallel construction ἐν κυρίῳ[7] or ἐν πνεύματι.[8] Alongside these Paul uses a few other terms that paraphrase the meaning of the new being.

---

[4] Cf. Romans 1:4; 1 Corinthians 1:24; 5:4, and elsewhere.

[5] The informative study of Udo Schnelle, *Gerechtigkeit und Christusgegenwart* 109ff, has shown that the early Christian baptismal tradition was the context from which the Pauline ἐν Χριστῷ formula originated. It was thus related to the baptismal concept of "putting on Christ" (Gal 3:27). The picture of putting on a garment supports the spatial understanding of the formula and points to a Hellenistic-syncretistic background. Cf. Odes of Solomon 8:22; 17:4, 13ff, and elsewhere. Cf. also W. Schmithals, *Gnosticism in Corinth: An Investigation of the Letters to the Corinthians* (Nashville & New York: Abingdon Press, 1971) 360–367, 402–406. E. Brandenburger, *Adam und Christus. Exegetisch-religionsgeschichtliche Untersuchung zu Röm 5:12–21 (1 Kor 15)* (WMANT 7) (Neukirchen-Vluyn: Neukirchener, 1962) 139–153.

[6] Cf. Romans 6:4; possibly an element of a prepauline baptismal tradition (U. Schnelle, *Gerechtigkeit und Christusgegenwart* 76–77); cf. also 1 Corinthians 12:13; Galatians 3:27–28; 2 Timothy 2:11.

[7] Cf. Romans 6:23; 8:39; 16:2, 8, 11ff; 1 Corinthians 4:17; 7:22, 39; 9:1–2; 11:11; 15:31, 58; 2 Corinthians 10:17; Galatians 5:10; Philippians 1:14; 2:19, 24, 29; 3:1; 4:1–2, 4, 10.

[8] Cf. Romans 2:29; 8:9; 9:1; 14:17; 15:16 (ἐν πνεύματι ἁγίῳ); 1 Corinthians 6:11 (θεοῦ); 12:3, 9; 2 Corinthians 6:6; Philippians 1:27; 1 Thessalonians 1:5. Pneuma and Christ/Kyrios may not be simply identified without further ado (cf. for example the expectation of the personal parousia of the coming Kyrios); on the other hand, there is an overlap of indicative and imperative statements. Cf. the data presented by F. W. Horn, *Angeld des Geistes* 342–343.

The word ἀπολύτρωσις vividly expresses "release" (by paying a ransom), often translated with "redemption" (which in this connection means "a freeing, a liberation"); cf. 1 Corinthians 1:30 ("He is the source of your life in Christ Jesus, who became for us wisdom from God, and righteousness and sanctification and redemption,..."); Romans 3:24 (where "redemption" = "to have liberation in Jesus Christ"). This also has a future-eschatological sense: Romans 8:23 refers to the redemption of the body at the eschaton. The acting subject of ἀπολύτρωσις is God; here is reflected Paul's "theocentric" thought.

Election, ἐκλογή, is a constitutive element of being ἐν Χριστῷ. The motif of "election" of the Christian community through the Spirit that works through preaching is already found in the early stage of Pauline theology. It does not stand in competition to the ἐν Χριστῷ concept but rather is concretized in the election that takes place in baptism and the believing acceptance of the gospel (1 Thess 1:4–5). The idea remains a marginal theme, however, and does not become a constant in the Pauline theology.[9]

Similarly, the conceptuality of "reconciliation" does not play a central role. Its secular meaning is illustrated in 1 Corinthians 7:11 but it has a theological function only in 2 Corinthians and Romans (καταλλαγή, 2 Cor 5:18–19; Rom 5:11; 11:15; καταλλάσσω, 2 Cor 5:18–21; Rom 5:10). In connection with expounding his apostolic commission Paul attempts to portray the δόξα that accompanies his office: in contrast to the human evaluation "according to the flesh" (2 Cor 5:16), Christian existence is a "new creation" (5:17). It is grounded in the "reconciliation" that God has brought into being through Christ. This was originally not identical with the "atonement" mediated through sacrifice;[10] it is rather the case that Hellenistic Judaism had already used the word καταλλάσσω for appeasement of God's wrath (2 Macc 1:5; 7:33). The sovereign and universal act of God is decisive. Second Corinthians 5:18 states "God ... has reconciled us," and 5:19 continues with "... in Christ God was reconciling the world to himself ... ", where κόσμος refers to the general world of humanity, in contrast to Romans 11:15, where it means the Gentile world. When juridical categories are applied this means that sins are not counted against one (2 Cor 5:19; cf. Rom 4:8; Ps 32:2). The apostle's mission is derived from this, namely to deliver "the message of reconciliation" (τὸν λόγον τῆς καταλλαγῆς, v. 19), thereby providing the basis for the human possibility of being reconciled to God (v. 20 "be reconciled to God"). In the letter to

---

9     Apart from 1 Thessalonians 1:4 the substantive is found only in the Israel section of Romans (9:11; 11:5, 7, 28). The verb is found only in 1 Corinthians 1:27. Differently J. Becker, *Paul: Apostle to the Gentiles* (Louisville: Westminster John Knox, 1993) 130–140.

10    Cf. C. Breytenbach, *Versöhnung. Eine Studie zur paulinischen Soteriologie* (WMANT 60) (Neukirchen-Vluyn: Neukirchener, 1989) 180–181.

the Romans the word stands for the first time in connection with the Pauline theology of justification (cf. Rom 5:1, 15; keywords are "faith" and "grace"), where it designates the comprehensive eschatological act of salvation. The event of reconciliation through Christ has "now" been received by believers (5:11). It thus corresponds in this context to the juxtaposition of Christ, the last Adam, and the dispenser of life and the first Man as the cause of death (5:12ff).

Thus the term "freedom" can also be used as a comprehensive term to designate the new being. The word ἐλευθερία and its derivatives is found in the New Testament predominately in the Pauline letters,[11] most of the occurrences being found in the "main" letters of Galatians and Romans that reflect the doctrine of justification. The occasional sociological aspect has an ethical-theological significance; thus in the juxtaposing of free and slave, the slave is paradoxically called the "freed person belonging to the Lord" and conversely the free person is called a "slave of Christ" (1 Cor 7:22). The eschatological body of Christ implies the bridging of social distinctions (Gal 3:28; 1 Cor 12:13). The interpretation of "theological" references must be understood in terms of their immediate context; the Pauline concept of freedom is not to be homogenized in a harmonizing manner but is developed exclusively with reference to the social or congregational situation presupposed in each case. In dependence on Gentile–Hellenistic tradition, Paul is concerned in the Corinthian correspondence for his independence as an apostle. This happens specifically in debate with his Corinthian opponents, especially with regard to his right to financial support (1 Cor 9:1ff) but also in view of the harassment of the Christian conscience by one's fellow human beings who are held captive in bondage (1 Cor 10:29). In the letter to the Galatians the Pauline consciousness of freedom attains a specific profile stamped with his doctrine of justification, in confrontation with the Judaistic opponents, their dependence on the elementary powers of the world (Gal 4:1ff) and their subjection to the Jewish law (Gal 4:4–5; cf. 5:1: circumcision as the "yoke of slavery"). The term "freedom" can also be replaced by "redeem" (Gal 4:5, ἵνα τοὺς ὑπὸ νόμον ἐξαγοράσῃ); in Romans it is connected to the Pauline tendency to systematize, as expressed for example in his doctrine of baptism and his pneumatology.

The Pauline concept of freedom concretizes the idea of "freedom from:" Christians know that in Christ they have been freed from the power of sin (Rom 6:18–22) and death (8:2). This "deliverance" from the body of death (Rom 7:24) at the same time means liberation from the power of the law and thereby from the human experience of alienation from one's self

---

[11] Of eleven instances of ἐλευθερία, seven are found in Paul; of 7 instances of ἐλευθερόω, 5 are in Paul; of 23 instances of ἐλεύθερος, 14 are in Paul; in addition, ἀπελεύθερος is found only once in the New Testament, 1 Corinthians 7:22.

(7:4ff), and beyond that from the fate of "mortality" (8:21 φθορά!). With this is bound up the idea of "freedom for," so that together they constitute a life grounded in and led by the Spirit, for where the Spirit of Christ prevails, there is freedom (2 Cor 3:17). In the sphere of the life-giving Spirit (Rom 8:2) the apostle practices his personal freedom. As illustrated by Old Testament typology (Gal 4:22ff, Sarah as prototype of freedom), the realm of Christ's lordship is the sphere of freedom (Gal 2:4). Corresponding to this, the *ethical imperative* is interlocked with the *indicative declaration* of the freedom established by Christ on which it is based. Since Christ has called us to freedom, there follows from this the demand to stand fast in this freedom and not to be made subject to δουλεία again (Gal 5:1), not to give opportunity to the flesh or to sin but to actualize the call to freedom in the mutual service of agape (Gal 5:13). While such freedom is a gift in the present (cf. 1 Cor 9:1; Gal 2:4, and elsewhere), it is at the same time a promise for the future, in which it will be realized as a universal gift of God comprehending the whole creation, comparable to the δόξα of the children of God (Rom 8:18–21).

As a comprehensive designation for the "salvation" accomplished by Christ and realized in Christ, Paul uses the term σωτηρία. Thus in the LXX the "nomen agentis" σωτήρ belongs to the frequently-used titles of God (e.g. Isa 12:2; Micah 7:7), without ever clearly being referred to the Messiah (in Zech 9:9; Isa 49:6; 4 Ezra 13:26 there are at most hints in this direction). A broad use of the term is found in the Greek-Hellenistic milieu of the New Testament. Greek mythology uses the word fairly often for deities (cf. Xenophon *An* I 8.16; Ζεὺς σωτὴρ καὶ νίκη), and in the adoration of Hellenistic rulers it is found as a title (θεὸς σωτήρ),[12] just as it is in the Roman Caesar cult. The only example in the Pauline letters is found in Philippians 3:20, perhaps adopted by him here from the tradition: Jesus Christ is invoked by his church as the "deliverer" or "savior" who as the Cosmocrator will change our mortal earthly bodies into his glorious body.

Just as the title "savior" is here understood in terms of future eschatology, the same is true for σωτηρία. The promise of salvation accepted in faith is primarily a reality of future hope. "Salvation" will take place at the parousia of the Kyrios (Rom 13:11); the apostle expects it for his own life (Phil 1:19; Job 13:16); it is the general object of Christian hope (1 Thess 5:8–9; cf. 2 Clem 1:7), the result of repentance (2 Cor 7:10) but also the goal of human striving (Phil 2:12). On the other hand, salvation is also a present reality. The "day of salvation" becomes present in the preaching

---

12   In an inscription honoring Caesar from Ephesus (48 B. C. E.) the title "The Visible Manifestation of God and the Universal Savior of Human Life" (τὸν ... θεὸν ἐπιφανῆ καὶ κοινοῦ τοῦ ἀνθρωπίνου σωτῆρα); cf. Dittenberger, *Sylloge*³ 760; *Umwelt des Urchristentums*, J. Leipoldt and W. Grundmann, eds. II (Berlin: Evangelische Verlagsanstalt, 1982⁶) 105.

of the apostle (2 Cor 6:2; Isa 49:8). "Salvation" happens "already" in the present in the calling of the Gentile world into the community of faith (Rom 11:11); it is an apostolic gift present in the church (2 Cor 1:6 alongside παράκλησις). The content intended by the word "salvation" can be said most clearly in negatives: it is the opposite of "destruction" (ἀπώλεια, Phil 1:28), just as it stands over against "death" (2 Cor 7:10) or the "wrath of divine judgment" (1 Thess 5:9; cf. Rom 5:9). The basis of this future salvation is the revelation of the righteousness of God through the apostolic preaching (Rom 1:16–17; cf. 10:10). Salvation is identified with the gift of ζωὴ αἰώνιος (Rom 5:21; 6:22–23; Gal 6:8).

So also the verb σῴζω essentially refers to the future. When Christians are designated as οἱ σῳζόμενοι, "those who are being saved," it is the future salvation promised to them that is being referred to (1 Cor 1:18; 15:2; 2 Cor 2:15; cf. 1 Thess 2:16: for the Gentiles). With regard to the people of Israel, the apostle expects that at the end of history the saving consummation of God's purpose will happen for them (Rom 11:26). For the Christian community, it is expected that salvation will come as the sequel to their confession and faith (Rom 10:9; cf. 1 Cor 1:21). It is promised to each individual Christian as the result of the apostle's struggle (1 Cor 7:16; 9:22; 10:33), even to the sinful member of the church whose flesh is handed over to destruction but whose spirit will find salvation on the day of the Lord (1 Cor 5:5; cf. 3:15 for the role of the preacher's work). While those who are "reconciled" have such a hope (Rom 5:9–10), the dialectic of salvation as a present experience and salvation as a future hope still applies (Rom 8:24 τῇ ἐλπίδι ἐσώθημεν).[13]

## 2. The Power of the Flesh

Brandenburger, E. Fleisch und Geist. Paulus und die dualistische Weisheit. WMANT 29. Neukirchen-Vluyn: Neukirchener, 1968.
Davies, W. D. "Paul and the Dead Sea Scrolls: Flesh and Spirit," K. Stendahl, ed., The Scrolls and the New Testament. New York: Harper, 1957. 157–182.
Dibelius, M. Paulus und die Mystik. Munich (1941); also in M. Dibelius. Botschaft und Geschichte II. Tübingen: J. C. B. Mohr (Paul Siebeck), 1956. 134–159; = K.H. Rengstorf. Das Paulusbild in der neueren deutschen Forschung. WdF 24. Darmstadt: Wissenschaftliche Buchgesellschaft, 1982³. 447–474.
Sand, R. Der Begriff 'Fleisch' in den paulinischen Hauptbriefen. BU 2. Regensburg: Pustet, 1967.
Jewett, R. Paul's Anthropological Terms. AGJU 10. Leiden: E. J. Brill, 1971.
Sasse, H. "κόσμος," TDNT III (1938) 867–896.
Schweitzer, A. The Mysticism of Paul the Apostle. New York: H. Holt and Company, 1931.
Schweizer E., F. Baumgärtel, and R. Meyer. "σάρξ," TDNT VII (1964) 98–151.

---

[13] The dialectic of present and future is seen in the use of the verb ῥύομαι, e.g. 1 Thessalonians 1:10; 2 Corinthians 1:10; Romans 7:24)

Strecker, G. "Befreiung und Rechtfertigung," *Rechtfertigung*. (FS E. Käsemann) Tübingen: J. C. B. Mohr (Paul Siebeck), 1976. 479–508; also in G. Strecker. *Eschaton und Historie. Aufsätze*. Göttingen: Vandenhoeck & Ruprecht, 1979. 229–259.

Paul adopts the Old Testament–Jewish tradition: σάρξ[14] is the material bodily existence of human beings. The term designates human beings as such, since they are earthly beings bound to a material bodily existence. Thus the combinations σάρξ καὶ αἷμα (בָּשָׂר וָדָם Gal 1:16)[15] or πᾶσα σάρξ (כָּל בָּשָׂר Rom 3:20; Gal 2:16 1 Cor 1:29) indicate in each case the bodily existence of the human person.

In addition, σάρξ refers to the sphere of the earthly-natural in general, to that which is temporal in distinction to that which does not pass away (e.g. Rom 2:28–29). Without further qualification, this can be understood in a neutral sense, so that the expression ἐν σάρξ means at first nothing other than that which happens or is present in the sphere of the earthly-natural (2 Cor 10:3; Gal 2:20; Phil 1:24).

The distinctively Pauline usage has a negative connotation; ἐν σαρκὶ εἶναι means for Paul not merely that one lives in the sphere of the earthly empirical world but more than that, that by being in this sphere of existence one is subject to the compulsions of the temporal world (Rom 7:5; 8:8–9). This goes beyond the horizon of the Old Testament-Jewish world of thought presupposed by Paul;[16] it is reminiscent of Gnosticism, in which the world is understood as the cosmos fallen away from God and delivered over to destruction. As in Gnosticism, where matter itself has the character of a power that holds human beings in prison, so Paul too can understand σάρξ as a power, an acting subject by which/whom human beings are overwhelmed and which/who is the cause of human sin (Rom 8:3; Gal 5:13, 17, 19). This is because human beings who are delivered over to the sarx are compelled to live according to the flesh. They stand within the dynamism of the φρόνημα τῆς σαρκός; they are oriented to the flesh and subject to it (Rom 8:6–7).

---

[14]   M. Luther translated σάρξ with *Fleisch* ("meat" or "flesh"); this translation is more subject to misunderstanding in German than in English, since English distinguishes more clear between "meat" and "flesh." In each instance, the translator must ask which theological association is connected with the term σάρξ.

[15]   Cf. Matthew 16:17. In 1 Corinthians 15:50 σάρξ καὶ αἷμα stand in parallel to φθορά and designates the substantial bodiliness of human existence that cannot enter into the ἀφθαρσία of the heavenly world. This excludes neither a somatic (personal) continuity between the earthly and the resurrected human being, nor the idea that the latter will be transformed into a σῶμα who has an essentially pneumatic mode of being (1 Cor 15:51–52).

[16]   A negative qualification of the Hebrew בָּשָׂר is sometimes found in the Qumran texts (e.g. 1QS 11.10–11; 1QH 4.29–30, 37). However, it is not a matter of a sinful or non-sinful sphere but of sinful deeds within the Qumran community. Cf. R. Meyer, σάρξ, TDNT 7:109–113; E. P. Sanders, *Paul and Palestinian Judaism. A Comparison of Patterns of Religion* (Philadelphia: Fortress Press, 1977) 270–284.

The situation of human beings under the power of the sarx is that of people who live κατὰ σάρκα. This expression κατὰ σάρκα is likewise not an unambiguous designation. When Abraham is called προπάτωρ ἡμῶν κατὰ σάρκα (Rom 4:1), σάρξ here refers primarily to natural origin without having any a priori negative connotation. The connection with a substantive lets it be understood widely in this neutral sense.[17] However, where κατὰ σάρκα is used in connection with a verb, the negative, anti-God character of the phrase is expressed: κατὰ σάρκα περιπατεῖν means that the world of the flesh has become the determining norm of human life.[18] Where a human being is confident or boasts κατὰ σάρκα, his or her confidence or boasting is not founded on God but places its trust in the destructive power of the flesh (2 Cor 11:18). Whoever practices γινώσκειν κατὰ σάρκα thereby shows that his or her judgment is exercised according to human, this-worldly standards and does not judge rightly but leads into error (2 Cor 5:16).

The life of those who have given themselves up to the flesh is without hope. They are unconditionally delivered over to the fate of ruin and nothingness. Their efforts to save themselves from this fate can only sink them more deeply in the world of flesh. This is about as realistic as the act of bravado of the Baron of Münchhausen, who claimed that he pulled himself out of the quagmire, horse and all, by the hair of his own head. Paul emphasizes that the possibility and reality of human beings in the world of nature are determined by the conditions that surround them, and that as beings of flesh they are condemned to hopeless existence in a world with no exits. The case is different for those who live in the realm of Christ's lordship: they have crucified the flesh along with its "passions" (παθήματα) and "desires" (ἐπιθυμίαι) (Gal 5:24), and are called to reject this slavery under the power of the flesh and its "desires" (Rom 13:14). Servitude to the flesh is the mark of the pagan world (1 Thess 4:5; Rom 1:24) but also accompanies the way of the Spirit-led community as a constant reality or potential danger (Gal 5:16).

The term κόσμος embraces a wide spectrum of meanings between a more positive or neutral content on the one side, and a negative interpretation on the other side. The word can have the general meaning of all that exists (1 Cor 3:22; 8:4; Phil 2:15), being used for example for everything created by God (Rom 1:20 ἀπὸ κτίσεως κόσμου). It can be used in a neutral sense to designate the place where human beings live, the earth,[19] or the world of humanity, i.e. the human race (Rom 3:6, 19). Here the contrast between God and humanity is already suggested, which also comes poign-

---

17  Cf. also Romans 9:3, 5; 1 Corinthians 10:18.
18  Cf. 2 Corinthians 10:2–3; Romans 8:4–5 (in contrast to κατὰ πνεῦμα περιπατεῖν); 2 Corinthians 1:17; 10:3, and elsewhere.
19  Cf. 1 Corinthians 14:10; Romans 4:13; 1:8: the faith of the Roman church is spoken of in the whole world (ἐν ὅλῳ τῷ κόσμῳ).

antly to expression in the distancing way of speaking of "this world" (κόσμος οὗτος, 1 Cor 3:19; 5:10; 7:31), which is used interchangeably with "this age" (αἰὼν οὗτος).[20] Even though the corresponding apocalyptic phrase "the future world" (αἰὼν μέλλων and the like) is not found in Paul, the connection with apocalyptic dualistic thought cannot be overlooked. It is suggested in such expressions as "to come into the world," "to be in the world," "to go out of the world."[21] The present world is contrasted with the coming kingdom of God (1 Thess 2:12; 1 Cor 6:9–10; 15:50; Gal 5:21) or juxtaposed to the future δόξα (Rom 8:18). Hostility to God is traced back to the sin that came into the world through the first human being, sin that brought death with it (Rom 5:12). All human beings (πᾶς ὁ κόσμος) are guilty before God (Rom 3:19) and have fallen under God's judgment (Rom 3:6; 1 Cor 6:2; 11:32). In a manner similar to sarx, the cosmos can also become a ruinous power and be thought of as an acting subject; it closes itself off to the wisdom of God (1 Cor 1:21); but the wisdom of the world is foolishness before God (1 Cor 3:18–19). "Worldly grief," which characterizes the essential nature of the world, brings death (2 Cor 7:10).

A not insignificant reason that human life is an endangered species in the realm of the world and the flesh is the fact that in the world there are demonic, anti-God powers that put their nature into practice. The "god of this world" (2 Cor 4:4) exercises his power in the world, just as do the "rulers" (1 Cor 2:6, 8), the different "principalities and powers" that dominate the world until at the eschaton they are stripped of their power (1 Cor 15:24, 26). Here are also to be counted the demons that appear in the pagan cults of the gods and goddesses (1 Cor 10:19–21 δαιμόνια, εἴδωλα) and who give anxiety to Christians with weak consciences. The opponent of God in the Old Testament, the Satan, is of course not comparable to an exponent of Gnostic dualism. He does not stand over against the creator God as an anti-God principle but it is not to be minimized that he is at work in this world through his servants, who appear in the church as false teachers (2 Cor 11:4; cf. Rom 16:17–20). He is encountered in the adversities of everyday life (1 Thess 2:18; 2 Cor 12:7), and as the "Tempter" he puts believers to the test and brings them into danger (1 Cor 7:5; 2 Cor 2:11). Just as his domination is characterized by death and ruin (cf. 1 Cor 5:5), so his own destruction is already promised (Rom 16:20).

While the Christian community is threatened by the anti-godly being of Satan and the demonic powers, it is still not delivered over to them. The Christian hope speaks of the eschatological dethronement of the Satanic powers (1 Cor 15:24ff; 1 Cor 2:6). Moreover, Christians have been converted from service to the demonic gods to the one God (1 Thess 1:9; cf. 1 Cor 12:2; 2 Cor 6:16). The believers' present experience of reality made possible by Christ affirms that the demons, gods, and goddesses no longer have any power in themselves (1 Cor 8:4, "we know that 'no idol in the world really exists, and that 'there is no God but one'"). The demonic world may still be influential in human affairs but only to the extent that its power is acknowledged by human beings, for neither meat sacrificed to idols nor the gods represented by the

---

[20]   Cf. e.g. Romans 12:2; 1 Corinthians 1:20; 2:6, and Galatians 1:4 "the present evil age."
[21]   Romans 5:12. Cf. also 1 Corinthians 1:12; 5:10; 8:4; 14:10.

idols mean anything in and of themselves; they only grasp their power on the basis of weak consciences (1 Cor 8:7; 10:19). Christians are called to protect themselves by struggle against the anti-God powers and to grasp what God's gracious promise has already declared to them (cf. 1 Cor 9:24–27; Phil 3:12).

Through the divine act of reconciliation in Christ the hostility that separated the world and God has been bridged (2 Cor 5:19; Rom 11:15), and the slavery under the elementary spirits of the cosmos has been broken (Gal 4:3). This means for the lives of believers: alienation in the world where Christians now live over against worldly values and distance from the given conditions of life in the flesh. Christians do not live by the "spirit of the world" but on the basis of the gift of the Spirit of God (1 Cor 2:12). They experience a reevaluation of those values that prevail in the world. God has not chosen the strong and the wise of the world but the weak and foolish (1 Cor 1:27–28). To be sure, Christians still live their life in the world but they are aware that it is passing away (1 Cor 7:31b), and do not let the world's rules become a norm that determines their lives (1 Cor 7:33–35). They do not conform themselves to this aeon but they let themselves be renewed and practice a "reasonable worship" in the every-dayness of the world (Rom 12:1–2). Here too the Pauline "as if not" applies: they make use of the world as those who are not using it (1 Cor 7:31a). A certain distance to the world is appropriate for Christian faith: "the world has been crucified to me, and I to the world" (Gal 6:14).

## 3. The Power of Sin and Death

Brandenburger, E. *Adam und Christus. Exegetisch-religionsgeschichtliche Untersuchung zu Römer 5,12–21 (1 Kor 15)*. WMANT 7. Neukirchen-Vluyn: Neukirchener, 1962.
Röhser, G. *Metaphorik und Personifikation der Sünde*. WUNT II 25. Tübingen: J. C. B. Mohr (Paul Siebeck), 1987.
Schunack, G. *Das hermeneutische Problem des Todes. Im Horizont von Römer 5 untersucht*. HUTh 7. Tübingen: J. C. B. Mohr (Paul Siebeck), 1967.
Wolter, M. *Rechtfertigung und zukünftiges Heil. Untersuchung zu Röm 5,1–11*. BZNW 43. Berlin: W. de Gruyter, 1978.

When Paul speaks of the liberation of human beings, he does this not primarily in regard to deliverance from the power of the flesh or from cosmic beings. It is rather the case that at the center of the Pauline idea of redemption stands the declaration that human beings are freed from the power of sin and death. The Pauline interpretation of the Adam myth is characteristic for this point, which binds the Adam/Christ typology to the eschatological reservation:[22] The new life that Christ brings is essentially

---

[22] Cf. above A. I. b. 3.

the reality of hope (1 Cor 15:49; Rom 5:17). The new being of the Christian is thus not given by fate but allows room for the freedom of human existence. Because this new life is a reality in history, the possibility always exists that it can be missed.

What is true of the new life is also true, mutatis mutandis, for the human existence of the person prior to and apart from Christ, for the one who does not (yet) believe. To be sure, all live ἐν σαρκί but this does not mean that human being as such is necessarily subjected to sin. This is indicated by Romans 5:12ff. The context speaks of the reality of the ζωή that is given with the Christ event. To illustrate what is new in Christ, Paul draws upon the example of Adam. As indicated above, Adam, the πρῶτος ἄνθρωπος, is not only the cause of death (1 Cor 15:21) but the cause of sin. Through Adam sin came into the world (5:12). The Adamic human history before Christ is the history of a humanity that stands under sin.[23] Adam is the antitype of Christ and in no way is his positive counterpart. As understood in the Lutheran tradition: Adam and Christ are related to each other as law and gospel. The question of how humanity as a whole participates in the fall of Adam into sin is answered by Paul not in mythological terms but in a "historical" sense. While in Gnostic mythology there is understood to be a physical unity between the primeval Man and the other human beings who are incorporated in his destiny, in Romans 5 (differently than in 1 Cor 15:20ff, 45ff) Paul does not argue on the basis of a physical connection. He does not refer to the notion that human beings are by nature characterized by original sin. To be sure, he acknowledges that flesh and death unavoidably determine human destiny but the idea of sin that is handed on by nature is foreign to him. Romans 5:12 says rather that, while the Adamic side of humanity was of course determined by sin, οὕτως εἰς πάντας ἀνθρώπους ὁ θάνατος διῆλθεν, ἐφ᾽ ᾧ πάντες ἥμαρτον

---

[23]   Differently K. Barth, *Christ and Adam: Man and Humanity in Romans 5* (New York: Collier Books, 1962), who applies the relation between Adam and Christ to the relation of law and gospel in such a way that indirectly Adam participates in the gospel. In the process the series Adam/Christ is so turned around that Christ as the first man includes all other human beings in himself, so that the history of humanity in relation to the history of Christ "in its essentials, can only be a copy and image of his" (p. 8). Thus in Romans 5 we have learned that "Jesus Christ is the secret truth about the *essential nature of man*" as such (p. 107).

Barth's interpretation is opposed by Bultmann in "Adam and Christ According to Romans 5," William Klassen and Graydon F. Snyder, eds., *Current Issues in New Testament Interpretation* (New York, Evanston and London: Harper & Row, Publishers, 1962) 143–165. Bultmann argues that Paul here distinguishes two periods in human history, the epoch of sin and the epoch of grace. Thus Adam, within the outline of the history of salvation presupposed by Paul, is the "type of the one who was to come" (Rom 5:14). In accordance with this, Paul's meaning is that "human existence received its essence only as Christian existence, i.e., by faith in the grace of God which has revealed itself in Christ." (164)

("so death spread to all *because* all have sinned").[24] With Adam, to be sure, the possibility of sin entered the world but this possibility does not mean a compulsion; it is rather the case that every human being availed himself or herself of this opportunity—both the people without the law, who lived form Adam until Moses, and people under the law, who have lived since Moses. From Adam on, sin has been a possibility; this possibility has been realized without exception. Every individual bears responsibility for this!

There is no situation of sinlessness for people prior to and apart from Christ. This is shown by Romans 1:18ff. Paul does not speculate about theoretical possibilities but ascertains the actual state of affairs: human beings are involved in sin, and thus are guilty. They thus need deliverance, liberation from their guilt. Even if Paul has the view that Adam as the first human being determines the destiny of the human race by anticipation, he never speculates about a primeval sinless state of humanity. He does, however, get into severe conceptual difficulties when he distinguishes two epochs ("without the law" and "under the law;" Rom 5:13–14; cf. Gal 5:18). In the context of the letter to the Romans, Paul presupposes that it is only the law that makes sin real sin; he develops this view in chapter 7. On the other hand, he cannot dispute that the reality of sin and death also existed in the time before Moses and cannot give up the theologoumenon of the universality of sin. This, of course, is the necessary negative presupposition for the proof in this context that salvation through Christ is a universal reality. Therefore the construction: sin also existed in humanity before Moses but it could not be "booked." The term λογίζεσθαι has the divine action as its content, which in the preceding chapter was related to the faith of Abraham, which was "reckoned ['booked'] as righteousness" to him (Rom 4:3ff). Here Paul is thinking of the divine judgment. God's judgment will be pronounced on the basis of human deeds as measured by the divine law and will condemn those who have transgressed the law. But also before the promulgation of the Sinai law there was punishment for sin and guilt, namely the universal fate of death for those who, even though they did not transgress the divine command in the same way as the first man,[25] still sinned, as was ascertained to be a universal reality already in 1:18ff.

That sin is in principal no unavoidable fate is seen from the distinction between σάρξ and ἁμαρτία. The fleshly existence of human beings is not

---

24  ἐφ᾽ ᾧ = ἐπὶ τοῦτο ὅτι: "because," "under the circumstance that" they all have sinned. Differently in the Latin translation: in quo omnes peccaverunt (in quo = in Adam). In this translation Adam is pictured as sinning in a representative fashion for all, so that human beings were determined by his act. To this was added the idea of inherited sin, according to which sin is thought of as an evil genetic trait that transplanted itself through the generations, so that it was ultimately Adam and not the human individual who is responsible for sin. The orthodox doctrine of the imputed transfer of the guilt of Adam on humanity (Formula of Concord I 9) can basically make use of either translation. On the one hand cf. Luther, *Lectures on Romans* (LCC 14. Philadelphia: Westminster Press, 1961) [...in quo omnes peccaverunt...], and on the other hand cf. Calvin *Commentarius in Epistolam Pauli ad Romanos* (ed. T. L. Parker) SHCT 22 (Leiden: E. J. Brill, 1981) 109: "...quandoquidem omnes peccaverunt."

25  The reading μή in 5:14 is omitted in a few minuscules and Old Latin manuscripts. This is in support of the understanding that inherited sin came into the world through Adam. However, the weight of the manuscript evidence for this reading is very small.

*eo ipso* sinful. Human beings are not sinful just by virtue of the fact that they live in the world, as of course Gnostics could formulate the case, since for them matter as such is evil. It is rather the case that, for Paul, human beings are sinful because they orient their lives to the world of flesh and the temporal things of the world take on a constitutive and normative character for them. People are sinners when they live κατὰ σάρκα, i.e. when they live their lives in a God-less manner and close themselves off to God's claim (cf. Rom 1:18ff). Such "disobedience" (Rom 11:32; cf. Gal 3:22) is the original sin, that can be expressed in different ways, for example in ἐπιθυμεῖν, when sin means being dominated by evil passions and desires. This means that the person has become subject to "desires" (ἐπιθυμίαι, Rom 6:12). Sin can also be concretized as μεριμνᾶν, in "care and anxiety" that is the signal that the person is not oriented to the Kyrios but to the cosmos (1 Cor 7:32ff; Phil 4:6). Sin can also be identified with "boasting, self confidence" (καυχᾶσθαι) as practiced by Paul's opponents at Corinth. For those who boast in themselves orient their lives to the flesh, to the givenness of empirical reality, but are not open to the will of God and oriented to the Kyrios (2 Cor 10:17–18).

Even though human beings are responsible for their sinful state of being, sin is still not merely something external and unessential. It is rather comprehensive and universal. Like the flesh, it is a universal, all-dominating power. Whoever is fleshly, and thus lives κατὰ σάρκα, is sold under sin, which is like a slaveholder who beats slaves while they are chained (Rom 7:14). When Paul in Galatians 5:1 speaks of the "yoke of slavery" (ζυγὸς δουλείας), it is sin that is meant. Despite (better: because of) their responsibility, human beings are still enslaved by sin. This is the state of affairs as determined by Paul, the point of departure for his preaching.

That humanity prior to Christ universally lived under sin is based in the first place on the fact that it is easy for people who live in the world of empirical reality to orient their lives to this world and the created cosmos but not to honor the creator. This is the case for all human beings, Gentiles and Jews (Rom 3:23). The universality of sin also results from the special function of the law for human beings, as expressed in those Pauline letters characterized by his doctrine of justification. The law entices to sin, precisely by erecting prohibitions (Rom 7:7), so that Paul can also say that sin without the law is dead (7:8).[26] The law thus has precisely as its

---

26   This statement may not be generalized but is to be understand from the context of this argument in which Paul is not concerned with the function of sin but with the law, and in which he wants to show the ruinous power of the law. That there was sin in the human world between Adam and Moses, even though human beings were not under the law, is indicated, of course, by Romans 5:13–14. In Romans 7:7 Paul says precisely that before the law came there was no *knowledge* of sin. That applies to people between Adam and Moses and indicates the universality of sin.

assignment to lead into sin. This too is the basis for the fact that humanity in general is enslaved to sin, for just as sin is a universal, all-comprehending reality, so also with the law; this is what Paul attempted to delineate in Romans 1:18–3:20. All this means that the domination of the power of sin is total.[27]

As in relation to the power of the flesh and the threat of cosmic beings, so also in relation to the power of sin human beings are dependent on extra-human help. Deliverance is brought by the Christ event, as is expressed in different frameworks of thought such as atoning death (e.g. 1 Cor 15:3) or substitutionary formulae (2 Cor 5:21). The incarnation of the sinless Christ (cf. Gal 2:17) is not only an entrance into the world of sarx but into the sphere of sin (Rom 8:3). The compulsion to sin is taken away through the liberating norm of the Spirit (Rom 8:2). This is the way the issue is expressed in Romans, where the forensic terminology of justification is used (cf. Rom 4:7–8: the Christ event means that sins are "not reckoned"), especially in connection with the problem of the law (Rom 3:20; 5:13; 7:5, 7–8).[28]

The conquest of the power of sin through Christ is not only promised to the church but is a reality that already is happening in the present. The Pauline baptismal doctrine affirms that believers have died with Christ to sin (Rom 6:2–11). But the church is not a "sin-free area."[29] While the power of sin is broken, sin is still a constant threat for Christians. Paul reckons with the fact of post-baptismal sin.[30] The apostolic parenesis is motivated by the reality that the church is not an ethically-perfect community. This is summarized in the statement, "Come to a sober and right mind, and sin no more" (1 Cor 15:34). Just as the apostle knows himself to be not always free from sin (2 Cor 11:7), the church too must draw the necessary consequences from the liberating indicative; it must take action with regard to the sinners in its midst, as illustrated for example by excluding the sexual offender at Corinth (1 Cor 5:1ff). The sacramental acts in general indicate that the church not only looks back on sins that lie in the past, now regarded as over and done with (as expressed in baptism, e.g. Rom 3:25; 4:25) but seeks to overcome sin and guilt within the fellowship (in the Lord's Supper: 1 Cor 11:23ff). The operational motto is, "whatever does not proceed from faith is sin" (Rom 14:23).

---

[27] For other comments on Romans 7 see below A. III. a. 4.

[28] Cf. below A. III. b. 1.

[29] Contra H. Windisch, *Die Entsündigung des Christen nach Paulus* (Leipzig: Hirschfeld, 1908) 94–95.

[30] Cf. I. Goldhahn-Müller, *Die Grenze der Gemeinde. Studien zum Problem der Zweiten Busse im Neuen Testament unter Berücksichtigung der Entwicklung im 2. Jahrhundert bis Tertullian* (GTA 39) (Göttingen: Vandenhoeck & Ruprecht, 1989) 117.

On conceptualization: in his own usage, including when he adopts Old Testament tradition (cf. Rom 4:8), Paul prefers the singular ἁμαρτία. It is incorrect to say, however, that the plural occurs only in quotations (Rom 4:7; 11:27; 1 Cor 15:3) or in traditional material (as possibly 1 Thess 2:16; Gal 1:4); it is also documented in Pauline formulations (1 Cor 15:17; Rom 7:5). Thus Paul does not only think of sin as a force field (as e.g. the use of the singular in Romans 6:1) but also refers in the plural to individual acts of sin. The enslaving power of sin becomes concrete reality in the present in individual human transgressions. This is expressed not only in the plural but in the singular (2 Cor 11:17; Rom 14:23). This is in accord with other terminology: ἁμάρτημα indicates the act of sin prior to faith (Rom 3:25 trad.) as also in the life of the Christian (1 Cor 6:18); similarly παράπτωμα: prechristian (Rom 4:25 trad.; 2 Cor 5:19 pl.) and Christian (Gal 6:1). So also ἁμαρτωλός is used both of prechristian existence (e.g. Gal 2:15; Rom 5:18, 19) as also for Christian conduct (Gal 2:17: returning to subordination under the Mosaic law). The same applies for the verb ἁμαρτάνω: it is not unusual for it to be used for life prior to faith (Rom 2:12; 3:23; 5:16) but also for the life of the believer, both as a potential possibility that has not been realized (Rom 6:15) and as actual sin by Christians against Christ (1 Cor 8:12; cf. 6:18). It is consistent with this that at the last judgment Christians will be judged according to their ethical conduct (2 Cor 5:10).

The situation of human beings prior to and apart from Christ is thus determined by the powers of flesh and sin. But it is also dominated by the reign of death (θάνατος). Death is a biological necessity, for as a person the human being is σάρξ; as an empirical human being he or she is part of the earthly-empirical reality, that which is mortal and passes away. But Paul sees death not only as the conclusion of bodily existence but understands it in accord with the traditional Adam myth as the historical consequence of existence ἐν σαρκί. Inasmuch as human beings belong to the sarx and are subject to its power, they are φθαρτοί, subject to temporality and decay (1 Cor 15:50; Gal 6:8). The being of humans, inasmuch as they are determined by the power of the sarx, is a being-toward-death. This is thought of in terms of destiny or fate, and allows the mythological thought-world to shimmer in the background: Adamic humanity is, along with the primal man, subject to the material world and must perish along with it.[31] If the final judgment is made according to one's works, then each will receive the deserved punishment, namely death (Rom 2:1ff). This is apocalyptic thinking. Deliverance can only come when the second Adam establishes the possibility of being-toward-life.

Alongside this Paul knows another forensic way of looking at this that is even more strongly emphasized: sin draws death behind it as a necessary consequence. Sin punishes those who transgress the law with death (Rom

---

[31]  This corresponds to the view of the Hylics in the Valentinian school, from whom the Gnostics and Psychics distinguished themselves as those who belong to the heavenly world, though the Psychics "could only expect a lower state of blessedness" (so A. v. Harnack, *Lehrbuch der Dogmengeschichte* [Tübingen: J. C. B. Mohr (Paul Siebeck), 1931⁷] 75.

1:32; 5:12, 17), for "the wages of sin is death," i.e., sin pays those who have been enslaved by it with death (Rom 6:23). Thus death is here again a physical, natural part of the givenness of the way things are (Rom 5:12ff). But as punishment for sin, natural death is at the same time an eschatological phenomenon: (eternal) death, from which there is no escape, is contrasted with ζωὴ αἰώνιος as the consequence of sanctification (Rom 6:21–22). Being-toward-death is executed at the last judgment, which both confirms and transcends natural death.[32]

But death as the punishment for disobedience, is also for Paul not only a future event. It already determines the present and past life of human beings. As Adamic humanity is oriented to the flesh, its being is totally dominated by temporality, decay, and futility. This is indicated by Romans 7:9–11: when sin came to life, the human being died, for sin deceived him about his true being and true goal, and killed him. Thus death was already prior to Christ a given eschatological reality in human life. And Adamic humanity, humanity apart from faith, was not only left in this situation by the proclamation of the gospel but fixed in it. The preaching of the Christian message is to unbelievers "a fragrance from death to death," it brings about in those who are already subject to death, nothing else than death (2 Cor 2:16). The radicality and totality of the enslavement of humanity prior to Christ under sarx, sin, and death cannot be overstated. From this slavery the only deliverance comes through the Christ event.

## 4. The "I" in Conflict

Althaus, P. *Paulus und Luther über den Menschen. Ein Vergleich.* SLA 14. Gütersloh: Gerd Mohn, 1958³.

Bornkamm, G. "Sin, Law, and Death," G. Bornkamm. *Early Christian Experience.* London: SCM, 1969, 87–104.

Bultmann, R. "Romans 7 and the Anthropology of Paul," *Existence and Faith: Shorter Writings of Rudolf Bultmann.* New York: Meridian, 1960, 147–157.

Eckstein, H.-J. *Der Begriff der Syneidesis bei Paulus.* WUNT II/10. Tübingen: J. C. B. Mohr (Paul Siebeck), 1983.

Kertelge, K. "Exegetische Überlegungen zum Verständnis der paulinischen Anthropologie nach Römer 7," *ZNW* 62 (1971) 105–114.

Kümmel, W. G. *Römer 7 und das Bild des Menschen im Neuen Testament.* Zwei Studien. TB 53. Munich: Kaiser, 1974.

Lichtenberger, H. *Studien zur paulinischen Anthropologie in Römer 7* Habilitionschrift, Tübingen 1985, privately printed.

---

[32] Is there also a final judgment for non-Christians? Second Corinthians 5:10 ("For all of us must appear before the judgment seat of Christ, so that each may receive recompense for what has been done in the body, whether good or evil") apparently applies only to believers, but Gentiles and Jews stand under the legal demand of the law and will be examined at the last judgment with regard to their works. See below under A. V.

Schmithals, W. *Die theologische Anthropologie des Paulus. Auslegung von Röm 7,17–8,39.* Stuttgart: Kohlhammer, 1980.

Schnelle, U. *The Human Condition: Anthropology in the Teachings of Jesus, Paul, and John.* Minneapolis: Fortress, 1987.

Theissen, G. *Psychological Aspects of Pauline Theology.* Philadelphia: Fortress, 1987.

Paul asks in Romans 7:24, "Wretched man that I am! Who will rescue me from this body of death?" He means here redemption from the power of flesh, death, sin, and law, and he himself gives the answer: "Thanks be to God through Jesus Christ our Lord!" (Rom 7:25a). The Christ event is deliverance from the powers that enslave human life. How this act of deliverance is thought of has already been stated: liberation is accomplished through the sacrificial death of the humiliated and then exalted Christ. While this liberation is not yet complete but anticipates the final deliverance at the eschaton in which it will be perfected, it is still possible to say that Christians already live in a new reality within historical time, because they are "in Christ."

Christian existence is accordingly determined by the dialectic of the "already" and "not yet" of eschatological salvation. Structures here become perceptible that already characterize the being of humanity prior to Christ. Romans 7:14ff gives Paul's views on this within the context of the Pauline theology of justification conceived within a forensic frame of reference.

This chapter is located within the corpus of Paul's letter to the Romans in the section in which Paul argues that the "righteousness of God," the new being in Christ, is already a present reality (Rom 5–8). Despite the powers that surround human life, eschatological salvation is not only a possibility but a present reality. Thus in Romans 5 Paul deals with the problem of freedom from death, introducing Adam as the antitype of Christ who brings this freedom, and in Romans 6 deals with freedom from sin, as made present by dying with Christ and rising in the hope of the resurrection. In Romans 8, freedom from death, like freedom from sin, is related to Paul's understanding of the Spirit: the new life as freedom from death and sin is a life ἐν πνεύματι; it stands under the guidance of the Spirit.

Thus Romans 5–8 is intended to demonstrate the reality of the new life. It is in this context that Romans 7 is placed, with its thematizing of the problem of the law. Just as the new reality means that humanity is freed from death and sin, so it also means that humanity is freed from the power of the law (7:1–6). This, however, raises the issue of the significance of the law, which is in fact an enslaving chain from which humanity must be freed. Alongside this question that is to be answered in what follows,[33] it is of great importance for Paul how human beings understand themselves under the claim of the law. It is here that the distinction between

---

[33]   On this, cf. below A. III. b. 1.

the "inner" and "outer" person arises (ἔσω ἄνθρωπος and ἔξω ἄνθρωπος), a distinction that cannot be limited to the relation of Adam and Christ but refers to human beings in general. For there is a split within each human being, who has two "I's" at the same time. There is the human self who does not do what he or she wants but the opposite (v. 15). The inner, true self wants the good and strives for life (v. 22); this corresponds to the intention of the law that wants to lead to life. But such a human being in fact stands under the law of sin, so that he or she is a slave, and the power of sin humiliates him or her, making him or her into an object. The external person is subjected to sin.

Since Augustine, whose interpretation was adopted by Martin Luther,[34] it has been thought that this passage reflects on the being of the Christian, the struggle of the Christian life. Luther concludes on the basis of this passage that the being of the Christian is at the same time sinful and justified ("simil iustus et peccator"). The Christian must constantly engage this internal struggle; it is a call to daily remorse and repentance.[35] For this interpretation, one must appeal to 7:25b ("So then, with my mind I am a slave to the law of God but with my flesh I am a slave to the law of sin"). This is preceded by thanksgiving to God through Christ (7:25a), so it appears that v. 25b refers to Christian existence. But 25b is apparently a secondary gloss (possibly also 8:1). The preceding section has spoken not of human life after Christ but of those who lived in the time before Christ. This is the only way to understand the fact that in Romans 7 Christ is not mentioned until 7:24–25a, where the Christ event is referred to as the goal of the preceding.

The alternative interpretation is thus to be preferred, namely that Paul is thinking of human life prior to and apart from Christ.[36] In favor of this understanding is the relation of v. 5 to v. 23: in v. 5 the imperfect tense is used ("While we were living in the flesh, our sinful passions, aroused by the law, were at work in our members to bear fruit for death"); this statement refers unambiguously to people of the past in the time before Christ. It is taken up again almost verbatim in v. 23 but now in the present tense ("but I see in my members another law at war with the law of my

---

[34] Augustine, *Contra Julianum* III 26.62. Luther, *Lectures on Romans* 330–331.

[35] So A. Nygren, *Commentary on Romans* (Philadelphia: Muhlenberg Press, 1949) 284–303): While the Christian, to be sure, belongs to Christ and the new aeon, he or she still lives in the old aeon, in the realm of the flesh. This is the basis for the tension between intention and deed in the life of the Christian as described by Paul.

[36] This is the interpretation of the Church Fathers and of Pietism. So also P. Althaus, *Paulus und Luther*; R. Bultmann, "Romans 7 and the Anthropology of Paul," in *Existence and Faith: Shorter Writings of Rudolf Bultmann* (Meridian Books, Inc.; New York, 1960) 147–157; W. G. Kümmel, "Römer 7 und das Bild des Menschen," as well as others.

mind, making me captive to the law of sin that dwells in my members").
Here the present tense also refers to human existence in the past, namely
as it now appears in the light of faith.

Does this mean that Paul is also making an autobiographical statement
in Romans 7? Is he documenting his life as a persecutor of Christians prior
to his conversion? From this point of view, one can see parallels to the life
of Luther. Martin Luther came to his reforming discovery of the justifying
righteousness of God after a time of anxiety and struggle in which the way
of the church and its law had become problematic for him. Did the same
thing happen to Paul, in that he, perhaps through the encounter with
Christian martyrs, began to doubt whether the way of the Jewish law was
right and was led by these doubts along the path toward conversion to the
Christian faith? In this case, Romans 7 would be a belated and supplementary documentation of the internal struggles of the prechristian Paul. But
in Philippians 3:5ff Paul speaks of his prechristian life as one in which as
a Pharisee he lived "according to the law" without any scruples of conscience. He takes pride in his Jewish past; it was a positive gain for him,
until for Christ's sake he considered it to be loss. Thus in this chapter Paul
is neither providing an autobiographical report nor picturing a subjective
state of affairs. It is rather an objectivizing representation of the state of
humanity before faith, as it appears from the perspective of faith. The "I"
has a generalizing sense. The person prior to faith is the unconverted
person as such. Such a person is characterized by the fact that two "I's"
struggle within him or her: the one I, the real self of the person that is
oriented toward life and intends the good, and the other I, the inauthentic
self, determined by the flesh and that wrongly thinks that it can gain life
in the way of the flesh. This I does not recognize that the original orientation of humanity to life has thereby been perverted and that life is not
to be expected from the temporality and decay of the fleshly world but that
in this realm only sin is powerful and leads the person to death.

The situation of humanity according to Romans 7 is for Paul not a
subjective but an objective state of affairs, and it lies in the past. Does this
mean that people prior to Christ were aware of this struggle within the
self?[37] There is no reflection here, however, on the state of human consciousness. That people prior to Christ were not aware of their situation

---

[37]  This question is also to be posed when 7:25b is excised as a postpauline interpolation, since 7:23 likewise speaks of the νοῦς, which in Paul is usually identical with
"understanding," "thought" (more specifically R. Bultmann, *Theology* 1:212–213,
"understanding volition"). The inner person agrees to the will of God, which is
identical with the norm τοῦ νοός μου, thus the "norm of my understanding." This
appears to presuppose that the person prior to Christ was aware of his or her situation before God. But here the term νοῦς obviously means only the inner person (cf.
7:22).

of despair is seen in 7:15 ("I do not understand my own actions"). The person apart from Christ is not clear about his or her own situation.[38]

From this point of departure, a critical stance is to be taken to the thesis of Paul Althaus,[39] according to which Romans 7 speaks of an "original revelation" (*Uroffenbarung*) of God, as if people before Christ—even if only to a limited extent—knew of a prechristian revelation of God. P. Althaus attempts to document this by a comparison with Romans 1–2, according to which it was possible for Gentiles to come to a knowledge of God on the basis of God's works in creation (Rom 1:20). But Paul is not speaking here in the abstract sense of an "original revelation," but with the intention of convincing people that everyone stands guilty before God. Even less can we appeal to Romans 7 to speak of an "original revelation" to prechristian humanity in general, since—as we have seen above—people prior to Christ were not aware of any split within their own "I." Instead of an "original revelation" one might speak more correctly of Romans 7 as affirming an "original hiddenness:" the person prior to and apart from Christ does not know his or her own situation, prior to having been told. People did not know that their orientation toward life did not lead to life but to death, because they were under the law. They needed this information about their own condition; this comes in the Christian proclamation. Whether this awareness comes by way of the gospel or by way of the law is an open question. In his missionary preaching Paul presumably began with the indicative proclamation of the gospel, even if his letters could suggest the contrary. The decisive matter is that the fallen situation of humanity enslaved to death prior to Christ can only be revealed through faith.

In accord with this, the believer, who lives "in Christ," is to be radically distinguished from the person prior to Christ without faith, for the believer no longer lives under the compulsion of the law that has called forth the split in the "I" of the person's selfhood. It is still the case, however, that the Christian life is lived within the tension of a specific dialectic. Since the Christian lives under the rule and norm of the Spirit, his or life stands over against the empirical world of the law of the flesh.[40] The state of faith is not that of having a certain attitude or deportment [*Habitus*], as shown by the paradoxical relation of indicative and imperative.[41]

---

[38]  Thus there is no suggestion here of a psychological reflection on Paul's state of consciousness before he became a Christian, especially since Romans 7 represents a later stage of Pauline theology that has been influenced by the problematic of justification (in regard to G. Theissen's view in *Psychological Aspects* 179–269).

[39]  P. Althaus, *Paulus und Luther* 44–45, note 3.

[40]  Cf. also the term cosmos, which is to be placed mostly on the negative side of Pauline dualism.

[41]  Cf. differently W. Schmithals, *Theologische Anthropologie* 39ff. He distinguishes between the σάρξ as the empirical reality in which sin dwells (= interpretation of the I) and the I of the person himself or herself; he points out that it is thus not said that Paul identifies the human person with sin. However, the I of the person before and apart from Christ is divided!

## b) Justification

Conzelmann, H. "Die Rechtfertigungslehre des Paulus: Theologie oder Anthropologie?," H. Conzelmann. *Theologie als Schriftauslegung.* BEvTh 65. Munich: Kaiser, 1974. 191–206.

Käsemann, E. "Justification and Salvation History in the Epistle to the Romans," E. Käsemann, *Perspectives on Paul.* Philadelphia: Fortress, 1971, 60–78.

Kertelge, K. *'Rechtfertigung' bei Paulus. Studien zur Struktur und zum Bedeutungsgehalt des paulinischen Rechtfertigungsbegriffs.* NTA 3. Münster: Aschendorff, 1971².

Lohse, E. "Die Gerechtigkeit Gottes in der paulinischen Theologie," also in E. Lohse. *Die Einheit des Neuen Testaments.* Göttingen: Vandenhoeck & Ruprecht, 1973. 209–227.

Schnelle, U. *Gerechtigkeit und Christusgegenwart. Vorpaulinische und paulinische Tauftheologie.* GTA 24. Göttingen: Vandenhoeck & Ruprecht, 1986².

Schweitzer, A. *The Mysticism of Paul the Apostle.* New York: H. Holt and Company, 1931.

Seifrid, M. A. *Justification by Faith. The Origin and Development of a Central Pauline Theme.* NT.S 68. Leiden: E. J. Brill, 1992.

Stuhlmacher, P. *Gerechtigkeit Gottes bei Paulus.* FRLANT 87. Göttingen: Vandenhoeck & Ruprecht, 1966².

Wernle, P. *The Beginnings of Christianity.* London: Putnam, 1903–1904.

Wolter, M. *Rechtfertigung und zukünftiges Heil.* BZNW 43. Berlin: W. de Gruyter, 1978.

Wrede, W. *Paulus.* RV 1. Halle 1904 (=1907²); also in K.H. Rengstorf, ed., *Das Paulusbild in der neueren deutschen Forschung.* WdF 24. Darmstadt: Wissenschaftliche Buchgesellschaft, 1982³. 1–97.

Since Martin Luther appealed to Pauline theology in his work at reforming the church, Paul has been thought of mostly as a theologian of justification by faith. Such a wholesale evaluation is in need of correction, and not only because criticism of Paul has been largely oriented to his doctrine of justification. Thus Paul Wernle described Paul's view of justification as "one of the most unfortunate creations" of the apostle, which in later times led to fanaticism, narrow mindedness and pettiness.[42] And when W. Wrede defined Paul's doctrine of justification as a "battle doctrine,"[43] this at least presented the danger of understanding the Pauline message of justification exclusively as an apologetic weapon, the significance of which was exhausted when it had freed the Christian faith from the shackles of its Jewish past, and does not speak of the positive function that the message of justification contributes to Pauline theology taken as a whole.

Albert Schweitzer is another critic of the Pauline theology of justification. He describes it as a "secondary crater" that stands alongside his other theological affirmations—such as his eschatology or his mystical doctrine

---

[42]  P. Wernle, *Anfänge* 185.
[43]  W. Wrede, *Paul* (K. H. Rengstorf, *Paulusbild* 67).

of redemption—so that the Pauline doctrine of justification is not to be accorded a central function in Paul's thought.[44]

This critique is justified in the sense that Paul should not be made exclusively into a theologian of justification. The oldest Pauline letter (1 Thessalonians) manifests no awareness of the doctrine of justification. This is an indication that this perspective did not stand at the beginning of the development of Paul's thought but was only later adopted and developed.[45] In the process the apostle could have made use of Jewish Christian tradition. The decisive motivating factor in the development of the Pauline doctrine of justification is the confrontation with his opponents. Paul's message of justification was occasioned for the first time by the Galatian crisis and developed in his letter to the Galatians. Here false teachers are opposed who require that members of the Christian communities observe the commandment of circumcision. These were nomistic Jewish Christians that may have had a connection with Jerusalem. To this extent W. Wrede was correct in describing Paul's message of justification as in fact a "battle doctrine."[46] Paul further developed his view of justification in the letter to the Romans. Here it is Gentiles who are addressed with regard to their stance to the law and who thus stand on the same theological plane as the Jews that strive to fulfill the law. Here the message of justification in Galatians is taken up and elaborated in a comprehensive presentation. One can describe it as the center of Paul's theology. But it is

---

[44]  A. Schweitzer, *Mysticism of Paul the Apostle* 220.

[45]  Neither does the Corinthian correspondence, which follows immediately after 1 Thessalonians, contain any real evidence of the Pauline proclamation of justification. If 1 Corinthians 15:56 is suspected of being a gloss (so F. W. Horn, "1 Korinther 15,56—ein exegetischer Stachel," *ZNW* 82 [1991] 88–105), there is in any case in this verse only a negative interpretation of the law but not the alternative characteristic of the message of justification, the faith/works contrast. So also the opposition between letter and Spirit in 2 Corinthians 3:6 does of course express an opposition to the Jewish law but without anticipating the doctrine of justification. Such "argumenta e silentio" are all the weightier, since there are no plausible historical grounds for considering Paul's conversion near Damascus to have been the beginning point for his doctrine of reconciliation (so Chr. Dietzfelbinger, *Die Berufung des Paulus als Ursprung seiner Theologie* [WMANT 58. Neukirchen-Vluyn: Neukirchener, 1985] 90ff; P. Stuhlmacher, "'The End of the Law,' on the Origin and Beginnings of Pauline Theology," *Reconciliation, Law, and Righteousness: Essays in Biblical Theology*. [Philadelphia: Fortress, 1986] 134–154; 140.

[46]  Accordingly, one cannot go along with W. Schmithals' argument that it was Paul who first introduced the issues of law and justification into the Galatian debate and that his opponents there were advocates of a Gnostic teaching (*Paul and the Gnostics* [Nashville & New York: Abingdon Press, 1972] 42–43. Even if one acknowledges a Gnostic element in Paul's opponents, then it still must have been the law that constituted their difference from Paul and was the point of dispute. This is still true even if the Pauline letters give a subjective picture of the events in Galatia.

not its foundation. The foundation is the doctrine of liberation or redemption, which is already presupposed in 1 Thessalonians, the message of the liberation of humanity enslaved by the sarx, sin and death that has been accomplished by God in the Christ event. This does not mean that the importance of justification for Paul is minimized but rather that it is thereby shown how it is to be understood: it is only against the background of the doctrine of liberation that the Pauline concept of justification can be interpreted aright. It is much more than merely a legal doctrine about punishment and grace; its forensic, juridical character has an ontological foundation. The point of departure for understanding Paul's doctrine of justification is given with his understanding of the law.

## 1. The Pauline Understanding of the Law

Bachmann, M. "Rechtfertigung und Gesetzeswerke bei Paulus," ThZ 49 (1993) 1–33.
Bornkamm, G. "Wandlungen im alt- und neutestamentlichen Gesetzesverständnis," G. Bornkamm. Geschichte und Glaube II, GAufs. IV. BEvTh 53. Munich: Kaiser, 1971. 73–119.
Dunn, J. D. G. "The New Perspective on Paul," J. D. G. Dunn. Jesus, Paul and the Law: Studies in Mark and Galatians. Philadelphia: Westminster, 1990. 183–214.
Ebeling, G. "Reflections on the Doctrine of the Law," Word and Faith. Philadelphia: Fortress, 1963, 247–281.
Hahn, F. "Das Gottesverständnis im Römer- und Galaterbrief," ZNW 67 (1976) 29–63.
Horn, F. W. "Paulusforschung," F. W. Horn, ed., Bilanz und Perspektiven gegenwärtiger Auslegung des Neuen Testaments. BZNW 75. Berlin-New York: W. de Gruyter, 1995. 30–59.
Hübner, H. Law in Paul's Thought. Edinburgh: T. & T. Clark, 1984.
Lambrecht, J. "Gesetzesverständnis bei Paulus," K. Kertelge, ed., Das Gesetz im Neuen Testament. QD 108. Freiburg-Basel-Wien: Herder, 1986. 88–127.
Luciani, D. "Paul et la Loi," NRTh 115 (1993) 40–68.
Moo, D. "Paul and the Law in the Last Ten Years," SJTh 40 (1987) 287–307.
Räisänen, H. Paul and the Law. WUNT 29. Tübingen: J. C. B. Mohr (Paul Siebeck), 1987².
Stendahl, K. "The Apostle Paul and the Introspective Conscience of the West," HThR 56 (1963) 199–215.
Wilckens, U. "Zur Entwicklung des paulinischen Gesetzesverständnisses," NTS 28 (1982) 154–190.
Zeller, G. "Zur neueren Diskussion über das Gesetz bei Paulus," ThPh 62 (1987) 481–499.

The distinction between law and gospel that became prominent in Reformation theology was unknown to the apostle Paul. When the apostle speaks of the εὐαγγέλιον, he thinks of the proclamation of the Christ event but not the juxtaposition of law/gospel or gospel/law.[47] So also for Paul the concept of νόμος is not made more precise by making it an alternative to gospel. What was intended by the later juxtaposition of law and gospel

---

[47]  Cf. G. Ebeling, "Reflections," Word and Faith 254–257.

was expressed by Paul through the contrast of "old and new διαθήκη"[48] or "letter (γράμμα) and Spirit (πνεῦμα)" (2 Cor 3:6ff; Gal 4:24). Thus the term "law" is understood from another set of connections.

When Paul uses the word νόμος he is referring primarily to the law of the Old Testament. He thereby adopts the usage of ancient Judaism, in which the תּוֹרָה means in the first place the Old Testament Torah (in distinction from the prophetic and narrative documents of the Old Testament), then the individual commandments, and finally the Old Testament as a whole. In addition, νόμος can have the general sense of "norm" or "restriction" (cf. Rom 7:2–3, 23–25). In place of the word νόμος Paul can also use the term ἐντολή, which mostly denotes an individual commandment (e.g. Rom 13:9; 1 Cor 7:19) but also can be equated with νόμος (Rom 7:8ff).

For Paul the "law" is therefore essentially identical with the Old Testament law as it was given to the Jewish people through Moses. As a summary designation for the will of God as revealed in the Old Testament, it contains both cultic and ethical requirements. It is the νόμος θεοῦ, the possession of which distinguished the Jewish people from other peoples, as the Christian Paul can still acknowledge with some pride (Rom 9:4). It is the law that constitutes the Jewish people as a people, for nation and religion are fused into a united whole by the Torah. The νόμος of the Old Testament, as presupposed in Paul's usage, is thus the national law of Judaism and the Jewish people. This is the sense in which Paul understands the concept of law held by his opponents in Galatia. It is their intention to establish the Torah of Judaism within the Christian communities by means of the circumcision commandment and to reestablish Jewish national unity that had been called in question by the apostle's preaching. It was this issue, seen in this light, that formed an essential part of the motivation for the Pauline doctrine of justification. Paul was debating with Judaistic teachers who wanted to establish the validity of the national Nomos of Judaism as normative for Christian faith.

In Paul's letter to the Romans he presents a broadened interpretation of his concept of the law. Here it is no longer only the Jews who have received the revelation of the will of God in their national law but Paul attempts to establish the universal, comprehensive significance of the justifying event.[49] This leads to the statement that the work of the law is

---

[48] On the term διαθήκη: while the word is the Septuagint translation of the Hebrew term בְּרִית (contract, treaty, covenant), in Greek it means merely "testament" in the sense of "will," or "arrangement, order, instruction" (cf. BAGD 183).

[49] On the relation of the understanding of the law in Galatians to that in Romans, cf. H. Hübner, *Law in Paul's Thought*, esp. 26ff and 36–37, who rightly contrasts the dynamic, direct debate in Galatians with the more systematic reflection in Romans. One may ask, however, whether Galatians 3:19 in fact contains the state-

written on the heart of the Gentiles, so that Paul can also say that the Gentiles observe the requirements of the law (Rom 2:26). (The ἔργον τοῦ νόμου of Romans 2:15 does not designate the law itself, and obviously not the fulfilling of its commands but the content of what the law demands.)[50] The apostle's intention is to establish that both Gentiles and Jews stand under the legal demand of God's law, a fact to which their conscience testifies (Rom 2:15). Therefore both Jews and Gentiles will be asked about their "works" in the last judgment (Rom 2:16; 2 Cor 5:10). By such a broadening of the concept of law, Paul has de-nationalized the Jewish understanding of Torah. This does not alter the fact that Paul from time to time can revert to the Jewish usage, as when he describes non-Jews as those who do not have the law (1 Cor 9:21; Rom 2:14). It is rather the case that he understands human existence as such as existence under the law (cf. Gal 5:18; Rom 2:12ff, 6:14–15).

The law is accordingly a "norm" by which the conduct of every human being is measured. It is not *eo ipso* negatively qualified; on the contrary: the law is the voice of God through which God's will is revealed. It is a binding, holy obligation that intends human good (Rom 7:12), for it is from God and its goal is life (Rom 2:7). Thus the law can also be understand as "spiritual," with which the "inner person" agrees (Rom 7:14, 22). It is a spiritual demand, because it is the gift of God and because of its orientation to life it does not belong to the world of flesh.

In Romans 7:10 Paul clearly states, however, that"... the very commandment that promised life proved to be death to me." The law has become a ruinous power that enslaves human life no differently than the powers of sin and the flesh and robs it of its authentic meaning, essence, and destiny. Those who involve themselves with the law stand under the curse of the law (Gal 3:10). Since both Jews and Gentiles have to do with the law, they are all subjected to the power of sin (Rom 3:9). Whoever

---

ment that the law was given through "demonic angelic powers," and whether Galatians 5:14 is in fact an ironic statement. On this topic cf. U. Schnelle, *Gerechtigkeit und Christusgegenwart* 89ff: the doctrine of justification found in Romans is different from that in Galatians by (1) the introduction of the *nomen actionis* δικαιοσύνη θεοῦ, (2) a new systematic evaluation of νόμος, and (3) the discussion of the relation of God's righteousness to the election of Israel.

50    Cf. M. Bachmann, "Rechtfertigung und Gesetzeswerke" 29, who points to 4QMMT. According to K. Stendahl, freedom from "the works of law" is not a matter of a conflict of conscience as understood in the wake of the Lutheran tradition but merely a concession to the Gentiles, in order to facilitate their admission to the Christian community. Similarly J. D. G. Dunn, according to whom the "works of the law" refer exclusively to the Jewish "identity markers" (circumcision, food laws, and Sabbath), thus not to the regulations of the Torah as a whole ("Perspective" 194). It should not be disputed, however, that when Paul is contending for the right of the Gentile mission he is dealing with the fundamental issue of how the Torah as a whole is to be understood. Cf. also J. Lambrecht, "Gesetzverständnis" 102.

serves the law, serves death (2 Cor 3:7, 9), for it leads to death (2 Cor 3:6; Rom 8:2). This is grounded in a two-fold manner: (1) Because the law provokes sin, when it sets up rules people are led to break the law and thereby placed under the power of sin and death (Rom 7:7ff; Gal 3:19).[51] (2) The deadly power of the law is achieved with the fact that fulfilling the law leads to self esteem in the sense of taking pride in one's own accomplishment, misleading people to trust in their own achievements, wanting to establish their own life and not to found it on God's gracious gift (Phil 3:3–6; cf. Rom 3:27; 4:2; 2:17, 23; 1 Cor 1:29). It follows from this that no real righteousness comes through the law; by the law one comes not to life but falls under the wrath of God (Rom 4:15). This makes it necessary that human beings must be freed from the power of the law, in a way that corresponds to their being freed from the powers of sin and death: τέλος γὰρ νόμου Χριστὸς εἰς δικαιοσύνην παντὶ τῷ πιστεύοντι(Rom 10:4). In the Christ event the power of the law is broken and the curse is removed; the one who is "in Christ" is free from the slavery of the law's demand.[52]

## 1. The Meaning of the Law for Unbelievers

The law is the παιδαγωγὸς εἰς Χριστόν (Gal 3:24, "disciplinarian" [previously in English translations, "schoolmaster"], "attendant," "guard," the one who educates us in the direction of Christ) but not in the sense of a pedagogue with the goal of gradually developing human potential in order finally to bring one to the greatest good, Christ. But the law is also not a pedagogue in the negative sense in which it helps us achieve the insight of the impossibility of attaining life by our own power and thus gets us ready for the proclamation of the Christ-event, since the view that the law leads

---

[51] Cf. R. Bultmann, "Romans 7 and the Anthropology of Paul," 147–157; 149.

[52] On the term τέλος (Rom 10:4): the Greek word has a wide spectrum of meanings, from "fulfillment" through "goal" to "end" (cf. U. Wilckens, Der Brief an die Römer [EKK 6/2. Neukirchen-Vluyn: Neukirchener, 1987²] 222; H. Hübner, τέλος EWNT 3:832–835; 832; C. E. B. Cranfield, Romans [ICC. Edinburgh: T. & T. Clark, 1981²] 2:516). For Romans 10:4 there are basically two translation possibilities, "goal" or "end." Christ is the "goal" of the Old Testament law, inasmuch as the righteousness for which the Old Testament law strove but could not attain has been made accessible in Christ. This corresponds to the understanding of the law as a "disciplinarian" (Gal 3:24–25). The other possibility is that Christ is the "end" of the law, since righteousness is no longer granted to human beings on the basis of keeping the law but only on the basis of faith. The immediate context favors the latter interpretation, in which Paul regards as exclusive alternatives the righteousness of the Mosaic law identified with ἰδία δικαιοσύνη (10:3, 5) to the righteousness mediated by the proclamation of the gospel and is accepted by faith for salvation (10:3, 6ff). Here it is not only the misuse of the law but the law itself that is done away with, to the extent that it was acknowledged to be and practiced as a way of salvation prior to and apart from Christ.

to sin is the insight of faith that is first achieved in retrospect from the point of view of the Christ event. "Disciplinarian until Christ came" means rather that the law kept human beings in bondage to what they were, in their fallen existence subject to and determined by sin and death. To say it pointedly: the law's pedagogical, disciplinary function consists in the fact that it has no positive or negative educational function, that its relation to the Christ event is characterized by the fact that it does not anticipate the Christ event, not even in a preparatory sense. When it is realized that the law cannot and should not have a soteriological meaning, then the will of God in the Old Testament law can be discussed.

## 2.  The Meaning of the Law for Believers

If Christ is the end of the law, then one would have to think that Paul sees no connection between the Christian and the law. But the term νόμος can also be used with reference to the Christian life. For example, Galatians 6:2 says, "Bear one another's burdens, and in this way you will fulfill the law of Christ."[53] The will of God as revealed in the Old Testament law remains unbroken and indispensable but it is modified: the "law of Christ" is the command of love, the mission to serve the neighbor and to be there for him or her. Not only is every casuistic legal ordinance abandoned but an essential element of the Old Testament law is preserved. In the Gentile Christian churches the ceremonial law is no longer binding. This documents Paul's fundamental freedom from the law.

In addition, the ruinous power of the law is broken by the Christ event. In faith Jews and Gentiles acknowledge that the law, in whatever manner they may have encountered it, is no means of salvation. The "norm of faith" is radically contrasted with the law of works (Rom 3:27). It is just as little to be paralleled to the demand of the Old Testament law, and represents just as little the demand for human accomplishment and merit, that νόμος can be used to sum up the meaning and effect of the Christ event on the individual Christian. When Romans 8:2 juxtaposes "the law of the Spirit of life in Christ Jesus" and "the law of sin and death," it is not so much the content of the law's demand in each case that is implied as what the Christ event represents for believers, namely *liberation*. This "law" comes to concrete realization in the substitutionary fulfillment of the law by Christ (cf. Rom 8:3–4). While the Christian is an ἔννομος Χριστοῦ (one who accepts the norm of Christ as binding for his or her life), Christians are not subject to a new law, since Jesus Christ is not understood as the

---

[53]  Cf. also 1 Corinthians 9:21; Romans 3:27; 8:2. Since in these references the term "nomos" is used directly or indirectly as an antithesis to the law of Judaism and has no negative nuance with reference to the state of believers, it is advisable in these places to translate with "norm." So also in Romans 7:21, 23.

bringer of a *nova lex* but Christians are understood as those who have been liberated. Since for him the power of the law has been broken, the apostle knows himself to be fundamentally more closely related to those without the law than those who have the law (1 Cor 9:20–21).[54] That includes responsibility in the world and for the world. The person who lives under the norm of the Christ event is called to serve; such a person is responsive to the demand of the commandment of love, which is the fulfillment of the law (Rom 13:8–10; Gal 5:14). The love commandment is no new law but the challenge to keep oneself in the freedom granted to the Christian, and to do whatever must be done in the moment to fulfill the demand of love. The one whose mind has been transformed is in the situation to judge what God requires, and what is that good, acceptable, and perfect will of God (Rom 12:2).

### 3. 'Epaggel...a and NÒmoj (Promise and Law)

The Old Testament mediates two words of God: the word of promise and the word of law. Paul makes a distinction between these two, even though he does not explicitly develop a hermeneutic of the Old Testament. As the law is a "disciplinarian until Christ came," it is the negative foil to Paul's message of justification. In contrast, the word of promise can be understood as the positive preparation for justification in Christ. It is shown typologically in the example of Abraham, who believed the promise made to him (Gal 3:16); he is thus the prototype of a justifying faith that does not rely on works of the law but on the promise of God alone. "Heirs of the promise" are those who belong to Abraham and like him stand under the promise, those who in the same way as Abraham trust the righteousness that comes from faith rather than righteousness that depends on works. They thereby travel a way that also has a temporal priority, since the promise to Abraham was given 430 years before the promulgation of the law on Sinai (Gal 3:17). As preparation for the justifying act of God, the promise had a universal significance; it is not limited to the national law of the Jewish people but promised to all peoples. This promise is fulfilled in Christ, for in him every one of God's promises finds its "Yes and amen"

---

54 Differently C. H. Dodd, ΕΝΝΟΜΟΣ ΧΡΙΣΤΟΥ in *Studia Paulina* (FS J. de Zwann. Haarlem: Erven F. Bohn, 1953) 96–110, who wants to understand the expression ἔννομος Χριστοῦ as parenetic instruction. However, the meaning of the Christ-"law" consists in the fact that, in contrast to the Old Testament law, it has a soteriological significance that nullifies the Torah as a way of salvation. The phrase ἔννομος Χριστοῦ is therefore to be interpreted in a strictly indicative sense. What is meant is of course not a separation from the will of God as expressed in the Old Testament but it is still the case that ἔννομος Χριστοῦ stands on the side of the ἄνομοι, so that every nomistic interpretation is excluded, including an interpretation in terms of Christian ethics.

(2 Cor 1:20). Thus the Christian also, who has been incorporated into this event, no longer stands under the Old Testament promise but in the time of fulfillment. This is true even though the ultimate realization of God's promise is still a reality of hope, reserved for its final fulfillment at the eschaton. Thus Paul can also make room for a future fulfillment of the promise made to the people of Israel as a particular people. But that the promises are first fulfilled in the church, and only later to Israel, poses a problem for understanding salvation history, a problem that Paul attempts to resolve by pointing in Romans 11:25–32 to the eschatological mystery.

In the relationship of promise and law, the promise has not only a chronological priority but also a priority in terms of its content, since it affirms the message of justification in an anticipatory way. But the promise is that of the Old Testament; along with the Old Testament-Jewish law, it is an element of God's revelation in the Old Testament. In Christ it is both fulfilled and brought to an end.

## 2.  The Victory over the Ruinous Power of the Law through Justification

### α) The Problem of Prepauline Traditions

Fitzmyer, J. A. "The Biblical Basis of Justification by Faith," J. Reumann. "Righteousness" in the New Testament. Philadelphia: Fortress, 1982. 193–227.
Schnelle, U. Gerechtigkeit und Christusgegenwart. Vorpaulinische und paulinische Tauftheologie. GTA 24. Göttingen: Vandenhoeck & Ruprecht, 1986².
Schnelle, U. Wandlungen im paulinischen Denken. SBS 137. Stuttgart: Katholisches Bibelwerk, 1989.
Strecker, G. "Befreiung und Rechtfertigung," G. Strecker. Eschaton und Historie. Aufsätze. Göttingen: Vandenhoeck & Ruprecht, 1979. 229–259.

Of the texts in the prepauline tradition that contain the basic elements of the Pauline doctrine of justification, to be named in first place is Romans 3:25:

|  |  |
|---|---|
|  | (Christ Jesus) |
| ὃν προέθετο ὁ θεὸς ἱλαστήριον | whom God put forward as a sacrifice of atonement |
| διὰ (τῆς) πίστεως ἐν τῷ αὐτοῦ αἵματι | by his blood, effective through faith. |
| εἰς ἔνδειξιν τῆς δικαιοσύνης αὐτοῦ | He did this to show his righteousness, |
| διὰ τὴν πάρεσιν τῶν προγεγονότων | because in his divine forbearance he had |
| ἁμαρτημάτων | passed over the sins previously committed |

The formula begins with v. 25. The preceding v. 24 belongs to the Pauline interpretation of justification, characterized by "as a gift" and "by his grace." The prepauline formula ends at v. 25, since v. 26 does not fit the grammatical structure of v. 25 (the genitive θεοῦ makes a rough connection with the preceding δικαιοσύνη αὐτοῦ) and is in part only a repetition of the preceding verse. While the context bears Pauline marks, v. 25 begins in characteristic liturgical style with a relative pronoun (ὅν, which refers back to ἐν Χριστῷ Ἰησοῦ). The phrase διὰ τῆς πίστεως can to be recognized as a Pauline interpretative addition, by means of which Paul brackets the formula with the preceding verse 24. The phrase ἐν τῷ αὐτοῦ αἵματι is also secondary, since the pronoun αὐτοῦ must refer, in contrast to the actual subject ("God"), to the ὅν and thereby to the to ἐν Χριστῷ Ἰησοῦ that lies still further back. It can remain an open question whether the phrase was added by Paul or by a pre- or post-Pauline tradent. Thus the following three line formula represents the original wording, which also manifests considerable unpauline vocabulary:[55]

ὃν προέθετο ὁ θεὸς ἱλαστήριον
εἰς ἔνδειξιν τῆς δικαιοσύνης αὐτοῦ
διὰ τὴν πάρεσιν τῶν προγεγονότων ἁμαρτημάτων.

This prepauline piece of tradition that obviously derives from a Hellenistic Jewish Christian context interprets the death of Jesus as the once-for-all atonement for sins committed in the past. Whether there is a connection here with the idea of the renewal of the Old Testament covenant cannot be decided on the basis of the term ἱλαστήριον. Nor can one infer that the piece had an original Sitz im Leben in the eucharistic celebration on the basis of the phrase "by his blood." It is probably a baptismal tradition. In it the death of Jesus, thought of as a once-for-all atonement for sins, is not contrasted with the Jewish law as a way of salvation. It is simply the case that in baptism the "sins previously committed" are now forgiven. There is no reference to overcoming the power of sin. This permits the conclusion that alongside the saving significance of baptism there was a complementary positive evaluation of the law. It is a different matter with the Pauline statement ἐν τῇ ἀνοχῇ τοῦ θεοῦ (v. 26a), which interprets the prepauline διὰ τὴν πάρεσιν. It understands the once-for-all act of the forgiveness of sins as the fundamental proof of the righteousness of God that has stripped the cosmic rulers of their power, the righteousness of God that determines the present life of the community.

Romans 4:25

| ὃς παρεδόθη διὰ τὰ παραπτώματα ἡμῶν | who was handed over to death for our trespasses |
| καὶ ἠγέρθη διὰ τὴν δικαίωσιν ἡμῶν. | and was raised for our justification. |

The two-line formulation of this piece of tradition stands out from the surrounding context as a good example of synthetic parallelism. The introduction with the relative pronoun ὅς makes clear that we are dealing

---

[55] Προέθετο is found elsewhere in the theological sense only in Ephesians 1:9 (in its secular meaning, Rom 1:13). Ἱλαστήριον is a *hapax legomenon* for Paul, elsewhere in the New Testament only in Hebrews 9:5. Πάρεσις is a *hapax legomenon* for the New Testament. On the other hand, ἔνδειξις is found more often in Paul (2 Cor 8:24 and Phil 1:28).

with liturgical tradition. This is also indicated by the formulaic language, which also recurs in Paul from time to time.[56] The interpretation is influenced by the way the doubled διά is understood. For the prepauline stratum an analogous causal interpretation of both lines is suggested ("for the sake of"). This would correspond to Romans 8:10. Here it becomes clear that despite the formal distinction between the death and resurrection of Jesus Christ, that which has been accomplished through the Christ event is one and the same: the forgiveness of trespasses is the justification of the sinner. Differently than in the comparable Pauline texts (Rom 5:21; 6:23; 8:10), the promised reality of salvation, the δικαίωσις, is not related to the future but to the once-for-all past event of the death and resurrection of Jesus. Corresponding to the prepauline understanding of the δικαιοσύνη Θεοῦ in Romans 3:25, the act of justification is referred to the past. The prepauline Hellenistic Jewish Christian tradition sees in the Christ event the promise of forgiveness of sins, which is limited to the past and is also not fundamentally opposed to the validity of the Jewish law in the future. From the adoption of the early Christian kerygma and the emphasis on the saving significance of Jesus' resurrection there are points of contact with the baptismal tradition (cf. esp. Rom 6:3ff), which suggests that one might suppose the piece originated as part of baptismal instruction.

An additional prepauline formula that belongs to the same cycle of tradition is found in 1 Corinthians 6:11b:

| | |
|---|---|
| ἀλλὰ ἀπελούσασθε, ἀλλὰ ἡγιάσθητε, | But you were washed, you were sanctified, |
| ἀλλὰ ἐδικαιώθητε | you were justified |
| ἐν τῷ ὀνόματι τοῦ κυρίου Ἰησοῦ Χριστοῦ | in the name of the Lord Jesus Christ |
| καὶ ἐν τῷ πνεύματι τοῦ θεοῦ ἡμῶν. | and in the Spirit of our God. |

Here too we have an independent prepauline unit of tradition that stands out from its context. The threefold ἀλλά construction and its explanation by the following synthetic parallelism represents a formally united structure. The partly unpauline linguistic usage[57] corroborates the text as prepauline tradition. The parallels to early Christian liturgical tradition suggests the same conclusion.[58] The content of this piece of

---

56   For παρεδόθη, cf. Galatians 2:20; Romans 8:32; 1 Corinthians 11:23. For παραπτώματα, cf. 2 Corinthians 5:19; Romans 5:15, 16, 18, 20. In addition, the prepauline origin is suggested by the reference to the kerygma of the death and resurrection of Jesus Christ (cf. e.g. 1 Thess 4:14), and by the word δικαίωσις, found elsewhere in Paul only at Romans 5:18.

57   Ἀπολούομαι is found only here in the Pauline corpus.

58   The verb ἁγιάζω also indicates its cultic background elsewhere in Paul, e.g. 1 Thessalonians 5:23; 1 Corinthians 1:2; Romans 15:16. Liturgical usage also stands behind ἐν τῷ ὀνόματι τοῦ κυρίου Ἰησοῦ Χριστοῦ; cf. 1 Corinthians 5:4; Philippians 2:10.

tradition is connected to baptism, which is understood as purification from sins, not in the sense of Jewish cultic law but as an act of initiation that incorporates the baptismal candidate into the community of those who call on the name of the Lord Jesus Christ. Despite the justification terminology, there is a difference from the Pauline doctrine of justification that is impossible to overlook. The verb ἐδικαιώθητε interprets baptism as an act that justifies, without however addressing the idea of freedom from the law. Differently than in Paul's interpretation, the justifying act is limited to the one-time act of baptism, and the law is not fundamentally called in question.

The Jewish Christian baptismal traditions discussed above are closely related to a Jewish Christian milieu that, despite its confession of Christ, sought to preserve a connection with Judaism related to the law. There is no indication here of a critique of the soteriological role of the law. It is rather the case that Torah and justifying event correspond to each other, in that justification is conceived as a supplement to and confirmation of Torah obedience.[59]

## β) The Righteousness of God

Bultmann, R. "ΔΙΚΑΙΟΣΥΝΗ ΘΕΟΥ," *JBL* 83 (1964) 12–16; also in R. Bultmann. *Exegetica*. Tübingen: Vandenhoeck & Ruprecht, 1967. 470–475.
Käsemann, E. "The 'Righteousness of God' in Paul," in E. Käsemann. *New Testament Questions of Today*. Philadelphia: Fortress, 1969.
Kertelge, K. "δικαιοσύνη," *EWNT* I (1980) 784–796.
Klein, G. "Gottes Gerechtigkeit als Thema der neuesten Paulus-Forschung," G. Klein. *Rekonstruktion und Interpretation*. BEvTh 50. Munich: Kaiser, 1969. 225–236.
Cf. also the literature to A.III.b.

In his programmatic essay on the righteousness of God, E. Käsemann brought the debate with his teacher R. Bultmann to a high point. The point at issue is whether Bultmann's anthropological view makes possible an adequate interpretation of Pauline theology. According to E. Käsemann, the term δικαιοσύνη θεοῦ shows that the anthropological approach unduly curtails Pauline thought, since for Paul the δικαιοσύνη θεοῦ has a dynamic character. The "righteousness of God" portrays a saving act that brings human beings under the divine lordship and assumes responsibility for them. The God of the Pauline message of justification is the God who acts in saving power, a way of thinking clearly connected to the Jewish world of thought. When Paul adopts this Jewish view, he radicalizes and universalizes it. He radicalized it by making the "righteousness of God" the ground of "justifying the ungodly," in contrast to the Old Testament-Jewish conviction that only the righteous could hope for the revelation of

---

[59] Cf. below under A. III. b.

God's righteousness. Moreover, Paul extended the Jewish way of speaking of the righteousness of God by making it universal, since God's revelation is no longer limited to the Jewish people of the Old Testament covenant but is also for the Gentiles.

It should not be disputed that E. Käsemann's critique of an exclusively anthropological approach to Pauline theology is justified. Bultmann, however, could respond to his critic by pointing out that δικαιοσύνη θεοῦ often has the character of a free gift, and thus means the righteousness of human beings they have received from God, the righteousness "that counts before God" (as Luther translated, i.e. that righteousness that counts as people stand before God as judge).[60] This, however, makes it necessary to ask about the understanding of human existence here presupposed, even if it is considerably influenced by the theocentric thought and thus the mythological conceptuality of Paul's anthropology.

How does Paul understand the term δικαιοσύνη θεοῦ? Grammatically, one must distinguish between two possibilities of translation and meaning: (1) *genetivus subiectivus* (subjective genitive) and (2); *genetivus auctoris* (genitive of the author; also sometimes inappropriately designated as objective genitive).

(1) *Subjective genitive*: One can name Romans 3:5 as an especially important example illustrating δικαιοσύνη θεοῦ as a subjective genitive ("But if our injustice ['unrighteousness'] serves to confirm the justice ['righteousness'] of God, what should we say?"). Here the phrase describes a quality of the being of God, God's own righteousness in the sense of a "nomen qualitatis." This is documented as authentic Greek usage.[61] The native speaker of Greek could connect the word δικαιοσύνη to the term for a specific quality or ethical conduct. This is also to be presupposed for Pauline usage; it is a matter of God's own conduct that is grounded in the very being of God. Similarly Romans 3:25: God demonstrates his righteousness in remitting the punishment for past sins. God is just; therefore he cannot simply ignore sin but must either punish it or forgive it. This view would place the Pauline concept of the righteousness of God as parallel to the satisfaction theory of the atonement as argued, for instance, by Anselm of Canterbury. In this theory, it belongs to God's essential being to require that sin be accounted for, that there be a "satisfaction," since the contradiction between the being of God's righteous nature and the existence of sin is an ontological conflict that is irreconcilable with the being of God. But Paul is not concerned with speculation about the being of God—though the ontological background of his thought is not to be absolutely excluded. It is rather the case that when Paul speaks of God, he

---

[60]   Cf. also G. Schrenk, δικαιοσύνη, TDNT 2:207–208.
[61]   Cf. Aristotle, Nicomachean Ethics 5.14.

speaks at the same time of humanity. This leads to the second possibility of understanding the genitive construction.

(2) *Genitivus auctoris.* In this view, δικαιοσύνη θεοῦ does not describe a quality that is attributed to God but a gift that comes from God. The following examples are especially illuminating of this usage:

*Romans 10:3* ("For, being ignorant of the righteousness that comes from God, and seeking to establish their own, they [the Jews] have not submitted to God's righteousness.") Here δικαιοσύνη Θεοῦ and ἡ ἰδία δικαιοσύνη are juxtaposed and contrasted. Thereby the expression "righteousness of God" is taken up by the phrase ἡ ἰδία δικαιοσύνη and interpreted by it in the opposite sense: the righteousness of God is not one's own, self-made righteousness but the righteousness received from God as a gift.

*Romans 1:17* ("For in it the righteousness of God is revealed through faith for faith.") That the righteousness of God is assigned to the realm of faith can be understood to say in effect that it is a gift given by God and accepted by human beings in faith.

*2 Corinthians 5:21* ("For our sake he made him to be sin who knew no sin, so that in him we might become the righteousness of God.") Here God's righteousness is unambiguously affirmed of human beings.

*Philippians 3:9* ("... and be found in him, not having a righteousness of my own that comes from the law but one that comes through faith in Christ, the righteousness from God based on faith.") In this text, one's own righteousness is the righteousness that comes from keeping the law; it is contrasted with righteousness that comes through faith, which is the righteousness of God. From this one may conclude that God's righteousness is a righteousness given to human beings as a gift.

The details of these examples can be interpreted in different ways. The issue of the grammatical classification of the genitive remains, when seen in isolation, as a theoretical affair. In any case, the genitive expresses the relation between δικαιοσύνη and θεός. The "righteousness" of which Paul speaks he places in relation to God. The manner of this relation must be determined from case to case by the context. Two extreme possibilities are to be excluded (a) Paul does not speculate about the aseity of God; the "righteousness of God" does not designate a quality of God that resides in the divine being. (b) Paul does not grant to human beings an authentic righteousness achieved by themselves. It is not a matter of an inner-worldly quality or of purely inner-worldly human conduct.

For the authentic Pauline understanding of the term "righteousness of God," one must take into account the theocentric point of departure for his theology, which is also manifest in other areas of his theology. It is a matter of *God's* righteousness, not only of a righteousness that human beings can have that makes them acceptable before God, even if this is conceived as a gift from God. This righteousness is not a static state but a vital, working power. It is revealed in the Christ event, which thereby becomes a justifying event, an event that makes human beings into righteous people.[62]

## γ) The Event of Justification

While E. Käsemann's interpretation of the term δικαιοσύνη θεοῦ (its "power" character) has found widespread acceptance, there can still be no doubt that when Paul speaks of God's righteousness he does so only in the interest of how this is related to human beings, for the righteous God requires righteousness from human beings. Here the demand of the law comes to expression, according to which human beings must present themselves as righteous through works of the law. If human beings are to attain life and experience God's saving will for humanity, then righteousness is a "conditio sine qua non," since no one can live in the presence of God without righteousness. But because—as Paul shows—human beings cannot attain to life on their own through the law, righteousness does not come through the law (Gal 3:21). Therefore the Christ event means that the law is done away with as a means of salvation. The soteriological function of the Christ event lies in the fact that it secures righteousness and thus can also secure life.

This new possibility means that the righteousness of God is revealed apart from the Law (Rom 3:21). This in turn means that God imposes no demand on human beings to produce works of the law. It is rather the case that the righteousness of human beings is henceforth a gift conferred upon them and not attained by human accomplishment. This is indicated by Romans 5:17 ("If, because of the one man's trespass, death exercised dominion through that one, much more surely will those who receive the abundance of grace and the free gift of righteousness exercise dominion in life through the one man, Jesus Christ"). The expression δωρεὰ τῆς δικαιοσύνης points to the gift that consists of righteousness/justification, a quality of human beings that is given by God. Thus the righteousness conferred on human beings can also be called the "righteousness of God" (cf. Phil 3:9, where δικαιοσύνη ἀπὸ θεοῦ is specifically contrasted with δικαιοσύνη ἐκ νόμου). Accordingly, it is not the law that constitutes the presupposition of attaining righteousness, but rather the χάρις θεοῦ; it justifies human beings freely, "giftwise," without works of the law (Rom

---

[62] It is striking that in the letter to the Galatians, in which Paul first delineated the foundations for his message of justification (cf. e.g. Gal 2:15–21), the expression δικαιοσύνη θεοῦ does not appear but only the noun (without the genitive), and is sometimes used of human beings (Gal 2:21; 3:21; 5:5). Here it is a matter of an anthropological quality, the reality of which is awaited in the eschatological future (Gal 3:5).

3:24). Here it becomes clear that the δικαιοσύνη θεοῦ is the righteousness/ justice of the judge who grants grace instead of demanding what the law requires, and who confers righteousness of human beings by his gracious act. Considered in this forensic aspect, the works of the law no longer pose a precondition that must be dealt with in order to be righteous. The only presupposition is faith, which is entirely different from a work, since it is not a matter of one's own achievement but is identical with renunciation both of requirements to be met and claims to have met them—without excluding human responsibility. Faith is accordingly no human "achievement," but a human "act!" This corresponds to the typological understanding of the story of the Old Testament patriarch Abraham, to whom faith was counted as righteousness (Gal 3:6).[63]

The structural elements of the justifying event are accordingly not law and works but grace and faith! The justified person does not live out of himself or herself but from an "extra nos" that has been manifested in the Christ event. Paul's doctrine of justification is his interpretation of the Christ event! It has been shown above that the Christ event could be interpreted in different ways, especially as the liberating act that delivers from the powers of sarx, sin and death. This is the basis for interpreting the Christ event as justification. As Christ is our "righteousness, sanctification, and redemption" (1 Cor 1:30), this means that with the establishment of the possibility of a new being and with the destruction of the power of the law, righteousness through Christ has become an attainable reality, a reality that can actually be put into practice "in Christ."

To the extent that such a conceptuality still moves in the world of thought conceived in terms of law, it still says nothing about the being of those who are justified. Paul's theology of justification as such implies no ontological structure but is to be understood juridically. But it still has an ontological foundation. As shown above, the being-character appropriate to the statements about justification are erected on the basis of the concept of redemption, the liberation from the powers of sarx, sin and death.[64] This corresponds to the statement that one who is in Christ is a καινὴ κτίσις (2 Cor 5:17). The new creation calls for a change in the old one. This opens up an approach to an ontological interpretation of the justifying event: that human beings are called into a new being comes to expression in the fact that God pronounced them to be righteous, for the justifying God is no other than the creator God, the one who "gives life to the dead

---

[63]  Cf. Genesis 15:6. In addition, cf. Romans 1:17, ὁ δὲ δίκαιος ἐκ πίστεως ζήσεται (Gal 3:11/Hab 2:4), where the adjective δίκαιος is not to be related to ζήσεται but to ἐκ πίστεως (= one who is righteous by faith), which affirms that being righteous comes from faith. In that the person lives by faith, he or she no longer stands under the law as a παιδαγωγός (Gal 3:25).

[64]  Cf. above A.III.

and calls into existence the things that do not exist" (Rom 4:17). Thus the act of justification is comparable to the act of creation, the act by which human beings are called out of death into life.[65]

From this perspective we may now assess the issue of *imputed* and *effective* (actual) righteousness, the distinction between the righteousness one has that has only been accounted to one, and the righteousness of a person who in fact possesses it, to whom it belongs in the sense of actually possessing it. On the basis of the above discussion, we may say that justification belongs originally within the world of thought in which it is conceived to be an imputed reality; it is a matter of that righteousness that is accounted to persons as if they had it (but do not really have it). It thus corresponds to the Jewish situation in which it originated, as expressed for example in Romans 2:13 ("For it is not the hearers of the law who are righteous in God's sight but the doers of the law who will be justified"— namely on the day of the last judgment, in which their works will be counted to them as righteousness). This is the terminological and material presupposition of the Pauline doctrine of justification, although Paul abrogates the Jewish way of thinking about justification, for it is faith that will be "reckoned ... as righteousness" (Gal 3:6). This too is to be understood in the sense of imputed righteousness but it does not exclude the connotation "being made righteous."[66] The result of the justification of the sinner is the fact that the sinner *is* justified. Thus imputed righteousness and effective righteousness are not alternatives in Paul's sense: whoever has been declared righteous is righteous, because the act of justification means nothing other than being incorporated into the realm of Christ, because justification is only another way of conferring the new being in Christ. The "being" in "being justified" that is conferred on those who are in Christ, is not a worldly, demonstrable reality but a pneumatic saving event. This is so because justification—as liberation from the power of sarx, sin and death—is an eschatological event (Rom 8:30, "And those whom he predestined he also called; and those whom he called he also justified; and those whom he justified he also glorified"). Those who have

---

[65] Differently E. Jüngel, *Paulus und Jesus. Eine Untersuchung zur Präzisierung der Frage nach dem Ursprung der Christologie* (HUTh 2. Tübingen: J. C. B. Mohr [Paul Siebeck], 1979[5]), who would like to understand the relation between statements about being and statements about justification from the opposite direction. To be sure, statements about being in Christ may not, in Paul's understanding of the matter, be separated from his teaching about justification but they are in fact first derived from this doctrine of justification. The doctrine of justification implicitly sets forth an ontological structure, so that it is the "announcement of a new being" (47). However, being in Christ is primary; this is seen already in the oldest Pauline letter, 1 Thessalonians, and is assumed in all the later Pauline letters.

[66] Cf. correctly H. Schlier, *Der Brief an die Galater* (KEK 7. Göttingen: Vandenhoeck & Ruprecht, 1989[15]) 126–131.

been baptized are also justified (1 Cor 6:11); by invoking the name of the Kyrios Jesus over them, they are justified and righteous. This is not a magical transformation but a reality brought about by being placed under the lordship of a new spiritual sovereignty.

If justification means being-incorporated-into-the-Christ-event, then this also means that the justification of the sinner participates in the dialectic in which the Christ was involved during the time of his earthly life. Those who have died have been justified from sin, i.e. they are freed from it (Rom 6:7). In faith, "righteousness" is already present (Gal 2:16–21). At the same time, it is a future reality, for it is also true of believers that the revelatory event to happen at the judgment seat of Christ is still in the future (2 Cor 5:10). The one who has been justified by Christ does not have justification at his disposal as though it were a possession that cannot be lost; it is at stake every day. There is no security. Believers are challenged to preserve their own being as those whom they actually are, to "be/come who you are!" Such "being/becoming" is not to be understood as a gradual growth but as a constantly new seizing and being seized by the possibility graciously given in the Christ event and that by faith is already now a reality in the salvation promised in Christ.

The justifying act thus means more than the once-for-all act of Jesus' sacrificial death. To be incorporated into the Christ event as the event of justification means not only that one looks back on the atoning death of Christ but affirms that one stands in a living reality determined by the justifying verdict already pronounced, and expects the gracious, acquitting pronouncement from God in the future. This means a radical break with earlier conditions of life, thus a break with the claims of the law, and taking one's stand in the reality of faith, which is as such the eschatological possibility for both Jews and Gentiles. For Paul, this justification is above all else the "iustificatio impiorum," i.e. renunciation of any human "praeparatio evangelica," a turning away from all well-meaning human preparations and preconditions, including religious and national rules and regulations that generally have the character of sanctity and inviolability. It is true of them without exception: they cannot lead to life, they belong to a past world, on the ruins of which a new world is being built, a world in which righteousness and holiness before God, freedom and love among human beings are the new realities of life.

In conclusion we look briefly at the relation of the Pauline understanding of justification to the parallel statements in the Qumran texts.[67] According to the Qumran texts too, human beings are sinful in their acts and being. In a way similar

---

[67] H. Braun, "Röm 7:7–25 und das Selbstverständnis des Qumran-Frommen," *ZThK* 56 (1959) 1–18; reprinted in *Gesammelte Studien zum Neuen Testament* (Tübingen, 1971³) 100–119.

to Paul's understanding, help and deliverance from sinful existence comes from divine grace.[68] By God's gracious saving act human beings are pronounced righteous. Despite such parallel statements, there are two decisive differences: (a) in Paul the justifying event is grounded on the saving event of God's action in Christ; in the Qumran sect there is no such place where God's grace becomes visible and concrete (unless entrance into the sect itself had such a function). (b) For Paul, the granting of eschatological salvation means freedom from the law; in contrast, at Qumran justification occurred without affecting the role and validity of the law. Justification there had a complementary relation to the demands of the Torah. Justification is in fact freedom for the Torah! The difference thus consists in the fact that Paul possesses a radical understanding of the law that goes all the way to the abolition of the law as a means of salvation, while the Qumran sect teaches that the way of grace and the way of the law are parallel tracks. This latter view stands close to the prepauline Jewish Christian theology of justification but not to the Pauline understanding.

## c)   The Granting of Freedom

### 1.   *Proclamation and Apostleship*

Dodd, C. H. *The Apostolic Preaching and its Developments*. New York: Harper, 1936 (1956[8]).

Grässer, E. "Freiheit und apostolisches Wirken bei Paulus," *EvTh* 15 (1955) 333–342.

Hahn, F. "Der Apostolat im Urchristentum," *KuD* 20 (1974) 54–77.

Hofius, O. "Wort Gottes und Glaube bei Paulus," M. Hengel und U. Heckel, eds. *Paulus und das antike Judentum*. WUNT 58. Tübingen: J. C. B. Mohr (Paul Siebeck), 1991. 379–406.

Klein, G. *Die zwölf Apostel. Ursprung und Gehalt einer Idee*. FRLANT 79. Göttingen: Vandenhoeck & Ruprecht, 1961.

Roloff, J. *Apostolat—Verkündigung—Kirche*. Gütersloh: Gerd Mohn, 1965.

Roloff, J. "Apostel, Apostolat, Apostolizität, I. Neues Testament," *TRE* 3 (1978) 430–445.

Schröter, J. *Der versöhnte Versöhner*. TANZ 10. Tübingen: Francke, 1993.

von Campenhausen, H. "Der urchristliche Apostelbegriff," K. Kertelge, ed. *Das kirchliche Amt im Neuen Testament*. WdF 439. Darmstadt: Wissenschaftliche Buchgesellschaft, 1977. 237–278.

After the delineation of the Pauline understanding of the Christ event, the question arises of how it is then possible that what has happened in the saving event can be made available and accessible to humanity at large. Paul's answer: people receive access to the saving event through preaching and the sacraments of baptism and the eucharist. Preaching and the sacraments are the "vehicula" through which the results of the saving event are mediated and granted to individual people.

Paul understands himself as apostle to the Gentiles, called to this ministry by a revelation. He pictures this in the style of the call to be a

---

[68]   E.g. 1QH 4.37; especially 1QS 11.12–14, "He will draw me near by His grace, and by His mercy will He bring me justification. ... Through his righteousness he will cleans me of the impurity...". Cf. also 1QS 11.2–3 and elsewhere.

prophet, in dependence on Jeremiah 1:5 and Isaiah 49:1, when he says that he "was separated from his mother's womb" to this ministry of *preaching* (Gal 1:15–16). This does not mean that Paul's self-consciousness was that of a prophet, especially since he never refers to himself as a "prophet," but rather that he knows he has received a commission just as did the prophets of the Old Testament. In distinction from Old Testament prophecy, his commission is determined by the cross and resurrection of Jesus.

Paul proclaims the "gospel," the message of salvation given to him by commission of the risen Christ (Gal 1:11; Rom 1:1; 2:16; 16:25). The εὐαγγέλιον Χριστοῦ can be understood in the sense of a *genetivus subiectivus*: the gospel whose patron is the Christ. But the genitive can also be understood as *genetivus obiectivus*: the gospel about Christ, the gospel of which Christ is the object.[69] The two possibilities are not to be kept separate but show the fluidity between the sender and the content of the message.

The content of the message is the Christ event, in both its redemptive and justifying functions. Such a message is the λόγος καταλλαγῆς (2 Cor 5:19). The "message of reconciliation" speaks of the fact that God has reconciled the world to himself so that the powers of sin and death can no longer prevail. He points back to the Christ event in which God acted once and for all in the reconciling event of the cross and resurrection. The kerygmatic formulae that Paul cites are for him summaries of his message—even though they are incomplete.

Alongside the word of reconciliation stands the word of justification. Through the gospel the δικαιοσύνη θεοῦ is revealed in the realm of faith (Rom 1:17). The righteousness of God is "revealed" through the message as a reality that punishes human transgressions in such a way that the sinner is pronounced righteous. This is what happened in the Christ event. The preaching of justification is thus christological preaching; its subject is the saving act of God in Christ that brings justification.

Such a message is not a mere report. It is not mere information about an event that lies only in the past but as kerygma it becomes present as a reality that leaps over time and space. The "gospel" proclaims the Christ event as the eschatological event. Thereby the act of preaching itself becomes an eschatological event, for the eschatological quality of the Christ

---

69 Alongside this meaning understood in terms of its content, whereby the "gospel" is the Christ event of past history (cf. e.g. 1 Thess 1:9–10), Paul also understands the term as a "nomen actionis," = the act of proclaiming the Christ event (e.g. 1 Thess 1:5). Such preaching of the gospel is the work of the Spirit and evokes pneumatic activity (cf. also 1 Cor 2:4). Presumably Paul found this idea in the context of confessional formulae (cf. 1 Cor 15:1ff; Röm 1:1–4.). Cf. G. Strecker, "Das Evangelium Jesu Christi," in G. Strecker, ed., *Jesus Christus in Historie und Theologie* (FS H. Conzelmann. Tübingen: J. C. B. Mohr [Paul Siebeck], 1975) 503–548; reprinted in *Eschaton und Historie* 183–228.

event is not separable from the word that interprets it. Not only the preacher but also the hearer of the message stands in an eschatological situation, for that which transpired in the Christ event also happens "now" in the promised word, the entrance of the eschaton into time (cf. 2 Cor 6:2, "See, now is the acceptable time; see, now is the day of salvation!"). The eschatological situation created by the word of preaching is reflected in 2 Corinthians 2:16 ("to the one a fragrance from death to death, to the other a fragrance from life to life"). This picture adopts the idea of the triumphal procession in which incense is scattered about, and makes clear that preaching as the eschatological event leads to either death or life, depending on the response of the hearers as to whether the proclamation generates faith or unbelief. In the message of the apostle, the eschatological judgment takes place in historical time. This is true even though the future judgment is still to come, for it will bring the ultimate confirmation of what is already happening in the event of preaching (cf. 2 Cor 5:10).

As preaching makes the Christ event present in historical time, the possibility is given to the individual of being incorporated into the body of Christ, or of being excluded from it. That the event of preaching is one in which crucial decisions are made is seen in the fact that for some it is a matter of a "stumbling block"(σκάνδαλον) and "foolishness" (μωρία) but for others it is the "power of God" (δύναμις θεοῦ). The eschatological consequence of acceptance or rejection in the last judgment is already demonstrated by the acceptance or rejection of the word by the hearers (1 Cor 1:18).

In order that the word can be either accepted or rejected, it must be understandable. Faith comes through the "hearing" of the word (Rom 10:17). The proclamation appeals to people's capacity to hear and understand. This is seen in the debate about spiritual gifts: glossolalia is usable in the worship service only to the extent that it is translatable speech (1 Cor 14:27–28); it is in need of "illumination" from the "translator" (διερμηνευτής) who stands by the tongue-speaker and transforms the unintelligible speech into understandable language (14:28). For preaching as intelligible speech Paul uses the term προφητεύω. Such "prophecy" (= authentic preaching) renounces the kind of pneumatic egoism that had appeared in the Corinthian church; it is oriented to one's fellow human beings in that it has "edification" (οἰκοδομή) as its goal (14:3). It requires perception and understanding from the community, especially through "encouragement" (παράκλησις) and "consolation" (παραμυθία). But it is addressed to the uninitiated and non-believing hearer. As intelligible preaching, it convicts the unbeliever, reveals his or her existence as inauthentic, and leads him to praise God (14:23ff).

In the last analysis, it is not the intelligibility of the speech that evokes this effect of preaching but it is the Spirit that brings about the conversion of the unbeliever.[70] The Spirit works through the word (1 Thess 1:6; Gal 3:2), and faith receives the Spirit as the eschatological gift of salvation (Gal 3:14) as it comes through the word (Gal 3:5). The Spirit is the "pledge" or "down payment."[71] This is one more way of saying that the proclamation continues the eschatological situation that had its beginning with the Christ event. As it results in the gift of the Spirit as an eschatological reality, so it is itself an eschatological event, for in and through it takes place in the present the saving act of God in Christ that transforms a world subject to chaos and sin into the new aeon, the ultimate end of which of course is still in the future but has nonetheless already begun in the event of preaching.

When the event of preaching is understood in this way it is to be expected that the apostle participates in the eschatological quality of the proclamation. The Kyrios Christ works through him (Rom 15:18). Paul is the "slave" (Rom 1:1) or the "servant of Christ," as 2 Corinthians 11:23ff declares in debate with his opponents. As such he is entrusted with the διακονία τῆς καταλλαγῆς (2 Corinthians 5:18) and acts in this capacity as the "ambassador of Christ" (2 Cor 5:20). As διάκονος Χριστοῦ (11:23) he represents Christ to the church, so that in relation to the church he serves as its helper, just as Christ served the church (2 Cor 4:5). Comparable to the lowliness of the earthly Kyrios, he carries out this ministry in a state of lowliness and suffering (2 Cor 4:10–12; Phil 1:20; 3:10). Just as Paul calls his hearers to imitate Christ (2 Cor 5:10), at the same time he instructs them to become imitators of Paul himself (1 Cor 4:16 μιμηταί μου γίνεσθε). Such admonitions are motivated by the statement "as I am [an imitator] of Christ" (1 Cor 11:1), for the apostle himself is an imitator of Christ. This is the basis of his claim to appear before the church with the authority of Christ. It is thus no accident that the apostle can sometimes refer to the content of his message as the "gospel of Christ" (Rom 15:19), and other times as "my gospel" (Rom 2:16; 16:25). To hear the word of the apostle is to hear the word of the Kyrios. The preacher does not derive his authority from the congregation, for it is authorized by Christ. With this point of departure, in the post-Pauline period there developed a direct line in the direction of a hierarchically structured formation of the tradition, along with the idea of an apostolic succession. This is already heralded in 2 Thessalonians. A certain foundation for this is in fact provided in the authentic letters of Paul, in which the apostle appeals to the authority of

---

70  On 1 Corinthians 14: glossolalia is a pneumatic phenomenon (1 Cor 14:4) in that it is a speaking to God, not to human beings (1 Cor 14:2). It is unintelligible to the hearers in the congregation (14:2, 11, 16). As a charismatic spiritual gift glossolalia belongs to the signs of the new aeon (1 Cor 12:10–13).

71  2 Corinthians 1:22, ἀρραβών = "down payment," "pledge," as guarantee that the rest will be paid; cf. 2 Corinthians 5:5; cf. also Romans 8:23 (ἀπαρχή).

the exalted Christ: it is from the Kyrios that he has received the authority with which he builds up the churches but which he can also use to destroy (2 Cor 13:2–3, 10). This authority, however, is related to the Spirit, which is not at human disposal, and not adjusted to a hierarchical system, even if such a system would appeal to a "lex divina."

The proclamation is thus closely related to the Christ event. The apostle represents the Christ. That is why his word can mediate the salvation established by Christ. The *vehiculum* is therefore the word. This word is comparable to the word of the Creator that calls being into existence from non-being. The word can call forth life, because it is the announcement of eschatological salvation, and it can bring death, since it is at the same time the word of judgment. The proclamation of the apostle anticipates the judgment and grace of the last day.

## 2. Baptism

Barth, G. *Die Taufe in frühchristlicher Zeit*. BThSt 4. Neukirchen-Vluyn: Neukirchener, 1981.

Betz, H. D. "Transferring a Ritual: Paul's Interpretation of Baptism in Romans 6," H. D. Betz. *Paulinische Studien, GAufs. III*. Tübingen: J. C. B. Mohr (Paul Siebeck), 1994. 240–271.

Bornkamm, G. "Baptism and New Life in Paul (Romans 6)," in G. Bornkamm. *Early Christian Experience*. London: SCM, 1969, 71–86.

Dunn, J. D. G. *Baptism in the Holy Spirit*. SBT 15. Naperville: Alec R. Allenson, 1970.

Frankemölle, H. *Das Taufverständnis des Paulus*. SBS 47. Stuttgart: Katholisches Bibelwerk, 1970.

Hahn, F. "Taufe und Rechtfertigung," *Rechtfertigung* (FS E. Käsemann). Tübingen-Göttingen: J. C. B. Mohr (Paul Siebeck), 1976. 95–124.

Hartman, L. *Auf den Namen des Herrn Jesus*. SBS 148. Stuttgart: Katholisches Bibelwerk, 1992.

Lohse, E. "Taufe und Rechtfertigung bei Paulus," *KuD* 11 (1965) 308–324; also in E. Lohse. *Die Einheit des Neuen Testaments. Exegetische Studien zur Theologie des Neuen Testaments*. Göttingen: Vandenhoeck & Ruprecht, 1973. 228–244.

Raeder, M. "Vikariatstaufe in 1 Cor 15,29?," *ZNW* 46 (1955) 258–260.

Schnelle, U. *Gerechtigkeit und Christusgegenwart. Vorpaulinische und paulinische Tauftheologie*. GTA 24. Göttingen: Vandenhoeck & Ruprecht, 1986². 33–145.

Wagner, G. *Pauline Baptism and the Pagan Mysteries: The Problem of the Pauline Doctrine of Baptism in Romans 6:1–11*. Edinburgh and London: Oliver and Boyd, 1967.

Wedderburn, A. J. M. *Baptism and Resurrection, Studies in Pauline Theology against its Graeco-Roman Background*. WUNT 44. Tübingen: J. C. B. Mohr (Paul Siebeck), 1987.

Although Paul had been baptized, he had hardly practiced baptism himself (cf. 1 Cor 1:13–17). It is therefore no accident that baptism is not an independent theme within the Pauline letters, however much it may be presupposed. In both the Pauline and prepauline churches it was accepted and practiced as self-evident. When Paul himself makes statements about baptism,[72] for the most part prepauline baptismal tradition stands in the background.

1. *Baptism is purification from sins.* So it is recorded in the prepauline formula of 1 Corinthians 6:11.[73] In a manner similar to the Jewish baths and washings of purification, baptism can free from sins.[74] Differently from them, it is motivated by the prior atoning act of Christ, which is conferred to the believer in baptism.

2. *Baptism is incorporation into the realm of authority of the Kyrios Jesus Christ.* This is affirmed by invocation of the "name."[75] In this regard it is also characteristic that baptism incorporates one into the spatial realm designated by being "in Christ" (ἐν Χριστῷ, e.g. Gal 3:26–28). Such incorporation means liberation from the powers of sin, sarx and death. Integration into the realm where the Kyrios is sovereign is reflected in the confession of Romans 10:9. This baptismal confession affirms that the baptismal candidate accepts the lordship of the Kyrios Jesus.

3. *Baptism brings about the conferral of the Spirit.* This is indicated by both 1 Corinthians 6:11 and 2 Corinthians 1:22, already mentioned in other connections. As the "down payment" (ἀρραβών), the Spirit is the guarantee of the eschaton. On this basis, baptism can also be interpreted as a "sealing." It is called a σφραγίς, because it impresses upon the person the mark that he or she belongs to the Kyrios.[76] The conferral of the Spirit at baptism means that the believer has been integrated into the body of believers that is the church; it is the Spirit that guarantees the unity of the church (cf. 1 Cor 12:13, "For in the one Spirit we were all baptized into one body—Jews or Greeks, slaves or free—and we were all made to drink of one Spirit"). The Spirit conferred in baptism overcomes the social distinctions and unites Christians of differing national, religious, and social

---

[72] This happened fairly often in connection with prepauline baptismal tradition, as in Romans 3:25; 4:25; 6:3–4a; 1 Corinthians 1:30; 6:11bc; 12:13; 2 Corinthians 1:21–22; Galatians 2:19–20; 3:26–28. Focal points of authentic Pauline statements about baptism are found in Romans 6 and 8; 1 Corinthians 1:13–17 and 10:1ff; Galatians 2:19–20. Cf. U. Schnelle, *Gerechtigkeit und Christusgegenwart* 33–145; G. Bornkamm, *Paul* (New York & Evanston: Harper & Row, 1979) 188–190.

[73] Cf. above A. III. b. 2; See also the prepauline traditional units in Romans 3:25; 4:25, and elsewhere.

[74] The Jewish baths of purification mediate ritual purity: Leviticus 14:8; 15:5ff, 11; Number 31:23; 2 Kings 5:14; Judith 12:6–8; Sirach 34:30. On proselyte baptism cf. Strack-Billerbeck I 102–103.

[75] On ὄνομα τοῦ κυρίου cf. also 1 Corinthians 1:10; 5:4. The classic treatment is W. Heitmüller, *Im Namen Jesu* (FRLANT 2. Göttingen: Vandenhoeck & Ruprecht, 1903).

[76] Cf. W. Heitmüller, "ΣΦΡΑΓΙΣ," *Neutestamentliche Studien für Georg Heinrici* (Leipzig, 1914) 40–59; W. Bousset, *Kyrios Christos* 295–296, note 186 (e.g. Diodorus XIV 30.7; Tertullian, *Heretics* 40)

origins into one body of Christ. In connection with the pneuma-motif, there is also another sacramental interpretation of what happens in baptism; the Spirit is a supernatural power;[77] it can also be thought of as a supernatural material element.[78] This is presupposed in the expression "spiritual body" (1 Cor 15:44 σῶμα πνευματικόν). The heavenly body is a body of pneumatic substance, in contrast to the earthly body composed of sarx.[79] This idea is of course used by Paul only in a fractured sense. The decisive thing for him is that the Spirit indicates a particular orientation of one's life; it is a power that brings about and influences a new life. It is an eschatological phenomenon set over against the world of sarx, so that to have the Spirit is identified with having the reality of a new life.

4. *Baptism is a dying and rising with Christ.* Romans 6:2ff declares that the reality of the new life is mediated by baptism is affirmed in connection with the Pauline doctrine of justification. Liberation from the power of sin does not occur by being subordinate to the law, is not attained by works of the law but only when one renounces every claim to one's own achievement. Baptism is understood as such a renunciation, for being baptized means dying with Christ, and thereby a liberation from the domination of sin and concern for justifying oneself (Rom 6:7). Such freedom does not mean that one is now able to attain what was previously impossible by one's own power, but happens only in such a way that the person who is baptized reenacts the destiny of Christ, dies and is buried with him. In this way the believers put on Christ (Gal 3:27; cf. Rom 13:14). They experience themselves as members of the body of Christ; their belonging to Christ is determined by the ἐν Χριστῷ εἶναι (Gal 3:28–29), which also includes having died with Christ. To be in Christ is identified with being incorporated into the Christ event.

While it is true that Paul's discussion of baptism in Romans 6 does appear to have "in the twofold sense of the word a subsidiary character" ("subsidiär und beiläufig,"

---

[77]    Cf. 1 Corinthians 15:45; 2 Corinthians 3:17, on which see F. W. Horn, *Angeld des Geistes* 147, 324–345.

[78]    According to E. Schweizer, πνεῦμα *TDNT* 6:413–436, 413, in the Greek and Hellenistic world pneuma was often considered a substantial element that belonged to the heavenly world. The Spirit is therefore not only a preliminary sign of the future eschaton. In contrast, in the Old Testament and Judaism the Spirit is a "power" that makes exceptional feats possible.

[79]    The connection to baptism presumably derives from the fact that the Spirit was combined with the water as a substantial unity; this is related to the command to baptize in flowing (living) water (e.g. Didache 7:1–2 [in connection with the triadic baptismal formula, which apparently presupposes literary dependence on Matthew 28:19] PsClem Diam 1:2: ζῶν ὕδωρ; cf. Rec III 67.4: in aquis perennibus; also VI 15.2). It seems that the "living Spirit" was connected to "living water." Examples are also found in Gnostic and Jewish-Gnostic tradition, e.g. Hippolytus Ref V 19.17 of the Gnostic Sethians; for the background cf. Genesis 1:2.

= "subsidiary and made in passing;" K. Barth, *Church Dogmatics* IV/4, 117), it is also true that it is fundamentally important for the connection between the preceding (chapter 5, freedom from the power of death) and the following (chapter 7, freedom from the power of the law). This discussion thus comes at a crucial place as expressing freedom from the power of sin (cf. 6:1). The first verse expresses the theme, followed by vv. 2–4 that gives the basis for Paul's answer to the question posed in v. 1 by referring to a christological creed. Vv. 5–7 then present an anthropological interpretation of the baptismal event which in turn is followed by a christological interpretation in vv. 8–10. V. 11 then provides a summary which is at the same time a transition to the following section, drawing the imperative consequence from the sacramental indicative.

There is no doubt that Paul is here utilizing older tradition. This is already suggested for 6:3b-4a. Even though the wording can now hardly be reconstructed, it is still clear that the opening ἣ ἀγνοεῖτε ὅτι (6:3a) introduces a tradition known to the Pauline churches (cf. also Rom 7:1), which suggests that in this tradition baptism had already been interpreted as dying and being buried with Christ.[80] Paul thus portrays baptism as the cultic location in which communion with the dead and risen Christ becomes real.

Of particular significance in this connection is the understanding of ὁμοιώματι. If one translates v. 5a with "for we have been fused together in the likeness of his death," one could then think that ὁμοίωμα means the death of Jesus into which believers are baptized and who thus die at the same time Jesus does (so G. Bornkamm, *Ende des Gesetzes* 42; U. Wilkens, *Der Brief an die Römer* [EKK VI/II. Neukirchen-Vluyn: Neukirchener, 1987²] 14). This appears to speak for the view that σύμφυτοι γεγόναμεν has occasioned the dative ὁμοιώματι (= *dativus sociativus*, dative of association). It may be asked, however, why Paul chose the word ὁμοιώματι in this context, since for Paul the word does not mean identity but "similarity," with a presupposed differentiation and distanciation (as e.g. Phil 2:7; cf. Rom 5:14; 8:3). For a christological interpretation one would have expected him to simply say τῷ θανάτῳ αὐτοῦ. It is thus more likely that τῷ ὁμοιώματι is to be understood as an instrumental dative and to translate, "For if we (with him) have grown together by means of the likeness of his death." In this case, ὁμοίωμα would describe baptism itself; it makes the death of Jesus Christ present to the individual who is being baptized. The one being baptized thus reenacts the destiny of the Crucified One in the act of baptism, and the old self is thereby crucified with Christ (6:6, 8).

Alongside 6:3b-4a, 6:4b also stands out as a traditional unit. Here we probably find a formula that has been preserved in a more original form in Colossians 2:12, "You have been buried with him [Christ] in baptism" and "you have been raised with him by faith...". Accordingly the following prepauline statement may be postulated for the text now found in Romans 6: "As Christ was raised from the dead through the glory of the Father, so also we (have been raised with him from the dead)." The same tradition is reflected in Colossians 3:1–4 under (deutero)Pauline influence. It may thus be the case that the Corinthian pneumatics had laid claim to this tradition on the basis of the close association between the crucified and risen Christ that they saw in it (cf. 1 Cor 12:13, as well as the prepauline tradition of Gal 3:27–28). In an understanding of baptism that sounds somewhat magical, baptismal candidates reenact not only the death but the resurrection of Jesus, so that their status of having been saved is an act that is already completed by the resurrection they have already experienced.[81]

---

[80]  Cf. U. Schnelle *Gerechtigkeit und Christusgegenwart* 75–76, 204–205.

[81]  Cf. also Ephesians 2:6; John 5:25; 1 Clement 23:1–27:7; Barnabas 11:1; Ignatius to Polycarp 7:1; 2 Clement 9:1; Justin Dial 80:4, and elsewhere.

In contrast to the tradition he had received, Paul did not speak of the resurrection as an event experienced in the present but argues in terms of an "eschatological reservation:" In the eschatological future the communion with Christ that Christians now have will be demonstrated so that dying-with-Christ becomes a living-with-Christ. The future tense (v. 5 ἐσόμεθα) indicates that the sacrament confers no magical quality but the actual realization of the event that happens in baptism is reserved for the eschatological future.[82] For the believer, the baptismal event participates in the dialectic of "already" and "not yet." Nonetheless, the presence of eschatological salvation as it is mediated by baptism is not only declared in the negative sense to be a dying-with-Christ and a being-buried-with-Christ but also affirms positively a new creation (2 Cor 5:17). Thus since baptism means an incorporation into the body of Christ, it is also the basis and realization of a new being in faith and in the Spirit.

The so-called "vicarious baptism" (1 Cor 15:29) has a special significance within the Pauline understanding of baptism. In the process of rejecting the denial of the resurrection of the dead by the Corinthian pneumatics, Paul bases the Christian hope on a future resurrection of the dead by pointing to the practice of the Corinthian church in which people were baptized for the dead:

> "Otherwise, what will those people do who receive baptism on behalf of the dead? If the dead are not raised at all, why are people baptized on their behalf?" (1 Cor 15:29)

If the hope for the resurrection of the dead is a vain hope, then it is meaningless to have people baptized for the dead. This stands in the same context as another challenge, also a Pauline rhetorical question: "And why are we putting ourselves in danger every hour?" (15:30).

The meaning of 1 Corinthians 15:29 has been bitterly disputed by exegetes. As the textual apparatus of the critical editions of the Greek New Testament shows, editors have often attempted to exclude the idea of vicarious baptism by punctuating the text differently. Vicarious baptism is documented outside the New Testament among Gnostic sects, e.g. by

---

[82]   That the baptismal act of dying with Christ and being buried with him has a future aspect is already clarified by Paul by the ἵνα clause (6:4b), which places the closure of the believer's worldly existence over against openness to the new life of the future. In Paul's understanding, the goal of participating in the resurrection of Christ still lies in the future. This is documented not only by the future tense of the verbs ἐσόμεθα in 6:5b ("we will share in the resurrection," which refers to the resurrection of Jesus Christ, which is itself the beginning of the general resurrection of the dead) and συζήσομεν (6:8) but also the construction of the following sentence (6:8 πιστεύομεν; cf. also the imperative λογίζεσθε of 6:11). The object of the church's hope is participation in the future resurrection. Cf. R. C. Tannehill, *Dying and Rising with Christ* (BZNW 32. Berlin: W. de Gruyter, 1967).

Epiphanius of Salamis for the Cerinthians,[83] who have themselves baptized in the name of those who have died in order to keep them from being rejected at the last judgment. Although Epiphanius cites our text in this connection, it is likely that vicarious baptism itself is of prepauline origin. It is not clear from 1 Corinthians 15:29 how the effect of baptism is supposed to apply to the dead. The comment in Epiphanius suggests a kind of magic associated with names. In any case, the idea of vicarious baptism is strongly flavored with magical ideas. For the Pauline understanding of baptism the significance of this idea is often minimized. But since Paul includes this practice in his line of argument, it is clear that he does not absolutely reject it, even if he himself never taught and practiced it. There are in fact points of contact between the understanding of the Spirit in the Pauline letters and the practice of vicarious baptism. If the Spirit intercedes for the saints and takes possession of them like an external force (Rom 8:26–27), the distance between this idea and the further step that the Spirit reaches beyond the barrier of death and can bring the dead to salvation is not so great. In Paul's understanding this does not lead to a magical understanding of what happens in baptism but in 1 Corinthians 15:29 we have an extreme form of the "extra nos" aspect of baptism that is present in Pauline theology. This is manifested in the baptismal event as incorporation of the one baptized into the body of Christ and has consequences for the issue of the baptism of children and infants.[84]

## 3.  The Eucharist

Bornkamm, G. "Lord's Supper and Church in Paul," G. Bornkamm. *Early Christian Experience*. London: SCM, 1969, 123–160.

Jeremias, J. *The Eucharistic Words of Jesus*. London: SCM, 1966³.

Käsemann, E. "Anliegen und Eigenart der paulinischen Abendmahlslehre," E. Käsemann. *Exegetische Versuche und Besinnungen* I. Göttingen: Vandenhoeck & Ruprecht, 1970⁶. 11–34.

Klauck, H. J. *Herrenmahl und hellenistischer Kult*. NTA 15. Münster: Aschendorff, 1982.

Kollmann, B. *Ursprung und Gestalten der frühchristlichen Mahlfeier*. GTA 43. Göttingen: Vandenhoeck & Ruprecht, 1990.

Lietzmann, H. *Mass and the Lord's Supper. A Study of the History of the Tradition*. Leiden: E. J. Brill, 1979.

Neuenzeit, P. *Das Herrenmahl, Studien zur paulinischen Eucharistieauffassung*. StANT 1. Munich: Kösel, 1960.

Schlier, H. "Das Herrenmahl bei Paulus," H. Schlier. *Das Ende der Zeit*. Freiburg: Herder, 1971, 201–215.

Schmithals, W. *Gnosticism in Corinth*. Nashville: Abingdon, 1971.

Schweizer, E. "πνεῦμα," *TDNT* VI (1959) 396–451.

---

[83]  Epiphanius, Heretics 28.6.4; Chrysostom, In Epist I Ad Cor Hom 40.

[84]  Cf. below B. III. c. e. β.

In the eleventh chapter of 1 Corinthians Paul cites a tradition that he explicitly says he had received from the Lord and had transmitted to the church, the words of institution of the Lord's Supper. This tradition comes from the collection of Jesus' words that we know was available to Paul.[85] It contains a chronological datum unique in the Pauline tradition: Jesus spoke the words of institution "on the night when he was betrayed" (1 Cor 11:23b). The tradition cited by Paul apparently began with these words. In addition to the chronological note, this tradition included the saying about the loaf and the saying about the cup (11:23b-26). Since it is a liturgical tradition, it can hardly be expected that Paul himself changed its wording. It had a fixed place in the congregational liturgy and must therefore have had a firm wording that would not be arbitrarily changed by individuals.

From the literary point of view the parallel tradition in the Synoptic Gospels is considerably later than this prepauline tradition.[86] This does not necessarily mean, however, that in every item the content of Paul's tradition represents the oldest form of the saying. The mutual relation of the two versions of the tradition cannot be reduced to a simple formula. It is clear at first, however, that Matthew (26:26-29) has for the most part simply taken over the Markan form of this tradition and thus represents the Markan type of tradition. Luke, on the other hand, appears to have a

---

[85]  Cf. above A. II. b. 3.

[86]  For comparison:

| | Mark 14:12-25 | Matt 26:17-19 | Luke 22:17-20 | 1 Cor 11:23b-26 |
|---|---|---|---|---|
| Situation located | 14:12 | 26:17 | 22:7, 15 | 11:23b "in the night in which he was betrayed" |
| Bread saying | 14:22 | 26:26 (φάγετε) | 22:19 (εἰς τὴν ἀνάμνησιν) | 11:24 (εἰς τὴν ἐμὴν ἀνάμνησιν) |
| Cup saying | 14:23-24 | 26:27 (πίετε) 26:28 (εἰς ἄφεσιν ἁμαρτιῶν) | 22:17,20 (μετὰ τὸ δειπνῆσαι) | 11:25 (μετὰ τὸ δειπνῆσαι ... εἰς τὴν ἐμὴν ἀνάμνησιν |
| Apocalyptic perspective | 14:25 | 26:29 | 22:16, 18 | 11:26 |

Additional verbatim agreements between Luke 22:15ff and 1 Corinthians 11:23bff are to be noted: ἡ καινὴ διαθήκη ἐν τῷ αἵματι (Luke 22:20; 1 Cor 11:25, vs. Mark 14:24/Matt 26:28: τὸ αἷμα μου τῆς διαθήκης); τὸ ὑπέρ ὑμῶν (Luke 22:19-20; 1 Cor 11:24); τοῦτο ποιεῖτε εἰς τὴν ἐμὴν ἀνάμνησιν (Luke 22:19b; 1 Cor 11:24-25). Instead of the "long text" found in Luke, or: Codex D it give a "short text" that omits Luke 22:19b-20, so that after the apocalyptic perspective (22:16) only the cup saying (vv. 17-18) and the bread saying (22:19a) are transmitted. On the relation of the Synoptic and the Pauline texts cf. also W. Schenk, "Luke as Reader of Paul: Observations on his Reception," in *Intertextuality in Biblical Writings* (FS B. van Iersel) (Kampen, 1989) 134-135. W. Bösen, *Jesusmahl, Eucharistiches Mahl, Endzeitmahl. Ein Beitrag zur Theologie des Lukas* (SBS 97. Stuttgart: Katholisches Bibelwerk, 1980).

special form of the words of institution that is substantially longer than Mark's (Luke 22:15ff). Here the apocalyptic perspective (Mark 14:25) of the saying about the cup is placed first. This is joined to the unit of 22:19–20, which has its own saying about the loaf and the cup, as familiar from 1 Corinthians 11. One can infer from this that the form of the tradition available to Luke presupposed both the Markan and Pauline traditions. Thus in order to answer the question of the oldest form of the words of institution, one must first clarify the relation of the Markan text to the Pauline text. This problem cannot be overcome with linguistic arguments alone.[87] A primitive Aramaic form cannot be reconstructed for the Markan text. The Evangelist Mark presents the words of institution in the form of a flawless parallelism (14:22, "This is my body;" 14:24, "This is my blood.") The Pauline tradition would certainly not have disrupted this parallelism if it had known it. This is an argument that the Markan form is secondary from the point of view of literary history, so that the unsymmetrical structure of the Pauline form would seem to be more original. But the Pauline text is not primary in every respect. The doubled command to repeat the ritual (11:24 and 25; anamnesis formula) goes back to liturgical influence, and is thus probably a secondary addition. In other respects the Pauline text should generally be considered to be closer to the earliest form than that of the Markan tradition.

At the beginning of the development of the tradition, was the last meal of Jesus with his disciples understood as a Passover celebration?[88] There is no doubt that in the Synoptic Gospels the institution of the Last Supper takes place within the framework of the Passover meal. However, this is obviously a secondary development. The matter is different in the Gospel of John, where Jesus' last meal takes place before the Passover.[89] It is especially important to note that in the words of institution themselves the essential elements of the Passover meal are lacking. There is no reference to the Passover lamb, nor of the unleavened bread and bitter herbs (cf. Exod 12:8). To the extent that the Lord's Supper derives from the time of the historical Jesus, it is not the Passover that is the point of departure but the last meal Jesus ate with his disciples, or his table fellowship with his followers in general.[90]

---

[87] Differently J. Jeremias, according to whom the Markan text goes back to an Aramaic original (*Eucharistic Words* 173–184), and three strands of tradition are postulated: Markan, Pauline-Lukan, and Johannine (*Eucharistic Words* 190).

[88] J. Jeremias has attempted to give detailed evidence why the last meal of Jesus must have originally been a Passover meal and why it is not the case that it was only later interpreted to be such (*Eucharistic Words* 15–88). Cf. in addition H. Patsch, *Abendmahl und historischer Jesus* (CThM.BW 1. Stuttgart, 1972; F. Hahn, "Die alttestamentlichen Motive in der urchristlichen Abendmahlsüberlieferung," *EvTh* 27 (1967) 337–374.

[89] See below.

[90] Cf. B. Kollmann, *Ursprung und Gestalten* 33.

But neither the prepauline nor the premarkan tradition is to be understood as simply Jesus' last meal; it is rather the case that other factors were more influential, factors that gave the meal the characteristics of a *sacred celebration*. It was not a normal meal understood to be for the satisfaction of hunger but the sacramental act that is the decisive factor; it confers the reality of eschatological salvation. It may well be that influences from the mystery religions were originally present. This does not mean, of course, that the fellowship meal is to be understood exclusively as an act of consecration but rather that the normal meal for nourishment and the sacred ritual act of celebration were connected. This may have come about in such a way that the saying about the loaf was originally spoken at the beginning of the meal, then followed the normal meal for nourishment, and then the saying about the cup came at the conclusion. It is possible that this twofold division is still recognizable in the Pauline form of the words of institution, since Paul begins the saying about the cup with the words "after supper" (μετὰ τὸ δειπνῆσαι); it could be that this merely refers to the ritual eating of bread as part of the eucharistic celebration but it could also refer to the more extensive regular meal that had preceded, the meal that had begun with the saying about the loaf.

If Paul was aware of the practice of reciting the words of institution in connection with a regular meal, then it was his intention to oppose the celebration of the holy ritual as the conclusion of an ordinary meal when he admonishes the Corinthians to satisfy their hunger at home before participating in the eucharist (11:22a). In prepauline earliest Christianity, the normal meal and the sacramental celebration were interwoven; there was no separate, purely liturgical celebration in which bread and wine were used. Paul himself contributed to this later development by his instruction in 11:22a.

On the basis of this distinction between normal meal and sacramental meal, H. Lietzmann derived his far-reaching thesis that there were originally two completely different types of communion meals in early Christianity:

(1) There was a "Jerusalem type" in which the earliest church celebrated the "breaking of bread" as the continuation of the table fellowship with the Lord of the church in a mood of eschatological joy (H. Lietzmann, *Messe und Herrenmahl* 252). As evidence for this type, which had no connection to Jesus' death, he cites the Lukan accounts of the fellowship meals of the earliest Jerusalem church (Acts 2:42–47; 20:7–12; 27:33–36; Luke 24:13–35), and additional texts from the post-New Testament period (PsClem Hom 14:1; Acts of John 85:106–110; Acts of Thomas 27, 29, 49–50, 120–121, 158; Acts of Peter 2, 5).

(2) There was the Pauline type, reconstructed on the basis of 1 Corinthians 10:1–22 and 11:17–34. It was presumably celebrated as a memorial of Jesus' last meal and his death. The breaking of bread was at the beginning of the meal, and the drinking of the cup at the end.

In support of this distinction, H. Lietzmann appealed to Didache 9–10. Since Didache 9.1–10.5 pictures a meal with no reference to the death of Jesus and without any sacramental character, not followed until 10.6 by a transition to the sacramental eucharist, he argues this shows that the combination of these two postulated types took place only secondarily. But the situation with regard to sources hardly permits one to postulate two such different basic types. The evidence for the "breaking of bread" found in the Lukan writings can hardly bear the burden of proof called for by this hypothesis, since it deals with an idealized picture of the Jerusalem church (especially in the summary of Acts 2:42–47). Moreover, the other evidence he introduces is from the apocryphal Acts of the Apostles, and is quite late. Neither does the expression "breaking of bread" mean that the sacred meal was practiced in the earliest church without the drinking of wine. "Breaking of bread" can be used in Hellenistic Christianity for the whole meal.[91] On the other hand, the founding of the purported Pauline type of eucharist through a direct revelation, as Paul is supposed to have advocated according to 1 Corinthians 11:23a, in not satisfactory. Finally, neither can the Didache be used as convincing evidence for the original existence of two independent forms of the eucharistic tradition. The author of the Didache presupposes—though with hesitation—what is also said in the tradition of the Lord's Supper found in the Synoptic Gospels.

It was not until postpauline times, possibly under the indirect influence of 1 Corinthians 11:20ff, that an independent agape meal appeared with a predominately charitable purpose (cf. Hippolytus, *Church Order* 27–28). Such "agape feasts" were important for providing for widows, and from the third century on were regarded as part of the care for the poor exercised by the church (cf. W.-D. Hauschildt, "Agapen," *TRE* 1 [1997] 748–753; 749).

The original connection between the normal fellowship meal and the sacramental meal is the point of departure for the problem that became acute in the Corinthian church (1 Cor 11:17–34). The order of the congregational gathering had obviously been disturbed by the different ways that people were conducting themselves during the celebratory meal: some had the ordinary meal in advance and were already drunk by the time the eucharist was celebrated (v. 21); they participated in the sacred celebration in an unworthy manner (11:27); they did not "discern" the body of Christ (11:29) and did not wait for their fellow Christians (11:33). Others came to the meal too late, since the others had not waited for them (11:33), and thus remained hungry (11:21).

W. *Schmithals*[92] relates this situation to the Gnostic opponents of Paul in Corinth who understood the Lord's Supper as an ordinary meal for nourishment; by introducing such a meal, the sacral eucharistic meal was profaned. The "eating and drinking in an unworthy manner" (11:27) thus consisted in their not distinguishing the eucharist from an ordinary secular meal. (Likewise, the Corinthian Gnostics would not have acknowledged that the meals connected to pagan sacrifices had any sacral character; here too they would have profaned an originally cultic meal, since as a result of their possession of true knowledge they could feel themselves free of its cultic-religious claims.)

G. *Bornkamm* has objected that there is no trace of a Gnostic argumentation in this section, and that Paul does not direct his argument against connecting the eucharist with an ordinary meal for nourishment.[93] Paul (and with him the Corinthian church) presupposes the unity of the two meals, i.e. that the eucharist was celebrated

---

91 See H. Lessig, *Die Abendmahlsprobleme im Lichte der neutestamentlichen Forschung seit 1900* (Bonn 1953) 134–135. G. Delling, "Abendmahl II: Urchristliches Mahlverständnis," *TRE* 1 (1977) 47–58; 56; G. Kretschmar, "Abendmahlsfeier I," *TRE* 1 (1977) 229–278; 231.
92 W. Schmithals, *Gnosticism in Corinth* 250–256.
93 G. Bornkamm, "Lord's Supper and Church in Paul" 127–129.

within the framework of an ordinary fellowship meal. According to Bornkamm, the abuse in Corinth did not consist in the profanation of a sacral act (the eucharist was in fact celebrated as a "most holy sacrament" at the end of the church's fellowship meal). It was in fact rather the case that the fellowship meal was being profaned by the conduct of some members of the community by separating it from the sacred meal. It was understood as a secular meal which then led to inappropriate conduct with regard to the sacrament.[94] The fellowship meal preceding the eucharist was held in such a way as to facilitate fellowship among relatives, friends, and insiders of various groups, with no consideration of the poor and those who had to come late.[95]

Paul is concerned to organize the fellowship meal and eucharistic celebration in such a way that the Corinthians would have to be considerate of the poor church members who had nothing to contribute to the fellowship meal. Social distinctions in the community should not be noticeable; this is the reason for his advise to eat at home (11:22). This does not mean a separation of the fellowship meal from the sacral meal but bringing them into the right relationship. Fellowship meal and eucharist[96] are united in a celebration that is organized with a concern for brotherly agape. Thus the fellowship meal must not become a gluttonous party; only so will the sacred celebration not become an expression of a sacramentalism that has withdrawn from the world but will continue to be related to the vital fellowship in which members are responsible for the welfare of one another, in a way that is supposed to represent the body of Christ and will in fact do so.

The words of institution refer to the past Christ event as an event of past history, in particular to the death of Jesus Christ. They do not interpret this event in an unambiguous way but imply different possibilities of interpretation, which do not contradict each other when understood in Paul's sense:

(1) *The Lord's Supper is grounded in the substitutionary or atoning death of Jesus.* Differently from Mark, Paul has transmitted an extended form of the bread saying. Τὸ σῶμα has been added τὸ ὑπὲρ ὑμῶν. This corresponds to the cup word in Mark (ὑπὲρ πολλῶν), and affirms that the body of the

---

94  Differently B. Bornkamm, *Paul* 193: there was an exaggerated sacramentalism in Corinth, since the members of the church knew themselves to be taken out of the world by their participation in the risen Christ, a participation mediated by the sacraments.

95  Cf. Bornkamm *Paul* 192. The social aspects of the Corinthian festive meals are further developed by G. Theissen, "Social Integration and Sacramental Activity; An Analysis of 1 Cor. 11:17–34," *The Social Setting of Pauline Christianity*, ed. J. H. Schütz (Philadelphia: Fortress, 1982) 145–174; 160.

96  The word εὐχαριστία in the New Testament has the general meaning "gratitude" (Acts 24:3) or "expression of thanks" (1 Thess 3:9; 2 Cor 9:11; Phil 4:6, and elsewhere). The exception in the variant reading of 1 Corinthians 10:16 is secondary. "Eucharist" and "eucharistic" as technical terms are post-New Testament (Did 9.1, 5; Ignatius Eph 13.1; Phld 4; Smyr 8.1).

Crucified One was delivered up as a sacrifice. It cannot be determined more precisely whether the main idea is that of substitution or atonement, since ὑπέρ can be understood and translated as "for" (in the sense of "atonement for sins") or as "instead of, in place of" (cf. 2 Cor 5:14).

(2) *In the Lord's Supper the death of Jesus is understood as a sacrifice that seals the "new declaration of God's will."* That the death of Jesus is the expression of the (last) will of God is also presupposed by the text of the words of institution in the Gospel of Mark (Mark 14:24). Although in the Synoptic Gospels setting the meal within the framework of the Passover celebration calls the Sinai covenant to mind, it is not a matter of a "covenant sacrifice," since διαθήκη is not to be translated with "covenant," but has the unambiguous meaning of "testament, will."[97] Similarly in Paul: the pouring out of Jesus' blood validates and puts in force the "new declaration of God's will." This is different from the promise of a "new covenant" in Jeremiah 31:31ff, which takes place without reference to a sacrifice. On the contrary, the new covenant is not to be like the old, for the law will be written in the hearts of the people. In contrast, the idea of a bloody sacrifice is reminiscent of the covenant-making activity of the God of Israel,[98] as this is more clearly the case in Mark. This means that in the sacrificial death of Jesus Christ God declares his new and at the same time the final declaration of his will. The saving reality of this new testament is promised to believers in the Lord's Supper.

(3) *The Lord's Supper means incorporation into the body of Christ.* So it is declared in 1 Corinthians 10:16–17. Here it can be seen how strongly Paul's thought is itself dependent on "Gnostic" ways of thinking:[99]

> The cup of blessing (εὐλογία) that we bless, is it not a sharing (κοινωνία) in the blood of Christ? The bread that we break, is it not a sharing in the body of Christ? Because there is one bread, we who are many are one body, for we all partake of the one bread.

Participation in the meals where food offered to idols is served means that one comes in contact with demons and places oneself within the realm where demons have authority. In contrast to this, the sacred celebration of the eucharist is understood as table fellowship with the Kyrios. This meal results in the participants are incorporated within the realm of Christ's lordship and thereby into the "body of Christ." Thus in the Lord's

---

[97] Cf. W. Wrede, "τὸ αἷμα μου τῆς διαθήκης," *ZNW* 1 (1900) 69–74; Bauer, διαθήκη, BAGD 183. Cf. also Hebrews 9:20 (Exod 24:8); 10:29.

[98] Cf. Genesis 15:9–10; Exodus 12:1–7, 21–23; 24:5–6; Jeremiah 34:18; Psalm 50:5.

[99] According to W. Schmithals, *Die Gnosis in Korinth* 234, 1 Corinthians 10:16–17 is a post-Pauline interpolation smuggled into Paul's letters by the Corinthian Gnostics. (Translator's note: Schmithals holds 10:16 to be from "gnostic tradition" which Paul "attaches to his saying...".)

Supper there is a real encounter between human beings and the Kyrios. The Kyrios is the exalted Lord of the community, who is identical with the Jesus of past history. On the basis of this christological foundation the eschatological reality of salvation (forgiveness of sins, the new declaration of God's will, the beginning of the new life) as it is realized in the Christ event also becomes a present possibility for those who participate in the sacrament. The mediation of the eschatological reality of salvation is christologically grounded and is made explicit ecclesiologically as incorporation into the body of Christ. Thus the question of whether Paul means the ἐστίν of 1 Corinthians 11:24 as real or symbolical does not address the Pauline intention. It is rather the case that Paul is concerned with the encounter with the Kyrios, as also expressed in the ἐν Χριστῷ εἶναι. A spiritualizing of the sacrament would not fit the Pauline understanding. In the sacrament, the Christ is not symbolically present but really present. This is not to be resolved rationally. The presence of the eschaton remains a *mysterium*, experienced in faith but a mystery that is not unraveled. Faith knows by experience that fellowship with the Kyrios means a real gift, an actual experience of the eschatological reality of salvation. On the other hand, the real presence of Christ in the sacrament implies no sacramental understanding. It presupposes neither a magical-natural uniting of the Christ with the elements nor a "transubstantiatio" (transformation) of the elements. It is rather the case that as believers eat and drink of the elements of the sacrament communion with the exalted Christ is made real. The sacramental understanding is not to be separated from its christological foundation.

It is thereby also made clear in this process that it is not faith but the exalted Kyrios who makes the sacrament into a sacrament. Thus one can speak in Paul's sense of a "manducatio impiorum." Also those who are unworthy, even unbelievers, who cannot distinguish the body of Christ from ordinary food (1 Cor 11:29), encounter the Christ at the Lord's Supper. The Pauline understanding is thus to be distinguished from both (a) interpreting the meal as a φάρμακον ἀθανασίας, a medicine of immortality (cf. Ignatius Eph 20:2), which places the elements of the sacrament in the foreground in an unpauline sense, and (b) from understanding the meal as a φάρμακον ἀπωλείας, a ruinous poison, although in Paul's understanding partaking of it in an unworthy manner can have visible consequences. That there are sick and weak people in the church, that some members have died before their time, Paul attributes to the inappropriate way they have been observing the Lord's Supper (11:30). This is understood as the consequence of God's judgment, the consequence of the fact that the Lord's gracious offer was refused, not as magical character of the sacramental elements themselves.

Since the Lord's Supper effects an encounter with the exalted Christ and incorporation into the body of Christ, the emphasis lies on the saving character of the sacrament in the present. In the here and now, in the celebration of the Supper, the community has communion with Christ. It is now one body in Christ (1 Cor 10:16–17). This includes a view toward the apocalyptic future, for there can be no certainty, not even when the sacrament is properly observed and when it is done in consideration of other members of the church. The pronouncement of final judgment is still reserved for the End. The celebration of the Lord's Supper in the prepauline churches was already determined by the expectation of the eschaton. The Kyrios, whose meal the church celebrates, with whom the community has table fellowship, is the same Lord who will meet them at the End. The Christian community celebrates the meal with a view toward the eschatological future, as declared in Mark 14:25. This is also presupposed by the text of the words of institution in 1 Corinthians 11:23ff, when it is said that at the eucharist the church proclaims the death of the Lord "until he comes" (11:26). The Kyrios is expected by the church as the One whom they at present encounter: the one who forgives sins, the one who is the guarantor of the new testament and who represents the saving act of God both now and in the future. It is in this sense that the community calls out "Marana tha," an acclamation that could be uttered at the observance of the Lord's Supper in the church's worship (1 Cor 16:22).

In the light of all this, the prepauline command to repeat the Supper ("do this in remembrance of me") cannot be understood in a purely intellectual sense. It is not a matter of a memorial to a dead person, as documented in the Hellenistic monuments to the dead,[100] but rather the case that the observance of the Lord's Supper makes the saving event a reality of the present. The *anamnesis* of Christ by believers is a reenactment of the saving significance of the Christ event. It is no accident that alongside the sacramental actions stands the statement τὸν θάνατον τοῦ κυρίου καταγγέλλετε (1 Cor 11:26). This is to be interpreted as indicative, not imperative. Proclamation takes place at and by means of the sacramental celebration, namely testimony to the eschatological significance of Jesus' death. The saving event is mediated into the present not only by the sacramental act but also by the word of preaching. Thus the same thing is true of the sacrament that is said of the apostolic message: it is "to the one a fragrance from death to death, to the other a fragrance from life to life" (2 Cor 2:16).

---

[100] Cf. the imperial grave monument from Bithynia with the words <ἐπὶ τῷ> ποιεῖν αὐτοὺς ἀνά<μ>νη<s>ιν μου; further evidence in B. Baum, *Stiftungen der griechischen und römischen Antike. Ein Beitrag zur antiken Kulturgeschichte, II. Urkunden* (Leipzig-Berlin, 1914); H. J. Klauck, *Herrenmahl und hellenistischer Kult* 83–86.

## d) Faith

Barth, G. "Pistis in hellenistischer Religiosität," *ZNW* 73 (1982) 110–126.
Binder, H. *Der Glaube bei Paulus*. Berlin: Evangelische Verlagsanstalt, 1968.
Deissmann, A. *Paul: A Study of His Social and Religious History*. New York: Doran, 1926.
Lohse, E. "Emuna und Pistis," *ZNW* 68 (1977) 147–163.
Lührmann, D. "Glauben," *RAC* XI (1981) 48–122.
Lührmann, D. *Glaube im frühen Christentum*. Gütersloh: Gerd Mohn, 1976.
Lührmann, D. "Pistis im Judentum," *ZNW* 64 (1973) 19–38.
Michaelis, W. *Rechtfertigung aus Glauben bei Paulus* (FS A. Deissmann). Tübingen: J. C. B. Mohr (Paul Siebeck), 1927. 116–138.
Schlatter, A. *Glaube im Neuen Testament*. Stuttgart: Calver, 1927⁴.
von Dobbeler, A. *Glaube als Teilhabe*. WUNT II/22. Tübingen: J. C. B. Mohr (Paul Siebeck), 1987.
Wissmann, E. *Das Verhältnis von Pistis und Christusfrömmigkeit bei Paulus*. FRLANT 40. Göttingen: Vandenhoeck & Ruprecht, 1926.

As we have seen in the above discussion, the saving event in which believers know themselves to be incorporated is mediated through word and sacrament. In what way can such a once-for-all event be mediated to the present? From the Christian side, what corresponds to the reality of eschatological salvation? At this point it is not enough to say that it is God who works in the saving event (cf. Phil 2:13), for the act of God on behalf of human beings needs a human response. In the Pauline understanding, how then do human beings respond to the gracious promise of God? His answer: by faith!

1. The apostle uses the term πίστις especially in the letters to the Galatians and Romans, and thus in the context of his message of justification. For Paul, faith is above all *justifying faith*. Romans 4 provides an example. The context is Paul's argument that righteousness has become a possibility for all people, both Jews and Gentiles. Paul's line of argument is that justification has been a possibility since the time that Abraham received the promise (of descendents) and responded to God's promise with faith, since the time that he trusted in God's promise without the security of the law or any accomplishments he could claim for himself. This faith, which is nothing more or less than trust in the word of God, was counted to Abraham as righteousness (Rom 4:3; Gen 15:6). Precisely thereby the way of works righteousness as a way of salvation was excluded; the only possibility for human beings was to allow their faith to be counted as righteousness; and people became righteous before God through such faith. The only possible way of salvation is accordingly justification by faith, not justification by works (Rom 4:11). This is the meaning of πίστις Χριστοῦ (Gal 2:16); for in the Christ event the possibility of being righteous before God was actually realized—independently of the judgment of the law, independently of the inadequacy of works.

Does this mean that faith is identical with eschatological salvation and not merely the precondition of salvation, but that rather the "experience of justification" is itself salvation?[101] That would mean that faith and justification are not distinguishable. However, the righteousness of faith is called δικαιοσύνη ἐκ πίστεως (Rom 1:17; 10:6). Righteousness comes from (literally "out of") but is not to be identified with faith, for faith is a "being toward something," an orientation of the self to the offered gift and at the same time the acceptance of the offer, as this is presented in the Christ event mediated by word and sacrament.

No less than in other New Testament authors, πίστις in Pauline theology is a relational term. The understanding of faith as the acceptance of an offered gift first becomes understandable from the perspective of this offer.[102] The offer of justification in Christ first requires the renunciation of one's own claims to accomplishment. Faith is not a supplement to works, as is the case in Jewish tradition, but is contrasted to works. As dependence on God's grace alone, not on human works, it is the counterpart of the gracious offer of God. All the same, faith is a human act, for human beings are called to faith by preaching; in faithful obedience human beings accept the salvation offered them. Thus "faith" appears as a synonym for "obedience" (ὑπακοή; Rom 1:5, 8; 16:9). Faith is the daring deed that opens itself to the offer present in the word. Thereby faith is the *conditio sine qua non* for the realization of salvation for human beings. Faith is a human act, the only precondition for salvation, without itself becoming a human accomplishment.[103]

2. As stated above, Paul's concept of faith has its essential function within the framework of the doctrine of justification; this is seen in the contrast of faith and works, of righteousness by faith and works righteousness. But also in *connection with the liberation of human beings from the power of sarx, sin and death,* i.e. in connection with Paul's doctrine of redemption as the foundation of his message of justification, faith is—even when not juxtaposed to works—the human correlate to the divine offer of salvation.

---

[101] Cf. W. Michaelis, "Rechtfertigung aus Glauben," in dependence on A. Deissmann, *Paul* 168–170.
[102] As a counter-example, cf. the theological position of Matthew: the offer is the eschatological demand that points the way to the community on its pilgrimage through time. Faith is the acceptance of this offer, and thus does not lead to a contrast between faith and works but is a faith that leads to works. From the Pauline perspective one would ask here whether faith has become a work itself.
[103] The paradox of Philippians 3:12–13 reflects both: the predestining act of God's deed, and the free act of the human being. From the point of view of faith, there is no contradiction in affirming both of these together. Elsewhere as well, Paul's statements about predestination are related to their context (cf. Rom 8:28–29; 9:18; 11:28–29; 1 Cor 11:26–29; cf. also Mark 4:11–12). Paul has neither an abstract concept of predestination nor an abstract theodicy.

In other words: πίστις within the framework of the Pauline concept of redemption is the expression for the acceptance of the new being as it is realized in distancing from the present aeon. This is true because those who believe, who ground their existence on the Christ event, are no longer subject to the powers of this world. First Thessalonians 4:14 ("For since we believe that Jesus died and rose again, even so, through Jesus, God will bring with him those who have died") is in toto a statement of faith, for the second clause of this statement also presupposes the premises of faith. A distinction is to be made here: faith in the kerygma of Jesus' death and resurrection is in the first place the ground of the salvation promised to the community in the present, and beyond that, the ground of its hope in a future existence. Romans 6:8 corresponds to this ("But if we have died with Christ, we believe that we will also live with him"). Apparently the first clause a statement generally known and accepted (cf. v. 9: εἰδότες; v. 3 already has ἤ ἀγνοεῖτε); the truth of the matter, however, is that the knowledge is a knowledge in faith, for faith implies a "knowledge," an understanding, of what it believes in, without it becoming "knowledge" in the secular sense.

Both passages witness to faith's orientation to the conquest of the powers of sarx, sin and death that has happened in the Christ event. It is the acceptance of the offer present in the victory over these powers. By faith the individuals can assert themselves over against these powers and withstand them. But such self-assertion (= the new being = being-incorporated-in-the-new-aeon = being-in-Christ) is not given as a possession. On the other hand, the idea of a faith that operates selectively, at some points in one's life but not at others, is foreign to Paul. It is obvious to him that Christians organized as a congregation are "the believers" (1 Cor 14:22). Paul does not presuppose that faith as such wavers back and forth between faith and doubt. It is still the case, however, that the believer stands in a dialectic conditioned by still being in the world. Even though faith is an element of "desecularized existence," since it is grounded on the breaking of the eschaton into time, it takes place in the world. Even though the power of the cosmos has been broken, the world and the conditions of worldly existence remain a reality to be reckoned with and a constant threat to believers.

3. *The dialectic experienced in faith.* Those who have been pronounced righteous on the basis of the Christ event, those who through the sacrifice of Jesus Christ know that they are freed from the powers of sarx, sin, and death, those who recognize the offer made to them through word and sacrament and receive it in faith, these receive and experience the gift of "adoption as God's children" (literally "sons;" Gal 4:5 υἱοθεσία). They are no longer slaves but regarded as sons and daughters of God (Gal 4:7). As "heirs," they find themselves in possession of all the rights of sonship (Gal

4:7b). They no longer live under the slavery of the law but from the grace of God (Rom 6:14). The freedom of the new life is a reality for them, so that Paul can say, "... all things are yours, whether ... the world or life or death or the present or the future—all belong to you" (1 Cor 3:21–22). However, Paul continues this statement and shows the ground and presupposition of such freedom: "you belong to Christ, and Christ belongs to God" (1 Cor 3:23).

The freedom of the Christian is not a boundless arbitrariness to do whatever one pleases but the freedom to live rightly in responsibility to the Kyrios. It is no magical phenomenon that belongs to the natural world but a reality within human history. It thus must be preserved and reaffirmed anew in each concrete situation. Here it is the standard of agape that is the point of orientation. As a dialectic reality, such freedom occurs in dialogue. When Paul, in discussion with the Corinthian pneumatics agrees with them in emphasizing the priority of freedom, he still adds the qualification, "...but not all things are beneficial" (1 Cor 6:12). Only that is beneficial which does not merely promote one's own consciousness of freedom but serves the neighbor (1 Cor 10:23–24).

There is also the possibility, however, that freedom can be lost and can become a new kind of slavery (cf. 1 Cor 7:23; 6:12b). The Christian's eschatological freedom appropriated by faith is a dialectical freedom; it participates in the movement of human beings in history, is not a static, fixed reality but risks itself in every new situation.[104]

This dialectic is reflected in the relation of indicative and imperative. Just as the "indicative" describes the believer's being-taken-out-of-the-world, so the "imperative" describes the believers being-placed-within-the-world. Paul leaves no doubt that for him the imperative, the ethical demand, derives from the indicative of the redemptive event (cf. 1 Cor 5:7–8; Gal 5:25). This existence in the world is an existence in the situation of being tested. Such an imperative arises from the fact that believers continue to live their lives in the sphere of the flesh; it affirms that being-in-Christ is a reality that must be concretely realized within the conditions of historical human existence.[105]

The extent to which the believer's being-in-the-world is determined by this dialectical movement is seen in the Christian's attitude to suffering. While the believer has died with Christ, is a member of the body of Christ and lives "in Christ," he or she is still one who lives a bodily existence in the empirical world and is subject to its conditions. Paul knows that he is threatened by bodily suffering (2 Cor 12:7). The treasure with which he is entrusted as an apostle of Christ is placed in an earthly vessel (2 Cor 4:7). This does not cancel out the other side of the statement that it is God's

---

[104] Cf. above A. III. a.
[105] On the problem of "indicative and imperative" cf. below under A. IV. b. 1.

own power that is at work in his human weakness. Differently than is the case for those who live prior to and apart from Christ (Rom 7:1ff), the Christian stands in the tension between the inner self and the outer nature: the outer nature that is delivered over to suffering, and the inner person, who is renewed from day to day, whose life is grounded not in what is visible but in what is invisible (2 Cor 4:16–18). The dialectical situation of being "in Christ" and "in the flesh" is expressed by Paul in the peristasis catalogue of 2 Corinthians 4:8–10:

> We are afflicted in every way but not crushed; perplexed but not driven to despair; persecuted but not forsaken; struck down but not destroyed; always carrying in the body the death of Jesus, so that the life of Jesus may also be made visible in our bodies. (cf. also 1 Cor 4:11–13; 2 Cor 6:9–10)

Those who are in Christ are not taken out of the world; they remain objects of the world, its suffering and persecution; they remain in the realm of the flesh and are assaulted by sickness, pain, and death. But their lives are not determined by weakness and death; they live with Christ by the power of God. Suffering too gives communion with Christ (cf. 2 Cor 1:5). Therefore the stance of the believer in the world is that of ὡς μή.[106] Believers are "desecularized," even though they still live their lives in the world. They are not of the world, although they do not withdraw from the world but they know themselves to be responsible in and for the world. They know that the σχῆμα of this world is passing away, that it is being replaced by a new world. Believing existence is a transitional existence.

# IV. The Community of the Free—The Church

## a) The Church as Community

Cerfaux, L. *The Church in the Theology of St. Paul*. New York: Herder and Herder, 1959.

Dahl, N. A. *Das Volk Gottes*. Oslo 1941.

Hainz, J. *Ekklesia. Strukturen Paulinischer Gemeinde-Theologie und Gemeinde-Ordnung*. BU 9. Regensburg: Pustet, 1972.

Hainz, J. *Koinonia. 'Kirche' als Gemeinschaft bei Paulus*. BU 16. Regensburg: Pustet, 1982.

Klaiber, W. *Rechtfertigung und Gemeinde. Eine Untersuchung zum paulinischem Kirchenverständnis*. FRLANT 127. Göttingen: Vandenhoeck & Ruprecht, 1982.

Roloff, J. *Die Kirche im Neuen Testament*. GNT 10. Göttingen: Vandenhoeck & Ruprecht, 1993.

---

[106] Cf. above on 1 Corinthians 7:29–31 in A. I. B. 2.

Schweizer, E. "Die Kirche als Leib Christi in den paulinischen Homologumena," E. Schweizer. *Neotestamentica*. Zurich-Stuttgart: Zwingli, 1963. 272–292.

Vielhauer, Ph. "Oikodome. Das Bild vom Bau in der christlichen Literatur vom Neuen Testament bis Clemens Alexandrinus," Ph. Vielhauer. *Oikodome. Aufsätze zum Neuen Testament Bd. 2*. G. Klein, ed. TB 65. Munich: Kaiser, 1979. 1–168.

von Campenhausen, H. *Ecclesiastical Authority and Spiritual Power in the Church of the First Three Centuries*. London: Adam and Charles Black, 1969.

## 1. Ecclesiological Predicates

The prescripts to the Pauline letters name the members of the churches as ἅγιοι (e.g. 1 Cor 1:2; 2 Cor 1:1; Phil 1:1). Christians are thus designated with the same term used in the Old Testament to describe priests.[1] The Old Testament-Jewish people, as the people of the covenant established by God, are characterized in this way.[2] קָדוֹשׁ is a cultic term in the Old Testament; it designates those who stand before God, who have access to the holy place or to the sacrificial ritual. They have undergone a "sanctification" that makes them holy, i.e. that removes them from the profane world of impurity.[3] Just as such sanctification is attained in the Old Testament through sacrifice and ritual washing, so the sanctification of the ἅγιοι in the New Testament is grounded in the cross and resurrection of Jesus. It is not unimportant in this regard that the Christ event is regarded as mediated through baptism (1 Cor 6:11). Thereby the Christian assembly is "desecularized" as a community prepared to approach God as were the priests. The members of the church are made holy in Christ (Phil 1:1). They are assigned to the Lord. Thus they are called "his" saints, i.e. those that belong to the Kyrios Jesus (1 Thess 3:13).[4] That the idea of "holiness" was current in early Christianity is seen, for example, in the fact that Paul refers to the members of the Jerusalem church as ἅγιοι (Rom 15:26; 1 Cor 16:1). It is not only the Jewish Christians, however, who are ἅγιοι but also Gentile Christians. The sanctification of the Gentiles is an important aspect of the mission of the apostle to the Gentiles. He provides a priestly ministry by means of which the Gentiles are both a sacrificial offering he delivers up to God and a people who are themselves sanctified through the Holy Spirit, a people made ready for God (Rom 15:16). The church as a whole is brought into the sanctified realm by the priestly ministry of proclamation. The word ἅγιοι thus applies to the church as a whole, to every individual Christian and every individual congregation (cf. Phil 1:1).

---

[1]  Exodus 28:41; 40:13; Leviticus 8:12; 1 Chronicles 15:14; 2 Chronicles 5:11.

[2]  Cf. Isaiah 4:3; Psalm 33:10 LXX; Daniel 7:18, 21.

[3]  Leviticus 10:10; 16:32; 2 Chronicles 23:6, 31:18; Ezekiel 42:13–14.

[4]  "Holiness" is a common idea in the secular Greek-Hellenistic world and had been connected since the fifth century B. C. E. in the Ionic and Attic cultic language with ἱερόν (cf. Herodotus II 41; 5.44). The term is used especially in the realm of Greek-Hellenistic mystery cults (cf. BAGD 9).

Just as preaching is important for the self-understanding of the community because it has an essential function as the means by which Christians are made into a holy community, this self-understanding also comes to expression in another predicate frequently used by Paul: the community is the congregation of the κλητοί; the members of the church are "saints who have been called" (1 Cor 1:2; Rom 1:7, κλητοὶ ἅγιοι). They have been reached by a call to which they have responded, and are thereby "called" and "chosen" (cf. Rom 8:33 ἐκλεκτοὶ θεοῦ). In their calling the πρόθεσις θεοῦ is realized, the decision made by God before the call was extended (Rom 8:28, 30). The church knows itself to be determined by a decision previously made by God. Paul understands himself in a similar manner, as a commissioned apostle, one who has been called to service (Gal 1:15). The call accordingly means commissioning and sending; it includes a separation from the world of impurity (1 Thess 4:7), is a call to community (1 Cor 1:9), to the kingdom of God and its δόξα (1 Thess 2:12).

The church can also be described as οἰκοδομὴ θεοῦ (1 Cor 3:9–15, "God's building"). The foundation stone of this building is Christ; this foundation is laid by the preaching of the apostle. The church is thus essentially related to the Christ event. Ecclesiological statements are not separable from their christological foundation. The preachers' work must be related to this christological foundation; they all build up the church on the same foundation. With all the differences that come to expression in the different preachers and their theologies, the Christian community has its unity on this common foundation.

This means for the situation of the Corinthian church that Apollos, Paul, and Cephas are God's coworkers, those who lay the foundation stone and then build up the church on this foundation. They do this in different ways, however. How well they have built, whether it will be preserved or not be preserved, will be decided in the final judgment (1 Cor 3:12–13).

The postpauline Letter to the Ephesians has modified this ordering of foundation stone (Christ) and the structure erected on it by the apostles: "built upon the foundation of the apostles and prophets, with Christ Jesus himself as the cornerstone. In him the whole structure is joined together and grows into a holy temple in the Lord" (Eph 2:20–21). Here it is not Christ but the preachers who are the foundation; Christ is the ἀκρογωνιαῖος, the "corner stone" or "key stone" placed at the peak of an arch and thus holding the whole structure together.[5] While the picture of a building is preserved, the function of the apostle has been changed. The apostles now have an essential role in the history of salvation; they themselves are part of the building (which in 1 Cor 3:9ff it was their task to build). This is a sign of the changed theological situation in which the apostolic office and the class of Christian prophets have solidified almost to the point of becoming institutions in their own right, institutions that are to guarantee the continuity of the church.

---

[5]    Cf. Isaiah 28:16; Psalm 118 (117):22. Cf. also J. Jeremias, "ἀκρογωνιαῖος" TDNT 1:792.

If Christ is the foundation stone, this means that the church as "the building constructed by God" does not derive its existence out of itself. If it is the "temple of God" (1 Cor 3:17), or "God's planting,"[6] then it is holy in God (1 Cor 3:17); its holiness does not derive from itself but from God. The apostles are nothing other than God's coworkers (1 Cor 3:9) who carry out the work that has already been decided upon by God. The God who has revealed himself in the Christ event is thus the founder and builder of the church, and finally also the one who brings it to completion. It is only this foundation that gives the church its eschatological quality as a community already separate from the world.

Finally, the term ἐκκλησία also plays a central role. It has been correctly understood in terms of its etymology, when it has been derived from ἐκ + καλέω (call out). The ἐκκλησία is accordingly "the community of those who have been called out." This originally referred to the assembly of the polis, or to the citizens who were called to war. The word pictures people being "called out" of their homes and their ordinary life.[7] However, it must be noted that in New Testament times this etymology was no longer known in secular Greek. In this period the word had already become a fixed term that described the political assembly of the citizens of a Greek city. Pre-pauline Christianity could apply this term to itself, perhaps because it was colorless enough to be used for any assembly of people. It is only secondarily that one should remember that in the Septuagint the word was used as a designation for the people of God (Hebrew קְהַל יהוה).[8]

The genitive θεοῦ makes clear that this "assembly" is not for a political purpose and does not have a secular character but is a fellowship of people

---

6   1 Corinthians 3:9; cf. also 1QS 8.5 ("When these are in Israel, the Council of the Community shall be established in truth. It shall be an Everlasting Plantation, a House of Holiness for Israel, an Assembly of Supreme Holiness for Aaron."); cf. also 1QS 11.8.

7   The adjective ἐκκλητός is found in Greek more frequently as a technical term in connection with the ἐκκλησία as an assembly of the people; cf. e.g. Xenophon, Hist 2.4.38 (soldiers), Plato Prot 319b (citizens). An extensive collection of references to ἐκκλησία arranged according to the nuances of how the term is used is found in C. G. Brandis, "ἐκκλησία," in RECA V (1905) 2163–2200.

8   Cf. L. Rost, TDNT 3:529, note 90. Alongside ἐκκλησία θεοῦ the LXX translates the same expression קְהַל יהוה with συναγωγὴ κυρίου. Since, however, at the time of Paul this expression had already been practically monopolized by Hellenistic Judaism, the Christian community had to use the less precise ἐκκλησία; cf. W. Schrage, "Ekklesia und Synagogue," ZThK 60 (1963) 178–202. Less likely is the derivation from the term קְהַל of apocalyptic Judaism (1QM 4:10; 1Qsa 1.25 conj), since for the oldest New Testament texts (e.g. 1 Thess 2:14; 1 Cor 1:2) a corresponding Hebrew basis cannot be documented (contra J. Roloff, "ἐκκλησία," EWNT 1:1000). The only instance of ecclesia in the New Testament that with some probability can be traced back to an Aramaic background (Matt 16:18) goes back neither to the historical Jesus nor can it be attributed to the linguistic usage of the earliest Palestinian community (rightly J. Roloff, Die Kirche im Neuen Testament 162–163).

who belong to God, since they have been "sanctified in Christ Jesus" (1 Cor 1:2). It is thus characteristic that ἐκκλησία can sometimes designate the church as a whole. When in Galatians 1:13 or 1 Corinthians 15:9 Paul says that he persecuted the "church of God," he is thinking of the church as a whole that had to suffer under this persecution. In this sense the expression "church of Christ" (Rom 16:16) means the universal church. At other times the term ἐκκλησία can refer to the individual congregation, as the plural usage makes clear (e.g. 1 Cor 11:16; 1 Thess 2:14; translator's note: since the usage in Rom 16:16 is also plural, this reference probably belongs here). Paul makes no terminological distinction between the universal church and the individual congregation. It is rather the case that since he uses the same term in these different ways, for Paul the local congregation represents the whole church.[9] The one church of God is present in different locations. In the Pauline understanding, the church is not an invisible reality but a reality that comes to concrete expression in the individual local congregations, but not in such a way that the eschatological claim represented by the church can be read off the surface of these local churches or be identical with their empirical concrete reality. The whole church, the local congregations, and the house churches each embody in different manifestations the "ecclesia visibilis" which is the one eschatological ἐκκλησία θεοῦ, the "ecclesia invisibilis," which is the object of faith, not of sight.[10]

## 2.  *sîma Cristoà*

Brandenburger, E. *Adam und Christus*. WMANT 7. Neukirchen-Vluyn: Neukirchener, 1962.

Gundry, R. H. *Soma in Biblical Theology with Emphasis on Pauline Anthropology*. MSSNTS 29. Cambridge: Cambridge University Press, 1976.

Käsemann, E. "The Theological Problem Presented by the Motif of the Body of Christ," E. Käsemann. *Perspectives on Paul*. Philadelphia: Fortress, 1971.

Käsemann, E. *Leib und Leib Christi. Eine Untersuchung zur paulinischen Begrifflichkeit*. BHTh 9. Tübingen: J. C. B. Mohr (Paul Siebeck) 1933.

Merklein, H. "Entstehung und Gehalt des paulinischen Leib-Christi-Gedankens," H. Merklein. *Studien zur Jesus und Paulus*. WUNT 43. Tübingen: J. C. B. Mohr (Paul Siebeck), 1987. 319–344.

Robinson, J. A. T. *The Body. A Study in Pauline Theology*. SBT 5. London: SCM, 1952.

Schweizer, E. "σῶμα," *TDNT* VII (1964) 1024–1094.

Schweizer, E. "Die Kirche als Leib Christi in den paulinischen Homologumena," E. Schweizer. *Neotestamentica*. Zurich-Stuttgart: Zwingli, 1963. 272–292.

The Pauline idea of the "body of Christ" has for a long time been seen in academic research as the locus classicus for the *influence of Gnostic ter-*

---

[9]  Contra K. Berger, "Kirche II. Neues Testament," *TRE* 18:201–218; 215.

[10]  Cf. also the Apostles' Creed, "I believe in ... one Christian church (εἰς ... ἁγίαν ἐκκλησίαν, *Die Bekenntnisschriften der evangelisch-lutherischen Kirche* [Göttingen: Vandenhoeck & Ruprecht, 1992[11]] 21).

*minology* and Gnostic thought on the theology of Paul.[11] According to E. Käsemann the body of Christ is thought of as a Gnostic aeon. This applies not only in the authentic Pauline letters but also in the deutero-Paulines (Colossians and Ephesians). Σῶμα Χριστοῦ is accordingly an ecclesiological-cosmological reality. Christians are members of this redeemer-aeon. For the soteriology presupposed in this conception, Käsemann relies on the redeemer myth of the *Urmensch*, the prototypical primitive man. This man is related to the "redeemed redeemer" by his "origin" (συγγένεια) and in fact is identical with him. This is the presupposition for the idea of the body of Christ and its soteriological importance. Human beings re-experience the destiny of the redeemed redeemer and are thereby led to salvation. This hypothesis suffers under the difficulty that the concept of the redeemed redeemer, i.e. the revealer who descends into the world of matter, frees himself from it, and by such an act of liberation also saves the other light sparks that are sunk in the material world, is not documented in pre-Christian times but first appears in the later Christian-Gnostic systems.[12]

On the other side, the *Jewish background* of the concept of the body of Christ is emphasized, especially in connection with the idea of the people of God.[13] The concept of the people of God is spiritualized as the idea of the body of Christ, as it were. According to E. Schweizer,[14] the Jewish background has been strongly modified by Christian tradition. Jewish tradition is acquainted with the idea that humanity can be represented as combined in one person.[15] Thus not only does Adam include all humanity in himself,[16] but in Jewish exegesis also the "Servant of Yahweh" is interpreted as a collective representing the Jewish people as a whole.[17] This is frequently related to other speculative interpretations of Adam in which as the patriarch of future generations Adam has a corresponding importance. One might also think of non-Jewish speculations about the archetypical

---

[11]  As examples one can name: R. Reitzenstein, *Die hellenistischen Mysterienreligionen* 335ff; H. Schlier, *Christus und die Kirche im Epheserbrief* (BHTh 6. Tübingen: J. C. B. Mohr [Paul Siebeck], 1930) 40–42; E. Käsemann, *Leib un Leib Christi* 105.

[12]  Cf. C. Colpe, *Die Religionsgeschichtliche Schule. Darstellung und Kritik ihres Bildes vom gnostischen Erlösermythos* (FRLANT 78. Göttingen: Vandenhoeck & Ruprecht, 1961) 173–175, 179–180, 185–186, 190–191; also his article "Gnostizismus," in RAC XI 538–659, 611–612.

[13]  L. Cerfaux, *The Church in the Theology of St. Paul* 282ff.

[14]  E. Schweizer, TDNT 7:1068–1072.

[15]  The concept of the "vine" (John 15:1ff) also seems to presuppose such an incorporation; cf. also Apocalypse of Abraham 5.

[16]  Cf. Romans 5:12ff. For Jewish exegesis, cf. 4 Ezra 3:7; 7:118; cf. also 2 Baruch 17:3; 23:4; Apocalypse of Moses 32 (Eve).

[17]  On the "servant songs" (Isa 42:1–4; 49:1–6; 50:4–9; 52:13–53:12) cf. the Targumim and other examples of Jewish exegesis (Strack-Billerbeck 1:483).

primitive man as parallels.[18] In this view the body of Christ concept is a view of the archetypical man that has been combined with the Jewish Adam mythology and speculation about the cosmic *Urmensch*. Paul has gone beyond such traditions in that the interprets the concept "body of Christ" in a specific way.[19]

From the point of view of the study of the history of religions, the question of the derivation of the concept of the body of Christ is more difficult than ever to resolve. What has been attained is that a series of analogies, at the most possible derivations, have been pointed out but research has not succeeded in presenting a genealogy of the body of Christ concept. While these issues are thus to be regarded as open questions, the general background can still be discerned, namely that a cosmic-mytho- logical world of thought is presupposed. The christological basis of the Pauline idea of the body of Christ is the concept of a preexistent being who descended, humiliated himself, and then was exalted as Kyrios, whose spiritual essence is not subject to the conditions of the earthly world, and which can also be an expression for ecclesial self-understanding, a self- understanding of the faith of the church that affirms that church in its essential being does not belong to this world.

The parenesis in 1 Corinthians 12:12–27 is illuminating for the Pau- line interpretation of the "body of Christ." The concern in this passage is with spiritual gifts (χαρίσματα), of which the church at Corinth possesses a great variety. That such variety need not lead to conflict and separation is affirmed by the picture of the body: the church is one body with many members. The variety of members points to the different origins and different functions of the members of the church. But that they are one body makes clear that they are oriented to one another, must be there for one another and care for one another, for every member has a special function that cannot be taken over by another. Each member has his or her own place, is irreplaceable and contributes to the functioning of the body as a whole. As *soma*, the church is an organism that is completely func- tional only when all the members together perform their appointed func- tions. This can be learned from Stoic ideas. The fable of Menenius Agrippa documents a similar view, when the cooperation of the individual mem- bers of the human body is used as the basis for the existing relations of political authority with the intent of promoting the communal life of human society without friction.[20] Within the framework of the Pauline

---

[18]  Cf. Philo Op 136–139, and further examples in E. Schweizer, *Die Kirche als Leib Christi* 274–277.

[19]  Cf. the following, and also E. Schweizer TDNT 7:1066, 1069, 1079.

[20]  The fable of Menenius Agrippa is transmitted in the Roman historian Livy (49 B. C. E.–17 C. E.) II 32.8, on which see W. Nestle, "Die Fabel des Menenius Agrippa," *Klio* 21 (1927) 350ff.

letter it is of course not a matter of representing a phenomenon that can be interpreted in sociological terms, however much the church may also come into view as a tangible organization. It is rather the case that its unity and awareness of belonging together does not have a this-worldly basis but consists in the fact that the church is the one body of Christ. (1 Cor 12:27: "Now you are the body of Christ and individually members of it [this body].") The authentic being and unity of the Christian community is given through its connection with Christ; it lives from the common temporal beginning and basis common to all, from the Christ event. From this there follows (formulated as an imperative) its external unity and authentic being.[21]

Romans 12:4–5 likewise locates the discussion of the body of Christ in the context of parenesis:

> For as in one body we have many members, and not all the members have the same function, so we, who are many, are one body in Christ, and individually we are members one of another.

The picture of the one body illustrates the unity and communion of the church. It may thus have at first been thought of metaphorically as in 1 Corinthians 10:17; 12:13, which speaks of the *one* body. But here too the concept of the *body of Christ* will have stood in the background: the unity of the church is given by the fact that it is the body of Christ; it is a matter not only of a sociological reality but of an eschatological identity. It thus means the dividing of Christ himself when divisions arise in the church; they tear apart the body of Christ.[22]

Accordingly, in the Pauline letters the concept of an organism is also in Paul's sense only an incomplete expression of Christian self-understanding. The prior understanding within which this concept is incorporated is that the church possesses its unity as the body of Christ. This unity is given in advance and is not constructed by the members of the

---

21 This signifies a clear distinction from Stoic material, for this grounding of the imperative in the Christ event and thus finally in being ἐν Χριστῷ (Rom 12:5) is a change from thinking on the model of an organism (cf. also Gal 2:20). While here the members can constitute the body, in Paul's modification of this idea the body of Christ is a reality that precedes the church. In 1 Corinthians 12:12 (οὕτως καὶ ὁ Χριστός) and 12:27 Paul leaves the metaphorical plane; the community is not *like* a body but *is* a body. Paul is thus not really interested in the analogy of an organism. In 12:13 he refers to the importance of the members in their unity on the basis of their belonging to Christ. The decisive expression is βαπτίζειν εἰς ἓν σῶμα, which, to the extent that it is understood in a spatial sense, implies being in Christ. By contrast, in the analogous thought in terms of the body as an organism, the existence of the body is first made possible by the members. Cf. also F. W. Horn, *Angeld des Geistes* 172–173 and elsewhere.

22 Cf. 1 Corinthians 1:13.

churches themselves. It is not an immanent, sociologically derivative unity, for the church as the "body of Christ" has an eschatological qualification. It is called into life through baptism (1 Cor 1:13; 12:13), for this means incorporation into the body of Christ (Rom 6:1ff), and thus a grounding of human existence on the crucified and risen Christ (Rom 7:4). The same is said by Galatians 3:26–28: in baptism one puts on Christ, and one is placed within the body of Christ. Something analogous happens in the Lord's Supper, in which communion with Christ and the unity of the community takes place through the encounter with the Kyrios, through which one's assignment to and incorporation into the body of Christ is constituted (1 Cor 11:24ff). Such indicative statements illustrate the presence of the reality of eschatological salvation. The community makes eschatological salvation a matter of its own existence. From this follows the imperative, the necessity, of representing the unity of the body.[23]

## 3.  Office and Spirit

Brockhaus, Ulrich. *Charisma und Amt: Die paulinische Charismalehre auf dem Hintergrund der frühchristlichen Gemeindefunktionen.* Wuppertal: Brockhaus, 1972.

Brosch, Joseph. *Charismen und Ämter in der Urkirche.* Bonn: Peter Hanstein Verlag, 1951.

Greeven, H. "Propheten, Lehrer, Vorsteher bei Paulus," *ZNW* 44 (1952/53) 1–43.

Kertelge, K., ed., *Das kirchliche Amt im Neuen Testament.* WdF 439. Darmstadt: Wissenschaftliche Buchgesellschaft, 1977.

Kertelge, K. "Der Ort des Amtes in der Ekklesiologie des Paulus," A. Vanhoye, ed. *L'Apôtre Paul.* BEThL 73. Leuven: Louvain University Press, 1986. 184–202.

Kertelge, K. *Gemeinde und Amt im Neuen Testament.* BiH 10. Munich: Kösel, 1972.

Roloff, R. *Apostolat—Verkündigung—Kirche.* Gütersloh: Gerd Mohn, 1965.

Roloff, R. "Apostel, Apostolat, Apostolizität, I. Neues Testament," TRE 3 (1978) 430–445.

Schweizer, E. *Das Leben des Herrn in der Gemeinde und ihren Diensten.* AThANT 8. Zürich: Calwer, 1946.

Sohm, R. "Kirchenrecht I. Die geschichtlichen Grundlagen," *Systematisches Handbuch der Deutschen Rechtswissenschaft, 8. Abteilung.* Leipzig 1892.

Sohm, R. *Wesen und Ursprung des Katholizismus.* Leipzig-Berlin 1912².

---

[23]  Whether the point of departure for the development of the body of Christ concept was the eucharistic tradition (so H. Conzelmann, *Theology* 262) is a disputed point. While the expression is found in the words of institution (1 Cor 10:16–17; 11:24), it is also used by Paul independently of this association (1 Cor 12:27), and the cosmic connotations of the statement are grounded pneumatically, not sacramentally. It is worth considering whether both the meaning of the term and its derivation within the history of the tradition owe more to the ἐν Χριστῷ concept and the associations of baptism as a "putting on Christ" interpreted as incorporation in the body of Christ (cf. Gal 3:27–28), even if it is admitted that the formula "in Christ" is not to be understood only in a spatial sense.

von Harnack, A. *Entstehung und Entwicklung der Kirchenverfassung und des Kirchenrechts in den zwei ersten Jahrhunderten.* Nebst einer Kritik der Abhandlung R. Sohms: "Wesen und Ursprung des Katholizismus" und Untersuchungen über "Evangelium", "Wort Gottes" und Das trinitarische Bekenntnis. Leipzig 1910.

The discussion carried on between the lawyer Rudolph Sohm and the church historian Adolf v. Harnack at the turn from the 19th to the 20th century is still important for the question of the relation of office and Spirit in early Christianity. Their discussion lets one see the beginnings of the two possibilities that developed in early Christianity for understanding the nature of church offices. Rudolf Sohm[24] advocated the thesis that law stands in essential contradiction to the essence of the church. The legal character of office and the essence of the church are related to each other as law is related to gospel. It belongs to the nature of law, and thus to church office, to realize its goals by compulsion. But the church lives by the Spirit; it does not follow the law that can be fixed in legal statements and executed by force but the "law" of love. The church accordingly has no law but at the most a charismatic order; its "law" is charismatic generosity and freedom. To the extent that the later church acquired legally-understood ordinances in the course of its development, it is to be thought of as falling into sin. In contrast, Adolf v. Harnack[25] affirmed that there had been legal ordinances in early Christianity from the very beginning. He distinguished charismatic officers who exercise authority in the whole church, and administrative officers, who are located in the local congregations. The origin of charismatic orders is attributed to the direct gift of the Spirit, while administrative officers are elected and installed by congregational vote. Spirit and office, Spirit and tradition, are no contradiction in Harnack's understanding, for it is rather the case that the Spirit works in the different ministries of the church.

It has become a commonplace of research to say that Spirit and tradition stand in no contradiction to one another, that charisma and office are not mutually-exclusive opposites.[26] But one should not too quickly, not even in a modified form, agree to Harnack's thesis, for there is a danger in affirming the identity of Spirit and office and their lack of contradiction, namely the danger of traditionalism and nomism, even of theological Pharisaism. To be sure, it is possible for office and Spirit to be complementary but in the history of the Christian church they have emerged fairly often as opposites. The order of the church does not guarantee the truth of this order. On the other side there is no less a danger that to prevent the Spirit from leading the church into fanaticism, enthusiasm and thus the

---

[24] R. Sohm, *Kirchenrecht* I 22–28, 475–476, and elsewhere.
[25] A. v. Harnack, *Entstehung* 36–44; cf. also 163–172 and 184–185.
[26] Cf. also E. Schweizer, *Das Leben des Herrn* 37 note 35, and p. 98.

denial of any order in the church, the freedom of the Spirit will be insti-tutionalized and reduced to official functions, so that the movement of the Spirit itself is extinguished.

In the fundamental sense, R. Sohm is thus still right today. The man-ner in which the Christian community understood and expressed its own identity according to the New Testament witness is that the essence of the church cannot be grasped in legal terms. It is accessible only to faith—in the language of Paul, it belongs to the sphere of the pneuma. Because the ἐκκλησία is an eschatological phenomenon, a discrepancy must emerge in every historical, worldly form of its manifestation. Thereby a critical dis-tance is also required to every legal system that is supposed to serve the church in its worldly existence, and in no case may be allowed to dominate the church. For what Paul says of the apostolic office is also true of the church: "But we have this treasure in clay jars, so that it may be made clear that this extraordinary power belongs to God and does not come from us" (2 Cor 4:7). The critical distance articulated by Paul over against the orders and regulations of the church becomes clear in the question of church offices that follow the apostolic office and are subordinate to it and that have validity for Christian congregations.

α) Prophets

In 1 Corinthians 12:28 Paul distinguishes three church offices:

> God has appointed in the church first apostles, second prophets, third teachers; then deeds of power, then gifts of healing, forms of assistance, forms of leadership, various kinds of tongues.

The prophets are distinguished from those who speak in tongues in that they are listed in the first place after the apostles as the bearers of church order. While the προφῆται are mentioned in a more personal way, the "various kinds of tongues" (γένη γλωσσῶν) are referred to impersonally. This corresponds to the manner in which prophecy is contrasted with glossolalia in 1 Corinthians 14. Both prophecy and glossolalia are "charis-mata," gifts of the Spirit; both are supposed to function for the edification of the church (1 Cor 14:26). But prophecy is a superior gift to speaking in tongues; it is proclamation, and thus intelligible speech (12:31), while glossolalia is unintelligible, and thus useful only to the tongue-speaker and not to the whole congregation. In contrast, prophecy occurs in accordance with the "analogia fidei" (Rom 12:6, κατὰ τὴν ἀναλογίαν τῆς πίστεως), i.e. within the sphere of πίστις that is for the good of the whole community. Thus prophecy can be evaluated by the other members of the church. The prophet's job is to give encouragement and consolation to the church (1 Cor 14:3, 31) and to bring hidden things to light by revelatory speeches (1 Cor 14:24–25).

On the basis of 1 Corinthians 14:40 (πάντα ... κατὰ τάξιν γινέσθω) it could be concluded that the prophets are a distinctive, independent group within the Pauline churches. Thus τάξις could be translated with "office." It is better, however, to translate "order" or "sequence." Paul is concerned that speaking in the church worship services be done in an ordered series (rather than chaotically).

That prophets did not constitute an established office in the church is seen in 1 Corinthians 14:37 ("Anyone who claims to be a prophet, or to have spiritual powers, must acknowledge that what I am writing to you is a command of the Lord"). In principle, every Christian, male and female, has the potential to prophesy,[27] i.e. every member of the church who senses the charisma of prophecy within himself or herself. This indicates that Paul considers prophecy to be a general gift of the Spirit to the church at large. It is no accident that in Romans 12:6 prophecy is listed as a charismatic gift to the church (alongside service, teaching, exhortation, and such). The special circumstances in Corinth had led to the beginnings of a prophetic *office*. This is suggested by the special emphasis Paul gives to prophecy, and his distancing it from glossolalia. First Corinthians 12:28 already is going in this direction. Obviously the initiatives taken by enthusiasts and others gave the occasion to look for a more carefully-defined and official church structure, which in the postpauline time did in fact pose a limitation on charismatic freedom.[28]

---

[27]  Cf. 1 Corinthians 11:5. Extensive evidence does not need to be given here for the fact that in the Pauline letters women have an almost unlimited participation in leadership roles in the church. This is clearly seen in the concluding greetings of Paul's letters, e.g. in Romans 16:3ff Prisca (Priscilla in Acts 18:2, 18, 26) is named (cf. also 1 Cor 16:19; 2 Tim 4:19). As the first woman convert in the Pauline congregation in Philippi, Lydia, a merchant in purple goods, had an important position of leadership (Acts 16:40, 44). All this apparently stands in contrast to the Pauline command for women to keep silent in the churches, so that the passage 1 Corinthians 14:33b-35 is often questioned as to whether it was really written by Paul (e.g. G. Fitzer, "Das Weib schweige in der Gemeinde," [TEH 110. Munich, 1963]; Hans Conzelmann, *1 Corinthians: a commentary on the First Epistle to the Corinthians* [Philadelphia: Fortress, 1975] 246). In this case it is possible, however, that since the verb used in 14:34, 35 is λαλέω rather than the more technical προφητεύω (in addition to 11:5, cf. especially 14:1ff), it should not be translated as "preach" but "speak in between" or "dispute." This would correspond to the overarching theme in the context (cf. vv. 33, 40, "... all things should be done decently and in order"), and would make unnecessary the alternative option of regarding this passage as a secondary insertion into this section.

[28]  Even though in the *Didache* prophets and teachers are (still) regarded as charismatics, it is still clear that the congregational officers of "bishops and deacons" gradually replaced the free charismatics; it is said of them that "they also perform for you the service of the prophets and teachers" (Did 15:1).

## β) Teachers

First Corinthians 12:28 names "teachers" (διδάσκαλοι) alongside "prophets." They do not have a general function in the church at large but a definite function within the structure of the local congregation. Paul could attach his own understanding to the tradition of a definite class of teachers within the synagogue.[29] In secular Greek the term διδάσκαλος described a teacher in general, so that what this teacher teaches must be specified more closely in order to distinguish him or her from other types of teachers. In contrast, in the Jewish Diaspora the διδάσκαλος was understood *eo ipso* to be a teacher of the law; this is presupposed in Romans 2:17ff and is also reflected in the term γραμματεύς (found in Paul only at 1 Cor 1:20; cf. the Christian γραμματεύς in Matt 13:52).

The teacher's job is to instruct the congregation. Such "instruction" (διδασκαλία) is not to be identified only with parenesis but above all affirms that the teacher is the one who hands on the oral tradition. Doubtless the kerygmatic formulae cited by Paul belong here. Thus no less than the prophets, teachers had responsibility for discerning and safeguarding the truth of the gospel. The matter should not be distinguished in such a way that prophets were responsible for the gospel, while teachers were responsible for the law, for the traditional material could not be sorted out in this way. Nor can one say that the prophets were advocates of the Spirit, while the teachers depended on tradition, since tradition only edifies the community when it is made relevant, i.e. when it is pneumatically empowered. On the other hand, the Spirit would be empty if it did not have the kind of content transmitted in the tradition. The distinction between prophets and teachers is not a matter of the material with which they work but rather consists of the fact that prophets proclaim in a way that actualizes their message to the current situation, while the teachers instruct in a representative capacity as interpreters of the tradition.[30] This is a distinction of their respective functions, with only relative importance, since obviously it cannot be excluded that instruction can modulate into preaching. This could easily happen due to the nature of the content of the kerygma.

While the parallel of the Jewish teacher in the Diaspora does suggest that there was a specific group of teachers in the Pauline churches, this

---

[29]  Cf. E. L. Sukenik, "Jüdische Gräber Jerusalems um Christi Geburt. Vortrag gehalten in der Archäologischen Gesellschaft," (Berlin-Jerusalem 1931) 17–18, which documented this from a Jerusalem ossuary from the beginning of the first century C. E.

[30]  Cf. H. Greeven, "Propheten, Lehrer, Vorsteher bei Paulus," 28–29: the teacher's task was to hand on tradition, especially as it was engaged with interpreting the Old Testament as prophecy of Christ. With the exception of catechetical and baptismal instruction as the exclusive task of the teachers, we should not think of a clear boundary between the functions of teachers, apostles, and prophets.

does not necessarily mean that Paul presupposes a teaching office with hierarchical authority. The fact of the matter is that the teachers exercised their functions only with reference to the church as the body of Christ, i.e. no differently than the prophets. Just as the prophet was subject to the διακρίνειν of the whole congregation (1 Cor 14:29), so also teaching was the responsibility of the congregation as a whole. What is presupposed is not an institution for private instruction, as was customary for wandering Hellenistic teachers and philosophers, for the concern was for the preservation of the community tradition and the right interpretation of Christian tradition, as well as for the responsible development and creation of new teaching material. In any case, prophets and teachers occupied a special position among the pneumatics but are still not fundamentally different from the other members of the congregation, since all knew that through baptism they had all received the gift of the Spirit.

*γ) Leaders (προϊστάμενοι)*

In Romans 12:8 the "leaders" or "presiders" stand alongside other charismatics.[31] According to 1 Thessalonians 5:12 they work in the community, admonishing and reprimanding the other members of the congregation (νουθετοῦντες). They have the responsibility of congregational leadership (1 Cor 12:28 κυβερνήσεις), so the other members of the congregation should be subject to them (1 Cor 16:15–16, "the household of Stephanas").

The persons who occupy prominent positions in congregational leadership have in part been appointed by Paul himself. This is not an anticipation of the later monarchial episcopate. On the contrary, it is not said that every congregation has only one leader but in larger cities it is to be supposed that there were several (house)churches, and thus that there were several leading personalities. Besides, it is not really possible to define the duties of the "leaders" over against the bearers of other charismatic gifts. It is possible that congregational leadership lay in the hands of men who were also prophets or teachers. There was no clearly defined office of leadership in the Pauline congregations. The reality of the body of Christ was the overarching concept, and the unity and unanimity of the church that had within it the functions of community leadership without needing

---

31  Cf. Romans 12:6–8: alongside teachers, prophets, diaconal ministers, exhorters, those who do deeds of compassion, and such. According to R. Banks, *Paul's Idea of Community. The Early House Churches in their Historical Setting* (Grand Rapids: Eerdmans, 1980) 37ff, the lack of the address "ἐκκλησία" in the prescript of Romans is understandable on the basis that in Rome there was no plenary gathering of Christians and thus no hierarchically structured "presiders" or "leaders." We should rather think of a number of house churches over which the προϊστάμενοι "presided." Cf. H.-J. Klauck, *Hausgemeinde und Hauskirche im frühen Christentum* (SBS 103. Stuttgart: Katholisches Bibelwerk, 1981) 21–41.

to make claims to hierarchical office, for the fundamental operative principle was: church leadership is a charisma, a gift of the Spirit. No one has the right to set this or that gift absolutely above the others in which the reality of the Spirit's presence in the congregation was experienced.

### δ) *Bishops and Deacons*

In the prescript to the letter to the Philippians, the congregation is addressed "with the ἐπίσκοποι and διάκονοι (Phil 1:1). For the first time in the history of the church, and the only time in Paul, the combination appears that was to play the dominant role in later church order. What is an ἐπίσκοπος? It is obvious that we should not presuppose that Paul identified the ἐπίσκοπος with the bishop of a particular church. The monarchical episcopate, in which a single ἐπίσκοπος exercised church leadership, did not appear until after Paul's time. It is no accident that Paul addresses the letter to the ἐπίσκοποι (plural). We should accordingly think of a small group, a "steering committee," that as a collective are called ἐπίσκοποι. In secular Greek the term ἐπίσκοπος means "overseer," "supervisor,"[32] especially in the political realm, so that administrative officials or financial commissioners could be so designated. They are also found in Hellenistic cultic communities, and it is from here, i.e. from the pagan Hellenistic milieu, that they found their way into the Pauline churches. From this linguistic usage one could suppose that in the Pauline churches the ἐπίσκοποι had primarily administrative functions.

So also the title διάκονος is documented in pagan-Hellenistic cultic associations, in part for employees charged with the arrangements for the sacral meals and had specific functions related to them.[33] From this one might surmise that in the Pauline churches too the "deacons" functioned in the benevolent work of the church. Διάκονος apparently appears as the designation for a particular class of church workers in Romans 16:1, where "our sister Phoebe," the διάκονος of the church at Cenchrea, is commended to the addressees. This is the first reference to a female deacon in Christian literature. Women too could fill the office of a deacon, just as women prophets were also acknowledged in the Pauline churches (cf. 1 Cor 11:5).

It is thus no accident that the letter to the Philippians speaks of "bishops and deacons." Since Paul was concerned about the administrative and charitable functions of the church, it was important for Paul to mention precisely these congregational leaders in his prescript, for the essential element of Paul's letter to the Philippians is Paul's expression of gratitude for the help the church had given the apostle (Phil 4:10–20). As indicated

---

[32] In 5/4 B. C. E. in Athens, ἐπίσκοπος was used as the title of a government official; cf. Aristophenes Av 1022ff. The term is also documented for the employee of a cultic association, e.g. IG II 1.731; 3.329 (care for the Apollo sanctuary on Rhodes).

[33] Numerous examples are listed in H. W. Beyer, "διάκονος" TDNT 2:91–92.

by the use of the words in the plural, one cannot speak of a hierarchical order of offices, including the relation between bishops and deacons. The primary thing is the function in the community, not a consciousness of individual offices and office-holders, and of course there is also no particular gift especially associated with each office. The development of church offices in the Pauline churches is at its very beginning stages—evidence of the freedom of the Spirit and the lack of rigidity given with the Pauline understanding of the Spirit. The Pauline doctrine of charismata is basic; from this point of departure the offices in the church are to be interpreted—not vice versa.

A. v. Harnack[34] distinguished two types of church polity:

(1) *The presbyterial type of church order,* in which church leadership is exercised by "elders." This is the way it is pictured in the account of Acts (15:2ff; 21:18; the account is of course secondary) as characteristic for the Jerusalem church, and represents the composition of the church according to Palestinian-Jewish presuppositions.

(2) *The episcopal form of church order;* this is first documented for the Pauline churches and has a Hellenistic background. It is no accident that Paul does not know the presbyterial form; it is the deutero-Pauline Pastoral Letters that first manifest such a development in the Pauline stream. First Timothy contains instructions for a bishop, for the presbyters, and for the deacons of the congregation (1 Tim 3:1–13; 5:17–19); here the presbyterial and episcopal understandings of church leadership are fused together (cf. Titus 1:5–9). Just how this amalgamation came about can no longer be discerned. Possibly within the college of presbyters there was an outstanding member who was good at preaching and teaching and who was installed as "bishop." First Timothy 5:17 could be a reference to this. It is certain that this development did not take place until post-Pauline times. It goes hand in hand with the formation of a legal system that established clear limits to the free sway of the Spirit.

In his essay "On the Origin of Luther's Concept of the Church" ["Zur Entstehung von Luthers Kirchenbegriff"], H. J. Iwand[35] declared his allegiance to R. Sohm, and adopted Sohm's statement "The church legal system contradicts the essential nature of the church" as *the* truth of Protestantism. It is in fact the case that the truth of the church is never expressed in a sentence of law, even if this legal sentence is re-coined as a "ius divinum," because the church lives from the truth of God and not from the solicitude of human beings. This is true because the Spirit works

---

[34]  Cf. A. Harnack, *Entstehung und Entwicklung.*

[35]  H. J. Iwand, "Zur Entstehung von Luthers Kirchenbegriff. Ein kritischer Beitrag zu dem gleichnamigen Aufsatz von. K. Holl," in *FS G. Dehn,* edited by W. Schneemelcher (Neukirchen-Vluyn: Neukirchener, 1957) 145–166; 146–147, note 5.

in the church and can never be identified with a legal form, no matter how responsibly it is chosen, and—if it must be so— the Spirit will sometimes annul such a legal form. This is seen in the Pauline doctrine of church offices. Church officials (or better, church functions) are inseparable from the Spirit that works within them, the same Spirit that grants spiritual gifts to members of the congregation in general. However much such a basic principle is misinterpreted, and however much it appears to promote and encourage the Protestant tendency to enthusiasm and fanaticism, it is actually against these, and on the other hand it is the appropriate power within the life of the church to keep it from hardening into a rigid institution. This is the thing that makes Pauline theology a "disturber of the church." The Christian church must resolve to live up to the motto "ecclesia semper reformanda" if it wants to consistently realize in practice the Pauline understanding of church leadership.

## b)   Church and World

Betz, H. D. "Das Problem der Grundlagen der paulinischen Ethik (Röm 12,1–2)," H. D. Betz. *Paulusstudien. GAufs. III*. Tübingen: J. C. B. Mohr (Paul Siebeck), 1994. 184–205.

Bultmann, R. "Das Problem der Ethik bei Paulus," R. Bultmann. *Exegetica*. Tübingen: J. C. B. Mohr (Paul Siebeck), 1967. 36–54.

Horn, F. W. "Wandel im Geist. Zur pneumatologischen Begründung der Ethik bei Paulus," *KuD* 38 (1992) 149–170.

Jüngel, E. "Erwägungen zur Grundlegung evangelischer Ethik im Anschluss an Paulus," E. Jüngel. *Unterwegs zur Sache*. BEvTh 61. Munich: Kaiser, 1972. 234–245.

Lohse, E. *Theological Ethics of the New Testament*. Minneapolis: Fortress, 1991.

Merk, O. *Handeln aus Glauben*. MThSt 5. Marburg: N. G. Elwert, 1968.

Schnackenburg, R. *Die sittliche Botschaft des Neuen Testaments*. HThK.S 2. Freiburg: Herder, 1988.

Schrage, W. *Ethics of the New Testament*. Philadelphia: Fortress, 1988.

Schulz, S. "Evangelium und Welt. Hauptprobleme einer Ethik des Neuen Testaments," *FS H. Braun*. Tübingen: J. C. B. Mohr (Paul Siebeck), 1973. 483–501.

Schulz, S. *Neutestamentliche Ethik*. ZGB. Zürich: Zwingli, 1987.

Strecker, G. *Handlungsorientierter Glaube. Vorstudien zu einer Ethik des Neuen Testaments*. Stuttgart-Berlin 1972.

Strecker, G. "Indicative and Imperative according to Paul," *ABR* 35 (1987) 60–72.

Strecker, G. "Strukturen einer neutestamentlichen Ethik," *ZThK* 75 (1978) 117–146.

## 1.   Indicative and Imperative in Ecclesiological Context

As we have seen, the term κόσμος in the Pauline understanding is by no means univocal. It can have a positive, neutral content (e.g. "the human world") but often has a negative tone.[36] Thus Satan can be described as

---

[36]   Cf. above A. III. a. 2.

"the ruler of this world" (2 Cor 4:4 ὁ θεὸς τοῦ αἰῶνος τούτου). He stands over against the creator of the world but remains subject to him, and so is not the absolute counterpart of God the creator in the sense of the Gnostic myth.[37]

Since the world is subject to the power of Satan, because it has been permeated by sin since the time of Adam (Rom 5:12), this means that to orient one's life to the world leads to death (2 Cor 7:10). The meaning of the saving event consists in the fact that through Christ the power of the ruler of this age is broken, and that with the conquest of sin and death so also the vanity and nothingness of the world has been set aside (2 Cor 5:19, "in Christ God was reconciling the world to himself..."; cf. also Rom 11:15).

God's act of the redemption of humanity must be actualized in the individual human being by faith. While God's redemptive act is universal, it does not happen automatically but calls for the decision of faith. To be sure, the individual believer does not exist apart from the community, and the Christian not without the church. Thus corresponding to the vanity of the world is the community of acceptance, the church. The counterpart of the collective reality of sinners is the collective reality of those who are justified. Here the same thing happens that is true of the faith of the individual believer: the dialectic of indicative and imperative.[38]

The ecclesiological indicative is already expressed in the designation of the church as the community of the ἅγιοι.[39] So also σῶμα Χριστοῦ designates a realm within the world oriented to Christ's lordship. The church is itself the realm of Christ's lordship, although the lordship of Christ is not congruent with the boundaries of the church and will not become de facto universal until the parousia (Phil 2:11; 1 Cor 15:23ff). Such indicative statements mean that the presence of the church in the world means the eschaton has entered into time.[40] That the church is an eschatological phenomenon within time does not mean that it is an institution of salvation in the sacramental sense, so that the relation of church and world

---

[37]  Cf. above A. III. a. 2. on the relation to this "present evil age" (Gal 1:4) or "this age" (e.g. 1 Cor 1:20). For the apocalyptic structure of this concept, which is to be presupposed despite the absence of the corresponding αἰὼν μέλλων in Paul, one must also consider the parallel expression βασιλεία θεοῦ; cf. 1 Corinthians 6:9–10; 15:50; Galatians 5:21; cf. also 1 Corinthians 15:24ff.

[38]  Cf. above A. III. d.

[39]  Romans 1:7 and elsewhere; see above A. IV. a. 1.

[40]  This is true even though for Paul the Christian community is not yet a mythological reality. Not until postpauline times will the church be personified as a preexistent heavenly reality, so that the distance between church and world will become a fundamental problem; cf. Colossians 1:15–20; Ephesians 5:29–32; 2 Clement 14 (R. Bultmann, *Theology* 179 asks whether Ephesians 5:32 polemicizes against the idea of the preexistence of the church).

would be without any connection. It is rather the case that what is true of
the individual Christian is also true of the church in the world: as a
corporation it must give account of its eschatological claim by its life in the
world, for it stands under the command to realize the being that has been
promised and declared to it by its actual existence in the world. Nothing
other than this is said in Philippians 2:15, according to which the members of the church are to "shine like stars in the world" (φωστῆρες ἐν κόσμῳ),
namely by the fact that they belong to the body of Christ. Such an existence
means to live without deceit and fraud in a hostile world. The world
continues to be the realm in which the dominating demonic powers are
still active,[41] although through Christ their lordship has been broken for
believers, and the existence of the church represents the victory of Christ
over the hostile powers. That the church participates in Christ's victory
over the hostile cosmic powers means that it lives under the imperative to
engage the world in a way that corresponds to the reality of the saving
event. That is to say: the church is called to live its life in a manner free
*from* the world in order to be free for service *to* the world, and implies the
demand that it put itself at the world's disposal because it has been called
to service. With the declaration that "all is yours," Paul includes the
cosmos as the Christian's property (1 Cor 3:22). This no more means a
call to theocracy and triumphalism than does the postpauline reflections
on the kingship of Christ (Col 1:13, 15ff). Neither is there any intention
of calling for an exploitation of the world, which would be a denial of
Christian responsibility and the love command. It is not a matter of
grounding an ecclesiastical claim to power over against the world but
rather that the relations of power have been reversed: it is no longer the
case that the world is powerful over against the believers but that believers
already participate in Christ's hidden victory over the worldly powers.
Here too the ὡς μή conceptuality (e.g. 1 Cor 7:31:... and those who deal
with the world as though they had no dealings with it. For the present form
of this world is passing away") testifies not only to the fundamental freedom from the world based on the fact that the world is passing away but
also to that freedom for the world exercised in Christian responsibility—
for the church's Lord is also the Cosmocrator. Even though the world does
not yet recognize this reality and will and must acknowledge it only at the
end of history (Phil 2:10–11), the church's unity with its Lord means that
it already participates in the lordship of Christ over the world.

## 2.   Faith and the Orders of the World

The concrete conduct of the church in the world and over against the
world may be illustrated by two particular texts.

---

[41]   Cf. Romans 8:38–39.

α) The Christian and the State (Rom 13:1–7)

Bammel, E. "Romans 13," E. Bammel and C. F. D. Moule (eds.). *Jesus and the Politics of His Day*. Cambridge: Cambridge University Press, 1984. 365–383.
Cullmann, O. *The State in the New Testament*. New York: Scribner, 1951.
Friedrich, J., Pöhlmann, W. and Stuhlmacher, P. "Zur historischen Situation und Intention von Röm 13,1–7," *ZThK* 73 (1976) 131–166.
Käsemann, E. "Principles of the Interpretation of Romans 13," E. Käsemann, *New Testament Questions of Today*. Philadelphia: Fortress, 1969, 196–216.
Käsemann, E. "Römer 13,1–7 in unserer Generation," *ZThK* 56 (1959) 316–376.
Pohle, L. *Die Christen und der Staat nach Röm 13. Eine typologische Untersuchung der neueren deutschsprachigen Schriftauslegung*. Mainz 1984.
Riekkinen, V. *Römer 13. Aufzeichnung und Weiterführung der exegetischen Diskussion*. AASF 23. Helsinki 1980.
Schrage, W. *Die Christen und der Staat nach dem Neuen Testament*. Gütersloh: Gerd Mohn, 1971.
Strobel, A. "Zum Verständnis von Röm 13," *ZNW* 47 (1956) 67–93.
Wilckens, U. "Römer 13,1–7," U. Wilckens. *Rechtfertigung als Freiheit. Paulusstudien*. Neukirchen-Vluyn: Neukirchener, 203–245.

In terms of its content, the section Romans 13:1–7 is composed of a unit set off from both the preceding and following sections of Romans. The overarching context is that of church parenesis. The beginning at 12:1–2 is characteristic of such parenesis: Paul challenges the church to demonstrate its eschatological existence in the concrete acts of everyday life. The obedience to earthly authorities here called for is accordingly a piece of Christian worship within the secularity of the world.[42]

The apostle commands that every one be subject to the ἐξουσίαι that are in power in their time and place (13:1). The understanding of the term ἐξουσίαι has become a much-discussed problem due to the thesis of O. Cullmann, according to which the expression is to be referred to both "the empirical state and the angelic powers" corresponding to Ephesians 3:10.[43] The earthly-political power is accordingly nothing else than the instrument of the angels, that is of the demonic powers that make use of the state for their purposes, even though under God's commission. These are the same cosmic powers that, according to Colossians and Ephesians, have been overcome by the cosmic Christ, so that they now exercise their office in the service of Christ. The power of the political authority accordingly has a christological foundation: Christ as the Cosmocrator both authorizes and limits the rights and requirements of the secular order, including the worldly political powers spoken of in Romans 13.

[42] Cf. E. Käsemann, "Römer 13,1–7 in unserer Generation" 374–376; cf. his "Principles of the Interpretation of Romans 13," *New Testament Questions of Today* (Philadelphia: Fortress Press, 1969) 196–216.
[43] O. Cullmann, *The State in the New Testament* (London: SCM Press Ltd., 1963) 62–66; 65.

Against such a christological grounding of this right, it is to be objected that the terminology of this section is that of the secular Greek administrative language.[44] From the point of view of the history of religions, the roots of this text do not lie in Christian tradition but in the Jewish synagogue. Hellenistic Jews probably spoke in a similar manner of the duties of Jews to the state.[45]

Romans 13 is not about a christological grounding of conformity to secular laws but about confirming that there is a given order in the world into which Christians must fit. Abstract propositions may not be derived from this. Paul is neither attempting to advocate a metaphysical doctrine of the state, nor does he intend to reflect on orders of creation and preservation; it is rather a matter of a concrete arrangement of God's that is realized in the secular authority and its claim.

Without intending to go into the details of this text, it is important here to state that Paul accepts the cultural conventions he has received but at the same time interprets them theologically. The governing "power" is a "servant of God;' it bears the sword at God's commission, in order to punish the evil and promote what is good (13:4). Christian faith is not identified with political-revolutionary enthusiasm. The attempt to conceive the kingdom of God in political terms and to establish it on earth must necessarily come to ruin along with the fanaticism in Münster. Faith is grounded in a transcendent reality and knows that it never can be identified with the being of this world even when it is filled with noble political ideals. Faith knows that it stands in diastasis (tension, separation) to the world and yet is called to service in and for the world as its daily worship of God.

The necessity of understanding its life in the world as worship to God is concretized according to Romans 13 in the call to obey secular authorities. Paul grounds this necessity in 13:5 with the words, "Therefore one must be subject, not only because of wrath but also because of conscience." The wrath of God that threatens the disobedient is manifested in the use of the sword by the secular authorities to punish evil. As this is the motivation for practicing obedience to the secular authorities, then this

---

44 Cf. A. Strobel, "Zum Verständnis von Röm 13," 90ff.
45 Cf. G. Stemberger, *Die römische Herrschaft im Urteil der Juden* (EdF 195. Darmstadt: Wissenschaftliche Buchgesellschaft, 1983) 107–108, 111 (Jewish "readiness to place themselves at the disposal of the Roman authorities" or the "willingness of the Jews to compromise"). G. Stemberger sees in this acknowledgment of Roman authority "even in the most difficult times ... [to be based on] theological foundations" (111). The Roman government was seen as God's punishment for Israel's unwillingness to serve God (107–108). This is expressed for example in the interpretation that Israel must not refuse to pay the Roman tax after it was unwilling to pay the smaller temple tax (107–108). Cf. also J. Maier, *Grundzüge der Geschichte des Judentums im Altertum* (Darmstadt: Wissenschaftliche Buchgesellschaft, 1981).

means that for the Christian the secular order is a binding command of God (cf. 13:4 θεοῦ γὰρ διάκονός ἐστιν). The second explanation says nothing different from this. Συνείδησις (13:5) points to the awareness of this demand. The fear of secular punishment and the knowledge of God's will both point to the one reality that the secular political order is binding for Christian faith.

The term συνείδησις appears fourteen times in the Pauline letters, three times in Romans and eleven times in the Corinthian letters.[46] The latter instance suggests that in the context of the debate Paul about eating food sacrificed to idols (1 Cor 8 and 10), Paul made use of the terminology already current in the Corinthian debate. In any case, he presupposes that the Corinthians already were familiar with the term. The word is documented relatively late in Greek literature, where it has the general meaning of "consciousness" (e.g. Democr 297) or also the more specific meaning of "conscience" (e.g. Pseudo-Lucian Amor 49). Paul gives no definition and can use the word in different senses in different contexts. Three perspectives may be distinguished:

1. Συνείδησις is attributed to *people who lived before Christ*. Thus in Romans 2:15, the "conscience" of Gentiles testifies with regard to those who live without the law and nonetheless know the law's demand that the work of the law is written in their hearts (cf. Rom 1:18ff). "Conscience" is accordingly a general human phenomenon that can be appealed to as an independent witness alongside the law and one's "thoughts" (cf. 2:16, with reference to the last judgment). "Conscience" thus does not mean the voice of God within human beings. The literal meaning of συνειδέναι should also be kept in mind ("knowledge about something"), so that "knowledge" and "conscience" are often not really to be distinguished. Paul's appeal, when his integrity has been challenged, has a universal orientation; he appeals to "the conscience of everyone" (2 Cor 4:2). Everyone, on the basis of the testimony of their own conscience, must acknowledge that the apostle and his message are in the right.

2. Paul can appeal to his *own conscience*. Alongside his testimony about himself he can call his conscience, as a separate witness, to testify in his behalf ("I am speaking the truth in Christ—I am not lying; my conscience confirms it by the Holy Spirit—" (Rom 9:1). Apparently an independent authority within human beings that expresses one's own accountability to oneself, it is not a "super-ego" and it is not the transcendent voice of God. Thus Paul by no means thinks of conscience in the modern liberal sense of subjective freedom of the individual. But it is still the case that the conscience has a function alongside the "I" of the apostle; it points to the grounding of Christian existence in something outside human potential, since the testimony of the conscience takes place "in the Holy Spirit, just as the apostle's speaking is not based on himself but happens "in Christ" (Rom 9:1).

On the same plane, Paul can cite his conscience as evidence for the sincerity of his life (2 Cor 1:12). Here too the conscience appears as something distinguishable from the person of the apostle himself, an authority that can present its own testimony and render its own decision—without abrogating the apostle's personal identity.

3. Finally, the word can refer to the conscience of the *Christian community* as a whole. In the Pauline understanding, the subordination of Christians to the political

[46] For bibliography, cf. M. Wolter, "Gewissen II. Neues Testament," TRE 13, 213–218. H.-J. Eckstein, *Der Begriff Syneidesis bei Paulus* (WUNT II 10. Tübingen: J. C. B. Mohr [Paul Siebeck], 1983).

power of the state is not only motivated by the threat of the eschatological-apocalyptic wrath of God but also "for the sake of conscience," i.e. on the basis of the general awareness of members of the Christian community that can be inferred from concrete facts. For example, the fact that church members are already paying taxes testifies to their awareness that they have a duty to the government authorities (Rom 13:5–6).

Paul shows that he can use the word in different senses during the debate about eating meat sacrificed to idols. Here a distinction is made between the attitude of those who possess knowledge, and others who have a "weak conscience" (1 Cor 8:7–13). In principle, Paul stands on the side of the pneumatics, for whom everything is permitted (though not everything is beneficial, 10:23) but he still calls for consideration of those who have a weak conscience. He is concerned to avoid offense and damaging the weak conscience of those who have scruples against accepting the practice of Christians who eat food sacrificed to idols. Accordingly the degree of weakness or strength is dependent on the degree of knowledge. As the authority charged with responsible conduct, it has a monitoring function. But it may not operate apart from the Christian ethic, the command of love and consideration for one's fellow human beings (cf. 1 Cor 10:23–11:1).[47] A firm concept that corresponds to a more elaborated Christian ethic is found in the deutero-Pauline Pastoral letters. Here the stereotyped expressions of "good conscience" (1 Tim 1:5, 19) or "pure conscience" (1 Tim 3:9; 2 Tim 1:3) have become predominate (cf. also Titus 1:15, corruption of conscience and mind).

The questions of whether there is a limit to the obedience to the state, and whether believers have a right to resist, are not raised by Paul. Conclusions can be drawn, however, from Paul's statement that the governing authority is "God's servant." The boundary is reached when the state no longer carries out the service to God with which it is charged, or when it refuses to do so. To be sure, the principle enunciated in Acts 5:29 ("We must obey God rather than any human authority") is not cited in either scope or content. Paul's intention is that the Christian community be subject to the Roman governing authority. This raises the question of the concrete situation addressed by Paul. Three possibilities present themselves:

1. Paul speaks to the situation in which the Roman church found itself as the result of the return of the Jews and Jewish Christians who had been driven out of Rome by Claudius. After Claudius' edict was annulled,[48]

---

47   Correctly also U. Schnelle, *The Human Condition* 97: "Conscience is thus a relational concept; it does not itself set norms but judges conformity to them."

48   Cf. Seutonius, *Life of Claudius* 25; Orosius, *historiae adversum paganos* VII 6.15 (which dates the expulsion of the Jews from Rome in the ninth regnal year of Claudius) = 49 C. E.). Dio Cassius LX 6.6 only reports a prohibition of assembly in the year 41. G. Luedemann construes the matter differently in favor of an early dating, by regarding the reports in Seutonius and Dio Cassius as referring to the same event in 41 C. E. (*Paul, Apostle to the Gentiles. Studies in Chronology* [Philadelphia: Fortress Press, 1984] 164–170; "Das Judenedikt des Claudius [Apg 18,2]," in C. Bussmann and W. Radl [eds.] *Der Treue Gottes trauen* [FS G. Schneider] (Freiburg: Herder, 1991] 289–298.) Cf. also F. F. Bruce, "Chronological Questions in the Acts of the Apostles," BJRL 68/2 (1986) 273–295.

those who had been expelled could return. The result would be the existence of two groups in the church: Jewish Christians and Gentile Christians. Paul's directive is addressed to this situation, instructing the returned Jewish Christians to conduct themselves in obedience to the Roman authorities, in order not to give them any occasion for a renewed attack on the Jewish and Jewish-Christian population.

2. Paul's stance is derived from the Jewish synagogue of the Diaspora. In contrast to Zealotism, this tradition adopted by Paul—with regard to its contents and to some extent even its language—was characterized by advocating obedience to the government authorities as a basic commandment. It is from this point of view that the generalizing "let every person be subject..." is to be understood.

3. Paul is on the way to Jerusalem; he sees in advance that his fate is to be persecution and imprisonment. While this was caused by his Jewish opponents, it was also actually carried out by the authorities of the Roman government. In this situation Paul resolved on being subject to Rome, since obedience to the governing authorities is a command established by God and binding on Christians. Summary: with regard to the secular government, it is not the right to resist but the duty to obey that is the task of Christian worship in the everydayness of the world.[49]

There is no necessity to consider these three possibilities of interpretation as mutually exclusive. The situation in which Romans was written is complex—especially since it can be reconstructed only in outline—but it is certainly the case that the goal of the letter was not to provide a "compendium christianae religionis." Paul's command to obey the secular government is intended concretely. Thus it has happened that in the history of the interpretation of this text that fairly often—as in the Third Reich—a suffering and persecuted church has put Paul's command to obey the government into practice to the very limit of even sacrificing their lives for the state, without being aware of the implied critical stance toward the state that also is present in Romans 13. Today it should need no particular justification to state that Paul's position cannot be applied without modifications within the framework of a democratic state, in which citizens understand themselves to be responsible participants in the government. But there is no doubt that the activity of political office holders of a democratic state can be understood as legitimated by God. They must give account to God for the way they have handled their responsibility. When these premises are assumed, Paul's instruction in Romans 13 can also claim our attention in both church and secular world.

---

[49] For details of the history of interpretation, cf. L. Pohle, *Christen und der Staat* 23–28 (who distinguishes four principal interpretations: theology of the orders of nature; concrete-charismatic, eschatological-realistic, and christocratic-political.)

β) Acceptance and Renunciation of the Legal System (1 Corinthians 6:1-11)

Dinkler, E. "Zum Problem der Ethik bei Paulus: Rechtsnahme und Rechtsverzicht," *ZThK* 49 (1952) 167–200; also in E. Dinkler. *Signum Crucis.* Tübingen: J. C. B. Mohr (Paul Siebeck), 1967. 204–240.

Fuller, R. H. "First Corinthians 6:1–11. An Exegetical Paper," *Ex auditu 2.* Kampen: Kok, 1986. 96–104.

Richardson, P. "Judgement in Sexual Matters in 1 Corinthians 6:1–11," *NT* 25 (1983) 37–58.

Vischer, L. *Die Auslegungsgeschichte von 1. Korinther 6,1–11. Rechtsverzicht und Schlichtung.* BGBE 1. Tübingen: J. C. B. Mohr (Paul Siebeck), 1955.

The context is concerned with a problem of Corinthian congregational life, responding to the question of how the church is to conduct itself when there are disputes among its members. Is it permitted to go to court with each other before pagan judges, or not? There were obviously cases in Corinth in which Christians had sought to settle disputes before pagan judges, including disputes in which the opponent was also a Christian. Paul's answer is that such disputes should not be taken into pagan courts but should be settled by the church itself, for the church, since it is the community of saints, will participate in the judgment of the world. This should exclude the possibility that they take their own disputes before pagan courts (6:2). The result should be not lawsuits but arbitration! (6:5!). Moreover, a fundamental principle should be that the Christian should rather suffer injustice than perpetrate injustice(6:7). While neither legal measures nor arbitration are forbidden in principle, both bring one close to actually doing injustice. Thus renunciation of one's rights is better than insisting on them by law or arbitration.

Here it is clear how the relation of faith to the world is regarded. A fundamental diastasis to the world is demanded. Christian existence calls for renunciation of worldly procedure and practice. This includes the basis of standing off from the world: Christians do not belong to the world, therefore they are not subject to inner-worldly conditions of existence. They did not find it necessary egoistically to claim the procedures of the world in order to promote their own cause. On the contrary, they are determined by *agape*. This works itself out in renunciation of one's own rights, and this means renouncing the claim on worldly procedures in order to promote oneself.

The difference in the stance toward the world in Romans 13 and that in 1 Corinthians 6 is easy to see. On the one hand stands the command to be obedient to the secular order, on the other side there is the demand to keep oneself free from the world and its legal procedures. The existence of Christians in the world cannot in principle be standardized and cannot be determined in advance once and for all. The Christian faith is fundamentally open to being expressed in a variety of different types of conduct.

Nonetheless, the common denominator that lies at the basis of both types of conduct can be recognized. The position of 1 Corinthians 6 is not abandoned in Romans 13. Precisely the "subjection," the renunciation of resistance, can be explained as an expression of Christian desecularization, of not allowing oneself to be determined by the world, of the "theologia crucis." In both cases, it is a matter of letting God be God. Without exception, the command of God in the world should be acknowledged as binding also for Christians. In both cases it is a matter of the concrete realization of what has happened for Christians who have been set free from the world for service to the world. The demand that is posed for Christians on the basis of the indicative is essentially the demand of love (cf. Rom 13:8–14), consideration for one's fellow human beings, even when the concrete shape of this demand remains the responsibility of the discerning and decision of the individual Christian. The demand of love does not tell us *what* is to be done in each case but rather *how* whatever is done must be done.

## c) Israel and the Church

Becker, J. *Paul: Apostle to the Gentiles*. Louisville: Westminster / John Knox, 1993.

Hahn, F. "Zum Verständnis von Röm 11,26a: '... und so wird ganz Israel gerettet werden'," M.D. Hooker-S.G. Wilson, eds. *Paul und Paulinism* (FS C. K. Barrett). London: SPCK, 1982, 221–236.

Horn, F. W. "Paulusforschung," F. W. Horn, ed. *Bilanz und Perspektiven gegenwärtiger Auslegung des Neuen Testaments*. BZNW 75. Berlin-New-York: W. de Gruyter, 1995. 30–59.

Hübner, H. *Gottes Ich und Israel. Zum Schriftgebrauch des Paulus in Römer 9–11*. FRLANT 136. Göttingen: Vandenhoeck & Ruprecht, 1984.

Lüdemann, G. *Paulus und das Judentum*. TEH 215. Munich: Kaiser, 1983.

Luz, U. *Das Geschichtsverständnis des Paulus*. BEvTh 49. Munich: Kaiser, 1968.

Müller, Chr. *Gottes Gerechtigkeit und Gottes Volk*. FRLANT 86. Göttingen: Vandenhoeck & Ruprecht, 1964.

Mussner, F. "'Ganz Israel wird gerettet werden' (Röm 11,26). Versuch einer Auslegung," *Kairos* 18 (1976) 241–255.

Mussner, F. "Gesetz—Abraham—Israel," *Kairos* 25 (1983) 200–222.

Niebuhr, K.-W. *Heidenapostel aus Israel. Die jüdische Identität des Paulus nach der Darstellung in seinen Briefen*. WUNT 62. Tübingen: J. C. B. Mohr (Paul Siebeck), 1992.

Sänger, D. *Die Verkündigung des Gekreuzigten und Israel. Studien zum Verhältnis von Kirche und Israel bei Paulus und im frühen Christentum*. WUNT 75. Tübingen: J. C. B. Mohr (Paul Siebeck), 1994.

Sänger, D. "Rettung der Heiden und Erwählung Israels. Einige vorläufige Erwägungen zu Röm 11,25–27," *KuD* 32 (1986) 99–119.

Schnelle, U. *Wandlungen im paulinischen Denken*. SBS 137. Stuttgart: Katholisches Bibelwerk, 1989. 77–87.

Strecker, G. "Das Christliche im jüdisch-christlichen Dialog," *LM* 35 (1993) 27–29.

Walter, N. "Zur Interpretation von Röm 9–11," *ZThK* 81 (1984) 172–195.

As has been shown above,[50] Paul grounds his theology on Jewish and Jewish Christian presuppositions but it is not to be understood as Jewish but as authentically Christian theology. For the relation of the apostle to Judaism, this would have to mean that Paul found himself in a clear discontinuity to Judaism. Thus he says in Philippians 3:7, "Yet whatever gains I had, these I have come to regard as loss because of Christ." The break with Judaism can hardly be expressed more radically. This statement stands in contrast to the widespread view that as an apostle Paul was carrying out a mission within the framework of salvation history and thus put his understanding of apostleship into practice only within a cohesive relationship with the people of Israel and its history.[51] In this view, there would be no discontinuity between Paul and his Jewish past, between the church and the synagogue, but a fundamental continuity. Paul would also stand in continuity with the earliest church's understanding of salvation history. There is, however, a clear hiatus: the Jewish Christianity of the earliest church understood itself to be in continuity with the particularistic message of Jesus and believed its mission had been directed first of all especially toward the Jewish people. The mission to the Gentiles was second both in time and in significance and was supposed to be carried out in agreement with the Jerusalem authorities. But Paul was sent to the Gentiles. Even if he—as portrayed in the Acts—[52] began his preaching in the Diaspora synagogues and was thoroughly familiar with the Jewish Christian schema "first to the Jews, then the Gentiles," as still echoed in Romans 2:10, his missionary experience and mission practice was in fact structured the other way: first to the Gentiles, then to the Jews (cf. Romans 11:25ff). Nevertheless, according to the statement of Romans 11, for Paul too the priority of Israel does not appear to be broken, so that the people of Israel have a special position in the history of salvation until the final goal of history is reached.

1. We first look back on the past of the people of Israel, as represented in Paul's understanding. Here it is to be noticed that the history of Israel in

---

[50]   See above A. I. a.

[51]   J. Munck, *Paul and the Salvation of Mankind* (London: SCM Press Ltd., 1959). Paul understands himself as "the instrument of an eschatological plan that comes from God" (41). Paul's preaching was "a sign that was to precede the messianic age" (40). Munck argues that the following plan for the history of salvation (taken from Rom 11) was behind Paul's theology: the "no" of the Jews was followed by the "yes" of the Gentiles (43). But the salvation of the Gentiles is not to be separated from the salvation of the Jews (43). The Gentile "yes" evokes the jealousy of the Jews, so that Israel too will be saved (43). Thus the "salvation of the Gentiles" and the "salvation of the Jews" are not "two isolated and mutually exclusive dimensions" (44). Accordingly Paul, whose preaching is part of this salvation-historical plan, can be seen as the precursor or the final prophet before the End, as in Jewish apocalypticism.

[52]   Cf. e.g. Acts 13:5, 14, 44; 14:1; 17:1–2, and elsewhere.

the Old Testament had the character of a promise; it points forward to its fulfillment in Christ. Thus Abraham is understood as the concretion of God's promise to Israel (Rom 4; Gal 3). He is a typological example of that faith that trusts in God's promise. In him justifying faith is manifested, the possibility of faith apart from works is set forth as the way of salvation but in such a way that the promissory character of faith is preserved: "in order that in Christ Jesus the blessing of Abraham might come to the Gentiles, ..." (Gal 3:14).

On the other side stands the history of Israel under the law. It is the epoch that manifests the lack of the reality of salvation, for while it is true enough that the Old Testament law is the revealed will of God to the Jewish people but (as stated in Rom 2:17ff) the Jews did not attain a righteousness that is valid before God by the law but they attempted to establish their own righteousness. Thus one cannot really speak of a "salvation history" in view of the past of the Jewish people but neither can one speak of an "'unsalvation' history,'" for Paul was not concerned to draw a continuous line from the past to the present, not even when he uses examples from history as understood and portrayed in the Old Testament, as happens for instance in 1 Corinthians 10. The history of Israel is rather a background on which Paul projects the statement that salvation is not attained through righteousness by works but that only righteousness by faith leads to salvation.

2. The line of thought in Romans 9–11 is different. This passage seems to deal with a problem of salvation history, namely the question of whether the saving offer made by God to Israel is still valid in light of the fact that the gospel has been rejected by Jews but accepted by Gentiles. In Romans 9–11 Paul answers this question in different ways.

(1) In *Romans 9:6–29* he ascertains that already in the Old Testament God's promise was not made to empirical Israel as a whole but only to a selection, since not all Abraham's descendents are really to be considered the children of Abraham (9:7). This is determined by God's gracious choice. The analogy of the potter appears in this context (9:20ff): God has the right to choose, just as the potter can shape his products according to his own will. God has the unlimited power to do what he has decided; God can predestine to salvation or to destruction. Paul is not here interested in metaphysical speculation about the essence of God, nor reflections on the theological topic of predestination, but wants rather to dismiss the question itself of the grounds for Israel's rejection. This question simply cannot be posed, just as little as the product of the potter's work can call the potter to account. God's dealing with the people of Israel is withdrawn from the realm of rational insight and remains hidden from human reasoning.

(2) In *Romans 9:30–10:21* the rejection of Israel is traced back to the guilt of the Jewish people. Israel has shown itself to be disobedient to the saving acts of God. Israel had the possibility of faith (10:18–19, Israel

heard the message!) but the word that generates faith found no response. Israel's rejection is the result of Israel's closing itself off to the message addressed to it.

The statements in Romans 9:6–29 and 9:30–10:21 are related to each other as divine predestination and human responsibility. The theocentric line of thought corresponds to an anthropological line of thought: the people for whom God acts are the same people who must act responsibly before God. Here Paul gives—obviously as the result of discussions within his own school—two different answers to the salvation-historical question. That they are not congruent with each other makes clear that for Paul the problem of salvation history is not really solvable. It will be answered in the apocalyptic future. Hope is directed to this future, a hope that is not grounded on rational bases.

(3) *Romans 11:1–36.* The mystery of Israel's history consists in the fact that the rejection is neither complete nor final. This is explained in the subsections of this chapter: Israel's rejection is not complete, for a remnant (of Jewish Christians!) shows by its acceptance of the gospel that it belongs to the elect (11:1–10). Moreover, Israel's rejection is not final. The revelation of this mystery of history declares that after the full number of Gentiles has come in, the people of Israel will also be saved (11:11–16, 25–32). An excursus is inserted into this section, a warning to Gentile Christians not to exalt themselves so that they look down on others, since they are a branch that has been grafted into an olive tree. Their election is due entirely to the grace of God (11:17–24).

The question is disputed, especially in the context of Christian-Jewish dialogue, whether in Romans 11:25ff Paul advocates a "special way" of salvation for the Jews that corresponds to the idea of a "permanent election" of the Jewish people. It is supposed that this idea could make Christian-Jewish dialogue easier. When the details of this section are examined, a whole series of questions is raised: What is the significance of the introductory passage 9:1–5 for understanding the larger section, including 11:25ff? What does the expression "all Israel" mean? How is this "salvation" to be thought of, in the context of the Pauline apocalyptic thought world as a whole?

For the understanding of this section, the introductory verses 9:1ff should not be overvalued. Paul addresses a concrete situation: the expectation of his return to Jerusalem and the issue of how he will be received there by the Jewish Christian church and its leadership, and his visit to Rome, where he will meet both Jewish and Gentile Christians. Consideration of these fellow Christians influenced by Judaism who were apparently distressed by the critical stance toward the law in his message occasioned Paul to introduce his discussion with a 'captatio benevolentiae' to gain the good will of his hearer/readers in advance, and to acknowledge the "saving gifts" from God that guarantee to empirical Israel their special position as chosen by God in relation to other peoples. Romans 9:1ff thus reflects the "assets" that have constituted the special quality of the Jewish people in its past history. Among these are the "promises" (9:4 ἐπαγγελίαι) made to the generations in the Old Testament period and which were fulfilled to the fathers and mothers of the faith (9:7–13; cf. 4:13). Here it already becomes clear that God's unbreakable promise is identical with the word that justifies by grace (cf. 9:12, "not by works but by his call"). The whole section Romans 9–11 cannot be interpreted apart from the preceding context of Romans 1–8, which presents in detail "justification apart from the works of the law, only on the basis of divine grace."

It should not be disputed, however, that the section 11:25ff plays a special role within the structure of Pauline theology. While in other passages Paul can apply the traditional term Ἰσραήλ to the church as the spiritual people of God (Gal 6:16), it is not to be denied that in this text it is exclusively the empirical Jewish people that is meant by "Israel."[53] This is the addressee of the threat of the Old Testament prophet Isaiah (9:27; 10:21); it was this people that was certified that, while it had striven after the "righteousness based on law" but it had not attained this law (v. l. "law of righteousness") (9:31). It was this people that was suspect of not understanding (10:19), that was "disobedient" and had not been reached by God's pleas (10:21; 11:2). These texts suggest that also the expression πᾶς Ἰσραήλ refers to empirical Israel, so that salvation is promised to this Israel as a whole, after the "full number of the Gentiles has come in" (11:25–26). To be sure, in this context Paul distinguishes between unconverted and converted Jews. While the former are subject to "hardening" (πώρωσις), the latter are explicitly distinguished from them. They belong to the "remnant" (λεῖμμα), on the basis of "election" (ἐκλογή) and are counted among the spiritual people of God (11:5). They are the "chosen" who have received the promised salvation not on the basis of works but by grace (11:6–7). There is no doubt that the idea of election must be interpreted in connection with the concept of a "holy remnant," and that this must be done in terms of a christocentric theology of justification.[54] This approach forbids the understanding of Romans 9–11 as promising a "permanent election" to empirical Israel as though a special way of salvation were granted to the Jewish people apart from the Christ event.[55] Neither can this be done by appealing to the validity of the promises made to Israel (we have seen that the term ἐπαγγελίαι cannot be abstracted from its christocentric content and its location within the Pauline doctrine of justification [9:8–9]). Likewise, the idea of a "permanent election" cannot be based on the "faithfulness of God," since it is the faithfulness of the sovereign Creator who disposes of his creation as he will and cannot be called to account at the court of human reason. The intention of the statement that God has not rejected his people (11:1–2) is not to establish a static consciousness of election but is grounded in the fact that a remnant of Israel has opened itself to the gospel (11:4ff).

In the light of what has been said above, it appears that the content of the mystery revealed by Paul cannot be understood as the authentic fruit of Pauline theology. It is obviously a concession born of the pressure of the political situation within the church according to which "all Israel will be saved" (11:26). Here it is clear that it is

---

53  Thus eleven times in Romans 9–11; cf. F. Mussner, "'Ganz Israel wird gerettet werden'" 241.

54  Differently Mussner, "'Ganz Israel wird gerettet werden'" 241–242.

55  The thesis of a "special way" has been interpreted differently; e.g. F. Mussner, "Gesetz—Abraham—Israel" 208: "There is a special way but it does not bypass Christ and his redemptive work." See also M. Theobald, "Bleibendes Nebeneinander der beiden Gotteszeugen Israel und Ekklesia," in *Die überströmende Gnade. Studien zu einem paulinischen Motivfeld* (fzb 22. Würzburg: Herder, 1982) 165. Differently B. Klappert, "Traktat für Israel (Röm 9–11)" in M. Stöhr, ed. *Jüdische Existenz und die Erneuerung der christlichen Theologie* (Münster, 1981) 58–137, according to whom Israel's special way is grounded in the fact that the election of Israel is subordinated to the gospel (85–86).

not only spiritual Israel, nor the remnant of empirical Israel but πᾶς Ἰσραήλ comprises Jews that have become Christians and Jews that have not. All are promised the eschatological σωτηρία[56] that through Christ will also include the Gentiles. How this is to happen, Paul does not explain. Whether a comprehensive "final preaching of the gospel" will lead to this goal,[57] is not said, just as it is not said whether and in what way conversion and faith are presupposed in Israel.[58] In any case, it cannot be affirmed that there is a special way of salvation apart from the Christ event. The decisive thing for Paul and his readers is that there is hope for a future in which there will be one people of God comprised of all peoples.

Just as is the case elsewhere, so also here Paul does not present a developed outline of the history of salvation. He is not concerned to present a demonstration of the divine saving work in history. It is rather the case that God's dealings with humanity remain hidden. The apostle has no intention of setting forth a systematic view of history divided into periods in which God acts by specific arrangements. Corresponding to the fact that the concept of election belongs to the Jews awareness of themselves as a particular nation, Paul speaks here as a native Jew for whom the national horizon of Judaism is taken for granted. While at the time of his conversion the bond between nation and religion was dissolved for him, in regard to the content of his faith and its manner of expression he is no longer a Jew but a Christian, just as he of course remained a Jew in terms of his national identity. From this point of view the Pauline expectation of the eschatological homecoming of Israel (Rom 11:25ff) remains a difficult hermeneutical problem for the Christian church. To be sure, Paul's statement has again and again been regarded as the authentically Christian standpoint of the problem of Israel. The prerogative of the Jewish people, which continues into the distant future, appears to be expressed here as something binding for Christian doctrine in general.

However, it must not be overlooked that in his earlier phase Paul himself advocated a different view. On the basis of his negative experience on the mission field he reached an unambiguous judgment that his own people were rejected to the extent that they hardened themselves in unbelief and persecuted the Christian community (1 Thess 2:16, "Thus they have constantly been filling up the measure of their sins; but God's wrath has overtaken them at last"). One cannot here be satisfied by saying only that Paul's statements are conditioned by the situation and bound to a particular time. They cannot be interpreted in an absolute sense as time-bound but they must be interpreted in terms of their relative connection to each other—cf. for example the different conceptions in 1 Thessalonians

---

[56]  Even if Paul is not concerned in general "from the very beginning with the σωτηρία of Israel," but his preaching is directed to both Jews and Gentiles, it is still true that in Romans 9–11 "σωτηρία ... [means] nothing else than the eschatological salvation of Israel" (F. Mussner, "'Ganz Israel wird gerettet werden'" 246–247).

[57]  So J. Becker, *Paul* 472.

[58]  So F. Hahn, "Zum Verständnis" 229–230.

2:16 and 2 Corinthians 3, by comparing which one can see a "development" in Paul's thought. If Romans 11:25–26 were to be considered the absolute conclusion of Paul's developing view, there would have to be indications that this is the goal of his theological development. In that case this passage would pose a problem for the unity of the New Testament. Alongside the Pauline assessment stands the theology of the Synoptic Gospels that not only make the Jewish people responsible for the death of Jesus but also leads to the statement that the election of Israel was valid up to the time of Jesus' death, but not after that; from the time of Jesus' death and resurrection on the priority of Israel is annulled and another people, the church of Jews and Gentiles, has taken the place of Israel and dissolved its special claim to be the people of God (cf. Matt 21:43; 27:25). These mutually exclusive answers symbolize two different kinds of interpretation that have led to divergent consequences for the problem of Israel in the history of Christian theology. An assessment of the matter in the sense of Romans 11:25ff has led to a philo-Semitic way of dealing with the issue that expects more from the Jewish people than is realistically to be expected of Jewish self-understanding. An assessment of the matter in the sense of the Synoptic Gospels has led to an anti-Semitism that has given a Christian seal to anti-Jewish feelings of different types and motives. A Christian assessment of the people of Israel will therefore have to proceed on the basis that according to New Testament understanding the Christ event is the turning point of history, that the word of the gospel calls for faith from every person without distinction of their national or religious background. When Paul attempts to resolve the issue that was an existential problem for him within the framework of an apocalyptic schedule and thus seeks to solve it by means of speculations about salvation history, this is a stepping over the boundaries of his own theology of justification, and is to be judged critically on this very basis.

# V. The Future of the Free

Baumgarten, J. *Paulus und die Apokalyptik*. WMANT 44. Neukirchen-Vluyn: Neukirchener, 1975.
Becker, J. *Auferstehung der Toten im Urchristentum*. SBS 82. Stuttgart: Katholisches Bibelwerk, 1976.
Beker, J. C. *Paul's Apocalyptic Gospel*. Philadelphia: Westminister, 1984[2].
Hoffmann, P. *Die Toten in Christus. Eine religionsgeschichtliche und exegetische Untersuchung zur paulinischen Eschatologie*. NTA NF 2. Münster: Aschendorff, 1978[3].
Hunzinger, C. H. "Die Hoffnung angesichts des Todes im Wandel der paulinischen Aussagen," B. Lohse und H. P. Schmidt, eds. *Leben angesichts des Todes, FS H. Thielicke*. Tübingen: J. C. B. Mohr (Paul Siebeck), 1968. 69–88.

Käsemann, E. "The Beginnings of Christian Theology," E. Käsemann. *New Testament Questions of Today*. Philadelphia: Fortress, 1969, 108–137.

Käsemann, E. "On the Subject of Primitive Christian Apocalyptic," E. Käsemann, *New Testament Questions of Today*. Philadelphia: Fortress, 1969, 108–137.

Klein, G. "Eschatologie IV. Neues Testament," *TRE* 10 (1982) 270–299.

Nebe, G. *'Hoffnung' bei Paulus. Elpis und ihre Synonyme im Zusammenhang der Eschatologie.* StUNT 16. Göttingen 1983.

Schade, H. H. *Apokalyptische Christologie bei Paulus.* GTA 18. Göttingen: Vandenhoeck & Ruprecht, 1984².

Schnelle, U. *Wandlungen im paulinischen Denken.* SBS 137. Stuttgart: Katholisches Bibelwerk, 1989. 37–48.

Vielhauer, Ph. and Strecker, G. "Apocalypses and Related Subjects. Apocalyptic in Early Christianity," W. Schneemelcher, ed. *New Testament Apocrypha* II. Louisville: Westminster / John Knox, 1989, 542–602.

Weder, H. "Hoffnung II. Neues Testament," *TRE* 15 (1986) 484–491.

Wiefel, W. "Die Hauptrichtung des Wandels im eschatologischen Denken des Paulus," *ThZ* 30 (1974) 65–81.

The question of whether or not Paul was an apocalyptist (E. Käsemann), i.e. whether he developed the future perspective of his theology in the thought world of apocalypticism, is essentially a matter of definition. If one understands the term "apocalyptic" in a literary sense, the question must be answered in the negative, since the apostle never wrote an apocalypse in the same category of the Jewish documents 1 Enoch, 2 Baruch, 4 Ezra, or the Christian Revelation of John.[1] The essential structural indications of apocalyptic as a literary category are: pseudonymity, vision reports, surveys of history in the form of prophecies. Woven into such literature are such specific formal elements as songs and prayers. While such formal elements are practically lacking altogether in the Pauline letters, characteristic items of apocalyptic content and themes such as the doctrine of two ages are in fact presupposed. The concept of the coming aeon is interpreted in personal terms; it deals with the coming one, the judge of the world. This means the parousia of Christ, who grants believers access to the heavenly world (1 Cor 15:23ff). There is no portrayal of the joys of the future world. Apocalyptic expressions are met only allusively, in code-like expressions that often are a part of the tradition Paul has received: βασιλεία τοῦ θεοῦ (Rom 14:17; 1 Cor 6:9–10; 15:50; Gal 5:21; 1 Thess 2:12); βῆμα τοῦ θεοῦ (Rom 14:10) or βῆμα τοῦ Χριστοῦ (2 Cor 5:10).[2] The futuristic-eschatological orientation is underscored by the frequent use of ἐλπίς (Rom 8:20, 24; 12:12; 15:4, 13; Gal 5:5). A more concrete point of reference is the resurrection of the dead. A distinction is to be made between the resurrection of believers at the return of Christ (1 Thess 4:16–

---

[1]   Cf. the apocalyptic documents in P. Riessler, *Altjüdisches Schrifttum ausserhalb der Bibel* (Darmstadt: Wissenschaftliche Buchgesellschaft, 1966²) and W. G. Kümmel and H. Lichtenberger (eds.) JSHRZ I-IV (Gütersloh: Gerd Mohn, 1973ff). For standard English translations, see James H. Charlesworth, ed. *The Old Testament Pseudepigrapha*, 2 vols. (Garden City, NY: Doubleday & Co., Inc., 1983, 1985).

17; 1 Cor 15:23) and the general resurrection of the dead, of which Paul speaks only indirectly at the most (1 Cor 15:24–27; Phil 3:21).

The universal presupposition of Paul's theology is the apocalyptic expectation of the near eschaton. Paul lives in the hope that the parousia of the Lord will take place soon. In one of his latest letters he still declares that "the Lord is near" (Phil 4:5 ὁ κύριος ἐγγύς). Clear traces of this near-expectation are found in Romans 13:11–12 ("Besides this, you know what time it is, how it is now the moment for you to wake from sleep. For salvation is nearer to us now than when we became believers; the night is far gone, the day is near") or 1 Corinthians 7:29 ("the appointed time has grown short") and in the cry heard in the worship of the earliest churches, "Marana tha" (1 Cor 16:22). The earliest extant Pauline letter, 1 Thessalonians, exhibits both the acute expectation of the nearness of the parousia and the problematic associated with this belief, as an awareness that the parousia would be delayed gradually dawned.

That Paul awaited the Kyrios as the coming eschatological ruler who will bring both judgment and salvation (cf. Phil 2:11; 1 Cor 15:23) presents him as a representative of a widespread Christian tradition. Already John the Baptist had understood his message as pointing to the one who is to come (Mark 1:7par), and Jesus is to be located in the same sphere when he, like John, appears as an eschatological prophet and announces the soon coming of the kingdom of God (Mark 1:14–15; Matt 12:28). The post-Easter church connected its message of the saving significance of Jesus' cross and resurrection with the expectation of the parousia, identifying Jesus as the risen and returning Son of Man (1 Thess 1:9–10; Mark 13:24ffpar; Luke 17:20par).

The awareness that the parousia was going to be delayed and that the original expectation of its nearness could not be maintained played an essential role in the development of early Christian theology—as elaborated by A. Schweitzer and his disciple M. Werner.[3] In their view, the "thoroughgoing eschatology" of earliest Christianity was replaced by the formation of the dogma of a church that was making itself into an institution. Paul stands at the beginning of this development, since his letters already indicate the first signs of an awareness of the delay of the parousia. A line can be drawn here that indicates the different solutions to what became an increasing problem, as time continued on and on and the parousia did not occur.

---

2   For the prepauline apocalyptic conceptuality, cf. also παρουσία (1 Thess 2:19); ἡμέρα (τοῦ) κυρίου, and others (1 Thess 5:2; 1 Cor 1:8), since "God's judgment" (Rom 2:2 κρίμα τοῦ θεοῦ) is expected at the end, this day will be a "day of wrath, when God's righteous judgment will be revealed" (Rom 2:5); on the other hand, the heavenly "glory" (δόξα) is promised to the believing community (Rom 8:18; 2 Cor 4:17).

3   M. Werner, *Die Entstehung des christlichen Dogmas* (Bern-Tübingen, 1953²) 105–125; cf. already A. Schweitzer, *Mysticism* 334–375.

(1) *1 Thessalonians 4:13–17.* In his earliest extant letter Paul states the question that had been raised in the church at Thessalonica he had founded: "What happens to Christians who have died before the Lord's parousia? Is there no hope for them?" This question presupposes that Paul's preaching that had founded the church had spoken of the near coming of the Lord but obviously had only made minimal reference to the future resurrection, if he had included it at all. Paul attempts to address the problem of the dawning awareness of the delay of the parousia with a "word of the Lord" (λόγος κυρίου 4:15; 16–17). This word of the Lord from the (Christian) apocalyptic tradition originally seems to have had the following wording:

| | |
|---|---|
| ¹⁶ ὅτι αὐτὸς ὁ κύριος ἐν κελεύσματι | ¹⁶ For the Lord himself, with a cry of command |
| ἐν φωνῇ ἀρχαγγέλου | with the archangel's call |
| καὶ ἐν σάλπιγγι θεοῦ | and with the sound of God's trumpet |
| καταβήσεται ἀπ᾽ οὐρανοῦ | will descend from heaven |
| ¹⁷ καὶ οἱ νεκροὶ … ἀναστήσονται | ¹⁷ and the dead … will rise first |
| ἁρπαγησόμεθα ἐν νεφέλαις | (and) will be caught up in the clouds |
| εἰς ἀπάντησιν τοῦ κυρίου εἰς ἀέρα· | to meet the Lord in the air |

Paul applied this "word of the Lord" from the apocalyptic tradition of Jewish Christianity to the situation of the church and to himself, in the process making some changes in its content. In the present context his message is that (a) there will be a resurrection of Christians who have died at the beginning of the parousia of the Kyrios, followed by (b) all Christians will be taken up together to meet the returning Lord. The hope for the eschatological reunion with the Lord Christ, a hope portrayed with strong apocalyptic coloration drawn from the tradition, is a hope that unites all Christians, so that it is immaterial whether they have died before the parousia or will still be alive then. Paul has no doubt that he will be among those still living at the coming of the Lord; Paul himself holds fast to the near expectation without modification, even if the time of the parousia is unknown (cf. 1 Thess 5:1–2).

(2) *1 Corinthians 15.* In distinction from 1 Thessalonians 4, where Paul applies the λόγος κυρίου to a given situation, in 1 Corinthians 15 Paul presents a rational line of argument in which there is systematic reflection on the future destiny of believing Christians. In contrast to the Corinthian pneumatics, who affirm the resurrection of Jesus but not the future resurrection of the dead, Paul attempts to argue not only for the "thatness" (*das Dass*) of the future resurrection but also for how it can be thought of (*das Wie*). The chapter may be outlined as follows:

1. Vv. 1–11 The tradition (the kerygma of the cross and resurrection of Jesus Christ, the witnesses)

2. Vv. 12–19 The actuality of the resurrection (that Christ was raised is the basis of the hope in the future resurrection)

3. Vv. 20–28 The order of the resurrection (Adam/Christ; the order of the eschatological events: Christ, resurrection of Christians at the parousia, the giving over of the kingdom of Christ to the Father)

4. Vv. 29–34 Further supporting arguments (v. 29: vicarious baptism; the sufferings of the apostle testify to his hope in the resurrection)

5. Vv. 35–58 The "how" of the resurrection (psychical and spiritual body; v. 51b: "We will not all die but we will all be changed").

The extensive rational argument focuses on specific points:

1. Adam/Christ typology (vv. 20ff: Adam as the author of death, with whom death entered the world; Christ the author of life; he is the first to be raised from the dead and is thereby an anticipation of the End).

2. The sequence of the eschatological drama (vv. 23–28).

3. A more precise description of the destiny of the living (in comparison with 1 Thess 4, the new idea in vv. 51–52 is the "change" of the living as well as the dead). The future existence is not without a σῶμα but the body will not be a σαρκικόν or ψυχικόν σῶμα but a σῶμα πνευματικόν (15:46). In agreement with 1 Thessalonians 4, Paul still counts himself among those Christians who will be alive at the parousia. For him personally the expectation of the near end is still unbroken, but it is still informative to compare 1 Thessalonians 4:17 ("Then we who are alive, who are left, will be caught up in the clouds together with them to meet the Lord in the air") and 1 Corinthians 15:51 ("we will not all die"). The way v. 51 is expressed suggests the possibility that some, perhaps many, will die before the parousia. In any case, however, in 1 Corinthians 15 too the equality of living and dead at the parousia is guaranteed.

3. *2 Corinthians 5:1–10.* According to v. 1 the Christian hope is that after the dissolution of the earthly tent in which we live, Christian believers will receive a heavenly house. Here statements about present reality are connected with statements about eschatological-future reality. Hellenistic-syncretistic influence is not to be missed in this formulation. Paul obviously does not exclude the possibility that he himself might die before the parousia; the goal of the future expectation is the judgment seat of Christ (5:10). Alongside this apocalyptic expectation, there appears the hope of having a house ("already now") with God (5:1). This presupposes that before the parousia one is "un-clothed" and "re-clothed" (5:3–4); it means separation from the earthly body and the conferral of a new bodily existence. As the "pledge" or "down payment" the Spirit guarantees the continuity between present and future (5:5). Paul reckons with the possibility that he himself might die before the parousia, which would mean a "being at home with the Lord" (5:8 ἐνδημῆσαι πρὸς τὸν κύριον). The relaxation of the expectation of the expectation of the near parousia does not mean the end of eschatological hope.

This passage already raises the question of the relation of the resurrection of the dead to the immediate reunion with the Lord after death. The influence of differing conceptual patterns can be discerned (on the one side, the apocalyptic expectation, on the other side, the ἐν Χριστῷ concept; cf. 1 Thess 4:16; 1 Cor 15:18). The expectation of an eschatological resurrection of the dead is more clearly expressed in 1 Corinthians 6:14; it is parallel to and derived from Jesus' resurrection.[4] Even more clearly 2 Corinthians 4:14 expresses the connection between the hope of the resurrection with the expectation of the parousia. Cf. also Philippians 3:10–11 (the resurrection as the goal of Paul's own hope). Both 1 Corinthians 6:14 and 2 Corinthians 4:14 document the theologoumenon of the hope of the resurrection of believers in general, without reflecting on Paul's own future. In contrast, Philippians 3:11 again gives Paul's own expectation with regard to himself but here too the general expectation stands in the foreground. The case is different in Romans 8:10–11, a passage that is to be understood as the extension of Galatians 2:20 (the life of Christ in one as overcoming the σάρξ), and can be interpreted from a double point of view: (a) the Spirit of God will be effective in your bodies (so Gal 2:20), or (b) God will raise you up through his Spirit (= hope in the resurrection for believers).

(4) *Romans 8:16–30.* The eighth chapter of Romans deals with "life in the Spirit." The Spirit is the ἀπαρχή (8:23) and the ἀρραβών (2 Cor 1:22), a pledge or "down payment" on the End. Its effectiveness is affirmed as something at work in the present (8:16–17). The Spirit is the community's help and support, encouraging us "that we are God's children." It follows from this that being accepted as children of God means acknowledgment as heirs.

The future eschatological orientation is underscored in 8:18–25. The Christian hope is motivated by suffering; κτίσις is the created world including all the forms of life in nature, not only the world of human beings. Like the children of God, the whole creation is characterized by "eager longing" (ἀποκαραδοκία) and awaits the future revelation, so that the present suffering of nature is the exact counterpart to the future glory (8:21). No less is true of the children of God, who are saved "in hope" (8:24). This ἐλπίς is the defining characteristic of those who believe.

8:26–27. The Spirit itself intercedes for believers in their weakness. The Spirit is present in the stammering prayer of the church that testify to the weakness of the Christian community. It thus becomes clear that such times belong to the weakness of this world and point to the fulfillment and redemption of the future world.

8:28–30. God's prior decision is the basis of the Christian hope, for it works in those who love God for their good. This is indicated by the picture of the Son who is the πρωτότοκος of many brothers and sisters (8:29a), who has preceded us on this way. His church knows itself to be determined by what is expressed in this inferential chain: foreknown—predestined (8:29) —called—justified—glorified (8:30). The final goal is δόξα; but this is also

---

4     Is 1 Corinthians 6:14 a gloss? Cf. U. Schnelle, "1 Kor 6,14—eine nachpaulinische Glosse," *NT* 25 (1983) 217–219.

already present in the Spirit. In all this there is no mention of the time of the parousia but it is clear that the expectation of the parousia is a presupposition that can be assumed.

(5) *Philippians 1:23.* Here Paul (presumably in a Roman prison) reckons with his death before the parousia. He will be reunited with Christ immediately after his death. An intermediate state after death is not presupposed,[5] but a direct reunification with the Lord. Apparently σὺν Χριστῷ (1:23) corresponds to the σὺν κυρίῳ (an obvious allusion to 1 Thess 4:17). The latter text, however, expresses the goal of the apocalyptic hope, the expectation of the near parousia; by contrast here the goal is the resurrection of the dead. Nonetheless, not even in Philippians does Paul abandon his earlier standpoint of near expectation (cf. 4:5). The hope in the resurrection also remains (Phil 3:10–11, ... "becoming like him in his death, if somehow I may attain the resurrection from the dead;" this refers not to a general resurrection of the dead but to the resurrection of believers; so also 1 Cor 15:23). With regard to himself, however, Paul reckons with his own death in the near future and his being with Christ directly thereafter.[6] Obviously the apostle expects, in accord with the Jewish idea of Paradise, that he will be received into the future residence of the righteous. This is a singular statement, found only here in one of the apostle's last letters. Although Paul can elsewhere speak of the state of affairs in the heavenly world after death (2 Cor 5:1), only here does he apply it concretely in view of his own death. In prior statements the predominant view was the apocalyptic, future-eschatological concept, the hope for meeting the Lord at his parousia.

In view of the relation of his own destiny to the parousia Paul's letters thus present more than one way of conceiving the future life: from an acute expectation of the parousia in the near future to a modification of this expectation in favor of the hope of being with Christ immediately after death. All the same, the expectation of the near parousia was not given up. That the parousia is to happen in the near future is a thesis to which Paul held firm from the beginning of his apostolic ministry until its end.

---

5   Contra W. Michaelis, *Der Brief des Paulus an die Philipper* (HThK 11) (Leipzig, 1935) 26–27; cf. on this text W. Schenk, *Die Philipperbriefe des Paulus* (Stuttgart: Kohlhammer, 1984) 154ff.

6   P. Hoffmann, *Die Toten in Christus* 321ff, esp. 327, disputes the thesis that there was a development in Paul's eschatological views between 1 Thessalonians 4 and Philippians 1:23. Philippians 1:23 belongs to Letter B, written in Ephesus about 54/55, so that the chronology of the eschatological passages would be: 1 Thessalonians 4—Philippians 1:23—1 Corinthians 15—2 Corinthians 5. Of course it is to be objected to this reconstruction that it strains the Acts account of Paul's stay in Ephesus. We know nothing of an imprisonment of Paul in Ephesus. In addition, the division of Philippians into fragments is problematic.

The future of the Christ who is coming, grounded in the Easter experience of the first disciples of Jesus, is the abiding goal of early Christian thought and life. For Paul, this is what motivates both that and how the presence of the eschatological time is apprehended. The dialectic of existence in faith, the "already" and "not yet" of salvation, has its real basis here. It is thus not of essential importance for the apostle whether such a future will be realized soon or whether it will be a longer period of time before Christ comes, so that in place of the expectation of the near parousia could be replaced by the expectation of meeting Christ immediately after death. Apocalyptic concepts and pictures could change—the decisive thing for the apostle and for earliest Christianity is that the Christian hope bears and holds on to this eschatological goal located in the transcendent world beyond time and space and provides the Christian consciousness of freedom that dimension that makes it Christian.

# B.
# Early Christian Tradition to the Composition of the Gospels

## I. The Proclamation of the Coming One—John the Baptist

Backhaus, K. *Die "Jüngerkreise" des Täufers Johannes. Eine Studie zu den religions-geschichtlichen Ursprüngen des Christentums.* PaThSt 19. Paderborn-Munich-Zürich-Wien: Schöningh, 1991.

Becker, J. *Johannes der Täufer und Jesus von Nazareth.* BSt 63. Neukirchen-Vluyn: Neukirchener, 1972.

Bultmann, R. *The Gospel of John.* Philadelphia: Westminster, 1971.

Bultmann, R. "Die Bedeutung der neuerschlossenen mandäischen und manichäischen Quellen für das Verständnis des Johannesevangeliums," in R. Bultmann. *Exegetica.* Tübingen: J. C. B. Mohr (Paul Siebeck), 1967, 55–104 (= First published in *ZNW* 24 [1925] 100–146).

Dibelius, M. "Jungfrauensohn und Krippenkind. Untersuchungen zur Geburtsgeschichte Jesu im Lukas-Evangelium," in M. Dibelius. *Botschaft und Geschichte. GAufs. Bd. 1: Zur Evangelienforschung.* G. Bornkamm and H. Kraft, eds. Tübingen: J. C. B. Mohr (Paul Siebeck), 1953, 1–78 (= First published in SHAW. PHK 4. Heidelberg, 1932).

Dibelius, M. *Die urchristliche Überlieferung von Johannes dem Täufer.* FRLANT 15. Göttingen: Vandenhoeck & Ruprecht, 1911.

Dobbeler, S. von *Das Gericht und das Erbarmen Gottes.* BBB 70. Bonn: Hanstein, 1988.

Ernst, J. *Johannes der Täufer, Interpretation—Geschichte—Wirkungsgeschichte.* BZNW 53. Berlin: W. de Gruyter, 1989.

Flusser, D. *Johannes der Täufer.* Leiden: E. J. Brill, 1963.

Hollenbach, P. "Social Aspects of John the Baptizer's Preaching Mission in the Context of Palestinian Judaism," ANRW II 19.1. Berlin-New York: W. de Gruyter, 1979, 850–875.

Hughes, J. H. "John the Baptist: The Forerunner of God Himself," *NT* 14 (1972) 191–218.

Kundsin, K. *Topologische Überlieferungsstoffe im Johannes-Evangelium.* FRLANT 22. Göttingen: Vandenhoeck & Ruprecht, 1925.

Lang, F. "Erwägungen zur eschatologischen Verkündigung Johannes des Täufers," in G. Strecker, ed. *Jesus Christus in Historie und Theologie* (FS H. Conzelmann). Göttingen: Vandenhoeck & Ruprecht, 1975, 459–473.

Laufen, R. *Die Doppelüberlieferungen der Logienquelle und des Markusevangeliums.* BBB 54. Königstein-Bonn: Hanstein, 1980.

Lindeskog, G. *Johannes der Täufer. Einige Randbemerkungen zum heutigen Stand der Forschung.* ASTI 12. Leiden: E. J. Brill, 1983, 55–83.

Lohmeyer, E. *Das Urchristentum, Vol. 1., Johannes der Täufer.* Göttingen: Vandenhoeck & Ruprecht, 1932.

Manson, T. W. *The Sayings of Jesus as recorded in the Gospels according to St. Matthew and St. Luke arranged with Introduction and Commentary.* London: SCM, 1949.

Rengstorf, K.H. "'Ιορδάνης," *TDNT* VI 608–623.

Sahlin, H. *Studien zum dritten Kapitel des Lukasevangeliums.* UUA 2. Uppsala: Lundequistska Bokhandeln, 1949.

Schenk, W. "Gefangenschaft und Tod des Täufers. Erwägungen zur Chronologie und ihren Konsequenzen," *NTS* 29 (1983) 453–483.

Schlatter, A. *Johannes der Täufer,* W. Michaelis, ed. Basel: Friedrich Reinhardt AG, 1956.

Schmithals, W. *Das Evangelium nach Lukas.* ZBK.NT 3.1. Zürich: Zwingli, 1980.

Schönle, V. *Johannes, Jesus und die Juden. Die theologische Position des Matthäus und des Verfassers der Redenquelle im Lichte von Matthäus 11.* BET 17. Frankfurt-Bern: Peter Lang, 1982.

Schütz, R. *Johannes der Täufer.* AThANT 50. Zürich-Stuttgart: Zwingli, 1967.

Scobie, Ch. H. H. *John the Baptist.* Philadelphia: Fortress, 1964.

Stegemann, H. *The Library of Qumran: on the Essenes, Qumran, John the Baptist, and Jesus.* Grand Rapids: Eerdmans, 1998.

Strecker, G. *Das Judenchristentum in den Pseudoklementinen.* TU 70,2. Berlin: Akademie, 1981[2].

Vielhauer, Ph. "Das Benedictus des Zacharias" (Lk 1,68–79), *ZThK* 49 (1952) 255–272; also in Ph. Vielhauer, *Aufsätze zum Neuen Testament.* TB 31. Munich: Kaiser, 1965, 28–46).

Vielhauer, Ph. "Tracht und Speise Johannes des Täufers," in Ph. Vielhauer. *Aufsätze zum Neuen Testament.* TB 31. Munich: Kaiser, 1965, 47–54.

Wink, W. *John the Baptist in the Gospel Tradition.* MSSNTS 7. Cambridge: Cambridge University Press, 1968.

The figure of John the Baptist plays an important role in the opening chapters of the canonical Gospels. From the outset, this is one important reason for beginning a section that traces the theological developments that led to the Gospels with a section on John the Baptist. Moreover, due to the historical location in which he stands, John can contribute to the understanding of the historical Jesus and the formation of the Jesus tradition.

## a)  Sources

The traditions about John the Baptist are extraordinarily disparate; not a few contradictions are found in the reports of his person and his work. The oldest *non-canonical* source is found in Josephus (*Ant* 18.116–119). According to Josephus, John's preaching had the purpose of leading the Jewish people in the way of virtue (ἀρετή) and to obligate them to live before God with justice and piety. John himself was distinguished by his ἀρετή. The baptism he performed on the Jews was for "purifying the body," since "the soul had already been purified by the practice of righteousness." Although in this connection Josephus provides some helpful historical information, by and large his report is tendentious. John receives the features of a Hellenistic wandering philosopher. Obviously Josephus introduces his own views as to what should be proclaimed as Jewish faith in his time. In his attempts to show that the tradition of Judaism is on a par with that of Graeco-Roman culture, he expresses the same tendency that dominates his historical work as a whole.

The later Slavonic Josephus tradition also belongs here; its report of the Baptist is of course legendary (2.7.2; 2.9.1), but still constitutes an "interesting sidetrack of the tradition."[1] The Mandean literature frequently mentions John (e. g. *Ginza* R 189: the baptism of Manda d'Haiyê by John). This baptist sect that has survived until the twentieth century in the region of the Euphrates has its own sacred writings that come from the seventh and eighth centuries C.E., though they contain older elements. It is striking that in these writings the baptismal water is called "Jordan," which, to be sure, is an expression that is also found among the Nestorian Christians of Syria and is widespread in the liturgy of the Orthodox Church.[2] The hypothesis that the Mandean sect represents a late branch of the disciples of John the Baptist is unproven.[3]

In contrast, the *New Testament sources* contain more extensive important material concerning the Baptist. The introduction to the Gospel of Mark pictures John baptizing and preaching in the wilderness, or at the Jordan (Mark 1:1–11). The Synoptics tell of his execution by Herod Antipas (Mark 6:17–29par). In a parallel stream of tradition the sayings source (Q) transmits the question of the Baptist to Jesus and Jesus' testimony to John in Matthew 11:2–19par (11:11: "among those born of women no one has arisen greater than John the Baptist"). The Gospel of John has reworked traditions about the Baptist that partly deviate from those in the Synoptics (1:35–36: John points to the "Lamb of God;" 3:22ff: John baptizes in Aenon, where he testifies "He (Jesus) must increase, but I must decrease."

A specifically Christian tendency is at work in the New Testament reports: John the Baptist is subordinated to Jesus. Thus Mark 1:9–11 tells of Jesus' baptism in the Jordan by John. The parallel in Matthew 3:13–17 portrays the event quite differently, especially by introducing a conversa-

---

[1] M. Dibelius, *Die urchristliche Überlieferung* 129. The most important passages are reprinted in F. F. Bruce in E. Güting, ed., *Ausserbiblische Zeugnisse über Jesus und das frühe Christentum* (Giessen-Basel 1991) 32–43; cf. "Literature zum slavischen Josephus" on p. 43.

[2] Cf. K. H. Rengstorf, *TDNT* 6.621–622.

[3] Contra R. Bultmann, *Exegetica* 100–101.

tion between John and Jesus after the introduction but before the combined event of baptism and epiphany: John at first refuses to baptize Jesus,
and is willing to perform the baptismal ceremony only after Jesus' response allays his reservations (3:14–15). The essential elements were
possibly already part of an expanded version of the Markan pericope in pre-
Matthean tradition. It shows that Christian tradition was at work on the
Baptist's image in a way that increasingly placed the figure of John in the
shadow of the person of Jesus by incorporating the Baptist into Christian
tradition as one who testifies to Jesus and his mission.

The portrayal of John as Elijah is another example that illustrates this.
Though this designation may originally have been a special title of honor
that John's disciples conferred on their master (cf. Luke 1:17, 76), in the
Synoptic tradition it is clearly placed at a lower point on the scale. According to the early Christian perspective, if John the Baptist is the returned
Elijah, this means merely that he was a prophetic forerunner, a precursor
of Jesus (Mark 9:12–13). This interpretation of the message and claim of
the Baptist is motivated by the fact that the early Christian communities
found themselves in competition with the *disciples of John*. Fragments of
this debate can still be recognized in the Synoptic tradition (Mark 2:18, the
question about fasting; Acts 11:16; John 3:22ff, baptism). As can be inferred from Acts 19:1–7, disciples of John also transferred into the Christian community.

From the demonstrable effort of the earliest Christian tradition to
Christianize the figure of John the Baptist, one can deduce a heuristic
factor in regard to reconstructing the Baptist tradition itself. In order to
recover its original form, the ways in which the Baptist has been portrayed
must be freed from the influence of the Christianizing process. The tradition that emanated from the disciples of John, which had the Baptist
himself as its subject, can be reconstructed only to a minimal extent.
According to M. Dibelius, authentic Baptist tradition is found in the
introductory stories of the Gospel of Luke (e.g. the "birth story" Luke 1:5–
25, 57–66).[4] The further research of Ph. Vielhauer led him to the view that
the song of Zechariah (the "Benedictus," Luke 1:68–79) quotes a psalm
that comes from the Baptist sect and proclaims the Baptist as the prophet
of the Most High (Luke 1:68–79).[5]

Later sources manifest a tendency in the opposite direction. For example, in the Κηρύγματα Πέτρου, a Jewish Christian source of the Pseudo-
Clementines, John the Baptist belongs to the series of false prophets that
extends through this age from the creation onwards (PsClem Hom II), and
thus is the antagonist of Jesus. In contrast, another Jewish Christian

---

4    M. Dibelius, "Jungfrauensohn und Krippenkind" 8–9; differently W. Wink, *John
     the Baptist* 60–72.
5    Ph. Vielhauer, "Benedictus" 267ff.

source, the Ἀναβάθμοι Ἰακώβου II, tells of a discussion in Jerusalem that involved "the Jews," the eleven disciples of Jesus and their Bishop James, and the disciples of John. It is reported that John's disciples regard their master John as the Christ (PsClem Rec I), citing Matthew 11:9, 11.[6] The figure of John the Baptist thus appears to have been understood more and more messianically in the course of the tradition, with the high point represented by the conferral of the title "Christ." During the same development on the Christian side the polemic against John's disciples became increasingly sharper.

## b) John's Message and Baptism

Despite the strong disparities in the traditions, a nucleus can still be sifted out from which a picture of John can be extracted. Old Synoptic tradition locates his appearance in the "wilderness" (Mark 1:4 ἔρημος). This is confirmed by the Q tradition (Matt 11:7). That John appeared in such an unusual geographical location apparently suggests that he saw himself in the stream of tradition associated with the Jewish Urzeit/Endzeit expectation, i.e. that the end of history would represent a cycling back to the original beginnings. Thus, just as at the beginning of Israel's history the people came out of Egypt into the wilderness, so there would be a second exodus that would lead Israel back into the wilderness (Hos 2:16–18 LXX; 12:10 LXX). The time of salvation was located in the wilderness, the place where the Jewish people would again be redeemed, the place where the eschatological hopes would be fulfilled. So also Christian apocalypticism later understood the wilderness typologically as the place of salvation (Rev 12:6, 14; Matt 24:26). From this perspective, John could accordingly be understood as the leader into the land of the exodus, as the one who calls for a new beginning and a refounding of Israel, as the gatherer of the holy remnant. However, such an extensive interpretation of the term "wilderness" can be no more than a supposition, since the Baptist tradition lacks both the concept of exodus and new beginning as well as the Endzeit/Urzeit schema.[7] Thus the term "wilderness" may mean nothing more or

---

6  Cf. G. Strecker, *Das Judenchristentum in den Pseudoklementinen* 189, 237–239, 241–243: PsClem Hom II 17, 23; Rec I 54, 60; also K. Backhaus, *Jüngerkreise* 275–298.

7  This is also to be said of the instructive study of Hartmut Stegemann, which interprets the appearance of John the Baptist as a prophetic sign to the people of Israel just prior to entering into the future age of salvation, like that of the wilderness generation of Israel before entering the Promised Land. (*The Essenes* 297). In this interpretation, however, both "wilderness" and "Jordan" receive an important place in salvation history, but this can also be seen without regard to the exodus typology and even interpreted negatively (cf. J. Ernst, *Johannes der Täufer* 278–279). So also J. Becker rightly disputes the connection to the exodus typology (*Johannes der Täufer*

less than a geographical datum, the historical setting of John's ministry. Other data connected with John (e. g. John 1:28, Bethany; John 3:23, Aenon, Salim) cannot be located geographically, since they refer to more than one place.[8] Moreover, we can infer that John led an ascetic lifestyle (cf. Mark 1:6). His clothing of camel's hair and leather belt and his diet of locusts and wild honey cannot definitely be interpreted in terms of either the Bedouin lifestyle[9] or the Old Testament prophet Elijah,[10] but have a

---

16ff); in his view the exodus tradition is never interpreted in John's preaching as an announcement of salvation. According to Becker, John was not a prophet of salvation but of repentance. The promise of salvation was only indirectly present, with the threat of destruction as the dominant note. It was not future salvation, but the wrath and judgment of God, the summons to remorse and repentance in which the exodus tradition played no role, that formed the content of his message (so also S. v. Dobbeler, *Gericht* 237ff). To be sure, one must take into consideration that the announcement of judgment implies salvation if the hearers repent, even if this is not explicitly expressed in the oldest layers of the Baptist tradition.

8    Cf. also the variant reading "Bethabara" at John 1:28, which E. Hirsch (*Das vierte Evangelium in seiner ursprünglichen Gestalt verdeutscht und erklärt* [Tübingen: J. C. B. Mohr (Paul Siebeck) 1936] 113) understands to represent an original τη Αραβια that was changed by the copyist into Βηθαραβα.

     J. Ernst supports the view that John "apparently baptized at the fords of the Jordan southeast of Jericho" and contemplates the alternative between a symbolic meaning and that the geographical locations had simply disappeared (281). According to K. Kundsin the place name at John 1:28 means that at the time of the Evangelist John there was a Christian community there that had originally been disciples of John (*Überlieferungsstoffe* 25–27, 73–75). All in all, it is very problematic to interpret the place name in John 1:28 as a historical datum referring to an actual place.

9    According to Ph. Vielhauer, "Tracht und Speise Johannes des Täufers." When Vielhauer also convincingly rejects (against M. Hengel, *The Charismatic Leader and His Followers* [Edinburgh: T. &. T. Clark, 1996] 36 note 71) the purported parallel between the clothing of the Baptist with that of Elijah, it is still questionable whether the clothing material is that of the Bedouins and whether for people who lived in the wilderness it represents an "eschatological demonstration (54)," i.e. a reflection of the wilderness typology (cf. also J. Becker, *Johannes der Täufer* 26). So also the Baptist's diet differs considerably from the normal food of nomads.

10   J. Ernst (*Johannes der Täufer* 284ff) also rightly rejects the view that John is imitating the clothing of Elijah and thereby clothing himself with Elijah's authority. There is nothing in the Old Testament that corresponds to the mantle of camels hair; 2 Kings 1:8 only speaks of a "hairy man." The mantle motif comes from Zechariah 13:4, and was first combined with 2 Kings 1:8 in the tradition about the Baptist of the New Testament period. Thus neither the clothing nor the diet of John can really be interpreted as referring to Elijah. This also answers the question of whether John understood himself to be the returned Elijah. Wherever pre-Christian ideas of John as Elijah redivivus are found in the New Testament traditions about the Baptist (e. g. Matt 11:14; Mark 8:28par; Luke 1:76 + 1:17), they reflect the faith of the Baptist community, not John's own understanding of himself. So also the lack of a political-national orientation and the break with the past is no evidence that the Baptist thought of himself as the "returning prophet Elijah." That such a connection is specifically rejected in John 1:21ff is of course the result of later reflection.

close parallel in the Jewish ascetic Banus.[11] In accordance with this, Matthew 11:18par says that John "came neither eating nor drinking;" and Mark 2:18 speaks of the fasts that were practiced in his circles. Finally, that John did not belong to those who "wear soft garments" (Matt 11:8par) is consistent with the ascetic lifestyle and corresponds to the frugal demeanor of the Old Testament prophets. According to 2 Kings 1:8 the prophet Elijah wore a leather belt, and Zechariah 13:4 describes prophets as wearing a hairy mantle. John's ascetic lifestyle is thus overlaid with these marks of the prophetic role (cf. Mark 11:32: "all regarded John as truly a prophet.")[12]

The content of John's message is the announcement of the Coming One (Mark 1:7: "The one who is more powerful than I is coming after me"). The earliest Christian community, and following it the Synoptic Gospels, understood this in the sense that John announced the coming of Jesus. But connecting the forerunner motif to Jesus is a Christian interpretation of the message of John. Jesus is not specifically named in Mark 1:7–8parr. The "one to come," also designated as the more powerful one, has no name and no title; he is the Unknown One.[13] But John defines his relation to him; he understands himself to be unworthy of performing the most menial duties of a slave for the Coming One (Mark 1:7). The Coming One is described only in visual imagery. He is like a farmer who separates the wheat from the chaff with his threshing shovel (Matt 3:12par). The Coming One is recognizable by his future function. He is the judge of the world, for in contrast to John he will not baptize with water but with fire.

---

[11] Cf. Josephus, *Vita* 2.11.

[12] The legendary Baptist traditions in the introductory section of the Gospel of Luke (Luke 1) presupposes that the Baptist was of priestly origins. This, of course, is not reliable biographical data. So also there is no serious basis for speculations that John belonged to a particular group of priests or even to the Essenes of Qumran. It is to be noticed that in the Baptist's preaching there are no visible elements of a critique against the temple. Cf. also J. Ernst, *Johannes der Täufer* 269ff; W. Schmithals, *Das Evangelium nach Lukas* 20ff.

[13] Differently J. Ernst, *Johannes der Täufer*, who supposes that by the "coming one" God was originally meant (e. g. 49–55; 305–308 and often). There is no limit to the imagination in the other proposals that have been made. J. Becker thinks of a political Messiah, supporting his hypothesis with material from the Old Testament, Psalms of Solomon, and the Eighteen Benedictions. But in view of the demonstrable variations of the messianic ideas of Judaism of the New Testament period, this is too thin a basis. So also the Son of Man hypothesis as the "most usable hypothesis to explain the mightier one" (J. Becker, *Johannes der Täufer* 36) remains too hypothetical. The messianic interpretation is widespread in the English-speaking world: cf. e. g. T. W. Manson, *Sayings* 41 and C. H. Scobie, *John the Baptist* 65–66. Similarly R. Laufen *Doppelüberlieferungen* 95; H. Sahlin, *Studien zum dritten Kapitel des Lukasevangeliums* 44–52; R. Schütz, *Johannes der Täufer* 82ff. O. Cullmann supposes that John announced the coming of an "endtime prophet" (*Christology of the New Testament* 25–26).

He will gather the righteous, but destroy the evil with fire (Matt 3:12par). In the face of the threatening judgment, there can be no appeal to belong to the elect people Israel. The judge will not ask about one's national connections, nor even about one's previous religious circumstances, but about each individual's deeds. His coming and his judgment stand in the immediate future; the ax is already (ἤδη) placed at the root of the trees (Matt 3:10par).

As illustrated by the announcement of the Coming One, John represents an expectation of the near eschatological end. This expectation is not related to the concept of the kingdom of God, for only later is there a forced linkage between the βασιλεία Θεοῦ conceptuality of the Christian tradition and John's original preaching. However, John's message was in fact concerned with the same reality comprehended by the idea of the kingdom of God: the future breaking into history of the eschaton that brings history to an end with both judgment and salvation, an eschatological event that already looms threateningly over the present. John is a prophet of the end time.

Since the expectation of the future demands concrete action in the present, the proclamation of the near end motivates the call to μετάνοια (Matt 3:7ff; 21:32; Mark 1:4, βάπτισμα μετανοίας). Μετάνοια literally means "change of mind;" however, it is not merely an intellectual change. Luther's translation "penance" is misleading, since it is not only a matter of feeling remorse. The word is more correctly rendered by "return," or "turn around" (Hebrew שׁוּבָה = a radical turning to God; cf. Isa 10:21; 30:15). John calls for a total reorientation of human existence, a radical change in human life, a turning from self to God. "Repentance" is not the same as "conversion" in the pietistic sense, but combines internal and external transformation. The meaning embraces a new obedience that becomes concrete in ethical acts (Matt 3:8: "Bear fruit worthy of repentance!").

John's baptism is to be seen from within this perspective. In Mark 1:4 it is called βάπτισμα μετανοίας (a baptism of repentance). Matthew speaks of a baptism into repentance (3:11: βαπτίζω ἐν ὕδατι εἰς μετάνοιαν) as though repentance were the result of baptism; this is a misleading expression that possibly results from the overlap of Mark and Q traditions in Matthew 3. Actually, being baptized is an expression of repentance (μετάνοια); the repentance which has already happened becomes concrete in the act of baptism, as illustrated by the confession of sins that precedes baptism (Mark 1:5).

The origin of the baptismal rite itself is disputed. Is John's baptism a development of the Jewish rite of initiation required of Gentile converts, the so-called "proselyte baptism?" First documented at the end of the first century C.E.,[14] the existence of proselyte baptism in John's time cannot be

---

[14]   Strack-Billerbeck, *Kommentar* 1:106–107.

demonstrated. Moreover, proselyte baptism functions to incorporate one into the Jewish religious community, while John's baptism has no such initiatory character. Parallels are apparently found in the Qumran literature. To the extent that the Qumran people practiced daily cultic washings of purification, one could call their community a baptismal sect, since such washing had the function of freeing from moral impurity.[15] John 3:25, where John's baptism is described as a καθαρισμός (purification), is another apparent parallel,[16] though the esoteric nature of the washings of the Qumran sect is not characteristic of John's baptism. It is particularly difficult to see John's own intention as being to found an esoteric community, even if after his death some of his followers did in fact form such a group. Moreover, the Qumran washings can be repeated an almost unlimited number of times. In contrast, John's baptism (like proselyte baptism) was a once-only act. Instead of being able to determine a precise derivation from the point of view of the history of religions, it is better simply to see John's baptism as emerging against a contemporary background that included several baptismal sects. From the viewpoint of the history of religions, John's baptism is one example of a complex pre-Christian baptist movement.[17] Despite these parallels, the independent character of John's baptism should be maintained. It is an eschatological sacrament performed a single time. It stands in closest connection with the Baptist's apocalyptic message, the announcement of the Coming One and his judgment. It is preparation for the end, for baptism saves one from the future judgment. It is oriented exclusively toward the future, so that John is exclusively the announcer of salvation to come, not himself the mediator of salvation in the present. The future turn of the ages stands in the immediate future, but is not yet present. John is only the voice calling in the wilderness, not the savior or judge.

According to the data of the Synoptic tradition, John's followers come primarily from the ranks of the socially marginalized (Matt 21:32; Luke 3:10ff). The movement that resulted from his preaching may have been the reason his preaching was regarded as political, and why Herod Antipas arrested John and had him imprisoned and executed in the fortress Macha-

---

[15] Cf. the "Community Rule" 1QS 3.4–12; 5.13–14.

[16] According to R. Bultmann, *Gospel of John* 171–172, this is an old, pre-Johannine tradition. It is also possible, of course, that here a typical Johannine expression is found as in 2:6, which wants to assign John's baptism to Jewish cultic practices and distinguish it from Christian baptism.

[17] Cf. SibOr 4.161ff: the call to baptism that purifies from immoral contamination and pacifies the wrath of God. Similarly the baptismal sect of the Elkesaites, that combined Jewish and Christian elements within an apocalyptic horizon. Cf. G. Strecker, "Elkesai," *RAC* 4.1171–1186 (reprinted in *Eschaton und Historie* 320–333); J. Irmscher, "The Book of Elchasai," in Hennecke-Schneemelcher, *New Testament Apocrypha* 2:745–750.

erus.[18] The advent of the Baptist, his preaching, the social structure of his hearers—these all have parallels in the early Christian tradition about Jesus and makes it easier to classify Jesus within the framework of the history of religions. At the same time, the contrasts between them allow Jesus' distinctiveness to be perceived.

### c)  John and Jesus

It is historically certain that Jesus was baptized by John (Mark 1:9–11parr). For the later tradition this was a problematic report that provided the occasion to moderate the account so that it was not so offensive.[19] For the rest, we must be content with suppositions. Jesus may have belonged to the circle of John's disciples. This is suggested by John 3:26 (the disciples of John speak to their master: "Rabbi, the one who was with you across the Jordan, to whom you testified, here he is baptizing, and all are going to him"), even if the claim that Jesus himself baptized is not confirmed by anything else in the Jesus tradition. A close connection between Jesus and John is indicated by the fact that Jesus defines his own position in terms of John (Matt 11:11). As portrayed in the Gospel of John, both worked alongside each other for awhile (John 1–3); in contrast, according to the Synoptic testimony Jesus' ministry did not begin until after John had been thrown into prison (Mark 1:14; Luke 3:19–20). This discrepancy is motivated in each case by theological considerations, so that it cannot be resolved historically. That the early church very early adopted baptism as the rite of initiation is to be traced back to the influence of John the Baptist and confirms the close connection between Jesus and his disciples on the one hand, and John and his disciples on the other. Thus the above already presents an essential part of the theological and historical context within which the historical Jesus appeared.[20]

---

[18]   Cf. Josephus *Ant* 18.116–119; Mark 6:27.

[19]   Cf. Matthew 3:14–15; GosNaz Fragm 2, Hennecke-Schneemelcher, *New Testament Apocrypha* 1:160: "Behold, the mother of the Lord and his brethren said to him: John the Baptist baptizes unto the remission of sins, let us go and be baptized by him. But he said to them: Wherein have I sinned that I should go and be baptized by him? Unless what I have said is ignorance (a sin of ignorance)." Cf. also Jerome, *Contra Pelagius* 3.2.

[20]   Since the circles around John the Baptist form an essential part of the complex religious-historical framework within which the historical Jesus appeared, this means that this framework included not only the so-called "official" Judaism represented by the priests and scribes, but also the "unofficial" Judaism represented by apocalyptic, zealotic, and other Jewish movements in Palestine of the first century C.E.

# II. The Kingdom of God—Jesus

Ben-Chorin, Sch. *Bruder Jesus. Der Nazarener in jüdischer Sicht*. Munich: List, 1979³.
Bornkamm, G. *Jesus of Nazareth*. New York: Harper, 1960.
Braun, H. *Jesus—der Mann aus Nazareth und seine Zeit*. Gütersloh: Gerd Mohn, 1988².
Bultmann, R. *Jesus and the Word*. New York: Scribner, 1958.
Conzelmann, H.: *Jesus*. Philadelphia: Fortress, 1973.
Dibelius, M. and W. G. Kümmel. *Jesus*. Berlin: W. de Gruyter, 1966⁴.
Flusser, D. *Jesus*. Philadelphia: Westminster, 1949, N.Y.: Herder and Herder, 1969.
Leroy, H. *Jesus. Überlieferung und Deutung*. EdF 95. Darmstadt: Wissenschaftliche Buchgesellschaft, 1978 (Lit.).
Niederwimmer, K. *Jesus*. Göttingen: Vandenhoeck & Ruprecht, 1968.
Reumann, J. *Jesus in the Church's Gospels: Modern Scholarship and the Earliest Sources*. Philadelphia: Fortress, 1968.
Schweizer, E.: "Jesus Christus," *TRE* 16 (1987) 671–726.
Schweizer, E. *Jesus Christus im vielfältigen Zeugnis des Neuen Testaments*. Gütersloh: Gerd Mohn, 1979⁵.
Stauffer, E. *Die Botschaft Jesu*. Bern-Munich: Franke, 1959.
Vermès, G. *Jesus the Jew*. Philadelphia: Fortress, 1981 (rev. ed.).

Every academic discipline that is not historically grounded is "in reality floating in the air."[1] This is also true of the quest of the historical Jesus, which has influenced the development of specific literary critical works on the Synoptic Gospels like no other discipline.

## a) Sources for the Historical Jesus

Bienert, W. *Der älteste nichtchristliche Jesusbericht. Josephus über Jesus*. TABG IX. Halle: Akademischer Verlag, 1936.
Hofius, O. "Isolated Sayings of the Lord," in W. Schneemelcher, ed. *New Testament Apocrypha* I Louisville: Westminster / John Knox, 1989², 88–91.
Jeremias, J. and O. Hofius. *Unknown Sayings of Jesus*. London: SPCK, 1964².
Jeremias, J. "Isolated Sayings of the Lord," in W. Schneemelcher, ed. *New Testament Apocrypha* I Louisville: Westminster / John Knox, 1963, 52–55.
Strack, H. L. and P. Billerbeck. *Kommentar zum Neuen Testament aus Talmud und Midrasch I*. Munich: Beck, 1986⁹, 36–39 (Rabbinic Texts on Jesus).

The main sources are the Synoptic Gospels, i.e. the reworked traditions they contain. These are the sayings collection (Q) and the Gospel of Mark

---

[1]   Cf. H. J. Holtzmann as remembered in the notes of a student in the practical theology college studying catechetics (summer semester 1871): The "substance ... of catechetical material" was mediated by Holtzmann "in closest connection with the general history of the church and the intellectual development of the Christian world." That was the beginning of my own conviction, if I understand the matter rightly, that every practical discipline that is not historically founded is in reality floating in the air, and is in any case bereft of the most interesting material" (H. Bassermann, "Heinrich Holtzmann als praktischer Theologe," *PrM* 6 [1902] 172–184).

as the oldest Gospel, and to a lesser degree the materials contained in the unique sources of each Gospel (*Sondergut*), and to an even lesser degree the Gospel of John, to the extent that it contains individual items of pre-Synoptic tradition.[2] Paul's quotation of "words of the Lord" does not contribute much to the study of the historical Jesus, since his citations are mostly understood as words of the exalted Lord.[3] The so-called agrapha, i.e. extra-canonical sayings of the Lord found in patristic texts, have been investigated several times,[4] but the extraction of authentic sayings of Jesus from this tradition remains problematic.

The non-Christian sources are not very numerous. The Talmud essentially offers late horror stories about Jesus, according to which Jesus appeared as a magician intent on deceiving the Jewish people, and was executed on these charges on the eve of the Passover. In this tradition Jesus was the illegitimate son of a Roman soldier named Pandera (possibly a satire or corruption of *natus ex virgine*, i.e. parthenogenesis). Such legends presuppose the Christian tradition and cannot be traced back to independent historical information.[5]

The matter is different with pagan-Hellenistic sources. Thus Tacitus, in the context of his report of the fire in Rome at the time of the emperor Nero, reports a persecution of Christians initiated by Nero. He explains the name "Christian" with the following statement:

> This name comes them from Christ, whom the procurator Pontius Pilate, under the rule of Tiberius, handed over to the torture. Repressed for the moment, this detestable superstition broke out anew, no longer simply in Judea, where the evil arose, but at Rome.[6]

This report portrays the situation about the year 60 and confirms the Christian tradition, but cannot be evaluated as a witness providing independent testimony.

The Roman author Suetonius, in his biography of the emperor Claudius, includes a comment about the expulsion of Jews from Rome in 49 C.E.:[7]

---

[2]    Thus C. H. Dodd, *Historical Tradition in the Fourth Gospel* (Cambridge: Cambridge University Press, 1963). The relation of the Gospel of John to the Synoptics is a controversial item among scholars; see under D. I.

[3]    Cf. A. II.b.2. above.

[4]    Cf. J. Jeremias, *Unknown Sayings of Jesus*, 1964; J. Jeremias and O. Hofius, *Unbekannte Jesusworte*; A. Resch, *Agrapha* (TU NF 15.3, 4. Berlin 1906² [= Darmstadt: Wissenschaftliche Buchgesellschaft, 1967]).

[5]    Cf. J. Maier, *Jesus von Nazareth in der Talmudischen Überlieferung* (EdF 82. Darmstadt: Wissenschaftliche Buchgesellschaft, 1978) 264–267; 274–275.

[6]    Tacitus, *Annals* 15.44.13.

[7]    On the dating cf. the discussion of Romans 13 above, as well as Acts 18:1–2, where

He [the emperor Claudius] expelled from Rome the Jews who, under the influence of Chrestus, did not cease to agitate.[8]

The similarity of the names (Chrestus instead of Christus) suggests that a dispute between Jews and Christians had occurred within the Jewish population of Rome, provoked by the confession of Christ by Jewish Christians.[9] Suetonius understood this in the sense that someone named Chrestus provoked these disturbances at the time, i.e. 49 C.E. This obscure note is not even adequate to confirm the historical existence of Jesus, since it is clear that Suetonius is dependent on reports of Jews and/or Christians who were involved.

More significant data is found in the Jewish historian Flavius Josephus in the so-called "Testimonium Flavianum:"

About the same time came Jesus, a wise man, if indeed we should call him a man. For he was a doer of miracles and the master of men who receive the truth with joy. And he attracted to himself many of the Jews and many Greeks. He was the Christ, and, when after his denunciation by our leading citizens, Pilate condemned him to be crucified, those who had cared for him previously did not cease to do so, for he appeared three days afterwards, risen from the dead, just as the prophets of the Lord had announced this and many other marvels concerning him. And the group which is called that of the Christians has not yet disappeared.[10]

This reference to Jesus reads like a Christian section. It contains the confession of the supernatural nature of Christ ("if indeed we should call him a man") and makes the clear confession "He was the Christ." It is hardly possible to distinguish within this text a Jewish original that has been later interpreted with Christian additions.[11] The extant text is inconceivable for the Jewish Josephus, since New Testament tradition clearly

Aquila and Priscilla are among those expelled and go to Corinth, where they receive Paul. Despite the efforts of G. Luedemann to show otherwise (Paul, *Apostle to the Gentiles. Studies in Chronology*. Philadelphia: Fortress, 1984, pp. 164–171), the reports in Dio Cassius (41 C.E.) and Suetonius or Orosius (49 C.E.) are not to be identified. It is more likely that Claudius issued two edicts against the Roman Jews, the first in 41 C.E. as a reaction to disturbing the peace or violation of Roman laws, the second in 49 C.E. as a response to the disturbances that also could have involved the Christian congregations. Cf. R. Jewett, *A Chronology of Paul's Life* (Philadelphia: Fortress Press, 1979) 57–62; F. F. Bruce, *New Testament History* (Garden City, NY: Doubleday & Co., Inc., 1971) 279–287.

8    Suetonius, *Claudius* 25.4. Translation from LCL.
9    Cf. P. Lampe, *Die stadrömischen Christen in den ersten beiden Jahrhunderten. Untersuchungen zur Sozialgeschichte* (WUNT 2.18. Tübingen: J. C. B. Mohr [Paul Siebeck] 1989² 1989) 6–8.
10   *Ant* 18.63–64, translation from LCL.
11   See J. Klausner, *Jesus of Nazareth. His Life, Times, and Teaching* (New York: Macmillan, 1944), 55–60; H. S. J. Thackeray, *Josephus—the Man and the Historian*, New York: Jewish Institute of Religion, 1929, 125–153.

stands in the background as godfather and sponsor.[12] Presumably this Christian testimony to Jesus has been interpolated into the original text of Josephus; it is also possible to extract the whole section from its context without leaving a gap. Perhaps the Christian author read something in this passage about Jesus, since in the context Josephus is speaking of the Roman administrator in Palestine, Pontius Pilate and has mentioned in this connection political disturbances that occurred at this time.[13] From this point of departure, it is conceivable that Josephus regarded Jesus as among those who had contributed to disturbing the political peace. The probability that Josephus in fact said something about Jesus in this passage is made more probable by the section in *Antiquities* 20.200. Here the stoning of James is mentioned, which apparently occurred in the year 62 C.E. James is referred to as "brother of Jesus who is called the Christ." Thus Josephus here presupposes that the name of Jesus was known, presumably because he had already spoken of him in another passage, namely *Antiquities* 18.63ff.

The non-Christian witnesses to Jesus can thus contribute nothing to our knowledge of the historical Jesus. They are mostly dependent on Christian reports. To be sure, they can confirm that in the second half of the first century C.E. it was doubted neither by Jews nor pagans that Jesus was an actual historical figure, but they are hardly adequate as the basis for a biography of Jesus. As M. Dibelius had already established,[14] within the framework of world history and the intellectual history of that time, Christianity was only a marginal phenomenon. It did not touch political life. There was no need to take note of it either historically nor in literature. Here one might add the further reflection that the real claim that was made by the appearance of the Christian faith did not find it necessary to clothe itself in the literary and historical forms customary in classical antiquity, since according to its own self-understanding it is not recognizable by historical analysis.

## b)   History of Research

Bultmann, R. *Das Verhältnis der urchristlichen Christusbotschaft zum historischen Jesus.* SHAW.PH 3. Heidelberg, 1960; also in R. Bultmann. *Exegetica.* Tübingen: J. C. B. Mohr (Paul Siebeck), 1967, 445–469).

---

[12]   A direct literary dependence cannot be demonstrated, of course, but there are parallels in content to New Testament tradition, e. g. εἴγε ἄνδρα αὐτὸν λέγειν χρή. (cf. Mark 15:39); ὁ Χριστὸς οὗτος ἦν (cf. Mark 8:29); ἐφάνη γὰρ αὐτοῖς τρίτην ἔχων ἡμέραν πάλιν ζῶν (cf. 1 Cor 15:3–7). According to H. Conzelmann, in *Ant* 18:63–64 even the kerygmatic schema of Luke can be recognized (*RGG*³ 3:622). Essential elements of Lucan theology are missing, however.

[13]   Josephus *Ant* 18. 52–62, 81–87.

[14]   M. Dibelius, "Urchristliche Geschichte und Weltgeschichte," *ThBl* 6 (1927) 213–224 (215).

Fuchs, E. "Das Neue Testament und das hermeneutische Problem," in E. Fuchs, *Glaube und Erfahrung. GAufs. III.* Tübingen: J. C. B. Mohr (Paul Siebeck), 1965, 136–173.

Fuchs, G. "Jesus' Understanding of Time" in *Studies on the Historical Jesus.* Naperville, IL. Alec R. Allenson, 1964, 104–166.

Fuchs, G. "The Quest of the Historical Jesus" in *Studies on the Historical Jesus.* Naperville, IL.: Alec R. Allenson, 1964, 11–31.

Fuchs, E. "Jesu Selbstzeugnis nach Matthäus 5," *ZThK* 51 (1954) 14–34; also in E. Fuchs. *Zur Frage nach dem historischen Jesus. GAufs. II.* Tübingen: J. C. B. Mohr (Paul Siebeck), 1960, 100–125.

Geiselmann, J. R. *Jesus der Christus I. Die Frage nach dem historischen Jesus.* Munich: Kösel, 1965.

Jeremias, J. *The Problem of the Historical Jesus.* Philadelphia: Fortress, 1964.

Kähler, M. *The so-called Historical Jesus and the Historic, Biblical Christ.* Philadelphia: Fortress, 1964.

Käsemann, E. "The Problem of the Historical Jesus," in *Essays on New Testament Themes.* SBT 41. London: SCM, 1964.

Kümmel, W. G. *The New Testament: The History of the Investigation of Its Problems.* London: SCM, 1964.

Leroy, H. *Jesus.* EdF 95. Darmstadt: Wissenschaftliche Buchgesellschaft, 1978, 1ff.

Noll, P. *Jesus und das Gesetz.* SGV 253: Tübingen: J. C. B. Mohr (Paul Siebeck), 1968.

Ristow H. and K. Matthiae, Eds. *Der historische Jesus und der kerygmatische Christus. Beiträge zum Christusverständnis in Forschung und Verkündigung.* Berlin: Evangelische Verlagsanstalt, 1961².

Schulz, S. "Der historische Jesus," in G. Strecker, ed. *Jesus Christus in Historie und Theologie* (FS H. Conzelmann). Tübingen: J. C. B. Mohr (Paul Siebeck) 1975, 3–25.

Schweitzer, A. *The Quest of the Historical Jesus.* New York: Macmillan, 1961.

Strecker, G. "Die historische und theologische Problematik der Jesusfrage," *EvTh* 29 (1969) 453–476 ; also in G. Strecker, *Eschaton und Historie. Aufsätze,* 159–182).

*Hermann Samuel Reimarus,* whose work was posthumously published as "fragments" by G. E. Lessing beginning in 1774,[15] contributed a new element in the quest for the historical Jesus (even if he had not intended to do so), by confirming that a dogmatic element was included in the traditional image of Jesus. After Reimarus it was no longer possible to ignore the question of the relation between faith in Jesus as the Messiah and the establishing of historical truth about Jesus. The reaction of the leading pastor of Hamburg, *Johann Melchior Goeze,* shows, however, that wide circles in both the church and the academic study of theology thought it was possible to hold fast to the supernatural interpretation of the Jesus tradition as it had been handed on in orthodox Christianity.[16] In contrast, one will have to grant to the advocates of the enlightened exegesis of the rationalists that they at least saw the fundamental problem which could no longer be avoided in the nineteenth century. This was the case, for

---

[15] *Lessings Werke,* Vol. 22: *Theologische Schriften 3. Lessing als Herausgeber der Fragmente,* Leopold Zscharnack, ed., Berlin-Leipzig.

[16] H. Reinitzer, ed., *Johann Melchior Goeze 1717–1786. Abhandlungen und Vorträge* (VB 8. Hamburg: Friedrich Wittig Verlag, 1987).

instance, for the Heidelberg New Testament scholar *Heinrich Eberhard Gottlob Paulus.*[17] He recognized that it was not feasible to convey the biblical testimony directly into the present in an unreflective manner, but that this raises question of what categories would make such a transfer of meaning possible. Rationalism believed it had found the appropriate category in human reason. This lead to a naturalistic explanation of miracles that is often named as the distinctive feature of rationalism: Jesus' stilling of the storm is to be traced back to an understandable natural event. The ship in which Jesus and his disciples were sailing during the story turned into the lee of a hilltop where the wind could not reach. The disciples thought that Jesus had commanded the storm to cease.[18] Or the miraculous feeding is explained by the fact that Jesus and his disciples divided the food they had brought along with those sitting nearby, which provided an example for others, so that soon everyone divided their supplies and there was enough for all.[19]

It is easy enough to caricature this type of explanation, but more difficult to do justice to the real concern of such exegesis. The old rationalists had a sure instinct for clear thinking, for unreserved honesty and integrity. It must nonetheless be recognized that the application of the categories of reason in the interpretation of the New Testament runs the risk of no longer being able to articulate the otherness, the mystery contained in the texts.

*David Friedrich Strauss* is to be credited with recognizing the weaknesses of rationalistic exegesis, the hiatus between its explanation and the text itself. To be sure, his *Life of Jesus* (1835)[20] is concerned not only with criticizing earlier rationalistic views, but with presenting his own attempt, by a new *"mythical interpretation,"* to raise the question of the essential content and meaning of Jesus' appearance in history and to go beyond previous results as to what was verifiable history. He followed a method he had developed from much reflection. Strauss's book followed the course of the life of Jesus as transmitted in the Gospels of the New Testament (3 sections: the story of Jesus' birth and childhood; the story of the public life of Jesus, and the story of the suffering, death, and resurrection of Jesus).

---

[17]  H. E. G. Paulus, *Das Leben Jesu als Grundlage einer reinen Geschichte des Urchristentums I-II* (Heidelberg: C. F. Winter, 1828).

[18]  Mark 4:35–41parr. See H. E. G. Paulus, *Philologisch-kritischer und historischer Kommentar über das neue Testament, in welchem der griechische Text, nach einer Recognition der Varianten, Interpunctionen und Abschnitte, durch Einleitungen, Inhaltsanzeigen und ununterbrochene Scholien als Grundlage der Geschichte des Urchristentums synoptisch und chronologisch bearbeitet ist,* Teil I (Lübeck: Bohn, 1800, 343–344).

[19]  Mark 6:30–44par; see H. E. G. Paulus, Part II (Lübeck: Bohn, 1801) 270–278.

[20]  D. F. Strauss, *Das Leben Jesu, kritisch bearbeitet,* I-II (Tübingen: Osiander, 1835–1836, 3rd ed. 1838–1839). Translated as *The Life of Jesus Critically Examined* (Lives of Jesus Series. London: SCM Press Ltd., 1972).

The subsections are likewise each divided into three parts. First the *supernatural explanation* of each pericope is presented and criticized. Supernaturalism understands the narratives in the Gospels as reliable reports that document the miraculous history of the Son of God on earth, narratives that basically agree with each other. Jesus' miracles are accordingly understood as supernatural incursions into earthly reality. Since the supernatural explanation regards the Gospel stories as reliable reflections of the historical reality, it is necessary to harmonize the contradictions between the Evangelists, or to deny them. Strauss ruthlessly exposes the inadequacy of such explanations. In the process, he does not hesitate to introduce rationalistic arguments. Thus when supranatural exegesis affirms the historical reality of the story of Jesus' temptations by Satan, Strauss points to the discrepancy between the reports in the three Synoptics, and argues alongside the rationalists when he asks how Jesus "could hunger after six weeks of abstinence from all food without having hungered [translator's correction: starved] long before; since in ordinary cases the human frame cannot sustain a week's deprivation of nourishment" (253), and expresses the same doubt as Julian the apostate emperor: "how the devil could hope to deceive Jesus, knowing, as he must, his higher nature?" (254). And the changes of location, the magical transportation through the air, represent a feature of the narrative "which seemed extravagant even to those who tolerated the personal appearance of the devil" (255).

Just as the supranaturalistic explanation wants to make "the inconceivable conceivable"[21] and thus must affirm a multitude of contradictions, so on the other side stands *rationalistic exegesis* that is likewise unwelcome since in interpreting the story of the temptation of Jesus, for example, it must resort to Jesus' "ecstatic mood," identifying the devil with someone sent by the Pharisees to test Jesus and the angels that appear at the end of the story to serve Jesus with a passing caravan that supplied him with provisions.[22]

Strauss's own explanation is neither the supernatural nor the natural, but the mythical. He adopts the threefold movement of Hegelian dialectic, with a thesis followed by an antithesis resulting in a synthesis. The *mythical explanation* is accordingly a higher level of development of the exposition of the New Testament than either the supernatural or the natural interpretations. Here Strauss takes up a hermeneutical approach that had already been applied to both the Old Testament and the New.[23] According

---

21   Strauss, *Life of Jesus* 1838[3] p. 1; cf. p. 39.
22   Strauss, *Life of Jesus* 257.
23   J. S. Semler, *Abhandlung von freier Untersuchung des Canon* I-IV (Leipzig 1771–75); G. L. Bauer, *Entwurf einer Hermeneutik des Alten und Neuen Testaments* (Leipzig 1799); *Hebräische Mythologie des Alten und Neuen Testaments, mit Parallelen aus der Mythologie anderer Völker, vornehmlich der Griechen und Römer,* 2. Teil (Leipzig 1802); W. M. L. de Wette, *Beiträge zur Einleitung in das Alte Testament I-II* (Darmstadt: Wissenschaftliche Buchgesellschaft, 1971 [= 1806, 1807]).

to the basic definition given by Strauss, New Testament myths are "a history-like clothing of early Christian ideas, formed unintentionally in the poetic creation of sagas."[24] To interpret the New Testament mythically thus means to show that New Testament narratives are the mythical clothing of early Christian ideas. This implies that the biblical story has no historical character to the extent that it is the product of the pious imagination of later Christian generations. Strauss did not dispute that the myth could have been occasioned by some historical event, such as the impression of Jesus' personality. But such a historical event has been mediated to us in such mythical forms that the extent to which the original nature and character of the original historical core can be reconstructed becomes very questionable. History is subordinated to myth; myth is independent of historical verification. This fundamentally distinguishes the mythical explanation from the natural, as it does from the supernatural, since it is characteristic of each of these approaches to affirm that their statements can be historically verified. Myth can claim to be basically superior to history. In regard to the person of Jesus it speaks of Jesus' uniqueness: in Jesus' self-awareness "the unity of the divine and the human first appeared with sufficient energy...to reduce to a disappearing minimum all hindrances of this unity in the whole range of his soul and life."[25] To be sure, the figure of Jesus does not transgress the boundaries of humanity, but is incorporated into the development of the human spirit; it would contradict the nature of the Absolute to be realized in a particular individual.[26] The concept of the Absolute is conceivable only with reference to humanity as a whole: "Humanity (not the human nature of Jesus) is the union of the two natures, God who has become man." It is clear that we here stand on the ground of Hegelian philosophy. Jesus is only—even if exceptionally so—an exponent of the development of the divine Spirit within human history. What distinguishes Strauss from Hegel is the consistent questioning of the Gospel texts with regard to their historical verifiability, an angle of questioning that could be immaterial to Hegel, because of his a priori conviction of the superiority of the idea in the philosophical sense to history. Strauss emulated him in his results, for after completing his *Life of Jesus* he too could feel quite at home in the left

---

[24]    Strauss, *Life of Jesus* (1835) 1:75. Cf. the fourth 1840 edition, p. 86: "We distinguish by the name *evangelical mythus* a narrative relating directly or indirectly to Jesus, which may be considered not as the expression of a fact, but as the product of an idea of his earliest followers."

[25]    Strauss, *Life of Jesus* (third edition) 802.

[26]    D. F. Strauss, *Streitschriften zur Vertheidigung meiner Schrift über das Leben Jesu und zur Charakteristik der gegenwärtigen Theologie*. Vol. III, *Die evangelische Kirchenzeitung, die Jahrbücher für wissenschaftliche Kritik und die theologischen Studien und Kritiken in ihrer Stellung zu meiner kritischen Bearbeitung des Lebens Jesu* (Tübingen: C. F. Osiander, 1838) 125–126.

wing of Hegelianism, leaving the theologians to worry about the ruins of what was once an imposing construction of the "life of Jesus"—this applies to the rationalistic as well as the supranaturalistic theologians. Strauss signifies the "embarrassment of theology," as Ernst Wolf once stated.[27] "Embarrassment" because Strauss's path finally ended in philosophy, since Strauss no longer answered, and could no longer answer, the question of why then Jesus is the beginning point and center of Christian faith. This is a question that, after all, is not to be answered definitively from the history of the human spirit. In other words: Strauss's Jesus book made the alternative unavoidable: history or myth? Strauss decided in favor of the latter. All this suggests that the mythologizing of the Jesus tradition can mean giving up the Christian faith as such, and that the danger exists that when the object of faith is separated from history it may be devalued to the point of being merely a philosophical idea. It is at this point that critique of Strauss must be addressed, raising the question of whether a way can be found beyond the "Hegelian" Christ back to the historical Jesus.

Scholarship on the Gospels as practiced in the second half of the nineteenth century was then essentially a dismantling of the philosophical-theological conception of Hegel and his school. Scholars wanted now to do sober, serious work, to ask what stands in the text, not least to deal with questions of detail. And since Strauss's *Life of Jesus* had ignored the Synoptic problem, i.e. the problem of the literary relation of the Synoptic Gospels to each other—he had based his presentation on individual pericopes, that for him basically stood in the text without any connection to each other—the newly awakened historical consciousness directed itself first of all to the literary critical problem of the Gospels: more precisely, to *source analysis*.

*Heinrich Julius Holtzmann* with his work *Die synoptischen Evangelien, ihr Ursprung und geschichtlicher Charakter* (1863) made a pioneering breakthrough. He compared the outlines of the Synoptic Gospels and concluded from the parallel course of the narrative that there was a common original written source (*Grundschrift*) which he found in the Gospel of Mark and designated Urmarkus or Quelle A ("Source A"). This *Grundschrift* is supposed to have contained a "first connected account of the Galilean activity of Jesus" including the "catastrophe in Jerusalem."[28] Mark's editorial work greatly abbreviated this *Grundschrift* in order to avoid everything "that could make the readers' view of the active work of Jesus less clear."[29]

---

[27]  E. Wolf, *Die Verlegenheit der Theologie. David Friedrich Strauss und die Bibelkritik*," in *Libertas Christiana*, ed. W. Matthias and E. Wolf (FS F. Delekat. BEvTh 26. Munich: Chr. Kaiser 1957) 219–239 (219).

[28]  H. J. Holtzmann, *Die synoptischen Evangelien, ihr Ursprung und ihr geschichtlicher Charakter* (Leipzig: Wilhelm Engelmann, 1863) 102.

[29]  H. J. Holtzmann, *Die synoptischen Evangelien* 385.

This assumption that there was an Urmarkus that contained narrative and speech material has not prevailed among scholars. But Holtzmann's contribution remains undisputed. Since his work the priority of Mark has become an indispensable element in contemporary New Testament scholarship. In addition, there is a second, no less important result of source analysis: the discovery of a second basic source of the Synoptic Gospels inferred from the material common to Matthew and Luke but absent from Mark. Holtzmann designated it "Source Λ" (= Urmatthew). This source document has become known in scholarship as the Q source. Holtzmann is thus the real founder and promoter of the two-source theory.

The occasion of this source-critical work was the debate over the problematic of writing a life of Jesus in the wake of D. F. Strauss. Holtzmann attempted on source-critical grounds, that is to investigate by historical means, "what the founder of our religion actually was like, the authentic image of his personality true to his own nature," and in fact to do this "by the application of the only legitimate means, namely by scientific, historical criticism." If this goal had been achieved, it would have meant that over against the mythical picture of D. F. Strauss the historical picture of Jesus would have been recovered. The figure and personality of Jesus would have to be placed on a relatively secure foundation by basing it on a secure determination of the state and relationship of the sources.

The image of Jesus obtained in this way was determinative for the liberal life-of-Jesus theory. On the basis of Mark as the earliest Gospel, a straight-line development of the life of Jesus could be constructed, a progressive development in his messianic consciousness that began with his baptism. A central point in this development was formed by Peter's confession at Caesarea Philippi (Mark 8:29), until—in the time of the passion predictions—the course of Jesus' life reached its end, "an end, that Jesus himself with ever-increasing clarity foresaw as divinely necessary and predicted as the only possible one, but also as the only one worthy of him."[30] Embedded within this narrative are Jesus' ethical instructions, which found their high point in the fundamental principle of "suffering love for the enemy."

For a long time it seemed as though after Holtzmann's work, history had won a clear victory over the Christ myth. His portrayal of Jesus based on historical and psychological study corresponds to his times. It was extraordinarily successful, although D. F. Strauss could hardly be countered with a psychologically-motivated life-of-Jesus theology. Strauss—in contrast to Holtzmann—was thoroughly aware of the character of the portrayal of Jesus in the Gospels that could not be captured within a

---

[30] According to W. G. Kümmel, *The New Testament: The History of the Investigation of Its Problems* (London: SCM Press Ltd., 1973) 154.

rational system, even though he interpreted the mythical element in philosophical terms, specifically those of Hegel. The dismantling of this liberal picture of Jesus first became possible when the history-of-religions school opened up the picture of how alien the New Testament traditions were to modern understandings. *Johannes Weiss*, in his work *Jesus' Proclamation of the Kingdom of God* (1892), had recognized the apocalyptic character of Jesus' preaching. Another result was that the interpretation of Jesus' message in the sense of a general human morality also became problematic.

William Wrede also challenged the Holtzmannian picture of Jesus, though he too worked with the historical-critical method. In *The Messianic Secret* (1901[1]) he shows that the application of psychological criteria to the Markan account encounters undeniable difficulties. The Gospel of Mark is essentially determined by the theory of the messianic secret through the dialectic of hiddenness and revelation of Jesus' messiahship. This dialectic results in a contradiction, in that a command to secrecy is placed alongside the public appearance of Jesus. This contradiction cannot be resolved by psychological means. Moreover, tracing a development of Jesus' messianic consciousness is not possible on the basis of the Gospel of Mark. From the very beginning, Jesus acknowledges himself as the Son of Man (Mark 2:10, 28), and so does not await a progressive development. Neither is it the case that the confession of Peter marks a turning point in Jesus' messianic self-understanding, since in the Markan portrayal Jesus had disclosed his identity to a few chosen disciples prior to the Caesarea Philippi episode.

Since the psychological interpretation of the life of Jesus cannot be supported on the basis of the Gospel of Mark, Wrede did not have much to say about the issue of the life of Jesus. Nonetheless, his work made a significant contribution to clarifying the problem of the life of Jesus. His book resulted in the thesis that the messianic secret in the Gospel of Mark did not originate from Mark himself but must have originated in the pre-Markan church. His "history-of-tradition solution" affirms that we must attribute an active role to the handing on of the Jesus tradition. Since Wrede, the scholarly investigation of the New Testament has had the irrevocable insight that between Jesus and the Evangelists lies an extensive field of active church theology, and that it is therefore not possible to make inferences about the life of Jesus directly from the Gospels. Since Wrede, life of Jesus research stands under the sign of a fundamental skepticism.

Form criticism made Wrede's awareness of the importance of an active church theology between Jesus and the Gospels into a fundamental principle. *Karl-Ludwig Schmidt* in his book *Der Rahmen der Geschichte Jesu* (1919) investigated the framework of the Gospel of Mark and arrived at the conclusion that the pre-Markan tradition circulated as individual isolated pericopes and that their chronological data is derived essentially from pre-

Markan tradition. Their use in worship was a decisive factor in their transmission, and in the course of this transmission process the individual pericopes were provided with a chronological framework.

This was a first step toward the development of *form criticism* as worked out by Martin Dibelius (1919[1]) and Rudolf Bultmann (1921[1]). This discipline investigates the traditions as they were handed on prior to the Gospels. They were analyzed according to their literary form and at the same time investigated with regard to their original, historical setting in life (Sitz im Leben). Here too the result was that the Christian community was the point of origin of a large number of oral and literary forms and individual pericopes.

For the question of the historical Jesus as it was studied up until the first half of the twentieth century, the result was an obvious skepticism with regard to the possibility of writing a generally-acknowledged life of Jesus. Albert Schweitzer had already seen this as the result of his study of two centuries of life of Jesus research: the program of reconstructing the historical Jesus was shattered. The mythical explanation of the Gospels led to a philosophical standpoint that abandoned the connection of the Christian kerygma to history and thereby gave up on the Jesus of the Gospels. The working out of the historical question led to skepticism in evaluating anything that could be called the historical Jesus, and this was based not only on what Wrede, Schmidt, and others had shown as the fragility of the literary foundations on which the liberal life of Jesus study had been built, but also because in the features of every reconstructed picture of Jesus the particular concerns of the historian could be recognized, so that the variety of authors was reflected in the variety of images of Jesus they projected. But even if it were possible to attain a historically-verifiable picture of Jesus, it would still be an open question as to what significance such a reconstructed Jesus could have for Christian faith. The achievement would be a "historian's Jesus," the theological relevance of which would still be an issue for further exploration. The question would remain whether a historical Jesus could or should legitimize Christian faith.

It appears to be a consistent response to this state of affirms when *Martin Kähler* challenged the different attempts to get back to the historical Jesus with his 1892 writing entitled *The So-called Historical Jesus and the Historical, Biblical Christ*.[31] He defended the fundamental independence of the biblical and churchly images of Jesus from historical research, making a sharp distinction between the earthly historical Jesus who at the most can only be reconstructed in rough outline by historical methods,

---

[31]    M. Kähler, *The So-Called Historical Jesus and the Historic, Biblical Christ* (Philadelphia: Fortress Press, 1964).

and the Christ who is the object of Christian faith, transmitted in the church's story and the Bible, the Christ who is proclaimed as the foundation of Christian faith and who encounters the believer in the word of the gospel. By this Kähler is affirming that the object of Christian faith can never be absorbed into history. To be sure, Kähler never really posed the question to himself as to how the Christ of faith is then related to the historical phenomenon of Jesus. Thus his contribution is to be understood only as an important corrective that raises the legitimate theological claim against every sort of historicism, but cannot itself be understood as the last word on the issue. It is rather the case that he posed the challenge for the future to find a way in which both the authenticity of the mythical (theological) interpretation and the validity of historical reconstruction could be affirmed, in other words a way in *both* the essential connection of the Christian faith to history and the person of Jesus *and* the eschatological significance of Jesus Christ for faith. This approach can be described as the *kerygmatic interpretation of Jesus*, in which the connection between the historical Jesus and the kerygma of the early Christian community is acknowledged and set forth.

*Rudolf Bultmann* understands himself to be essentially a Pauline theologian, and thus does not think that Christian faith means faith in the person of Jesus, much less the Jesus as reconstructed by historical research. He appeals to 2 Corinthians 5:16 ("even though we once knew Christ from a human point of view [lit. "according to the flesh"], we know him no longer in that way").[32] From this point of view is not possible for a *historia Jesu* to play a legitimate role for Pauline theology, not to speak of a legitimizing role in the Christian kerygma. It is the exalted Christ, not the earthly Jesus, who is present in the kerygma. Thus to the extent that scholarship investigates the history of Jesus, at the most it can uncompromisingly shatter false sources of security, so that faith does not attempt to rest on the foundation of a reconstructed life of Jesus as its secure basis.

Just the same, Bultmann himself wrote a Jesus book (1926[1]), and the first section of the first part of his *Theology of the New Testament* gave a reconstruction of the message of Jesus (1948[1], ET 1951, 1955), just as did his *Primitive Christianity in its Contemporary Setting* (1949, ET 1956). But the first sentence of his theology of the New Testament is characteristic: "The message of Jesus is a presupposition for the theology of the New Testament rather than a part of that theology itself."[33] This corresponds to his book about earliest Christianity in its history-of-religions context, in which the message of Jesus is presented as a subsection within the larger

---

[32]  R. Bultmann, "Die Christologie des Neuen Testaments," in *Glauben und Verstehen* I 259.
[33]  R. Bultmann, *Theology* 1:3.

context of "Judaism." This means that, just as M. Kähler had already made a sharp distinction between the historical Jesus and the Christ of faith, and as A. Harnack had differentiated the proclaimer (Jesus) and the proclaimed (Christ) ("Not the Son, but the Father alone, belongs within the gospel as it was preached by Jesus"[34]), so also R. Bultmann juxtaposed Jesus as a member and exponent of Judaism to the Christ as the object of Christian faith.

The image of Jesus developed by Bultmann positions Jesus in the religious context of Judaism. Jesus proclaimed the soon coming of the kingdom of God, and did it in such a manner that his own person was the sign of the times (Luke 10:23–24). His preaching makes an end of all securities that interpose themselves between the individual human being and the radical demand of God. He protests against a Jewish understanding of God in which belonging to the chosen people and keeping the Law is a guarantee of eschatological salvation. The God of Jesus is not the God of the Torah, but the God who makes a new claim on the whole person in a way that transcends fulfilling the Old Testament law (Matt 5:21–48). He calls for love of God and neighbor in a way that challenges the traditional pattern of law observance. But this preaching does not make Jesus identical with the Messiah; he has no messianic self-consciousness, but as eschatological prophet he points to the future coming of the Son of Man as the bringer of judgment and salvation. Bultmann attempted to show, on the basis of Mark 8:38, that Jesus did not identify himself with the future Son of Man, but made a distinction between himself and the coming eschatological Son of Man.

As an eschatological prophet, Jesus belonged within the context of Judaism. Jesus the proclaimer first became the proclaimed Christ in the Easter faith of the earliest Christian community that believed in him and expected him to return as the Son of Man. The earliest Christian kerygma was permeated by this hope. It was not founded on the events of the life of Jesus, but on the event of the cross and resurrection. Christian faith is not Jesus-faith (neither in the sense of Jesus' own faith or faith in Jesus), but faith in the saving word made present in the Christ event. This faith permeated the Jesus tradition, a state of affairs that considerably inhibits the possibilities available to the historian to write a life of Jesus or even to reconstruct the message of the historical Jesus. Consequently, Bultmann held the view that the historical content of the kerygma is not the historical reconstruction of the life of Jesus, but only the "That" of the historical Jesus. The verifiable historical information found by the historian who analyzes the Christian kerygma turns out to be no more than the bare historical fact of Jesus.

This view is to be qualified, since the statement that Jesus died on the cross is more than the mere historical confirmation of the "thatness" of Jesus' existence. Bultmann too, in fact, knows more to say about Jesus

---

[34]   As cited in Kümmel, *The New Testament* 183.

than the mere fact that he lived.[35] It is still the case, however, that the kerygmatic interpretation of the person of Jesus unites both of the lines named above: the historical factor, by the affirmation of the historical "that," and the—in the terminology of D. F. Strauss—"mythical character" of the Jesus narrative of the Evangelists, that could also be conceived as the "eschatological" or "kerygmatic" element. The Jesus of the Gospels is conceptualized from the point of view of faith. In the testimony to Jesus in the Gospels we do not meet historical argumentation, but the Christian kerygma and its eschatological claim.

At this point the interest of scholars turned again to the kind of research that attempted a more positive historical evaluation of the message and ministry of Jesus. To be sure, *Ernst Käsemann* responded to the attempted renewal of the quest for the historical Jesus with a certain skepticism, since the image of the earthly Jesus had been almost completely absorbed into that of the exalted Lord.[36] This, however, is no reason for resignation,[37] since in any case it is the unanimous opinion of exegetes that the first, second, and fourth antitheses of the Sermon on the Mount have preserved authentic Jesus material.[38] With this as the point of departure, a picture of the historical Jesus is reconstructed in which the authority of Jesus that surpasses Moses' authority plays a central role. With a radical claim to authority that surpasses even that of the Baptist, Jesus shatters the sphere of Jewish piety. He is more than a Jewish Rabbi or some Jewish prophet or other; he has a messianic self-consciousness.[39] He proclaims the kingdom of God as beginning already in his own present (Matt 11:12-13). This claim makes it impossible to fit Jesus into the categories of either history or the history of religions; he remains a riddle that cannot be solved by the historian alone.

We ask: with this presupposition, what is the motivation for making Jesus the object of historical study? Is "the continuity of the gospel within the discontinuity of the times"[40] really the only thing that saves faith from falling over the cliff into moralism or mysticism? Is there not also a moral or mystical continuity? The danger of losing the gospel in the discontinu-

---

[35] Bultmann's holding fast to the mere "that" of the historical Jesus is to be explained by his hermeneutical interest. Cf. R. Bultmann, *Das Verhältnis der urchristlichen Christusbotschaft zum historischen Jesus*, (SHAW.PH 3. Heidelberg: C. W. Winter, 1960) 13, 21, 25. Cf. also E. Biser, "Hermeneutische Integration. Zur Frage der Herkunft von Rudolf Bultmanns hermeneutischer Interpretation," in B. Jaspert, ed. *Rudolf Bultmanns Werk und Wirkung* (Darmstadt: Wissenschaftliche Buchgesellschaft, 1984) 220.

[36] E. Käsemann, "The Problem of the Historical Jesus," *Essays on New Testament Themes* (SBT 41. London: SCM Press, 1964) 46.

[37] E. Käsemann, "Problem of the Historical Jesus" 25-26.

[38] E. Käsemann, "Problem of the Historical Jesus" 37.

[39] E. Käsemann, "Problem of the Historical Jesus" 37, 43.

[40] E. Käsemann, "Problem of the Historical Jesus" 46.

ity of the times is not to be met only by returning to the quest for the historical Jesus. One could also return to the early church's confessions of faith, as has in fact been done in the past. And furthermore: what criteria are available for reconstructing the message of Jesus? Käsemann affirmed against Bultmann that Mark 8:38 had originated as a prophetic saying of the risen Jesus within the Palestinian church. The same has been claimed for other Jesus material once regarded as authentic. At this point the issue of the criteria to be utilized in the reconstruction of Jesus' message attains a particular importance.

*Gerhard Ebeling* indicates that it is the task of Christology to give an accounting for the statement "I believe in Jesus." In this connection he investigates Jesus' own concept of faith, for if historical study should in fact prove that faith in Jesus had no point of contact with Jesus himself, then that would be the end of Christology. The result of the detailed investigations of the concept of faith in the Gospels is that Jesus wanted to awaken faith, and put his own faith on the line in the effort to bring others to faith. "It is faith that relates to Jesus only because it is faith awakened by Jesus himself."[41] Ebeling later modified this by distinguishing between the historical Jesus as the witness to faith and the Risen One as the ground of faith.[42] The "rise of faith" is attributed to "encounter with witnesses of faith."[43] In this way the "word event" occurs, the existential appropriation of what had happened in Jesus.[44]

In "Das Verhältnis der urchristlichen Christusbotschaft zum historischen Jesus," a document composed late in his life, *R. Bultmann* expressed himself once again on the issue of the historical Jesus and objected against Ebeling that by making the personal attitude of Jesus into an object of academic research he had exchanged the existential encounter that results from the kerygma with objectifying observation. Christian faith, however, does not come from such objectifying observation but by responding in obedience to the call of the word. Moreover, it must be asked whether Ebeling has not overestimated the significance of Jesus' own faith. The Synoptic Gospels say little about the faith of Jesus, and the few references cannot be consistently claimed to belong to the oldest layer. Hebrews 12:2 does speak of Jesus as the one who begins and completes faith, but this refers to the preexistent Christ who is identified with the Crucified and Risen One, not to the historical Jesus. Christian faith occurs only under the material presupposition of the cross and resurrection.

[41] G. Ebeling, "Jesus and Faith," in *Word and Faith* (Philadelphia: Fortress Press, 1963). 201–246 (235).
[42] G. Ebeling, "The Question of the Historical Jesus and the Problem of Christology," *Word and Faith* 288–304.
[43] G. Ebeling, "Jesus and Faith," 244.
[44] *Ibid.*

Finally, *Ernst Fuchs* is to be mentioned. Like G. Ebeling, E. Fuchs thinks that the essence of Christian faith can be derived from the historical Jesus. Differently from Ebeling, however, he does not focus on Jesus' faith, but on Jesus' personal conduct, his love for sinners and his readiness to forgive. By his conduct, Jesus radicalized the message of John the Baptist; as Jesus sees himself as already standing within the realm of the kingdom of God, he brings to bear the voice of love and therefore God himself. He himself is the "language event." This interpretation is based on Jesus' parables, analogies, and aphorisms as transmitted in the Synoptic Gospels. They reflect Jesus' own conduct as the framework for interpreting his message. Against this one should ask with R. Bultmann, however, whether—quite apart from individual aspects of Fuch's interpretation that are worthy of consideration—whether the person of Jesus is not psychologized in this process, so that what we have here is a historical adjustment of Jesus' person to the categories of psychology, the theological significance of which would remain to be raised. Moreover, one must ask who this Jesus is who comes to speech here. It is not the historical Jesus but (at least primarily) the Jesus of the Gospels. E. Fuchs himself admits as much.[45] Finally, but not least in importance, it is disputed which parables (if any) may be utilized in reconstructing the message of the historical Jesus. Taken as a whole, Fuchs' Jesus-interpretation has greater significance for understanding the portrayal of Jesus in the Synoptic Gospels than for understanding the historical Jesus.

## c) Reconstructing Pictures of the Historical Jesus—Four Models

### 1. The Apocalyptic Model

Hermann Samuel Reimarus had had a polemical goal in mind when he attempted to make the figure of Jesus understandable by setting him against the background of the thought world of contemporary Judaism, and by calling attention to the necessity of distinguishing between the historical event of Jesus' appearance and the interpretation of this event by the Christian community.[46] According to Reimarus, the original connection between the message of the historical Jesus and Jewish tradition consists in the near expectation of the end typical of Jewish apocalypticism, which Jesus and his disciples shared. Jesus is accordingly a proclaimer of the nearness of the kingdom of God and coupled this announcement with

---

[45] Cf. E. Fuchs, "Jesu Selbstzeugnis" 31.

[46] Cf. Fragment 1. Von Duldung der Deisten. "Fragment eines Ungenannten," in G. E. Lessing, *Sämtliche Schriften 12*, ed. K. Lachmann (Leipzig: Göschen, 1897³) 254–271.

the call to conversion.[47] The apocalyptic type of preaching anticipated by Reimarus thus affirms that Jesus was portrayed as a prophet of the end-time. Foundational for this view is Mark 1:15: in the fullness of time Jesus announces the soon arrival of the kingdom of God that will appear amid cosmic catastrophes, which will be the realization of the Old Testament promises, and will bring grace and judgment to humanity.[48] Through this proclamation the kingdom of God not only becomes present, but by Jesus' message is projected into time. Therefore the time of Jesus' ministry is the time of decision; the response to Jesus' message is decisive for salvation or condemnation of the individual at the eschatological judgment. While the life and message of Jesus as that of the eschatological prophet are un-messianic in the strict sense,[49] the message of Jesus so conceived still belongs to the apocalyptic horizon, including the expectation of a future Messiah-Son of Man, as appears to be affirmed in Mark 8:38. Alternatively, this type of portrayal of Jesus is associated with the idea that Jesus himself expected his own exaltation by which he would become the apocalyptic Son of Man and judge of the world, analogous to the Similitudes of Enoch, in which the installation of Enoch as the Son of Man is predicted.[50]

## 2.  *Jesus as Wisdom Teacher*

A different non-apocalyptic understanding of Jesus which still interprets him in the context of his Jewish surroundings is that of a sage or a teacher of Torah. The "enlightened" interpretation of the person of Jesus by Gotthold Ephraim Lessing had already portrayed Jesus as a divine teacher who appeared for the instruction of the human race, who had made the subject of his instruction the three pillars of natural religion, namely God,

---

[47]  Cf. Fragment 7: "Von dem Zwecke Jesu und seiner Jünger (Lessing, *Sämtliche Schriften 13*, 215–327). Translated as "Concerning the Intention of Jesus and His Teaching," in Charles H. Talbert, ed. *Reimarus: Fragments* (Philadelphia: Fortress, 1970).

[48]  Cf. e. g. R. Bultmann, *Theology* 1:4–6. An apocalyptic exposition of the message of Jesus is the basis for other Jesus-books, e. g. K. Niederwimmer (*Jesus* [Göttingen: Vandenhoeck & Ruprecht, 1968]), in which the author also gives a psychological interpretation of the person of Jesus. (53ff: Jesus introduced an "adjustment of consciousness").

[49]  Cf. e. g. R. Bultmann, *Theology* 1:27, and "Verhältnis" 11: "Thus a prophetic consciousness, even a consciousness of having great authority, is to be ascribed to him [Jesus]."

[50]  1 Enoch 70–71. Cf. W. Baldensperger, *Das Selbstbewusstsein Jesu im Lichte der messianischen Hoffnungen seiner Zeit*, (Strassburg: J. H. Ed. Heitze, 1892², 200ff; A. J. B. Higgins, *The Son of Man in the Teaching of Jesus* (SNTSMS 39. Cambridge: Cambridge University Press, 1980; R. Kearns, *Das Traditionsgefüge um den Menschensohn* (Tübingen: J. C. B. Mohr [Paul Siebeck], 1986); J. Theisohn, *Der auserwählte Richter* (StUNT 12. Göttingen: Vandenhoeck & Ruprecht, 1974).

virtue, and immortality.[51] And wherever the work of Jesus was interpreted "according to reason" and as oriented to the practice of everyday life, his message was understood as essentially a summary of "common sense rules,"[52] similar to the manner in which the liberal life-of-Jesus theology presented ethical instruction as the core of Jesus' teaching.[53] In recent studies this type is recognizable where the Gospel tradition's designation of Jesus by his disciples and the people as "Rabbi" or διδάσκαλος[54] is understood in terms of the content of Jesus' teaching. Unlike the rabbinic style of the Talmud, but still in accord with the tradition of Jewish pedagogy, Jesus' instruction made use of aphorisms and parables and taught the "will of God"[55] by pointing his hearers toward the right path of life by giving directions in terms of concrete details. In view of the boundless goodness of the Creator he prohibits anxiety (Matt 6:25ff). One's obligation is rather to be concerned for the welfare of the other, even if it means the violation of the rules of purity and the Sabbath.[56] The demands for ethical conduct such as those set forth in the Decalogue are fundamental (Mark 10:19par), at the top of which are the commands to love God and neighbor, including love for enemies (Matt 5:44). Even when these instructions are expressed in terms of individual ethics, they are not limited to the group of Jesus' followers but have a universal horizon.[57] In this connection the crucial issue is how Jesus' conduct is to be evaluated with regard to the Old Testament-Jewish Torah. Fairly often a distinction is made between Jesus' critical stance toward the oral tradition of Judaism and his own teaching, which does not abrogate the written Law but is its fulfillment.[58] On the other hand, it appears from some statements in the Gospels that Jesus was no less critical of the Old Testament law itself

---

51  Cf. G. E. Lessing, "Die Erziehung des Menschengeschlechts" 1780 (= *Sämtliche Schriften 13* [Leipzig 1897[3], 413–436]).

52  E. g. H. E. G. Paulus, *Das Leben Jesu als Grundlage einer reinen Geschichte des Urchristenthums* (2 vols.), Heidelberg: C. F. Winter, 1828.

53  William Wrede was no longer able to elaborate the teaching of Jesus as he had imagined it, as the beginning point of the history of the Christian tradition (cf. his "Über Aufgabe und Methode" passim), but the indications in his book on Paul point in this direction (cf. W. Wrede, *Paulus* 89ff). See also W. Heitmüller, *Jesus* (Tübingen: J. C. B. Mohr [Paul Siebeck], 1913) 118ff.

54  Rabbi: Mark 9:5; 10:51; 11:21; 14:45par; διδάσκαλος (as translation of Rabbi: John 1:38; 20:16); Mark 4:38; 9:17, 38; 10:17, 20, 35; 12:14, 19; 13:1par; cf. also J. Schniewind, "Der Verkündigungscharakter der theologischen Wissenschaft," *ThLZ* 72 (1947) 167.

55  Cf. R. Bultmann, *Jesus and the Word* 57–132.

56  Mark 2:23ff; 7:1ff; cf. P. Noll, *Jesus und das Gesetz* 5; E. Käsemann "Problem" 38.

57  P. Noll, *Jesus und das Gesetz* 15ff.

58  Matthew 5:17; on the distinction cf. D. Daube, *The New Testament and Rabbinic Judaism* (JLCR II. London: Athlone, 1952, 1956) 55ff; W. D. Davies, *The Setting of the Sermon on the Mount* (Cambridge: Cambridge University Press, 1964) 99ff; B. Gerhardsson, "Memory and Manuscript," in H. K. McArthur, ed. *In Search of the Historical Jesus* (New York: Harper, 1969) 33–40.

than he was of the oral tradition, and that he at least sharpened the requirements of the Old Testament.[59] In the antitheses of the Sermon on the Mount he expressed a claim that greatly transcends that of a wisdom teacher,[60] so that if Jesus is understood from this point of view he is not merely a secular facilitator of good ethical conduct, but should rather be seen as the Messiah of the Torah.[61]

## 3. The Pauline-Lutheran Model

Such an ethical interpretation of the message of Jesus does not yet transgress the boundaries of the range of Judaism that can be verified by study of the history of religion, all the less since—as pointed out by Gerhard Kittel— there is not a single item of Jesus' ethical instruction that can be considered absolutely unique within the framework of Judaism.[62] But the preaching of Jesus achieves the rank of an independent message, a conception that can no longer be derived from Jewish premises, as soon as it is no longer regarded under the summary aspect of individual ethical instructions but is expressed as absolute demand and is thereby made an "outrageous" claim.[63] The direction of interpretation that is thereby indicated can hardly deny its basis in theological dogmatics; it approximates the Pauline-Lutheran approach to the issue in which the thesis that the demand of Jesus, if not impossible to fulfill, at least is not in fact fulfilled, and so functions as the *usus elenchticus legis*, is a fundamental theological presupposition. For understanding the message of Jesus this means that the authority absent from the words of the scribes but manifest in the words of Jesus (Matt 7:29par.) is the authority of God's promise of unconditional acceptance. It is the authority of God's love for human beings, a love that also calls for love in return. Thereby the word of Jesus becomes a call to decision; the command "love your neighbor as yourself" gives no excuse whatever for selfish love for oneself;[64] it is rather the case that it makes the individual aware of his or her guilt. But this word would be incomplete if, alongside the demand of love, it did not also promise God's forgiveness.

---

[59]  H. Braun, *Spätjüdisch-häretischer und frühchristlicher Radikalismus II. Die Synoptiker* (BHTh 24/2. Tübingen: J. C. B. Mohr [Paul Siebeck] 1969[2]) 28, 33, and elsewhere.

[60]  Cf. E. Käsemann, "Problem" 37–38.

[61]  Cf. W. D. Davies, *Torah in the Messianic Age and/or the Age to Come*, (JBLMS 7. Philadelphia, 1952) passim; *Setting* 93ff; E. Käsemann *ThLZ* 81 (1956) 547–548; R. Riesner, *Jesus als Lehrer* (WUNT II 7. Tübingen: J. C. B. Mohr [Paul Siebeck], 1993[4]; M. Hengel, "Jesus als messianischer Lehrer der Weisheit und die Anfänge der Christologie," in *Sagesse et religion* (Paris: ed. Pr. Univ. de France, 1979) 148–188.

[62]  G. Kittel, "Die Bergpredigt und die Ethik des Judentums," ZSTh 2 (1925) 555–594.

[63]  E. Käsemann, "Problem" 38.

[64]  S. Kierkegaard, "You Shall Love Your Neighbor," *Works of Love: Some Christian Reflections in the Form of Discourses* (New York: Harper, 1978) 67–69.

Thus the call to decision is made with an unsurpassable sharpness, since now the "no" to this demand is at the same time a "no" to God's forgiveness.[65] If the cry "Abba" was an original element in Jesus' own speech,[66] and if—as formulated by Bousset, though with a different theological intention—Jesus' faith in the fatherly love of God was his most characteristic act,[67] then it appears to be necessary to see the message and life of Jesus as a unity[68] and also—without trying to read christological predications back into the life of Jesus—to interpret the person of Jesus christologically. Jesus' conduct is then the real framework for his message.[69] His conduct as seen in his fellowship with publicans and sinners, his acceptance of the socially and religiously disenfranchised, (in a word: in his love for sinners) is the meaning and claim of his advent. Consequently, Jesus' preaching in parables is essentially the demonstration of his own life. In the parable of the lost son Jesus defends his own conduct as the conduct of the one who—in that he draws and accepts sinners into his own presence—acts in God's place.[70] Thus the Christology claimed to be implicit in Jesus' proclamation is here no longer identical with the call to decision,[71] but is constituted by the life of Jesus as such. This also means that the Pauline interpretation of the saving event, namely the distinction normative for Paul between indicative and imperative, the Pauline idea of the manifestation of judgment and grace in the Christ event, would accordingly have been basically anticipated by the historical Jesus.[72]

## 4. Jesus as Revolutionary

Already Reimarus was of the opinion that Jesus had hoped to be proclaimed a political Messiah and to be able to establish a secular messianic kingdom,[73] and Ernest Renan's famous *Life of Jesus* portrayed the second

---

[65] K. E. Løgstrup, *Die ethische Forderung* (Tübingen: J. C. B. Mohr [Paul Siebeck], 1968²) 236–237.

[66] J. Jeremias, *The Prayers of Jesus* (Naperville, IL: Alec R. Allenson, Inc., 1967) 95–98.

[67] W. Bousset, *Jesu Predigt in ihrem Gegensatz zum Judentum* (Göttingen: Vandenhoeck & Ruprecht, 1892) 41ff.

[68] Cf. among others P. Althaus, *Der gegenwärtige Stand der Frage nach dem historischen Jesus* (SBAW.PPH 6. Munich: Bayerischen Akademie der Wissenschaften 1960) and G. Bornkamm, *Jesus of Nazareth* 23.

[69] E. Fuchs, "Quest of the Historical Jesus" 21.

[70] *Ibid.*

[71] As in R. Bultmann, *Theology* 1:43, who, however, says this in the context of "Jesus' Meaning to the Faith of the Earliest Church" (42), and thus is not really speaking of an implied Christology in the preaching of Jesus.

[72] E. Käsemann, "Blind Alleys in the Jesus of History Controversy," in *New Testament Questions of Today* (London: SCM, 1969) 23–65; 56; H. Braun, *Gesammelte Studien zum Neuen Testament und seiner Umwelt* (Tübingen: J. C. B. Mohr [Paul Siebeck], 1971³) 296, 315.

[73] Fragment 7; cf. *Reimarus: Fragments*, C. Talbert, ed., (Philadelphia: Fortress, 1970) 135–150.

period of Jesus' ministry as "in the highest degree revolutionary."[74] The Marxist reconstructions of the life of Jesus[75] have made popular the revolutionary type of Jesus picture; and the liberal disputing of Jesus' own historicity corresponds in content to its portrayal of early Christian community life as the life of a revolutionary, Communist-proletariat group. Both views reflect the times; neither view laster very long.[76]

Jesus as revolutionary: this means not only the attempt, with or without violence, to force cultural or social changes; this does not at all mean only a verbal protest of love against the injustice and lovelessness in the existing social state of affairs, but describes the attempt by all available means to replace a perverted power structure by a different and better one, as required by the most extreme definition of the word "revolution." The basis for a political interpretation of the life of Jesus is the fact established by the agreement of all the accounts of the New Testament Gospels that Jesus was executed by crucifixion by the Roman occupational authorities—obviously as a political agitator, as shown by the placard on the cross (Mark 15:26). From this point of departure, Jesus' life is understood as a unity: like John the Baptist, so Jesus as his disciple also stands in opposition to the ruling groups of his time. But differently than John, he does not withdraw into the desert but turns to the people in order to effect his revolutionary plan and to introduce the kingdom of God by his own actions. He is like the other Jewish patriots who resisted the Romans and their Jewish collaborators.[77] Thus the nicknames of some of his disciples suggest that they belonged to the Zealot resistance movement,[78] and the saying about the sword (Matt 10:34; Luke 22:36; cf. Luke 12:49) is interpreted to mean that Jesus had an armed strike force at his disposal. Accordingly Jesus' march into Jerusalem and the cleansing of the temple that immediately follows are to be seen as political events, so that Jesus' arrest by armed soldiers and his crucifixion are only the consistent outcome of a revolutionary life. It was only after his death that the church in process of formation attempted to understand his life and ministry in a spiritualizing sense; then the authors of the Gospels likewise modified and eliminated the original political thematic.[79]

---

[74]  E. Renan, *Life of Jesus* (Boston: Little, Brown, & Co., 1923) 174.

[75]  E.g. K. Kautsky, *Foundations of Christianity* (New York: T. A. Russell, 1953).

[76]  E. g. A. Kalthoff, *Das Christusproblem. Grundlinien zu einer Sozialtheologie* (Leipzig: Eugen Diederichs, 1902) and *Die Entstehung des Christentums. Neue Beiträge zum Christusproblem* (Leipzig: Eugen Diederichs, 1904).

[77]  J. Carmichael, *The Death of Jesus* (London: Macmillan, 1963) 159; cf. 179–180.

[78]  *Ibid.* 156–158.

[79]  *Ibid.*, 212ff. On this model cf. M. Hengel, *Was Jesus a Revolutionist?* (Philadelphia: Fortress, 1971) and *Victory Over Violence: Jesus and the Revolutionists* (Philadelphia: Fortress, 1973).

## d) The Possibility and Theological Importance of Reconstructing the Life and Message of Jesus

While the older studies were primarily concerned with reconstructing the external and internal course of the development of Jesus' life so as to write a life of Jesus, in more recent New Testament scholarship this attempt has been by and large abandoned, seeking instead to rediscover the message of Jesus. The common element in both quests is that Jesus is understood as the object of historical research. They both presuppose decisions about criteria that can facilitate such historical research.

1. Rudolf Bultmann, in his *History of the Synoptic Tradition* named three criteria that can be applied in deciding on the authenticity of Jesus traditions: (1) Statements in the Jesus tradition that contradict Jewish moral teaching and the practices of Jewish piety can be claimed for the historical Jesus. (2) Statements in the Jesus tradition that are characterized by the lack of specific Christian traits, and accordingly cannot be attributed to the post-Easter Christian community with any probability, can be attributed to Jesus. In contrast, other passages that contain genuine Christian statements cannot be considered authentic sayings of Jesus. (3.) Related to the two criteria just named (which together are often called the "criterion of dissimilarity") is the "criterion of coherence," according to which Jesus material can be considered authentic whose content substantially agrees with material established by the criterion of dissimilarity. On this basis, the "intense eschatological consciousness" found in Jesus material is understood as a mark of its authenticity.[80]

It must be said as a critique of these criteria that while the contrast between the message of Jesus and contemporary Jewish thinking does correspond to the Jesus tradition in the Gospels, it can by no means guarantee that such material is from Jesus, for anti-Jewish traits are also found in other layers of the Gospels, since the Christian community, especially in its early phase, was subject to persecution by Jewish authorities. Moreover, we can identify Jewish or anti-Jewish elements in Jesus' life and message only on the basis of our fragmentary knowledge of Judaism at the time of Jesus. Since Bultmann's time the discovery of the Qumran community and its literature has considerably extended the basis for the scholarly investigation of first-century Judaism.[81]

So also the elimination of specifically Christian characteristics from the Jesus tradition presupposes a particular pre-understanding, such as the view that Jesus did not consider himself to be the Messiah. Here R.

---

[80]  R. Bultmann, *History of the Synoptic Tradition* 126 and elsewhere.

[81]  Cf. the brief summary and the bibliography given by J. Maier, "Antikes Judentum," in G. Strecker and J. Maier, *Neues Testament—Antikes Judentum* (GKT 2. Stuttgart: Kohlhammer, 1988) 172–173.

Bultmann depends on the results of W. Wrede's *Messianic Secret*, whose analysis of the Markan and pre-Markan tradition contrasted the unmessianic tradition of the life of Jesus with the faith in the resurrected Jesus Christ, must now be modified.[82]

With regard to the "intense eschatological consciousness," it can now hardly be doubted that a similar eschatological mood was also present in the environment of the New Testament, as documented in the Jewish apocalyptic writings. Thus the eschatological consciousness as such cannot be understood as inherent only in sayings of Jesus, but is found both in Jewish and Christian materials of the time.

All this means that one must reckon with a significant degree of uncertainty in the application of these criteria. It is only consistent with this when H. Conzelmann was unwilling to distinguish between the oldest layer of the Synoptics and authentic Jesus tradition.[83] Thus the results attained in such a Jesus book must share the same uncertainty inherent in the effort to reconstruct the message of Jesus. The problematic is deepened by the intentional lack of distinction between the theology of the Synoptic Gospels and the message of Jesus.[84] Moreover, the fact that the early church tradition consisted primarily of isolated units of material also contributed to this uncertainty, since such individual pieces of tradition were later fitted together into different patterns as in a mosaic. The result is a variety of differing images of Jesu, each made according to the prior understanding that shapes the reconstruction. The "sense of direction of Jesus' message" (E. Fuchs) is subordinated to the subjective judgment of the observer. In addition, the active role of early church theology can hardly be overestimated. Ernst Käsemann called attention to the significance of early Christian prophets who both modified existing traditions and created new ones. This means that "our questioning has sharpened and widened until the obligation now laid upon us is to investigate and make credible not the possible inauthenticity of the individual unit of material but, on the contrary, its genuineness,"[85] or, better said: neither the claim of "authenticity" nor the claim of "inauthenticity" of each element of the Jesus tradition can be assumed, but each must be argued on the basis of evidence.

The inadequacy of the criteria available for this task is seen in the large number and wide variety of proposed reconstructions. However, the re-

---

[82] Cf. G. Strecker, "Zur Messiasgeheimnistheorie im Markusevangelium," in *Eschaton und Historie* 33–51; W. Wrede, *The Messianic Secret* (Cambridge & London: James Clarke & Co. Ltd., 1971).

[83] H. Conzelmann, *Outline* 97–98; differently G. Bornkamm, *Jesus of Nazareth* 17–26; 215–220

[84] This is also the case in H. Merklein, *Die Gottesherrschaft als Handlungsprinzip* (fzb 34. Würzburg: Echter, 1984³).

[85] E. Käsemann, "Problem of the Historical Jesus" 34.

sulting justifiable skepticism should not have the last word. The uncertainty of the reconstruction can be reduced by application of the "criterion of development." This method understands the text analogously to the growth rings of a tree. The older a text is, the more it is surrounded or even overgrown by secondary traditional material. The more clearly such secondary tradition can be identified as formations of the Christian community, the more probably the original kernel of the tradition can be attributed to the authentic sayings of Jesus. This can be illustrated by study of the Sermon on the Mount.[86]

2. While the reconstruction of the message and ministry of Jesus is a necessary task for the historian if the history of the church is to be understood in the light of its beginnings and presuppositions, the question of the *theological significance* of such a reconstruction is also to be posed. At the beginning of the recent debate concerning the historical Jesus, Karl Barth declared in view of the approach of the "leading New Testament scholars who, much to my amazement, have armed themselves with swords and staves and set off on a new quest of the historical Jesus, to which I have the same response as before, namely that I do not want to participate in it."[87] Nevertheless, we ask how it came to be that a "new quest" was launched? E. Käsemann based the theological necessity of such a quest with the claim that otherwise history would be replaced by myth and a heavenly being would replace the man of Nazareth.[88] Precisely for this reason it would be indispensable to hold fast to the identification of the exalted Christ with the historical Jesus. Accordingly, the danger arises that the Christ event would become an unhistorical abstraction, and that the location of Christology in the conflict between Ebionism and docetism the scale would seem to be tipping in the latter direction, or that at the most one would still be concerned with the name of Jesus, but not with the person of Jesus, and would finally have to agree with the statement of the liberal P. W. Schmiedel: "My most personal religious faith would not be damaged if I found it necessary on historical evidence to acknowledge that *Jesus had never lived*.[89] Here one must object: the affirmation of the historical existence of Jesus is inseparably bound to the early Christian kerygma and could be eliminated only with damage to the original structure of Christian faith. On the other hand it belongs to the basic principles of this kerygma that faith in Christ can never be handed over to historical study and that with regard to its essence it can never be dependent on the

---

[86]  Cf. G. Strecker, *The Sermon on the Mount: An Exegetical Commentary* (Nashville: Abingdon, 1988) 11–15 and passim.

[87]  K. Barth, "How My Mind Has Changed," *EvTh* 20 (1960) 104.

[88]  E. Käsemann, "Problem of the Historical Jesus," 25.

[89]  P. W. Schmiedel, "Die Person Jesu im Streite der Meinungen der Gegenwart," *PrM* 10/7 (1906) 281.

results of historical study, since the claim that the person of Jesus is the eschatological sign for the world is an affirmation that cannot be established by historical research. The significance of Jesus for faith is visible only in the light of the resurrection event. It was so understood by Paul (cf. 1 Cor 15). So also the witness to Christ presented by the New Testament Evangelists is by no means to be understood as a reflection of the message or life of the historical Jesus but has grown from the testimony to Jesus of the early Christian community, and is accordingly determined by the Easter faith.

But is it not in the interest of faith itself to show its continuity with the past? Is it not necessarily interested in understanding itself in the context of history, and all the more so as it knows of the discontinuity and disparity of the Christian message? Here it must be clearly said: while it is important that faith remains identical with itself as a matter of faith, its foundation is in fact a contingent event, something that is not derivable from history, namely the eschatological promise of the word of God as it has occurred in the Christ event. In its essence it is without any historical analogy, because it opens itself only to acceptance by faith. Faith is oriented only to the testimony of the early Christian kerygma. The question of continuity would at the most show the external side of this event, therefore proving nothing with regard to faith itself. For the essential nature of faith is not a matter of researching its historical basis, for faith bears its evidence within itself, even when it is oriented to the faith of others. A falling back on evidence about the historical Jesus could neither add nor take away anything from this. The attempt to legitimate the Christian faith by salvation history was still possible in the nineteenth century under the influence of Hegel's philosophy, since he thought he stood at the end of history in the sense that its secrets had become transparent to him. The person of today, under the influence of two world wars, knows that this was an illusion, and that it is futile to seek for a demonstrable meaning of history. The theologian is here in no better situation than the secular historian, and should express his solidarity with the secular world by acknowledging his ignorance. His ignorance includes the impossibility of being able to explain why it is that precisely this Jesus of Nazareth, of all people, has been constituted the eschatological sign for the world. If historians, including those among the theologians, want to argue about what Jesus of Nazareth in himself was or was not, the faith that Jesus Christ is the word of God to church and world can neither be proved nor disproved by historical study. This faith rests on the Easter message as proclaimed at the first by the witnesses of the resurrection. Historical inquiry as to what lies behind the early Christian kerygma is not only not necessary for faith, but also inappropriate in terms of its own subject matter (just as out of place as the question of what God was doing before the creation of the world.—Luther's answer: God sat in the forest and cut switches for those who asked such questions.) Here the saying is true: believe that you have it, and you have it. That means, believe in what is proclaimed to you, and do not attempt to legitimize it by some other means. The only possible legitimization is found in faith itself, not outside faith in some other realm, including not in the historical Jesus!

Nonetheless, historical inquiry necessarily belongs to an exegetical discipline that seeks to pursue the issue by combining the historical and theological perspectives on the issues. It will thus be necessary in the following to sketch the "basic structure of Jesus' message," and all the more so since the "criterion of development" sketched above can help to overcome destructive skepticism, and also because the reconstruction of the message of Jesus in its first-century ambience can prepare the way for a model of theological significance by which contemporary faith can be both ignited and measured.

### e) The Basic Structure of Jesus' Message

*1. The Time and Location of Jesus' Life*

The date of Jesus' birth is unknown. The representation of the census under Caesar Augustus (Luke 2:1) points to the year 6/7 C.E., for this was the first census in Judea. But this (Lucan) note originated later and presupposes the birth of Jesus in Bethlehem. The Lucan synchronism in Luke 3:1–2 refers to the appearance of John the Baptist and locates this in the fifteenth year of Tiberius Caesar, which would be 28 C.E. It is not clear, however, how the chronological connections between the appearance of John and that of Jesus are to be understood. According to Luke 3:23, Jesus was about thirty years old at the beginning of his ministry; according to John 2:20, Jesus was active in the forty-sixth year of the Herodian temple (= 27/28 C.E.).

The year of Jesus death can be determined more accurately. Pontius Pilate was procurator of Judea in the years 26–36; Jesus was crucified on a Friday. According to the Synoptics this was the first day of the Passover festival (= 15th Nisan). According to the tradition in the Gospel of John the crucifixion occurred on the day of Preparation for the Passover, on which the Passover lambs were slaughtered (= 14th Nisan). If the beginning of the month Nisan is exactly calculated according to the phases of the moon, then the fifteenth of Nisan would have fallen on a Friday in the year 30 C.E, which would have been the 4th of April.[90]

The location of Jesus' ministry: The Gospels are determined by the geographical schema "from Galilee to Jerusalem." The geographical details

---

[90] Detailed discussion of the chronology is found in O. Betz, "Probleme des Prozesses Jesu," *ANRW* 2.25.1: 565–647.

of the tradition correspond to this, especially the appearance of Jesus at the Sea of Gennesaret (and the city of Capernaum). Jesus' home town is not far distant (Mark 1:9; Matt 2:23). Jesus' identifying name Ναζαρηνός (Mark 1:24 and elsewhere) or Ναζωραῖος (Matt 2:23; 26:71) is derived from the Greek form of Nazareth (= Nazara). The hypothesis of H. H. Schaeder,[91] that Ναζωραῖος is derived from the Greek Ναζιραῖος (Judges 13:5, 7 LXX = one dedicated to God) breaks down on the difference between omega and iota; so also other derivations from Hebrew or Aramaic (נצר "keep, observe") from which the name Nazareth could be inferred are too hypothetical. The purported birthplace Bethlehem was connected to the Son of David Christology of the pre-Synoptic tradition by its material associations and has no historical value.

The temporal span of Jesus' activity: According to the Synoptic Gospels Jesus made only one trip from Galilee to Jerusalem (the extent of his ministry was then one year?), while the Gospel of John identifies several trips to the Passover festival in Jerusalem. Exact information cannot be derived from these references. It may well be that the ministry of Jesus included at least the years 27–30.

## 2.  History-of-Religion Perspectives

Jesus was a Jew. This statement needs to be made more precise, for Palestine at the beginning of the first century was not only inhabited by Jews. Especially Galilee was the homeland of a mixed population where Jewish, Hellenistic, and Oriental influences overlapped.[92] These influences would have already had an effect on Jesus in his youth. But it was also the case that on the streets of Jerusalem one heard not only Aramaic, but Greek and Latin. Not only linguistically, but also theologically, the Judaism of Jesus' time was a complex structure. The Qumran texts present an outstanding illustration of this complexity. The scribes that Jesus confronted are not to be identified with the Rabbis of the Talmud, but belong to an early Rabbinic or pre-Rabbinic stage of scribal development.[93] The Pharisees as a group of "separatists" stand alongside the Sadducees who were

---

[91]  H. H. Schaeder, Ναζαρηνός TDNT 4:874–979.
[92]  Cf. W. Bauer, "Jesus der Galiläer," in Aufsätze und Kleine Schriften, ed. G. Strecker (Tübingen: J. C. B. Mohr [Paul Siebeck], 1967) 91–108; 92–97. U. Schnelle, "Jesus, ein Jude aus Galiläa," BZ 32 (1988) 107–113; W. Bösen, Galiläa als Lebensraum und Wirkungsfeld Jesu (Freiburg: Herder, 1985). S. Freyne, Galilee from Alexander the Great to Hadrian (Notre Dame: Notre Dame University Press, 1980).
[93]  Cf. R. Riesner, Jesus als Lehrer. Eine Untersuchung zum Ursprung der Evangelien-Überlieferung (WUNT II 7. Tübingen: J. C. B. Mohr [Paul Siebeck] 1981) 173–176; G. Strecker, Johannine Letters xxxvi note 55. Cf. also P. Schäfer, "Der vorrabbinische Pharisäismus," in M. Hengel, ed., Paulus und das antike Judentum (WUNT 58. Tübingen: J. C. B. Mohr [Paul Siebeck], 1991) 125–175.

consciously open to Hellenistic and Roman influences. Thus the thesis that Jesus was a member of the Jewish people does not say much in itself; it must be nuanced and filled with some particular content.

Jewish literature about Jesus considers "Brother Jesus" as one of their own and understands Jesus as "a central figure of Jewish history and the history of Jewish faith."[94] They do this by emphasizing the tensions that exist between Jesus and later Christianity. However, the conflicts that existed between Jesus and his own Jewish contemporaries must not be ignored. Thus the Jewish charges against Jesus as being an agitator led to his crucifixion under the Roman procurator Pontius Pilate. To whatever extent the history of Jesus, considered externally, is to be reckoned as belonging to Jewish intellectual and theological history, it is still the case that he stands alone within this history. From the point of view of the historical study of religions, Jesus must be understood even within his Jewish context as a singular figure.

## 3. The Proclamation of the Kingdom of God

Already in the work of H. J. Holtzmann the point of departure for the reconstruction of the message of Jesus was Mark 1:14–15 (Jesus came "proclaiming the good news of God, and saying, 'The time is fulfilled, and the kingdom of God has come near; repent, and believe in the good news'"). Here we have a Markan summary, the historical accuracy of which can be disputed.[95] However, the second petition of the Lord's Prayer, "Your kingdom come" (Matt 6:10par), agrees with this Markan summary, as does the introduction to Jesus' parables of the kingdom (e. g. Mark 4:26, "The kingdom of God is as if someone would scatter seed on the ground,..."].

The term βασιλεία θεοῦ[96] can mean the territory ruled by God ("God's kingdom") as well as the exercise of divine power ("God's rulership"). Jesus adopts the usage of Jewish apocalyptic, i.e. the expectation of an "eternal

---

[94] So Sch. Ben-Chorin, Bruder Jesus 12.

[95] Cf. G. Strecker, "Literarkritische Überlegungen zum εὐαγγέλιον-Begriff im Markusevangelium," in Eschaton und Historie 76–89 (78–82).

[96] Cf. U. Luz, βασιλεία, EWNT I 481–491 (483). In addition: H. Merklein, Jesu Botschaft von der Gottesherrschaft (SBS 111. Stuttgart, 1989³; U. Bejick, Basileia. Vorstellungen vom Königtum Gottes im Umfeld des Neuen Testaments (Diss. Heidelberg, 1990 [Microfische]); D. Kosch, Die Gottesherrschaft im Zeichen des Widerspruchs. Traditions- und redaktionsgeschichtliche Untersuchung von Lk 16:16; Mt 11, 12f bei Jesus, Q, und Lukas (EHS.T 257. Bern, 1985); J. Schlosser, Les logia du règne: étude sur le vocable,Basileia tou theou' dans la prédication de Jésus (Strassbourg: J. Gabalda, 1982); H. Merkel, "Die Gottesherrschaft in der Verkündigung Jesu," in M. Hengel and A. M. Schwemer, eds. Königsherrschaft Gottes und himmlischer Kult im Judentum, Urchristentum und in der hellenistischen Welt (WUNT 55. Tübingen: J. C. B. Mohr [Paul Siebeck], 1991) 119–161; Th. Schmeller, "Das Reich Gottes im Gleichnis," ThLZ 119 (1994) 599–608.

kingdom that shall never be destroyed" established by the God of heaven (Dan 2:44; 7:27).[97] Such a futuristic-eschatological idea corresponds to Mark 1:15 (ἤγγικεν), as it does to Mark 14:25:

> I will never again drink of the fruit of the vine until that day when I drink it new in the kingdom of God!

or Luke 17:21:

> The kingdom of God will all at once be "in your midst" (ἐντὸς ὑμῶν).

It can not be calculated in advance by observing its signs.[98]

Jesus promises the coming kingdom of God to the poor, hungering, and crying as the saving gift of God (Luke 6:20–21par). The announcement of the kingdom of God is thus essentially paraclesis. Jesus makes a helpful promise. Thereby a connection is made between his appearance as announcer and the future advent of the kingdom of God. This is what is pointed to by the parables of growth: while the beginning in the preaching of Jesus is unobservable, the final result will indeed be wonderful. The "contrast" that is thus expressed means that the presence of Jesus, his preaching and his miracles, are an anticipation of the coming kingdom. Cf. Matthew 12:28par:

> But if it is by the Spirit of God that I cast out demons, then the kingdom of God has come to you.

Even though Jesus may be rejected by his opponents in the present, they have also encountered the presence of the kingdom in him. This is the meaning of the original form of the saying about those who take the kingdom by force:

> The Law and the Prophets (are valid) until John; from then on the kingdom of God suffers violence (βιάζεται) and the violent ones are trying to seize it by force (Matt 11:12par.; Luke 16:16).

The kingdom of God is present in persecution and suffering.

But the announcement of the kingdom of God is not only a gracious promise, but the threat of judgment is also included in it. This corresponds to the apocalyptic tradition of Judaism, according to which the establishment of the eternal kingdom of God means the destruction of all powers hostile to God (Dan 2:44; 7:27). Therefore Jesus connects the call to repentance to the announcement of the kingdom of God (Matt 11:21–

---

[97]    Cf. also 1 Enoch 84:2; 92:4; 103:1, where מַלְכוּת שָׁמַיִם means the "rulership of God" (not the "kingdom of God"); so C. Westermann and G. Schille, "Reich Gottes," *BHH* 1966, 3:1573–1577 (1575).

[98]    The other possibility of interpretation: "It is within you," on which see U. Luz, βασιλεία, *EWNT* I 489. The future orientation is also expressed in Matthew 6:10par.

22): the unrepentant cities of Chorazin, Bethsaida and Capernaum are promised destruction, in comparison to Tyre, Sidon, and Sodom; cf. also Matt 12:41). Grace and judgment cannot be separated in Jesus' preaching of the kingdom of God. With his advent, the time of decision has come. Jesus calls his hearers to decide for or against the offer he presents. This is concretized in the call to discipleship (Luke 9:60):

> "Let the dead bury their own dead; but as for you, go and proclaim the kingdom of God!"

Just as the "kingdom of God" is an apocalyptic concept, the content of which corresponds to the "age to come," the "new creation" or the "new heaven and new earth," so also the title "Son of Man" is originally an element of the apocalyptic thought world.[99] Three groups of sayings are to be distinguished in the Synoptic tradition: (1) the future (coming), (2) the presently active, and (3) the suffering Son of Man. How these are related to the historical Jesus continues to be disputed. Alongside the conservative view that Jesus used the designation "Son of Man" of himself,[100] Ph. Vielhauer has advocated the thesis that the concepts of kingdom of God and Son of Man are mutually exclusive from the point of view of the history of tradition, and that Jesus therefore could not have used the term "Son of Man," since originally kingdom of God and Son of Man belonged to separate streams of tradition.[101] This view that all the Son of Man sayings are secondary formations of the early church has had a great influence on the discussion. However, among the christological titles applied to Jesus in the New Testament, there is at least a possibility that Jesus himself used the term "Son of Man." To be sure, the group of sayings about the suffering Son of Man are formations of the early church (vaticinium ex eventu), but the situation is different with the first two groups. According to Mark 8:38 Jesus distinguished between himself and the coming Son of Man/judge of the world. Unless the third-person speech here is only a stylistic variation without any meaning with regard to the content,[102] then Jesus is pointing to a figure distinct from himself. This would then not only correspond to the focus of the message of John the

---

[99] Cf. Daniel 7:13; 1 Enoch 37–71; 4 Ezra 13.

[100] A. J. B. Higgins, *Jesus and the Son of Man* (London: Lutterworth, 1964) 185–209; C. C. Caragounis, *The Son of Man. Vision and Interpretation* (WUNT 38. Tübingen: J. C. B. Mohr [Paul Siebeck], 1986) 145–243, 245–250.

[101] Cf. Ph. Vielhauer, "Gottesreich und Menschensohn in der Verkündigung Jesu," in *Aufsätze zum Neuen Testament I* (TB 31. Munich: Kaiser, 1965) 55–91.

[102] M. Dibelius, "Evangelienkritik und Christologie," in G. Bornkamm, ed. *Botschaft und Geschichte I* (Tübingen: J. C. B. Mohr [Paul Siebeck], 1953) 293–358 (320); E. Haenchen, *Der Weg Jesu. Eine Erklärung des Markus-Evangeliums und der kanonischen Parallelen* (Berlin: Töpelmann, 1968²) 299–300.

Baptist,[103] but can appeal for support to the expectation of the Son of Man in Jewish apocalyptic.

According to the Similitudes of 1 Enoch (1 Enoch 37–71), the author of the book of Enoch understands himself to be the "Son of Man" who has been transported to the presence of God (1 Enoch 70–71). It has fairly often been supposed that Jesus understood himself as the Son of Man who would be taken into God's presence in the future.[104] It seems that one could appeal for support to the Son of Man sayings placed in Jesus' mouth in which he speaks of the Son of Man as already present. However, the Aramaic equivalent for υἱὸς τοῦ ἀνθρώπου (Dan 7:13) means the same as "human being" in general (cf. Job 25:6; Ezek 2:1). Thus the group of sayings about the present Son of Man could refer to Jesus in the sense of "human being."[105] To be sure, several of these sayings presuppose the titular use of the phrase with reference to the present work of the Son of Man, and are secondary formulations. It appears possible, however, on the basis of Mark 8:38 to suppose that Jesus announced the future advent of one called the "Son of Man," and defined his own role in close relation to this future figure. To begin with, this would correspond to the message of John the Baptist who announced the "Mightier One" who would come after him. Moreover, it is significant that both Q and the Markan apocalypse contain the idea of the coming Son of Man, in each case without it being immediately clear that this Son of Man is identified with Jesus. Furthermore, the general apocalyptic character of the message of Jesus is reflected in the fact that the Easter kerygma then expected Jesus as the Coming One, the first one to have been raised from the dead (1 Cor 15:20).[106]

---

103  Cf. also R. Bultmann, "Die Frage nach der Echtheit von Mt 16,17–19," in *Exegetica* 255–277 (275–276); H. E. Tödt, *The Son of Man in the Synoptic Tradition* (Philadelphia: Westminster Press, 1965) 195–196.

104  So e. g. E. Schweizer, "Der Menschensohn (Zur eschatologischen Erwartung Jesu) in *Neotestamentica* (Zürich-Stuttgart 1963) 56–84 (78 and elsewhere).

105  Cf. e. g. Ch. Burchard, "Jesus of Nazareth" in J. Becker (et al) (eds) *Christian Beginnings. Word and Community from Jesus to Post-Apostolic Times* (Louisville: Westminster John Knox, 1993) 15–72. The idea of a "Human One" as a designation of the eschatological bringer of salvation is placed by W. G. Kümmel already in early Judaism, an idea that Jesus could have adopted with reference to himself. Cf. Kümmel, "Jesus der Menschensohn?" SbWGF XX 3 (Wiesbaden 1984) 147–188 (165–166). In addition: G. Vermès, *Jesus the Jew: A Historian's Reading of the Gospels* (London: Collins, 1973) 163–168.

106  On this cf. also W. Schmithals, who regards the crucifixion of Jesus by the Romans in the context of Jesus' apocalyptic preaching of the kingdom of God ("Jesus und die Apokalyptik," in G. Strecker, ed. *Jesus Christ in Historie und Theologie* (FS H. Conzelmann. Tübingen: J. C. B. Mohr [Paul Siebeck], 1975) 59–85 (67–68). On the problem of implied soteriology, cf. Ph. Vielhauer and G. Strecker, "Apokalyptik des Urchristentums," in W. Schneemelcher, ed. *NTApo* II⁵, 516–517 [Schneemelcher's original chapter translated in "Apocalyptic Prophecy of the Early Church," *New Testament Apocrypha* 2:684–750]. On implicit Christology, cf. Bultmann, *Theology* 1:9, 42-43.

## 4. The Ethic of Jesus

Hoffmann P. and V. Eid. *Jesus von Nazareth und eine christliche Moral.* Freiburg-Basel-Wien: Herder, 1976[2].

Merklein, H. *Die Gottesherrschaft als Handlungsprinzip, Untersuchung zur Ethik Jesu.* fzb 34. Würzburg: Echter, 1984[3].

Merklein, H. *Jesu Botschaft von der Gottesherrschaft. Eine Skizze.* SBS 111. Stuttgart: Katholisches Bibelwerk, 1989[3].

Schnackenburg, R. *Die sittliche Botschaft des Neuen Testaments.* HThK.S 1. Freiburg-Basel-Wien: Herder, 1986.

Schrage, W. *The Ethics of the New Testament.* Philadelphia: Fortress, 1988.

Strecker, G. *The Sermon on the Mount.* Nashville: Abingdon, 1988.

If the content of Jesus' ethical demand "was *not* based on the nearness of the kingdom,"[107] it is still the case that the announcement of the coming kingdom of God and the approaching judgment played a motivating role in his message. Those who expect the kingdom of God and see themselves as facing the threat of God's judgment cannot remain unaffected in their conduct. They must "already" orient themselves to the eschaton in terms of concrete events that constitute the way they live their lives. The answer to the question of what they are concretely to do is given by Jesus by adopting the wisdom tradition of Judaism, which originally only repeated common sense rules for daily life. For example:

> For with the judgment you make you will be judged, and the measure you give will be the measure you get. (Matt 7:2)

Or:

> So do not worry about tomorrow, for tomorrow will bring worries of its own. Today's trouble is enough for today. (Matt 6:34)

Ethical instruction can be oriented to God's own actions that show concern for the lives of both humans and animals (Matt 6:25–33). God's goodness is a model for human conduct, for he causes the sun to rise on bad and good alike, and makes it rain on the just and on the unjust (Matt 5:45). However, this pointing to God's own conduct is not the central motif of Jesus' ethic. More important is the expectation of the coming kingdom of God that necessitates ethical conduct today. Above all, it is Jesus' ἐξουσία, his unconditioned eschatological claim acknowledged by his disciples, that provides the motivation for Jesus' ethical teaching. Jesus' authority is seen in his stance toward Old Testament-Jewish law, in that he interprets the Torah concretely and radically. While Jesus finds the will of God expressed in the Mosaic Law, he does not hesitate to criticize its details, nor to transcend or cancel some of its commands.

---

[107] H. Conzelmann, "Zur Methode der Leben-Jesu-Forschung" in H. Conzelmann, ed. *Theologie als Schriftauslegung* (BEvTh 65. Munich: Kaiser, 1974) 18–29 (27).

One example of Jesus' understanding of the Law is found in the *antitheses of the Sermon on the Mount* (Matt 5:21–48par). According to a widely-accepted view, the six antitheses of the Sermon on the Mount go back to pre-Matthean tradition. This is certainly true with regard to the antitheses now found in a Matthean redactional frame, but which are to be attributed to Q on the basis of their parallels in Luke: Matthew 5:31–32par Luke 16:18 (divorce), Matthew 5:38ffpar Luke 6:29–30 (retaliation), Matthew 5:43ffpar Luke 6:27–28, 32–35 (love for enemies), but also for the antitheses of the material unique to Matthew, which presumably were found by Matthew in the tradition already formulated as antitheses: 5:21ff ("you shall not kill"), 5:27–28 ("you shall not commit adultery") and 5:33–37 ("you shall not swear falsely"). By the "criterion of development" the original Jesus material may be sifted out: (a) a radicalization of the Torah, as in the first antithesis, where the Old Testament prohibition of murder is sharpened to a prohibition of anger. In Matthew 5:27–28 the prohibition of adultery becomes a prohibition of lustful looks; in Matthew 5:43–44 the command of love for the neighbor becomes a command to love the enemy. (b) Alongside this, in the antitheses of the Matthean special material is found a critique of the Torah that intends not only a heightening of the traditional Old Testament-Jewish command, but actually nullifies specific commands of the Mosaic Torah.[108] The third antithesis (5:31–32) in its original form speaks of an absolute, radical prohibition of divorce (thus corresponding to the pre-Pauline tradition in 1 Cor 7:10–11). The offense of adultery already presupposes that a man divorces his wife and marries another woman; the marriage of a divorced woman is also covered by this verdict, since this is identified as adultery within a marriage that is still considered valid.

Also the fourth antithesis (Matt 5:33–34a), with Jesus' absolute prohibition of oaths, includes a critique of both the Old Testament law and the Jewish practice of giving oaths.[109] One cannot say with H. Conzelmann that Jesus here does not prohibit the institution of taking oaths, but only forbids swearing as such, for where could one document such a meticulous distinction in Jesus' context?[110] In his own concrete attitude with regard to specific Old Testament commands, Jesus also shows a lack of respect,

---

[108] A different view is still represented by H. Conzelmann, *Outline* 119: "Jesus' criticism is not of the law, but of legalism." However: to the extent that legalism can appeal to the Torah itself, Jesus' critique applies also to the law itself. Cf. Mark 10:5–6: the permission of divorce in Deut 24:1 is a concession of Moses "because of the hardness of your hearts," but according to the plan of creation divorce contradicts the original will of God.

[109] Contra G. Dautzenberg, "Eid IV," *TRE* 9:379–382 (380–381); on this cf. Strecker, *Sermon on the Mount* 77–80.

[110] H. Conzelmann, *Jesus: The Classic Article in the RGG Expanded and Updated* (Philadelphia: Fortress Press, 1973) 65.

e. g. in his stance toward Sabbath observance (Mark 2:23ff; 3:1ff). This independence over against the Jewish law is a factor to be taken into consideration when one considers the conflicts he had with strict Torah-observant Jews, especially the religious leaders of the Jewish people.

By his radical interpretation of the Torah ("But I say to you...") Jesus intends to express the original, unqualified will of God. Thus he does not approach the issue with the question of whether or not his demand can be fulfilled. His hearers are simply confronted with the absolute will of God. This results in the disclosure of the theological meaning of the law (usus theologicus or elenchticus legis). That no human being can stand before God with a claim about his or her own achievement, but must be dependent on God's grace alone, is the content of Jesus' critique and radicalization of the Torah. It is nothing other than a concrete call to repentance that shatters every human claim before God. But the proclamation of the theological meaning of the law does not exclude the demand for ethical action. Jesus addresses people in their actual situation, which means he spoke to the situation of Jews who lived under Roman occupation. The pericope about paying taxes has a particular scope: "Give to Caesar what belongs to Caesar, and give to God what belongs to God" (Mark 12:17). This means that both God and Caesar have valid claims. It is a matter of deciding from case to case which is the right way. Jesus is thus no Zealot or revolutionary. In his conduct he seeks to let God's will come to concrete expression. He steps forth in society as "friend of publicans and sinners" (Matt 11:19). His conduct manifests the command to love, as expressed in the parable of the Good Samaritan (Luke 10:29–37), as do his numerous teachings that reflect the provenance of wisdom ethics.[111]

## 5. Jesus and the Church

"Jesus preached the kingdom of God, and what came was the church." This state of affairs was so formulated by the French modernist A. Loisy at the turn of the century.[112] If the nucleus of the message of Jesus is the kingdom of God, then the status quo's institutional system of coordination is placed in question. The call to repentance shatters theological order and social barriers, all the security systems that human beings have established for themselves. So also the post-Easter church, to the extent that it claims such a function of establishing security for itself, is struck by this call to repentance. To be sure, it was not Jesus' intention to estab-

---

[111] Cf. the thorough presentation by Ch. Burchard, "Jesus von Nazareth" 41–50 as well as R. Schnackenburg, *The Moral Teaching of the New Testament* (New York: Seabury Press, 1973).

[112] A. Loisy, *The Gospel and the Church* (Lives of Jesus Series. Philadelphia: Fortress Press, 1976) 166: "Jésus annonçait le royaume, et c'est l'Eglise qui est venue."

lish a church. The consistent focus of his message on the imminent arrival of the kingdom of God excludes such an intention. It is also the case that he probably never intended a mission to the Gentiles; the New Testament pericopes that report a ministry of Jesus in Gentile territory or to "Gentiles" (e. g. Matt 8:5–13par, John 4:46–53; Mark 7:24–30par) are secondary, and originated in a Gentile Christian context. The preaching of the historical Jesus was directed to the people of Israel (cf. Matt 10:6; 15:24).[113] This people is called to repentance; even where Jesus' message transcends these boundaries, it is still the people of Israel who are the real addressees, for example in Matthew 8:11–12:

> I tell you, many will come from east and west and will eat with Abraham and Isaac and Jacob in the kingdom of heaven, while the heirs of the kingdom will be thrown into the outer darkness.

This is also documented by the circle of disciples that Jesus gathered about himself. The number "twelve" for his disciples is independent of the contradictory lists of disciples (Mark 3:16–19; Matt 10:2–4; Luke 6:14–16; instead of Thaddeus, Luke has the name Judas son of James), and goes back to Jesus himself, since this tradition was already known to Paul (1 Cor 15:5b). This number has a factual basis in that the message of Jesus was directed to the twelve tribes of Israel, and all the more so in view of the logion Matthew 19:28par, in which the future judgment of the twelve tribes is entrusted to the twelve disciples. Jesus' calling a circle of twelve does not mean, however, that Jesus wanted to establish a "new Israel." The content and goal of the preaching of Jesus' disciples—like that of Jesus himself—is the call to repentance, the preparation of the Jewish people for the coming kingdom of God. This has parallels in the message of John the Baptist and remains bound to the context of the Jewish people of that time. Only after Jesus' death was the call to repentance made universal, the Gentile mission launched, and the church of Jews and Gentiles established.

There can be no doubt that the radicality of Jeus' claim made his appearance in history an event without analogy. Jesus can also be designated an apocalyptic prophet within the categories used in the study of the history of religions, so that his appearance—like that of John the Baptist—signaled and introduced the eschatological times. It is still the case, however, that with the radicality of his message of the coming kingdom of God, especially the critique of the Law that was bound up with it, Jesus was a unique figure within the Judaism of his times, and all the more so since with charismatic authority he defined anew the will of God.

---

[113] So also G. Lohfink, *Wie hat Jesus Gemeinde gewollt? Zur gesellschaftlichen Dimension des christlichen Glaubens* (Freiburg-Basel-Wien: Herder, 1982[6]) 28.

# III. The Palestinian and the Hellenistic Church

Becker, J. ed. *Christian Beginnings*. Louisville: Westminster/John Knox, 1993.
Bultmann, R. *Primitive Christianity in Its Contemporary Setting*. New York: Meridian Books, 1956.
Conzelmann, H. *Gentiles-Jews-Christians. Polemics and Apologetics in the Greco-Roman Era*. Minneapolis: Fortress, 1992.
Dobschütz, E. von. *Probleme des Apostolischen Zeitalters*. Leipzig: J. C. Hinrichs, 1904.
Fischer, K. M. *Das Urchristentum*. KGE I/1. Berlin, 1985.
Goppelt, L. *Apostolic and Post-Apostolic Times*. Grand Rapids: Baker, 1970.
Koester, H. *Introduction to the New Testament*. Vol. 1 *History, Culture, and Religion of the Hellenistic Age*, New York: W. de Gruyter, 1995²; Vol. 2 *History and Literature of Early Christianity*. Philadelphia: Fortress, 1982.
Lietzmann, H. *A History of the Early Church*, Vol. I.: *The Beginnings of the Christian Church*. New York: Charles Scribners Sons, 1949.
Schneemelcher, W. *Das Urchristentum*. UB 336. Stuttgart: Kohlhammer, 1981.
Vouga, F. *Geschichte des frühen Christentums*. UTB 1733. Tübingen-Basel: J. C. B. Mohr (Paul Siebeck), 1994.

## a)   The Origin of Christian Faith as Faith in the Resurrection of Jesus

Campenhausen, H. von. *Der Ablauf der Osterereignisse und das leere Grab*. SHAW.PH. Heidelberg: C. Winter, 1977⁴.
Grass, H. *Ostergeschehen und Osterberichte*. Göttingen: Vandenhoeck & Ruprecht, 1970⁴.
Hübner, H. "Kreuz und Auferstehung im Neuen Testament," *ThR* 54 (1989) 262–306.
Lüdemann, G. *The Resurrection of Jesus. History, Experience, Theology*. Minneapolis: Fortress, 1994.
Marxsen, W. *The Resurrection of Jesus of Nazareth*. Philadelphia: Fortress, 1970.
Schenke, L. *Auferstehungsverkündigung und leeres Grab*. SBS 33. Stuttgart: Katholisches Bibelwerk, 1968.
Wilckens, U. *Resurrection: Biblical Testimony to the Resurrection: An Historical Examination and Explanation*. Atlanta: John Knox, 1977.

As we have seen,[1] 1 Corinthians 15:3b-5a contains a pre-Pauline tradition that possibly derives from the Hellenistic Jewish Christianity at Antioch. This formula connects the affirmation of the death and resurrection of Jesus with the further statement that the Risen One appeared to "Cephas" (= Peter). From this oldest written Easter tradition we may infer that in the pre-Pauline Christian community Simon Peter was acknowledged as the first witness of the resurrection. The additional witnesses to the resurrection that Paul has obviously drawn from oral tradition directly link these traditions with those found in the Synoptic Gospels, and documents the existence of an even more extensive store of Easter traditions.

---

[1]   See above A. I. C.3.

## The Petrine Tradition

Brown, R. E., Donfried, K. P. and Reumann, J. eds. *Peter in the New Testament.* Minneapolis: Augsburg, 1973.

Cullmann, O. *Peter, Disciple, Apostle, Martyr; a Historical and Theological Study.* Philadelphia: Westminster, 1962².

Grappe, Ch. *D'un Temple à l'autre. Pierre et l'Église primitive de Jérusalem.* EHPhR 71. Paris: 1992.

Lietzmann, H. *Petrus und Paulus in Rom.* AKG 1. Berlin-Leipzig: Marcus and Weber, 1927².

The blessing of Simon bar Jonah and his commission to lead the *ecclesia* is probably based on a very old resurrection tradition (Matt 16:17–19). As suggested by a comparison with 1 Corinthians 15:15a, but also with John 20–21, we probably have here a tradition in which Simon, who is always named first in the lists of disciples,[2] was given the symbolic name Cephas on the basis of this Easter experience and was installed as leader of the new Christian community (cf. also Gal 1:18). This tradition was inserted into this context by the redactor Matthew and connected to the confession of Peter at Caesarea Philippi (cf. Mark 8:27–30).[3] The linguistic form lets an earlier Aramaic nucleus be recognized: thus the form of the name "bar Jonah" (= son of Jonah), as well as the wordplay with Cephas ["rock"] ("You are rock, and on this rock...").[4] Moreover, there are linguistic features that probably go back to the pre-Matthean church tradition; these features permit the inference that Matthew received this traditional unit from the oral tradition. It confirms the tradition of 1 Corinthians 15:5a: the first resurrection appearance to Peter had a constitutive significance; Peter was thereby established as leader of the earliest Christian community. The thoroughly Semitic character of the language speaks for an original unit of tradition that was originally at home in the earliest Aramaic-speaking church.[5]

So also the story of the sinking Peter (Matt 14:28–31) evidences Petrine resurrection tradition. Inserted into the Markan context by the Evangelist

---

[2]    Mark 1:16–20parr; Mark 3:16–19parr; Acts 1:13.

[3]    Differently O. Cullmann, *Peter* 170–212, who argues that Peter was given his authoritative commission at the last supper. His argument is based on an unpersuasive combination of Matthew 16, Luke 22, John 6 and 21.

[4]    The Greek terms πέτρος / πέτρα apparently go back to the same Aramaic form Kepha כֵּיפָא.

[5]    Cf. G. Strecker, *Weg der Gerechtigkeit* 202 note 4. Differently P. Lampe, "Das Spiel mit dem Petrusnamen—Matt. XVI. 18, *NTS* 25 (1979) 227–245, who disputes that there was an older Aramaic source for Matthew 16:17–19 and would like to trace the tradition back to a Greek-speaking Hellenistic-Jewish community. However, "Cephas" in the language of the Aramaic Bible can have the meaning not only of "stone, clod, clot," but also "rock, crag, cliff."

Matthew, it possibly goes back to a more extensive pre-Matthean tradition parallel to Mark 6:45–52 (the "walking on the water"). That it deals with an original resurrection tradition can be supposed on the basis of John 21:7–8, where the narrative of Peter's walking on/through the water is connected with a resurrection appearance.

A different form of the Petrine resurrection tradition is found in Luke 5:1–11. Here it is in the form of a call story that tells of the call of Simon as the first disciple. That it is based on earlier Easter tradition can be supported by the obviously secondary tradition in John 21:15–17 (the Risen One commissions Peter at the Sea of Galilee) and by John 21:1–14 (the miraculous catch of fish by Peter and his companions, and the appearance of the Risen One). John 20:1–10 also contains an Easter tradition connected with Peter: Simon Peter and the other disciple see that the grave is empty.

The motifs are thus not homogeneous. Their common denominator is their emphasis on the outstanding significance of Peter as the first witness to the resurrection. Luke 24:34 is also to be noted here: "The Lord has risen indeed, and has appeared to Simon." This is also the case with the apocryphal Gospel of Peter, which probably concluded with an appearance to Peter.[6]

While the Petrine tradition represents a particular type of Easter tradition, in that it revolves around the person who was the first witness to the resurrection, the Easter stories focusing on the empty tomb can be distinguished in terms of their content from those stories that focus on the appearance of the Risen One. As will be seen, both types are found in the Petrine tradition.

## Stories of the Empty Tomb

The oldest testimony to the empty tomb is found in Mark 16:1–8par. The report of the women who came to the tomb on the first day of the week in order to anoint the body of Jesus has its center of gravity in the message of the angel about the resurrection of Jesus (16:6). This is followed by the commission to tell the disciples to go to Galilee. While this latter command (16:7) is clearly secondary and points to a conclusion of the Gospel of Mark that is no longer extant, Mark 16:1–6, 8 is a pre-Markan unit of tradition that testifies to the empty tomb and was originally confined to

---

6   The Gospel of Peter concludes with the comment that the disciples remained grieving in Jerusalem until the end of the Feast of Unleavened Bread, without Jesus appearing to them (58–59). Accompanied by Levi, Peter and Andrew go toward the Sea of Galilee (60). Here the fragment breaks off, but it was probably followed by a story of an appearance at the sea.

Jerusalem (cf. also Luke 24:23).[7] The tradition of Mark 16:1–8 is presupposed in Luke 24:23 when the Evangelist reports that the women came to the tomb, "but they did not find his body."

So also the other reports of the empty tomb are limited to Jerusalem. This is the case in John 20:1–10,[8] just as in Matthew 28:11–15, when the Jews want to conceal the fact of the empty tomb and thus the reality of Jesus' resurrection by spreading the rumor that Jesus' disciples stole his body from the tomb. Accordingly, this tomb tradition has an anti-Jewish apologetic tendency.[9]

## 1. Appearance Stories

The Gospel of John provides extensive accounts of resurrection appearances: to Mary Magdalene (20:11–18), to the disciples (20:19–23), and the theologically weighty epiphany to the disciple Thomas (20:24–29). Here too an anti-docetic tendency becomes visible: that the doubter Thomas could place his hands in the wounds should convince him of the living reality of the Risen One. And when the risen Jesus eats a meal with his disciples (John 21:12–14), this too shows that the resurrection is a matter of material reality. Already Luke 24:36–43 reports an appearance of the Risen One to the disciples in which the reality of the resurrection body is demonstrated by the risen Jesus' command that his disciples touch him, and by eating a piece of fish before their eyes.

Other appearance stories give the occasion for interpreting the way of Jesus, as when it is stated that Jesus' suffering and entering into his glory

---

[7] Mark 14:28, like 16:7, shows that the second Evangelist intended a conclusion to his Gospel in which the encounter of Peter and the other disciples with the risen Lord in Galilee was described, or was to be described (cf. above A. II. c). This is the view of W. Marxsen, *Mark the Evangelist* (Nashville: Abingdon, 1969) 111–116; 182–189, according to which the Gospel of Mark was composed in view of the parousia expected to occur immediately in Galilee (a view he himself retracted in *Einleitung in das Neue Testament* [Gütersloh: Gerd Mohn, 1978⁴] 144; cf. English translation of the 1964 4th edition: "It is possible that Mark's references are meant to point to the parousia..." [*Introduction to the New Testament* (Philadelphia: Fortress Press, 1970) 142]), and cf. already E. Lohmeyer, *Das Evangelium nach Markus* (KEK I/2. Göttingen: Vandenhoeck & Ruprecht, 1967¹⁷, 356]. Marxsen's view is improbable since such an expectation, connected with the commission to the disciples that they should await the coming of the Son of Man in Galilee, would have made the composition of the Gospel superfluous.

[8] The pericope already mentioned, about Peter and the other disciple at the empty tomb, manifests an antidocetic tendency; cf. U. Schnelle, *Antidocetic Christology in the Gospel of John* 17.

[9] Thus for example from Justin, *Dialogues* 108:2. The same tendency is found in the apocryphal Gospel of Peter 45–49: the soldiers were witnesses of the resurrection and report to Pilate what they have seen. But Pilate commands them to be silent about it, in order not to "fall into the hands of the Jewish people" (48).

was a course of events necessitated by the Scriptures (Luke 24:26). Thus the story of the epiphany of the risen Lord to the disciples on the road to Emmaus is more a didactive narrative told for purposes of edification (Luke 24:13–35).

The conclusion of the Gospel of Matthew poses a special problem. The risen Lord meets his eleven disciples on a mountain in Galilee (Matt 28:16–20). The pre-Matthean tradition of this appearance scene was apparently originally located in the baptismal liturgy. The ἐξουσία of the Risen One is made present in the act of baptism. In contrast, the Matthean redactor is interested in the idea of the Gentile mission and intentionally places this tradition at the conclusion of his Gospel: the church's missionary path into the world is commanded by the appearance of the risen Lord. The church is instructed to baptize and to teach what Jesus has taught; the presence of the risen Lord is promised within this missionary activity.[10] Another appearance scene is found in Matthew 28:9–10. The women returning from the tomb meet the risen Christ; they worship him and receive the instruction to announce what has happened to "the brothers" (obviously a secondary expansion of Mark 16:7).[11]

The content of what each of the resurrection traditions wants to affirm is different, depending on its location in the history of the tradition. If we ask which type is primary, that of the empty tomb or that of the appearance of the Risen One, there can be no doubt: at the beginning stood the idea of the appearance of the risen Jesus, as already documented in 1 Corinthians 15:3b-5. The stories of the empty tomb have a different point of view, seen in their interest in showing the earthly reality of the resurrection in a manner that can be demonstrated, a concern that was foreign to the original tradition.[12] But the appearance stories also changed their original character in the course of their transmission. They tend more and more to emphasize the bodily reality of the Risen One, and to rework the way the stories are told into more didactic or liturgical formulations. At the beginning, however, stood the confession of the direct or mediated testimony of the appearance of the Risen One: "Christ died and was raised" (as also in the pre-Pauline tradition Rom 10:9; cf. e. g. 1 Thess 4:14; Acts 2:23–24).[13]

---

[10] On the layers of tradition involved, cf. still G. Strecker, *Weg der Gerechtigkeit* 208ff. Matthew 28:16–20 contains a pre-Matthean revelatory saying with three members that speak (1) of the authority of the Risen One, 28:18b, (2) his command to baptize, 28:19b, and (3) of his promise, 28:20b.

[11] Cf. also the secondary Markan conclusion 16:9–20, which has an appearance to Mary Magdalene (16:9), to two disciples (16:12–13; cf. Luke 24:13–35), and to the eleven (16:14–18; cf. Matt 28:16–20).

[12] Cf. above A. II. C.

[13] It is hardly the case that at the beginning there stood a concept of exaltation derived from Psalm 110. Contra F. Hahn, *Titles of Jesus in Christology* 129–133; cf. Phil 2:9.

## 2.  The Historical Location of the Origin of the Resurrection Tradition

Even though the view argued by Hans Grass that all the resurrection appearances occurred in the Jerusalem area has now lost a lot of ground, it is still repeatedly advocated, including by Hans Conzelmann.[14] In this view the Galilean and Jerusalem traditions are mutually exclusive, with priority given to the Jerusalem tradition. Then a flight of the disciples from Jerusalem to Galilee[15] after the crucifixion would have to be regarded as legendary.[16] However, we know nothing about the chronology of the resurrection appearances. Precisely where the revelations named in 1 Corinthians 15:3b-5 are to be located is not given in the tradition itself. The datum "raised on the third day" (1 Cor 15:4) is a theological datum, possibly derived from Hosea 6:2, and is thus not the date of the first resurrection appearance. The Synoptic tradition that locates appearances in Galilee cannot be understood without presupposing that it is based on decisive events such as one or more resurrection appearances. Since Jerusalem was the place of the crucifixion, the tomb of Jesus, and especially the location of the earliest Christian community, it is more likely that Jerusalem later became the focus of the tradition of resurrection appearances. On the other hand, the foundational first appearance to Peter is located in Galilee.[17] Accordingly, we may reconstruct the following historical sketch of the events:

After the death of Jesus the disciples returned to their home territory. The texts do not speak of a "flight" to Galilee, so such a flight should not be presupposed. Here in Galilee the first appearance to Peter took place, which was also the occasion when Simon received his new name "Cephas." This name signifies Peter's fundamental role in the foundation of the church, without intending anything like an apostolic succession.[18] Then followed other appearances, including the appearance to the Twelve (1 Cor 15:5b). However, that after the first appearances of the Risen One Jesus' disciples went back to Jerusalem is not unlikely, for this was where the majority of Jesus' following was to be found. The epiphany to the five hundred (1 Cor 15:6), which is not to be identified with the Pentecost

---

[14]  H. Conzelmann, "Auferstehung Christi," *RGG*³ 1:698–700 (699).

[15]  Cf. Mark 14:50. H. Grass, *Ostergeschehen und Osterberichte* 119–120 considers a flight of the disciples to be probable.

[16]  The disciples, H. Conzelmann says somewhat casually, would have to have marched at double speed back and forth between Galilee and Jerusalem in order to have been in both places at almost the same time ("On the Analysis of the Confessional Formula" *Interpretation* 20/1 [January, 1966] 22).

[17]  John 21; cf. Luke 5:1–11, as well as the lost or only intended conclusion of the Gospel of Mark. Cf. also Matthew 28:16–20 (11 disciples).

[18]  Differently P. Dausch, *Die drei älteren Evangelien* (HSNT II. Bonn, 1932²) 241–243; J. Lambrecht, "'Du bist Petrus'. Mt 16,16–19 und das Papsttum" SNTU 11 (1986) 5–32, esp. 28–29.

phenomena (Acts 2), is presumably to be located in Jerusalem. This is also the case with the appearance to James the Lord's brother (1 Cor 15:7), since James later becomes the leader of the Jerusalem church (cf. Acts 21:18; Gal 2:9). While this reconstruction relies primarily on the pre-Pauline tradition in 1 Corinthians 15, it is confirmed by the later reports of appearances to Peter. The accounts of the discovery of the empty tomb cannot be fitted into this outline; their structure already bears the marks of their secondary, legendary origin. Although localized in Jerusalem, they probably did not originate there, but mostly grew out of the creative retelling of the Easter stories that occurred in the early Christian tradition in the interest of edification.[19]

Both the older and later resurrection traditions narrate the event with a certain naiveté, not distinguishing between what is said and what is meant; they do not reflect on or give an account of the concepts and frame of reference that are employed in order to tell the story. Thus it is the task of the exegete who is interested in history to investigate what really happened. In this process it must be acknowledged: with the employment of historical categories a system of coordinates is brought into play that determines both the way the question is asked and the kind of answer that can be found. Thus what does the historian see? He does not see the empty tomb, for this is not documented in the oldest traditions of the resurrection, but is a secondary supplement. Moreover, this supplement is more a hindrance than a help on the way to theological understanding, since a variety of interpretations, including contradictory ones, have attached themselves to the concept of the empty tomb, as illustrated, for example, by Matthew 28:11-15.

Thus what does the historian see? He does not see the resurrection. W. Marxsen has rightly emphasized that the New Testament does not narrate *how* the resurrection took place.[20] It is only narrated *that* the disciples saw the Risen One. But neither does the historian see the Risen One. Neither the resurrection event as such, nor the person of the Risen One are phe-

---

[19]   On the other hand, the historicity of the empty tomb is argued by F. Mussner, *Die Auferstehung Jesu* (BiH VII. Munich: Kaiser, 1969) 128–133; M. Hengel, "Ist der Osterglaube noch zu retten?" ThQ 153 (1973) 252–269 (264); "Maria Magdalena und die Frauen als Zeugen," in O. Betz et al (eds.) *Abraham unser Vater* (FS O. Michel. AGJU 5. Leiden: E. J. Brill, 1963) 243–256, who argues on the basis of the secondary Markan conclusion that it is probable that the resurrection appearances to the women represent the oldest traditional material); P. Stuhlmacher, "Kritischer müssten mir die Historisch-Kritischen sein!", ThQ 153 (1973) 244–251 (246–248); E. L. Bode, *The First Easter Morning. The Gospel Account of the Women's Visit to the Tomb of Jesus*, (AnBib 45. Rome: PBI, 1970) 173–175; E. Schweizer, *Jesus Christus im vielfältigen Zeugnis des Neuen Testaments* (Munich-Hamburg: Siebenstern, 1968) 50–51; J. Jeremias, *New Testament Theology* 304–306.

[20]   Willi Marxsen, *The Resurrection of Jesus of Nazareth* 66–78.

nomena that can be grasped by the methods available to the historian. The historian only sees the testimony to the resurrection as it has precipitated out into our documents; it is possible for the historian to investigate this deposit on the basis of the categories and methods with which historians work, and to sort it out into the available historical categories. The historian will accordingly trace the testimony to the resurrection back to a visionary event. The oldest historically verifiable basis for the resurrection faith is the fact that after the death of their teacher the disciples of Jesus had visions in which the crucified one appeared to them as alive. At this point historical knowledge reaches its boundary. What the vision amounts to, and especially whether the interpretation the disciples gave to their visionary experience was correct or not—such a judgment cannot be made by the historian. He can deal with the historical event, i.e. the vision, but not the interpretation of this event, since the interpretation the disciples gave to this event extends beyond the realm of the historian's competence—which means that the interpretation of the event cannot be dealt with in terms of psychology.[21]

## 3.  Theological Interpretation

While the problem may thus be settled for the historians, at the most they can inform us of the witness to the resurrection connected to the visionary events in Galilee and Jerusalem and the task of theological interpretation remains. What does it mean in the theological context that the disciples of Jesus had visionary experiences that they interpreted as an encounter with the risen Jesus? Thereby is posed the question of the theological meaning of the primal testimony, "Jesus died and was raised," coined by Jesus' disciples as the result of this experience.

The question of the theological context of the New Testament testimony to the resurrection is not to be separated from implications for issues of the history of tradition and the history of religions that are bound up with the transmission of the testimony to the resurrection.

1. It is suggested that the oldest interpretation of the resurrection event is the concept of exaltation that has an essential function in the Christ hymn of Philippians 2:9, namely of marking the separation between the earthly and heavenly existence of the exalted Lord. Thus F. Hahn at-

---

[21]   The attempt to cast light on the psychic state of the disciples after the death of Jesus with the help of the tools of different schools of depth psychology (S. Freud, C. G. Jung) and to explain the vision of the resurrected Jesus by the psychic depression of his disciples (cf. G. Lüdemann, *The Resurrection of Jesus* [Minneapolis: Fortress, 1995] 98–99) can only be convincing to those who are determined by a "depth psychology credo." The eschatological character of the early Christian witness to the resurrection is not even touched by such an approach.

tempts to ground this interpretation by an appeal to Psalm 110:1.[22] However, the citation of Psalm 110 in a christological context occurs only late in the history of the tradition and is not related to the resurrection of Jesus. In Mark 12:36 it stands in the context of the issue about the Son of David and in Mark 14:62 it has a future eschatological significance without naming the resurrection. Psalm 110 is not interpreted in terms of the exaltation of Jesus Christ until Acts 2:34, where it is applied to the ascension. There is no direct citation in 1 Corinthians 15:25, which in any case only deals with the lordship of Christ during the transitional eschatological period.

2. It is also not possible to grasp the resurrection of Jesus from the perspective of the past reality of Jesus' life. The resurrection kerygma of the earliest Christian community contains no reference to the life of Jesus, apart from the bare fact of the cross. When it is said in 1 Thessalonians 4:14 that "Jesus died and rose again," this is an independent formula that does not merely interpret the resurrection event as the continuation of the life of Jesus. Nor can it be interpreted in psychological terms, as though Jesus foresaw his death and expected the resurrection as the exaltation and confirmation of his life.[23] When predictions of the suffering and resurrection of Jesus appear in the Synoptic Gospels, these are to be identified as formulations of the church and thus vaticinia ex eventu (Mark 8:31; 9:31; 10:32–34parr). Since we have only inadequate information on Jesus' self-consciousness, it is pointless to try to establish a continuity between the life of Jesus and the resurrection event.

3. The resurrection of Jesus is also not to be identified as a prodigy within the realm of nature, the resuscitation of a dead person as illustrated by elements in the Synoptic tradition (Luke 7:11–17: the widow of Nain's son; Mark 5:21–43par, the daughter of Jairus), and also included in the stories in Acts (9:36–43, Peter awakes a Christian named Tabitha from death; 20:7–12, Paul brings Eutychus back from the dead). This kind of amazing deeds, which of course contradicted the laws of nature already known in antiquity, belongs to the kind of narratives represented by folk tales. They are not oriented to apocalypticism,[24] but represent an inter-

---

[22]  As already discussed above (note 13). Cf. also the critique of Ph. Vielhauer, "Ein Weg zur neutestamentlichen Christologie? Prüfung der Thesen Ferdinand Hahns," in Ph. Vielhauer, Aufsätze zum Neuen Testament (TB 31. Munich: Kaiser, 1965) 1:141–198.

[23]  Cf. e. g. H. Schürmann, "Wie hat Jesus seinen Tod bestanden und verstanden? Eine methodische Besinnung," in P. Hoffmann, ed. Orientierung an Jesus. Zur Theologie der Synoptiker (FS J. Schmidt. Freiburg-Basel-Wien: Herder, 1973) 325–363; cf. 360, note 155; J. Jeremias, New Testament Theology 272; R. Pesch, "Zur Entstehung des Glaubens an die Auferstehung Jesu," ThQ 153 (1973) 201–228 (220).

[24]  Neither is the story in Luke 16:19ff (v. 31: "If they do not listen to Moses and the prophets, neither will they be convinced even if someone rises from the dead").

ruption in the natural course of things. This is obviously also the case
with the resurrection of Jesus. But it is still more than a "normal" coming
back from the realm of the dead, since it is witnessed to as having an
eschatological quality.[25]

4. Is the oldest interpretation of the resurrection of Jesus apocalyptic? This
would correspond to the thesis of Ernst Käsemann, that apocalyptic is the
mother of all Christian theology.[26] In any case, it should not be disputed
that the resurrected Christ was expected by the disciples as the one to come
in the future (1 Thess 1:10). However, this is not explicitly connected with
statements about Jesus' resurrection.[27] A visionary experience, as represented by the encounter with the Risen One, is as such not yet an apocalyptic event, however much apocalyptic authors may have had charismatic-
visionary experiences. Therefore, however much the resurrection of Jesus
in the understanding of the New Testament became the material foundation for Jesus' exaltation and parousia and represents the transition from
earthly to heavenly existence of the Risen and Coming One, it was still not
originally connected with the apocalyptic world of thought.

5. That the resurrection of Jesus dealt with the transition from an earthly
to a heavenly existence is also close to the concept of being taken bodily
into the heavenly world while still alive, an idea that was widespread in
the ancient oriental-Jewish world, just as it was in the Greek-Hellenistic
world. In the first place this was only a matter of change of location.[28] The

---

[25]    On this cf. the interpretation of the resurrection testimony by Paul, above A. II. c.,
especially 1 Corinthians 15, where the hope for the resurrection of the dead is based
on faith in the one who is already risen.

[26]    E. Käsemann, "The Beginnings of Christian Theology," in *New Testament Questions of Today* (London: SCM Press, 1969)82–107. With regard to the apocalyptic
horizon of Jesus' resurrection cf. also the apocalyptic "schedule" in 1 Corinthians
15:23, according to which the resurrection of Christ introduces the resurrection of
those who belong to him at his parousia (so also 1 Thess 4:14). A future eschatological orientation is also included in the affirmation of the resurrection in Acts
3:15, when Jesus is designated the ἀρχηγὸς τῆς ζωῆς and his being taken up into
heaven (the ascension) is connected with the expectation of his return (Acts 3:21).
The resurrection of Jesus thus means the dawn and anticipation of the coming aeon.

[27]    Thus the passion and resurrection prediction of Mark 8:31par has hardly any connection with the parousia expectation of Mark 8:38par. Mark 9:1par and Mark
9:11–13par presuppose only the parousia, while in contrast the story of the Transfiguration of Mark 9:2–10 contains only the idea of the resurrection. It is not until
Matthew 17:12b that the Transfiguration story is supplemented with the motif of
the suffering Son of Man. So also Luke 17:23–25 combines the suffering motif with
the expectation of the parousia; compare Luke 17:23–25 with Matthew 24:26–27.

[28]    Cf. e. g. the Gospel of the Hebrews about Jesus: "Even so did my mother, the Holy
Spirit, take me by one of my hairs and carry me away on to the great mountain
Tabor" (Schneemelcher, *New Testament Apocrypha*, 1:177.

idea in Acts 8:39–40 is also conceived in the most realistic terms: the evangelist Philip was snatched away by the Spirit of the Lord to Ashdod. Nearer to our subject are those accounts of being snatched away to the other world that at the same time affirm the conquest of death. Thus the Old Testament tells of the translation of both Enoch (Gen 5:24) and Elijah (2 Kings 2:11) to heaven. The New Testament still knows of the return of the translated prophet Elijah (Mark 9:11–13par). It was told of the apocalyptist Baruch that he was taken from the earth so that he could be preserved for the end of time and then give his testimony (2 Baruch 13:3). There are many similar stories in Greek mythology. On the one hand one can point to the cult of Urania and its display of the empty grave. Thus the Thebes tell that Alcmene, the mother of Hercules, was taken by the god Hermes from the funeral bier to the Island of the Blessed, so that she has no grave in Thebes (Pausanias 9.16.7). On the other hand the connection with the chthonic cult and evidence of the grave is also documented: Amphiaraus is taken away to live under the earth, where he continues to live and has a cultic shrine near Thebes.[29] The idea of being snatched away to heaven is also apparently behind the story of the ascension that Luke gives in his two volume work (Luke 24:50–53; Acts 1:9–11). A temporal factor also plays a role here, namely the Lucan view of the life of Jesus. The resurrection of Jesus marks a temporal transitional stage in the Jesus story, inserted into a series arranged according to the concept of salvation history: from the earthly life and death of Jesus through the resurrection, understood as the reappearance of Jesus from the world of the dead, until the ascension occurs forty days later. That is, the ascension is the final departure of Jesus to heaven, Jesus' farewell to the material world. The idea of the ascension is a pre-Lucan concept (cf. Barnabas 15:9); it corresponds to the same interest that resulted in the development of the idea of the empty tomb, namely the interest in the empirical reality of the Risen One. This is a secondary development within the history of tradition. The original resurrection faith identified resurrection and ascension: originally, resurrection meant exaltation; the one risen from the dead is the one who has been exalted to the divine world. At his resurrection, he entered the heavenly glory, his place at the right hand of God (cf. Heb 1:3). It is this idea of exaltation, not the concept of ascension, that is presupposed in the stories of Jesus' resurrection appearances (cf. 1 Cor 15:3ff, Matt 28:16ff, as well as in the pre-Pauline hymn Phil 2:6–11).

According to the earliest Christian understanding, the resurrection was therefore by no means a segment of a timeline. It is to be grasped neither psychologically nor in terms of salvation history from the past, the life of

---

[29] Pindar, *Nem* 10:8. For discussion of the phenomena of "rapture" in the ancient world in general, cf. G. Strecker, "Entrückung," *RAC* 5:461–476.

Jesus, nor from the immediately following future, but the statement "Jesus died and arose" (1 Thess 4:14) means that the Christ event is a salvific, living present. That Jesus Christ lives thus means not only that Jesus has come back from the dead. This would mean nothing more than a continuation of his past life. It is therefore also inadequate to express the essential content of the resurrection concept with the statement "the cause of Jesus continues," as does W. Marxsen.[30] Instead, the resurrection of Jesus declares: only now, only in the event of the encounter with the exalted Lord, does it become clear what the "cause of Jesus" amounts to. Here for the first time not only is it revealed that Jesus is the eschatological prophet of Judaism, but also that his death has saving significance. Even if during his lifetime people had talked about him as a phenomenon within the history of Jewish religion—it was as the Risen One that he became the object of Christian preaching. The proclaimer could become the proclaimed because "Jesus Christ is risen" means that in him, God has acted. For, since God did not leave him in death, Jesus means God's eschatological "Yes" to human beings, God's unswerving promise to and acceptance of humanity. The salvation of humanity is inseparably bound to the person of Jesus Christ, the crucified and risen one.

Early Christianity interpreted and set forth this confession of the resurrection in different ways. They could speak of the Lord Jesus Christ as the cosmic Lord of the church and the powers of history, or of the future Son of Man who would appear as the judge of the world, or of the Son of God, chosen by God and sent for the salvation of humanity. Thus, in their way they did what theology in every age has as its task, namely, to bring to expression in ways that correspond both to the subject matter itself and to the modes of understanding of its own time the faith that the one testified to as Jesus Christ, the crucified and risen one, means salvation for humanity.

As we have seen,[31] the cross and resurrection of Jesus are placed alongside each other. The meaning of the cross of Jesus is thus not to be grasped in any other way than from the perspective of the resurrection. The history of Jesus' passion and death remains as mere events of the past if they are not seen from the post-Easter point of view. The resurrection faith interprets the cross: the suffering one is the exalted Lord of the church. The paradox of suffering and exaltation is the characteristic feature not only of the Christ who is believed in, but is just as much the mark of the community that believes in him. One can therefore only speak of the suffering of Jesus as the way that leads to resurrection. It must also be said the other way around: this inseparable combination of cross and resurrection pro-

---

[30]   W. Marxsen, *The Resurrection of Jesus of Nazareth* 78, 141
[31]   Cf. A. I. C.3. above on Romans 10:9; 1 Corinthians 15:3ff.

vides the Evangelists with the justification for projecting the resurrection faith back into the life of Jesus, not with the goal of narrating a "historia Jesu," but in order to testify to the Christ who is believed on in the community. Thus Jesus in the understanding of the New Testament is not only a "factum historicum brutum," but is the Christ of faith. What he was in himself can only be learned from the kerygma. Rudolf Bultmann coined the statement, "Jesus rose into the kerygma."[32] This means that we can learn who Jesus really is not by historical investigation but from the Easter kerygma alone. Jesus, the word of God, the word of truth, of love and justice, and not least the word of hope, is encountered only in the word that testifies to him. In the encounter with the witnesses, the meaning and significance of the Christ event is opened up and made available. The theology of the New Testament is a matter of these witnesses and their testimony.

## b) The Palestinian Church

Bihler, J. *Die Stephanusgeschichte im Zusammenhang der Apostelgeschichte*, MThS I 16. Munich: M. Hueber, 1963.
Conzelmann, H. *History of Primitive Christianity*. Nashville: Abingdon, 1973.
Dunn, J. D. G. *Unity and Diversity in the New Testament*. London-Philadelphia: Westminster, 1990².
Filson, F. V. *A New Testament History*. Philadelphia: Westminster, 1964.
Goppelt, L. *Apostolic and Post-Apostolic Times*. Grand Rapids: Baker, 1970.
Haenchen, E. *The Acts of the Apostles*. Philadelphia: Westminster, 1971.
Lüdemann, G. *Early Christianity According to the Traditions in Acts*. Minneapolis: Fortress, 1989.
Malherbe, A. J. *Social Aspects of Early Christianity*. Philadelphia: Westminster, 1983².
Schenke, L. *Die Urgemeinde. Geschichtliche und theologische Entwicklung*. Stuttgart: Katholisches Bibelwerk, 1990.
Schlatter, A. *Die Geschichte der ersten Christenheit*. Stuttgart: Calwer, 1983⁶.
Schmithals, W. *Paul and James*. Naperville: A. R. Allenson, 1965.
Schneemelcher, W. *Das Urchristentum*. UB 336. Stuttgart: Kohlhammer, 1981.
Simon, M. *St. Stephan and the Hellenists in the Primitive Church*, London-New York: Longmans, Green, 1958.
Vouga, F. *Geschichte des frühen Christentums*. UTB 1733, Tübingen-Basel: J. C. B. Mohr (Paul Siebeck), 1994.

## 1. Sources

The *tradition of the ancient church* regarding the history and theology of earliest Christianity does not preserve a great deal of information. The most helpful source is still the church historian Eusebius, who in his

---

[32] R. Bultmann, "Das Verhältnis der urchristlichen Christusbotschaft zum historischen Jesus," in *Exegetica* 445–469 (469).

"Ecclesiastical History" preserves quotations from older sources such as Hegesippus and Clement of Alexandria. Among non-Christian sources we may mention again the note in Josephus about James the Lord's brother (Ant 20.200).[33] More important are the *New Testament data*, which must of course be evaluated with caution. Acts 1–12 presents an outline of the history of the earliest church that is mostly a Lucan construction which, to be sure, contains older traditions.[34] Alongside these, we may place the Synoptic Gospels as historical sources for early Christianity, since the individual units of tradition gathered by the Evangelists derive in part from the early Palestinian church and reflect its situation (e. g. Matt 10:5–6; 16:17–19). The Letters of Paul provide an additional source to the extent that they contain the apostle's references to his relation to the Jerusalem church (cf. especially Gal 1–2). The New Testament apocrypha offer relatively little material. They transmit a variety of "acts of the apostles," but they only document how extensively legendary material about the Jerusalem apostles had already been formulated in the second century.[35]

## 2. Historical Situation

The origin and formation of the theological traditions in the New Testament is found in the historical situation of the earliest Jerusalem church. At the beginning stands not only the testimony of Peter to the resurrection, but also the fact that he was the first leader of both the Jerusalem church and of the Twelve—independently of the issue of whether the group of the Twelve can be traced back to the life of Jesus and the extent to which the story of the choice of Matthias as the twelfth disciple to replace Judas goes back to reliable tradition (Acts 1:15–26).[36] It was in this period that the christological and ecclesiastical thinking of the church was first developed.

The external events, especially those of the year 44, led to a radical change in the leadership structure. Under Herod Agrippa I, James the son of Zebedee, a member of the circle of the Twelve, was executed (Acts 12:2). E. Schwarz supposes that his brother John suffered the same fate.[37] As one

---

[33]   Cf. above B. II., on sources for the life of Jesus.
[34]   Cf. G. Luedemann, *Early Christianity according to the Traditions in Acts* (Minneapolis: Fortress Press, 1989) 9: "...Luke's activity as a writer consists in linking traditions together, i.e. of composing a consecutive narrative on the basis of traditions...".
[35]   Cf. W. Schneemelcher, *New Testament Apocrypha*, vol. 2.
[36]   According to W. Schneemelcher, *Urchristentum* 98, Peter would have been the presiding member of the apostolic circle; at least it is so reported by Paul (Gal 1:18).
[37]   E. Schwarz, "Ueber den Tod der Söhne Zebedaei. Ein Beitrag zur Geschichte des Johannesevangeliums," in E. Schwarz, ed. *Gesammelte Schriften V* (Berlin: W. de

consequence of this persecution, Peter had to leave Jerusalem (Acts 12:19). This meant the virtual dissolution of the institution of the Twelve, even if Peter reappeared in Jerusalem at the Apostolic Council, this time as a member of the circle of three στῦλοι ("Pillars:" James, Peter, and John, Gal 2:9) which by then had taken the place of the circle of the Twelve. At the Apostolic Council the three "Pillars" had exercised the leadership in dealing with the issues focused on Paul and Barnabas; this can also be presupposed for the parallel account in Acts 15. It is to be noted that in Galatians 2:9 Cephas no longer occupies the leading position of this group; leadership has passed to James the Lord's brother. Obviously James has gradually stepped into the foreground and thereby became the successor of Peter in Jerusalem.[38] This state of affairs is confirmed by the account of the collision between Peter and Paul in Antioch (Gal 2:11ff). There were "some (people) who came from James" who gave Peter and his group occasion to break off table fellowship with the Gentile members of the Christian community. The expression "some who came from James" is an indication that soon after the Apostolic Council the institution of the "Pillars" was also disbanded and that James alone was the leader of the earliest Jerusalem church. This agrees with the testimony of the ancient church that describe James as "Bishop of Jerusalem."[39] According to Josephus, James was executed in the year 62 at the instigation of the high priest Ananias (Antiquities XX 9.1.200).

This does not conclude the story of the earliest Jerusalem church, which endured beyond the Jewish war (66–70) and did not disappear until the catastrophe of the rebellion under Bar Cochba in 135 C.E. In any case, this is what is presupposed by the list of Jerusalem bishops transmitted by Eusebius.[40] It should thus not be supposed that, for instance, the Jerusalem church migrated across the Jordan to Pella before the first Jewish war began in 66 C.E., as Eusebius also reports (HE 3.5.3). Luke does not know of this tradition, although he refers to the Jewish war in chapter 21 of his

---

Gruyter, 1963) 48–123. This is presumed on the basis of Jesus' prediction in Mark 10:39, which announced the martyrdom of both sons of Zebedee. Such a chronological reconstruction of events, however, is an unlikely combination. It would require that the Apostolic Council occurred before the year 44, since according to Galatians 2:9 John had participated at the Council as the third member of the directorate called the στῦλοι. Such an early dating is in fact advocated by, for example, A. Suhl, Paulus und seine Briefe. Ein Beitrag zur paulinischen Chronologie (StNT 11. Gütersloh: Gerd Mohn, 1975) 339; Ph. Vielhauer, Geschichte der urchristlichen Literatur 78.

[38]  On James, cf. W. Pratscher, Der Herrenbruder Jakobus und die Jakobustradition (FLRANT 139. Göttingen: Vandenhoeck & Ruprecht, 1987).

[39]  Eusebius, HE 4.5.1ff; 22.4—based on earlier sources (the writings of Hegesippus and the Jerusalem lists of bishops). Cf. also the Pseudo-Clementines, the letters of 1 and 2 Clement, and other such documents.

[40]  Eusebius, HE 4.5.1ff; 5.23.3.

Gospel, and the Jerusalem list of bishops also presupposes an unbroken chain of bishops until the year 135. The Pella tradition is consequently a legend, perhaps originating among the Jewish Christians in Pella, deriving from an interest in documenting an episcopal succession or perhaps from a theological conviction that God was guiding the history of early Christianity.[41]

## 3. Theology

The history of the earliest Jerusalem church can be presented as a particular line of theological development. As the leadership of the community came increasingly into the hands of James the Lord's brother, it is clear that the Jerusalem church increasingly turned its mind back in the direction of its Jewish roots. To that extent the history of early Jewish Christianity is the history of a growing nomism. This means that at the beginnings, the consciousness of Torah was not the foundation of early Christian self-understanding. At the beginning stood rather the resurrection faith, the testimony to the resurrection of Jesus Christ. The encounter with the risen Jesus meant the foundation of the church. The resurrection faith called for explication; what did it mean that Jesus lives as the resurrected one and that this faith becomes the foundation of the church? There is a sense in which the apocalyptic interpretation of the resurrection of Jesus is right. The earliest Christian community understood the Risen One as the one who would reappear at his parousia. They understood God's "yes" that had been spoken to it in Jesus Christ in no other way than that this divine "yes" was coming to them and they were going to meet it at the near parousia of the risen Lord.

### α) Christology

Earliest Christianity expected the parousia of the Risen One. The pre-Markan sayings tradition testifies that the exalted Lord is expected "in this generation," i.e. in the generation of the eyewitnesses (Mark 9:1, 13:30). The faith of the earliest Christians was essentially hope for the

---

[41] Cf. W. Schneemelcher, *Urchristentum* 52–53, 164–165; G. Strecker, *Das Judenchristentum in den Pseudoklementinen*, (TU 70. Berlin: Akadamie Verlag, 1981², 229ff, 283ff; differently M. Simon, *Le Christianisme antique et son contexte religieux*, (Scripta Varia II, WUNT 23. Tübingen: J. C. B. Mohr [Paul Siebeck], 1981) 477–494; H. Lietzmann, *A History of the Early church* (New York: World Publishing Co., 1961), 1:177–190; J. J. Gunther, "The Fate of the Jerusalem Church," *ThZ* 29 (1973) 81–94. The first account of this event in Epiphanius, *de mens* 15, is already harmonizing, picturing the Jerusalem church that had fled to Pella during the war as returning to Jerusalem near the end of the war. Cf. C. Andresen, *Geschichte des Christentums I. Von den Anfängen bis zur Hochscholastik* (ThW 6. Stuttgart: Calwer, 1975) 1; H. Conzelmann, *History of Primitive Christianity* 137.

encounter with the resurrected Christ in the immediate future. This is also indicated by the Aramaic prayer "Marana tha."[42] What did the earliest Christians expect from the future? They expected the advent of the Risen One as the Son of Man. They utilized the savior figure and judge of Jewish apocalypticism as a means of interpreting the resurrection event. They took up a term from the Jewish eschatological expectation that had already become "canonical" in Jewish tradition in Daniel 7:13 (cf. Mark 13:26; 14:62).[43] The point of departure for the discussion must be that already in the Aramaic-speaking earliest Palestinian church, the title בַּר אֱנָשׁ had been applied to Jesus as the object of the resurrection faith.

As indicated above,[44] the Synoptic tradition transmitted three different groups of Son of Man sayings: (1) sayings about the suffering and rising Son of Man, as in the context of the passion and resurrection predictions of Jesus in Mark (Mark 8:31; 9:31; 10:32–34; cf. also Mark 9:12b). This group has no parallels in the Q-tradition and is clearly secondary, dealing with *vaticinia ex eventu*. These sayings originated in the Hellenistic-Jewish church in order to interpret the destiny of Jesus as the fulfillment of Scripture. (2) Sayings about the present activity of the Son of Man,[45] in which the situation of the church outside Palestine can be perceived. This is the case, for example, in the discussion about the validity of the Sabbath (Mark 2:28) or the forgiveness of sins (Mark 2:10; Matt 12:32par). They belong within the milieu of the Christian wandering charismatics, who retroject their own situation into the life of Jesus (Matt 8:20par), and who found themselves in debates with other groups (e. g. Matt 11:19par, where the debate partner is the group of John the Baptist's disciples). It is not probable that this group of sayings goes back to the earliest church, since they presuppose the idea of the present and/or past of the Son of Man. The earliest church confessed its faith in the Son of Man to come, not the present or past Son of Man. (3) Sayings about the future Son of Man of

---

[42] 1 Corinthians 16:22: μαράνα θά ("our Lord, come!"); see above A. II. a. 3.

[43] In his sixth semester of university studies H. Lietzmann composed as his first published article, "Der Menschensohn. Ein Beitrag zur neutestamentlichen Theologie," (Freiburg-Leipzig, 1896), in which he attempted to trace the term "Son of Man" back to the Hellenistic world. He considered it a Greek translation that had misunderstood the Aramaic בַּר אֱנָשׁ (= a human being) (87); in his view the Messianic title "Son of Man" was never known to the Palestinian church, but was an invention of Hellenistic Christianity (95). In view of the clear examples of the term in Jewish apocalypticism, this thesis cannot be sustained.

[44] See above B. II. d. 3.

[45] R. Bultmann traces this group back to a linguistic misunderstanding of the Aramaic בַּר אֱנָשׁ, following J. Wellhausen *Einleitung in die drei ersten Evangelien* (Berlin: Georg Reimer, 1911²) 123–130, and H. Lietzmann, "Der Menschensohn" 87. This, however, is unlikely. The term is found in such key passages that one can hardly interpret it in the general sense (of "human being" or "I"). These passages are rather to be understood as Messianic declarations.

whom Jesus speaks (Mark 8:38; 14:62; 12:8–9par; Matt 10:23).[46] Earliest Christianity was confident that the image of the Son of Man was closely connected with the kingdom of God. They expected the coming kingdom of God in no other way than that Jesus, the crucified and risen one, is the Son of Man and thus the one who will bring in the kingdom of God (Matt 19:28par; Luke 22:29–30).[47]

Earliest Christianity identified the coming Son of Man with the risen Christ. Just as Jesus, in his testimony before the high priest announced the future appearance of the Son of Man in power, coming on the clouds of heaven (Mark 14:62), so the community knows that this coming one is the past and present Lord (*Mar*) Jesus who has been raised from the dead. The earliest Christians confessed that the future salvation they expected was inseparable from the person of their Lord. They therefore expected the coming βασιλεία τοῦ θεοῦ (מַלְכוּת יהוה) in such a way that the breaking in of the kingdom of God coincided with the advent of the Son of Man with which it was identified. The coming of the kingdom of God is the breaking in of the new aeon that will bring world history to an end (Mark 10:29–30). The appearance of the Son of Man means judgment for the world and the destruction of the cosmos (Matt 24:3) and/or the introduction of the End (cf. 1 Cor 15:23–28; 1 Thess 4:15–17). With this is connected the expectation of the destruction of the temple.[48] The church will be preserved through the catastrophe, for the destructive judgment will mean liberation for them, and the gathering of the elect (Mark 13:20–23). It will bring consolation and compensation (Mark 10:29–30), so that they may enter into the wedding hall (Matt 22:10) and attain to ζωὴ αἰώνιος (Mark 10:30; Matt 25:46). The fulfillment of the Christian hope is realized in table fellowship with the exalted Lord (Mark 14:25). This community has the promise that they, together with the Son of Man, will judge the people of Israel (Matt 19:28).

---

[46] Authentic Jesus material is found only in this group by R. Bultmann, *Theology* 1:29–30; H. E. Tödt, *Son of Man* 40 (according to Tödt, only Mark 8:38 can be attributed to Jesus). For the contrary view, see Ph. Vielhauer, "Gottesreich und Menschensohn in der Verkündigung Jesu," 55–91, in *Festschrift für G. Dehn* (Neukirchen-Vluyn: Neukirchener), 1957, 51–79 (71); reprinted in Ph. Vielhauer, ed., *Aufsätze zum Neuen Testament* (TB 31. Munich: Kaiser, 55–91).

[47] Although it includes editorial reworking from both Matthew and Luke, Matthew 19:28par is probably an old saying that emphasizes the special function of the circle of the Twelve.

[48] Mark 13:2. The saying about the temple probably goes back to Jesus, in view of the variegated and widespread criticism of the temple in the Old Testament and Judaism, and since it fits the context of the prophetic ministry of Jesus. Cf. e. g. E. Lohmeyer, *Das Evangelium des Markus* (KEK I/2. Göttingen: Vandenhoeck & Ruprecht, 1967[17]) 268. Differently J. Lambrecht, *Die Redaktion der Markus-Apokalypse. Literarische Analyse und Strukturuntersuchung* (AnBib 28. Rome: PBI, 1967) 68–79; R. Pesch, *Naherwartungen. Tradition und Redaktion in Mk 13* (KBANT. Düsseldorf: Patmos, 1968) 83–93.

The concept of the Son of Man is accordingly the central christological predication of the earliest Christian community; its Christology was essentially a Son-of-Man Christology. The other christological predicates recede.[49] At the most, one might suppose that the title "Son of David" had a special significance. But here too the general principle for all the christological titles applies: they were filled with content mainly in the Hellenistic church, more precisely, in Hellenistic Jewish Christianity.

β) Ecclesiology

The earliest church's Son of Man Christology paved the way for the understanding of its ecclesiology. The church fellowship understood itself as the eschatological congregation. The term "eschatological" is here used in its original sense, as meaning that this community was genuinely oriented to the end time.

This is seen, for example, in the "Lord's Prayer," the "Our Father," which goes back to Jesus[50] and came to the Evangelists Matthew and Luke in independent formulations (Matt 6:9–13par Luke 11:2–4). When Matthew inserted it into its present context he added an "application," an admonition about the readiness to forgive others, motivated by the promise that then the heavenly Father would be willing to forgive. This is

---

[49] The situation with regard to the history of traditions is too complex to attain even a probable solution with regard to the other christological titles. The view that the earliest church had "identified the 'Risen One' with the expected Messiah of the seed of David and the transcendent 'Son of Man'" (so L. Schenke, *Urgemeinde* 127) can hardly appeal to older texts. On the contrary, a community in a Jewish milieu that was concerned with an eschatological recompense most likely would have found the political character of the Jewish Son of David Messiah difficult to use in its own Christology. So also, just how the earliest church thought of the exaltation of Jesus Christ as the Risen One can no longer be determined. The supposition that alongside the expectation of the parousia, the concept of preexistence also played a role (so L. Schenke, *Urgemeinde* 121) is improbable. A developed Christology cannot be documented. This is also true for the issue of how the practice of baptism was interpreted, especially how its relation to the forgiveness of sins was grounded. Presumably a Christology that included a complete doctrine of the atonement had not been developed in the earliest church. It obviously sufficed that the baptismal ritual was practiced as a sign of admittance to the new community, as in the circle around John the Baptist.

[50] For support for this view, see G. Strecker, *Sermon on the Mount* 107–113. Differently e. g. S. Schulz, *Q Die Spruchquelle der Evangelisten* (Zürich: Theologischer Verlag, 1972), who supposes that in the Lord's Prayer we have "the pattern of prayer of the oldest Palestinian Christian Q-community," (87) even if there "old, indeed oldest tradition" is used (86). M. D. Goulder, "The Composition of the Lord's Prayer," *JThS* 14 (1963) 32–45, proceeds on the basis of the hypothesis that Jesus had provided his disciples a model of prayer, which was taken up by Mark. Matthew then composed this into a formulaic prayer, which Luke then shortened and modified (35ff). S. v. Tilborg, "A Form-criticism of the Lord's Prayer," *NT* 14 (1972) 94–105 (104), sees in the Lord's Prayer "a liturgical reflection upon the Gethsemane story" (Mark 14:32–42) that originated in the Jewish Christian community.

occasioned by the parenetic context of the Sermon on the Mount, which also influences the understanding of the fifth petition (Matt 6:14–15; cf. v. 12).[51] A comparison of the Synoptic parallel shows that Matthew has seven petitions, while Luke has only five. Luke is doubtless closest to the original. Matthew makes use of a church tradition characterized by heptadic formation. So also Matthew has expanded the address πάτερ by the addition of ὁ ἐν τοῖς οὐρανοῖς. That the Lord's prayer was used in the earliest Palestinian church is indicated by the Semitic linguistic character at the base of the composition, recognizable for example in the passive verb forms (first and second petitions: circumlocution for the name of God). In addition, the parallels in Jewish prayers, especially the Eighteen Benedictions, point to a Jewish background.

By praying the Lord's Prayer, the earliest Christian community articulated its eschatological self-consciousness. The first petition ("Hallowed be thy name") presupposes that God's name has been profaned by the sins of his people.[52] Here the confidence is affirmed that God will remove this profanation by the judgment that he will execute on sinners and his foes. The second petition for the coming of the kingdom likewise corresponds to the eschatological-apocalyptic self-understanding of the community: the kingdom for which the community hopes and prays, God's own rulership, will bring the present age to an end.

The first two petitions of the Lord's Prayer ("thou petitions") speak theologically of God and correspond to each other as judgment and grace. They provide the essential foundation of the Lord's Prayer. They are followed by the second section of "we-petitions," which are concerned with human needs.

The third petition (following the original enumeration) speaks of the "bread that we need;" ἐπιούσιος means "necessary for existence," "what is essential," which is asked for daily. This petition is thus concerned with the necessities of life for each day. The prayer is not for some sort of supernatural bread but for what it takes to survive in the face of earthly, physical poverty.

The content of the fourth petition deals with the forgiveness of sins. The prayer for forgiveness (as in Luke 11:4; apparently Matt 6:12 is more original: τὰ ὀφειλήματα ἡμῶν = "our debts") is bound up with the understanding that the one who prays is willing to forgive. Here, differently than in the third petition, the eschatological judgment resonates in the background of the prayer: if forgiveness begins in the present, this petition is still oriented to the last judgment in which the final pronouncement will be made about the transgressions of the individual.

---

[51]   The contrary thesis occasionally advocated neglects the redactional context in favor of an isolated evaluation of its liturgical origin.

[52]   This corresponds to the Old Testament idea, e. g. Isaiah 43:25; 48:11 and elsewhere.

The fifth petition ("and lead us not into temptation") asks for preservation from that which can take one off the right way. Whoever falls by the wayside now has already made a decision about his or her final destination; thus here the eschatological tone is not to be denied. It is only the third petition, the prayer for daily necessities, that appears to violate the eschatological orientation of the whole prayer. But it stands under the same sign as the whole second section. The prayer for the coming of the kingdom is placed before all else. Thus the third petition too is bounded and relativized by the apocalyptic horizon that was characteristic of the self-understanding of earliest Christianity in general. The reality of everyday life is understood within the framework of eschatological expectation.

The Lord's Prayer makes it clear that earliest Christianity understands itself to be the eschatological congregation. They can thus describe themselves as the congregation of the ἐκλεκτοί. They are the "chosen" not because they already have an existence outside of history, but because their eschatological quality will be revealed along with the end of the world. They are "called out," inasmuch as the Son of Man will confess them at his coming. In the present age, of course, their lot is suffering and persecution (cf. Mark 13:19, 22), but the terrors of the endtime will be shortened for their sakes (Mark 13:20). God will hear their cries, will destroy their persecutors, and send the Son of Man as their savior (cf. Luke 18:7–8) and will gather those who are now scattered throughout the world from the ends of the earth (Mark 13:27). The hope for such a glorious future supports them in the present and carries them through its trials.

An additional predication of the eschatological community is expressed in the designation ἅγιοι. Here we are dealing with a term characterized by its usage within the Old Testament cultus, where the "holy ones" are those who are permitted to enter the sacred area—such as the priests of the Old Testament sacrificial cult—and who thus have access to the holy place and can stand before God.

Paul uses this term to designate the church, especially in reference to the Jewish Christians in Jerusalem (Rom 15:25–31; cf. e. g. 1 Cor 16:1, 15; 2 Cor 8:4; 9:1 and elsewhere.). This ecclesiological predication is to be understood primarily in a proleptic sense: the members of the community are holy inasmuch as they have the promise. They know that on the day of the parousia of the Son of Man access to God will stand open before them. They are marked off from the world, ἐπ᾽ ἐλπίδι (Rom 8:20 v. l.; Tit 1:2); they are saints "in regard to hope," in regard to the promise that one day the sacred realities of heaven will be given them.[53]

---

[53] One often finds the term οἱ πτωχοί considered to be an additional ecclesiological predication. It is found in the Pauline letters especially in the context of the collection for the "saints" in Jerusalem (cf. Rom 15:25–29), and apparently portrays the Jerusalem church as characterized by the Jewish ideal of poverty as an expression of religious conviction. Accordingly, the Jerusalem church would have practiced a

If we compare the two predicates ἐκλεκτοί and ἅγιοι with Pauline theology, we see that in Paul's letters they reflect the dialectic of present and future salvation.[54] While Paul teaches the dialectic between the "already" and the "not yet," it is clear that the earliest Christian community emphasized the "not yet." It has not yet come out of this aeon, but rather expects everything from the coming day of the Son of Man; it expects its salvation in the near future. That it understands itself in the present as the eschatological community is grounded in the fact that it has this hope.

However, the orientation of the community to the future needs one other qualification. The community knows itself to be in possession of the Spirit, the divine pneuma, which in the Jewish view is the eschatological gift (cf. Joel 3:1–2). Here it stands in contrast to the idea widespread in apocalyptic and rabbinic literature, according to which the Spirit was restricted to preceding times when it appeared in the prophets but is now extinct.[55] As

---

kind of community of property (as Acts 2:44–45 and 4:32–35 seem to indicate). One is tempted to see this as the basis for the designation that Jewish Christians received in the writings of the Church Fathers, "Ebionites," (the Hebrew word for "poor"), as for example in Irenaeus *Against Heresies* 1.26.2; 3.11.7; 3.21.1; 4.33.4; 5.1.3; Origen, *De Principiis* 4.3.8; *Against Celsus* 2.1; Eusebius *HE* 3.27.1, 6 and elsewhere. Here it is a matter of a Jewish Christian self-description, which was possibly connected with the ideal of religious poverty in some streams of Judaism. This designation, however, does not reach back to New Testament times. The Acts accounts of the community of goods in Jerusalem are secondary, presumably representing Luke's generalizing of episodes that were not characteristic of the Jerusalem church as a whole. The expression οἱ πτωχοί in the Pauline letters is a sociological term, not a religious predicate. Cf. F. W. Horn, *Glaube und Handeln in der Theologie des Lukas* (GTA 26. Göttingen: Vandenhoeck & Ruprecht, 1986²) 36–49.

54   Cf. A. IV. a. l. above. With regard to the expression ἅγιοι, it should be noted that there are Jewish analogies to this self-description of the earliest Christians. The Qumran community described itself as the "Community of the Saints" or the "Saints of the People of God," as for example in 1QM 6.6; 1QS 5.18, 20; 11.8 and elsewhere. Contra H. Balz, ἅγιος *EWNT* 1:38–48 (44: "…presupposes the language and theology of Hellenistic Judaism.")

55   Cf. 1 Maccabees 4:46; 2 Baruch 85:1ff. So also W. Bousset in H. Gressmann, ed., *Die Religion des Judentums im späthellenistischen Zeitalter* (HNT 21. Tübingen: J. C. B. Mohr [Paul Siebeck], 1966⁴) 394. Differently R. Meyer, "Prophecy and Prophets in the Judaism of the Hellenistic Roman Period" (TDNT 6:812–828), who sees in 2 Baruch the "dogma of the canonical period of salvation, as advocated by Josephus *Apion* 1.41 and the Rabbis" (816). But in its basic tendency, 2 Baruch "by no means excludes the circulation of oracles and thus the appearance of prophets in the time of Vespasian" (*ibid.*). Thus 2 Baruch 48:34–37 "refers to the charismatic phenomena at the time of the destruction of the temple." The promises mentioned there, some of which turned out to be true and others did not, are references to the prophetic messages of deliverance and destruction of that time (*ibid.*, note 225). Meyer interprets 1 Maccabees 4:46 in connection with 9:27 and 14:41: the whereabouts of the stones of the ancient altar could be determined by the high priest John Hyrcanus, since he has charismatic authorization to decide on matters concerning the temple (816). On this "dogma," cf. F. W. Horn, *Das Angeld des Geistes* 26–40.

in contemporary Judaism,[56] so also in earliest Christianity, people emerged who were endowed with the Spirit, who delivered prophetic utterances. The prophet Agabus of Jerusalem is an example (Acts 11:28; 21:10).[57] And when Mark 3:29 warns against blaspheming the Holy Spirit, this may refer to the Spirit at work in early Christian prophets.[58]

It is not to be doubted that earliest Christianity knew itself to be in possession of the Spirit and thereby also experienced the corresponding spiritual manifestations. The class of early Christian prophets is clear evidence of this; the formation of the pre-Synoptic tradition can hardly be explained otherwise. If the earliest church possesses the Spirit, that means that it has the eschatological gift. The presence of the Spirit testifies that the eschaton has entered into time. The church is accordingly not exclusively oriented to the "not yet," but rather—to use Pauline language—with the spirit has the ἀπαρχή ("first fruits," Rom 8:23), the ἀρραβών ("down payment," 2 Cor 1:22; 5:5), the sign and pointer to what is still to come. The pneuma does not effect any sacramental quality, does not create a "character indelebilis," but remains a "deposit" on what is to come. The Spirit is no guarantee of acceptance in the future final judgment but is a preliminary sign. Though it points beyond itself, it is still a sign in the present that reflects the future glory.

This sign is mediated by *baptism*, which was presupposed as the given practice in earliest Christianity.[59] Baptism mediated the Spirit. This also appears to be the meaning of Matthew 3:11parr: John the Baptist announces the Coming One as the one who will "baptize with the Holy Spirit and fire." This characterization of the Coming One, however, is probably a Christian interpretation. The Baptist presumably did not speak of bap-

---

[56] Cf. W. Schneemelcher, *New Testament Apocrypha* 2:601–607; D. E. Aune, *Prophecy in Early Christianity and the Ancient Mediterranean World* (Grand Rapids: Eerdmans, 1983) 103–152; M. E. Boring, *Sayings of the Risen Jesus: Christian Prophecy in the Synoptic Tradition* (MSSNTS 46. Cambridge: Cambridge University Press, 1982) 23–25 and passim.

[57] One may ask whether the earliest Christian table fellowship was permeated with eschatological jubilation effected by the Spirit (ἀγαλλίασις; as in Acts 2:46), or whether this portrayal does not rather go back to Luke's idealization of the early Christian congregational life. So also the ecstatic phenomena such as happened in the congregational worship at Corinth (1 Cor 14) are not to be projected directly back into earliest Palestinian Christianity. It is particularly questionable whether the Pentecost event can be traced back to a Jerusalem experience of the Spirit. The story of Pentecost in Acts 2 is certainly secondary, an account reflecting Luke's own theology.

[58] Even if the situation in Corinth (1 Cor 14) may not be presupposed for the earliest Palestinian church, it is still the case that Paul understood himself to be a Spirit-endowed charismatic; see the above chapter "Office and Spirit" A. IV. a. 3.

[59] Cf. the relation of Jesus to the baptism of John (see above B. I. c.). By the line John—Jesus—members of the community, baptism came into the early church and became the sacrament of entrance ("initiation rite").

tism in the Spirit but only of the coming baptism in fire. Already in the Q tradition, the expression πνεύματι ἁγίῳ will have been added, which is then found exclusively in Mark 1:8. The church understands the preaching of the Baptist to refer to its Lord, to Jesus as the coming Son of Man. He will not only bring the future baptism of fire but has already brought a baptism, namely baptism in the Spirit. The community not only looks forward to the baptism of fire, the final judgment, but at the same time it knows itself already to be determined by the water rite, which mediates the Spirit. This binding together of baptism and conferral of the Spirit has thus found an early expression in Matthew 3:11parr. This corresponds to the general consciousness of early Christianity of being in possession of the Spirit. Thus Acts 2:38 later documents what Paul had already spoken of, that "in the one Spirit we were all baptized into one body" (1 Cor 12:13).

Baptism in earliest Christianity was therefore not only a baptism of repentance like that of John. To be sure, like John's baptism it conferred the forgiveness of sins and was likewise oriented toward the future, for the final confirmation of the forgiveness received in baptism will not happen until the end of history. However, early Christian baptism was not only a "bath of purification ... for the coming reign of God,"[60] but by the conferral of the Spirit baptism itself signified that something had happened. It had the ἀπαρχή character of mediating participation in the Spirit, and all the more so as it placed the baptized person in relation to Jesus as the coming Son of Man, since it is probable that even in the earliest times Christian baptism was administered in the "name of Jesus, even if this is not documented prior to Acts (e. g. 2:38; 8:16; 19:5) and is reflected in the letters of Paul (Rom 6:3; [13:14]; Gal 3:27). No other baptismal formula has been preserved from earliest Christianity, and baptism in the name of Jesus corresponds to the Marana tha cry of Aramaic-speaking Christianity.

These considerations do not fundamentally alter the sign-character of baptism in early Christianity. Its proleptic orientation is preserved, such that in the real sense of the word baptism represented something provisional, as was characteristic of the eschatological self-understanding of the earliest church.

To summarize: baptism possessed three functions in earliest Christianity: (1) forgiveness of sins, (2) conferral of the Spirit, and (3) establishing a relation to the coming Son of Man, Jesus Christ. All three functions are constitutively oriented toward the future. In contrast, for Paul it is characteristic that while he too knows these three functions, even if partly in a different linguistic expression, he also adds a fourth: dying and rising with Christ, which happens in the act of baptism according to Romans

---

[60]     So R. Bultmann, *New Testament Theology* 1:39.

6:1ff. Thereby the significance of baptism for the present is strongly emphasized. This corresponds to Paul's context in the Hellenistic world, especially the cultic piety of this world. Earliest Christian baptism, in contrast, is constitutively oriented to the apocalyptic future and cannot be separated from this sense of eschatological existence. It goes beyond the meaning of John's baptism in that it is an eschatological sacrament.

With regard to the *fellowship meal* of earliest Palestinian Christianity, one can use the Synoptic accounts (Mark 14:22–24parr) or the Pauline tradition (1 Cor 11:23–25) of the institution of the Lord's Supper only with great caution. To be sure, these texts can be traced back to a very early form.[61] It is also clear that the attempt to understand this tradition as deriving from the setting of a Passover meal cannot be convincing. The differences between them and a Jewish Passover celebration are too serious for this hypothesis ever to be generally accepted. This is still true even though the context in the Synoptic Gospels is that of a Passover celebration.

R. Bultmann has vigorously advocated a Hellenistic background for this tradition, based especially on supposition that the shorter form of the words of institution represents the oldest form: "This is my body, this is my blood," so that the additional explanatory words are to be considered secondary interpretations. In this view the tradition originated within Hellenistic Christianity, where the risen Lord was celebrated as a mystery deity in a manner analogous to the Hellenistic mystery cults. This reconstruction still leaves open questions.[62] There can be no doubt, however, that a sacramental interpretation of the words of institution would simply be without analogy in the world of Jewish thought, so that an approach that looks for parallels within Judaism from the point of view of the history of religions must be abandoned.[63] The Synoptic reports of the institution of the Lord's Supper thus reflect the thought world associated with the Hellenistic church, not that of earliest Palestinian Christianity. Stating this does not mean that the principle of analogy in the study of the history of religions is accepted as the "last word" on the issue.[64] It is simply a matter of asking the question from the point of view of historical criticism, which of course makes it impossible to draw firm conclusions from the New Testament accounts of the institution of the Lord's Supper with regard either to the meals celebrated in earliest Palestinian Christianity or the last meal of Jesus with his disciples.

---

[61] Cf. above A. III. c. 3.

[62] It is to be noted, for example, that this hypothesis must presuppose that the reconstructed parallelism must be seen as having been later spoiled.

[63] So also L. Goppelt, *Apostolic and Post-Apostolic Times* (New York: Harper & Row, 1962) 47 note 24.

[64] Contra L. Goppelt, *ibid.*

The consequence for historical interpretation is that at the most we can speak of a "Lord's Supper" in earliest Christianity with reference to the Aramaic *Mari* title, since the *Kyrios* idea that is presupposed later, like that of the accounts of the institution of the Lord's Supper, belong to the realm of Hellenistic Christianity. In contrast, the fellowship meal of earliest Christianity is oriented primarily to the future. Our sources are inadequate to describe it more precisely. Two possible textual bases are to be distinguished:

(a) Acts 2:42–47, the summary report of the community life of the first Christians (with breaking of bread and prayer), places the emphasis on the ἀγαλλίασις, the eschatological joy of the community. It remains questionable, however, whether the fragmentary Lucan account contains a historical kernel that the historian can take seriously, even if the earliest church's awareness that it possessed the Spirit means it cannot be completely excluded.

(b) Mark 14:25par are Jesus' parting words referring to the future table fellowship in the kingdom of God. While in both texts it is uncertain whether they reflect tradition from the earliest community, they still have in common the eschatological orientation. Since this is documented elsewhere as characteristic of the earliest church, it may well have been the case that the table fellowship of the earliest Christians was permeated with this eschatological-apocalyptic mood. This table fellowship accordingly had no sacramental character. Perhaps it was the continuation of Jesus' own table fellowship, or made a specific connection with Jesus' last meal. Doubtless Jewish mealtime customs prevailed at these gatherings, but in distinction to Jewish usage the festive meal was characterized by an eschatological prospect: the earliest Christians celebrated their meal as the eschatological congregation of their coming Lord.[65]

γ) Stance towards the Law

The question of how the earliest Christian community understood itself in relation to the Jewish law is of decisive importance for understanding its faith. The Torah is God's gift to his people Israel.[66] Jewish piety and Jewish faith are constitutively bound to the law given on Sinai. Whoever lives according to the law established by God will live.[67] This self-evident premise of Judaism was also operative in the context in which early Christianity originated. If we ask how the earliest Christian community con-

---

[65]   Cf. the reconstruction of B. Kollmann, *Ursprung und Gestalten der frühchristlichen Mahlfeier* (GTA 43. Göttingen: Vandenhoeck & Ruprecht, 1990).

[66]   E. g. Leviticus 26:46; Ezekiel 20:11.

[67]   Leviticus 18:5; Psalm 1; (19:8); 119; Proverbs 4:4; Nehemiah 9:29; Ezekiel 20:11, 21.

ducted itself in a situation where this was the given state of affairs,[68] after it had encountered the Risen One who had grounded the hope that he would return as the Son of Man, there can be no doubt that from the point of view of the history of religions the church presented itself as "an eschatological sect within Judaism."[69] After the experiences of the epiphanies of the risen Jesus and the constituting of early Christian community life associated with these experiences, this cohesion with Judaism was maintained.

Thus Christians continued to observe the Sabbath (Matt 24:20; Acts 16:13), visit the temple (cf. Acts 2:46; 5:12), to pay the temple tax (Matt 17:24–27), participate in the sacrificial cult (Matt 5:23–24), and to take pride in the Jewish initiation practice of circumcision (Gal 2:3). So also the institution of the Twelve points to a close relationship to Judaism, since it makes the claim of representing the twelve tribes of Israel (Matt 19:28par). The missionary enterprise was directed to the Jewish people, not primarily to Gentiles. This particularistic limitation of the earliest Christian mission is explicitly confirmed by Matthew 10:5–6 and 15:24.

Continuity with Judaism is thus preserved. In its appearance and external character, this association belonged within Judaism. But this does not yet grasp the real essence of this movement, its own affirmation of the early Christian faith. On the contrary, early Christian faith in the resurrection of Jesus implies a break with the past and understands itself to stand in discontinuity with its Jewish context. This is still true, even if the earliest Christian community was apparently itself not yet aware of this new self-understanding, i.e., even if there was no consciously articulated self-awareness parallel to this new self-understanding. Even if the early Christian self-understanding had not found adequate expression in its theological and ecclesiological statements, it still stood in essential discontinuity with its Jewish environment, since in contrast to its Jewish contemporaries this community knew what its future held. The witnesses of the resurrection knew the one who would return as the Son of Man. That meant a fundamental breaking of the bond of that Jewish legal observance which continued to bind the Christian community externally with Judaism, since it is not on the basis of law observance, but on the basis of their eschatologically-grounded hope that it is the congregation of the "elect" and the "saints." They are distinguished from their Jewish

---

[68] It would obviously be a short-circuit to try to interpret the stance of the Judaism of Jesus' day to the Torah in only one sense, a narrowly legal one (cf. on this correctly E. P. Sanders, *Paul, the Law, and the Jewish People* [Philadelphia: Fortress, 1983]). Neither is Paul's contrast between faith and works to be introduced into the problematic of earliest Christianity. Nevertheless, it should not be disputed that the question of the basis of eschatological salvation touches on the problem of whether keeping the law is "necessary for salvation."

[69] R. Bultmann, *New Testament Theology* 1:42.

environment because they possess the ἀπαρχή, the Spirit, the beginning of the future fulfillment. While they may have continued to keep the law as a matter of external observance, their existence as the eschatological congregation rests on their faith in the identity of the Risen One with the coming Son of Man. In later Jewish Christian writings[70] Jesus is identified with the Christ, the one expected in Judaism as the bringer of salvation. Therefore the description of earliest Christianity as an eschatological sect within Judaism is not adequate for comprehending its own self-understanding. It makes its confession on the basis of its experiences, on the foundation of its encounter with the Risen One and the hope thereby established on which the future will be constructed, a future that will also bring about the fulfillment of Israel—not on a foundation built on law or an understanding of salvation history. It is only consistent with this self-understanding that this community knew itself to be called to a mission to Israel and that the content of this mission is the call to repentance, a call to repentance in view of the approaching advent of the community's Lord.

The history of earliest Christianity shows that the stance to the Jewish law, like the relationship to Judaism in general, did not remain constant. At the latest, a change seems to have taken place with the transition of the leadership of the community to James. The Lord's brother is described as "the righteous" in the Gospel of the Hebrews.[71] In Jewish Christian tradition he is regarded as the one who advocated and practiced in his own life an especially strict observance of the law. One might suppose that during the time of his leadership of the community, sayings were formulated that express this intention.[72] The variable stance toward the Gentile mission that may be perceived for the earliest time appears to have been influenced by James' own conduct. Galatians 2:9 indicates that the agreement of the "pillars" with Barnabas and Paul was that the latter should go to the Gentiles, while the Jerusalem group would conduct a mission among the Jews. When Luke, in Acts 15 speaks of the same council, he adds in 15:20, 29 the "Apostolic Decree" that is explicitly directed to Gentile Christians and contains four requirements: to abstain from meat sacrificed to idols, from fornication, from whatever has been strangled, and from eating blood. But this Apostolic Decree was not promulgated at the council, since Paul remained unaware of it. This list of minimal legal requirements possibly reflects the later stance of the Jerusalem church to the issue of the Gentile mission and thus also the stance of James. In any

---

70   Pseudo-Clementine AJ II (Rec 1:39–40).
71   *Gospel of the Hebrews* 7; cf. also *Gospel of Thomas* 12.
72   E. g. Matthew 5:18: "For truly I tell you, until heaven and earth pass away, not one letter, not one stroke of a letter, will pass from the law until all is accomplished."

case, it fits in with this view that according to Acts 21 James the Lord's brother asks Paul to sponsor some men in Jerusalem who had made a Nazarite vow (Acts 21:18–26). Finally, this also corresponds to Galatians 2:12, in which it was the authority of James that stood behind the demand that Jewish Christians not participate in table fellowship with Gentile Christians, a demand that carried the day in Antioch.

The developing history of earliest Christianity is thus shaped by an increasingly nomistic tendency. The beginning is characterized by the all-consuming faith in the Risen One who will return as the Son of Man. Thereby the significance of the law as a way of salvation was fundamentally relativized. The later development, in contrast, took up the law again as an expression of its goal of demonstrating that the new movement was holding fast to the unity of the Jewish religion and nation.

1. At the beginning stands the encounter with the Risen One. It does not signify the confirmation of the Jewish law, but a shattering of the identification of the Jewish law with the law of God. The earliest Christian faith is, in terms of its origin, a being called out of the given structure of things because it opens itself radically to the One who transcends all. The origin and destiny of the community is not identical with the content of the teaching of the Pharisees and scribes. At the beginning stands the experience of being overcome by the revelation of God, which is essentially a historical revelation, which means an encounter with a particular Thou. Such a revelation is not to be derived from history, but as the disclosure of the absolute God can only stand in a paradoxical relation to history. It is therefore concretized in the paradoxical sign, in the identity of the Crucified One and the Risen One, an identity that cannot be grasped in human terms.

2. But at the beginning there stands not only the realization that the Risen One is identical with the Crucified One, but also that the Risen One is the One to come in the future. The community expects the one who will come to it from the realm beyond history. The Christ of faith is for the believers not the end of history in such a manner that the community would exist in an ahistorical realm. It does not confess its faith in a Christ who is now the end of history, but expects him as the one to come in the future, who will appear from beyond the cosmos and bring the being of this world to an end. Faith accordingly directs itself to the future end of history in which the community will meet its Lord. Such faith means "openness to the future;" it relativizes the present, and all the more so since faith in the crucified and risen one has already called in question the powers that operate in history. Inherent in earliest Christian faith is the knowledge that the believer will encounter the One who has already been present as the Crucified and Risen One. Such faith likewise knows that the future will confirm what it already apprehends in the present.

3. Therefore this "eschatological sect of Judaism," as it is called from the perspective of the history of religions, manifests in its very existence the risk inherent in Christian faith. This faith is constrained to seek its way between revelation and history, the Jewish law and the law of God, order and freedom. Christian faith stands constantly before the task of preserving the one without losing the other, for faith is not ahistorical, as though it could feel itself to have been delivered once and for all from the demands of historical structures. It is rather the case that the Christian faith is a faith oriented to history; its structure points it to being in the world, and it must maintain itself within the world. But its being is not determined by the world and therefore may not be exchanged with a philosophical doctrine, a world view, or a humanitarian ideal. At its essential core this faith is rather an openness to the "Wholly Other." That allows the absolute barriers erected in history to be broken, and relativizes the nature of faith as being-in-the-world. It poses the task to believers of guarding their life in the world from its seductive offers. The history of earliest Christianity makes the essence of Christian faith paradigmatically clear.

### c)   The Hellenistic Church

Bauer, W. "Der Wortgottesdienst der ältesten Christen," SGV 148, Tübingen: J. C. B. Mohr (Paul Siebeck), 1930; also in G. Strecker, ed. *W. Bauer, Aufsätze und Kleine Schriften.* Tübingen: J. C. B. Mohr (Paul Siebeck), 1967, 155–209.

Dautzenberg, G. et al, eds., *Zur Geschichte des Urchristentums.* QD 87. Freiburg: Herder, 1979.

Georgi, D. *The Opponents of Paul in Second Corinthians.* Philadelphia: Fortress, 1986.

Hahn, F. *Mission in the New Testament.* London: SCM, 1965.

Hengel, M. *Between Jesus and Paul. Studies in the Earliest History of Christianity.* Philadelphia: Fortress, 1983.

Hengel, M. *Acts and the History of Earliest Christianity.* Philadelphia: Fortress, 1980.

Müller, U. B. "Zur Rezeption gesetzeskritischer Jesusüberlieferung im frühen Christentum." *NTS* (27) 1981, 158–185.

Theissen, G. *Social Reality and the Early Christians: Theology, Ethics, and the World of the New Testament.* Minneapolis: Fortress, 1992.

On the term itself: the phrase "Hellenistic Church" is a generic term, a collective noun. In the following it refers to Christianity in the non-Palestinian pagan environment of the first Christian generation. This includes a variety of types of early Christianity in terms of both time and space. Here belong both Hellenistic Jewish Christians that played a decisive role in mediating both Scripture and ways of interpreting it to the developing church, as well as native Gentiles who, at least in the early stages, stood in a close relation to the synagogue. This is the religious context from which Paul received the initial stimuli for the early phase of his theology. In this section, therefore, in order to avoid repeating the matter here, the reader is referred to the chapter on Paul.

## 1.   Sources

The Book of Acts gives information about the growth of Christianity on Gentile-Hellenistic soil; especially Acts 6:1–8:4, the Stephen tradition, gives an account of a kind of Christianity that developed in a Hellenistic setting. This also applies to the portrayal of the church in Antioch (Acts 13:1), as well as for the descriptions of the mission of Paul or Barnabas in general (Acts 11:19ff). Additional sources are available within the pre-Synoptic tradition: since the Gospels were written within the realm of Hellenistic Christianity, they reflect first the traditions current in the Hellenistic church as they are reworked by the Evangelists. They thus provide information on the question of the theology of this church prior to the writing of the Gospels. In addition, the pre-Pauline tradition that can be extracted from the Pauline letters provides relevant data, since it draws material from the kerygma of the Hellenistic Christian churches, a kerygma that can in part be presupposed by the churches he addresses, for example in Rome. Finally, to the extent that traditions earlier than the Pauline letters and the Gospels can be recognized in them, later sources transmit an impression of the religious situation in the Hellenistic churches. This is the case with the "Apostolic Fathers" (1 Clement, Ignatius, and others), as well as New Testament writings (e. g. Hebrews) and non-Christian documents (e. g. the letters of Pliny such as *Ep* 10.96). A comparison of these sources facilitates the emergence of a picture of a Christianity that existed in Gentile territory independently of the earliest Jerusalem church. In this Hellenistic Christianity lie the decisive impetuses and motivating factors that led to the formation of the faith, doctrine and organization of the later mainstream early catholic church, the "Great Church."

## 2.   Historical and Theological Prior Questions

In relation to the outstanding significance of Hellenistic Christianity for the formation of the church, the possibilities of attaining a clear picture of the course of its historical development and the transmission of its traditions are extraordinarily small. Acts alone, in connection with the name of Stephen, reports one item concerning the historical development of the "Hellenists." According to Acts 6:5 Stephen was the leading member of a college of seven men charged with the care of the needy, the widows and orphans of the Jerusalem church. The "Seven" are the representatives of the Ἑλληνισταί. This group is contrasted to the Ἑβραῖοι in the earliest church (Acts 6:1).[73]

---

[73]   On the different interpretations of the Ἑλληνισταί cf. M. Hengel, "Between Jesus and Paul: The 'Hellenists', the 'Seven,' and Stephen (Acts 6:1–15; 7:54–8:3) in M.

It has sometimes been supposed that members of the Qumran community were included among the Ἑλληνισταί.[74] This is improbable; the thought world of the Qumran group cannot be harmonized with that of the Stephen tradition (Acts 7). There is more to be said for the supposition that "the Ἑλληνισταί" were people who practiced a Hellenistic lifestyle, i.e. who lived in an un-Jewish manner independently of the Jewish law. They would then have been the law-free group among the Jerusalem Christians. Possible evidence for such an understanding would be the "speech of Stephen" (Acts 7), which is intended as a critical debate with the Jewish cult and thereby renews the prophetic critique of the temple and sacrificial system. However, the speech of Stephen very likely derives from an independent, Jewish-Christian tradition; it is a composition that reflects scribal learning, which Luke has secondarily inserted into this context. This speech was editorially bracketed with this context by 6:13; the connection between the figure of Stephen and the motif of freedom from the Law is secondary; it corresponds to Luke's compositional technique in Acts.[75] The probability that the "Hellenists" of Jerusalem were not law-free Christians is increased when one reflects on the fact that their residence in Jerusalem was supposedly

Hengel, ed. *Between Jesus and Paul: Studies in the Earliest History of Christianity* (Philadelphia: Fortress, 1983) 1–29; 132–156.

Literature on the Problem of the Hellenists: E. Baumgartner, "Zur Siebenzahl der Diakone in der Urkirche zu Jerusalem," *BZ* 7 (1909) 49–53; G. P. Wetter, "Das älteste hellenistische Christentum nach der Apostelgeschichte," *ARW* 21 (1922) 397–427; W. Grundmann, "Das Problem des hellenistischen Christentums innerhalb der Jerusalemer Urgemeinde," *ZNW* 38 (1939) 45–73; E. Lohse, *Die Ordination im Spätjudentum und im Neuen Testament* (Berlin: Evangelische Verlagsanstalt, 1951) 74–79; H. Zimmermann, "Die Wahl der Sieben (Apg 6,1–6)," in *Die Kirche und ihre Ämter und Stände*, (FS J. Frings. Köln, 1960) 364–378; A. Strobel, "Armenpfleger ‚um des Friedens willen'," *ZNW* 63 (1972) 271–276; U. Borse, "Der Rahmentext im Umkreis der Stephanusgeschichte (Apg 6,1–11,26)," *BiLe* 14 (1973) 197–204; S. G. Wilson, *The Gentiles and the Gentile Mission in Luke-Acts*, (MSSNTS 23. Cambridge: Cambridge University Press, 1973) 129–153; J. T. Lienhard, "Acts 6:1–6: A Redactional View," *CBQ* 37 (1975), 228–236; D. Daube, "A Reform in Acts and Its Models," in R. G. Hamerton-Kelly and R. Scroggs (eds.) *Jews, Greeks and Christians*, (FS W. D. Davies. Leiden: E. J. Brill, 1976) 51–163; S. Dockx, "L'ordination des "sept" d'après Actes 6,1–6," in *Chronologies néotestamentaires et Vie de l'Église primitive*, (Paris-Gembloux: Duculot, 1976) 265–288; E. Richard, *Acts 6,1–8,4. The Author's Method of Composition*, (SBL.DS 41. Missoula: Scholars Press, 1978); R. Pesch et al., "'Hellenisten' und 'Hebräer'. Zu Apg 9,29 und 6,1," *BZ* 23 (1979) 87–92; N. Walter, "Apostelgeschichte 6,1 und die Anfänge der Urgemeinde in Jerusalem," *NTS* 29 (1983) 370–393.

[74]  Thus for example A. F. J. Klijn, "Stephen's Speech—Acts VII.2–53," *NTS* 4 (1957/ 58) 25–31, who regards it as quite probable that the Hellenists belonged to the Dead Sea Qumran group; O. Cullmann, "Der Rätsel des Johannesevangeliums," in *Vorträge und Aufsätze 1925–1962*, ed. K. Fröhlich (Zürich: Zwingli Verlag, 1966) 260–291, regards the stance of Stephen ("radical rejection of the temple and sacrifice") as not identical with that of the Qumran sect, but clearly prepared for by the views of the Dead Sea group (278–279). For critique, cf. E. Haenchen, *Acts of the Apostles* 266.

[75]  Cf. U. Schnelle, *Gerechtigkeit und Christusgegenwart. Vorpaulinische und paulinische Tauftheologie* (GTA 24. Göttingen: Vandenhoeck & Ruprecht, 1983) 99. Cf. also E. Richard, *Acts 6:1–8* 4, 89 (according to whom it is a matter of Lucan composition; like the context, so the whole Stephen story comes from the Lucan composer).

influenced by the same motives that led Diaspora Jews to Jerusalem in the first place, namely, participation in the Jewish cult, strengthening the ties that bound Diaspora Judaism to the religion of the homeland.[76] Thus a third interpretation is more probable: Ἑλληνισταί were identical with "Greek-speaking Jewish Christians."[77] Because the Ἑλληνισταί came from the Greek-speaking Diaspora, they are distinguished by their language and culture from the "Hebrews," who spoke Hebrew or Aramaic. It is thus no accident that they had contacts with the Jerusalem synagogue associations of Hellenistic Jews.[78]

The group to which Stephen belonged thus represents early Hellenistic Jewish Christianity. This group thus had its beginnings in Jerusalem. It was first located within the theological context of the earliest church. It is the bearer of the message that went forth from Jerusalem to the Gentiles. This Hellenistic Jewish Christianity was the bridge by which the kerygma passed into the world of the Gentiles. From this it follows that at first there were no purely Gentile Christian communities that were independent of Jewish or Jewish Christian influences. The Gentile Christianity of the earliest period was characterized by Jewish or Jewish Christian elements. This is seen in the use of the Old Testament. This is initially the Holy Scripture of Gentile Christianity no less than of Jewish Christianity. The theological affirmations of Hellenistic Christianity were developed under the usage of the language and thought world of the Old Testament because the teachers of the Gentile Christian learned what Christian faith is only as it was mediated by Jewish Christianity.

Finally, it follows from the fact that a Hellenistic Jewish Christianity stood at the beginning of the Hellenistic Christian churches, that at first there was no problem with regard to the law. The Hellenistic Jewish Christians assumed as obvious that the Jewish law was a sign of their belonging to the Jewish people. The acceptance of Gentile Christians was a matter that happened gradually. The intermediate stage was formed by the group of φοβούμενοι, Gentiles who were interested in Judaism and who had been accepted as marginal "associate members" of Jewish synagogues (Acts 13:16). The observing of Jewish legal prescriptions was not an *articulus stantis et cadentis ecclesiae*. The conduct of Paul may be taken as an example, which according to our extant reliable reports was actually contradictory:

---

[76] Cf. S. Safrai, *Die Wallfahrt im Zeitalter des Zweiten Tempels* (FJCD 3. Neukirchen-Vluyn: Neukirchener, 1981) 65–93, "Wallfahrt aus den Ländern der Diaspora." The author shows that there were many reasons for Jewish pilgrimages to Jerusalem (purification sacrifices and ablutions, offerings of wood, and such), as well as the fact that firm connections already existed between the Diaspora and the Jewish holy land (cf. the temple tax!).

[77] So already Chrysostom, Hom 14.1 on Acts 6:1 (PG 60.113); Hom 21.1 on Acts 9:29 (PG 60.164).

[78] Cf. Acts 6:9: Alexandrians, Cyrenians.

(a) According to Galatians 2:3 he affirmed freedom from the Law. His associate Titus was not circumcised, although he was a Gentile by birth.

(b) On the other hand Acts 16:3 reports that Paul had another of his associates, Timothy, whose father was a Greek "circumcised because of the Jews that were in those places." The primary motive is obviously not to place any unnecessary hindrances in the path of the Apostle's mission. Paul was fundamentally open with regard to observance of the Jewish law, as Acts 21 also shows. After all, he was prepared to be a Jew to the Jews, a Greek to the Greeks.[79] The matter of whether or not to observe the Jewish law could have for him the character of an *adiaphoron*. Legal observance then first became a problem when it becomes a *status confessionis*, when the question arises as to the source and basis of faith's understanding of itself and whether the freedom of faith is itself at stake in legal observance. Then such a *status confessionis* is given when the church grows beyond the bounds of Jewish Christianity and becomes a purely Gentile community, but only there when those who keep the Jewish inheritance interpret the law as the basis of faith and dispute its character as an adiaphoron.[80]

This fundamental freedom from the law is the presupposition for the formation of a Gentile Christian church. But it is not its foundation, because in the Hellenistic church there were both Jewish Christians and Gentile Christians, people who were obligated to keep the Jewish law, and others, who had never known it before. The unifying bond between Jewish and Gentile Christians is a specific interpretation of the early Christian kerygma. Foundational and typical for the Hellenistic Christian churches is the incorporation of the kerygma of the crucified and risen Lord within the Hellenistic framework, by which are to be distinguished: (a) Hellenistic Jewish Christian congregations, which still stand with relative clarity within the Jewish stream of tradition, and (b) Hellenistic Gentile Christian congregations composed primarily of ethnic Gentiles. The development began with Jewish Christian congregations being in the majority and resulted in a Gentile Christian majority.[81] Even in the later stages of development, the Jewish element was a component of Gentile Christian theology. A clear separation between Jewish and Gentile factors was not possible until the time of the patristic theology.

Given all these factors, it becomes clear that the Hellenistic church is a complex entity. This is further conditioned by the fact of the different

---

[79]    1 Corinthians 9:20–21; 10:33; Acts 21:20–26.

[80]    Cf. the collision between Paul and Peter in Antioch, Galatians 2:11–21.

[81]    An overlapping of Jewish Christian and Gentile Christian elements is seen, for example, in the Matthean church, which had an original Jewish Christian foundation, but then developed in a Gentile Christian direction. So also the church in Rome, composed primarily of Gentile Christians, but which was familiar with the theological problematic of Jewish/Jewish Christian relations.

ways in which elements of Judaism and the Gentile world were mixed in Jewish Christianity and Gentile Christianity respectively, corresponding to the environment in which each church lived. Moreover, the Greek and Hellenistic culture is an urban culture. The sociological reality of the πόλις (the city-state) had determined Greek thought from its beginnings. The Greek individual thought of his or her life within the enclosed area of the city; he or she was a ζῶον πολιτικόν ("political animal"), as for example has been shown by A. A. T. Ehrhardt in his study *Politische metaphysik*.[82] The human spirit lives in the cities, at first in the cities of Greece, then later, in the Hellenistic age, in the cities of Greater Greece and the Roman Empire. Flavius Josephus illustrates in his portrayal of the Jewish war of the years 66–70, to what a great extent the culture and political situation of Galilee was shaped by the coexistence alongside the Galilean villages of πόλεις, i.e. of social units each of which represented a relatively closed world. It was under this presupposition and under these conditions that Hellenistic Christianity was formed. The Hellenistic Christian church thus participated in the πόλις-structure of its world. It was one element in a closed *societas* that was small enough to be surveyed as a whole and was compelled to relate to it and to develop within it. This could happen in dependence on the Jewish synagogue that already represented an accepted religious institution within the Hellenistic framework, but also—to the extent that the Gentile element was dominant—in correspondence to the numerous religious associations of Hellenism, such as the mystery cults. More important than the question of particular models from within the contemporary religious world is the awareness that these too took place within the framework of the πόλεις, i.e. that every local congregation was constrained to attempt to give appropriate expression to its faith in its own situation. The local Christian congregations, including the house churches within them, represented the whole church, for the designation ἐκκλησία θεοῦ was used for both the local congregations and the universal church. This means, on the one hand, that every local congregation had a high measure of independence and a solid supply of local leadership, but on the other hand that it preserved its contacts and unity with other churches through wandering charismatic teachers (Did 11:3). In such a context there emerged different forms of local church life as they worked out their faith theologically and developed their understanding of the church within the framework of a limited framework that can be described sociologically, while still claiming to represent the whole church and to carry on the work of Christ. The Risen One was encountered in no other way than in the variegated witness of the individual congregations. Because Christ's claim

---

[82] A. A. T. Ehrhardt, *Politische Metaphysik von Solon bis Augustin, Band I, Die Gottesstadt der Griechen und Römer* (Tübingen: J. C. B. Mohr [Paul Siebeck], 1959) 55–58.

is concrete, this means for the theology of the Hellenistic church that its theological affirmations are disparate. The multitude of individual congregations corresponds to the multiplicity and disparity of their theologies. The Hellenistic church thus demonstrates *in nuce* what is to be said for the New Testament in general: it is a multiplicity of theological conceptions. Thus the question is posed with which every theology of the New Testament sees itself to be confronted: the question of the unity which stands at the basis of the variety of the theological conceptions within the New Testament.

## 3.  Theological Conceptions in the Hellenistic Church

### α)  Christology[83]

Though the Hellenistic church also proceeds on the basis of the original kerygma, "Jesus died and was raised" (cf. 1 Cor 15:3–5; Rom 10:9), it is nevertheless at variance with the situation in the earliest church, since the Son of Man Christology no longer plays an essential role in the interpretation of the resurrection message.[84]

The resurrection kerygma is interpreted in the Hellenistic church by means of the Kyrios Christology. To be sure, the earliest Palestinian church could also designate Jesus as "Lord" by using the Mari title, but they were referring to the Mari—Son of Man who was to appear in the future. In contrast, the Hellenistic term "Kyrios"—as already presupposed by Paul[85]—placed the accent on the presence of the Risen One, in accord with the understanding of the pagan cults, where the initiates encountered cultic deities called κύριοι, because they exercised lordship over the initiates. The Kyrios is the god who has power and authority, and who determines the destiny of the individual.[86]

When Paul in 1 Corinthians 8:5–6 says,

---

[83]   In the following we will basically go into those developments that led to the writing of the Gospels. We will not here repeat what was said in the section on "The Theology of Paul" above, especially what has already been said with reference to the pre-Pauline tradition, christological titles, and such. From time to time the reader will be referred to that section for more detailed information.

[84]   The Son of Man title is found in Acts 7:56, and then several times in the Gospel of John. These secondary witnesses underscore the fact that a vital Son of Man Christology was no longer present in the Hellenistic church. This is also indicated by the usage of the Son of man title in the Markan community, where in the immediate pre-Markan tradition the Son of Man Christology was essentially interpreted in terms of the suffering and rising Jesus, and the original apocalyptic understanding was no longer central (Mark 8:31parr).

[85]   Cf. A. II. a. 3. above.

[86]   Cf. W. Foerster, κύριος, *TDNT* 3:1039–1097, esp. 1039–1057; S. Schulz, "Maranatha und Kyrios Jesus," *ZNW* 53 (1962) 125–144.

Indeed, even though there may be so-called gods in heaven or on earth—as in fact there are many gods and many lords—yet for us there is one God, the Father, from whom are all things and for whom we exist, and one Lord, Jesus Christ, through whom are all things and through whom we exist,

he thereby expresses that the κυριότης of this Lord is radically different from the sphere of influence in which other κύριοι exercise their power and authority. Here it is not a matter of a Lord of a particular cultic association but the Lord who stands at the origin of the universe, and who reigns over his church. In the kerygma of the crucified and risen Lord, one encounters this Kyrios, whose sphere of influence is the whole cosmos, who rules heaven and earth by his power, and who calls for unconditioned faith and obedience.

In the Hellenistic church the proclamation of the Risen One has as its goal that Jesus be acknowledged and confessed as Lord, that honor be given to him, not to the "many Lords." This implies the demand that one's own existence be grounded in the authority and power of this Lord. Thus faith means to place oneself under the sovereignty of the Lord Jesus and to let one's life be determined by his Lordship. The pre-Pauline Christ hymn in Philippians 2:6–11 demonstrates the cosmic power of the Lord Christ and at the same time shows that the resurrection kerygma could be interpreted by the Kyrios Christology with the scheme "preexistence, incarnation, exaltation." The inthronization to the rank of Kyrios is associated with the giving of a new name, an understanding resonant with the Hellenistic significance of "naming," as found also in the magical papyri.[87] If Jesus has received the name and function of the Kyrios, this means that he has been installed into a corresponding sphere of power and authority. By confessing Jesus as the one who has been exalted to receive the title "Lord," the Hellenistic church confessed him as the one who has power and authority over the world. This is what it experiences in faith, not in sight, for the final revelation of his Lordship is still in the future. The inthronization of the Kyrios is not identical with the all-embracing proclamation, the universal acknowledgment of his lordship by the cosmic powers. This universal acknowledgement of his lordship will happen in the future, as part of the eschatological events (cf. Phil 2:11–12). This testifies to the fundamentally apocalyptic orientation of the pre-Pauline hymn in Philippians and documents the transition in the history of the tradition from the futuristic eschatological Mari-proclamation of earliest Palestinian Christianity to the Kyrios predication of the Hellenistic church.

---

[87] K. Preisendanz, *Papyri Graecae Magicae. Die Griechischen Zauberpapyri I, II.* (Leipzig-Berlin: Teubner, 1928, 1931); ἐξ ὀνόματος (ZP 4.2973); τὸ ἅγιον ὄνομα or τὰ ἅγια ὀνόματα (ZP 3.570, 627; 4.1005, 3071); μέγα καὶ ἅγιον ((ZP 5.77; 13.561; cf. 12.257); ὄν. μέγα καὶ ἅγιον καὶ ἔνδοξον (ZP 13.183–184, 504–505).

The designation υἱὸς θεοῦ stands very close to the Kyrios title, for κύριος is essentially an appellative, "Son of God," in contrast not to a functional description, but an expression of his being. Whether and to what extent earliest Christianity had already applied this title to Jesus is still an open question. There is no doubt that in Jewish Messianic understanding the ascription "Son of God" could be applied to the king of the Jewish people (cf. e. g. Ps 2:7), but in New Testament usage such a reference cannot be demonstrated, despite incidental echoes (Acts 13:33; Heb 1:5). It would have required a reinterpretation as its presupposition, namely the elimination of the political connotations of the term. In Hellenistic Christianity, on the other hand, the title has a genuine place: the inthronization as Kyrios has a close parallel in the concept of adoption as the Son of God, as represented for example in the baptism of Jesus (Mark 1:9–11). Thus in the earliest times the adoption of Jesus as Son of God was connected with the concept of resurrection or exaltation. This is illustrated in Romans 1:4, which still bears traces of this understanding. The concept of adoption is documented in broad areas of Hellenism.[88] Adoption of Jesus as Son of God underscores his presence as the one who as been exalted to this rank. The Kyrios, by virtue of being the Son of God, participates in the divine status. Within the realm of Hellenism, this is thought of in physical terms.[89] As the Son of God, the risen Christ has a superhuman nature; God's own being is what is appropriate for such a being. This comes to expression in the pre-Synoptic tradition especially in the theologoumenon of the virgin birth, which apparently originated in Hellenistic Jewish Christianity (Matt 1:18–25; Luke 1:26–38). Jesus' divine, supernatural quality is already expressed in stories about his earthly activity beginning with his birth (contra Mark 1:9ff).

The application of specific Hellenistic titles of honor to Jesus made the Jesus tradition transparent to Hellenistic Christians who could then understand the faith in their own terms. If the Risen One is the Son of God, then he demonstrates in his own person the paradoxical unity of the divine

---

[88]  The Egyptian Pharoah was called "Son of God;" thus since the fourth dynasty among the Pharoah's titles was "Son of (the sun god) Re;" in the Greek realm individuals could be adopted as sons of a god, e. g. Alexander the Great (FGrHist IIb 645, υἱὸς τοῦ ἡλίου; cf. Mitteis-Wilcken I 2, No. 109.11; OGIS 90.3; DittOr I 90.3). Thus Plato was considered son of Apollo, Pythagoras as son of Zeus, and Aristotle as son of Asclepius. Probably the most well-known examples are the heroes (Dionysius, Heracles, and Asclepius). Cf. also P. Pokorný, *Der Gottessohn. Literarische Übersicht und Fragestellung* (ThSt[B] 109. Zürich: Theologischer Verlag, 1971) 14–15.

[89]  On the basis of statements in the "Gospel of the Hebrews,", the Ebionites denied the virgin birth of Jesus (*Gospel of the Hebrews*, fragment 3, cited in Epiphanius *Heresies* 30.13.7–8); Schneemelcher, *New Testament Apocrypha* 1:177–178) Jesus' divine authority is not thought of in terms of his divine conception and miraculous birth but as the union of the Holy Spirit with him at his baptism.

and human, of the supernatural and the natural. This is then reflected in the way his earthly life is portrayed by the New Testament Gospels. These documents testify to the "paradoxical fact" that God has become a human being and that thereby human beings are given the possibility of a life not determined by this world, i.e. the possibility of participation in the realm of God's power and authority.

In his own person the Son of God is God's turning toward the world in love and compassion. This conviction allows the ideas associated in the Hellenistic world with divine-human beings to be applied to Jesus, such as the concept of the θεῖος ἀνήρ.[90] These ideas that were already current in Hellenistic Judaism[91] are applied to the heroes of Jewish history, i.e. to inspired persons such as Moses, who as a teacher of wisdom participates in the divine glory (ἰσόθεος τιμή). He competes with Egyptian magicians and defeats them at their own game. His works manifest the power of the true God. The giving of the Law becomes the high point of this divine power. The end of Moses' life on earth is portrayed in accordance with this view: his being raptured to heaven, or his ascension (*Assumption of Moses*). So also traditions are found in pagan Hellenism in which people are endowed with special, supernatural knowledge and possess miraculous powers by which they heal the sick, cast out demons, and perform wonders that violate the usual laws of nature. They identify themselves with the god who sent them, speak by divine authority, and represent the claim of this god. Thus the way one responds to the θεῖος ἀνήρ is identified with the way one responds to the god who sent him. Lines of connection between the portrayal of the "divine man" Jesus in the Gospels cannot be overlooked.[92]

On Hellenistic soil the θεῖος ἀνήρ motif was associated with the Jesus stories of the pre-Synoptic tradition. This was a first step in the direction of Gospel composition. Another step was taken when the christological predication υἱὸς Δαυίδ was incorporated into the traditional material. Here the background was not pagan-Hellenistic, but Jewish-Hellenistic. Appar-

---

[90] Cf. A. II. a. 2. above.

[91] Cf. Philo *Virt* 177: the sinless person as θεῖος ἀνήρ; Josephus *Antiquities* 3.180 (Moses); 10.35 (Isaiah).

[92] On the discussion of the role of the θεῖος ἀνήρ in New Testament studies, cf. the thesis of L. Bieler, ΘΕΙΟΣ ΑΝΗΡ. *Das Bild des "göttlichen Menschen" in Spätantike und Frühchristentum.* (2 vols. Göttingen: Vandenhoeck & Ruprecht, 1935, 1936), according to whom the figure of Christ is fundamentally different from the other θεῖοι ἄνθρωποι of the surrounding Hellenistic world. However, Bieler does arrive at the conclusion that antiquity, especially in its later phase, and early Christianity were acquainted with the same picture of the divine man (145). See also H. Koester, *Introduction to the New Testament* 1:173, 264, 276, 290, 296–297, 300, 302, 315, 367–368; 2:127–128, 174, 184, 314; Ph. Vielhauer, *Urchristliche Literatur* 399. Cf. also the critique of the concept "aretalogy", e. g. in G. Strecker, *History of New Testament Literature* 107–108.

ently in Hellenistic cities such as Damascus, Antioch, and Alexandria this Jewish traditional material was worked into the developing Christian doctrine. The background was thus formed by a "liberated," i.e. a liberal Diaspora Judaism,[93] that was openly available to the Christian congregations within developing Gentile Christianity.

The faith of these Jewish Christians was expressed in the Son of David Christology. While it is questionable whether earliest Palestinian Christianity had ever applied this title to Jesus,[94] we may be confident that the ascription was used in Hellenistic Christianity. Here the *process of amalgamation* in which (Jewish) Hellenistic Christianity found itself becomes clear, since the Son of David title was combined with other christological titles. A characteristic example is the pre-Pauline kerygmatic formula in Romans 1:3–4.[95] Another combination of the Son of David predication with a christological title is reflected in the pericope about the Son of David question in Mark 12:35–37par. Here the Son of David predication is juxtaposed with ὁ Χριστός or κύριος. This implies the idea that the Son of David title is not appropriate or adequate to express Jesus' Messiahship, so that it is subordinated to the title "Christ" or "Lord." This tradition has a critical stance toward the Son of David title. On the other hand, the appeal back to the Old Testament promise (12:36–37; Ps 110:1) becomes clear: in Hellenistic-Jewish tradition "Son of David" essentially describes the "Messiah" as the heir and fulfiller of the promises given to the people of Israel.

A further example of the Hellenistic *process of amalgamation* is seen in the connection between the Son of David predication and the θεῖος ἀνήρ motif. Thus in the context of the narrative of the healing of Bartimaeus (Mark 10:46–52parr; cf. Matt 9:27–31), Bartimaeus attracts the attention of Jesus the miracle worker with the cry, "Jesus, Son of David, have mercy on me." As a Θεῖος ἀνήρ who functions as a thaumaturge, Jesus bears the title "Son of David," as documented more frequently in Matthew.[96]

"Son of David" was originally a matter of physical descent. The descendents of David had, by virtue of their genealogy, a claim to the title and dignity of a "Son of David." This idea is related to the messianic expectation of the Jewish people.[97] The genealogies of Jesus presuppose this connection between physical descent and claim to messianic office (Matt 1:1–17par; Luke 3:23–38). This is also the case in the formula "Jesus

---

[93]  Cf. W. Bousset, *Kyrios Christos* 367–370.
[94]  Cf. above B. III. 3.
[95]  Cf. above A. I. c. 1.
[96]  Cf. e. g. Matthew 15:22 (healing the daughter of the Syro-Phoenician woman); cf. also Matthew 12:23; 21:9, 15. The Kyrios designation is also sometimes added, e. g. Matthew 20:30–31: the Son of David is the Kyrios.
[97]  Cf. Jeremiah 23:5–6; 33:14–16.

Christ, raised from the dead, a descendant of David" (2 Tim 2:8; possibly related to Rom 1:3–4). The Jewish messianic expectation was related to the descendents of David, which occasioned Hellenistic-Jewish faith to apply the title to Jesus. It claims the truth expressed in Judaism for itself. That which was expressed in the Old Testament and Jewish messianic hope finds its fulfillment in Jesus. "Judaism ... reached its completion in preaching the coming of the Messiah, Jesus Christ."[98] To be sure, such a fulfillment means at the same time a modification; for this "Messianology" is not political, since Jesus was not the expected military hero Ben David, but the crucified and risen Christ of the community's faith. As such, he brings the history of Israel to fulfillment, and at the same time makes an end of the traditional understanding by his own person. Connected with this are the logical implications concerning the understanding of salvation history and the ecclesiological self-understanding of the community as the new Israel.

The christological titles of the Hellenistic church[99] basically set forth a Christology that emphasizes the presence of Christ. Jesus as the Risen One is the present Lord, the *Christus praesens*. This aspect is strengthened when narratives present him as a figure of the past. Thus in the case of the Son of David or θεῖος ἀνήρ concepts: such narratives are oriented to no one else than the crucified and risen one, who as the exalted Lord is the same figure who appeared on earth: the appearance in history of the act of God.

The affirmations of the presence of Christ made by the Christology of the Hellenistic church include the claim that the risen one is also the one to come in the future. The church at first expected the eschatological catastrophe in the very near future, when the world would be brought to an end by the coming of its Lord. An instructive example is found in the tradition that Paul includes in 1 Thessalonians 4:13–18.[100] Just as in the earliest Palestinian church, so also at the beginning of Hellenistic Christianity stood an expectation of the parousia in the immediate future. This expectation did not so much speak of a future "day of the Son of Man" (as still in Luke 17:24, 26), but of the ἡμέρα (τοῦ) κυρίου (1 Thess 5:2; 1 Cor 1:8; 2 Thess 2:2). This expression is dependent on the Old Testament concept of the "Day of the Lord" (Joel 3:1–5; Acts 2:20). The expectation was for the "Day of Christ" (Phil 1:6, 10; 2:16; 1 Cor 1:8), the "coming"

---

[98] M. Dibelius, *From Tradition to Gospel* 30.
[99] On the title ὁ Χριστός cf. above A. II. a. 4., especially the distinction between the titular use and "Christ" as a proper name. The development was clearly from the titular usage toward its replacement by "Christ" as a proper name. But the awareness that Χριστός is the translation of the Hebrew הַמָּשִׁיחַ also lasted for some time; cf. John 1:41; 4:25ff.
[100] Cf. further Philippians 4:5; 1 Corinthians 7:29; 15:51–52; Romans 13:11.

(παρουσία) of the Kyrios Jesus Christ (1 Thess 2:19; Matt 24:3; 2 Pet 1:16). The Risen One was in fact expected to appear with a twofold function: as the judge of the world who would pronounce God's judgment on human beings,[101] and as the savior (σωτήρ) who would transform our lowly bodies and thereby bring freedom from death (Phil 3:20–21). He is the one who saves from the future wrath by appearing at the end as the church's deliverer (1 Thess 1:10). The judgment of the world and the deliverance of the church—precisely this is the establishment of the kingdom of God and the ultimate confirmation of the sovereignty of the Kyrios (cf. Eph 5:5), which affirms the resurrection of the dead and entrance into a life without death (2 Clem 9:1; Acts 17:18).

Thus the Hellenistic church too lives within the apocalyptic horizon of the earliest Christian proclamation. The orientation to the end, to the future that would confirm their present faith, forms an essential motif of their conduct within history. But differently from that of the earliest Palestinian church, alongside the "not yet" of eschatological fulfillment stands the "already:" as we have already seen within the world of christological thought and will be confirmed when we examine their understanding of the sacraments, the presence of salvation in the here and now plays an important role in their thinking. The dialectic between the "already" and "not yet" of salvation is thus pre-Pauline; it was then developed by Paul with reference both to the church and to his own life.

Alongside the Lord Jesus, the Hellenistic church proclaimed the "one God." Εἷς θεός is a fundamental motif of Jewish mission preaching. Judaism knew itself to be distinguished from, and superior to, the surrounding pagan world by its monotheistic faith. Hellenistic Jewish Christianity took over this faith in the one God as it began its own mission in the Hellenistic world. While it was the christological creed that stood at the beginning (e. g. 1 Cor 15:3–4), this may be explained by the Jewish context of the earliest Christians, where monotheistic faith was presupposed. A further step was taken when the two-member confession of faith was developed (e. g. 1 Thess 1:9–10), in which the confession of Christ was joined to the confession of the one true and living God.

Thus as the monotheistic faith in God became an essential element of the missionary preaching of the Christian community in the Hellenistic world, it was joined to the call to repentance, namely to forsake the other Kyrioi and to follow the one Lord Jesus, which also meant the demand to give up the θεοὶ πολλοί and to believe in the one God. This God is the creator of the world, as it is affirmed in unity with the Jewish tradition (Acts 4:24; Rev 4:11). This God demands faith and acknowledgment of his

---

[101] Acts 17:31; 2 Timothy 4:1; 2 Clement 1:1. The concept of Christ as eschatological judge was included in the three main creeds of the later church, namely the Apostles' Creed and the Nicene and Athanasian confessions (BSLK 21–30).

omnipotence, since he is the God who raises the dead and calls the creation into existence from non-being (Rom 4:17). He is the "Demiurge," the Creator and Lord of all things (1 Clem 33:2; 35:3); all that exists is from him and through him and to him (Rom 11:36). This God comprehends the universe but is himself incomprehensible (Herm Mand 1.1). Such formulae are reminiscent of the Stoic doctrine of deity, especially on the natural theology of the Stoa, in which divine providence (πρόνοια) is inferred from the cosmic order and the creator is inferred from the cosmos itself. From this it becomes clear—as Paul already indicates in Romans 1:18–32—that the non-pagan and specifically Christian elements can be recognized both by their adoption of and tension with such Hellenistic ideas as were already present. This becomes concrete in the call to repentance: the knowledge of the one God must lead to an acknowledgement of his power and authority, and thus must lead to repentance.

In this connection it is not unusual for a portrayal of the immorality of the pagan world to emerge (cf. Rom 1:18–32). The Christian apologetes of the second century developed this motif extensively, using pagan immorality as the dark foil against which to portray the superiority of Christian faith in God and Christian morality.[102] We may here put aside the question of the extent to which such judgments are realistic, and how many of them represent unrealistic generalizations. It is clear that the proclamation of the Hellenistic Christian churches was oriented to the three basic themes of pagan immorality, the call to repentance, and faith in the one God, but that these were only different ways of expressing their unconditioned faith in Christ. They were thus concrete expressions of their conviction that in the Crucified and Risen One, the one God had spoken to humanity.

β) Ecclesiology

According to 1 Corinthians 1:2, Christians designate themselves as οἱ ἐπικαλούμενοι τὸ ὄνομα τοῦ κυρίου ἡμῶν Ἰησοῦ Χριστοῦ: Christians are those who call upon the name of the Lord Jesus Christ. In accord with this, Romans 10:13 says, "Everyone who calls on the name of the Lord shall be saved" (citing Joel 3:5). This ecclesiological designation became widespread. It is also found in 2 Timothy 2:22, and shows that community prayer was directed to the Lord Jesus. Thus Matthew picks up on this, when he has people who call out for help cry out κύριε σῶσον (Matt 8:25; 14:30). In these texts it is not a matter of a plea for mercy, or doxologies or confessions in which Jesus name is expressed, but a call to the Kyrios for help, a prayer. That which had been modeled in earliest Christianity as the Marana tha prayer is developed in Hellenistic Christianity with

---

[102] Cf. e. g. Aristides, *Apology* 9.8; 15.3–12; 16.1–6; 17.2

reference to the present: the Kyrios Jesus is the Lord who is present and active within the community of faith. To call on the name of the Lord Jesus thus means to have one's life determined already now, in the present, by the power and authority of the Lord Jesus, and to experience the salvation of which this Kyrios is the manifestation. The Christian community that calls on the Kyrios knows itself to be secure within the realm of the power and authority of Jesus Christ.

With this point of departure, a new understanding of the traditional ecclesiological predications could be attained. While the earliest Palestinian church had understood itself to be the community of the ἐκλεκτοί, because it looked forward to the event of the "election" that was to happen at the eschaton and lived in the certainty of this future ἐκλογή,[103] the Hellenistic church saw itself as already the elect,[104] which was only consistent with its understanding of the Kyrios Christology. Where the name of the Lord is pronounced, there occurs the event of decision and separation, of being chosen and elected.

The case is similar with the ecclesiological predication ἅγιοι. The church is the "community of saints" not only from the perspective of the future, in which its members will be presented as the "holy ones," but already in the present they are what they will be, because they are already united with their Lord: the community of those who have been taken out of the world, who have entered into the sacred realm. "Already now" they are "God's chosen ones, holy and beloved" (Col 3:12).

These predications are fundamentally made of the whole church. As far as the local congregation is concerned, they declare that the individual congregations are bound to one another and indicate the unity of the one church. This solidarity is also expressed in the understanding of the church as the "new Israel." "Not all Israelites truly belong to Israel," says Paul in Romans 9:6, and thereby expresses the claim that the church as a whole is the true Israel, the Ἰσραὴλ κατὰ πνεῦμα.[105] The Israel that corresponds to God's expressed intention (Heb 8:8–13; cf. Jer 31:31–34) is the λαὸς (τοῦ) θεοῦ, the people of God, as is now said of the church as it takes over the biblical designations for the people of Israel chosen by God in the Old Testament (Heb 4:9; 1 Pet 2:10). No differently than as we determined above for earliest Palestinian Christianity do we have here a break in the relation to empirical Israel. The turning point is constituted by the saving event in Christ on which the kerygma of the community is based. Here too, it is not

---

103 See above B. III. b. 3.

104 Cf. Mark 13:20: ἐξελέξατο; more decisively, Ephesians 1:4: "just as he chose us in Christ before the foundation of the world;" here the divine ἐκλογή appears as preexistent, and thus the church itself as a preexistent reality.

105 The term itself is not found in Paul, but is to be presupposed as the counterpart to empirical Israel, Ἰσραὴλ κατὰ σάρκα. Cf. also Galatians 6:16 Ἰσραὴλ τοῦ θεοῦ.

continuity, but discontinuity, that stands in the foreground. This community emphasizes that it has entered into the promised inheritance and is the new Israel (cf. Matt 21:33–43). The author of the Epistle of Barnabas emphasized this discontinuity in an especially extreme manner.[106]

So also the Hellenistic Christian tradition of the words of institution of the *Lord's Supper* presuppose discontinuity with empirical Israel. Even though (1) the oldest traditional layer of the words of institution cannot be reconstructed with certainty, we are still justified in supposing that at the beginning the body and blood of Jesus was identified with the saving elements given to the participants during the eucharistic celebration. This tradition is not to be traced back to the earliest Palestinian church where the central aspect of the table fellowship was the expectation of the coming Son of Man. In contrast, the meals of the Hellenistic Christian communities manifest close contacts to the table celebrations of the mystery cults where the living presence of the Lord was celebrated. In Hellenistic Christianity, this meal signifies participation in the destiny of the crucified and risen Lord Jesus, and incorporation into his death and life. In it is grounded the certainty of being ἅγιος and ἐκλεκτός.

So also the two additions that were apparently made successively to the text of the short form of the words of institution are to be understood from within the framework of the Hellenistic Christian church: (2) the addition τῆς διαθήκης (Mark 14:24) affirms that Jesus' death was interpreted as a sacrifice of the new covenant, which seals this (final) declaration of God's will.[107] As Jesus' death founded the new Israel, so the celebration of the meal facilitates the incorporation of individual Christians as members of this new people of God. The promises given to old Israel are now promises that apply to the new people of God and are fulfilled in it. The covenant promised in Jeremiah 31:31–34 has been realized in the saving act of God, the Christ event.

(3) An additional interpretation is given by the addition of the words τὸ ἐκχυννόμενον ὑπὲρ πολλῶν (Mark 14:24; similarly 1 Cor 11:24: τὸ ὑπὲρ ὑμῶν—in connection with σῶμα, however, not with αἷμα). The death of Jesus is understood as a sacrifice for sins. The human being Jesus is compared to a sacrificial animal whose blood is poured out on the altar and whose death takes away sins. In this way Jesus made atonement by offering his own blood. The further addition in Matthew 26:28 (εἰς ἄφεσιν ἁμαρτιῶν), derived perhaps from the liturgy of the Matthean church, is a clarification that rightly understood the preceding words.

---

[106] It is thus his theological intention to show that the "Scripture," the Old Testament, is the exclusive property of Christians. He affirms, for example, that to say that the Mosaic covenant was made with Israel is sinful—it applies only to Christians (4.6–8; 14).

[107] Cf. 2 Corinthians 3:6; Hebrews 8:8; 9:15; 12:24.

Such a stratification of the tradition might seem to suggest an understanding of the Lord's Supper in the sense of a sacrifice in which the church so to speak offers Jesus to God as a sin offering or as a sacrifice that renews the covenant. But no such idea is actually found here. It is rather the case that the sacrificial terminology points to table fellowship with the Lord realized in the sacred meal. The basic reality is the encounter with the community's Lord who is present and active. It is no accident that Paul describes the meal as the κυριακὸν δεῖπνον (1 Cor 11:20). The fellowship with the Lord established by the meal thus affirms the believer's incorporation in the new people of God and participation in the forgiveness created and guaranteed through the Lord. Despite the terminological difference and the successive layers of tradition, the original meaning of the celebration of the meal was basically preserved. In any case, the meal is the realization of God's promise. It mediates the meaning of God's act in Christ for the believer, the realization in the present of eschatological salvation.

No less than the Lord's Supper, *baptism* makes concrete of the encounter with the exalted Lord. It mediates (1) forgiveness of sins[108] and (2) the gift of the Spirit.[109] This also agrees with the views of earliest Palestinian Christianity, but in Hellenistic Christianity is also understood in an ecstatic sense, for the Spirit is the power that leads to ecstatic experiences and is experienced in ecstasy (cf. 1 Corinthians 14:1ff). In addition, baptism results in (3) being placed within the community of the lordship of Jesus. This accords with the fact that baptism is administered "in the name of the Lord Jesus" (Did 9.5; Acts 8:16). This is different from earliest Palestinian Christianity, in which baptism in the name of Jesus was primarily oriented to the coming of the Son of Man. Finally, in Hellenistic Christianity, baptism was interpreted (4) as dying and rising with Jesus Christ.[110] On the basis of this interpretation of baptism, the term "rebirth" can be used with reference to what happens in baptism (cf. Titus 3:5: λουτρὸν παλιγγενεσίας): by dying and rising with Christ the believer puts aside the old existence and is reborn into a new life.

At this point, several aspects with regard to the *problem of infant baptism* emerge.[111] The results of an intensive discussion of scholarly research is mostly negative. Neither the thesis that early Christianity practiced infant baptism (J.

---

[108]  Cf. 1 Corinthians 6:11 ("... you were washed, you were sanctified"—the pre-Pauline understanding of "sanctification" meant the forgiveness of sins).

[109]  Cf. 1 Corinthians 12:13 ("For in the one Spirit we were all baptized into one body— Jews or Greeks, slaves or free—and we were all made to drink of one Spirit").

[110]  Cf. Romans 6:1–4. Here too Paul is going back to pre-Pauline baptismal tradition.Cf. above A. III. c. 2.

[111]  Cf. the discussion between J. Jeremias and K. Aland: J. Jeremias, *Infant Baptism in the First Four Centuries* (Philadelphia: Westminster, 1960); K. Aland, *Did the Early Church Baptize Infants?* (Philadelphia: Westminster Press. 1963); J. Jeremias, *The Origins of Infant Baptism; a Further Study in Reply to Kurt Aland* (Naperville, Ill.:

Jeremias), nor the opposite thesis that infant baptism did not yet exist in the first century (K. Aland), can be demonstrated from the sources with adequate confidence. If one proceeds from the different theological conceptions of early Christianity, then one must reckon not only with adult baptism, which of course would have been the predominant practice in the missionary situation, but also with the baptism of children and babies. Since in Hellenistic Christianity different soteriologies existed alongside each other, the possibility must be affirmed that in some contexts baptism was limited to adults, while in other contexts both adult and infant baptism were practiced. In favor of the former possibility is the fact that a baptismal confession (ὁμολογία) was connected with the act of baptism (1 Tim 6:12). Baptismal candidates make their confession of faith in the Lord Jesus on the basis of instruction they had received prior to baptism. The possibility and necessity of confession excludes infants from such a baptism; it was only later as a secondary development that a representative might have made such a confession in behalf of the one being baptized. This means, accordingly, that to the extent that the homologia-character of baptism was emphasized infant baptism was excluded. On the other hand, the more strongly the sacramental character of baptism comes to the foreground, the greater the possibility that children, even infants, were subjects of baptism. A sacramental, possibly even physical or magical interpretation of the element (baptismal water) does not inquire about the predisposition of the baptismal candidate on matters of faith or understanding. Already Ignatius understood the Lord's Supper as the φάρμακον ἀθανασίας (medicine of immortality), which was also described as ἀντίδοτος (antidote)—in an almost magical sense—that had the capacity to bestow immortality (Ignatius, *Eph* 20:2). Similar things are documented with regard to early Christian baptism. The vicarious baptism mentioned by Paul (1 Cor 15:29), which functioned by baptizing representatives for those who had already died thus enabling them to participate in salvation, suggests a magical character for the ritual.[112] The encounter with the presence of the Lord in baptism was accordingly interpreted in very different ways in the Hellenistic church. It could be connected closely with the element of water and thereby presuppose an "objective" gift in advance of any action on the part of the one being baptized. On the other hand it could be bound to the individual's confession of faith as a "subjective" condition. Correspondingly, the question of infant baptism can be only decided in regard to concrete cases, on the basis of the operative theological understanding. In any case, it is possible that the baptism of children and infants was already practiced in the Hellenistic church. It is possible wherever baptism is understood in sacramental terms, i.e. where the transsubjective aspect of baptism is emphasized. And it is theologically impossible where baptism is conceived exclusively on the basis of the individual's faith and confession. Infant baptism is possible wherever there is more confidence in the power and authority of the Lord than in the ability of the individual.

---

A. R. Allenson. 1963); K. Aland, *Die Säuglingstaufe im Neuen Testament und in der alten Kirche. Zweite, durchgesehene Auflage, vermehrt durch einen notwendigen Nachtrag aus Anlaß der Schrift von J. Jeremias "Nochmals: Die Anfänge der Kindertaufe. Eine Replik auf Kurt Alands Schrift ,Die Säuglingstaufe im Neuen Testament und in der alten Kirche'"*, Munich: Kaiser, 1963[2] = TEH NF 86); K. Aland, *Die Stellung der Kinder in den frühen christlichen Gemeinden—und ihre Taufe* (TEH NF 138. Munich: Kaiser 1967).; A critical response to both arguments is found in A. Strobel, "Säuglings- und Kindertaufe in der ältesten Kirche," in O. Perels, ed., *Begründung und Gebrauch der heiligen Taufe* (Berlin-Hamburg: Lutherisches Verlagshaus, 1963) 7–69.

[112] As in the practice of Marcionites, Cerinthians, and Montanists; cf. the discussion and documentation in H. Lietzmann-W. G. Kümmel, *An die Korinther I/II* (HNT 9. Tübingen: J. C. B. Mohr [Paul Siebeck], 1969[5]) 82.

# IV. Directives of the Son of Man—
# The Sayings Collection

Bergemann, Th. *Q auf dem Prüfstand*. FRLANT 158. Göttingen: Vandenhoeck & Ruprecht, 1993.

Edwards, R. A. *A Theology of Q*. Philadelphia: Fortress, 1976.

Harnack, A. von. "Sprüche und Reden Jesu," in *Beiträge zur Einleitung in das Neue Testament* II. Leipzig: Hinrichsche Buchhandlung, 1907.

Hoffmann, P. *Studien zur Theologie der Logienquelle*. NTA 8. Münster: Aschendorf, 1982³.

Kloppenborg, J. S. *The Formation of Q*. Philadelphia: Fortress, 1987.

Laufen, R. *Die Doppelüberlieferungen der Logienquelle und des Markusevangeliums*. BBB 54, Königstein-Bonn: Hanstein, 1980.

Lührmann, D. *Die Redaktion der Logienquelle*, WMANT 33, Neukirchen-Vluyn: Neukirchener, 1969.

Polag, A. *Die Christologie der Logienquelle*, WMANT 45, Neukirchen-Vluyn: Neukirchener, 1977.

Polag, A. *Fragmenta Q*, Neukirchen-Vluyn: Neukirchener, 1982².

Robinson, J. M. "LOGOI SOPHON: On the Gattung of Q," in *Trajectories through Early Christianity*, J. M. Robinson and H. Koester, eds. Philadelphia: Fortress, 1971, 71–113.

Sato, M. *Q und Prophetie*. WUNT II 29. Tübingen: J. C. B. Mohr (Paul Siebeck) 1988.

Schulz, S. *Q—Die Spruchquelle der Evangelisten*. Zürich: Theologischer Verlag, 1972.

Schürmann, H. Beobachtungen zum Menschensohn-Titel in der Redequelle, in R. Pesch-R. Schnackenburg, eds. *Jesus und der Menschensohn*, (FS A. Vögtle) Freiburg-Basel-Wien: Herder, 1975, 124–147.

Streeter, B. H. *The Four Gospels. A Study of Origins*. London: Macmillan, 1924.

Tödt, H. E. *The Son of Man in the Synoptic Tradition*. Philadelphia: Westminster, 1965.

Wanke, J. *Bezugs- und Kommentarworte in den synoptischen Evangelien*. EThS 44. Leipzig: St. Benno-Verlag, 1981.

Wernle, P. *Die synoptische Frage*, Freiburg/Leipzig: J. C. B. Mohr (Paul Siebeck), 1899.

Zeller, D. *Die weisheitlichen Mahnsprüche bei den Synoptikern*. fzb 17. Würzburg: Echter, 1977.

Zeller, D. *Kommentar zur Logienquelle*. SKK.NT 21. Stuttgart: Kohlhammer, 1984.

## a)  Reconstruction and Origin of the Q Source

In addition to the Gospel of Mark, Matthew and Luke used in common a second source in the composition of their Gospels, the sayings collection (Q). Generally speaking, Q is inferred from the common traditional material found in Matthew and Luke but not in Mark. But Q is also recognizable in doublets, i.e. in passages where Matthew and/or Luke adopt material from both their Markan and their Q sources.

The extent of Q is not to be strictly limited to parallel texts in Matthew and Luke not found in Mark. Q material is also found in texts peculiar to Matthew or Luke, depending from case to case on how the Evangelists have edited the Q source. It is not to be presupposed that Matthew and Luke incorporated all the Q material available to them or that they edited the material in the same way. It is rather the case that (similar to their different procedures in adopting and editing material from the Gospel of Mark), we must reckon with the possibility of abbreviations corresponding to the individual character of each Gospel's redaction, so that on the other side there is a "surplus," usually attributed to the special material of the respective Evangelist, but which may have been in Q. Moreover, the material in the Q source was subjected to several different influences in the process of its transmission, not the least significant of which was the variety of situations in which the oral tradition was transmitted. It is thus not possible to speak of *the* Q-source; more precisely, we may establish only that there were different phases of the tradition and layers of the sayings collection.[1]

If we look for the theological structures presupposed in the sayings collection, then in the following we proceed on the basis of the stratum of the Q source that may be inferred from the comparison of Matthew and Luke. It can be recognized from the parallel traditions that the Q source followed a simple chronological order: it begins with the speech of John the Baptist (Matt 3:5, 7–12 par), proceeds to the temptation of Jesus,[2] and then via different groups of sayings to the apocalyptic speech.[3] Within this chronological framework three groups of sayings material have been

---

[1]   In contrast to the redaction-critical perspective that distinguished between tradition and redaction and with this approach could only attribute a few words to the redaction and thus saw the redactional work principally in the arrangement of the materials (D. Lührmann, *Redaktion*), several recent publications have distinguished between (a) the oldest traditional material (essentially words of Jesus and the first commentary on them) (J. Wanke, *Bezugs- und Kommentarworte*), (b) the first thematic collections (c) the main collection, (d) the redaction of the main collection and (e) the transitional editions used by the Evangelists. The latter versions are inferred from the fact that Q seems to have come to Matthew and Luke in slightly different forms. This layer may be traced out in exemplary fashion by observing the different use of theological statements (cf. e. g. H. Schürmann, "Beobachtungen zum Menschensohn-Titel"; D. Zeller, "Redaktionsprozesse und wechselnder 'Sitz im Leben' beim Q-Material" in J. Delobel, ed., *Logia* (BEThL 59. Leuven: Leuven University Press, 1982) 395–409; F. W. Horn, "Christentum und Judentum in der Logienquelle," *EvTh* 51 (1991) 344–364. M. Hengel, "Aufgaben der neutestament-lichen Wissenschaft," *NTS* 40 (1994) 336 n. 45, emphasizes over against these "in part absurd hypotheses," that "behind the Q tradition there stood not a collective... [but the] theological mind of a disciple of Jesus."

[2]   Matthew 4:3–10par; an adoptionistic baptismal pericope may be presupposed here; cf. Matthew 4:3par, "Son of God."

[3]   Matthew 24:26ffpar, 37ffpar, with the concluding Parable of the Talents: Matthew 25:14–30; one might consider whether Luke 22:28–30 formed the conclusion; cf. E. Bammel, "Das Ende von Q," in Otto Böcher and Klaus Hacker (eds.), *Verborum Veritas* (FS G. Stählin. Wuppertal: Brockhaus, 1970) 39–50.

placed: (1) basic instructions for the community and its missionaries. This material is found above all in the Sermon on the Mount/Plain (Matt 5:3ff; Luke 6:20ff and elsewhere); in addition the "mission discourse" is to be cited especially Matthew 9:37–10:15par; sayings about discipleship (Matt 8:19–22par), the woes pronounced on the Galilean cities (Matt 11:20–24par), Jesus' thanksgiving to the Father (Matt 11:25–27par), and the blessing pronounced on the disciples (Matt 13:16par). (2) Debates with the community's opponents. The words of Jesus about John the Baptist belong in this category (Matt 11:2–19par), as well as the Beelzebul charge, the demand for a sign (Matt 12:22–45par) and the anti-Pharisee speech (Matt 23:1ffpar). (3) Words of apocalyptic admonition and instruction: words about prayer (Matt 6:9–13par, the Lord's Prayer, 7:1-11par, on judging and the hearing of prayer), on anxiety (Matt 6:19-34par), parables of the kingdom of God (Matt 13:31–33;[4] 13:44–46par), words about steadfast confession and discipleship (Matt 10:26–39; 18:7, 12–22), the Parable of the Great Supper (Matt 22:1ffpar) and the parousia speech (Matt 24:26–28, 37–41; 25:14–30par).[5]

It is thus by no means the case that the "sayings source" contained exclusively sayings material. Narratives were included alongside sayings. Thus the story of the nobleman of Capernaum was joined to the Sermon on the Mount/Plain (Matt 8:5–13; Luke 7:1–10). The temptation story (Matt 4:1–11; Luke 4:1–13) is also to be counted among the narrative material; in addition, the sayings about John the Baptist are presented in the form of a report presupposing a narrative framework (Matt 11:2–19; Luke 7:18–35), as is the Beelzebul charge (Matt 12:22–28).

If the Q source in this reconstructed pre-synoptic stratum is a conglomeration of speech and narrative material in which the speech tradition played the dominant role, and if there was neither passion story nor resurrection tradition, then Adolf Jülicher was correct in designating Q as a "semi-Gospel." The Evangelists Matthew and Luke found the sayings collection already present in their Hellenistic Christian context. This is indicated by, among other things, the fact that the Old Testament citations are mostly from the Septuagint. On the other hand, a number of sayings have preserved an earlier linguistic form, so that a nucleus of the Q source can with certainty be located on Aramaic-speaking ground, which means it reaches back to the time of the earliest Palestinian church and

---

4   Whether Matthew 13:31–32par belonged to the Q source is disputed. It can be seen as a double parable in connection with Matthew 13:33par, but the "minor agreements" can also be taken as evidence that Matthew and Luke used a slightly different version of the Gospel of Mark as their source (Deutero-Mark; so F. Kogler, *Das Doppelgleichnis vom Senfkorn und vom Sauerteig in seiner traditionsgeschichtlichen Entwicklung* [fzb 59. Würzburg: Echter, 1988).

5   Cf. the synoptic display in G. Strecker and U. Schnelle, *Einführung in die neutestamentliche Exegese* (UTB 1253. Göttingen: Vandenhoeck & Ruprecht, 1994[4]) 60–62.

into the life of Jesus. The Q tradition thus combines Semitic and Hellenistic elements. It has preserved reflections of the theological thinking of the community from the very beginnings up to the time of the pre-Synoptic Hellenistic church. This complexity is to be taken into account when one inquires after Q's characteristic theological traits.

## b) The Person of Jesus

The sayings source ended with Jesus' apocalyptic speech. Although it contained neither a passion narrative nor a resurrection account, it would nonetheless be misguided to conclude from this that the tradents of the Q source ignored the passion and resurrection of Jesus and belonged to an independent branch of early Christian tradition.[6] Palestinian and Hellenistic Christians, from the very beginning, confessed their faith in the crucified and risen Jesus. This faith is foundational for the tradition behind the Q source and also to a considerable extent for the formation of Q itself. That the confession of the crucified and risen one is presupposed is seen in the saying about following Jesus on the way to the cross in Matthew 10:38par ("whoever does not take up the cross and follow me is not worthy of me"). The technical term σταυρός presupposes the early Christian kerygma of the crucifixion of Jesus.[7] The absence of passion and resurrection narratives from the sayings source is to be explained from the intention of gathering this particular group of traditional material, namely that Q had an essential parenetic function, intended to guide the Christian community along the right ethical way. The passion and resurrection narratives were not so appropriate for this purpose. An additional consideration is that the nucleus of the collection derives from the pre-Easter period. This did not lead naturally to the adding of passion and resurrection narratives that originated after Easter and were formed in a different manner than the collection of parenetic-ethical collection of sayings and stories.

Although the Jesus of the sayings collection is not explicitly designated the Crucified and Risen One, in the post-Easter tradition this is presup-

---

[6]  For S. Schulz, a particular community stands behind Q that had no contact with the theology of the pre-Markan community, or perhaps even protested against it (S. Schulz, *Q. Die Spruchquelle der Evangelisten* (Zürich: Theologischer Verlag, 1972) 31, 42, 433. W. Schmithals also thinks in terms of an independent religious community separate from the rest of early Christianity (W. Schmithals, *Das Evangelium nach Markus* [ÖTK 2/1. Gütersloh: Gerd Mohn, 1979] 24; *Einleitung in die drei ersten Evangelien* (Berlin: Evangelischer Verlagsanstalt, 1985) 402.

[7]  Dinkler's hypothesis that the saying points to the early Christian practice of marking with the sign of a cross is less probable; cf. E. Dinkler, "Jesu Wort vom Kreuztragen," in *Siglum Crucis. Aufsätze zum Neuen Testament und zur Christlichen Archäologie* (Tübingen: J. C. B. Mohr [Paul Siebeck], 1967) 77–98. For critique see H.-W. Kuhn, "Jesus als Gekreuzigter in der frühchristlichen Verkündigung bis zur Mitte des 2. Jahrhunderts," *ZThK* 72 (1975) 1–46.

posed. Thus it is the exalted Lord of the community who speaks in the sayings tradition. This community and its tradition bear witness to the reality it has experienced in the event of Jesus' cross and resurrection, thereby expressing its post-Easter ecclesial self-understanding.

The community encounters the reality of the Risen One in the linguistic form of the *Son of Man Christology*. The Lord of the community is the Son of Man who is to come in the future; his advent will be a startling event without advance warning. The situation of the community will be like that of the house owner in the parable: he does not know when the thief might come; he lives in danger of being burglarized. So also the community lives in view of the parousia of the Son of Man (Matt 24:43–44par). It is in this light that the parenesis γίνεσθε ἕτοιμοι is to be understood; this does not mean "Don't let yourself be surprised," but points to the surprising suddenness of the advent of the Son of Man and draws the consequence: live in such a way that expresses your conviction that the Son of Man could appear at any time!

On the other hand, the sayings collection speaks of the past, earthly Son of Man: Matthew 8:20par (the Son of Man has no place to lay his head); Matthew 11:19par (the Son of Man, in contrast to the ascetic conduct of John the Baptist, is considered a glutton and drunkard; he is a friend of tax collectors and sinners; cf. also Matthew 11:25ffpar).

Moreover, the sayings source contains a *Son of God Christology*. According to Matthew 4:3par the temptations are aimed at the υἱὸς θεοῦ. The primary issue dealt with in this connection is not that of the "Messianic" quality of Jesus, as though the community confesses faith in Jesus as the Son of God who has overcome the testing of his Messianic nature and mission and through this victory over the tempter has confirmed his status as Son of God. It is more probable that instead of specifically Messianic temptations Jesus is pictured as subject to general human ones, temptations that illustrate the dangers that threaten the community on its own path of discipleship. By handing on this pericope in the tradition, the community confesses its faith in the one who, as representative and model, has withstood the dangers and thereby has shown it a new way.

In addition, in the sayings source the community confesses its faith in the one who is the "Son."[8] As the "Son" Jesus has access to the "Father." By the address "Father" in the Lord's Prayer he makes it possible for the

---

8    Cf. Matthew 11:27par. Only here does Q use the υἱός title absolutely. Even if it is to be distinguished formally from the "Son of God" predication, the absolute usage still presupposes the relation of God the Father and the Son of God, since the reciprocal relation of πατήρ and υἱός is expressed in this text. This shows the Hellenistic background of the cry of jubilation in Matthew 11:25ff and at the same time lets it be recognized as late tradition within Q—despite the fact that that the absolute usage of the term υἱός is also used in early Christian apocalyptic (1 Cor 15:28).

community to approach the Father and to be a fellowship of "sons" (Matt 5:45). As the "Son," Jesus is the revealer (Matt 11:25ffpar); there is no knowledge of the Father apart from the Son. The philosophical question of the Father's being-in-and-for-himself is far removed from the theological conception of the sayings collection, for through the Son the being of the Father is a being-for-the-community. The Son has been given authority over all (Matt 11:27par), thus also the authority to represent the Father in himself. In the advent of the Son the Father reveals himself; in and through the Son it is the Father who is known.

The epitome of the Son's identity as revealer is the βασιλεία Θεοῦ. The kingdom becomes present where the Son makes himself known. Thus Matthew 11:12–13par says, "All the prophets and the law prophesied until John came; from the days of John the Baptist until now the kingdom of heaven has suffered violence, and the violent take it by force." The "kingdom of God" is accordingly not yet present with the advent of the Baptist, but comes with the advent of the one John announced, namely Jesus. It is present only as an attacked and threatened reality. Therein is reflected the lowliness and threatened nature of the presence of the Son of God. In the Q context the βιασταί ("violent") are presumably the Jewish persecutors, especially the scribes and Pharisees (cf. Matt 23:1ffpar). The βασιλεία is thus present in a paradoxical way. It is really present, as the kingdom that suffers, in that it is subjected to being in time. As the earthly, suffering one, the Son of God represents the eschatological kingdom of God, as the Son of Man who finds no place among human beings (Matt 8:20par Luke 9:58). The kingdom of God also comes near in the unpretentious appearance of the human messengers (Matt 10:7). With it the promise is given that the small beginnings will lead to a magnificent, successful end (cf. Matt. 13:31-32) and the kingdom of God will permeate everything like leaven. Already here in the earliest proclamation, the universality of the beginning is set forth (Matt 13:33par). That is why it can be said that the time of salvation has "already, in the present" broken in, and salvation can already be granted to those who see it (Matt 13:16–17par).

## c)   The Message of Jesus

The "Son" represents the kingdom of God.[9] His appearance means:

1. *The call to repentance.* The Baptist had also called for μετάνοια (Matt 3:8), but with Jesus the Coming One himself steps forth as the caller. His call to repentance leaves no other way open. After him there is only the possibility of the End, of judgment or grace. His call therefore is a radical

---

9   H. Schürmann, "Das Zeugnis der Redequelle für die Basileia-Verkündigung Jesu," in *Gottes Reich—Jesu Geschick* (Freiburg: Herder, 1983) 65–152.

call to decision and results in dividing his hearers. This is seen in the concluding parable of the Sermon on the Mount/Plain (Matt 7:24–27par). Thus Jesus' preaching included an absolute threat of the coming judgment; it pointed to the sign of Jonah (Matt 12:39–42): this "evil generation" will receive no other sign than this, the appearance of the Son of Man for judgment. The warnings to the cities of Galilee are also radical threats of coming judgment (Matt 11:21–24par; cf. also Matt 10:34–39par).

2. *The promise of salvation.* According to the oldest tradition of the blessings of the Sermon on the Mount/Plain, the consoling promise of eschatological salvation is made to the poor, the hungering, the crying (or lamenting) (Luke 6:20–21par). An expansion of the series of Q-beatitudes in the second stratum of the tradition (Matt 5:5, 7–9) contains ethical blessings that call for right conduct in the church and world, but also still have the character of consoling eschatological promise. The message of Jesus promises salvation. Such encouraging words that mediate the promised eschatological blessings apply especially to the persecuted: the suffering church stands in the situation of the Old Testament prophets. The suffering endured in persecution is the occasion of joy, for it is the ground of hope (Matt 5:11–12; cf. also Luke 14:16–24).

3. *Instruction in doing right.* The emphasis of the sayings collection lies on the hortatory and monitory sayings. Of decisive importance is the command to love one's enemies, which refers to those who are persecuting the community. Such love is measured by the constant, impartial goodness of the heavenly Father (Matt 5:44–48par). This corresponds to the radical nature of other instructions (e. g. Matt 5:39: "...if anyone strikes you on the right cheek, turn the other also"). The comprehensive command to love God and neighbor (Matt 22:34–40par) had apparently come to Matthew and Luke not only in a Marcan but in a Q form. Love of the neighbor and unconditional love of God belong together, for love of God becomes actual in no other way than in love for the neighbor.

4. *Mission to the World.* The connection with Jesus' own preaching meant for the early Christian missionaries in the first place a mission to Israel. This is presupposed in Jesus' lament over Jerusalem (Matt 23:37–39par); also the sending out of the disciples (Matt 10:5–6: not to the cities of the Samaritans; Matt 19:28: the disciples of Jesus as judges over the twelve tribes of Israel). Such preaching is directed to Israel as a call for faith, a challenge to conversion. The national and religious limitations of Judaism are overcome; even the Gentile centurion is numbered among those who are accepted (Matt 8:5–13par).

5. *Preparation for the End.* Even though Jesus' message contained a dialectical tension between the experience of salvation in the present and the

hope of future salvation, according to the tradition of the earliest church the center of gravity lay on the hope for the future consummation of salvation, the parousia (Matt 24–25par). Thus accepting the message of Jesus implies an understanding of living "between the times;" it is the time of the absence of Jesus (Matt 23:39). In such a time one must be always ready for the parousia, rejecting false teaching and resisting the claims of the false Messiahs. The parousia of the Son of Man cannot be discerned from signs and miracles given in advance; it cannot be diagnosed in terms of apocalyptic doctrine but will come like a flash of lightning in the night, but then no one will be able to elude it (Matt 24:27; Luke 17:24).

### d)   The Community's Understanding

It accords with the history of the sayings collection that we cannot discern *one* understanding of the church within it. On the contrary, the history of the traditions incorporated in Q lets us trace the path from particularism (Matt 10:5–6: preaching exclusively to the Jewish people) to a universal understanding of the church's mission (Matt 8:5ffpar: the mission to the Gentiles; also Matt 22:1ffpar). According to S. Schulz a distinction must be made between the kerygma of the Palestinian-Syrian region and the kerygma of the later Q communities of Syria, but one must ask whether the matter is not more complex than this. Moreover, it is not at all clear that "Q communities" ever existed. Doubtless, the images of the church that may be extracted from Q are incomplete. There are neither baptismal nor eucharistic traditions. This, however, was determined by the subject matter, since the content of Q is mainly parenesis. The community that used this parenetic collection for instruction within the life of the church understood itself to be en route. It is on the way toward the parousia of the Son of Man. While this future orientation motivates its conduct in the present, it also looks back to the cross as a salvific past event. Three distinctive perspectives are generated by this understanding:

*1. Discipleship under the sign of the cross.* According to Matt 8:19–22par, discipleship calls for a complete abandonment of worldly entanglements. Discipleship to the Son of Man leads to homelessness. It presupposes radical separation, abandoning father and mother. It calls for a willingness to place one's life on the line (Matt 19:37–39par).

*2. Orientation to the future: uncertainty about the time of the End.* The conclusion of the Q source is marked by the parables of the return of the Son of Man (Matt 24:37–41par). Here the uncertainty of the time of his appearance is emphasized. The Christian community has no advantage over the generation of Noah's time. The End will mean a radical separation, in which one will be accepted and another rejected (Matt 24:40–

41par Luke 17:35). This is the basis for the challenge to do what is right today, for the parousia will occur without warning (Matt 24:42–44 par Luke 12:39–40).

3. *The journey through time is made with confidence and trust.* This is seen in the Lord's Prayer, that characteristically begins with the address to God as "Father" (Matt 6:9–13par). The confidence in God's act in the present and future is based on the sonship of the believers (Matt 5:9, 45par). This means that in their journey through time they can be relieved of anxiety and can place their trust in the goodness of the Father (Matt 6:25–34par). This community, however, looks not only to the future end of history that will reveal them to be the ἐκλεκτοί, but also to the Christ event as something that has already happened in history; for at the beginning of its history stands the Son of Man as the one who has already come. Confession of him results in his confession of them as belonging to his community (Matt 10:32par).

# C.
# The Way of Jesus Christ—
# The Synoptic Gospels

Bultmann, R. *The History of the Synoptic Tradition*. New York: Harper & Row, 1963, 319–374.

Conzelmann, H. "Literaturbericht zu den Synoptischen Evangelien, "*ThR* NF 37 (1972), 220–272; 43, 1978, 3–51.321–327.

Ellis, E. E. "New Directions in Form Criticism," *Jesus Christus in Historie und Theologie* (FS H. Conzelmann), G. Strecker, ed. Tübingen: J. C. B. Mohr (Paul Siebeck), 1975, 299–315.

Epp E. J. and MacRae, G. W., eds. *The New Testament and its Modern Interpreters*, SBL.SP 3. Philadelphia-Atlanta: Scholars Press, 1989.

Güttgemanns, E. *Candid Questions Concerning Gospel Form Criticism*. Pittsburgh: Pickwick, 1979.

Hahn, F., ed. *Der Erzähler des Evangeliums. Methodische Neuansätze in der Markusforschung*. SBS 118/119. Stuttgart: Katholisches Bibelwerk, 1985.

Koch, K. *The Growth of the Biblical Tradition; the Form-Critical Method*. New York: Scribners, 1969.

Koester, H. "Formgeschichte/Formenkritik II," TRE 11 (1983) 286–299.

Lindemann, A. "Literaturbericht zu den Synoptischen Evangelien," ThR 49 (1984) 223–276.311–371.

Riesner, R. *Jesus als Lehrer. Eine Untersuchung zum Ursprung der Evangelienüberlieferun*. WUNT II 7. Tübingen: J. C. B. Mohr (Paul Siebeck), 1993[4].

Rohde, J. *Rediscovering the Teaching of the Evangelists*. Philadelphia: Westminster, 1968.

Roloff, J. *Das Kerygma und der irdische Jesus*. Göttingen: Vandenhoeck & Ruprecht, 1973.

Roloff, J. *Neues Testament*. Neukirchen-Vluyn: Neukirchener, 1985[4].

Schmithals, W. *Einleitung in die drei ersten Evangelien*, Berlin-New York: W. de Gruyter, 1985.

Schmithals, W. "Evangelien, Synoptische," TRE 10 (1982) 570–626.

Schmithals, W. "Kritik der Formkritik," ZThK 77 (1980) 149–185.

Schneemelcher, W. "Introduction A. Gospels: Non-Biblical Material about Jesus," W. Schneemelcher, ed. *New Testament Apocrypha* I. Louisville: Westminster John Knox, 1991[2], 77–87.

Schulz, S. *Die Stunde der Botschaft. Einführung in die Theologie der vier Evangelisten*. Hamburg: Furche, 1982[3].

Strecker, G. "Redaktionsgeschichte als Aufgabe der Synoptikerexegese," G. Strecker, ed. *Eschaton und Historie. Aufsätze*. Göttingen: Vandenhoeck & Ruprecht, 1979, 9–32.

Strecker, G. "Schriftlichkeit oder Mündlichkeit der synoptischen Tradition? Anmerkungen zur formgeschichtlichen Problematik," *The Four Gospels* (FS F. Neirynck) BEThL 100. Leuven: Leuven University Press, 1992, 159–172.

Stuhlmacher, P., ed. *The Gospel and the Gospels*. Grand Rapids: W. B. Eerdmans, 1991.
Talbert, C. H. *What is a Gospel? The Genre of the Canonical Gospels*. Philadelphia: Fortress, 1977.
Taylor, V. *The Formation of the Gospel Tradition*. London: Macmillan, 1933.
Vorster, W. S. "Der Ort der Gattung Evangelium in der Literaturgeschichte," *VF* 29 (1984) 2–25.
Zimmermann H. and Kliesch, K. *Neutestamentliche Methodenlehre*. Stuttgart: Katholisches Bibelwerk 1982, 223–266.

The following is an effort to determine the theological conceptions of the authors of the Synoptic Gospels. This manner of posing the question is usually the approach of "redaction history" (Redaktionsgeschichte, usually translated "redaction criticism," i.e. "editorial analysis") or "composition criticism." The expression "redaction history" is open to misunderstanding; for redaction-critical analysis does not intend to reconstruct a "history" of the redaction but rather to set forth the theological conceptions of the editors of the respective Gospels. "Redaction history/criticism" is subject to the same kind of misunderstanding as the expression "Form history/criticism," since "form history/criticism" does not have as its goal the delineation of the history of a form but rather to study the process of the oral transmission of various literary genres or forms. Though the term "redaction history/criticism" does not refer to a historical account of the editing of the Gospels, it can call attention to the fact that every "redaction" stands in a particular historical context. It is the task of redaction criticism to present this context. More precisely said, redaction criticism investigates the relation of tradition and redaction by comparing the redactional work of the Evangelist (the "redactor") to the tradition that came to him in order to determine what was typical of him and the principle by which he was guided in the adoption and adaptation of traditional material. The redactional work of the Evangelist can be determined only to the extent that the tradition that came to him can be isolated. This means that redaction criticism is useful only in comparison with other approaches that are concerned with the history of the tradition. One of its methodological presuppositions is that of "form criticism," which investigates primarily the laws of oral tradition, for the redactors of the Gospels stand on the same sociological foundation as the bearers of the pre-Synoptic tradition. As exponents of the faith of the community and thus of the community theology, redactors can be interpreted only in relation to their communities and their traditions. This is still the case even though they have made substantial contributions by their elaboration and structuring of the theological conceptions of the early Christian communities and thereby to the process by which Christian life and thought found its own proper orientation in the second and third Christian generations.

In addition to the results of form criticism, redaction criticism presupposes the source analysis of the Synoptic Gospels. The Two-Source-Theory documents the stable element of the tradition. Its concern with the comparison of written traditions serves to clarify the Evangelists' manner of composing and the results of their Gospel composition.

# I. Fundamental Problems of Gospel Composition

Bultmann, R. "Die Erforschung der synoptischen Evangelien, "*Glauben und Verstehen* IV. Tübingen: J. C. B. Mohr (Paul Siebeck), 1975, 1–41.
Dormeyer, D. *Das Evangelium als literarische und theologische Gattung.* EdF 263. Darmstadt: Wissenschaftliche Buchgesellschaft, 1989.
Dormeyer, D. *The New Testament among the Writings of Antiquity.* Sheffield: Sheffield Academic Press, 1995.
Dormeyer, D. and Frankemölle, H." Evangelium als literarische Gattung und als theologischer Begriff," ANRW II. 25.2 (1984), 1463–1542.
Strecker, G. *History of New Testament Literature* (Harrisburg: Trinity Press International, 1997) 123–148.

## a) The Relation of Kerygma and History as a Redaction-critical Problem

Ebeling, G. *Theology and Proclamation; dialogue with Bultmann.* Philadelphia: Fortress, 1966.
Käsemann, E. "The Problem of the Historical Jesus," E. Käsemann, ed. *Essays on New Testament Themes.* Naperville: Alec R. Allenson, Inc., 1964, 15–47.
Schmidt, K. L. "Die Stellung der Evangelien in der allgemeinen Literaturgeschichte, ΕΥΧΑΡΙΣΤΗΡΙΟΝ, (FS H. Gunkel) FRLANT 36/2. Göttingen: Vandenhoeck & Ruprecht, 1923, 50–134.
Vögtle, A. "Die historische und theologische Tragweite der heutigen Evangelienforschung," *ZKTh* 86 (1964) 385–417.

The redactors of the Gospels presuppose the Easter faith and the Easter kerygma of the early Christian community. The Gospels they composed are testimonies of faith and should not be confused with historical biographies. It is to the credit of form-critical investigation that the kerygmatic element in the Synoptic tradition has been made clear. Though R. Bultmann speaks of the "myth of the kerygma" that gives the Gospel of Mark its unity,[1] he concedes that the Gospels have "the form of a coherent, historical, biographical story,"[2] since they begin with the appearance of

---

[1]   R. Bultmann, *History of the Synoptic Tradition* 371.
[2]   Ibid. 370. Cf. the analogies in the ancient biographical literature, e. g. the Life of Homer: D. E. Aune, *The New Testament in its Literary Environment* (LEC VII) (Philadelphia: Westminster, 1987) 63–64; D. Dormeyer, *Das Evangelium als literarische und theologische Gattung* 159.

the Baptist, (Matthew and Luke even have the story of Jesus' birth and childhood), and end with the narrative of the death and resurrection of Jesus Christ. They are concerned to provide at least an elementary outline that represents the chronological and geographical flow of the narrative. Such a "double character" of the Gospel is not to be differentiated by the terms "form and content" but raises the question of how the kerygmatic and historical are to be related to each other. What does it mean that the early Christian community did not stop at the transmission of the kerygma, that they did not align their tradition strictly to Pauline theology and also did not let their tradition determine the shape of the proclamation of the present and future Kyrios? What is the reason for the new evaluation of history in the Gospels? There were certainly historical motifs already at work in the tradition prior to Mark. This is seen, for example, in the fact that the sayings collection transmitted a series of chronological and geographical data. So also some of the individual units of the pre-Synoptic tradition contained chronological or geographical statements that could be classified as "historical." Since Mark was the first to create the literary genre "Gospel," this raises the question of how history and kerygma fit together in the Gospel.[3] The origination of the Gospel genre signifies a reevaluation and upgrading of the history mediated by the kerygma with a possible emphasis on history over against the kerygma. What then was the occasion that gave rise to the formation of the Gospel genre?

According to R. Bultmann ("Das Verhältnis der urchristlichen Christusbotschaft zum historischen Jesus," in *Exegetica* [Tübingen: J. C. B. Mohr (Paul Siebeck), 1967] 453), the "combination of historical report and kerygmatic Christology in the Synoptics does not mean to legitimize the Christ kerygma by means of history but the other way round: the story of Jesus is so to speak legitimized as messianic by placing it in the light of kerygmatic Christology." Accordingly, it would not be the historical but the kerygmatic aspect that was the decisive factor in the composition of the Gospels. However, according to the dominant scholarly view this would not be true at least for Luke, who is considered the "historian" among the Evangelists. This scholarly view attributes to Luke not only the intention to interpret faith but also ascribes a demonstrative function to his historical writing. This, however, cannot be excluded from the purpose of the other Evangelists. — The position of Bultmann contradicts G. Ebeling (*Theology and Proclamation* 132): "one does not legitimate the history of Jesus messianically, simply because people still retain memories of it, but clearly because one is not merely interested in the *That* of the historicity of Jesus but also in the *What* and *How* of his appearance—of

---

3    Contra W. Schmithals, *Einleitung* 409, who argues that Mark cannot be the First Evangelist but found a Gospel writing already in existence before him (the "foundation document") which he revised.

course not as critical historians but because faith is concerned with the concretion of the kerygma." This opens up the question of what it was that gave the Evangelists the occasion to reach back behind the kerygma to the story of Jesus.

A variety of answers:

1. *The anti-docetic interest*. To a considerable extent this means the same as the buzz word "antignostic" interest. According to the gnostic-docetic view, the idea of "Christ" could not be united with that of the earthly Jesus. Since the gnostics alone had access to the truth by their knowledge, they knew themselves to be separated from the world of human-earthly existence. Thus the person of Jesus, the redeemer who came into the world, is not understood in terms of flesh and blood but only as one who seemed to be a part of this-worldly reality. In contrast, what became the orthodox theology of the Great Church at an early date emphasized the reality of the incarnation of Jesus Christ. Though this could also represent one motive in the composition of the Gospels, this approach remains hypothetical, however, since a confrontation with gnosticism and docetism is not demonstrable for any of the Synoptic Gospels, including even Luke. In Paul's farewell speech to the elders at Miletus (Acts 20:17–36) the departing apostle warns the church against "people with false doctrine"— a concrete warning against heretics but their false teaching is not specified, and in Luke's sense cannot be narrowed down to one particular error. It is not specific heretical groups that are the objects of the apostolic admonition but the general possibility of "false teachers." Thus docetic or gnostic opponents cannot be claimed as the motive for Luke's historical writing.

We come nearer to answering the question of what it was that motivated the composition of the Gospels, when we note:

2. The composition of the Gospels reflects the *transition in the development of the history of early Christian tradition from Jewish Christianity to Gentile Christianity*. The form "Gospel" corresponds to the Gentile Christianity's own native orientation. This does not, however, exclude Jewish or Jewish-Christian factors in the process of Gospel composition. Nonetheless, it is still true that there are no authentic Jewish parallels to the Gospel genre. The closest Jewish analogies are rabbinic anecdotes and collections of sayings, which are related to the wisdom literature and thus are similar to the Q source but not to the Gospels themselves. K. L. Schmidt had already shown in his essay "The Place of the Gospels in General Literary History" that the Greek-Hellenistic parallel phenomena to the New Testament Gospel literature are instructive. To be sure, the literary claim of ancient biographical writings distinguishes them in form and content from the New Testament Gospels. Since the Greek-Hellenistic biographies sketched literary portraits, K. L. Schmidt was correct

when he numbered them among the "high-class" literature (*Hochliteratur*), while classifying the Synoptic Gospels, in contrast, as "cult books for ordinary folk" (*volkstümliche Kultbücher*).[4] Yet the parallels are not to be overlooked: as in ancient biography, a "hero" stands at the center of the Gospel narratives; in both cases an extensive "life story" is presented, even if in part by inadequate means; chronological and geographical details are provided in both instances.[5] The formal differences can be explained for the most part from the popular, congregational orientation of the Gospel tradition. These observations do not nullify the fundamental similarity but do mean that the composition of the Gospels reflects the adaptation of the Christian faith to the ethos of the Hellenistic world. The operative motif is faith's finding its own proper orientation within the Hellenistic world. This, of course, is only acknowledging an external motif that can be incorporated within the history of ideas. As a result, the issue of the theological basis for the composition of the Gospels would only be partially answered from this perspective.[6]

3. The theological motive for the composition of the Gospels is the Gospel redactors' *interest in salvation history*. The term "salvation history," used in a variety of ways, denotes that history in and through which salvation occurs. The Evangelists portray such a saving event. Their narrative of Jesus has as its subject matter a past event that possesses saving power which is to be mediated to the present and future. The Evangelists' Jesus-narrative is thus not identical with the "kerygma," the direct word of address; it is not preaching in the specific sense but address refracted through the medium of history. Only through the insight of what has happened in history is it possible to perceive that this event is of significance for the present, and how this is so. The Evangelists' Jesus-narrative does not therefore intend merely to rehearse historical data. It is not satisfied merely to report the "brute facts" of the events of Jesus' life but presupposes and brings to expression the conviction that the past event is an eschatological event whose actual reality is not available within the temporal categories of historical perception. Eschatological and historical

---

[4]  K. L. Schmidt, *Neues Testament—Judentum—Kirche. Kleine Schriften*, G. Sauter, ed. (TB 69. Munich: Kaiser, 1981) 118.
[5]  Cf. here the definition by D. E. Aune, *The New Testament in its Literary Environment* 29: ("a discrete prose narrative devoted exclusively to the portrayal of the whole life of a particular individual perceived as historical"). On the following cf. also C. H. Talbert, *What is a Gospel?*; G. Strecker and U. Schnelle, *Einführung* 91ff; G. Strecker and J. Maier, *Neues Testament—Antikes Judentum* 55–57; G. Strecker, "Biblische Literaturgeschichte II," TRE 21, 338–358.
[6]  For additional attempts to explain the form of the Gospel from Old Testament-Jewish tradition, as midrash or apocalyptic drama: G. Strecker, *History of New Testament Literature* 104–112.

interest are combined in the Evangelists' Jesus-narrative. This is what the term "salvation history" intends to convey.

By the connection to history as presented in the Jesus-narrative of the Gospels, the "what" and "how" of the kerygma is concretized. In the Gospels' presentation of the Jesus-story, faith extends itself beyond the bare announcement of the kerygma and gives account of itself. In the narrative mirror of Jesus' past, faith sees its own reflection in order to come to itself and to understand itself. This could also happen by means of myth and was set forth mythologically, e. g. in the theology of Paul, and to some extent in the pre-Synoptic Gospel tradition. Yet the Evangelists did not basically attach themselves to the mythological elements of the tradition but to its more historical components. They thereby provided the basis for the widespread assumption that their interpretative presentation is a historical report in the modern, objective sense. Since the category "history" appears to fit our times better than that of "myth," the redactors of the Gospels give an occasion for the misunderstanding that they are narrating a story subject to demonstration and that they intended to provide historical proof for the truth-content of the kerygma. And it is not to be denied that they have themselves sometimes fallen victim to this misunderstanding. This state of affairs, in which a reality not subject to proof is narrated in the form of historical facts so that faith is thereby re-coined into knowledge and thereby falsified, constitutes the problematic of salvation history and thus also the problematic of the composition of the Gospels.

While historical grounding is a significant element in the construction of the narrative, it is also the case that the conjunction of eschatological and historical orientation reveals the *theological concern of the Gospel writers*.

(1) The concretion of the "what" and "how" of the kerygma means above all an emphasis on the ἐφ᾽ ἅπαξ of the Christ event. The flow of the narrative in terms of salvation history does not mean that the Jesus-event was a random point on the time line. On the contrary, in the understanding of the Gospel redactors Jesus is the "midst of time." The unrepeatable once-for-all character of the Christ-event comprehends both its continuity and discontinuity with reference to the course of history, since the salvation-historical mode of thinking affirms that the saving will of God has adjusted the course history with reference to this central event. This becomes clear in regard to the course of history prior to Christ in the way Old Testament prophecy is understood as referring to Jesus. And this means that the time following the Jesus-event is understood to be determined by him. As the orientation point for all of history, the Christ-event is a discontinuous event in the course of time but it is still incorporated within history, participating in the continuity of history. The salvation-historical aspect of the Christ-event expressed in the juxtaposition of

continuity and discontinuity is somewhat restrained with reference to the concept of the contingency of the revelation in Christ, which is not to say that it altogether excludes this idea. From this standpoint questions may be addressed to the issue of the origin of the Gospels, as well as to the misunderstanding that has emerged from it that the saving event is a demonstrable event within history. Although the attempt to present proofs on the level of actual historical events is condemned in advance to fail, one must at least acknowledge that the theological conviction that the Christ-event is not derivable from history, but is an event grounded alone in the sovereign will of God, does not stand at the midpoint of the Gospel writers' conception of what they were doing. Salvation-historical demonstration cannot—one could even say, contrary to the intention of the Evangelists— wipe out the contingency of the Christ-event.

(2) In the second place, the concretion of the "what" and "how" of the kerygma in the process of Gospel composition means an emphasis on the *extra nos* of the Christ-event. The very existence of the Gospels testifies to the fact that Christian faith cannot be grounded in subjectivity. That to which faith appeals is not something that human beings can say to themselves; on the contrary, faith is grounded on something prior to and apart from the believer. Here too the danger exists that Christian faith will be dissolved in a system of historical coordination and that a historical fact would become the ground of Christian faith. In fact the story of which the Evangelists speak, a story qualified by its eschatological content, affirms that the *extra nos* of faith is a reality that has come into the world in the Christ-event but cannot be grasped on the basis of this-worldly presuppositions. It deals with a historical event that cannot be apprehended in subject-object categories, even if the Evangelists themselves have sometimes given occasion for this misunderstanding.

(3) Finally, the concretion of the "what" and "how" of the kerygma in the process of Gospel composition affirms the *paradoxical nature* of the Christian faith. The Evangelists bring the paradox of Christian faith to linguistic expression by portraying the Christ-event as a paradoxical event that consists of the eschaton breaking into history. This means: the possibility of faith exists in a world that denies this possibility not only theoretically but in practice. Over against such a worldview, the Gospel is a witness for the fact that faith is a possibility given to human beings, that being in the world but not of the world is a real possibility.

The Synoptic Gospels bear witness to this paradox by presenting Jesus as the Christ, portraying him not as one human being among others but as the Christ who is accepted by faith, the coming Kyrios-Son of Man who has already come. By the presentation of this story, the saving story of Jesus as the Christ qualified by its eschatological content, the Evangelists declare nothing else than that which was proclaimed in the early Christian kerygma from the beginning: "the Word became flesh" (John 1:14), or, in the traditional words of the early Christian kerygma: "Jesus has been raised" (1 Cor 15:4). The composition of the Gospels draws out from this kerygmatic sentence the consequence in view of the past, when it brings to expression: the Kyrios-Christ is a historical reality that can be presented in the literary form of the Gospel.

## b) The Problem of the Delay of the Parousia

Bornkamm, G. "Die Verzögerung der Parusie," In Memoriam Ernst Lohmeyer. Stuttgart: Evangelisches Verlagswerk, 1951, 116–126 also in G. Bornkamm, ed. Geschichte und Glaube I. Munich: Kaiser, 1968, 46–55).

Conzelmann, H. "Geschichte und Eschaton nach Mc. 13," ZNW 50 (1959) also in H. Conzelmann, ed., Theologie als Schriftauslegung. BEvTh 65 Munich: Kaiser, 1974, 62–73.

Grässer, E. Das Problem der Parusieverzögerung in den synoptischen Evangelien und in der Apostelgeschichte. BZNW 22. Berlin: W. de Gruyter, 1977 (Bib.).

Hölscher, G. "Der Ursprung der Apokalypse Mrk 13," ThBL 12 (1933) 193–202.

Kümmel, W.-G. Promise and Fulfillment: the Eschatological Message of Jesus. London: SCM, 1957.

Lambrecht, J. Die Redaktion der Markus-Apokalypse. AnBib 28. Rome: Biblical Institute Press, 1967.

Pesch, R. Naherwartungen. Tradition und Redaktion in Mk 13. Düsseldorf: Patmos, 1968.

Vielhauer Ph. and Strecker, G. "Apocalyptic in Early Christianity," W. Schneemelcher, ed. New Testament Apocrypha II. (rev. ed.). Louisville: Westminster John Knox, 1984, 569–602.

Walter, N. "Tempelzerstörung und synoptische Apokalypse," ZNW 57 (1966) 38–49.

Zmijewski, J. Die Eschatologiereden des Lukas-Evangeliums. BBB 40. Bonn: Hanstein, 1972.

According to Albert Schweitzer's work *The Mystery of the Kingdom of God: The Secret of Jesus' Messiahship and Passion* (originally published 1901; English translation London: Darton, Longman & Todd, 1914) and corresponding to his basic principle of "consistent eschatology," the proclamation of Jesus was essentially an announcement of the near end of the world, i.e. the imminent breaking in of the Kingdom of God. Moreover, Schweitzer concluded that Jesus had understood himself as the future, immediately-expected Messiah. This is also the basis for the messianic secret, the hiddenness of Jesus' Messiahship in his public ministry as presented in the Gospel of Mark. Furthermore, since Jesus wanted to induce the final events by means of a moral renewal, the teaching of Jesus, especially in the Sermon on the Mount, was nothing else than an "interim ethic," instruction devised for the transitional period between the two ages, an "ethical eschatology".[7] It follows from this that with the disap-

---

[7]    A. Schweitzer, *Das Messianitäts- und Leidensgeheimnis, eine Skizze des Lebens Jesu* (Tübingen: J. C. B. Mohr [Paul Siebeck], 1956) 28; cf. G. Strecker, "Strukturen

pointment of the near expectation and the refutation of Jesus' message that the end would come in his own generation, the substance of Christian faith had to be changed. While Martin Werner in his work *The Formation of Christian Dogma* attempted to draw the consequences for the history of dogma and advocated the thesis that the development of theological thinking in the course of history has meant essentially a de-eschatologizing of Christian faith,[8] one may also raise counter-questions. Much in early Christian tradition that has been attributed to reflection on the delay of the parousia is doubtless nothing other than the result of the historicization of Christian faith. After the dynamic beginnings, early Christianity in the course of its history had increasingly to deal with the problems of the time and the world. Nonetheless, one cannot doubt that the awareness of the delay of the parousia was not an insignificant element in the formation of early Christian tradition.

## 1. The Presynoptic Tradition

The importance of the themes "near expectation" and "delay of the parousia" should not be underestimated for the development of early Christian theology. The earliest Palestinian church existed in an atmosphere of acute near expectation, as indicated by the cry "Marana tha." So also the Hellenistic church in its beginning phase lived in the expectation that the end stood immediately before them, as illustrated by 1 Thessalonians 4. Thus originally the eschatological existence of the community, like that of the individual Christian, was conceived within the framework of the expectation of the near parousia. The eschaton was considered to be essentially a future reality, expected in the near future as an event bringing both threat and grace.

About the turn of the first to the second Christian generation at the latest, the problem of the delay became acute for the Christian communities. The question of when the expected end and the advent of the Kyrios-Son of Man would occur became unavoidable. This question became all the more burning to the extent that the community interpreted its eschatological existence in terms of the future, and less important to the extent

---

einer neutestamentlichen Ethik," ZThK 75 (1978) 117–146; 133 note 39; E. Grässer, *A. Schweitzer als Theologe* (BHTh 60. Tübingen: J. C. B. Mohr [Paul Siebeck], 1979); W. G. Kümmel, *The New Testament* 300: "As repentance in view of the coming Kingdom of God, the ethic of the Sermon on the Mount is also an interim ethic" (quoted from Schweitzer, *Messianitäts- und Leidensgeheimnis* 19); finally, directly appropriate: E. Grässer, "Zum Stichwort ‚Interimsethik'. Eine notwendige Korrektur," *Neues Testament und Ethik* (FS R. Schnackenburg) (Freiburg: Herder, 1989) 16–30.

8   M. Werner, *The Formation of Christian Dogma; An Historical Study of Its Problem* (New York, Harper. 1957).

that it was aware of the present, effective power of the Kyrios in its midst. It was thus especially the Palestinian church, and the churches on Hellenistic soil that contained a strong Palestinian Jewish-Christian impact, for whom the problem of the delay became important. This happened at the point in time when the death of the first generation leaders made questionable whether the first generation would in fact experience the parousia.

The problematic of the delay is reflected in some pericopes of the pre-Synoptic tradition. The parable of the ten bridesmaids (Matt 25:1–13) is a story tailored to the problem of the parousia. The distinction between the wise and foolish virgins corresponds to two possible attitudes in view of the parousia: the one group is not ready but the others are prepared to meet the bridegroom. V. 5 speaks explicitly of the delay of the bridegroom (χρονίζοντος δε τοῦ νυμφίου) and shows that the community which handed on this parable was plagued by the effort to find an answer to the pressing problem of the delay of the parousia. The answer: Be ready at any time! The arrival of the Kyrios must not find you unprepared. The delay of the parousia thus led to the formation of ethical admonitions. Correspondingly, the Synoptic apocalyptic tradition contains a series of parables and challenges to vigilance. Even if in individual cases the intent is not entirely clear, these parables and admonitions could have been generated by the problematic of the delay of the parousia.

A further example of this problematic is the saying

> When they persecute you in one town, flee to the next; for truly I tell you, you will not have gone through all the towns of Israel before the Son of Man comes (Matt 10:23).

This logion stands in the context of the mission speech of Jesus to his disciples. Two possibilities of interpretation present themselves: (1) It is a matter of a *mission logion* that describes the missionary situation of the Christian community, as already in Matthew 9:37–38. The saying would then mean that the mission to Israel would not be brought to a successful conclusion before the Son of Man comes—so near is the parousia! This interpretation, however, is less probable, for although Matthew does speak at the beginning of the chapter of the mission of the disciples, this is incorporated into the narrative of the past history of Jesus, and in Matthew 10:17 the Evangelist turns to the persecution situation of the church. The immediate context thus deals not with mission but with persecution. (2) Accordingly, what we have here is a *persecution logion*. The persecuted community is promised eschatological consolation. The flight from the persecutors will not have proceeded through all the cities of Israel before the Son of Man appears! The saying presupposes a Palestinian-Jewish situation. The near expectation is expressed relatively unambiguously but the reference to the coming of the Son of Man suggests the problem of the delay. The expectation of the near parousia of the Son of Man promises consolation for the persecuted community. In this manner early Christian prophets dispensed encouraging words.

Differently than in this logion, the consciousness of the delayed parousia obviously comes to acute expression in the saying:

> And he said to them, "Truly I tell you, there are some standing here who will not taste death until they see that the kingdom of God has come with power." (Mark 9:1; cf. Matt 16:28; Luke 9:27).

"Seeing the kingdom of God" is not to be spiritualized, and is not identical with "insight,"[9] but is to be interpreted realistically as meaning "see with one's own eyes." It is apparently a saying of an early Christian prophet. Here the delay of the end becomes tangible. If the community had originally expected that its generation as a whole would go forth to meet the returning Lord at his parousia, now it is only "some" (τινες) who are promised what the whole community originally expected: the experience of the parousia. Before the end comes, many will die. This community has already experienced the delay of the parousia but this does not mean that it has given up hope. The date of the end can be adjusted but the eschatological orientation of the community remains constant.

A similar situation is reflected in the saying found at the close of the Markan apocalypse:

> Truly I tell you, this generation (γενεὰ αὕτη) will not pass away until all these things have taken place (Mark 13:30; cf. Matt 24:34; Luke 21:32).

The expression γενεὰ αὕτη describes "this generation." Even though the expectation of the parousia is still maintained in this saying, it is clear at the same time that the expectation is no longer intact. The parousia is still expected for "this generation," but nothing is any longer said about everyone participating in it.

These examples show that the pre-Synoptic tradition reflected the problem of the delay of the parousia in different ways. With the passing of time the expectation of the parousia also experienced changes: from an unbroken near expectation to reflection on the appointed date. This conclusion regarding the pre-Synoptic traditional strata is to be distinguished from the situation of the Gospel redactors themselves.

## 2.   Mark

The Evangelist Mark essentially takes over the "Markan apocalypse" (Mark 13:5b-37) from the tradition. Apparently the nucleus of this chapter goes

---

[9]   C. H. Dodd, *The Parables of the Kingdom* (New York: Charles Scribners Sons, 1961) 37–38.

back to an original Jewish document[10] that originated in the first half of the first century C. E. This source was probably comprised of 13:7–8, 12, 14–20, 24–27. In view of the threatening events of the present, a pointer to the approaching end was explicitly expressed, a pointer to the advent of the Messiah—Son of Man who in dependence on the tradition in the book of Daniel was expected to appear as the savior of the Jewish people. This source document was reworked by adding a second traditional layer of Christian origin, comprised of 13:5b-6, 9, 11, 13, 21–22, 28–32, 34–36. This intermediate Christian layer included not only the portrayal of the terrors of the end time and the coming of the Son of Man but also warnings against false teaching, the announcement of persecutions that were to break in just before the end, warnings against false Messiahs and false prophets, concluding with the question of the date of the parousia. It is to this context that 13:30 ("this generation") belongs. The problem of the delay of the parousia is already recognizable in the Christian re-editing of the Jewish source. Precisely for this reason, the pre-Markan apocalypse obviously received a Christian editing in order to address this problem. The various images of the different preliminary signs of the parousia give the expectant community not only the necessary information but provide encouragement and motivate the admonition to remain alert (13:34–36).

The Evangelist Mark took over and reworked this tradition. The verses 13:10, 13, 23, 33and 37 are to be regarded as Markan. Differently than the parallel references,[11] Mark distinguishes two epochs: the present (13:5–13) and the future (13:14ff). Within the future epoch H. Conzelmann[12] demarcates two periods of time. While 13:14–23 portrays the final epoch of world history with its great terrors, the verses 13:24–27 have the cosmic catastrophe in view, with which the real eschaton, the supranatural parousia begins.[13] Among the redactional supplements named above 13:10 receives fundamental significance by its location and content:

And the good news must first be proclaimed to all nations.

This verse belongs to the epoch of the present, which is determined by the proclamation of the gospel to all nations. This proclamation is not related to the parousia in such wise that by the preaching of the gospel the

---

[10] G. Hölscher, *Ursprung*, speaks of a "Jewish leaflet;" cf. also R. Pesch, *Naherwartungen* 207–223.

[11] Synoptic comparison:

| Mark 13 | Matthew 24: future | Luke 21 |
|---|---|---|
| 5–13 present | 5–8 "beginning of the woes" | 8–24 past ("signs from heaven") |
|  |  | 9–28 "distress" |
| 14ff future | 29ff parousia | 25–28 future |
|  |  | ("signs in heaven") |

[12] Cf. H. Conzelmann, "Geschichte und Eschaton nach Mc. 13" 62–73.

[13] Cf. Ph. Vielhauer-G. Strecker, "Apocalyptic in Early Christianity" 579–581.

arrival of the parousia could be accelerated, but is to be taken literally: the present is distinguished from the coming parousia by the proclamation to all nations. The preaching of the gospel requires time for the message to be heard throughout the whole earth. This time has been extended. The end no longer stands in the immediate future; in any case, it is not so close as to make the worldwide preaching of the gospel impossible.

The present time is the time of persecution. Persecution breaks over the community because they belong to the Kyrios (13:13). Thus the admonition to remain steadfast to the end (13:13b). The awareness that the end is delayed leads to the formation of the parenetic instruction. The ethical instruction is determined by the delay of the parousia.[14]

The failure of the parousia to appear as originally expected leads to the instruction to attend to the signs of the times (13:23). As time continues to pass, the saying of Jesus gives direction on bridging the time of expectation to the very end. The time of the end is uncertain (13:33); it could be near but also could lie in the distant future. Thus the admonition: "Stay alert!" (γρηγορεῖτε) (13:37).

The influence of the consciousness of the delay is seen clearly in the redactional reworking of the Markan apocalypse. For Mark, the time of the end is undetermined. This makes it possible for Mark to take over the statements of 9:1 and 13:30, which originally specified "this generation," as the time appointed for the parousia, but also already reflected an uncertainty regarding the date and thus lets the problem of the delay be recognized.

It can hardly be determined to what extent the redactor has understood these sayings in their literal sense or reinterpreted them so that their meaning to him can no longer be reconstructed. It is possible that for Mark "this generation" (13:30) no longer referred to the contemporaries of Jesus but to the human race in general. In any case, Mark is no longer primarily oriented to a particular point in time but to the uncertainty of the date of the end. This enables him to integrate sayings into his Gospel that express both the expectation of the near end and those that indicate only a distant expectation.

## 3. Matthew

The First Evangelist understood the Synoptic apocalypse essentially as a succession of two epochs: Matthew 24:5–8 speaks of the ἀρχὴ ὠδίνων ("the beginning of the labor pains"), 24:9–28 of the epoch of θλίψις ("persecu-

---

[14]  The term τέλος (13:13) perhaps designates in the Markan understanding not the "end" of the world but possibly the end of human life, so that an indefinite future prior to the coming of the Kyrios could be in view.

tion") followed by the parousia (24:29ff). In contrast to the Markan parallel it is striking that the Matthean apocalypse does not refer to the present and does not reflect Matthew's own time.[15] This becomes clear from the rearrangement made by the First Evangelist: Mark 13:9b, 11–12 has been transferred to Matthew 10:17–21. The distress and challenge of the present is no longer explicated in the Matthean apocalypse. The "beginning of the labor pains" (Matt 24:8) no longer refers, as in Mark, to the present situation of the community but has a purely future character. This corresponds to the future tense μελλήσετε (24:6): the signs of the parousia (wars and rumors of wars) still lie in the future. By viewing apocalyptic events as distinct from the present, the Matthean community understands itself as no longer living in the time of the final apocalyptic drama.

Matthew 24:14 takes up Mark 13:10 but replaces the Markan δεῖ ("it is necessary") with the verb form κηρυχθήσεται ("will be preached"). This use of the future tense confirms that the events spoken of still lie in the future and emphasizes that the preaching of the gospel is an event that must continue in the future. In addition, the universal scope of this proclamation is explicated by the phrase ἐν τῇ ὅλῃ οἰκουμένῃ ("in the whole world"). This corresponds to the commission given by the Risen One to the disciples to make disciples of all nations (28:19). This assignment will be achieved before the end of the world. This corresponds to the Matthean εἰς μαρτύριον πᾶσιν τοῖς ἔθνεσιν (24:14): the proclamation results in a witness for or against all nations. The proclamation of the church is oriented toward the time of the end. Judgment and grace, salvation and disaster will be manifested over the world of nations at the end time.

Matthew has accordingly emphasized the pure futurity of the eschatological events. Time marches on, the end no longer stands in the immediate future. To be sure, Matthew, like Mark, was also able to incorporate sayings in which the near expectation can be perceived, partly in connection with the problematic of the delay: the saying about the flight of persecuted missionaries through the cities of Israel (10:23) has already been mentioned. The question here is, what does this saying mean in the context of the theology of the First Evangelist? Is Matthew perhaps not thinking of the cities of Palestine but more generally of the cities with a Jewish population throughout the world? If so, then this saying too allows for an extension of time. Obviously the possibility also exists that in such

---

[15] It is characteristic for Matthew that he also makes temporal distinctions in the introductory verses. Jesus does not respond directly to the disciples question "When will this be?" (24:3b), which refers to the prediction of the temple's destruction but speaks only of the coming of the Son of Man and the end of the age (24:3c). For Matthew, the destruction of the temple is an event that already lies in the past (cf. 22:7).

sayings the redactor merely included them as part of the larger context without associating any specific interpretation with them.[16]

Alongside these instances that document the original near expectation stand others that clearly express that the community must reckon with a continuation of history for some time. Thus the parable of the talents says "After a long time (μετὰ δὲ πολὺν χρόνον) the master of those slaves came and settled accounts with them" (Matt 25:19; contra Luke 19:15). This is a redactional addition of Matthew, who along with his community reckons with the possibility that the parousia will not occur for a long time to come. This is made clear by the arrangement of the Gospel as a whole, in which a tendency toward institutionalization of the church can be detected (e.g. 18:15–18). Of course it is also the case that here too the date itself is still unknown: "Keep awake therefore, for you know neither the day nor the hour" (25:13). As in Mark, the uncertainty of the date leads to a combination of the views that the end can be expected in the near or distant future. However, Matthew's method of composing his Gospel demonstrates that he has adjusted much more than Mark to the prolongation of time.

### 4. Luke

The Gospel of Luke contains two portrayals of the apocalyptic events. Luke 17:20–37 has extensive parallels in Matthew 24:26–28, 37ff (= the Q apocalypse) and contains announcements about the future just as does the Matthean parallel. The passage 21:8–36 (par Mark 13:5–32) is different. Here Luke has intervened to make changes in the Markan apocalypse by historicizing the main part of Jesus' apocalyptic speech. The decisive intervention is located between verses 24 and 25: Luke, in contrast to Mark, refers the preceding portrayal neither to the events of the present, nor to future events but to the past—concretely to the events immediately preceding the destruction of Jerusalem and the catastrophe itself. Luke 21:20–24 is a description of the fall of Jerusalem in the form of a "vaticinium ex eventu." Though the Third Evangelist includes that event, which lies in his own past, in Jesus' apocalyptic speech, the circumstances that led to the fall of Jerusalem are in any case for him not eschatological events but belong to the historical past to which Luke looks back: messianic pretenders, wars, famines and other worldly terrors (21:8–11), persecution of the Christian community (21:12–19). And while these are all "signs," even signs "from heaven" (21:11 ἀπ᾽ οὐρανοῦ σημεῖα μεγάλα), they

---

[16] Here possibly only in the sense of the general motif of encouragement: the Son of Man will come, and distress and persecution play a role in preparing for the end. A similar problem is posed by the logia 16:28 (par Mark 9:1) and 24:34 (par Mark 13:30).

are still earthly phenomena that can be interpreted as signs that precede and lead to the destruction of Jerusalem. Among these signs are false prophets who claim to be Christ and try to persuade folk that the end is near (21:8). In contrast, Luke views this period of history as a time which has not yet come and the final period of history is still future.

The portrayal of the parousia does not begin until 21:25–28. Cosmic signs in the sky (21:25 σημεῖα ἐν ἡλίῳ καὶ σελήνῃ και ἄστροις) introduce the final drama. Here Luke brings forth a "locus de novissimis" (ultimate temporal period) according to which Luke structures his apocalyptic tradition. But it is still the case that such a perspective on the future has implications for responsibility in the present in that it provides motivation for ethical parenesis and grounds the admonition to be alert (21:36).

Such historicization of the original apocalyptic tradition is based on the fact that Luke, more strongly than the other two Synoptic Evangelists, reckons with the continuation of history. This is seen, for example, in Luke 20:9, where the owner of the vineyard leaves the country "for a long time" (χρόνους ἱκανούς). Luke thereby interprets his Markan source, reckoning with the possibility of an extended period before the end. He thus agrees with the general Synoptic view. Since the date of the end is unknown, the challenge is still valid: "You also must be ready, for the Son of Man is coming at an unexpected hour" (12:40).

From all the above two inferences may be made for understanding the problem of the delay of the parousia in the Synoptic Gospels:

(1) For the Synoptic Gospels there is no acute problem of the delay of the parousia. The layer of tradition that reflects a struggle concerning the problem of whether the promises were true and whether the earliest Christian eschatological expectation was true or false reflects a time that is now past. Though this concern did come to expression in the pre-Synoptic tradition, the redactional element of the Synoptics gives no indication of being pressed or plagued by the question of the delay of the parousia. The problematic of the delay is the presupposition, not the subject matter, for the composition of the Synoptic Gospels. It is rather the case that the Synoptic Evangelists hold fast to the conviction that the time of the parousia is unknown. In their conception there is room for both the near and distant expectation. Since the Synoptics presuppose the problematic of the delay, that of course means at the same time that they are also indirectly affected by the problem of the parousia. For early Christian faith, the fact of the delay brings into view the question of "time" and "space." If the earliest Christian hope for the near end of history could ignore the matter of time (and in a certain sense also the "world"), then with the awareness of the continuation of history there came the task of orienting itself within time and space. Faith thereby faced the question of how its original orientation to the eschaton could still be affirmed even though it is now compelled to live in the historical arena of world and time. This

task, the question of the right relation of history and eschaton, had not been settled in the pre-Synoptic tradition. It was to this task that the redactors of the Gospels set themselves.

(2) The literature often expresses the achievement of the Evangelists with regard to the delay of the parousia by explaining that the Synoptics, or at least Luke, apparently brought about a deeschatologization of the traditional material. Is the incorporation of the original apocalyptic-eschatological traditional material into history in fact appropriately described as "de-eschatologization?" Although Luke has especially emphasized the historical dimension, one cannot ascertain that he has also carried out a deeschatologization of the tradition. On the contrary, Acts 2:17 shows that Luke understands the church to be existing "in the last days." The eschatological element is thus not to be bracketed out either for the past or for the present but orientation to the eschaton remains constitutive for Christian existence despite the change in the expectation of the parousia. The Evangelists did not want to eliminate the eschatological element in the testimony of faith (i.e., they did not want to write only history) but they wanted to interpret it. This means that the Synoptic Evangelists let us perceive a structural change in eschatological self-understanding. It is not the elimination of eschatological self-understanding, but its restructure, that is characteristic for the time of the Gospel writers. Despite the change that had occurred, faith remained true to itself, and faith's claim continued to be what it in fact is—an eschatological phenomenon. We must now inquire how this claim has been given shape in the Gospels.

c)  The Term εὐαγγέλιον

Dormeyer, D. *Evangelium als literarische und theologische Gattung.* Darmstadt: Wissenschaftliche Buchgesellschaft, 1989.
Frankemölle, H. *Evangelium. Begriff und Gattung.* SBB 15. Stuttgart: Katholisches Bibelwerk, 1988.
Friedrich, G. "εὐαγγελίζομαι" etc.., TDNT II, 705–735.
Marxsen, W. *Mark the Evangelist; Studies on the Redaction History of the Gospel.* Nashville: Abingdon, 1969.
Schniewind, J. *Euangelion, Ursprung und erste Gestalt des Begriffs Evangelium.* BFChTh.M 13.35. Gütersloh: Gerd Mohn, 1927, 1931.
Strecker, G. "εὐαγγέλιον," EWNT II, 176–186.
Strecker, G. "Das Evangelium Jesu Christi," G. Strecker, ed. *Jesus Christus in Historie und Theologie* (FS H. Conzelmann) Tübingen: J. C. B. Mohr (Paul Siebeck), 1975, 503–548; also in G. Strecker, ed., *Eschaton und Historie*, 183–228.
Strecker, G." Literarkritische Überlegungen zum εὐαγγέλιον-Begriff im Markusevangelium," (FS O. Cullmann) H. Baltensweiler and B. Reicke, eds. *Neues Testament und Geschichte.* Zürich: Theologischer Verlag, 1972, 91–104; also in G. Strecker, *Eschaton und Historie*, 76–89.
Stuhlmacher, P. *Das paulinische Evangelium, I. Vorgeschichte.* FRLANT 95. Göttingen: Vandenhoeck & Ruprecht, 1968.

## 1. The Presynoptic Tradition

(α) The term εὐαγγέλιον was already present in the Hellenistic world prior to the beginning of Christianity. With the transition from Palestinian to Hellenistic Christianity the pagan term was adopted by Christian faith. It thus corresponds to faith's belonging to the world that faith must speak the language of the world in order to make itself understood. In the process of doing so, the specifically Christian element in distinction from secular usage becomes recognizable, which can be emphasized by juxtaposing New Testament statements with the use of the word in nonchristian contexts.

In secular Greek usage εὐαγγέλιον was originally the "victory message," i.e. the announcement of victory from the battlefield. The bearer of such a message received a reward. This led to the derived meaning "reward" for the one who brought the message (as in Hom Od 14.152–153).

In the honors paid to Hellenistic rulers, and following them the Roman emperors, εὐαγγέλιον received an additional cultic meaning. As a θεῖος ἄνθρωπος ("divine man"), what the emperor did and said could become the content of the εὐαγγέλιον. Thus the announcement of his having come of legal age, or his ascent to the throne, and especially the birth of the successor to the throne, could be considered εὐαγγέλιον. This is what is referred to in the famous inscription from Priene 105.40–41 (Asia Minor):

ἦρξεν δὲ τῶι κόσμωι τῶν δι᾽ αὐτὸν εὐανγελίων ἡ γενέθλιος τοῦ θεοῦ (OGIS 458).
The birthday of the god was for the world the beginning of the good news that has gone forth because of him.

Afterwards the term referred to the announcement of the emperor's birthday as the "message of good news." This message had a universal significance; it was valid throughout the empire; even the cosmos was influenced by this message, for it meant peace and well being for the whole world.

When early Christian faith took up this term it was in order to express its own characteristic message: the content of the faith is good news, like the content of the honors paid to the emperor in the cult of the divine Caesar. It refers to a divine event that is valid for the whole world. A distinctive characteristic, however, is that in the New Testament the term is never found in the plural but only in the singular. The Caesar cult can speak of different εὐαγγέλια related to the advent of the ruler and that from case to case can refer to different times and be attached to different persons. The Christian tradition is different; it uses the term in a singular manner. Faith knows and acknowledges only one εὐαγγέλιον, only one message that is founded on the Christ event. At the same time, in individual instances is to be asked whether the prefix εὐ- is still thought of as influencing the meaning of the word, for the message announces not only grace but also judgment (cf. Mark 1:14–15).

(β) In the Masoretic text of the Old Testament the linguistic term nearest to the religious usage of εὐαγγέλιον in Hellenism is the verb בָּשַׂר, which has primarily a secular meaning but can also be translated as "proclaim" (the message of Yahweh). Correspondingly the derived substantive מְבַשֵּׂר (Isaiah 41:27; 52:7 = "good news"). It was thus taken up by New Testament authors (e. g. Luke 4:1:18; Matt 11:5 par Luke 7:22). This applies only to the verb, however. The substantive בְּשֹׂרָה does not have a theological significance in the Old Testament but merely a neutral meaning (cf. 2 Sam 4:10: "reward for the messenger;" 2 Kings 7:9: "good news"). The term εὐαγγέλιον appears in the LXX with the same meaning as its Hebrew equivalent but only in the plural (2 Kings 4:10 LXX). The feminine ἡ εὐαγγελία is also found with the meaning "good news" (2 Kings 18:20, 22, 25, 27 LXX; 4 Kings 7:9 LXX: "good news"). These linguistic data provide no possibility for deriving the usage of the New Testament exclusively from the Old Testament.

(γ) The word appears in the Pauline letters 52 times, more than half of which are used absolutely. Frequently the meaning is qualified by adding the genitive τοῦ Χριστοῦ (e. g. 1 Cor 9:12; Rom 15:19). In such cases it is essentially a matter of an "objective genitive" (the message about Jesus Christ), even when this cannot be absolutely separated from the "subjective genitive" (the message of the Risen One who has commissioned his apostles).[17]

Paul uses a terminology which had already been shaped in the missionary enterprise of the Hellenistic church. Accordingly the content of the gospel is the bipartite confession of the "living and true God" united with the expectation of the coming Son of God as the "savior" (cf. 1 Thess 1:5 with 1:9b-10). So also according to 1 Corinthians 15:1–2 the (christological) confession, namely the saving significance of the death and resurrection of Christ, is to be regarded as an essential element of the "gospel" (1 Cor 15:3b-5a). The content of the "gospel of God", which is identical with the "gospel of the Son" (Rom 1:1, 9), is the Davidic sonship of the earthly Jesus and the divine sonship of the Risen One; thus it has been previously announced by God's prophets in the Holy Scriptures (Rom 1:2–4).

Thus if the christological interpretation of the term is to be presupposed as already present in the pre-Pauline Hellenistic Christian missionary churches, this corresponds to the usage in the Pauline letters themselves: εὐαγγέλιον describes the doctrinal content of the gospel that was entrusted to the apostle to be proclaimed (1 Thess 2:4). This is referred to from case to case according to the context in each letter by the expression ἐν κυρίῳ/Χριστῷ, which contains the tension between the "already" and the "not yet." This phrase announces eschatological salvation that already happens in an anticipatory manner in the gift of the Spirit (1 Thess 1:5;

---

[17]   Cf. also A. III. c. 1 above.

4:8; 5:19). While in 1 Corinthians the instances of εὐαγγέλιον are mostly subordinated to the parenetic-ethical goal (cf. 1 Cor 9:12ff), 2 Corinthians basically reflects Paul's commission to preach the gospel in comparison with the claims of his opponents (cf. 11:1ff). In Galatians, however, Paul develops his gospel as the message of justification, namely that the Christ-event as the content of the gospel overcomes human legal righteousness and grounds life in the "grace of God" (Gal 1:11; 2:19–21). The "truth of the gospel" is experienced as the justification of the sinner (2:5, 14). The Letter to the Romans further develops the link between the gospel and the preaching of justification that had been made in Galatians. While Paul's preaching is grounded on the Christ kerygma (in addition to Rom 1:3–4 cf. also 15:19), the gospel still has not only an salvation-history horizon (1:1–2) but also has a universal orientation: for every believer God's justifying act has a saving reality by the εὐαγγέλιον (1:16–17). Alongside this, the proclamation of judgment according to one's works is also included in the content of the gospel (2:16). Finally, the two prison letters to the Philippians and Philemon show that inherent in the gospel is the power to create fellowship between the apostle and the church; the suffering of the apostle serves to spread the gospel (Phil 1:5, 12; 2:22; 4:3, 15; Phlm 13). The gospel provides the norm for the conduct of the church and maintains the unity of the faith (Phil 1:27). In general it must be stated that εὐαγγέλιον in the Pauline letters denotes not only a doctrinal content but also as a "nomen actionis" (noun of action) portrays of the church-founding preaching of Paul in action (cf. 1 Thess 1:5 and elsewhere!).

## 2. Mark

The term εὐαγγέλιον plays a central role in the Gospel of Mark. If one disregards the secondary titular superscription[18] and the post-Markan conclusion (Mark 16:15), then all seven instances are to be attributed to the redactor Mark (1:1, 14–15; 8:35; 10:29; 13:10; 14:9).[19] For Mark also,

---

[18] The titular superscripts of the Synoptic Gospels, e. g. εὐαγγέλιον κατὰ Μᾶρκον, are secondary, since it was only after the New Testament period that a book was designated by the word "Gospel" (Iren Haer 4.20.6; Diogn 11.6; ClemAlex Strom 1.136.1–2). Contra M. Hengel, "The Titles of the Gospels and the Gospel of Mark," in *Studies in the Gospel of Mark* (Philadelphia: Fortress, 1985) 64–84. Cf. F. Bovon, "The Synoptic Gospels and the Non-Canonical Acts of the Apostles," *HThR* 81 (1988) 19–32; 22–23, who also opposes Hengel's view.

[19] This is especially disputed with regard to Mark 1:14–15. The terms are used in a manner unusual for Mark (1:14c εὐαγγέλιον τοῦ θεοῦ; 1:15c πιστεύετε ἐν τῷ εὐαγγελίῳ); however, one should also reckon with the influence of the LXX on Mark. Cf. G. Strecker, "Literarkritische Überlegungen" 94ff; cf. also Strecker, *History of New Testament Literature* 92–95; contra G. Dautzenberg, "Der Wandel in der Reich-Gottes-Verkündigung in der urchristlichen Mission," in Dautzenberg et al., eds., *Zur Geschichte des Urchristentums* (QD 87) Freiburg: Herder, 1979) 11–32.

it is clear that the term εὐαγγέλιον and the person of Christ belong most closely together and that the christological tradition of the Hellenistic church stands in the background (cf. esp. 1:1; 14:9). If accordingly the genitive τοῦ Χριστοῦ is to be understood primarily in the objective sense in the tradition of the Hellenistic church and Paul, Mark in contrast interprets the genitive primarily in the subjective sense: Jesus is the preacher of the gospel (1:14–15). The first sentence of the Second Gospel ἀρχὴ τοῦ εὐαγγελίου Ἰησοῦ Χριστοῦ should accordingly be understood as "The beginning of the good news brought by Jesus Christ." There can hardly be any doubt that the sentence refers to the (good) news that Jesus brings (= "subjective genitive"), since according to 1:14–15 Jesus is the preacher of the gospel, which has as its content that the time is fulfilled and the kingdom of God has come near. The challenge to repentance and faith follows from this. Just as the Markan Jesus is the preacher (rather than the content) of the good news, so this good news has as its content the eschatological fulfillment of time and the near approach of the eschaton. The appearance of John the Baptist prepares for this proclamation of Jesus Christ, and is thus its beginning (1:1). If accordingly 1:1 is primarily to be understood in the subjective genitive sense, in 13:10 and 14:9 an objective sense is not to be excluded as also present. Mark 8:35 and 10:29 can be understood as expressing both the preaching of Christ and the preaching of Christians.

Mark's teaching presents a "sharp curve" away from Christ's own preaching toward the church's preaching of Christ, in order to allow the church to orient itself to the picture of the Son of God/Son of Man who has already accomplished his ministry in the historical past.[20] In the Gospel of Mark, however, the concept εὐαγγέλιον is not only incorporated into history but is also interpreted in an apocalyptic sense. It is not Jesus' preaching taken by itself that is the "fulfillment of time;" it is rather the case that Jesus' preaching announces the future kingdom of God (1:15 ἤγγικεν = "has come near"). So also 8:35 has an apocalyptic orientation. Since one's conduct with regard to Jesus is identified with one's conduct with regard to the gospel, this equation is decisive for one's acceptance or rejection at the last judgment.

If Mark makes no terminological distinction between the gospel preached by Jesus and the post-Easter gospel proclaimed by the church, it is still the case that he regards the church's preaching of the gospel (13:10; 14:9) as originating in the word of Jesus. This includes the challenge to take up one's cross and follow (8:34). Thereby the cross of Jesus does not become the exclusive criterion for interpreting the εὐαγγέλιον but the concretion of the comprehensive motif of the hiddenness of the revealer, a hiddenness that is partially resolved at Easter and points for its final

---

[20]  Compare 8:35 with 8:38: "Whoever is ashamed of me and my words...".

resolution to the parousia (cf. 9:1, 9 and elsewhere). The persecuted disciples are promised an eschatological future (10:29–30), and the gospel that according to 13:10 is made the church's assignment, as an element of the "eschatological woes" (13:8) is itself an apocalyptic event. After the cross and resurrection of Jesus it is proclaimed to Jews and Gentiles; it is realized precisely in the suffering and persecution of the community as anticipation and announcement of the coming kingdom of God.

## 3.  Matthew

In most instances, the First Evangelist follows Mark's usage of the εὐαγγέλιον terminology in both frequency and content. To the extent that deviations are present at all, these are motivated by the subject matter: Mark 1:1 is replaced as the beginning of the Gospel by the genealogy and birth story; Mark 8:35 and 10:29 would have softened the Matthean emphasis on the person of Jesus; the content of Mark 1:14–15 recurs in Matthew 4:23 and 9:35. Unlike Mark, Matthew never uses the term εὐαγγέλιον absolutely but adds the genitive τῆς βασιλείας (4:23; 9:35; 24:14) or augments the term by the demonstrative pronoun τοῦτο (24:14; 26:13). Matthew appears to have found the term already in public use, and reflects the Greek-Hellenistic usage:

> According to W. Marxsen,[21] however, the difference between the Matthean and Markan usage is explained by the fact that for Matthew εὐαγγέλιον does not mean the message of Jesus but "speech complex." For example the Sermon on the Mount is a εὐαγγέλιον. This modification of the concept would have occasioned the addition of the demonstrative pronoun. Against this explanation is the fact that Matthew never uses the plural εὐαγγέλια. In addition, the final example (26:13) does not stand in the context of a speech complex but in the passion story and has a "narrative" connotation.

Moreover, the First Gospel also uses the term to mean the (good)news in the same way as Mark, without defining it any more precisely. By combining it with the term κηρύσσω (4:23; 9:35; 24:14; 26:13 par Mark 14:19), the word is related to the preaching of Jesus even more strongly than in Mark. It deals with Jesus' message of the coming kingdom of God. No distinction is to be made between the preaching and teaching of Jesus. The proclaimer is at the same time the subject of the message. This is inserted into the temporal frame of the life of Jesus, for the eschatological salvation of which this message speaks has come into history within the time framed by the birth and resurrection of Jesus—a salvific past that points to a salvific future. The gospel preached by Jesus contains ethical demands *and* eschatological instruction, and addresses both church and world (cf. 28:18–20).

---

[21]   W. Marxsen, *Mark the Evangelist* 124 and elsewhere.

## 4.  Luke

It is characteristic of the Third Evangelist that the term εὐαγγέλιον is
avoided in his Gospel. It is found only twice in Acts, where it is a technical
term for the apostolic preaching and refers to the proclamation of the
apostles among the Gentiles (Acts 15:7; 20:24). This modification excludes the possibility of using the term for the preaching of Jesus, all the
more so since the apostolic preaching in Acts is not understood as a repetition of the preaching of Jesus but as grounded on and determined by the
cross and resurrection of Jesus Christ. Luke thus makes a terminological
distinction between Jesus' own preaching and the church's preaching about
Jesus. He is conscious of the distance between his time and the time of
Jesus. Historical time has continued, the traditional material is dismantled, and distinctions can be made between different epochs of the proclamation.

This is also reflected in the usage of the verb εὐαγγελίζομαι.[22] This
term, which the Q-source had already used for the preaching of Jesus (Luke
7:22 par Matt 11:5), is taken over by Luke and developed in an independent fashion. In Luke, when the verb is used with reference to Jesus, it refers
to Jesus' preaching, not to his advent (e. g. Luke 4:18, 43; 8:1; 20:1). Only
in Acts does the life of Jesus become the subject of "preaching" (e. g. Acts
17:18). Here too there is accordingly a distinction made between Jesus and
the community, the preaching of Jesus and the preaching of the church.
The Synoptic Evangelists do not want simply to reproduce the preaching
of the church but they present a report, a narrative about Jesus. As the
Third Evangelist shows in the example of Acts, from this point of view a
starting point for the preaching of the church is provided, with regard both
to its time and its content.

The Synoptic Evangelists agree in their claim that what they report has
an eschatological significance. They present a message that extends beyond the world and history, even though it has appeared within history.
It deals with the message of the Christ, which has Christ himself as its
subject matter. The report of the Evangelists contains this message, and
the message appears in the form of report. In both, the word binding on
the community occurs as event.

---

[22]  Passive: Luke 16:16; predominately with accusative object: Luke 1:19; 2:10; 3:18
and elsewhere.

# II. Secret Epiphany—The Evangelist Mark

Brandenburger, E. *Markus 13 und die Apokalyptik*. FRLANT 134 Göttingen: Vandenhoeck & Ruprecht, 1984.

Dschulnigg, P. *Sprache, Redaktion und Intention des Markus-Evangeliums*. SBB 11. Stuttgart: Katholisches Bibelwerk, 1986.

Fendler, F. *Studien zum Markusevangelium*. GTA 49. Göttingen: Vandenhoeck & Ruprecht, 1991.

Gnilka, J. *Das Evangelium nach Markus*. EKK II/1+2. Neukirchen-Vluyn: Neukirchener, 1986[2], 1989[3].

Hahn, F., ed. *Der Erzähler des Evangeliums. Methodische Neuansätze in der Markusforschung*. SBS 118/119. Stuttgart: Katholisches Bibelwerk, 1985.

Kertelge, K. *Die Wunder Jesu im Markusevangelium*. StANT 23. Munich: Kösel, 1970.

Koch, D. A. *Die Bedeutung der Wundererzählungen für die Christologie des Markusevangeliums*. BZNW 42. Berlin-New York: W. de Gruyter, 1975.

Kuhn, H.-W. *Ältere Sammlungen im Markusevangelium*. StUNT 8. Göttingen: Vandenhoeck & Ruprecht, 1970.

Kuhn, H.-W. "Neuere Wege in der Synoptiker-Exegese am Beispiel des Markusevangeliums," *Bilanz und Perspektiven gegenwärtiger Auslegung des Neuen Testaments*, F. W. Horn, ed. BZNW 75. Berlin-New York: W. de Gruyter, 1995, 60–90.

Lührmann, D. *Das Markus-Evangelium*. HNT 3. Tübingen: J. C. B. Mohr (Paul Siebeck), 1987.

Marxsen, W. *Mark the Evangelist:Studies in the Redaction History of the Gospel*. Nashville: Abingdon, 1969.

Pesch, R. *Das Markusevangelium*. HThK II/1+2. Freiburg: Herder, 1989, 1991.

Pokorný, P. "Das Markus-Evangelium," ANRW II 25.3 (1985) 1969–2035.

Rau, G. "Das Markus-Evangelium," ANRW II 25.3. (1985) 2036–2257.

Robinson, J. M. *Messiasgeheimnis und Geschichtsverständnis*. TB 81. Munich: Kaiser, 1989.

Robinson, J. M. *The Problem of History in Mark. Studies in Biblical Theology*. London: SCM Press Ltd., 1962.

Robinson, J. M. *The Problem of History in Mark and Other Marcan Studies*. Philadelphia: Fortress Press, 1982.

Schmithals, W. *Das Evangelium nach Markus*. ÖTK 2/1+2. Gütersloh: Gerd Mohn, 1986[2].

Vielhauer, Ph. "Erwägungen zur Christologie des Markusevangeliums," Ph. Vielhauer, ed. *Aufsätze zum Neuen Testament*. TB 31. Munich: Kaiser, 1965, 199–214.

Weeden, Th. J. *Mark—Traditions in Conflict*. Philadelphia: Fortress, 1971.

## a) The Messianic Secret Theory

Blevins, J. L. *The Messianic Secret in Markan Research, 1901–1976*. Washington: University Press of America, 1981.

Ebeling, H. J. *Das Messiasgeheimnis und die Botschaft des Markus-Evangelisten*. BZNW 19. Berlin: W. de Gruyter, 1939.

Horstmann, M. *Studien zur markinischen Christologie*. NTA 6. Münster: 1973.

Kingsbury, J. D. *The Christology of Mark's Gospel*. Philadelphia: Fortress, 1983.

Luz, U. "Das Geheimnismotiv und die markinische Christologie," ZNW 56 (1965) 9–30.

Räisänen, H. *The "Messianic Secret" in Mark*. Edinburgh: T. & T. Clark.
Räisänen, H. *Die Parabeltheorie im Markusevangelium*. SFEG 26. Helsinki: Finnische Exegetischen Gesellschaft, 1973.
Schweizer, E. "Die theologische Leistung des Markus," *EvTh* 24 (1964) 337–355.
Schweizer, E. "Zur Frage des Messiasgeheimnisses bei Markus," *ZNW* 56 (1965) 1–8.
Strecker, G. "Zur Messiasgeheimnistheorie im Markusevangelium," G. Strecker, ed. *Eschaton und Historie. Aufsätze*. Göttingen: Vandenhoeck & Ruprecht, 1979, 33–51.
Tuckett,Ch. M. *The Messianic Secret*. Philadelphia-London: Fortress, 1983.
Weber, R. "Christologie und ‚Messiasgeheimnis' im Markusevangelium. Eine redaktionsgeschichtliche Untersuchung," Diss. theol., Marburg 1981.
Weber, R. "Christologie und ‚Messiasgeheimnis': Ihr Zusammenhang und Stellenwert in den Darstellungsintentionen des Markus," *EvTh* 43 (1983) 108–125.
Wrede, W. *The Messianic Secret*. Cambridge and London: James Clarke, 1971.

## 1. The Textual Data: Revelation and Hiddenness

Martin Dibelius described the Gospel of Mark as the "book of secret epiphanies."[1] In fact the Gospel of Mark is indeed characterized by a specific theory that sets it apart from all the other Gospels: the idea of the messianic secret. The Markan Jesus is the hidden Christ; his proclamation occurs far from the public's hearing. His intention is to remain hidden. The reaction of those who hear his words corresponds to this; they hear but do not understand. That is also true of Jesus' own disciples; in Mark's story they stand in the presence of Jesus' preaching and teaching without comprehension. This is what is affirmed by the theory that affirms that along with all this concealment, revelation nonetheless occurs: the twin motifs of revelation and hiddenness are the structural elements of the secrecy theory.

The *revelatory motif* is expressed in different ways. It occurs for the first time in the heavenly voice at the baptism (1:11 "you are my beloved Son") and continues with the preaching of Jesus: "The time is fulfilled, the kingdom of God has come near" (1:15), is taken up by the confession of Peter (8:29 "You are the Christ"), and is further portrayed in, for example, the epiphanic event of the transfiguration (9:2ff), miraculous healings (2:1ff; 10:46ff), and teaching in parables (4:1ff and elsewhere). The revelatory event is expressed in a variety of ways, conditioned by Mark's adoption of individual traditions. The revelation of the Messiah is not determined by a particular form of expression but varies from case to case depending on the perspective and intent of each unit. The constant factor, however, is the basic confession: this one is the Christ!

In contrast, the *secrecy motif* is expressed more formally, in material that may be arranged under topical headings. Especially important are Jesus' commands to silence. In the narrative traditions that report the

---

[1]    M. Dibelius, *From Tradition to Gospel* 230.

healing of people possessed by demons who recognize him as the Son of God, it is said that Jesus did not permit the demons to speak "for they knew him" (1:34). In confronting the demons who recognize him, Jesus uses his power as exorcist to command silence (3:11–12). While this can be a stylistic element of stories of exorcisms and thus supposedly belongs to the pre-redactional tradition, this same motif is found in the redactional work of Mark: the hiddenness of the Messiah may not be penetrated either by demons or by the disciples. Thus epiphany scenes are followed by commands to silence: after Peter's confession at Caesarea Philippi (8:30 "he sternly warned them not to tell anyone about him"), or after the transfiguration on the mountain (9:9 "he ordered them to tell no one about what they had seen, until the Son of Man had risen from the dead"). The commands to silence addressed to the disciples—like those addressed to those who had been healed—are to be attributed to Markan redaction;[2] they accompany the epiphany of the Christ and give it its distinctive character. Although one may distinguish between broken commands to silence in the context of healing stories and unbroken commands to silence in the exorcism stories,[3] the emphasis remains on the unity of the motif.

Parallel to Jesus' intention to maintain the secret nature of his revelation stands the disciples' misunderstanding. Though this misunderstanding is in part pre-redactional (8:32–33; 9:5–6; 14:37ff), found alongside these are redactional insertions of this motif (9:10; 14:40b). A clear example is the comment on the disciples lack of understanding in the story of walking on the water (6:52 "for they did not understand about the loaves, for their hearts were hardened").[4]

The predictions of Jesus' passion and resurrection are an example of how the two structural elements of the secrecy theory are woven together (8:31–33; 9:30–32; 10:32–34), forming a structuring principle for the Gospel as a whole. In each case Jesus' declaration is made in the presence of his disciples and expresses the messianic revelation (8:31; 9:31; 10:33–34). But alongside this stands the secrecy motif (8:30, command to silence; 9:30, Jesus' intent to remain hidden; 10:32, the separation of the twelve). The motif of the disciples lack of comprehension also belongs here (8:32, Peter's menacing response to Jesus, because he fails to comprehend the meaning of Jesus' declaration; 9:32, general lack of understanding; 10:35ff, redactional addition to the pericope with the request of the sons of Zebedee).

---

[2]   On the attempt of H. Räisänen to prove that the commands to silence belong to the pre-Markan tradition, cf. F. Fendler, *Studien* 126–127, 133 and B. Kollmann, "Jesu Schweigegebote an die Dämonen," *ZNW* 82 (1991) 267–273.

[3]   On U. Luz "Secrecy Motif" cf. also F. Fendler, *Studien* 129–130.

[4]   Cf. also 7:18; 8:17–21 (disciples lack of understanding); 10:24 (dismay of the disciples).

## 2. Topological Conceptions; the Parable Theory

It is not rare for the messianic secret to be expressed in Mark by means of specific topological conceptions that articulate the secrecy theory in a stereotypical manner. Thus ἡ ἔρημος τόπος indicates Jesus' place of prayer (1:35), or the place of testing (1:12), or the place where Jesus has withdrawn but where people go in order to come in contact with him. It is accordingly a matter of a place where an epiphany occurs, and the same is true of the term ὁδός. It thus follows that Peter's confession occurred ἐν ὁδῷ; in 9:33–34 the disciples are portrayed as with Jesus "on the way;" and in 10:52 it is said of the blind Bartimaeus who had been healed that he "followed him (Jesus) on the way." At the same time the word characterizes the life of Jesus as a wandering from place to place, it distinguishes him from the settled residents. Jesus finds himself in a "boundary situation," that is not to be psychologized in the sense of Jesus' feeling of loneliness but is to be understood in the eschatological sense. So also the term ὄρος describes Jesus' place of prayer as a place of revelation (6:46). On a "mountain" Jesus manifests his authority and calls the disciples into his service (3:13). On the "mountain" the epiphany of the transfiguration takes place (9:2). Likewise the term οἶκος has the connotation of both epiphany and distanciation. The "house" separates disciples and crowd (especially 7:17). Within a house the Christ's special revelation is made to his followers (also 9:28, 33; 10:10). That we are here dealing with a topos of the secrecy theory is seen from the fact that the "house" appears without any prior reference, and without the reader's being able to locate it geographically. The "house" is there wherever it is needed by the secrecy theory. It not a matter of geography but is a topological (i.e. theological) concept.[5]

Mark's topological conceptuality extends beyond the items named above. Thus the people around Jesus also represent a topos for the setting in which revelation occurs, especially so in the case of the twelve disciples. No differently than the geographical terms, the circle of the twelve forms a place where revelation occurs, not only in the context of sending out the disciples on a missionary tour (6:7) but also at the institution of the Lord's Supper (14:17). That we here have a topological concept is seen from the way the ὄχλοι, the crowds of Jewish people, are juxtaposed to the disciples: crowds and disciples are separated. Despite the preaching of Jesus to the crowds, the crowds and the disciples are related to each other as concealment and revelation. So also πλοῖον is important for the topological train of thought: the "boat" separates Jesus and his disciples from the crowds

---

5    The word οἰκία, on the other hand, is only used in the neutral sense (6:10; 10:29–
     30; 12:40; 13:15, 35).

(4:1, 36; 6:32; 8:14).[6] The same is true for πλοιάριον, which according to 3:9 had protected Jesus from the crowds that pressed in on him. It is not only the twelve that are witnesses of the revelation but at times a special group of three disciples is marked off (e.g. 9:2), while at other times the boundary is extended to a larger number (4:10 "those who were around him along with the twelve"). The circle of the witnesses to the revelation is thus of variable size. This is also seen in 3:31ff: while Jesus relatives are among those who stand "outside," the disciples and the crowd belong to the inner circle. The decisive element is not the number of people concerned but the concept of marking off a special group, the distinction between the place of revelation and the places of concealment. It has become clear that the revelatory event creates its own place.

So also Mark's "parable theory" belongs in this context. The fourth chapter of his Gospel presents a series of parables, which are obviously based on a written source that he has elaborated by bringing other pre-Markan traditions into this context and by redactional additions of his own. The pre-Markan parable source was comprised of 4:3–(9), 10*, (13)-20, 26–29, 30–32. It thus contained three parables, the first of which, the Parable of the Sower, had been provided with an interpretation. A transition was then provided by the pre-Markan form of 4:10, i.e., the question about the meaning of the preceding parable. This pre-Markan collection was concluded with the statement that Jesus' teaching in parables was adjusted to the understanding of his hearers (4:33).

Mark has reworked this source. He inserts an introduction (4:1–2) and expands the transitional 4:10 (ὅτε ἐγένετο κατὰ μόνας, ἠρώτων αὐτὸν οἱ περὶ αὐτὸν σὺν τοῖς δώδεκα τὰς παραβολάς). He further expands elements of 4:11–13, and adds 21–25, 34. It is of theological importance that in expanding 4:10 and adding 4:11–12 Mark has altered the transition from the parable to its interpretation so that it becomes a question about the meaning of Jesus' teaching in parables as such. The Markan 4:34 affirms that the interpretation of the parables to the disciples preserves intact the topos of their being witnesses of the revelation. This is also undertaken in 4:13. The interpretation of the Parable of the Sower is given to a limited circle, named in 4:10 and addressed in 4:11–12, the larger circle around Jesus and his twelve disciples. They are contrasted with those who are "outside" (τοῖς ἔξω, 4:11). These do not receive the interpretation; instead, the Isaiah quotation (6:9–10) is applied to them:

> "they may indeed look but not perceive,
>     and may indeed listen but not understand".

---

6   On the other hand, "boat" has a non-theological meaning in 1:19–20; 5:2, 18, 21; 6:45, 47, 51, 54; 8:10.

As the Isaiah text deals with God's commission to the prophet to harden the heart of the people, so in the Gospel of Mark this is the meaning and goal of Jesus' teaching in parables. The Markan ἵνα[7] and the corresponding μήποτε may not be explained away.[8] Mark harshly emphasizes the "praedestinatio in malum." The parabolic teaching of Jesus facilitates the hardening of the people, confirming rather than eliminating the distinction between those who are outside and the witnesses of revelation.

Mark's parable theory is essentially determined by the Isaiah quote on which it is based. There is no analogy to it in the Gospel of Mark itself. It is therefore not constitutive for the Markan secrecy theory. Nonetheless, it is to be interpreted in relation to this theory. As in the case of the topological conceptions, it is an expression of the messianic secret. Mark emphasizes the motif of hiddenness. Even more than the topological statements, the parable theory strengthens the motif of the hidden character of the revelation. While Jesus' revelatory activity marks itself off over against those who "stand outside," his parabolic teaching leads to the hardening of the people as an expression of the secret that is inherent in the person and proclamation of Jesus. Thus between hiddenness and revelation a dialectical tension exists such that the revelation of Christ is not without hiddenness, and the hiddenness is not without its revelation.

### 3.  The Tradition-history Explanation

What is the significance of the fact that Mark has structured his Gospel by the motif of the messianic secret? What does it mean for the Markan understanding of the person and work of Jesus, and to what extent has the confession of the Markan community affected this process? In answering this question we must begin with W. Wrede, who in his epoch-making work on the messianic secret in the Gospels distinguished between the faith of the early Christian community and the original Jesus tradition. According to this view, the post-Easter faith of the community was determined by its conviction that Jesus was the Messiah and by its orientation to the future Messiah and judge of the world; within this context the figure of Jesus was interpreted messianically. It was different matter, however, with the original Jesus tradition. Wrede inferred from the contrast

---

[7]   Contra Isaiah 6:9. Isaiah 6:9a includes an imperative but ἵνα is not found in the LXX text of Isaiah. One cannot appeal to the Isaiah Targum, which is late. On the other hand, it cannot be excluded that Mark here uses an independent tradition. Cf. J. Gnilka, *Die Verstockung Israels. Isaias 6:9–10 in the Theology of the Synoptics* (StANT 3. Munich 1961).

[8]   Cf. differently Matthew, who in 13:13 reads ὅτι instead of ἵνα, so that the parable speech is motivated by the people's refusal to hear, thus preserving the accountability of the hearers and even appealing to the responsibility of the individual Christian.

between the revealed Messiahship of Jesus and the hiddenness of this Messiahship that the latter reflected the actual unmessianic life of Jesus, so that the original Jesus tradition had not been marked by messianic traits. The secrecy theory was thus the attempt of the community to harmonize the messianic and unmessianic traditions with each other, with the result that Jesus was then understood as have revealed his identity in secret. In other words, Wrede explained the theory of the messianic secret in terms of the history of traditions. It combined two pre-Markan traditions so that Mark, as it were, stood under a certain constraint. He reproduced what the church tradition had already worked out before him. Wrede based his understanding that the messianic secret was of pre-Markan origin on two observations: (1) the theory in itself is complex and contradictory, so that it can hardly be laid at the door of the author of the Second Gospel, and (2) it is also found in the Gospel of John, which in Wrede's view originated independently of Mark.[9]

Wrede's thesis is no longer advocated today for two reasons: (1) Wrede underestimated the formative power of the church. The Easter faith had so controlled the earlier Jesus tradition that the unmessianic Jesus tradition posited by Wrede must have been absorbed very early by the earliest Christian community. (2) The statements about the messianic secret in the Gospel of Mark belong for the most part to the redactional material. They represent the authentic work of the Second Evangelist himself and therefore cannot be interpreted in terms of the history of the pre-Markan tradition but only in terms of redaction criticism. They are a genuine element of Mark's own theological conception, who certainly never knew an unmessianic Jesus tradition.

## 4. Apologetic Explanation

According to widespread opinion[10] the Evangelist Mark created the messianic secret in order to confront his opponents in the Christian community. The messianic secret would thus represent an apologetic motif. The impetus for this theory would then be a Jewish objection to the Christian confession. When Christian faith affirmed that the Messiah was Jesus, the Jews opposed this by pointing to the unmessianic character of the life of Jesus and declared that the affirmations of the church's faith contradicted the historical facts of the life of Jesus. Mark responded to this with the theory of the messianic secret: the life of Jesus appeared to be unmessianic because Jesus had intended it so and revealed his messianic

---

[9] On this cf. G. Strecker, "W. Wrede," in G. Strecker, ed., *Eschaton und Historie* 335–359.

[10] E. Haenchen, *Der Weg Jesu* (Berlin: Evangelische Verlagsanstalt, 1966) 132–135; W. Bousset, *Kyrios Christos* 107. Cf. the critique of R. Bultmann, *History of the Synoptic Tradition* 346.

identity only in secret. The following response is to be made to this apologetic explanation: (1) Since Mark did not know an unmessianic Jesus tradition, he could not have responded to such a charge from Jewish opponents of the Christian community. (2) Furthermore, the Gospel of Mark was not written as an apologia for the Christian faith; it was rather the case that the Evangelists wanted to offer to church and world a positive testimony to the Christian faith. Apologetic literature emerged first in the second century. (3) Even when Christian faith did enter into debate with the intellectual and religious streams it confronted, the apologetic element in the New Testament must not be overestimated. Faith does not only come to articulate expression where it is challenged from outside. It is rather the case that the intention to enter into discussion with the surrounding world and to debate with its views is inherent in the faith itself. Consequently, it is not defense against hostile attacks but faith's own orientation of itself in the world that provides the fundamental task by which the authors of the Gospels know themselves to be challenged.

### 5.   The Hiddenness Motif as a Historical Formative Element

The hiddenness motif is an essential factor in the formation of the theory of the messianic secret. Of decisive significance is the command to silence in 9:9, "Jesus ordered them to tell no one about what they had seen, until after the Son of Man had risen from the dead." If according to W. Wrede's explanation in terms of the history of traditions the resurrection of Jesus is the point of intersection between two epochs, namely the epoch of the unmessianic Jesus tradition and the messianic church tradition, in fact the historical character of this notice is not to be overlooked. While it is true that the resurrection of the Son of Man does not separate a messianic from an unmessianic epoch, it does separate a time of the secret, in which the Son of Man exercised his ministry on earth, and a time when this secret is annulled. The hiddenness of the "Messiahship" of Jesus is most closely bound up with the temporality of the Christ. To what a great extent the secrecy motif is determined by its temporal character is also indicated by the predictions of the passion and resurrection in the Gospel of Mark. They point in advance to a definite temporal terminus, the death and resurrection of Jesus. They are in effect prior to this temporal point but afterwards are only of "historical" significance. The hiddenness associated with them applies only until the time of the resurrection. The faith of the post-Easter community will understand what was said then, in contrast to the uncomprehending witnesses during the time of Christ's revelation.

The messianic secret thus has a temporal limitation in the Gospel of Mark. The earthly course of Jesus' life, his "way," can be portrayed from the perspective of the secret. It belongs to the temporality, thus to the hiddenness of the Messiah, that he appeared in Galilee and from there came to Jerusalem. It is no accident that the topological predications are oriented in a temporal-historical framework. Other predications emphasize spatial considerations as the locus of Christ's revelation. Time and space constitute the framework for the messianic revelation that is revealed in such hiddenness.

## 6.   *The Paradox of Faith*

According to E. Schweizer the messianic secret in the life of Jesus is to clarify that Jesus' messianic being is to be understood from the perspective of the kerygma of Jesus' passion and resurrection. The way of Jesus prior to his death and resurrection was a hidden way; after that it was revealed.[11] Thus Peter shows his lack of understanding especially when confronted with the suffering of Jesus (8:32–33).[12] In Schweizer's perspective it was only after Easter that the truth of Jesus' person was revealed to his disciples and thus could be perceived by them.[13] However, the secret is not only a matter of an incomplete statement about the person and being of Jesus that points to his death and resurrection, after which it is then dispensed with; nor is it to be interpreted in an epistemological sense. On the contrary, it is an essential expression of the faith that eschatological salvation has entered into history through Jesus Christ. The messianic secret is a concrete expression of the paradox that the earthly Jesus is the Son of God, or (better) said the other way round: the one acknowledged by God as Son has appeared in history as a human being. The paradox is to be conceived not only "horizontally" but also "vertically." It affirms that the Messiahship of the Revealer belongs to that realm that is not at human disposal, and that this event, although it happened in the world of time and space, transcends the categories of time and space. As the eschatological event, it stands in tension with history. It is a dialectic event, marked by the self-revelation of the Christ and by his self-concealment. Revelation and hiddenness are dialectically related to one another. This is seen especially in the fact that, despite the intentional hiddenness of the Messiah, his concealment is repeatedly broken through. The revelation breaks through the framework of hiddenness.[14] The enclosing space that surrounds and veils the revelation is broken through by the Christ event

---

[11]   Cf. Mark 9:9; E. Schweizer, *Good News according to Mark* 185.

[12]   Cf. E. Schweizer, *Jesus* (Richmond: John Knox, 1971) 130–131.

[13]   Cf. E. Schweizer, *Good News according to Mark* 216.

[14]   Cf. 7:36: the healing of a person impaired in both speech and hearing (= an epiphany of the Christ) is concluded by a command to silence, which, however, is not kept ("but the more he ordered them, the more zealously they proclaimed it"). The revelation breaks through the concealment! Similarly 7:24 with reference to the οἶκος-motif: "He entered a house and did not want anyone to know he was there. Yet he could not escape notice,…".

itself. If Mark, the creator of the Gospel genre, had attempted to compose his work without the theory of the messianic secret, then his work would have become a "history of Jesus" that would not have allowed its eschatological claim to be perceived. The dialectic of hiddenness and revelation makes clear that the Christ event was not dissolved into history. However much it occurs in the hiddenness of time, it is not immanent in time. It occurs within the confines of a certain space, and yet it cannot be contained in space. For Mark the secrecy theory was a constitutive element of his writing of the Gospel. It is the foundation of the Markan christological conception but of course not the only characteristic element involved.

## b) The Person of Jesus

Breytenbach, C. "Grundzüge markinischer Gottessohn-Christologie," *Anfänge der Christologie* (FS F. Hahn). Göttingen: Vandenhoeck & Ruprecht, 1991, 169–184.
Horstmann, M. *Studien zur markinischen Christologie*. NTA 6. Münster: Aschendorff, 1973.
Kazmierski, C. R. *Jesus, the Son of God. A Study of the Markan Tradition and its Redaction by the Evangelist*. fzb 33. Würzburg: Echter, 1979.
Perrin, N. "Die Christologie des Markus-Evangeliums. Eine methodologische Studie," R. Pesch, ed. *Das Markusevangelium*. WdF 411. Darmstadt: Wissenschaftliche Buchgesellschaft, 1979, 356–376.
Schreiber, J. "Die Christologie des Markusevangeliums," *ZThK* 58 (1961) 154–183.
Schreiber, J. *Die Markuspassion. Eine redaktionsgeschichtliche Untersuchung*. BZNW 68. Berlin-New York: W. de Gruyter, 1993.
Schreiber, J. *Theologie des Vertrauens. Eine redaktionsgeschichtliche Untersuchung des Markusevangeliums*. Hamburg: Furche, 1967.
Strecker, G. "Die Leidens- und Auferstehungsvoraussagen im Markusevangelium (Mk 8,31; 9,31; 10,32–34)," G. Strecker, ed. *Eschaton und Historie. Aufsätze*. Göttingen: Vandenhoeck & Ruprecht, 1979, 52–75.
Vielhauer, Ph. "Erwägungen zur Christologie des Markusevangeliums," Ph. Vielhauer, ed., *Aufsätze zum Neuen Testament*. TB 31. Munich: Kaiser, 1965, 199–214.
Zmijewski, J. "Die Sohn-Gottes-Prädikation im Markusevangelium. Zur Frage einer eigenständigen markinischen Titelchristologie," *SNTU* 12 (1987) 5–34.

## 1. Basic Issues

The concrete formation of the messianic secret theory results from its christological connection. In this regard J. Schreiber has presented a specific exegetical proposal, according to which the messianic secret in Mark is to be interpreted in terms of the concept of the Gnostic redeemer. Philippians 2:6–11 and 1 Corinthians 2:8 are considered to be parallel texts and are presented as evidence for this thesis: "As in Phil 2:6–11 and 1 Cor 2:8, so also in Mark's portrayal the redeemer remains unrecognized prior to his death, in order by means of this death ... to attain his exaltation and victory over the cosmic powers."[15] In this way Mark takes up the

---

[15]  Schreiber, "Christologie" 157.

Hellenistic christological kerygma, which he supplements by adopting the θεῖος- ἀνήρ tradition, which likewise is derived from the Hellenistic Christology of the pre-Markan church. It is this combination that gives the Gospel its specific unity. The cross means the ultimate victory of Christ over the Satanic powers. The θεῖος- ἀνήρ tradition of the Jesus stories is recycled and transformed by the Christ myth derived from Gnosticism. Both traditions are combined in the theory of the messianic secret: Jesus is concealed as in the Gnostic redeemer myth, and he strides across the earth as a θεῖος ἀνήρ.

The decisive problem is not so much whether a θεῖος ἀνήρ tradition was reworked in the Gospel of Mark, since regardless of how this issue may be judged with respect to individual stories, in any case the pre-Markan tradition presupposes the idea that Jesus did wonderful deeds of power like a "divine man." The crucial issue is whether alongside this Mark has placed a redeemer myth like that of Gnosticism, and thus whether Jesus is in fact presented as the Gnostic "redeemed redeemer" (*salvator salvandus*). Did the Second Evangelist know a preexistence Christology, so that Jesus, like the redeemer in the Gnostic systems, came down from heaven and then returned? In support of this thesis Schreiber appeals to Mark 1:11 (the heavenly voice at Jesus' baptism addresses him as "Son of God") and to 12:1ff (the designation υἱὸς ἀγαπητός is found in the Parable of the Wicked Husbandmen, 12:6).[16] However: the concept of a "descent," in which the redeemer comes down from heaven and returns there is absent from the Gospel of Mark. Nor does the Second Gospel know a cosmic interpretation of the person of Christ comparable to those in Gnosticism. And especially Mark 1:11 speaks of the adoption of Jesus to become the Son of God, of an epiphanic event in which divine revelation occurs to and in Christ. It is not necessary to associate this with the idea of preexistence. It is rather the case that at baptism Jesus is adopted as Son of God. This inauguration into the status of Son of God at baptism speaks against the understanding that the epiphanic event of Jesus' baptism presupposes that Jesus was already Son of God. It is informative to note that the heavenly voice at the Transfiguration states "This is my beloved Son" (9:7) and thereby confirms that Jesus has been Son of God since the baptism. That Mark advocates an adoption Christology, not a preexistence Christology, makes it impossible to incorporate his Christology into the framework of the Gnostic redeemer conceptuality as Schreiber proposes, all the more so since genuine Gnosis ("Gnosticism") emerged after the beginning of Christianity.[17]

---

[16]   Schreiber, "Christologie" 166–167.
[17]   Cf. G. Strecker, Excursus "Γινώσκειν," in *The Johannine Letters* (Hermeneia. Minneapolis: Fortress, 1995) 222–227. K. Berger, "Gnosis/Gnostizismus I," *TRE* 13, 519–535; R. McL. Wilson, "Gnosis/Gnostizismus II," *TRE* 13, 535–550; C.

## 2.  Christological Titles

If neither a preexistence Christology nor a Gnostic redeemer myth is to be presupposed for Mark, then one must ask what are in fact the central concepts that determine the Markan Christology.

(α) Significantly, the Son of David title only stands in the background. It is found only once in connection with a healing story, in the outcry of the blind man Bartimaeus (10:47). Nor is the remainder of the narrative characterized by the Son of David Christology. This distinguishes Mark from Matthew and Luke, who have taken up this traditional title especially in their birth stories, and permits the supposition that Mark and his tradition have only been slightly influenced by the Jewish Christian stream of tradition. The title appears once again in the pericope "About David's Son" (12:35–37). Here, however, one notes that the Son of David title is relegated to secondary status, and since the pericope belongs to the pre-Markan tradition can be considered one reason why the title plays only a minor role in Mark's own Christology.

(β) The title ὁ Χριστός is more characteristic of Mark himself. Though Mark can use Χριστός as a proper name (1:1; 9:41), the titular use occurs more frequently, as in Peter's confession: "You are the Christ" (8:29), and in 12:35, where the title "Christ" is given priority over "Son of David." It appears also in the high priest's question (14:61) "Are you the Christ, the Son of the Blessed One?", and in 15:32 (with the supplement "the king of Israel"). It is thus characteristic that a christological predication is added, since ὁ Χριστός alone is a generic designation of the eschatological savior.

(γ) Especially significant is the question of whether or not Mark knew the title Κύριος as a Septuagintal designation for God. In any case, he uses the word in this sense in 5:19; 12:29; 13:20, though he can also employ it as a secular term (e. g. 13:35, the master of the house). Moreover, in three passages Mark understands κύριος in the christological sense. Especially to be noted is the pericope of the entry into Jerusalem (11:3: "The Lord needs it [the colt]"). This story presupposes the Old Testament messianic tradition of Zechariah 9:9 and probably originated on the basis of this text.[18] We may therefore conclude that the title ὁ κύριος has a messianic

Colpe, *Die religionsgeschichtliche Schule* (FRLANT 78. Göttingen: Vandenhoeck & Ruprecht, 1961); K. Rudolph, *Gnosis: The Nature and History of Gnosticism* (San Francisco: Harper & Row, 1977); K. Rudolph, ed. *Gnosis und Gnostizismus* (WdF 262. Darmstadt: Wissenschaftliche Buchgesellschaft,1975); H. Jonas, *The Gnostic Religion*, 2nd rev. ed. (Boston: Beacon Press, 1963); K. W. Tröger, ed., *Gnosis und Neues Testament* (Gütersloh: Gerd Mohn, 1973); K. W. Tröger, ed., *Altes Testament—Frühjudentum—Gnosis* (Gütersloh: Gerd Mohn, 1980).
[18]  This understanding is to be preferred despite the essay of W. Bauer, "The 'Colt' of Palm Sunday (Der Palmesel) *JBL* 72 (1953) 220–229, which argues that πῶλος does

significance. It is also possible that the address ὁ κύριος in the mouth of the Gentile woman from Syrophoenicia is to be understood as a christological title (7:28), since the address is used without qualifiers. And finally, in the pericope about the Son of David in 12:35–37, David calls the Christ "Lord" (in accordance with the quote from Ps 110:1), where the unqualified usage suggests a titular understanding (12:37). Summary conclusion: Mark presupposes, if only sporadically, the Kyrios-Christology. This connects him with the Hellenistic kerygma and distances his Christology from that of the Palestinian-Jewish church.

(δ) With regard to the title ὁ υἱὸς τοῦ ἀνθρώπου, we have already noted that in the Gospels a distinction is to be made between sayings that deal with the coming, the present work, and the suffering Son of Man. Mark knows all three groups, and preserves the original apocalyptic content of the expression "Son of Man" (cf. 13:26). Moreover, the tradition that came to Mark had already incorporated the concept of the apocalyptic Son of Man into the life of Jesus (group 2: 2:10, 28). Accordingly, the connection between the θεῖος ἀνήρ concept and the Son of Man terminology had already been made prior to Mark and obviously originated on Hellenistic soil, which facilitated the portrayal of the "divine man" Jesus as the one already equipped with eschatological power, the Son of Man who demonstrates such power and authority during his earthly ministry. In this regard, however, the characteristic feature of the Gospel of Mark is its emphasis on the third group of Son of Man sayings. Here too, however, the portrayal of the Christ as the suffering Son of Man was in part already present in the pre-Markan tradition; thus in 8:31 Jesus' prediction of the passion and resurrection of the Son of Man was presumably already included in the Caesarea Philippi pericope prior to Mark,[19] just as 10:45 is also pre-Markan ("For the Son of Man came not to be served but to serve, and to give his life a ransom for many.") In the pre-Markan tradition this λύτρον-saying had a primarily soteriological meaning; it testified to the ministry of the Son of Man who acted in behalf of human beings to take away their troubles. This verse is related to the Pauline conceptual world and documents a "Pauline component" in the tradition that came to Mark. An additional saying about the suffering Son of Man is found in 14:21 ("For the Son of Man goes as it is written of him, but woe to that one by whom the Son of Man is betrayed!"). This woe-cry probably originated in the theological reflection of the early Christian community. It was prob-

---

not refer to a donkey's colt but to a young horse. Cf. also Bauer's essay "Der Palmesel," in W. Bauer, *Aufsätze und Kleine Schriften* (Tübingen: J. C. B. Mohr [Paul Siebeck], 1967) 109–121. Cf. K. G. Kuhn, "Das Reittier Jesu in der Einzugsgeschichte des Markusevangeliums," *ZNW* 50 (1959) 82–91.

[19] Cf. G. Strecker, "The Passion-and Resurrection Predictions in Mark's Gospel" *Interpretation* 22/4 (Oct 1968) 421–442.

ably never transmitted as an independent element of the tradition but as an element of the story of Judas' betrayal and was of pre-Markan origin.

However, Mark not only found sayings about the suffering Son of Man in the tradition but extensively reformulated and expanded them himself. The second and third passion predictions are Markan (9:31; 10:33–34), in dependence on the pre-Markan tradition to which 8:31 belongs. The secondary influence of the passion story can be seen especially in 10:33–34. Jesus is here the Son of Man who goes forth to meet suffering, death and resurrection. Moreover, 14:41b is a redactional transition; it speaks of the betrayal of the Son of Man, who is given over into the hands of sinners.[20]

Two observations result from this survey:

1. *Concerning the history of the tradition:* Mark found sayings about the suffering of the Son of Man in the tradition of his community; they are not to be assigned to a particular written source document but—so far as we can determine—also never existed in written form independently of the Markan tradition; they are unknown to the Q-tradition, for example. This interpretation of the Son of Man concept is to be placed late in the history of the tradition. It is to be understood as a secondary combination of the first two groups of Son of Man sayings with the christological kerygma. This group of sayings originally had a soteriological orientation, as can be recognized from 10:45.

2. *Concerning the redaction:* Mark intentionally took up his community's tradition of the suffering Son of Man, reworked it and incorporated it into his Gospel. He interpreted it in relation to his messianic secret theory. Jesus, the suffering Son of Man, is the hidden Messiah. The suffering of Christ is an expression of the humiliation and hiddenness of the revealer. This is not to be understood in the Gnostic sense (since the Gnostic redeemer is subject to suffering in this world due to his "descent" from heaven to earth understood in a cosmological sense) but in the sense of the Christian kerygma. The Christ of faith conceals his exalted status in suffering; it is broken in the passion and then shines forth unconcealed at the resurrection.

(ε) In the Gospel of Mark, of even greater importance than the Son of Man terminology is the christological predicate υἱὸς τοῦ θεοῦ. This is true even though all the references are of pre-Markan origin. The Markan editorial work is essentially compositional rather than a matter of creating new independent statements. The manner in which Mark has arranged the individual units of tradition and "edited" them brings what is characteristic of his own theology clearly into focus. Thus the term "Son of God"

---

[20]   Mark 9:12b does not belong to this category but can be recognized as a post-Markan interpolation already present in the copy of Mark used by Matthew.

has something decisive to say about the understanding of the person of Jesus in the Gospel of Mark. It is interpreted in different ways:

1. The question of the high priest, "Are you the Messiah, the Son of the Blessed One?" (Mark 14:61) is answered by Jesus' pointing to the coming of the Son of Man on the clouds of heaven (14:62). The high priest's question thus receives a positive answer but the understanding it presupposes is modified by Jesus' reference to the coming of the eschatological Judge. The Son of God, who Jesus in his earthly reality in fact is, as he confesses himself to be, is no other than the future judge of the world, the Son of Man. The term "Son of God" thus has in Mark an eschatological dimension; it is oriented toward the future, in contrast to the presupposed Jewish idea of the Son of God as the king of Israel.

2. A different framework of thought is the background for 3:11. The demons acknowledge Jesus' authority by falling before him and crying out "You are the Son of God." This belongs to the context of Jesus' exorcisms and is in any case of pre-Markan origin (cf. also 5:7). This passage also expresses another tradition than that just named, namely that of the θεῖος ἀνήρ, which portrays Jesus as the divine man endowed with power, in particular as a worker of miracles. This means: the one thus portrayed does not belong to the world of earthly reality; he has divine power, because he is a divine being. His divine nature is manifest in his earthly appearance and is characteristic of the exalted claims he makes.

3. The three following references are of greater significance: 1:11 (the adoption of Jesus as Son of God through his baptism); 9:7 (designated as Son of God at the Transfiguration on the mountain); 15:39 (the confession of the centurion at the cross: "Truly this man was the Son of God"). There are parallels to these references in the ancient Egyptian ritual of inthronization, according to which the king ascended to the throne according to a fixed ritual:[21] 1. *Exaltation* (apotheosis). The king is awarded divine qualities by his heavenly Father, and thereby becomes a divine being himself. 2. *Presentation.* The divinized king is presented to the circle of the gods and is made equal to them in dignity. 3. *Inthronization.* Power and authority to rule are conferred on the divine king.

This inthronization schema has also been applied to New Testament texts, e. g. to the 1 Timothy 3:16 hymn; cf. also Hebrews 1:5–13 and Matthew 28:16–20. While the analogy is questionable in matters of detail, it is still clear that for interpreting the Gospel of Mark the comparison with the ancient Egyptian inthronization schema is illuminating: the *apotheosis* of the divine king can be seen to reappear in the adoption of Jesus as Son of God in the baptismal pericope (Mark 1:11). Similarly, the Trans-

---

[21]  Cf. E. Norden, *Die Geburt des Kindes* 118–123.

figuration pericope can be understood as the presentation of Jesus as the Son of God (9:7), in that Jesus is presented as having a rank equal to heavenly beings, namely Elijah and Moses. And finally, it appears possible to interpret the crucifixion as the *inthronization* of the Son of God, in that lordship over the world is conferred on the Crucified One, as is apparently indicated by the centurion's confession (15:39).

It must be acknowledged, however, that the purported parallels are not without free from objections. In particular, the centurion's confession says nothing explicitly about an inthronization; on the contrary, by saying "This one was (ἦν) the Son of God," it makes an evaluative declaration about a past event, the death of Jesus.[22] It would be more correct to understand the centurion's confession in relation to the θεῖος ἀνήρ tradition; it testifies that Jesus the Son of God was endowed with divine power during his earthly life. If the inthronization schema is applied consistently to the Gospel of Mark, then it must be supposed that the lost conclusion of Mark also contained the predicate υἱὸς τοῦ θεοῦ. In fact, the possibility is not to be excluded that the inthronization of Jesus as Son of God was declared in the context of a resurrection appearance to Peter. This would correspond to the extant resurrection texts: the Risen One is the one who has been enthroned, the one exalted to "the right hand of God" (cf. Matt 28:16–20).[23]

First of all, the comparison with the ancient Egyptian inthronization schema illuminates the Christology of the Gospel of Mark in that Mark presents Jesus as the future eschatological king who is already present and active. This is what is referred to by the title placarded on the cross.[24] It is the typical misunderstanding that does not recognize the truth and is unwilling to accept it, the truth that the Crucified One is not a ruler in the political sense. Here the hiddenness of Jesus' Messiahship is manifested by being inappropriately conceived in terms of a political Messianism. In reality, however, it is a matter of the Messiahship of the eschatological king. It is no accident that cosmic signs accompany his earthly way (the heavenly voice in 1:11 and 9:7; darkness and the tearing of the temple curtain in 15:33, 38). The appearance of this king has a universal, cosmic meaning.

If one presupposes that the Markan portrayal of the life of Jesus is comparable to an inthronization drama, then one must conclude that Mark intended to portray the earthly event of Jesus' life as the saving event. Characteristic of this portrayal is the connection between the Son of God tradition and the Son of Man tradition. The Son of God presents himself as θεῖος ἀνήρ (for the former cf. 1:11 and 9:7; for the latter 3:11 and 15:39). The eschatological divine king is at the same time the divine man

---

[22]   Ph. Vielhauer, "Erwägungen" 199–214; 211, 213.

who acts on earth, endowed with wonder-working power. Mark intentionally places the church's confession of Jesus as the eschatological king within the framework of history; he is concerned to present a linear historical narrative. The saving event is represented as salvation history.

## 3.  The Way of Jesus

If one attempts to outline the Markan presentation, three periods of salvation history may be distinguished: (1.) the time of hiddenness, i.e. the time of prophetic prediction looking forward to Jesus, including the appearance of John the Baptist, (2.) the time in which the presence of the eschatological event is both hidden and revealed in the person of Jesus, and (3.) the post-Easter time, i.e. the time of the mission of the church that lasts until the end of the world. The time of Jesus may thus be located in a unilinear temporal movement.

(α) This can be demonstrated in *the relation of Jesus to the Jews*. In the Gospel of Mark, the representatives of the Jewish people, like the Jewish people itself, do not belong to the Judaism contemporary with Mark and his community. The Second Evangelist does not reflect primarily his own time but is concerned to portray the sacred past. The Jewish leaders and people he portrays are presented as the contemporaries of Jesus, even if they also to some extent mirror the Judaism of Mark's own time. The Markan Jesus stands over against Judaism; he preaches in *their* synagogues (1:39), and thus seems no longer to be numbered among the Jews himself. Similarly, Jesus distances himself from the teaching of the Pharisees and scribes as "your tradition" (7:9, 13). The portrayal of the Jewish authorities and parties, and to some extent that of the Jewish people, is subordinated to the secrecy motif of the messianic revelation. The revelation of the Christ breaks like a wave against their misunderstanding and opposition. The appearance of Jesus takes place as the counterpoint to the history of the Jewish people; it is oriented to the history of this people and has an influence on it. The parable of the Wicked Husbandmen is a characteristic illustration of this point (Mark 12:1–12). The servants who are sent to the vineyard keepers to bring back the owner's share of the harvest are mistreated or killed—an allegory of the Old Testament prophets. The sending of the "beloved son" is the mission of Jesus. He too is killed by the vineyard workers; the result is that the vineyard will be given to others. This is in accord with the Old Testament prediction (Ps 118:22: "The stone that the builders rejected has become the cornerstone"). In harmony with such allegorizing of salvation history, the history of the Jewish covenant people is portrayed as an unholy past devoid of salvation, a history of murder of the prophets. It comes to its high point and end with the crucifixion of Jesus. The result is the rejection of the Jews and the election of another people, i.e. the formation of the church to which all who respond to the call of Jesus belong. While on the one hand in Mark the Jews represent the hardening and lack of understanding that the revelation of the Christ encounters, on the other hand they are made responsible for their attitude. They bear the responsibility for the death of Jesus (15:6–15). However much this passage later became the basis for antijudaism among Christians, Mark himself hardly has any fundamental antijewish orientation. The standpoint for one's theological perspective is more important for the Second Evangelist than any concrete opposition to his Jewish contemporaries. This theological standpoint is not articulated in terms of some cheap apologetic but in the church's confession of the truth given to it. Since the truth of such faith cannot be separated from the person of the believer, historical writing oriented to salvation history goes beyond the boundary of believing confession when it is detached from the person of the believer and objectivizes and historicizes the confession of faith and attempts to demonstrate that the way of others is not the way of truth. This transgression of the boundaries that are set for the truth that is confessed by faith can already be recognized in Mark and is developed more consistently in the Matthean and Lucan parallels. This is the path taken by the effort to demonstrate the truth of faith in terms of salvation history. With this comes the danger that the truth of faith degenerates to a matter of correctness and that the object of the confessed faith becomes a demonstrable "historical fact."

(β) Along with Jesus, the *disciples of Jesus* are on the road. They follow Jesus on the road (e. g. 1:18) and accompany him to the cross (10:32; 14:54; 15:40–41). When Mark speaks of the disciples of Jesus, he thinks primarily not of the Christian community but of those who accompanied the earthly Jesus. To be sure, there is no observable development in the faith of the disciples. It is neither the case that Peter's confession (8:27ff) marks a division point between two periods, as though a period of incomprehension or misunderstanding were thereby separated from a period of understanding, nor is it the case that a period characterized by lack of understanding that Jesus is the Messiah is distinguished from a period of misunderstanding that Jesus is the suffering Messiah. The portrayal of the disciples is intended to show that discipleship is a matter of dialectical existence. Confession of faith and misunderstanding are woven together; they confess Jesus as the Christ and still do not grasp the secret of his way.[25] Precisely as

---

23    In the words of the Apostles' Creed: "I believe...in Jesus Christ...[who] rose again from the dead; ...he ascended into heaven, and sitteth on the right hand of God the Father Almighty."

24    15:26: the Gentiles name Jesus as "King of the Jews;" cf. also 15:32: the Jewish chief priests and scribes speak ironically of Jesus as "the Messiah, the King of Israel."

25    On the disciples lack of understanding prior to Peter's confession cf. 5:41–42; 6:51–52; 8:14ff; 8:31ff.

uncomprehending, doubting, suffering people plagued by worries (cf. 14:50) they are called to be witnesses of the revelation (9:9) who find their task in the post-Easter mission to the nations (13:10).

(γ) Differently than in the case of the disciples, a line of development can be perceived in the Markan depiction of the *person of Jesus*. The disciples are nothing else than witnesses of the revelation and therefore their existence is inseparable from the revealer. They are incorporated into the history only to the extent that they are related to the figure of Jesus. This figure determines the layout of the Gospel throughout: the way of Jesus begins with his baptism by John (1:9–11) or with his first public appearance in Galilee (1:14–15) and ends in Jerusalem with his crucifixion and resurrection. The Gospel is accordingly divided into two major sections: the Galilean period (1:14–9:50) and the Jerusalem period (10:1–15:37); Jesus' journey to Jerusalem begins at 10:1. This structure is characterized in its details by the dialectic of the hiddenness and revelation of the Christ and shaped by the concept of inthronization. Jesus is presented as a "divine man" in word and deed, whose way is a way through time and space. This is documented by the different chronological and geographical data; in the passion story this is extended even to delineating the days and hours. A turning point is marked by the story of Peter's confession in 8:27ff and the first passion prediction that follows. From then on, the way of Jesus is the way to the cross (8:31). This is a path through space, namely through the Galilean countryside and within the city of Jerusalem. Neither case is to be understood typologically,[26] but strictly geographically. It is a path that leads through time and space to the resurrection, and then points beyond itself to the parousia of the Christ-Son of Man.

## 4. The Significance of the Person of Jesus for Faith

Mark has so composed his work as to make it unmistakably clear that his intention is to understand the time of the church as the sequel to the time of Jesus (cf. Mark 9:9). However, he did not develop his own ecclesiology. This is based on the fact that that he does not intend his work as preach-

---

[26] Contra E. Lohmeyer, *Das Evangelium des Markus* (KEK I/2. Göttingen, [17]1967), who understands Galilee as "the land of eschatological fulfillment" (356); cf. also Lohmeyer, *Galiläa und Jerusalem* (FLRANT 52. Göttingen: Vandenhoeck & Ruprecht, 1936) 31 and passim; similarly W. Marxsen, *Mark the Evangelist: Studies in the Redaction History of the Gospel* (Nashville: Abingdon, 1957) 57 and passim; P. Parker, "Mark, Acts, and Galilean Christianity," *NTS* 16 (1970) 295–304 (303–304); W. H. Kelber, *The Kingdom in Mark: A New Place and a New Time* (Philadelphia: Fortress Press, 1974). On this topic cf. the critical debate by H. R. Preuss, *Galiläa im Markus-Evangelium* (theol. Diss. Göttingen, 1966) 57ff.

ing to the community but primarily as a portrayal of the history of Jesus that lies in the past. The Gospel of Mark does not explicitly raise the question of the significance of Jesus for the faith of the community. The answer to this question can probably be inferred, however, from Mark's statements with regard to the relation of believers to the historical figure of Jesus.

α) Atoning Death

Martin Kähler's well-known definition that the Gospels are "passion stories with extensive introductions" has been often repeated.[27] This definition cannot be applied to Mark, however, either from the perspective of the pre-Markan tradition or the Markan redaction. From the point of view of the history of tradition, the passion story represents a traditional unit that presumably lay before Mark as an detached element complete in itself.[28] As such it was Mark who first combined it with other components of the Jesus tradition. From the perspective of tradition history therefore, the passion story cannot be understood as the beginning point of a development that led to the formation of the Gospels.

But neither is Kähler's thesis viable from the point of view of redaction criticism: (1.) To be sure, the goal of Jesus' way in the Gospel of Mark is the passion and resurrection, but the way of Jesus leads beyond that to the resurrection and points to the parousia. Jesus' passion is therefore only a section, not the final goal of Jesus' way, and does not determine the shape of the Gospel as a whole. (2.) Kähler's thesis implies the presupposition that the decisive orientation point and goal of the Gospel is the sacrificial or atoning death of Jesus on the cross. This, however, is not a genuine Markan idea. Here a sharp distinction must be made between tradition and redaction, since the concept of the atoning death of Jesus belongs to the pre-Markan tradition, as can be seen from the two most important examples in Mark. As has been shown above, the λύτρον-saying (10:45) contains different traditional layers of pre-Markan origin. Already in the pre-Markan tradition but also by Mark, it was no longer understood in a soteriological sense but ethically, as is suggested by the introductory καὶ γάρ: Jesus is the model for service to the neighbor.

A second affirmation of the atoning death of Jesus is found in the words of institution in the pre-Markan Last Supper pericope that speak of Jesus' blood being poured out for many (14:24). Here too, the interpretation of the death of Jesus as an atonement or substitutionary offering is not a part

27  Martin Kähler, The So-called Historical Jesus and the Historic Biblical Christ (Philadelphia: Fortress, 1964) 80.
28  Cf. G. Strecker, "Die Passiongeschichte im Markusevangelium," in F. W. Horn, ed., Bilanz und Perspektiven gegenwärtiger Auslegung des Neuen Testaments 218–247.

of Mark's redactional work. This means that the Markan church not only was familiar with the idea of the atoning effect of the suffering and death of Jesus but had adopted this understanding as their own in the celebration of the Lord's Supper. The decisive point, however, is that the sacramental practice of the community is not grounded in the portrayal of the person and work of Jesus in the Gospel of Mark itself. The death of Jesus appears in Mark primarily as a fact, a segment in the time line, a necessary transition from the time of Christ's hiddenness to the revelatory event of the resurrection. This fact is incorporated into salvation history and legitimized by appeal to Old Testament prophecy (14:21). It stands under the transcendent δεῖ that signals the divine necessity inherent in salvation history (8:31). Christ accepts this as his "destiny" (14:32ff). He affirms it and by his supernatural knowledge elevates it to a higher plane than that of a merely secular human event (14:8, 18, 27). With the exception of the pre-Markan eucharistic narrative the Markan Jesus does not attribute an atoning effect to his death. The question of the soteriological significance of the person of Jesus, as Mark understands it, is to be answered from a different perspective.

β) The Jesus-event as Saving Event

According to Mark, the significance of Jesus for faith consists in the fact that Jesus represents the incursion of the eschaton into time. On the one hand, this means that the εὐαγγέλιον that Mark sets forth in his book is the message of Jesus and at the same time has Jesus himself as its content. On the other hand, this signifies that the Jesus of past history can be interpreted through a variety of christological predicates and that his supernatural authority is manifested in mighty eschatological acts.

The Jesus of the saving event demands faith of human beings. His appearance in history declares that people are divided by his person, and that the two possibilities of human conduct in response to him are faith and unbelief. This faith is more than not doubting the supernatural power of the miracle worker—this latter kind of faith is clearly illustrated in Mark 5:34; 10:52: "your faith has made you well". It is rather πίστις θεοῦ (11:22), faith that recognizes in Jesus the eschatological claim. It can therefore expect from Jesus liberation from sin and guilt (cf. 2:5). Mark, however, sets forth no corresponding theory of the atonement; the concretion of the saving event remains faint. Thus the decisive thing for the Second Evangelist is not the question, "What is the significance of Jesus for faith?" but the affirmation *that* Jesus is significant for faith. Jesus expects faith in response to him, because by his existence he makes faith possible. For Mark, the decisive thing is not the "what" but the "that" of the saving event. With Jesus the eschaton has become a historical reality. He is a "fact"; not as an objective datum but veiled in the hiddenness of history, both a demand for faith and perceptible by faith.

γ) The Authority of the Jesus-event

As the saving event the Jesus event includes a demand: it requires obedience. Christology and ethics belong most closely together. The Jesus event is not only to be acknowledged in faith; it must also become concrete acts in human life. The followers of Jesus know that faith calls for action. As the dispute about handwashing shows, the Markan Jesus declares the Jewish ritual law in both the rabbinic oral tradition and in its Old Testament form to be abolished (7:1–23).[29] This tradition presumably did not originate on Palestinian soil but in the realm of Gentile Christianity. The action to which faith is called does not consist in ritual observance but in ethical integrity, for it is not ritual impurity but ethical impurity that "defiles" (7:21–22). Faith proves itself in rejecting the bad and doing the good. This component of faith is also addressed in those passages where Jesus calls for service to the neighbor (Mark 10:44: "whoever wishes to be first among you must be slave of all"). The paradigm of such service is the Son of Man, who so served others (10:45). The obedience called for by the Jesus event is realized in taking up the cross, the desisting-from-one's-self in order to walk the way of Jesus (8:34ff), for paradoxically, giving oneself up leads to gaining oneself. The loss of one's life means the gaining of one's life! Eschatological reality is set over against this worldly "reality." Its δόξα is found precisely where, from a human point of view, nothing is to be expected, in suffering and death. To follow Jesus means to share his own hiddenness, in order also to share his eschatological revelation. The promised future comes only by taking up the cross.

# III. The Way of Righteousness— The Evangelist Matthew

Betz, H. D. *Studien zur Bergpredigt.* Tübingen: J. C. B. Mohr (Paul Siebeck), 1985.

Betz, H. D. *Essays on the Sermon on the Mount.* Philadelphia: Fortress Press, 1985.

Bornkamm G., Barth, G. und Held, H. J. *Tradition and Interpretation in Matthew.* Philadelphia: Westminster, 1965.

Davies, W. D. *The Setting of the Sermon on the Mount.* Cambridge: Cambridge University Press, 1966.

Davies, W. D. and Allison, D. C. *The Gospel according to Saint Matthew.* ICC. Edinburgh: T. & T. Clark, I 1988; II 1991.

Eichholz, G. *Auslegung der Bergpredigt.* BSt 46. Neukirchen-Vluyn: Neukirchener, 1984.

---

[29]    Cf. H. Hübner, "Mark VII 1–23 und das 'jüdisch-hellenistische' Gesetzverständnis," *NTS* 22 (1976) 319–345.

Frankemölle, H. *Jahwebund und Kirche Christi*. NTA 10. Münster: Aschendorff, 1984².

Gnilka, J. *Das Matthäusevangelium*. HThK I/1+2. Freiburg: Herder, I 1988; II 1988.

Gundry, R. H. *Matthew. A Commentary on his Literary and Theological Art*. Grand Rapids: W. B. Eerdmans, 1982.

Hummel, R. *Die Auseinandersetzung zwischen Kirche und Judentum im Matthäus-evangelium*. BEvTh 33. Munich:Kaiser, 1966.

Kilpatrick, G. D. *The Origins of the Gospel according to St. Matthew*. Oxford: Oxford University Press, 1950.

Kramer, W. *Christ, Lord, Son of God*. Naperville: A. R. Allenson, 1966.

Lange J., ed. *Das Matthäus-Evangelium*. WdF 525. Darmstadt: Wissenschaftliche Buchgesellschaft, 1980.

Luz, U. *Das Evangelium nach Matthäus*. EKK I/1+2. Zürich-Einsiedeln-Köln-Neu-kirchen-Vluyn: Neukirchener, I 1985; II 1990; III 1997.

Luz, U. *Matthew 1–7: A Commentary*. Minneapolis: Augsburg Fortress, 1989.

Luz, U. *The Theology of the Gospel of Matthew*. Cambridge: Cambridge University Press, 1995.

Sand, A. *Das Matthäus-Evangelium*. EdF 275. Darmstadt: Wissenschaftliche Buch-gesellschaft, 1991.

Schenk, W. *Die Sprache des Matthäus*. Göttingen: Vandenhoeck & Ruprecht, 1987.

Schlatter, A. *Der Evangelist Matthäus, seine Sprache, sein Ziel, seine Selbständigkeit*. Stuttgart: Calver, 1957.

Schweizer, E. *Matthäus und seine Gemeinde*. SBS 71. Stuttgart: Katholisches Bibelwerk, 1974.

Stanton, G. "The Origin and Purpose of Matthew's Gospel," ANRW II 25.3. (1985) 1889–1951.

Stendahl, K. *The School of St. Matthew and its Use of the Old Testament*. ASNU 20. Uppsala 1954 (Philadelphia: Fortress, 1968).

Strecker, G. *The Sermon on the Mount*. Nashville: Abingdon, 1988.

Strecker, G. "Das Geschichtsverständnis des Matthäus," *EvTh* 26 (1966) 57–74; also in G. Strecker, ed. *Eschaton und Historie* 90–107).

Strecker, G. *Der Weg der Gerechtigkeit. Untersuchung zur Theologie des Matthäus*. FRLANT 82. Göttingen: Vandenhoeck & Ruprecht, 1971.

Trilling, W. *Das wahre Israel. Studien zur Theologie des Matthäusevangeliums*. StUNT 10. Munich: Kösel, 1964.

v. Dobschütz, E. "Matthäus als Rabbi und Katechet," *ZNW* 27 (1928) 338–348.

Walker, R. *Die Heilsgeschichte im ersten Evangelium*. FRLANT 91. Göttingen: Van-denhoeck & Ruprecht, 1967.

## a)  Historicizing the Traditional Material

As we have shown above, the writing of Gospels grew out of the interest of Christian faith to orient itself in the world and to give an account of itself in the world of time and space in which it lives. The faith of the Evangelists is attuned to the world and thereby integrally related to history. The Evangelists themselves make this clear. Mark writes his work with a view toward the past, to the life of Jesus, that comprises a specific segment of time. Faith is grounded and confirmed with reference to the Jesus event.

Matthew has proceeded more consistently than Mark. The space/time orientation of faith has become more specific and intentional. This is already seen in the outline of the First Gospel. In distinction from Mark, Matthew begins with a genealogy and birth story (1:1–2:23). The time line is traced back to the beginning of Jesus' life and beyond. The lost ending to the Gospel of Mark was also unknown to Matthew. This provides him the occasion to formulate his own conclusion. In 28:9–20 Matthew has added resurrection appearances that reach their high point in the mission command of the Resurrected One to the disciples to teach all nations and make them his followers.

Matthew has also adopted Mark's geographical outline. The introductory stories are followed by the first major section, the Galilean period of Jesus' ministry (4:12–18:35), which is then followed by the journey to Jerusalem, where Jesus performs his final acts and is put to death (19:1–27:66). The life of Jesus is a reality qualified by its existence in a particular space. As such it is localized geographically and thereby strictly distinguished from other-worldly myths. Moreover, the life of Jesus is a temporal reality that begins with his birth and leads through his first appearance and ministry in Galilee and Jerusalem to its conclusion in death and resurrection.

1. One example of the spatial orientation of the First Evangelist is represented by the οἰκία motif. As shown above, in Mark this motif represents a theological statement that reflects the dialectic of hiddenness and revelation, and thus is a sub-topic within the messianic secret theme. In Matthew too the distinction between the hiddenness and the revelation of Jesus' Messiahship, between Jesus and the people, can still be recognized. According to 13:36 the parables are interpreted to the disciples after he had entered εἰς τὴν οἰκίαν. Matthew thereby adopts the Markan parable theory according to which a sharp separation is made between the parables and their interpretation, between the people who receive only the parabolic instruction, and the circle of disciples to whom the interpretation is given. It is characteristic for Matthew, however, that he has placed the theological motif in a geographical framework. The "house of Peter" (8:14) is localized in Capernaum, as the whole section 8:5–34 reports incidents in and around Capernaum (see below). The οἰκία motif found in this context is thus entirely related to Capernaum (8:9, 10, 28, 32). This can also be shown to be the case in other passages (cf. the sea situation in 13:1–36). So too the question about the temple tax (17:25) mentions a house in which Peter and Jesus meet and that is specifically located in Capernaum. Thus Matthew, differently than Mark, thinks of a particular house—Jesus' residence—when he makes use of this motif. Accordingly, Jesus' move from Nazareth to Capernaum is specifically mentioned and supported with a reflection citation (4:13: from now on Jesus lives in Capernaum). It is characteristic that Capernaum is now considered to be ἡ ἰδία πόλις, Jesus' own city (9:1). This raises the question of whether Matthew always thinks of Peter's house in Capernaum that also serves as

Jesus' residence, or of Jesus' own house in Capernaum. In any case, it is clear that Matthew has utilized Mark's theological-topological category in terms of geography. It is located firmly in history; the traditional material has been historicized.

2. A further example is provided by the temporal perspective of the First Evangelist. At three prominent points in his composition, Matthew has redactionally added the temporal formula ἀπὸ τότε, a formula not found elsewhere in the New Testament except for the exceptional text Luke 16:16. In Matthew 4:17 this formula signals the beginning of Jesus' preaching ministry. "From then on," i.e. from the time when Jesus located his residence in Capernaum, began the public ministry of Jesus. In 16:21 this same formula marks the beginning of the series of passion and resurrection predictions; it introduces the final phase of the way of Jesus and characterizes it as the way of suffering, death, and resurrection. Finally in 26:16 Matthew inserts this formula at the beginning of the story of the betrayal by Judas. Even though Matthew portrays no development in the life of Jesus, he does present a narrative time line. What he sets forth is not direct address to the reader but history, a report of something that happened in the past.

3. We come a step further when we consider the Matthean *reflection citations*. These are preceded by a specific introductory formula (the full form of which is found in 1:22: Τοῦτο δὲ ὅλον γέγονεν ἵνα πληρωθῇ τὸ ῥηθὲν ὑπὸ κυρίου διὰ τοῦ προφήτου λέγοντος). These quotations are found in 1:23; 2:6, 15, 18, (23); 4:15–16; 8:17; 12:18–21; 13:35; 21:5 and 27:9–10. In 2:23, a text sometimes included in this list, there is no direct quotation but presumably a redactional allusion to the familiar designation of Jesus as Ναζωραῖος. The citation in 3:3 (par. Mark 1:2–3) is also to be bracketed out, since the source here is the text of Mark, and 13:13–14 is to be excluded as a post-Matthean interpolation. By and large, however, the reflection citations belong to the same traditional layer, presumably a collection of such quotations.

As indicated by the underlying textual form, which differs from the LXX otherwise used by Matthew, this collection of texts lay before Matthew in written form and was edited by him into his other traditional materials. Matthew used this testimony collection with pointed, telling effect: each stage of the birth story is concluded with a reflection citation (1:18–2:23). So also Jesus' change of residence to Capernaum is documented in the same way (4:15–16). The citations highlight a geographical line: Bethlehem, Egypt, Nazareth, Capernaum. Biographical details of Jesus' life are also emphasized in this manner: his miracle-working ministry (12:18ff), his entry into Jerusalem (21:5), and his betrayal by Judas (27:9–10). The documentation of such events by citations from Scripture means that the predictions made by the Old Testament prophets are seen to be fulfilled in the life of Jesus. The Jesus event is incorporated into the history of the Jewish people by regarding it as the fulfillment of the prophecy given to the Jewish people. The "Erlangen school" (J. Chr. K. von Hoffmann) identified such interpretation as "salvation history" thinking, and correctly so to the extent that it sees Matthew as having integrated the eschatological message into a historical account. The reflection quotations speak both of the fact that in the life of Jesus the *eschatological event* is fulfilled, and that the eschatological event is fulfilled *in the life of Jesus*. They are referred to a specific segment of time, which for Matthew lies in the past. As constitutive elements of the portrayal of the life of Jesus they both interpret the narrated event and make the interpreted event discernible as something that happened in the past.

The life of Jesus is presented as a discrete epoch of past history. It belongs to the nature of past events that they are unrepeatable. Matthew knows no Eastern, cyclical pattern of history in which the final period is a repetition of primeval beginnings (Endzeit = Urzeit) but pursues a linear understanding of history. The time of Jesus was a discrete segment of time in the course of history, an unrepeatable, unique time.

4. This may be clarified by taking the topic *Israel in the Gospel of Matthew* as an example. The First Evangelist is the only Synoptics author to include the saying "I was sent only to the lost sheep of the house of Israel" (15:24), a pre-Matthean word of the Lord that presumably came to Matthew as an isolated unit of tradition. The same saying is reflected in the context of Jesus' mission discourse in which the disciples are directed to go only to "the lost sheep of the house of Israel" (10:6).

A discrepancy exists between these sayings and Matthew's own conception as presented elsewhere in his Gospel, according to which the one church consists of Jews and Gentiles (21:33ff; 22:1ff) just as it does in the Gospel of Mark. Above all, the missionary command given by the Risen One points beyond the boundaries of Judaism and includes the whole world as the goal of the church's missionary preaching (28:16–20). This prohibits our accepting a popular interpretation according to which the sayings that limit the preaching of Jesus or the disciples to Israel are supposed to reflect a Jewish Christian position of Matthew himself. This view does not really explain the discrepancy between particularism and universalism in the message. It is also not possible to suppose that Matthew thought in terms of two concentric circles, with the Jewish mission being his primary concern and the Gentile mission as next most important, for there is no hint in Matthew of a qualification or limitation of either the Jewish or the Gentile mission.[1] On the contrary: while for the Evangelist Mark one may postulate on the basis of 7:27 a temporal or

---

[1]    Cf. differently Romans 11:25ff, and the discussion in A. IV. c. above.

functional ordering of the Jewish and Gentile missions (7:27: "Let the children *first* be fed," from which it could be inferred that "the dogs" will also receive bread) but in the Matthean parallel 15:26 the key word πρῶτον has been omitted.

W. D. Davies attempted to resolve the discrepancy between the particularistic Jewish mission and the universalistic Gentile mission by supposing that "Matthew's loyalty to the original Jesus tradition" allowed the Evangelists to tolerate such polarities.[2] In this view, accordingly, Matthew included the Jewish-Christian particularism of 10:6 and 15:24 not on the basis of his own reflection but only the result of a mechanical repetition of the tradition. This interpretation underestimates Matthew's own redactional contribution. Clearly, Matthew intentionally placed each saying in its present context. The difference between particularistic and universalistic orientation to the church's mission is thus to be explained redactionally. It is a matter of a genuinely Matthean construction. The Evangelist makes a distinction between the time of Jesus and the time of the church. The statements in 10:6 and 15:24 were valid for the time of Jesus: the people of Israel were called to repentance. Jesus' preaching, like that of his disciples, was directed exclusively to the Jewish people. Thereby the promises given to the Jewish people are realized. This is also indicated by the reflection citations. The eschatological event takes place within the space occupied by the Jewish people: the offer is made to it alone. The First Evangelist indicates that the Jewish people rejected this offer. This corresponds to his Markan source. The parable of the Wicked Husbandmen in Mark already had the meaning that the Jewish people had lost its special preferred status and that the "vineyard," i.e. its special place in salvation history, would be given to others (Mark 12:9). Matthew developed this idea even more consistently: the "other tenants" will deliver the fruits of the vineyard to the owner—in contrast to the Jewish people, who brought forth no fruit (Matt 21:41). This corresponds to the threatening pronouncement directed to the chief priests and the Pharisees, "the kingdom of God (ἡ βασιλεία τοῦ θεοῦ) will be taken away from you and given to a people that produces the fruits of the kingdom" (21:43, Matthean redaction). The Jewish people loses its position of pre-eminence as it loses its participation in the kingdom of God. Thus 21:43 is expressed in the future tense (ἀρθήσεται); it does not deal with the eschatological future but with the historical future, and thus describes something that had already happened in the time of Matthew. The kingdom of God has been taken from the Jews and transferred to another people, the church.

---

[2]    Cf. W. D. Davies, *Setting* 330: "The 'particularism' of Matthew is not a sign of a Jewish-Christian, anti-Pauline current but of his loyalty to the historic tradition of Jesus' ministry and of the early Church." On this point cf. G. Strecker, *Weg der Gerechtigkeit* 262–263.

This assessment of the Jewish people has had an extensive effect on the way Matthew has composed his Gospel. As was the case in Matthew's Markan source, so also for Matthew himself—the Pharisees and scribes, who appear in the story as constant opponents of Jesus are not to be interpreted as representing the Jewish contemporaries of the Evangelist but are set in the historical past, the time of Jesus. To be sure, Matthew presents the Jewish people as at first an approving chorus that responds to Jesus' mighty deeds with applause, admiration, amazement, and shock. But it is characteristic of Matthew's point of view that at the end of Jesus' life "the whole people" join with the chief priests and elders in demanding the death of Jesus (27:20), with the terrible consequence, "His blood be on us and on our children!" (27:25, Matthean redaction). Matthew intentionally emphasizes that it is the Jewish people as a whole that is involved in the cry for Jesus' crucifixion and invokes on itself the destruction of Jerusalem that was to happen in the near future as its punishment (22:7; 24:2). Here a decisive event of salvation history occurs, in the sense that the salvation history of the Jewish people, as it came to expression in the election of the people of Israel, reaches its high point which is at the same time its conclusion. The preferential position of Israel comes to an end with the crucifixion of Jesus, and the gift of the kingdom of God is given to another people. Matthew has given a terminological indication of this datum of salvation history by using the term "Israel" in his Gospel for the Jewish people,[3] i.e. a title of honor for the chosen people of God but after the crucifixion of Jesus he replaces it with the word Ἰουδαῖοι, a term used elsewhere by Gentiles to designate the Jewish people as one people among others, a people that can no longer claim any special position (28:15).

As documented by the geographical and chronological data, the reflection citations, and not least by the portrayal of the relation of Jesus to the Jewish people, the Gospel of Matthew is not to be understood as though it were the direct address of a sermon. From his own later perspective, Matthew consciously writes the story of Jesus as a figure of the past. What is the meaning of narrating such story from the past? The Evangelist would doubtless not have told the story of Jesus in this fashion if the narrative form, and not merely the content, had not been important to him. It is meaningful to narrate the Jesus event in this manner because it is something that has already been given to the Christian community and in it something is portrayed that has happened "extra nos." That which comes to speech in the Jesus event is not something that human beings can say to themselves but something that can only be said to them. It is not the product of subjective feelings, of human wishes and hopes but is a basis for human hope and faith that transcends human potential. It

---

3    Cf. 2:20–21; 8:10; 9:33; 10:6, 23; 15:24, 31; 19:28; 27:42 (in addition to the reflection citations 2:6; 27:9).

precedes faith in the same way that the human being Jesus precedes the Christ of faith, in such a manner that the Christ who is believed in would not be the object of faith if he did not point believers to the person of Jesus as a human being. The human Jesus, however, is to be interpreted neither subjectively nor merely to be made into an objectivization of human being in general. On the other hand, it would be wrong to attempt to understand Jesus objectively as though it were a matter of a "fact" that is provided as a basis for faith. The story is not reported for its own sake, the history is not presented historically but the Jesus-narrative is set forth from faith and for faith—as a story about a past event and therefore as preceding faith as its presupposition but still is not presented as a story that can be separated from faith as though the story of this event were dispensable. Just as any statement that has to do with faith is inseparable from the person of the speaker, so also for the story of Jesus as told by Matthew, that in its form as a story of a past event, apparently adequate in itself, is still a believed story, a story of faith. The result of historicizing the story is thus not to be interpreted merely in terms of the historian's craft but can be grasped only by faith as the "extra nos" and ἐφ᾽ ἅπαξ of the Christ of faith. This is the decisive theological content that is indispensable for the Evangelists, even when they portray its object in an apparently objectivizing and historicizing fashion.

## b) The Person of Jesus

### 1. Idealization

Differently than in his Markan source, Matthew speaks of Jesus in a specific manner. Mark, for example, in the pericope where Jesus blesses the little children mentions that Jesus "was indignant" to his disciples (Mark 10:14 ἠγανάκτησεν) but Matthew eliminated this picture of Jesus' emotions (19:14). A further example: according to Mark 1:43 Jesus angrily "scolded" (ἐμβριμησάμενος) the man whom he had healed; this too was omitted by Matthew (8:3; but cf. 9:30), just as in 12:13 he has eliminated the περιβλεψάμενος αὐτοὺς μετ᾽ ὀργῆς of Mark 3:5. In addition, the First Evangelist avoids using the verb ἐξίστημι of Jesus (12:23; differently Mark 3:21, "for they were saying, 'He has gone out of his mind'"). Neither is this verb applied to the disciples; cf. Matthew 14:32par. The same is true of θαυμάζω ("to be amazed;" 13:58 in contrast to Mark 6:6) or ἐκθαμβέω ("to be distressed and agitated;" 26:37 in contrast to Mark 14:33). The comparison of Mark 6:5 with the parallel Matthew 13:58 also reveals something characteristic. According to Markan tradition Jesus "could do no deed of power there [Nazareth]" because of the unbelief of the people, although the redactor adds the qualification, "except that he laid his hands on a few sick people and cured them." Differently Matthew 13:58, "and he did not do many deeds of power there, because of their unbelief." While Mark speaks of Jesus' inability, even if he then qualifies it, Matthew avoids even the appearance of portraying Jesus as unable to work miracles. That he in fact did not do many might deeds there is attributed to his own decision.

In other passages Matthew demonstrates the power of Jesus. While according to Mark 14:58 Jesus is said to have predicted, "I will destroy this temple (καταλύσω)... and in three days I will build another," Matthew replaces the future with a δύναμαι καταλῦσαι: Jesus has the power to destroy the temple and to rebuild it in three days (Matt 26:61). Thereby Matthew demonstrates the power of Christ, at the same time avoiding picturing Jesus as having made a prediction about the destruction and reconstruction of the temple that did not in fact take place. The same Matthean redactional modification of traditional material is seen in Matthew 19:17. In contrast to the Markan parallel (Mark 10:18), the Matthean Jesus does reject the address ἀγαθός but has fundamentally altered the question, "Why do you ask me about what is good?" The Matthean *Kyrios* can claim basically any designations that contribute to the dignity and honor of his office.

The miracles Jesus accomplishes are also enhanced. The First Evangelist often adds to the tradition the comment that "in that hour" or "from that hour on" the healing was effective (8:13; 9:22; 15:28; 17:18). The word of Jesus has super-human, miracle-working qualities. The power of this word is demonstrated when Matthew emphasizes the comprehensive scope of Jesus' miracle working activity: "all" were healed (4:23; 8:16; 9:35; 12:15; 14:35–36), or "all" ate and were satisfied (15:37). The latter example also enhances the number of those who were fed, since it is calculated "not counting women and children" (14:21; 15:38).

Even if such modifications of the literary sources by the redactor Matthew are not always carried through consistently, and even though Luke in part presents notable parallels, so that while every instance is not distinctly Matthean, it is nevertheless the case that the Matthean tendency [*Tendenz*] to edit the tradition in the way presented above is clearly recognizable and calls for an explanation. Matthew does not place the accent on the dialectic of the lowliness and exaltation of Jesus, as can be shown in detail for Mark. It is rather the case that in the First Gospel the intention can be recognized to let the traditional elements that expressed Jesus' lowliness recede in order to emphasize those that express Jesus' exalted status. Matthew presents Jesus as the Kyrios who has been given universal power for his earthly work. This is the reason for the idealizing redaction of the figure of Jesus.[4]

---

4    Cf. G. Strecker, *Weg der Gerechtigkeit* 120–122.

## 2.   Christological Titles

### α) Son of David

The Gospel of Matthew designates Jesus as Son of David, who is also Son of Abraham, at the very beginning (1:1). The genealogy is conceived basically as certification of Jesus as the Son of David who is also son of Abraham. Both show that Jesus is rooted in the Jewish people and its history and that in a messianic sense, since postulating the Davidic descent of Jesus corresponds to the Jewish messianic expectation. As the Son of David, Jesus is the one through whom "God gives Israel's history its fulfillment."[5] Jesus is Son of David as the heir and fulfiller of the promises given to the empirical people of Israel.

This is seen in the birth story of Jesus (1:18–2:23). Joseph too belongs to the descendents of David (1:20). The birth story of Jesus is essentially structured in the style of a throne succession narrative and designates Jesus as the one who as Son of David has authentic claim to sovereignty (2:1–23). Moreover, Jesus the miracle worker is also called "Son of David" in the cry of the blind who call out for healing (9:27). It is thus taken up in the choral conclusion that marks the end of the ten miracle stories Matthew has put together (8:1–9:34). When the Jewish crowds cry out, "Never has anything like this been seen in Israel" (9:33), Jesus' miracle working activity is clearly oriented toward the Jewish people. Since Jesus' mission in word and deed is directed to the Jews, the title "Son of David" is appropriate. When after the healing of a demoniac the question broke out from the amazed crowd, "Could this be the Son of David?" (12:22–23), this is no longer thought of in the Jewish sense—the Jewish messianic Son of David is a political messiah, not primarily a miracle worker (Zech 9:9–10; Isa 11:1–10; PsSol 17). Thus it is truly Christian tradition that here comes to expression. The title "Son of David" has been depoliticized by linking it to the θεῖος ἀνήρ tradition. As Son of David Jesus is the divine man, who strides across the earth working miracles.

The inference from what has just been said is that the title "Son of David" in Matthew cannot be considered historical data. This title cannot be fitted into the framework of what was possible in the Palestinian Judaism of Jesus' time; it reflects the confession of Christian faith and derives originally from a Jewish Christian context. Matthew, of course, used the term in a historicizing sense. In 15:22 the Gentile woman also uses this predication. That which can be explained neither psychologically nor historically becomes clear within the theological concerns of Matthew: the Syrophoenician woman uses the title in order to express the Matthean conception that Jesus is sent to Israel. Jesus' miracle on behalf of the

---

[5]   A. Schlatter, *Der Evangelist Matthäus* 1.

woman stands out all the more as an exception which at the same time presents the faith of the Gentile woman as a positive example in contrast to the unbelief of the Jews.

The title is also found in 21:9. The Markan parallel of the individual pericope reflects the political messianic expectation—to be sure, without mentioning the title "Son of David." Accordingly, the Jewish people connect Jesus' entrance into Jerusalem with the expectation of the restoration of David's kingdom. It thus belongs to the Markan motif of misunderstanding; in this way the ὄχλοι let it be seen that they do not understand the revelation of the Christ (Mark 11:9-10). The matter is different in Matthew, in that he no longer orients his usage of the term as a "via negativa" to its original political understanding but pictures the entrance of the righteous Son of David who embodies the attitude of "gentleness and humility" (πραΰτης, 21:5; cf. 11:29). He is the one whose intention it is to call the Jewish people to repentance. That the pericope of the temple cleansing also contains the Son of David title (21:15) is no accident. The introductory scenes of the passion story thus show the setting for which this occurrence is characteristic. The execution of Jesus is made the responsibility of the Jewish people and means that they have rejected their own elected status within the history of salvation, because it is the Son of David promised to the people Israel.

It is from this perspective that the problem of why the Son of David question is limited to Matthean redaction is to be clarified (22:41-46). Here the two titles υἱὸς Δαυίδ and κύριος are juxtaposed. In Matthew's understanding these two titles are not mutually exclusive. In his view, "Son of David" should not be rejected as a christological title of lesser importance than "Kyrios." A widespread opinion among scholars is that "Son of David" refers in Matthew to the earthly Jesus, while Kyrios denotes the future enthroned Christ. But such an interpretation cannot be sustained in Matthew, where the earthly Jesus already bears the title Kyrios. It is thus a simultaneous juxtaposition.[6] The simultaneous juxtaposition of the titles Son of David and Kyrios means in the first place that Jesus' sending as Son of David to Israel was a historically unique and unrepeatable event. The title Kyrios, on the other hand, points to the eschatological quality of Jesus. To be sure, such a quality is not to be excluded for the Son of David (cf. Rom 1:3); its connection with the Kyrios name gives it a

---

[6]  According to G. Bornkamm, "End-Expectation" 32-38 it is a matter of the juxtaposition of humility and exaltation; while "Kyrios" emphasizes the exalted divine status of Christ, "Son of David" denotes his earthly lowliness. This is not satisfying. Matthew is more interested in setting aside the statements about Jesus' lowliness and emphasizing those that point to his exalted majesty. Furthermore, it is as Son of David that Jesus is the miracle worker; this is not an expression of earthly lowliness but of divine sovereignty.

special significance by its orientation of the mission of Jesus to the Jewish people. Therefore this title represents an essential element in the historicizing of the traditional material by the redactor Matthew.

β) Lord

In Matthew's Christology the title κύριος has a very high rank, as can be seen in the pericope dealing with the Son of David (22:41ff; cf. also the connection with "Son of David" in 15:22 and 20:30–31). This designation is derived from the secular title used in respectful address ("Lord," "Sir"), which is also found in the First Gospel (21:29; 27:63). It is difficult to decide whether Jesus is ever addressed in this secular sense. However, two theological directions are clear in the usage. In the first place, Κύριος refers to the God of the Old Testament; this is especially clear in the introductory formulae to the reflection citations (1:22; 2:15; also in quotations: 4:7; 5:33). Moreover, the word has a christological significance, as in the address Κύριε to the Son of Man as the world's eschatological judge (25:37, 44). The One who comes again is the "Lord" (24:42), i.e. the "Son of Man" (24:44). He is expected, even if his advent is delayed (24:45–51). This address thus refers primarily to the community's Lord whose future advent is awaited.

The earthly Jesus also bears the Kyrios title. Here a distinction appears: the disciples and those who seek healing address Jesus as Κύριος (e. g. 8:2; 9:28; 14:28, 30), while his opponents use the term διδάσκαλος or ῥαββί. A good example is provided by the description of Judas the betrayer at the last supper (26:20–25). Here Matthew differs from his Markan source: the disciples address Jesus with Κύριε but the traitor Judas uses the address ῥαββί ("teacher"). This distinction is carried out so consistently that it can be used as an exegetical criterion. Wherever Jesus is addressed as Κύριε, someone is speaking who has become a follower of Jesus. In contrast, whenever the term διδάσκαλος appears one may assume that opposition is also present (e. g. 8:12–22).

With this title the community's confession of the exalted Lord Jesus is projected back into the life of Jesus. This story deals with the one who in the present and future is the community's Lord. It's meaning is not to be limited to an element or function in the course of Israelite salvation history. It is rather the case that already during his earthly life he possessed an "authority" surpassing that of the Pharisees and scribes (7:29) that is given to him as the Exalted One (28:18). Since the earthly Jesus already possesses eschatological authority, it is only appropriate that human beings honor him in a worshipful manner (προσκυνέω e. g. 2:2, 8, 11; 8:2; 9:18) or approach him with the cry for mercy (ἐλέησον 9:27; 15:22; 17:15; 20:30–31) or when they encounter him call out "save" (σῶσον 8:25; 14:30)—acclamations that were used in the community's worship. They are applied to the earthly Jesus, since he had been clothed in the colors of the eschatological Lord, because his power and exalted status were that of the eschatological Lord.

γ) Other Christological Predicates

With regard to the term "Son of Man," Matthew takes over almost all the references in Mark (exception: Matt 16:21 in contrast to Mark 8:31). Elsewhere he adopts the usage of his other traditions (Q and his special sources). There are no characteristic redactional statements. The only peculiarity is the expression "kingdom of the Son of Man" (13:41; 16:28; 20:21) that is found in ecclesiological contexts.

So also the First Evangelist has for the most part taken over the term "Son of God" as used in his sources. In the redactional material υἱὸς τοῦ θεοῦ plays a special role as an element in confessional formulations (14:33; 16:16); Matthew has also inserted it into the passion story (27:40, 43). The change in the baptismal story is of fundamental importance, where 3:17 has Οὗτός ἐστιν ὁ υἱός μου ὁ ἀγαπητός, ... (in contrast to Mark's Σὺ εἶ ὁ υἱός μου ὁ ἀγαπητός, ...). The adoptionistic meaning of the Markan baptismal story is here set aside. The heavenly voice does not pronounce Jesus now to be God's adopted Son but proclaims him as the Son of God. This accords with the birth story, which already designates Jesus as Son of God (2:15). Jesus' divine sonship begins with his birth. Accordingly the whole life of Jesus has a salvific character. Thus in Matthew the physical components associated with the term "Son of God" are expressed much more strongly than in Mark. That Matthew has taken over the Hellenistic Christian theologoumenon of the virgin birth is no accident (1:18ff). Here is an advance announcement of something that became very important in the life of the later church, the issue of the "nature" of Christ. It is of course more important that Matthew incorporates the physical components of Christ's divine sonship into the portrayal of Jesus' preaching ministry.

Only occasionally is Χριστός found as a christological title, as can be recognized from the use of the article (e. g. 16:16, 20).[7] The tendency is clear, however, to use "Christ" as a proper name (cf. 1:1 "Book of the origin of Jesus Christ"). The redactional "Jesus who is called Christ" (Ἰησοῦς ὁ λεγόμενος Χριστός 1:16; 27:17, 22) is characteristic of Matthew.

In addition, Jesus is called βασιλεύς; either as βασιλεὺς τῶν Ἰουδαίων (2:2; 27:11, 29, 37) or βασιλεὺς Ἰσραήλ (27:42). As in Mark, a distinction is here consciously made: the Gentiles describe Jesus as "king of the Jews," while Jews speak of him as "king of Israel." While Matthew with this

---

[7] In contrast, W. Kramer, *Christ, Lord, Son of God* 212, concludes that it is impossible to generalize the issue of the connection between the use of the article and christological usage. But cf. M. de Jonge, "The Earliest Christian Use of Christos," *NTS* 32 (1986) 321–343; 328–329.

predicate emphasizes the connection of Jesus' advent with history and his mission to the Jewish people, there is still a characteristic connection with the motif of misunderstanding. What Matthew portrays is not the story of a king but of the eschatological Kyrios. The sovereignty of the earthly Jesus is a paradoxical reality, visible only to eyes of faith but hidden from unbelievers.

### 3.  The Message of Jesus

α) Didache and Kerygma

Vocabulary statistics show that the verb διδάσκω does not occur any more often in Matthew than in Mark; the same is true of its derivatives. Yet this does not tell us much in regard to Matthew's conception of the person and work of Jesus; on the contrary the Matthean redactor's overarching perspective has eliminated several references from Mark. On the other hand, it is indisputable that the statements about Jesus "teaching" have a central place in the Gospel of Matthew. Thus Matthew specifically warns against the διδαχή of the Pharisees (16:12, redactional). He is the only Evangelist to take over the logion that deals with the importance of right doctrine (5:19), and the missionary command of the Risen One calls for the "teaching" of all nations (28:20). Moreover, Jesus is regularly portrayed as "teaching" (e. g. 5:2; 7:29).

The verb κηρύσσω is often placed alongside διδάσκω (4:23; 9:35; 11:1). A distinction can be made: διδάσκω refers to Jesus' teaching on the subject of law and basic principles; in contrast κηρύσσω has the essential character of a proclamation and portrays direct address to the hearers that call them to decision, repentance, or refusal. But this distinction is appropriate only on first glance, for examination of the teaching of Jesus shows that it also has the character of address (cf. 7:24ff). And on the other hand, when Jesus "preaches" (κηρύσσω) the kingdom of God, the proclamation does not occur without instruction; the address contains a doctrinal content. Thus there is an extensive overlap in the contents of didache and kerygma, between teaching and preaching. This is clear from a comparison of 10:7 and 28:19–20. According to 10:7 Jesus commissions his disciples to "preach" (κηρύσσω) the nearness of the kingdom of God, while the missionary command of the Risen One charges the eleven disciples to "teach" all nations (διδάσκω, 28:19–20). Preaching the kingdom of God and ethical instruction are bound closely together.

The "beatitudes of the Sermon on the Mount" (5:3–12) throw light on the problem of the relation of didache and kerygma. Matthew found the pronouncement μακάριος in his tradition. It is familiar from the Jewish wisdom literature (e. g. Sir 25:8–9). There the word has a general, non-specific meaning (well-being, wholeness). Accordingly the beatitudes are to be understood as wisdom instruction, and Jesus is presented as a wisdom teacher. On the other hand, the New Testament μακάριος has throughout an eschatological significance. In the New Testament they primarily introduce a pronouncement that promises eschatological salvation (Luke 10:23–24; 14:15). The beatitudes of the Sermon on the Mount include as their final clause a clear eschatological assurance, the promise of the βασιλεία τῶν οὐρανῶν, that is, the kingdom of God that is to appear at the end of time. The beatitudes of the Sermon on the Mount are thus to be understood as eschatological proclamation.

The interpreter can typically swing back and forth between the two exegetical possibilities. This observation is relevant for understanding this aspect of Matthean theology: in the Gospel of Matthew wisdom instruction can be set forth as eschatological proclamation, and conversely eschatological statements can appear in the form of wisdom teaching. Neither can be separated from the other. Jesus is the teacher who speaks with eschatological authority; his teaching bears the promise of the kingdom of God, and the promise of the kingdom of God is accomplished in his teaching.

### β) The Ethicizing of the Traditional Material

Matthew has compiled five speech complexes in his Gospel, each of which is recognizable by its redactional concluding formula (7:28; 11:1; 13:53; 19:1; 26:1).

The fact that speech tradition has a prominent place in the Gospel of Matthew has led some scholars to speak of a *church catechism* that Matthew wants to set forth in his Gospel. In support of this thesis one can unquestionably point to the "church order" (18:1ff), which especially reflects the problems of church discipline in the Matthean community. But Matthew is concerned first of all with the narrative of Jesus' life and work, and the speeches are worked into the temporal and geographical situation of the life of Jesus.[8] In addition, the practical aims of the Gospel of Matthew may not be narrowly limited. The Jesus narrative is not only valuable for catechetical purposes but also for liturgical, since the early Christian congregations took over from the synagogue the practice of scripture exposition as a part of worship. As the Gentile element became independent, it became necessary to fall back on their own Christian writings. This too was doubtless an occasion for the origin of the Gospels, so that a liturgical goal cannot be juxtaposed to a catechetical goal as though these were alternatives.

The proclamation of Jesus in the Gospel of Matthew has an essential parenetic-ethical character. In comparing Matthew's redactional work with the tradition that came to him one notes an ethicizing of the tradition. Three examples:

1. The *beatitudes of the Sermon on the Mount* are mainly traditional material. Three layers of tradition are to be distinguished:

---

[8]     Differently than the extra-canonical "Teaching of the Twelve Apostles," written in the first half of the second century and addressed directly to the Christian community. On this cf. K. Niederwimmer, *The Didache* (Hermeneia) (Minneapolis: Fortress, 1998).

a) The *oldest tradition* documented by Luke 6:20–23 (par Matt 5:3–4, 6, 11–12). These pronouncements of blessing on the poor, the hungry, the crying and the persecuted go back to the Q tradition. According to them, the kingdom of God is promised to those who suffer; those who passively persevere receive the promise of victory over distress and persecution.

b) In an *intermediate layer of tradition* seven beatitudes were compiled, all having the same form (5:3–9), concluded by the blessing on the persecuted (5:11–12). Septads are found frequently in the pre-Matthean tradition (1:1ff, the genealogy of Jesus; 6:9ff, the Lord's prayer); seven is a theologically significant "round number." In terms of their content, this means that with 5:7–9 blessings on those who do the word are placed alongside the announcement of salvation for those who suffer. The person's active conduct, the deed of concern and compassion, of purity and peacemaking now become the object of blessing. An ethicizing development is here suggested that finds its conclusion in the final layer in the history of the tradition, the redactional work of Matthew himself.

c) The *Matthean redaction*. The First Evangelist reaches back to the intermediate layer but modifies this text in the process of adopting it. In 5:3 the addition τῷ πνεύματι leads to a spiritualizing of the traditional blessing of the poor and declares that the Matthean Jesus extols the "meek."

In 5:6 the phrase τὴν δικαιοσύνη is added (perhaps also the preceding καὶ διψῶντες). The blessing now no longer refers to those who physically hunger, promising them satisfaction with material food but in a spiritualizing manner praises those who hunger for righteousness, i.e. who intensively strive after a righteous attitude. This too is an ethicizing of the traditional material, that contains an indirect challenge to do righteousness. The promise is made to those who do righteousness.

Finally, Matthew has independently created 5:10 by excerpting from v. 11, or by reusing material from 5:3b. Here too the typical Matthean δικαιοσύνη concept appears. Here too it concerns the ethical conduct of the community, which is the occasion for persecution and thus the basis of the promise. The beatitudes as a whole are in the Matthean redaction an example of the ethicizing of the traditional material. They contain indirect demands, and may be described (with H. Windisch) as "entrance conditions into the kingdom of God." They appear as a "table of virtues" (M. Dibelius), although to be sure not in the secular sense but with an eschatological claim.

2. The so-called *adultery clause* appears in Matthew 5:32 and 19:9. The issue of divorce had already been dealt with by both Q and Mark. Here too different layers of tradition can be distinguished.

a) The oldest layer is found in 1 Corinthians 7:10–11 (a pre-Pauline version), and, in a different form, in the conflict story about divorce in Mark 10:1–9. This oldest stratum of the tradition contains an absolute prohibition of divorce (cf. Mark 10:9, "What God has joined together, let no one separate"). This has been the will of God from the very beginning. The provision in the law of Moses for divorce is accordingly only a secondary accommodation to the hardness of human hearts. When this demand speaks against any divorce, the Old Testament law is also criticized. As the oldest Christian tradition on the problem of divorce, this saying presumably contains authentic words of Jesus.[9]

b) The next stratum in the history of the tradition is represented by a two-fold form: by the Q tradition, which may be inferred from Luke 16:18 par Matthew 5:32, and by the logion Mark 10:11–12, which likewise goes back to old Jesus tradition, even though Mark presumably did not know the sayings collection used by Matthew and Luke. Here we no longer find an absolute prohibition of divorce but the concern is to define and to differentiate: "adultery" (μοιχεία) occurs when there is divorce *and* remarriage. This corresponds to the (pre-Pauline?) addition to the original saying of the Lord in 1 Corinthians 7:11a. The marriage is considered to still exist even after the divorce; it is first broken when one of the partners marries a second time. Thereby the original absolute indissolubility of marriage is placed in question. It is now possible to think of the marriage partners as separating without this being considered adultery and without the necessity of the church having to intervene with disciplinary measures. The canon law of the Roman Catholic Church knows a corresponding "separation from bed and board" that accepts this possibility, in order to avoid a definitive dissolution of the marriage. If this possibility from classical Roman Catholic exegesis of Matthew 5:32par is placed in the foreground, then such an interpretation can appeal to the intermediate tradition but not to the oldest form of this saying. This intermediate layer of the tradition lay before Matthew but was edited by him in a characteristic manner:

c) *Matthean redaction* has formally changed 5:32, in that (1.) the saying has been reformulated into an antithesis and (2.) a phrase has been added, παρεκτὸς λόγου πορνείας ("except on the ground of unchastity"). Accordingly, divorce and remarriage are permitted in the exceptional case of πορνεία. That this interpretation is characteristic for Matthew is seen in his reworking of the Markan text. In 19:9 Matthew adds (contra Mark 10:11–12) μὴ ἐπὶ πορνεία ("except for unchastity"). This exception clause also affirms that "unchastity" removes the prohibition of divorce and remarriage.

Matthew reflects the tradition of his community. What is presented here as marital law represents the actual practice of the Matthean church. A parallel to these legal arrangements is found in the rabbinic discussion. The school of Rabbi Hillel wanted to permit divorce for any reason, even minor ones (even the wife's burning supper could be the occasion for giving

---

[9]     Cf. above B. II. e. 4.

her a certificate of divorce). In contrast, Rabbi Shammai permitted divorce only for sexual offenses (= πορνεία). The tradition of Matthew's church is nourished from Jewish roots. Thus in the predominately Gentile Christian community of Matthew himself, these rules are brought into harmony with the Jewish Christian foundations of his church and handed on as an element of the tradition. It is characteristic of Matthew's understanding of Jesus' message that he hands on this tradition within the framework of the Sermon on the Mount and the conflict stories. This is to be understood with reference to ethics: as the eschatological teacher Jesus gives instructions that are both binding on the community and can be put into practice.

We see that the history of the tradition can be traced as the history of increasing accommodation of Jesus' original apodictic prohibition of divorce to the actual situations in the churches. At the beginning stood the maxim of the indissolubility of marriage. In the preaching of Jesus, it was bound to the proclamation of the kingdom of God and the call to repentance. The absolute demand of the call to repentance—as seen in the history of the tradition of this saying—does not do away with the relativity of the world. Church teaching adapts the radical statement originally made in Jesus' situation to the realities of human life. This is theologically legitimate, if such adjustments do not intend to annul the fundamental demand for repentance and if church teaching does not itself become a "ius divinum," a divine, unchangeable law. Admittedly, it appears that the Matthean redaction comes close to such an understanding, for the speaker is the eschatological Teacher whose instruction claims absolute validity. It is thus set forth as a practicable demand, as indicated by the Matthean insertion of the unchastity clause, and at the same time a radical demand, since as a practicable law it simultaneously represents an eschatological teaching. The path from here to the idea of church law as divine law is not very far. Matthew gives expression to the self-understanding of the church of his time, by projecting it back into the life of Jesus and by interpreting the person and work of Jesus from the situation and self-understanding of his church. Such an interpretation of the message of Jesus can not anticipate and replace the decisions that later Christian generations must make. To be sure, the eschatological qualification of Matthew's answer makes clear that every Christian's ethical decision has an ethical dimension and must be made "sub specie aeternitatis."

3. In this context we will briefly introduce only one final example, the question of *oaths*. In 5:33–37, within the framework of the Sermon on the Mount, there is an antithesis with an apparently pre-Matthean structure. Here Jesus opposes the prohibition of perjury, as it was given to those in ancient times, with his own absolute prohibition of swearing: "Do not swear at all" 5:34a). This counter thesis is illustrated by examples that are in part also documented in James 5:12. The concluding verse 37 has been

heavily edited by Matthew; not only is 37b Matthean but also 37a. In distinction from James 5:12, where "yes" is to mean "yes" and "no" mean "no," and which is thus a demand for truthful speech, the First Evangelist reads: "Let your word be 'Yes, Yes' or 'No, No'" (5:37a). Thereby a formula is transmitted that presumably was used in the Matthean church. The doubled yes or no is documented in Jewish literature as a formula used for solemn vows (e. g. Slavonic Enoch 49:1 and elsewhere). By this means the Matthean church avoids violating Jesus' absolute prohibition of oaths in that in investigative legal situations they do not use an oath but rather this form of solemn vow, in order to establish testimony as valid. Again, Matthew has adjusted the Jesus tradition to the requirements of community life in his time. The original absolute prohibition of oaths is broken, and the proclamation of Jesus becomes ethical instruction.[10]

γ) Δικαιοσύνη and Ἀγάπη

A comprehensive statement of the content of the message of the Matthean Jesus is contained in the term δικαιοσύνη, which appears seven times in the Gospel, five of which are in the Sermon on the Mount (3:15; 5:6, 10, 20; 6:1, 33; 21:32). That all these references have been added by the redactor Matthew indicates the supreme importance the Evangelist attributes to this term as a summary of the content of Jesus' message. It is hardly a matter of "God's own righteous rule."[11] On the contrary, it is characteristic that only in 6:33 does Matthew add a genitive modifier that refers to God. The usage in this passage, however, is to be explained from the fact that here Matthew closely follows his source, that originally had spoken of his (= God's) kingdom (cf. Luke 12:31). Most of the Matthean passages either use δικαιοσύνη either without an appositional genitive or with the genitive ὑμῶν. The term thus has an anthropological orientation. "Righteousness" is the comprehensive term for the right conduct of the disciples in general, and thus for the whole Christian community. Such righteousness must be different from that of the Pharisees and scribes (5:20). It can be seen in the individual actions that people do (cf. 6:1 as the title and summary of the good works "giving alms, prayer, and fasting"). This righteousness is the reason and occasion that provokes persecution against the community (5:10). When the community strives for the heavenly rule of God, it thereby is striving for "righteousness" (6:33). It is this righteousness that must be the object of human striving (5:6). The words of Jesus can be understood as the exposition of this comprehensive de-

---

10   Thus in Matthew 5:33–37 three layers of tradition may be distinguished: (1.) 5:33–34a is from Jesus; (2.) 5:34b-36 is from the pre-Matthean church; (3.) 5:37 is Matthean, i.e. it is composed or heavily edited by Matthew.

11   P. Stuhlmacher, *Gerechtigkeit Gottes bei Paulus* (FRLANT 87. Göttingen: Vandenhoeck & Ruprecht, 1966²) 189.

mand for righteousness, a striving that has as its object standing before God with attitude and actions that God vindicates as right. This righteousness takes as its model God's own conduct, who causes the sun to rise on bad and good, righteous and unrighteous (5:45).

The essence of "righteousness" is developed in contrast to that of Pharisaism. When the Pharisees are portrayed as the opponents of Jesus and his preaching, it is characteristic that Jesus warns against the teaching of the Pharisees and Sadducees (16:11–12, Matthean redaction). But it is not only the doctrine of the Pharisees that is presented and caricatured as a negative example; their actions are presented in the same way (6:1ff).[12] As theological representatives of Judaism they are considered to be ὁδηγοὶ τυφλοί (23:16, 24). Their unbelief is manifested in ὑπόκρισις and ἀνομία, both of which are antithetical concepts to δικαιοσύνη. Thereby Pharisaic "hypocrisy" is not thought of as an "objective self-contradiction," as though the Pharisees were not aware of the contradictory nature of their conduct. It is rather the case that the expression ὑπόκρισις portrays a conscious pretense. The intentional acts of the Pharisees, for which they are held responsible, stands in contrast to the responsible, intentional acts of the followers of Jesus. Their "hypocrisy" reveals the contradiction between the way they present themselves in public and their real inner attitude (6:1ff; 23:1ff).

The way the observance of Jewish practices is portrayed in the Gospel of Matthew is also informative. The Jewish ceremonial law is considered to be essentially a matter of external forms. Thus the possibility is provided for a person to acquire the reputation for a special piety that does not correspond to the person's inner attitude (23:5, 23). In contrast to this Jesus demands the realization of an ethical righteousness in actual practice. The ceremonial law is set over against the moral law (cf. 15:19–20; in contrast to Mark, the ethical requirement is tightened up and oriented to the Decalogue). Yet the non-ritual conduct of the Pharisees also falls under the verdict "hypocrisy," for here too they are characterized by the contrast between "outer" and "inner," the contradiction between what they do and their real inner attitude. Even when their external deeds are good, they do not represent their internal attitude, for the decisive criterion for realizing "righteousness" is that deeds be done as before God, not with a view to what other human beings think about them. That means: (a) Quantitatively, righteousness must be done totally. It is typical of Matthew to use πᾶς-statements in the context of presenting ethical requirements (3:15; 23:5; 28:20). It is a matter of realizing "perfection" (5:48),

---

[12]  Here there is an apparent contradiction to 23:3, where the words of the Pharisees are to be followed but not their actions; this is an introduction to the anti-Pharisaic speech that was already present in the tradition and is less characteristic of Matthew himself.

which leaves no area of human life out of consideration. Human righteousness must be complete.[13] Moreover, (b) "righteousness" in the Matthean sense is not only a quantitative increase in contrast to a non-Christian lifestyle but the Pharisaic tradition is confronted with an independent "law" of Jesus. This requirement is qualitatively different from the ethics of Jewish or Gentile law, because it is spoken by the Kyrios with eschatological authority.

In addition to the above considerations, it is important to note that Matthew presents the message of Jesus in summarizing formulae. The "Golden Rule" appears at the conclusion of the Sermon on the Mount (7:12—" In everything do to others as you would have them do to you; for this is the law and the prophets"). In dependence on Hosea 6:6 the Matthean Jesus calls for "mercy, not sacrifice" (9:13; 12:7). Of special importance is the double commandment to love God and human beings (22:34–40; cf. Deut 6:5 and Lev 19:18; cf. also the command to love the neighbor in Matt 19:19). A high point is represented by the command to love the enemy (5:44). A tendency toward fundamental principles is clearly recognizable. The demand for perfection, mercy, and especially love is intended to represent the message of Jesus.

In this network of associations the Matthean love commandment is not to be understood as though ἀγάπη stood in contrast to δικαιοσύνη. The commandment to love God and the neighbor does not nullify the demand for righteousness. It is rather the case that the love command is fulfilled in the practice of righteousness. To conduct oneself righteously in relation to one's fellow human beings means to love them and to let them have what is rightfully theirs. Conversely, this also means that righteousness is not to be separated from love. To deal with one's fellow human being in righteousness means to open oneself to others and to accept them as those whose existence is also willed and affirmed by God. The extent to which righteousness and love are bound to each other is seen in the way in which the Decalogue is paired with the love commandment. In 19:19 the love commandment is included as the last of the laws of the Decalogue, with the result that it appears as a fundamental principle summarizing the Decalogue. Like the individual commands of the Decalogue, so also the love commandment is a command that can be put into actual practice. Matthew does not think of it as though it were basically impossible really to fulfill it (in the sense of an "usus elenchticus legis"), but for Matthew and his church it is understood to be practicable. Its goal and intention is to be fulfilled. This does not exclude taking it in a radical sense but the radical interpretation of the command is oriented to the concrete situa-

---

[13]  Cf. also the pleonistic περισσεύσῃ … πλεῖον, which is to be understood primarily in a quantitative sense (5:20).

tion. The right attitude of love and the right practice of righteousness are at one and the same time both radical and concrete.

When the Matthean Jesus is presented as preaching righteousness and love, he is thereby understood as the turning point of the history of salvation, the fulfillment of the Law and the Prophets, as the goal of the Old Testament. The relation of Jesus to the Old Testament in the First Gospel, understood mainly in terms of his relation to the Old Testament law, is characterized by an antinomy: on the one hand Jesus' message is characterized by a positive affirmation of the Old Testament law (cf. 5:18 "For truly I tell you, until heaven and earth pass away, not one letter, not one stroke of a letter, will pass from the law until all is accomplished"). On the other hand, Jesus' preaching can deal critically with the Old Testament law: (Matt 19:8: "It was because you were so hard-hearted that Moses allowed you to divorce your wives but from the beginning it was not so"; in 5:21ff the antitheses of the Sermon on the Mount include a clear critique of not only the oral tradition of Judaism but of the written Mosaic law itself; cf. especially the prohibition of divorce and oaths. Not of least importance in this regard is the fact that the rejection of the ceremonial law implies a critical stance over against the wording and practice of the Old Testament law; cf. 15:19-20). From both of the above considerations we may conclude that the preaching of Jesus is not a "nova lex;" it rather understands itself to be in continuity with the Old Testament law and prophets. On the other hand, the proclamation of Jesus does not mean simply a repetition of the Old Testament law but unites in itself both a fundamental affirmation and a critical stance toward the Old Testament. Precisely this coexistence of the two stances is the "fulfilling" of the law and the prophets (5:17; cf. 7:12; 22:40). Jesus is the true interpreter of the Old Testament; his authority as the eschatological Kyrios stands fundamentally over the Old Testament, since he not only proclaims the will of God (6:10; 7:21) but also realizes it in his own conduct in exemplary form (26:42).

δ) The Grounding of the Message of Jesus

If the essential content of the message of Jesus is the ethical demand of righteousness and love, and if this can be described as the "law of the Lord", not least on the basis of the Sermon on the Mount,[14] then the question cannot be avoided as to whether Matthew hereby places himself on the side of nomism, somewhat alongside the author of the Letter of James, according to which righteousness by works would stand at the

---

[14]   Cf. G. Strecker, "Das Gesetz in der Bergpredigt—Die Bergpredigt als Gesetz," in T. Veijola, ed. *The Law in the Bible and in its Environment* (SFThL 51. Helsinki-Göttingen: Vandenhoeck & Ruprecht, 1990) 109-125; 121.

center of Christian teaching and thus would constitute an obvious contrast to the Pauline-Lutheran doctrine of justification. There can be no doubt that the comparison with Paul reveals that it would be entirely artificial to postulate for Matthew the Pauline distinction between indicative and imperative. To be sure, scholars such as A. Schlatter[15] or G. Schrenk[16] have understood the Matthean concept of righteousness in the Pauline sense primarily as "gift," obtained for human beings by Jesus' suffering understood as atonement or by his substitutionary death. Such a gift would have to be followed by the demand for righteousness that would be an appropriate response to such a gift. The human actions called for in the Gospel of Matthew would have to be understood in no other way than the human answer to the redemptive act of God. We have seen, however, that according to the Matthean understanding in the preaching of Jesus δικαιοσύνη is not understood as gift but as demand. This demand is not qualified by the atoning death of Jesus, which plays no larger role in Matthew than it does in Mark. It is also not the case that the ethical demand is only "an implication of Christology,"[17] for conversely Christology and ecclesiology are permeated by the ethical demand.[18]

The basis for Jesus' demand in Matthew's understanding is in the very first place the apocalyptic future which is not at human disposal. The First Evangelist has elaborated the apocalyptic materials of his sources. As argued above, the Markan apocalypse has been redactionally modified to focus more sharply on the future. The Matthean Jesus announces the coming judgment, the judgment over which he will preside as Son of Man. Eschatological judgment and reward are held before the reader's view. This is thought of in apocalyptic-realistic terms: the redactional formula ὁ κλαυθμὸς καὶ ὁ βρυγμὸς τῶν ὀδόντων is found often (8:12; 13:42, 50; 22:13; 24:51; 25:30), describing the final state of the unrighteous. Not infrequently, the expression τὸ σκότος τὸ ἐξώτερον is found as a designation for the place of punishment (8:12; 22:13; 25:30). The eschatological reward for the righteous is described with the term μισθός (6:1–2, 5, 16; 10:41–42, 20:8); Matthew explicitly emphasizes the transcendent reward.[19] Such orientation to future "reward" affirms that the community of Jesus' followers is oriented to the future "eternal life," which is identical with the

---

15  A. Schlatter, *Evangelist Matthäus* 136–137.
16  G. Schrenk, "δικαιοσύνη," TDNT 2:195–225; esp. 198–199, 202–210.
17  Ph. Vielhauer, *Literaturgeschichte* 364.
18  Other attempts to correlate indicative statements in Matthew to imperatives are no more persuasive; cf. G. Strecker, "Das Gesetz in der Bergpredigt" 123.
19  Since μισθός is his term for heavenly reward, Matthew avoids this word with reference to earthly compensation; cf. 10:10 (τῆς τροφῆς) in contrast to Luke 10:7 (τοῦ μισθοῦ), since differently than in the wisdom literature the doing of righteousness is not reimbursed on earth. For Matthew, in this world believers receives persecution as their earthly compensation.

eschatological "joy" (χαρά; 13:44; 25:21, 23). If the realization of right-eousness and love in the present leads to persecution, the bearing of such suffering is still meaningful. It has a promise that is not fulfilled in the realm of history. This perspective provides th basis for Jesus' ethical demand. Ethical responsibility is grounded in eschatology, namely the necessity of bringing the "here and now" into conformity with what is demanded.

Yet the proclamation of Jesus does not only point beyond itself to the eschatological future but is also grounded in the fact that the future kingdom of God has already become present in the proclamation of Jesus. Even if the βασιλεία suffers violence with the advent of Jesus (11:12), this means that it is already salvifically present in Jesus' word. Eschatological salvation is announced today to the church of Jews and Gentiles (21:43; cf. 28:20). This reality happens in the present wherever the claim of Jesus is articulated; therefore the content of the proclamation of Jesus can be described not only as an ethical demand but as an eschatological claim.

## 4. Jesus as Model

The Gospel of Matthew binds the words and deeds of Jesus most closely together. Alongside the connection between κηρύσσω and διδάσκω stands θεραπεύω: Jesus *preaches* the gospel and *heals* every sickness among the people (4:23–24; 9:35; 10:7–8). It is also significant that following the Sermon on the Mount, ten mighty acts of Jesus are narrated (8:1–9:34). The word of Jesus is confirmed by his messianic acts. The Messiah of word is also the Messiah of deed (J. Schniewind). It is not only his miraculous acts, however, that verify the word of Jesus but his deeds as such.

This is seen in the "call of the savior:"

> Come to me, all you that are weary and are carrying heavy burdens, and I will give you rest. Take my yoke upon you, and learn from me; for I am gentle (πραΰς) and humble(ταπεινός) in heart, and you will find rest for your souls. For my yoke is easy, and my burden is light.

Even if these verses are of pre-Matthean origin (to mention only one item, there are six *hapax legomena*) and the ἀνάπαυσις concept is dependent on Jeremiah 6:16, it is still the case that this traditional unit has been intentionally placed in this context by the redactor. Corresponding to the situation presupposed, this text deals with the burden of those who are oppressed by Pharisaic regulations. To these people Jesus promises, by the call to personal discipleship to himself—and that means at the same time to his ethical-eschatological demand—a "rest," which illuminates the present aspect of salvation found in the imperative word of Jesus. Moreover, it is emphasized that Jesus points people to himself; he himself is "gentle and humble in heart." Jesus is the model for the ethical attitude and conduct demanded by his preaching.

This is also seen in the tradition dealing with Jesus' baptism (3:13–17). In contrast to the Markan parallel (Mark 1:9–11), Matthew (possibly from pre-Matthean oral tradition) has inserted into the narrative a conversation between Jesus and John the Baptist (3:14–15). But in the fixation of this tradition the redactor has reformatted the text; in particular, the words in v. 15 πληρῶσαι πᾶσαν δικαιοσύνην are his work. Here we see that, by being baptized by John the Baptist, Jesus fulfills the requirement of righteousness in attitude and deed. He thereby becomes a model to the church, which lives from the instruction of its Lord.

That the Matthean Jesus himself lives out the instruction he give to others in his own conduct as an example to them is also seen in the passion story (26:2ff). Matthew portrays Jesus in the divine sovereignty of the eschatological Kyrios also in the passion story. In the Matthean understanding, the story of Jesus' passion is not so much an expression of his lowliness as of his divine sovereignty. Such a "theologia crucis" is at the same time a "theologia gloriae:" Christ is the one who triumphs over suffering and death. It is no accident that it is constantly emphasized that Jesus "knowingly" goes forth to his destiny (cf. 26:2). Jesus speaks of his καιρός as the hour of his death (26:18), and he specifically designates Judas as the traitor (26:25 Matthean redaction).

Moreover, the exalted status of the suffering Christ is expressed in his obedience. This point is illustrated by the Gethsemane pericope (26:36–46). The Matthean version of the story is determined by Jesus' two acts of prayer, and Jesus' giving himself over to God's will is dramatically enhanced. Jesus here puts into practice the third petition of the Lord's Prayer (6:10); his attitude and conduct is a model for the believing community, which is not only to repeat this prayer but to live it out in their own conduct.

The λύτρον saying (Matt 20:28) also belongs in the context of the passion. When Matthew, in contrast to Mark 10:45, introduces the saying with "just as" (ὥσπερ), Jesus' attitude and life of service to others that is ultimately expressed in the passion story becomes a model to be imitated by his followers. Jesus' life provides directions for the church's own way. This is seen finally in the summarizing statements about Jesus' suffering: the persecuted community orients itself by the model that Jesus gave to his church once and for all in his passion (16:24; 23:34).

### c)  The Church

#### 1.  The Foundation

Since the Gospel of Matthew presents primarily a Jesus narrative, the focus is on Christology rather than ecclesiology.[20] To be sure, in his Jesus

---

[20]  Contra W. Trilling, *Das wahre Israel*, who—as indicated by the title of his work—

narrative Matthew distinguishes between past and present, for he tells his story for his community. This means that, consciously or unconsciously, the self-understanding of the Matthean church is reflected in the Jesus narrative.

The temporal and functional foundation is located in the missionary command of the Risen One (28:16–20), which presumably goes back to a pre-Matthean baptismal tradition in which the Risen One is celebrated as the Cosmocrator (28:18b). In this tradition the risen Lord gave his baptismal command with the triadic form (Father, Son, Holy Spirit, 28:19b) and in the concluding line promised the continuing presence of the Risen One with the church (28:20b). The redactor Matthew preserved the form in the tradition but expressed his own conception by supplementary additions: the piece of liturgical tradition is now incorporated into Matthew's temporal scheme. It marks the conclusion and high point of the life of Jesus and the foundation of the epoch of the church that now follows. The baptismal tradition is modified into a missionary command that, in distinction from the sending of the disciples to Israel during the time of Jesus, is now directed to all nations. The content of the mission is baptism and teaching. Both refer back to the life of Jesus, for the words and deeds of Jesus, the story of Jesus Christ as a whole is foundational for the being and self-understanding of the church.

## 2. The Church as Institution

Just as the church is called into being by the advent of Jesus as pictured by Matthew in his Gospel, so it is essentially determined by the content of Jesus' message. It orients itself to the eschatological-ethical imperative, which it proclaims and realizes in its own life, thereby making manifest the present rule of the Kyrios. The church of Matthew's time is portrayed as a "corpus mixtum." The church is an eschatological reality in the present world; it is the ἐκκλησία of the Lord Jesus (16:18; cf. 18:17). It proclaims Jesus' word and deed, and through its proclamation participates in the

---

interprets the theology of Matthew in connection with the experiences of his contemporary church, even if this is seen along with the theological presuppositions of the First Evangelist. Cf. with the same tendency G. Lohfink, *Jesus and Community: The Social Dimensions of Christian Faith* (Philadelphia: Fortress, 1984) and the response by G. Strecker *ThLZ* 111 (1986) 24–27; U. Luz, *Das Evangelium nach Matthäus*, EKK 1/2 (Neukirchen-Vluyn: Neukirchener, 1990), on Matthew 8–9, and "Die Wundergeschichten von Mt 8–9" in G. F. Hawthorne and O. Betz, eds. *Tradition and Interpretation in the New Testament* (FS E. E. Ellis) (Grand Rapids-Tübingen: Wm. B. Eerdmans, J. C. B. Mohr [Paul Siebeck], 1987) 149–165. That Matthew is able to distinguish between "biographical" and ecclesial goals of his work is seen in the mission discourse (10:5–42): first it is tailored to the idealized portrayal of the disciples situation (10:5–16) but from v. 17 on the situation of the church in the time of the First Evangelist is reflected.

eschatological quality of its Lord. The church realizes in its own life the demand of Jesus and is thereby not merely a secular reality that can be grasped in sociological terms, as it appears to the external observer, but by realization of the word of Jesus it has been lifted out of secular history. On the other hand, the Christian church is a combination of bad and good people. Although the ethical imperative places it under the demand to live in the world as the perfectly fulfilled eschatological community, within its ranks are found concrete evils and corruptions. Only at the End will the final separation between righteous and unrighteous be made (cf. 21:43–44; 22:9ff).

Inasmuch as the Christian community is the representative within temporal history of the eschatological-ethical demand, this can also be seen in the Christian institution of penance, which is documented only here in the Gospels (18:15–20). The church accordingly possesses the eschatological authority "to bind and loose."[21] The local congregation has the right to exclude members from the fellowship and to readmit them. The claim and authority of the whole church is thereby expressed. This action is accompanied by the promised presence of the exalted Lord (18:20). This is more than the Jewish practice of banning, with its measures for "binding and loosing," was able to do or claimed to do, for there it was a matter of an inner-synagogue disciplinary procedure that was applied gradually and for a limited time, and did not result in excommunication from the community as such.[22] In Matthew, however, the church acts as the authorized eschatological congregation in order by such action to realize "righteousness" in its own ranks.

This already makes clear that Matthew's church is to be understood as an "institution." However unclear the particular form of church order of the Matthean church may be,[23] it is very clear that the church itself has a firmly structured organization. Thus the understanding of the *sacraments* reflects the institutional understanding of the church. *Baptism* (cf. 3:13–17) is understand essentially as a legal act; it is a "rite of initiation" by which the believer is made a part of the community, and precisely thereby corresponds to the command of the Lord Jesus who instituted the

---

[21]   The terms δέω and λύω go back to Jewish models; cf. F. Büchsel, "δέω" *TDNT* 2:60–61; Strack-Billerbeck *Kommentar* 1:738–742.

[22]   Cf. Strack-Billerbeck, *Kommentar* 1:792–793.

[23]   The office of "scribe" (13:52; cf. also 23:8ff). Cf. G. Strecker, "Das Geschichtsverständnis des Matthäus" 105; D. Zeller, "Zu einer jüdischer Vorlage von Matt 13:52," *BZ* NF 20 (1976) 223–226; R. Schnackenburg, "Jeder Schriftgelehrte, der ein Jünger des Himmelsreiches geworden ist (Mt 13,52)," in K. Aland and S. Meurer, eds., *Wissenschaft und Kirche* (FS E. Lohse) (Bielefeld: 1989) 57–69; O. Betz, "Neues und Altes im Geschichtshandeln Gottes," in *Jesus. Der Messias Israels* (WUNT 42. Tübingen: J. C. B. Mohr [Paul Siebeck], 1987) 285–300; U. Luz, *Das Evangelium nach Matthäus* 1/2: 361–366.

rite. The act of baptism is itself an act of obedience. As such it mediates forgiveness of sins, which is preceded by the repentance of the baptismal candidates (cf. 3:2ff). However much forgiveness of sins is acknowledged to be the effect of baptism, the sacrament does not take precedence over the institution of the church itself but is incorporated into it.[24]

So also the *Lord's Supper* (26:26–28) illustrates the church's authority to forgive sins. The understanding of the eucharist is adjusted to the understanding of the church as the eschatological community; it actualizes participation in the eschatological future. It takes place within the framework of the institution of the church, as an element of carrying out the command of Jesus. This becomes clear in the imperative form of the words of institution (26:26: φάγετε; 26:27: πίετε; contrast Mark 14:22ff). The Lord's Supper is the fulfillment of the eschatological-ethical command of Jesus. Here too—as in the baptismal sacrament—obedience to the word and deed of Jesus is realized; here too there is no reflection on the atoning effect of Jesus' death. The decisive thing is not the "why" but the "that" of the atoning work. The decisive thing is the church order of which the Lord's Supper is an element and which gives it legitimacy.

The sacraments of baptism and the Lord's Supper, like the disciplinary procedures of the church, have their real reference point in the word of Jesus. This word charges the church to understand itself as the community of the "righteous" and to realize this understanding in its life. However little this charge can be realized in the present, where the church understands itself as a mixed community of good and bad, so much the more is the eschatological-ethic demand of Jesus the norm that is also valid for the future. It has a universal validity, because it is the command of the Lord of the whole world (28:16–20), and because the Son of Man who is the judge at the Last Judgement will ask about the fulfillment of these commands (25:31–46). This judgment involves not only the church but the whole world. Church and world will be judged according to the standard of the one eschatological-ethical norm. Here we see how Matthew in his own way realizes the solidarity of the church with the world: all humanity stands under the one demand of the one Lord.[25]

---

[24]  This is also seen in a linguistic observation: Matthew uses the term βάπτισμα only with reference to the baptismal sacrament but not however in a metaphorical sense (contrast Mark 10:38–39 with Matt 20:22).

[25]  That church and world are pictured in matching ways is seen in the observation that not only is the church portrayed as a corpus mixtum but so is the world. Cf. in this regard the Parable of the Weeds (13:36–43), where the world is equated with the "kingdom of the Son of Man," within which the doers of unrighteousness will be separated from the righteous (13:41, 43). Similarly the Parable of the Net (13:47–50), which analogously portrays righteous and unrighteous living side by side in the world, with the final sifting taking place in the Last Judgment.

# IV. The Midst of Time—The Evangelist Luke

Bovon, F. *Das Evangelium nach Lukas*. EKK III/1. Zürich-Neukirchen-Vluyn: Neu-kirchener, I 1989; II 1996.

Bovon, F. *Luke the Theologian: Thirty-three Years of Research (1950–1983)*. Allison Park, PA: Pickwick, 1987.

Braumann, G. ed., *Das Lukasevangelium*. WdF 280. Darmstadt: Wissenschaftliche Buchgesellschaft, 1974.

Bultmann, R. "Zur Frage nach den Quellen der Apostelgeschichte," R. Bultmann, ed. *Exegetica*. Tübingen: J. C. B. Mohr (Paul Siebeck), 1967, 412–423.

Burchard, Ch. *Der dreizehnte Zeuge. Traditions- und kompositionsgeschichtliche Untersuchungen zu Lukas' Darstellung der Frühzeit des Paulus*. FRLANT 103. Göttingen: Vandenhoeck & Ruprecht, 1970.

Bussmann C. und Radl, W. eds. *Der Treue Gottes trauen. Beiträge zum Werk des Lukas* (FS G. Schneider). Freiburg: Herder, 1991.

Conzelmann, H. *The Theology of St. Luke*. New York: Harper & Bros., 1960.

Conzelmann, H. "Geschichte, Geschichtsbild und Geschichtsdarstellung bei Lukas," *ThLZ* 85 (1960) 241–250.

Dibelius, M. *Studies in the Acts of the Apostles*. New York: Scribners, 1956.

Ernst, J. Lukas. *Ein theologisches Portrait*. Düsseldorf: Patmos, 1985.

Fitzmyer, J. A. *The Gospel According to Luke*. AncB 28–28a. New York: Doubleday, 1981, 1985.

Flender, H. *St Luke: Theologian of Redemptive History*. Philadelphia: Fortress, 1967.

Goulder, M. D. *Luke. A New Paradigm*. 2 vols. JSNT.S 20. Sheffield: Sheffield Univ. Press, 1989.

Grässer E., *Das Problem der Parusieverzögerung in den synoptischen Evangelien und in der Apostelgeschichte*. BZNW 22. Berlin: W. de Gruyter, 1977.

Haenchen, E. *The Acts of the Apostles*. Philadelphia: Westminster, 1971.

Horn, F. W. *Glaube und Handeln in der Theologie des Lukas*. GTA 26. Göttingen: Vandenhoeck & Ruprecht, 1986.

Korn, M. *Die Geschichte Jesu in veränderter Zeit*. WUNT II 51. Tübingen: J. C. B. Mohr (Paul Siebeck), 1992.

Lohfink, G. *Die Sammlung Israels*. StANT 39. Munich: Kösel, 1975.

Lohse, E. "Lukas als Theologe der Heilsgeschichte," *EvTh* 14 (1954) 256–274; also in E. Lohse, ed. *Die Einheit des Neuen Testaments*. Göttingen: Vandenhoeck & Ruprecht, 1973, 145–164.

Maddox, R. *The Purpose of Luke-Acts*. FRLANT 126. Göttingen: Vandenhoeck & Ruprecht, 1982.

Nebe, G. *Prophetische Züge im Bilde Jesu bei Lukas*. BWANT 127. Stuttgart: Kohl-hammer, 1989.

Rese, M. *Alttestamentliche Motive in der Christologie des Lukas*. StNT 1. Gütersloh: Gerd Mohn, 1969.

Rese, M. "Das Lukas-Evangelium. Ein Forschungsbericht," ANRW II 25.3 (1985) 2258–2328.

Schneider, G. *Lukas, Theologie der Heilsgeschichte*. BBB 59. Königstein-Bonn: Han-stein, 1985.

Schürmann, H. *Das Lukasevangelium*. HThK III/1+2. Freiburg: Herder, I 1984, II 1994.

Schürmann, H. *Traditionsgeschichtliche Untersuchungen zu den synoptischen Evan-gelien, Beiträge*. KBANT. Düsseldorf: Patmos, 1968, 159–309.

Strecker, G. "Die sogenannte Zweite Jerusalemreise des Paulus (Act. 11,27–30)," *ZNW* 53 (1962) 67–77; also in G. Strecker, ed. *Eschaton und Historie* 132–141.

Taeger, J.-W. *Der Mensch und sein Heil. Studien zum Bild des Menschen und zur Sicht der Bekehrung bei Lukas.* StNT 14. Gütersloh: Gerd Mohn, 1982.

Vielhauer, Ph. "On the Paulinism of Acts," *Studies in Luke-Acts,* L. E. Keck and J. L. Martyn, eds. Philadelphia: Fortress, 1980.

Wilckens, U. *Die Missionsreden der Apostelgeschichte. Form- und traditionsgeschichtliche Untersuchungen.* WMANT 5. Neukirchen-Vluyn: Neukirchener, 1974.

Wilson, S. G. *Luke and the Law.* MSSNTS 50. Cambridge: Cambridge University Press, 1983.

## a)   The Lucan Understanding of History

The point of departure for grasping the theology of Luke must be the observation that Luke alone among the Evangelists composed not only a Gospel but also the Acts of the Apostles. Each work presupposes the other (Acts 1:1–14 takes up Luke 24:50–53). The prologue of the Gospel, to which Acts 1:1 refers, makes clear that the author is concerned to pursue a single line that does not end with the Gospel but continues into the history of the church. Gospel and Acts form one historical work that identifies Luke as a "historian." It appears to be a significant datum that M. Dibelius provided one of his essays with the title "The First Christian Historian:" Luke is a writer of history who, differently than Matthew and Mark, is familiar with the literary methods of ancient historiography and knows how to make use of them within his own literary intentions. As a historian who puts stories together into a connected history by taking the individual traditional units and composing them into a united whole and thereby giving the history of the church a "sense of direction," he maintains his concern of pointing to that which is typical of the events he reports, and to their significance.

1.   The Lucan Prologue (1:1–4).

| | |
|---|---|
| 1  Ἐπειδήπερ πολλοὶ ἐπεχείρησαν ἀνατάξασθαι διήγησιν περὶ τῶν πεπληροφορημένων ἐν ἡμῖν πραγμάτων, | Since many have undertaken to set down an orderly account of the events that have been fulfilled among us, |
| 2  καθὼς παρέδοσαν ἡμῖν οἱ ἀπ᾽ ἀρχῆς αὐτόπται<br><br>καὶ ὑπηρέται γενόμενοι τοῦ λόγου, | just as they were handed on to us by those who from the beginning were eyewitnesses and servants of the word |
| 3  ἔδοξε κἀμοὶ παρηκολουθηκότι ἄνωθεν πᾶσιν ἀκριβῶς καθεξῆς σοι γράψαι, κράτιστε Θεόφιλε, | I too decided, after investigating everything carefully from the very first, to write an orderly account for you, most excellent Theophilus, |
| 4  ἵνα ἐπιγνῷς περὶ ὧν κατηχήθης λόγων τὴν ἀσφάλειαν. | so that you may know the truth concerning the things about which you have been instructed. |

Luke's historical intention is expressed in the prologue to the Third Gospel in a unique manner. The author refers to the attempts of other writers who have reported "the events that have been fulfilled among us." He is at least referring to the Gospel of Mark and the Q source, possibly to other unknown gospel writings. The personal pronoun in the phrase ἐν ἡμῖν ("among us") contains an ecclesial "we." The Jesus event is an event in which the community believes, verifiable within the community of faith. Continuity with the history of Jesus also means a high degree of contemporaneity with the Jesus event.

The community knows of this event through eyewitnesses (1:2) who have "have handed it on to us." Luke presupposes a firm concept of tradition. The community stands in the tradition founded by eyewitnesses "from the beginning" and "ministers of the word" who have handed it on.[1] It is important to note that Luke does not claim to be directly dependent on eyewitness tradition, which will have characterized the "attempts" of his predecessors, but he independently undertakes the task of inquiring and documenting: ἄνωθεν ("from the beginning") πᾶσιν ("all," i.e. comprehensively), ἀκριβῶς (with precision, carefully). Thus his presentation is καθεξῆς ("in order"). Luke stands in the tradition of ancient historiography. This is indicated by the dedication κράτιστε Θεόφιλε.[2] As in ancient historiography[3] Luke is aware of doubts about the current tradition; like it, he expresses the intention to portray the events as they really happened, not just according to their appearance. Thus Luke wants to get back to the "bruta facta historica." There is, of course, justifiable doubt as to whether the historical intention as here expressed really succeeded in the production of an objective historical account. So also the other ancient historians, e. g. Thucydides and Tacitus, were far removed from being objective historians. Despite their declared intentions, they were not in the situation to describe events "sine ira et studio." On the contrary, clearly tendentious perspectives and prejudiced opinions and conceptions influenced their results, intentionally or unintentionally. This is no less the case with Luke. He presents neither the Jesus story nor that of the apostles just as

---

[1]  The use of the article here (one article that applies to both nouns) probably indicates a hendiadys; cf. G. Klein, "Lukas 1:1–4 als theologisches Programm," in *Rekonstruktion und Interpretation. Gesammelte Aufsätze zum Neuen Testament* (BEvTh 50. Munich: Kaiser, 1969) 237–261; 245–249; F. Bovon, *Das Evangelium nach Lukas* 37.

[2]  Cf. Acts 1:1; it is an open question whether or not Luke in fact dedicated his work to an actual prominent member of the Romen equestrian class (κράτιστος as designation of a member of the Roman equestrian order in Josephus *Ant* 20.12). A critique of this thesis is given by F. Bovon, *Das Evangelium nach Lukas* 37.

[3]  Cf. also the dedication in Josephus, *Apion* 1.1ff. In *Apion* 1.3 Josephus expresses an outspokenly skeptical evaluation of the reliability of the Greek tradition he utilizes.

it happened but as it should have happened according to his understanding. In that he attempts to trace the meaning and direction in which history unfolded, he constructs his outline of history from the point of view of the last stage, in which he himself stands.

The intention that guides Luke's presentation is clarified in 1:4. The expression "traditions" (NRSV "things," λόγοι, literally "words") refers to the content of Christian instruction. The goal of the Lucan writing of history is thus to allow the content of the Christian faith, as it is transmitted in catechetical instruction, to become unmistakable certainty. Faith obtains "reliability" from history. The question "how it really happened" is answered by the way in which the question "what should I believe" is posed and answered. The truth claim of faith and the process of historical study are indissolubly bound together, and thus the question is here raised of whether truth has not become dependent on historical study. Luke, however, in that he attempts to answer this question in his own historical work, gives to history its due; he is not telling a secular story but the story of what happened in history as the foundation for faith, and thus what is historically significant with regard to the truth claim of faith. However much Luke is to be recognized as a "historian" in dependence on ancient models, the product of his work is not a secular account but a qualified story, a history in which the effective influences of the eschaton can be ascertained. Although Luke is not primarily preacher but narrator, it is still the case that the orientation of his work toward faith is perceptible in every verse. Luke is no more and no less a historian than the other synoptic Evangelists but he is in addition a theologian who presents history as the foundation, legitimization, and even the proof of the truth claim of faith. In this regard Luke stands on the same ground as the other Synoptic Gospels. Matthew and Mark of course make no claim to be literature in the same way as Luke, but just the same each is motivated by a historical orientation to the tradition and the salvation-history connecting line that directs the flow of the narrative. Even though Luke, and even Matthew, go beyond Mark in this, they are all still united in the intention to present a Jesus narrative informed and motivated by salvation history. When Luke proceeds more consistently than Matthew and Mark by continuing the Gospel history into the Acts of the Apostles, he is only explicating what was already present "in nuce" in the theology of the other two synoptic Evangelists. The prologue Luke 1:1–4 does not thus fundamentally separate Luke from Mark and Matthew, but points to the common intention of the synoptic Evangelists' literary activity directed to ἀσφάλεια.

As indicated by the Lucan prologue, the Evangelist distinguishes between the early Christian tradition that came to him and his own redactional work. By wanting to go back through the tradition to the historical facts themselves, a somewhat critical stance toward tradition is inherent in his historical approach. This corresponds to the intention of

Hellenistic historiography. The result of Luke's redaction, however, is a confirmation of the tradition. This is seen from the way in which the continuity of church history is guaranteed by a chain of witnesses. Thus at the beginning stand the eyewitnesses as ministers of the word, on whom others are dependent. The latter group includes, as portrayed in Acts, the apostle Paul, who after his conversion was incorporated in the "chain of succession" by the disciple Ananias (Acts 9). This idea of tradition is also expressed in the story of the selection of Matthias to be the twelfth apostle (Acts 1:15ff), as also in picturing the extension of the mission as remaining strictly under the apostolic authority in Jerusalem (cf. Acts 8:14ff; 15:1ff). The result of Luke's redactional work turns out to be not critical analysis of the tradition but its affirmation and confirmation. This is in accord with his announced intention to confirm the truth of the catechetical Christian tradition. When Luke declares that by his literary work he wants to establish "the truth" (1:4), he is referring to the content of Christian instruction as handed on in the oral and written tradition of the Christian community. Finally, it is not to be doubted that Luke is himself an exponent of church tradition. Despite the claim that reflects his secular education, the author of the Lukan two volume work does not write with the objectivity of the historian but as exponent of the church and its faith. He is thereby in fundamental agreement with the first and Second Evangelists. The result of his work is more like the other synoptic Gospels, and less distinctively Lucan, than is widely assumed.

## 2.  The Periodization of Salvation History

Luke writes a qualified history; he constructs a narrative outline that includes the dialectic of history and eschaton, which we have also observed in Mark and Matthew. The question to be pursued is the extent and manner by which this dialectic is articulated. The distinctive aspect of the Lucan narrative is its historical framework that is structured according to a succession of several historical epochs.

(α) H. Conzelmann entitled his influential study of the theology of Luke the "The Midst of Time" [*Die Mitte der Zeit*; English translation *The Theology of St. Luke*], thereby designating the life of Jesus as portrayed by Luke as the central epoch of all history. For distinguishing "the midst of time," Conzelmann points to Luke 16:16, "The law and the prophets were in effect until John came; since then [ἀπὸ τότε] the good news of the kingdom of God is proclaimed, and everyone tries to enter it by force." If the phrase ἀπὸ τότε is understood in an exclusive sense,[4] then John the Baptist does not belong to the kingdom of God, and thus not to the time

---

4     Conzelmann, *Theology of St. Luke* 16.

of Jesus as the time of the kingdom, but only has the task of announcing the time of Jesus. This corresponds to the geographic distinction that John the Baptist teaches and baptizes at the Jordan but Jesus avoids the Jordan region (contra Mark 10:1). The result is that there is a clear demarcation between John the Baptist and Jesus; the time of Jesus as the midst of time begins "after John."

This thesis, however, needs to be qualified. The temporal phrase ἀπὸ τότε not only has an exclusive meaning but can also be understood in an inclusive sense. John is also classified within the time of Jesus, namely as the eschatological prophet who prepares the way for the Messiah. In the Lucan understanding John too is an eschatological figure.[5] Luke identifies him explicitly with Elijah, who was expected to appear at the endtime (1:17); he is "Elijah redivivus," who is more than an ordinary prophet (7:26–27). However much in Luke's understanding John is subordinate to Jesus, is not clear that he belongs only to the preceding historical epoch of the Law and the prophets. He is a transitional figure who leads into the time of Jesus as the time of fulfillment.[6]

It is not so clear when the conclusion of the time of Jesus is to be located. If the midst of time is the Jesus event, then the end of Jesus' life must signal the end of this period.[7] The end point, however, is not clearly marked. It may be identified with the resurrection or the ascension. Pentecost as the beginning of the church is also possible. Luke himself does not designate a clear boundary line. Presumably the turning point coincides with the end of the Gospel of Luke but since this overlaps with the narrative in Acts 1, it is clear that Luke was not concerned to fix the line of demarcation between the periods with exact precision.

Regarding the internal structure of the time of Jesus, it seems that Luke 23:5 suggests a geographical outline: "He stirs up the people by teaching throughout all Judea, from Galilee where he began even to this place

---

5   For further discussion see the section B. I. above on John the Baptist.

6   Stereotypical formulae that Luke uses for the beginning of the time of Jesus are also characteristic for explaining the transitional function of John the Baptist: (a) Acts 10:37–38; 13:24–25; 19:4: the time of Jesus begins "after John;" (b) Acts 1:22: "beginning from the baptism of John." Here the prepositions μετά and ἀπό can be used interchangeably. This signals the transitional function of John, who sometimes is included in the time of Jesus as the eschatological forerunner, and other times is excluded, since he is a prophet but not the Messiah.

7   It is conceivable that this period is delimited by the two παρουσίαι of Jesus, his birth and his return as the Son of Man. This would mean that Luke sees himself as living in the midst of time, which would be identical with the time of the church as the central period of history. But the term παρουσίαι is not found in the Lucan historical work (παρουσία is found in the New Testament Gospels only Matt 24:3, 27, 37, 39). Since the "midst of time" is a normative period, it is to be identified with the time of Jesus and limited to that period; cf. e. g. Acts 3:13–15; 4:10–12; 13:27–31.

(Jerusalem)." Thus the ministry of Jesus took place within the geographical limits of Palestine. Corresponding to the Markan outline, Luke too has
Jesus work begin in Galilee but then contrary to Mark includes an extensive travel narrative that pictures Jesus on the way to Jerusalem, and
concludes in Jerusalem as the scene of the suffering, death, and resurrection of Jesus Christ.

This external framework of the story of Jesus has as its internal content
a geographical movement, the way of Jesus. Moreover, this way is comprised of juxtapositions of Jesus' epiphanies as the Kyrios and Jesus' rejection. Thus Jesus' baptism is followed by the rejection at Nazareth (3:21–
22; 4:15ff), the epiphany story of the transfiguration is followed by the
rejection in the Samaritan village (9:28ff, 51ff), and the epiphany scene of
Gethsemane is followed by the rejection of Jesus in the passion and crucifixion (22:39ff, 47ff). However, Luke did not attempt to subject the
account of the time of Jesus to psychological categories, as though he
wanted to portray an internal development of Jesus' psyche.[8] The truth of
the matter is that he did not want to picture the inner itinerary of Jesus'
life but its external course [*Weg*], which is conditioned by time and space
and leads into the way [*Weg*] of the church.

(β) The time of Jesus is preceded by a *preliminary, provisional period*.
This is the time when Israel is addressed with the demand and promise
of the will of God. The time line leads straight to Jesus; the Law and the
prophets wrote about Jesus (24:27, 44). The Old Testament Law (= the
Pentateuch) has no less a predictive character than the Old Testament
prophets, for the patriarchs, like king David, looked ahead to the time of
Jesus and his resurrection and saw it in advance as the resurrection of the
Messiah (Acts 2:30ff; Ps 110:1). From the point of view of salvation
history, the time of Israel was interpreted not only positively but negatively. This is seen in the "speech of Stephen" (Acts 7:1–53), which represents Hellenistic Jewish Christian tradition, according to which the
preceding period, the time of Israel, was a history of rejecting the will of
God, an "unholy salvation history." It is the history of the murder of the
prophets, the repudiation of the salvific claim of God (cf. Luke 11:47ff;
20:9ff). Especially in the mission sermons of Acts the idea is found that
the Jewish people are responsible for the death of Jesus (Acts 7:52). The
predominant factor here is not so much an apologetic, since it is not really
a matter of a Christian defense against Jewish attacks, but a missionary

---

[8]    It is obvious that Luke's story of the twelve-year-old Jesus in the temple (Luke 2:
      41–52), the only such story in the Synoptics, cannot be considered evidence for a
      psychological development of the person of Jesus in the Third Gospel. Contra O.
      Glombitza, "Der Zwölfjährige Jesus," *NT* 5 (1962) 1–4; K. H. Rengstorf, *Das Evan-
      gelium nach Lukas* (NTD 3. Göttingen: Vandenhoeck & Ruprecht, 1978[17]) 51.

offensive that is concerned to seek Jewish understanding and to relegate the conduct of Jews in the past to a time of "ignorance" (Acts 3:17; 13:27). Such an unholy history ended with the destruction of Jerusalem at the latest: "... so that this generation may be charged with the blood of all the prophets shed since the foundation of the world..." (Luke 11:50–51); "... Jerusalem will be trampled on by the Gentiles, until the times of the Gentiles are fulfilled" (Luke 21:24). The date of the destruction of Jerusalem lies outside the time of Jesus. Luke's periodizing of salvation history presupposes fluid transitions. The distinction between the time of Jesus and the preceding time of the election of the Jewish people within God's plan for history, the period of history that pointed forward to the time of Jesus which brought the time of Israel to both its high point and its end, cannot be fundamentally nullified by such lack of sharp boundaries; this lack of precision within the general scheme in fact strengthens the case that Luke has divided the history of salvation into distinct periods

(γ) Following the time of Jesus comes *the historical epoch of the church*. Even though the temporal beginning of this period is not clearly marked, the distinction itself needs no further justification. In Acts, Luke provides an impression of how he thought of this period. He places great weight on the continuity of salvation history. The development of church history proceeds without gaps; one phase follows in a straight line immediately after the other. It thus develops as a contrast to continuing Jewish history, for the history of the church is the story of the gradual separation of Christianity and Judaism.[9] This is seen in the chronological outline of Acts: from the ascension of Jesus (Acts 1:4–14) to the arrival of Paul in Rome (Acts 28:14). This corresponds to the geographical structure of the narrative: the framework of the movement of history in Acts is marked out by the Jerusalem and Rome.

The final destination "Rome" points to the greatest possible difference from Judaism. It is no accident that the work ends with the rejection of Paul by the Jews in Rome (Isa 6:9–10 is quoted: "...this people's heart has grown dull...") and with the announcement that salvation is sent to the Gentiles (Acts 28:25–28). Already at the beginning point the close connection between the earliest Jerusalem church and Jerusalem is seen. The community worships in the temple and observes the Jewish Law (Acts 3:1; 5:12; 15:1ff; 21:20ff). Although they are distinguished from official Judaism by their confession of faith and by their life together as a Christian community (especially by their sharing of property, 4:32ff; 5:1ff), they still knew that they

---

9    That Luke portrays the history of the church as a contrast to continuing Jewish history makes it obvious that he was not a Jewish Christian—no more so than the author of the Gospel of Matthew or the author of the Epistle of Barnabas. It is rather the case that Luke's portrayal shows that the problem of Judaism was given to the church at the very beginning. The gradual separation of Christianity and Judaism meant that Gentile Christians had to develop a mode of thought that could stand on its own and an independent Christian theology.

were not separated from Judaism. But two factors led to the gradual dissolution of this unity: (a) the expansion of Christianity beyond the area of Palestine (mentioned for the first time in Acts 6: the naming of the Hellenistic part of the earliest church represented by the Stephen circle; these Hellenistic Jewish Christian missionaries carried on a mission among their compatriots in non-Jewish areas; cf. 8:4ff). (b) Persecution by the Jews was the direct occasion for the scattering of the church among the Gentiles and the dissolution of the original connection with Judaism. Thus after the death of Stephen and the persecution of his circle (Acts 7), the church expanded beyond Jerusalem. The evangelist Phillip, a member of the Stephen circle, carried on a mission in neighboring, semi-Jewish Samaria (Acts 7–8). Thereby continuity with the Jerusalem church was preserved, since although Phillip preached and baptized, the power to confer the Spirit remained with the Jerusalem apostles (8:14ff). An additional important step of the church from the Jews to the Gentiles occurred in the conversion of Paul (Acts 9). But the Gentile mission too was opened by a Jerusalem apostle, by Peter, through the conversion of the centurion Cornelius in Caesarea (Acts 10); he was the first Gentile convert.[10] Then follows the founding of the church in predominately Gentile Antioch (Acts 11) and the missionary travels of Paul and Barnabas, with Barnabas at first being named as the principal figure and the link to the Jerusalem church (Acts 13:1ff), until Paul steps forth in his triumphalistic world mission as the outstanding apostle to the Gentiles, with James remaining as the representative of the connection with Jerusalem (15:1ff; 21:18ff). A chronological and geographical straight-line development! The history of the church is incorporated into a transparent and continuing historical movement. Such a construction is theologically significant: here the saving plan of God is fulfilled, which points to the eschatological future, from which the community's Lord is expected (Luke 17:22ff; Acts 10:42).

## 3.  Salvation History and World History

While the extent to which Mark and Matthew are interested in the issue of the relation of salvation history to secular history is not obvious, it is clear that this question may be addressed to Luke, who is the only one of the Evangelists to exhibit an extensive reflection on the incorporation of the saving event within the framework of human history in general. The synchronism of Luke 3:1 dates the appearance of John the Baptist in the fifteenth year of the reign of the emperor Tiberius, while Pontius Pilate was governor of Judea and Herod was tetrarch of Galilee. This synchronism contains some imprecise factual data (3:2: "during the high priesthood of Annas and Caiaphas"—as though two high priests were in office at the same time); nonetheless, from this data the appearance of John the Baptist may be dated in the year 28/29 C. E. In addition, other temporal data are given: John the Baptist was born in the days of Herod (Luke 1:5ff); a census took place during the reign of the emperor Augustus, while Quirinius was governor of Syria (2:1ff). The connection between salvation

---

[10]  The status of the Ethiopian eunuch converted by Phillip is left by Luke "in the twilight zone." Haenchen, *Acts* 314.

history and secular history is also reflected in Acts, when for instance Paul is brought as a prisoner before the highest political courts in the land (Acts 23–24, the governor Felix; Acts 25–26, the governor Festus and king Agrippa).

The references to secular history do not indicate that Luke advocates a specific theological point of view with reference to secular history. He does not reflect on the metaphysical aspects of history. Neither is it the case that the Jesus event is set within the framework of a time in secular history that is identified in some special way in contrast to preceding and following times. Nevertheless, the interlocking of secular history and the events of salvation history shows that the history of salvation that Luke intends to write is closely connected with secular history. The history that Luke is concerned to portray did not happen in a ghetto but in confrontation with and assimilation to world history and it brings to light the universalistic orientation of Luke's theology. The events of salvation history participate in the historical character of world history. The interlocking with secular history underscores the historical element in the history of salvation. The eschatological event that Luke portrays happens in space and time. On the other hand, this means that secular history too is not to be understood apart from its counterpart, salvation history. In it too the saving will of God is realized, for God the creator has not left himself without witness among the Gentiles; he has always been near to them by his gifts (Acts 14:15ff); he determined periods and boundaries of the peoples in advance (17:24ff). Such a "theologia naturalis" affirms that the Gentiles could recognize and acknowledge God in his works. This is reminiscent of Paul's dependence on the Stoic understanding of God (Rom 1:18ff). But Luke is no more concerned than Paul to place such statements within an abstract theological system but to place them within the framework of missionary preaching. The reference to the general revelation of God in the world motivates the call to repentance; it is the basis for the admonition to turn away from idols and turn to the one God (Acts 17:30), the God who has revealed himself in Jesus Christ. By pointing beyond itself to God the creator, the world and its history is also pointing to the revelatory event in Christ. The world and its history has no value "in itself" (*an sich*); considered by itself the world and its history stands under God's judgment, for the history of the secular world is the time of ignorance and disobedience over against the revelation of God the creator. The time of ignorance is overcome and superceded by the revelation in Christ and has become the time in which knowledge and obedience are possible. Therefore universal history has its real goal in Christ.

Luke has expressed this idea in still another way, namely in the genealogy of Jesus (Luke 3:23ff). This genealogy traces Jesus' ancestry through Joseph as Jesus' father—also presupposed in the Matthean genealogy. But differently that Matthew, Luke does not trace Jesus' genealogy only back as far as Abraham, but to Adam. Here too the principle of round numbers is at work. As Matthew counts three times fourteen members (= series of sevens!), so Luke counts seventy-seven members from Jesus to Adam. The intention is to affirm that human history has its secret goal in Jesus Christ.

### b)   The Time of Jesus (Christology)

#### 1.   Christological Titles

Since Luke's theology as a whole is embedded within the conception of history discussed above, this obviously applies to his understanding of Christology as well.[11] In the process he uses the christological titles also known to the other New Testament authors.

(α) Of the christological titles mentioned in Luke and Acts, Χριστός has a central position. Used without the article as a proper name, the word is found especially in combination with Ἰησοῦς (Acts 2:38; 4:10; 10:36). Luke's frequent titular usage is an exception to the tendency of the historical development to replace the original titular understanding of the word by its use as a proper name. The titular use is found often in Luke. Thus already at the beginning of the Gospel ὁ Χριστὸς κυρίου is the object of the aged Simeon's expectation and thereby the final goal in the hope of the pious of Israel (Luke 2:26). The title is thus intentionally connected to the promise and expectation of the Jewish people. This is also seen in Acts: Jesus is Israel's previously appointed Christ (Acts 3:20). His passion was also predicted in the Scriptures of Israel (4:26–27/ Ps 2:2). As the fulfiller of Old Testament prophecy and the guarantor for salvation still to come, Jesus stands in the center of salvation history as the Christ. In accordance with this, at Caesarea Philippi Peter confessed Jesus to be τὸν Χριστὸν τοῦ

---

[11]   H. Flender, *St. Luke, Theologian of Redemptive History*, advocates the thesis that at the basis of the Lucan Christology lies the idea that has been transmitted in the formulae of 1 Timothy 3:16 and Romans 1:3–4, and in the pericope about the Son of David question in Mark 12:35–37b par Luke 20:41ff. In this view characteristic for Luke's Christology would be a two-stage schema that implies the dialectic juxtaposition of the earthly and heavenly modes of existence of the Christ (pp. 37–38). The postulated scheme, however, is not to be found in Luke, including Luke 20:41ff, where it appears to be echoed. Luke has taken over this pericope from his source, without either working this theme in or elaborating what was already there. Luke's intention is to write a clear, understandable history of salvation that develops along a single line, a history that emphasizes not two christological layers but the christological continuum (cf. Acts 2:22–36; 10:34–43).

θεοῦ (the Christ of God; in contrast to the absolute ὁ Χριστός of Mark 8:29): in Christ is fulfilled the promise and plan of God.

(β) The title κύριος is used more frequently by Luke than by the two other Synoptics.[12] The pagan Hellenistic Kyrios cult contributed to the use of the title for the risen Christ. This is also seen in the usage in Acts: as the deeds of the ancient Kyrios are proclaimed as an act of praise, so the Christian community proclaims its Lord Jesus (Acts 11:20). And as the ancient Kyrios demanded faith from his followers, so the faith of the Christian community is directed to the Lord Jesus (Acts 11:17; 16:31; 20:21). Just as prayers were addressed to the Kyrioi in pagan religion, so in the Christian community prayers are addressed to the Lord Jesus (Acts 7:59–60).[13] In contrast to the pagan Kyrioi, the Kyrios Jesus possesses universal authority and power. He is the πάντων κύριος, the Cosmocrator (Acts 10:36).

From the community's confession of faith in the risen Lord the Kurios-concept is projected back into the life of Jesus. This is indicated by the frequent use of the term in the absolute. ὁ κύριος is found frequently referring to Jesus (e. g. Luke 11:39; 13:15; 17:5–6). The Kyrios sends out the seventy disciples and thereby makes use of the eschatological authority that belongs to the exalted Lord (Luke 10:1). So also the faith of the community in the exalted Lord is expressed in numerous acclamations (cf. especially the vocative κύριε in Luke 9:54, 59, 61; 10:17, 40; also 11:1, "Lord, teach us to pray).

The two predications Χριστός and Κύριος are both exalted titles of majesty, titles that can also be used together. Thus in Acts 2:36: "Therefore let the entire house of Israel know with certainty that God has made him both Lord and Messiah, this Jesus whom you crucified." If it is assumed that in the pre-Lukan tradition this was an adoption formula that spoke of the adoption of Jesus as Son of God at the resurrection,[14] Luke himself uses both titles in reference to the earthly Jesus (Luke 2:11; 10:17; 23:2; cf. also Acts 4:26 = Ps 2:2!). In the Lucan understanding, Jesus had already revealed himself as Lord during his earthly life, and this was confirmed by his resurrection from the dead (Luke 7:22).

(γ) The title υἱὸς Θεοῦ presents nothing new. For Luke, as for Matthew, Jesus is Son of God from his birth on (Luke 1:32, 35). Thus 3:22 is to be understood from this point of view and read "You are my Son, the Be-

---

12  Mark 18x; Matthew 80x; Luke 104x; Acts 107x.
13  Cf. H. Lietzmann, *An die Römer* (HNT 8. Tübingen: J. C. B. Mohr [Paul Siebeck], 1971) 97–101; also W. Boussett, *Kyrios Christos* (Nashville: Abingdon, 1970) 121–148; R. Bultmann, *Theology* 1:124–126; W. Fauth, "Kyrios, Kyria," *KP* 3:413–417.
14  For the pre-Lucan tradition cf. e.g. J. Roloff, *Die Apostelgeschichte* (NTD 5. Göttingen: Vandenhoeck & Ruprecht, 1988[18]) 60; differently U. Wilckens, *Missionreden* 170–174, who regards 2:36 as a Lucan formulation.

loved; with you I am well pleased."[15] The whole life of Jesus is eschatologically qualified by the divine sonship.

The Son of God is at the same time the παῖς θεοῦ; he is the one chosen by God, who takes the place in history that God has assigned him (Acts 3:26; 4:27).[16] It is significant that the title "Servant of God" can be used in a non-christological sense, with reference to David (Luke 1:69; Acts 4:25).

(δ) In the Christmas message of the angels to the shepherds, Jesus is announced as the σωτήρ (Luke 2:11, "The Savior, who is Christ, the Lord, in the city of David..."). The title here has the same meaning as Kyrios and Christ. As is the case with Kyrios, so also σωτήρ comes from the Hellenistic realm—more precisely, from those Hellenistic cults in which this title was used for the cult deities, including the emperor. In contrast, Judaism does not describe the Messiah with the term σωτήρ (at the most, there may be hints in the LXX of Zech 9:9 and Isa 49:6).[17] Luke, like the tradition he inherited, is obviously dependent on Hellenistic Jewish Christianity, since for him Jesus is in the first place the σωτήρ of Israel. This is indicated by the connection with the Davidic sonship (2:11) but also by its usage in Acts (twice in the missionary preaching to the Jews, 5:31; 13:23). As the "Savior" promised to the Jewish people Jesus is also the ἀρχηγός ("pioneer," "scout"), the one who opens up the way to salvation and guides others to it.[18] Since Jesus leads to faith, the right response to his person is "turning around," repentance as the presupposition of forgiveness of sins and thus of σωτηρία (Luke 1:69, 71, 77; 19:9; Acts 4:12; 7:25; 13:26, 47; 16:17; 27:34).

The Davidic sonship of Jesus is touched upon in the Lucan birth story (Luke 1:27, 32, 69; 2:4) in the sense of the flow of the line of salvation history. Jesus is traced back to David as a principal member of his genealogy (cf. also 3:31). The birth of the child is thus the fulfilling of the promise. Luke 1:32 is not a reference to the eschatological work of Jesus.

## 2. The Way of Jesus

Although Luke distinguishes between the earthly Jesus and the exalted Christ, the christological titles are assigned to Jesus in both his earthly

---

[15] With א, B, A, and others, against D it, which cite Psalms 2:7: "You are my Son, today I have begotten you." This Old Testament, adoptionistic form of the text is clearly secondary. Cf. differently Acts 13:33, where the same quote is used with reference to the resurrection of Jesus.

[16] Isaiah 53 is cited only once, without using the term παῖς θεοῦ (Acts 8:32–33).

[17] G. Fohrer, σωτήρ B. (σωτήρ in the Old Testament) TDNT 7: 1012–1013; cf. also H. Conzelmann, New Testament Theology 86.

[18] Acts 5:31; similarly Hebrews 12:2, the pioneer of faith; 2 Clement 20:5, pioneer of immortality.

and heavenly existence. The way of Jesus is the way of the community's Lord but is also the way of the earthly Jesus, bound to an unrepeatable and non-transferable concrete historical situation. Luke expresses this conviction when, for example, in contrast to Mark he inserts into the outline of the Second Gospel a "travel narrative" (9:51–18:14). The two geographical blocks in Mark (Galilee and Jerusalem) are thus extended to become three extensive sections. The course of Jesus' ministry is thus summarized in 23:5 ("from Galilee where he began even to this place [= Jerusalem]"). It is debatable whether one can infer from this passage that Luke had the erroneous geographical conception that Galilee and Judea shared a common border, so that all the scenes within the "travel narrative" took place within one of these two locations.[19] In any case, it is clear that Luke's geographical knowledge of Palestine is imperfect. This does not alter the fact, however, that Luke intends to set the way of Jesus in a geographical context. Jesus' ministry is pictured as a wandering (13:33: "Yet today, tomorrow, and the next day I must be on my way, because it is impossible for a prophet to be killed outside of Jerusalem"). The "way" terminology is characteristic for Luke, which shapes not only the story of Jesus but that of the disciples. They accompany Jesus on his way to Jerusalem and do not return to Galilee (in contrast to Mark and Matthew) but encounter the Risen One in Jerusalem. The way of Jesus and his disciples is irreversible, and leads in a straight line to the founding of the church.

(α) *The way of Jesus stands under the divine* δεῖ. Already at the age of twelve, Jesus "must" be about his Father's business in the temple (2:49). Later he says, "I must proclaim the good news of the kingdom of God ... for I was sent for this purpose" (4:43). The passion and resurrection predictions of the wandering Jesus consistently refer to the divine δεῖ (9:22; 17:25; 24:7, 26). So also the exaltation to heavenly δόξα corresponds to the divine necessity (24:26). The whole destiny of Jesus is the fulfillment of God's plan. Even the end of the story is divinely determined (22:22: "For the Son of Man is going as it has been determined..."). Beginning and end, life and ministry of the earthly Jesus are altogether the expression of the divinely-willed eschatological event.

(β) *The way of Jesus is an anticipation of the time of salvation.* Even though the story of Jesus is part of the comprehensive story of salvation, it is still a uniquely salvific segment of time—for the time of Jesus is a Satan-free period.[20] After the temptation the devil leaves Jesus ἄχρι καιροῦ (4:13: "until the opportune time"). This kairos occurs at the beginning of the story of Jesus' passion: Satan takes possession of the betrayer Judas Iscariot (22:3). The passion of Jesus is the time of terrible testing by the

---

[19]  So Conzelmann, *Theology of St. Luke* 41 n. 1.
[20]  Conzelmann, *Theology of St. Luke* 9, 16, 28.

Tempter. The time in between (4:13–22:3) is free from Satan's temptations and from Satan himself. It is an eschatologically charged time; for what was expected for the endtime happens in the historical segment of the life of Jesus. The time of Jesus anticipates the time of salvation.

This is also indicated by the βασιλεία–conceptuality and terminology. On the one hand, the "kingdom of God" is the future reality of salvation; it is expected in the future (13:28–29). The preaching of Jesus announces the nearness of the future kingdom of God (10:9). This preaching is communicated with the verb εὐαγγελίζομαι (4:43; 8:1; 16:16). On the other hand, the βασιλεία becomes a present reality in the time of Jesus. The statement in 17:21 is often interpreted in this sense: ἡ βασιλεία τοῦ θεοῦ ἐντὸς ὑμῶν ἐστιν. According to current exegesis this would mean that in the person of Jesus the kingdom of God appeared "in the midst" of human beings, i.e. among them, in their presence. The present tense ἐστίν appears to support this view. The context, however, refers to the apocalyptic events of the endtime. It is thus more likely that ἐστίν is to be translated in a futuristic sense: the kingdom of God will appear among you suddenly, at one stroke, without one seeing it coming or knowing about it in advance. On the other hand, Luke (along with the sayings collection Q and the Gospel of Matthew) understood Jesus' exorcisms as a sign of the presence of the βασιλεία (11:20: "But if it is by the finger of God that I cast out the demons, then the kingdom of God has come to you"). The βασιλεία is present as the presence of the eschatological fulfillment, the steadfast commitment and promise of God to humanity. This is illuminated by the fact that Jesus appears as the bearer of the Spirit (3:22; 4:18; 10:21).

That in the person of Jesus the eschatological time of salvation appears as a given fact within history can be perceived in the story of Jesus' appearance in Nazareth (4:16–30). In characteristic deviation from the Markan pericope (though probably not in dependence on Q),[21] Luke tells of the content of Jesus' sermon in the synagogue: the combination of quotations from Isaiah 58:6 and 61:1–2 (the commission of the prophet to announce the year of Yahweh's favor) is interpreted by the Lucan Jesus as a prophetic prediction of his own advent. "Today" (σήμερον) the prophecy is fulfilled. With the advent of Jesus comes good news to the poor, the proclamation of freedom to prisoners and the oppressed and the giving of sight to the blind. Such an advent means the ἐνιαυτὸς κυρίου δεκτός (= "the year of the Lord's favor," as translated by Luther). The temporal indication σήμερον is to be understood literally—to be sure, the "year of God's grace" is also made present in the preaching of the church but only as the continuation of that which happened in Jesus of Nazareth. Σήμερον thus describes in the first place the historical hour of Jesus' own appearance.

---

[21] Differently Schürmann, *Lukasevangelium* 3/1: 242–243.

Here is the fulfillment of hope, the realization of God's promise. The time of Jesus is the time of the eschatological reward, the time of eschatological salvation.

(γ) The realization of the time of salvation in the advent of Jesus is an expression of *God's love for those whose rights have been denied, the socially degraded and despised*. In the presence of Jesus that which by human standards is considered undeserving is revalued; every individual is acknowledged to be valued in the sight of God. Thus Jesus' preaching and acts are directed to the publicans, the sinners, the poor. This eschatological love and care of God is concretized in Jesus' table fellowship (5:27–32; 19:1–10), and is reflected in the table fellowship of the Risen One with the disciples on the road to Emmaus (24:13–35).[22] This event of God's love and compassion means "Today salvation has come to this house" (19:9). From the human side, the human response to this divine turning toward (*Zuwenden*) humanity in love and grace is μετάνοια, turning away (*Abwendung*) from one's previous orientation to life, and the realization of a new manner of existence made possible by Jesus (5:8, 32). This repentance ("turning around") is the only condition for participation in eschatological salvation. It means acknowledging one's own nothingness in the face of the eschatological claim, namely that human beings cannot generate salvation from within or among themselves but must let it be given to them. This is expressed especially in the parables that belong to the Lucan special materials (15:11–32; 16:19–31; 18:9–14).

(δ) Juxtaposed to the offer of salvation and the demand for repentance that it implies is the *call to discipleship*. To accept the word of Jesus means to practice self denial (9:23–27) and to make the command to love God and neighbor a reality in one's own life (10:25–28). This is what is presented in the example story of the Good Samaritan (10:29–37: the disciple of Jesus does not ask "Who is my neighbor?" but "To whom am I neighbor?" 10:36). To be a disciple of Jesus means: to practice mercy and compassion to others (10:37). This is what happens in obedience to the claim of the Kyrios, in hearing the word of Jesus: the hearing of this word is itself a part of discipleship; it is placed over against anxiety and concern (10:38–42). Discipleship is realized in prayer (cf. 11:5–8, the parable of the Friend at Midnight; 11:1–4, the Lord's Prayer). Luke portrays Jesus as the model of incessant prayer (3:21; 5:16; 6:12; 9:18, 28–29; 11:1–2; 18:1; 22:41, 44).

The presence of salvation thus happens in Jesus' compassionate turning to the outcast *and* in the call to discipleship. The relation between

---

[22] Cf. also Jesus' blessing and promise to the poor in Luke 6:20–21, as well as the presumably Lucan, harshly expressed woes against the rich (6:24–25). Several Lucan parables have a similar orientation; on this latter point cf. F. W. Horn, *Glaube und Handeln*; L. Schottroff and W. Stegemann, *Jesus von Nazareth—Hoffnung der Armen* (Stuttgart, 1990³).

these two may be understood as indicative and imperative. But Luke himself gives no accounting of how he relates the two. He is not concerned with the Pauline question of what is right and wrong with the Law. For Luke, it is a matter of the two sides Jesus' life and ministry taken as a united whole, which does not find its unity in a theological synthesis but in the historical location of Jesus' appearance. In the life of Jesus the proclamation of the eschatological time of salvation occurs, in his words but likewise in his table fellowship with sinners. So also his miracle-working activity is a demonstration of his eschatological claim. Here the Old Testament promise comes to its fulfillment and is made present as the kingdom of God (7:18–23; Isa 29:18–19; 35:5–6; 61:1). Just as the kingdom of God is manifest in the exorcisms (11:20), so Jesus' advent was accompanied by miraculous deeds of power and itself had an eschatological consequence (6:47–49), just as did the preaching of the disciples (10:10–12). All this means that in such an event God visits and redeems his people (7:16), a visitation in the service of peace but that also is an anticipation of God's judgment (19:37–40).

### 3. The Death and Resurrection of Jesus

(α) If the life of Jesus is understood as the time of eschatological salvation, it would then appear that the *death of Jesus* would be portrayed in eschatological terms in a special way, and that it would be seen as the eschatological event in which the old aeon comes to an end and the new world begins. Although this corresponds to Pauline theology, for the Lucan understanding of the Christ event the death of Jesus is not as such the turn of the ages but is the decisive event within the historical continuum. The life of Jesus proceeds in a straight line through death and resurrection to ascension and Pentecost and is continued in the history of the church. Thus it is not discontinuity but continuity that characterizes the Lucan understanding of the death of Jesus. To the extent that this possesses an eschatological significance, it is incorporated within this temporal movement. Within the framework of the Lucan conception, the death of Jesus is interpreted as a fact of salvation history.

Both the historical and the eschatological aspects correspond to this understanding of salvation history. From the historical point of view the death of Jesus is the result of a "miscarriage of justice among the Jews."[23] They are the betrayers and murderers of Jesus (Acts 7:52); they delivered Jesus over to the Romans even though they could produce no capital charges against him (Acts 13:28). Taken by itself, such a death has no

---

[23] Vielhauer, "On the 'Paulinism' of Acts" 35–36. Cf. also J. R. Wilch, "Jüdische Schuld am Tode Jesu—Antijudaismus in der Apostelgeschichte?" in W. Haubeck and M. Bachmann, eds. *Wort in der Zeit* (FS K. H. Rengstorf) (Leiden: E. J. Brill, 1980) 236–249.

salvific meaning. It is thus only consistent with this that, as is the case with the other Synoptics, there is no reflection on the atoning significance of Jesus' death.[24] Just as the Jews are responsible for the death of the promised Messiah (Acts 2:22–23; 4:28), so the destruction of Jerusalem is the result of this outrageous act (Luke 13:34–35; 19:42–44; 23:27–31)[25] Thereby the realm of historical categories is abandoned and the eschatological aspect of such an event comes to light.

In the death of Jesus the saving plan of God becomes an event in this world; it is the transitional event to Jesus' exaltation. This event was determined by God in advance (Acts 2:23; 4:28); it was willed by God and predicted by the Old Testament prophets (Acts 3:18). Thus the Jewish opponents of Jesus cannot be made ultimately responsible for this event. The antinomy is not to be denied: on the one hand, the Jews are described as guilty of Jesus' death; on the other hand, it is not the Jews but the divine plan of salvation that is the determining power at work in the event. Since the Jews act κατὰ ἄγνοιαν, they are at least not considered to be guilty in the subjective sense (Acts 3:17; 13:17). Luke has not attempted to resolve this antinomy. Within the framework of the church's mission preaching both aspects have one and the same assignment: the appeal to acknowledge and confess one's guilt grounds the call to repentance. On the other hand, the recourse to the ignorance of the Jews has the assignment of letting repentance emerge as a real possibility. Not until the call to repentance is rejected does the definitive situation emerge that excludes from salvation those who are unwilling to repent. In the salvation-historical interpretation of the death of Jesus both aspects are emphasized as facts: the human act of rejection and the saving act of God. The antinomy is thus to be explained from the historical and eschatological aspect of the Christ event and is an expression of the understanding of the death of Jesus as a salvation-historical event.

(β) If one wants to understand the Lucan conception of the *resurrection of Jesus* rightly, it is to be understand in an analogous way as Jesus' death, namely as a factual event in salvation history. Thereby the death and resurrection of Jesus are closely bound to each other, as is made clear by stereotyped formulae: "...Jesus Christ of Nazareth, whom you crucified, whom God raised from the dead..." (Acts 4:10; cf. among other texts 3:13–15; 5:30; 10:39–40; 13:28–30). Even if a clear distinction cannot always be made,[26] it is striking that Luke's terminology for the resurrection of

---

[24] It is revealing that the Third Evangelist has reformulated the λύτρον saying in Mark 10:45 (cf. Luke 22:27). A traditional formula is found in Acts 20:28; it has a devotional purpose and is not systematically elaborated within the Lucan conception.

[25] Cf. M. Bachmann, *Jerusalem und der Tempel* (BWANT 109. Stuttgart: Kohlhammer, 1979).

[26] Cf. J. Kremer, *EWNT* 1:210–221.

Jesus uses the transitive (ἀνέστησα = "to raise") or ἐγείρω (= "raise," "wake up"), not the intransitive ἀνέστην (= 2. aorist) or the middle forms of ἵστημι, all of which are intransitive (= "rise"). The Lucan usage points to the act of God in Christ. The relation between Father and Son is one of subordination. At the center stands the saving plan of God, not the sovereign power of the Son. Moreover, the eschatological aspect of Jesus' resurrection is seen in the fact that Jesus is called "the first to rise from the dead" (Acts 26:23). The resurrection of Jesus is the first step in the general resurrection, understood in connection with the apocalyptic hope of Judaism. Thus in Acts 2:25ff, citing Psalms 16:8–11, it is said "You will not abandon my soul to Hades" (2:27). The Jewish hope for the resurrection of the dead is fulfilled in the Jesus event. That the resurrection of Jesus is predicted in the Old Testament indicates the eschatological character of this event.

On the other hand, for Luke it is not only a matter of demonstrating the saving plan of God but also a matter of historical fact. The preaching of the post-Easter church has the resurrection of Jesus as its decisive theme. The circle of the apostles is limited to eyewitnesses. This includes testimony to the resurrection, for the apostles have the assignment of confirming that the testimony is based on actual fact (Acts 1:21–22). Their task is to make the resurrection of Jesus believable as an event that happened in the past in an "objective" manner, i.e. as observable event that can be supported with evidence, namely that the Risen One appeared to those who are now witnesses—this in the interest of the truth claim of the faith. Thus the resurrection of Jesus becomes a reasonable phenomenon. So too the "empty grave" becomes an argument that can be presented by eyewitnesses for the truth of the faith (cf. Luke 24:1–11). Such a historical line of argument need not exclude the eschatological aspect of the resurrection event. This means that Luke understands the resurrection of Jesus in a salvation-historical sense, as something that happened in history that is at the same time an eschatological event. Thus it is inserted into the historical time line. The immediate continuation is formed by the exaltation of Jesus, the ascension (Luke 24:51–52; Acts 1:9–11). The death and resurrection of Jesus are no longer seen as the decisive saving events per se but merely as salvific occurrences alongside others. They can be portrayed in a distancing, reporting style, because it is a matter of actual events that happened in the past.

## c) The Time of the Church (Ecclesiology)

Luke no more presents a developed ecclesiology than the other Evangelists, since his intention is not to portray the essence and self-understanding of the contemporary church but the past events of salvation history.

The question of the nature of the church is answered by Luke in the way that he describes the church in history.

## 1. The Apostolic Office of the Twelve

At the beginning of Acts, Luke has placed the account of the replacement of Judas by Matthias to complete the story of the institution of the Twelve (Acts 1:21ff). The view that twelve apostles stood at the beginning of the history of the church is a secondary development. Paul could use the term "apostle" in a considerably wider sense (ἀπόστολος = Christian missionary). In the Lucan narrative, in contrast, the term is essentially limited to the Twelve. This is presumably not Luke's own construction but was already found by him in the tradition; otherwise he would have carried out this understanding with complete consistency and would have avoided the discrepancy that emerges in Acts 14:4, 14, where—in contradiction to Luke's usage elsewhere—Paul and Barnabas are named "apostles." Even if Luke did not create the idea of the Twelve Apostles (the limitation to the term "apostle" to the Twelve is already suggested by Mark 6:7, 30), it is still for him extremely important. According to Luke's understanding, the church rests on the pillars of the twelve apostles of Jesus who were eyewitnesses of the resurrected Christ, and who had accompanied Jesus from the beginning. Such apostolic tradition has the assignment of guaranteeing the truth of the faith. The truth that is believed is validated by a reliable tradition. Such an idea of tradition had the function of limiting the freedom of pneumatic authority and of advocating the right of church order over against pneumatic arbitrariness.[27]

The extent to which Luke emphasizes this principle of tradition is illustrated by the manner in which Luke portrays Paul in the Acts narrative. Paul does not belong to the circle of the (twelve) apostles, because he belongs neither to the group of eyewitnesses of the life of Jesus nor to the witnesses of the resurrection. This includes both a temporal and factual distinction: Paul is placed both after the circle of the Twelve, and below them in rank. In this regard it is significant that he is inserted into the "chain of succession" by Barnabas, the middle man between Paul and the Jerusalem church (Acts 9:27). It is not accidental that on the first missionary trip, Barnabas is named before Paul as occupying the leading place, so that Paul becomes the dominant figure only after a probationary period. This coincides with the change of names used by Luke (Acts 13:9, 13, "Paul" replaces "Saul").[28] In relation to the Twelve, Paul represents a

---

[27] Cf. J. Roloff, *Apostolat—Verkündigung—Kirche. Ursprung, Inhalt und Funktion des kirchlichen Apostelamtes nach Paulus, Lukas und den Pastoralbriefen* (Gütersloh: Gerd Mohn, 1965) and "Apostel/Apostolat/Apostolizität I," *TRE* 3, 430–445.

[28] Cf. above A. I. a.

second link in the chain of tradition and is of secondary importance. This corresponds to the salvation history pattern of thinking, which has continuity as its first principle. It is indisputable that here the position of Luke—doubtless against his own will—is similar to the antipaulinism of Paul's opponents (who had also been Jesus' opponents), and does not do justice to the freedom of Paul the pneumatic as an apostle of Jesus Christ.

## 2. The Way of the Church

### α) The Church and Judaism

Corresponding to the continuity of salvation history, the relation of church and Judaism is determined by a gradual, step-by-step detachment.[29] Luke does not teach an abrupt break in the salvation-historical election of Israel, as is seen not only in Matthew but also in Mark. It is rather the case that after the death and resurrection of Jesus the church continues to be associated with Judaism. Its preaching applies to the Jews. This is shown by the Pentecost story (Acts 2:1–13), in which the catalogue of nations (2:9–11) does not refer to Gentiles but to the Jewish Diaspora scattered in many nations outside the Palestinian homeland. After the conversion of the first Gentile, the centurion Cornelius (Acts 10), the church continues both to be confronted with Judaism and continues to be associated with it. This is seen in the way the *Jewish Law* is evaluated. The Law problematic originates with the expansion of the Gentile church. The Gentile mission raises the question of whether Gentile Christians, like Jewish Christians, must keep the whole Jewish law. The "Apostolic Decree" (Acts 15:20, 29; 21:25), with the regulations to refrain from things polluted by idols, from fornication,[30] from what is strangled, and from blood sets forth the minimal requirements of the Jewish ritual law as also binding on Gentile Christians. This decree also serves to secure the unity of the church within the context of the developing story line of Acts.

It is of course not to be assumed that Luke and his church actually practiced the Apostolic Decree in a legal sense. For Luke, it represents a transitional rule in the history of salvation that could be left behind as the church's situation in history changed. It is nonetheless significant that Luke pictures the relation of the early church to the Jewish law in this way. He is unaware of the real problematic of the law—despite his portraying the contrast between Pharisee and publican (Luke 18:9–14). That the Law

---

[29]   Cf. above C. IV. a.

[30]   The concept πορνεία (= sexual immorality, fornication) is not to be identified with "incest," or with marrying someone too closely related, as is sometimes suggested. Cf. e. g. H. Baltensweiler, *Die Ehe im Neuen Testament* (AThANT 52. Zürich: Zwingli, 1967) 93, 101. The coordination with εἴδωλον/εἰδωλόθυτον also speaks for a more general understanding of the term.

does not lead to life but to death is a Pauline idea that was never grasped by Luke. On the contrary, it is no problem for Luke to picture Paul himself as a pious, Torah-observant Jew (Acts 21:26). From the theological point of view, Luke is not a disciple of Paul and thus is probably not to be seen historically as a companion of Paul. That means for the Lucan understanding of the relation of church and Judaism that in the step-by-step disengagement from Judaism the church should nevertheless be understood as the legitimate continuation of Judaism and thus as having taken over the Jewish law (even if only to a limited degree). This is also made clear in the stereotyped form that the missionaries went first to the Jews, then to the Gentiles (Acts 13:46; 28:28). The rejection of the missionary preaching by the Jews creates an independently existing church of Jews and Gentiles that knows itself to be connected with the Jewish people of God in the history of salvation, and thereby understands itself to be the real preserver of the heritage of Judaism.

β) The Proclamation

Corresponding to this movement in the history of salvation, Acts focuses attention on the Christian message as first being preached to the Jews. In his composition of the missionary sermons, Luke follows a uniform scheme: (1) a comprehensive kerygmatic declaration of the passion and resurrection of Jesus is followed by (2) the testimony of the apostles, then (3) proof from Scripture and (4) the call to repentance. This schema appears in the missionary preaching addressed to the Jews.[31] Luke uses a different tradition in Acts 7 (outline of the unholy salvation history of Israel) and Acts 17 (the "sermon on Mars Hill" presents a developed "natural theology" in place of the schema used elsewhere). Each case is a matter of mission preaching that sets the message within the context of salvation history. The schema can be adjusted to the concrete situation. The basic principle is always that of making contact with the given situation. The message is understandable only if it proceeds from within the presuppositions of the circle of intended hearers, and only in this way can a call to repentance be heard. The motivation for repentance is adapted to the variety of situations. While in the case of the Jews the call to repentance is grounded in their outrageous act against Jesus the elect Servant of God, Gentiles are challenged to repent on the basis of their failure to respond to the revelation of God in nature and history. In addition, the missionary message is incorporated within a history that is oriented to its final end, to the judgment and grace of the eschatological Judge of the world. This perspective is the ultimate, decisive motivation for the call to repentance addressed to both Jews and Gentiles (Acts 10:42; 13:40–41; 17:31).

---

[31]   Scriptural proof and the call to repentance are missing from Peter's sermon in Acts 10:34–43 but it is delivered to Gentiles in the house of Cornelius, not to Jews.

γ) The Spirit

While the time of Jesus was a Satan-free time, the church knows of no such liberation for its own time. But even if it is subject to persecution and testing, it is still not merely a phenomenon to be understood in sociological terms. The Christian community acts in the name of the exalted Kyrios. Its messengers heal in the name of Jesus (Acts 3:6, 16; 4:10, 30; 19:13), and they proclaim the name of the Lord Jesus (4:12, 17–18; 5:28–30), just as they endure persecution in his name (5:41; 9:16; 21:13). For Luke and his community this is the confirmation that the power of the Kyrios is effective in their community.

Moreover, the pneuma is given to the Christian community, corresponding to the fact that Jesus was the bearer of the Spirit during the course of his earthly life. How is the Lucan conception of the gift of the Spirit to be understood? According to H. Conzelmann and E. Haenchen, due to the delay of the parousia and the continuation of history, as portrayed by Luke's historical composition the Spirit was a "substitute" for the delayed realities of eschatological salvation. In the history of the church, therefore, the gift of the Spirit would accordingly emphasize the fact that the End had not yet come and that the church is not to understand itself in history as an eschatological reality. This would then be an indication of the deeschatologization of the tradition. The Spirit given to the church would then merely have the assignment of bridging the interim period until the End comes, but it would be a link, not itself an element of the eschatological reality of salvation.[32]

Such an interpretation could appeal to Acts 2:17, if the μετὰ ταῦτα of Codex Vaticanus is accepted (against the majority of MSS).[33] However, this reading is probably a secondary harmonizing of the text to Joel 3:1–5 from which Luke is citing. Originally the pouring out of the Spirit on the day of Pentecost was connected to the statement "In the last days it will be..." (ἐν ταῖς ἐσχάταις ἡμέραις). This reading conflicts with the Old Testament source and is accordingly to be seen as Lucan interpretation: the Spirit is a reality of eschatological salvation. The gift of the Spirit guarantees the fact that the church already lives in the end time. By virtue of the possession of the Spirit, the church is itself an eschatological phenomenon.

Such an eschatological quality does not stand in contradiction to the incorporation of the Christian community within history. To be sure, the gift of the Spirit is not bound to the sacraments, as will be the case in later theology (e. g. Tertullian, Cyprian of Carthage, Augustine); the Spirit is not given in the sacraments "ex opere operato" but remains a free gift. It is not legitimized institutionally, as is possible within the context of a

---

[32]   Conzelmann, *Theology of St. Luke* 184; 195–196.
[33]   So E. Haenchen, *The Acts of the Apostles: A Commentary* 179.

church that understands itself to be an institution that dispenses salvation. But the Spirit is still bound to the institution, namely to the apostolate of the Twelve.[34] Moreover, the Spirit is also related to history in that it is the moving power operative in the continuing historical course of the church's development. The Spirit constantly intervenes in the ongoing course of history, to correct and guide the developing church. This is not to be understood as an incidental part of the Spirit's work,[35] but rather it is by this activity that the Spirit guarantees that the course of church history develops in accord with the God's eschatological plan. The Spirit is something like a "deus ex machina" that corrects missteps in the church's movement through history (cf. Acts 16:6ff: at the direction of the Spirit Paul's stay in Asia Minor is broken off and the European mission is begun). By such leadership of the Spirit the divine plan of salvation is thus realized, the divine δεῖ that had already determined the way of Jesus in the days of his earthly life. Through the Spirit the divine "providence" (πρόνοια) becomes effective as the church makes its own way through history. Precisely by this means the history of the church becomes salvation history. In the sense that the Spirit is related to history in this way, the Spirit in Luke's understanding is also a reality of eschatological salvation.

In conclusion, however, we must observe that Luke did not grasp the radicality of the tension between history and eschaton as it is found for example in Paul. Luke certainly does not yet know the sacramental identification of the church with Christ as expressed in the Deuteropauline letters that would mean an absolute eschatologizing of history and make the church into an institution that dispenses salvation. In Luke's understanding the Spirit is thoroughly integrated into the dialectic of history and eschaton. However, an absolute break in time, the end of history, the radical juxtaposition of history and eschaton are not comprehended in the Lucan concept of the Spirit. From the dynamic juxtaposition of Spirit and history, as was characteristic for the earliest Christian experience of the Spirit, Luke has constructed a view in which the Spirit and history can be placed side by side without tension. By being placed within the scheme of salvation history, the Spirit has been demoted from its place as a reality of eschatological salvation.

## 3. The Apocalyptic Future

Here we need only to refer to Luke 17:20–37 and 21: (5–6), 8–36, since the details have already been dealt with above.[36] The factual and theological

---

[34] Cf. Acts 8:15ff; not Philipp the evangelist but only members of the circle of the Twelve can mediate the gift of the Spirit by laying hands on those who have been baptized.

[35] So H. Flender, *St. Luke, Theologian of Redemptive History* 126–131.

[36] Cf. above on the problem of the delay of the parousia (C I b).

questions are not fundamentally different from the other Synoptics. The characteristic item is the continuation of temporal history. More strongly than the other two Synoptics, Luke reckons with history in terms of an extensive future. This has led to a modification of the original apocalyptic view, as illustrated for example that the destruction of Jerusalem is looked back upon as a historical event (Luke 21:20–24). On the other hand the fundamental eschatological orientation of the church's existence, like that of the individual Christian, has been preserved (cf. Acts 24:25).

## Concluding Remarks

As the author of this two volume work, Luke is more strongly influenced by his tradition than is often supposed. He was not always interested in smoothing out theological discrepancies in his work, even though these tensions cannot be overlooked (e. g. the juxtaposition of Jesus' love for sinners and his ethical demands, conflict with and victory over the Pharisees and affirmation of the Jewish law, the guilt of the Jews but also excusing them because they acted in ignorance, and others). However much these differences may include a theological dynamic, they are not to be evaluated as foundational for Luke's theological conception. The central conception of Luke's theology is without doubt the outline of salvation history, which made Luke into the most consistent historian among the Synoptic authors, though not their greatest theologian.

How Luke's "character" has been thought of through the years has swung back and forth. On the one hand Luke's salvation-historical perspective has fallen under the verdict that the Third Evangelist has delivered the Christian faith over to history, that he has unforgivably neglected the contingency of revelation for the sake of the continuity of the course of history. In contrast to such a negative judgment of Lucan theology there exists a theology of history, not to speak of a metaphysic of history, that has made Luke into the prototype of a theologian who adequately testifies to God's action in universal history, a theology that portrays history as the essential place of God.[37]

It is not appropriate here to foment a kind of ostracizing that would finally prove to be unfruitful. But on the other side it is also not possible to repristinate the Lucan theology, but it must soberly be stated that it was not without good grounds in church tradition that the Lucan theology was placed in the New Testament canon. It may be seen as a preliminary indication of the task that belongs to the church throughout its history; it raises questions for the church that can never become obsolete.

---

[37]  Cf. U. Wilckens, *Missionsreden* 92–96.

The questions that the theology of Luke presents us with—still today—are: How is it to be understood that there is a church in this world within the confines of space and enduring through continuing time? How is the transhistorical, eschatological assignment entrusted to the church to be fulfilled within the framework of history? And above all: How is the eschatological claim of the Jesus event to be expressed, an event that happened within an uneschatological segment of the course of history? Luke attempted to answer these questions in behalf of the church; his answer cannot be repeated in the form in which he expressed it. He attempted a synthesis between history and eschatology that is certainly questionable and, when measured by the theology of Paul, appears as more than problematical. This, however, casts no doubt on the magnitude of his theological and historical achievement. His outline of salvation history testifies forcefully and irrevocably to the "thatness" of the eschatological event, as it happened once for all in the event of Jesus Christ. It is the source of the church's message in which this event is ever realized afresh.

# D.
# Truth and Love—The Johannine School

*Preliminary Remarks on Chronology*

Brown, R. E. *Community of the Beloved Disciple*. New York: Paulist, 1979.
Cullmann, O. *The Johannine Circle*. Philadelphia: Westminster, 1975.
Culpepper, R. A. *The Johannine School*. SBL.DS 26. Missoula: Scholars Press, 1975.
Hengel, M. *The Johannine Question*. London: SCM Press, 1989.
Langbrandtner, W. *Weltferner Gott oder Gott der Liebe. Der Ketzerstreit in der johanneischen Kirche*. BET 6. Frankfurt: Peter Lange, 1977.
Müller, U. B. *Die Geschichte der Christologie in der johanneischen Gemeinde*. SBS 77. Stuttgart: Katholisches Bibelwerk, 1975.
Schnelle, U. "Die johanneische Schule," in *Bilanz und Perspektiven gegenwärtiger Auslegung des Neuen Testaments*," F. W. Horn, ed. BZNW 75. Berlin-New York W. de Gruyter, 1995, 198–217.
Schüssler-Fiorenza, E. "The Quest for the Johannine School: The Apocalypse and the Fourth Gospel," *NTS* 23 (1977) 402–427.
Strecker, G. "Chiliasmus und Doketismus in der Johanneischen Schule," *KuD* 38 (1992) 30–46.
Strecker, G. "Die Anfänge der Johanneischen Schule," *NTS* 32 (1986) 31–47.
Taeger, J. W. *Johannesapokalypse und johanneischer Kreis*. BZNW 51. Berlin: W. de Gruyter, 1988.
Vouga, F. "The Johannine School: A Gnostic Tradition in Primitive Christianity?," *Bib* 69 (1988) 371–385.
Cf. also the monographs on the Gospel of John and especially those on 1 John.

The close relationship in language and conceptual world that can be observed between the Johannine Letters and the Gospel of John has led scholars to speak of a "Johannine circle" or "Johannine school."[1] The

---

[1] On the basis of the Papias reference, already in 1914 W. Heitmüller, "Zur Johannes-Tradition," *ZNW* 15 (1914) 189–209, attempted to show the existence in Asia Minor of a Johannine circle or school that used the honorary title "Elder," a school whose circle of ideas was in contact with the Gospel of John and the Apocalypse. Heitmüller considered the founding authority to be the presbyter John, the figure (whether real or imagined) met in 2 and 3 John and in Revelation 1–3 (201–204). O. Cullmann, *The Johannine Circle*, attempts to trace a line of development in the history of theology to which the Johannine school belongs, a line that had its ultimate origins in a marginal heterodox Judaism, through the Johannine disciples of Jesus (the Beloved Disciples), through a Hellenistic group within the earliest Jerusalem church, to the Johannine community. These groups are characterized by common community structures, missionary interest, polemic against false teachers, and a concern for the legitimization of their own group.

similarities and differences manifest by this group of writings enable scholars to recognize school traditions and the teacher/student relationship
that is basic for the definition of an ancient school. The comparison with
ancient schools in the Jewish and Hellenistic context of early Christianity, as well as other New Testament tradition, makes clear that the activities and processes of a school were involved in the creation and transmission of literary and especially pre-literary units of sayings and speeches.

One criterion for the existence of a school is its derivation from a
founder who establishes its independence over against other groups. Since
the "Beloved Disciple" of the Fourth Gospel is more an ideal figure than
a historical person, i.e. the reflection of the founding personality of the
Johannine school projected into the life of Jesus,[2] the indication of the
sender ὁ πρεσβύτερος (2 John 1; 3 John 1) is the only self-designation of an
author in the Johannine writings. The unqualified manner of expression
presupposes that the author of these letters was known to the addressees,
and that they acknowledged his authority. There are points of contact
between the "presbyter tradition" documented by Eusebius for Bishop
Papias of Hierapolis in Asia Minor:

> And I shall not hesitate to append to the interpretations all that I ever learnt well
> from the presbyters (παρὰ τῶν πρεσβυτέρων) and remember well, for of their truth
> (ἀλήθεια) I am confident.
> For unlike most I did not rejoice in them who say much but in them who teach
> the truth, nor in them who recount the commandments (ἐντολάς) of others but in
> them who repeated those given to the faith by the Lord and derived from truth itself;
> but if ever anyone came who had followed the presbyters (τοῖς πρεσβυτέροις), I inquired
> into the words of the presbyters (τοὺς τῶν πρεσβυτέρων λόγους), what Andrew or Peter
> or Philip or Thomas or James or John or Matthew, or any other of the Lord's disciples
> (τις ἕτερος τῶν τοῦ κυρίου μαθητῶν) had said, and what Aristion and the presbyter John,
> the Lord's disciples, were saying (οἱ τοῦ κυρίου μαθηταὶ λέγουσιν).[3]

---

[2]  Cf. H. Thyen: in the texts about the Beloved Disciple by the author of John 21 "a
literary monument ... has been erected to the author of the two small Johannine
letters." ("Entwicklungen innerhalb der johanneischen Theologie und Kirche im
Spiegel von Joh. 21 und der Lieblingsjüngertexte des Evangeliums," in M. de Jonge,
ed., *L'Évangile de Jean. Sources, rédaction, théologie* (BEThL XLIV) (Leuven: Leuven
University Press, 1977) 259–299; 296. On the other hand, it is less likely that the
Beloved Disciple is to be identified as a historical figure who founded the Johannine
school, as argued by R. A. Culpepper, *The Johannine School* 288, based on the term
ἀπ᾽ ἀρχῆς (1 John 2:7, 24; 3:11; 2 John 5–6). C. K. Barrett considers an early apocalyptic theologian on whom the author of Revelation was dependent to have been the
founder of the Johannine school, cf. *The Gospel according to St. John* (2nd ed. 1978)
62. Cf. also Barrett's essay "School, Conventicle, and Church in the New Testament," in K. Aland-S. Meurer, eds., *Wissenschaft und Kirche* (FS E. Lohse) (TAzB 4.
Bielefeld, 1989) 96–110.
[3]  Eus *HistEccl* 3.39.3–4.

This tradition exhibits a clear connection with the Johannine language world.[4] In addition, there are agreements in the apocalyptic manner of expression. Moreover, there are points of contact between the "presbyter" of 2 John 1 / 3 John 1 and the "presbyters" of Papias. The latter distinguishes on the one hand the πρεσβύτεροι who are identified as the Twelve Disciples, with whom for reasons of chronology Papias could not have been acquainted, and, on the other hand, Aristion and the presbyter John as "disciples of the Lord." In this connection it is to be noticed that the presbyter title is not attributed to Aristion but is restricted to John. It is presupposed that both were still alive at the time of Papias, indicated both by the present tense λέγουσιν and by Eusebius' testimony,[5] so that one can probably infer that the Presbyter of 2 and 3 John is the same as the presbyter John to whom Papias refers.

If now the relation of the Johannine writings to each other is investigated, the result is that the arrangement commonly assumed (Gospel, then 1 John, then 2–3 John) is by no means likely. As the presentation of the theology of the presbyter's letters will show below, not only is there no lack of the Johannine motifs and thought world in the two smaller letters but they manifest an older stage in the history of tradition as well. This observation provides valid grounds for affirming the hypothesis that 2–3 John are to be recognized as the oldest writings of the Johannine school. The sequence of the writings likewise speaks in favor of regarding these works as writings of the founder of the school, which owe their transmission in the tradition and eventual acceptance into the New Testament canon to the high regard in which the presbyter was regarded as the founding authority of the Johannine school. Likewise, the thrice-repeated aorist ἔγραψα in 1 John 2:14 suggests the order 2 John—3 John—1 John. The understanding often advocated, that the present tense γράφω and the aorist ἔγρψα (1 John 2:12–13) represent merely a stylistic variation, is not persuasive. It is more likely that we have here an indication that 1 John presupposes 2 and 3 John. The objection to this inference, that there is nothing explicitly corresponding to this feature in the two smaller letters, turns out to be too sweeping. The author of 1 John has no intention of quoting a previous document but does want to place himself in the tradition of these writings. To this corresponds the further observation, that there are in fact echoes of the presbyter's letters in 1 John.[6] Even though the identity of the author of 1 John with the author of the earlier letters is to be excluded on temporal grounds and because of the advanced development of the tradition in comparison with them, it is still the case that the author of 1 John intentionally takes over the tradition of the Johannine school and attempts to identify his own authority with that of the presbyter, or to attach himself to it. The presupposition of such identification is the author's description of himself as ear- and eyewitness (1 John 1:1–4), so that possibly an identification of the presbyter John and apostle of the same name had already occurred, as is documented later in Irenaeus (*Haer* 3.16.5).

---

4    Thus the absolute use of ἀλήθεια is reminiscent of 2 John 1; 3 John 1, 8, 12; ἐντολάς reminds one of 2 John 4-6.
5    Eus *HisEccl* 3.39.7: "The Papias whom we are now treating confesses that he had received the words of the Apostles from their followers but says that he had actually heard Aristion and the presbyter John."
6    Cf. e. g. 1 John 2:14a (ἐγνώκατε τὸν πατέρα) with 2 John 1-3 (οἱ ἐγνωκότες τήν ἀλήθειαν ... εἰρήνη παρὰ θεοῦ πατρός).

1 John is often described as a "Johannine Pastoral Epistle,"[7] in connection with the presupposition that 1 John was written later than the Gospel. It is important first to be clear that the Gospel and 1 John share common linguistic elements; cf. for example the key Johannine words ἀλήθεια and ἀγάπη. But this in itself by no means indicates a literary connection; the common elements are to be traced back to the school tradition on which both Gospel and Epistle are based. Moreover, significant differences are to be noted, the first of which is the formal distinction between letter and gospel. Along with this is the observation that 1 John betrays no awareness of a life-of-Jesus tradition, while the Gospel of John in contrast presents a "life of Jesus" which has given attention to the narrative beginning and ending points—even if less complete and less consistent than we find in the Synoptics.[8] In contrast to 1 John, which as a "letter-like homily" is aligned to ecclesiological issues, the Gospel is oriented to Christology. There are also terminological divergences. Thus the word παράκλητος in 1 John refers to Jesus Christ (1 John 2:1) but in the Gospel to the Holy Spirit. Differences in eschatology are also to be noted, since in the Fourth Gospel futuristic eschatology recedes differently than in 1 John. While the atoning character of the death of Jesus is presupposed in John 1:29 and 36, it is only in 1 John that it has become a major theme (1:7, 9; 2:2; 4:10). If the independence of both documents is to be presupposed, then one must reckon with different authors. Apparently the Gospel of John was written later than 1 John, since at the time of the composition of the Fourth Gospel the sharp internal disputes that were present when 1 John was written appear to lie in the past.

The tradition of the ancient church locates the composition of the Johannine writings in Asia Minor. On the one hand, this corresponds to the writing of the Apocalypse on the island of Patmos just off the coast of Asia Minor, and on the other hand 1 John is first documented about the middle of the second century by Polycarp of Smyrna. The Papias reference likewise points to Asia Minor. Irenaeus also indicates an awareness of Asia Minor as the homeland of the Johannine tradition, when he says that the Fourth Gospel was published by John son of Zebedee in Ephesus.[9]

In accordance with the above discussion, the delineation of the theology of the Johannine writings must begin with the presbyter's letters. Then the discussion of 1 John and the Gospel will follow, corresponding to the historical development. The conclusion will be formed by the Apocalypse of John. The Apocalypse deserves special attention, not least because its independent character presents a problem with regard to its relation to the other Johannine writings in terms of both the history of tradition and of its theology.

---

[7]  H. Conzelmann, "Was von Anfang war," in H. Conzelmann, *Theologie als Schriftauslegung. Aufsätze zum Neuen Testament* (BEvTh 65. Munich: Kaiser, 1974) 207–214; 214. Already A. Neander had described 1 John as a "circular pastoral letter" (*Geschichte der Pflanzung und Leitung der christlichen Kirche durch die Apostel* [Gotha 1862²] 490).

[8]  On the literary form of the Gospel of John, cf. G. Strecker, *History of New Testament Literature* 161ff; on the relation of John to the Synoptics, pp. 165ff of the same volume.

[9]  Iren *Haer* 3.11; Eus *HistEccl* 5.8.4. This is in accord with the contacts with the Asia Minor heretical leader Cerinthus to the Johannine tradition, as is also the case with the disputes about the Fourth Gospel and the contention over the Apocalypse between Montanists and the Alogoi in the second half of the second century, all of which were centered in Asia Minor.

# I. The Presbyter's Letters

Bauer, W. *Orthodoxy and Heresy in Earliest Christianity*. Philadelphia: Fortress, 1971. (With a supplement by Georg Strecker.)

Bergmeier, R. "Zum Verfasserproblem des II. und III. Johannesbriefes," *ZNW* 57 (1966) 93–100.

Böcher, O. "Antichrist," *TRE* 3 (1978) 21–24.

Bornkamm, G. πρέσβυς, *TDNT* VI (1959) 651–683.

Bousset, W. *The Antichrist Legend: A Chapter in Jewish and Christian Folklore*. London: Hutchinson, 1896.

Brown, R. E. *The Epistles of John*. AncB 30. Garden City-New York: Doubleday, 1982.

Bultmann, R. *The Johannine Epistles*. Hermeneia. Philadelphia: Fortress Press, 1973.

Dodd, C. H. *The Johannine Epistles*. MNTC. London: Hodder and Stoughton, 1946.

Käsemann, E. "Ketzer und Zeuge," *ZThK* 48 (1951) 292–311, also in *Exegetische Versuche und Besinnungen* I. Göttingen: Vandenhoeck & Ruprecht, 1970, 168–187.

Klauck, H.-J. *Der zweite und dritte Johannesbrief*. EKK XXIII/2. Zürich-Neukirchen-Vluyn: Neukirchener, 1992.

Klauck, H.-J. *Die Johannesbriefe*. EdF 276. Darmstadt: Wissenschaftliche Buchgesellschaft, 1991.

Lieu, J. *The Second and Third Epistles of John*. Edinburgh: T. & T. Clark, 1986.

Lieu, J. *Theology of the Johannine Epistles*. Cambridge: Cambridge University Press, 1991.

Lohmeyer, E. "Antichrist," *RAC* 1 (1950) 450–457.

Malherbe, A. J. "The Inhospitality of Diotrephes: God's Christ and his People," *Studies in Honour of N.A. Dahl* (Oslo: Universitetsforl, 1977, 222–232.

Schnackenburg, R. *The Johannine Epistles*. New York: Crossroad, 1992.

Schnackenburg, R. "Zum Begriff der 'Wahrheit' in den beiden kleinen Johannesbriefen," *BZ* 11 (1967) 253–258.

Strecker, G. *The Johannine Letters*. Hermeneia. Minneapolis: Fortress, 1996.

von Harnack, A. "Über den dritten Johannesbrief," *TU* XV 3, Leipzig-Berlin: Hinrichs (1897) 3–27.

Vouga, F. *Die Johannesbriefe* (HNT 15/3. Tübingen: J. C. B. Mohr (Paul Siebeck) 1990.

Wendt, H. H. *Die Johannesbriefe und das johanneische Christentum*. Halle: Buchhandlung des Waisenhauses, 1925.

The letters of the presbyter present an even less systematically structured theology than the other writings of the New Testament.[1] The letters are brief occasional writings whose content was determined by the specific situation that evoked their composition. This fact, along with their usual

---

[1]  The information about the Asia Minor presbyter tradition in Eusebius (*HistEccl* 3.39) as documentation of particular results in the reconstruction of the theology of the presbyter can be used only with restraint (as in the question of eschatology). The opposite approach, however, hardly promises success. This approach would like to use the Papias reference to establish connections in the history of early Christian theology or information about the authors of New Testament documents (as for instance M. Hengel, *Studies in the Gospel of Mark* [Philadelphia: Fortress, 1985, passim], and D. Guthrie, *The Gospels and Acts* [London: Inter-Varsity, 1965, 65ff).

placement at the end of the Johannine writings may be responsible for the shadowy life that these letters have experienced at the hands of New Testament scholars.[2]

The author identifies himself as ὁ πρεσβύτερος (2 John 2; 3 John 1), apparently a title of honor given on the basis of age and life experience. While the term may also refer to the congregational office of a "presbyter," it is still not a matter of a church office structured within a firm official hierarchy. However the elder may have obtained his distinctive title, in any case it expresses a high-ranking authority with claims beyond the congregation from which the letter (2 John) is sent and wants to be acknowledged as such—though this claim is not undisputed. Obviously neither the claim nor importance of the presbyter is restricted by ecclesiastical regulation.

Insights into the early history of the Johannine school are provided by the presumed order 2 John → 3 John, especially the dispute between the presbyter and Diotrophes (3 John 9–10). This controversy has been evaluated very differently in the history of exegesis. On the basis of the formal similarity of the two letters, and the relative order named above, it would be a priori very unlikely that the attempt to ward off the false teachers as described in 2 John 7–11 would not have been important to the church addressed in 3 John. To be sure, the identity of the heresy has been an object of scholarly debate. If one presupposes the dominance of the "heretics" in extensive sections of the church in Asia Minor, then one could easily suppose that Diotrophes, the leader of his congregation, should be described as a "leading heretic."[3] On the other hand, if one is of the view that the presbyter himself is a "Christian gnostic" and is also the author of the Fourth Gospel,[4] then Diotrophes becomes an advocate of the orthodoxy of what was to become the mainstream church. The following will show that the presbyter was something of an outsider in comparison to the doctrinal development underway that would lead to the early catholic church, while on the other hand Diotrephes was possibly inclined in the direction of the docetic teachers of the Johannine school tradition. When Diotrephes is labeled as φιλοπρωτεύων (3 John 9: "who wants to be first [among you]), this is not necessarily a reference to the office of the monarchical bishop but does show that Diotrephes occupied an influential position in the congregation.[5] The presbyter's doctrine of Christ (2 John 9) represents the nucleus of the later christological developments of the

---

[2]  An examination of the index of New Testament passages in the standard reference works on New Testament theology makes clear that they do not grant independent significance to the presbyter's letters.

[3]  W. Bauer, *Orthodoxy and Heresy* 93.

[4]  E. Käsemann, "Ketzer und Zeuge" 178.

[5]  G. Bornkamm, "πρέσβυς," TDNT 6: 670.

Johannine school. As it will be worked out in the formation of both docetic and antidocetic traditions, this development has later fallout in 1 John and the Gospel of John.[6]

These events are also reflected in the structure of the short letters, which are to be outlined as follows:

2 John
|  | 1–3 | Letter introduction |
|---|---|---|
| I. | 4–6 | Admonition to mutual love |
| II. | 7–11 | Warning against deceivers |
|  | 12–13 | Letter conclusion |

The outline of 3 John, a personal letter to an otherwise-unknown Gaius, is as follows:

3 John
|  | 1–2 | Letter introduction |
|---|---|---|
| I. | 3–8 | Praise of Gaius |
| II. | 9–10 | Warning against Diotrephes |
| III. | 11–12 | Commendation of Demetrius |
|  | 13–15 | Letter conclusion |

With regard to the relation between presbyter and the church addressed in 2 John, the respectful introductory greeting (2 John 1) suggests that the addressees are not assumed to be a congregation dependent upon and subordinate to the presbyter. The Johannine school obviously lives in the context of autonomous congregations that cultivate contact with each other.

## a) The Apocalyptic Horizon

That the theology of the presbyter is developed within an apocalyptic horizon is seen from 2 John 7–11, a key passage for understanding of the presbyter's two letters:

Many deceivers have gone out into the world, those who do not confess that Jesus Christ will come [so Strecker; NRSV "has come"] in the flesh; any such person is the deceiver and the antichrist! Be on your guard, so that you do not lose what we have worked for, but may receive a full reward. Everyone who does not abide in the teaching of Christ but goes beyond it, does not have God; whoever abides in the teaching has both the Father and the Son. Do not receive into the house or welcome anyone who comes to you and does not bring this teaching; for to welcome is to participate in the evil deeds of such a person.

This is different from 1 John 4:2 ("Every spirit that confesses that Jesus Christ has come in the flesh [ἐληλυθότα] is from God"), since in 2 John 7

---

[6]   Cf. G. Strecker, "Chiliasmus und Doketismus."

the present participle ἐρχόμενον is used, which contains no statement about the past but can only be understood as referring to the present or future.

When interpreted as referring to the present, the deceivers dispute Jesus' "coming in the flesh" and thereby deny the real presence of Jesus Christ in the sacrament. 1 John 5:6-8, as well as the emphatically realistic interpretation of the eucharist in John 6:51b-58, let us overhear the disputes within the Johannine school and on its margins as to how the sacrament should be understood. These disputes documented in 1 John and the Fourth Gospel point to the presence of spiritualistic teachers that deviated from the christological and sacramental teaching of the Johannine school. Yet the presbyter's letters do not yet reflect this dispute.

Thus the futuristic interpretation is more likely, according to which the opponents deny that "Jesus Christ will come in the flesh."[7] Obviously the presbyter himself expects the parousia of Jesus Christ "in the flesh." In 1 Corinthians 15:23ff Paul had already reckoned with the unfolding of three phases of the eschatological drama, according to which before the final end of history there would be a messianic reign of Christ on earth inaugurated by the parousia. Such a conception is widespread in apocalyptic Judaism. The duration of this reign is often considered to be 1000 years; thus this teaching is often designated "chiliasm" or "millennialism" ("1000" = Greek χίλια; Latin *mille*). This designation is retained for the idea of a future earthly messianic reign before the final End, even when the period is not considered to be a thousand years.[8] A precise millennialism is documented in the New Testament itself: according to Revelation 20 Satan, the Dragon, will be bound by an angel for a thousand years; this is interpreted as the first resurrection of Christians, who will reign with Christ on earth for a thousand years.[9] Hebrews 4:1ff portrays the motif of the κατάπαυσις, the expected "sabbath rest for the people of God," the advent of which is identical with the coming of the messianic kingdom of

---

7    So also B. F. Westcott, *The Epistles of St. John*, London: Macmillan, 1886² (= Grand Rapids: Wm. B. Eerdmans, 1966) 218; Ch. Gore, *The Epistles of St. John*, (London: John Murray, 1920), 226–227 and elsewhere; cf. G. Strecker, *The Johannine Letters* 234, note 9. The future interpretation referring to the parousia is also considered by D. F. Watson, "A Rhetorical Analysis of 2 John according to Greco-Roman Convention," NTS 35 (1989) 104–130, note 4, but finally rejected in favor of the incarnational interpretation, since he postulates 1 John as the earlier document.

8    Cf. P. Volz, *Die Eschatologie der jüdischen Gemeinde*, 1934 (reprinted Hildesheim 1966), 143–144.

9    This idea may also be reflected in John 9:4 ("We must work the works of him who sent me while it is day; the night is coming when no one can work"). Cf. also O. Böcher, "Chiliasmus I. Judentum und Neues Testament," TRE 7, 723–729 (bib.). Böcher adopts the idea that for John 9:4 the world Sabbath begins with the death of Jesus. Then the judgment would not come until *after* the 1000 years.

peace. Also related to the presbyter's world of ideas is the expectation of the eschatological counterpart of Christ in 2 Thessalonians. There the antichrist plays the role not only of the apocalyptic tyrant but also is described as the false prophet. He will lead people astray by the power of Satan with "signs and lying wonders" and by "every kind of wicked deception." Because he is present within the community, he holds back the parousia of Christ. As the negative counterpart to Christ he introduces the future reign of Christ (2 Thess 2:3–12).

The expectation that with the parousia of Christ a messianic reign "in the flesh" would be established was widespread in the province of Asia Minor in the second century.[10] Long before the Montanists near the end of the century advocated a rigorous chiliasm,[11] one already finds chiliastic ideas in Justin (*Dial* 81:1–3; it is not accidental that the Dialogues are located in Ephesus), in Irenaeus the student of Polycarp (*Haer* V 23.33), and, according to Gaius of Rome, in the Asia Minor resident Cerinthus.[12] As Eusebius reports (HE 3.39.12), Papias of Hierapolis was also a chiliast— an additional argument for identifying the presbyter of the letters with the presbyter John, whose student Papias had been.

So also the pseudepigraphical letter of Barnabas supports the thesis that the presbyter was a chiliast. The author of this document concludes on the basis of Old Testament texts that the world will come to an end after 6000 years, at which time the peaceful reign of Christ will dawn (Barn 15:4–5). This coming of Christ is described as ἐν σαρκί (Barn 6:9). The author hopes

"for the one who will be manifested to you in the flesh."[13]

If the theology of the presbyter is characterized by a future-eschatological expectation oriented to a messianic kingdom to be realized on this earth, then quite consistently the earthly reality of the coming one is emphasized. The identification of the deceivers, who have denied the reality of the apocalyptic expectation, with an apocalyptic figure, the antichrist, confirms that the presbyter stands in a broad apocalyptic horizon. The word ἀντίχριστος, which occurs in the New Testament only 2 John 7;

---

10  For the detail provided under D. IV. (Apocalypse of John) cf. G. G. Blum, "Chiliasmus II. Alte Kirche," TRE 7, 729–733; see also G. Kretschmar, *Die Offenbarung des Johannes. Die Geschichte ihrer Auslegung im 1. Jahrtausend*, CThM.BW 9, Stuttgart 1985. 71–72.

11  Cf. Apollonius in Eusebius HE 5.18.2; Epiphanius *Haer* 48.14.1–49.1.3.

12  Eusebius HE3.28.2.

13  ...ἐπὶ τὸν ἐν σαρκὶ μέλλοντα φανεροῦσθαι ὑμῖν Ἰησοῦν. Similarly Barn 7:9: "'they will see him' on that day with the long scarlet robe 'down to the feet' on his body (περὶ τὴν σάρκα). For the interpretation cf. H. Windisch, *Der Barnabasbrief*, HNT ErgBd. III, Tübingen: J. C. B. Mohr (Paul Siebeck), 1920 346; G. Strecker, *Johannine Letters* 235–236, note 16.

1 John 2:18, 22; 4:3 (singular) and 1 John 2:18 (plural), was possibly coined by the presbyter. He takes up an idea widespread both in Judaism and in early Christianity. The coming Christ will be opposed by a hostile ruler who will overwhelm the people of God with war and persecution. At the end of time, before the establishment of the messianic kingdom of peace, this figure (who can also be thought of as the "false prophet," Mark 13:2; 2 Thess 2:9–10; 1 John 4:1–3; Rev 13:11–18; 16:13; 19:20; 20:10; indirectly also John 5:43) will be defeated. The presbyter follows a tradition according to which at the end of time the Messiah's counterpart, represented by a single false prophet or a group of them, appears and inaugurates the final drama by his false teaching. In this apocalyptic situation the eschatological warning βλέπετε ἑαυτούς (2 John 8 "be on your guard") sounds forth. In the advent of the deceivers the very existence of the community is at stake. It is called to decide whether it wants to lose what it has and is—its standing in the faith, its being in the truth (2 John 2, 4; 3 John 3–4) and in love (2 John 6)—, or whether it will obtain the "full reward."[14] In agreement with Jewish and early Christian apocalyptic tradition, according to which the righteous and unrighteous will be separated at the beginning of the messianic reign, and the righteous will receive their reward, the presbyter expects the heavenly reward, which is identical with eternal life, the future fellowship with Christ.[15]

The apocalyptic horizon of the presbyter's letters indicates that the Johannine school from the beginning had access to early Christian apocalyptic traditions. Furthermore, this observation means that the Apocalypse of John by no means stands over against the Johannine school as something foreign to it, even though the presbyter had no intention of writing an apocalypse. Despite the future-eschatological orientation of his theology[16] he is no more to be considered an apocalyptist than is Paul. His remarks are not geared towards speculative apocalyptic ideas but have as their goal the preservation of Christian existence in the unity of the church grounded on love and truth.

## b) The Doctrine of Christ

The presbyter attaches a special importance to the doctrine of Christ he advocates:

> Everyone who does not abide in the teaching of Christ but goes beyond it, does not have God; whoever abides in the teaching has both the Father and the Son. (2 John 9)

---

[14] Rev 11:18; 22:12; Barn 20.2; 21.3 Cf. Dan 12:1–2; PsSol 3:12; 9:5; 13:11 1 Enoch 37:4; 40:9; 4 Esr 14:35; syrBar 14:13; see also H. Preisker-E. Würthwein, "μισθός κτλ.," TDNT 4 695–728; 724.

[15] The entrance of the believer into the kingdom of Christ can be identified with the promised reward; cf. Matt 25:21, 23, and elsewhere.

Fellowship with God is then only given when the obligatory doctrine of Christ advocated by him is maintained. This doctrine has the testimony about Christ as its subject matter and content (objective genitive), even if it is thought of as being authorized by the exalted Christ. This doctrine is determined by the triad: (1) fellowship with God, (2) truth, and (3) love, each of which is a key concept in the theology of the Johannine writings.

## 1. Fellowship with God

The doctrine of Christ mediates fellowship with God, for it can be said of those who abide in the teaching, that they "have God" (2 John 9). Those who accept the doctrine of Christ and comply with it are "from God," and have "seen God" (3 John 11). Here the author is dependent on Greek models as well as on Hellenistic-Jewish tradition, when he interprets and Christianizes the theological expressions "have God" or "have the Father" by "have the Son" (2 John 9).[17] Even though the Father and the Son are distinguished as persons, the theological and christological worlds of imagery to which each belongs still overlap each other. The presbyter makes no real distinction between fellowship with God and fellowship with Christ[18] but rather places the two ideas more strongly parallel to each other than in the analogous statements in 1 John. The content of fellowship with God is characterized by walking or being in the truth.

## 2. Truth

A central concept of Johannine theology is ἀλήθεια. The presbyter is an advocate of "knowing the truth" (2 John 1), and sends out "the brothers" in order to spread it (cf. 3 John 3, 10). By "knowledge of the truth" the presbyter does not mean a critical perception or observation of information from the spectator's point of view, in the light of which one then decides whether to accept or reject it as true. Instead, the Johannine γινώσκω[19] is like the Hebrew ידע[20] in that it includes not only a theoretical

---

16 This corresponds to the fact that the beginnings of Christian theology were largely characterized by apocalyptic.
17 Philo *Op* 170–172; *Som* 2.248; *Post* 122; *Gig* 28; *SpecLeg* 4.49; LXX supplements to Esther 4:17; 2 Macc 8:36; 11:10; 3 Macc 7:16; Test XII (e. g. *Test Dan* 5; *Test Iss* 7); Jos *Ant* 8.227 <ἔχει τὸν θεόν>; cf. 10.250; cf. also below D. II. d.
18 Cf. also 2 John 3
19 On the concept "knowing" in the Johannine writings, see the excursus γινώσκειν in Strecker, *Johannine Letters* 222–226.
20 Although "knowing" is related primarily to being, what-is (ὄν) and the truth (ἀλήθεια) as "the reality underlying all appearances of reality" (Bultmann, γινώσκω κτλ. TDNT 1:692; cf. e. g. Plato *Resp* 9.581b), γνῶσις and γινώσκω in Greek-Hellenistic thinking express an experiential knowledge, a being-affected by something, and can represent the presupposition to ethical action. In Stoicism the knowledge of God leads to the demand of obedience (Epictetus, *Ench* 31.1).

knowledge but also an experiential acknowledgement. The knowledge intended by the presbyter is possible only as one gives oneself to the truth.

"The truth" means the revealed reality of God, in which one can participate because it takes hold of one (cf. 2 John 2) or one finds oneself "in" it or "walking" in it (cf. 2 John 4; 3 John 3–4). When the presbyter writes that he loves the addressees "in (the) truth" (2 John 1; 3 John 1), he presupposes that their mutual relationship is determined by the reality of God. The "truth" can also be thought of in personal terms (3 John 8; cf. v. 12).[21] It is not to be identified with the doctrinal content of the Christian proclamation.

As a reality that is not at human disposal, the truth grasps the believers, and as long as they abide in the realm of truth, they continue as believers in Christ. Thus the truth is both a christological and an ecclesiological reality. It is said of Christians in an almost mystical speech, that they "love in the truth," and that at the same time the truth "abides in us." But the Christian community is embraced by the truth not only in a spatial sense; the truth that embraces them is also a reality with a temporal dimension: ἔσται εἰς τον αἰῶνα (2 John 1–2).

Through its being in the truth the community experiences today and in the future a saving reality:

Grace, mercy, and peace will be with us from God the Father and from Jesus Christ, the Father's Son, in truth and love. (2 John 3)

This formulation based on the greeting form of earlier Christian letters is not to be taken as a blessing *wish* but declares as a *promise* that the saving gifts μεθ᾽ ἡμῶν (with us) *will* be present. Since the community already lives in the present in the realm of the truth and the knowledge/acknowledgement of God, the promised saving gifts apply not to the distant future but are already present. In the first place they are a matter of the fellowship between human beings and God but are not to be separated from the anthropological aspect. This is especially suggested by the term "peace." The reality of salvation has ethical consequences and works itself out in person to person relationships.

The correlation of knowledge and action is an essential aspect of Johannine theology. Corresponding to this, fellowship with God and the knowledge of the truth embraced in it calls not only for theoretical acknowledgement but the ethical action that necessarily follows from it. When the eschatological truth prevails in the life of believers, they stand under the demand of walking in *the* truth (2 John 4; 3 John 3–4). Thus when truth and doctrine are also closely bound to each other, this still does not mean that the concept of truth is an element of an early catholic doctrinal

---

development.[22] Even though it is the case that the "teaching" distinguishes between heretics and the church, the understanding of "truth" is still not determined by doctrine alone. As the teaching of Christ is not something at one's disposal and does not become objectifiably apparent in the realm of the church, so also the truth derived from it is not identical with an "orthodox" doctrinal content. It is rather the case that truth happens in the acts in which agape becomes real. This is indicated in the portrayal of the Gaius to whom 3 John is written, described as one who "walks in the truth" (3 John 3). Corresponding to this, the members of the community are called on to be "co-workers with the truth" (3 John 8). Working together for the truth is the goal (ἵνα!) laid on each individual Christian.[23] This means rejection of evil and doing the good (3 John 11).

## 3. Love

The stereotyped relative clause that recurs at the beginning of each of the presbyter's letters οὓς/ὃν ἐγὼ ἀγαπῶ ἐν ἀληθείᾳ (whom [pl./s.] I love in truth, 2 John 1; 3 John 1) serves to describe the relationship between the presbyter and the addressees and indicates the special significance of the content of the term *agape*. "Love" as the attitude of the presbyter toward the community is determined by the reality of God. Doubtless the presbyter would have been able to paraphrase the meaning of the reality of God with the term *agape*, even though a comparable theological identification of love with God (1 John 4:8, 16 ὁ θεὸς ἀγάπη ἐστίν) is not found in the shorter Johannine letters. This is seen in the author's placing together ἀλήθεια and ἀγάπη in the salvific words of promise that function as the customary blessing formula of early Christian letters: the eschatological gifts of saving grace, mercy and peace have their reality "in truth and love" (2 John 3). Corresponding to his concept of truth, so also the presbyter's understanding of *agape* is not determined by dogma or church law.

Although the later technical term "brotherly love" (e. g. 1 John 2:9–10) is not yet used in the smaller Johannine letters, the command to love each other (ἀγαπᾶν ἀλλήλους) is emphatically and sharply present: as the commandment "from the beginning" (2 John 5) it is at the same time the commandment of the διδαχὴ τοῦ Χριστοῦ. It attains a concrete point of reference in the dispute with the lying prophets who want to mislead the community (cf. 2 John 7, 9). This command is of divine origin (2 John 4b); the keeping of it means walking in the truth and corresponds to the commands of God in general (vv. 4a, 6). In such an ethical obedience the

---

[22] Contra R. Bergmeier, "Zum Verfasserproblem," and *Glaube als Gabe nach Johannes* (BWANT 112. Stuttgart: Kohlhammer, 1980) 200ff.

[23] Cf. ὀφείλειν 3 John 8a; cf. also 1 John 2:6.

community's way of life is fulfilled. The severity of the charge against the "deceivers" consists in their violating the truth and the love commandment by attempting to split the community. In contrast, the presbyter admonishes his addressees to practice love among one another and thereby to preserve the unity of the community. Gaius is a model for such love; he is praised for his love because he has been concerned to provide for the "brothers" visiting from other communities and to send them on their way (3 John 5–6). In comparison with the early Christian tradition, the independence of the presbyter's ethical admonition is indicated by the fact that he does not relate the *agape* commandment as the command to mutual love either to the Old Testament command to love the neighbor (cf. Lev 19:18) or to the double commandment of love known from the Synoptic tradition (Mark 12:28–34 parr).

### c) Dualism

Although the sharply-defined dualism of 1 John and the Fourth Gospel is still absent from the presbyter's letters,[24] the basic elements of a specific dualism can still be recognized, a dualism that can be described as an ontologically motivated dualism of decision. Thus in 3 John 11 Christian existence is characterized as a "being from God" (ἐκ τοῦ θεοῦ εἶναι). This ontological formulation does not denote a sharing of God's essence or a habitual mode of existence; the parenetical context indicates that individual Christians have the freedom to decide whether they will live in a manner responsible to the truth-event or not. The being of the Christian as described above is inseparably bound up with the responsibility of the individual to do the good, just as truth and love are most closely related to each other. The one who has known the truth (2 John 1) has not only "seen God," but will also do the good and practice love. Such as person is "from God." Others however, who practice evil, disclose by their deeds that they have not seen God and do not know the truth, and therefore are not from God (3 John 11).

The eschatological orientation of the theology of the presbyter sharpens the ontologically-motivated dualism of decision. "Being from God" is very important for understanding the present but is also to be understood in terms of the future and therefore is to be oriented to the coming of God: in the life of the believer the truth given by God is realized as love that is "already now" practiced in the present. Alongside this stands the "not yet"

---

[24]   2 John 7 (cf. 1 John 4:1 reflecting a later influence of this text) documents a neutral concept of the cosmos. The cosmological dualism of John 1:9–10, 1 John 2:15ff; 4:5 (the false teachers are "from the world"); the understanding of the world in 1 John 4:9 is not yet present in the presbyter's letters.

of Christian existence that is directed toward the coming Lord of the community. Christian existence in time is realized and experienced dialectically.

The concept of truth (2 John 1), the formulation "to be from God" (3 John 11) or to "have God" (2 John 9) prepares the way for the Johannine writings' later contrast of truth and lie, "from God" or "from Satan." So also the contrast between "truth" and "cosmos" as the negation of the world (cf. John 14:17) is not yet found, just as is the case with the light/darkness contrast (John 1:5; 1 John 1:5) or the ethical antithesis of lie and truth, according to which the false teaching is identified with the lie because it is not from the truth (so e.g. 1 John 2:21). However, an antithetical linguistic form is already present which is a common characteristic of the Johannine school tradition (2 John 9–11; 3 John 11).

### d) The Community's Self-understanding

The congregation to whom the presbyter writes, like the congregation from which he is writing, is described more precisely by the adjective ἐκλεκτός (2 John 1, 13). The congregations in the circle influenced by the Johannine school understand themselves as "elect," because they know themselves to be grasped by the Christ event in which God's grace that "calls out" from the world has been manifested (2 John 3). It is presupposed that there are autonomous congregations who can be addressed by the presbyter through the common self-understanding grounded on the truth of the Christ event. This is also evinced by the address "beloved" (Ἀγαπητέ) applied to the fellow Christian Gaius (3 John 2, 5, 11), which indicates that both individual and community stand together under the one love. The unity of Christians grounded by love is threatened by the "deceivers" who endanger the continued existence of the community. The "elect" are thus not as such withdrawn from the grip of the world and thereby "taken out of the world," but they are challenged to hold on to that which they themselves once grasped and constantly to actualize it anew. Thus when "love" seems at first to be limited to the circle of fellow Christians, this still does not mean that the community of the presbyter understood itself as "ecclesiola in ecclesia, as the form of community that sustains the church."[25] It is rather the case that the addressees of the smaller Johannine letters agree with the missionary intent of the presbyter that serves as the impetus for his sending out "brothers" and promoting his "doctrine of Christ" in other congregations. The Johannine school in its early stage is by no means an exclusive group closed in on itself but is

---

[25] So E. Käsemann, "Ketzer und Zeuge" 179.

determined by a missionary attitude. And that it cannot be described as sectarian is seen from the interpretation of the *agape* concept, which is basically to be understood no differently than in 1 John: this community lives out of the unlimited love directed to the whole cosmos that has become manifest in the Son of God.

# II. The First Letter of John

## a)  Introduction

Bultmann, R. "Die kirchliche Redaktion des ersten Johannesbriefs," *In Memoriam E. Lohmeyer*, W. Schmauch, ed. Stuttgart: Evangelische Verlagswerk, 1951, 189–201; also in R. Bultmann, *Exegetica*. Tübingen: J. C. B. Mohr (Paul Siebeck), 1967, 381–393.

Conzelmann, H. "'Was von Anfang war'," *Neutestamentliche Studien für R. Bultmann*, W. Eltester, ed.. BZNW 21. Berlin: W. de Gruyter, 1954, 194–201; also in H. Conzelmann, *Theologie als Schriftauslegung*. BEvTh 65. Munich: Kaiser, 1974, 207–214.

Dodd, C. H. "The First Epistle of John and the Fourth Gospel," *BJRL* 21 (1937) 129–156.

Heise, J. *Bleiben. Menein in den johanneischen Schriften*. HUTh 8. Tübingen: J. C. B. Mohr (Paul Siebeck), 1967.

Klauck, H.-J. *Der erste Johannesbrief*. EKK XXIII/1. Neukirchener-Vluyn: Neukirchener, 1991.

Klein, G. "'Das wahre Licht scheint schon'. Beobachtungen zur Zeit- und Geschichtserfahrung einer urchristlichen Schule," *ZThK* 68 (1971) 261–326.

Lieu, J. M. "Authority to Become Children of God'. A Study of I John," *NT* 23 (1981) 210–228.

Lohmeyer, E. "Über Aufbau und Gliederung des ersten Johannesbriefes," *ZNW* 27 (1928) 225–263.

Malatesta, E. *Interiority and Covenant*. AnBib 69. Rome: Biblical Institute Press, 1978.

Minear, P. S. "Diversity and Unity. A Johannine Case-Study," *Die Mitte des Neuen Testaments*, C. Breytenbach-H. Paulsen, eds. FS E. Schweizer. Göttingen: Vandenhoeck & Ruprecht, 1983, 162–175.

Minear, P. S. "The Idea of Incarnation in First John," *Interp.* 24 (1970) 291–302.

Nauck, W. *Die Tradition und der Charakter des ersten Johannesbriefes*. WUNT 3. Tübingen: Tübingen: J. C. B. Mohr (Paul Siebeck), 1957.

O'Neill, J. C. *The Puzzle of 1 John*. London: SPCK, 1966.

Schnelle, U. *Antidocetic Christology in the Gospel of John*. Minneapolis: Fortress, 1992.

Smalley, S. S. *1, 2, 3 John*. WBC 51. Waco: Word, 1984.

Stegemann, E. "'Kindlein, hütet euch vor den Götterbildern!'," *ThZ* 41 (1985) 284–294.

Strecker, G. "Die Anfänge der Johanneischen Schule," *NTS* 32 (1986) 31–47.

Strecker, G. *The Johannine Letters*. Hermeneia. Minneapolis: Fortress Press, 1996.

von Dobschütz, E. "Johanneische Studien I," *ZNW* 8 (1907) 1–8.

Weiss, K. "Orthodoxie und Heterodoxie im 1. Johannesbrief," *ZNW* 58 (1967) 247–255.

Wendt, H. H. "Der 'Anfang' am Beginne des I. Johannesbriefes," *ZNW* 21 (1922) 38–42.

Wengst, K. *Der erste, zweite und dritte Brief des* Johannes. ÖTK 16. Gütersloh: Gerd Mohn, 1990.

Wengst, K. *Häresie und Orthodoxie im Spiegel des ersten Johannesbriefes*. Gütersloh: Gerd Mohn, 1976.

In order to determine more closely the literary character of 1 John it is necessary first to notice that, differently from the presbyter's letters, the most important formal indicators of a "letter" are lacking. There is neither prescript, proömium, nor concluding greetings. So also, the prologue 1 John 1:1–4 cannot be identified as the beginning of a letter. Despite the frequent direct address to the readers, the document lacks the information about sender and addressees customary in ancient letters. Neither can 5:13 be interpreted as an epistolary postscript, since further admonitions follow and the essential elements of the letter's conclusion (greetings, blessing) are absent. In view of the character of the document as direct address, one can thus better understand its literary genre as "letter-like homily." The outline[1] indicates an alternation between the themes of fellowship with Christ and mutual love of the brothers and sisters. Thereby is to be noted that the dispute with the opponents plays a significant role. Alongside the parenetic discussions that address the readers directly in order to deepen their knowledge and present concrete instructions helpful for their Christian life are found polemical sections especially concerned with the doctrine of the opponents and thus oriented to theological teaching.[2] Their goal is to establish the Christian community in their knowledge and faith (5:13), including its ethical dimension understood concretely as the actualization of *agape* in the Christian life. The document is determined by the Johannine school tradition. One must also take account of the meditative style, not least because of the breaks and jumps in the train of thought. On closer examination, however, the significance of these rough transitions need not be exaggerated, so that we should proceed on the assumption of the document's basic literary unity.[3]

## b) The "Apostle" and the Tradition ἀπ᾽ ἀρχῆς

A distinguishing feature for the theology of 1 John is its specific consciousness of tradition. The author refers to an ἀρχή that is constitutive for both his preaching and his writing (1 John 1:1; cf. 2 John 5–6; John 1:1ff). This "beginning" is identical with the λόγος τῆς ζωῆς, which can be

---

[1] Cf. already Th. Haering, *Die Johannesbriefe* (Stuttgart: Calver, 1927) 6, 9–10.
[2] Thus after the introduction (1:1–4) the composition can be understood as an alternating series of parenetic and theological sections (parenesis: 1:5–2:17; 2:28–3:24; 4:7–5:4a; 5:13–21; theological expositions: 2:18–27; 4:1–6 and 5:4b-12).
[3] With the exception of the "Comma Johanneum," a later addition to 5:7–8.

translated "word of life" and is identical with the Christian message but also understood in the sense of a "genitive adiectivus" as "life-giving word" and thereby personified and refers to the Logos as a person (alongside 1 John 1:1, cf. also 1 John 2:13–14; John 1:1ff). The beginning by which both author and community know themselves to be determined is identical with the Christ-event. The author also declares that eternal life is revealed in Jesus Christ (cf. 1 John 5:11–12). Such a consciousness of tradition is expressed in the claim to be an ear- and eyewitness of the beginning event. This means—as indicated by the characteristic, historically-oriented witness terminology in 1:1–4—that the claim here presented appears as that of an "apostle," who bears witness to the hearers of a later generation to the reliability of the beginning of the Christian church, namely to the factuality of the Christ-event that now stands in the past. This event encompasses the grand sweep of time from preexistence (1:2 "with the Father") through the advent of the earthly Jesus (1:1 "what we have heard and seen with our eyes") to the resurrection of Jesus Christ (1:1 "what we have seen and our hands have handled") and is now mediated through the preaching of eyewitnesses in order to establish a comprehensive "fellowship" that includes Father, Son, witness, and community (1:3) so that Christian joy may extend to its eschatological fulfillment (1:4). As made clear by the juxtaposition of the authorial "we" to the "you" (pl.) of the addressees (1:3), the author does not want to speak of a general experience available to all Christians but as a member of the first Christian generation who is a witness to the actual encounter with the incarnate and risen Christ, he wants to distinguish himself from the readers, so that his testimony can guarantee the foundation and certainty of the faith for all Christians.

Even though the author's claim to authority corresponds to that of an apostle of the first generation, it is nonetheless revealing that the term "apostle" is not used by him. His claim does not authorize any historical conclusions with regard to his being a contemporary of Jesus. So also the presbyter, who writes prior to him (2 John 1; 3 John 1), as the teacher of Papias was no eyewitness of the life of Jesus. The supposition that the author of 1 John was a pupil or advocate of John the son of Zebedee (R. Schnackenburg) cannot be supported with evidence. Distinct from the blessing pronounced in John 20:29 on those who do not see, we find in 1 John a realistic perspective that corresponds to the eyewitness testimony presupposed by the document (cf. 1 John 4:14). This perspective doubtless stands in an apocalyptic horizon, as already indicated in the presbyter's letters, but is made concrete in the letters combative debate with the opponents.

## c)   The Opponents in the First Letter of John

In contrast to the presbyter's letters, in 1 John there is no longer any trace of a dispute about chiliasm. The motif itself is missing from the author's presentation. Nevertheless, the apocalyptic worldview has been preserved as documented by the continuing expectation of Christ's parousia (2:28), the concept of ἐλπίς (3:3) that defines the community in terms of the hope for the future vision of God (3:2), and other future-eschatological statements (3:2; 4:17: the concepts of the eschatological παρρησία[4] and ἡμέρα τῆς κρίσεως, the latter unique in the Johannine corpus). To extract such statements from their context and attribute them to an ecclesiastical redaction would be to ignore an essential component of the theology of 1 John and thereby to diminish it.

At the center of the dispute stands a different question, which can be traced back to the dispute displayed in the presbyter's letters. Over against the emphasis on the realistic eschatology and Christology advocated by the presbyter, his opponents are to be located in a Hellenistic Christianity oriented to the Spirit. The opponents in 1 John are to be classified as under the influence of the same milieu. They once belonged to the Johannine circle but have now separated from it (2:19). The essential point of difference, according to the author of 1 John, is that they deny that Jesus is the Christ (2:22):

> Who is the liar but the one who denies that Jesus is the Christ? This is the antichrist, the one who denies the Father and the Son.

The inference that hereby the opponents of 1 John are identified as Jews, who deny the Messiahship of Jesus,[5] is not persuasive. The opposition party described by the presbyter as "antichrists" is to be sought on the basis of the docetic ideas described in 4:2–3:

---

[4]   This idea is also known in the wisdom literature of Hellenistic Judaism. Cf. Wis 5:1, "Then (at the final judgment) the righteous will stand with great confidence (ἐν παρρησίᾳ πολλῇ) in the presence of those who have oppressed them."

[5]   This view was already taken by A. Wurm, *Die Irrlehrer im ersten Johannesbrief.* BSt(F) 8, 1 (Freiburg, 1903) 24–52, who not only rejected the view that there were different groups of opponents in 1 John but identified this united group as Jews that deny the Messiahship of Jesus. Cf. further J. C. O'Neill, *The Puzzle of 1 John;* H. Thyen, "Johannesbriefe," TRE 17, 186–200; 191–195; J. A. T. Robinson, "The Destination and Purpose of the Johannine Epistles," NTS 7 (1960/61) 56–65, describes the Johannine letters as "necessary correctives to deductions drawn from the teaching of the Fourth Gospel by a gnosticizing movement within Greek-speaking Diaspora Judaism (65; see also 60: "The question is … whether Jesus is the 'Messiah.'") K. Weiss, without wanting to disregard any possible connection with (proto-) Gnosticism, points to an opposing group that has its home in a Jewish context ("Die 'Gnosis' im Hintergrund und Spiegel der Johannesbriefe," in K. W. Tröger, ed., *Gnosis und Neues Testament. Studien zur Religionswissenschaft und Theologie* (Gütersloh: Gerd Mohn, 1973) 341–356.

> By this you know the Spirit of God: every spirit that confesses that Jesus Christ has come in the flesh is from God, and every spirit that does not confess Jesus is not from God. And this is the spirit of the antichrist, of which you have heard that it is coming; and now it is already in the world.

As indicated by the perfect participle ἐληλυθότα, the Christ-event is understood as an event of the past that has continuing significance into the present. The opponents' criticism is thus focused on the incarnation of Christ; this leads to the well-founded hypothesis that the issue here is docetism.

The designation "docetism" is derived from the Greek term δόκησις/δοκεῖν.[6] The group designated by this term disputed the possibility of reconciling the earthly being Jesus of Nazareth with his divine origin. They could grasp the Christian confession of the saving significance of Jesus only to the extent that they could make a strict distinction between the heavenly Christ, whom they acknowledged, and the earthly human Jesus. It was only the latter, in their understanding, who had suffered and died on the cross, while the former only "appeared" to be identical with Jesus. Docetism disputed the concept of the incarnation on the basis of the premise that the divine and heavenly could not unite with the human and earthly.

This conception is derived from a Greek way of thinking, not from Jewish or authentic Jewish-Christian thought.[7] It could be articulated within the framework of different systems, so that the possibility of a Gnostic docetism is given. To be sure, gnosticism and docetism are not necessarily to be identified, since the latter is often lacking a soteriology conceived in cosmological terms.[8] Apart from their docetic Christology, little concrete data can be provided concerning the opponents in 1 John. Since they dispute that Jesus is the Christ and the Son of God, we may suppose that they made a distinction between the person "Jesus" and the "Christ." Although the terminological details can no longer be discerned, it is still likely that the distinction between the earthly Jesus and the heavenly Christ involved a dualism. Although less developed, such a dualism is also already evident at the beginnings of the Johannine school (3

---

[6] On the problem of docetism cf. e. g. N. Brox, "'Doketismus'—eine Problemanzeige," ZKG 95 (1984); J. G. Davies, *The Origins of Docetism.* StPatr VI, TU 81 (Berlin 1962) 13–35; U. Schnelle, *Antidocetic Christology* 63–70; M. Slusser, "Docetism: A Historical Definition," *The Second Century* 1 (1981) 163–172; P. Weigandt, *Der Doketismus im Urchristentum und in der theologischen Entwicklung des 2. Jahrhunderts.* Diss. theol. Heidelberg 1961.

[7] Cf. e. g. P. Weigandt, "Der Doketismus im Urchristentum" 29; differently Brox, "Doketismus" 313–314, who attempts to derive docetism from Jewish Christianity.

[8] Thus Brox "Doketismus" 313 rightly states, "Non-gnostic docetic christologies were apparently no rarity in the early second century."

John 11). This dualistic orientation is further reflected in the contrast between light and darkness, life and death, God and world (1 John 1:5–7; 2:8b-11, 15–17; 4:4–6; 5:4–5). The docetic Christology obviously implies a devaluation of the material world and presupposes a prophetic and gnostic self-understanding. Finally it should be noted that the original meaning of "gnosticism" had to do with knowledge as the knowledge and experience of God and is thus not to be defined solely in terms of mythological knowledge. A gnostic system as found especially in the disputes of the Church Fathers in the second century can not be discerned in the texts of 1 John.

In debate with this hostile front, the author emphasizes that Christ lived on the earth as visible, audible, and touchable. In contrast to the dehistoricizing and spiritualizing way of looking at things advocated by his opponents, he is thus concerned to emphasize the "graspable," "empirical" reality of the Christ event. It is at this point that the "pseudepigraphical" motif plays a role: under the fictitious sign of apostolic authority claimed by the author for himself, he seeks to repudiate the opposing teaching.

The expression ἔγραψε, understood as a reference to the presbyter's letters, corresponds to the emphasis on tradition.[9] In contrast to the opponents, whose docetic tradition is presupposed by the author of the Fourth Gospel, the author of 1 John understands himself to be standing in the tradition of his own school. His claim goes beyond that of the presbyter in that he represents himself as an eyewitness of the life of Jesus, without giving any indication that he knows events from the life of Jesus in his writing. The author of the Gospel of John was the first to write a "life of Jesus" within the framework of the Johannine school.

The common ground represented by the tradition has been abandoned by the opponents (2:19):

> They went out from us but they did not belong to us; for if they had belonged to us, (then) they would have remained with us. But by going out they made it plain that not all are from us.

When the opposing teachers withdrew from the Johannine community, then their real nature became visible. They never really belonged to the community. It therefore belongs to the essence of the community that their members remain together and preserve the unity of the Christian fellowship. It is precisely the splitting of the community that reveals the antichrist character of the false teaching and shows a deficiency of love.

In summary we may say that in 1 John, independently of the Gospel of John, the Johannine thought world has been taken up and recast in an

---

9   2:14, 21 (cf. discussion above); on the other hand, the references in 2:26; 5:13 are to the present writing, as are the present-tense verb forms: 1:4; 2:1, 7–8, 12–13; 2 John 5.

independent manner. The author places himself in the tradition ἀπ' ἀρχῆς that is still as valid as ever, emphasizing on the one hand the physical perceptibility of the saving event that can be verified christologically, on the other hand tracing his claim to authority back to the beginning in a way that goes beyond the presbyter. As a witness who has seen, heard, and touched, he opposes the docetic opponents whose false teaching has been revealed by the fact that they have split the community. In the following we will see that the author of 1 John opposes the spiritualistic view of the opponents by emphasizing the atoning power of the death of Jesus (1:7) and the spiritual mediation of salvation by baptism and the eucharist (5:6–8). This also corresponds to the picture of the docetic teachers, for hostility to the sacraments was regarded by the Church Fathers as an indication of docetism.[10]

### d)  Fellowship with God

#### 1.  "Abiding in God" and Other Designations for Fellowship with God

The theme "fellowship with God" represents a central element of the theology of 1 John. This is what is represented by the phrase μένειν ἐν, as well as what is expressed in the phrases "begotten by God," "being from God," and "have God."

As was already the case in Greek literature, so also in the New Testament the term "abide" (μένειν) has to do with location.[11] The usage of the term in a spatial sense can become a metaphorical paraphrase meaning "to abide in a particular sphere" (1 John 2:10, "in the light;" 3:14, "in death") and portray the relation of God to human beings or that of human beings to God or Christ. While this usage is reminiscent of the terminology of the Greek mysteries,[12] it is nevertheless not to be understood in a mystical sense. The phrase μένειν ἐν does not attest a mystical dwelling of God in the believer but rather implies a personal encounter between God and humans. This is what is indicated by the reciprocal *immanence formula*, as found for instance in 1 John 3:24:

All who obey his commandments abide in him, and he abides in them.

The formula μένειν ἐν expresses a continuing unity between God/Christ and human beings (cf. also 2:6; 3:9, 15; 4:12–13, 15–16). This corresponds to the idea of begetting by God or being a child of God. In terms of content, the believer's fellowship with God is interpreted as keeping the commandments. It is thus concretized in the ethical acts of "brotherly love," i.e. by believers who abide in the love of the Father.

The primary sense of the term "abiding" is that it represents the state of the community in the indicative mood. By virtue of its possession of the

---

[10]   Cf. IgnSm 7.1; IgnPhld 4; Epiph Haer 30.16.1.

"anointing" (χρίσμα) it knows that it is thereby led to the truth and is separated from the "seducers" (2:27). Along with the affirmation that each member of the community abides "in him" it is further said, also in the indicative mode, that they do not sin, even that they cannot sin (3:6, 9), just as conversely the being of the unbeliever is characterized as an abiding in death (3:14; cf. v. 15). Most such passages are located in a parenetic context, so that the transition to the imperative is fluid. That is especially true for the indicative statements that presuppose a condition. Thus the confession that Jesus is the Son of God not only indicates that one belongs to the church in contrast to the false teaching, but making this confession is the presupposition for the fact that the Christian abides in God and God abides in him or her (4:15).

Alongside the spatial component of the term, the temporal component is also to be considered. The author of 1 John exhorts his readers to "abide in" the Son in view of the future parousia (2:28). Fellowship with God, i.e. the abiding of human beings in God and God in them, has as its goal the perfection of love that will finally be fulfilled on the day of the last judgment (4:16–17). If the perfection of love is thought of spatially as the place where the divine and human love fully interpenetrate (4:12), then this also has a future-eschatological orientation. The author of 1 John does not dispute the reality of a future judgment for himself and his church but knows that he is already incorporated in the perfection of love that is happening here and now. That such love is already being realized among Christians is sufficient ground for the certainty that on judgment day the Christian community will have boldness and will be able to stand before the judgment of the One who judges the whole world (4:17).

There are certainly close material connections between the theology of Paul and that of 1 John as seen in the concepts of fellowship with God expressed by the Johannine immanence formula and the Pauline ἐν Χριστῷ statements.[13] While this observation may be taken as an indication that the Johannine circle originally had a Pauline basis,[14] a distinctive feature

---

[11] Cf. Plato Ep 358c: "in the customs;" Resp 360b: "in righteousness." 1 Tim 2:15 "abide in faith and love;" 2 Tim 3:14: "abide in what you have learned." It is also documented in this sense in the Johannine corpus (1 John 2:24, 27).

[12] Cf. R. Reitzenstein, *Die hellenistischen Mysterienreligionen* 396–400 (on 1 John 2:20ff).

[13] Cf. on the one hand "in Christ:" 1 Thess 1:1; 2:14; 4:16; 5:18; Gal 1:22; 3:28; 5:6 and elsewhere; on the other hand "Christ in me:" Gal 2:20; "the truth of Christ in me:" 2 Cor 11:10; "Christ in you" 2 Cor 13:5; Rom 8:10.

[14] A connection between Pauline and Johannine ideas in the history of the tradition also appears to be reflected in the use of the noun δικαιοσύνη in 1 John 2:29 (cf. Rom 1:17; Gal 2:17). This is also the case when the noun does not refer to God but describes the object of the community's action (cf. 1 John 3:7, 10). Especially the Johannine coupling of salvific indicative and ethical imperative is informative regarding the relation to the Pauline tradition (1 John 2:1–6; cf. Rom 6:1ff; Gal 5:25).

of the theology of 1 John (and that of the Fourth Gospel) is provided by the motif of divine begetting, which defines human existence by its connection with divine being.[15] These anthropologically-constructed statements give a basis for Christian existence that does not lie in human beings themselves but is given to them from elsewhere. Thus the content of the idea of being begotten by God can be identified with that of being a child of God (3:9–10; 5:1–2), though the two ideas can be distinguished terminologically and in terms of the history of their respective traditions. Like the phrase μένειν ἐν, both express a continuing ontic fellowship between human beings and God.

While the idea of divine begetting had its original setting in the baptismal tradition (cf. John 3:3ff), it is also thought of in connection with the reception of the word or the attainment of knowledge.[16] This suggests that the docetic opponents of 1 John claimed "divine begetting" for themselves, especially since this idea had not yet appeared in the presbyter's letters. Thus a docetic Christology could be combined with a dualistic-spiritualistic anthropological concept. This was taken up in a positive sense in the vocabulary and theology of the Johannine community (cf. John 1:13; 3:3, 5–8). Distinctions may be noted within this transferred use of the language: born/begotten of God (1 John 2:29; 3:9; 4:7), by the Spirit (John 3:6, 8; cf. 3:5: of water and the Spirit) or begetting "from above" (John 3:3, 7). The history-of-religions background is not that of Old Testament Judaism.[17] Although this Jewish tradition knows the motif of being children of God,[18] this is never identified with a divine begetting. For this one must rather look at the Hellenistic-syncretistic background. Already in Cleanthes' Hymn to Zeus, the human race is derived from God the Fa-

---

[15]  Cf. also the use of γεννᾶσθαι in 1 John, almost exclusively in the passive sense: 2:29; 3:9; 4:7; 5:1, 4, 18; cf. John 1:13; 3:3ff.

[16]  Thus the Coptic *Gospel of Truth* states that "If one has knowledge, he is from above. If he is called, he hears, he answers, and he turns to him who is calling him, and ascends to him. And he knows in what manner he is called. Having knowledge, he does the will of the one who called him … He who is to have knowledge in this manner knows where he comes from and where he is going. He knows as one who having become drunk has turned away from his drunkenness, (and) having returned to himself, has set right what are his own." *NHC* I 3:22.2–10, 13–19. Cf. K. Rudolf, *Gnosis: The Nature and History of Gnosticism* (San Francisco: Harper &Row, 1977) 227.

[17]  Cf. R. Schnackenburg, *Johannine Epistles: Introduction and Commentary* (New York: Crossroad, 1992) 164–166 (contra O. Michel–O. Betz, "Von Gott gezeugt," in W. Eltester, ed. *Judentum, Urchristentum, Kirche* (FS J. Jeremias). (BZNW 26) (Berlin: W. de Gruyter, 1960) 3–23). The use of the verb ("bear," "beget") in Ps 2:7 refers to the adoption or legitimization of the king of Israel, and also in Deut 32:18 (the rock that bore / begot you) remains entirely in the sphere of metaphor (about the chosen people). The same is true for 1Qsa II 11 (-12) and 1QH IX 35–36.

[18]  Cf. Mal 3:17–18; Wis 2:18; 5:5 and elsewhere.

ther,[19] in Epictetus one finds the worshipper acknowledging before God, "You have begotten me,"[20] and Plato had already identified the creator of the world with the divine Father.[21] When Philo speaks of God as ὁ γεννήσας or as the γεννητὴς πατήρ who "begat" human beings at the creation of the world, it is the result of this Greek influence, especially Stoicism.[22] Moreover, Philo connects the idea of the divine begetting with the ethical ideas of the adoption of the virtuous person by God as his "son."[23] While the issue of whether the concept of divine begetting was influenced by the mystery cults remains disputed,[24] in any case it is clear that in 1 John the idea is not to be understood either physically or in terms of a theology of creation but ontologically. That is, the author articulates the "extra nos" of existence in faith, the confession of the believing community that it owes its faith not to its own achievement but gives thanks for it to the "Wholly Other."

Such "predetermination according to one's origin" is not only a claim made by the opponents but is an affirmation that can be applied to the Christian community as a whole. This community believes in Jesus Christ as the Righteous One and confesses faith in him by its deeds. Only when their deeds harmonize with their confession of faith are they numbered among those who are begotten by God (2:29) and have confidence that in the future too they will be acknowledged as "children of God" (3:1).

This line of thought has already been met in the descriptions for fellowship with God found in the presbyter's letters. ἐκ τοῦ θεοῦ εἶναι ("to be from God" 3 John 11; 1 John 4:2, 4, 6; also in the negative sense: 3:10; 4:3, 6) as a distinguishing feature of the Christian community comes to expression in the confession of "Jesus Christ who comes in the flesh" (4:2). This leads to the distinguishing of spirits, the spirit of truth and the spirit

---

19 Stob Ecl 1.25.3ff (v. Arnim 1.121.37ff) ἐκ σοῦ γὰρ γένους ἐσμέν (for we are of your race).
20 Epict Diss 4.10.16: με σὺ ἐγέννησας
21 Cf. Plato Tim 37c (ὁ γεννήσας πατήρ) R. Reitzenstein–H.H. Schaeder, *Studien zum antiken Synkretismus aus Iran und Griechenland.* Leipzig-Berlin 1926 (reprinted Darmstadt: Wissenschaftliche Buchgesellschaft, 1965). JBW 7, 142ff; G. Schrenk," πατήρ κτλ." *TDNT* 5. 945–1022; 956–958.
22 Philo Op 84; Spec Leg II. 30–31; III 189.
23 Sobr 56: "He [the human being] is in fact the only one of distinguished ancestry, because he has been chosen by God the Father and only he has been adopted by God as his son (γεγονὼς ... υἱός).
24 F. Büchsel, "γεννάω" *TDNT* 1.665–675 speaks against such an influence. R. Schnackenburg, *Johannine Epistles* 166–167, sees a terminological contact between 1 John and the piety of the mystery cults. R. Bultmann, *A Commentary on the Johannine Epistles* argues that there was even a material connection between gnostic and Christian preaching, a view that is relativized by M. Vellanickal, *The Divine Sonship of Christians in the Johannine Writings* (AnBib 72. Rome: PBI, 1977) 234ff, and R. E. Brown. *The Epistles of John* (AncB 30. New York: Doubleday, 1982.) 385ff.

of error (4:3, 6), and between those who belong to the world and therefore are not from God, and the children of God who know that they have overcome the cosmic powers (4:4). However much such distinctions are expressed in ontological terms, they still have a historical import; it is articulated in the doing or not doing of righteousness and love for the brothers and sisters (3:10). The content of the term θεὸν ἔχειν ("to have God") is not far removed from this, a term that is not specifically Christian but has models in Greek[25] and Hellenistic Jewish[26] literature. In the Johannine writings a supplementary Christianization has taken place, in that they speak not only of "having God" or "having the Father" (2 John 9; 1 John 2:23) but also of "having the Son" (2 John 9; 1 John 5:12). Differently than in the presbyter's letters, in 1 John a series of steps can be perceived that proceeds from the Son to the Father (2:23; cf. 5:12). "Having" is not understood as "possessing" but within the framework of present eschatology is a periphrastic expression for fellowship with God and Christ. Such fellowship remains dependent on the advocacy of the Paraclete (2:1). It is not only "known" by human beings in a theoretical sense but their knowledge is bound to an acknowledgment of the Father and the Son (2:3ff) and implies the demand that what has once been grasped not be lost (cf. the use of μένειν in the imperative, 2:24–28).

Fellowship with God is characterized by and grounded by ἀγάπη. Just as the Christian community is determined by its "being from God," the same is true of its "existence in love." Whether this love is directed to God or to human beings, in each case it is related to the divine begetting of those who love. On the other hand, "being begotten/born of God," which is identical with "being from God" (4:7b), expresses itself in agape. The divine love is the foundation for the community of believers' fellowship with God (4:16). In contrast, loveless people who do not acknowledge God are excluded from fellowship with God (4:8; cf. 2:5).

The love of God is made concrete by the Son, who entered into earthly reality.[27] Here the divine love delivered itself over to human perception and shows its reality in a concrete event by entering history in the "only Son" (4:9). The object of the revelation of God's love in the Son is the cosmos. As the "world of human beings" this world stands under the domination of sin and is characterized by nothingness and hostility to God

---

[25] E. g. Epict Diss 2.18.17.

[26] E. g. 2 Macc 8:36; 11:10; 3 Macc 7:16; Jos Ant 7.227 and elsewhere. Cf. also above D. I. b. 1.

[27] According to H. Schlier, *Das Ende der Zeit. Exegetische Aufsätze und Vorträge* III, Freiburg: Herder, 1971, 125, we might suppose that here is a rejection of gnostic ideas. Over against the docetic dissolution of the figure of the historical Jesus it is emphasized that life has appeared in Christ, that in Christ God's love can be experienced concretely.

(1 John 2:2, 15ff; 3:1; 4:4–5, 14). The revelation of the love of God provides a clear alternative to being in the worldly realm of domination. The goal of sending the Son is ζῆν or ζωή, which has the identical meaning as "eternal life" (1 John 4:9; cf. 2:25; 5:16). The revelation of the love of God in the Son is also represented as the act of reconciliation between God and human beings. Such an "atoning sacrifice" (ἱλασμός), namely God's act of forgiveness, is bound up most closely with the person of Jesus Christ (4:10; cf. v. 15), for Jesus Christ is the divinely sent saviour of the world (4:14). His saving mission frees from sin (cf. 2:2), saves from the nothingness of the cosmos (2:15) and from death (3:14) and confers the gift of life (1:1–2; 3:14; 5:11ff). Therefore the Son of God is not only the ground and source of life but also of love, which is revealed in him and provides the example of love for others. His act of reconciliation and salvation is attributed solely to the act of God motivated by love (4:10).

When the abiding nature of fellowship with God is presupposed in the themes discussed above, it is still not a matter of a static essence but rather of a historical event. Abiding in the Father or in the Son becomes concrete in human life in different ways. On the one hand, it is realized in freedom from sin, on the other hand in brotherly love.

## 2.  The Realization of Fellowship with God in Freedom from Sin

That the believers understand themselves as begotten by God gives the occasion for the author of 1 John to make an extraordinarily strong statement about freedom from sin (1 John 3:9–10):

> Those who have been born of God do not sin, because God's seed abides in them; they cannot sin, because they have been born of God. The children of God and the children of the devil are revealed in this way: all who do not do what is right are not from God, nor are those who do not love their brothers and sisters.

The statement of this text that Christians are not able to sin ("non posse peccare") appears to me to stand in absolute opposition to 1:8 ("If we say that we have no sin, we deceive ourselves, and the truth is not in us.") and to 3:4, which presupposes that sinful acts exist within the Christian community.[28] There is thus a heightening in comparison with the absence of sin in 3:6, 9a ("non peccare"). These statements cannot be brought within a single consistent system but are to be understood as determined as a whole by a parenetic perspective with the goal that the community is to have no active participation in sin. The author proceeds from the assumption that members of the community are begotten by God and are essentially one with God. As the eschatological community the

---

[28]  Cf. also 1 John 2:1–2; 5:16, 18.

Christian church is delivered from all sinful activity. It is constantly called back to this point of orientation, for the "not-to-sin" perspective portrays its true eschatological reality from which it has lived since its origin. Nevertheless, the earthly reality is not set aside. Sin remains a threatening power; it must be constantly resisted and overcome until the end of the world.

The saving reality of the community is thus not separated off to itself. It finds itself in a dualistic force field, for salvation can be lost if the power of darkness attains dominance or if life is oriented in conformity to the world. This is why ethical instruction (e. g. 2:12–17; 3:17–18) is indispensable. The promised salvation already present in Christ must determine the present. The community stands under the obligatory challenge: "Become/be what you are."

Although the cosmos as the "human world" can be evaluated positively (1 John 2:2; 4:9, 14) or in a neutral sense (1 John 4:3), the term is also interpreted negatively in the sense of a power hostile to God (5:4–5). The expression ἀγαπᾶν τὸν κόσμον (2:15) portrays the categorizing of a person within the world in such a way as to imply an essential belonging within the world. This stands in diametrical opposition to fellowship with God, since the world is ruled by the πονηρός (5:19). Those who are like the false teachers in not only living ἐν τῷ κόσμῳ but at the same time are also ἐκ τοῦ κόσμου (4:5) have turned their existence over to the worldly powers. Christians know that they have been delivered from being determined by the world. Wherever people are begotten by God and live on the basis of their faith, the world is overcome (5:4–5), there the "love of the world" has no chance (2:15–17). Of course, wherever people love God and keep his commandments (5:3), the admonition remains nevertheless necessary not to fall out of the fellowship and lose salvation by coming under renewed subjection to the power of the cosmos.

This understanding is also documented in a future-eschatological perspective by the admonition in 2:28–29:

> And now, little children, abide in him, so that when he is revealed we may have confidence and not be put to shame before him at his coming.
> If you know that he is righteous, you may be sure that everyone who does right has been born of him.

The phrase "abide in him" makes clear the necessity that the community and Christ must remain closely bound to each other. Christ is so to speak a space, in which the community with all its expressions of life is incorporated. As is also the case in the theology of Paul, the local and spatial understanding of fellowship with Christ does not exclude the idea of a personal encounter (cf. 1 Thess 4:16–17). Present and future eschatology are juxtaposed in a tensive relationship. The expectation of the eschatological revelation is equated with the "arrival" of Christ. Without reflecting on the date of the parousia, believers expect the "that" of the coming of the Son of God, the one who has already come. In view of his coming, the appropriate attitude of the community that abides "in him" is that of παρρησία, "boldness" or intrepidity that is demanded of it in the present. That their confidence is justified can and will be demonstrated on the day when Christ returns, i.e. on the day of judgment (1 John 4:17). Now what is required is to realize freedom from sin in the tensive force-field of the world by "abiding in him," with the goal that such abiding will continue into the future when Christ shall come.

### 3. The Realization of Fellowship with God in Brotherly Love

For the author of 1 John it is unthinkable that fellowship with God, "abiding in God," is realized without the responsible "deed" of human beings that is still not to be equated with a human "achievement." Thus in 1 John 4:12 the indicative statement that God abides in us is bound directly to the condition that we love one another. It is the practice of love that lets the mutual relation of abiding in God and God's "abiding in us" become visible (cf. also 4:16). Similarly, "abiding in the light" presupposes that one loves his brothers and sisters (2:10). It is the person who practices the commandment of mutual love to whom the statement applies that God abides in them and they in God. The indicative of "abiding in the light" or "being in the light" (2:9) implies the indirect demand of realizing the eschatological situation in concrete acts by practicing love rather than hatred toward one's brothers and sisters (cf. 2:11). Whoever hates a brother or sister is still subject to the powers of darkness. So also the promise that one will "live forever" is conditioned on fulfilling the will of God (2:17). The "children of God" are accordingly recognized by doing what is right (2:29). This follows necessarily from their being from God and is identical with their practice of love with regard to their brothers and sisters (cf. 3:10). If this is not done, then fellowship with the devil replaces fellowship with God, and those without love are recognized as children of the devil (3:7–10).

The understanding of agape is determined by the tensive force field in which the love of God and love for the brothers and sisters are operative. In 1 John the concept ἀγάπη τοῦ θεοῦ can have an objective or subjective meaning. Both God's love for human beings, which defines God's reality (4:8), and the love of human beings for God[29] stands in an unconditioned and indissoluble relation to love for the brothers and sisters. Among and

---

[29] 1 John 4:20–21; 5:1–3; differently in the Gospel of John, where on the basis of the christological conception love for God is affirmed only of Jesus (John 14:31) and the "upward directed" love of the disciples is affirmed only in relation to Jesus (John 14:15, 21, 23; see also 21:15–16).

within those people who are begotten by God and know God (4:7), there comes into being the comprehensive and inclusive agape. The Johannine school tradition teaches and practices not only the "upward directed" love for God by humans or God's "downward directed" love for humans but above all mutual love (2 John 5), the love of brothers and sisters for each other (1 John 2:7–11). While such love is "from God," it is not a static ontic givenness in the nature of things or a magical sphere but presupposes human action and responsibility. The Christian knowledge of God (γι-νώσκειν τὸν θεόν) does not refer to some theoretical or informational knowledge of certain facts (cf. 4:2; 5:2) but means "to acknowledge God" in an experiential sense. When a Christian does deeds of practical love, this means that precisely in this act he or she acknowledges God in this sense (2:13–14; cf. 5:20), while the world demonstrates its denial of God by its lovelessness (3:1, 6, 13). Those who, in contrast to worldly people, acknowledge God, keep God's commands (2:3ff), the highest of which is agape (2:7ff). As a specific characteristic of Johannine theology, found elsewhere neither in New Testament documents nor in its religious environment, the author coins the formula "God is love," which has both a christological (4:8) and an ecclesiological (4:16) orientation. That God himself is identical with agape was revealed through Christ (4:9) and has as its consequence that fellowship with God must be determined by love (4:8, 16). Conversely, it is also true that the ethical actions of Christians are repeatedly to be traced back to the reality of the love of God, for it is an objective reality beyond human subjectivity that meets the Christian in acts of love. The statement "God is love" thus does not merely describe an anthropological givenness in the nature of things (= a kind of fellow-feeling for other human beings), nor can it be tautologically reversed ("love is God" or "where love is, there is God"). Of decisive importance is rather the claim that in Jesus Christ God is revealed as the One who loves.

It is to be noted that, in distinction from the presbyter's letters, where only the term "love one another" appears (2 John 5), 1 John speaks not only of mutual love (ἀγαπᾶν ἀλλήλους; 3:11, 23; 4:7, 11–12) but also of "brotherly love" (2:10; also 3:10; 4:20–21 and elsewhere: ἀγαπᾶν τὸν ἀδελφόν). The designation ἀδελφός ("brother," [but also generically "brother or sister"]) suggests that the Johannine circle is essentially represented by men (cf. 3 John: presbyter, Gaius, Diotrephes, Demetrius); but "sisters" may be excluded no more than is the case in the Pauline churches. Another indication of the independence of the Johannine school is provided by the fact that it obviously does not know the command to love the enemies (cf. Matt 5:44) and is not related to the Jewish wisdom tradition (Prov 25:21–22, quoted in Rom 12:20). Nor is either the double command of love (Mark 12:28–31 par) or the command to love the neighbor documented (Lev 19:18). Decisive for understanding the Johannine love commandment is that the ἀγάπη τοῦ θεοῦ is directed not merely to the church as a community closed in on itself but to the world of human beings as a whole (cf. John 3:16; 1 John 4:9). The universality of the love of God is reflected in the absolute agape-concept (cf. 1 John 4:18–19).

## e) Ecclesiology and Ethic

In 1 John the "apostolic" authority of the author is emphasized more strongly than in the presbyter's letters. This can be seen, for example, in one of the *ecclesiological predicates*. The term τεκνία[30] is used to address the readers[31] which points to an advanced stage in the history of the Johannine circle. This address, which alternates with παιδία (1 John 2:14, 18), emphasizes the distance between the author and his readers. The diminutive "my little children" expresses the author's sense of authority and apostolic claim he had already registered in 1:1–4. With this address the author turns not only to the circle of his own community but to all Christians who are willing to be addressed by his writing.

Thus this phrase is to be distinguished from the designation τέκνα (τοῦ) θεοῦ which, although separate from the idea of divine begetting in the history of tradition, determines the relation of believers to God in a similar way (1 John 3:1–2, 10; 5:2; cf. John 1:12; 11:52). The idea involved in being "children of God," however, extends beyond that of the divine begetting and is related to the finality of God's love (cf. 1 John 3:1, ἵνα τέκνα θεοῦ κληθῶμεν). It is oriented to the future, in which those who have been born of God will have the pronouncement spoken over them that they are indeed God's children. To be sure, that which shall become finally manifest in the future is already a present reality (cf. in the same verse, καὶ ἐσμέν!). At the same time, the term "children of God" defines the believers in contrast to the world. In both future and present they belong to God; thus the chasm between them and the world cannot be bridged. This corresponds to the Johannine dualism in which believers who belong to God are distinguished from unbelievers who belong to the world. The idea of being children of God that was widespread in the Hellenistic world[32] here receives a negative counterpart in the term τέκνα τοῦ διαβόλου that originated in Jewish apocalyptic thought.[33] Accordingly in the eschatological perspective two historical possibilities for human existence were set forth. The revelation of the Life (1:2) has as its result the separation of humanity into "children of God" and "children of the devil." The author

---

[30] In place of τέκνα in the presbyter's letters; cf. 2 John 1, 4, 13; 3 John 4.

[31] Cf. 1 John 2:1, 12, 28; 3:7, 18; 4:4; 5:21. The address τεκνία (μου) is found in the New Testament only in John 13:33. Here too the term serves to increase the claim of authority. Just as Jesus in the Fourth Gospel is designated as the decisive authority, so in 1 John the author claims, as an eyewitness, to function as providing a norm for the tradition.

[32] Cf. the Cynic Diogenes (Dio Chrys Or IV.21–23) address to Alexander the Great, spoken with an ethical purpose, since Alexander described himself as son of Zeus.

[33] Cf. the distinction expressed in Jewish documents by a different terminology between the "children of light" and the "children of darkness" (1 QS 1.10; 1QH 6.29–30; Jub 15.26ff; Apoc Abr 13–14; Test Dan 4:7).

does not speak of the devil's children in the same manner as of the children of God. There can be no talk of having been begotten by the devil, obviously because, differently than in the case of being children of God, belonging to the devil does not have an (un)saving event or sacramental act as its presupposition but is dependent on what human beings themselves have done. The criterion of whether one is a child of God or a child of the devil is an ethical criterion (3:10).

So too the term "brothers and sisters" (ἀδελφοί) describes those who are fellow Christians. In connection with statements about brotherly love (cf. 2:10–11, 3:10, 13ff; 4:20, and elsewhere), the community of believers is characterized in contrast to the world. They are different from the world in that they are the community of those begotten by God and thereby participate in life and put love into practice, while for the world it is characteristic that they hate the brothers and sisters (cf. 2:9, 11, and elsewhere). Such rejection is not caused by the practice of brotherly love in the Christian community but the world's hatred of the church is grounded in the fact that the cosmos is fallen under the power of death (3:14) and can generate neither love nor life. On the other hand, those who do not draw conclusions for their own selves from the saving event (4:20) fall out of the realm of fellowship with God. The address ἀδελφός therefore makes the reader aware that life in the community of faith must have consequences for the practice of love in a way that explicitly marks one off from the world.

The appellation ἀγαπητοί (2:7; 3:2, 21; 4:1, 7, 11; cf. 3 John 2, 5, 11) designates the readers not only as the object of the author's love. Rather, the believers are beloved by God, since they have experienced God's love for them, a love that has brought them into fellowship with God in the present and will continue to do so into the future (1 John 3:1–2). They understand themselves in the context of the revelation of the love of God in contrast to the love of both church and world (1 John 3:16; cf. John 3:16–17) and know themselves to be placed under the command of mutual love (3:17–18). This surpassing significance of agape determines the uniqueness of Johannine theological thought in comparison with the use of this term by other New Testament authors (sing. Phlm 16; plur. 1 Thess 2:8; 1 Cor 10:14 and elsewhere).

A further characterization of the community consists in the encouraging declaration that they *possess* the χρῖσμα τοῦ ἁγίου (1 John 2:20, 27).[34] While it is possible to make a grammatical distinction between the anointing that comes from God/Jesus (cf. v. 27: ἀπ᾽ αὐτοῦ = God or Jesus) and the anointing that comes from the Holy Spirit (cf. John 1:33; 14:26; 20:22), there is still no contradiction between the two possibilities of

---

[34]   On the term χρῖσμα cf. G. Strecker, *Johannine Letters* 65–66.

understanding the phrase. The anointing effected by God presupposed in possessing the anointing has the same function attributed to the Paraclete in the Fourth Gospel: the instruction of the Christian community so that they recognize and know the truth, walk in the way of truth and can abide in God (cf 1 John 2:27). The Evangelist traces the Spirit of God back to its divine origin (John 15:26). From the perspective of 1 John the community, which is addressed as true in contrast to the false teachers, possesses the anointing inasmuch as it has right knowledge. Thus what is meant here is the possession of the Spirit of Truth, which is not conferred automatically by the sacraments but is the gift of God that requires faith (1 John 4:1–3, 13). Precisely this is what the author presupposes for his readership as a whole, in contrast to the opponents who threaten the community and to whom the possession of the χρῖσμα is denied. The conferral of the χρῖσμα is thus paralleled with the effect of proclamation, which likewise presupposes the decision of faith. The Spirit of Truth—identical with the χρῖσμα conferred on the community of believers by faith—leads to the knowledge of the truth, just as does the Paraclete of the Gospel of John. Nothing is closed off to such knowledge. It is active in the discernment of critical judgments, is able to distinguish between "truth" and "lie," and to the identification of dangerously different doctrine. The community is aware that the gift of the Spirit has been given it as an abiding gift (1 John 2:27; cf. 4:13) and that this gift carries with it an obligation. Thus the challenge to abide in the χρῖσμα means that believers must constantly actualize anew the truth that has been given them by the Spirit.

The *Sacraments* play a special role in the author's understanding of the church, since both theory and practice of the churchly community are stamped with a sacramental theology. It should not be necessary to introduce particular evidence that both baptism and the eucharist were practiced in the Johannine circle. According to the Gospel of John, rebirth is bound to baptism in water (3:5), and the Revealer's discourse on bread culminates in the (antidocetic) command to eat the flesh of the Son of Man and to drink his blood.[35] Here too 1 John presupposes baptismal tradition that connotes, among other things, the idea of the divine begetting (1 John 2:29; 3:9; 4:7). In contrast to the docetic doctrine, the reality of the incarnation had to be emphasized by a corresponding interpretation of the sacraments. This is seen in 5:6–8:

> This is the one who came by water and blood, Jesus Christ, not with the water only but with the water and the blood. And the Spirit is the one that testifies, for the Spirit is the truth. There are three that testify: 8 the Spirit and the water and the blood, and these three agree.

---

[35] John 6:53; cf. also 19:34: "water and blood" are often interpreted as symbols for baptism and the eucharist; cf. below under D. III. b.

The elements water and blood refer to the baptism and death of Jesus as the two components of the Christ event. Presumably the opponents of 1 John acknowledged Jesus' baptism and even practiced baptism themselves. It is possible that they interpreted Jesus' baptism as "adoption," the means by which the heavenly Christ was united to the earthly Jesus. This could be inferred from the polemical verse 6b ("not by water alone"). But the author wants to assert that the Jesus-event is constituted not only by Jesus' baptism in water but also the atoning death of Jesus, just as the blood of a sacrificial animal effects atonement (cf. 1:7; 2:1–2; 3:16; 4:10). Accordingly, the community of 1 John, in contrast to the docetic opponents, confesses the saving significance of the passion and death of Jesus. The sacraments are grounded in the reality of the event of the incarnation. The fact that Jesus Christ came "through" water and blood, i.e. in his baptism and in his death on the cross and thus "in the flesh" (4:2), is the decisive saving event. This is the basis for faith's victory over the world (5:4), and the soteriological significance of this event is mediated to the community through the sacraments of baptism and the eucharist and appropriated by faith. That the sacraments confer salvation does not mean that it is conferred through the practice of baptism and the celebration of the eucharist in and of themselves. The sacraments receive their true significance only in conjunction with the Spirit, so that believers are freed from the temptation to understand the effect of the sacraments as working "ex operato" or to degrade them to the level of magic. The Spirit is the third witness who, alongside water and blood, i.e. in and through the sacraments, vouches for the reality of eschatological salvation to the Christian community. As it knows by means of the χρῖσμα that it is in possession of the Spirit (2:20, 27), it is the Spirit that actualizes in the sacrament the given truth of God. This is what is affirmed in the "witness terminology:" the witness given by the Spirit keeps the community in the knowledge of the truth (2:27; 4:13), for it is the divine testimony that has as its content the sending of the Son. Whoever confesses faith in this testimony experiences the truth of the confession of the incarnation of Christ, namely that the Father has granted eternal life through his Son (5:11).

The confession of faith in the incarnate Christ has effects that concern the whole life of the believer. Even if relatively seldom, 1 John does contain *ethical instructions* pregnant with meaning (2:12–14):

I am writing to you, little children, because your sins are forgiven on account of his name. I am writing to you, fathers, because you know him who is from the beginning. I am writing to you, young people, because you have conquered the evil one. I write to you, children, because you know the Father. I write to you, fathers, because you know him who is from the beginning. I write to you, young people, because you are strong and the word of God abides in you, and you have overcome the evil one.

Differently from the household codes (Col 3:18–4:1; Eph 5:22–6:9) or social codes (1 Pet 2:13–3:7) of the New Testament, this passage is not bound to the situation of the house and is not arranged in pairs that present an ascending line. The thrice-repeated γράφω (vv. 12–13) and thrice-repeated ἔγραψα (v. 14) gives this table its independent structure. Presumably it is not only a matter of an author's stylistic variation but with the aorist ("I have written") the author intentionally refers back to the presbyter's letters. He wants to say that at that time (as the presbyter) he wrote to the community on the basis of the presupposition that it was in possession of the eschatological knowledge, and that this declaration is still valid as he writes 1 John. Thereby the address τεκνία or παιδία indicates that the Johannine community has grown beyond the boundaries given in the presbyter's letters. The diminutive form also makes the author's claim to authority more clear and allows the reader to perceive that the author writes with a sense of apostolic authority. While all members of the community are thereby addressed without distinction, two groups are explicitly named: "fathers" and "young men." As 3 John shows, men are the ones responsible for the life of the community. These can be addressed by the author's words in 1 John because they are within the redeemed community, purified by the atoning effect of the death of Jesus (1:7, 9) and have been claimed by the word of God (cf. 1:10; 2:5). This still does not mean, however, that Christian existence is something that can be given once and for all, with no further ado. It is rather the case that the community, like the individual Christian, stands in a tensive force field. Even though the powers of darkness have been overcome by faith, they can spring to life again in hatred of the brothers and sisters of the community and become a renewed threat. This is why believers must still keep their distance from the world and not let it mislead them into false paths by its offers ("desires," "riches") but direct all its energies toward doing the will of God and practicing the commandment of love. The agape-command finds its clearest expression in the love for the brothers and sisters of the community, even to the point of giving one's life for the other (3:16). The love command also takes concrete shape in not ignoring the distress of the brothers and sisters but in helping them by sharing one's own possessions. In this way the love one has experienced from God is shared with others, and being a Christian is not a matter of words alone but is realized in concrete acts that are appropriate to the truth that has been accepted in faith (3:17–18).

Even though in 1 John *prayer* does not stand at the center of the community's vital signs, the Johannine circle nonetheless knows of experiences of answered prayer and is equipped with a resolute assurance that its prayers are heard. This is seen, for example in 3:22, where the confidence that the Christian can address God with "boldness" (παρρησία) and the prayers of believers will be heard is most closely connected with the necessity of keeping God's commandments. The unity between the confidence of being heard and keeping God's commands is not harmonized in some rationalistic manner but motivated parenetically. The admonition is simply given to realize both in practice: the confidence that prayers are heard and the doing of God's will.

The concluding part of the letter, which has unjustifiably been suspected as being a secondary addition (as though the letter actually closed with 5:13), contains a further statement demonstrating the power of prayer. We have here a logical development of thought in which first the intention of the author is made known to nourish the knowledge of eternal life among his readers (5:13; cf. 1:2, 4). This leads to the challenge to exercise "boldness" in prayer according to God's will (5:14). This challenge is grounded by referring to the experience of prayer the community has already had (5:15). To this is then added an individual example of right prayer (5:16–17):

> If you see your brother or sister committing a sin (that does) not (lead) to death, you will ask, and God will give life to such a one —to those whose sin is not to death. There is sin that is to death; I do not say that you should pray about that. All wrongdoing is sin but there is sin (that does) not (lead to) death. (Author's translation.)

There can be no doubt that here the subject is intercessory prayer, while in the preceding the verb αἰτεῖν has been used in the general sense of "ask" (5:14). Prayer should be for the benefit of one's fellow Christians. The Christian community is—as has been constantly presupposed throughout 1 John—a community threatened by sin and that must take care not to continue in sin (cf. 1:8; 2:1). In this community, prayers are made for brothers and sisters who have committed sins. But a distinction is made: such prayer should be made only for the brother or sister who has committed a sin that does not lead to death but not for those who have transgressed with a "sin unto death." The sin to death is such a serious transgression that it separates one irretrievably from the eschatological community. The author thus knows of a definitive separation that does not have to await the future last judgment but has already occurred in the community and is made effective in the prohibition against praying for those who have sinned unto death. The Johannine theology does not advocate an Origenesque concept of the ἀποκατάστασις πάντων.[36] With the offer of eschatological salvation not only is there the possibility given of accepting it in faith but also of rejecting it in unbelief and thereby missing its promise of eternal life. To be sure, it is not said to which transgression the expression "sin to death" refers. Since the author is not concerned to

---

[36] "Restoration of all" (Origen Princ 3.6.1). On this cf. TDNT 1.391–393.

provide a definition, it is obvious that the passage cannot determine once and for all the boundary between forgivable and unforgivable sins. While intercessory prayer is made for Christian brothers and sisters without distinction, it is not necessarily presupposed that committing the sin unto death is something of which only the "false teachers" can be guilty. It is rather a matter of an instruction valid for the church of all times; in the prohibition against praying for the brother or sister who has committed the sin unto death, the church always sees itself confronted by the unlimited claim and demand of God.

# III. The Gospel of John

Barrett, C. K. *The Gospel According to St. John*. 2. ed. Philadelphia: Westminster, 1978.

Bauer, W. *Das Johannesevangelium*. HNT 6. Tübingen: J. C. B. Mohr (Paul Siebeck), 1933.

Becker, J. *Das Evangelium nach Johannes*. ÖTK 4. Gütersloh: Gerd Mohn, I 1985²; II 1984².

Beutler, J. *Martyria. Traditionsgeschichtliche Untersuchungen zum Zeugnisthema bei Johannes*. FTS 10. Frankfurt: Peter Lang, 1972.

Blank, J. *Krisis. Untersuchungen zur johanneischen Christologie und Eschatologie*. Freiburg: Herder, 1964.

Blinzler, J. *Johannes und die Synoptiker. Ein Forschungsbericht*. SBS 5. Stuttgart: Katholisches Bibelwerk, 1965.

Bornkamm, G. "Zur Interpretation des Johannes-Evangeliums. Eine Auseinandersetzung mit E. Käsemanns Schrift ‚Jesu letzter Wille nach Johannes 17‛," G. Bornkamm, ed. *Geschichte und Glaube I*. BEvTh 48. Munich: Kaiser, 1968, 104–121.

Braun, F. M. *Jean le Théologien*. Paris: J. Gabalda, 1959; 1964; 1966.

Brown, R. E. *The Gospel According to John*, AncB 29.29A, Garden City-New York: Doubleday, 1966; 1970.

Bühner, J.-A. *Der Gesandte und sein Weg im 4. Evangelium*. WUNT 2/2. Tübingen: J. C. B. Mohr (Paul Siebeck), 1977.

Bultmann, R. *The Gospel of John*. Philadelphia: Westminster, 1971.

de la Potterie, I. *La vérité dans Saint Jean* I, II. AnBib 73,74. Rome: Biblical Institute Press, 1977.

Dodd, C. H. *The Interpretation of the Fourth Gospel*. Cambridge: Cambridge University Press, 1968.

Fortna, R. T. *The Gospel of Signs*. MSSNTS 11. Cambridge: Cambridge University Press, 1970.

Haenchen, E. *John: A Commentary on the Gospel of John*. 2 vols. Hermeneia. Philadelphia: Fortress, 1984.

Hengel, M. *Die johanneische Frage*. WUNT 67. Tübingen: J. C. B. Mohr (Paul Siebeck), 1993.

Hengel, M. *The Johannine Question*. London: SCM Press, 1989.

Käsemann, E. *The Testament of Jesus*. Philadelphia: Fortress, 1968.

Lattke, M. *Einheit im Wort*. StANT 41. Munich: Kösel, 1975.

Martyn, J. L. *History und Theology in the Fourth Gospel*. Nashville: Abingdon, 1979.

Müller, U. B. *Die Geschichte der Christologie in der johanneischen Gemeinde.* SBS 77. Stuttgart: Katholisches Bibelwerk, 1975.

Onuki, T. *Gemeinde und Welt im Johannesevangelium.* WMANT 56. Neukirchen-Vluyn: Neukirchener, 1984.

Rengstorf, K. H. *Johannes und sein Evangelium.* WdF 82, Darmstadt: Wissenschaftliche Buchgesellschaft, 1973.

Richter, G. *Studien zum Johannesevangelium.* BU 13. Regensburg: Pustet, 1977.

Ruckstuhl, E. *Die literarische Einheit des Johannesevangeliums.* NTOA 5. Freiburg-Göttingen: Vandenhoeck & Ruprecht, 1987.

Schmithals, W. *Johannesevangelium und Johannesbriefe.* BZNW 64. Berlin: W. de Gruyter, 1992.

Schnackenburg, R. *The Gospel according to St. John.* 3 vols. New York: Crossroad, 1968, 1980, 1982.

Schnelle, U. *Antidocetic Christology in the Gospel of John.* Minneapolis: Fortress, 1992.

Schnelle, U. "Die johanneische Schule," *Bilanz und Perspektiven gegenwärtiger Auslegung des Neuen Testaments,* F. W. Horn, ed. BZNW 75. Berlin-New York: W. de Gruyter, 1995, 198–217.

Schottroff, L. *Der Glaubende und die feindliche Welt.* WMANT 37. Neukirchen-Vluyn: Neukirchener, 1970.

Schulz, S. *Untersuchungen zur Menschensohn-Christologie im Johannesevangelium.* Göttingen: Vandenhoeck & Ruprecht, 1957.

Schweizer, E. *Ego Eimi. Die religionsgeschichtliche Herkunft und theologische Bedeutung der johanneischen Bildreden.* FRLANT 56. Göttingen: Vandenhoeck & Ruprecht, 1939 (= 1965²).

Thüsing, W. *Die Erhöhung und Verherrlichung Jesu im Johannesevangelium.* NTA 21. Münster: Aschendorff, 1970.

Thyen, H. "Johannesevangelium," *TRE* 17 (1988) 200–225.

Windisch, H. "Johannes und die Synoptiker. Wollte der vierte Evangelist die älteren Evangelien ergänzen oder ersetzen?," *UNT* 12, Leipzig 1926.

## a)   Introduction

The Gospel of John exhibits a series of breaks and seams that present almost insoluble problems for any attempt to clarify the issue of the literary integrity of the document. Yet, making a literary-critical judgment about the pericope 7:53–8:11, the woman taken in adultery, is still relatively simple. A large number of manuscripts (including P⁶⁶, ⁷⁵; אB) do not have this text at all; others place it in a different context.[1] It is found after 7:52 only in M, D, and primarily in Latin MSS—partly with asterisks or obelisks as an indication of the uncertainty of the textual tradition. The context in John does not presuppose this section (a loose connection is made first at 8:15). It is thus a matter of a later insertion, which documents the expansion of the Gospel material after the composition of the Gospel of John.

---

[1]   Minuscule 225 at 7:36; f¹ after 21:25; f¹³ after Luke 21:38.

The "supplementary chapter" (ch. 21) that narrates appearances of the Risen One at the Sea of Galilee is to be considered a separate composition from that of the original Gospel. It was obviously added as a secondary addition after the conclusion of 20:30–31, and is not a literary unity in itself, since vv. 1–23 reflect a competitive relationship between Petrine and Johannine traditions, while in vv. 24–25 the Beloved Disciple is identified as the author of the Gospel.[2] It is less probable that the note about the Beloved Disciple as eyewitness[3] in 19:35 was added secondarily. In addition it is to be remembered that R. Bultmann attributed a number of pericopes and verses to the "ecclesiastical redaction,"[4] including the allusions to the sacraments (6:51b-58; 19:34; 3:5 "water"), affirmations of future eschatology (e. g. 5:28–29; 6:39–40; 44b, 54; 12:48), also references dependent on the Synoptic tradition (e. g. 1:22–24, 26b, 27, 33 "with water," 34; 3:24; 4:2; 11:2; 16:5b; 18:9, 13b, 14, 24, 32).

However, the rough literary transitions in the Gospel of John that doubtless exist are not so much to be accounted for by a secondary redaction as by the combination of different layers of tradition, which can be identified with written sources only to a minimal extent. Bultmann's hypothesis that the major part of the speeches of the Johannine Jesus were derived from a "revelatory discourse source" has not prevailed in further study. Only the supposition that there was a written σημεῖα-source has found significant scholarly acceptance. This hypothetical source has been mainly grounded on the enumeration of the first (2:1–11 wine miracle at Cana) and second miracles (4:43–54, the healing of the nobleman's son as the second sign Jesus did after he had come from Judea to Galilee); in addition the conclusion of the Gospel (20:30–31) seems not really to fit the Gospel as a whole, which presents mainly discourses of Jesus and not only miracle stories. Thus it has been supposed that 20:30–31 was originally the conclusion of the σημεῖα-source, from which it is inferred that this source document wanted to call its readers to faith (cf. also 12:37). Accordingly Jesus' miracles are transparent "signs," revelations of the glory of the Son of God (2:11; 11:4), and in this sense included by the Evangelist in his composition. However, the language of the "σημεῖα-source" cannot be distinguished from that of the Evangelist or the Johannine school.[5] Also,

[2]  Additional arguments are the I-form in v. 25 and the linguistic character. Cf. also W. G. Kümmel, *Introduction to the New Testament* 207–208. Differently E. Ruckstuhl, *Die literarische Einheit des Johannesevangeliums* 134–149, who considers chap. 21 to be original.
[3]  In 19:35 the linguistic and material affinity to 21:34 appears especially to indicate a secondary origin; however, the agreement can also be explained if one assumes that the author of 21:24 utilized the description in 19:35. Cf. also the discussion of the Beloved Disciple below.
[4]  R. Bultmann, *Gospel of John, passim.*
[5]  Cf. Schnelle, *Christology* 154–160.

the life of Jesus as a whole is presented in the Fourth Gospel as a series of signs, so that this term is not restricted to the miracles. Thus the units attributed to the σημεῖα-source are more correctly ascribed to the traditions of the Johannine school, which are of disparate origins, including an undeniable element of influence from the Synoptic Gospels.

Moreover, there are tensions in the text that cannot be convincingly solved by source criticism. For example, it is striking that the events of 6:1ff take place on the sea of Galilee, even though there is no geographical transition from the preceding chapter's location of Jesus in Jerusalem (5:1). The farewell discourse appears to come to an end in 14:31, although 15:1ff continues this discourse (to 18:1!).[6]

These contradictions and tensions have led to the supposition that the original order of the composition later fell into disarray.[7] Thus R. Bultmann undertook the project of restoring the original order (18:1ff as the original continuation of 14:31; 6:1 as the continuation of 4:54, and other such adjustments). The result, however, is adventurous reconstructions (e. g. the insertion of chap. 17 between 13:30/31; of 15:1–16:33 between 13:35/36). In addition, the cause of the disarray remains unexplained. The theory that it occurred through a "rearranging of pages" that happened soon after the composition of the Gospel is unsatisfactory, since the exchanged pages must then have been of unequal sizes. And despite the ingenious rearrangements, a unified result free of contradictions cannot be reconstructed. One must then more correctly assume that the original composition of the fourth Evangelist was not an impeccable model. This may be an indication that the Gospel was left incomplete, and a final editing was intended but never carried out.

The conception of the Evangelist indicates much more interest in the material content of the revelation that came through Christ than in presenting a clearly outlined historical course of the life of Jesus. However, one may detect—though less clearly than in the Synoptic Gospels—a flow of the narrative line that gives the work the external form of a "life of Jesus." Of fundamental significance for the composition is the dividing line at 12:50/13:1 (the beginning of Jesus' way to the passion, crucifixion, and resurrection). From this point of view the following outline emerges:

---

[6]   Cf. also the discrepancy between 3:27–30 (testimony of the Baptist) and 3:31–36 (which describes the relation between God the Father and the Son of God in the style of the Johannine revelatory discourses).

[7]   This is also the presupposition of the widespread "basic document hypothesis" (*Grundschriftshypothese*), according to which it is up to the shrewdness of the exegete to reconstruct this basic document that was reformulated by the Evangelist in a number of different ways (thus e. g. W. Schmithals, *Johannesevangelium und Johannesbriefe*)—a hypothesis that already F. Overbeck, *Das Johannesevangelium* (Tübingen: J. C. B. Mohr [Paul Siebeck], 1911) 105 assigned to the category of "game" ("a source-critical game"). Cf. also G. Strecker–M. Labahn, "Der johanneische Schriftenkreis," *ThR* 59, 1994, 101–107; G. Strecker, *History of New Testament Literature* 162–165.

| A. | 1:1–18 | Prologue: Jesus the preexistent Logos |
|----|--------|----------------------------------------|
| B. | I. 1:19–12:50: | The Ministry of the Logos in the World |
|    | II. 13:1–20:29: | The Return of the Logos to the Father |
|    |        | a) 13:1–17:26: The Revelation before the Disciples |
|    |        | b) 18:1–20:29: Passion and Resurrection |
| C. | 20:30–31: | Conclusion of the Gospel |
|    | 21:1–23, 24–25: | Appendix |

This outline is reminiscent of the Synoptic Gospels. As there, a simple chronological and geographical scheme lies at the base, in which the way of the Logos is portrayed from his first appearance to the cross and resurrection, in the regions of Galilee and Judea/Jerusalem. One notes material agreements as well. The Gospel begins with a Prologue (1:1–18, cf. Luke 1:1–4), then with the advent of John the Baptist (cf. Mark 1 parr). The narrative contains pericopes about the calling of disciples and miracle stories, the latter partly parallel to those in the Synoptics (6:1ff: feeding of the five thousand followed by walking on the water, the same order as Mark 6:32–52). Among the parallel narratives are Peter's confession (6:66ff; cf. Mark 8:27ff parr), the entry into Jerusalem (12:12ff; Mark 11:1ff parr), the passion story (chaps. 18–19; Mark 14–15 parr). In addition there is a series of parallel individual sayings (e. g. 2:19/Mark 14:58; 3:35/Matt 11:27; 4:44/Mark 6:4; 5:8–9/Matt 9:6; 9:1ff/Mark 8:23; 13:16/Matt 10:24–25).

On the other hand, the Gospel of John has a character distinct from the Synoptics, that comes to expression especially in the discourses of the Son of God, but not only there. There are also numerous differences in detail, especially in connection with the question of the length of Jesus' ministry: the Synoptics report only one Passover festival, which Jesus celebrated with his disciples at the beginning of the passion in Jerusalem. The Gospel of John likewise connects the passion of Jesus with a Passover in Jerusalem (11:55; 12:1; 18:28) but mentions other Passovers as well (2:13; 6:4; cf. 5:1 "a festival"). Thus at least two and one-half years must be allowed for the public ministry of Jesus (in contrast to one year in the Synoptics). So also the date of the day of Jesus' death is represented differently. The Synoptic Evangelists identify it with the Passover itself (= 15th Nisan); according to "John," Jesus did not die on Passover day but on the day of Preparation for the Passover (= 14th Nisan), i.e. on the day on which the Passover lambs were killed. This suggests that the death of Jesus should be interpreted as the sacrifice of the Passover lamb.[8] In the framework of the Synoptic narrative, on this day Jesus celebrated the Last Supper with his

---

[8] This would fit in with the lamb Christology (cf. John 19:36/Exod 12:46) of the Apocalypse (cf. Rev 5:6; 7:9–10, 14; 12:11 and elsewhere) and the atonement theology of 1 John (1:7; 2:2 and elsewhere), and is not to be attributed to the theological conception of the Evangelist but to his tradition (cf. also 1 Cor 5:7; 6:11).

disciples (Mark 14:12ff). In contrast, the fourth Evangelist gives no report of the institution of the Eucharist, and no corresponding festival meal with his disciples, but indicates his awareness of eucharistic tradition only in 6:51ff, while 13:1ff portrays Jesus' last meal and the designation of the betrayer but no institution of the Eucharist.

Exegetes have come to different conclusions on the basis of these agreements and differences. R. Bultmann and C. H. Dodd were of the opinion that it is possible to solve the problem before us with the hypothesis that the fourth Evangelist was dependent on pre-Synoptic tradition.[9] In fact, it should not be doubted that especially in the discourse material traditions are documented that could suggest this conclusion. However, specific conceptions such as elements of the "messianic secret" theory, the idea of the suffering Son of Man, and others indicate that "John" knew at least the final redaction of Mark, possibly through intermediary links.[10] According to C. K. Barrett and W. G. Kümmel, the fourth Evangelist used not only Mark but also Matthew, and perhaps even Luke as well.[11] The problem is not to be solved by posing false alternatives; one must give attention to the layers of tradition that "John" presupposes and to the temporal connections, which would suggest that the Johannine school had contact with the developing Synoptic traditions at a particular stage.

The question whether the author intended his work to "supplement" or "replace" the Synoptic Gospels[12] is misplaced. It proceeds from the presupposition that the Johannine communities had made extensive use of the Synoptic Gospels as sacred texts. The fact of the matter is that the extensive absence of allusion to Synoptic materials in the Johannine letters permits the inference that most of the Johannine circle was unaware of the Gospel literature, or at least did not consider it essentially impor-

---

[9]  Cf. C. H. Dodd, *The Interpretation of the Fourth Gospel* 444–453; cf. also *Historical Tradition in the Fourth Gospel* (Cambridge: Cambridge University Press, 1963).

[10]  The differing order of parallel pericopes is also important for the connection between John and the Synoptics. Cf. the Johannine placing of the temple cleansing in relation to the first appearance of the Logos in the narrative (John 2:13ff; in Mark 11:1 parr at the beginning of the Jerusalem period) and the Johannine placing of the story of the anointing in Bethany prior to Jesus' entry into Jerusalem (John 12:1ff; in Mark 14:3ff at the beginning of the passion story). Here the independent composition of the fourth Evangelist is clear.

[11]  Cf. C. K. Barrett, *Gospel according to St. John* 42–54, who also considers it likely that John knew Luke. In addition, cf. F. Neirynck, *Jean et les Synoptiques* BEThL XLIX (Leuven: Leuven University Press) 1979; M. Sabbe, "The Footwashing in John 13 and its Relation to the Synoptic Gospels," *EThL* 58 (1982) 279–308; K. Th. Kleinknecht, "Johannes 13, die Synoptiker und die 'Methode' der johanneischen Evangelienüberlieferung," *ZThK* 82 (1985) 361–388; G. Strecker, *History of New Testament Literature* 165–168.

[12]  Cf. H. Windisch, *Johannes und die Synoptiker* 134, who favors the replacement theory.

tant. The fourth Evangelist wanted neither to supplement nor replace the
Synoptic Gospels but intended, by making a limited use of fragments of
Synoptic tradition, to write *the* Gospel of the Johannine circle. With this
presupposition and interest, namely the transmission of "gospel" narrative and sayings material within his community, the Johannine Evangelist
as author and theologian is different from both the author of 1 John and
from the presbyter who authored the two small Johannine letters. Together with the linguistic differences, this is an indication that the author
of the Fourth Gospel is not identical with the presbyter nor with the writer
of 1 John but is an independent representative of the Johannine school
tradition. This alone makes it necessary to date the composition of the
Gospel of John *after* the time of the presbyter,[13]—an important argument
against the tradition of the ancient church that the author had been an
eyewitness of the life of Jesus, as of course the author of the appendix
chapter presupposes in 21:24 and is first documented in the Muratorian
Canon (lines 9ff).[14] The supposition that the Evangelist had been an
eyewitness becomes improbable when one realizes that the defective representation of items of Jewish law,[15] like the interpretation of the Old
Testament,[16] can hardly be attributed to a Palestinian Jew such as John the
son of Zebedee is portrayed to be in the New Testament. In addition, the
favorite early dating of the Fourth Gospel at the turn of the first to the
second century can no longer be supported by the testimony of Egerton
Papyrus 2 and P[52], since no more can be inferred from them than that the
Gospel was known in Egypt near the end of the second century C. E.[17]

---

[13] Thereby the significance of the "strong, resolutely individual life" of the fourth
Evangelist (A. Schlatter, *Zur Theologie des Neuen Testaments und zur Dogmatik*
[TB 41. Munich: Kaiser, 1969] 226) is not disputed. This happens, however, first
within the framework of the Johannine school.

[14] Cf. 19:35; Iren Haer 3.1.1; 3.3.4; 3.11.1. Especially to be noted is the identification
of John the Apostle, the son of Zebedee, with the Evangelist John in Eusebius HE
3.23.1; 3.24.1–2. A different conclusion was advocated by the Roman presbyter
Gaius and by the Alogoi, who thought both the Gospel and the Apocalypse of John
had been written by Cerinthus (cf. Epiph Pan 51).

[15] Cf. 7:32, 45, according to which the Jewish High Council consisted of ἀρχιερεῖς and
Φαρισαῖοι; apparently the author exchanged the Jewish Pharisees with the scribes,
who were a constituent part of the Sanhedrin. In 11:49 Caiaphas is described as
ἀρχιερεὺς ὢν τοῦ ἐνιαυτοῦ ἐκείνου ("High Priest that year"); in reality Caiaphas was
in office 18–36 C. E. The author apparently presupposes the High Priest's term
lasted one year, corresponding to the Hellenistic-Roman administrative practice.

[16] Cf. 19:23–24, which interprets the parallelism of Ps 21:10 LXX all too literally; cf.
similarly Matt 21:5! On the interpretation of *parallelismus membrorum* cf. M.
Hengel, "Zur matthäischen Bergpredigt und ihrem jüdischen Hintergrund," *ThR*
52 (1987) 327–400; 342–343.

[17] Contra F. G. Kenyon–A. W. Adams, *The Text of the Greek Bible* (London: Duck-
worth, 1975) 206–207. Egerton Papyrus 2 contains fragments of four narratives
that deal with Jesus. As indicated in the edition of H. I. Bell and T. C. Skeat,

In this context the question of the "disciple whom Jesus loved," i.e. the Gospel of John's *Beloved Disciple*, constitutes an issue that has often been overrated in terms of its historical importance but theologically neglected.[18] Apart from the Appendix (21:7, 20–24), this figure is mentioned only at the beginning of the passion story (13:23–26), then alongside the mother of Jesus at the cross (19:26–27) and as a witness of the empty tomb alongside Simon Peter (20:2–8). The latter passage connects the designation "the disciple whom Jesus loved"[19] with the expression (ὁ) ἄλλος μαθητής (20:2, 3, 8), which is also used for the disciple who was acquainted with the high priest and facilitated Peter's entrance into the high priest's court (18:15–16). He is the true "eyewitness" (19:35), who is obviously identical with the Beloved Disciple beneath the cross (cf. 19:26–27).

Who is meant by this designation? The answer to this question calls first for a clarification of the relation of the Beloved Disciple to the author of the Gospel. In the Appendix this disciple is unmistakably identified with the fourth Evangelist (21:24), and this became the basis in later church tradition for accepting the same identification in the other passages where the Beloved Disciple is mentioned.[20] However, only 19:35 could support such an inference, and only then if one holds the view that this verse was first added to the Gospel at the time of the ecclesiastical redactor, who thereby wanted to characterize the Beloved Disciple as both eyewitness *and* author of the Gospel.[21] But 19:35 is not necessarily to be ascribed to the redactor; the language, style and conceptual world are quite Johannine, just as are the preceding references in 19:34b to history (= the fact of Jesus' death) and the sacraments (water and blood = baptism and Lord's Supper). But if 1934b is an original part of the Gospel, then the disciple beneath the cross represents for the Evangelist an important guarantor for the truth of the tradition but he is not to be identified with the

---

*Fragments of an Unknown Gospel and other Early Christian Papyri* (London: British Museum, 1935), palaeographic study of Egerton Papyrus 2 provides some indication of coming from the end of the first century but others that point to the beginning of the third century as its time of origin. Furthermore, it is not clear whether the section that concerns the Gospel of John, with partly-identical wording to John 5:39, 46; 7:30; 8:59; 9:29 represents the Gospel of John or an older tradition.

P[52] documents John 18:31–33, 37–38 and manifests similarities to the script of Egerton Papyrus 2. But here too palaeographic research has not confirmed the dating suggested by the publisher, "the first half of the second century" (C. H. Roberts, *An Unpublished Fragment of the Fourth Gospel in the John Rylands Library* [Manchester: Manchester University Press, 1935] 11). Cf. also A. Schmidt, "Zwei Anmerkungen zu P.Ryl. III 457," *Archiv für Papyrusforschung* 35 (1989) 11–12.

18    Cf. R. E. Brown, *The Gospel according to John* xcii-xcviii; E. Haenchen, *John* 2:236–238.

19    20:2: ἐφίλει; also ὃν ἠγάπα ὁ Ἰησοῦς: 13:23; 19:26; 21:7, 20.

20    For the older literature cf. W. Bauer, *Johannesevangelium* 173–175.

21    Cf. Bultmann, *Gospel of John* 678.

fourth Evangelist. The other references to the Beloved Disciple do not give the slightest reason for such an identification.[22]

The attempts to understand the Beloved Disciple as intended by the Evangelist to represent a historical figure can appeal to the fact that concrete statements referring to events in the life of Jesus are associated with this figure. The Beloved Disciple appears to have been an eyewitness (19:35) and companion of Jesus (13:23ff). According to the incident reported in the Gospel of John, he was well acquainted with the high priest (18:15–16). After the death of Jesus, he took Jesus' mother to his own home (19:27) and alongside Peter became one of the most important witnesses to the empty tomb (20:1ff). Which outstanding personality in the life of Jesus is concealed behind this anonymous figure, of whom the Synoptics seem not at all to be aware? The opinion is widespread that the Beloved Disciple is *John* the son of Zebedee, who according to Mark 5:37; 9:2; 14:33 belonged to the three most trusted of Jesus' disciples.[23] However, the text on which this hypothesis has been based can hardly be used for support. According to John 1:40–41 *Andrew*, the former disciple of John the Baptist, "first" (πρῶτον) found his brother *Simon Peter* and brought him to Jesus—from the little word πρῶτον it is inferred that there is an allusion to the second pair of brothers, namely to James and John the sons of Zebedee, and that from this the identity of the Beloved Disciple can be inferred.[24] The situation is no better with the other suppositions, as in the effort to identify the Beloved Disciple with *Lazarus*, of whom it is said in 11:3, 5 that the Lord loved him.[25] However, the characterization of Jesus as the "one who loves" is distinctive of his mission as such and in

---

[22]   The attempt to eliminate all the references to the Beloved Disciple as secondary was already made by E. Schwarz, *Aporien im vierten Evangelium* (NGWG.PH. Göttingen, 1907) 342–372 and by W. Bousset, "Ist das vierte Evangelium eine literarische Einheit?" *ThR* 12 (1909) 1–12, 39–64. But these attempts are not convincing. Neither are the more recent attempts, e. g. H. Thyen, "Entwicklungen innerhalb der johanneischen Theologie und Kirche im Spiegel von Joh. 21 und der Lieblingsjüngertexte des Evangeliums," in M. de Jonge, ed. *L' Évangile de Jean. Sources, rédaction, théologie* (BEThL XLIV. Leuven: Leuven University Press, 1977) 259–299.

[23]   Cf. 13:23–24; 18:15–16; 19:27, 35; 20:1ff. So P. Feine-J. Behm, *Einleitung in das Neue Testament* (Heidelberg: Quelle und Meyer, 1956[11]) 102; W. Michaelis, *Einleitung in das Neue Testament* (Bern: B. Haller,1954[2]) 99, and others.; cf. on this and the following points the critical observations of W. G. Kümmel, *Introduction* 202–204, and A. Kragerud, *Der Lieblingsjünger im Johannesevangelium* (Oslo: Osloer Universitätsverlag, 1959) 42ff.

[24]   Cf. e. g. W. Michaelis, *Einleitung* 98.

[25]   Cf. 11:36; so e. g. F. V. Filson, "Who Was the Beloved Disciple?" *JBL* 68 (1949) 83–88; 84, and K. Eckardt, "Der Tod des Johannes als Schlüssel zum Verständnis der Johanneischen Schriften," *SRRG* III (Berlin 1961) 20, who then identifies Lazarus with John the son of Zebedee.

any case is not to be limited to the disciple who was closest to him.[26] Just as hypothetical is the claim that concealed behind the figure of the Beloved Disciple stands *John Mark*, whose mother according to Acts 12:12 placed her house at the disposal of the new community as its meeting place.[27]

The efforts to identify the Beloved Disciple with a historically concrete figure have not been successful,[28] so that it is understandable that other interpretations have abandoned the attempt to find a historical referent and would like to think instead of a symbolic figure. Thus R. Bultmann, on the basis of 19:26–27, supposes the reference is to an ideal figure who is intended to embody Gentile Christianity, "insofar as it is the authentic Christendom which has achieved its own true self-understanding," who was then first made into a historical figure by the author of the Appendix (ch. 21).[29] A. Kragerud would like to infer from all the references to the Beloved Disciple a unified symbol for early Christian prophecy that found itself in competition with the official church offices represented by Peter.[30] Similarly, E. Käsemann, who designates the Beloved Disciple as the "right witness," who as "eye witness and ear witness of the Christ experienced as present (*Christus praesens*)" was projected back into the Gospel story by the author of the Gospel, so that then in the Fourth Gospel the *Christus praesens* "virtually absorbs" the historical Jesus.[31]

Historical and symbolic interpretations of the figure of the Beloved Disciple apparently stand in irreconcilable conflict with each other. But is it really a matter of these two alternatives?

1. Over against understanding the Beloved Disciple exclusively as a symbol for positions within the spectrum of church theology we must observe

---

[26]  Cf. 11:5; 13:1; 14:21; 15:9.

[27]  So P. Parker, "John and John Mark," *JBL* 79 (1960) 97–110.

[28]  The same applies to the position of R. Schnackenburg, according to whom the Beloved Disciple came from Jerusalem and was an "honorable witness, still from the time of Jesus, whom the Johannine Church honored as their authority, bearer of the tradition and interpreter of Jesus' deeds and words" (*Gospel according to St. John* 3:387.) Cf. also W. G. Kümmel, *Introduction* 235, according to whom the Evangelist for his passion story had an authoritative witness who bore the honorary title "*the disciple whom Jesus loved.*" According to the letter bishop Polycrates of Ephesus sent to the Roman bishop Victor (end of the second century) the disciple "who lay on the breast of Jesus" (John 13:23; NRSV "reclined next to him") was for the first time identified with the "John" who was buried in Ephesus (Eusebius HE 3.23.3; 31.2–3). This is a secondary construction, for that the "Lord's disciple John" had been an eyewitness was unknown to Papias, and that the Fourth Evangelist had personally known an eyewitness whom he used as his authority is unlikely in view of the time elapsed.

[29]  Bultmann, *Gospel of John* 483–484; cf. the 1957 Supplement to the German edition, p. 55); so also A. Loisy, *Le quartrième Évangile* (Paris: Emile Noutry, 1903).

[30]  A. Kragerud, *Lieblingsjünger* 123; cf. also Vielhauer, *Geschichte* 483.

[31]  Käsemann, "Ketzer und Zeuge" 181.

that the Evangelist intentionally incorporates this figure within the framework of his work as a *Vita Jesu*. As a companion of Jesus, he is an integral part of the past history of the life of Jesus as it is portrayed in the Fourth Gospel.

2. In opposition to the unsuccessful attempt to identify the Beloved Disciple with an actual companion of Jesus, on grounds of temporal distance it is clear that the Evangelist writing in the second century could not have personally known any of the eyewitnesses of Jesus' ministry. Thus the Beloved Disciple must be a projection of a theological claim back into the history of Jesus. But what does the Evangelist intend to say by means of the figure of the Beloved Disciple? In order to answer this question, 19:35 must be the point of departure.

(a) The primary function of the Beloved Disciple is that of *witnessing*. He bears witness to the reality of the death of Jesus and the reality of salvation grounded in the Christ event and mediated by the sacraments of baptism and the Lord's Supper. In addition to these references and by means of them, he testifies to the reality of the passion, cross, and resurrection of Jesus. Even though the Evangelist does not directly connect an antidocetic purpose with such testimony,[32] he does articulate a nondocetic position and takes up the stream of tradition that had developed within the Johannine school in opposition to the Docetists (cf. 1 John 5:5–13).

(b) Moreover, the testimony of the Beloved Disciple *guarantees the truth of the tradition*. In that he is portrayed as eyewitness and earwitness of the life of Jesus including witnessing the empty tomb, the Beloved Disciple exercises the function that, according to the formulation of earliest Christianity, belongs to the apostles as witnesses of the resurrection (cf. 1 Cor 15:3ff). By making it clear that he writes his Gospel on the basis of the testimony of the Beloved Disciple, the Evangelist establishes his Gospel as true and as the foundation for Christian faith. The Evangelist places himself as a member in a series of witnesses that goes back to the life of Jesus and is legitimized precisely by this link. This is not fundamentally different from what the author of 1 John does, even though he makes a greater claim than the Evangelist, since he places himself on the same level as the eyewitnesses and earwitnesses (1 John 1:1ff). In comparison with 1 John, the work of the Fourth Evangelist represents a more advanced level of historical reflection, since he bases his work on the testimony of the Beloved Disciple.

(c) The coordination of the Beloved Disciple to Jesus as the suffering and risen Son of God implies a fundamental theological perception: *Christian witness and Christian faith have their origin in the revelation of the*

---

[32] Contra U. Schnelle, *Antidocetic Christology* 228. The docetic/antidocetic struggle within the Johannine school belongs to an earlier phase (see below).

*Son of God.* The testimony of the Son of God is bound to confession of faith in him. By bearing witness to the reality of the divine Sonship of Jesus Christ, the Beloved Disciple provides an example of the right confession of faith in Christ as the Son of God and thereby an example of right faith (cf. 1 John 4:15).

3. If then the Beloved Disciple is not to be understood as an actual historical figure, the question arises as to how this figure is related to *the historical person of the "Presbyter"* as the founder of the Johannine circle. Already E. Käsemann called attention to the closeness of the subject matter of 3 John 12 to John 19:35. The testimony of the "Presbyter" was also directed to Christ (2 John) and includes the intention to establish an authoritative tradition and corresponding truth claim.[33] This is in no way different from the way the testimony of the Beloved Disciple is presented in the Fourth Gospel. Although the Beloved Disciple is not literally to be identified with either the Presbyter or the author of the Gospel, it may still be supposed that the tradition of the Johannine community derived from its founder, the Presbyter who established the tradition and mediated it by his authoritative testimony, has found an expression in the figure of the Beloved Disciple. This hypothesis is made all the more probable by Papias' report of the Ephesian John, who is presumably identical with the Presbyter, and who was described as the "Lord's disciple."

4. A late situation in the tradition of the Johannine community is reflected in the Appendix (John 21). Here the Beloved Disciple is not a witness of the empty tomb (as in 20:1ff) but along with the other disciples is a witness of the appearance of the Risen One (21:1ff). Moreover, there is a perceptible competitive relation to Peter[34] that clearly is decided in Peter's favor, since he, and not the Beloved Disciple, is charged by the risen Christ to "shepherd my sheep" (21:15ff). Here the position of the developing early catholic church may be recognized, as it is found especially in the Roman Petrine tradition and becomes dominant over the special tradition of the Johannine circle. Alongside this catholic tradition, the Johannine community preserved its specific heritage, which also comes to expression in John 21, when Peter has to be informed by the Beloved Disciple of the identity of the figure on the beach (21:7). Also, differently from Peter, whose previous denial of Christ is presupposed (21:15ff; cf. 13:37–38; Mark 14:26–31par), no new confession of faith is required from the Beloved Disciple. All this, of course, is more like a personal legend than a meaning in terms of church polity. At the time of the composition

---

[33] Cf. Käsemann, "Ketzer und Zeuge" 180 n. 40; cf. especially the first person plural of 3 John 12.

[34] Cf already John 20:1ff (the Beloved Disciple arrives at the empty tomb before Peter but lets Peter be the first to enter); differently 18:15ff.

of the Appendix, the Johannine circle had already been forced onto a side-track as far as church polity is concerned.

In conclusion, with regard to 21:24–25: As said above, here the Beloved Disciple is identified with the Fourth Evangelist. Here we have a secondary addendum, which itself perhaps betrays the hands of two different authors, as may be indicated by the change of persons (21:24 "we;" 21:25 "I"). Verse 24 points back to 19:35 in both its language and subject matter, and is probably dependent on this verse.

We see: the Fourth Evangelist is a member of the chain of tradition within the Johannine school, followed by other members. This justifies the inference that it was as an exponent of the Johannine community that he composed his work for this community.

## b) Christology

### 1. The Prologue (1:1–18)

Barrett, C. K. "The Prologue of St. John's Gospel," *New Testament Essays*, London: SPCK, 1971.

Bultmann, R. "Der religionsgeschichtliche Hintergrund des Prologs zum Johannes-Evangelium," *Eucharisterion* (FS H. Gunkel) Vol. 2. Göttingen: Vandenhoeck & Ruprecht, 1923, 3–26; also in *Exegetica*. Tübingen: J. C. B. Mohr (Paul Siebeck), 1967, 10–35.

Bultmann, R. "Die Bedeutung der neuerschlossenen mandäischen und manichäischen Quellen für das Verständnis des Johannesevangeliums," *Exegetica*. Tübingen: J. C. B. Mohr (Paul Siebeck), 1967, 55–104.

de la Potterie, I. "Structure du Prologue de Saint Jean," *NTS* 30 (1984) 354–381.

Haenchen, E. "Probleme des johanneischen 'Prologs'," *ZThK* 60 (1963) 305–334; also in *Gott und Mensch. GAufs. I*, E. Haenchen, ed. Tübingen: J. C. B. Mohr (Paul Siebeck), 1965, 114–143.

Hofius, O. "Struktur und Gedankengang des Logos-Hymnus in Joh 1,1–18," *ZNW* 78 (1987) 1–25.

Hofrichter, P. *Im Anfang war der 'Johannesprolog'. Das urchristliche Logosbekenntnis—die Basis neutestamentlicher und gnostischer Theologie*. BU 17. Regensburg: Pustet, 1986.

Käsemann, E. "The Structure and Purpose of the Prologue to John's Gospel," *New Testament Questions of Today*. Philadelphia: Fortress, 1969, 138–167.

Painter, J. "Christology and the History of the Johannine Community in the Prologue of the Fourth Gospel," *NTS* 30 (1984) 460–474.

Schnackenburg, R. "Logos-Hymnus und johanneischer Prolog," *BZ* NF 1 (1957) 69–109.

Theobald, M. *Die Fleischwerdung des Logos. Studien zum Verhältnis des Johannesprologs zum Corpus des Evangeliums und zu 1 Joh*. NTA.NF 20. Münster: Aschendorff, 1988.

Theobald, M. *Im Anfang war das Wort*. SBS 106. Stuttgart: Katholisches Bibelwerk, 1983.

Tobin, Th. H. "The Prologue of John and Hellenistic Jewish Speculation," *CBQ* 52 (1990) 252–269.

Wengst, K. *Christologische Formeln und Lieder des Urchristentums*. StNT 7. Gütersloh: Gerd Mohn, 1972, 12.

1 Ἐν ἀρχῇ ἦν ὁ λόγος,
και ὁ λόγος ἦν πρὸς τὸν θεόν,
και θεὸς ἦν ὁ λόγος.

2 οὗτος ἦν ἐν ἀρχῇ πρὸς τὸν θεόν.

3 πάντα δι᾽ αὐτοῦ ἐγένετο,
και χωρὶς αὐτοῦ ἐγένετο
οὐδὲ ἕν.
ὃ γέγονεν

4 ἐν αὐτῷ ζωὴ ἦν,
και ἡ ζωὴ ἦν τὸ φῶς τῶν ἀνθρώπων

5 και τὸ φῶς ἐν τῇ σκοτίᾳ φαίνει,
και ἡ σκοτία αὐτὸ οὐ κατέλαβεν.

6 Ἐγένετο ἄνθρωπος
ἀπεσταλμένος παρὰ θεοῦ,
ὄνομα αὐτῷ Ἰωάννης·

7 οὗτος ἦλθεν εἰς μαρτυρίαν,
ἵνα μαρτυρήσῃ περὶ τοῦ φωτός,
ἵνα πάντες πιστεύσωσιν δι᾽ αὐτοῦ.

8 οὐκ ἦν ἐκεῖνος τὸ φῶς,
ἀλλ᾽ ἵνα μαρτυρήσῃ περὶ τοῦ φωτός.

9 Ἦν τὸ φῶς τὸ ἀληθινόν,
ὃ φωτίζει πάντα ἄνθρωπον,
ἐρχόμενον εἰς τὸν κόσμον.

10 ἐν τῷ κόσμῳ ἦν,
και ὁ κόσμος δι᾽ αὐτοῦ ἐγένετο,
και ὁ κόσμος αὐτὸν οὐκ ἔγνω.

11 εἰς τὰ ἴδια ἦλθεν,
και οἱ ἴδιοι αὐτὸν οὐ παρέλαβον.

12 ὅσοι δὲ ἔλαβον αὐτόν, ἔδωκεν αὐτοῖς
ἐξουσίαν τέκνα θεοῦ γενέσθαι,
τοῖς πιστεύουσιν εἰς τὸ ὄνομα αὐτοῦ,

13 οἳ οὐκ ἐξ αἱμάτων οὐδὲ ἐκ θελήματος
σαρκὸς οὐδὲ ἐκ θελήματος ἀνδρὸς
ἀλλ᾽ ἐκ θεοῦ ἐγεννήθησαν.

14 Καὶ ὁ λόγος σὰρξ ἐγένετο
και ἐσκήνωσεν ἐν ἡμῖν,
και ἐθεασάμεθα τὴν δόξαν αὐτοῦ,
δόξαν ὡς μονογενοῦς παρὰ πατρός,
πλήρης χάριτος καὶ ἀληθείας.

15 Ἰωάννης μαρτυρεῖ περὶ αὐτοῦ και
κέκραγεν λέγων, οὗτος ἦν ὃν εἶπον,
ὁ ὀπίσω μου ἐρχόμενος ἔμπροσθέν
μου γέγονεν, ὅτι πρῶτός μου ἦν.

16 ὅτι ἐκ τοῦ πληρώματος αὐτοῦ
ἡμεῖς πάντες ἐλάβομεν
και χάριν ἀντὶ χάριτος·

17 ὅτι ὁ νόμος διὰ Μωϋσέως ἐδόθη,
ἡ χάρις καὶ ἡ ἀλήθεια
διὰ Ἰησοῦ Χριστοῦ ἐγένετο.

18 θεὸν οὐδεὶς ἑώρακεν πώποτε·
μονογενὴς θεὸς ὁ ὢν εἰς τὸν κόλπον
τοῦ πατρὸς ἐκεῖνος ἐξηγήσατο.

---

1 In the beginning was the Word,
and the Word was with God,
and the Word was God.

2 He was in the beginning with God.

3 All things came into being through
him, and without him came into
being not one thing.
What has come into being

4 in him was life,
and the life was the light of all people.

5 The light shines in the darkness,
and the darkness did not overcome it.

6 There was a man
sent from God,
whose name was John.

7 He came as a witness
to testify to the light, so that
all might believe through him.

8 He himself was not the light,
but he came to testify to the light.

9 The true light,
which enlightens everyone,
was coming into the world.

10 He was in the world, and
the world came into being through him;
yet the world did not know him.

11 He came to what was his own,
and his own people did not accept him.

12 But to all who received him, he gave them
power to become children of God,
(those who) who believed in his name,

13 who not of blood or of the will of the
flesh or of the will of man,
but of God were born,

14 And the Word became flesh
and lived among us,
and we have seen his glory,
the glory as of a father's only son,
full of grace and truth.

15 John testified to him and cried out,
"This was he of whom I said,
'He who comes after me ahead
of me ranks because he was before me.'"

16 From his fullness
we have all received,
grace upon grace.

17 The law indeed was given
through Moses; grace and truth came
through Jesus Christ.

18 No one has ever seen God.
It is God the only Son,
who is close to the heart of the Father,
who has made him known.

## Structure

Scholarship is almost unanimous that in these verses[35] the Evangelist cites a hymn[36] that came to him in the tradition. The use of a source is already indicated by the fact that only in 1:1 and 1:14, and nowhere else in the Gospel, the term λόγος appears as a christological term. This is confirmed by the observation that the text is composed of rhythmic verses, and by the presence of *hapax legomena*,[37] although on the other hand it must be said that the whole section is characterized by a thoroughly Johannine linguistic style.[38]

A variety of attempts have been made to reconstruct the original form of the hymn. They mostly proceed from the observation that in vv. 6–8 and 15 John the Baptist is spoken of directly, without any transition. These verses doubtless function to prepare the reader for the following section (cf, 1:19ff) and cannot be counted as an integral part of the quoted hymn. The verb ἐξηγήσατο and thus all of v. 18 could also have the same function. Furthermore, the alternation between the third person plural and the first person plural is striking (vv. 13–14). In addition, with the aid of stylistic considerations it is possible to ascertain the underlying metrical structure as well as perspectives on the hymn's content.[39] When one takes into account the necessary subjective element in weighing different criteria, it is understandable that the attempts at reconstruction have resulted in considerable variety:

R. Bultmann[40] arrives at the following results: the cultic community hymn was based on dyadic verses, with both members either expressing a single thought (vv. 9, 12, 14b) or as parallelism (v. 3) or as antitheses (vv. 5, 10, 11), or the second member supplements the thought of the first member and takes it further (vv. 1, 4, 14a, 16). The pre-Johannine hymn contained the verses 1, 3–5, 9–12b (without ἐξουσίαν and τοῖς πιστεύουσιν ... αὐτοῦ), 14 and 16. This text was originally a "song of the Baptist

---

35 On the problem of punctuation, cf. K. Aland, "Eine Untersuchung zu Joh 1, 3.4, ZNW 59 (1968) 174–209, also printed in *Neutestamentliche Entwürfe* (TB 63. Munich: Kaiser, 1979) 351–391).

36 Differently P. Hofrichter, "Johannesprolog" 41, who speaks of a "creedal text."

37 Especially φωτίζω, (v. 9), σκηνόω (v. 14; only 4x elsewhere in the NT, in Revelation), πλήρωμα (v. 16; in the NT especially in the Pauline corpus); χάρις (only vv. 14, 16, 17; but cf. 2 John 3), τέκνα θεοῦ (v. 12; elsewhere in the Gospel only 11:52; but cf. 1 John 3:1, 2, 10; 5:2), κόλπος (v. 18; elsewhere in the Gospel only 13:23), ἐξηγέομαι (v. 18; otherwise in the NT only Luke 24:35 and 4x in Acts).

38 ἴδια (also 8:44; 16:32; 19:27) or οἱ ἴδιοι (also 13:1), elsewhere often used adjectivally; θέλημα (also 4:34; 5:30; 6:38–40; 7:17; 9:31 [cf. 1 John 2:17; 5:14]). The theological conceptuality is particularly Johannine: φῶς, ζωή, σκοτία, ἀλήθεια, ἐξουσία, δόξα, σάρξ, μαρτυρέω, μονογενής, θεὸν ὁρᾶν.

39 Cf. R. Bultmann, *Gospel of John* 13–18.

40 Cf. Bultmann, "Der religionsgeschichtliche Hintergrund" 3–26; *Gospel of John* 15ff.

community."[41] It was edited by the Evangelist. Among the redactional additions of the Evangelist are vv. 12c, 13 (as explanation of 12b), 17,[42] 18.[43] Critique of Bultmann's reconstruction includes the observation that, despite his basic argument for the metrical structure of the hymn, he reckons with lines of differing length[44] and postulates a pre-Johannine Baptist song with a strong Johannine ring to it, which cannot be considered probable due to the late origin of the Mandean literature.

E. *Käsemann*[45] distinguishes two strophes in the pre-Johannine traditional unit: (1) vv. 1–4 (without v. 2?) (2) vv. 5 and 9–12, while asking "whether v. 9, too, ought not to be ascribed to the Evangelist."[46] Impetus is provided especially by the final member (v. 9c: ἐρχόμενον εἰς τὴν κόσμον), which as a "rabbinic twist" strikes one as "prose." Furthermore, the adjectival ἀληθινόν (v. 9a) is "typical of the Evangelist," and finally v. 10 can be easily understood as the continuation of v. 5.[47] Accordingly, the first part of the hymn consists of seven or eight lines respectively, the second part "up to the end of v. 11 would also contain seven lines."[48] Critical questions must be raised here: the ambiguous delineation of the two strophes does not evoke confidence in this attempt at reconstruction. Furthermore, vv. 14 and 16 are not considered part of the pre-Johannine hymn; thereby the origination of vv. 14–18 becomes an unsolvable riddle with regard to the work of the Evangelist.[49] Finally, Käsemann's reconstruction contains a material problem: already at the beginning of the hymn, at the latest in v. 5, the epiphany of Jesus Christ as the Logos appears to be affirmed, a tension arises with v. 10b, where testimony is apparently given to the cosmic function of the Logos, therefore not yet the incarnation.

K. *Wengst* proposes yet another view.[50] Following E. Käsemann, he would like to find an inconsistent alternation between two-line and three-line strophes but he takes on the twofold division of strophes in another way: (1) vv. 1, 3–5, 9–11; (2) vv. 14 and 16. Here the basis is more clearly the metrical disposition. V. 2 is attributed to the

---

[41]   *Ibid* 15.
[42]   *Ibid* 13–15.
[43]   Here Bultmann reads, in agreement with the presupposed confession of the Evangelist, μονογενὴς υἱός instead of μονογενὴς Θεός (*Gospel of John* 81–83).
[44]   Already v. 1 is not composed in triadic lines rather than dyadic. The same is true of vv. 9–10. Cf. E. Käsemann, "Structure and Purpose" 142; K. Wengst, *Christologische Formeln* 204–205.
[45]   Käsemann, "Structure and Purpose" 138ff.
[46]   *Ibid.* 151.
[47]   *Ibid.*
[48]   *Ibid.* 168; v. 12 would then be regarded as a "culmination" or "resumé" statement (*ibid.*).
[49]   Cf. also E. Haenchen, "Probleme des johanneischen 'Prologs'" 305–334, according to whom the hymn consisted of vv. 1–5, 9–11, 14, 16–17; v. 18 is attributed to the Evangelist, vv. 6, 8, 12–13, 15 to a redactor after the Evangelist. Problematic here is the separation of the Baptist material (vv. 6–8, 15) from the work of the Evangelist.
[50]   K. Wengst, *Christologische Formeln* 200–208; here too a debate with E. Ruckstuhl, *Die literarische Einheit des Johannesevangeliums. Der gegenwärtige Stand der einschlägigen Forschungen* (SF NF 3. Freiburg: Herder, 1951) (= NTOA 5, Göttingen-Fribourg: Vandenhoeck & Ruprecht, 1988) 69–97; W. Eltester, "Der Logos und sein Prophet. Fragen zur heutigen Erklärung des johanneischen Prologs," in W. Eltester and F. H. Kettler, eds., *Apophoreta* (FS E. Haenchen) (BZNW 30. Berlin: W. de Gruyter, 1964) 109–134, which champions the unity of the Johannine Prologue.

Evangelist as a "prosaic" summary of v. 1. He also finds it acceptable that vv. 14 and 16 are basically pre-Johannine material. On the other hand, one must observe that already in v. 9 the proposed metrical structure is irregular (the participle ἐρχόμενον is not on a par with the preceding lines). The same is true for v. 14 (direct joining of the δόξα clause without transition; the πλήρης-clause is also grammatically difficult) and for v. 16 (beginning with ὅτι; elliptical καί-postscript).

An unequivocal reconstruction of the source of the Johannine Prologue can obviously not be presupposed. In any case, one must reckon with additions by the Evangelist, which are not easily recognized. Furthermore, the possibility cannot be dismissed that prior to the composition of the Gospel, the hymn had already been edited in the Johannine school. Finally, one must ask whether the change from third person to first (at v. 14) can be made the basis for two different strophes (which results in considerable difference in the length of the two units in Wengst's reconstruction), or whether we must not be much more modest in answering the question of the strophic arrangement of the tradition that came to the Evangelist.

While v. 2 is presumably the work of the Evangelist[51], the remainder of the hymn in vv. 1, 3–5 appears to be cited relatively verbatim. Vv. 6–8 form the secondary interpretation of the preceding verses, and already connect the Christ theme with the appearance of the Baptist. The keyword φῶς (v. 9) is taken up v. 5. Whether the adjectival ἀληθινόν is possibly an addition by the Evangelist, since it appears to presuppose the secondary v. 8 as its antithetical counterpart,[52] cannot be decided with certainty, since the expression τὸ φῶς τὸ ἀληθινόν is also found in 1 John 2:8 independently of the Evangelist, and presupposes there σκοτία as the counterpart as in John 1:5. The two final parts of v. 9 make no confident impression: the relative clause must not be original (v. 12 is comparable!); in the present context it is just as unlikely that the final element with the participle ἐρχόμενον is to be referred to φῶς but as a participial construction and with the change of subject it does not fit the speech rhythm of the sentence. Possibly at this point in his source the Evangelist had a statement that combined the essential being of the Logos as light with its/his connection to the world, and thus provided the transition to v. 10.

The unevenness in the present structure may be the result of the insertion of the previous section (vv. 6–8), which at the same times makes it clear that by no means may we expect an exclusively conservative reproduction of his source. This also applies to what follows: although v. 10a ("he was in the world") is joined seamlessly to the preceding text (v. 9c: "coming into the world"), v. 10 in its present form is still apparently not original. The logical ordering of the series would call for: creation of the world through the preexistent Logos (v. 10b), his/its being in the cosmos (v. 10a), and the failure of the cosmos to recognize/acknowledge him/it (10c). Even if one

---

[51] It is a matter of simply repeating v. 1ab. The introductory οὗτος is characteristic of the Evangelist (cf. 1:7, 15, 30, 34; cf. K. Wengst, *Christologische Formeln* 201; R. Schnackenburg, *Gospel according to St. John* 236; "Logos-Hymnus und johanneischer Prolog," *BZ* NF 1 (1957) 69–109; 79).

[52] Cf. E. Käsemann, "Structure and Purpose" 151; differently K. Wengst, *Christologische Formeln* 202.

concedes that the hymn contained three-liners alongside two-liners,[53] the original order remains in doubt, and all the more so since v. 11 with a clearly antithetical two-liner appears to presuppose a corresponding metrical arrangement of the preceding (resumed by v. 11b from v. 10c). If v. 11 belonged to the source, the same cannot necessarily be said for v. 12 without further ado. To be sure, there is no material contradiction to v. 11, as though v. 11's "all rejected the Logos" is contradicted by v. 12's "however, some did acknowledge him/it,"[54] but still the correlative ὅσοι as well as the adversative δέ are unusual for the song.[55] Even if one does not share Bultmann's linguistic views and reflections on the content of the expression ἐξουσίαν διδόναι,[56] v. 12c is in any case to be recognized as a secondary explanation which—in that it corresponds to the train of thought of the verse as a whole—makes one skeptical of the whole of v. 12, especially since the expression τέκνα θεοῦ anticipates v. 13, which is almost universally acknowledged as hardly the component of a hymn. One must ask whether v. 14 can be understood as the beginning of a second strophe that continues the preceding hymn. To be sure, such a judgment is made difficult by the serious possibility that in place of v. 12 there could originally have stood a positive statement. Furthermore, the irregularity of the structure mentioned above not only for v. 14 but for v. 16 does not speak for the thesis that the Evangelist was here concerned to reproduce his source exactly. There remains, therefore, hardly any other conclusion than to suppose that of the added verses 14–18 the main ideas contained in vv. 14 and 16, and perhaps also v. 18, should be traced back to the source, since they give the impression of older material on both linguistic and material grounds. But whether they formed the "second strophe" of a hymn, as perhaps the response of the community to the "Angel's Song" (= the first strophe)[57], can only be mentioned here as a possibility.

However successful the reconstruction of the Evangelist's "source" may turn out to be, with the associated continuing uncertainty about factors of greater or lesser importance in detail, it is relatively certain that the author of the Gospel of John was dependent on a source for the material in the Prologue, and that we thereby encounter an old layer of the

---

[53]   Differently R. Bultmann, *Gospel of John* 54 note 2.

[54]   According to K. Wengst, *Christologische Formeln* 202, in the source ἴδιοι (v. 11) and ὁ κόσμος (v. 10) refer to humanity as a whole. The Evangelist, however, referred these terms to unbelievers and placed them in contrast to believers (v. 12). One can well imagine, however, that the comprehensive κόσμος concept (v. 10) is also pre-supposed when οἱ ἴδιοι (v. 11) is understood in a restricted sense and suppose (with K. Wengst) that the original continued with v. 14 ("we" = the church!). Under-standing ἴδιοι as the Jewish people is not persuasive because of the context (contra H. Thyen, "Das Heil kommt von den Juden," in D. Lührmann and G. Strecker, eds., *Kirche* (FS G. Bornkamm) (Tübingen: J. C. B. Mohr [Paul Siebeck], 1980) 163–184; 171.

[55]   Cf. in contrast καί used adversatively (vv. 5, 10).

[56]   Cf. R. Bultmann, *Gospel of John* 57 note 5. For the revealer, the simple δίδωμι is supposed to be characteristic (4:14; 6:27, 33–34, 51–52; 10:28; 14:27; 17:2, 7, 22) so that ἐξουσία (in the Greek sense of "power," "authority," is probably the Evangelist's addition (1:12, 5:27; 10:18; 17:2; 19:10–11 are "all sentences from the Evangelist."

[57]   So Chr. Demke, "Der sogenannte Logos-Hymnus im johanneischen Prolog," *ZNW* 58 (1967) 45–68; 64.

Johannine school tradition. A comparison with 2 and 3 John, and also with 1 John, can show that the traditional ideas in it are "early Johannine." Thus the Johannine "key concepts" ἀλήθεια, (vv. 14, 17; 2 John 1–3; 1 John 1:6, 8, and elsewhere); ἀρχή (vv. 1–2; not in this absolute sense: 2 John 5–6; 1 John 1:1), κόσμος (vv. 9–10; cf. 2 John 7; 1 John 2:2), γινώσκειν (christological: v. 10; 1 John 1:2–4; 3:1; the "truth:" 2 John 1), the opposition of σκοτία and φῶς (vv. 5, 9; 1 John 1:5ff; 2:8); the unity between the Logos and the Father (vv. 1–2, 18; cf. 2 John 3; 1 John 1:2 and elsewhere), "seeing God" (v. 18; cf. v. 14; 3 John 11; 1 John 4:20; cf. 3:2, 6). Likewise, the Prologue manifests structural elements of the Johannine world of thought, which are determined by dualistic traits more strongly than in 2 and 3 John but on the other hand are presupposed by the author of 1 John as familiar and thus can be considered early Johannine.

The subject of the hymn is the *divine Logos*, who is portrayed as the preexistent mediator of creation (vv. 1–3, 10). He is further described as the revealer, with which the idea of a descent from heaven is connected (vv. 9–11, 14, 18). Included in this is his soteriological function, in that he is understood as the representation and bringer of life and light and the δόξα θεοῦ (vv. 4, 9, 14). The term "Logos" and the concept associated with it have a history that extends far into the time prior to the composition of the Gospel of John. The problem of its derivation from the point of view of the history of religions has generated different suggestions:

1. The Prologue's beginning with the words ἐν ἀρχῇ ἦν ὁ λόγος is reminiscent of the first words of the Old Testament Genesis (1:1: בְּרֵאשִׁית). Is the Johannine Logos thus to be understood from the *Old Testament*? Is it a counterpart to the powerful creative word of God, that separates light and darkness, consolidates and sustains heaven and earth, calls the animate creation into being as portrayed in the creation story of the "priestly document" and is documented later as an expression for the creative power of God (Ezek 37:5–6; Isa 40:26; 44:24ff; 48:13)? In fact one can find a parallel here to the Johannine Logos, inasmuch as the Logos indicates the beginning, is thought of as the originating cause of the cosmos, and is itself of cosmic significance. However, in the Old Testament idea of creation the word of God is not personified. It is not a hypostasis but a function of God's speaking that make's known God's sovereign power. The Logos of the Johannine Prologue is different: he has the characteristic features of a heavenly being described in mythological terms, who has existed from the primeval beginning. He is not designated as λόγος τοῦ θεοῦ but absolutely as ὁ λόγος.

2. The Johannine Prologue stands closer to the *Jewish wisdom literature*. Wisdom ("Chokhma") can be understood as a personified figure (Prov 8:22ff): she is preexistent, mediator of creation, comes into the world in order to share herself with human beings but in the cosmos experiences

the destiny of rejection.[58] The parallel to the Johannine Logos-concept is near to hand, especially with regard to the relation of logos and cosmos, and also in the fact that in both cases it is a matter of a mythological personification of the claim of God on the world. However, in contrast to the Johannine Prologue, in the authentic Jewish tradition personified wisdom is not designated with the title "Logos" (ὁ λόγος).[59] Furthermore, Old Testament–Jewish wisdom is identified with the Torah;[60] in contrast, the Johannine Logos is not an interpretation of the Law of God or identical with it.

3. The Jewish wisdom speculation is not an authentic outgrowth of Judaism but stands under Hellenistic influence, as made clear by its ethical-rational orientation. That is also true of the mythical *Chokhma*, especially for the idea of its descent from heaven and for its characteristically timeless message. With this as a beginning point it is probable that the origin of the Johannine λόγος tradition is to be sought in the Greek-speaking realm, even if there are possible overlapping points of contact with non-Greek, oriental-Jewish settings. A related area is the *gnostic thought* world to which R. Bultmann sought to trace back the Johannine Logos-understanding. In the classical Christian gnosticism of the second century the *Nous*[61] is the "redeemed Redeemer," the revealer sent by God who became human, the one who undertook the salvation of the "sparks of light" that had fallen into the material world, in accordance with the gnostic doctrine of the origin of the world (soteriology as reversal of cosmology). The fact that the saving event involved a mythical being, his nearness to God (to be sure, thought of as an emanation), his function as revealer and redeemer, and not least the explicit identification with Christ—all this lets the revealer figure of the gnostic systems of the second century appear to be related to the Logos concept of the Johannine prologue. However, the system found there that led to a speculative number symbolism, and the combination of cosmology and soteriology, are not

---

58   For the details cf. A. I. a. 2. above.
59   Philo is an apparent exception: ἡ δέ (sc. σοφία) ἐστιν ὁ θεοῦ λόγος (All 1.65); even here, however, λόγος is not used in the absolute sense.
60   Cf. G. Kittel, λέγω κτλ. TDNT 4:132–133, who of course would like to infer from such a parallel that there was a connection between the Johannine Prologue and rabbinic Torah speculation (133). The rabbinic passages introduced as support must be dated later, however. Likewise, the consideration that perhaps the Prologue was originally written in Aramaic so that the term λόγος would be secondary, is unhelpful (133), since the literature of the Johannine circle, despite the occasional emergence of Semitisms, certainly is based on the presupposition of Greek as the primary language.
61   Occasionally also the λόγος: Irenaeus Haer 1.15.3 for the gnostic doctrine of Markus (the Tetrad of Anthropos, Ecclesia, Logos, and Zoe).

found in the Gospel of John.[62] From this perspective one is prompted to suppose that the Johannine Logos tradition represents a preliminary form of later gnosticism (= "pre-gnostic," "proto-gnostic," or the like). Since the Christian-Gnostic texts belong to the post-New Testament age, this conclusion is the more probable.[63]

4. These examples at least make it clear that the concept of a revealer figure is by no means found only among Christians but—as also seen in the Jewish wisdom speculation—comes to expression in various non-Christian systems. *Hellenistic Judaism* is especially to be mentioned here as a locus for the idea of a divine Logos figure. Thus Philo of Alexandria, for whom the λόγος τοῦ θεοῦ or the θεῖος λόγος stands beside God as God's εἰκών, as the mediator of creation, and also as μονογενής (cf. John 1:14, 18; 3:16, 18), simply as mediator between God and humanity. This figure represents the divine reason over against the world.[64] The dualistic thinking at the base of this philosophical doctrine, like the rational conception of the Logos as the world reason is reminiscent of Pythagoreanism and Neo-Platonism, where λόγος in the absolute sense appears as the power that gives meaning and form to everything, permeating time and space, matter and spirit.[65] It is also obvious that the Johannine Prologue has no direct genetic connection to these last named systems. But they make visible the setting in which the Johannine Logos-concept could originate, namely Hellenistic and Jewish ideas, the philosophical and religious syncretism of the first century as a whole. These made available the structural elements from which the Christ-hymn of the Johannine Prologue could be created. The close relationship with the tradition of the Johannine school makes it probable that prior to the Evangelist there was a characteristically formed christological unit that had already identified the Logos concept and terminology with the Christ.

---

[62] This also separates the Prologue from the Poimandres tractate of the Corpus Hermeticum, where the Ur-man is understood as a cosmic principle (1.12–19).

[63] Also the Mandean literature—especially the *Ginza*; the Mandean *Book of John*, and others—belong to a later time (7/8 cent.). Furthermore, they are marked by Christian (Nestorian) tradition; cf. H. Lietzmann, "Ein Beitrag zur Mandäerfrage," SPAW.PH (Berlin 1930) 596–608. Also found here are specific citations from the Gospel of John; therefore the inference that the baptist sect of the Tigris and Euphrates area goes back to the school of John the Baptist, which was originally located in the area east of the Jordan, despite various attempts cannot really be substantiated (so also K. Rudolph, *Die Mandäer* [FRLANT 74. Göttingen: Vandenhoeck & Ruprecht, 1960)] 80, 253; *Gnosis: The Nature and History of Gnosticism* (San Francisco: Harper & Row, Publishers, 1977).

[64] See also the revealer figure of the Pseudo-Clementines, the "true prophet," who journeys through world history making appearances from Adam onwards (PsClem Hom 3.20.2); cf. G. Strecker, *Das Judenchristentum in den Pseudoklementinen* TU 70 (Berlin: Akademie Verlag, 1981²) 145–153.

[65] Cf. Plot Enn 3.2.15: Ἀρχὴ οὖν λόγος καὶ πάντα λόγος.

*Interpretation*

α) The Universal Cosmic Significance of the Logos

For both the Evangelist and his source, the Logos, Jesus Christ, is thought of as a preexistent heavenly being who is also the Revealer. The Ἀρχή of 1:1 describes the absolute beginning, in contrast to the predominant us-age of the Johannine letters, where the ἀρχή is identified with the Christ event of the past or with the founding of the Christian community.[66] Differently than in the letters, the ἀρχή of the Logos is grounded in his/its connection to God, and, like God, has an eternal character. Since the Logos existed from the primeval beginning, this means that he was present before the creation. Thus it can not only be said of him that he is a second divine person "with God," but also that "the Logos was God" (1:1c). Ob-viously this statement does not intend to emphasize that God and the Logos are two different "persons," but it is clear that the preexistent Logos is a divine being, a different "person" from God but not different in essen-tial being.[67] Since this statement applies to the preexistent one, neither the incarnation nor the revelatory function of the Logos has yet come in the purview of 1:1c.

That the Evangelist does not intend a personal identification between God and the Logos is accented in 1:2, which corresponds almost verbatim to 1:1b and underscores not only the unity but also the difference between the two persons (1:3).[68] The divine, preexistent being of the Logos is seen in his function as the mediator of creation (1:3). Since everything "be-came" through him, i.e. was created by him, then not the least item in the universe is independent of him. Everything that exists was called into life through him.[69] His being is oriented to the cosmos. As the preexistent one, the activity of the Logos has a universal concern. It has a cosmic breadth, as appropriate to the mediator of creation. His appearance within the cosmos is also determined by this: he steps forth into the world as one who possesses a pre-cosmic existence, who does not belong to the cosmos, is not dependent on the cosmos, and yet turns mercifully toward the cosmos. The life (ἡ ζωή) that presents itself in him (cf. 6:35; 11:25) and is symbol-

---

[66]  Cf. above 1 John 1:1; 2:13, 14; 3:11.

[67]  This conclusion cannot be avoided by taking θεός as a predicate nominative rather than the subject (despite the word order), as though the meaning were "the Logos was divine," since for this sense one would expect the adjective θεῖος rather than the noun θεός. On the sense presupposed here, cf. also 1:18 and 20:28.

[68]  Cf. the emphasis on the unity between Father and Son in 5:21ff, 10:30, and else-where, which also includes the differentiation between the two persons (cf. 6:38; 14:28, and elsewhere).

[69]  On the separation of ὃ γέγονεν (1:3c), that is to be connected to 1:4, cf. the manu-script documentation in Nestle-Aland[27] (among others, P[75]), as well as the inves-tigation of K. Aland cited in note 35.

ized by the light (φῶς) is the gift of God to humanity (1:4). As light stands over against darkness as mutually exclusive opposites (1:5), so also the life-giving Logos is set over against the power of death (1:5; cf. 5:24; 8:51). Thus the event of the incarnation means that the Logos as a non-cosmic being reveals himself and the Father to the world of humanity.

However, at what point in the Prologue this event is first spoken of remains an open question. The two extreme positions: (a) The incarnation is not spoken of until 1:14; everything prior to that is the preliminary way of the Logos through history (cf. the pseudo-Clementine doctrine of "yoked pairs," and Mani). (b) Already from 1:4–5 on the hymn speaks of the incarnation ("the light was the life of all people ... the light shines [present tense!] in the darkness..."). In any case, 1:5 speaks primarily about the nature of the Logos, who is identical with "light," but stands over against the "darkness" (cf. also 3:19; 8:12; 9:5; 12:46).

## β) The Johannine Adaptation

It is certain that in 1:6–8 the Evangelist intends to point to the revelatory event. The figure of John the Baptist is introduced in solemn language with an ancient, Hebraizing tone that both reveals and veils his identity. Thereby the author can appeal to traditions that he also uses later (1:19ff), traditions that have parallels in Mark, Matthew, and Luke (Mark 1:2ffpar). The purpose of John's appearance is to bear witness to the Light, i.e. the Logos-Revealer. The goal of his preaching is faith, which is available to all (cf. John 20:31; 1 John 5:13). Just as the mission of the Revealer is universal, so also the goal of the "witness." The testimony he gives, however, is subordinate to the revelation. The narrator's assertion that "he [John] was not the Light" (1:8) shows that the Baptist's proclamation was only provisional and temporary, and pointed to what was to follow. To this extent the term "forerunner" is appropriate (cf. Luke 1:17). Even if he is not chronologically anchored in history, as he is in Luke, he is still given a particular place within the temporal story line. Just as the appearance of the Logos occurs in a specific segment of the timeline, so also in the case of his precursor the Baptist. A direct anti-Baptist polemic cannot be read out of such "subordination" statements. Neither is such a polemic to be inferred from the subordination statements of the Synoptics (e. g. Matt 3:14–15). Apparently in the older pre-Synoptic layers of the tradition there was a sharp debate between the followers of Jesus and the Baptist sect over the issue of the relation of the Baptist to Jesus. But the Evangelists are concerned neither with polemic nor apologetic but to strengthen the faith that the Revealer is greater than the witness and that the witness fulfilled his function only with reference to the Revealer. This also applies to 1:15: John the Baptist points to the preexistent one whose advent had been predicted. Mark 1:7–8par Matthew 3:11 provides an important parallel with reference to the one who had been predicted. This tradition is also taken up in John 1:27, 30. The Gospel of John refers to familiar material from the Synoptic tradition, where John the Baptist appears as the precursor of Jesus.

On the other hand, there is no prophecy/fulfillment schema; the one who is sent as the "forerunner" and the one whose sending is the "real thing" are not related to each other in a straight chronological timeline. On the contrary, a presumed temporal chain of cause-and-effect is broken by 1:30: "After me (ὁ ὀπίσω μου) comes a man who ranks ahead of me (ἔμπροσθέν μου) because he was before (πρῶτος) me." The temporal designations ἔμπροσθεν and πρῶτος are to be taken literally, so that it is expressed paradoxically that the one who follows John is ahead of him. This is no longer to be interpreted chronologically but affirms: the Preexistent One precedes all human preaching and all human action. It thus agrees with the term πλήρωμα (1:16): his "fullness" is not limited by space or time; it is inexhaustible, a source of χάρις and ζωή that can never run dry.

Further lines of interpretation developed by the Evangelist: in the remainder of the Prologue the Evangelist's adjustments and "interpolations" can also be seen, where he connects the preceding text with the following one. This is the reason for the emphasis on "faith in his name" (1:12; cf. 1 John 5:13), which anticipates the Gospel's assignment of awakening faith (20:31). The statement about the coming of the Logos "into the world" (1:9c) points ahead to 3:16 and is to be understood in the sense of emphasizing God's gracious turning to the world in his Son. And when in 1:17 the Mosaic Law and the "grace and truth" revealed through Jesus Christ are juxtaposed, this suggests and points ahead to the typology constantly used in the following narrative in which the Jews appear as representatives of unbelief (cf. 1:19ff; 5:16, 18; 7:1; 10:31, 33; 11:8, and elsewhere).

γ) The Incarnation

The incarnation is first named in a way that cannot be misunderstood in 1:14. According to E. Käsemann the first half of the hymn already speaks of the incarnation, e.g. in 1:5.[70] According to R. Bultmann, the first part of the "source" spoke of the revelation in creation. From 1:5 on the Evangelist at the most hints at the incarnation, which is then clearly affirmed in 1:14. However, if one assumes that 1:4–5 belonged to the source, then a distinction between source and Evangelist cannot be made on this point, and the statement of 1:4–5 also corresponds to the intent of the Evangelist. Moreover, if a conscious distinction between the Logos before the incarnation and the manner in which the earthly Christ appeared had been made, then one would expect that there exists a material relation between the two forms of existence, i.e. that the λόγος ἄσαρκος would display basically nothing different in regard to the world in its creation

---

[70] Käsemann, "Structure and Purpose" 151, according to whom the hymn ended with 1:12. Cf. also J. Becker, *Das Evangelium nach Johannes* (ÖTK 4/1. Gütersloh: Gerd Mohn, 1979) 71.

than does the λόγος ἐν σαρκί; for the idea is essentially that of the personal identity of the Logos; it is independent of the form of his appearance.

It is likely that the hymn (and even more so the author of the Gospel) already had the incarnation in view when the initial ἀρχή was written. This is made clear in 1:4: the essence of the Logos consists in his activity as revealer! His revelation is recognizable in that he manifests himself as Light and Life for human beings. That this is affirmed in 1:4–5 already anticipates the content of 1:14, although a more clear statement of "coming into the world" is not made until 1:9–10. In other words: as in 1:14–15 the affirmation of preexistence breaks through the temporal scheme, limiting it and interpreting it with reference to the Logos (especially 1:15b). On the other hand, the affirmation of the incarnation is already transparent in the idea of the Logos as the mediator of creation at the beginning of the hymn. The decisive statement for the whole context is ὁ λόγος σάρξ ἐγένετο (1:14). The declaration about the incarnation addresses the issue that had already been applied to the Logos in universal and cosmological categories in the preceding section of the text. His universalism is oriented to the incarnation, and the incarnation is interpreted by his universalism, because the being of the Incarnate One is none other than that of the Preexistent One, and conversely the preexistence of the Logos can and should only be affirmed in such a way that it includes the being of the Incarnate One who discloses himself for the sake of humanity. Therefore the appearance of the Logos in and for the world is already affirmed at the beginning of the hymn—and not merely as a hint—even though the specific assertion of the incarnation is not made until 1:14.

Moreover, it is possible that, in the view of both the source and the Evangelist, the connection between the pre-Christian being of the Logos and the incarnation was developed in such a manner that the "coming into the world" of the Logos (1:9–10) did not occur first with the Jesus event but also happened in human history prior to Christ (cf. already 1:5, the present tense φαίνει). Similarly, in Jewish thought the Wisdom of God revealed herself continually throughout the history of the world,[71] or, according to a Jewish Christian view, the "true prophet" wandered through history from the time of Adam, appearing in a continuous series of incarnations and mediating the divine word to humanity in accord with his universal mission.[72] In the post-apostolic age, following the Platonic line

---

[71] Proverbs 1:20–33; Sirach 24:6–7; Baruch 3:10ff; 1 Enoch 42:1ff.

[72] Pseudo-Clementine Homilies 2:15–18:2; CMC 18ff; 23:4ff (L. Koenen and C. Römer, *Der Kölner Mani-Kodex. Über das Werden seines Leibes* (ARWAW, Sonderreihe Papyrologica Coloniensia XIV, 1988); Pseudo-Clementine Homilies 3.20.2. Cf. HippRef 9.14.1 (for Elkesai); also the logion of the Gospel of the Hebrews, according to which the Firstborn Son had been awaited as "requies mea" in all the prophets (Jerome, in Isa 11:2).

of thought, the λόγος σπερματικός, a universal figure in pre-Christian and para-Christian thought, allowed humanity as a whole to benefit from divine revelation.[73] Not only could 1:11 ("He came to what was his own, and his own people did not receive him,...") be understood as referring to such pre-Christian history but already 1:10 as well as 1:4b-5 could be thought of as the coming of the Logos into the world. From this point of departure 1:12–13 would not refer directly to the Christian community but to those people who accepted the revealer prior to the Jesus event, believed in his name, and thus became τέκνα θεοῦ.[74] In such a context the verses 1:6–8 do not stand in isolation but the "witness" John is numbered among the "children of God" who recognized and acknowledged the Logos (1:12). Nevertheless, it is clear that, however much he may be concerned with the revelation of the Preexistent One, the intention of the Evangelist is not focused on the time before Christ but is oriented to the revelation in Jesus Christ.

In whatever manner the details of the relationship between the pre-Christian being of the Logos and his incarnation in Jesus Christ are conceptualized, it is clear that 1:14 contains the real affirmation of the incarnation. Here for the second and last time in the Gospel of John the term λόγος occurs. Luther translated the Greek term with "word," as it at first seemed appropriate from the Greek linguistic tradition. It is clear, however, that the absolute use of λόγος in Johannine usage refers to a person, which is not adequately conveyed by the translation "word." When Goethe warned against letting the pen hurry too quickly past this text, his warning is all the more important for an academic discipline that must work through the results of the study of the history of religion. Dr. Faustus had good reasons for considering the translation "word" too weak to represent the event it intends. But is his suggestion, that the term be translated with "deed," any more appropriate? That everything depends on "action" corresponds to the activistic striving of the modern age. However, the One sent by the father is not only more than human language can express; he is also more than human action can accomplish; he is a mythical heavenly being who paradoxically assumes human σάρξ; his being is essentially divine, as is affirmed by 1:1–2, and he represents cosmic and pre-cosmic reality. All this indicates that the term Logos, precisely because it means "the only God" (1:18), cannot be definitively translated, for it points to one whose existence is before and outside the world. It is not accidental that even in this locus classicus of the incarna-

---

[73]   Cf. Justin Apol 1.46; Protev James 11.2.

[74]   It is no accident that the term τέκνα θεοῦ is mentioned elsewhere only in John 11:52, in reference to the Jewish people. Cf. also R. Bultmann, *Gospel of John* 59, note 2: the "source" in 1:12 "spoke of the few individuals who had received the revelation and who thus were exceptions in the different generations."

tion doctrine a gap becomes visible between the person of the Logos and his appearance in history; for the Logos is only recognized in the reflection of his divine essence, namely his δόξα (1:14b). The word Logos is untranslatable in the same way that a myth is untranslatable. But since a myth can and must be interpreted, it must be asked what the Evangelist means when he speaks of the λόγος: he thereby describes Jesus Christ the only one born from the Father.

Is the Johannine Logos "vere homo et vere deus" or— in the words of the Athanasian creed, "perfectus Deus, perfectus homo?"[75] It is clear that neither the terminology nor the conceptual world of the later christological dogmas of the ancient church can be presupposed for the Gospel of John. Yet it is here that the question which has received controversial answers in scholarly investigation is raised—the question of the *Docetism* of the Gospel of John.

From the perspective of E. *Käsemann*, 1:14a is to be interpreted on the basis of 1:14b:[76] In his view, the doxa-Christology is decisive for understanding the Johannine Son of God Christology. The Johannine Jesus is "a god who strides across the earth." His earthly life is no more than the "foil" for his heavenly revelation. His obedience is accomplished in his return to the Father. Thus the descent and deployment, the mission and return of the Son are the central motifs of the Christology of the Fourth Gospel. From this point of departure Jesus' miracles are understood as manifestations of his δόξα, as are the "monologue-like" speeches of Jesus which are thus also not to be interpreted in a soteriological sense but represent dogmatic reflections on the inner divine relation between Father and Son.

In such a perspective the "church under the Word" is also not to be seen within the framework of the usual ecclesiology of the New Testament church. If the non-worldly δόξα is the decisive content of the advent of the Son of God, so too the church is a non-worldly quantity unrelated to history. It thus lives as a convential-like branch of Christianity with a Hellenistic-enthusiastic character, which interprets the sending of Jesus in terms of a "naive docetism." It is the "relic of a branch of early Christianity that had been forced into a corner." The "Christian unity" with which it is concerned is based on the unity of Father and Son, that is on the divine love. This separates it from the world. The Johannine love commandment also has a similar anti-world and esoteric character. This difference is precisely what distinguishes it from the Synoptic command to love the neighbor. The inference seems to lie near at hand that the canonicity of the Fourth Gospel is problematic, that this Gospel is to be designated neither apostolic nor orthodox. The above is Käsemann's understanding of the Fourth Gospel, and accords with his judgment that the author of 3 John is to be considered a "heretic and witness."

*Günther Bornkamm* devoted an extensive and thoroughly critical review to Käsemann's book.[77] Bornkamm acknowledges that, to be sure, there are traces of a docetic-gnostic theology and the image of a god striding across the earth is to be found

---

75  BSLK 29.46.
76  Käsemann, *The Testament of Jesus* 6. Cf. also L. Schottroff, *Der Glaubende und die feindliche Welt* 295–296.
77  G. Bornkamm, "Zur Interpretation des Johannesevangeliums," *EvTh* 28 (1968) 8–25 (= *Geschichte und Glaube 1, Gesammelte Aufsätze III* (BEvTh 48) (Munich: Kaiser, 1968) 104–121); F. Hahn, *Der Prozess Jesu nach dem Johannesevangelium*

in the Gospel of John; they are, however, elements of the pre-Johannine tradition. The Gospel itself is interpreted "backwards" from the testimony of the Paraclete. In this testimony it is not so much the earthly Jesus who is presented but the "one who completed his mission on the cross." This implies a critique of the pre-Johannine docetic tradition. It thus corresponds to the process of the formation of the Johannine circle, since 1 John also argues in an antidocetic fashion. "Gnosticism" is therefore the presupposition of the Fourth Gospel, which is itself anti-Gnostic, as can be seen in 1:14 (with 14a taken as determinative). But it also includes the idea that God turns graciously to the world which is understood as God's own creation. Also supporting this conclusion is the fact that the Gospel of John otherwise exhibits no Gnostic dualism (the heavenly origin of the redeemed, gathering of the sparks of light out of the world, and such).[78]

In contrast to 1 John, the Fourth Gospel contains no polemic against current docetics or docetic doctrines that are directed to an actual situation. The theology of the Evangelist spans different streams that have both struggled against and mutually influenced each other in the history of the Johannine school. In that the Evangelist seeks to bring these together into a unity, his work includes views that do tend in the direction of docetism, as well as ideas that are more antidocetic. An original *docetic tendency* may be supposed to have stood behind the doxa-Christology (already in 1:14b),[79] in the negative evaluation of the κόσμος (e. g. 9:39; differently 3:17; 12:47!; and then 12:31; 14:17, and elsewhere) or in the affirmation that the eschatological events are already present (the presence of the resurrection in the Logos, 11:25; the judgment, 3:19; 16:8, 11). Moreover, this original docetic tendency may be seen in the interpretation of the cross as "exaltation" (e. g. 3:14: ὑψόω = docetic concept of ascension from the cross?). In addition, the question is to be posed concerning the extent to which the language of Johannine dualism (light and darkness, life and death, truth and lie, and such) have been influenced by the debate with docetism.[80] Over against all this there appears to have been an original *antidocetic tendency* at work in the massive appreciation for the sacra-

---

(EKK-Vorarbeiten 2. Zürich-Einsiedeln-Köln-Neukirchen-Vluyn: Neukirchener, 1970) 23–96; E. Schweizer, "Jesus der Zeuge Gottes. Zum Problem des Doketismus im Johannesevangelium," in *Studies in John* (FS J. N. Sevenster). (NT.S 24. Leiden: E. J. Brill, 1970) 161–168. For critique of L. Schottroff, *Der Glaubende*, cf. K.-W. Tröger, "Ja oder Nein zur Welt. War der Evangelist Johannes Christ oder Gnostiker?" *ThV* 7 (1976). On M. Lattke, *Einheit im Wort*, cf. die discussion by N. Walter in *ThLZ* 102 (1977) 580–583.

[78] Bornkamm, "Interpretation des Johannesevangeliums" 23.

[79] Still valuable is the presentation of material on this subject by W. Schmithals, *Neues Testament und Gnosis* (EdF 208. Darmstadt: Wissenschaftliche Buchgesellschaft, 1984) 116–118.

[80] Docetic motifs may also be assumed to have affected the motif of "abiding in Christ" (14:20; 15:4ff) and the preexistence Christology (3:13, 31; 8:23). However, J. Becker, "Beobachtungen zum Dualismus im Johannesevangelium," *ZNW* 65 (1974) 71–87 overestimates the possibility of evaluating the dualism of the Gospel of John by literary-critical methods.

ments (6:51ff; 19:34), as also in the miracle tradition (2:1ff; 11:1ff).[81]
Additional pointers in the direction of a realistic, non-docetic theology are
the passion and resurrection traditions (chaps. 18–19; 20–21), the apocalyptic elements in the Gospel of John (e. g. βασιλεία, 3:3, 5; a future κρίσις,
5:24, 29; the futurity of the resurrection, 11:24; cf. 6:39–40, 44, "I will
raise that person up on the last day," and other such statements), and the
general fact of the composition of the Gospel itself, which—even if to a
smaller degree than in the Synoptics—results in a historicization of the
life-of-Jesus tradition (cf. 1:45).

At the level of the Gospel composition the author unifies these different tendencies. The Evangelist understands his conception to be able to
unite both *distance from the world* of the Logos and his own (1:10; 8:23;
9:39; 14:17ff; 18:36: "my kingdom is not from this world") and *gracious
turning toward the world* (3:16 "For God so loved the world...;" 12:47: "I
came not to judge the world but to save the world"). The same is true of
the question of present versus future: the *judgment* is expected as a future
reality (κρίσις, 5:24, 29) but it is "already now" present in the person of the
Revealer (12:31ff). So also the resurrection: the apocalyptic expectation of
the resurrection of *the* dead (pl.) is taken over from the tradition (11:24)
but at the same time is affirmed for the presence of the Christ (11:25).
Doubtless, the Evangelist's emphasis falls on present eschatology. Such
eschatological statements oriented to the present—differently than would
have been conceivable in the docetism of the Johannine school tradition—
are provided with "historical" characteristics. This goal is also served by
the incorporation of the miracle tradition into the Gospel which provides
a historical framework for the appearance of the Revealer. By depicting the
dialectic of eschaton and history, the present and future of eschatological
salvation, the objective reality of salvation and spiritualizing interpretation, the Evangelist fundamentally affirms the dialectic inherent in the
revelatory event.

Such a dialectic is programmatically set forth in 1:14. Even if it is
argued that this verse represents the pre-Johannine tradition of the Logos
hymn, it should be acknowledged that it receives a key function in the
context of the theology of the Evangelist,[82] since it is here that are found
the opposing pair of concepts σάρξ and δόξα and the dialectic between

---

[81]    The judgment about how to classify the Johannine miracle tradition is dependent
on the question of whether this tradition possessed in the Johannine circle a docetic
function analogous to the pre-Synoptic miracle tradition that made Jesus' deeds
transparently revelatory of his deity, or whether they must be understood in terms
of their own realism as representing the work of Jesus in an antidocetic manner.
Cf. W. Schmithals, *Neues Testament und Gnosis* 117.

[82]    Differently J. Becker, "Beobachtgungen zum Dualismus" 77 note 17: "1:14 remains
an isolated citation in the Fourth Gospel. One would be well advised to ignore it
in discussing the Christology of the Evangelist."

eschaton and history that are united in the person of the Logos. For the author this is no docetic statement—1:14a is unthinkable in a docetic system!—but it is also not a matter of an antidocetic polemic, since it cannot be shown—as said above—that the situation in which the Fourth Gospel was written was influenced by docetic "opponents." The truth is that 1:14 is a genuine expression of the Evangelist's own theology. The historical and eschatological dimension articulated here characterizes the Gospel's whole presentation of the Christ: the paradox of the unity of God and humanity in the person of Jesus Christ as the Logos. Of course, it is not a matter of an absolute paradox in the sense of the *Athanasianum*.[83] It should rather be asked whether a "docetic remnant" remains. However much the advent of the Incarnate One in the empirical world has the character of an instructive pointer, his essential being, namely that he is the Son from the Father, is only recognized by his eschatological doxa. To express this state of affairs, the expression "naive docetism" is certainly too strong. Nonetheless an indispensable *Prae* of the transcendent is appropriate for revelatory thought, however much the Evangelist strives for a dialectical balance. Other christological texts (e. g. Phil 2:6–11; Heb 1:1ff) give evidence of a corresponding way of thinking. Even the Synoptic Jesus and the Christology of Paul make it clear that the "Son" as the "Sent One" by the Father (cf. e. g. Gal 4:4; 1 John 4:9) cannot be recognized as such on the basis of empirically demonstrable "facts," but only through a "sending" activated from beyond that is the event of eschatological salvation. In this manner the Johannine concept of revelation distinguishes itself from an acute docetic or antidocetic problematic and brings it into harmony with the christological understanding of revelation of the New Testament in general.

## 2. The Christological Titles

The priority of the eschatological dimension, the special significance of the Son's having been "sent," becomes clear from the christological titles used by the Evangelist. A distinctive title is the adjective μονογενής (1:14), which Luther translated as "eingeboren" ("native;" "innate;" "hereditary;" KJV "only begotten;" NRSV "only"). The meaning is "only," "unique." The background of the expression in the history of religions covers a broad spectrum.[84] The title appears for deities in Orphic tradition, especially in Greek cosmological tradition documented by Plato and the Neoplatonists, according to which the cosmos itself in relation to God is a μονογενής. It is also found in this sense in (Christian) Gnostic literature.[85] It is striking

---

83    BSLK 29.46–48.

84    Cf. G. Strecker, *Johannine Letters* 150–151; J. A. Fitzmyer, μονογενής *EWNT* 2:1081–1083; R. Bultmann, *Johannine Epistles* 67 note 13.

85    E. g. Basilides according to Clement of Alexandria, Strom 5.11.74.3.

that Sophia is also designated πνεῦμα μονογενές.[86] Both examples in the Johannine prologue (cf. in addition to 1:14 also 1:18 μονογενής Θεός)[87] testify to the unity of the Logos with God the Father. This harmonious divine unity reflects the nature of the Logos and thereby also characterizes the nature of Jesus' mission as the "Sent One" as portrayed by the Evangelist.

Similarly, the title υἱὸς τοῦ Θεοῦ articulates the transcendent element in the appearance of Jesus Christ in this world. John adapts the term from early Christian tradition (11:27; cf. Mark 1:11; 9:7; 15:39 and elsewhere). This early Christian tradition, not the Old Testament description for the king of Israel, is the immediate background for the term from the perspective of the history of traditions. Both Jewish and Hellenistic influences are present in the broader context of the term. In the Gospel of John the title is used in connection with the Prologue (as in the preaching of John the Baptist, 1:34), and must be understood in relation to the λόγος concept. This means that in the Gospel of John, Jesus the "Son of God" is incorporated in a different coordination system than is the case in the Synoptics (cf. Mark 1:11: adoption at baptism; Matthew and Luke: Son of God by being born "ex virgine"). For the Fourth Gospel, Jesus is the Preexistent One: "Before Abraham was, I am" (8:58); thus John the Baptist also testifies to this (1:15). Preexistence is the appropriate category not only for Jesus as the Logos but also as Son of God, as indicated by the concept of "being sent" used in this connection (10:36). As "Son of God" he came into the world (11:27), exists in the glory of his Father (11:4; 17:1ff), and it is because of this claim that he is persecuted by the Jews and accused before Pilate (10:36; 19:7), although at the same time he is the "King of Israel," as confessed by Nathanael (1:49). As Son of God he has the quality not only of preexistence but eschatological existence, since in accordance with apocalyptic ideas the resurrection of the dead will be initiated by "the voice of the Son of God" (5:25).

The absolute designation ὁ υἱός ("the Son") is to be distinguished from the above titles. Except for the variant in 1:18 it is found only in the mouth of Jesus. As shown by Matthew 11:27par and Mark 13:32par, this usage is pre-Johannine.[88] It is also documented in 1 John 2:22–24; 4:14; 5:12 and 2 John 9. The Father/Son relationship is characterized by the sending

---

[86] WisSol 7:22. The term μονογενής is not found in Philo but he can describe the λόγος as the πρωτόγονος υἱὸς (θεοῦ) (Agric 51), i.e. the firstborn, who stands in first place, and thus approaches the Johannine usage of μονογενής.

[87] As an adjective also in 3:16 (υἱόν) and 3:18 (υἱοῦ τοῦ θεοῦ); cf. 1 John 4:9; in the rest of the New Testament the phrase is not found in the christological sense but only in with its ordinary natural meaning of an only son (Heb 11:17; similarly Luke 7:12; 8:42; 9:38).

[88] Cf. also 1 Corinthians 15:28; Hebrews 1:2, 5, 8 and elsewhere.

of the Son by the Father (3:17), the love of the Father for the Son (3:35; 5:20), or the unity of Father and Son (5:19, 23; 7:16ff; 12:44ff). The unity of the Son with the Father, as well as his preexistence, are manifested in Jesus' knowledge of the future (e. g. 13:1, 3, 27, 38 and elsewhere), and in the manner in which Jesus goes to meet his destiny of his own free will (13:21; 19:11). Moreover, that the Son has a commission from the Father is clear: the Father has given the authority to judge over to the Son (5:22, 27); he has conferred on the Son to have life in himself (5:26; cf. 3:36). In the care with which this commission is carried out by the Son, the Father is glorified (14:13; 17:1). Thereby Jesus is distinguished from the δοῦλοι, who are subject to sin. In contrast to them he is "the Son" who abides forever, and whose distinguishing sign is freedom (8:35–36). Such statements about himself stand in the larger context of the preexistence idea and the descent from heaven, as does that of the concept of the return of the Revealer to the Father (cf. 3:13; 6:62; 8:21; 16:28).

Instead of using Χριστός as a proper name, the Fourth Evangelist prefers the titular usage ὁ Χριστός, especially when used in relation to "the Jews" (4:29; 7:26ff) but of course also as a general christological title (20:31: the Christ = Son of God; see also 11:27). The Evangelist is fully aware that ὁ Χριστός ("the anointed") was originally a Jewish messianic title; he knows that this title is the translation of Μεσσίας (1:41; cf. 4:25: ὁ λεγόμενος Χριστός; also Matt 1:16; 27:17, 22). From these data it already comes to light in the Christology of the Gospel of John that "the Jews" have a special significance. This is seen also in the Johannine discussion of Jesus as *Son of David*, which calls forth a "division" among the people and brings to light the double meaning of the "Jewish" christological titles (7:42): on the one hand this conceptuality points out the empirical location of Jesus' advent within salvation history but on the other hand "the Jews" stand for unbelievers as such; the rejection of the Revealer by the world is illustrated by their conduct. To the extent that the christological titles reveal such a "Jewish" background, they also include the idea that the appearance of the Logos means rejection by the world and the world's *krisis*.

From Christian tradition the Evangelist takes over the term υἱὸς τοῦ ἀνθρώπου, which has its roots in Jewish apocalyptic.[89] Thus the function of the Son of Man as the final judge can still be seen (5:27). That means that the three groups of Son of Man sayings found in the Synoptic tradition (1. future 2. present work 3. suffering, dying and rising Son of Man) are all found in the Gospel of John. The first group is the most weakly attested, just as the apocalyptic element in general recedes in the Fourth Gospel. The others are reformulated in typical Johannine fashion: the present work of the Son of Man is characterized by the fact that Jesus opens the

---

[89]   Daniel 7:13; 1 Enoch 46:2–4; 48:2; 62:7, 9, 14; 63:11; 69:26–27; 70:1; 71:17; 4 Ezra 13:3, 5, 12, 25, 32, 51.

eyes of the blind—in contrast to the world's inability to see (9:39); the present work of the Son of Man is at the same time the time of the promise of bread from heaven, namely eternal life (6:27; cf. 6:53), as also the time of heavenly epiphanies (1:51). The present activity of the Son of Man is incorporated into the mythological schema of descent and ascent to heaven (3:13; 6:62). Moreover, the Fourth Evangelist emphasizes that the person of the suffering and rising Son of Man forms a unit, as expressed by connecting the statements about divine glory with the passion (12:23; 13:31), and especially by interpreting the cross as the exaltation of the Son of Man (3:14; 8:28; 12:34). This final group is of particular significance in the Gospel of John; it is characteristic of the late composition of John in comparison with the Synoptics. In the Gospel of John the concept of the Son of Man is extensively developed and Christianized in the Johannine sense.

The ἐγώ εἰμι sayings constitute the outstanding self-interpretations of the Logos-Revealer. They can be formally classified in four categories: (1) extended metaphors (6:35; 8:12; 10:11, 14; 11:25; 14:6; 15:1, 5) (2) indirect sayings (with reference to the preceding: 6:41); (3) absolute "I am" (8:24, 28); (4) "I am he" (from an originally secular recognition formula: cf. 6:20; Mark 6:50; also John 18:5b-6, where 18:5a = Ἰησοῦς ὁ Ναζωραῖος.[90]

The origin of this terminology is disputed from the perspective of the study of the history of religions. Parallels are found (1) in Mandean or Gnostic literature, as well as in the magical papyri (therefore in relatively late sources),[91] (2) in the Old Testament (where, however, here is no connection between an "I am" [Yahweh] and a "metaphor;"[92] (3) in Oriental tradition (Babylonian, Egyptian [Isis]).[93] In the context of the Fourth Gospel the interpretation is clear: the ἐγώ εἰμι sayings manifest the claim of Jesus Christ as the Logos-Revealer. The metaphors are transparent; they

---

[90] The formula appears with a substantival participle or prepositional phrase in 4:26; 8:18, 23. John 6:35 provides an example of an ἐγώ εἰμι saying as an extended metaphor. This category includes further distinctions: (1.) the "recognition formula" in which a revelatory saying is expressed in the order (a) presentation ("I am") and (b) metaphor ("the bread of life"); to this is joined (2.) an additional soteriological clause or phrase or a promise with (a) invitation ("whoever comes to me... and whoever believes in me...") and (b) a promise ("will never hunger... and will never thirst").

[91] Cf. Left Ginza 3.47; Right Ginza 2.3 (texts in M. Lidzbarski, *Ginza. Der Schatz oder Das grosse Buch der Mandäer* [QRG 13, Gruppe 4, 1925; reprinted 1979] ). English translation in Werner Foerster, *Gnosis*, vol. 2 (Oxford: Clarendon, 1974).

[92] The formula setting forth sayings and speeches אני יהוה (LXX ἐγὼ κύριος) is especially frequent in Ezekiel (e. g. 15:7; 36:36). The LXX of Ezek 28:9 has a polemical εἰμι ἐγώ. The expression ἐγώ εἰμι is often found in ordinary speech between human beings (e. g. Judges 6:18 LXX; Job 33:31 LXX).

[93] Cf. A. Deissmann, *Light from the Ancient East* 136–145.

are not to be understood literally but utilize a symbolic language that articulates the claim of the Revealer to be the true Life. The sayings therefore have a christological-soteriological point. The required response is faith that does not need a legitimizing sign (cf. 6:35).

### c)  The Revelation

Bultmann, R. "γινώσκω," *TDNT* I 1964, 688–719.
Bultmann, R. "The Concept of Revelation in the New Testament," *Existence and Faith: Shorter Writings of Rudolf Bultmann*, Schubert M. Ogden, ed. New York: Meridian, 1960, 58–59.
Bultmann, R. and Lührmann, D. "φανερόω," *TDNT* IX, (1973) 4–6.

*Conceptuality*

Revelation terminology is not found nearly as often as one would have expected on the basis of the Prologue. The verb ἀποκαλύπτω appears only once (12:38, in a quotation), γνωρίζω only twice (15:15; 17:26), which is paralleled by the more frequent φανερόω (compare 17:6 with 17:26; eight times in the Gospel, seven times in 1 John). These instances are mostly connected with the speeches of Jesus: his function consists in revealing the Father to the world. His revelation is not merely the communication of hitherto unknown information or new rules for correct conduct. The content of the revelation of Jesus Christ is rather the "Truth," which is represented by the person of the Revealer himself (14:6). The revelation of Jesus Christ as the one sent by the Father appeals to the insight of human beings; it challenges them to recognize him for who he is, and through him the Father (γινώσκω stands beside πιστεύω: 6:69; 10:38; 17:8; cf. 1 John 4:16). Since it is oriented to the Truth, such a "knowledge" (Erkennen) is at the same time an "acknowledgement" (Anerkennen), that means surrendering the whole person to God. Thus the opposite possibility also becomes clear wherever people close themselves off to the offer of the Revealer and do not acknowledge him (1:5, 10: in the world).

*1.  The World (Cosmos)*

As the one sent from the Father, the Logos-Revealer is fundamentally separate from the world (cf. 8:23). The being of the world is contrary to the heavenly being of the Logos. The world's being is determined by the ἄρχων τοῦ κόσμου, who dominates the world and imprisons it within its anti-God nature (12:31; 14:30; 16:11). In contrast, the kingdom of Jesus Christ is not from this world (18:36); it includes renunciation of claims to power and self assertion by force. It thus corresponds to the fact that the Logos is a preexistent heavenly being who existed in unity with the Father before the foundation of the world (17:5; cf. 1:15).

On the other hand, in the Johannine understanding the cosmos is not "per se" fallen under the power of the Evil One and is not simply to be equated with it. Differently than in the Gnostic systems,[94] it is not understood primarily in terms of substance; on the contrary, as God's creation it was originally oriented to God (cf. 1:10). To the extent that it is now in rebellion against God, this is to be seen in terms not of nature but of history. It leaves room for actions for which human beings themselves are responsible. This is in harmony with the view of the Fourth Gospel that the cosmos is not primarily identified with the world of "nature," but with the world of human action and history (cf. 12:19). Humanity, to the extent that it stands under the domination of the devil, shares his evil nature (8:44). Precisely for this reason it needs liberation. This is the point of departure for understanding the sending of the Son of God into the world. He came into the world not to condemn the world but to save it (3:17; 12:47). This salvation takes place as God turns to the world in love (3:16).

The comparison of the Logos-Revealer with the Light (1:4–5; cf. 8:12; also 9:5; 12:46) is an element of the Johannine "light/darkness" dualism, which has deep roots in the history of religion.[95] In regard to understanding the Johannine view of the cosmos, this means that the world is located within the framework of this dualistic system. It stands on the negative side, corresponding to the "darkness" (σκοτία), for the Son of God comes into the world as light into the darkness (12:46). Alongside such metaphorical identification with darkness, the cosmos is also to be understood as the realm of the "lie" (ψεῦδος, 8:44), for there is no recognition and acknowledgment of the truth within it. Thus it is the realm of servitude under sin; it is the sphere of those who commit sin and thereby become slaves to sin (8:34; cf. Rom 6:16–17). Whoever sins has also fallen under the power of death (8:21, 24). The Fourth Evangelist does not reflect on the cause of humanity's state of un-salvation. He does not take up the Jewish tradition of the fall of Adam into sin or the corresponding idea of "original sin." Neither is it a matter of a fate, as though humanity had been unconditionally delivered over to this destiny as in Gnosticism but it is a matter of a historical event, even if it is not presupposed that each person has made a conscious decision against the truth. On the contrary: the example of "the Jews" in the Gospel of John shows that they understand themselves as the descendents of Abraham and on this ground claim to be free from any servitude. Nevertheless they do not understand; they reject the claim of the Revealer Jesus Christ, who wants to bring them into true freedom (8:31ff); they claim they are able to see and precisely for this reason they remain in the blindness of sin (9:41). Life in falsehood, sin,

---

94   Cf. Corp Herm 6.4; see also NHC 2.4.94 (142), 5–13; NCH 2.5.99 (147), 2–22.
95   Cf. Diog Laert 8.26; Philo Abr 205; 1QS 3.13ff; 1QM 13.10–12

and subjection to death points to a situation that is objectively hopeless but of which the individual is not aware. This does not remove the responsibility of human beings for their own destiny but this makes clear that the problematic with which their situation is burdened transcends a purely intellectual understanding and concerns the reality of their existence. There is no escape hatch from one's being in this world of untruth; it is total. And this situation is all the more hopeless, since the worldly human being takes untruth for truth, darkness for light, and death for life (cf. 9:40–41).

## Excursus: The "Jews" in the Gospel of John

Barrett, C. K. *The Gospel of John and Judaism.* London: SPCK, 1975.

Grässer, E. "Die antijüdische Polemik im Johannesevangelium," *NTS* 11, (1964/65) 74–90; also in *Text und Situation, Gesammelte Aufsätze zum Neuen Testament,* E. Grässer, ed. Gütersloh: Gerd Mohn, 1973, 50–69.

Grässer, E. "Die Juden als Teufelssöhne," *Antijudaismus im Neuen Testament,* W. Eckert et al., eds. Munich: Kösel, 1967, 157–170, 210–212; also in *Text und Situation.* Gütersloh: Gerd Mohn, 1973, 70–83.

Meeks, W. A. "Am I a Jew? Johannine Christianity and Judaism," *SJLA* 12 (1975) 168–186.

Neuhaus, D. (ed.) *Teufelskinder oder Heilsbringer—die Juden im Johannesevangelium.* ArTe 64. Frankfurt: Peter Lang, 1990.

Thyen, H. "'Das Heil kommt von den Juden'," *Kirche* (FS G. Bornkamm), D. Lührmann and G. Strecker, eds. Tübingen: J. C. B. Mohr (Paul Siebeck), 1980, 163–184.

Wrede, W. *Charakter und Tendenz des Johannesevangeliums.* SGV 37. Tübingen: J. C. B. Mohr (Paul Siebeck), 1933.

Apart from Acts, which thematically presents the gradual separation of Christianity from Judaism as a historical development, in no New Testament book does the word Ἰουδαῖος occur so frequently as in the Gospel of John (71 instances). It is used mostly in the plural, and always refers to members of the Jewish people. To be sure, the Evangelist is also acquainted with the respected name Ἰσραήλ (1:31, 49; 3:10; 12:13; cf. 1:47), so that the use of the expression "the Jews" already connotes a certain distancing, since in Judaism it is used mainly not as a theological self-description (as is Ἰσραήλ) but is the usual designation of Jewish people by non-Jews (cf. 18:33ff).

Moreover, the Evangelist John distinguishes different groups within the Jewish people. Particularly significant are the "Pharisees," who, as in the Synoptic Gospels, are Jesus' counterparts in critical debate (8:13; 9:13, 15–16 [alternate with "the Jews" 9:18, 22]; 9:40; 12:19); they pursue him and seek to arrest him (7:32; cf. 4:1); they do not themselves come to faith (7:47–48) and prevent the people from believing (12:42). The Synoptic tradition had already known Pharisees (and Sadducees) as those addressed by John the Baptist (Matt 3:7). Analogously, also at the beginning of the

Fourth Gospel, Pharisees appear as those sent to the Baptist by the "Jews of Jerusalem" (1:24; alongside "priests and Levites" 1:19). That the picture is not uniform but that also in this Jewish "party" it is possible to find followers of Jesus, is illustrated by the Pharisee Nicodemus (3:1; cf. 7:50; 19:39).

When Nicodemus is described as a ἄρχων τῶν Ἰουδαίων (3:1) he is counted among the "upper class" (ἄρχοντες) of whom "many" stand on Jesus' side but "because of the Pharisees" do not confess him publicly (12:42; cf. 7:26, 48). In contrast the "high priests" (ἀρχιερεῖς)[96] are often named alongside the Pharisees (7:32, 45; 11:47, 57); like the Pharisees, they participate in pursuing Jesus and his disciples (7:23, 45; 11:47ff; cf. 12:10). But they do not represent the opinion of the people in general, even though they claim to act in behalf of the people (cf. with regard to ἔθνος: 11:48–52; 18:35). "The people" often provide a neutral background for Jesus' work (e. g. as ὄχλος 5:13; 11:42). They follow Jesus (6:2, 5, 22, 24; cf. Matt 14:13; also John 12:9ff). But they vacillate in their attitude; even if "many of the people" come to faith (7:31), there is still "division among the people" in regard to their relationship with Jesus (7:43).

A similar uneven usage may be confirmed for the word Ἰουδαῖοι. When it is used in contrast to Gentiles, then it means a member of the Jewish people.[97] A value judgment is not recognizable in this use of the term but it becomes clear that the author does not consider himself a member of the Jewish people but speaks of "the Jews" rather distantly as his story locates them either in the past life of Jesus (e. g. 10:19; 11:19, 31, 33, 36, 54; 12:9; 19:20–21), or when he looks back at their customs (2:6; 5:1; 18:20; 19:40, 42) or festivals ("Passover of the Jews," 2:13; 6:4; 11:55; "the Jewish festival of Booths," 7:2). While narrating these events he also mentions the "division among the Jews" (10:19; cf. 9:16, "among the Pharisees," so that the complexity of the way the Jewish people are presented by the Evangelist is confirmed when he can also report that "many of the Jews ... believed in him" (11:45; 12:11). Nonetheless, the majority of references point to their hostility toward Jesus and their rejection of his mission. While several texts are ambiguous, that the Jews demand a sign early in the story (2:18, 20) already implies a critical stance to Jesus and brings the Jewish opposition into focus as the specific horizon of the work of Jesus in the Fourth Gospel. As "disciples of Moses" (9:28), they are obligated to keep the Mosaic law (8:17), yet they do not actually keep it (7:19). And however much the individual commandments of the Old Testament/Jewish Law

---

[96]  In the singular also = "high priest;" Caiaphas 11:49: high priest "that year;" cf. 11:51; 18:13, 19, 22, 24.

[97]  E. g. 4:9, in distinction from the Samaritans. In distinction from the Romans, cf. the relation of Pilate to the Jews: 18:33, 35–36, 38–39. So also in the placard on the cross: 19:19, "king of the Jews;" cf. e. g. 19:3, 21.

may determine the life of the Jewish people (7:22–23: circumcision and Sabbath command), it is said just as clearly that "Moses in the Law, and the prophets" pointed to no one other than Jesus of Nazareth, and also that Moses' actions were typological anticipations of what is fulfilled in Jesus Christ (3:14: lifting up the snake as a model for the crucifixion of Jesus). Just as the Evangelist does not doubt that Mosaic faith should rightly lead to Jesus and must generate faith in Jesus, so also the lawgiver of the Old Testament, on whom the Jewish people set their hope, will become their accuser, since "he wrote about me" (5:46). There is thus a *line of salvation history* that leads from the history of Israel to Jesus: Abraham had already seen the day of the preexistent Son of God, even if the Son was before him (8:56–58). The "prophecy and fulfillment" schema is applied to the story of Jesus (e. g. 12:14–15, 37–41; 13:18; 19:24). This basic temporal feature also characterized the portrayal of the Jews in that their lack of understanding or misunderstanding of Jesus' mission is constantly emphasized (6:41, 52; 8:22, 57) and their rejection of Jesus (cf. even 5:10) with the reproach that he was possessed by a demon (8:48) eventuates in persecution (5:16; cf. 15:20). The hostile attitude of the Jews to Jesus is also seen in the fact that Jesus' disciples have "fear of the Jews" (7:13; 9:22; 19:38; 20:19) and that Jesus keeps his distance from them (11:54). One factor integral in the Gospel's construction is the intention of the Jews to put Jesus to death (5:18; 7:1, 19, 30; 8:37ff; 10:31ff; 11:8). In accord with this tendency is the fact that alongside the Roman "cohort" there were "police" from the high priests and Pharisees who came to arrest Jesus (18:3), and that "the Jews" asked for the acquittal of the bandit Barabbas instead of Jesus, that "the high priests and their police" joined in calling for Jesus' crucifixion, that "the Jews" demanded Jesus' death on the basis of their Law (18:38–40; 19:6–7). Furthermore, their concern that the corpses of those who had been executed not remain on the cross on the Sabbath, so as not to profane the Passover (19:31), is only consistent with this tendency.

The portrayal of the Jews in the Fourth Gospel is inserted within the framework of a "life of Jesus" and—as is also the case in the Synoptic gospels—interpreted in terms of (un-)salvation history. From this point of view, the attempts to trace the opposition between Jesus and the Jews to contemporary confrontations between Jewish leaders and the Evangelist and his community are to be evaluated with caution.[98] There is no direct polemic, which in any case would not have been impossible within a

---

[98]  Differently W. Wrede, *Charakter und Tendenz*; K. Wengst, *Bedrängte Gemeinde und verherrlichter Christus. Der historische Ort des Johannesevangeliums als Schlüssel zu seiner Interpretation* (BThSt 5. Neukirchen-Vluyn: Neukirchener, 181) 37–44; J. L. Martyn, *History and Theology in the Fourth Gospel* (New York, rev. 1979).

historical framework (cf. Matt 28:15). A detailed knowledge of the Judaism of the New Testament period is obviously not present. The Evangelist "John" owes the whole picture of the opposition of the Jewish people to Jesus to the Synoptic tradition, even if this is only articulated indirectly, in the alienated Johannine manner. In this process, the tendency to generalize stands out, since in contrast to the Synoptic Gospels individual groups are not distinguished within the people as a whole.[99] On the other hand, the prominent position of the Pharisees as opponents of Jesus known from the Synoptics is emphasized even more sharply. In particular, the shifting of responsibility for the death of Jesus to the Jewish people is a consistent extension of the line of (un-)salvation history of the Synoptic Gospels (cf. Matt 27:25). In John, no more than in the Synoptics, is it presupposed that the Jewish people could resume its special place within the history of salvation (differently Rom 11:25ff).

Such a historicizing and generalizing approach does not necessarily exclude the possibility that authentic historical elements are also included in the way the history is portrayed. They consist only of details, however (e. g. the reference to Caiaphas and Annas, 18:13, 24), so that the general evaluation must be that the Evangelist, who is distant from the actual historical facts, sought to express his own theological convictions. Since "historical" thinking predominates, it is not probable that the relation of church and synagogue of his own time is reflected in the story. On the contrary, even those passages where influences from the author's own situation have been supposed are by no means clear.

An outstanding example that is used as evidence for a sharp debate between the Fourth Evangelist and his community on the one side and contemporary Judaism on the other is provided by the ἀποσυνάγωγος-passages (9:22; 12:42; 16:2). The word ἀποσυνάγωγος is not found prior to the Fourth Gospel, either in pagan Greek authors or in the LXX. This suggests that it is an invention of the Evangelist himself. The first two references are entirely in the service of his portrayal of Jesus: *9:22* provides the motivation for the parents of the healed man, who decline to provide an explanation for the miraculous healing of their blind son because of their fear of the Jews. The magnitude of Jewish hostility is illustrated by the fact that "the Jews" wanted to exclude from the synagogue anyone who confessed faith in Jesus. In fact, the healed man was later "excluded" (probably to be understood literally, = "pushed out;" cf. 9:34–35 [NRSV "drove him out"]).

Similarly in *12:42*. High-ranking Jews do not confess their faith in Jesus "because of the Pharisees," since they fear being excluded from the synagogue. In the Evangelist's portrayal this is the fulfillment of Isaiah 6:10; the Jewish authorities are made blind because they honor human beings rather than God (12:43).

*16:2* is different in that it contains Jesus' prediction about his disciples that they are supposed to remember in the later time of persecution. The persecution will

---

[99] Missing from John are the "Sadducees" found frequently in the Synoptics, along with "tax collectors," "scribes," "Zealots," "Herodians;" nor are social distinctions mentioned.

include not only expulsion from the synagogue but the attempt to kill the disciples, which the persecutors will suppose is a service to God. The latter reference may allude to persecutions by Gentiles, since the Jews of the Roman Empire did not have the right of capital punishment. The unusual expression λατρείαν προσφέρειν could refer to the offering of sacrifice before the image of the emperor that was performed by lapsed Christians as evidence of their loyalty—as reported by Pliny.[100]

What is meant by ἀποσυνάγωγος? It is clearly not a matter of the Jewish ban that could be imposed by the synagogue in two different degrees; according to rabbinic tradition this was disciplinary measure internal to the synagogue that was intended to keep those who had violated the traditional rules within the synagogue or to restore them to it, and thus is explicitly not to be identified with excommunication.[101]

One can more likely suppose that the reference to exclusion from the synagogue is to a "consequence of the *Birkat ha-Minim*, namely a result of the curse pronounced against heretics in the Eighteen Benedictions, a liturgical prayer of the synagogue. Thus the Twelfth Benediction says: 'As for the Nazarenes [= Christians] and the Minim, may they perish immediately.'" However, this addition is found only in the Palestinian recension of the Eighteen Benedictions. The tradition is unstable, and "this text should be regarded as approximately the oldest but not as the prayer dating to the beginning of the second century A.D."[102] In the writings of the Church Fathers there is a clear reference to the persecution of Christians in the synagogue that can be interpreted as reflecting the Eighteen Benedictions, first in Epiphanius (Heresies 29:9), then in Jerome (in his commentary on Isa 5:18–19; 49:7; 52:4ff). In contrast, Justin only refers very generally to the fact that Christian believers "were cursed in the synagogue" (Dial 16.4 and elsewhere). On these grounds, it is improbable that at the time of the composition of the Fourth Gospel the cursing of Christians was already a part of the Eighteen Benedictions. In no case is such cursing identified with exclusion from the synagogue. It is also questionable whether this may be seen as a "consequence" of the Eighteen Benedictions; it is more probable that the cursing of "Christians and heretics" already presupposes a separation of church and synagogue. Against this is Luke 6:22, one of the oldest Christian witnesses that affirms a separation of Jews and Christians, according to which "hatred" of members of the Christian community is connected to defamation and disfellowshiping (lit. "cast out your name as evil"). However, it is not here a matter of a legal act of excommunication from the synagogue. Neither is this the case in 1 Thess 2:14–16, where the persecution of members of the Christian community by the Jewish people of Judea is mentioned. Regardless of how the question of whether there were conflicts with "the Jews" in the tradition of the Johannine school that immediately precedes the Fourth Gospel may be answered, it is quite likely that the origin of the word ἀποσυνάγωγος

---

[100] Cf. Pliny Ep 10.96.5–6 (Pliny to Trajan); *Ep* 10.97.1 (Trajan to Pliny).

[101] Cf. Strack-Billerbeck 4.1.329–333; W. Schrage, ἀποσυνάγωγος, *TDNT* 7:848–852.

[102] E. Schürer, *The History of the Jewish People in the Age of Jesus Christ*, rev. and ed. G. Vermès, F. Millar and M. Black, eds. (Edinburgh: T. & T. Clark, 1979) 2:462.

On the one hand, a distinction must be made within the text of the Eighteen Benedictions, between (1) a curse against the "heretics" (Minim). This is supposed to have been added to the Eighteen Benedictions by Rabbi Samuel the Small (ca. 100 C. E.) at the instigation of Rabbi Gamaliel II (ca. 90 C. E.) (b Ber 28b) and (2) the reference to the "Nazarenes", which is found only in a secondary, singular recension of the text, the Geniza version (cf. Schürer, *History of the Jewish People*, 2:461–463, and J. Maier, *Jüdische Auseinandersetzung mit dem Christentum in der Antike* [EdF 177. Darmstadt: Wissenschaftliche Buchgesellschaft, 1982] 136–141; esp. 140–141).

is to be derived from the tendency of the Fourth Evangelist to portray "the Jews" as prototypes of the general rejection of the Revealer's appearance in the world.

In addition to the role played by "the Jews" as a component of the Johannine portrayal of salvation-history, they also have a significant place in the framework of Johannine dualism. As this is determined by the opposition of God and cosmos, light and darkness, truth and lie, as representatives of the cosmos they are assigned a place in the Johannine scheme as exemplifying the unbelieving world of humanity. They stand on the side of darkness (8:12), lie (8:44–45) and death (8:51); since they are "of this world," their origin is "from below" (8:23), since they did not recognize the One who is "from above" and "not of this world." Therefore they must die in their sins (8:24). If they take offense at Jesus' calling God his Father and making himself equal with God (5:18), and that he claims to have existed before Abraham (8:58; cf. 8:53), they thus show that they are ignorant of where the Revealer comes from and where he goes (7:33–34; 8:14). His appearance in this world does not fit their image of the Messiah, in which the Messiah is to come from Bethlehem, the city of David, not from Galilee (7:41–42). They know that Joseph is his father (6:42; cf. 1:45). There can be no doubt that this is not a dispute between different Jewish messianic expectations but concerns the radical contrast between the heavenly origin of the Son of God and the earthly orientation of his Jewish hearers. Their orientation challenges the truth claim of Jesus to be the light of the world (8:12–13). Because the Jews "judge by human standards" (literally "according to the flesh," 8:15) they remain in slavery—despite their descent from Abraham which, they believe, makes them free, for only the Son can make one truly tree (8:33ff). All of this means that they not only do not know the Son, they do not know the Father, and thus do not really believe in God (8:14, 19, 42). Salvation does indeed come from the Jews (4:22) but this statement is valid only in a preliminary sense in that it applies to the historical appearance of Jesus as a Jew, for true worship is a matter of Spirit and truth (4:23). Because the Jews do not consider the word of Jesus as the word of the Truth, they show themselves to be "children of the devil" and do not participate in being "from God" (8:44–47).

It is hardly the case that with this judgment the Evangelist is pursuing anti-Jewish or anti-Semitic goals. As has been shown, his concern is not to defeat concrete Jewish opponents. It is rather the case that he stands at the junction of two powerful streams of tradition: on the one hand the docetic-antidocetic tradition that has as its object the radical opposition of God and world, Spirit and flesh, truth and lie and uses the figure of "the Jews" as symbolic representatives of the world of unbelief, and on the other hand the Synoptic tradition of salvation history, according to which the Jesus event is embedded in the history of Israel that extends from the Old

Testament prophecies to its fulfillment in the cross and resurrection of
Jesus Christ, a history that results in Israel's loss of their privileged place
by the Jewish rejection of the Son of God. Both these different branches of
the tradition have in common that they are intended to facilitate the self-
orientation of the community and establish it in faith in the Son of God
Jesus Christ (cf. 10:27–28; 20:31).

## 2. The Judgment (Crisis)

Blank, J. *Krisis. Untersuchungen zur johanneischen Christologie und Eschatologie,*.
    Freiburg: Herder, 1964.
Bultmann, R. "The Eschatology of the Gospel of John," *Faith and Understanding* I, R.
    W. Funk, ed. New York: Harper & Row, 1969, 165–183.
Richter, G. "Präsentische und futurische Eschatologie im 4. Evangelium," *Studien zum
    Johannesevangelium*, J. Hainz, ed. BU 13, Regensburg: Pustet, 1977, 346–382; also
    in *Gegenwart und Kommenden Reich*, P. Fielder and D. Zeller, eds. SBB. Stuttgart:
    Katholisches Bibelwerk, 1975, 117–152.

The Gospel of John contains both future-apocalyptic and present-eschato-
logical sayings alongside each other, without harmonizing them. Past
scholarship has drawn a clear line of demarcation between them. Thus R.
Bultmann attributed all the passages in the Gospel of John that speak of
*future eschatology* to a redactor. This is correct in the case of 21:22. Here
it is the author of the Appendix who is speaking, and one may call him the
redactor. The parousia expectation in this passage is secondary. It is hardly
possible, however, to consider the whole complex of passages that affirm
future eschatology as secondary. Thus the words of Jesus that speak of his
"going ahead" to prepare a dwelling place for his own (14:2–3; 16:28;
17:24) fit smoothly into the Johannine conception and do not deny an
original future-eschatological component. With this point of departure, a
convincing argument cannot be made that denies that the statements
about a future resurrection of the dead belong to the theology of the Evangelist (5:21, 27, 28–29; 6:39ff; 11:24).

The *present eschatology* stands alongside the future. "Very truly, I tell
you, the hour is coming, and is now here, when the dead will hear the voice
of the Son of God, and those who hear will live (5:25)". With the advent
of the Son, the resurrection has already come into the world, and with the
resurrection, the judgment (9:39). The Lazarus story is a good illustration
of the juxtaposition of future and present eschatology (11:1ff). In 11:24
Martha is the advocate of the traditional future eschatology ("I know that
he will rise again in the resurrection on the last day."), to which Jesus
answers (11:25), "I am the resurrection and the life. Those who believe in
me, even though they die, will live, and everyone who lives and believes
in me will never die."

Present eschatology interprets future eschatology! But this means no
elimination of future statements but necessarily includes a tension in

terms of the content. Within this tension the Johannine emphasis is clearly on the side of the presence of the eschaton.[103] The temporal tension, the orientation to the future, has not been lost; it belongs to the universality of the Logos but it has lost its original importance.

The new element in the Johannine theology is that the eschaton has been made radically present in the Jesus event. This means that the content of the early Christian apocalyptic expectation has been extensively transformed, namely by appropriating these realities as already present. Thus it can be said in the sense of the Evangelist: the eschatological crisis, the event of the last judgment, already happens in the Jesus event.

Of course, it is also the case that the Synoptic Evangelists connected the this-worldly realization of salvation and disaster with the person of Jesus. In the Johannine conception, however, the present realization of the final judgment stands in a starker confrontation to the world, which is understood more negatively than in the Synoptics:

> And this is the judgment, that the light has come into the world, and people loved darkness rather than light because their deeds were evil. (3:19)

The coming of Jesus into the world is the eschatological event; it discovers (*ent-dekt* = discovers and removes the cover from) the true being of the cosmos. Accordingly, the meaning is not that the being of the world in the realm of falsehood is caused by the advent of the Revealer in that his message generates sin as its reaction but that the Revealer reveals the sinful being of the world for what it already is, a fallen world of sin and death. Thus it is said in 9:39:

> Jesus said, "I came into this world for judgment so that those who do not see may see, and those who do see may become blind."

People who encounter the Revealer are disclosed for what they really are; although they appear to see, in truth they are blind. The coming of Jesus pronounces the verdict that is irrevocably final, and confirms the world in its ungodly state of being. This will also be the function of the promised Paraclete, when he proves that "the ruler of the cosmos (already) is judged" (16:11).

Not only does the word "crisis" (κρίσις) mean "judgment," it can mean "division" as well. By appearing in this world as the incarnate Logos, Jesus

---

[103] With regard to the term "present eschatology," the intended meaning is the incursion of the eschaton into the present through the Christ-event. Since for the Evangelist the center of gravity of the Christ event already lies in the past, the term "present eschatology" in this context means that the salvation grounded in the past appearance in history of the Revealer Jesus Christ has become present and remains a present reality for the community after him (cf. the function of the Paraclete, and the Excursus on this below).

holds judgment, and the division takes place between faith and unfaith, between truth and lie, between life and death:

"Very truly, I tell you, anyone who hears my word and believes him who sent me has eternal life, and does not come under judgment but has passed from death to life." (5:24; cf. 1 John 3:14)

The division that results from the appearance of Jesus in this world leads the one to life, and leaves the other in death. The crisis of the cosmos that has become a present reality by the coming of the Logos in Jesus Christ means the execution of the final judgment (3:18; 12:31, 48). It brings the latent, already present condition of the world to light and to a "crisis," which results in confirming unbelievers in their state of untruth and death and establishes them there permanently as their real existence. Believers experience the opposite result: the possibility of a new life, and this is the goal of the revelatory ministry of the Son of God (cf. 1 John 4:17).

## 3.  Life

Bultmann, R., et al., "ζάω/ζωή," *TDNT* 2, (1964) 833–877.
Mussner, F. ΖΩΗ. *Die Anschauung vom ‚Leben' im vierten Evangelium unter Berück-sichtigung der Johannesbriefe*. MThS.H I/5. Munich: Kösel, 1952.
Schottroff, L. "ζῶ/ζωή," *EWNT* 2 (1981) 261–271.

The term ζωὴ αἰώνιος is a traditional "technical term" for the apocalyptic reality of salvation, "eternal life."[104] As the apocalyptic gift of salvation, this must not be misunderstood in a biological sense; it is not identical with βίος as the biological reality of physical existence. But it should also not be simply spiritualized, as though the gift of salvation were only a spiritual matter to be understood in some idealistic or spiritual sense. Rather, the apocalyptic gift of salvation, "eternal life," is a comprehensive concept that concerns the whole of human life. It is bound to the person of Jesus and to that extent is already a reality within the world of time. In the encounter with this reality, the terrors of death disappear, for the Revealer speaks:

I am the resurrection and the life. Those who believe in me, even though they die, will live, and everyone who lives and believes in me will never die. Do you believe this? (11:25–26)

The appearance of the Revealer in this world is an eschatological event; it makes the eschaton present, for it makes what was expected to happen at the eschaton already a present reality: the resurrection of the dead and eternal life.

---

[104] Cf. Daniel 12:2; 1 Enoch 37:4; 40:9.

On this basis, in the Johannine understanding, Jesus is more than a prophet. He is the prophet who is to come into the world (1:19ff; 6:14; 7:40).[105] Jesus is *the* prophet, because he brings the truth and the life that absolutely surpasses all preceding salvation (and un-salvation) history. He himself is the Life and the Truth, because he is the Way to the Father, and he is the Way to the Father, because in him *the* Life and *the* Truth are revealed (14:6). By surpassing the miraculous gift of the manna provided for the Exodus community, he himself is the Bread of God that comes down from heaven and gives life to the world, the "Bread of Life" (6:32ff).

The idea of the "bread of life" is not freed from the future aspect of death, for the reality of biological death is not negated; θάνατος is finally overcome and destroyed at the future eschaton. But "Life" is a reality "already now" present in Jesus and his community, not as an elixir of life but as an eschatological event that grounds human existence anew. The Fourth Evangelist has thus freed the church-apocalyptic idea of "eternal life" (as a reality of the Endtime) from its link to apocalyptic; the churchly apocalypticism is the presupposition for the Johannine conception in regard to tradition history but is no longer the substantial and functional center. For the Johannine understanding of death, this means: death has lost its power; it has been disarmed by the new all-pervasive power of life encountered in Jesus, the power that Jesus is in his own person. That applies to death in the comprehensive sense, as a spiritual and biological phenomenon which is at the same time a cosmic reality. Along with the cosmos itself, death is revealed for what it is and overcome as one of the powers that belong to the world of untruth and darkness.

The "Life" that the Revealer has brought into the world could in the Johannine understanding also be designated by other words: it is the σωτηρία, the "rescue" from death and ultimate fallenness (3:16–17).[106] This life is also the ἀλήθεια, that which is no longer concealed, that which is disclosed, the "Truth," which at the same time is turning away from the lie (14:6). Above all, this life is identical with ἀγάπη; this love cannot be attained by the world, for it is the love of the Father, who loves the Son, in order that the Son might love the world and his community (13:1; 15:9; 17:23). It is thus the love of the Father that encounters the world in the incarnate Son of God and which the Son mediates to the world. The love of God is not defined in a timeless, theoretical sense,[107] but is experienced in Jesus and is something that happens in encounter with Jesus.

If we ask how the event of the Father's love that is realized in Jesus becomes a reality in human life, we make a distinction that the subject matter itself does not allow: *Jesus' action*, which on the one hand represents the love of the Father, and on the other hand the *faith* of Jesus'

---

[105] In this regard cf. the revelatory figure in Gnosticism, of which at least the "true prophet" of the Pseudo-Clementines is reminiscent: Kerygmata Petrou H 3.17–21.

[106] Thus the Revealer can also be called "savior of the world" (4:42 σωτὴρ τοῦ κόσμου; cf. 1 John 4:14), or the "Door" (10:9, ἡ θύρα).

[107] That is only apparently the case in 1 John (4:8, 16: "God is love").

disciples who know themselves to be addressed, grounded, and determined by this event.

*Jesus' action*, which represents and makes present ἀγάπη and ζωή that become the foundation of authentic life, is carried out within the framework of the incarnation and exaltation of Jesus Christ. In this framework, which is more reminiscent of the myth of a Gnostic redeemer, with his descent from heaven and return there, than it is of the life of Jesus as portrayed in the Synoptics, is the manifestation of ζωή. In the first place, it becomes reality in the *word of Jesus*. In this word Jesus calls people to himself, and promises the gift that he himself is (6:35, the Bread of Life; 8:12, the Light; 11:25, the Life). In his word Jesus makes the claim to be the One he really is, the Son sent from the Father to give life to the world. Through his word Jesus calls for the decision of faith, the byproduct of which is unbelief, misunderstanding, and rejection.

But ζωή is manifest not only in the word of Jesus Christ as the Revealer. It is also met in Jesus' miraculous deeds. The Fourth Evangelist portrays the Son of God as a "divine man" who works miracles by the supernatural power with which he is endowed. It is significant that Jesus' miracles are not placed in the category of δυνάμεις but are designated as σημεῖα. As "signs" they make Jesus' earthly activity transparent, pointing to his δόξα as the "glory" of the preexistent Logos (2:11). They point to Jesus himself, who is more than any wonder worker; he is the bringer of truth and love. No differently than the word, so also the "signs" of Jesus are a call to the Revealer himself and to that which he brings.

The character of the σημεῖα as pointing beyond themselves not only comes to expression in the fact that Jesus' miraculous works as a whole direct the viewer's gaze to the one who does them but also in the manner in which they symbolically represent the eschatological salvation that Jesus brings. The wonderful "sign" of the multiplication of the loaves (6:1ff) expresses the faith that the Son of God himself is the Bread of Life. The miracle of healing the blind man (9:1ff) makes it clear that in Jesus the Light of the world is encountered. And the raising of Lazarus (11:1ff) has the symbolic meaning that Ζωή is salvifically present in the person of Jesus.

Moreover, this ζωή is revealed in the *death and resurrection of Jesus*. The *passion of Jesus* is the consummation of the sending of the Son, because in it the highest ἀγάπη of the Father comes to expression in the Son. The cosmos and its ruler cannot find any falsehood or sin in Jesus (cf. 7:18; 8:46; 1 John 3:5; he is without sin!). Nevertheless, the Son accepts suffering in order to fulfill the Father's command and thereby to bring ἀγάπη to reality. The death of Jesus is the expression of the Father's love. Therefore in the cross of Jesus the Father is glorified by the Son (17:4, "I glorified you on earth by finishing the work that you gave me to do."— the farewell discourses with the concluding "high priestly prayer" refer directly to the passion and death of Jesus). The crucifixion of Jesus means a "being glorified" (δοξασθῆναι) not only in regard to the Father but also to the Son, for "being crucified" is identical with "being lifted up/exalted" (ὑψω-θῆναι).[108] Through death on the cross Jesus returns to the glory that he had at the beginning as the Preexistent One. In this too, the "Life" he represents is manifested (cf. 12:32).

### d) The Church

Bull, K. M. *Gemeinde zwischen Integration und Abgrenzung.* BET 24. Frankfurt: Peter Lang, 1992.
Lindemann, A. "Gemeinde und Welt im Johannesevangelium," *Kirche* (FS G. Bornkamm) D. Lührmann and G. Strecker, eds. Tübingen: J. C. B. Mohr (Paul Siebeck), 1980, 133–161.
Onuki, T. *Gemeinde und Welt im Johannesevangelium.* WMANT 56. Neukirchen-Vluyn: Neukirchener, 1984.
Schnelle, U. "Johanneische Ekklesiologie," *NTS* 37 (1991) 37–50.
Schweizer, E. "Der Kirchenbegriff im Evangelium und in den Briefen des Johannes," E. Schweizer, *Neotestamentica.* Zürich-Stuttgart: Zwingli, 1963, 254–271.

As indicated above, the intention of the Fourth Evangelist is to report that the sending of th Logos means "Life" for humanity, that in the appearance of the Christ in this world the eschatological crisis happens "already now" and the eschaton as the pronouncement of judgment and salvation is near at hand. Accordingly, if the Gospel as a whole is oriented to a christological conception, then the question of the Johannine ecclesiology becomes problematic, just as in the case of the Synoptics. The history of the Johannine community, its problems and its challenges, are not the theme of the Gospel, for the time of the church begins after Easter, outside the narrative framework constructed by the Evangelist.

On the basis of the christological conception set forth by the Gospel of John, we may make the following basic statements concerning the ecclesiology that is presupposed but not explicated: Like the Evangelist's presentation of Christ, his presentation of the church is determined by a horizontal and a vertical dimension. The *horizontal dimension* of Johannine thought affirms that the history of the community is joined to the *vita Jesu.* The Johannine community understands itself on the basis of the Christ event that happened in its past and constitutes its foundation, and it is oriented toward the coming of the Son of God "on the last day," the time of the general resurrection of the dead (6:39ff; 11:24). In the horizontal time line, the time of Jesus is set off from the time of the church at the

---

[108] Cf. 3:14; 8:28. On the identity of "be crucified" and "be glorified" cf. 12:23, 28; 13:31–32; 17:1, 5, and elsewhere.

point when the gift of the Spirit, the Paraclete, is given (cf. e. g. 7:39;
14:16–17, 26; 15:26). This connects the Johannine ecclesiology with that
of the Synoptics, in which also the Spirit has the function of bridging the
time of Jesus to the time of the End.[109] It is not, however, filled in to the
same extent as in the Synoptics, in which after Easter the church of Jews
and Gentiles becomes the heir of the Jewish heritage and the plan of God
expressed in salvation history continues to be realized in the history of the
Christian community.

Moreover, the church of the Synoptic Gospels is also aware of a *vertical
dimension*, knowing that in every phase of its history it is directly related
to God, to the exalted Christ, or to the Spirit. It is not unimportant that
this understanding is correlated to the Synoptics' conception of salvation
history. In the Fourth Gospel such an eschatological vertical dimension is
determined by the manifestation of the preexistent Logos, who means for
the world the offer of ζωή and the reality of the κρίσις.

Should we assume that the community likewise knows itself to be
addressed in the same way by such a manifestation of the Logos? In order
to be able to answer this question, we must look at the Johannine characterization of the μαθηταί, the disciples of Jesus, who in the Gospel of John
are not only presented as the irreplaceable historical companions of Jesus
but also as prototypes of the members of the Christian community, and
thus of the church that is joined to the Jesus event. There can be no doubt
that in the first place the "disciples" are those who accompanied Jesus: the
five who are called first (1:35ff), then the twelve disciples of Jesus (6:67),
whose call is presupposed (corresponding to Mark 3:14, 16par; 6:70–71).
With them Jesus comes into Judea and baptizes (3:22);[110] Jesus opens the
way to the passion by his exemplary service of washing the disciples feet
(13:1ff). Within the more narrow circle of those who follow Jesus are also
found his mother (2:1ff), whose name is never explicitly given (so also in
19:25–27, beneath the cross!), his brothers (2:12; 7:3ff) and other relatives
(19:25). The Beloved Disciple is numbered within the circle about Jesus
(13:23ff; 19:26–27; 20:2ff). Joseph of Arimathia did not belong to the
circle of the twelve, "who was a disciple of Jesus, though a secret one
because of his fear of the Jews" (19:38).

---

[109] Cf. in this regard also the dialectic that determines the Synoptic understanding of
the outline of history (see above C IV, on Luke).

[110] This is "corrected" in 4:2, "not Jesus...'. The interpretation is disputed in terms of
source- and tradition analysis. E. Linnemann, "Jesus und der Täufer," in G. Ebeling,
E. Jüngel, and G. Schunack, eds. *Festschrift für Ernst Fuchs* (Tübingen: J. C. B.
Mohr [Paul Siebeck], 1973) 219–236; 226, sees in 3:22–4:3 two independent units
of tradition, both of which rest on historical facts, while R. Bultmann, *Gospel of
John* 167, considers it doubtful "that this scene (vv. 22–26) is a *literary construction*." For Bultmann, John 4:2 stands under the "strong suspicion of being a redactional gloss" (168 note 1).

From these examples it becomes clear that the Fourth Evangelist does not restrict the term μαθητής to the members of the circle of the Twelve. Jesus' appearance in the world has as its general purpose "to make disciples," and the number of his disciples is in fact larger than that of the Baptist (4:1). The possibility of becoming disciples of Jesus is also open to the Jews (8:31). The healed blind man becomes Jesus' disciple, in contrast to the Pharisees, who call themselves disciples of Moses (9:28). The term μαθητής thus is more comprehensive than the circle of the Twelve.[111] This justifies the interpretation of the term in a more general frame of reference. We may distinguish four points:

1. *The disciples believe the word of Jesus.* After the resurrection of Jesus they remember the Scripture and the word that Jesus had spoken to them, and they believe it (2:22). Such faith is identical with "abiding in the word of Jesus" (8:31; cf. 2 John 9). Since it is not "blind faith," it implies "recognition", which at the same time means "acknowledgement" (Erkennen/Anerkennen).[112] Thus the disciples believe and confess not only that Jesus is the διδάσκαλος and κύριος (13:14) but that as the Christ Jesus is the Holy One of God (6:69), as well as that Jesus is from God (16:27ff) and thus is the One sent by the Father.[113] They are therefore representatives and examples of what right faith is, of which it is said that all who believe in Jesus have eternal life and do not come into judgment (3:15, 18; cf. 20:31).

2. *The disciples are representatives of lack of understanding, even to the point of denying Jesus.* They are included among the characters in the Johannine story who typically misunderstand what Jesus is about (4:33–34; 11:11–12). Their failure to understand is expressed even in direct questions they pose (14:5; 16:7; also 9:2 and elsewhere). Their being disciples does not protect them from taking offense and falling away (6:60ff). Above all, the disciples' lack of understanding is documented by the story of Peter's denial (18:17, 25ff; it is presupposed in the Appendix chapter 21, cf. vv. 15ff). On the other hand, their lack of understanding during the time of Jesus is removed after the resurrection (2:22; 12:16).[114]

---

[111] Some of the details remain unclear. Thus with regard to 7:3 one may ask whether the reference is to the disciples of Jesus or—as Bultmann believes, *Gospel of John* 290–291, note 9—to Jesus' followers in a more general sense? On the Johannine understanding of the disciples cf. also R. Schnackenburg, *Gospel according to St. John* 3:203–217.

[112] On the relation of γινώσκω and πιστεύω, cf. 6:69 (cf. also 1 John 4:6).

[113] Thus in the high priestly prayer of Jesus: "Now they know that everything you have given me is from you; for the words that you gave to me I have given to them, and they have received them and know in truth that I came from you; and they have believed that you sent me" (John 17:7–8).

[114] Cf. the Messianic secret in Mark 5:43; 8:29–30; 9:9 and elsewhere.

3. *The disciples stand under the requirement of the love command-ment, i.e. the command to bring forth fruit.* Faith in the Son affirms not only that the disciples of Jesus are incorporated into the realm of δόξα and eternal ζωή but thereby implies that the believers stand under an ethical demand. This is what becomes visible in the love command (13:34–35). Mutual love is the mark of discipleship; it means to let oneself be deter-mined by the ἀγάπη θεοῦ, and leads to a way of living one's life, as illus-trated by the image of "bearing fruit." The fulfillment of the ethical de-mand is identified with glorifying the Father (15:8; cf. 15:4–5, 16).

4. *As eyewitnesses and earwitnesses of the life of Jesus, the disciples play an irreplaceable role.* Just as Jesus is portrayed as the preexistent Son of God who has entered into a specific segment of human history, the disciples are witnesses of the Jesus event that occurred in this particular segment of time. They are eyewitnesses of Jesus' deeds, and they are promised that they will see greater things than these (1:50–51). Such seeing leads to faith (20:8). It is thereby clear, however, that the seeing of the works and the person of the Son of God does not compel one to believe; for the world too sees Jesus' works but they close themselves off to his claim and persecute him with hatred (15:24). Nevertheless, the Evangelist is enough of a realist to interpret the seeing of Jesus deeds as assisting in the process of coming to faith. That is true of the people (6:2, 30ff; cf. 4:45), just as it is true of the disciples (2:11), particularly with regard to seeing the Risen One, which compels the disciple Thomas to the confes-sion, "My Lord and my God." At the same time, the value of such a confession is relativized: "Blessed are those who have *not* seen and yet believe" (20:28–29). This points precisely to the situation of the post-Easter community, which lives "by faith, not by sight" (cf. 2 Cor 5:7).

The special feature in the relation of the disciples to Jesus with regard to the post-Easter community is seen in the fact that the disciples have direct access to the Jesus event. In this regard they play an irreplaceable role, however much in other ways they may be depicted as anticipating the later Christian community. That the Evangelist acknowledges the special historical position of Jesus' disciples is seen in his concept of *witness*. As historical companions of Jesus they are able to bear authoritative testi-mony to the revelation of the Son; they are the guarantors of the church's tradition, which is measured by its faithfulness to the Christ event. For not only does Jesus testify to what he has seen (3:11, 32),[115] but also the disciple beneath the cross sees and bears witness to the event (19:35). So also the Paraclete as the "Spirit of Truth" will give his testimony about Jesus, as will all the disciples who have been with Jesus "from the begin-

---

[115] Cf. already the portrayal of John the Baptist, who *sees* the Spirit of God descend on Jesus and testifies, "This is the Son of God" (1:33–34).

ning" (15:26–27). The community knows itself to be borne along by this testimony, knows that its message is thereby legitimized, and knows itself bound to the role of a continuing witness (21:24; cf. 17:20; 1 John 1:1ff).

*Excursus: The Paraclete in the Gospel of John*

Becker, J. *Das Evangelium nach Johannes.* ÖTK 4,2. Gütersloh: Gerd Mohn, 1985.

Bornkamm, G. "Der Paraklet im Johannesevangelium," *FS R. Bultmann.* Stuttgart-Köln, 1949, 12–35; also in *Glaube und Geschichte* I. Munich: Kaiser, 1968, 68–89.

Brown, R. E. "The Paraclete in the Fourth Gospel," *NTS* 13 (1966/67) 113–132.

Johnston, G. *The Spirit-Paraclete in the Gospel of John.* MSSNTS 12. Cambridge: Cambridge University Press, 1970.

Müller, U. B. "Die Parakletenvorstellung im Johannesevangelium", *ZThK* 71 (1974) 31–77.

Mussner, F. "Die johanneischen Parakletsprüche und die apostolische Tradition," *Praesentia Salutis.* Düsseldorf: Patmos, 1967, 146–158.

Richter, G. "Zur Formgeschichte und literarischen Einheit von Joh 6,31–58,"*ZNW* 60 (1969) 21–55; also in G. Richter, *Studien zum Johannesevangelium*, J. Hainz, ed. BU 13. Regensburg: Pustet, 1977, 88–119.

Wilckens, U. "Der Paraklet und die Kirche," *Kirche* (FS G. Bornkamm) D. Lührmann and G. Strecker eds. Tübingen: J. C. B. Mohr (Paul Siebeck), 1980, 185–203.

Windisch, H. *The Spirit-Paraclete in the Fourth Gospel.* Facet Books Biblical Series—20. John Reumann, general editor. Philadelphia: Fortress Press, 1968.

Five separate Paraclete sayings can be distinguished, all in the farewell discourses (1) 14:16–17; (2) 14:26; (3) 15:26–27; (4) 16:4, 6–11; (5) 16:12–15 (cf. 1 John 2:1–2). The brief form of the first two sayings modulates into the more expansive ones that follow. In the process there is also a shift in statements about the sending of the Paraclete: Nos. 1 and 2: the Father (however, No. 2 has the supplement "in my name"); Nos. 3 and 4, "I" (with No. 3 adding "from the Father").[116] The Paraclete is more accurately described as the "Holy Spirit" (No. 2) or as the "Spirit of Truth" (Nos. 1, 3, 5), who stands over against the world. The world cannot recognize it but the Spirit is promised to the disciples as an abiding gift (No. 1). His function is to remind them of the teaching of Christ (No. 2) or the testimony of Christ (No. 3), and especially the anticipation of the final judgment of the world; for his appearance means that sin, righteousness, and judgment will be revealed (No. 4). Such leading "into all the truth" makes present the sending of Christ, for the Paraclete will speak with the authority of the Risen One; he will also announce future events which he will hear from the Risen Christ (No. 5).

---

[116] According to U. B. Müller, "Die Parakletenvorstellung" 66, in ch. 14 *the Father* sends the Spirit, while in chaps 15–16 Jesus does this himself. However, the inseparable bond between Father and Son is presupposed throughout.

The Greek term παράκλητος means "counselor" (in the legal sense) or "helper" (Luther's translation "Tröster" = comforter, encourager or "Fürsprecher" = intercessor, mediator, advocate). It is documented in the rabbinic literature as a loanword from Greek. The author of the Gospel of John presupposes that his readers know and understand the term. In contrast to the Gospel, in 1 John 2:1 the Paraclete is identified with Jesus Christ and is there to be translated as "advocate" (with the Father).

Since the word does not appear in the LXX but is used in rabbinic literature as a loanword, a derivation from the Old Testament-Jewish realm is virtually excluded. An attempt such as that of G. Bornkamm to interpret the Johannine Paraclete in terms of the Jewish precursor-completer scheme (according to which the relation of Jesus to the Paraclete would parallel the relation of John to Jesus and thus would be connected to the Old Testament Messianic expectation)[117] does not do justice to the fact that in the Johannine understanding Jesus is more than a precursor. This is also seen in the Son of Man sayings that are transferred to Jesus as the Johannine Revealer. S. Mowinckel and N. Johannsson think of the idea of the eschatological advocate in Judaism, according to which advocate-angels take over an intercessory function at the last judgment,[118] an idea that, to be sure, can be applied to 1 John 2:1 but not to the sayings in the Fourth Gospel.

Unanswered questions also arise from the suggestion of U. B. Müller that the Paraclete is to be explained from the Jewish genre of "farewell discourse," namely that here an "authorization of tradition" would result by designating a "successor." Against this suggestion one must ask whether the connection between Paraclete and farewell discourses is not secondary, created by the (pre-) Johannine tradition, and also, whether the Paraclete is in fact comparable to an earthly "successor" who needs to be authorized by some such transfer of authority.

On the other hand, a derivation from Gnosticism, according to which the Paraclete is identified with a Gnostic revealer figure,[119] is not probable, since this ignores the temporal differentiation between Jesus and the Paraclete.[120]

---

[117] So G. Bornkamm, "Der Paraklet im Johannesevangelium" 98–99.

[118] Jesus represents the δικαιοσύνη of God. As representative and revealer of the righteousness of God, he places the community under obligation to be "righteous" as he is righteous. But sin, that continues to be an undoubted reality in the life of the community, is no reason for despair and the abandonment of hope, since the community can appeal to Jesus Christ as the Paraclete.

[119] So Bultmann, *Gospel of John* 567–568.

[120] One must take account of this, if one with A. Kragerud, *Lieblingsjünger* 92, identifies the Paraclete with the Beloved Disciple—which is in any case excluded on grounds of content. One might more correctly say, with U. Wilckens, "Der Paraklet und die Kirche" 203, that there is a mutual relation between the two, when the Beloved Disciple is the authority and representative of the community that is founded anew

In contrast, as the basis for understanding the term in 1 John 2:1 one must in fact adopt the meaning of the Greek word for (legal) "counselor" and the Hellenistic Jewish idea of a Paraclete-intercessor[121] that has been applied to Jesus, and for the Paraclete sayings of the Gospel the idea of the Spirit of God that functions as counselor to the community.[122] In the interpretation of the Fourth Gospel a time line is thereby connected that was already suggested in the Synoptic and pre-Synoptic tradition about the Holy Spirit,[123] but is now brought to specific expression in continuity with the Gospel genre (cf. also John 20:22–23).

From the point of view of tradition history, the tradition in 1 John 2:1 can claim priority in comparison with the Paraclete sayings found in the Gospel of John, since it is closer to the usage of the term in pre-Christian materials. In distinction from the Paraclete's function in 1 John where the exalted Christ as the Paraclete serves as eschatological intercessor before God, in the Fourth Gospel the Paraclete as "counselor" has the mission of accompanying the disciples on their future way. This means that in the post-Easter situation, in the time after the death and resurrection of Jesus Christ, the Paraclete stands by the community throughout its history as guide and encourager. While the apocalyptic foundations of the early Johannine tradition are still clearly recognizable through the Paraclete's association with the judgment of the world (esp. John 16:8ff), it is still the present function of the Paraclete that is of definitive importance. The Paraclete makes the revelation of the Logos-Christ present for the post-Easter community. It is not by accident that in the first reference to the Paraclete the expression ἄλλος παράκλητος is used (14:16), which implies that Jesus Christ himself was the first Paraclete, whose role is then continued by the Paraclete who follows. The pneumatic foundation of the church is incorporated within a particular course of history. In a way that is not dissimilar to the theological intention of the "historian" Luke, who strongly emphasizes the connection between Spirit and church in the course of time, the Fourth Gospel's understanding the Paraclete functions

---

by the Paraclete: "...the Paraclete gives and preserves its picture for the post-Easter church in the pre-Easter "Beloved Disciple." However, a distinction must still be made between the Paraclete and the Beloved Disciple. It is the Evangelist who composes the picture of the Beloved Disciple (see above). Of course, behind the figure of the Beloved Disciples stands the authority of the "Presbyter" as the founding authority of the Johannine circle, so that this community experiences in such a figure, as also in its own present experience, the working of the Paraclete.

[121] For the pagan-Hellenistic background, cf. Demosth Or 19:1; Dion Hal, AntRom 11.37.1; also Aug JohEvTract 94.2, also JohEpistTract 1.7–8 ("advocatus"); Jewish-apocalyptic: 1 Enoch 47:2; 104:1; Targum Job 33.23; TestDan 6:2 ("intercessory angelic being").

[122] Cf. Mark 13:11par (with R. Schnackenburg, *Gospel according to St. John* 3:142, 148).

[123] Cf. Mark 1:8par; Acts 1:5; 11:16; Matt 28:19.

so as to bridge the period from the Christ event to the End. This function guarantees that the present experience of the Christian community is in continuity with the foundation of church history, the Christ event of the past. In accordance with the theology of the other Evangelists, the final goal of history thus continues to be pictured as the future parousia of the Son of God as judge of the world.[124]

Just how the leadership of the Johannine community was structured and organized cannot be determined from the Fourth Gospel. This is not surprising, since of course the Gospel portrays the revelatory event that lay in the past. Thus that the community had no church order or officials at all cannot be affirmed merely on the basis of the silence of the Gospel on these matters.[125] Third John manifests at least the rudiments of an official structure, as in the designation "presbyter," and also in the action of Diotrephes; and 1 John concludes with a church ruling that distinguishes two classes of sins, which presupposes a corresponding disciplinary procedure in the Johannine community at the time the letter was written (1 John 5:16). This has a functional equivalent in the Gospel of John, when the authority to forgive sins is conferred on the disciples (20:22–23), in a text that speaks not only of the "forgiveness" of sins but also of their "retention."[126]

The Johannine circle accordingly found itself in a situation that was characteristic for the churches of the late New Testament period. Like them, the Johannine community stood at the threshold of the developing early catholic church. For this reason, the supposition is unlikely that the Johannine school did not have any *sacraments*. In fact, there are clear pointers to baptism and the Lord's Supper not only in 1 John (5:6–8) but also in the Gospel. Even if the Johannine healing stories are not inter-

---

[124] 5:28–29 (without using the "technical term" παρουσία); also 16:16, where not only the Easter events but also the parousia events are meant; in addition 16:22–23 (contra Bultmann *Gospel of John* 576–595). On source and literary analysis: since 14:31 is continued in 18:1, the problem arises as to whether chapters 15–17 are secondary additions. This difficulty can hardly be resolved by positing an "ecclesiastical redactor." One should rather think in terms of the Evangelist's standing within the stream of the Johannine school, so that the Johannine farewell discourses were already somewhat firmly-fixed elements of the tradition that were inserted by the Evangelist into this context. The Paraclete sayings can by no means be isolated from their context (contra H. Windisch, *Spirit-Paraclete in the Fourth Gospel* 35) but are constituent elements of the speech complex in which they are presently embedded (so also U. Wilckens, "Der Paraklet und die Kirche" 186–190).

[125] Cf. E. Schweizer, "Der Kirchenbegriff im Evangelium und in den Briefen des Johannes," StEv I (= TU 73) Berlin: Akademie Verlag, 1959, 363–381; 373. See the critique of R. Brown, *The Gospel according to John* cix. On the whole subject, cf. K. Haacker, "Jesus und die Kirche nach Johannes," ThL 29 (1973) 179–201.

[126] Cf. also the function of the Spirit-Paraclete according to 16:8–9, who will "convict" the world of sin.

preted as disguised references to sacramental theology,[127] the attribution of all the sacramental texts to the "ecclesiastical redactor" is still unfounded.[128]

It is evident that the Johannine community practiced baptism. With the idea that the Spirit is given through an anointing (χρῖσμα), 1 John presupposes a corresponding practice of baptism that was combined with a ceremony of anointing (1 John 2:20, 27). This document also has other clear indications of the baptismal sacrament (especially 1 John 5:6–8, as well as "being begotten by God" and other such references). From this point of departure it is probable that the Fourth Evangelist also proceeds on the basis that baptism had an important function in the community's life and self-understanding. To be sure, the references are relatively few. In the conversation with Nicodemus it becomes clear that conversion presupposes a new birth (3:3 ἄνωθεν). This rebirth happens through "water and Spirit" (3:5). The textual transmission of this verse is virtually unanimous, so that the omission of ἐξ ὕδατος ("from water")[129] cannot be based on text-critical arguments. The fact that in the remainder of the Nicodemus conversation baptism with water is mentioned neither directly nor indirectly is not due an ecclesiastical redactor's having introduced it secondarily into the text but is the result of the dualistic Johannine conception that juxtaposes flesh and Spirit (3:6), presupposes the ritual of water baptism as the assumed practice of the community and interprets it in the specific Johannine sense named above, so that the center of gravity of the argument rests on the interpretation of the meaning of baptism, not on the fact of it. This interpretation affirms that the person is reborn in the act of water baptism, by the interaction of water and Spirit. The person is taken into the realm of the Spirit by means of water baptism, and given the possibility of a new existence that also is oriented toward the future of the kingdom of God (cf. 3:5–6).

In this connection the interpretation of 13:10 is difficult. The use of the verb λούω is striking, since in the context νίπτω is used. Λούω is found only here in the Gospel of John; translated literally it means "immerse" or "bathe;" it also has the meaning "baptize" (cf. Acts 22:16; 1 Cor 6:11 ἀπολούω; Heb 10:22 λούω). The perfect participle λελουμένος could refer to a prior act of baptism. How is the relation to footwashing to be seen? This is often identified with the Lord's Supper but the vocabulary of the text has no suggestion of this. Neither is it likely that footwashing is an additional requirement after baptism that means "the partial forgiveness which follows and as

---

127 O. Cullmann, *Salvation in History* (New York & Evanston: Harper & Row, 1967) 279–280.

128 Contra R. Bultmann, *Gospel of John* 219; J. Becker, *Das Evangelium nach Johannes* 219–221 (on 6:51c-58). For the whole subject see also H. Klos, *Die Sakramente im Johannesevangelium* (SBS 46. Stuttgart: Katholisches Bibelwerk, 1970).

129 Thus for example H. H. Wendt, *Das Johannesevangelium. Eine Untersuchung seiner Entstehung und seines geschichtlichen Wertes* (Göttingen: Vandenhoeck & Ruprecht, 1900).

it were continues baptism."[130] More correctly one should understand the words εἰ μὴ τοὺς ποδός νίψασθαι in v. 10 as part of the presupposed scene, so that καθαρός would be identified with the baptismal bath: the disciples have received (complete) cleansing by following Jesus. Perhaps the Evangelist is thinking in this regard of the baptism of the disciples by Jesus or John the Baptist. In any case baptism is not the problem here; it is more likely that here too the reference is to baptism into the community. It has the function of purifying and implies the demand of mutual service among the disciples, just as Jesus has done for them (cf. 13:34–35).

The statement that when the crucified Jesus was stabbed by the soldier's lance, immediately "water and blood" came out (19:34) also belongs to the original composition of the Gospel of John, and reveals the hand the Evangelist with particular clarity.[131] In this context, when the eyewitness testifies that after the lance thrust blood and water came forth from Jesus' crucified body, the statement is certainly intended to document the reality of the passion and death of Jesus (19:35).[132] Presumably there was an antidocetic purpose in the background, which was especially characteristic of the pre-Johannine tradition. This docetic challenge was opposed by citing the illustration named above as documentation of the reality of Jesus' suffering and death. But in addition to this, the symbolic manner in which the Fourth Evangelist constructs his scenes is to be taken into consideration. Just as in the case of the miracle stories of the Son of God which point beyond the actual events they report and portray the salvation made available by Christ, so water and blood from the side of the crucified Christ represent the sacraments of baptism and the Lord's Supper that are made possible by the death of Christ as their foundation. As the death of Jesus makes atonement for the world (1:29; 11:50–51; 18:14), so the sacraments established by Jesus' death have a soteriological sense for human beings. Both baptism and the Lord's Supper mediate the eschatological reality of salvation. The appropriate response to salvation mediated by the sacraments is faith, which appeals to the seeing, knowing, and testifying of the eyewitness (19:35).

The discourse on the Bread of Life (6:26–59) is particularly significant for understanding the Lord's Supper. The discourse by Jesus occurs in dialogue with the Jewish people in connection with the stories of feeding the multitudes and walking on the water (6:1–15, 16–21), following a geographical transition (6:22–25). The section 6:51c-58 is often seen as a later insertion and attributed to the so-called ecclesiastical redactor.[133] In

---

130 So A. Oepke, *TDNT* 4:306.
131 So U. Schnelle, *Antidocetic Christology* 209; cf. E. Schweizer, "Das johanneische Zeugnis vom Herrenmahl," *EvTh* 12 (1953) 341–363; 349.
132 Cf. 4 Maccabees 9:20: "bloody water" (ἰχώρ); further documentation in E. Schweizer, "johanneische Zeugnis" 350–351; Strack-Billerbeck 2:582–583.
133 According to Bultmann, *Gospel of John* 174, G. Bornkamm attempted to make this thesis probable ("Die eucharistische Rede im Johannesevangelium," *ZNW* 47 [1956]

fact, it cannot be disputed that this section differs from its context in both language and content. In the context of the Bread of Life discourse, the Revealer Jesus Christ is identical with the Living Bread that has come down from heaven. According to 6:51c-58, however, it is the flesh and blood of Jesus that is equated with the heavenly bread. Though there the eating of the bread can be understood only symbolically, here "eating" (φάγομαι) and "chewing up" (τρώγω) are meant literally. And there the heavenly origin of Jesus stands in the foreground, while here it is his incarnation. There the response demanded from people is faith, while here nothing is said about faith but only the necessity of eating the flesh and drinking the blood. All this suggests that this passage is a secondary insertion that intends a sacramental interpretation in very realistic terms, similar to the identification of the Lord's Supper with the φάρμακον ἀθα- νασίας, as taught by Ignatius of Antioch.[134]

The opposing view is that the section 6:51c-58 was an original part of the Bread of Life discourse.[135] In fact, there are a number of connections to the context, including the term "Son of Man," which in the preceding is portrayed as the giver of food (6:27), in this section as the food itself (6:53), and in the following as returning to his heavenly existence (6:62). In the Johannine understanding, it is a matter of a united christological concept, since the heavenly giver can be thought of as identical with his gift. There are also other links to the context. Thus 6:51c can be under- stood as a direct continuation of 6:51a-b,[136] and it is not to be denied that both Johannine language and the Johannine world of ideas are also present.[137] This is only apparently contradicted by the summarizing state- ment, "It is the Spirit that gives life; the flesh (σάρξ) is useless" (6:63), as

161–169; reprinted in *Geschichte und Glaube* 1 [Munich: Kaiser, 1968] 60–67]. Cf. G. Richter, "Zur Formgeschichte und literargeschichtlichen Einheit von Joh 6,31–58," in *Studien* 88–119; J. Becker, *Das Evangelium nach Johannes* 219–221; L. Wehr, *Arznei er Unsterblichkeit* (NTA NF 18. Münster: Aschendorff, 1987) 188–277.

[134] IgnEph 20.2. However, Ignatius could also interpret the Lord's Supper in a spiritua- lizing sense. Cf. IgnTrall 8.1: The "Lord's flesh" is understood as faith, and the "blood of Christ" is love (cf. E. Haenchen, *John* 1:294).

[135] So H. Klos, *Die Sakramente im Johannesevangelium* (SBS 46. Stuttgart: Katho- lisches Bibelwerk, 1970); U. Wilckens, "Der eucharistische Abschnitt der johan- neischen Rede vom Lebensbrot (John 6,51c-58), in J. Gnilka, ed. *Neues Testament und Kirche*. Freiburg: Herder, 1974) 220–248; H. Schürmann, "Die Eucharistie als Repräsentation und Applikation des Heilsgeschehens nach Joh 6,53–58," in *Ursprung und Gestalt* (Düsseldorf: Patmos, 1970) 167–187; cf. B. Kollman, *Ursprung und Gestalten der frühchristlichen Mahlfeier* (GTA 43. Göttin- gen: Vandenhoeck & Ruprecht, 1990) 109–125.

[136] Cf. also βρῶσις in 6:27 and 55; δώσει/δώσω in 6:27 and 6:51c.

[137] Cf. the immanence formula in 6:56 (cf. 14:20; 15:5; 17:21 and elsewhere); the typical Johannine misunderstanding by "the Jews" in 6:52 (cf. 2:20; 6:41–42; 7:35; 8:22, 57, and elsewhere).

if this stood against the eating of the flesh of the Son of Man (6:54–55). Actually, 6:54–55 makes a christological statement, while 6:63 has an anthropological orientation that indicates "the real conditions of faith and unbelief"[138] and thereby attaches itself to the motif of "the Jews" (6:41, 52) and the present world.

All in all, it appears unlikely that the section 6:51c-58 is a secondary addition of a redactor. It is more probable that it was placed in the context of the Bread of Life discourse by the original Evangelist who undoubtedly used older traditions—as suggested by the colors of the Johannine language. Thus it is possible to recognize an early docetic branch of the Johannine school tradition, while for the second phase an antidocetic orientation can already be perceived on the basis of parallels to the Ignatius texts (especially in 6:51c, 54, and 56). In the Evangelist's understanding, both belong alongside each other: the statement that Jesus has appeared in this world as the Bread of Life and life comes by faith in him, as also the other statement that the eucharistic celebration effects participation with Christ and that such sacramental participation mediates the transcendental reality of salvation. The living bread that came down from heaven not only became an empirical reality in the incarnation of Christ but no less so in the sacramental elements. It belongs to the paradox of the incarnation (1:14) that the eschaton is made present in the empirical events of baptism in water and in the eating of bread and drinking of wine. The present sacramental experience of salvation is the object of the faith of the individual Christian just as it is of the liturgical practice of the Johannine community. Such an empirically oriented faith cannot ignore the ethical problematic within which Christians are aware that they live, since discipleship is not an ahistorical neutral stance but an engagement with good and evil.

From this point of view it is clear that the Gospel of John, no less than the Johannine epistles, can ignore the *problem of ethics*. The central term is the word "agape." To be sure, the Gospel of John is different from 1 John, in that (1) it contains no definition comparable to 1 John 4:8, 16 ("God is love") and (2) that nothing is said of human beings' love for God (differently 1 John 4:20, 5:1ff); (3) also, differently than 1 John, the word "brotherly love" is not used (as in 1 John 2:10, 3:14; 4:20); however, the "new commandment" of "mutual love" (13:34–35) corresponds in content. The special significance attached to agape is explained by the Gospel's focus on the Christ, since the whole Gospel is oriented to the fact that the Father's love is revealed in the Son. The foundation for the ethic of the Gospel of John is accordingly the ἀγάπη θεοῦ manifest in the Son. This love has a

---

[138] U. Wilckens, "eucharistische Abschnitt" 245; cf. U. Schnelle, *Antidocetic Christology* 214; see also the similar understanding of σάρξ in 1:13, 3:6.

cosmic breadth, for the cosmos as such is the object of God's love.[139] It is concretized in the unity of the Father with the Son; it is witnessed to by the love of God for the Son before time began (17:24). The present of the Christ is determined by this (5:20[140]; cf. also 15:10; 17:26). The love of the Father for the Son presupposes that the Son gives his life for others (10:17), and the Son of God responds to the love of God by giving his life for human beings.[141] Of course, a direct love of God for humanity is also affirmed,[142] but the decisive thing is that the love of God is mediated to humanity by the Son (17:26). The essential content of the power and authority that the Son receives from the Father is his making the love of God real to human beings (cf. 3:34–36). This is not only the basis of the sending of Jesus into the world in order to save it (3:16–17) but also the basis of Jesus' love for his own (15:9–10). Therefore, the love of God mediated by Jesus is the foundation for the community's own self-understanding and calls for the community to respond to Jesus in love (14:21, 23; 16:27). Is such love to be understood in a non-ethical perspective? Is the Evangelist's concern only to establish the unity in the word which must determine the life of the community? If one understands by "ethics" only a system of norms that provide obligatory instructions for concrete individual cases, then one will seek in vain for an ethic in the Gospel of John. The Fourth Evangelist distinguishes himself from the Synoptics as well as from the authors of the New Testament letters by the fact that he gives no ethical instruction for particular cases. One should not conclude from this, however, that his theology excludes any positive relationship to ethical requirements. To be sure, one cannot derive too much from the frequent occurrence of the terms ἐντολή/ἐντολαί in the mouth of Jesus, since ἐντολή mostly has the general meaning of "assignment," "direction,"[143] so that from this point of

---

[139] Cf. 3:16—The term κόσμος refers to "humanity;" this corresponds to the theological conception of the Evangelist, since this Christ is described as σωτήρ of the world (4:42; cf. 3:17). The claim of M. Lattke, that the love of God applies exclusively to the group of believers (Einheit im Wort 52, 84–85 and elsewhere; cf. E. Käsemann, Testament of Jesus 59, 72–73; the same applies to the so-called ecclesiastical redaction: J. Becker, Das Evangelium nach Johannes) stands in contradiction to the texts named above.

[140] Here the verb φιλέω which in the Gospel of John is synonymous with ἀγαπάω; cf. M. Paeslack, "Zur Bedeutungsgeschichte der Wörter φιλεῖν, lieben', φιλία, Liebe', ,Freundschaft', φίλος, Freund' in der LXX und im Neuen Testament unter Berücksichtigung ihrer Beziehungen zu ἀγαπάω, ἀγάπη, ἀγαπητός," ThViat 5 (1954) 51–142 (esp. 64–65). For John's use of these words as equivalents, in addition to 5:20 and 10:17 (Father/Son) cf. 14:23 and 16:27 (God/humans) and 11:5 and 3 (Jesus), 15:19 and 12:43 (cosmos).

[141] 15:9; cf. 13:14 ("as I have loved you"); 11:5, 36 (φίλει); 13:1.

[142] 14:21, 23; 16:27 (φιλεῖ); 17:23.

[143] In Jesus' preaching the word ἐντολή is used to describe the Father's commission to the Son (10:18; 12:49–50; 15:10) and also for the Son of God's instruction to the

departure the only the question that can be posed is whether this word, or
the Son of God's appearance in this world as such, as it is portrayed in the
Fourth Gospel, implies any ethical requirements at all. But that the unity
of Father and Son in regard to discipleship does not limit itself merely to
this unity, i.e. the obligation to remain in the word of love but calls for
concrete loving acts, is seen from the fact that the Evangelist portrays Jesus
as the "model."[144] Jesus' service is giving himself for his own, as is clarified
in the form of a saying.[145] From the disciples side, following is the means
by which such service takes place (12:26). Whoever follows Jesus is called
to do what the Son of God has done (13:14–15; cf. 8:12; 10:4–5, 27).

It is already clear from the above that the advent of Jesus as the Son of
God, with his deeds of love as the concrete realization of his unity with the
Father, is not without a concrete point of reference. The truth he reveals
is concrete, since the obedience of the Christ is a concrete reality, confirmed by his suffering and death (15:10). By giving his life for his own, he
becomes for the disciples the supreme model of the meaning of love.
Therefore the demand for mutual love as expressed in the "new commandment" (13:34) is not to be understood only in an esoteric sense and not as
oriented exclusively to preserving one's relation to God. It is rather the
case that agape calls for concrete realization in the realm of empirical life.
Also the admonition to bring forth "much fruit" (15:5), while it presupposes unity with the Son (as indicated by the imagery of the vine), has as
its goal that by such bearing of fruit the Father is glorified and the reality
of discipleship is experienced (15:8, 16). The existence of the community
can only be rightly understood as a historical existence. Those who are
taken possession of by the truth of the Revealer go forward to the resurrection of life, while others stand under the threat of judgment (5:29). This
functions to pose the question of doing either good or evil. This constant

---

disciples (13:34; 14:15, 21; 15:10, 12), in which singular and plural can alternate.
The ἐντολαί reflect the one ἐντολή; keeping them is the sign of one's love for Jesus
(cf. 14:15 and elsewhere).

[144] 3:15 (the service of Jesus to his disciples as ὑπόδειγμα) cf. 1 John 3:16.

[145] 15:13 ("No one has greater love than this, to lay down one's life for one's friends")
interprets v. 12, according to which the love of Jesus for his own is the model for
love among the disciples. Differently M. Dibelius, "Joh 15,13. Eine Studie zum
Traditionsproblem des Johannesevangeliums," *Botschaft und Geschichte* (Tübingen: J. C. B. Mohr [Paul Siebeck], 1953) 1:204–220, who interprets the Johannine
concept of agape in terms of the Gnostic myth of the Primal Human as a cosmic-
metaphysical participation in being; v. 13 is supposed to have come to the Evangelist as tradition, since it does not correspond to the Evangelist's own idea of
sacrifice. This necessarily infers that additional statements about agape (e. g. Jesus'
love for the Beloved Disciple, for Lazarus, and also 3:16) cannot be acknowledged
as original with the Evangelist. It is characteristic of the Evangelist John, however,
that elsewhere he can also coordinate the idea of self-giving love with his interpretation of the sending of Jesus (cf. 10:1ff, 15, 17).

demand can never be avoided by the community as long as it lives in the world.

The agape to which the community knows itself to be called is not to be defined on the basis of mutual love (13:34), for it is entirely a matter of reflecting the comprehensive love of God manifest in the Son, a love that is directed to the world. However much the world may close itself off against such love, the ἀγάπη θεοῦ is stronger than the hatred of the world and more inclusive than the "brotherly" love practiced in the world, which always remains fragmentary. It is from this point of departure that the often-posed question must be answered, namely, the question of why the Fourth Evangelist speaks neither of love for the neighbor, which by definition extends beyond the circle of disciples, nor of love for enemies. This silence is not to be explained on the basis of the esoteric orientation of the mutual love commanded to the disciples but from the fact that the ἀγάπη θεοῦ precedes all human action. Wherever people let themselves be determined by this love, they stand completely under its claim, and are called to love even to the point of giving their lives. Every limitation is excluded. The love of neighbor and love of enemies are both therefore implied in the agape-command, for whoever stands in unity with the Father and the Son is determined by the comprehensive and universal deed of love.

It has become clear that the agape-command requires concrete action in individual cases, and is the basis for such action. When the Evangelist himself gives no concrete instructions, this is based on the conviction that the gift of agape includes the gift of freedom and responsibility to those who believe. Christians know that they are called to do the right thing at the right time, the time of every new situation in which they are called upon to decide what action is appropriate to that love that proceeds from the Father through the Son and has brought them near to God.

# IV. The Coming of the Lamb—The Apocalyptist John

Aune, D. E. "The Apocalypse of John and the Problem of Genre," *Semeia* 36 (1986) 65–96.

Beagley, A. J. *The "Sitz im Leben" of the Apocalypse with Particular Reference to the Role of the Church's Enemies.* BZNW 50. Berlin-New York: W. de Gruyter, 1987.

Böcher, O. *Die Johannesapokalypse.* EdF 41. Darmstadt: Wissenschaftliche Buchgesellschaft, 1988.

Böcher, O. *Kirche in Zeit und Endzeit. Aufsätze zur Offenbarung des Johannes.* Neukirchen-Vluyn: Neukirchener, 1983.

Boring, M. E. "Ἀποκάλυψις Ἰωάννου as Προφητεία: A religionsgeschichtlich and Theological Perspective," Η. Β. Οικονομου, ed. 1900 ΕΤΗΡΙΣ ΤΗΣ ΑΠΟΚΑΛΥΨΕΩΣ ΙΩΑΝΝΟΥ· ΠΡΑΚΤΙΚΑ ΔΙΕΘΝΟΥΣ ΔΙΕΠΙΣΤΗΜΟΝΙΚΟΥ ΣΥΜΠΟΣΙΟΥ (Ἀθῆναι- Πάτμος, 17–26 Σεπτεμβρίου 1995) (Athens: ΕΚΔΟΣΙΣ ΤΗΣ ΕΝ ΠΑΤΜΩ ΙΕΡΑΣ ΠΑΤΡΙΑΡΧΙΚΗΣ ΜΟΝΗΣ ΑΓ. ΙΩΑΝΝΟΥ ΤΟΥ ΘΕΟΛΟΓΟΥ, 1999).

Bornkamm, G. "Die Komposition der apokalyptischen Visionen in der Offenbarung Johannis," *Studien zu Antike und Urchristentum*, G. Bornkamm, ed. BEvTh 28. Munich: Kaiser, 1970[3], 204–222.

Bousset, W. *Die Offenbarung Johannis*. KEK XVI. Göttingen: Vandenhoeck & Ruprecht, 1906 (1966 reprint ed.).

Feuillet, A. *The Apocalypse*. Staten Island, NY: Alba House, 1965.

Hadorn, W. *Die Offenbarung des Johannes*. ThHK 18. Leipzig: Deichert (Scholl), 1928.

Hahn, F. "Die Sendschreiben der Johannesapokalypse. Ein Beitrag zur Bestimmung prophetischer Redeformen," *Tradition und Glaube* (FS K.G. Kuhn) G. Jeremias et al., eds. Göttingen: Vandenhoeck & Ruprecht, 1971, 357–394.

Hellholm, D. (ed.) *Apocalypticism in the Mediterranean World and the Near East*, Proceedings of the International Colloquium on Apocalypticism. Uppsala, August 12–17, 1979. Tübingen: J. C. B. Mohr (Paul Siebeck), 1983.

Horn, F. W. "Zwischen der Synagoge des Satans und dem neuen Jerusalem. Die christlich-jüdische Standortbestimmung in der Apokalypse des Johannes," *ZRGG* 46 (1994) 143–162.

Karrer, M. *Die Johannesoffenbarung als* Brief. FRLANT 140. Göttingen: Vandenhoeck & Ruprecht, 1986.

Kraft, H. *Die Offenbarung des Johannes*. HNT 16a. Tübingen: J. C. B. Mohr (Paul Siebeck), 1974.

Lambrecht, J. (ed.) *L'Apocalypse johannique et l'Apocalyptique dans le Nouveau Testament*. BEThL 53. Leuven: Leuven University Press, 1980.

Lohmeyer, E. *Die Offenbarung des Johannes*. HNT 16. Tübingen: J. C. B. Mohr (Paul Siebeck), 1970.

Lohse, E. *Die Offenbarung des Johannes*. NTD 11. Göttingen: Vandenhoeck & Ruprecht, 1988.

Müller, U. B "Apokalyptik im Neuen Testament," *Bilanz und Perspektiven gegenwärtiger Auslegung des Neuen Testaments*, F. W. Horn, ed., BZNW 75. Berlin-New York: W. de Gruyter, 1995, 144–169.

Müller, U. B. *Die Offenbarung des Johannes*. ÖTK 19. Neukirchen-Vluyn: Neukirchener, 1984.

Müller, U. B. "Literarische und formgeschichtliche Bestimmung der Apokalypse des Johannes als einem Zeugnis frühchristlicher Apokalyptik," in D. Hellholm, *Apocalypticism in the Mediterranean World and the Near East*. Tübingen: J. C. B. Mohr (Paul Siebeck), 1983, 599–619.

Müller, U. B. *Messias und Menschensohn in jüdischen Apokalypsen und in der Offenbarung des Johannes*. StNT 6. Gütersloh: Gerd Mohn, 1972.

Οικονομου, Η. D. (ed.) 1900 ΕΤΗΡΙΣ ΤΗΣ ΑΠΟΚΑΛΥΨΕΩΣ ΙΩΑΝΝΟΥ· ΠΡΑΚΤΙΚΑ ΔΙΕΘΝΟΥΣ ΔΙΕΠΙΣΤΗΜΟΝΙΚΟΥ ΣΥΜΠΟΣΙΟΥ (Ἀθῆναι- Πάτμος, 17–26 Σεπτεμβρίου 1995) (Athens: ΕΚΔΟΣΙΣ ΤΗΣ ΕΝ ΠΑΤΜΩ ΙΕΡΑΣ ΠΑΤΡΙΑΡΧΙΚΗΣ ΜΟΝΗΣ ΑΓ. ΙΩΑΝΝΟΥ ΤΟΥ ΘΕΟΛΟΓΟΥ, 1999)

Schüssler-Fiorenza, E. "Apokalypsis und Propheteia. The Book of Revelation in the Context of Early Christian Prophecy," J. Lambrecht, ed. *L'Apocalypse johannique et l'Apocalyptique dans le Nouveau Testament*. BEThL 53. Leuven: Leuven University Press, 1980, 105–128.

Schüssler-Fiorenza, E. "Composition and Structure of the Book of Revelation," CBQ 39 (1977) 344–366.

Schüssler-Fiorenza, E. *Revelation. Vision of a Just World*. Proclamation Commentaries. Minneapolis: Fortress, 1991.

Vanni, U. "L'Apocalypse johannique. État de la question," J. Lambrecht, ed. *L'Apocalypse johannique et l'Apocalyptique dans le Nouveau Testament*. BEThL 53. Leuven: Leuven University Press, 1980, 21–46.

Vielhauer, Ph. and Strecker, G. "Apocalyptic in Early Christianity. Introduction." *New*

*Testament Apocrypha* II, rev. ed., W. Schneemelcher (ed.). Louisville: Westminster John Knox, 1992.

Yarbro Collins, A. "Early Christian Apocalyptic Literature," *ANRW* II 25.6 (1988) 4665–4711.

Yarbro Collins, A. *The Combat Myth in the Book of Revelation.* HDR 9. Missoula: Scholars Press, 1976.

## a) Introduction

The last book of the Bible has the special character of an "apocalypse." The key word ἀποκάλυψις is found in the first sentence (1:1: "The revelation of Jesus Christ, which God gave to him..."). This word indicates that the book is intended to represent what was revealed by God through an angel to the "servant John"—even if it contains literary units selected by the author from tradition or created by John himself. He understands his message as "words of prophecy" (1:3; cf. 19:10; 22:7, 19, 18–19). Encouragement and admonition are constituents of the prophetic mission, and echoes of the structures of prophetic speech can be discerned.[1] The author does not refer to himself as a "prophet," however; he appears rather to be a Christian apocalyptist, who distinguishes himself from other prophets by the book he writes (cf. 10:7; 11:10, 18; 16:6; 18:20, 24; 22:6, 9).

### 1. Relation to Jewish Apocalyptic

That the Revelation to John belongs to the category of apocalyptic literature is seen in its points of agreements with Jewish apocalyptic literature.[2] The following general characteristic features may be observed:

*Formal*

1. *Pseudonymity.* The apocalyptist does not write under his own name but either remains anonymous or uses the name of some great figure of the past (e. g. Baruch, Ezra, Elijah, Enoch). The author's name "John" (1:1, 4, 9; 22:8) accordingly apparently points to the founder of the Johannine school, who was regarded as an authority in the author's area of Asia Minor.

2. *Reports of visions and auditions.* In apocalyptic literature, the revelation is received in a dream or vision, more rarely as an audition. The Revelation of John accordingly begins with a call vision (1:9–20), which goes beyond the Old Testament vision reports (e. g. Isa 6; Jer 1) by virtue of the motif of "ecstasy" (= carried away "in

---

[1]  Cf. F. Hahn, according to whom the messages to the churches of chapters 2–3 belong to a distinct but complex genre consisting of the messenger formula, an οἶδα-section, a call to alertness, and a saying about conquering (Hahn, "Sendschreibung der Johannesapokalypse). The repeated formula "thus says the (τάδε λέγει) + christological predication" supports this view.

[2]  For the following cf. Ph. Vielhauer, *Geschichte* 487–494; Ph. Vielhauer, in Schneemelcher, *New Testament Apocrypha* 2:608–641; G. Strecker, *History of New Testament Literature* 207–219.

the Spirit," 1:10; cf. 4:2; 17:3; 21:10). That which the apocalyptist "sees" (visions: 1:12ff; 5:1–2, 6; 6:2 and elsewhere; and what he "hears" as interpretation of what he has seen (audition: 1:10; 6:3, 5, 7; "seeing and hearing:" 4:1; 5:11; 6:1 and elsewhere) is the subject of his mission, namely to write out what he has seen and heard and to communicate it to the seven churches in Asia (1:4, 11; cf. 10:8ff and elsewhere).

3. *Pictorial language.* That which has been seen, and also that which has been heard, is clothed in pictorial imagery. The announced events are mysteriously concealed by symbols or allegories. In this way traditional motifs receive a new meaning by their context in the book.

4. *Explanations.* An essential aspect of apocalyptic vision is the interpretation of the imagery. This is done by God himself but it is also not uncommon for it to be done by one or more interpreting angels (angelus interpres) (cf. 1:19–20; 5:5; 7:13; 17:1ff; 21:9ff; 22:6ff). It often is the case that the essence of what is explained still remains in the realm of the mysterious, even when it is concretized in the breaking of seals (6:1ff).

5. *Systematizing.* The events portrayed are typically systematized by number symbolism. Preference is given to "round numbers" that can be found in the unfolding of the course of history. Thereby a structural order imposed on history by God's wisdom is perceived by the apocalyptist (cf. the septad scheme of the Revelation of John; also 13:18, 666 as the "number of the beast;" 7:1 four angels on the four corners of the earth; the four points of the compass 4:6; 7:1; 20:8; on the number seven cf. also 10:3, the seven thunders; 17:7, the seven heads of the beast; 4:5, seven torches of fire = seven spirits of God; 17:7: 10 horns = 10 kings; 12:1: crown of 12 stars on the head of the woman who appears in the sky as the symbol of the twelve tribes of the people of God; 7:4ff: 144,000 < 12 x 12,000 > sealed, who represent the new people of God; 21:12: 12 gates of the New Jerusalem; 21:17: the walls of Jerusalem are 144 < 12 x 12 > cubits high; 4:4, 24 elders).

6. *Mixture of forms.* From the point of view of form, an apocalyptic work is not a unity. It contains different literary formulations, e. g. surveys of history in the form of predictions, images picturing the transcendent world, throne room visions, as well as liturgical forms (prayers, doxologies, and others) that originally had no apocalyptic orientation but were adapted to the apocalyptic framework and fairly often indicate the key points of the subject matter (e. g. 15:3, the Song of the Lamb; 19:1–2, 6–7, the praise of the heavenly multitude). The epistolary framework contributes to the formal disparity (1:4–5: prescript; 1:4, 11: addressees; 22:21: concluding greeting; cf. also the messages to the seven churches, 2:1–3:22). But taken as a whole the apocalyptic (revelatory) motifs are dominant, and constitute the primary content of the Revelation of John.

In comparison with Jewish apocalyptic, the Revelation of John is characterized by a strong Christianizing of the apocalyptic thought world. It is not God's final judgment but the parousia of the exalted Christ that is the final goal of the apocalyptic events (cf. 22:20). There is also no survey of history in the form of predictions of the future[3] that would establish the date of the "seer" and the readers at the point of transition from the fictive to the factual view of the future.[4] Revelation lacks *ex eventu* prophecies

[3]   Cf. e. g. 4 Ezra 14:11–12; Daniel 2:7; 2 Baruch 53–71 (with reference to the whole of world history); cf. further Daniel 8–12 (esp. 10:11–11:45); 2 Baruch 35–40; Assumption of Moses 2–10; Apocalypse of Abraham 27–30; Sibylline Oracles 4:47ff; Testament of Levi 16–18.
[4]   Cf. Ph. Vielhauer in *New Testament Apocrypha* 2:584–586.

and the sealing of the revelations which are to be "preserved" for the supposed future time for which they are intended. However, the author can arrange future events in a particular chronological order (e. g. 20:4–15: the thousand year messianic kingdom, two resurrections) that lead to the final christological goal. The definitive aspect in his understanding of history, however, is the dialectic of the presence and future of the eschatological event that also determines the interrelatedness of the revealed times.[5] Moreover, Revelation contains typical (Jewish) items of apocalyptic content, in partially modified form.

### Content

1. *The doctrine of the two aeons.* To be sure, the Revelation of John has no explicit juxtaposition of the present evil aeon and the coming good aeon but Christian hope is nonetheless oriented toward the idea that the present unredeemed age determined by evil powers under which the church suffers will be replaced by the coming age of salvation brought by Christ (cf. 11:15ff; 12:10; 18:1ff: the fall of the city of Babylon; 20:2–3: the binding of the dragon for a thousand years; 21:1ff: new heaven and new earth). This understanding of history is thus characterized by an apocalyptic dualism, namely by the opposition between the Christian community and the political powers, the opposition between Christ and Satan.

2. *Pessimism and transcendent hope.* The pessimistic apocalyptic self-understanding assumes as its point of departure that the present world is dominated by evil powers (e. g. by the activity of Satan: 2:9, 13, 24; 3:9; 12:9; 20:2 and elsewhere). In this world demons are worshipped, and sorcery and fornication prevail (9:20–21; cf. 21:8; 22:15). The Christian community is constantly faced with the dangers of apostasy, lack of love, and unwillingness to repent (2:4–5, 14–15, 20–21, and elsewhere). This situation is addressed by the hope that God will establish his kingdom and the marriage supper of the Lamb will be celebrated (19:6–7), that the 144,000 elect will be united with the Lamb (14:1), and the New Jerusalem will descend from heaven (21:2).

3. *Universalism and individualism.* The apocalyptic expectation of a new heaven and a new earth (21:1; cf. Isa 65:17; 66:22) exhibits the essentially universal orientation characteristic of apocalyptic. It is not merely a matter of the redemption of an elect people but of a cosmic event that spans the beginning and end of the world, heaven and earth (21:6; cf. also the christological self-designation A and Ω in 22:13). The city of Jerusalem is no longer the capital of an earthly realm but the symbol of a renewed world (3:12; 21:2, 10). Such universalism has a corresponding concept of time: the apocalyptic event transcends the boundaries of space and time; it has a trans-temporal, eternal dimension (cf. 14:6: "eternal gospel;" also 1:18; 4:9–10; 11:15; 22:5, and elsewhere). National boundaries are also dismantled; salvation is not a matter of belonging to a particular nation but is promised to the individual person, who can be sure of heavenly reward because of their "works" (14:12: steadfastness in faith and keeping the commandments of God; cf. 12:17), for "each one will be rewarded according to his or her works" (22:12; cf. 11:18). In contrast, the wrath of God awaits those who worship the beast and his image (14:9–11). Evil doers are promised they will be repaid double "according to their works" (18:6; cf. 20:12ff), just as the devil that seduced them, and the beast and false prophet will receive terrible punishment for ever (20:10). The universal extension of the eschatological event is complemented by the individualizing of the reception of salvation or punishment.

---

5    Cf. G. Bornkamm, "Komposition" 204–222.

4. *Determinism and near expectation.* According to the Jewish-apocalyptic understanding of history, the whole course of the world takes place just as God the Lord has
predetermined (4 Ezra 4:37; 6:1ff, and elsewhere). A corresponding deterministic view
of history in a systematic, reflective form is not found in the Apocalypse of John.
Revelation also lacks a schema of periodization on the basis of which the eschatological incursion of God into history could be calculated. (The data of 3 1/2 years, 42
months, or 1260 days <11:2–3; 12:6, 14; 13:5> do not play this role but merely
function as apocalyptic "round numbers.") Neither does the announcement of heavenly "signs" (12:1, 3; 15:1) have this function (differently e. g. Luke 21:11, 25). It is
recognized, however, that God is at work in earthly history (cf. 17:17: God placed it
into the hearts of kings to carry out the will of the beast; cf. also 10:7), even if the
victory of God will first become visible in the future, and the promise of God that this
will happen in the near future conditions the present. The near expectation of the end
of the world and the coming of Christ permeates the whole work from beginning to
end (3:11; 22:20: "Surely I am coming soon!").[6]

## 2. Provenance and Date of Composition

The problem of the provenance of Revelation appears to be resolved by the
data given by the author himself, according to which the work was written
on the island of Patmos (1:9). This is confirmed by the addresses of the
seven messages in chapters 2–3, all of which are located in the western
part of Asia Minor. The problem of dating is more complicated. The widespread view that places the writing in the time of the emperor Domitian
(81–96 C. E.) can appeal to Irenaeus *Haer* 5.30.3 (adopted and elaborated
by Eusebius *HistEcc* 5.8). However, for apologetic reasons Irenaeus in-
clines toward a harmonizing perspective that causes him to emphasize
the age and apostolic dependability of the New Testament writings.[7] Thus
we must rely primarily on data from Revelation itself. There are no clear
allusions within the text of Revelation to the time of Domitian. And
though Eusebius also names Domitian as the second emperor (after Nero)
to persecute the Christians (*HistEccl* 3.17), there is no evidence in the
ancient sources themselves that Domitian persecuted the church in Asia
Minor.[8] This passage names the island of Pontia in the western Mediterranean as the place of banishment, which is not identical with the Patmos
of Asia Minor. Even if one interprets the statement of 1:9, that "John" was

---

[6]   For discussion of the details cf. P. Volz, *Die Eschatologie der jüdischen Gemeinde
im neutestamentlichen Zeitalter* (Hildesheim 1966 [= Tübingen: J. C. B. Mohr
(Paul Siebeck), 1934²] 4–10.

[7]   Cf. his identification of the author of 1 John with the Evangelist: Irenaeus *Haer*
3.1.1; also 16.5.8.

[8]   Eusebius merely reports that Domitian "had given many proofs of his great cruelty
and had put to death without any reasonable trial no small number of men distinguished *at Rome* by family and career..." (*HistEcc* 3.17) and that among the number
of persecuted Christians was Flavia Domitilla, a niece of the Roman Consul Flavius
Clemens (*HistEcc* 3.18.4).

banished to Patmos "because of the word of God and the testimony of Jesus Christ" (cf. 6:9; 20:4), to indicate a persecution of Christians, this still does not necessarily point to the time of Domitian. Thus Tertullian (*AdvHaer* 36) could place John's banishment in the time of Nero, and Epiphanius (Haer 51.12, 33) in the time of Claudius. All this confirms the widespread patristic tendency to date New Testament documents early but does not presuppose any real knowledge of the facts.

There are indications within the inner history of the Johannine school, however, that point not only to connections between Revelation and the other Johannine writings but also can suggest a particular chronological relationship. Thus the Revelation of John, as the only apocalyptic writing in the New Testament canon, takes over the world of ideas that not only characterized the theology of earliest Christianity in general but also the Johannine school in its beginning phase. One can draw lines of connection between the millennial ideas of Revelation (20:2, 7) and 2 John 7. The concept of judgment and the expectation of the parousia (20:11ff) are also current to the author of 1 John (2:28; 3:2–3; 4:17), and also the Gospel of John contains old Christian-apocalyptic tradition.[9] Particular ideas and terminology also speak for a common traditional basis, e. g. the "Lamb" (ἀρνίον: Rev 5:6, 12 and often; but ἀμνός in John 1:29, 36); God and Christ as interchangeable figures (21:1ff; 22:6ff), the term "word of God" (19:13; John 1:1ff) or "water of life/living water" (21:6; 22:1, 17; John 4:10ff; 7:38); and not of least importance, the "witness terminology," which is documented not only in the Apocalypse (μαρτυρέω: 1:2; 22:16, 18, 20; μαρτυρία: 1:2, 9; 6:9; 11:7; 12:11 and elsewhere); μάρτυς: 1:5; 2:13; 11:3; 17:6) but also for the Johannine letters and the Gospel of John (μαρτυρέω: e. g. 3 John 3, 6; 1 John 1:2; 4:14; John 1:7–8; μαρτυρία: 3 John 12; 1 John 5:9ff; John 1:7, 19; 3:11, 32–33).

That the Apocalypse of John contains no evidence of opposing a (docetic) challenge to hope for a real parousia places it not at the end but more likely in the middle period of the development of the Johannine school tradition, which began with the Presbyter's letters of 2 and 3 John.[10]

---

9    Cf. John 11:24 (resurrection on the last day); 3:3,5 (expectation of the kingdom of God); also the κρίσις terminology.

10   There are a variety of arguments for a common Johannine tradition, which however do not establish literary dependence: O. Böcher, "Johanneisches in der Apokalypse des Johannes," *Kirche in Zeit und Endzeit* (Neukirchen-Vluyn: Neukirchener, 1983) 1–12; E. Schüssler-Fiorenza, "The Quest for the Johannine School: The Apocalypse and the Fourth Gospel," *NTS* 23 (1977) 402–427; J. Frey, "Erwägungen zum Verhältnis der Johannesapokalypse zu den übrigen Schriften des Corpus Johanneum," in M. Hengel (ed.), *Die johanneische Frage* (WUNT 67. Tübingen: J. C. B. Mohr [Paul Siebeck], 1993) 326–429.

## 3.  Sources

In comparison with the rest of the Johannine school tradition, the independence of the author is seen not only in the fact that he has composed a Christian apocalypse,[11] but also by the manner in which he has taken over traditions that are unique in New Testament literature. From case to case one may ask whether the author incorporates fragments of written documents (as perhaps 7:1–8; 11:1–13; ch. 12; perhaps also in chaps. 13–14; 17–18; 21–22) and thereby makes use of Jewish and/or Christian apocalyptic tradition, or whether the primary factor to be reckoned with is "oral tradition." There is no case where we may be certain about longer sections. It is clear, however, that the Old Testament represents an essential "source" which the author has used in an independent way, often alluding to its imagery and language. Especially numerous are allusions to Ezekiel (e. g. 4:3ff: cf. the throne vision in Ezek 1 and elsewhere) and Daniel (e. g. the "Son of Man" in 1:7, 13; 14:14: Dan 7). Much of this may have already been formed in previous Christian tradition (e. g. Mark 13par). The author's composition is also influenced by materials from Christian worship, prophetic and wisdom tradition, and traditions from the Pauline and early Johannine streams.

## 4.  Composition

John has created a carefully-composed work of exceptional unity. Following a letter-like opening (1:1–8) that concludes with a portrayal of his call vision (1:9–20), the author fulfills the assignment given him (1:19) by first sending messages to seven churches in Ephesus, Smyrna, Pergamum, Thyatira, Sardis, Philadelphia, and Laodicea, thereby addressing the churches of his time (2:1–3:22). Then follows the real apocalypse, in which is portrayed "what must take place" (4:1; cf. 1:19). It is structured in septads: visions of seven seals, trumpets, and bowls (5:1–8:1; 8:2–11:19; 15:1–16:21). Seven visions may also be discerned in chapter 14. Given the reference to the "book with seven seals" (5:1), it is striking that that the contents of only the first six seals are described, while the seventh seal leads directly to the visions of the seven trumpets (8:1). It is obvious that the idea in the background is that the contents of the book are visibly listed on the outside (6:1–8:1), while the contents of the book itself are presented in 8:2–22:5 after the opening of the seventh seal. Then chapters

---

[11]  Revelation is the only apocalypse accepted into the New Testament canon; elsewhere, units of apocalyptic tradition are incorporated into other documents, as in 1 Thessalonians 4–5; 1 Corinthians 15; 2 Corinthians 5:1–10; 2 Thessalonians 2; Mark 13par.

12–14 and 17–19 can be seen as inserted into this framework as supplementary materials that go beyond the scope of the hebdomadal structure.[12]

### b) Christology

Boring, M. E. "Narrative Christology in the Apocalypse," *CBQ* 54 (1992) 702–723.
Boring, M. E. "The Voice of Jesus in the Apocalypse of John," *NT* 34 (1992) 334–359.
de Jonge, M. "The Use of the Expression ὁ Χριστός in the Apocalypse of John," J. Lambrecht (ed.), *L'Apocalypse johannique et l'Apocalyptique dans le Nouveau Testament.* BEThL 53. Leuven: Leuven University Press, 1980, 267–281.
Holtz, T. *Die Christologie der Apokalypse des Johannes.* TU 85. Berlin: Akademie Verlag, 1971.
Müller, U. B. *Messias und Menschensohn in jüdischen Apokalypsen und in der Offenbarung des Johannes.* StNT 6. Gütersloh: Gerd Mohn, 1972.

A survey of the *christological titles* in the Revelation of John gives the following picture: the designation Χριστός is found seven times. Only three times is it clearly a proper name (1:1–2, 5, alongside Ἰησοῦς); otherwise it is used as a title, as indicated by the definite article (11:15; 12:10; 20:4, 6). The author adopts the Old Testament-Jewish usage (11:15 is based on the LXX of Ps 2:2), so that the Old Testament royal title can be translated literally (= "the Anointed"). The idea of the eternal sovereignty of the Anointed One also comes from the Old Testament royal ideology (11:15; cf. Ps 10:16), a sovereignty that is identical with God's own rule (11:17;

---

[12] The view of G. Bornkamm, "Komposition," is important in that it shows the parallelism of the portrayal of eschatological events in 8:2–14:20 and 15:1–22:5, especially the parallelism between chaps. 12–14 and 17–19. It is not a matter of chronological progression but supplements to what has been presented in the framework of septads. This is to be evaluated more in terms of the history of the tradition than as a matter of literary criticism. In consideration of the hebdomadal structure for the composition of the whole work, the following outline may be proposed:

| | | |
|---|---|---|
| A. | 1:1–20 | Introduction |
| I. | 1:1–3 | Foreword |
| II. | 1:4–8 | Messages to the Seven Churches in Asia |
| III. | 1:9–20 | Call Vision |
| B. | 2:1–3:22 | First Major Section: Seven Messages to the Churches of Asia Minor |
| C. | 4,1–22:5 | Second Major Section: Revelation of the Future Events |
| I. | 4:1–11 | Opening Vision |
| II. | 5:1–8:1 | Vision of the Seven Seals |
| III. | 8:2–11:19 | Vision of the Seven Trumpets |
| IV. | 12:1–14:20 | Struggle against the Enemies of God |
| V. | 15:1–16:21 | Vision of the Seven Bowls |
| VI. | 17:1–19:10 | Babylon is Judged |
| VII. | | 19:11–22:5   The Coming of the Lord |
| D. | 22:6–21 | Concluding Section: Final Instructions, Announcement of the Coming of Jesus. |

19:6; cf. also Ps 97:1; 99:1; Dan 3:33 and elsewhere). The Old Testament-Jewish roots of this way of thinking is also visible in the derivation of the Messiah from the "tribe of Judah" as the "root of David" (5:5; cf. 22:16). The title "Son of David" is not found, however. And when the Messiah is designated "the holy one, the true one, who has the key of David" (3:7), this echoes not only Isaiah 22:22 but also the idea that Jesus Christ has the keys to the kingdom of heaven (Matt 16:19). Thus the meaning of the title "Christ" is not determined by the nationalistic royal concept of Jewish tradition but by the Christian confession of the exalted Lord. The sovereignty of Christ will—this is the expression of genuine Christian apocalyptic hope—prevail against the anti-godly powers of this world (12:10). It is therefore not to be understood in a this-worldly political sense. This is also seen in the portrayal of the eschatological expectation that Christ's community will participate in the future lordship of Christ over the world (20:4, 6).

The majority of examples of κύριος refer to God; only four passages point clearly to Christ (11:8; 14:13; 22:20–21). Doubtless the dominant reference to God is a result of adopting the LXX usage, in which יהוה is replaced by κύριος. This is also seen in the Old Testament citations in the Apocalypse (cf. 1:8 with Amos 3:13; 4:8 with Isa 6:3). It is still an open question, however, whether the author in this or that instance really wanted to understand the title only in a strictly *theo*logical sense. One can ponder, for example, whether with the phrase κύριος τῆς γῆς, before whom the two olive trees and the two lampstands stand (11:4), has God or Christ in view. If, on the basis of the allusion to Zechariah 4:3, 11–14, one decides for the former possibility, one must still not overlook that 5:6 points back to the same text (Zech 4) but interprets it christologically in terms of the "Lamb." Obviously the alternative, whether the Old Testament text speaks of God or Christ, is not appropriate in every case. Even in passages where God and Christ are placed grammatically alongside each other (11:15, "Lord and Christ"), one may ask whether the author is not thinking of one and the same person, namely the one who "will reign forever and ever" (15b), and all the more so since elsewhere Old Testament predicates of God are referred to Christ.

On the other hand, there is no ambiguity in 22:20–21 ("come, *Lord* Jesus"), where the title κύριος clearly refers to Jesus. This is an instance of the Greek form of the Aramaic acclamation used in worship, "Marana tha" (cf. 1 Cor 16:22), which indicates that the author stands in the realm of early Christian apocalyptic tradition (cf. also Did 10:6). In *11:8* κύριος is linked to the possessive genitive αὐτῶν (referring to the "great city ...where also *their* Lord was crucified"). Since the reference here is to the cross of Jesus Christ in Jerusalem, it is striking that "their Lord" refers exclusively to the two witnesses mentioned in the context. The absolute use ("the Lord") is thus applied to a specific situation. Obviously secular usage is also echoed, which is also found in the address to the *angelus interpres* in 7:14 ("my Lord" = "Sir"). Also different is the blessing of "the dead who die in the Lord" (14:13). This is reminiscent of Pauline texts (ἐν κυρίῳ: 1 Cor 7:22; Gal 5:10; Phil 2:24, 29; 4:2, and elsewhere), and is particularly close to 1 Corinthians 15:18 and 1 Thessalonians 4:16 ("the dead in Christ"). This makes clear the christianizing of the use of κύριος in the Apocalypse. In conclusion we note that this is documented by the Greek adjective κυριακός, which cannot be translated into Hebrew or Aramaic, which describes the "Lord's Day" (ἡ κυριακὴ ἡμέρα) on which John the Seer receives his vision (1:10), and thus strengthens the christological orientation of the Apocalypse.[13]

The term familiar from Jewish apocalyptic, υἱὸς τοῦ ἀνθρώπου appears only twice (in vision reports: 1:13; 14:14). The difference from the Synoptic tradition is easily recognizable: there the "Son of Man" is not only the one expected in the future but the earthly, and in particular, the suffering Christ, while the Apocalypse understandably makes only limited use of the term, even though the author was probably not totally unacquainted with the Synoptic tradition.[14] So also the Pauline school, which shared a substantial number of traditional elements with the Johannine school,[15] did not use the title "Son of Man." The Old Testament background is definitive for the usage in Revelation, just as it is in the Synoptic apocalypse Apokalypse (cf. Mark 13:26parr; 14:62parr). Both are based on Daniel 7:13. This is suggested by the use of ὅμοιον that occurs twice (Dan 7:13, ὡς) and by the missing article. Additional evidence for this background is the fact that motifs from Daniel 10 are echoed in the context.[16] Since the image taken over from Daniel is part of a vision report and serves to emphasize the transcendent nature of what is reported, it cannot be in-

---

[13]  It is less likely that the use of κύριος expresses an antithesis to the Roman Caesar cult, though this is supposed by E. Lohmeyer, *Die Offenbarung des Johannes* 47, commenting on 4:11 (*dominus et deus noster*).

[14]  Cf. E. Schüssler-Fiorenza, "Quest" 420 (a kind of synopsis of Rev 1:7a; Dan 7:13 LXX; Matt 24:30c; Mark 13:26; Luke 21:27); also 420–421, on the parousia of the Son of Man; 421, the "exhortation to watch;" on which see Mark 13:35–37 and Matthew 25:13. Compare also Revelation 3:2–3; 16:15 with Matthew 24:42; Luke 12:39–40. Revelation 3:5c-8 is supposed to be dependent on the eschatological Q-tradition, which also is reflected in Matthew 10:32 and Luke 12:8. On confessing and denying, cf. the comparison of Revelation 3:21 (the promise to all Christians) with Luke 22:28–30; Matthew 19:28 (promise to the disciples); so also the call to alertness of Revelation 13:9, 18 may be compared with Mark 13:14 and Matthew 24:15c.

[15]  On the connections between the Pauline and Johannine school traditions, cf. E. Schüssler-Fiorenza, "Quest" 425: there are linguistic connections, even an affinity of Revelation for Pauline "language, tradition, and form."

[16]  Cf. T. Holtz, *Christologie* 15, 116–117; G. Dalman, *The Words of Jesus Considered in the Light of Post-Biblical Jewish Writings and the Aramaic Language* (Edinburgh: T. & T. Clark, 1909) 241–242.

ferred that it functioned for the apocalyptist as a christological *title*,[17] but rather serves to paint the vision of the Exalted One with the colors of Daniel, so as to represent the extraordinary, supernatural, unapproachable aspect of the Revealer, whose authority is represented in the following seven messages to the churches (1:13), and to demonstrate his incomparable authority as judge (14:14; cf. 1:18b).

The christological predicate υἱὸς τοῦ θεοῦ appears only once (2:18). That it is only in the messages to the churches that the Exalted One is described as "Son of God" may be due to the fact that a relatively free citation of Psalm 2:8–9 is found in 2:26–27. Since this psalm affirms the installation of the king of Israel into the realm of divine honor (Ps 2:7), this could have suggested its christological appropriation. That this title appears nowhere else in the Apocalypse need not necessarily mean that its christological usage was unfamiliar to the author; it is more likely that the frequent πατήρ predications (e. g. 1:6; 2:28; 3:5) presuppose that a Father-Son relationship existed between God and Christ. To be sure, there is no further reflection on this; it is not a matter of speculation about the internal relationships of the Trinity but an affirmation of the eschatological authority turned toward humanity, an authority independent of worldly claims to power.

The name Ἰησοῦς is found more frequently (14x), but not with any christological overtones (there is no recognizable allusion to the Hebraic meaning "Yahweh is salvation"). As in the rest of the New Testament, Ἰησοῦς simply functions as a proper name. This is seen in its combination with Χριστός (1:1–2, 5) or κύριος (22:20–21). Just as most of the passages named portray Jesus as acting, so it can also be said of "Jesus" that he sends his angel (22:16). "Jesus" is also often the object of the community's action. Thus the testimony of the apocalyptist (1:2) or the martyrs (17:6; 20:4) has "Jesus" as its object (objective genitive). There can be no doubt that here the early Christian confession is meant, the confession that is being made and must be held fast in the community's situation of persecution (1:9; 12:17: μαρτυρία Ἰησοῦ; also 14:12: πίστις Ἰησοῦ).

*Summary*: With the exception of the proper name "Jesus," the christological terminology is determined by Old Testament usage in a way unique in the New Testament. The christological terms are given a Chris-

---

[17] Contra J. Schneider, ὅμοιος, *TDNT* 5 186–188 ("messianic designation"); according to T. Holtz, *Christologie* 17, the title "Son of Man" originated in "apocalyptic circles of Judaism ..., from which it was taken over by Jesus or the church." On the basis of the Apocalypse, one can only say that the "apocalyptic circles of Judaism" are identical with the Old Testament book of Daniel. Cf. U. B. Müller, *Messias und Menschensohn* 196–199. The supposition that the Son of Man Christology is related to the idea of the Servant of Yahweh (O. Cullmann, *Christology of the New Testament* 179ff) cannot be documented in the Apocalypse, nor is it likely for 1 Corinthians 15:45ff or Romans 5:12ff.

tian interpretation within the framework of the tradition provided by the Old Testament. This does not happen by applying the "prophecy and fulfillment" schema but by appropriating the Old Testament conceptuality within the linguistic and theological purpose of the Apocalypse. The Christology of the New Testament tradition is presupposed much more strongly than is obvious simply by the observing the author's use of particular christological titles.

The formula in 1:5–6 is revealing with regard to the manner in which the conceptual worlds of the Old Testament and the Christian tradition are interwoven. Here primarily three predicates portray the exalted Christ; they can be traced back to Psalm 88 LXX (89 MT), in that a salvific declaration is made about David and his descendent.

1. "The faithful witness" (ὁ μαρτὺς ὁ πιστός). The same phrase is found in Psalm 88:38 LXX; there it refers to the constant existence of the moon in the sky that is called as a witness to the faithfulness of the promises of God. Even though μαρτύς in the Apocalypse of John is not exclusively a christological title (cf. 2:13, where it is used of Antipas), it is still the case that here as in 3:14 Christ is not designated "the faithful witness" with reference to his earthly activity but as the Exalted One who makes himself known to his servant and commissions him with the revelatory message. The Exalted One himself stands behind the reliability of the revelations he gives.

2. "The firstborn of the dead" (ὁ πρωτότοκος τῶν νεκρῶν); cf. Psalm 88:28 LXX: "firstborn" as an expression for the promise to the royal descendent of David. The Messiah has preceded the community in the resurrection; as the Risen One he is the guarantor of their own resurrection. His resurrection and exaltation constitute the event that grounds his promise to the community (cf. 1 Cor 15:20; Col 1:18).

3. "The ruler of the kings of the earth" (ὁ ἄρχων τῶν βασιλέων τῆς γῆς); cf. Psalm 88:28 LXX. Like the Davidic king but in a transcendent manner, the exalted Christ assumes an incomparable position of authority over all earthly rulers (cf. 17:14; 19:16: "king of kings"). He is also superior to the hostile supernatural powers that affect world history. Implied in this is the promise to the community that they will share in his position of power. This already implies that the destiny of the community is related to the position of the exalted Christ, which is further developed in the three following designations:

4. "The one who loved us" (τῷ ἀγαπῶντι ἡμᾶς). That the love of Christ is a fundamental element in his relationship to the community is also affirmed in other traditions of the Johannine school (cf. John 13:1, 34; 14:21; 15:9; in a soteriological sense also in the love of God implied in the "divine condescension" of 1 John 4:9–11) and found as the description of the relationship of the exalted Christ to the church in Philadelphia (Rev 3:9). The present participle indicates the enduring nature of the love of Christ. It is developed in the following two theses:

5. "The one who freed us from our sins by his blood" (λύσαντι ἡμᾶς ἐκ τῶν ἁμαρτιῶν ἡμῶν ἐν τῷ αἵματι αὐτοῦ). In conjunction with traditions from the Old Testament (cf. Psalm 129:8 LXX; Isa 40:2) and early Christianity (cf. Rom 3:25; Eph 1:7; Heb 9:12; 1 Pet 1:19), the author interprets the saving work of Christ, represented by the pouring out of the blood of Jesus, as a liberation from sins. A similar idea is familiar to other Johannine traditions (cf. e. g. 1 John 3:5, 9). The rare λύω (v. l. λούσαντι = "washing," a reflection of the baptismal tradition) has the meaning of "ransom" (cf. 5:9: "You have <them> ransomed them for God with your blood <ἠγόρασας>). The image of slave traffic is suggested, in which a purchase price is paid for a slave. In our passage the purchase price for the community is the blood of Jesus, without the image being developed to the extent that one must ask to whom the price

was paid. Since Christ is presupposed as the "ruler," the ransoming of sinners is identified with the change of rulership (cf. also the related terms ἀπολύτρωσις, Col 1:14; Eph 1:7; λύτρωσις: Luke 1:68; 2:38; Heb 9:12; λύτρον, Mark 10:45par; λυτρόομαι, Luke 24:21; Titus 2:14; 1 Pet 1:18 and elsewhere).

6. "...and made us to be a kingdom, priests serving his God and Father" (ἐποίησεν ἡμᾶς βασιλείαν ἱερεῖς τῷ θεῷ καὶ πατρὶ αὐτοῦ). The steadfast love of the "faithful witness" Jesus Christ and the liberation from the burden of sin accomplished by him have as their result that the Christian church can have the designations applied to it that were applied to the people of Israel or the Sinai generation (Isa 61:6; Exod 19:6 LXX: kingdom of priests; cf. 1 Pet 2:9). That which is to happen in the future, the reigning of the redeemed in the millennial kingdom (20:4; cf. 5:10 βασιλεύσουσιν ἐπὶ τῆς γῆς) is happening "already." Each one who is addressed by this message and responds to it in faith participates in this kingdom.

The christological predicates envisioned here are accordingly characterized by Old Testament and Christian perspectives, without the latter being limited exclusively to baptismal and eucharistic traditions. Their contents point primarily to the exalted Christ; they portray his actions that encompass the whole world and focus on the community as determined by love. By placing the appearance of his book under the authority of the exalted Lord, the author attempts to mediate the confidence that Christ has assumed lordship over all the earth and grants to the community promises and warnings that they have every reason to take seriously.

The most frequently used christological predication is the term ἀρνίον (28x). This word appears elsewhere in the New Testament only in the supplementary chapter of the Gospel of John (21:15, where it is not used in a christological but an ecclesiological sense). This is particularly close to the christological title ἀμνός in the Gospel of John (1:29, 36; elsewhere in the New Testament only Acts 8:32 and 1 Pet 1:19).

There are two possibilities of interpretation: (1.) "Lamb," "sheep," as in the LXX (Ps 113:4, 6; Jer 11:19); also Ps Sol 8:23; Philo (*Spec Leg* 1.169; 4.105; *Leg Gai* 362); Jos (*Ant* 3.226–249); as a picture of weakness: 2 Clem 5.2ff.[18] This interpretation suggests itself in view of the Old Testament-Jewish idea of the "Passover lamb" (cf. Exod 12:4–5 LXX: πρόβατον; John 19:36; 1 Cor 5:7). The supplementary term ἐσφαγμένον points in this direction (5:12; 13:8). As the "slaughtered lamb" his blood functions to ward off the death angel (Exod 12:7, 13). So also the blood of Jesus, the eschatological Passover lamb, has a liberating effect (Rev 7:14; 12:11; cf. 1 Pet 1:19).[19]

---

[18]  Derivation from Isaiah 53:7 is not to be supposed for ἀρνίον but is to be assumed for ἀμνός. Thus Jeremias, ἀμνός, ἀρήν, ἀρνίον TDNT 1.338–341, which assumes a double meaning for the Aramaic expression טַלְיָא דֶּאֱלָהָא for John 1:29, 36: (a) "lamb" (b) "boy" or "servant of God" = *agnus dei* who takes away the sins of the world. That John 1:29, 36 presupposes an Aramaic model or source continues to be only a disputed possibility, however. Moreover, in Isaiah 53:7 the expression ὡς ἀμνός is parallel to ὡς πρόβατον and is only an element in the imagery, is not used as a title, and the genitive θεοῦ is missing.

[19]  There are parallels to the portrayal of the passion in the Gospel of John, according to which Jesus' crucifixion took place on the "Day of Preparation" before the Passover, the day on which the Passover lambs were slaughtered (John 19:14, 31, 42).

Thus, although as the tradition of the Passover lamb who brings protection by its powerlessness and death stands clearly in the background of the ἀρνίον-concept of the Apocalypse, this imagery breaks down when the connotations of the image that suggest "power" are taken into account. (2.) These traits suggest the second translation possibility, "ram." Seven horns and seven eyes demonstrate the all-embracing power and knowledge of the exalted Christ (5:6). As the guide who brings his sheep to pastures and springs of water (7:17; cf. 14:1, 4), he fulfills the function of the leader of the flock. His power is manifest in his "wrath" (6:16) and in his victory over his enemies (17:14). If one can describe him as the "Messianic Ram,"[20] that can still not obscure the fact that the portrayal of the powerful advent of the ram is mingled with the imagery of the Passover lamb and thus it is not a Jewish image but the Christian image of the exalted and coming Christ that is presented.[21]

Even though the details are disputed of just how the author's "lamb terminology" relates to the sources of this imagery in the background and historical context—the later Jewish tradition is to be taken into consideration alongside that of the Old Testament—[22], this terminology is still to be understood as a united whole within the framework of the Apocalypse. The tensive juxtaposition of weakness and power, of the lowliness and exaltation of the Lamb, functions to prevent the christological image from being directly and immediately appropriated, keeping its individual elements in an unresolved, unharmonized state. Nonetheless, two complementary fundamental declarations can be extracted:

1. *The Lamb signifies redemption for the followers of Christ* (cf. 14:4). Even though his transcendent appearance is connected with the idea that he is a preexistent heavenly being,[23] the reference to a particular past

---

[20] Thus O. Böcher, *Die Johannesapokalypse* 47; so also F. Boll, "Aus der Offenbarung Johannis. Hellenistische Studien zum Weltbild der Apokalypse," in ΣΤΟΙΧΕΙΑ. *Studien zur Geschichte des antiken Weltbildes und der griechischen Wissenschaft* 1. (Leipzig-Berlin: B. G. Teubner, 1914) 44 (equated with Aries, the astrological symbol).

[21] Even if there are elements of astral mythology in the background of the apocalyptic thought world, there is no evidence in the text that the author of the Apocalypse is thinking here of the astrological symbol "Aries" (cf. the reflections of C. Clemen, *Religionsgeschichtliche Erklärung des Neuen Testaments. Die Abhängigkeit des ältesten Christentums von nichtjüdischen Religionen und philosophischen Systemen* [Giessen: Töpelmann, 1924² = Berlin 1973] 383–384); cf. F. Boll, "Aus der Offenbarung Johannis" 44–45.

[22] So U. B. Müller, who attributes the statements in texts that portray the Christ or Son of Man as engaging and destroying the powers of the world to a Jewish tradition (*Messias und Menschensohn* 189, 214ff). Critique of this view: T. Holtz, *Christologie* 245–246. Whether "lamb" was already a Jewish messianic designation is also a disputed point; cf. Test Jos 19:8 (the Armenian version is traced back to Egyptian models by B. Murmelstein, "Das Lamm in Test.Jos. 19,8," *ZNW* 58 (1967) 273–279; differently E. Lohse, *Die Offenbarung des Johannes* 42. Lohse sees in Test Jos 19.8 the only example of contemporary Judaism where "the coming redeemer is pictured as a lamb" (42) but here it is a matter of a later Christian insertion into the text; see in detail T. Holtz, *Christologie* 249.

[23] Cf. 1:8, 17–18; 21:6; 22:13.

event is presupposed even more strongly: the pouring out of his blood refers to his violent death in the historical past (e. g. 12:11). When the death of Jesus is interpreted by means of the Old Testament Exodus tradition, the result for the present and future is that people are "ransomed" from slavery "from every tribe and language and people and nation." Thereby the foundation for the new Israel is laid (5:9–10; cf. 14:3–4).

2. *The Lamb signifies the judgment of the powers hostile to God and the reign of the kingdom of God forever.* With the manifestation of God's sovereignty (19:4–6), which is also celebrated as the "marriage of the Lamb" (19:7–9), the promise of Psalm 2:9 is fulfilled: judgment is executed on the enemies of God (19:15; cf. 12:5). Although the name of Christ is the "Word of God" (19:13) and the "sharp sword that came from his mouth" (19:15, 21), the reference is not only to the spiritual conquest of the evil powers through the Word (cf. Heb 4:12) but the picture of the "divine meal", in which the birds of the sky eat the flesh of kings and military commanders (19:17–18), is painted in drastic colors and means the total annihilation of the "beast" and those who have helped him (19:20–21). At the end of history the lasting kingdom of God and of the Lamb is established, in which "there will be no more night" (22:3–5; cf. 12:10).

### c)  Ecclesiology

Böcher, O. *Kirche in Zeit und Endzeit. Aufsätze zur Offenbarung des Johannes.* Neukirchen-Vluyn: Neukirchener, 1983.
Satake, A. *Die Gemeindeordnung in der Johannesapokalypse.* WMANT 21, Neukirchen-Vluyn: Neukirchener, 1966.
Schüssler-Fiorenza, E. *Priester für Gott. Studien zum Herrschafts- und Priestermotiv in der Apokalypse.* NTA 7. Münster: Aschendorff, 1972.
Wolff, Chr. "Die Gemeinde des Christus in der Apokalypse des Johannes," *NTS* 27 (1981) 186–197.

John the Seer received the commission to write "what you have seen, what is, and what is to take place after this" (1:19). This is not an outline of the document, although there is an anticipation of basic motifs that will constantly reappear in the following: the Seer reports his visions and the interpretation given to him (especially by the angel). The subject matter of his imagery is indeed current events, the situation of the church of his time but future events are also portrayed, though both present and future are presented in such a way that the reader must often decide which is which. The real goal of the work is the future end of history, to which all visions and events in the world are directed. Here they find their final fulfillment (cf. chaps. 21–22). Since the presentation of present and future history is concerned with the whole Christian community, it comes within the purview of the author even where it is not directly or indirectly addressed (as e. g. in the picture of the seven lampstands of 1:12–13, 20; 2:1 or in the messages addressed to the seven churches of chaps. 2–3).

## 1. Situation

The church's present is portrayed as a situation of persecution. The seer John finds himself on Patmos "because of the word of God and the testimony of Jesus" (1:9). He looks back on persecutions in which a number of victims had given their testimony in their own blood (6:9), and expects that further persecutions will follow (6:11; cf. 12:17).[24] Despite these frequent allusions to persecution, which however remain within the realm of Revelation's visionary imagery, the historical circumstances of the persecution presupposed cannot be clearly discerned. The worship of the beast (13:8, 15), like the mark on the right hand or the forehead as the requirement for participation in economic life (13:16–17), point to the Roman emperor cult. The Christians' refusal to worship the emperor as divine and to sacrifice to his image in the Caesar temple was punished severely, including the death penalty.[25] Even though the details of the persecution remain obscure, there can be no doubt of the fact itself, nor can it be doubted that the attitude of the government authorities placed the very existence of the Christian community in danger.

## 2. Predications

The author knows that he has been called to address the Christian community in this situation.[26] He summons the community to an awareness of itself as already a community separated from the world by the liberating act of the Lamb: they understand themselves as ἅγιοι. Of the 23 references in the Apocalypse, almost half (11) are constructed in the plural with the article ("the saints").[27] In the Greek world and in the Old Testament, "holy" is a cultic concept that indicates something withdrawn from secu-

---

[24] Cf. also 13:1ff: God's enemy, the beast that arises from the sea, is the Antichrist, whose characteristic traits are the antithetical counterpart of Christ: 13:3, 12, 14: the mortal wound of the beast and its healing can be understood as the counterpart of the death and resurrection of Christ.

[25] Cf. Pliny Ep 10.96–97. W. Foerster, *Neutestamentliche Zeitgeschichte* (Hamburg: Furche Verlag, 1959³) 1:199–201; H. Koester, *History and Literature of Early Christianity* II, 334–338 773–777; B. Reicke, *Neutestamentliche Zeitgeschichte* 292–295.

[26] Cf. the messages to the seven churches (2:1–3:22); the churches are symbolically represented by the seven golden lampstands, with the Son of Man in their midst (1:12–13, 20; 2:1).

[27] The other references: to God (4:8; 6:10), to Christ (3:7), or to angelic beings (14:10); also adjectival, "the holy city" (11:2; 21:2, 10; 22:19); parallel to μακάριος: 20:6; substantive singular: 22:11 ("let the holy still be holy").

lar use and that belongs to the divine sphere. Correspondingly, the term when used as a Christian self-description indicates that believers understand themselves as made holy, sanctified, by the saving act of Jesus Christ (1 Cor 1:2). It was thus already a Christian "terminus technicus" that was adopted by the author of the Apocalypse.[28] There are no explanatory reflections but the context indicates the christological reference: the "prayers of the saints" are joined with the praises of the 24 elders as the representatives of the heavenly church before the throne of the Lamb. They praise the sacrifice of the Lamb that has brought a universal redemption (5:8–9). Their prayers ascend before God from the hand of the angel like the smoke of incense, and are heard (8:3–4). It is the persecuted church of Jesus Christ that prays to God. Just as the Lamb was slaughtered, so his followers are delivered over to suffering: the "beast" makes war "with the saints" (13:7; cf. Dan 7:21). As the blood of the Lamb was poured out, so also the blood of the saints (16:6; 17:6; 18:24).

The persecution is due to the fact that the saints are "witnesses of Jesus" (17:6). In this situation they are called to steadfastness and keeping the faith (13:10). Their endurance is manifest in their "keeping the commands of God and the faith of Jesus" (14:12). Those who keep faith receive the promise that they will share in the first resurrection (20:6). The "reward" is given to them (11:18; 22:12). Such an expectation is reason for joyful celebration: God's victory has prevailed over Babylon (18:21) and the righteous judgment of God is executed on his enemies (16:6–7). Even if Gog and Magog besiege the military camp of the saints, these will still be saved by fire (20:9).

The self-understanding of the community is also interpreted by the expression "those who fear the name of God" (11:18; cf. 19:5), which is rooted in an Old Testament background (cf. Micah 6:9; Ps 60:6 LXX). Members of the church in general are designated with this term, to the extent that they obey God's commands and hold fast to the faith.[29] Their names are written in the "book of life" (cf. 21:27; 3:5; the negative counterpart for the followers of the beast: 13:8; 17:8; 20:15).

The eschatological community is also portrayed with the picture of the 144,000 "virgins" (παρθένοι, 14:4). The "round number" is a picture of heavenly fullness (similarly in a symbolic sense 7:4: 144,000 martyrs) and can no more be interpreted literally than the statement that they "have not defiled themselves with women" (14:4). Virginity is not here identical with

---

[28] The term is found only rarely in Jewish apocalyptic tradition; but cf. Daniel 7:21 and especially the Similitudes of 1 Enoch (38:4–5; 39:1, 4–5); also rare in the Qumran literature (e. g. 1QM 3:5; 6:6).

[29] Differently O. Böcher, "Bürger der Gottesstadt," in *Kirche in Zeit und Endzeit* 164 note 21: the basis is the Jewish tradition according to which "God-fearers" (proselytes) become "saints" by martyrdom.

asceticism (renunciation of marriage or sexual activity) but is a general description that the saints have not been overcome by the tests and temptations that have broken upon them in the persecution. Their ethical purity is expressed in their description as "firstfruits" (ἀπαρχή) for God and the Lamb and that they have kept themselves "blameless" (ἄμωμοι), as expressed in the language of the sacrificial cult (cf. also 2 Cor 11:2). That they bear the name of the Lamb and his Father on their foreheads signifies their eschatological quality. This is not dependent on a particular religion, race, or nation but on the fact that they have been called together out of all humanity, "the redeemed from (the inhabitants) of the earth" (14:3).

That the community belongs to God and Christ is also indicated by the term δοῦλος. As in the Old Testament Moses can be understood as the "servant of God" to attest that he acts as one commissioned by God (Josh 1:2, 7), so also the seer John can signify his relation to Jesus Christ with the term δοῦλος. He delivers the message to the community, reporting what he has seen and heard, not on his own authority but at the command of the exalted Lord (1:1). The whole Christian community is described as the fellowship of the "servants" of Jesus Christ (1:1; 22:6). The ecclesial usage prevails, for even in the passages where the term is associated with "prophets" (10:7; 11:18) the meaning "believers in Christ" is present. The martyrs too, whose blood is avenged against the harlot Babylon, are named "his servants" (19:2), which refers to the whole church in general. As the new people of God it joins in the praise of God and thereby demonstrates its service to God (19:5). Despite the danger of being misled by false prophecy that would cause it to lose its relation to God, the church has the promise that it will attain the restored paradise of God, where before the throne of God and the Lamb it will both serve and rule (22:3, 5).

## 3.   Office and Spirit

Among the official roles in the church that cannot be exercised by all members of the community belongs the word προφήτης. Even though the author does not use this designation of himself, and his work as a whole has the character of an apocalyptic writing rather than that of a prophetic book,[30] he still considers the revelations given to him as λόγοι τῆς προφητείας (1:3; 22:7, 10, 18–19), and considers his mission to be such that his words are to be interpreted as prophetic predictions for the nations (10:11: προφητεύω). Thus he can describe himself as "brother of the prophets" (22:9). It is more significant, however, that "prophets" are named alongside saints and apostles, and accordingly refer not to Old Testament figures but to Christian prophets (11:18; 16:6; 18:20, 24). Thus the author knows a prophetic office within the church (cf. also Did 11:8–12).

---

[30]   Correctly A. Satake, *Gemeindeordnung* 73.

Even though this office is not described more precisely, it is still clear that he ascribes great importance to this office, since it is placed on the same level as that of the angels (22:9, the revelatory angel as "a fellow servant with the prophets"), and also that the prediction of future events is included in the mission of Christian prophecy (cf. 10:11; 22:6; Acts 11:28; 21:10: Agabus). The "two witnesses," who "speak as prophets" (11:3), appear as a special example of Christian prophecy (11:10). They are not described more closely, however, so that an identification of them with Moses or Elijah (cf. Mark 9:4par) remains hypothetical despite the fitting echoes of an Old Testament background in 11:5–6 (cf. 2 Kings 1:10; 1 Kings 17:1; Jer 5:14; Exod 7:19). In the author's understanding it refers to a picture of the future. The two witnesses have the mission to "torment" the inhabitants of the earth, i.e. to announce their coming judgment (11:10). If this is understood as a description of the function of Christian prophets, their more detailed description (their struggle with the Antichrist in which they are killed but are later raised from the dead, 11:7, 11–12; cf. Ezek 37:5, 10) reflects not only the destiny of Christian prophets but that of the persecuted church as a whole, which is promised that after the persecution of the end times they will be victorious over the powers hostile to God.

Ἀπόστολος is named as a church office alongside the prophets. This term is, of course, also to be understood in a purely historical sense, as a designation of the Twelve Apostles that form the foundation of the church (21:14; cf. Luke 6:13; Matt 10:2) but their being listed between saints and prophets (18:20) makes it likely that it refers to a church office analogous to that of the prophets. Like them, the apostles are subjected to persecution as Christians. This is also indicated by 2:2, according to which *false apostles* have appeared in the church at Ephesus. Accordingly this office is not bound to a particular place but it is rather a matter of wandering missionary preachers, even though we are not able to say anything more precisely about their function or their relation to Christian prophets.

The case is different with the term πρεσβύτερος. It is found 12 times, exclusively in the second major section of the Apocalypse, and only with reference to the 24 heavenly elders (4:4, 10; 5:5 and elsewhere). In his vision, the Seer beholds them near the throne of God, endowed with heavenly attributes (sitting on 24 thrones, clothed in white garments, golden crowns on their heads). Twice, one of the 24 elders functions as *angelus interpres* (5:5; 7:13ff). There is no hint that this portrayal reflects a churchly office of presbyter. Their significance is rather that the 24 elders participate in the transcendent worship.

The antithetical counterpart of the Christian prophets is the "false prophet" (ψευδοπροφήτης). As one of God's enemies along with the "beast," the false prophet persecutes the Christian community and attempts to mislead it by "signs" (19:20; cf. 16:13–14). He suffers the same fate as the beast, the Antichrist (19:20; 20:10). More specifically, the prophet (προφῆτις) Jezebel appears, who is said to beguile the church at Thyatira (2:20). The connection with Old Testament tradition is not to be overlooked (1

Kings 16:31: Jezebel seduces king Ahab into idolatry). The content of her seduction is also derived from this Old Testament tradition.[31] Thus if the picture of false prophecy remains somewhat pale and traditional, it is still clear that the dispute between true and false prophets reflected in the Apocalypse was not unfamiliar to the churches of Asia Minor (cf. also 1 John 4:1; in addition Matt 7:15; 24:11, 24par and elsewhere).

The fact that the structure of the churches represented in the Apocalypse includes a prophetic office might suggest that the term πνεῦμα refers to this office in particular or that the gift of the Spirit was accordingly limited to it. But actually the author never speaks of the Spirit of God working in or through the prophets.[32] On the other hand, it is also not said that the church's existence is constituted by the power of the Spirit of God or Christ, as though the church is founded on a general function of the πνεῦμα among church members (cf. John 16:13); it is rather the case that the genitive phrases "Spirit of God" or "Spirit of Christ" are absent from the Apocalypse, as is the term "Holy Spirit." If one disregards the texts that refer to a specific, limited function of the Spirit,[33] two remaining conceptual spheres remain:

1. The vision of the *seven spirits* has a variety of roots in the history of religion, among which is the Old Testament-Jewish tradition of the seven archangels (Tob 12:15). There is also the identification with or parallel to the seven stars[34] or the seven torches (4:5) in the non-Jewish world of ideas.[35] The seven spirits, like the seven angels (8:2), stand before the throne of God, and are thus part of the heavenly court (4:5). Not only God but also the angels bestow the salvific gifts of grace and peace pronounced upon the churches (1:4). As the "seven spirits of God" they are sent forth to all the earth (5:6). Although their particular functions remain unclear— neither their identification with the Spirit of God nor with the angels of the seven churches is made explicit (1:20)—the symbolic connotation of "seven" shows that they are representations of the incomparable divine

---

[31] Cf. Numbers 25:1-2; there is no compelling evidence for an allusion to the "apostolic decree" (Acts 15:20, 29; 21:25).

[32] Cf. rather 19:10: the "spirit of prophecy," i.e. the testimony of the prophets, is equated with the "testimony of Jesus;" in 22:6 God is the Lord over the "spirits of the prophets," i.e. those who hold the Christian prophetic office.

[33] "Spirit" as "breath of life" (11:11; 13:15); in the plural: unclean spirits, i.e. demons (16:13-14; 18:2); also being "in the Spirit" as opposed to bodily existence as an expression of ecstasy or rapture (1:10; 4:2; 17:3; 21:10).

[34] 1:20, angels of the seven churches; cf. 3:1. The identification of the angels of the churches (2:1, 8 and elsewhere) is disputed. Are they the earthly congregational leaders? It is more likely that each church is thought of as having its angel that represents it before the heavenly throne. On the messenger character of the angels, cf. Malachi 2:7; 3:1; Haggai 1:13.

[35] Cf. W. Hadorn, *Die Offenbarung des Johannes*, Excursus 3, 31-32; E. Schweizer, πνεῦμα, πνευματικός, *TDNT* 6:449-451.

fullness and perfection that is promised to the churches and at the same time is already given and present.

2. The absolute term *the Spirit* appears especially in the context of the messages to the seven churches in the identical *call to alertness formula* "Let anyone who has an ear listen to what the Spirit is saying to the churches" (2:7, 11, 17, 29; 3:6, 13, 22). The obvious meaning is that the exalted Christ, the Son of Man (1:13) addresses the churches through these messages. Still, an explicit identification of Christ and the Spirit is not made; against this is especially the passage in *22:17*, where the Spirit and "the bride" (= the heavenly Jerusalem and/or the heavenly church; cf. 19:7-8; 21:9-10) address the earthly church and pray for the coming of Christ (cf. 22:20). That the author sometimes distinguishes Spirit and Christ from each other, and at other times approaches what appears to be their identification, corresponds to the mysterious style of the Apocalypse that intentionally leaves what is said in the realm of what cannot finally be grasped. Nonetheless, the mission of the Spirit can be clearly recognized: *The Spirit is the speaker of divine revelations addressed to the Christian community.* The human person of John the seer recedes, even when the Spirit's speech is articulated by the apocalyptic author (cf. 2:7; 14:13). Without binding his function as speaker to a specific class within the church (e. g. that of prophets), and without conferring a pneumatic character on the church as a whole, the Spirit addresses and works within the churches. Through words of encouragement and admonition it orients the church in the present and guides it along the way that leads to the ultimate fulfillment of human history (cf. 14:13; 22:17). The Spirit is the reality that characterizes and directs the church in the present and into the future.

### 4.  *Encouragement and Warning (The Messages to the Seven Churches)*

The seven messages (2:1-3:22) are not real letters but products of literary artistry that express the author's theological intention and self-understanding. Within the structure of the work as a whole, they function as a preparatory transition to the second major section with the real revelatory visions (4:1-22:5; see note 12 above).[36] On the other hand, the connection with the preceding vision of Christ (1:9-20) is significant, since several of its motifs recur in the messages to the churches.[37] The messages to the seven churches in Asia Minor are accordingly grounded in the authority of the exalted Christ who is both savior and judge, so that in what

---

[36]   Cf. W. Popkes, "Die Funktion der Sendschreiben in der Johannes-Apokalypse," ZNW 74 (1983) 90–107.

[37]   Cf. Chr. Wolff, "Die Gemeinde des Christus in der Apokalypse des Johannes" 186–197.

follows both the ecclesial-anthropological indicative and the ethical imperative are based on the reality of the exalted Christ.

The surpassing greatness of the power of the Christ/Son of Man is portrayed in the introductory vision in vivid colors: the beginning and end of time, death and life are subject to his domain (1:17–18). So also in the messages to the churches the absolute power of the exalted Lord is emphasized: he was dead and is alive (2:8), he is prior to God's creation (3:14); he has the "key of David" and is able to open a "door" or to close it (3:7–8).

The content of the message includes both promise of salvation and announcement of judgment. The *word of promise* applies to the churches and their members if they overcome the onslaughts of the devil and in the persecutions hold fast to their faith in the exalted Christ. They will receive the "crown of life" and will be delivered from the second death (2:10–11). They will share in Christ's own realm of lordship, sit on his throne, and receive the "morning star" (3:21; 2:28).

On the other hand, a *word of judgment* is pronounced against the churches addressed. The exalted Christ threatens to knock down the lamp stands of the churches if they do not repent (2:5). Those who are not willing to repent are threatened with the "sharp two-edged sword" (2:12, 16; cf. 19:21). The one who "searches minds and hearts" (2:23) will rule the nations with an iron rod and shatter the godless like clay pots (2:26–27). It thereby becomes clear that only the Exalted One will execute violence against the enemies of God; for the inhabitants of the earth, the maxim applies, "if you are to be taken captive, into captivity you go; if you kill with the sword, with the sword you must be killed" (13:10 v. l.).

The churches addressed in the seven messages not only look back on persecutions they have already endured (e. g. 2:2–3, 13, 19; 3:8) but are presently experiencing "affliction" (2:9; cf. 1:9) and anticipate that they must also do so in the future (2:10, 22). In view of this situation, they are addressed with words of encouragement and admonition, as in the promises to "those who conquer,"[38] to which corresponding makarisms are found in the second major section.[39] Promises and makarisms announce future salvation to the suffering churches, as well as to individual Christians, if they have not "soiled their clothes" (3:4), for the victory of the Lamb stands at the end of history (17:14). For all who conquer with him, a glorious "inheritance" is prepared (21:7; cf. 2:7; 3:12, 21).

Alongside the encouraging pronouncements, the messages to the churches contain warnings that presuppose that the churches as a whole have by no means already given a good account of themselves. On the contrary, some have abandoned "the love they had at first" and have

---

[38]  The "conqueror" sayings are found in 2:7, 11, 17, 26; 3:5, 12, 21 and in 21:7.
[39]  14:13; 16:15; 19:9; 20:6; 22:7, 14, and in 1:3. That there are exactly seven is striking!

"fallen away" (2:4–5). Others tolerate false teachers in their midst, who lead them into error.[40] The church at Laodicea is reproached that it is "neither hot nor cold" but "lukewarm" (3:15–16). It has not made adequate use of the new existence and the gifts that have been given to it; its satisfaction is evidenced by its boasting of its (spiritual) riches, without knowing how poverty-stricken it really is. It thus is counseled to accept the gifts of salvation provided by Christ that it may be truly rich (3:17–18).

## 5.   Present and Future

Günther, H. W. *Der Nah- und Enderwartungshorizont in der Apokalypse des heiligen Johannes.* fzb 41. Würzburg: Echter, 1980.
Rissi, M. *Was ist und was geschehen soll danach. Die Zeit- und Geschichtsauffassung der Offenbarung des Johannes.* AThANT 46. Zürich: Zwingli, 1965.

### Present Salvation

Even if the admonitions are not made concrete in their particulars, it is still clear that in the Apocalypse taken as a whole the center of gravity lies on the admonitions to perseverance and steadfastness.[41] That the community knows of a presently-experienced salvation that can be expressed in the indicative is reflected in its confession of sharing the "testimony of Jesus"[42] or the "faith of Jesus,"[43] but also in its eschatological self-understanding according to which it understands itself to be the present and future fellowship of kings and priests (1:6; 5:10; cf. 20:6). Moreover, traces of the celebration of the community's *sacramental practice* can be perceived. Even if the details remain disputed, it still seems that the apocalyptist's futuristic view of the heavenly worship (7:9–17; 22;3–5) reflect elements of the baptismal and/or eucharistic traditions of the Johannine churches. They declare that the saving effect of the pouring out of the blood of the Lamb (1:5; 5:9; 7:14; 12:11) are sacramentally mediated to the believers. Thus the "washing of their garments in the blood of the Lamb" could be a reflection of early Christian baptismal tradition,[44] espe-

---

[40]   2:14–15, 20. The warning against the teaching of Balaam utilizes Old Testament vocabulary (especially from Num 31:16), which makes a precise identification of the opposing propaganda impossible. Neither can the "teaching of the Nicolaitans" be interpreted with confidence (2:15), a teaching that is to be distinguished from that of the Balaamites, as is indicated by the additional reference in the message to the church at Ephesus (2:6).

[41]   In a particular manner in 13:10 and 14:12.

[42]   1:2, 9; 12:17; 19:10; 20:4; cf. 17:6.

[43]   14:12; cf. 2:13. The decision between subjective or objective genitive is problematic in each case.

[44]   Cf. J. Roloff, *The Revelation of John: A Continental Commentary* (Minneapolis: Fortress, 1993) 99.

cially since being clothed in white garments was a common baptismal practice in the early church. So also the act of "sealing" (7:2–3, 9:4) may point to Christian baptism (cf. 2 Cor 1:22; Eph 1:13; 4:30). In addition we might suppose there is a sacramental background for the image of the "water of life" (21:6; 22:17). Although the imagery deals with God's future gift to the redeemed, the christological framing of this imagery in the Gospel of John (John 4:10–11, 13–14) still shows that this image was understood to have a present reference within the Johannine school. To be sure, the problem of the connections within the history of tradition are not clearly resolved,[45] but John 3:5 also documents that the sacrament of baptism with water was connected with the (life-giving) Spirit.

If one sees a connection between the "Bread of Life" (John 6:35) and the "Water of Life,"[46] then one could easily imagine that eucharistic traditions are reflected. It is a disputed point whether the author alludes to the Lord's Supper in his picture of the "open door" and the future table fellowship of Christ with his own (3:20). The primary idea, at least, is that of the coming of the Kyrios Jesus and the receiving of his church into heavenly glory. The announcement that evil doers and the godless will be excluded from the coming city of God (22:15) could refer to the practice in early Christian worship in which only members of the congregation but not catechumens or non-Christians, could participate in the eucharistic celebration (cf. Did 9:5). This would fit in with the liturgical acclamation "Marana tha," which is echoed in the prayerful call "Amen, come Lord Jesus" (22:20) that was probably at the beginning of the eucharistic service (cf. Did 10:6).

The presence of eschatological salvation is more clearly expressed in the christological affirmations that the Christ/Son of Man has "already in the present" assumed his sovereign power (1:5, 18), and also in the fact that—as the ecclesiological predicates also indicate—the Christian community understands itself to be "not of this world." Therefore the churches are admonished in the seven messages with the call to repentance to return to their "first love" they had at the beginning (2:4) and to do their "first works" (2:5) in a renewed manner. They are also reminded of "what you have received and heard" (3:3). Since the call to repentance means that the churches of the Apocalypse were not in a state of perfection but had to be constantly challenged anew to remember the salvation they have received and to give concrete expression to the eschatological dimension

---

[45]  For a derivation from Gnosticism cf. J.-W. Taeger, *Johannesapokalypse und johanneischer Kreis. Versuch einer traditionsgeschichtlichen Ortsbestimmung am Paradigma der Lebenswasser-Thematik* (BZNW 51. Berlin: W. de Gruyter, 1989). Apocalyptic roots are discovered by F. Hahn, "Die Worte vom lebendigen Wasser im Johannesevangelium," in J. Jervell and W. A. Meeks, eds., *God's Christ and His People* (FS N. A. Dahl) (Oslo-Bergen-Tromsö: Universitetsforl, 1977) 51–70.

[46]  So F. Hahn, "Die Worte vom lebendigen Wasser" 52–54 and elsewhere.

of their being in right ethical conduct, on the other hand a group is highlighted that stands immediately before the ultimate completion:

The term μάρτυς appears five times in the Apocalypse; with the exception of 17:6, it does not yet have the special meaning of "martyr" as one who testifies to the truth by shedding his or her blood, the meaning it received in later church terminology. Here it indicates one who testifies to something, an announcer or preacher.[47] Of course, the testimony can result in the witness being persecuted and suffering a violent death. This is the case with the "faithful witness" Antipas, who held fast to his testimony "to the point of death" (2:13), and for the two witnesses who—after they had given their testimony—were defeated and killed by the beast from the underworld (11:3, 7). So also saints and prophets suffer the death penalty for the sake of Christ but without the martyr/witness terminology being applied to them (18:24). But even though the witness terminology does not always appear, it is still the case that it is generally presupposed (not only in 17:6) that confession of Christ results in being persecuted and killed. For—as the vision of the fifth seal shows—those who are executed were "slaughtered for the word of God and for the testimony they had given" (6:9; cf. 20:4). They are promised that they will conquer the "Accuser" "by the blood of the Lamb and by the word of their testimony, for they did not cling to life even in the face of death" (12:11). This promise is graphically illustrated (6:11: clothed with white garments); its fulfillment is awaited at the first resurrection, with the establishment of the thousand year reign of peace (20:4).

*Future Salvation*

The Apocalypse of John was written in the context of persecution of Christians. The connection to the Johannine school suggests that this persecution occurred not under Domitian but in the time of the emperor Trajan (98–117). In favor of this view is the oracular saying about the eighth king who is also one of the seven who preceded him, since Trajan was the eighth emperor after Nero and could be seen in terms of the "Nero redivivus" myth.[48] This dating remains hypothetical, however, especially since the influence of the oracle tradition on the composition of the Apocalypse must be taken into consideration. Independently of its precise dating, it is clear that the Apocalypse advocates the expectation of the near parousia.[49]

---

[47] This is also the meaning when used of the exalted Lord as the "faithful witness" (1:5; 3:14).

[48] Domitian was the seventh emperor after Nero. Cf. also the problem of the number 666 or 616 in 13:18.

[49] Cf. 1:1, "what must soon take place" (ἐν τάχει) is revealed to the seer by the exalted Christ. So also 1:3, "the time is near" (ἐγγύς); 3:11 "I am coming quickly;" also 22:7, 10, 17, 20.

It is clearly a fresh revival of near expectation, since the motifs of suddenness and surprise ("I will come like a thief," 3:3; cf. 16:15) appear to presuppose a previous problematic awareness that the parousia had been delayed (cf. 1 Thess 5:2; Matt 24:43). Both the beast from the abyss (11:7, 17:8) and the beast from the sea (13:1–10, 18) appear at the end of the series of trumpet visions or bowl visions to persecute the Christian community (6th trumpet: 9:13; 11:7; 6th bowl: 16:12ff), after which the "heavenly Messiah" appears (11:15; 12:10; 19:11ff).

The portrayal of the final drama follows within the framework of two cycles of motifs: the final cosmic catastrophe and the victory over the anti-God worldly power. These two motifs overlap. The cosmic catastrophe is unleashed by the seventh trumpet (10:6–7; 11:17). The Creator will bring an end to the present heaven and earth (20:11); time ($\chi\rho\acute{o}\nu o\varsigma$)will also disappear (10:6), and a new heaven and new earth will appear.[50] The cosmic upheaval is introduced by earthquakes, floods, hailstorms, and by the fall of the city of Babylon (16:17–21). Interwoven with this picture is the second, dominant aspect, the victory over the anti-God powers. These have different names that are not to be identified with each other:[51] alongside the "beast from the sea" that makes war with the saints (13:1ff) is named "another beast that rose out of the earth;" it has the same features as the false prophet, since it does "great signs" and makes the earth and its inhabitants worship the first beast (13:11ff). To be distinguished from both is "the beast that comes up from the bottomless pit," that makes war with the two witnesses (11:7). More frequent reference is made to the "dragon," who pursues the woman and the newborn child (12:1ff; 13ff) and is combated by Michael and his angels (12:7ff); he is also called the "great dragon," the primeval serpent, the devil, and Satan (12:9; 20:2). These images are congealed into a Satanic triad of "dragon, beast, and false prophet." All of these belong to the demonic world (16:13–14); they assemble for a final cosmic battle at the place Harmagedon (16:16). The Son of Man stands over against the anti-God powers (14:14ff). As the "Lord of Lords" he will conquer them (17:14), will destroy the godless with his sword and at the hour of harvest execute God's righteous judgment on them (19:15).

Even though there is no calculation of the time of the end of the world and the events seen in the visions cannot be organized into a temporal scheme but rather are complementary and supplementary interpretations of one and the same event, namely the struggle between God and Satan, between the Messiah—Son of Man and the anti-God powers, there is still one place in the Apocalypse where a temporal schema appears: chapter

---

[50]  21:1; cf. Isaiah 65:17; 66:22; 2 Peter 3:13.
[51]  Cf. R. Schnackenburg, *Johannine Epistles* 138; G. Strecker, *Johannine Letters* 238–242.

twenty clearly distinguishes between a first and second resurrection, separated by a thousand-year reign of peace (20:1–15). Four phases can be
distinguished:

1. The sovereign appearance of Christ begins, and the first act of his reign
on the earth is the binding of the Satanic trio who have been terrorizing
the earth after the dragon's expulsion from heaven (12:9ff). In accord with
the apocalyptic perspective the reign of peace will last 1000 years; it is
portrayed realistically as an earthly reign (cf. Dan 2:44; 7:22; also Rev
5:10: "They will reign *on earth*").

The chiliastic expectation of a thousand year reign is rooted in Jewish apocalypticism. 4 Ezra 7:28–28 (end of the 1st century C. E.): the Messiah will reign for 400
years. Then he will die along with his contemporaries; after seven days there follows
a resurrection for judgment (4 Ezr 7:30–33), which results in eternal salvation for the
pious, eternal torture in Gehenna for the godless (4 Ezr 7:34–38), and the New
Jerusalem will appear in glory (4 Ezr 10:27, 44–55).
   2 Baruch (beginning of the 2nd cent. C. E., perhaps presupposing 4 Ezra): the
divine judgment is executed on the whole earth (2 Bar 24–28), the Messiah comes
(29), who returns to heaven after a brief period on earth (30:1a). Then follows the
resurrection of the righteous (30:1b-3) and the destruction of the ungodly (30:4–5).
Then Jerusalem is rebuilt (32:2) but destroyed again "after some time" (32:3a).
Finally, the general resurrection of the dead and the judgment of the world arrives,
bringing the righteous to eternal salvation and the unrighteous into torment (50:2–
51:16).
   While the duration of the Messianic kingdom is set at various lengths (Rev: 1000
years; 4 Ezr 400 years; 2 Bar "some time"), in each instance it is still the case that
we have a periodization of the final events in which the eschatological intermediate
kingdom plays an important role. The thousand year period is also documented in
*Testament of Isaac* (prior to 70 C. E.?), which speaks of a thousand year festival
(10:12) or banquet (8:11, 20) in which the pious participate.[52]
   Millennialism was widespread in early Christianity, and was already present in
the New Testament. In addition to 1 Corinthians 15:20–28, there are traces in the
Gospel of John (5:17–18; 9:4 = "world Sabbath"?). This conception is clearly documented in Justin's interpretation of Isaiah 7:14 and 8:4: the goal of the millennial
hope is accordingly the rebuilding of Jerusalem and the establishment of a reign of
peace in which the church will live together with Christ (Dial 80:1–2). So also Papias
of Hierapolis, who was close to the Presbyter John, was a chiliast (Eusebius HE
3.39.12; Irenaeus Haer 5.33.3–4; 36.1–2). And it was said of the Gnostic Cerinthus
that angels had revealed to him that after the resurrection the kingdom of Christ
would be established on earth and that those who had been restored to bodily life
would dwell in Jerusalem; for a period of 1000 years people could surrender themselves to every possible delight, spending this time as at a wedding celebration
(Eusebius HE 3.28.2, 4–5).
   Also the author of the Epistle of Barnabas (ca 130–135 C. E.) calculated that after
6000 years of world history, at the beginning of the seventh millennium Christ's
peaceable kingdom would be established (Barn 15.4–5), and a second creation will be
made like the first (6:13). This means that the seventh millennium will correspond

---

[52]   Cf. further references in O. Böcher, "Das tausendjährige Reich," in *Kirche in Zeit
und Endzeit* 136ff.

to the seventh day of creation, the Sabbath of creation (cf. 15.8–9: Jesus Christ arose on the eighth day and thereby laid the foundation for the new creation; cf. Isa 65:17; Rev 21:1). The second coming of Christ is expected as the foundation for the seventh millennium, the time when Christ will be revealed "in the flesh" (Barn 6.9; 7.9). This is an expectation that the coming kingdom of Christ will take place in the real world of time and space, as indicated in the parallel in 2 John 7 (see above).

Summary: Chiliasm is a product of Jewish apocalyptic, presumably originating as a combination of the Jewish-nationalistic hope for the reestablishment of the Davidic kingdom with the specific concept of history according to which world history is divided into a world week of 1000–year days, at the end of which stands a world Sabbath of 1000 years (cf. Gen 1:31; 2:1–3; Ps 90:4). At the beginning of the second century C. E. this view was widespread not only in Jewish apocalyptic literature but also in the Christian hope for the parousia, which contributed to the revival of earliest Christianity's expectation that the end of history lay in the immediate future.

2. At the beginning of Christ's kingdom of peace the martyrs and confessors will be raised from the dead (= the first resurrection). They will rule with Christ (cf. Matt 19:28par); 1 Cor 15:20–28; 6:2–3; Dan 7:22, 27) in his messianic kingdom as "priests of God and of Christ" (20:4–6). Since they had existed previously only as "souls" in an intermediate state (6:9; 20:4), it is presupposed that at the first resurrection they will be reclothed with bodies (cf. Ezek 37:1–14). This thus corresponds to the realistic millennial expectation of the coming thousand year reign.

3. There follows for a "short time" (20:3) the final threat, which is portrayed with echoes of Ezekiel 38–39 (20:7–10). Satan deceives the nations one last time but the saints and their city are saved. The anti-God Gog and Magog are defeated, the Satanic trio are overcome and thrown into the place of damnation (cf. 19:20; 20:2–3).

4. After the first resurrection, in which only the martyrs and confessors had been brought to life, comes the second resurrection in which all the dead are raised and stand before the last judgment that includes all humanity (20:11–15). This event includes the dissolution of earth and heaven, the destruction of death and the realm of the dead, as well as all who are not found in the Book of Life. The appearance of the new heaven and new earth is identified with the descent of the new Jerusalem from heaven (21:1–22:5; cf. Ezek 40–48). The marriage of the Lamb with his bride, the holy city Jerusalem, is celebrated (21:9–10; announced 19:7–9), and a worship service begins that will last forever (22:3–5).

## d) Ethics

The ethical admonitions of the Apocalypse are oriented to the existence of the church in history, especially in the situation of persecution that is presupposed. Written as a book of encouragement and warning for the persecuted church, the Apocalypse is directed in particular to the relation to the state. Corresponding to this situation—in contrast to that of the Pauline ethic—it is not a positive attitude but a withdrawal from the Roman political authority that is definitive for the document's ethical parenesis (cf. e. g. 14:9ff; 20:4). It must be acknowledged that the apocalyptic genre is almost devoid of concrete information, so that the interpretation of the meaning of these statements in their own historical context is burdened with severe difficulties and cannot achieve really satisfactory results. This also applies to the question as to whether references to "fornication" and "food sacrificed to idols" (2:14) castigate sexual misconduct in the churches. It is more likely a metaphorical and exaggerated manner of speaking that refers to apostasy from the faith.[53] The references to "virgins" are also to be interpreted metaphorically.[54] This is a way of expressing the purity and blamelessness demanded of Christ's followers, who are to keep themselves from every contamination of apostasy and denial.

At the most, it is only in a few passages that the ethical problem of "poverty and wealth" seems to emerge. Thus in the message to the church at Smyrna (2:9), "poverty" (πτωχεία) is named alongside "affliction" (θλίψις) and "slander" (βλασφημία). These are all different expressions of the oppressive situation of the church. "Poverty" may be the effect of the prohibition of commercial activities directed at those who confess their faith by refusing to worship the beast, i.e. participate in the imperial cult (13:16–17). That there were also Christian congregations that had good financial means at their disposal is seen in the message to Laodicea, which was warned against a false sense of security based on their wealth (3:17). When the harlot Babylon is portrayed as, along with other attributes, having great wealth and living in luxury (17:4), this underscores her unlimited power that she directed against the oppressed without restraint. There is no trace, however, of a strict ideal of poverty or a rigorous poverty ethic.[55] The author's concern is rather that the Christian community—whether poor or rich is unimportant—remains faithful and never loses sight of the final goal of history, the coming of its Lord (cf. e. g. 2:10–11).

So also the vice catalogues of 21:8 and 22:15,[56] similar to each other in content and language, are themselves part of the early Christian catalogue tradition (cf. esp. Rom 1:29–31; 1 Cor 6:9–10; Gal 5:19–21), so that no inferences can be made from them regarding the actual situation in the

---

[53] This is the way the polemic against the "harlot Babylon" is to be understood (14:8; 17:1ff; 18:2–3, 9; 19:2).

[54] Contra S. Schulz, *Neutestamentliche Ethik* (ZGB) Zürich: Theologischer Verlag, 1987) 551.

[55] Contra S. Schulz, *Neutestamentliche Ethik* 553.

[56] Cf. 9:20–21, where analogous offenses are listed. On the vice catalogues cf. O. Böcher, "Lasterkataloge in der Apokalypse des Johannes," in *Leben lernen im Horizont des Glaubens* (FS S. Wibbing) (Landau 1986) 75–84.

churches, especially since 9:20–21 refer to "the rest of humankind," i.e. not particularly to Christians. An exception is the first element of the catalogue in 21:8, which speaks of the "cowards and faithless" (δειλοῖς καὶ ἀπίστοις) and alludes to the situation of persecution. Those who have closed themselves off from the claim of Christ and have denied their faith during the persecution may expect the "lake that burns with fire and sulfur" as the "second death" (21:8).

Instead of presenting concrete and detailed instructions for the conduct of the community, the author's main concern is to challenge the churches to steadfastness and faithfulness. So also the call to "turn around" ("repentance" = μετανοέω), which is expressed especially frequently in the messages to the churches (2:5, 16, 21–22; 3:3, 19), means of course with reference to the unconverted that they should turn away from an unethical, immoral life (9:21; 16:9, 11), but in reference to the Christian community that they should regain their earlier level of faith (cf. 2:4–5, "your first love," "your first works").

Thus in contrast to 1 John or Hebrews, the possibility of a (second) repentance is offered to members of the Christian community, while images of the terrible judgment of God is held before the eyes of those who fall away (21:8). As shown especially by the messages to the seven churches of Asia Minor, the content of the ethical demand is faithfulness expressed in doing right.[57] Though the decision at the last judgment is made on the basis of works (2:23; 20:12–13; 22:12), this is done without making faith into a work or making good deeds into self-justifying achievements. That faith could be misunderstood as a "virtue" and an achievement with which one could be self-satisfied may well be excluded by the fundamental reference to the prior love of Christ and his reconciling act (1:5–6; 5:9–10). However, in comparison with the theology of Paul, Revelation lacks the penetrating understanding of sin and a dispute with the Old Testament-Jewish concept of law.[58] The author does not advocate the understanding of justification found in the late phase of Paul's thought. But in the correlation of Christology and ecclesiology, as in the author's ecclesiology, the distinction between indicative and imperative can be perceived. Eschatological salvation as the gift of Christ (1:5; 5:9) calls for concrete deeds in the life of the churches, above all the Christian stance of "endurance" (13:10, ὑπομονή).

---

[57]  2:13, 19; cf. also 13:10; 14:12 ("the faith of Jesus"); 19:8 ("the righteous deeds of the saints").

[58]  The word νόμος is found neither in Revelation nor in 1–3 John.

# E.
# On the Way to the Early Catholic Church—
# the Deuteropauline Literature

Not only did Paul and his coworkers stand in a relationship of teacher and student, but also after the death of the apostle there is evidence of a "Pauline school" in a broader sense. In the following generations the Pauline world of thought was elaborated, handed on, and interpreted in different ways under the authority of Paul the teacher. Some of the results of this development are found not only in the Deutero-Pauline letters (Colossians, Ephesians, 1 Timothy, 2 Timothy, Titus, 2 Thessalonians), but also in letters not written under his name but which still show the influence of his theology (Hebrews, 1 Peter).

It would, of course, also be possible to treat the Deutero-Pauline literature in connection with the section dealing with the theology of Paul, instead of the arrangement chosen here. The effects of Paul on the theological conceptions of the "school" that grew out of his work could be presented in this way.[1] Such a procedure, however, implies that important New Testament writings that in any case are to be attributed to the broader circle of the Pauline school would have to be presented separately under the heading of "other early Christian preachers."[2] However, within the realm of Pauline thought are also found such theologically-rich documents as 1 Peter and 2 Thessalonians, and at a certain distance, also the letter to the Hebrews. In each case their differing theological models are to be seen in their relation to authentic Pauline theology, without applying a theory of the "decline" of Paul's theology. The situation and unique approach of each document is to be appreciated no less than the theological frontiers of these models. For these reasons in this chapter we limit ourselves to the epistolary literature explicitly ascribed to the apostle though not written by him.

---

[1]  E. g. R. Schnackenburg, *Die sittliche Botschaft des Neuen Testaments*. HThK.S. II. (Frieburg: Herder, 1988) 10. Schnackenburg places the Deutero-Paulines (Colossians, Ephesians, Pastorals) immediately after Paul.

[2]  So R. Schnackenburg, *Die sittliche Botschaft* 11: 1 Peter, Hebrews, Jude and 2 Peter, Revelation.

# I. Christ, the Head of the Church—The Letter to the Colossians

Bornkamm, G. "The Heresy of Colossians," in F. O. Francis and W. A. Meeks (eds.) *Conflict at Colossae* (Missoula: SBL, 1973) 123–145.

Bujard, W. *Stilanalytische Untersuchungen zum Kolosserbrief als Beitrag zur Methodik von Sprachvergleichen.* StUNT 11. Göttingen: Vandenhoeck & Ruprecht, 1973.

Burger, C. *Schöpfung und Versöhnung. Studien zum liturgischen Gut im Kolosser- und Epheserbrief.* WMANT 46. Neukirchen-Vluyn: Neukirchener, 1975.

Gabathuler, A. J. *Jesus Christus. Haupt der Kirche—Haupt der Welt.* AThANT 45. Zürich: Zwingli, 1965.

Gnilka, J. *Der Kolosserbrief.* HThK 10,1. Freiburg: Herder, 1980.

Grässer, E. "Kolosser 3,1–4 als Beispiel einer Interpretation secundum homines recipientes," ZThK 64 (1967) 139–168; also in: E. Grässer. *Text und Situation,* Gütersloh: Gerd Mohn, 1973, 123–151.

Käsemann, E. *Leib und Leib Christi.* BHTh 9. Tübingen: J. C. B. Mohr (Paul Siebeck), 1933.

Lähnemann, J. *Der Kolosserbrief. Komposition, Situation und Argumentation.* StNT 3. Gütersloh: Gerd Mohn, 1971.

Lindemann, A. *Der Kolosserbrief.* ZBK.NT 10. Zürich: Zwingli, 1983.

Lohmeyer, E. *Die Briefe an die Philipper, an die Kolosser und an Philemon.* KEK IX. Göttingen: Vandenhoeck & Ruprecht, 1964.

Lohse, E. *Colossians and Philemon.* Hermeneia. Philadelphia: Fortress, 1971.

Lona, H. E. *Die Eschatologie im Kolosser- und Epheserbrief.* fzb 48. Würzburg: Echter, 1984.

Ludwig, H. "Der Verfasser des Kolosserbriefs—ein Schüler des Paulus," Diss. theol., Göttingen (masch.) 1974.

Merklein, H. "Paulinische Theologie in der Rezeption des Kolosser- und Epheserbriefs," in K. Kertelge (ed.), *Paulus in den neutestamentlichen Spätschriften.* QD 89. Freiburg: Herder, 1981, 25–69.

Percy, E. *Die Probleme der Kolosser- und Epheserbriefe.* SVSL. Lund: Societatis Humaniorum Litterarum Lundensis, 1946.

Pokorný, P. *Der Brief des Paulus an die Kolosser.* ThHK 10,1. Berlin: Evangelische Verlagsanstalt, 1987.

Schenk, W. "Der Kolosserbrief in der neueren Forschung (1945–1985)," ANRW II 25.4. (1987) 3327–3364.

Schweizer, E. *The Letter to the Colossians.* Minneapolis: Augsburg, 1982.

Steinmetz, F. J. *Protologische Heils-Zuversicht. Die Strukturen des soteriologischen und christologischen Denkens im Kolosser- und Epheserbrief.* FTS 2. Frankfurt: Peter Lang, 1969.

Wolter, M. *Der Brief an die Kolosser. Der Brief an Philemon.* ÖTK 12. Gütersloh: Gerd Mohn, 1993.

Zeilinger, F. *Der Erstgeborene der Schöpfung. Untersuchungen zur Formalstruktur und Theologie des Kolosserbriefes.* Wien, 1974.

## a)    Introduction

The Letter to the Colossians[3] is regarded as a genuine letter of Paul by conservative scholars. As evidence for this they can appeal to the fact that the letter claims to have been written by Paul (and "Timothy our brother," 1:1), and that the concluding greeting has Pauline traits, including the signature "with my own hand" (4:18a; cf. 1 Cor 16:21; 2 Thess 3:17). As additional evidence of authenticity, it is pointed out that the letter was written during an imprisonment of Paul (4:18b) on the occasion of sending Tychicus (4:7) and Onesimus (4:9). The points of contact with the letter to Philemon are striking (cf. 4:18a with Phlm 19a, and especially the list of greetings in 4:10ff with Phlm 23–24). This suggests the question of whether Colossians was written at the same time and within the same imprisonment situation as Philemon, or whether an unknown author used the letter to Philemon as a source and model, and thus whether a special connection is presupposed to the churches in Colossae and Laodicea, churches not founded by Paul (cf. 2:1). If one decides that the letter to the Colossians is pseudepigraphical, then it is to be assumed that the letter was written after the death of the apostle (cf. 1:24) and is a product of the post-apostolic Pauline school.

The theology of Colossians has close connections to Paul's own theology, but in some ways stands at some distance from it. Agreements are seen in the basic letter structure of the classical Pauline letters (Galatians, Romans) that are composed of two major units, a theological section and an ethical section. However, the ponderous linguistic style already sets the document apart from the language of the authentic Pauline writings. There are not only lengthy and complicated periodic sentences but also numerous unpauline expressions.[4] While the author may have adopted traditional materials, and may have been engaged in a debate with oppo-

---

[3]    Outline of Colossians:
    A.      Introduction
            1:1–2 Prescript
            1:3–14 Proömium
    B.      1:15–2:23 Theoretical Part
        I.     1:15–23 Christ, the firstborn of creation and the firstborn of the dead
        II.    1:24–2:5 The message of the apostle
        III.   2:6–23 Defense against false teaching
    C.      3:1–4:6 Practical Part
        I.     3:1–17 Taking off the old person and putting on the new
        II.    3:18–4:1 The Christian *Haustafel*
        III.   4:2–6 Instructions regarding prayer and right conduct in relation to non-Christians
    D.  4:17–18 Conclusion
[4]    For details, cf. the thorough presentation of the evidence in W. Bujard, *Stilanalytische Untersuchungen*.

nents that influenced his vocabulary, this still does not completely explain the linguistic differences between Colossians and the undisputed Pauline letters. In terms of the content, it is striking that Paul's doctrine of justification is hardly reflected at all, although the position of the opponents who call for the observance of food laws and regulations connected with festival days and the Sabbath would seem to call for it. So also in the letter's Christology and ecclesiology there are characteristic differences from Paul's theology. These differences are so considerable that they can hardly be explained as the result of Paul's own personal development but point rather to the postpauline position of the author. This author attempts to come to terms with the theological situation of his own time with the triad of "Christ—apostle—church," whereby the apostle is the connecting link between Christ and church, not as an eyewitness, but as proclaimer.

## b) Christology

### 1. The Christ Hymn Colossians 1:15–20

Aletti, J. N. *Colossiens 1.15–20.* AnBib 91. Rom: PBI, 1981.

Burger, C. *Schöpfung und Versöhnung. Studien zum liturgischen Gut im Kolosser- und Epheserbrief.* WMANT 46. Neukirchen-Vluyn: Neukirchener, 1975.

Fossum, J. "Colossians 1.15–18a in the Light of Jewish Mysticism and Gnosticism," NTS 35 (1989) 183–201.

Käsemann, E. "Eine urchristliche Taufliturgie," FS R. Bultmann. Stuttgart: 1949, 133–148; also in E. Käsemann, *Exegetische Versuche und Besinnungen* I. Göttingen: Vandenhoeck & Ruprecht, 1970, 34–51.

Schweizer, E. "Kol 1,15–20," *EKK Vorarbeiten* 1. Neukirchen-Vluyn: Neukirchener, 1969, 7–31.

Further literature on the Colossian hymn is found in M. Wolter, *Der Brief an die Kolosser* 70–71.

I.

1.15 ὅς ἐστιν εἰκὼν τοῦ θεοῦ τοῦ ἀοράτου,
πρωτότοκος πάσης κτίσεως,
1.16 ὅτι ἐν αὐτῷ ἐκτίσθη τὰ πάντα
ἐν τοῖς οὐρανοῖς καὶ ἐπὶ τῆς γῆς,
τὰ ὁρατὰ καὶ τὰ ἀόρατα,
εἴτε θρόνοι εἴτε κυριότητες
εἴτε ἀρχαὶ εἴτε ἐξουσίαι·
τὰ πάντα δι' αὐτοῦ καὶ εἰς
αὐτὸν ἔκτισται·
1.17 καὶ αὐτός ἐστιν πρὸ πάντων
καὶ τὰ πάντα ἐν αὐτῷ συνέστηκεν,
1.18 καὶ αὐτός ἐστιν ἡ κεφαλὴ
τοῦ σώματος τῆς ἐκκλησίας·

I.
(Jesus Christ)
15 He is the image of the invisible God,
the firstborn of all creation;
16 for in him all things in heaven and on
earth were created,
things visible and invisible,
whether thrones or dominions
or rulers or powers
—all things have been created
through him and for him.
17 He himself is before all things
and in him all things hold together.
18 He is the head of the body,
the church;

II.

ὅς ἐστιν ἀρχή, πρωτότοκος
ἐκ τῶν νεκρῶν,
ἵνα γένηται ἐν πᾶσιν αὐτὸς πρωτεύων,

1.19 ὅτι ἐν αὐτῷ εὐδόκησεν
πᾶν τὸ πλήρωμα κατοικῆσαι

1.20 καὶ δι' αὐτοῦ ἀποκαταλλάξαι
τὰ πάντα εἰς αὐτόν,
εἰρηνοποιήσας
διὰ τοῦ αἵματος τοῦ σταυροῦ αὐτοῦ,
(δι' αὐτοῦ) εἴτε τὰ ἐπὶ τῆς γῆς
εἴτε τὰ ἐν τοῖς οὐρανοῖς.

II.

he is the beginning, the firstborn
from the dead,
so that he might come to
have first place in everything.

19 For in him all the fullness
of God was pleased to dwell,

20 and through him God was pleased
to reconcile to himself[5] all things,
by making peace
through the blood of his cross.
[with everything][6] whether on earth
or in heaven.

Although the details of the reconstruction remain uncertain,[7] there is good reason to believe that the author cites a Christian hymn composed of two strophes. Both parts begin with a relative construction (ὅς ἐστιν, vv. 15, 18b) and are oriented to the term πρωτότοκος. The different terms that then follow (v. 15 εἰκὼν θεοῦ; v. 18b, ἀρχή) are important for the meaning of the whole. The first strophe deals with the cosmological significance of Christ as the firstborn of creation and the mediator of creation, while the second strophe presents the soteriological significance of Christ as the "firstborn of the dead," the mediator of eschatological salvation. The hymn is set off from what precedes by its two part structure[8] and from what follows by the transition to the second person, where the readers are addressed with ὑμᾶς (v. 21). The transmitted text in the letter is to be seen by and large as the unedited text received by the author in the tradition. At the most it may be asked whether the genitive τῆς ἐκκλησίας is a redactional comment on "head of the body," even though it has a transitional function,[9] since this term is taken up in the second strophe neither directly nor indirectly—though the second strophe does deal with the salvation now made present in Christ. Since in 1:24 the author does equate the body of Christ with the church, it is possible that the phrase in the hymn also expresses his own specifically redactional interest.

The matter is different with regard to the expression διὰ τοῦ αἵματος τοῦ σταυροῦ (v. 20), which is likewise often considered a secondary addition. The overlap with the following δι' αὐτοῦ is noticeable, if the latter is regarded as a secondary reading (see above). To be sure, the death of Jesus (on the cross) is also mentioned in the context (1:22; 2:14). This, however, may be understood as an adoption of the received tradition (v. 20). Placing the resurrection (v. 18b) prior to the crucifixion of Jesus (v. 20) does not of course fit the historical sequence, but is suggested by the formal structure (anticipation of the πρωτότοκος), and is thus no indication of its being

---

5  Cf. the conjecture of Griesbach (ἑαυτόν).
6  The reading δι' αὐτοῦ is taken not to be original, on the basis of the reading of many MSS.
7  There is no denying, for example, that the change of subject between v. 19 and v. 20 is awkward.
8  Differently E. Lohmeyer, *Briefe an die Philipper* 41–54, according to whom the hymn begins with 1:13.
9  With E. Käsemann, "A Primitive Christian Baptismal Liturgy" 150–152.

secondary.[10] That the death and resurrection of Jesus are understood as the saving event corresponds to the Pauline tradition (cf. 1 Thess 4:14; 1 Cor 15:3ff; Rom 6:3–4), but could have become part of a hymn in the Pauline circle.

## Content

Both strophes of the hymn celebrate Christ as the εἰκών of the invisible God (1:15a). This is not only the image ([Ab-]Bild), but rather the "archetype" or "Platonic idea" of God (Urbild). As a divine hypostasis, the person and being of Jesus Christ represents God's reality. He is thus rightly thought of as having a preexistent essence.[11] He existed before the creation of the world,[12] in which he participated as the mediator of creation (1:16a). This is the basis for his sovereignty over the cosmic powers, who are essentially oriented to him, who exist only through him (1:17). The redactor has arranged an impressive conclusion for the first strophe: Christ is the head of the church, which is his body (1:18a).

As the first strophe points to the cosmic authority of Christ, the second expresses a soteriological perspective. The sovereignty of Christ over the world is manifest in his overcoming death by his resurrection. He is the first to step across the threshold that separates death and life, and thereby makes faith and hope in eternal life possible for his church (1:18b). That the divine fullness has become present in his person means that the universe and the whole of human history is comprehended in him as the ultimate expression of God's will (1:19). The picture of "reconciliation" has as its object this unification with the divine pleroma (1:20a). The same is meant by the "establishing of peace" that comes about by the death of Jesus Christ on the cross: all powers, however hostile they may be to God's will, are overcome by this divine incursion into history (1:20b).

## Location in the History of Religions

The assumption that the hymn is a pre-Christian composition[13] is opposed by the clear references to the Christ kerygma in the second strophe

---

10   Differently W. Schenk, "Christus, das Geheimnis der Welt, als dogmatischen und ethisches Grundprinzip des Kolosserbriefes," *EvTh* 43 (1983) 138–155; 150: the baptism of Jesus was the earthly resurrection of Jesus; this is why the text speaks first of the resurrection (v. 18) and then of the crucifixion (v. 20). He supposes that this is the mystery of which the author speaks in 2:2. He further supposes a similar view is to be found in the Gospel of Mark. This, however, is an over-interpretation of the Markan baptismal pericope, and has no real point of contact in Colossians, even if "baptismal theology" is reflected. For a critique of this view see also Pokorný, *Kolosserbrief* 60–61, note 85.
11   So also in the Christ hymns of Philippians 2:6–11; John 1:1–18; Hebrews 1:3–4; cf. also 1 Timothy 3:16.
12   Like the expression "firstborn of creation" (1:15), the "divine passive" ἐκτίσθη (1:16) can include some distance from God the Creator.
13   Thus for example E. Käsemann, "Primitive Christian Baptismal Liturgy" 154–159.

(1:18b, "firstborn from the dead;" 1:20b, "through the blood of his cross"). And not only the concept of preexistence (cf. Gal 4:4) but also the participation of the Son of God in creation belongs to early christological tradition (1 Cor 8:6; Rom 11:36; cf. John 1:3). Thus if the author has worked an early Christian hymn into this passage, the question arises of which religious streams influenced its content and form. The influence of the *Old Testament* is minimal. The designation εἰκὼν θεοῦ ἀοράτου does go back ultimately to Genesis 1:26–27, but has obviously been transformed in a Hellenistic direction. Thus the Hellenistic Jew Philo has the invisibility of God as a fundamental presupposition.[14] In any case, 2 Corinthians 4:4 shows that Paul could already identify Christ with the "image of God," so that presumably here too early Christian christological tradition is to be presupposed. The speculation that the concept of reconciliation points back to the image of the servant of Yahweh of Isaiah 52:13–15 or 53:10–12 is likewise hardly correct.[15] It is the cosmic dimension that is basic to the whole image. This is found in the Jewish *wisdom tradition*, according to which the preexistent wisdom of God (Prov 8:22ff; Sir 1:1ff) is the mediator of creation,[16] also described as the image of God's goodness (Wis 7:26), who dwells among the people of God (Sir 24:3–8). To be sure, against a too exclusive derivation from wisdom speculation[17] stand the facts that in Judaism wisdom is basically identified with the Torah, and that in any case the Jewish view of wisdom has been extensively influenced by Greek and Hellenistic thought. The *logos understanding* of Philo is nearer, according to which the λόγος can be identified with the wisdom of God (*All* 1.65), and like wisdom can also be called the εἰκὼν θεοῦ (*SpecLeg* 1.81) as well as ἀρχή and εἰκών (*All* 1.43). While distinguished from God, the Logos is still a divine being (*All* 2.86) and a mediating figure of the created world (*Op* 24). The Logos stands between God and the world, or between God and humanity (*Gig* 52; *VitMos* 2.133). The Logos permeates, forms, shapes, and gives order to the visible world and encompasses all the creative forces within itself.[18] Philo is an example of the fusion of Jewish and Greek-Hellenistic thought in Judaism outside Palestine, a kind of Jewish thought that was open to Greek and Hellenistic philosophical

---

[14]   Cf. Philo *Post* 15 and elsewhere (ἀόρατος); cf. G. Strecker, *Johannine Letters* 156 n. 12; W. Michaelis, ὁράω κτλ. TDNT 5:319–324. The idea of God's invisibility is already present in Homer, *Od* XVI 161 and elsewhere.

[15]   Contra Pokorný, *Kolosserbrief* 75.

[16]   Cf. F. Christ, *Jesus Sophia. Die Sophia-Christologie bei den Synoptikern* (AThANT 57. Zürich: Zwingli, 1970) 34, 158. Cf. also A.I.a.2. above on the Sophia tradition.

[17]   Advocates: J. N. Alletti, "Colossiens 1.15–20; E. Schweizer, "Die Kirche als Leib in den paulinischen Antilegomena," in *Neotestamentica* (Zürich-Stuttgart: Zwingli, 1963), 293–316, on which see Pokorný *Kolosserbrief* 56–58.

[18]   Philo, *Fug* 101; *Her* 188; for details cf. H. M. Kleinknecht, λέγω κτλ. B., TDNT IV 77–91; P. Pokorný, *Kolosserbrief* 57 and note 62 (with bib.).

thought. In particular, Philo's understanding of the Logos is to be explained in terms of its connection with Platonic thought and later Middle Platonism. Parallels are also found in the Hellenistic mysteries.[19] To be mentioned in this connection is also the Hermetic literature, which was in part nourished by the Greek and Hellenistic philosophical tradition.[20]

It is to be asked whether the notion of *"Gnosticism"* [*Gnosis*] can be applied to the conceptuality of this text. It has been so transmitted in the tractate "Trimorphic Protennoia," one of the texts found at Nag Hammadi (NHC XIII 1; 35.1–50.24). This text resembles the Barbelo and Sethian Gnosticism of the second century, and develops philosophical and theological speculations into a cosmology and soteriology. Here Protennoia, the "primal thought" of the Father, appears in a threefold form: The heavenly redeemer is Father, Mother, and Son all in one. The whole universe coheres in him/her/it (35:4); as the Preexistent One the Protennoia is the "firstborn" of all things (35:5), the "image of the invisible Spirit," through whom the All was given form (38:11–12), the coming aeon and the "fulfillment of the All" (45:9). Especially the cosmological interpretation manifests points of contact with the Colossian hymn (for the soteriology, cf. 48:20: spring of the <water of> life). In neither case is there any sharp dualism between God and the world. Nor is there any model of cosmological emanations. The essential trademarks of the Gnostic systems of the second century are missing (a doctrine of the origin of the world, the descent and ascent of the heavenly redeemer, among others). One must thus be hesitant to call the Colossian hymn "Gnostic."[21] It rather belongs to the realm of Hellenistic syncretism (including its Jewish components), which is also to be considered the background of the theology of Paul and the Johannine school.

## The Author's Interpretation

Since the hymn implies no dualistic opposition between God and the world, the question of whether the text is to be understood in a cosmological or theological sense is misplaced.[22] Neither may a Trinitarian concept be introduced, for instance by identifying the "fullness" with the

---

[19]   Osiris, for example, in Plutarch *Is* 54 is the spiritual archetype of the world.
[20]   On the Corpus Hermeticum cf. e.g. TDNT 4:87–88. The Hermetic Logos theory is further documented in Cornutus *TheolGraec* 16 ggA; cf. Diogenes Laertius VII 1.36 (49); preliminary stages in Plato *Crato* 407eff; in Stoicism Ag 14:12; for logos theology one could also point to Plutarch *Is* 53 (II 373a, b, d), and cf. further Clement of Alexandria *Strom* V 14.94.5; Origen *Contra Celsus* 6.60.
[21]   On the definition cf. G. Strecker, "Judenchristentum und Gnosis," in K. W. Tröger (ed.) *Altes Testament–Früchristentum–Gnosis* (Gütersloh: Gerd Mohn, 1980) 261–282.
[22]   Contra J. Gnilka, *Kolosserbrief* 72–73.

Holy Spirit. The fact is that the church hymn is directed to Christ. Both its cosmological and theological dimensions have the task of communicating the meaning of the Christ event.[23] There is a direct line from this to the ἐκκλησία; the world-body of the Christ is interpreted as the "church" (1:18a). The meaning: the Christ who is addressed in the church's prayer and proclaimed by the church's preaching, the one who bears and encompasses the whole created world, the one who is sovereign over all authorities and powers in heaven and on earth, the one who has come near to the world of humanity as the Crucified One, and who as the Exalted One has gone before it on the way to divine fulfillment—this one is to the church as the head is to the body, and his church belongs to him in the same way.

In a way similar to the prepauline hymn to Christ in Philippians 2:6–11, the Colossian hymn represents the indicative of the Christ event. It is only in the context that it becomes clear that the Christian community, if it praises Christ as the agent of universal reconciliation, must at the same time be aware what the implications of this event are. To be sure, it is significant that in both the preceding and following the indicative of the nature of the community, its being, is named: in the thanksgiving it confesses that it participates in the "inheritance of the saints," has been transferred into the kingdom of the Son, and that through the Son has received forgiveness of sins (1:12–14). Eschatological salvation is experienced not only in baptism[24] but also in faith in the proclaimed word (cf. 1:23). The meaning is that the church is founded by the reality of reconciliation accomplished by the cosmic Christ, who has led it back home from the far country, from alienation to authentic being (1:21–22). From the presence of the saving reality there follows the imperative of ethical action. The church is aware that not only the promised salvation expressed in the indicative, but also the "fruit bearing" demanded of it, i.e. its good works, are to be attributed to God's act and God's work (1:9–11, 22). So also the form of the conditional sentence ("provided that you continue securely established and steadfast in the faith") is not the opening the door to a new works-righteousness, but does make clear that the "conditio sine qua non" for the church's continuing experience of the reality of salvation and its remaining free from harm continues to be its firmness, certainty, and faith in the gospel.

---

[23]   In v. 19 θεός is to be added, for "God," not πλήρωμα, is the subject. Only this way can a double change of subject in vv. 18–20 be avoided; εἰρηνοποιήσας requires a masculine subject (= θεός), which is therefore also to be presupposed for εὐδόκησεν (in response to J. Gnilka, *Kolosserbrief* 59, 72).

[24]   The idea of reconciliation in 1:22 (corresponding to 2:11) can refer to baptism. According to E. Schweizer, *A Theological Introduction to the New Testament* (Nashville: Abingdon, 1991) 33, 93, in 1:25–26 there is a "revelation schema" that juxtaposes there-and-then and here-and-now.

Doubtless the Christology of the letter to the Colossians is strongly shaped by the cosmological orientation documented by the hymn to Christ. The author can here appeal to Paul, for whom Christ will be the Lord of all cosmic powers (Phil 2:10–11), and—in accord with the church's own confession of faith—has "already in the present" received universal sovereignty, even if the final fulfillment of this confession still lies in the future (cf. 1 Cor 8:6; Rom 11:31ff). If the church of the Colossian letter confesses its faith in such a cosmic event, this means that the world-encompassing reality of Christ is the ground and goal of its faith. It knows that it has been incorporated into the realm of Christ's sovereignty over the world; it is no accident that the cosmological affirmation comes first, and then the soteriological function of Christ is expressed in the hymn. All the hostilities encountered in this world (the sufferings of the apostle himself, for example [1:24ff]) are abrogated in and through Christ; the church must orient itself to him as the image of God and the head of his body the church.

## 2.  Christological Titles

The titles for Christ in the letter to the Colossians are to be understood with these cosmological-soteriological premises, especially when the Pauline influence is also unmistakable. Even less than in the authentic Pauline letters is Χριστός used in a titular sense (= "the Christ," "the Messiah") (3:1, 3, 4, 15). The development in the direction of a proper name appears to have proceeded further than in Paul's own usage (absolute Χριστός: 2:2, 5, 8; 3:11; Ἰησοῦς Χριστός: 1:3 or Χριστὸς Ἰησοῦς, 1:1, 4; 4:12; cf. Phil 3:12, 14). So also Pauline influence is present in the frequent ἐν Χριστῷ (1:2, 28; cf. 1:4), ἐν κυρίῳ 3:18, 20; 4:7) or σὺν Χριστῷ (2:20; cf. 3:3). Not to be minimized is the alternation between "in Christ" and "Christ in you" (1:27, 28), which is also reminiscent of Paul (cf. Gal 2:20).

That the tradition has become even more christologically-oriented than it is in Paul is seen in the use of the κύριος title. A reference to God (frequent in Paul, reflecting his dependence on Old Testament usage) could at the most be found in Colossians in the traditional formula "fearing the Lord" (3:22). The textual tradition has already understood it unambiguously as referring to Christ, and this corresponds to the context: κύριος is consistently a designation for Christ (including 1:10, 3:13). This is confirmed by the connection with the understanding of Christ as the exalted Lord (4:1 "... you also have a Master [Lord = κύριος] in heaven") and in its combination with the proper name "Jesus Christ" (1:3; 2:6).[25]

---

[25]  Son of God Christology is documented only in 1:13; ὁ υἱὸς τῆς ἀγάπης is unusual, apparently a reflection of the familiar ὁ υἱὸς ὁ ἀγαπητός (Mark 1:11par; 9:7par). Is it a "Hebraizing Greek construction (so E. Lohse, *Colossians* 38)? But cf. also PsSol

## c) Ecclesiology

Lohse, E." Christusherrschaft und Kirche im Kolosserbrief," *NTS* 11 (1964/65) 203–216.

Löwe, H. "Bekenntnis, Apostelamt und Kirche im Kolosserbrief," in: Kirche, FS G. Bornkamm, hg. v. D. Lührmann u. G. Strecker, Tübingen 1980, 299–314.

Schweizer, E. "Die Kirche als Leib Christi in den paulinischen Antilegomena," in E. Schweizer, *Neotestamentica*. Zürich-Stuttgart: Zwingli, 1963, 293–316.

### 1. The Body of Christ

The distinctive character of the Letter to the Colossians in comparison with Paul's own writings comes to expression most clearly in its under-standing of the body of Christ. Although a preliminary form of this con-cept was present in the theology of Paul, a comparison reveals character-istic differences. Paul speaks of the body of Christ only in parenetic contexts (1 Cor 6:15–16; 12:12ff; Rom 12:4ff). The influence of the Stoic idea of the human community as an organism can be recognized in Paul (members of the Christian community, like members of the human body, must consider the balance and interplay of the body as a whole, since only in this way can the church "function"). While an ontological background for Paul's thought need not be denied, it is not emphasized. In contrast, the author of the Letter to the Colossians has understood the body of Christ primarily as an ontic phenomenon, which gives a somewhat preju-diced perspective of the way the Christian community is understood.

In terms of the history of tradition, two lines may be distinguished:

1. *The early Christian confessional tradition.* This tradition declares the saving reality of the cross and resurrection of Jesus Christ (cf. e.g. 1 Cor 15:3b-5a). Deviating from this, Colossians considers the decisive saving event to be not only Jesus' death but the incarnation (2:9, "for in him the whole fullness of deity dwells bodily [σωματικῶς])." This corresponds to the statement that the death of Jesus is explicitly connected with the "body of his flesh" (1:22). The Pauline kerygma is elaborated: it is the somatic reality of Jesus' appearing in the flesh, the event as a whole, that possesses saving significance, not only his death on the cross.

2. In addition, the *Christology of the Colossian Christ-hymn* has exercised a decisive influence on the letter's concept of the body of Christ.

These two presuppositions form the basis of the independent concept of the body of Christ found in Colossians. It is distinguished from that of the Pauline letters in three ways:

---

13:9: υἱὸς ἀγαπήσεως. The genitive has a more solemn ring than the mere adjective; since the context (possibly) goes back to baptismal tradition, we should perhaps presuppose a liturgical background (so P. Pokorný, *Kolosserbrief* 45).

1. While in Pauline thinking Christ is identical with his body, the author of Colossians contrasts *Christ the head* (κεφαλή) and the church as the body of Christ (σῶμα). This does not cancel out the idea that the cosmic Christ permeates the universe (cf. 1:16–19), but clarifies the idea that the universal church as the body of Christ participates in the lordship of Christ over the cosmic powers (cf. 2:10). This is the result of the union of Christians with their Lord (2:19).

2. This coordination of church and cosmic Christ goes beyond the Pauline model of the church as organism. The Christian community is not understood as a sum of individual human beings who exercise charismatic functions and thus function as one body of Christ (1 Cor 12:12), but, corresponding to the cosmic Christ, is understood as a *universal ontic reality*. Differently from Paul, ἐκκλησία is not primarily the local congregation but the church as a whole. The ground and goal of its being is the incarnate and exalted Christ. Its belonging to the preexistent and cosmic Lord implies the interpretation of the church in spatial terms, a realm that is free from the assaults of the cosmic powers, an interpretation that can later be understood in terms of the preexistence of the church (Eph 5:29–32); 2 Clem 14:1ff). The universal character of the church becomes concrete in the position of the apostle and his mission to the Gentile world (1:24–29).

3. Finally, a new element in contrast to the Pauline soma-conception is the idea of *growth*, which applies the picture of the growth of the human body to the church as the body of Christ in relation to its head, Christ. The God-given growth of the body takes place with regard to the head (2:19). The unity between Christ and church is hereby affirmed, at the same time calling attention to the necessary consequences including the mission to the Gentiles, since the gospel "is bearing fruit and growing in the whole world" (1:6). No distinction is made between individual church members and the church as a whole; it is rather the case that growth in the knowledge of God in individual Christians is part of the growth of the universal church (1:10; contrast 2 Cor 10:15, only individual growth in faith).

## 2. The Apostle

The apostle Paul is mentioned three times by name.[26] The influence of Pauline tradition is seen when the apostolic office is traced back to "the will of God" (1:1; verbatim agreement with 2 Cor 1:1; cf. only 1 Cor 1:1), and when reference is made to the apostle's past activity as a "servant of the gospel" (1:23; cf. 1:25). The stance asserting universal teaching stands out (1:28 "... warning everyone and teaching everyone in all wisdom, so

---

[26]  1:1, 23; 4:18—a clear emphasis in comparison with the authentic Pauline letters; cf. only once each in Romans (1:1) and Philippians (1:1).

that we may present *everyone* mature in Christ"); its goal is being "established in the faith" (2:7). This teaching should facilitate the capacity and responsibility of every member of the church to teach and admonish one another (3:16).

The content of the apostolic teaching and preaching (cf. 1:28 καταγγέλλομεν νουθετοῦντες ... διδάσκοντες) is the "gospel" (εὐαγγέλιον), which alongside "faith" (πίστις) is reckoned among the foundation stones on which the church is built (1:23). The proclamation of the church is based on the encompassing reality of Christ (1:15–20). Adopting the triad of "faith, hope, and love," the gospel as the "word of truth" concentrates on the hope "laid up for you in heaven" and is now made known through the apostle (1:4–5). According to Colossians 1:24, the sufferings of Christ are not yet filled up to their full measure. These are now being fulfilled by the apostle Paul. The sufferings of Christ are continued in the destiny of the apostle. The apostle has been commissioned to preach the word of God (1:25; cf. 3:16, "word of Christ"), which is identical with the "mystery" (μυστήριον) that, though once concealed, has now been "revealed" by the apostle (1:26; 4:3–4). The revealed mystery is identical with Christ as the lord of the church (1:27; 2:2). Paul makes a distinction between himself and Christ, since he refers back to the Christ event as a reality of the past.[27] This thus corresponds to "God's commission" (lit. "God's plan," 1:25) which legitimizes, as further elements in the chain of proclamation, the apostles' coworkers (e.g. Epaphras, 1:7; 4:12) and the members of the church (4:7–11) who work along with the apostle in spreading the message. That the proclamation is to reach out beyond the church addressed in the letter is seen in the charge to deliver the letter to the church in Laodicea (4:16).

The apostle is portrayed as primarily the servant and teacher of the church, against the background of the imprisonment situation (4:3, 18). This is what makes it necessary for the apostle to be "absent in body," but "in the Spirit" he has fellowship with his readers (2:5; cf. 1 Cor 5:3). The "sufferings" of the prisoner are not, however, determined by the awareness of separation and oppression, but the struggle that must be carried out in the place where he is imprisoned to encourage the church and to strengthen it in love (2:1–2; cf. 2 Cor 1:4ff). As the apostle shows himself thereby to be a "servant of the church" (1:25), he can find joy in this painful situation; for in his sufferings (παθήμασιν) for the church as the body of Christ he completes "what is lacking in Christ's afflictions" (τὰ ὑστερήματα τῶν θλίψεων τοῦ Χριστοῦ, 1:24). The postpauline theological position is here expressed in a twofold respect:

(1) The apostolic suffering happens "for" the church (ὑπὲρ ὑμῶν). While the historical apostle can also think of his sufferings in such a way that

---

[27]    Cf. 1:13–14, 23.

they mean encouragement for the church, it is still the case that he never speaks of his sufferings as happening "for" the church. This is reminiscent rather of the ὑπέρ formula[28] used to express Jesus' act for sinful human beings. That the affliction of the apostle's imprisonment is analogous to the passion of Jesus as suffering for others, and that thereby Paul himself is understood as *Christus prolongatus*,[29] so that the picture of apostleship in Colossians is on the way to portraying Paul as a saint removed from the general company of Christian believers, is seen (2) in the fact that the apostle's functions as continuing of the Christ event and as a substitution for the other members of the church is clearly articulated.[30] Even though the atoning effect of the death of Jesus is not thereby minimized,[31] it is still the case that the author understands the apostle's sufferings in prison as the continuation and completion of the sufferings of Jesus.[32] This is based on the idea that the realm of the cosmic Christ and the church as his body includes the person of the apostle and his sufferings.[33]

Can the message of the apostle and thereby the theological conception of Colossians be more clearly profiled by a comparison with the *opposing "philosophy"* (2:8)? It should be admitted that the author hardly names more than a few details that can only be pieced together into a picture of the whole with great difficulty. Even the basic question is disputed as to

---

[28] Cf. Romans 5:6, 8; 8:32; 14:15; 1 Corinthians 5:7 v. l.; 11:24; 15:3 and elsewhere.

[29] Here the author can attach himself to authentic Pauline ideas; thus the distress of the church (θλίψεις) or the apostle (2 Cor 1:4–5) in reverse word order in Colossians 1:24 are interpreted as the outflow of the sufferings of Christ (παθήματα). Paul himself understood himself to be a participant in the sufferings of Christ (e.g. Phil 3:10) and bears the "marks of Jesus" on his body (Gal 6:17).

[30] Ἀνταναπληρόω has the meaning "fill up or complete as a substitute for someone else" (cf. Bauer, *Lexicon* 73); the expression "what is lacking in Christ's afflictions" points to Jesus' passion as not being complete, and is not to be interpreted in terms of sociology, as though "what is lacking" meant the material poverty and lowly estate of the apostle; cf. U. Wilckens, TDNT 8:598. More correctly H. Merklein, "Theologie" 30. Cf. also the understanding of this passage in Bauer, *Lexicon* 73: "… he supplies whatever lack may still exist in its (the church's) proper share of suffering." But this contradicts the genitive τοῦ Χριστοῦ; it is to be presupposed that "what is lacking in Christ's afflictions," is not the sufferings of the church, which in fact according to the understanding of the Colossian letter can be described as "fullness" (2:10).

[31] Cf. rather 1:14, 20, 22—to be sure, the Colossian letter, in contrast to Hebrews 7:27; 9:12; 10:10, never speaks of the ἐφάπαξ of the Christ event!

[32] With H. Schlier, TDNT 3:143, the παθήματα of the apostle and the θλίψεις of Christ have identical content.

[33] Cf. 1:17–18, 27. According to P. Pokorný, *Kolosserbrief* 83, there is a paralleling of statements here. "Completing what is lacking in the messianic woes still to come" is supposed to correspond to "making the word of God fully known" (1:24–25). But the latter is not identical with the prisoner's suffering fate but refers to the apostle's preaching. What is common to both statements is that they each refer to fulfilling something that has not yet come to an end (cf. differently Rom 15:19).

whether we are dealing with a Christian or non-Christian teaching; only in the first case can lines of connection be drawn to the Christ hymn (1:15–20) that might be helpful in reconstructing the heretical teaching. In addition, it must be taken into consideration that the polemic of the author by no means reflects only the terminology of the opponents, but introduces his own interpretation including elements derived from Paul himself. Thus the designation of the opposing philosophy as "human tradition" (2:8) is influenced by Paul (cf. 1 Thess 2:13; Gal 1:11–12), and the "terminus technicus" στοιχεῖα τοῦ κόσμου (2:8, 20) can very probably be traced back to the (Pauline)[34] designation of the Galatian heresy (cf. Gal 4:3, 9). From this point of view it is not improbable that the juxtaposition of "elementary spirits of the cosmos" and "Christ" goes back to the author's own interpretation of Pauline materials. Since specifically Christian elements cannot be established for the rest, the juxtaposition may not have an inclusive sense, but an exclusive one, and the Colossian heresy may be of non-Christian origin. This could be true even though it is presupposed that they had a special attractiveness to Christians (2:20).

The structural elements, so far as we can tell, are not limited to Hellenistic syncretism but point to Jewish foundations. The "worship of angels" (2:18 θρησκεία τῶν ἀγγέλων) appears to have been an essential element. These demonic powers require humble subjection. From this a certain "legal" conduct follows: circumcision (2:11); asceticism (2:23), the observation of food laws, fasts, new moons, and Sabbaths (2:16, 21). While the honoring of transcendent powers does open up access to higher worlds (cf. 2:10, 15), the author places against this the confession of the cosmic Christ, who is the ruler of all powers. The required cultic practices are nothing other than "self-imposed piety" (2:23), to be considered at the most as oriented to something that was only preliminary. In contrast, Christ's victory over the cosmic powers is reenacted in the faith of the community (2:20) and has the promise of the victor's prize (2:18). Such a debate can make use of the weapons provided by the Christ hymn, without it offering a basis for agreement with the philosophically-educated "robbers" (2:8).[35] At most, the community of the Christ hymn and the Colossian heresy have in common an affinity for the same cosmic elements; but the church and the author know that these have found Christ to be their master.

---

[34] On this cf. Ph. Vielhauer, "Gesetzesdienst und Stoicheiadienst im Galaterbrief," in J. Friedrich, W. Pöhlmann and P. Stuhlmacher (eds.), *Rechtfertigung* (FS E. Käsemann) (Göttingen: Vandenhoeck & Ruprecht, 1976) 543–555.

[35] Contra E. Schweizer, *Kolosserbrief* 104, according to whom the opponents were also able to sing this hymn. Cf. also Ph. Vielhauer, *Geschichte* 193: Christ would accordingly be ranked by the Colossian heresy as at the highest level of the cosmic hierarchy.

## 3. Baptism and the New Life

Baptism is mentioned in Colossians only at 2:12,[36] where it is understood as "being buried with Christ" and "being raised with Christ." Comparison with Romans 6:4 shows that in Paul's understanding church members are baptized into the death of Christ and buried with Christ, and that just as Christ was raised from the dead so also believers will participate in the resurrection (Rom 6:5).

> Even though it has not yet been possible to mark off a prepauline unit in Romans 6:3–4,[37] it should still not be doubted that here Paul adopts and adapts a tradition that has also been used in Colossians 2:12 (and 3:1–4). The bases for this judgment are:
>
> (a) The inner logic of the argument makes it likely that at the beginning of the history of the tradition there stood a traditional unit that spoke of "being buried and raised with Christ" in an unbroken manner and that was secondarily modified by Paul on the basis of his "eschatological reservation," for this is foundational for the following parenesis (Rom 6:12ff).
>
> (b) Early Christian tradition made a connection between baptism and the resurrection (1 Cor 15:29; cf. 1 Pet 3:18–22). The term "rebirth" also corresponds to the idea that resurrection happens in baptism.[38]
>
> (c) A pneumatically or enthusiastically grounded present soteriology probably existed in the Corinthian church. This resulted in the denial of the future resurrection (1 Cor 15:12; cf. 2 Tim 2:18, anticipation of the resurrection). It should not be assumed, however, that in Romans 6 Paul is marking himself off from such a group.
>
> (d) The milieu of the history of religions offers numerous parallels to the idea of a resurrection that happens in the present (e.g. NHC II 3; the Gnostic Menandros in Irenaeus *Heretics* I 23.5 is supposed to have identified baptism with resurrection).
>
> The counter-objection is not persuasive, since for this piece of tradition the alternative "not temporal but ontological"[39] cannot be claimed, for it is rather the case that the ontology of present salvation is incorporated within the temporal horizon.[40]

"Rising with Christ" is accordingly a prepauline description of the experience of new life that happens in the present as an anticipation of the future, as this is also to be presupposed for the Corinthian pneumatics. Paul himself does not fundamentally dispute the present experience of salvation by placing it under the eschatological reservation. That the author of the Colossian letter knows an ontologically-flavored interpretation of the Christ-kerygma is indicated not only by 2:12, but also in 3:1–4,

---

[36]    The rare word βαπτισμός is used here; other texts have βαπτίσματι.

[37]    Cf. above A.III.c.2; on this cf. U. Schnelle, *Gerechtigkeit und Christusgegenwart. Vorpaulinische und paulinische Tauftheologie* (GTA 24. Göttingen: Vandenhoeck & Ruprecht, 1986²) 77.

[38]    John 3:3, 5; cf. also Ephesians 5:14; further documentation in Pokorný, *Kolosserbrief* 109.

[39]    Cf. G. Sellin, "'Die Auferstehung ist schon geschehen'. Zur Spiritualisierung apokalyptischer Terminologie im Neuen Testament," *NT* 25 (1983) 220–237, 222.

[40]    Example: Gospel of Phillip NHC II 3, 73.1–5, "If one does not receive the resurrection while still living, one will receive nothing at death."

where—if the Pauline formulation had been its Godfather—there would be more evidence of the eschatological reservation. In contrast, however, with his "you are risen with him" the author here makes use of the resurrection ontology a second time (3:1). This corresponds to the "you are dead" (3:3); here too the hiddenness of dying and rising with Christ is clearly articulated, now not primarily as a description of the baptismal event but as point of departure for the ethical demand. From the indicative statement that the resurrection with Christ has already happened, and the dialectic tension according to which the future life is now hidden in Christ and later will be revealed in glory (3:4), there follows the obligation that Christians are to live their lives in such a manner as one who understands that they are accepted (2:6; 3:5ff). The new life of Christians is thus understood on the basis of the revelation of Christ. In connection with the praise of the cosmic Christ it has already been stated that—as the revelatory schema affirms—"evil works" are to be rejected and that the goal of the reconciling act of Christ is the holiness, blamelessness, and good record of the Christian community (1:22). Since believers have died with Christ to the cosmic powers (2:20), the necessary consequence is "to kill" whatever is considered to belong to the earthly world (3:5). It thus corresponds to the given fact that the old self has been taken off and the new self has been put on that believers must adjust to the image of the Creator.[41]

In the process of adopting Hellenistic-Jewish tradition the Christian community formulated catalogue-like lists that contain ethical demands, such as catalogues of virtues and vices.[42] Twice in Colossians a list of five "vices" appears. The first catalogue names the immoral kinds of conduct that characterize the Gentile world (3:5, fornication, impurity, passion, evil desire, and greed [which is idolatry]," while the second lists evil practices that interfere with the life of the Christian community (3:8, "... anger, wrath, malice, slander, and abusive language"). Over against these are placed five virtues (3:12, "... compassion, kindness, humility, meekness, and patience").

The first appearance of a Christian *Haustafel* in the New Testament appears in the Letter to the Colossians (3:18–4:1; cf. then the parallel text in Ephesians 5:22–6:9, dependent on this text). In comparison to the Pauline letters, such household codes manifest a new ethical situation for the Christian community. Obviously under the influence of the waning expectation of the near parousia, a more positive attitude to the "world" had developed. In the generation after Paul it was no longer possible to ignore the question of how different social strata within the Christian

---

[41]  Cf. 3:9–10, corresponding to 3:11, which obviously presupposes the baptismal tradition of Galatians 3:26–28.

[42]  Cf. Pseudo Phocylides, *Sentences*, esp. 132–152; already Galatians 5:19–21; Romans 1:29–31, and elsewhere.

community were to relate to each other. The smallest social unit is the "house" (οἶκος). The Christian *Haustafel* deals with conflicts that could originate in the Christian household [43] (husbands and wives, children and parents, slaves and masters), instructing them in obedience and mutual consideration. Presupposed is the patriarchal household structure that had characterized Greek culture from its beginnings. The roots of this tradition are already found in the "unwritten laws" (νόμιμα ἄγραφα), i.e. in the traditional ethics of the common people of early Greek culture. They were systematized by Greek philosophy and incorporated within the duties taught by Stoicism on the basis of natural law. Hellenistic Judaism preceded Christian tradition in this regard by combining Stoic and Old Testament–Jewish materials (the Decalogue, monotheistic faith). Colossians is dependent for its materials on a preceding (oral) layer of Christian tradition, a few basic features of which can be reconstructed by comparing it with 1 Peter. In contrast, the author of Ephesians manifests a literary dependence on the Colossian *Haustafel*, which he develops in the direction of a timeless Christian ethic. Common to both writings is the tension between the present eschatology of the Christ event and concrete application to the world. Against the background of the debate with the opposing "philosophy," the existing social relations are both confirmed and made transparent to their connection with the cosmic Christ (cf. 3:18, 20, 22–24; 4:1).

It corresponds to the present *eschatology* of Colossians that its ethic is mainly determined by the vertical dimension. Since the Christian community as the body of Christ is "in Christ" (cf. 2:10), ethical conduct is a matter of keeping one's distance from the world and turning toward the cosmic Christ (cf. 3:1, "... seek the things that are above"). Those who have died with Christ are called to put to death those things that are earthly in them (3:5). This does not mean, however, that the traditional horizontal perspective determined by the apocalyptic worldview is forgotten. While there is no talk of an expectation of the near parousia, it is still the case—as has already become clear—that the gospel proclaimed by the apostle is bound most closely to the concept of "hope" (1:5, 23). The regulations imposed by the Colossian heresy can be dismissed by pointing out that they are only "a shadow of what is to come," and thus that the

---

[43]  In the narrow sense only Colossians and Ephesians; in contrast, 1 Peter 2:13–3:7 already goes beyond the boundaries of the household and includes the Christian's relation to the state. Analogously, the "congregational code" of 1 John 2:12–14 is not limited to the situation of the household, but deals with the relation of old and young people as well as children; cf. G. Strecker, "Die neutestamentlichen Haustafeln," in H. Merklein (ed.) *Neues Testament und Ethik* (FS R. Schnackenburg) (Freiburg: Herder, 1989) 349–375. Partial parallels are found in 1 Timothy 2:8–15 (instructions for men and women), Titus 2:1–10 (old men and young men, women, slaves).

final victory over the heretical view will be manifest at the future appearance of Christ (2:17). So also the idea of growth, when related to the imagery of sowing the gospel (1:6), while it is realistically oriented to "fruit bearing" in the Christian community of the present, is also open to the eschatological future (1:10, 2:19). So also the completing of the "afflictions of Christ" by the apostle (1:24) has this dimension, for the idea of "Christ in you" implies for believers the hope for a consummation in glory (1:27). Thus for the present the admonition applies that one should "redeem the time" (4:5; cf. the addition in the parallel in Eph 5:16, "for the days are evil"). This means that now is the time for using God's gracious gift, so that the coming revelation of Jesus Christ will be a time "in glory" for the church (3:4).

# II. Attaining the Maturity of Christ— The Letter to the Ephesians

Best, E. "Recipients and Title of the Letter to the Ephesians: Why and When the Designation 'Ephesians'?," *ANRW* II 25.4 (1987) 3247–3279.

Ernst, J. *Pleroma und Pleroma Christi* BU 5. Regensburg: Pustet, 1970.

Fischer, K. M. *Tendenz und Absicht des Epheserbriefes*. Berlin-Göttingen: Vandenhoeck & Ruprecht, 1973.

Gnilka, J. *Der Epheserbrief*. HThK X/2. Freiburg: Herder, 1982.

Hegermann, H. *Die Vorstellung vom Schöpfungsmittler im hellenistischen Judentum und Urchristentum*, TU 82. Berlin: Evangelische Verlagsanstalt, 1961.

Käsemann, E. "Das Interpretationsproblem des Epheserbriefes," in E. Käsemann., *Exegetische Versuche und Besinnungen* II, Göttingen: Vandenhoeck & Ruprecht, 1970, 253–261.

Lindemann, A. *Der Epheserbrief*. ZBK 8. Zürich: Zwingli, 1985.

Lindemann, A. *Die Aufhebung der Zeit. Geschichtsverständnis und Eschatologie im Epheserbrief*. StNT 12. Gütersloh: Gerd Mohn, 1975.

Lona, H. E. *Die Eschatologie im Kolosser- und Epheserbrief*. fzb 48. Würzburg: Echter, 1984.

Merkel, H. "Der Epheserbrief in der neueren Diskussion," *ANRW* II 25.4 (1987) 3156–3246.

Merklein, H. *Das kirchliche Amt nach dem Epheserbrief*. StANT 33. Munich: Kösel, 1973.

Mitton, C. L. *The Epistle to the Ephesians. Its Authorship, Origin and Purpose*. Oxford: Clarendon, 1951.

Mussner, F. "Epheserbrief," *TRE* 9 (1982) 743–753.

Pokorný, P. *Der Brief des Paulus an die Epheser*. ThHK X/2. Berlin: Evangelische Verlagsanstalt, 1992.

Pokorný, P. *Der Epheserbrief und die Gnosis*. Berlin: Evangelische Verlagsanstalt, 1965.

Rohde, J. *Urchristliche und frühkatholische Ämter*. TABG 33. Berlin: Evangelische Verlagsanstalt, 1976.

Schlier, H. *Christus und die Kirche im Epheserbrief.* BHTh 6. Tübingen: J. C. B. Mohr, 1930.

Schlier, H. *Der Brief an die Epheser.* Düsseldorf: Patmos, 1971.

Schnackenburg, R. *Ephesians.* Edinburgh: T. & T. Clark, 1991.

The literary dependence of Ephesians on Colossians is especially evident in their common outline and in the presupposed situation (the apostle as prisoner: Eph 3:1; 4:1; 6:20), even to the point of minor details.[1] To be sure, differently from Colossians the first major section of Ephesians has an extended proömium (praise of God, thanksgiving, intercession); there is space within this framework, however, for theoretical discussions about Christ and the origin and unity of the Christian church (1:3–3:21). The second major section (4:1–6:20) is dedicated to apostolic instruction and admonition, just as in Colossians. The *Haustafel* occupies a large section (5:22–6:9); it elaborates the Colossian source in a christological sense and applies the ethical instructions to the church of all times.

The independent character of Ephesians is indicated by the fact that it not only reflects extensive use of the Colossian Christ hymn (in 1:3–14), but also has worked in other traditional liturgical materials not derived from Colossians (e.g. 1:20–23; 2:4–10, 14–18, 19–22; 5:14). With the help of these pre-redactional traditions, but also by the author's own activity, Ephesians represents an independent development of Pauline theology that goes beyond Colossians. This is also seen in the independent adoption of specific Pauline expressions;[2] but the temporal and theological distance from Paul is also visible in the author's terminology and conceptuality.

## a) Christology

In a more comprehensive way than either the authentic Pauline letters or Colossians, Ephesians articulates the *cosmic dimension* of the Christ event. The term τὰ πάντα, which already in Colossians designates "the universe" seen as God's creation (Col 1:16–17, 20; Eph 3:9), is structured into its individual elements. Thus "in the heavenly places" (ἐν τοῖς οὐρανοῖς) is named as the place that Christ has taken at the right hand of God (1:3, 20; cf. 6:9, "the same Master in heaven," ἐν οὐρανοῖς), and in which also the redeemed community has already taken its place (2:6). This expression is also applied to the place where the "rulers and (angelic) au-

---

[1]    Cf. the synopsis in C. L. Mitton, *The Epistle to the Ephesians* 279ff.

[2]    Cf. the frequent use of the term χάρις: 1:6–7; 2:5, 7–8; 3:2, 7–8; 4:7, 29; especially 2:5 "by grace you have been saved"; also 2:15 "He has abolished the law with its commandments and ordinances…;" 2:8–9, the contrast of faith and works; 3:8 is to be compared with 1 Corinthians 15:9–10 (the least of all the saints).

thorities" as well as the evil spirits (3:10; 6:12). Moreover, the "realm of the air (ἀήρ) designates the home territory of demonic powers (2:2). A distinction is also made between the "heavens" (οὐρανοί) traversed by the redeemer at his ascension (4:10) and the "earth" (γῆ) as the lowest part of the universe that Christ entered at his descent from heaven.[3] The individual spheres are generally not clearly distinguished from one another.[4] Still, the formulaic way in which "heaven and earth" is used (1:10; 3:15) shows that in Ephesians *the whole visible and invisible universe is the scene of the redemptive event.* A spatial orientation dominates the author's conceptuality. But the juxtaposition of "this age" and "the age to come" (1:21; cf. 2:2, 7) documents that there is also a temporal orientation; it affirms the *eternal significance* of the Christ event in a way that the older Pauline school had not yet done.

As in Colossians, the *Christ event is interpreted as the central act of salvation* by the adoption of traditional terms and concepts.

1. *The cross of Jesus* is the church's point of origin. Here is where the hostility between Gentiles and Jews as well as the wall that separated humanity and God are overcome (2:16) and an all-embracing peace is established (2:15, 17). The death of Jesus is also interpreted in conjunction with the cultic thought world, sometimes as the sacrificial gift presented to God by Christ because of his love for the church (5:2), sometimes as the pouring out of his blood that effects redemption and forgiveness of sins (1:7; cf. 2:13). The author is no more committed to a "theology of the cross" than is the author of Colossians; it is rather the "flesh" (σάρξ) of Christ that makes it possible for there to be one church of Jews and Gentiles, in the sense that it was not only Jesus' death, but the *incarnation of Christ* that is the decisive saving event (2:14). This is the basis of citizenship in the new Israel (2:12), as it is of the establishment of the holy temple on the "cornerstone" (ἀκρογωνιαῖος) of Jesus Christ (2:20–21).[5]

2. Corresponding to the early Christian kerygma, the unity of Jesus' death on the cross and the resurrection is maintained, and the resurrection is identified with the exaltation (1:20; cf. 1 Pet 3:22 / Ps 110:1). Such *exaltation Christology* presupposes the idea that Christ descended from heaven. Thus the preexistence Christology is also implied (1:4, the election of the church "in him" before the foundation of the world), but in distinction to Colossians it is not emphasized (the word πρωτότοκος of Col 1:15, 18 is

---

[3]  Ephesians 4:9; another interpretation is "realm of the dead;" cf. J. Gnilka, *Epheserbrief* 209.

[4]  Contra F. Mussner, *Christus, das All und die Kirche* (TThSt 5. Trier, 1968²) 28; see also his article "Epheserbrief" 744. In the above sense cf. also H. Schlier, *Der Brief an die Epheser* 45–46.

[5]  On this problem cf. F. Mussner, "Epheserbrief" 750 note 1. Differently J. Jeremias, "Der Eckstein," *Angelos* 1 (1925) 65–70.

missing from Ephesians). It is rather emphasized that the Christ event is the result of God's decision before all time (1:9, 11; 3:11), and that it was God who was active in the Christ event (1:20). After his earthly life Christ ascended "above all the heavens" in order to free the prisoners and to fill all in all (1:23; 4:8–10/Ps 68:19). By his exaltation he assumed his *cosmic lordship*. God gave him his place at God's right hand (1:20) so that he could exercise his lordship over all powers and authorities and so that everything would finally be subject to him (1:21–22). Such a "saving plan" directed by God has as its goal the "fulfillment of the times," which is present and future at the same time, for "all things are gathered up" in Christ.[6]

3. The statement that all things are gathered up in Christ does not contradict the declaration that *Christ as head* of the church is distinguished from his body, as the author can also formulate the matter in dependence on Colossians (1:22; 4:15; 5:23). As Christ as head is placed over the church, so thereby his lordship over all is reflected. As is the case with the church, so also with the universe: Christ is lord. This is what is spoken of in the "mystery of God" that has been revealed in Christ (1:9–10). Christ's position of cosmic authority is oriented to the ultimate revelation in the future (cf. the term "hope" in 1:18; 4:4). This is also indicated by the ecclesiological growth terminology: as the head, Christ is the goal of the church's growth. The Christians' relation to each other is a matter of their orientation toward Christ (4:15–16).

The relation of the church to Christ is also interpreted by the *picture of marriage*. The "mystery" of Genesis 2:24 is interpreted as referring to Christ and the church. As is the case in a marriage partnership, so also the relation of Christ and the church is determined by love (5:31–32). In the elaboration of the Colossian *Haustafel* (Col 3:18–19), the relation of men and women is measured by the fundamental unity of Christ and the church. Just as the church knows it is subordinate to Christ, so wives should be subordinate to their husbands, and husbands are admonished to love their wives "just as Christ loved the church and gave himself up for her" (Eph 5:22–25).

### b) Ecclesiology

The Letter to the Ephesians represents the church as the goal of the Christ event in a way that is unique in the New Testament. It can be described

---

[6]   The word ἀνακεφαλαιόω is found in the New Testament only in Ephesians 1:10 in the christological sense. It originally comes from rhetoric (cf. Rom 13:9, = "recapitulatio"), and is to be distinguished from the idea of the "reconciliation of all things"(ἀποκαταλλάξαι) in Colossians 1:20.

as "the New Testament Song of Solomon—to the Church." Only here is there a New Testament statement about the preexistence of the church (1:4), and going beyond Colossians in an unparalleled manner, not only Christ but *the church is celebrated as a cosmic reality*. It not only participates with Christ in his lordship over the cosmic powers, but as his body it shares the same essential reality with him; it is the "fullness" of the one who "fills all in all" (1:23). However much humanity is threatened and oppressed in the world by evil powers, in the church the "fullness" represented through Christ and the peace established by him have become a reality that cannot be empirically observed. Thus the church confesses its faith in the one Lord, even though it does not overlook the reality of the world and it is acknowledged that the promised "all-embracing fullness" of the church is still a promise for the future (3:19).

While the universality and wholeness of the Christian church is an eschatological reality, the "already" of Christian existence is seen in that the church is presented as a *universal, interethnic reality* (2:13 "But now in Christ Jesus you who once were far off have been brought near by the blood of Christ;" cf. also 2:17). Jews and Gentiles have been reconciled to God in one body (2:16). This is reflected in the author's ecclesial self-understanding: whoever belongs to the Christian community is no longer counted among the "strangers and aliens" (πάροικοι 2:19) but belong to the "household of God" (οἰκεῖοι τοῦ θεοῦ). As "belonging to the body" (σύσσω-μος) all Christians are blessed heirs of the promise grounded in Christ (3:6). The close union of the church as Christ's body to the head, Christ, is illustrated and clarified by the term "structure" (οἰκοδομή, 2:21); Christ is the "keystone" that crowns the whole structure of the church (2:20); everyone who has responsibility in the church and who cooperate in the "work of ministry" (4:12) is oriented to him.

The distinctive perspective of Ephesians with regard to *church offices* can be seen in shifts from the theology of Colossians and from Paul's theology. No church offices are mentioned in Colossians. Instead, a direct union between the church and Christ is affirmed (2:7, Christians are "rooted and built up in him"). In contrast, *Ephesians 4:11* indicates a developed stage of church structure, listing "apostles, prophets, evangelists, pastors and teachers." Paul too knows a coherent ordering of church functions in which apostles and prophets are named first (1 Cor 12:28). However, his "church polity" is charismatically determined,[7] but a clear

---

[7]  Cf. 1 Corinthians 12:28, deeds of power, gifts of healing, forms of assistance, forms of leadership, various kinds of tongues. That according to Ephesians 4:7 "each of us was given grace according to the measure of Christ's gift" is not related to the matter of church offices, but rather communicates the apostolic self-understanding to every baptized Christian (1 Cor 3:10; Rom 12:3).

distinction is found in Ephesians: the apostles and prophets[8] belong to the
"foundation" (θεμέλιον) of the church in a previous generation of Christians,[9] while evangelists, pastors, and teachers have responsibility in the
present for the church's preaching, leadership, and teaching. Differently
than in the Pauline tradition, which presupposes that leadership functions
in the church are gifts of God, while appointment to office in Ephesians
is attributed to the exalted Christ. The all-encompassing sovereignty of
the cosmic Christ is concretely expressed in his lordship over the church
exercised by his appointed leaders.[10]

The task entrusted to the church officers is especially concerned with
proclamation. Its content is the *message that establishes peace and brings
salvation*. The proclamation of peace refers not only in the external sense
to a political peace or the establishment of a realm of human relations free
from conflict, but to the cosmic resolution of peace that brings all things
together in a reconciled and reconciling unity on the plane of both the
macro-cosmos and the micro-cosmos (2:17; cf. also 3:8–10). Since such
oneness is not only already given by God, but must be attained again and
again on the human level, the church can be compared to a "mature
person" who has reached an advanced level of maturity but is still growing.
Such a one is oriented to Christ and thus to the attainment of the "measure of the full stature of Christ" (4:13).

The message of the church can also be summed up in the term εὐαγγέλιον. The "gospel" is related to Christ, for its content is "the mystery
of Christ" (3:4ff; 6:19). As the "word of truth" it mediates eschatological
salvation (1:13) and a share in the promise (3:6). On the basis of its
universal orientation that establishes unity and encompasses the beginning and end of the Christian life, it can be called the "gospel of peace"
(6:15).

So also *baptism*, as the act of initiation that incorporates the life of the
individual believer in the church, is an essential responsibility of the
church officers. It is explicitly named once, in connection with a triadic
formula that possibly derives from the congregational liturgy, "one Lord,
one faith, one baptism" (4:5). The Christian community is accordingly
constituted by the exalted, cosmic Christ, by the faith that is a response

---

[8]   "Prophets" are also named in 3:5 alongside apostles as those who received the
revelation of the mystery, in contrast to Colossians 1:26, according to which the
revelation of the mystery has been given generally to "all the saints." Ephesians is
referring to Christian prophets, not the prophets of the Old Testament, as indicated
by the word order "apostles and prophets."
[9]   Ephesians 2:20; differently 1 Corinthians 3:11, where Christ is the only foundation; cf. also 1 Corinthians 3:10, where Paul lays the foundation as a "skilled
master builder."
[10]  On the christocentricity of Ephesians cf. also 2:16, where reconciliation is the act
of Christ, in contrast to Colossians 1:20.

to the proclaimed word, and not least by baptism, for in the baptismal confession the candidate confesses his or her statement of faith, and at baptism the name of Jesus Christ is invoked (Acts 2:38; 10:48; cf. Matt 28:19). The designation "sealing" (σφραγίζω) apparently goes back to early Christian baptismal tradition,[11] even though Ephesians speaks only of "sealing by the Spirit" (1:13; 4:30), since in the early Christian understanding the Spirit is given at baptism.[12] On this basis, the whole life of the church is the product of the Spirit (cf. 1:13, "spiritual blessing," 5:19, "spiritual songs"). The Spirit conferred at baptism is the basis of authentic prayer (6:18); it directs the proclamation of the Word of God, which is described as the "sword of the Spirit" (6:17), just as the historical foundation of the church's proclamation by apostles and prophets was a work of the Spirit (3:5). The Spirit generates wisdom and knowledge in all Christians and enlightens their hearts (1:17–18). In particular, the Spirit is the guarantor of the unity of the Church, which is challenged to keep the unity of the Spirit in the bond of peace (4:3). The unity of the body of Christ must correspond to the one Spirit (4:4); this is a challenge to the church that must constantly be renewed, for the Spirit opens the way to the future. As the "pledge of our inheritance" (1:14, ἀρραβὼν τῆς κληρονομίας) the Spirit mediates access to God's dwelling place (2:22).

The connection between Spirit and baptism is manifest in the way the new life of the believer is portrayed and explained, when this is pictured as the changing of one's clothing, removing the old self and putting on the new (4:22ff in dependence on Col 3:9ff). Baptismal instruction stands clearly in the background here. Paul had already understood baptism as the crucifixion of the old self with Christ (Rom 6:6), and knew the conclusion for the life of the one baptized that was to be drawn from this, namely "... be transformed by the renewing of your minds" (Rom 12:2). In Ephesians it is the Spirit of God that effects this renewal of the inner person (4:23–24, 30). Thereby the new creation comes into being (cf. 2 Cor 5:17), i.e. the "clothing yourselves with the new self" (4:24; cf. Gal 3:27; Rom 13:14, "putting on Christ"). The new life is accordingly only possible on the basis of a new beginning constituted by baptism. Baptism begins the renewal effected by the Spirit, a change of lordships from triviality to a meaningful existence, from immorality to a pure life, from ignorance to the knowledge of God, from lie to truth.[13]

---

[11] In post-New Testament tradition, "seal" (σφραγίς) is a "terminus technicus" for baptism: 2 Clement 7.6; 8.6; Hermas *Similitudes* VIII. 6.3; IX. 16. 3ff.

[12] Cf. Acts 2:38; 8:15ff; 10:47–48; John 3:5; Titus 3:5.

[13] The apparently similar formulation, that "He has abolished the law with its commandments and ordinances, that he might create in himself one new humanity in place of the two" (2:15), is not to be understood in an anthropological sense, does not refer to baptism, but has an ecclesiological meaning. It reflects the overcoming of hostility between Gentiles and Jews (2:11ff; cf. 2:16 "that he might reconcile

So also the quotation in 5:14 comes from baptismal tradition, although the precise literary origin of the citation has not yet been adequately explained:

| | |
|---|---|
| Ἔγειρε, ὁ καθεύδων, | "Sleeper, awake! |
| καὶ ἀνάστα ἐκ τῶν νεκρῶν, | Rise from the dead, |
| καὶ ἐπιφαύσει σοι ὁ Χριστός. | and Christ will shine on you." |

In Ephesians this text is a wakeup call to Christians who already experience the new life. They are called to break loose from the past and to orient themselves to Christ (cf. 5:15ff). In his parenesis Paul also uses the picture of awaking from sleep, though with a sharp eschatological focus (Rom 13:11–12; 1 Thess 5:5ff). The background is not mythological-Gnostic, but Hellenistic-syncretistic under the influence of both similar Gnostic texts and traditions from the mystery cults.[14] In the present context it is a matter of church parenesis that no longer evokes the specific connection with baptism.[15]

Ethical issues are handled in a relatively free adaptation of the material from Colossians.[16] As in Colossians, Ephesians includes *vice catalogues:* 4:18–19 (the immoral life of the Gentiles); 4:28–31 (admonition to the church not to grieve the Holy Spirit but to live a righteous life); 5:3ff (church parenesis). There are also *catalogues of virtues* in 4:32 and 5:9 (on the latter, cf. Gal 5:22). As already discussed, the *Haustafel* (5:22–6:9) is elaborated on the basis of Colossians 3:18–4:1; here one sees both the christocentrism of Ephesians and the tendency to timelessness that is developing in late New Testament ethics. An original element within the framework of New Testament ethics is the elaborated picture of the *armor of God* (6:10–20).

*Vice catalogues:* Ephesians 4:31 modifies Colossians 3:8 by expanding the series so that it becomes two units of three members each. The additions are πικρία ("bitterness," "resentment," "spite") and κραυγή ("clamor," "angry shouting"). The latter word replaces αἰσχρολογία of Colossians 3:8, making vivid reference to the goings-on in congregational life.

---

both groups to God in one body through the cross, thus putting to death that hostility through it"). Although elements of Pauline thought stand in the background (cf. "new creation" in 2 Cor 5:17; Gal 6:15), in Ephesians one must think not only of the separation between Gentiles and Jews but of the cosmological schema. Also the breaking down of the "dividing wall" (2:14) has an echo of the victory over the cosmic powers that took place at the resurrection/ascension of Christ (4:8ff).

14 Cf. E. Norden, *Agnostos Theos* 258 note 1.

15 On the history of the later influence of this idea, cf. the further development in Clement of Alexandria Prot 9.84, which could confirm the baptismal liturgy as the place of origin. Cf. also Syr Did 21.

16 On the ethics of Ephesians, cf. U. Luz, "Überlieferungen zum Epheserbrief und seiner Paränese," in H. Frankemölle and K. Kertelge (eds.) *Vom Urchristentum zu Jesus* (FS J. Gnilka) (Freiburg: Herder, 1989) 376–396.

Each case points to sins against the Christian fellowship that make congregational fellowship difficult. The author wants to affirm that the interpersonal relations of church members must be free from tensions that can be caused by bad attitudes or verbal aggression. This is an appeal for congregational unity (4:25).

Ephesians 5:3–8 is formulated in close dependence on Colossians 3:5. Some words such as "disgraceful behaviour" (αἰσχρότης), "silly talk" (μωρολογία), and "vulgar talk" (εὐτραπελία) are not found elsewhere in the New Testament and obviously are inserted into this context. Truth, not lie, must prevail in the congregation (4:25; cf. Zech 8:16); moreover, no evil talk should "come forth" from your mouth (4:29). The following verses also warn against "empty words" that deceive (5:6). In comparison with Colossians 3:5 the warning is made more sharply not only to avoid wrong actions, but also to attend to the reputation of the church. The health of the community includes the obligation to do what is commanded (5:3–4), for the "saints" (5:3) are called to imitate God (4:32; 5:1ff). The concluding eschatological warning that the sinner will have no share in the kingdom of Christ and God (5:5), is appropriate for the tradition of early Christian vice catalogues (cf. 1 Cor 6:9–10; Gal 5:21; cf. Rev 21:8), and shows that the author has not surrendered the future aspect of eschatology; he knows that the cosmic Christ hides the eschatological inheritance in his presence (1:14; cf. 1:11).

*Virtue Catalogues*: The virtue catalogue of Colossians has been specifically reworked in Ephesians when in 4:2 only the three terms "humility," "gentleness," and "patience" are itemized. At the beginning of the parenetic, second major section, the initial thematic admonition to "lead a life worthy of the calling to which you have been called" (4:1) points back to the christological grounding of this call (1:18; cf. 4:4). As in Colossians, the virtue catalogue makes concrete the demand to draw the necessary consequences from the calling Christians have received and stands in close connection with the admonition to members of the church to be considerate of each other and to tolerate one another in love (4:2b). It is a matter of the "love" that lives from the ἀγάπη θεοῦ manifested in the saving Christ event and in the pre-temporal election (2:4; 1:4). In a way that is basically no different than the author of Colossians, the author of Ephesians aims at the unity of the church. A material difference is suggested, however, already in the terminology each uses: Ephesians does not designate love as the "bond of perfection" but speaks rather of the "bond of peace" that guarantees the "unity of the Spirit" (4:3). Thereby the ideas of Colossians are taken up. Just as the cosmic Christ is "our peace" (2:14; cf. 2:17), so also the Christ event manifests this peace and both grounds and effects the unity of the Christian community, while Colossians speaks of the hearts of believers in which the peace of Christ should rule. While Colossians is more strongly focused on the individual-ethical, Ephesians emphasizes the ecclesial-ethical. Both correspond to the Pauline tradition.

Ephesians 4:32 could also be counted among the virtue catalogues, though it does not present a series of virtues in a list, but is part of the parenesis into which it is incorporated in both language and content. The relation to Colossians 3:12 is striking: after the abbreviated adoption of Colossians' virtue catalogue in Ephesians 4:2, the other pieces of the parenetic source are used here. The nouns of Colossians 3:12 appear here as adjectives. The admonition to be kind, loving, and ready to forgive and thereby to "walk in love" is grounded, as in Colossians, by the forgiveness experienced in Christ (4:32b; 5:2). It points to the paradigm of the gracious God as manifest in the Christ event, and back to the "grace of God" (1:6–7; 2:5ff). Here the basic Pauline idea comes to expression that the grace of God revealed in the Christ event must determine the ethical life of believers.

Independently of Colossians, in Ephesians 5:9 the triad "good, right, and true" is named. The contents are known from the Pauline letters (cf. e.g. Gal 5:22; Phil 4:8). From the point of view of the history of religions, parallels are found both in Hellenism (Luc Piscator 16) and in Jewish literature (1QS 8.2); one need only note Micah 6:8. The triad has a special weight in this context. It is the "fruits of light" that are being described. Despite the descriptive form, the catalogue is intended parenetically; it follows directly after the imperative "live as children of light" (5:8). The health of the Christian community demands a distancing from the "useless works of darkness." Christian life stands constantly under the demand to make distinctions and to discern what is evil and what is pleasing to God (5:10–11).

*The Haustafel (5:22–6:9):*[17] A Christianizing of the Haustafel's presentation of the relation of husband and wife is offered in Ephesians 5:22–24, when the admonition to the wife to be subordinate is explicitly referred to Christ as head of the church and this is made the basis of subordination to the husband (cf. 1 Cor 11:3). The instruction to the husband to love the wife is consistent with this, placed in a christological and ecclesiological context (5:25, 28). The attitude called for is motivated by the love of Christ for the church and made analogous to it (v. 25 "as Christ..."; cf. v. 23).

On the relation of parents and children (Col 3:20–21 and Eph 6:1–4), Ephesians adopts the christological formula "in the Lord," which Colossians had already taken over from Paul's own usage. The traditional elements of family order receive a new meaning in the realm of the Kyrios. Right conduct of children happens within the responsibility expected of them as Christians whose lives are based on the Christ event and lived in the context of the Lord's church. Ephesians 6:1–4 is a clear expansion and modification of Colossians 3:20–21. The universal aspect of the admonition is reduced (Col 3:20a, "in everything" is omitted), and instead of the theological grounding of Colossians 3:20b ("...for this is your acceptable duty in the Lord") appeal is made to doing what is "right." The focus is on what is generally acknowledged as right, including within the secular realm. The Old Testament law is significant as a basis for ethical argument (6:2–3/Exod 20:12). The obedience children owe their parents respects the Old Testament law, and has God's promise attached to it. The address to fathers is strengthened (in comparison to Col 3:21) with the prohibition of provoking the children to anger (Eph 6:4). The positive task of the father is to bring up the children "in the discipline and instruction of the Lord" (ἐν παιδείᾳ καὶ νουθεσίᾳ κυρίου), which on the one hand means the discipline of the smaller children, while on the other hand an appeal is made to the insight and capacity for understanding that the older sons or daughters have. An upbringing is called for that is carried out in the authority of the Kyrios, but also in the manner presented by the Kyrios.

Ephesians 6:5–9 likewise adopts the sequence of Colossians 3:22–4:1 and turns to the relation of slaves and masters. This is preserved despite the detailed nature of the original passage: the command that the slaves obey their "earthly masters" (6:5) and the correlative command to the masters to conduct themselves in the same obedience to the Lord (6:9). The christological aspect is expressed more clearly and insistently than in Colossians 3:22: the obedience of the slave should be offered to their masters "as to Christ" (6:5). The focus is more clearly concentrated on Christ as the Lord of the church (cf. 6:6, "slaves of Christ"). Moreover, the parenesis is sharpened when the slaves are instructed to perform their service "with fear and trembling." The main thing is the slave's obligation to what is good; here too as elsewhere in the Ephesian *Haustafel* the reciprocal nature of the admonition is

---

17   G. Strecker, "Die neutestamentlichen Haustafeln (Kol 3:18–4:1 und Eph 5:22–6:9)," in H. Merklein (ed.) *Neues Testament und Ethik* (FS R. Schnackenburg) (Freiburg: Herder, 1989) 349–375.

explicitly underscored (cf. 6:4, 9). Both, slaves and masters, are pointed to the apocalyptic consequences of their acts. The existing social relations are at the same time both confirmed and made transparent to their relation to Christ, and in this way are relativized. The *Haustafeln* of both Colossians and Ephesians contain an eschatological tension, which is grounded on the one side by the Christology of the present on which an ecclesiology is then based, and on the other side has as its object concrete attention to the world. In Ephesians the *Haustafel* is characterized by a stronger tendency toward timelessness, which prepares the way for a theological ethic in which generally valid ethical instruction can be given independently of the changes of history.

*The armor of God (Ephesians 6:10–20)*: Following the extensive *Haustafel* of Ephesians 5:22–6:9 there follows a parenetic section,[18] in which the addressees are called to "put on the whole armor of God" (6:11, 13), in order to withstand the cunning attacks of the devil (6:11). In the background stands the mythical idea of an "armor of God," with which the members of the community carry on the eschatological battle against the demonic foes of the endtime.[19]

In this section are found numerous echoes of Old Testament motifs (WisSol 5:15ff; Isa 11:5; 59:17), but Paul had already spoken of a spiritual armor (1 Thess 5:8; 2 Cor 6:7; Rom 6:13; 13:12). In Ephesians' use of the picture, a shift in the eschatological perspective in comparison with Paul can be discerned. In 1 Thessalonians 5:8 Paul speaks—differently than Ephesian 6:17's "helmet of salvation"—of the "helmet of the hope of salvation." Hope belongs to the armor of God; Paul's eschatological reservation is clearly visible. With this discussion of the armor of God that introduces the conclusion of the letter, the author of Ephesians wants give the community a final reminder of the structure of the Christian life as a constant demonstration and putting into practice of the gift it has received from God. The section then flows into 6:18–20 and its call to prayer.[20]

## c) Eschatology

A. Lindemann[21] advocates the view that the author of Ephesians radicalized Pauline eschatology by transforming the temporal dimension into the spatial dimension.[22] According to him, there is no real future dimension of Ephesians' eschatology. He acknowledges that, to be sure, there are echoes of traditional futuristic eschatology;[23] but these are subordinated to the author's conception of present eschatology. Thus the αἰών

---

18  J. Gnilka, *Epheserbrief* 305 sees "baptismal parenesis" here (as he does in 4:24).

19  On the background from the point of view of the history of religions, cf. the excursus in M. Dibelius, *An die Kolosser. Epheser. An Philemon* (HNT 12. Tübingen: J. C. B. Mohr [Paul Siebeck], 1953³) 96–97; so also H. Schlier, *Der Brief an die Epheser* 291–294.

20  Thus the close dependence on the Colossian source can be seen in the structure of Ephesians 5:21–6:20: while in Colossians 4:2–4 the command to pray follows closely after the *Haustafel* (Col 3:18–4:1), Ephesians inserts between the *Haustafel* and the prayer parenesis (Eph 6:18–20) the passage about the "armor of God" (6:10–17).

21  A. Lindemann, *Die Aufhebung der Zeit*.

22  A. Lindemann, *Die Aufhebung der Zeit* 209–210: "… the future aspect of Pauline theology is replaced by an undifferentiated affirmation of the present. So also the victory over the cosmic powers is no longer understood as an event in time but is seen only in terms of its spatial aspect.

23  *Die Aufhebung der Zeit* 193.

μέλλων of Ephesians 1:21b is not the "'coming age' as in apocalyptic,"[24] but designates a "'personal' power whose ruling authority is over a certain space, not a rulership thought of in terms of time."[25] Ephesians 4:30, which speaks of the "day of redemption," is understood by Lindemann in such a way "that the Christians on the 'day of redemption' are acknowledged to be already redeemed through the seal."[26] The author of Ephesians thus is supposed to undertake an "intentional de-eschatologization."[27]

However much present eschatology is dominant in Ephesians, it must be objected against Lindemann's thesis that futuristic eschatology is not completely eliminated. As 6:10ff shows, the church is not yet to its final goal. It must be challenged to equip itself for the struggle. Ephesians 1:12, 18 and 4:4 show that the eschatological hope is still a basic point of orientation for the Christian life. Ephesians 2:21–22; 4:16 make it just as clear that the church is in the process of growth and construction. One must also ask whether the "day of redemption" (Eph 4:30) is not after all best regarded as evidence for Ephesians' having preserved some elements of futuristic eschatology. The challenge to make the most of the time because the days are evil (Eph 5:16) can be seen as a preservation of futuristic eschatology, since the characterization of the last period before the parousia as a time of special threat was a common topos of apocalyptic thought (2 Thess 2:3–12; Matt 24:15–22). Some passages at least permit more than one interpretation. Despite the emphasis on present eschatology, the author of Ephesians does not want to eliminate completely the future aspect.[28]

# III. Sound Doctrine—The Pastoral Letters

Brox, N. *Die Pastoralbriefe*. RNT 7,2. Regensburg: Pustet, 1969.

Dibelius, M. and Conzelmann, H. *The Pastoral Epistles*. Hermeneia. Philadelphia, 1972.

Donelson, L. R. *Pseudepigraphy and Ethical Argument in the Pastoral Epistles*. HUTh 22. Tübingen: J. C. B. Mohr (Paul Siebeck), 1986.

Fiore, B. *The Function and Personal Example in the Socratic and Pastoral Epistles*. AnBib 105. Rome: PBI, 1986.

Holtz, G. *Die Pastoralbriefe*. ThHK 13. Berlin: Evangelische Verlagsanstalt, 1980.

Roloff, J. *Apostolat—Verkündigung—Kirche*. Gütersloh: Gerd Mohn, 1965.

Roloff, J. *Der erste Brief an Timotheus*. EKK XV. Zürich-Einsiedeln-Köln-Neukirchen-Vluyn: Neukirchen, 1988.

Schenk, W. "Die Briefe an Timotheus I und II und an Titus (Pastoralbriefe) in der neueren Forschung (1945–1985)," *ANRW* II 25.4 (1987) 3404–3438.

---

[24]    *Die Aufhebung der Zeit* 210.

[25]    *Die Aufhebung der Zeit* 210.

[26]    *Die Aufhebung der Zeit* 231–231.

[27]    *Die Aufhebung der Zeit* 236.

[28]    In contrast to A. Lindemann, H. E. Lona, *Eschatologie* 442, speaks of the future as an epiphany of the present: "The presence and futurity of salvation is spoken of only in connection with the reality of the church."

Schlarb, E. *Die gesunde Lehre. Häresie und Wahrheit im Spiegel der Pastoralbriefe.* MThSt 28. Marburg: Elwert, 1990.

Spicq, C. *Saint Paul. Les Épîtres Pastorales* I-II. EtB. Paris: Gabalda, 1969.

Trummer, P. *Die Paulustradition der Pastoralbriefe.* BET 8. Frankfurt: Peter Lang, 1978.

v. Lips, H. *Glaube—Gemeinde—Amt. Zum Verständnis der Ordination in den Pastoralbriefen.* FRLANT 122. Göttingen: Vandenhoeck & Ruprecht, 1979.

Wolter, M. *Die Pastoralbriefe als Paulustradition.* FRLANT 146. Göttingen: Vandenhoeck & Ruprecht, 1988.

## a) The Situation

The incorporation of the Pastoral Letters into the theology of the New Testament presupposes a decision on the issue of whether the two letters to Timothy and the letter to Titus are authentic writings of the apostle Paul, as claimed by the prescripts. If one gives an affirmative answer to this question, then one is compelled, because of the undeniable tensions with the chronology of Paul's life as we otherwise know it, to place them after the account of Acts 28 and to postulate a second Roman imprisonment. This imprisonment would have followed after a renewed period of missionary activity in Asia Minor not documented in Acts (cf. 1 Tim 3:14; 2 Tim 4:13; Titus 3:12), which would have been the setting and occasion for these writings, with the formal and material differences between the Pastorals and the undisputed letters of Paul accounted for by the development in Paul's thought that took place in the meantime. The extensive prescripts of 1 Timothy 1:1–2; 2 Timothy 1:1–2 and Titus 1:1–4 as well as the linguistic and theological peculiarity would in this case be indications for an advanced level of Paul's theology. However, a developmental theory or a psychological explanation is hardly adequate to bring the independence of the Pastoral Letters into line with the other documents of the Pauline corpus. Especially the statements that reflect the Pauline linguistic and thought world suggest rather a firm body of traditional material that was already well-worn; they belong to a later time and illustrate the fact that the author draws upon a secondary stream of tradition of the Pauline school that was becoming independent, that he obviously is to be included in this stream of tradition himself, and that he could expect his readers in the churches of Asia Minor who are indirectly addressed to understand this literary development of the Pauline structures with which they had been familiar. The qualifying assumption expressed fairly often, that a "secretary" of the apostle wrote these documents in the name of Paul, does not really solve the problem presented by the texts. The secretary hypothesis merely confirms that we are not dealing with letters composed by Paul himself.

The names of the letters' addressees are known from New Testament tradition. According to the picture in Acts, *Timothy* came from Lystra in Lycaonia; he was the son of a Greek father and Jewish mother; his mother had become a Christian (Acts 16:1; cf. more extensively 2 Tim 1:5). He was converted by the preaching of Paul (1 Cor 4:17), who chose him to accompany him on his missionary journeys, and is supposed to have circumcised him for this reason (Acts 16:3). In Acts (17:14–15; 18:5; 19:22; 20:4) he is named as the constant companion of Paul; he is the co-sender of several Pauline letters (1 Thess 1:1 par 2 Thess 1:1; 2 Cor 1:1,19; Phil 1:1; Phlm 1), and accordingly found himself with Paul in the places where Paul was imprisoned (cf. also the mention in Rom 16:21, greetings from his fellow worker Timothy), and was commended by the apostle to the church at Philippi with high praise (Phil 2:19ff).

The picture of Timothy in the Pastoral Letters is different; it belongs to the post-apostolic generation. If according to the testimony of the Pauline letters to the church at Thessalonica Timothy had helped the church in Thessalonica get established (1 Thess 3:2–3) and had taught in Corinth in a manner similar to Paul himself (1 Cor 4:17; 16:10–11), in the Pastorals he becomes the recipient of apostolic instruction, one who is completely subordinate to the authority of the apostle (1 Tim 1:3–4; 6:11ff). He is presented as an exemplar of the church's faith (1 Tim 1:18; 2 Tim 1:5ff), the transmitter and model advocate of the normative church organization (1 Tim 3:15; 5:1ff), a contender for true doctrine against the heretics (1 Tim 4:6ff; 2 Tim 1:13, and elsewhere).

*Titus* is not mentioned in Acts, although he accompanied Paul to the Apostolic Conference (Gal 2:1–2) and stood on the apostle's side during the debates with the Corinthian church (2 Cor 2:13; 7:6–7, 13ff; 8:23). The silence of Acts is presumably to be explained by the harmonizing interest of its author and his interest in seeing things from a salvation-historical perspective. But contrary to the portrayal of Acts, it is certain that Titus participated in the gathering of the collection for the original church in Jerusalem (2 Cor 8:6, 16ff; 12:18). As a native Greek (Gal 2:3) he belonged to the first generation of Gentile Christians who were to constitute the beginning of the Gentile Christian church that was in the process of formation as an independent community over against Jewish Christianity. According to statements in the Pastorals, Titus was converted or ordained by Paul (Titus 1:4 "... my loyal child in the faith we share;" cf. 1 Tim 1:2). Titus is active in Dalmatia (2 Tim 4:10) and on Crete, in order to establish or strengthen the proper structures in the congregations (Titus 1:5). Like Timothy, he is charged with the propagation of "sound doctrine" (Titus 1:9; 2:1; cf. 1 Tim 6:3, 20; 2 Tim 1:13). The claim to authority represented by his doctrine and admonition is to be supported by his own example (Titus 2:7), but also through the solidarity of the apostle with his coworkers (2:15). All this means that in the Pastoral Letters the addressees Timothy and Titus are figures of the post-apostolic period, through whose example the author attempts to solve the problems of orthodoxy and heresy by going back to the apostolic tradition.

Paul's imprisonment in Rome is presupposed as the place of writing (2 Tim 1:8). Here the apostle has to come before the court but "was rescued from the lion's mouth" (2 Tim 4:16–17). Nonetheless, he is still staring death in the face (2 Tim 4:6). Since a second Roman imprisonment is nowhere mentioned, including in the Pastorals, the pseudonymous author obviously is thinking of the imprisonment of Paul in Rome narrated in Acts. The details cannot be harmonized with the historical reality—evidence that it was pious imagination that provided the materials for the author's pen. While a (three year) residence of Paul in Ephesus is documented in Acts (19:1ff; 20:31), and also that the apostle journeyed from there to Macedonia (Acts 19:21; 20:1–2), the statement that Timothy had been left behind in Ephesus (1 Tim 1:3ff) contradicts the way the story is told in Acts 19:22, according to which Timothy along with Erastus was sent ahead from Ephesus to Macedonia (cf. also 2 Cor 1:1, where Timothy is with Paul in Corinth and Acts 20:4, where he is among those who accompanied Paul on the trip to Jerusalem).

Also the note that Paul left Titus behind on Crete so that he could establish proper offices in the churches and combat the heretics (Titus 1:5), and then rejoin Paul in Nicopolis (in Epirus?) (Titus 3:12), cannot be verified historically, since, although Paul's journey from Caesarea to Rome did in fact sail to the island of Crete en route, this was only a transitory contact, and instead of landing in Phoenix because of the stormy conditions ended up on Malta (Acts 27–28). Therefore, despite Titus 1:5, there were probably no churches founded by Paul on Crete.

That the addressee of 2 Timothy was to bring items Paul had left behind in Troas (2 Tim 4:13) is likewise unlikely, since according to Acts Timothy had accompanied the apostle on the trip to Jerusalem (Acts 20:4), and with other travelling companions was even sent ahead to Troas, where he was later reunited with the rest of the party (Acts 20:5–6). According to this same tradition, Trophimus was also with Paul (Acts 20:4); as a Gentile Christian from Ephesus he was the immediate occasion for the apostle's arrest (Acts 21:29–30); differently in 2 Timothy 4:20, where he remained behind in Miletus due to sickness.

There is no doubt that these data cannot be harmonized with the historical picture reconstructed from statements of the authentic Pauline letters and Acts. They rather have the function of mediating the person of the apostle to later Christian generations, especially for the purpose of claiming the authority of Paul that was acknowledged in the churches for the teaching of a later church that saw itself as facing new challenges.[1]

---

[1] For introductory issues cf. especially N. Brox, *Pastoralbriefe* 9ff; on the other side see e.g. G. Holtz, *Pastoralbriefe* 19–20; J. Jeremias, *Die Briefe an Timotheus und Titus* (NTD 9. Göttingen: Vandenhoeck & Ruprecht, 1985¹²) 7–10.

## b) Christology

### 1. The Christ Hymn 1 Timothy 3:16

Deichgräber, R. *Gotteshymnus und Christushymnus in der frühen Christenheit. Untersuchungen zu Form, Sprache und Stil der frühchristlichen Hymnen.* StUNT 5. Göttingen: Vandenhoeck & Ruprecht, 1967.

Fowl, St. E. *The Story of Christ in the Ethics of Paul. An Analysis of the Function of the Hymnic Material in the Pauline Corpus.* JSNT.S 36. Sheffield: Sheffield Academic Press, 1990, 155–194.

Metzger, W. *Der Christushymnus 1. Timotheus 3,16, Fragment einer Homologie der paulinischen Gemeinden.* AzTh 62. Stuttgart: Calwer, 1979.

Stenger, W. "Der Christushymnus 1 Tim 3,16," TThZ 78 (1969) 133–148.

Stenger, W. *Der Christushymnus 1 Tim 3,16. Eine strukturanalytische Untersuchung.* RSTh 6. Regensburg: Pustet, 1977.

Wengst, K. *Christologische Formeln und Lieder des Urchristentums.* StNT 7. Gütersloh: Gerd Mohn, 1973, 156–160.

Like the authentic Pauline letters, the Pastorals also take up church traditions with which the author seeks to illustrate his own christological views.[2] Thus 1 Timothy 3:16 transmits some lines of hymnic tradition:

|  |  |
|---|---|
|  | (Christ Jesus) |
| ἐφανερώθη ἐν σαρκί, | was revealed in flesh, |
| ἐδικαιώθη ἐν πνεύματι, | vindicated in spirit, |
| ὤφθη ἀγγέλοις, | seen by angels, |
| ἐκηρύχθη ἐν ἔθνεσιν, | proclaimed among Gentiles, |
| ἐπιστεύθη ἐν κόσμῳ, | believed in throughout the world, |
| ἀνελήμφθη ἐν δόξῃ. | taken up in glory. |

The hymnic character is evident in the six lines structured as three antithetic parallelisms, the chiastic structure (ab/ba/ab) juxtapose the heavenly (Spirit, angel, glory) and the earthly (flesh, peoples, world) spheres. Beginning the first line with the relative pronoun ὅς is a stylistic feature typical of such hymns; it points to a presupposed "Christ Jesus" as the object of the hymn's praise (cf. Phil 2:6; see 1 Tim 3:13). The structure is disputed. E. Norden suggested that the outline corresponds to his reconstruction of an ancient Egyptian inthronization ritual: (1) endowment with the divine life, (2) presentation and (3) installation.[3] However, the first and last lines at the most can be incorporated into a linear series of temporal events (inthronization as ascent to heaven). Nor does the first line say anything about an "endowment with divine life" but presupposes

---

[2]   See below. To be distinguished from these are the biographical notes that correspond to the pseudepigraphical letter situation and are to be attributed primarily to the literary intention of the author. Cf. P. Trummer, *Paulustradition* 114–116.

[3]   E. Norden, *Die Geburt des Kindes* 116–128; cf. Ph. Vielhauer, *Geschichte* 42.

the preexistence of Christ and refers to the incarnation, which is interpreted as an epiphany.[4] There are two possibilities for interpreting the text from this point of view:

(1) After the affirmation of the incarnation (line 1), from line 2 on the heavenly Christ is the subject (God declares the judgment "vindicated" about Christ; this portrays his new heavenly existence "in the Spirit;" cf. 1 Cor 15:44; 1 Pet 3:18b). Against this is to be objected that the idea of the ascension is not clearly articulated until line 6.[5]

(2) If one proceeds on the basis of the last-named possibility, then lines 1– 5 would have to describe the being of the Incarnate One before the ascension—likewise a difficult idea, even if one can point to parallel texts in the Synoptic Gospels (on line 3, cf. Mark 1:13).

In fact, lines 2–5 do not permit an alternative between the earthly and heavenly existence of the Preexistent One. His being "in the Spirit," his "vindication" as the divine demonstration of his eschatological integrity (line 2) already takes place in his earthly advent as the revealer (John 6:63; differently John 16:10: ascension to the Father as demonstration of the righteousness of the Son). The decisive point for determining the proper interpretation is the universality of the Christ event that embraces earth and heaven, as expressed for example in lines 1 and 2 or lines 1 and 6. The appearance to the angels, the proclamation of Christ among the nations, and the fact that the proclamation calls for faith, are not to be limited to distinct temporal phases of the ascension, but express the universal significance of the Christ event as a whole. The reality and claim of the preexistent, earthly, and exalted Christ are all-embracing. There is nothing that can withdraw itself from his mysterious presence (3:16a).

If the Christ hymn is a fragment of early Christian hymnic material that came to the author as part of his tradition, then only speculations can be proposed for the implied theological contents of the original that go beyond the Christology here expressed.[6] The presupposed soteriology (in a manner similar to Phil 2:6ff) may be inferred from the contrast between flesh and Spirit or flesh and glory. The question of redaction criticism as to the function of the hymn in the context of 1 Timothy,

---

[4]   Cf. John 1:5, 14ff. The idea of the "revelation" appears to resemble the revelatory scheme as expressed for example in 1 Corinthians 2:7–10; Colossians 1:26; Ephesians 3:4–6:8; cf. also 2 Timothy 1:9–10; Titus 1:2–3; 1 Peter 1:20–21. Cf. W. Stenger, "Christushymnus" 129ff; E. Schlarb, *Gesunde Lehre* 151–160. However, the "once/now" juxtaposition is not found in our text, even indirectly.

[5]   That line 6 is "a comprehensive counterpart to the opening line" (H. Conzelmann, *Theologie* 99; the note is missing from the 1969 English translation of an earlier edition) is not likely, since the phrase "was taken up" refers concretely to Christ's being taken up into the divine glory.

[6]   Mark 16:12–19 cannot be considered a parallel, since there it is a matter of several (post-Markan) reports of resurrection appearances (vs. Spicq, *Saint Paul. Les Épîtres Pastorales* 1:231).

cannot be easily answered, since it is difficult to draw lines of connection between it and its immediate context, and the preceding verses correspond to the train of thought of the letter as a whole.

(a) Reflection of the situation in which the letter was written: announcement of the apostle's coming, with instructions about what to do until he arrives (3:14–15a).

(b) Ecclesiological framework: the instructions refer to right conduct in the "household of God," which is "the church of the living God" and the "pillar and bulwark of the truth" (3:15b).

(c) Christological transition: Jesus Christ is the "great mystery of our religion" (3:16a). This designation takes up the terms "mystery of the faith" (3:9) and "truth" (3:15) without intending any differentiation. What is meant is that the Christ who is invoked and praised in the hymn is the true object of Christian faith. What follows speaks of the apostasy of the heretics, without making any perceptible connection with the content of the Christ hymn (4:1ff).

First Timothy combines admonitions about the personal conduct of Timothy with elements of church order, and—partly overlapping with these—instructions for resisting the heretics. It is not unusual to find Christological statements made in a parenetical context (e.g. 1:15–16; 2:5–6; 3:13; 4:6; 5:11; 6:14). These are inserted into the parenesis in a relatively unconnected manner. Reflections on the connection between Christology and ethics, indicative and imperative, are practically non-existent. This indicates that the ground, standard, and goal of ethical conduct is the Christ who came into the world to save sinners (cf. the tradition reflected in 1 Tim 1:15).[7]

## 2.   God and Christ

As illustrated by the Christ hymn of 1 Timothy 3:16b, the author of the Pastorals adopts and adapts traditions that had been used in early Christian worship. This is also true of his concept of God. Liturgical tradition is doubtless represented by the two-member confessional statement that has the one God and the one "Mediator" Jesus Christ as its object (1 Tim 2:5–6; cf. 1 Tim 1:1; Titus 2:13; 3:4–7). The author's *theocentric* orientation already perceptible here becomes clearer in the affirmations that praise God as the "King of kings" (1 Tim 6:15b-16) or as the "Savior" (σωτήρ) who has called the church into being (2 Tim 1:9–10). The non-christological statements about God have not so much an Old Testament-Jewish[8] as a

---

[7]   St. E. Fowl correctly argues that in 1 Timothy 3:16b it is God's act in Christ that is emphasized, and that thereby the contrast between Creator and creation is bridged. Thus ascetic practices are not necessary in order to overcome the barrier between humanity and God (*The Story of Christ in the Ethics of Paul* 185–187; cf. also 207–209, "A Suggestion for Recasting the indicative/imperative problem in Paul").

[8]   But cf. the terms "name of God" (1 Tim 6:1), "household of God" (1 Tim 3:15), which entered Christian vocabulary at an early date.

Greek-Hellenistic flavor.[9] That God is the subject of eschatological salvation for humanity is indicated by his function as the giver of fearlessness (2 Tim 1:7) and of "repentance to come to a knowledge of the truth" (2 Tim 2:25). God is the court before which human conduct must stand to give account (2 Tim 2:15). God is not only the Creator, whose works are good (1 Tim 4:4), but the foundation of right doctrine (2 Tim 2:19), and it is only consistent with this that hope (1 Tim 5:5; 6:17), faith (Titus 3:8), and confession (Titus 1:16) are offered to him.

Accordingly, when God is called σωτήρ[10] and his sovereign act of salvation for humanity is described, from the point of view of the history of religions it is not so much the Old Testament-Jewish as the Greek-Hellenistic world of thought that should form the basis of comparison. God's saving act happens in Jesus Christ, is realized in the life of the church (Titus 3:5, baptism), and is valid for all human beings (1 Tim 4:10; cf. 2:4; Titus 2:11). Such a universalistic dimension can be understood without appealing to the hypothesis that the author is here combating an opposing doctrine that teaches "salvation is not for all."[11] It is also the case that the Hellenistic ruler cult only stands in the distant background of the author's theology. The term "savior" has been Christianized in the Pastoral Letters, and made into an authentic expression of the theology of Christian redemption. In harmony with early Christian tradition, the saving act of God is not an isolated object of theological reflection; it is not separated from the Christ event but is included within it. This is seen not only in the text just mentioned, but especially in Titus 3:4–7, which speaks of "... when the goodness and loving kindness of God our Savior appeared, he saved us," and poured out the Holy Spirit on us "through Jesus Christ our Savior." Jesus Christ can be spoken of as σωτήρ, the same predicate applied to God (2 Tim 1:10; Titus 1:4; 2:13; 3:6), for the purpose of his coming is "to save sinners" (1 Tim 1:15).

That the center of gravity of the theological thought of the Pastorals rests on the Christ event is also made clear by the ἐπιφάνεια/ἐπιφαίνω terminology. To be sure, God is the subject of the "revelation," for it is the "grace of God" that has "appeared" as the saving reality for all people (Titus 2:11; cf. 3:4), and the "God who never lies" who brings to pass the promise expressed before all ages, in that he has "revealed" his word and has entrusted the message to his apostle (Titus 1:2–3). The church also awaits

---

9   Cf. the terms σωτήρ, ἐπιφάνεια (see below), μακάριος (1 Tim 1:11), ἄφθαρτος, ἀόρατος (1 Tim 1:17), σωτήριος (Titus 2:11), ἀψευδής (Titus 1:2); μέγας (Titus 2:13), and others. V. Hasler rightly emphasizes that the "enlightened Hellenism" here comes to expression ("Epiphanie und Christologie in den Pastoralbriefen," *ThZ* 33 [1977] 193–209, 197).

10  Six instances in the Pastorals refer to God, while four refer to Christ; cf. W. Foerster, σωτήρ C. D., *TDNT* 7: 1013–1018.

11  Foerster, σωτήρ 1017.

the future "revelation of the glory of the great God," which is at the same time the revelation of the glory "of our savior Jesus Christ" (Titus 2:13). This is integrated into the schema of the history of salvation, according to which the time of salvation (terminus technicus καιροῖς ἰδίοις = "at the right time") was first revealed in the earthly appearance of Jesus Christ (Titus 1:3)[12] and will be completed by God at the parousia "of our Lord Jesus Christ" (1 Tim 6:14–15). The structure in terms of salvation history is recognizable from the fact that the revelation of God as the saving event[13] is realized in the two appearances of Jesus Christ, in his earthly advent and his future advent from heaven. It thus has a christological focus: the earthly appearance of Jesus Christ "who has destroyed death" (2 Tim 1:10) and likewise the coming parousia. This expectation motivates the ethical instruction (1 Tim 6:14; 2 Tim 4:1, 8); its object is the fulfilling of Christian hope (Titus 2:13).

The way the earthly advent of Jesus Christ is portrayed is also oriented to interpreting his person in terms of salvation history. Following the Gospel tradition[14] not only is the incarnation affirmed (1 Tim 3:16), but also Jesus' descent from David (2 Tim 2:8; cf. Matt 1:6, 17ff; Rom 1:3), the confession before Pontius Pilate (1 Tim 6:13), the atoning death (e.g. 1 Tim 2:6; Titus 2:14 and elsewhere), Jesus' resurrection from the dead (2 Tim 2:8), and the expectation of Jesus Christ as the judge of the living and the dead (2 Tim 4:1; Titus 2:13–14; cf. Acts 10:42; Rom 2:16).

This interest in the person of the earthly Jesus points to a widespread christological tradition in the postpauline churches, without our being able to say much about it beyond what is presented above. In comparison with Paul's own letters, the *christological titles* also manifest a more advanced state of development.[15] In place of the title "Christ," not uncommon in Paul (the titular ὁ Χριστός only in 1 Tim 5:11), the predominate usage is Χριστὸς Ἰησοῦς (1 Tim 1:1, 15; 2:5; 4:6; 5:21; 6:13 v. l.; 2 Tim 1:10; 2:3; 4:1; 2:13 v. l.); alongside which is also found Ἰησοῦς Χριστός

---

[12]   Cf. also 1 Tim 2:6; differently V. Hasler, "Epiphanie und Christologie" 199, "who will 'show' to his time … the epiphany of Jesus Christ."

[13]   Cf. D. Lührmann, "Epiphaneia. Zur Bedeutungsgeschichte eines griechischen Wortes," in G. Jeremias, H. W. Kuhn, and H. Stegemann (eds.) *Tradition und Glaube. Das frühe Christentum in seiner Umwelt* (FS K. G. Kuhn) (Göttingen: Vandenhoeck & Ruprecht, 1971) 185–199; 196, 198.

[14]   There are echoes of the Synoptic Gospels; cf. 1 Timothy 5:18 with Matthew 10:10; Luke 10:7; 1 Timothy 1:15 with Luke 5:32; 19:10; 2 Timothy 2:12a with Matthew 10:22; 2 Timothy 2:12b with Matthew 10:33; Luke 12:9, and others as well; C. Spicq, *Saint Paul, Les Épîtres Pastorales* 1:128ff; F. W. Horn, *Glaube und Handeln in der Theologie des Lukas* (GTA 26. Göttingen: Vandenhoeck & Ruprecht, 1986²) 87, 223, 256–257.

[15]   An unresolved problem in the history of tradition follows from the observation that in distinction from both early Christian liturgy and the Pauline tradition the Pastoral Letters do not use the title "Son of God."

(1 Tim 1:16; 6:13; 2 Tim 1:8; Tit 2:13). The ἐν-conceptuality and terminology is an indisputable connection with the Pauline tradition: the use of ἐν Χριστῷ Ἰησοῦ is reminiscent of the "in Christ" terminology of the Pauline letters (cf. 1 Thess 2:14; 4:16), also because in the author's portrayal of the apostolic sufferings, fellowship with Christ is emphasized.[16] It is clear that, as is the case with Paul, the Christ predication refers not only to the earthly Jesus but to the exalted Lord (cf. 1 Tim 3:16; 2 Tim 1:10ff). However, the Pastoral Letters know no formula that speaks explicitly of being "in Christ" or "with Christ." It is rather the case that they combine the Pauline "in Christ" idea not with personal existence but with abstract concepts. While Paul uses "faith" and "in Christ" in an almost tautological sense, the Pastorals use the expression πίστις ἐν Χριστῷ (1 Tim 1:14; 3:13; 2 Tim 1:13; 3:15) in order to affirm that the faith and religion of the church have their ground and continued existence in Jesus Christ. The linguistic differentiation between "faith" and "in Christ" (or "through Christ") reminds one of the likewise postpauline manner in which faith and works are differentiated in the Letter of James (James 2:14ff), without intending to surrender the basic Pauline idea of the unity of faith and fellowship with Christ. It is rather the soteriological aspect that is emphasized: The "promise of life" (2 Tim 1:1) and "grace" (2 Tim 1:9; cf. 2 Tim 2:1) are conferred "in Christ Jesus." "Through Christ" or "in Christ" the elect receive salvation and are endowed with "eternal glory" (2 Tim 2:10). The unity of being determined through Christ and one's ethical conduct is expressed in the phrase "… live a godly life in Christ Jesus" (εὐσεβῶς ζῆν ἐν Χριστῷ Ἰησοῦ 2 Tim 3:12); it combines Christian elements with authentic pagan (Greek) conceptuality and thereby makes visible the location of the author in the history of thought.

Regarding the κύριος *title*: The use of "Lord" with reference to God is especially visible in those places where an Old Testament text is cited, including when this is done indirectly (2 Tim 1:19/Num 16:5 [MT יהוה]; also 2 Tim 2:7/cf. Prov 2:6) or stands in the background (2 Tim 4:14; cf. Ps 62:13; Prov 24:12—sometimes without an explicit mention of the κύριος). While here the world of Old Testament thought is adopted, where God is designated as creator or judge by the title "Lord," in the authentic Pauline letters there is a fluid transition to Christology, since Paul can often use predicates of God with reference to Jesus. Thus one may ask whether it is God or Christ who is praised as the "Lord" who delivers from persecution (2 Tim 3:11), and whether the Lord who stood by Paul and will rescue him from every evil attack is God or Christ (2 Tim 4:17–18). It is uncontestable, however, that when the author uses the term Kyrios he thinks primarily of Jesus Christ. This is suggested by the concluding blessing (2 Tim 4:22 "The Lord be with your spirit;" cf. the v. l. "the Lord Jesus Christ;" cf. also Gal 6:18 "our Lord Jesus Christ"), and is confirmed by combinations such as "Lord Jesus Christ" (κύριος Ἰησοῦς Χριστός, 1 Tim 6:3, 14) or "Christ

---

[16] 2 Timothy 2:9–10; see 2 Corinthians 13:4; Phil 1:12ff; cf. also the σύν-constructions in 2 Timothy 2:11–12.

Jesus our Lord" (Χριστὸς Ἰησοῦς ὁ κύριος ἡμῶν, 1 Tim 1:2; 2 Tim 1:2). Just as the Christian community is the fellowship of those who "call on the Lord" (2 Tim 2:22), here it is doubtless the name of Jesus Christ that is meant (cf. 1 Cor 1:2). It is to him that the apostle knows he is obligated (2 Tim 2:24 δοῦλος κυρίου; cf. also James 1:1), and the community expects him as the "righteous judge" who will give the victor's crown to all who have loved his appearing (2 Tim 4:8).

## c) Ecclesiology

### 1. The Apostle

Just as the Christology of the Pastorals is not limited to the repetition of formulaic material but draws upon a living, progressing Pauline tradition and develops it even further, so also the ecclesiology of the Pastoral Letters is not merely a matter of "instruction about church offices." It is rather the case that the instructions to the clergy suggest an ecclesial self-understanding, inasmuch as the church officers are thought of as part of the church and the admonitions directed to them also provide insight into the author's understanding of the theological and ethical horizons that form the ideal and reality of the church's life. We are clearly on the way to the Great Church of the second century. By adopting the pseudepigraphical form that orients the historical and functional beginnings of the church to the apostolic generation, the author indicates the specific consciousness of history of the Pastoral Letters. To be sure, it is not the group of apostles as a whole that forms the foundation of the church (differently than Eph 2:20), but the person of Paul who is the norm for the church's faith and order. Only he bears the title "Apostle of Jesus Christ;"[17] as "herald and apostle, teacher of the Gentiles" (1 Tim 2:7), he has been commissioned with the proclamation of the "glorious gospel of the blessed God" (1 Tim 1:11). He has fulfilled this commission in a global manner that embraces the whole church.[18] As indicated by the epigonic formula "according to my gospel" (κατὰ τὸ εὐαγγέλιόν μου),[19] the Christ kerygma is the content of his message. The "gospel" is identical with "sound doctrine,"[20] which is oriented to what is good and reasonable (cf. 1 Tim 3:2; Titus 1:8; 2:2, 5, 12). In debate with the unhealthy doctrine of the heretics, it is the apostle's

---

[17] 1 Timothy 1:1; 2 Timothy 1:1 v. l.; 2 Corinthians 1:1; Galatians 1:1.
[18] 1 Timothy 1:3: Ephesus, Macedonia; 2 Timothy 1:15: Asia; 1:17: Rome; 4:20: Corinth, Miletus; Titus 1:5: Crete; 3:12: Nicopolis.
[19] 2 Timothy 2:8; cf. Romans 2:16; 16:25—both presumably postpauline.
[20] 1 Timothy 1:10–11 ἡ ὑγιαίνουσα διδασκαλία, also 2 Timothy 4:3; Titus 1:9; 2:1; cf. the expression "sound words" (ὑγιαίνοντες λόγοι) in 1 Timothy 6:3,; 2 Timothy 1:13; cf. also Titus 2:8 (singular) λόγος ὑγιής; "sound teaching (καλὴ διδασκαλία) 1 Timothy 4:6. The term διδασκαλία appears 21 times in the New Testament, 15 of which are in the Pastoral Letters.

concern to hand on the "body of doctrine"[21] with which he has been entrusted, so that it can continue to be preserved for the future. His teaching is intended to bring about "piety" (εὐσέβεια), which characterizes the Christian life of the individual as well as that of the church as a whole,[22] and is manifested in such Christian virtues as faith, love, patience, and humility (1 Tim 6:11).

The person of the apostle serves as a model for the Christian life. He is an example of, and realizes in his own life, the kind of conduct that is expected of Christians in the present, and that will be expected for all generations to come.[23] For the postpauline time the apostolic model is important not only for the rejection of heresy but especially for the establishment and proper maintenance of church order. While the law is "good" (1 Tim 1:8), a reflection of the adoption of Pauline tradition (Rom 7:12, 16), his interpretation reflects the later stages of the Pauline school and is not the same as Paul's. Here, the point is in contrast to false doctrine and immoral actions (cf. 1 Tim 1:3–4, 9–10), so that the law is the οἰκονομία θεοῦ experienced in faith (1 Tim 1:4 "divine training" or "divine plan") as the divinely willed goal of Christian life and church organization. On this point the author presents a series of concrete instructions: The apostle vouches for the necessity of abiding church structures; he himself established something like a "successio apostolica" by laying his hands on Timothy (2 Tim 1:6). To be sure, this is restricted to the results of Paul's own apostolate and is not yet developed along the lines of the later ecclesiastical idea of apostolic succession (cf. differently 1 Clem 42:1–5; 44:2–3, 5), since laying on of hands and the charismatic gifts that are thereby bestowed on the disciples of the apostles also reside in the presbytery (1 Tim 4:14; cf. 5:22; Heb 6:2). And however much the apparently firmly-structured παραθήκη appears to determine the content of the commission to teach with authority, the pneumatic element is still not excluded, since the "good treasure entrusted to you" is to be guarded with the help of "the Holy Spirit living in us."[24]

---

21  Παραθήκη is really a juristic term = that which has been deposited; that which has been entrusted to the apostle's disciple for safekeeping (1 Tim 6:20; 2 Tim 1:14); cf. 2 Tim 1:12, παραθήκη μου, and the verb παρατίθημι: 1 Timothy 1:18 (to "entrust" the commandment); 2 Timothy 2:2: the apostle's disciple is to entrust the apostolic teaching to "trustworthy" or "believing" men, who will be able to teach others (= the beginning point of the idea of an authorized chain of teaching).
22  Cf. the expression ἡ κατ᾽ εὐσέβειαν διδασκαλία: 1 Timothy 6:3; cf. 1 Timothy 2:2; 4:7, and other such texts.
23  Cf. 1 Timothy 1:16: The apostle is a model (ὑποτύπωσις) for all who will live a Christian life in the future. 2 Timothy 1:13, "Hold to the standard of sound teaching that you have heard from me, ...".
24  2 Timothy 1:14; cf. on the concept of the Spirit, 1 Timothy 3:16; 4:1; 2 Timothy 1:7; Titus 3:5.

The stable element in the constitution of the church is found in the essential ecclesial orders of the ministry. The *bishop* (1 Tim 3:1–7; Titus 1:7–9), whose qualifications for office are generally accepted ethical criteria, is to be blameless, sober, sensible, dignified, and hospitable. He is also to fulfill special duties: skilled in teaching, not a recently baptized convert, held in high respect by outsiders, "a man of [only] one wife." If he presides over his own household well, one may suppose that as "God's steward" (Titus 1:7, οἰκονόμος θεοῦ) he will also be concerned to manage well the affairs of the church. His office is characterized by teaching (proclaiming the word), leadership of the congregation, and service; there is no reference to sacramental functions. Whether the Pastoral Letters know the concept of a monarchial bishop, or whether the bishop is on the same level as the presbytery and at most a "first among equals," is a disputed point.[25] In favor of the latter view is that the list of qualifications for bishop and presbyters are about the same. But since the Pastorals speak of the bishop only in the singular, but of the presbyters only in the plural, at least a step has been taken in the direction of the monarchial episcopacy of the later Catholic Church.[26]

The personal qualifications of the *presbyter* (1 Tim 5:17–19; Titus 1:5–6) correspond to those of the bishop. Presbyters too must bring to this teaching office definite personal qualities of a moral and intellectual nature. They too are installed in office by the laying on of hands (1 Tim 5:22) and receive a salary from the church (1 Tim 5:17–18; Deut 25:4). Thus "presbyter" refers to an office, not to the age of the persons concerned (in distinction from 1 Tim 5:1).

The same criteria are applied to the *deacons* (1 Tim 3:8–13) as are applied to elders. They too must have a good reputation, should be married, and should preside over their households in an exemplary manner. Going beyond what is said of presbyters, ethical qualifications are also given for their wives.[27] Timothy, disciple of the apostle, who elsewhere, like Titus, is directly entrusted by the apostle with the teaching office and the authority to organize the church and who thus has an intermediate function between the apostle and the bishop / presbyters (cf. 1 Tim 1:3ff, 18–19; 2 Tim 4:1ff; Titus 1:5), is himself described as a "good deacon of Jesus Christ", whose food is "the words of faith and the sound teaching" (1 Tim 4:6). It is striking that the three church offices of bishop, presbyter,

---

[25] So H. v. Campenhausen, *Ecclesiastical Authority and Spiritual Power in the Church of the First Three Centuries* (London: Adam & Charles Black, 1969) 107–124.

[26] Cf. already Ignatius, Eph 3–6. The argument that the singular "the bishop" of the Pastorals is to be understood in the generic sense does not persuade, since there is no similar generic use for the offices of presbyter and deacon.

[27] 1 Timothy 3:11; it is not likely that here "deaconesses" are meant; cf. rather the analogous ethical standards that refer to the older women of the church in Titus 2:3.

and deacon are only mentioned separately: either bishop and deacons (1 Tim 3:1–13) or the presbyters alone (1 Tim 5:17–19), or the presbyters with an appended list of qualifications for the bishop (Titus 1:5–9). This suggests that the Pastorals document for the first time the amalgamation of what had been two different types of organizational structure: on the one hand, the presbyterial structure that grew out of the Jewish synagogue, on the other hand the episcopal structure whose home was originally in the Hellenistic churches. Their beginnings are already documented in Paul, when these are mentioned as "supervisors" and "servants" as persons holding official roles, obviously charged with the collection of funds for subsidies (Phil 1:1; 4:10–20). The threefold official structure of bishop-presbyter-deacon is first clearly documented for Asia Minor in the letters of Ignatius at the beginning of the second century (e.g. Ign Phil 7:1).

## 2. The Church

Although church order is strongly emphasized, in the description of the various church offices the self-understanding of the church as such already comes to expression. Moreover, church structures are recognizable that limit the development toward a "church hierarchy" and remain open to the free working of the Spirit (e.g. 2 Tim 1:14 and elsewhere). An intermediate position between office and congregation is occupied by the class of *widows* (χήρα; 1 Tim 5:3–16). While in the general ethics of New Testament times the widows stand at a lower level on the social scale and, along with orphans, are the object of special care (James 1:27; Acts 6:1ff), the Pastoral Letters in contrast for the first time presuppose the existence of a class of widows in the congregational life that plays a special role (Viduat). This group is frequently documented in the later church.[28] Early Christian tradition can here attach itself to an Old Testament-Jewish tradition according to which widows and orphans stand in a special way under God's protection (Exod 22:22; Deut 24:17ff). So also in the Pastoral Letters the benevolent perspective is noticeable when a distinction is made between widows who are wealthy, who have relatives, or who live in the household of other Christians who support them financially, and others who are limited to their own resources and who "set their hope on God" (1 Tim 5:5). A distinction is also made between older and younger widows. While the latter group are to marry, bear children, and manage the household and thus should not rely on support from the church, the older widows (60 and above) who have been married to only one husband and who have a good reputation in other respects, may be entered in the offi-

---

[28] Pseudo-Clementine Recognitions 3:11; it is not likely that here "deaconesses" are meant; cf. rather the analogous ethical standards with regard to the older women in Titus 2:3.

cial list of widows (1 Tim 5:9–10). The task of those who are accepted into this congregational class of "real widows" (1 Tim 5:3) is to continue constantly in supplications and prayers.[29] As explicitly established by later church orders, they are not thereby fundamentally separated from the congregation, but carry out the kinds of duties incumbent on all Christians (cf. *Egyptian Church Order* 7:6).

The origin of the class of widows is to be interpreted as essentially the result of Christian social action, for the essence of the church comes to expression in such benevolent concern for the welfare of others. This "essence" is also expressed in the traditional terms such as "saints" (1 Tim 5:10 ἅγιοι), "beloved" (1 Tim 6:2 ἀγαπητοί), "elect" (2 Tim 2:10; Titus 1:1 ἐκλεκτοί), and especially as the community of "believers" (πιστοί).[30] There is no reflection on the basis and meaning of these terms. They have often lost their original meaning and are transmitted in a homogenized sense. Thus the community's self-description as "elect" has lost its original apocalyptic character, for while it is oriented to eschatological salvation, it no longer includes an awareness of the presence of the eschatological saving event (2 Tim 2:10). So also the term πιστοί does not so much mean believing acceptance of the promised salvation as it does being loyal or dependable ("faithful" rather than "believing"), in accord with understanding the Christian life as piety and ethics.[31] That this lifestyle is not without its dangers is seen from the comparison of the church with a "household." Just as the bishop is to administer his household in an exemplary manner, so he must preside over the "church of God" in the same way (1 Tim 3:5, ἐκκλησία θεοῦ; cf. also 1 Tim 3:15). This is also expressed in the rules laid down for how the apostolic disciple Timothy is to conduct his life. He is to know how one properly conducts himself in the "household of God" (οἶκος θεοῦ) (1 Tim 3:15). Here the "church of God" is understood as the "pillar and ground of the truth", in contrast to 1 Corinthians 3:11 (Christ is the only foundation), and thereby suggests a confrontation with the false teachers (cf. 1 Tim 4:11ff). This image is developed in 2 Timothy 2:19–21, when the church is compared to a large house that contains both valuable and less valuable objects, pure and impure vessels. The labeling of the false teaching as "gangrene" (2:17) does not exclude that the relation

---

29   1 Timothy 5:5; cf. also Const Ap 21; Didask III 5.1.
30   1 Timothy 3:11; 4:3, 10, 12; 5:16; 6:2; 2 Timothy 2:2; Titus 1:6.
31   Cf. 1 Timothy 1:12; 3:11; 2 Timothy 2:2. Correspondingly, πίστις means not only the Christian's stance as a believer (1 Tim 1:2, 4–5, 19b; 4:1; 5:8; 6:10, 12; 2 Tim 1:5 and elsewhere) or the content of the faith (1 Tim 4:1, 6), but also the faithfulness and dependability manifested by Christians (1 Tim 1:19a) that stands alongside other Christian traits (such as "love" and/or other ethical qualities: 1 Tim 4:12; 6:11; 2 Tim 2:22; 3:10; Titus 2:2). The modification of the Pauline triad "faith, hope, and love" (1 Cor 13:13) to "faith, love, holiness and modesty" (1 Tim 2:15) is also revealing.

to the heretics is to be characterized by coolness and sobriety (2:20); but the emphasis is on the command to keep one's distance from impurity (2:21).

A central concern of the Pastoral Letters is the struggle against *false teachers*. Here for the first and only time in the New Testament the term "Gnosticism" (γνῶσις) is used as a heresiological term (1 Tim 6:20 ἀντι-θέσεις τῆς ψευδωνύμου γνώσεως). The conjecture already made by F. C. Baur, that there is a reflection here of the title of Marcion's book "Antith-eses,"[103] has no basis in the text, so that (in accord with the preceding expression "profane chatter") one should more correctly translate "contra-dictions of what is falsely called 'knowledge'." Nor is it clear that the author sees himself as confronted by a specifically Gnostic concept of knowledge (despite Titus 1:16), or that a specific Gnostic system is in view. A mythological Gnosticism as represented in the second century by Saturninus, Basilides, or Valentinus is not (yet) visible. But concrete infor-mation is given about the opposing teaching. It contains clear Jewish elements. Thus the author of the Letter of Titus speaks of "deceivers, especially those of the circumcision" (Titus 1:10), and knows that they are spreading abroad Jewish myths and human commandments (1:14; cf. 1 Tim 4:7; 2 Tim 4:4). A Jewish background for this teaching could also be indicated by the expectation that "teachers of the law" (1 Tim 1:7) will appear and that disputes about the (Old Testament?) law will break out (Titus 3:9), as well as references to disputations about "genealogies" (1 Tim 1:4; Titus 3:9) or ascetic practices (1 Tim 4:3), especially the prohibition of certain foods (1 Tim 4:3; cf. Titus 1:15; but cf. also Rom 14:20; Luke 11:41).

On the other hand, when the opponents forbid marriage (1 Tim 4:3; on which cf. the positive commendation of marriage in 1 Tim 2:15; 3:2, 12; 5:14; Titus 2:4), or explain that the resurrection has already happened (2 Tim 2:18; cf. Justin *Apology* I 26.4; Irenaeus *Heretics* I 23.5; II 31.2), one may think more readily on Gnostic sectarians who on the basis of a dualistic conceptuality affirm that by "knowledge" they have already over-come the world. Their description as "deceitful spirits" or advocates of "teaching of demons" (1 Tim 4:1) cannot be identified so clearly. In por-traying the opposing group, the author uses a traditional arsenal of weap-ons used against heretics, including materials he has adopted from the Pauline school. An example is the critical statement that these opponents use their "religious practices" as a means of gain (1 Tim 6:5; Titus 1:11; cf. 1 Pet 5:2; 1 Thess 2:5; 2 Cor 7:2; 12:17–18; 2 Pet 2:3), or in the shrill

---

32   F. C. Baur, *Die sogenannten Pastoralbriefe des Apostels Paulus aufs neue kritisch untersucht* (Stuttgart-Tübingen 1835) 26–27. So also W. Bauer, *Orthodoxy and Heresy* 226; Ph. Vielhauer, *Geschichte* 228, 237.

charges that they are "puffed up" (1 Tim 6:4; cf. 2 Tim 3:4), "have a morbid craving for controversy" and for "disputes about words" (1 Tim 6:4; 2 Tim 2:14), that they operate as hypocrites who spread lies (1 Tim 4:2)—statements that are usually found in the parenetic vice catalogues (cf. 1 Tim 1:9–10; 2 Tim 3:2ff; Titus 1:12 has a quotation from the Cretan poet Epimenides), but which could also be used in the struggle against heretics (1 Tim 6:4–5; cf. 2 Tim 3:2–4 and 3:5, 13). The idea that heretics necessarily live an immoral life became an established topos of heresiology. It appears in the Pastorals with the admonition to the apostolic disciple to remain in the right, sound doctrine and to advocate this in accord with his commission (1 Tim 4:12ff; 2 Tim 3:14ff; Titus 1:5ff; 2:1ff); by contrast the teaching of the opponents is unsound and sick (1 Tim 6:4). Also to be included within the early Christian anti-heretical topos is the allusion to the hypocritical "speakers of lies" who will appear "in the last days."[33] This is already happening in the church's present experience. The false teaching is a harbinger of the final events. Because the warning against false teaching is open-ended in view of the future events, it is not possible, nor is it the author's intent, to give a precise description of the heresies to appear in the future (cf. also Acts 20:29–30). This excludes the possibility of restricting the heresiological statements of the Pastoral Letters to a particular group such as "Jewish Gnostics," but rather places the author's anti-heretical statements on the plane of general exhortations, and thus points to the readers' responsibility to be alert for the appearance of heresy in their own times, in whatever concrete forms it may appear.

The apostle is to be the standard and model for the lifestyle of the community. If it, like the apostle, is persecuted (2 Tim 3:11–12), it is to orient itself by the model provided by the apostle (1 Tim 1:16 and elsewhere; cf. 1 Cor 4:16, where this note already appears). This is impressively illustrated by the section 2 Timothy 2:11–13, which is formulated in a hymnic manner, and possibly in vv. 11–12 goes back to an older tradition expressing the dialectical relationship of suffering and glory:

> The saying is sure: If we have died with him, we will also live with him;
> if we endure, we will also reign with him;
> if we deny him, he will also deny us;
> if we are faithless, he remains faithful—for he cannot deny himself. (2 Tim 2: 11–13).

Fellowship with Christ is promised not only to the apostle but to all Christians (v. 10). This works itself out in the manner in which the apostle accepts his lot as a prisoner "for the sake of the elect," in order that thereby the spread of the gospel is furthered (2 Tim 1:8; cf. Phil 1:12ff). The

---

[33]  1 Timothy 4:1–2; 2 Timothy 3:1ff; cf. Mark 13:21–23 par Matthew 24:23ff; 1 John 2:18; 4:3; 2 Peter 2:1ff; Jude 4ff.

interpretation of apostolic suffering takes place within the framework of the adoption of the Pauline baptismal tradition (Rom 6:4ff, 8). It is applied to all Christians (1. person plural). As fellowship with Christ is grounded in martyrdom, so the hope for eternal life is placed on the same foundation. The dialectic of the Pauline baptismal theology is preserved (Rom 6:4; cf. differently Col 2:12). The new element is that the christological orientation is primary: judgment (2 Tim 2:12b; cf. Matt 10:33) and salvation (2 Tim 2:13).[34] Each is included in the preaching of Christ and is a component of the "faithful saying,"[35] by which the persecuted community threatened by heresies (2 Tim 3:12) is called to patience and loyalty to the proclaimed word of truth (2 Tim 2:15). That the church of the Pastoral Letters is aware of both the external and internal threats in its situation makes it impossible for it to sink into a satisfied bourgeois existence and to understand the "godliness"[36] demanded of it as an introverted, self-satisfied pious lifestyle. The "quiet and still life" for which it prays in its prayers for the government (1 Tim 2:1–2) is not to be confused with a superficial middle-class peace and quiet. It is rather a goal that has not been attained and factually cannot be attained, that it must hold constantly before its eyes. To be sure, the community is concerned when possible to live without offense and to practice what is considered in its Hellenistic environment to be "reasonable" (cf. Titus 2:12, "self-controlled") and "respectable."[37] However, this does not in principal mean a life conformed to the world. Despite the accommodation to the present age (1 Tim 6:17ff; Titus 2:12) which is also seen, for example, in the establishment of church offices, the unworldly distinctiveness of the eschatological message, although legitimized by apostolic tradition and churchly institution, is not given up and is affirmed over against both heresy and the world.[38] Not the least factor here is the contribution made by Pauline tradition, still perceptible in the distinction between indicative and imperative,[39] or in the conviction that the "grace of God" ($\chi\acute{\alpha}\rho\iota\varsigma$) that repre-

---

[34] The distinction between "denial" (= "falling away") and "unfaithfulness" (= "relapse" into the state prior to baptismal grace; cf. C. Spicq *Les Épîtres Pastorales* 2:750 [on 2 Tim 2:13] is unclear; the confession of Christ's faithfulness can be related to Old Testament picture of the faithfulness of God (cf. Deut 7:9; Rom 3:3–4).

[35] Πιστὸς ὁ λόγος also in 1 Timothy 1:15; 3:1; 4:9; Titus 3:8; on the formulaic character of this expression, cf. N. Brox, *Pastoralbriefe* 112ff (on 1 Tim 1:15).

[36] 1 Timothy 4:7–8; 6:3, 5–6; 2 Timothy 3:5; Titus 1:11. The German translation "Frömmigkeit" ("piety," "religion," translated in the NRSV as "godliness") designates the manner of thinking and acting appropriate to believers, corresponding to the original meaning of the world.

[37] Σεμνότης: 1 Timothy 2:2; 3:4; Titus 2:7.

[38] Cf. also 2 Timothy 4:10: ὁ νῦν αἰών = "the present age;" 1 Timothy 6:7, κόσμος = "world."

[39] Cf. 1 Timothy 2:1–7; 2 Timothy 1:13–14; 2:19; Titus 3:7–8, 14.

sents the main principle of Christian action[40] has played a role in the formation of the theological profile typical for the Pastoral Letters.[41]

# IV. Against the False Eschatological Teachers— Second Thessalonians

Best, E. *A Commentary on the First and Second Epistles to the Thessalonians.* HNTC. New York: Harper & Row, 1977.

Braun, H." Zur nachpaulinischen Herkunft des zweiten Thessalonicherbriefes," ZNW 44 (1952/53) 152–156; also in H. Braun (ed.). *Gesammelte Studien zum Neuen Testament und seiner Umwelt.* Tübingen: J. C. B. Mohr (Paul Siebeck), 1971, 205–209.

Cullmann, O. "Der eschatologische Charakter des Missionsauftrages und des apostolischen Selbstbewusstseins bei Paulus. Untersuchung zum Begriff des κατέχον (κατέχων) in 2. Thess. 2,6–7," in O. Cullmann, *Vorträge und Aufsätze 1925–1967,* K. Fröhlich (ed.). Tübingen: J. C. B. Mohr (Paul Siebeck), 1967, 305–326.

Dibelius, M. *An die Thessalonicher I.II. An die Philipper.* HNT 11. Tübingen: J. C. B. Mohr (Paul Siebeck), 1937.

Hartman, L. "The Eschatology of 2 Thessalonians as Included in a Communication," in R. F. Collins (ed.), *The Thessalonian Correspondence.* BEThL 87. Leuven: Leuven University Press, 1990, 470–485.

Holland, G. S. *The Tradition that You received from us: 2 Thessalonians in the Pauline Tradition.* HUTh 24. Tübingen: J. C. B. Mohr (Paul Siebeck), 1988.

Holtzmann, H. J. "Zum zweiten Thessalonicherbrief," ZNW 2 (1901) 97–108.

Hughes, F. W. *Early Christian Rhetoric and 2 Thessalonians.* JSNT.S 30. Sheffield: Sheffield Academic Press, 1989.

Jewett, R. *The Thessalonian Correspondence. Pauline Rhetoric and Millenarian Piety.* Philadelphia: Fortress Press, 1986.

Krentz, E. "Traditions Held Fast: Theology and Fidelity in 2 Thessalonians," in R. F. Collins (ed.), *The Thessalonian Correspondence.* BEThL 87. Leuven: Leuven University Press, 1990, 505–515.

Lindemann, A. "Zum Abfassungszweck des Zweiten Thessalonicherbriefs," ZNW 68 (1977) 35–47.

Marxsen, W. *Der zweite Thessalonicherbrief.* ZBK 11.2. Zürich: Zwingli, 1982.

Merk, O. "Überlegungen zu 2 Thess 2,13–17," in C. Mayer, K. Müller, G. Schmalenberg (eds.), *Nach den Anfängen fragen.* GSTR 8. 1994, 405–414.

Müller, P. *Anfänge der Paulusschule: dargestellt am 2. Thessalonicherbrief und am Kolosserbrief.* AThANT 74. Zürich: Zwingli, 1988.

---

[40]    Titus 2:11–12; cf. 1 Timothy 1:14; 2 Timothy 1:9; 2:1.

[41]    The text 2 Timothy 2:11–13 indicates that the relation to Paul cannot be oversimplified by relating it to the key expression "theology of the cross" supposed to be present in Paul but absent from the Pastorals. For literature, cf. A. Schlatter, *Die Kirche der Griechen im Urteil des Paulus. Eine Auslegung seiner Briefe an Timotheus und Titus* (1983³ (1958², 15); P. Trummer, *Paulustradition* 116–141; W. Schenk, "Die Briefe an Timotheus" 3416ff.

Rigaux, B. *Saint Paul. Les Épîtres aux Thessaloniciens.* EtB. Paris: Gabalda, 1956.

Schmithals, W. "The Historical Situation of the Thessalonians Epistles," in W. Schmithals. *Paul and the Gnostics.* Nashville: Abingdon, 1972, 123–218.

Schmithals, W. "Die Thessalonicherbriefe als Briefkompositionen," in E. Dinkler (ed.), *Zeit und Geschichte.* (FS R. Bultmann). Tübingen: J. C. B. Mohr (Paul Siebeck), 1964, 295–315.

Schweizer, E. "Der zweite Thessalonicherbrief ein Philipperbrief?," *ThZ* 1 (1945) 90–105.

Trilling, W. *Der zweite Brief an die Thessalonicher.* EKK XIV. Neukirchen-Vluyn: Neukirchener, 1980.

Trilling, W. "Die beiden Briefe des Apostels Paulus an die Thessalonicher. Eine Forschungsübersicht," *ANRW* II 25.4 (1987) 3365–3403.

Trilling, W. *Untersuchungen zum zweiten Thessalonicherbrief.* EThSt 27. Leipzig: St. Benno, 1972.

v. Dobschütz, E. *Die Thessalonicherbriefe.* KEK X. Göttingen: Vandenhoeck & Ruprecht, 1909 (Reprint 1974 with additional bibliography by O. Merk).

v. Harnack, A. "Das Problem des zweiten Thessalonicherbriefes," SPAW.PH 31, Berlin (1910) 560–578.

Vielhauer, Ph. and Strecker, G. "Apocalyptic in Early Christianity. Introduction." W. Schneemelcher (ed.) *New Testament Apocrypha* II (Louisville: Westminster, 1992[2]) 569–603.

Wrede, W. *Die Echtheit des zweiten Thessalonicherbriefes.* TU NF 9.2. Leipzig: J. C. Hinrichs, 1903.

## a) The Question of Authenticity

Since at the beginning of the nineteenth century J. E. Chr. Schmidt[1] set forth the thesis that 2 Thessalonians could not be an authentic letter of Paul on the basis of the different eschatology it contains, the question of the authenticity or inauthenticity of 2 Thessalonians has been constantly raised afresh, and has been given differing answers. The following discussion presupposes that the document was not composed by Paul himself, but originated within the Pauline school (in the broad sense of that term).[2] In favor of this view is above all the fact that—as W. Wrede has shown in a penetrating analysis—1 and 2 Thessalonians are to a great extent parallel to each other in their outlines.[3] Each letter names Silvanus and Timothy as co-senders, reports persecutions and distresses of the church; they presuppose that the church situation in Thessalonica has remained by and large the same. The main topic of each letter is eschatology, and both

---

[1] J. E. Chr. Schmidt, "Vermutungen über die beiden Briefe an die Thessalonicher," in *Bibliothek für Kritik und Exegese des Neuen Testaments* II (Hadamar 1801) 380–386 (cf. the reprint in W. Trilling, *Untersuchungen* 159–161).

[2] Cf. Ph. Vielhauer, *Geschichte* 95–100; W. Trilling, *Der zweite Brief an die Thessalonicher* 22–26.

[3] W. Wrede, *Echtheit* presents tables that show in detailed fashion the agreements between the two letters.

address "disorderly" members of the congregation. Apart from a few exceptions (though these are significant), 2 Thessalonians corresponds structurally to 1 Thessalonians:

| 1 Thess | 2 Thess | |
|---------|---------|--|
| 1:1–10 | 1:1–12 | Prescript; Proömium |
| 2:1–3:10 | | Personal notes; founding of the church; sending of Timothy |
| 3:11–13 | 2:13–17 | Blessing |
| 4:1–12 | 3:1–5 | General parenesis |
| 4:13–5:11 | 2:1–12 | Instruction about the parousia |
| 5:12–15 | 3:6–12 | Against the disorderly |
| 5:16–28 | 3:13–18 | Conclusion and greetings |

In addition, theological arguments must be considered that speak for the secondary nature of 2 Thessalonians with regard to the authentic letters of Paul.[4] This will make it unnecessary to consider the numerous attempts to explain the existence of two letters of Paul of essentially identical content by postulating different addressees or by division into various sources.[5] The literary dependence is not in every case as close as Ephesians is to Colossians, but verbatim parallels can be seen (cf. e.g. 2 Thess 1:1–2/1 Thess 1:1, or 2 Thess 3:8 with 1 Thess 2:9). It is revealing that the personal sections of 1 Thessalonians (2:1–3:10), including Paul's specific longing to see the church again (3:10), are not taken over by the author of 2 Thessalonians. Instead, the parenetic and apocalyptic contents of 1 Thessalonians are extensively elaborated, with the result that 2 Thessalonians has received the character of a monitory and didactic letter.[6]

---

4  H. Braun, "Die nachpaulinische Herkunft."
5  So e.g. A. v. Harnack, *Das Problem*, who argues that the two letters are directed to different groups in the same church: 1 Thessalonians to Gentile Christians, 2 Thessalonians to Jewish Christians. According to M. Dibelius, *An die Thessaloniker* 49, 1 Thessalonians is addressed to a particular group within the church in Thessalonica. E. Schweizer, "Der zweite Thessalonikerbrief," assumes that 1 Thessalonians and 2 Thessalonians were sent to different churches. The second letter was sent to Berea (Goguel) or Philippi (Schweizer), and reached Thessalonica by a later exchange of letters. But 2 Thessalonians makes it clear that an earlier letter to Thessalonica is presupposed. The attribution to Philippi rests on what is supposed to be a quotation of 2 Thess 1:4 and 3:15 in Polycarp's *Letter to the Philippians* 11:3–4. This hypothesis has been rightly challenged by A. Lindemann, "Abfassungszweck." W. Schmithals reconstructs from the two Thessalonian letters four different letters to Thessalonica, all by Paul himself (in dependence on W. Lütgert, *Die Vollkommenen in Philippi und die Enthusiasten in Thessalonich* [BFChTh 13. Gütersloh: Gerd Mohn, 1909]); W. Hadorn, *Die Abfassung der Thessalonicherbriefe in der Zeit der dritten Missionsreise des Paulus* [BFChTh 24,3/4, Gütersloh: Gerd Mohn, 1919]).
6  According to W. Trilling, *Untersuchungen* 157, 2 Thessalonians is "no 'letter' to a concrete church, but a general 'apostolic' monitory and didactic writing." To be sure, one must take into consideration that even if the specific statements regarding

The intention of the author can also be seen in the redactional apocalyptic section 2:1–12, which stands out from the rest of the outline of 1 Thessalonians. It is presupposed that there are teachers representing a conflicting point of view, whose doctrine is "the day of the Lord is already here / is imminent."[7] This opposition attempts to legitimize its teaching with "prophecy, word, or letter" (2 Thess 2:2). The details are not clear. Is the intention to identify the "letter as from us" (ὡς δι᾽ ὑμῶν) with 1 Thessalonians? Then the author of 2 Thessalonians would be claiming that 1 Thessalonians is a forgery[8] in order to take it away from the oppo-

---

eschatology and ethics with regard to the ἄτακτοι were provided by 1 Thessalonians, it is still the case that 2 Thessalonians shows "the will to interpret and explain to members of the church who are already acquainted with 1 Thessalonians and the issues raised by its subject matter" (O. Merk, "Überlegungen" 412).The result is that "in 2 Thessalonians we meet an author who must be acquainted with the church known from 1 Thessalonians, and that this author writes to interpret and develop what the apostle Paul had said in a supportive manner" (413).

[7] This first translation of the perfect tense corresponds to BAGD 266. The precise interpretation of this statement must be decided by the context. Scholars have understood it in either a Gnostic or an apocalyptic sense. W. Schmithals, *Gnosticism in Corinth* 146–150 sees connections to the enthusiasts in Corinth and to the comparable interpretation of the resurrection in 2 Timothy 2:18. The opponents were advocates of a radically realized eschatology. To this it can be objected (Ph. Vielhauer, *Geschichte* 94) that ἐνίστημι can also mean "be imminent" (also as a perfect participle or as aorist in 1 Cor 7:26; Jos *Ant* 4.209). Then one could understand the saying in the sense of an acute apocalyptic near expectation. W. Wrede, *Untersuchungen* 49–50, had already pointed to the interesting parallels of the bishop in Pontus, who announced the judgment within a year with the words ὅτι ἐνέστηκεν ἡ ἡμέρα τοῦ κυρίου (Hipp, Comm in Dan IV 18–19). When he thereby refers to 2 Thessalonians 2:2, he had in any case understood this text as an apocalyptic announcement of the near end. It is also problematic for the gnosticizing understanding that the apocalyptic term "day of the Lord" is not elsewhere documented in a spiritualizing sense for realized eschatology. It may be that the persecutions of which 2 Thessalonians 1:4 speaks belong to the traditional preliminary signs of the apocalyptic drama, which encouraged the acute near expectation. This is not certain, since 1 Thessalonians 2:14 had already spoken of sufferings (to be sure, not with the key words διωγμός, διώκω). In any case, 2 Thessalonians 1:5 attributes—quite apart from any direct parallel in 1 Thessalonians—a "sign-like" character to the persecutions in connection with the events of the endtime. Likewise, it is not certain whether the avoidance of work mentioned in 2 Thessalonians 3:6–12 is to be interpreted in connection with apocalyptic exuberance. R. Russell, "The Idle in 2 Thess 3,6–12: An Eschatological or a Sociological Problem?," NTS 34 (1988) 105–119, presents an alternate interpretation in terms of social history to explain the contrast between wealthy and working-class Christians in Thessalonica.

[8] So A. Hilgenfeld, "Die beiden Briefe an die Thessalonicher," ZWTh 5 (1862) 249–251, a view to which A. Lindemann has returned in "Abfassungszweck." It is irrelevant whether one refers ὡς δι᾽ ἡμῶν to prophecy, word, or letter together, or limits it exclusively to letter; in any case the author of 2 Thessalonians warns his church of the danger that the "opponents" are arguing their case with Pauline authority understood in their sense. (Thereby, inasmuch as the letter alluded to in 2:2 is our

nents as a basis of their argument. Had then some people taken up 1
Thessalonians and reintroduced it into the discussion as proof for their
view that the day of the Lord "is imminent"? In any case, the author of 2
Thessalonians does not wish to suppress 1 Thessalonians nor disqualify
it as a forgery but specifically does want to correct his opponents interpretation of it.[9] Thus, analogous to the procedure of his opponents, he makes
the content of 1 Thessalonians the basis of his own exposition.

### b)   Eschatology

Since the Pauline letters fundamentally and consistently presuppose that
the parousia will occur soon or even in the immediate future, this unfulfilled expectation must have become a pressing problem for the following
generations. The delay of the parousia was obviously the reason, alongside
the appearance of his opponents, for the author's insertion of an *apocalyptic timetable* into the outline of 1 Thessalonians that lay before him (2:1–
12). His intention is to oppose the misunderstanding that the Day of the
Lord stands in the immediate future. Here it appears we have a difference
within the Pauline school, more than merely different understandings of
what the appropriate reinterpretation of the Pauline heritage should be.
Although the "opponents" set forth their teaching on the basis of a Pauline
letter (2 Thess 2:2), so also does the author of 2 Thessalonians, who
makes his connection with Paul clear by his dependence on 1 Thessalonians and by his concluding greetings (2 Thess 3:17–18).[10] That the

---

1 Thessalonians, then this letter is rejected as a forgery brought forth by the opponents; so BAGD 898, "a quality wrongly claimed, in any case objectively false ...
a letter (falsely) alleged to be from us"). Or the reference may be to the interpretation that claims support from this letter, but the interpretation is misleading and
a delusion (2:3), since it leads to eschatological anxiety and bewilderment. Among
other problems with the hypothesis that 2 Thessalonians is trying to discredit 1
Thessalonians as a forgery is that 2 Thessalonians 2:15 refers to the earlier letter
in a positive manner. The personal concluding greeting in 2 Thessalonians 3:17
cannot be taken without further ado as an argument for the discrediting hypothesis.
To be sure such a greeting is missing from 1 Thessalonians (as it is from Rom, 2
Cor, Phil), but it is found in Galatians 6:1; Philemon 19; Colossians 4:18, and 1
Corinthians 16:21, so that the author here follows an often-documented convention of the Pauline school. If 2 Thessalonians wants by means of this identifying
mark mentioned in 2 Thessalonians 2:2 to "discredit" 1 Thessalonians, and thus
expose it as a forged document, then we would have to speak of 2 Thessalonians
as a "counter-forgery" (cf. W. Trilling, *Der zweite Brief an die Thessalonicher* 158–
160).

9   W. Trilling, *Der zweite Brief an die Thessalonicher* 158–160, argues this persuasively.
10  Differently W. Trilling, *Der zweite Brief an die Thessalonicher* 27: "The unknown
*author* probably does not come from a 'Pauline school'...".

church must adjust to a waiting period of undetermined length is indicated by the different stages of the apocalyptic future.[11]

The author opposes the view that the Day of the Lord is imminent, or already present, with the following argument: There must first come the great apostasy (2:3a),[12] so that—chronologically preceding the great apostasy—the Antichrist ("the lawlessness one, the one destined for destruction") must first appear (2:3b), and only then will Christ return. To be sure, the "mystery of lawlessness" is already at work and with it the nearness of the final events (2:7); but the parousia of the Antichrist will itself be delayed through a retarding figure or factor (τὸ κατέχον 2: 6; ὁ κατέχων 2:7), and cannot take place until this restraining influence is set aside. All the features of this picture are traditional, the new element here being the accenting of the traditional materials in the direction of the dampening of apocalyptic enthusiasm. The retarding power, expressed once with the neuter participle τὸ κατέχον and once with the masculine participle ὁ κατέχων, thus receives special attention in this passage.[13] The political interpretation, apparently documented for the first time in Irenaeus, sees the Roman Empire as "that which restrains." Thereby the fourth world empire of Daniel 2 and 7 is also understood to be the Roman Empire, with the Emperor himself identified as the κατέχων. This interpretation, however, has been mostly abandoned, since both Jewish and Christian apocalyptic saw the Roman Empire not as a mechanism to hold eschatological evil in check, but an element of the final coalition of powers hostile to God. The political aspects are first thematized in our text in 2:4 with the figure of the Antichrist, and are not associated with the Katechon. Over against this stands the interpretation of O. Cullmann in terms of salvation history: τὸ κατέχον means the gospel and its proclamation, which must be preached to the nations before the end comes (cf. Mark 13:10), and ὁ κατέχων refers to Paul himself, whose death will be the prelude for the appearance of the Antichrist.[14] Finally, A. Strobel has seen in "kate-

---

[11] W. Trilling, *Der zweite Brief an die Thessalonicher* 71–72, finds two layers of tradition in 2:1–12. In this view the author in 2:3b-4, 8–10a gives "a view of the Antichrist that was already 'traditional' for the author and his readers." (71) In vv. 5–7, 10b-12 the author himself highlights the relevant aspects with in the apocalyptic timetable. P. Müller, *Anfänge* 43, thinks there are two layers of tradition but opposes the attempt to disentangle them so clearly.

[12] Cf. the motif of the final attack of the enemy against the people of God (Dan 11:31–39; Jub 23:14–23; 1 Enoch 91:7; AssMos 5; 4 Ezra 5:1–2; CD 1.20; 5.21; 8.19; 19.6, 32; 1QpHab 2.1–6).

[13] Cf. the informative excursus "Die ‚aufhaltende Macht'" in W. Trilling, *Der zweite Brief an die Thessalonicher* 94–105.

[14] This interpretation has already been often opposed, especially by the commentary of B. Rigaux, *Saint Paul* 276–277. This view cannot be held if 2 Thessalonians is considered deutero-Pauline; the Antichrist did not arrive after the death of Paul.

chon" a terminus technicus for the delay of the parousia calculated into God's plan, so that God himself is ultimately the katechon.[15]

But if one stays with the words κατέχον / κατέχων and its usage in the literature, then one finds for example that in an Egyptian prayer the god Horus is called ὁ κατέχων δράκοντα, and in a magical papyrus the archangel Michael is called ὁ κατέχων, ὃν καλέουσιν δράκοντα. The reference is thus to mythical figures who keep the transcendent antagonist bound until the proper time (cf. also Rev 20:1–10). But can the author of 2 Thessalonians really presuppose that his readers know what or who is referred to by the "katechon" (cf. v. 6 "you know...")? It is conceivable that the author intentionally uses a mysterious allusion. However, since the katechon like the Antichrist is a part of the mystery of lawlessness that will be removed (2:7), this retarding factor must be a negative power. That does not mean that the katechon may be a person or power determined by God himself, without of course being identical with God. The function of the katechon is thus to delay the appearance of the Antichrist until a predetermined point in time (2:6b). As far as that goes, it can be said of this functional role that the term "katechon" stands for the necessity of the delay of the parousia as such, and "has no more specific content."[16] A differentiation between the neuter and masculine forms would no longer be relevant for this exegesis.[17]

The dating of this little apocalypse 2 Thessalonians 2:1–12 (apart from the so-called secondary layer) is uncertain. The motif of desecration of the temple (2:4) cannot be taken as evidence for a composition before 70 C. E. Apart from the fact that it is a matter of traditional motifs that have been combined—both, "taking his place in the temple," and "declaring himself to be God" are traditional—the temporal setting of the writing prior to 70 included in the fiction of Pauline authorship means that the reference to the temple cannot be used as evidence for dating the piece.

To now turn our attention back to the apocalyptic timetable itself, we note that after the katechon is removed prior to the great apostasy, then comes the revelation of the man of sin, the son of lawlessness. This last period is characterized by ἀνομία (2:3, 7, 8), ἀδικία (2:10, 12), ψεῦδος (2:9, 11). Finally the Lord Jesus comes to oppose the adversary and destroys him, in order to grant salvation to those who have been chosen from the beginning (2:13–14). In 2 Thessalonians 2:3–12 there is a fusion of the

---

[15] A. Strobel, *Untersuchungen zum eschatologischen Verzögerungsproblem auf Grund der spätjüdisch-urchristlichen Geschichte von Habakuk 2,2ff* (NT.S 2) (Leiden 1961); similarly R. D. Aus, "God's Plan and God's Power: Isaiah 66 and the Restraining Factors of 2 Thess 2:6–7," JBL 96 (1977) 537–553.

[18] A. Strobel, *Untersuchungen* 101.

[17] P. Müller, *Anfänge* 50, to the contrary: "... the neuter is to be understood as an influence caused by God, and the masculine as its representative. The neuter thus means God's timetable and the delay of the parousia included within it."

two Antichrist traditions into one figure. Verse 4 uses the motif of the violent and arrogant ruler from Daniel 11:36, while 2:9–10 takes up the tradition of the lying prophet that goes back to Deuteronomy 13:2–6. The top priority in 2 Thessalonians 2 is the threat of false doctrine that leads to apostasy. The eschatological conception of 2 Thessalonians has been directly evoked by the appearance of prophets who appeal to Paul and announce the imminent parousia, but probably not that the day of the Lord is already present. The author of 2 Thessalonians presents an explanation for the delay of the parousia that both confutes these "opponents" and provides a theoretical basis for the spreading consciousness of the delay.

In comparison with 1 Thessalonians, a sharpened sense of determinism is found within the framework of apocalyptic thought. Over against the eschatological group of believers who have been "elected" by God through the preaching of the gospel as the "firstfruits" (ἀπαρχή) of eschatological salvation (2:13–14) stands the group of the "lost", who have been destined by God himself through a "powerful delusion" to "believe the lie" (2:10–12). In this strictly theocentric hardening theory there is also an echo of the response to the question of why the evangelistic mission of the church has not been successful and why the church continues to suffer. The coming judgment will bring a reversal of the present in which suffering will be relieved and the persecutors will suffer punishment (1:5–9).[18]

## c) The Apostolic Norm

A characteristic identifying mark of 2 Thessalonians is that readers of the letter are to find their point of orientation in the authority and tradition of Paul as the apostolic norm. This can already be seen in the fact that the author has structured his letter according to the outline and content of 1 Thessalonians. Thus 1 Thessalonians is thereby neither discredited or supplemented,but taken up in a specific manner and elaborated in view of the opposing teaching, of course without directly citing 1 Thessalonians as a source.[19] One indication of this post-apostolic commitment to the apostolic norm is visible from the surface of the letter itself, namely from the observation that 2 Thessalonians contains no personal data whatever (travel plans, greetings, personal circumstances, references to the place from which it is written). The concluding greeting "with my own hand"

---

[18] Paul never uses this motif of apocalyptic reversal elsewhere with the function of encouraging the church.

[19] Cf. O. Merk, *Überlegungen* 413. Against the "discrediting theory" is the fact that it would apply at the most to the eschatological statements of 1 Thessalonians, while leaving all its other themes of the preceding letter untouched.

(2 Thess 3:17) functions—differently than in 1 Cor 16:21; Gal 6:11; Phlm 19—as a claim to authenticity, and thus points to the pseudepigraphical situation. The commitment to the apostolic norm mentioned above can be seen in the several reformulations of material from the Pauline letters. The church is pointed exclusively to τὸ εὐαγγέλιον ἡμῶν (2:14), it is the normative παράδοσις (2:15; 3:6) transmitted by Paul orally and by letter (2:15 certainly presupposes 1 Thessalonians). The expression "the traditions that you were taught by us, either by word of mouth or by our letter" (2:15) is without parallel in the authentic Pauline letters. The combination "word of mouth and letter" stands for the Pauline oral and written tradition that had become the norm for authentic faith. It can be referred to in a way approaching a binding legal standard (3:14). The heightened binding force of the Pauline norm is thus seen in the increased use of παραγγέλλομεν (2 Thess 3:4, 10, 12; in Paul only 1 Cor 11:17; 1 Thess 4:11 and in 1 Cor 7:10 with reference to the Kyrios) and παρελάβοσαν παρ' ἡμῶν (3:6) as terms for the transmission of tradition, in contrast to παρακαλοῦμεν (1 Thess 4:1, 10; 5:11, 14). First Thessalonians had also called for imitation of Paul (1:6), but now Paul as such is the absolute model to be imitated (2 Thess 3:9, in dependence on 1 Thess 1:7), the model Christians "must" follow (2 Thess 3:7).

By way of conclusion we consider the accenting of particular items of the apostolic norm. In dealing with a brief writing directed to a particular situation, it is only possible to point out the highlights. Here we only note that dominant themes of Pauline theology such as the doctrine of justification, the theme of the role of Israel, the theology of the cross, the soteriological interpretation of the death and resurrection of Jesus are all missing, although some of these are partly addressed in 1 Thessalonians. The christological title that is presupposed and most used is obviously κύριος (1:1, 7, 8, 12; 2:1, 8, 13, 14, 16; 3:3, 5, 6, 12, 16, 18). The present status of the Risen One hardly comes in view; all attention is focused on his eschatological function in the apocalyptic events of the end (1:5, 8; 2:1), on the parousia and the victory over the eschatological Adversary (2:8). Only a few differences in the use of the κύριος title in comparison with 1 Thessalonians are noticeable: attributes of God are transferred to Christ. Thus in 1 Thessalonians 1:4 (ἠγαπημένοι ὑπὸ [τοῦ] θεοῦ becomes ἠγαπημένοι ὑπὸ τοῦ κυρίου in 2 Thessalonians 2:13. Second Thessalonians 1:9, 12; 2:14 speak of the δόξα κυρίου, while 1 Thessalonians 2:12 and the other Pauline literature reserve δόξα predominately for God, and can at the most speak of the δόξα κυρίου in a derivative sense (2 Cor 3:18; 4:4, 6). Second Thessalonians 3:16 speaks of Christ as the "Lord of peace," 1 Thessalonians 5:23 of the "God of peace." This transfer of God's attributes to Christ is, as H. Braun has shown,[20] typical of the second

---

[20]   H. Braun, "Zur nachpaulinischen Herkunft."

Christian generation. In contrast, the strictly theological statements appear to stay close to the pattern of 1 Thessalonians, the election theology of which is adopted and interpreted.[21] The church stands in a present relation to God, who gives it grace, mercy, and peace (1:2), the God who has chosen it and sanctified it in the Spirit (2:13), the God who loves it and has given it comfort and good hope (2:16).

A concrete application of the apostolic norm is seen in the command, "in the name of our Lord Jesus Christ, to keep away from believers who are living in idleness and not according to the tradition that they received from us" (2 Thess 3:6). Orthodoxy and orthopraxy are both provided by the apostolic model. Second Thessalonians 3:11a (cf. also 3:6) proceeds on the basis of what the author has heard:[22] there are some in the church who "are living in idleness, mere busybodies, not doing any work." The motivation of these church members, as well as the details of their lifestyle, can hardly be brought into focus.[23] Second Thessalonians addresses this situation with an apostolic order in 3:7–9 that thematizes the apostolic model and sets it forth as obligatory. The knowledge that Paul had voluntary served in his churches, refusing any payment, and earning his living by his own work (1 Cor 9) is made into an intentional example of the apostle, a παράδοσις that is now a timeless example for the work ethic of the church. It is summarized in a sentence probably taken from Jewish tradition, "Anyone unwilling to work should not eat" (2 Thess 3:10), which is now promulgated as apostolic instruction, with the result that "the occasion and the step taken against it no longer stand in a balanced relationship."[24] This is understandable within the conditions of the pseudepigraphical situation: orientation for the changed circumstances are sought, found, and given by appeal to Paul as the apostolic norm.

---

[21] Cf. F. W. Horn, *Das Angeld des Geistes* 148, on 1 Thessalonians: "It is not the Kyrios Christ who is presently at work in the church, but God himself. The Kyrios in 1 Thessalonians is the eschatological deliverer (1:9) but exercises no present functions as the church's Lord."

[22] W. Trilling, *Der zweite Brief an die Thessalonicher* 144, supposes it is the intention of this section "also by this example to demonstrate in a formal way the 'principle' and the dignity of apostolic tradition." But his statement on 152 opposes this: "That some sort of 'abuse' is present and that the whole passage is not completely artificial (a view to which I have been inclined for some time) can hardly be doubted."

[23] That work-shyness was the result of expectation of the soon coming of the end or of a Gnostic attitude has been repeatedly claimed. This would mean that the preaching of the opponents had already persuaded some members of the church. But the instruction that they should do their work μετὰ ἡσυχίας (3:12) should not be over-interpreted, since it is dependent on 1 Thessalonians 4:11.

[24] Rightly W. Trilling, *Der zweite Brief an die Thessalonicher* 152.

# F.
# A Message with a Universal Claim— The Catholic Letters

## I. Christ, the True High Priest—The Epistle to the Hebrews

Bornkamm, G. "Das Bekenntnis im Hebräerbrief," ThBl 21 (1942) 56–66, also in G. Bornkamm. *Studien zu Antike und Christentum*. GAufs. 2. BEvTh 28. Munich: Kaiser, 1963, 188–203.

Braun, H. *An die Hebräer*. HNT 14. Tübingen: J. C. B. Mohr (Paul Siebeck), 1984.

de Jonge, H. J. "Traditie en exegese: de hohepriester-christologie en Melchizedek in Hebreën," NedThT 37 (1983) 1–19.

Grässer, E. *An die Hebräer*. EKK XVII 1+2. Neukirchen-Vluyn: Neukirchener, 1990, 1993.

Grässer, E. *Aufbruch und Verheissung. Gesammelte Aufsätze zum Hebräerbrief*. BZNW 65. Berlin-New York: W. de Gruyter, 1992.

Grässer, E. *Der Glaube im Hebräerbrief*. MThSt 2. Marburg: Elwert, 1965.

Hegermann, H. *Der Brief an die Hebräer*. ThHK 16. Berlin: Evangelische Verlagsanstalt, 1988.

Hofius, O. *Katapausis. Die Vorstellung vom endzeitlichen Ruheort im Hebräerbrief*. WUNT 11. Tübingen: J. C. B. Mohr (Paul Siebeck), 1970.

Käsemann, E. *The Wandering People of God: An Investigation of the Letter to the Hebrews*. Minneapolis: Augsburg, 1984.

Laub, F. *Bekenntnis und Auslegung. Die paränetische Funktion der Christologie im Hebräerbrief*. BU 15. Regensburg: Pustet, 1980.

Loader, W. R. G. *Sohn und Hoherpriester*. WMANT 53. Neukirchen-Vluyn: Neukirchener, 1981.

Löhr, H. *Umkehr und Sünde im Hebräerbrief*. BZNW 73. Berlin-New York: W. de Gruyter, 1994.

Nomoto, S. "Herkunft und Struktur der Hohenpriestervorstellung im Hebräerbrief," NT 10 (1968) 10–25.

Rissi, M. *Die Theologie des Hebräerbriefes*. WUNT 41. Tübingen: J. C. B. Mohr (Paul Siebeck), 1987.

Schierse, F. J. *Verheissung und Heilsvollendung. Zur theologischen Grundfrage des Hebräerbriefes*. MThS.H 9. Munich: Karl Zink, 1955.

Schröger, F. *Der Verfasser des Hebräerbriefes als Schriftausleger*. BU 4. Regensburg: Pustet, 1968.

Theissen, G. *Untersuchungen zum Hebräerbrief*. StNT 2. Gütersloh: Gerd Mohn, 1969.

Vanhoye, A." L'Épître aux Ephésiens et l'Épître aux Hébreux," *Bib* 59 (1978) 198–230.

Vanhoye, A. *La structure littéraire de l'Épître aux Hébreux.* SN 1. Paris: Desclée de Brouwer, 1976.

Vanhoye, A. "Literarische Struktur und theologische Botschaft des Hebräerbriefs," *SNTU* 4 (1979) 119–147; 5, 1980, 18–49.

Weiss, H. F. *Der Brief an die Hebräer.* KEK XIII. Göttingen: Vandenhoeck & Ruprecht, 1991.

Zimmermann, H. *Das Bekenntnis der Hoffnung. Tradition und Redaktion im Hebräerbrief.* BBB 47. Köln-Bonn: Hanstein, 1977.

## a)   The Christological Prelude: The Cosmic Exaltation of the Preexistent Son of God

1  Πολυμερῶς
   καὶ πολυτρόπως πάλαι
   ὁ θεὸς λαλήσας
   τοῖς πατράσιν ἐν τοῖς προφήταις
2  ἐπ᾽ ἐσχάτου τῶν ἡμερῶν τούτων
   ἐλάλησεν ἡμῖν ἐν υἱῷ,
   ὃν ἔθηκεν κληρονόμον πάντων,
   δι᾽ οὗ καὶ ἐποίησεν τοὺς αἰῶνας·

3  ὃς ὢν ἀπαύγασμα τῆς δόξης
   καὶ χαρακτὴρ τῆς ὑποστάσεως αὐτοῦ,
   φέρων τε τὰ πάντα
   τῷ ῥήματι τῆς δυνάμεως αὐτοῦ,
   καθαρισμὸν τῶν
   ἁμαρτιῶν ποιησάμενος
   ἐκάθισεν ἐν δεξιᾷ
   τῆς μεγαλωσύνης ἐν ὑψηλοῖς,
4  τοσούτῳ κρείττων
   γενόμενος τῶν ἀγγέλων
   ὅσῳ διαφορώτερον παρ᾽ αὐτοὺς
   κεκληρονόμηκεν ὄνομα.
5  Τίνι γὰρ εἶπέν ποτε τῶν ἀγγέλων,
   Υἱός μου εἶ σύ,
   ἐγὼ σήμερον γεγέννηκά σε;
   καὶ πάλιν,
   Ἐγὼ ἔσομαι αὐτῷ εἰς πατέρα,
   καὶ αὐτὸς ἔσται μοι εἰς υἱόν;

1  In many and various ways
   long ago God spoke
   to our ancestors
   by the prophets,
2  but in these last days
   he has spoken to us by a Son,
   whom he appointed heir of all things,
   through whom he also created the worlds.

3  He is the reflection of God's glory
   and the exact imprint of God's very being, and he sustains all things
   by his powerful word.
   When he had made purification for sins, he sat down at the right hand of the Majesty on high,
4  having become as much superior
   to angels as the name
   he has inherited
   is more excellent than theirs.
5  For to which of the angels did God
   ever say, "You are my Son;
   today I have begotten you"?
   Or again, "I will be his Father,
   and he will be my Son"?

The weighty, formally structured prelude to the Letter to the Hebrews[1]

---

[1]   In Hebrews we do not have a letter but a tract, even if one considers the epistolary conclusion (13:18, 22–25) to be original. It is striking, however, that in the body of the document there are no epistolary features, and that only in this conclusion is it necessary to see elements of Pauline tradition. Thus the thesis is still worthy of consideration that the epistolary conclusion—perhaps on the occasion of the canonization of the document—was added secondarily. Cf. W. Wrede, *Das litera-*

is composed in a hymnic style.[2] This style is augmented by parechesis or alliteration of the Greek text (1:1),[3] the heaping up of relative pronouns (1:2-3) and participles (1:3). The linguistic level is elevated in 1:4 by the correlatives ("as much superior ... as ... is more excellent"). The center of gravity of this grand periodic sentence is located in this verse. The declaration that the Son "is superior to angels" is anticipated in 1:3d ("he sat down at the right hand of the Majesty on high"). The special status of the Son of God is illustrated through statements from four different perspectives that at the same time present the comprehensive framework that has fundamental significance for the christological thought of the Letter to the Hebrews.

## 1. Temporal Aspects (1:1-2a)

The Christ event is part of a long history. God's speaking, with which it is identical, already was happening in Old Testament times, in the word of the prophets of Israel directed to our ancestors in the faith (cf. 11:2, 4ff). At the end of this epoch of salvation history, and that means at the same time at the end of this aeon, the definitive revelatory word of God took place in the Son. This means for the Christian community that it is addressed and called into life by this word, that it stands with Christ at the turn of the ages, even if it is aware that time goes on, and is especially aware of its increasing distance from the earthly Jesus (cf. 2:3).

## 2. Cosmological Aspects (1:2b-3b)

The Son stands at the beginning and end of the cosmos:

(α) As the "heir of all things" (κληρονόμος πάντων) he is the goal of world history. This is grounded in the God's act of enthroning him (cf. 1:3d, 4b) and is the motivation of the hope "that those who are called may receive the promised eternal inheritance" (9:15; cf. 1:14; 6:12).

(β) He stands as the mediator of creation at the beginning of the cosmos, for God created the worlds (αἰῶνας) through him. He is thus a preexistent being, as the wisdom of God is understood in Jewish tradition

rische *Rätsel des Hebräerbriefes* (FRLANT 8. Göttingen: Vandenhoeck & Ruprecht, 1906) 68–70; A. Vanhoye, *La structure littéraire* 219ff; and *Prêtres anciens, Prêtre nouveau selon le Nouveau Testament* (Paris 1980) 82–263; G. Strecker, *History of New Testament Literature* 44–45, 48.

[2]    On the following, cf. E. Grässer, "Hebräer 1,1–4. Ein exegetischer Versuch," (EKK Vorarbeiten 3. Neukirchen-Vluyn: Neukirchener, 1971) 55–91; reprinted in E. Grässer, *Text und Situation* (Gütersloh: Gerd Mohn, 1973) 182–228.

[3]    "Parechesis" = phonetic echoes of different words. Alliteration = several words begin with the same letter, which happens here five times. Cf. also Matthew 5:3–6; 2 Corinthians 6:10; cf. Blass-Debrunner-Funk §485; 488.1b, c, 2.

[4]    Cf. Philo All III 96; SpecLeg I 81; Migr 6; Sacr 8.

(Wis 9:2) or as in Philo's understanding of the divine Logos.[4] This mediating role is not essentially intended to maintain God's sovereignty and distance to the world but is grounded in the christological interest of emphasizing the superiority of the Son.[5]

(γ) He manifests the being of God in the cosmos. The expression "reflection of God's glory" (ἀπαύγασμα τῆς δόξης) and "exact imprint of God's very being" (χαρακτήρ [also "stamp," "impression"] τῆς ὑποστάσεως) derive from the Hellenistic Jewish doctrine of emanations (for Wisdom, cf. Wis 7:25–26); for the divine Logos, cf. Philo Conf 97; Fug 12); they illustrate the nearness of the Son to the highest being, his unity with God: in him God's glory is encountered.[6]

(δ) He maintains the creation. Spanning the distance between God and the world was often achieved in the thought world of antiquity by intermediate beings who not only were involved in the formation of the world but also preserve it; thus divine Wisdom (Wis 8:1; 10:4), "the power of the (preexistent, divine) oath" (1 Enoch 69:15, 25), the eternal Logos that permeates all things (Philo, Fug 112; Agr 51; Her 188). The designation of the created world as "the All" (τὰ πάντα) reveals a Hellenistic structure.[7] That such a maintenance and preserving function is ascribed to the powerful divine Word not only suggests that as in Genesis 1:3, 6 and elsewhere God's powerful word is the cause of the created world but also that the Son can be thought of as identical with precisely this word (cf. Philo Conf 97), and that the "word spoken through angels" shows itself to be at work in the church (Heb 2:2; 4:12).

### 3. Soteriological Aspects (1:3c)

The Son has effected purification for sins. In the Old Testament perspective "purification" (καθαρισμός) makes possible the integrity of the cult, access to the holy place and belonging to the holy people of God (Exod 30:10). The reference to purification in 1:3 is already thinking on the earthly advent of the Son of God and is an anticipation of his atoning high-priestly act (cf. Heb 9:11ff. By the offering of his blood, through his perfect self-sacrifice,[8] liberation from sin and the holiness of his people is

---

5   On preexistence Christology cf. N. Walter, "Geschichte und Mythos in der urchristlichen Präexistenzchristologie," H. H. Schmid (ed.), *Mythos und Rationalität* (Gütersloh: Gerd Mohn, 1988) 224–234; H. Hegermann, *Die Vorstellung vom Schöpfungsmittler im hellenistischen Judentum und Urchristentum* (TU 82. Berlin: Evangelische Verlagsanstalt, 1961) 95–96.110ff; G. Schimanowski, *Weisheit und Messias* (WUNT II 17. Tübingen: J. C. B. Mohr [Paul Siebeck] 1985).
6   Cf. the analogous use of the εἰκών concept in Colossians 1:15par.
7   Cf. JosAs 8:3; Corp Herm 13.17; Herm Sim 7.4; note already in 7.2b. Further documentation in BAGD 631.
8   Cf. 9:14; on the purifying significance of blood, cf. Leviticus 16:14ff, 30; 17:11.

effected. While Jesus' death on the cross is not mentioned, it and its atoning effect are still presupposed (cf. 9:12; 10:10, 12–14; 12:2; 13:12).

## 4. Inthronization (1:3d-5)

The Letter to the Hebrews does not know the idea of the rising or resurrection of Jesus from the dead. The exaltation of the Son follows directly from his death on the cross. This accords with the statement that the heavenly High Priest Jesus entered the heavenly sanctuary through his blood (9:12; cf. 10:20). This exaltation is affirmed by adopting the early Christian liturgical tradition (Mark 14:62; Rom 8:34; 1 Pet 3:22), especially Psalm 110:1 (109:1 LXX), with the affirmation, "he sat down at the right hand of the Majesty on high."[9] The reference is to the preexistent Son of God, so it is not the adoption but the inthronization, the (re-) installation to his position of cosmic authority, which includes the superiority of the Son to the angels.

This is established by a citation from Scripture (1:5, Ps 2:7 LXX; cf. also Heb 5:5), which begins a series of seven Old Testament quotations from the Greek Bible and in the use of the (round) number seven expresses a feature of scribal hermeneutic. After the exaltation of the Son of God is proven and elaborated by scriptural evidence (cf. on 1:5b 2 Sam 7:14a), v. 6 follows with a new beginning. The reentry of the Firstborn into the world (εἰς τὴν οἰκουμένην) contains an echo of the role of the preexistent Son of God as mediator of creation (1:2b-3b; cf. Col 1:15) but like the following quotation refers to the future parousia. The Preexistent One is the Postexistent One (Heb 1:10–12; cf. 1:2ba). To be sure, in his scriptural interpretation the author can adopt the allegorical methods of Hellenistic-Jewish exegesis but still in his "messianic" interpretation he is operating within the realm of authentic Christian tradition.[10] He confesses his faith that the preexistent Son of God demonstrates his superiority in his future

---

9    Cf. further Mark 12:36par; 16:19; Colossians 3:1; Ephesians 1:20. See also Hebrews 1:13; 8:1; 10:12; 12:2. On the use of Psalm 110, cf. F. Hahn, *The Titles of Jesus in Christology* 129–135; M. Hengel, "Psalm 110 und die Erhöhung des Auferstandenen zur Rechten Gottes," in H. Paulsen-C. Breytenbach (eds.), *Anfänge der Christologie* (FS F. Hahn) (Göttingen: Vandenhoeck & Ruprecht, 1991) 43–73; and "'Setze dich zu meiner Rechten!' Die Inthronisation Christi zur Rechten Gottes und Psalm 110,1," in M. Philonenko (ed.), *Le Thrône de Dieu* (WUNT 69. Tübingen: J. C. B. Mohr [Paul Siebeck], 1993) 108–194; Ph. Vielhauer, "Zur Frage der christologischen Hoheitstitel," ThLZ 90 (1965) 569–588, esp. 577–578 on Psalm 110:1.

10   Cf. above note 9. The Jewish-messianological interpretation is altogether late. There is no early Jewish parallel to v. 5b. The Psalms of Solomon (17.26, 31, 41) refer Psalm 2:8–9 to the Messiah ben David (cf. Heb 1:13) but not Psalm 2:7 (Heb 1:5a). On 1:13 cf. also Testament of Job 33:3 (dated in the first century B. C. E. to the second century C. E.)

advent not only over the angels but will establish his lordship over all cosmic powers.[11]

That at the core of this interpretation is a traditional early Christian pattern is seen by a comparison with the Christ hymn in the Letter to the Philippians:

| Philippians 2 | | Hebrews 1 |
|---|---|---|
| V.6 | Preexistence | V.1–2a.2b-3b |
| V.7 (-8) | Humiliation | V.3c |
| | (Death on the cross) | |
| V.9 | Exaltation | V.3d-5 |
| V.10–11 | Parousia | V.6–13 |

### b)   Christology: The Heavenly High Priest[12]

The 17 references in the Letter to the Hebrews that designate Jesus as a "High Priest" (ἀρχιερεὺς μέγας) all derive from the author of Hebrews (2:17; 3:1; 4:14, 15; 5:1, 5, 10; 6:20; 7:26, 27, 28; 8:1, 3; 9:7, 11, 25; 13:11). The contrary view, that this christological title comes from an older early Christian confession, can only apparently appeal to 3:1 and 4:14–15, where the term ὁμολογία is used. It is improbable, however, that the author is citing a traditional formula in these passages,[13] since the expression here has the active sense of a *nomen actionis* (= the act of confessing, not its content; so also in 10:23; so also the verb in 11:13 and 13:15), referring to the confessional act of the church. This confession is directed to the "apostle and high priest" Jesus Christ, without this being a fixed confessional formula.

If the title was used at an early time in Christian liturgical tradition,[14] and even though there were points of contact in the thought world of

---

[11]   Cf. esp. 1:13–14. The text cited is Psalm 109:1 LXX; in this sense also 10:12–13. Cf. also the counterpart in the future-eschatological orientation of 1 Corinthians 15:23–28.

[12]   On the Christology of Hebrews, cf. E. Grässer, "Zur Christologie des Hebräerbriefs," in *Neues Testament und christliche Existenz* (FS H. Braun) (Tübingen: J. C. B. Mohr [Paul Siebeck], 1973) 195–206; F. Laub, "Schaut auf Jesus' (Hebr 3,1)," in *Vom Urchristentum zu Jesus* (FS J. Gnilka) (Freiburg: Herder, 1989) 417–432; H. Hegermann, "Christologie im Hebräerbrief," in *Anfänge der Christologie* (FS F. Hahn) (Göttingen: Vandenhoeck & Ruprecht, 1991) 337–351; J. Roloff, "Der mitleidende Hohepriester," in *Exegetische Verantwortung in der Kirche* (Göttingen: Vandenhoeck & Ruprecht, 1990) 144–167.

[13]   So for example G. Bornkamm, "Bekenntnis;" S. Nomoto, "Herkunft und Struktur" 11–12; H. Braun, *An die Hebräer* 71.

[14]   Cf. the usage in 1 Clement 36:1; 61:3; 64:4; Ign Phld 9:1; Polycarp 12:2 (*sempiternus pontifex*); MartPol 14:3.

Hellenistic Judaism,[15] it is the author's own exegesis that is responsible for the theological elaboration of the title, for he is the one who explicitly takes up Psalm 110 (cf. the reference to Ps 110:4 in 5:6; 7:21, though of course the term here is "priest," not "high priest"). It is the author who connects the title with the traditional christological schema, especially the Christology of descent and exaltation, and it is the author who interprets the high-priestly office of the Son of God by contrasting it with the earthly high priest of the Old Testament.

The picture of the heavenly high priest is elaborated by means of typological exegesis of the Scripture, applying the categories of "correspondence, superiority, and difference." This is done not by dealing with particular texts of the Old Testament but by allowing the general picture of the office of the Old Testament high priest to stand in the background (Exod, Lev, Num), as in the chiastically structured argumentation of 5:1–10 and in the parallel structure of 7:27–28, as can be clarified by this comparison:

Chapter 5:

| Old Testament High Priest | Heavenly High Priest |
|---|---|
| V.4 called by God | V.5 begotten by God (Ps 2:7) |
| V.(1), 3 brings offerings | V.7 prayers and supplications |
| V.2 weakness (cf.7:28) | V.8 suffering |
| V.1b installed for human beings | V.9 for all who are obedient to him |
| V.1a taken from among humans | V.10 named by God as high priest according to the order of Melchizedek (cf. v. 6 / Ps 110:4) |

Chapter 7:

| | |
|---|---|
| V.27a daily sacrifice offered for his own sins | V.27b once for all (ἐφάπαξ) (4:15; 7:26: without sin) |
| V.28a installed through the law as a weak human being | V.28b installed through an oath (of God) as a Son perfected forever |

Analogous to Aaron, the Old Testament high priest, the heavenly high priest is also called by God (5:5). He too must offer sacrifice but this means something different or superior in relation to the earthly high priest when it is said of his sacrifice that it is not a matter of gifts and sin offerings but is his own prayers and supplications, as these are portrayed in Gethsemane (5:7). While the Aaronic-Levitical priesthood is bound to human "weakness," the Christ "in the days of his flesh" was obedient to his father and submitted himself to his destiny of suffering (5:7–8). While the earthly

---

[15]   Cf. Philo Fug 108–109; Som 1.214, 219; 2.188–189, and elsewhere; in Judaism the concept of a messianic or heavenly priesthood was widespread (more rarely, a heavenly high priesthood); cf. the critical survey and documentation in H. Braun, *An die Hebräer* 73–74.

high priest is installed for human beings in order to facilitate their forgiveness, and is himself of human origin, so the heavenly high priest is the cause of eternal salvation for all those who obey him; he is the "high priest according to the order of Melchizedek" (5:9–10). One difference between the heavenly high priest and his earthly counterpart is that the heavenly high priest, as a sinless being, offered himself "once for all," while the Aaronic-Levitical high priests had to offer daily sacrifice both for their own sins and for the sins of the people (7:26–27). While they as weak human beings are installed in their office through the Mosaic law, the heavenly high priest is installed in eternity as the Son by the divine oath (7:28).

The author also makes his own independent interpretation of the high priestly office of Christ in terms of the Old Testament-Jewish Melchizedek tradition. At the high point of the argumentation of Hebrews, at the beginning of the λόγος τέλειος, the "perfect word/complete doctrine" (7:1–10:18), *Melchizedek* is presented as king of Salem and priest of the Most High God (7:1–28). Genesis 14:18–20 is brought up in order to show the superiority of Melchizedek to Abraham and Levi (7:4–5), and thereby to illustrate the superiority of Christ the heavenly high priest. While Christ, like Melchizedek, did not have a priestly genealogy, and has his office not on the basis of the law but by virtue of the divine oath, so he is also not subject to death but on the basis of the power of an indestructible life is the true high priest for ever (7:16–17, 26–28).

The wide range of interpretations connected with the Melchizedek tradition manifest a fascinating variety. The figure of Melchizedek in the Old Testament is connected with the rulership of Jerusalem—Psalm 110 speaks of the inthronization of the Davidic king—and in the course of Jewish and Christian tradition had experienced a medley of interpretations.[16] This was already true in the pre-Christian period. The interpretation of the tradition not only attached itself to the Genesis text but presupposes relatively old Jewish exegesis, especially that of Hellenistic Judaism; in 7:3 there may be a particular reflection of a non-Christian piece of tradition (hymn fragment?). In Hellenistic Judaism Melchizedek was already occasionally identified as a "high priest" (Philo Abr 235, ὁ μέγας ἀρχιερεὺς τοῦ μεγίστου θεοῦ). The double interpretation of the name is also found in Philo (on Heb 7:2 cf. Philo All 3.79–80; Jos Ant 1.180–181). The idea of Melchizedek's being without father and mother (7:3) also reflects the perspective of Hellenistic interpretation, and is not derived directly from the Old Testament text (although presumably inferred from the fact that Melchizedek's parents are not mentioned there) but corresponds to the methods of Hellenistic-Jewish biblical interpretation (cf. Philo Ebr 61 on Gen 20:12: the ancestral mother Sara was ἀμήτωρ). Similarly, the Greek tradition refers to the goddess Athena with the designation "motherless" (cf. Philo Op 100; Lact Inst 1.7.1) and Hephaistos with the term "fatherless" (ἀπάτωρ: Pollus Onom 3.26; cf. Anthol Palat 15:26; PGM 6:282), in order to affirm their divine origin. The same is true of Melchizedek, who was not subject to earthly conditions but was of divine origin. His supernatural

---

[16]  Cf. H. Windisch, *Der Hebräerbrief* (HNT 14. Tübingen: J. C. B. Mohr [Paul Siebeck], 1931²) 61–63; H. Braun, *An die Hebräer* 136–140.

character is also affirmed by the term "without genealogy" (ἀγενεαλόγητος, documented for the first time in Hebrews). This does not mean only "without a priestly genealogy," although in the Jewish-Samaritan Melchizedek tradition a latent anti-Levitical point was already present, but in general declares the impossibility of deriving Melchizedek's origin from human ancestors. Thus it is also said in the parallel to the Son of God. That he "was made like to the Son of God" (7:3 ἀφωμοιωμένος δὲ τῷ υἱῷ τοῦ θεοῦ) makes it clear that Melchizedek was not a type of the Son of God but that conversely the preexistent reality of the heavenly high priest is inherent in the priest-king Melchizedek. This interpretation has a parallel in Philo's identification of Melchizedek with the "true Logos" or the "priestly Logos" (Philo All 3.80.82).[17]

Alongside the Melchizedek tradition, the concept of the high priesthood of Christ is filled in with content from *additional units of tradition*. The schema of descent from heaven and re-ascent to heaven is foundational, as presented in the christological prelude (1:1–5). Moreover, the early Christian tradition of the atoning death of Jesus is known (compare 5:3; 7:27 with Rom 3:25). So also the concept of exaltation ("sitting at the right hand of God," 1:3; 8:1; 10:12; 12:2) is not only derived from Psalm 110:1 but from early Christian tradition (cf. Rom 8:34). Connected with this is the "intercession" of the exalted Christ for his own (2:17; 7:25; cf. 1 John 2:1). In contrast, references to the tradition of the *earthly Jesus* are rare, as is true for the New Testament letters in general.[18]

Only 2:9 and 5:7–8[19] even raise the question of whether a tradition of Jesus' passion stands in the background (cf. Matt 26:38–46parr, Gethsemane). It may be that the connection between Jesus' suffering and his temptation (2:18) is also to be included here. However, it is not a matter of real information about the historical Jesus. So also the statement that Jesus suffered "outside the gate" (13:12), even if it could be influenced by an old tradition, is not intended as a historical comment but is deduced from Leviticus 16:27 (cf. 13:11). And the information that Jesus comes "from Judah" (7:14) does not go beyond the kerygmatic tradition of Jesus as the Son of David (cf. Rom 1:3; Rev 5:5). To the extent that these statements refer to the earthly Jesus, they are incorporated into the mythological schema according to which the earthly Jesus is the incarnate, preexistent Son of God.

---

[17]   Cf. on Hebrews' exegesis of the Old Testament in general and of the Melchizedek passage in particular: F. Schröger, *Der Verfasser des Hebräerbriefes*; H. Löhr, "'Heute, wenn ihr seine Stimme hört ...'. Zur Kunst der Schriftanwendung im Hebräerbrief und in 1 Kor 10," in H. Löhr and M. Hengel (eds.), *Schriftauslegung* (WUNT 73. Tübingen: J. C. B. Mohr [Paul Siebeck], 1994) 226–248.

[18]   On this cf. F. Laub, "'Schaut auf Jesus';" J. Roloff, "Der mitleidende Hohepriester."

[19]   On the disputed textual tradition and its interpretation cf. A. v. Harnack, *Zwei alte dogmatische Korrekturen im Hebräerbrief* (SPAW.PH. Berlin 1929) 62–73; for a detailed treatment, cf. H. J. de Jonge, *Traditie* 11–12; W. R. G. Loader, *Sohn und Hoherpriester* 97ff.

That a developed christological tradition is here presupposed is seen in the *christological titles*. The absolute "Son" (υἱός 1:2, 8; 3:6; 5:8; 7:28) is reminiscent of Johannine usage. Differently than in the Gospel of John, however, the relation to the Father is not developed, just as the motif of the "sending of the Son" is missing.[20] Formally, this usage is to be distinguished from "my Son" (υἱός μου), which appears only in the quotation from Psalm 2:7 LXX and refers to the inthronization (1:5; 5:5). Taken as a whole, "(the) Son" and "my Son" mean the same as "Son of God" (υἱὸς τοῦ θεοῦ 4:14; 6:6; 7:3; 10:29), and both are interchangeable with the term "high priest" (cf. on the one hand 5:8–10; 7:28; on the other hand 4:14; 5:5–6; 7:3). The "Son" terminology is accordingly determined by the schema of descent from and re-ascent to heaven (cf. 1:2), as he is then also called the exalted "Son of God" (10:29).

In contrast, other New Testament designations of Christ recede. As is also the case with Paul, "Son of Man" is lacking (2:6 is only an apparent exception, since the quotation from Psalm 8:5 LXX does not use the phrase in the titular sense); neither is the title "Son of David" present. "Lord" (κύριος) can be used of either God or Christ (7:21; 12:14 and elsewhere); when used of Christ this can be indicated with the genitive pronoun "our" (7:14) or connected to the personal name "Jesus" (13:20) in reference to the earthly Jesus (2:3; 7:14). Alongside this usage, the simple designation "Jesus" can stand in the foreground as the designation for the one sent from heaven, the heavenly high priest (3:1; also 4:14 alongside "Son of God"), and thus points not only to the historical Jesus but to the Incarnate One (his suffering and death: 2:9; 10:19; 13:12), the one who begins faith and brings it to its conclusion (12:2), the guarantor and mediator of the new order (7:22; 12:24), who has gone into the heavenly sanctuary (6:20). "Christ" is also used as a personal name (3:6; 9:11, 24) but the relatively frequent use of the article also shows that the titular usage predominates (nominative, 5:5; 9:28; genitive, 3:14; 6:1; 9:14; 11:26). The combination "Jesus Christ" designates the preexistent, earthly, and exalted one as the mediator of the saving event who comprehends all time in himself (10:10; 13:21; esp. 13:8, "Jesus Christ, the same yesterday, today, and forever").

*The work of Christ* is developed on the basis of the concept of covenant (διαθήκη). The word διαθήκη does not designate a relationship of contract or treaty between God and human beings but juxtaposes two "orders:" that of the Sinai Law and the "better order" of Christ.[21] The old order of the

---

[20]    A further formal correspondence is found in 1:8–9; as in John 1:18 and 20:28, Jesus is named "God," but of course only in the quotation from Psalm 44:7–8 LXX.

[21]    The technical term διαθήκη (LXX translation for בְּרִית) is found 17x in Hebrews (of 33 instances in the New Testament). It designates the "testament" that becomes effective on the death of the one who has made a will (9:16ff) but especially is used

Levitical priesthood, erected on the foundation of a weak and useless law, stands over against the order represented by the heavenly high priest, Jesus Christ, who has brought about a change of the law (7:12, 18). This "priest forever" opens access to God for human beings (7:24–25). Differently than the shadowy, flawed worship of God represented by the tabernacle, which functioned as a type (τύπος) for the right worship of God to come in the future, the prototype that Moses had seen while on the mountain (8:5–6), the new order introduced by the heavenly high priest fulfills the prophecy of Jeremiah 31:31ff (cf. 8:8–13). The first sanctuary (9:1) with its blood sacrifices was only preliminary. The whole history of the people of God, Old Testament and New Testament, is implicitly determined by the term "promises" (ἐπαγγελίαι). The promise, however, cannot be demonstrated by a historical course of events or shown to be true by a chain of succession. The heroes of the people of Israel are regarded as the exemplary bearers of this promise. Abraham received it directly from God (6:13; 7:6; 11:17; cf. 11:33). In steadfast trust (πίστει) in the promise given him, he dwelt for some time in the "promised land" (11:9) but like the other Old Testament witnesses of faith, he did not experience the fulfillment of the promise (11:13).

It is at this point that the work of the heavenly high priest comes in. Christ is "the mediator of a better declaration of God's will (testament)," the "new testament." He is the "pioneer of salvation" (2:10; cf. 5:9); he is the founder of the "better promises" (8:6; cf. 7:22; 9:15). Since his ministry is developed in comparison and contrast to that of the Old Testament high priest, two streams of tradition are combined in the interpretation of Jesus' death:

1. The Old Testament tradition, such as Leviticus 16, according to which the Old Testament high priest on the Day of Atonement offered sacrifice both for himself and then for the sins of the people, and must offer this sacrifice yearly (9:7; cf. 7:27; 10:3). In contrast to this the interpretation of the Letter to the Hebrews, according to which the heavenly high priest Christ offered himself as the sacrifice and thereby once for all obtained "eternal redemption" (9:12; cf. 13:20).

2. The Christian tradition, in which the death of Jesus was generally interpreted as a sin offering, an idea also known to Hellenistic thought. Thus in the idea of the *blood of Jesus Christ*, that purifies the conscience (9:14) and opens up access to the holy place (10:19; cf. 9:12). While this

---

for the "declaration of God's will" given by God, the "order." The latter understanding is the dominant one in Hebrews, in which the old order instituted at Sinai (9:20) is juxtaposed to the new order established by Christ (8:8; 9:15; 10:29 v. l.; 12:24; cf. 7:22; 8:6; 13:20). The translation found fairly often, "covenant" or "contract," is generally incorrect. Only in Hebrews 9:4 (and Rev 11:19) does the traditional translation "covenant" come into consideration in connection with the "ark of the covenant" (cf. Bauer BAGD 183).

idea has a background that stretches back quite far into early Christian history (cf. Luke 22:20; Rom 5:9; Eph 1:7; 1 John 1:7), the same is true of the *concept of sacrifice*, as implied in the ὑπέρ construction: Christ died *for* sins (ὑπὲρ ἁμαρτιῶν) as a sacrifice offered once for all (10:12; cf. 7:25; 9:24). This corresponds to early Christian formulations (cf. e.g. 1 Thess 5:10; Titus 2:14 and elsewhere); cf. also the means of atonement in Romans 3:25 (ἱλαστήριον). The redemption brought about by the high priestly work of Christ includes his life on earth and continues to be effective in the present life of the church.[22]

The church that harkens to the word of the heavenly high priest is not perfect. It finds itself on the way, following the example of Abraham and all the other witnesses of faith (6:12) and by its endurance (ὑπομονή) it persists in the will of God (10:36; 12:1).

### c)  Ecclesiology: The Wandering People of God

The Christian community of Hebrews can be presented as "wandering" (E. Käsemann, *The Wandering People of God*) and as the "waiting people of God" (O Hofius, *Katapausis*).[23] The community of the heavenly high priest *waits* for the announcement of salvation since it is oriented toward the "future world" (2:5 οἰκουμένη μέλλουσα); it understands itself as the heir of "better promises" (8:6), for it is the community of those who "are called to an eternal inheritance" (9:15) and that is to inherit salvation (σωτηρία, 1:14; cf. 5:9). The concrete goal of this hope is "rest" (κατάπαυσις), that is, the heavenly reward God has promised to his people as an eternal inheritance (4:1ff). The substance of such hope can also be described as the "Sabbath rest" or "Sabbath celebration" (σαββατισμός, 4:9), as the "Fatherland" or "native country" (11:14), as the (heavenly) city (11:16) or as an "unshakable kingdom" not subject to the changing currents of history (12:28). It is the eschatological future that is expected, in accordance with the apocalyptic drama of history connected to the idea of the heavenly reward (10:35), the resurrection of the dead and eternal judgment (6:2; 11:35b), but corresponding to the presupposed christological view is primarily the saving encounter with the returning Christ (9:28).

---

[22]  Conditioned by the divergent elements of christological tradition (preexistence, incarnation, exaltation), the question at what point in time the saving work of Christ took place is not answered precisely in Hebrews. The overarching category is that of the heavenly high priest, who combines past, present, and future in his person, and as such "has obtained eternal redemption" (9:12; cf. H. Braun, *An die Hebräer* 32–33, Excursus "The Chronological Aporias of the Christology of Hebrews").

[23]  Cf. now E. Grässer, "Das wandernde Gottesvolk—Zum Basismotiv des Hebräerbriefs," ZNW 77 (1986) 160–179.

The Christian community, however, is not only portrayed as waiting for the coming reality of salvation but it understands itself as the eschatological community of the endtime that also is *wandering* through time. The promise given to it concerns not only the final goal of history but accompanies it on its journey through time. This is what determines the understanding of history in the Letter to the Hebrews. It looks back on the constitutive eschatological event, to the once-for-all atoning act of the heavenly high priest Jesus Christ who has come "in these last days" (of the Old Testament prophets, 1:2) and "... has appeared once for all at the end of the age to remove sin by the sacrifice of himself" (9:26). On the other hand, it looks ahead for the final realization of its hope of salvation and thus stands in the dialectic of the "already" and "not yet" of salvation. The promise of salvation is effective in the present, and does not only point back to the Christ event of the past. This definitive event has rather an ecclesiological and anthropological consequence. It affirms that the Christian community understands itself as the "household of Christ" (3:6). Through the sacrificial death of Christ it is "sanctified," and precisely thereby it is bound to Christ as a brother (2:11, 17). As a community of brothers and sisters, which it really is in its own self-understanding (cf. the address ἀδελφοί, 3:1, 12; 10:19; 13:22), it knows itself to be in possession of the promise and holds fast to this, its "confession of our hope" (10:23). This confident hope (cf. 6:11) of entering into the heavenly sanctuary, is grounded christologically, for it has been freed from its transgressions through the blood of Jesus has received the forgiveness of sins. Precisely for this reason it can "already now" affirm for itself an event that has "perfected for all time those who are sanctified" (10:14; cf. 16ff). That such a presently-experienced salvation is not something the community itself has appropriated for itself is also indicated by the sacrament of baptism and by the laying on of hands, which are named alongside "repentance from dead works" and "faith toward God" as elementary items of Christian instruction (6:1–2). Therefore the community can have "confidence" in God's help and can live its life among its fellow human beings without fear (13:5ff).

Alongside the awareness of the presence of salvation, the community's journey is determined by the "not yet" of the consummation of salvation. The question of whether a near or distant prospect is presupposed is not to be answered as though these were alternatives. There is no doubt that the church of Hebrews looks back on an extensive history of the Christian community that has already transpired—as the presumed date of the document in the last quarter of the first century also makes probable—, and the admonition to practice perseverance points to the painful experiences of th past (10:32ff; cf. 6:12). So also dangers of growing tired of the Christian life (10:25) or of apostasy (3:13) are to be numbered among the indications of the congregational reality. It is at this point that the emphatic reaffirmation of the traditional near-expectation of the parousia is made: "... as you see the Day approaching" (10:25).[24] "For yet 'in a very little while, the one who is coming will come and will not delay'" (10:37; the quotation is from Isa 26:20 and Hab 2:3). As is the case in the Synoptic Gospels, such near-expectation presupposes that it is impossible to calculate the coming of the Lord in advance. His coming will be a surprise. The urgent announcement of the breaking in of this event has the function of motivating right Christian conduct in the here and now. While the horizontal-eschatological dimension has priority (9:28; 12:26), the vertical-eschatological perspective is also brought into play: the heavenly high priest Jesus "always lives to make intercession for them" (7:25; cf. 4:14–15; 9:24). Every individual segment of time that the church traverses on its journey through history is determined by the liberating, redemptive event that is both out ahead of them and is at the same time present with them, the reconciling event that the heavenly high priest embodies in his own person.

In the "already now" of the reality of eschatological salvation, the Christian community differentiates itself from the Old Testament people of God. It has found access to "Mount Zion and to the city of the living God, the heavenly Jerusalem" (12:22), for the blood of Jesus has mediated to it the ultimate, new declaration of God's will, the "New Testament."[25] The eschatological quality of its church consciousness is normative for the way every Christian must live his or her life. While the Pauline distinction between indicative and imperative (Gal 5:25) is missing, it is still the case that Christian ethical conduct is based on the eschatological dimension conceived in both horizontal and vertical perspectives at the same time.[26] It is only under the presupposition of sanctification by the Christ event of the past effected by Christ the heavenly high priest who qualifies the life of the community in the present, and the expectation of future judgment and salvation that it is understandable that and how the ethical imperative of Hebrews is shaped. The exodus generation thereby becomes the negative foil against which the parenesis directed to the Christian community stands out by contrast. Because of its unbelief and disobedience (4:2, 6, 11) the exodus generation received the proper retribution for its transgressions (2:2); it did not attain perfection (9:9; 10:1). Against this background the Christian community receives the warning not to disdain the offer of salvation, to harken to the message and not to lose sight of the goal (2:1, 3). They should leave behind the elementary items of instruction and turn to the teaching about right conduct (5:13–14). Included in this is the

---

[24]  Hebrews 10:25. The reference is to the coming day of judgment; cf. 10:30. ἡμέρα is already a technical term for the final judgment day in the oldest Christian literature: 1 Thessalonians 5:2, 4; Philippians 1:6, 10; 2:16; cf. also Matthew 7:22; 10:15; Luke 21:34ff and elsewhere.

possibility of discerning between good and evil (5:14), the warning against the "evil heart of unbelief" (3:12), the admonition to produce love and good works (10:24; cf. 6:10). Such parenesis is all the more important since the Christian community, differently than what is said of ancient Israel, is freed from an evil conscience (10:2, 22; cf. 9:14), and knows that it has a "good conscience."[27] But it is still not perfect; it is called to put aside the "sin that clings so closely" and to persevere in the competitive struggle (ἀγών) in which it is engaged (12:1). In view of the many troubles and challenges the church faces, which are not to be limited to some particular situation of persecution, they must concern themselves with steadfast endurance (ὑπομονή) and constantly put themselves at the disposal of the "will of God" (10:36). It learns this also in the "discipline" (παιδεία) imposed on it (12:4ff). The Old Testament-wisdom background (cf. 12:5–6/ Prov 3:11–12) reveals the ethical perspective. While it is not a matter of moral instruction, it is still a "discipline" effected by God, to which suffering and persecution make their contribution. Such discipline has no atoning effect in regard to sins; the suffering of Jesus on the cross has already done this (cf. 5:8–9; 2:9–10). It corresponds to the picture of competitive athletic struggle that the divine "pedagogy" is not itself the goal but the means to the goal, which is "eternal life" (12:9). This way not only involves joy but also trouble and struggle. But the consequence of such endurance is full of blessing: "the peaceable fruit of righteousness" (12:11).

A key aspect of the understanding of human life found in Hebrews is expressed by the term πίστις.[28] While "faith" is "the assurance of things hoped for, the conviction of things not seen" (11:1), it is not a theoretical matter but an aspect of everyday life, of which there are many examples among the "great cloud of witnesses" in the course of past history (11:1–12:1). In contrast to the Paulinizing concluding section (13:18, 22–25), faith is not "justifying faith" in the Pauline sense, something that happens by God's grace without human achievement but more of an attitude, a way of living, as is familiar from the Hellenistic-Jewish tradition of "virtues."[29] It thus has a close connection with the concept of righteousness (cf. 11:7, "righteousness, that is in accordance with faith"). To be sure, the faith

---

25    Hebrews 12:24; on the term διαθήκη see above F. I. b.
26    The indicative-imperative sequence is hinted at in, for example 3:7 (διό) —→ 3:6; also 4:14a (15) —→ 4:14b, (16). On the incorporation of ethical statements into the theology of Hebrews, cf. H. Löhr, *Umkehr und Sünde im Hebräerbrief.*
27    Hebrews 13:18. — To be sure, it is striking that the expression καλὴ συνείδησις occurs only here in Hebrews—an indication that 13:18, 22–25 belongs to the secondary epistolary conclusion of the document.
28    For extensive treatments, cf. E. Grässer, *Der Glaube im Hebräerbrief;* Th. Söding, "Zuversicht und Geduld im Schauen auf Jesus. Zum Glaubensbegriff des Hebräerbriefs," ZNW 82 (1991) 214–241.
29    Cf. Philo Migr 44; Virt 215–216; Her 93–94; Mut 181–182; Conf 31; Abr 268.

called for and practiced in the Christian community is oriented to Christ and stands under the presupposition of the christological-soteriological indicative of the saving event enacted by the heavenly high priest, the forgiveness of sins (12:2).

A focal point of Hebrews' parenetic instruction is found in the statement that excludes a second repentance. Neither apostates nor wanton sinners can "be restored again to repentance" (6:4–6; 10:26–31; 12:16–17). The once-for-all character of Christ's sacrifice leaves no room for a repeated forgiveness of flagrant sins. The necessity of mutual admonition and unconditional ethical conduct is to be seen against this background. This reflects the post-apostolic situation, in which the disciplinary problems of congregational life were growing in importance, and opens the door to the later rigorous penitential practice, the beginnings of which can already be seen in Paul (1 Cor 5:1–13) and Matthew (18:15–18), which have a parallel in 1 John 5:16–17, and which found a consistent realization in the refusal of Montanists (2 century) and the Roman presbyter Novatian (3 century) to receive lapsed Christians back into the congregation.

# II. Suffering with Christ—The First Letter of Peter

Beare, F. W. *The First Epistle of Peter. The Greek Text with Introduction and Notes.* Oxford: Blackwell, 1970.

Brox, N. *Der erste Petrusbrief.* EKK XXI. Neukirchen-Vluyn: Neukirchener, 1986.

Bultmann, R. "Bekenntnis- und Liedfragmente im ersten Petrusbrief," *CNT* 11 (1947) 1–14; also in R. Bultmann. *Exegetica.* Tübingen: J. C. Mohr (Paul Siebeck), 1967, 285–297.

Cothenet, E." La Première de Pierre: bilan de 35 ans de recherches," ANRW II 25.5 (1988) 3685–3712.

Delling, G. "Der Bezug der christlichen Existenz auf das Heilshandeln Gottes nach dem ersten Petrusbrief," in *Neues Testament und christliche Existenz* (FS H. Braun) H. D. Betz and L. Schottroff (eds.), Tübingen: J. C. Mohr (Paul Siebeck), 1973, 95–113.

Elliott, J. H. *A Home for Homeless. A Sociological Exegesis of 1 Peter. Its Situation and Strategy.* Philadelphia: Fortress, 1981.

Feldmeier, R. *Die Christen als Fremde. Die Metapher der Fremde in der antiken Welt, im Urchristentum und im 1. Petrusbrief.* WUNT I 64. Tübingen: J. C. Mohr (Paul Siebeck), 1992.

Frankemölle, H. *1. Petrusbrief, 2. Petrusbrief, Judasbrief.* NEB NT 18, 20. Würzburg: Echter, 1987.

Goldstein, H. *Paulinische Gemeinde im Ersten Petrusbrief.* SBS 80. Stuttgart: Katholische Bibelwerk, 1975.

Goppelt, L. *A Commentary on First Peter.* Grand Rapids: W. B. Eerdmans, 1993.

Lohse, E. "Parenesis and Kerygma in 1 Peter," *Perspectives on First Peter.* Charles Talbert, ed. Macon: Mercer, 1986, 37–59.

Millauer, H. *Leiden als Gnade. Eine traditionsgeschichtliche Untersuchung zur Leidenstheologie des ersten Petrusbriefs.* EHS.T 56. Frankfurt: Peter Lang, 1976.

Perdelwitz, R. *Die Mysterienreligionen und das Problem des 1. Petrusbriefes. Ein literarischer und religionsgeschichtlicher Versuch*, RVV 11.3. Giessen: A. Töpelmann, 1911.
Prostmeier, F. R. *Handlungsmodelle im ersten Petrusbrief.* fzb 63. Würzburg: Echter, 1990.
Reichert, A. *Eine urchristliche Praeparatio ad Martyrium.* BET 22. Frankfurt: Peter Lang, 1989.
Schelkle, K. H. *Die Petrusbriefe. Der Judasbrief.* HThK XIII/2. Freiburg: Herder, 1988.
Schröger, F. *Gemeinde im 1. Petrusbrief. Untersuchungen zum Selbstverständnis einer christlichen Gemeinde an der Wende vom 1. zum 2. Jahrhundert.* Passau, 1981.
Schutter, W. L. *Hermeneutic and Composition in 1 Peter.* WUNT II/30. Tübingen: J. C. B. Mohr (Paul Siebeck), 1989.
Schweizer, E. "Zur Christologie des ersten Petrusbriefes," in C. Breytenbach and H. Paulsen (eds.) *Anfänge der Christologie, FS F. Hahn,* Göttingen: Vandenhoeck & Ruprecht, 1991, 369–381.
Selwyn, E. G. *The First Epistle of St. Peter.* London: Macmillan, 1947 (repr. 1974).
Windisch, H. and Preisker, H. *Die katholischen Briefe.* HNT 15. Tübingen:: J. C. B. Mohr (Paul Siebeck), 1951.
Wolff, Chr." Christ und Welt im 1. Petrusbrief," ThLZ 100 (1975) 333–342.

The following discussion presupposes that in 1 Peter we have a pseudepigraphical circular letter from the last years of the first century to the Christian community of Asia Minor that intends to offer them hope amid the increasing social pressures under which they live and to do so in concrete, everyday terms. The central focus is thus neither on christological statements nor on description of the Christians situation of suffering. Rather, the community is to find courage and hope in their distress by accepting the conduct of Christ as the model for their own lives.[1]

The theme that occupied scholarship for a long time, the discovery by means of literary criticism of a "baptismal sermon" as the basis for 1 Peter, can here be left out of consideration, since the critical objections to this hypothesis have repeatedly been convincingly presented elsewhere. Beginning with R. Perdelwitz's history-of-religions studies in 1911, in the course of which he claimed to have discovered 1:3–4:11 to be a baptismal sermon,

---

[1] This understanding of the theme of 1 Peter accords with N. Brox, *Der erste Petrusbrief* 17. In contrast, K. H. Schelkle, *Die Petrusbriefe* 3, regards the theme of the letter to be "a message to the church in view of the severe distress of the church that has already begun and will worsen in the future." L. Goppelt, *Theology of the New Testament* 2. 164 has energetically disputed this, finding the sole theme of 1 Peter to be the issue of "Christian responsibility in society," a view he had already argued in "Prinzipien neutestamentlicher Sozialethik nach dem 1. Petrusbrief," in *Neues Testament und Geschichte* (FS O. Cullmann) (Zürich/Tübingen 1972) 285–296. His *Commentary on 1 Peter* entitles the second major section 2:11–4:11 "The Realization of Christian Existence in the Structures of Society." Brox, *Der erste Petrusbrief* 17–18 rightly criticizes this view: "But 1 Peter, which clearly speaks the insider language of an insignificant minority regarded from the sociocultural perspective, does not go beyond the situation and possibilities of the early Christian scene in such wise as to discover 'society' as a field of Christian responsibility."

there followed a "rapid escalation"[2] of form-critical studies and analyses of the motifs of 1 Peter that made Perdelwitz's theory more and more precise. While it is not to be doubted that baptismal material belongs in the traditions upon which 1 Peter draws, it is off-target to understand 1 Peter as basically a liturgical text inserted into a minimal epistolary framework.[3]

## a) Authorship

The prescript designates the author of the document as Πέτρος ἀπόστολος Ἰησοῦ Χριστοῦ (1:1), who later introduces himself as μάρτυς τῶν τοῦ Χριστοῦ παθημάτων (5:1). Even if 5:1 is not necessarily to be taken as a claim to have been an eyewitness of the passion of Jesus, it is still clear that both statements intend to be understood as referring to the disciple of Jesus, Simon Peter. Nevertheless, there are several objections to the assumption of Petrine authorship.

1 Peter is written in a refined Greek (cf. among other features, the rhetorical questions in 2:20; 3:13; 4:18; the participial construction in 1:3–12; antitactic and syntactic word-plays in 1:8, 10; 2:2, 25; 3:4, 6; the parallelisms in 1:14–15, 18–19, 23; 2:16; 5:2–3; the use of the optative in 3:14, 17 and elsewhere). These features, as well as the exclusive use of the LXX, would be remarkable for a writing by Peter the disciple of Jesus, since according to Acts 4:13 he was uneducated and according to Mark 14:70 was recognizable by his Galilean dialect of Aramaic.[4] Whether in addition one should have expected Simon to have used his real name in the pre-

---

2    Brox, *Der erste Petrusbrief* 20.

3    H. Preisker's Supplement to H. Windisch's commentary (*Die katholischen Briefe* 156-162) finds 1:3-4:11 to be remnants of the order of service for the baptismal liturgy of the Roman church. The act of baptism itself occurred between 1:21 and 1:22. W. Bornemann, „Der erste Petrusbrief—eine Taufrede des Silvanus?" *ZNW* 19 (1919-1920) 143-165 proceeds from the assumption that the baptismal sermon was based on Psalm 34, and was preached by Silvanus in a small town in the province of Asia about 90 C. E. M. E. Boismard, „Quatre Hymnes Baptismales dans la Première Épître de Pierre," *LeDiv* 30 (Paris 1961) detected in the texts with hymnic characteristics (1:3-5; 2:22-25; 3:18-22; 5:5-9; 1:20; 4:6) elements of a baptismal liturgy. Finally, F. L. Cross, *I. Peter. A Pascal Liturgy* (London: Mowbray, 1954), argued idiosyncratically that the repeated πάσχω in 1 Peter has the connotation of πάσχα (Passover) and that 1 Peter is therefore a Passover baptismal eucharistic sermon that was delivered at an Easter worship service.

    The scholarly criticism of Perdelwitz and his followers is reviewed by Brox, *Der erste Petrusbrief* 19-22, and critiqued also by G. Strecker, *History of New Testament Literature* 48.

4    This argument has of course only a relative value, since Galilee in New Testament times was bilingual. Andrew, the brother of Peter (Mark 1:16), like Simon himself (Σίμων), bore Greek names. Only Acts 15:14 and 2 Peter 1:1 give the Semitic form Συμεών.

script may be explained by the possibility that he had become known in the Christian world only by his official name Peter or Cephas. Although the letter appeals to the suffering of Christ, there is no personal reference by the author to Jesus' passion, the witness of which he claims to be (5:1).[5] In addition, one misses any reference to the time when the author was a disciple of Jesus. It also strikes one as strange that Peter, who at least to some degree was the antipode of Pauline theology, is claimed to be the author of a writing so characterized by "Paulinism."[6] A final consideration is that 1 Peter is addressed to churches (1:1) that, so far as we know, stand more in the Pauline mission area than the Petrine.[7]

The information regarding the letter's sender in 5:13, Ἀσπάζεται ὑμᾶς ἡ ἐν Βαβυλῶνι συνεκλεκτή should also be discussed in connection with the authorship question. "Babylon" could be a cryptogram for Rome, as in SyrBar 67.7; SibOr 5.143, 159; Rev 14:8; 16:19; 17:5, 9; 18:2, 10, 21, first equated with Babylon after the first Jewish war.[8] Since Peter's martyrdom is probably to be dated prior to 70, 5:13 accordingly cannot be understood in the sense that by documenting the presence of Peter in Rome it supports Petrine authorship. But does 1 Peter, which calls for loyal, respectful conduct with regard to the emperor (2:13–17), intend that 5:13 be read as part of an apocalyptic message, i.e. as a cryptogram? That is not very likely. A metaphorical sense, not a cryptographic meaning, is primary: "Babylon" probably does stand for Rome but in addition stands for what Rome means to the Christians of Asia Minor. Just as the recipients of the letter are addressed as "aliens/exiles" (1:1; 2:11), so the reason for this existence-in-exile is the superpower Babylon/Rome "as ... the place where faith is

---

5  N. Brox, "Zur pseudepigraphischen Rahmung des ersten Petrusbriefes," *BZ* 19 (1975) 78–96; 80–81 is critical of the view that this passage claims to be an eye-witness of the passion.
6  The key word "Paulinism" is here initially mentioned without prejudice one way or the other, and without presupposing any particular content connected with it (cf. below F. II. d). H. Hübner, *Biblische Theologie des Neuen Testaments* (Göttingen: Vandenhoeck & Ruprecht, 1993) 2:387ff represents 1 Peter as "the high water mark of the influence of Pauline theology."
7  It is a pure assumption when C. P. Thiede, *Simon Peter: From Galilee to Rome* (Exeter: Pater Noster, 1986) 155 postulates a Petrine mission in the provinces or geographical areas named in 1:1 in the period prior to the Apostolic Conference.
8  On this cf. C.-H. Hunzinger, "Babylon als Deckname für Rom und die Datierung des 1. Petrusbriefes," in H. Reventlow (ed.) *Gottes Wort und Gottes Land* (FS H.-W. Herzberg) (Göttingen: Vandenhoeck & Ruprecht, 1965) 65–67. In contrast, C. P. Thiede, "Babylon, der andere Ort. Anmerkungen zu 1. Petr 5:13 und Apg 12:17," *Bib* 67 (1986) 532–538, in the interest of providing evidence for Petrine authorship, has pointed out that already in Petronius, *Satyricon* (written at the latest 61 C. E.) "Babylon" was already found in common conversation as a symbol of the moral decay of Rome.
9  Brox, *Der erste Petrusbrief* 43. This thesis is taken up and developed further by F.-R. Prostmeier, *Handlungsmodelle* 123–126.

placed in an extreme situation."[9] The greeting from the "Roman" church possibly presupposes the tradition that Peter had spent time in Rome (cf. 1 Clem 5:4; Ign Rom 4:3) but in the light of what has been said above it must remain doubtful whether the point is to claim Petrine authorship.[10]

Some of the objections to accepting Petrine authorship need not be considered very weighty evidence, however, if the recommendation in 5:12 Διὰ Σιλουανοῦ ὑμῖν τοῦ πιστοῦ ἀδελφοῦ, ... ἔγραψα is understood in the sense of the "secretary hypothesis." In this view the letter was actually written at Peter's commission by Silas/Silvanus, Paul's companion on the second missionary journey (Acts 15:40; 2 Cor 1:19), who came from Jerusalem (Acts 15:22), and was Peter's interpreter just as was Mark, also mentioned in this connection (5:13; on Mark cf. Eusebius HE 3.39.15).[11] On the one hand the self-recommendation of Silvanus in 5:12 is disconcerting to the secretary hypothesis.[12] On the other hand, the expression γράφειν διὰ τίνος need not necessarily refer to a secretary, since the phrase is usually used to refer to the one who delivers the letter (so Ign Rom 10:1; Ign Phil 11:2; Ign Smyr 12:1; Pol 14:1; Acts 15:23 of Silvanus).[13] In addition, 2 Peter 3:1 does not mention a secretary but exclusively Peter as the author of the first writing. It is thus quite possible that in this pseudepigraphical writing those traditions are represented that have been brought together under the names of Peter and Silvanus.[14] Nevertheless, we are dealing with a pseudepigraphical writing from the end of the first

---

[10]   In contrast, M. Karrer, "Petrus im paulinischen Gemeindekreis," ZNW 80 (1989) 210–231; 226 has reaffirmed the old hypothesis that συνεκλεκτή refers to a person, i.e. a Christian woman present in Rome with Peter.

[11]   A full presentation of the "secretary hypothesis" is given by Goppelt, and cautiously evaluates it as "conceivable," *Commentary on 1 Peter* 10–15 and in his *Theology of the New Testament* 2:162. According to Goppelt Silvanus writes "sometime after Peter's death" (*Commentary on 1 Peter* 370). The names "Peter" and "Silvanus" are "unlikely to be a simple postulate of pseudonymous authorship" (*Commentary on 1 Peter* 51). Rather, the letter represents a particular application of the tradition for which both names stand. At the same time, the juxtaposition of the names Peter and Silvanus (a disciple of Paul) testifies to the synthesis of traditions that had been achieved in the church's development. K. H. Schelkle, *Die Petrusbrief* 134, assumes that Silvanus contributed "a considerable part" of the present form of the letter.

[12]   Goppelt, *Commentary* 370 considers it possible that this recommendation need not be understood as a self-recommendation, nor even the recommendation of the (already dead) Peter but transmits the recommendation of the Roman church.

[13]   Brox, *Der erste Petrusbrief* 242–43; differently BAGD 180. According to Goppelt, *Commentary* 369, δι' ὀλίγον, which refers to the content of the letter, excludes this understanding. Besides, it is not conceivable that the letter was delivered to all the churches in the provinces named in 1:1 by a single messenger.

[14]   At the present there is an increasing number of voices speaking in favor of a "Petrine school" in Rome and regarding 1 Peter as a product of this school: cf. M. L. Soards, "1 Peter, 2 Peter, and Jude as Evidence for a Petrine School," ANRW II 25.5, 1988, 3827–3849; O. Knoch, "Gab es eine Petrusschule in Rom?" SNTU 16 (1991) 105–127; J. H. Elliott, *Home for the Homeless* 270ff.

century, which (a) adopts the contemporary picture of Peter as Roman martyr, (b) knows of his connection to Mark (Acts 12:12), and (c) appropriates the picture preserved in Acts 15:22 of Silvanus as a faithful deliverer of letters.[15] In this regard an ecumenical claim of the writing should not be overlooked. The author adds to the information about the sender the names of two able exponents of the Pauline mission (Silvanus, Mark), and his letter is the first great writing that, according to its own claim, is directed from Rome to the Christian community of Asia Minor.[16]

The letter is addressed to the elect sojourners of the Diaspora in Pontus, Galatia, Cappadocia, Asia, and Bithynia" (1:1). Just as the author presents himself as writing from the perspective of Rome (5:13), so in 1:1 the names refer not to geographical areas but to the current designations of Roman provinces.[17]

A number of different topics are subsumed under the concept "suffering" (πάσχω), which is used twelve times (2:21, 23; 3:18; 4:1 in reference to Christ; 2:19, 20; 3:14, 17; 4:1, 15, 19; 5:10 in reference to Christians, in addition to 5:9 παθήματα). The range of topics extends from the unjust suffering of Christian slaves (2:19–20) to suffering ὡς Χριστιανός because of one's identity as a Christian (4:16). The statements in 1 Peter are not to be taken as the direct reflection of a persecution that has just broken out. Rather, the experiences of the community are already reflected to the extent that they can be clearly connected to the sufferings of Christ (2:21–25; 3:18; 4:1), conceived as the necessary expression of the diaspora situation of Christian existence (1:1:2:11), and accepted in an apocalyptic perspective as the final but brief time of testing (1:6–7; 5:4, 8, 10), since

---

[15] The case for pseudonymity is made convincingly by N. Brox, "Zur pseudepigraphischen Rahmung."

[16] If 1 Peter is in fact a pseudepigraphical writing, then it cannot simply be assumed without further ado that it was actually composed in Rome (so Goppelt, *Theology of the New Testament* 2:162. *Commentary on 1 Peter* 48 and elsewhere). It could just as well represent a claim to have been written in Rome (so Brox, *Der erste Petrusbrief* 42). Walter Bauer, *Orthodoxy and Heresy in Earliest Christianity* (Philadelphia: Fortress Press, 1971) 106–107; 217–219 perceives 1 Peter to be a manifesto of the Roman church to the Christians of Asia Minor.

[17] Among the problematic aspects of the province hypothesis is the division of Pontus and Bithynia into two provinces, since in the Christian period Pontus had been united with Galatia or Bithynia into a single province. To be sure, the older state parliaments had been retained. Also, in 72 C. E. Galatia was combined with Cappadocia. Since 1 Peter 1:1 does not reproduce the correct names of the provinces, it cannot be used as evidence in the issue of the date of the letter. Neither can the travel route of the deliverer of the letter be inferred from the order of the names, since no cities are named (contra R. Riesner, *Paul's Early Period* [Grand Rapids: W. B. Eerdmans, 287 note 38]). Altogether missing are the provinces of Lycia, Cilicia, Pamphylia or respectively the geographical areas Phrygia, Pisidia, Lycaonia. The author has in view almost the whole of Asia Minor, which is essentially identical with the Pauline mission territory.

they derive ultimately from the will of God (1:6; 3:17).[18] Because the Christians set themselves off from their environment by their manner of life (2:11–18; 3:1–4, 7, 16), they are presently suffering verbal abuse (κακαλαλέω 2:12; 3:16), are subject to mistreatment and unjust suffering (2:19; the general nature of the statement is not to be limited to the parenesis to slaves), and are defamed (ἐπηρεάζω 3:16). Their pagan neighbors are truly alienated by their changed life style (cf. the vice catalogue in 4:3) but can respond only with insults (βλασφημέω 4:4). For the Christian community this means pain (1:6; 2:19) and testing (1:6; 4:12). The contrast between the Christian community and the world is described at the close of the letter in ever more dramatic terms,[19] so that the question must be posed, whether alongside social discrimination from their neighbors one can also discern a related response from the authorities. 4:12 speaks of a "fiery ordeal" (πύρωσις)[20], 5:8 of an "adversary" (ἀντίδικος).[21] If one looks for contemporary indications of a sharpened persecution situation for the Christian church in Asia Minor, the only possibility is provided by the decades of the Roman emperors Domitian and Trajan. Especially the correspondence between Trajan and Pliny (Pliny Ep 10.96–97), the governor of Bithynia/Pontus, seems to provide parallels to the situation reflected in 1 Peter. Christians were denounced by their fellow citizens and had to provide a defense of their Christian identity before the governor (1 Pet 4:15–16; Pliny Ep 10.97).

In view of this situation the author sets before his churches a Christology that emphasizes both the saving work of Christ that has called the churches out of the world and a discipleship ethic of suffering with Christ.

### b)  Christology

The christological predicates of 1 Peter: Χριστός appears in the titular sense in 1:11, 19; 2:21; 3:16, 18; 5:10, 14; with the definite article in

---

18    Cf. here the discussion by F.R. Prostmeier, *Handlungsmodelle* 136, which emphasizes the "triadic calculation of 1 Peter," namely pragmatism, apocalyptic scheme of articulation, and authorial fiction.

19    N. Brox, *Der erste Petrusbrief* 33: "The oppressive ... humiliations ... are portrayed on the large screen: as the attack of the great Adversary himself (5:8–9), as a global event (5:9b), as part of the events of the divine judgments that bring history to an end (4:17)." A. Reichert, *Eine urchristliche Praeparatio* 46–59, rejects the hypotheses that regard 4:12 as the author's beginning a new literary unit.

20    While this apocalyptic term in Revelation 18:9, 18 means the eschatological destruction of Babylon by fire, in 1 Peter 4:12 it refers to the testing of the faith of the believers, which is in actual truth a sharing of Christ's sufferings (cf. v. 13).

21    The term generally refers to one's opponent in a legal suit (*BAGD* 74). When 1 Peter 5:8 attributes this designation to the devil, then possibly interrogations before pagan judges on account of the Christian name (1 Pet 4:16) are in view, in which the devil is perceived as the ultimate opponent acting through the human court.

4:13; 5:1; in the phrase Ἰησοῦς Χριστός in 1:2, 3, 7, 13; 2:5; 3:21; 4:11. The usage in 1:19; 2:21; 3:18; 4:1, 13; 5:1 is determined by the context of passion terminology and theology. In 1 Peter 3:15 τὸν Χριστόν is added to the LXX citation (Isa 8:13). The phrase ἐν Χριστῷ in 3:16 and 5:14 is probably to be taken as an unspecific christological formula. Κύριος (1:3, 25; 2:3, 13; 3:12, 15) clearly refers to the exalted Christ only in 1:3 and 3:15; the other instances are probably a matter of conventional theological usage. Although there can be no doubt that Isaiah 53 is cited in 1 Peter 2:24, the author makes no use of the title "servant of the Lord."

Additional christological predicates are ποιμήν (2:25), λίθον ζῶντα (2:4), λίθον ἀκρογωνιαῖον ἐκλεκτὸν ἔντιμον (2:6), ἀμνός (1:19), δίκαιος (3:18). The installation of Christ at the "right hand" of God is announced in 3:22. Whether in 4:5 God or Christ is to be thought of as "judge of the living and the dead" can hardly be decided with certainty. In any case, this affirmation found its way into the Apostles' Creed as a christological predication.

Using terminology mostly from church tradition and the metaphors of blood (1:2, 19) and wounds (2:24), the author addresses the topic of the vicarious suffering (2:21; 3:18) and the salvific, substitutionary death of Christ. The resurrection of Jesus is named in 1:3 and 3:21, his being raised by God in 1:21. 1:7–8, 11, 13, 20; 4:13, 5:1, 4, 10 look forward to the parousia of Christ, which perhaps is more clearly in the author's vision than Christ's lordship in the present. This corresponds to the emphasis on the believers' "hope" (1:3, 13, 21; 3:5, 15) in view of the day of the parousia, which also signals the imminent end of the time of suffering.[22]

It is characteristic of the Christology of 1 Peter that a positive correlation exists between Christ's substitutionary role and Christ as a model to be imitated. In 2:21 the "for you" of Jesus' suffering is directly linked with the "example" so that you "should follow in his steps."[23] Thus in 1 Peter many predications about Christ have a direct connection with ecclesiological affirmations:[24] Christ as "lamb" (1:19) pours out his blood and thus establishes the "flock," (5:2–3; cf. also 2:25 "sheep" as ecclesiological term), just as Christ is at the same time the "shepherd" (2:25) and "chief shepherd" (5:4) of the church. Christ is the "righteous one" (3:18), just as the church consists of "righteous" (2:19; 3:14, 18; 4:18). They are "living stones" (2:5), just as Christ is the "living stone" (2:4).

Positive correlations are found above all, of course, in the passion theology. Although the suffering of Christ is substitutionary (2:21; 3:18),

---

[22] N. Brox, *Der erste Petrusbrief* 22 rightly emphasizes that 1 Peter is oriented more to eschatology, with the keyword "hope," than to statements about baptism.

[23] E. Schweizer, "Christologie" 376–377: "A Christology that portrays the 'for us' of Jesus thus also grounds a Christology in which Jesus is example or better the 'trace' to be followed by his disciples ... such that as a rule the christological statement is formally subordinate."

[24] For the following cf. Schweizer, "Christologie" 374–376.

it is still the case that he (2:21, 23; 3:18; 4:1) and the church (2:19–20; 3:14, 17; 4:1, 15, 19; 5:10) are united in suffering to the extent that suffering is the necessary way to δόξα for both Christ (1:11) and the church (4:13; 5:1, 10). To the ascent of Christ into the heavens (3:22) corresponds the exaltation of believers (5:6), and the Spirit plays a role in both ascension and exaltation, though precisely what its function is in each case is not easy to say (3:18; 4:6). It is clear that the parallels extend far beyond the realm of an ethical *imitatio Christi* and include the saving event as a whole. In this regard the most extensive parallel is found in the understanding of sin. Christ's original sinlessness is presupposed in 2:22. Only so does he fulfill the conditions of a perfect sacrificial offering and thus can bear "our sins" on the cross (2:24). Neither sinlessness nor substitutionary suffering are merely human possibilities. But the author of 1 Peter apparently expects that in view of Christ's attitude, it can also be said in the church, "whoever has suffered in the flesh has finished with sin" (4:1).[25]

## 1. The Christological Traditions

In 1:18–21; 2:21–25 and 3:18–19 (-22) the author combines christological formulae with discussions of the meaning of Christian existence. It is hardly possible to reconstruct these fragmentary elements into their original hymns or songs.[26] The author makes use of an independent stream of early Christian christological tradition and arranges it in relation to the parenesis and paraclesis of his composition.

1 Peter 1:18–21

| | |
|---|---|
| 18 εἰδότες | 18 You know |
| ὅτι οὐ φθαρτοῖς, ἀργυρίῳ ἢ χρυσίῳ, | that you were ransomed from the futile |
| ἐλυτρώθητε ἐκ τῆς ματαίας | ways inherited from your ancestors, not |
| ὑμῶν ἀναστροφῆς πατροπαραδότου | with perishable things like silver or gold |

---

[25]  It is not entirely clear what the author intended by the coordination of the aorist in the initial clause with the perfect middle in the final clause. The difference from Paul's exposition in Romans 6:7 consists in the fact that for Paul it is death, not suffering, that frees from sin. The parallel to Christ is also less than complete, since he of course suffered as the sinless one. The connection to v. 2 shows the line of the author's argument: "the flesh" is understood as a negative element, as the location of evil desires that cannot correspond to the will of God. In view of Christ's own attitude, the insight dawns that suffering suppresses the desires of the flesh. Thus 1 Peter 4:1–2 wants finally to interpret the experience of suffering positively, not to propose a theory of sinlessness. The author's statement about sin from a soteriological perspective is found in 2:24 (ἁμαρτία in the singular). 4:1 shows that the church is in fact not a realm free from sin but that by suffering sins (in the sense of evil desires; ἁμαρτίαι in the plural) come to an end. For this interpretation, cf. L. Goppelt, *Commentary on First Peter* 278–284; K. H. Schelkle, *Die Petrusbriefe* 114.

[26]  R. Bultmann's attempt at reconstruction, "Bekenntnis- und Liedfragmente" involves a considerable amount of rearranging the text. 1:20 is placed at the beginning of 3:18–19, 22, "although that must remain a mere supposition." (295)

19 ἀλλὰ τιμίῳ αἵματι
ὡς ἀμνοῦ ἀμώμου καὶ ἀσπίλου Χριστοῦ,

20 προεγνωσμένου μὲν
πρὸ καταβολῆς κόσμου
φανερωθέντος δὲ ἐπ᾽ ἐσχάτου
τῶν χρόνων δι᾽ ὑμᾶς

21 τοὺς δι᾽ αὐτοῦ πιστοὺς
εἰς θεὸν
τὸν ἐγείραντα αὐτὸν ἐκ νεκρῶν
καὶ δόξαν αὐτῷ δόντα,
ὥστε τὴν πίστιν ὑμῶν
καὶ ἐλπίδα εἶναι εἰς θεόν.

19 ut with the precious blood of Christ,
like that of a lamb without defect or
blemish.
20 He was destined
before the foundation of the world
but was revealed
at the end of the ages for your sake
21 Through him you have come to trust
in God,
who raised him from the dead
and gave him glory
so that your faith
and hope are set on God.

*Exegesis:* The hypothesis that a complete hymn is preserved in the present text must be excluded because of the lack of stylistic consistency. The prose of vv. 18–19, 21 disrupts the parallelism of v. 20. The individual statements of the text follow differing early Christian traditions, which the author presupposes as known to the churches (εἰδότες). So also the revisions of the redactional hand of the author is not to be overlooked,[27] so that we must distance ourselves from the notion of a fixed hymn or song. The term λυτρόω[28] expresses metaphorically the idea of the purchase of freedom by paying a ransom.[29] The use of the passive voice presupposes that God is the one who has paid the ransom, which of course is not a matter of money but of the blood of Christ. Thereby the text combines the idea of ransom with that of the reconciling power of sacrificial blood, a view of the meaning of Christ's death documented in the New Testament independently of the ransom concept (John 19:36; 1 Cor 5:7: Christ as the Passover lamb) but also appears in 1 Corinthians 6:20 and Revelation 5:9 in combination with it. After all, Jesus is named the "lamb" here as in both John 1:29, 36 (ἀμνός) and Revelation 5:6, 8, 12–13; 6:1, 16 and elsewhere (ἀρνίον), the lamb which fulfills the Torah's requirement of being without defect (Exod 29:1; Lev 23:12–13; Ezek 43:22).[30] It is not said why a sacrificial lamb is needed as the ransom price. A previous lapse in the

---

27 Of the thirteen instances of ἀναστροφή in the New Testament, eight are found in the Petrine letters (1 Pet 1:15, 18; 2:12; 3:1, 2, 16; 2 Pet 2:7; 3:11) with the sense of "way of life" (N. Brox, *Der erste Petrusbrief* 80).

28 The word group from λυτρόω is frequently found in the New Testament in a soteriological sense: λύτρον (Mark 10:45); λυτρόω (1 Pet 1:18; Tit 2:14); λύτρωσις (Heb 9:12); ἀντίλυτρον (1 Tim 2:6); ἀπολύτρωσις (Rom 3:24; 1 Cor 1:30; Eph 1:7; Col 1:14; Heb 9:15). Thus from the context λύτρον is not to be understood in the general sense of redemption but as ransom. As parallel concepts cf. λύω (Rev 1:5) and ἀγοράζω (1 Cor 7:23; Rev 5:9).

29 Alongside the Greek / Hellenistic ransom terminology, there is also a possible allusion to Isaiah 52:3 LXX (καὶ οὐ μετὰ ἀργυρίου λυτρωθήσεσθε).

30 ἄμωμος is used both for the blemish-free condition of the sacrificial animal (Lev 23:12–13; Num 6:14) and for the human moral life (Eph 1:4; 5:27 and elsewhere). The term refers to Christ in both 1 Peter 1:19 and Hebrews 9:14. ἀσπίλος has no Old

believer's conduct is not directly addressed. The ransom has freed believers from their past history, spoken of as the fateful destiny of their previous pagan life.[31] It may be that the parallelism of v. 20 reflects a fragment of an early Christian hymn.[32] From the point of view of the chronology of the Christ event, it does not fit as the conclusion of vv. 18–19, since after the redemption through Christ's blood it is the preexistence of Christ that next comes into view. In the background of the statement stands the revelatory schema according to which the present, eschatological revelation corresponds to a divine determination made before the beginning of time (cf. Rom 1:25–26; 1 Cor 2:7, 10; Col 1:26; Eph 3:5, 9–10; 2 Tim 1:9–10).[33] The saving event reaches its goal (v. 20 "end") in the Christian community (δι' ὑμᾶς), which directs its faith and hope entirely to the God who raised Jesus from the dead (v. 21).[34] This community stands at the end of time and participates in the end-time events.

### 1 Peter 2:21–25

| | |
|---|---|
| 21 εἰς τοῦτο γὰρ ἐκλήθητε, | 21 For to this you have been called, |
| ὅτι καὶ Χριστὸς ἔπαθεν ὑπὲρ ὑμῶν | because Christ also suffered for you, |
| ὑμῖν ὑπολιμπάνων ὑπογραμμὸν | leaving you an example, |
| ἵνα ἐπακολουθήσητε τοῖς ἴχνεσιν αὐτοῦ, | so that you should follow in his steps. |
| 22 ὃς ἁμαρτίαν οὐκ ἐποίησεν | 22 "He committed no sin, |
| οὐδὲ εὑρέθη δόλος ἐν τῷ στόματι αὐτοῦ, | and no deceit was found in his mouth." |
| 23 ὃς λοιδορούμενος οὐκ ἀντελοιδόρει | 23 When he was abused, he did not return abuse; |
| πάσχων οὐκ ἠπείλει, | when he suffered, he did not threaten; |
| παρεδίδου δὲ τῷ κρίνοντι δικαίως | but he entrusted himself to the one who judges justly. |
| 24 ὃς τὰς ἁμαρτίας ἡμῶν αὐτὸς ἀνήνεγκεν | 24 He himself bore our sins |
| ἐν τῷ σώματι αὐτοῦ ἐπὶ τὸ ξύλον, | in his body on the cross, |
| ἵνα ταῖς ἁμαρτίαις ἀπογενόμενοι | so that, free from sins, |
| τῇ δικαιοσύνῃ ζήσωμεν, | we might live for righteousness; |
| οὗ τῷ μώλωπι ἰάθητε | by his wounds you have been healed. |

---

Testament counterpart in the legal corpus; but cf. in the New Testament as ethical concept: 2 Pet 3:14 (alongside ἄμωμος), James 1:27. Both terms portray Christ as (a) sacrificial lamb without blemish, since he fulfills the prescriptions of the Torah, and (b) as an ethical model to which the community members can orient their own lives.

[31] In addition to "vain, empty," μάταιος can also describe the pagan past, the pagan world, and sometimes refers to idols (Acts 14:15).

[32] R. Bultmann, "Bekenntnis- und Liedfragmente" 293 supposes that 1:20 represents the beginning of the Christ hymn of 3:18–19, 22, with δι' ὑμᾶς as a redactional addition.

[33] While in general the revelatory schema speaks of the revelation of the mystery of the Spirit, of wisdom, of grace, it is here referred to Christ. Since the final goal of the revelatory schema is the eschatological revelation, speculations are not permitted about the preexistence of Christ mentioned in 1 Peter 1:20.

[34] V. 21 also takes up a traditional early Christian statement; as parallels cf. the resurrection formulae in Romans 8:11; 2 Corinthians 4:4; Galatians 1:1; Colossians 2:12, among others.

25 ἦτε γὰρ ὡς πρόβατα πλανώμενοι,
ἀλλὰ ἐπεστράφητε νῦν ἐπὶ τὸν ποιμένα
καὶ ἐπίσκοπον τῶν ψυχῶν ὑμῶν

25 For you were going astray like sheep,
but now you have returned to the shepherd
and guardian of your souls.

*Exegesis*: Directly connected to the parenesis to slaves we find a "Christ hymn" (vv. 21–25), which in this context is intended to provide the basis for the thesis of v. 19, that unjust suffering is the grace of God. In this text, too, we may speak only in a limited manner of a hymn or song, since at the most the original tradition can only be approximately reconstructed.[35] A certain structure is provided by the four relative clauses, which are related to v. 21b ("Christ also suffered for you"). Vv. 22 and 23a each are constructed of two parallel members. V. 24ab deviate from the context by speaking in the first person plural rather than the second person plural. Finally, there is a noticeable reference throughout to the fourth Servant Song of Deutero-Isaiah (cf. v. 22/Isa 53:9; v. 23/Isa 53:7, 12; v. 24ab/Isa 53:4, 12; v. 24c, 25/Isa 53:5–6). Vv. 21acd and v. 25 may be considered redactional additions with relative certainty, and possibly also v. 23c, 24cd).

The occasion for connecting this Christ hymn with the slave parenesis could have been provided both by the superscript "Christ suffered" (v. 21)[36] and by the statements of v. 23 that point to the passion of Jesus.[37] The "Christ hymn," as a traditional text not composed just for this situation, goes beyond the concrete concern that causes it to be introduced here (cf. only v. 24). Its distinctiveness must be seen on the one hand by the christological exposition of the Servant Song of Isaiah 53, to which the present passage is connected via the ὑπέρ-formula[38] (v. 21 illustrated by v. 24). This is the only New Testament text to make this connection.[39] In the suffering servant of Deutero-Isaiah, Christ is recognized, the one who bears the sins of humanity on the cross, the one whose wounds effect salvation. On the other hand, the exemplary traits of the innocent suffer-

---

[35] L. Goppelt, *Commentary on 1 Peter* 208 excludes the possibility of delineating the original traditional form. Cf. the Excursus "Structure and Origin of the Christ Hymn 2:22–225" (204–207).

[36] According to N. Brox, *Der erste Petrusbrief* 135, the key word ἔπαθεν triggered the adoption of this tradition in this context of the letter. This means at the same time that the text critical problem is resolved on the basis of the content.

[37] So L. Goppelt, *Commentary on 1 Peter* 208.

[38] On the ὑπέρ- formula, cf. G. Barth, *Der Tod Jesu Christi im Verständnis des Neuen Testaments* (Neukirchen-Vluyn: Neukirchener, 1992), 41–47.

[39] If, with L. Goppelt, *Der erste Petrusbrief* 208–209, one understands the ὑπέρ- formula and its connection with the Servant Song as Jesus' own interpretation of his imminent passion, then one must explain why this interpretation first appears in a late New Testament document but was passed over by the rest of early Christianity. This question is also to be posed to Goppelt's hypothesis (203) that Paul's unusual christological use of the verb πάσχω goes back to the Palestinian church, possibly to Jesus himself.

ing of Jesus (vv. 22–23ab), which do not characterize the Christ hymn taken as a whole, are intentionally applied to the distressed situation of the slaves (and the church as a whole). The way of Christ is regarded as the example left behind for slaves (ὑμῖν ὑπολιμπάνων ὑπογραμμόν) that must shape their own way of life. Here the author utilizes (ἐπ-) ἀκολουθεῖν, the technical term for discipleship in the Synoptic Gospels, found elsewhere in the New Testament only here and Revelation 14:14. It is thus not here a matter of an *imitatio*-ethic. On the one hand, after the death of Jesus the concept of "following" could be maintained only in a metaphorical sense anyway,[40] and on the other hand the christological-soteriological orientation of the Christ hymn excludes a complete human *imitatio*, in that it points to a unique figure.

1 Peter 3:18–19, 22

| | |
|---|---|
| 18 ὅτι καὶ Χριστὸς ἅπαξ<br>περὶ ἁμαρτιῶν ἔπαθεν,<br>δίκαιος ὑπὲρ ἀδίκων,<br>ἵνα ὑμᾶς προσαγάγῃ τῷ θεῷ<br>θανατωθεὶς μὲν σαρκὶ<br>ζῳοποιηθεὶς δὲ πνεύματι | 18 For Christ also suffered<br>for sins once for all,<br>the righteous for the unrighteous<br>in order to bring you to God.<br>He was put to death in the flesh,<br>but made alive in the spirit, |
| 19 ἐν ᾧ καὶ τοῖς ἐν φυλακῇ<br>πνεύμασιν πορευθεὶς ἐκήρυξεν, | 19 in which also he went and made<br>a proclamation to the spirits in prison, |
| 22 ὅς ἐστιν ἐν δεξιᾷ (τοῦ) θεοῦ<br>πορευθεὶς εἰς οὐρανὸν<br>ὑποταγέντων αὐτῷ ἀγγέλων<br>καὶ ἐξουσιῶν καὶ δυνάμεων | 22 who is at the right hand of God,<br>having gone into heaven<br>with angels, authorities,<br>and powers made subject to him. |

*Exegesis:* Those analyses that have reconstructed a traditional Christ hymn from 3:18–22 have usually detected its beginning in 1:20 (preexistence of Christ) or 3:18a (suffering of Christ), and its conclusion in 3:22b (subordination of the powers). What other christological affirmations the source that is quoted in 3:18–22 intended to make, and in what order they are to be understood, are questions that exegesis has answered in a variety of ways.[41] If one attempts to reconstruct a chronology of christological development, the one will supposedly see in 3:18–19, 22 a tradition comparable to 1 Timothy 3:16. It reads like a preliminary stage of the later second article of the Apostles Creed: "suffered," "died" (v. 18), "descended to the realm of the dead" (v. 19), "was raised" (v. 21), "ascended into heaven," "sits at the right hand of God" (v. 22). The effect of this way of Christ applies not only to believers but extends even to the realm of the dead (v. 19) and achieves its final goal in the subjection of all powers to Christ (v. 22). Contemporary research has mostly given up the attempt to

[40] So also ἴχνος is used in a metaphorical sense in all New Testament instances (Rom 4:12; 2 Cor 12:18; 1 Pet 2:21).
[41] Cf. the survey in Goppelt, *Commentary on 1 Peter* 247–250.

reconstruct the precise form used by 1 Peter and tends to speak rather of a combination of traditional chains of statements. They have their own traditional history, since the original statements are not conditioned by the themes of 1 Peter.

We may say the following with regard to the individual affirmations of the Christ hymn: The suffering of Christ[42] was unique and once-for-all (on ἅπαξ cf. Rom 6:10: τῇ ἁμαρτίᾳ ἀπέθανεν ἐφάπαξ). His death was a substitutionary atonement for the sins of the unrighteous, so that Christ himself, who was brought to life in the Spirit,[43] brings the believers to God (v. 18).[44] In v. 19–21 the author takes up a complex of motifs already traditional in early Judaism and interprets it in terms of the work of Christ and of baptism. The decisive matter is the proclamation to the spirits in prison (cf. F. II. b. 3). Already in the early Jewish traditions about Noah and Enoch, there was a connection between "prison, proclamation, flood." This facilitated the transition to the typological interpretation of the deliverance from the flood at the time of Noah as baptism in the present. The sacrament portrays in an external fashion the removal of bodily uncleanliness but confers more than that. Baptism saves (σῴζει) through the resurrection of Jesus Christ. In v. 21 the author is possibly expressing with the words συνειδήσεως ἀγαθῆς ἐπερώτημα εἰς θεόν not only a specific understanding of baptism but also a liturgical form. The hapax legomenon ἐπερώτημα can in this context hardly be translated with "request" or "question".[45] Thus the term is often connected to the Latin *stipulatio* ("binding element of a contract") and related to a baptismal vow obligating one to a

---

[42]    The reading ἀπέθανεν found in important MSS corresponds to early Christian confessional statements (Rom 6:10; 1 Cor 15:2). If the author of 1 Peter has modified this statement of the meaning of Jesus' *death* in the direction of his own theology of *suffering* (ἔπαθεν), then these witnesses to the text have later readjusted them to correspond to statements about Jesus' *death*.

[43]    A precise interpretation of the parallelism θανατωθεὶς μὲν σαρκὶ ζωοποιηθεὶς δὲ πνεύματι is difficult. Regarding it as a bipartite rendering of Christ in flesh and Spirit (thus once again K. H. Schelke, *Petrusbriefe* 103–104) stands in tension to the resurrection statement in v. 21. However, if one intentionally sets ζωοποιηθείς apart from the resurrection statement of vv. 21–22 (so H. Windisch-H. Preisker, *Die katholischen Briefe* 71), then there could be a temporal transitional period in view, in which Christ as a living spirit freed from death preaches in the underworld, and then is resurrected. In this case ἐν ᾧ would have to refer back to πνεύματι. That is unlikely, however, since ἐν ᾧ in 1 Peter is used as a temporal conjunction, "thereby" 1:6; 2:12; 3:16, 19; 4:4; so N. Brox, *Der erste Petrusbrief* 170; differently BAGD 261). There is thus probably a semantic shift within the parallelism: death occurred in the flesh but the act of making alive occurred instrumentally through the Spirit (of God); cf. F. W. Horn, *Das Angeld des Geistes* 101–102.

[44]    Since Christ himself does the leading, 1 Peter 3:18 differs somewhat from Hebrews 10:19–22 (Christ opens the way into the Holy of Holies to God) and Romans 5:2 (Christ brings about access to God's grace).

[45]    W. Schenk, EWNT II 53–54; L. Goppelt, *Commentary on 1 Peter* 269.

634     A Message with a Universal Claim—The Catholic Letters

changed life.[46] On the other hand, some scholars have been reminded of the *abrenuntiatio* (the renunciation of the devil, the idols, the old life), traces of which are found in the Jewish Christian baptismal theology.[47] In both cases it is a matter of the baptismal candidate's acceptance of new duties, with a "good conscience" as the hoped-for goal. The Christ hymn concludes with the affirmation of Christ's resurrection (v. 21) and enthronement at the right hand of God.[48] When the "ascension" is here spoken of again, after the resurrection was already declared in v. 21, it may be understood as meaning that it was during the ascension of Christ that the "angels, authorities, and powers" were subjected to him.[49]

## 2. The Descent of Christ into the Realm of the Dead

Bieder, W. *Die Vorstellung von der Höllenfahrt Jesu Christi. Beitrag zur Entstehungsgeschichte der Vorstellung vom sogenannten Descensus ad inferos.* AThANT 19. Zürich: Zwingli, 1949.

Dalton, W. J. *Christ's Proclamation to the Spirits. A Study of 1 Peter 3:18–4:6.* AnBib 23. Rome: PBI, 1965.

Dalton, W. J. "The Interpretation of 1 Peter 3,19 and 4,6: Light from 2 Peter," *Bib* 60 (1979) 547–555.

Grillmeier, A. "Der Gottessohn im Totenreich. Soteriologische und christologische Motivierung der Descensuslehre in der älteren christlichen Überlieferung," in A. Grillmeier (ed.), *Mit ihm und in ihm. Christologische Forschungen und Perspektiven.* Freiburg: Herder, 1978, 76–174.

Gschwind, K. *Die Niederfahrt Christi in die Unterwelt. Ein Beitrag zur Exegese des Neuen Testaments und zur Geschichte des Taufsymbols.* NTA II/3–5. Münster: Aschendorff, 1911.

Jeremias, J. "Zwischen Karfreitag und Ostern. Descensus und Ascensus in der Karfreitagstheologie des Neuen Testaments," ZNW 42 (1949) 194–201; also in J. Jeremias. *Abba.* Göttingen: Vandenhoeck & Ruprecht, 1966, 323–331.

Reicke, B. *The Disobedient Spirits and Christian Baptism. A Study of 1 Pet. III. 19 and its Context.* ASNU 13. Copenhagen: Munksgaard, 1946.

Spitta, F. *Christi Predigt an die Geister (1 Petr 3,19ff). Ein Beitrag zur neutestamentlichen Christologie.* Göttingen: Vandenhoeck & Ruprecht, 1890.

Vogels, H. J. *Christi Abstieg ins Totenreich und das Läuterungsgericht an den Toten. Eine bibeltheologisch-dogmatische Untersuchung zum Glaubensartikel 'descendit ad inferos'.* FThSt 102. Freiburg: Herder, 1976.

---

[46]  So Brox, *Der erste Petrusbrief* 178–179.

[47]  Goppelt, *Commentary on 1 Peter* 269–270.

[48]  Cf. Ephesians 1:20; Hebrews 1:3; 8:1; 10:11; 12:2; Romans 8:34; Acts 2:34. The statement is based on Psalm 110:1 (cf. F. Hahn, *The Titles of Jesus in Christology* 103–113).

[49]  Thus while 1 Corinthians 15:23–28 and Hebrews 2:5–9 still look forward to Christ's subjection of the spirit-powers in the future, Colossians 2:10–15, Ephesians 1:20–22, and PolPhil 2:1 (or the source to which he appeals with πιστεύσαντας) and 1 Peter 3:22 regard these powers as already subdued. Bultmann, "Bekenntnis- und Liedfragmente" 290: "It is the characteristic Gnostic understanding of salvation as a cosmic redemptive work that is the basis of all these statements. This is different from the older view of earliest Christianity, which derived from Jewish apocalyptic."

The affirmation of the Apostolic Creed that Christ "descended to the realm of the dead" is probably derived from 1 Peter 3:19–20 (4:6) but was first acknowledged as an article of faith in the "Fourth Creed of Sirmium" in the year 359.[50] Precisely what 1 Peter 3:19–20 intends to proclaim can hardly be determined from the elements of the individual statements. That the introductory ἐν ᾧ probably refers not to πνεῦμα (3:18) but is to be understood as a conjunction (as in 1:6; 4:4) has already been mentioned in the exegesis of 3:18–22. This implies that the descent of Christ into the realm of the dead, into the prison[51] to preach to the πνεύματα was done by the resurrected Christ but chronologically not between Good Friday and Easter by Christ in his "existence as a spirit."

In contemporary exegesis two interpretations stand over against each other, depending on their respective understandings of πνεύματα:

a) The spirits in prison refer to the unrepentant contemporaries of Noah.[52] Πνεῦμα would then here mean the same as ψυχή, as it does in 4:6, and would refer to the souls of those who died in the flood but who continued to live and found themselves in a place of punishment beyond this world (so also 2 Clem 6:8). Since according to rabbinic interpretation the flood generation "has no share in the resurrection," (Sanh 10.3a), in 1 Peter 3:19–20 the saving efficacy of Christ's death would extend even to this part of human history.[53] Christ would be the evangelist to those who have died, as on this interpretation 4:6 shows even more clearly.

b) The second exegetical approach follows the lead from the history-of-religions school of F. Spitta's work "Christi Predigt an die Geister," which reflects on the influence of the book of Enoch on early Christian literature (e. g. Jude 6, 13; 2 Pet 2:4). Here the πνεύματα are the fallen angels of Genesis 6:1–4.[54] The myth that lies behind this text is often reflected in Jewish literature (1 Enoch 10–16; 19; 21; Jub 5.6; 2 Baruch 56:13; 1QGen-Apk 2:1, 16; CD 2:16–21) and is also to be presupposed as known in some

---

[50] Cf. here the Excursus in Brox, *Der erste Petrusbrief* 182–189 (which reprints some of the relevant texts), which also makes clear on the basis of linguistic differences that the formation of the Apostles Creed was not based on the statements of 1 Peter.

[51] Φυλακή stands for the "underworld as prison of the dead," without permitting us to make this concept any more precise by appealing, for instance, to Jewish speculations about transcendent locations for the "intermediate state" or for the damned.

[52] This interpretation is to be distinguished from the tradition of the ancient church which regarded the contemporaries of Noah as the righteous ones of the Old Covenant who were converted prior to the Flood.

[53] So especially Goppelt, *Theology of the New Testament* 2:177; *Commentary on 1 Peter* 258–259.

[54] This identification of πνεύματα and angels is documented for the New Testament period: Hebrews 1:14; Luke 10:20; Revelation 1:4; 3:1 and elsewhere; 1 Enoch 10:15; 13:6; 15:11; 19:1.

streams of early Christianity.[55] According to 1 Enoch 18:11–19:1; 21:10; 2 Baruch 56:13 and elsewhere, the fallen angels were confined to a prison. Enoch received the assignment of going to them to announce that they would never be forgiven (1 Enoch 12:5). In several places in Jewish literature a direct connection is made between the interpretation of Genesis 6:1–4 and their guilt for causing the flood, which is of course related to the fact that this text is part of the larger context of Genesis 6–8 (1 Enoch 10:2, 22; 67:4–13; Wis 14:6; Jub 5, among others). While the connection between the spirits in prison and the flood story was already made in Jewish tradition, we must recognize in the typological interpretation of the flood with reference to Christian baptism (reminiscent of 1 Cor 10:1–13) a Christian biblical hermeneutic proceeding from sacramental theology.

In the Christian reception of the Jewish interpretation of the fall of the angels and its connection with the flood, Christ steps into the place of Enoch as the one who preaches in the underworld. In the process, however, there is obviously here no emphasis on the content of his message[56] or on the cosmological aspect that makes Christ into Lord of the underworld.[57] Therefore we must consider seriously the possibility that the principal factor in the adoption of this Jewish tradition is the typological correspondence between the flood and baptism, since this is the only aspect in the application to the church's life to which the author's interpretation attributes contemporary relevance. The few saved in Noah's ark—eight souls in the midst of a world hostile to God and condemned to destruction—stand symbolically for the harassed churches of Asia Minor. In any case, it is clear that the author is far removed from any speculative interest in Christ's journey to the realm of the dead.[58]

---

[55] Cf. especially the commentary by N. Brox, *Der erste Petrusbrief* 168–176, which also provides linguistic agreements that constitute the evidence for the Jewish myth and its reworking in 1 Peter 3:19–20. Cf. O. Merk, EWNT 2:719–720, who agrees.

[56] Κηρύσσειν (only here in 1 Peter) is not bound to any particular content in New Testament usage. Whether Christ, like Enoch, preached condemnation, or in contrast to him preached salvation, cannot be decided on the basis of the word itself. That interpretation which dates the descent of Christ into the realm of the dead between Good Friday and Easter may not in the strict sense speak of a message of salvation.

[57] This is considered in connection with the first aspect by Brox, *Der erste Petrusbrief* 175. The superiority of Christ to Enoch is emphasized by Goppelt, *Theology of the New Testament* 2:177 and Schelke *Die Petrusbriefe* 107.

[58] 1 Peter 4:6 may not be harmonized with 1 Peter 3:19–20. The idea of the "descent" is in any case only weakly presupposed. The proclamation is directed to the "dead," not to spirits or angels. Against the background of suffering, is there an appeal to a theodicy in which God is vindicated by a righteous judgment beyond the boundary of death?

## c)  Ecclesiology

The author addresses the readers as ἐκλεκτοῖς παρεπιδήμοις διασπορᾶς (1:1), ὡς παροίκους καὶ παρεπιδήμους (2:11; cf. also 1:17). This existence as resident aliens already comes in view as social marginalization. To this sociological state of affairs corresponds election by God as the theological cause of their life as aliens (1:1–2; 2:4–10; 5:10, 13).

Originally the description πάροικοι καὶ παρεπίδημοι should be thought of as referring to a social rather than a spiritual status. Thus Luke uses the term to refer to Abraham (Acts 7:6) and in reference to Moses (Acts 7:29) as foreigners residing in a land where they have no rights of citizenship (cf. also Wis 19:10; 3Macc 7:19; Acts 13:17). The term διασπορά added in 1:1 strengthens this social understanding, since it originally had in view Jews who were scattered among the Gentile nations. But a spiritualizing of the concept had already taken place in early Christian literature (Heb 11:13; Eph 2:19; Diog 5:5). A tradition of interpretation had already been grounded, as a result of which 1 Peter could address Christians as such as "those elect who no longer belong to the world." "It belongs to the nature of the church always to exist in the world as a repressed minority."[59] In contrast, especially N. Brox and J. H. Elliott[60] have taken these terms not primarily as describing the spiritual status of the readers but as social descriptions that portray the empirical reality of their worldly situation. Their alien status is not a matter of being distant from their heavenly homeland but the experience of distance and separation from their pagan environment. It is true, of course, that 1 Peter 1:4 speaks of the heavenly inheritance but this statement is not related to their present existence as foreigners. It is thus God's call into the Christian community that is the basis of their experienced alienation from the surrounding world, which comes to concrete expression in marginalization, verbal abuse, and suffering.

To be sure, the boundaries between the readers and their hostile environment do not seem to have been so tightly closed as to exclude "missionary conduct." 1 Peter 3:1 addresses the concrete case of the marriage between a Christian woman and pagan man, while 2:18–25 deals with the situation of a Christian slave under a pagan master. The task of bearing witness to the faith in word and deed before the pagan environment is emphasized in 2:15 and 3:15.

A thorough discussion of the two leading ecclesiological aspects mentioned above—election by God and marginalization by the pagan environment—is found in 2:4–10.[61] The exposition is oriented to the traditional

---

59  Schelke, *Die Petrusbriefe* 20.
60  Brox, *Der erste Petrusbrief* 56–57; Elliott, *Home* 21–49.
61  As indicated by the Old Testament citations, motifs, and key words, it is again a matter of a text strongly influenced by tradition, even though we are not able to reconstruct a literary form prior to the writing of 1 Peter itself.

pictures of the "stone" and/or "sacred house" (vv. 6–8) and the "people of God" (vv. 9–10).

Three Old Testament passages are foundational for 2:6–8: Isaiah 28:16; Psalm 118:22; Isaiah 8:14. These texts are usually found in the New Testament in the context of scriptural proof of christological claims and in the dispute with Israel. Verses 4–5 anticipate the interpretation intended by the author of the following series of quotations. In vv. 9–10 he adds a midrash-like exposition of Old Testament motifs (especially Exod 19:6). VV. 4–6, 9–10 address the Christian community directly, while vv. 7–8, within the context of the "Scripture citation" (vv. 6–8) speaks of the unbelievers.

The ecclesiological predications correspond to Christ, the "living stone" (v. 4), the "elect, precious cornerstone" (v. 6): the believers are themselves "living stones," a "spiritual house," a "holy priesthood" (v. 5). To be sure, in the following the building and growth metaphors are not pursued further, in contrast to the usual usage of this metaphorical realm. The emphasis is rather placed on the fact that Christ as the cornerstone has become a "stone of stumbling and rock of offense" for unbelievers (vv. 7–8 with Ps 118:22; Isa 8:14). This interpretation does not exclude a parallel ecclesiological point: Christ and Christians stand together against a hostile world.

1 Peter 2:5 names ἱεράτευμα ἅγιον as an ecclesiological predicate, while 2:9 names βασίλειον ἱεράτευμα. Both texts have been claimed as documentation for the "priesthood of all believers,"[62] but this understanding is probably incorrect. This text was intended to say nothing on the issue of clerical authority but to use priestly pictorial material to address Christians in general as a chosen group. In any case, the author's instruction to his community about official structures is found in 5:1–4.

The right of transferring the Old Testament predicates "chosen race," "royal priesthood," "holy nation," "God's own people" to the church is grounded in their call (v. 9), which is like a new creation that has brought the erstwhile pagans from darkness to light. In the process, the Old Testament citation Hosea 2:25 is separated entirely from the issue of Israel and is applied to the church: it is that entity which God's gracious choice has made into a people, in contrast to the pagan Gentiles.

The author speaks only allusively with regard to the external form of the church. The only office named is that of the "elders" (5:1–5).[63] Their task is to "tend the flock" (5:2). There is no reference to the Pauline order of ἐπίσκοποι/διάκονοι. On the other hand, the reference to the χάρισμα that

---

[62] Cf. the Excursus in Brox, *Der erste Petrusbrief* 108–110.
[63] An extensive discussion of this text is found in J. Roloff, "Themen und Traditionen urchristlicher Amtsträgerparänese," in H. Merklein (ed. ) *Neues Testament und Ethik* (FS R. Schnackenburg) Freiburg: Herder,1989, 507–526.

each one has received (4:10) can only be understood as a later influence of the Pauline understanding of church leadership. It is noticeable that the charisms are limited to preaching and serving, and thus that the charismatic gifts that were decisive in the earlier period (1 Cor 12:28b) are not longer mentioned.

### d)  On the Paulinism of 1 Peter

Goldstein, H. *Paulinische Gemeinde im Ersten Petrusbrief.* SBS 80. Stuttgart: Katholische Bibelwerk, 1975.
Lindemann, A. *Paulus im ältesten Christentum. Das Bild des Apostels und die Rezeption der paulinischen Theologie in der frühchristlichen Literatur bis Marcion.* BHTh 58. Tübingen: J. C. B. Mohr (Paul Siebeck), 1979.

First Peter manifests a large number of contacts with the Pauline corpus: (a) The introductory formula of 1 Peter follows the model of the Pauline letters. (b) The Silvanus and Mark mentioned in 5:12 are coworkers in the Pauline mission. (c) The command to greet with the kiss (of love) (5:14) corresponds to the instruction in the conclusion of Pauline letters (holy kiss: Rom 16:16; 1 Cor 16:20; 2 Cor 13:12; 1 Thess 5:26). (d) 1 Peter has verbal agreements especially with Romans and Ephesians. But they are never so extensive that one must speak of literary dependence.[64] (e) 1 Peter uses the formula ἐν Χριστῷ found in other early Christian literature but originated by Paul (3:16; 5:10, 14). (f) 1 Peter uses, as did the Paul, the "once/now" schema (1:14–15) and the "revelation schema" (1:20). On the basis of these and other data, the question of the "Paulinism" of 1 Peter has been rightly raised.

The great commentary by E. G. Selwyn[65] has presented a comprehensive body of data supporting the view that 1 Peter draws from a broad stream of early Christian tradition that cannot be restricted to the Pauline stream. We still need more precise analyses of how this body of tradition is to be categorized and 1 Peters relation to it. However, we are in a position to make the following statements with regard to the "Paulinism" of 1 Peter. The comparison of 1 Peter and the Pauline corpus can by no means be based on the authentic Pauline letters alone. If 1 Peter is a relatively late document coming from the end of the first century, then by this time the picture of Paul and the standard Pauline theology was represented by the deuteropauline letters and by Acts. The observation that

---

[64]  Cf. the listing in Goppelt, *Commentary on 1 Peter* 28–30. In contrast, H. Hübner, *Biblische Theologie* 2:387, holds fast to the view that 1 Peter "knew the writings of the Pauline corpus."
[65]  E. G. Selwyn, *The First Epistle of St. Peter.*

characteristic features of the theology of the primary Pauline letters are not found in 1 Peter can be seen as analogous to their fading away in the deuteropauline letters and in Acts, just as it can also be an indication of a pre-Pauline or early Pauline theology (in 1 Peter) in which these characteristic features were not yet determinative.[66]

1 Peter is not a witness to the Pauline doctrine of justification. Lacking is not only the term δικαιοσύνη θεοῦ (δικαιοσύνη in 2:24; 3:14 in other expressions; δικαιόω is missing completely) but any critique of the law. 1 Peter does contain a wealth of expressions involving πίστις (1:5, 9, 21; 5:9) and πιστεύω (1:8; 2:7), some of which are reminiscent of Paul: 1 Peter 1:8/ 2 Corinthians 5:7; 1 Peter 1:21 on Romans 4:24; 1 Peter 2:7 on 1 Corinthians 1:18. On the other hand, the statement of 1 Peter 1:9 that one receives the salvation of one's soul as the outcome of one's faith presents an aspect foreign to Paul. A clear indication of the historical location of the author and his distance from Pauline theology is that the Israel thematic has completely fallen away. The author is concerned neither with the church's rootage in Israel, nor the contrast between Israel and the church but with the relation of the church to its pagan environment (cf. 2:4–10). Sarah and Abraham provide a timeless ethical example for Christian women and men. Finally, the author of 1 Peter presents a different picture of church structure (presbyterial/episcopal) from that of Paul.

Thus while "the language of the letter is more Pauline than its content,"[67] one can speak of 1 Peter's "Paulinism" only in a limited sense. In any case, the focal points of 1 Peter's theology, the suffering thematic and Christ-as-model, have no direct antecedents in Pauline theology. We must accept the view expressed by Lindemann that the author is best seen as "witness to a type of Christianity not fundamentally oriented to Paul," but who has been influenced by Pauline tradition and possibly by Pauline letters.[68]

---

[66] Rightly Brox, *Der erste Petrusbrief* 51: "This lack can, however, be taken in a completely different way, as an indication that we have a post-Pauline writing that contains elements of a pre-Pauline tradition…, which had not (yet?) been touched by the dispute about the Law.

[67] Brox, *Der erste Petrusbrief* 50.

[68] A. Lindemann, *Paulus* 260.

# III. Orientation to the Beginnings—The Letter of Jude and Second Peter

Bauckham, R. J. *Jude and the Relatives of Jesus in the Early Church*. Edinburgh: T. & T. Clark, 1990.

Bauckham, R. J. *Jude, 2 Peter*. WBC 50, Waco: Word, 1983.

Berger, K. "Streit um Gottes Vorsehung. Zur Position der Gegner im 2. Petrusbrief," in *Tradition und Re-Interpretation in Jewish and Early Christian Literature*. (*FS J.C.H. Lebram*), StPB 36. Leiden: E. J.Brill, 1986, 121–135.

Dschulnigg, P. "Der theologische Ort des Zweiten Petrusbriefes," BZ 33 (1989) 161–177.

Fornberg, T. *An Early Church in a Pluralistic Society. A Study of 2 Peter*. CB.NT 9. Lund: Libera/Läromedel/Gleerup, 1977.

Hahn, F. "Randbemerkungen zum Judasbrief," ThZ 37 (1981) 209–218.

Heiligenthal, R. *Zwischen Henoch und Paulus. Studien zum traditionsgeschichtlichen Ort des Judasbriefes*. TANZ 6. Tübingen: Francke, 1992.

Käsemann, E. "An Apologia for Primitive Christian Eschatology," *Essays on New Testament Themes*. Naperville: Alec R. Allenson, 1964, 169–195.

Paulsen, H. *Der zweite Petrusbrief und der Judasbrief*. KEK XII/2. Göttingen: Vandenhoeck & Ruprecht, 1992.

Schelkle, K. H. *Die Petrusbriefe. Der Judasbrief*. HThK XIII/2. Freiburg: Herder, 1988.

Schrage, W. "Die Briefe des Jakobus, Petrus, Judas," in H.R. Balz, *Die ,katholischen' Briefe*. NTD 10. Göttingen: Vandenhoeck & Ruprecht, 1993.

Sellin, G. "Die Häretiker des Judasbriefes," ZNW 77 (1986) 206–225.

Vögtle, A." Christo-logie und Theo-logie im zweiten Petrusbrief, "in C. Breytenbach and H. Paulsen (eds.), *Anfänge der Christologie. FS F. Hahn*. Göttingen: Vandenhoeck & Ruprecht, 1991, 383–398.

Watson, F. *Invention, Arrangement and Style. Rhetorical Criticism of Jude and 2 Peter*. SBL.DS 104 Atlanta: Scholars Press, 1988.

Windisch, H. and Preisker, H. *Die katholischen Briefe*. HNT 15. Tübingen: J. C. B. Mohr (Paul Siebeck), 1951.

Among the New Testament writings, Jude and 2 Peter are the documents that have most decisively been addressed in the history of exegesis by critical analysis of their subject matter, and whose acceptance into the canon has thereby been most often seen as problematic.[1] If one wants to do justice to these two brief letters in the present situation, then their specific concerns must be lifted above all critical analysis. The two docu-

---

[1] After the hesitations expressed in the criticism of the ancient church (cf. only Eusebius HE III 3.4; 25:2), the middle ages and the reformation (on which see H. Paulsen, *Der zweite Petrusbrief* 42–43), the sharpest reservations have been formulated in this century especially by E. Käsemann in connection with the debate about "early catholicism." Cf. his "The Canon of the New Testament and the Unity of the Church," *Essays on New Testament Themes* (London: SCM Press Ltd., 1964) 95–107; "An Apologia for Primitive Christian Eschatology," *Essays on New Testament Themes* 169–195; "Paul and Early Catholicism," *New Testament Questions of Today* (London: SCM Press Ltd., 1969) 236–251. Extensive agreement with Käsemann's argumentation is presented in W. Schrage's commentary on Jude and 2 Peter.

ments are here dealt with together because of their literary connection, since most of Jude was incorporated into 2 Peter, but also on grounds of their contents: Jude and 2 Peter, in opposition to other Christian teachers at work in the churches in late New Testament times, advocate a fundamental orientation to apostolic beginnings, and do so on specific items of doctrinal substance.[2]

## a)  Literary-Historical Presuppositions

The literary character of *Jude* corresponds most closely to that of a tract for a particular situation,[3] even though no passage in the document can be limited to one particular congregation. After the prescript (vv. 1–2) and presentation of the occasion and theme (vv. 3–4) to which the warning (vv. 20–23) is related, vv. 5–19 sets forth a polemic against false teaching in the style of a midrash. This section combines Old Testament-Jewish traditions (vv. 5–7, 9, 11, 14–15) and early Christian prophecy (vv. 17–19) with specific interpretations of the author (vv. 8–10, 12–13, 16, 19) that deal with the false teachers (Οὗτοι).[4] The author of the tractate presents himself as "Jude, servant of Jesus Christ, brother of James" (v. 1). There can be no doubt that this is intended to be understood as referring to Jude the brother of Jesus (cf. Matt 13:55; Mark 6:3; Eus Hist Eccl III 19–20.1), who is also possibly to be counted among the missionary "brothers of the Lord" named by Paul in 1 Corinthians 9:5. Even though once again arguments for interpreting Jude as an authentic letter written by Jesus' brother have emerged in the current discussion, arguments worthy of being taken seriously,[5] the indications in the document that point to pseudepigraphical authorship are still overwhelming. Among these is especially the statement of v. 17, which refers to a time predicted by the apostles, expressed in such a way that distinguishes their words from the words available in the memory of the real author, Jude, who does not consider himself an apostle.[6] The au-

---

[2]  H. Paulsen, *Der zweite Petrusbrief* 91, in regard to the return to the authority of the past in 2 Peter: "What this means theologically, the author has pointedly expressed in the concept of remembering."

[3]  G. Strecker, *History of New Testament Literature* 49, in agreement with M. Dibelius, *Geschichte der urchristlichen Literatur* (TB 58. Munich 1975 reprint).

[4]  On the structure of the text: R. Bauckham, "Jude, Epistle of," in *ABD* 3:1098–1103.

[5]  Cf. again the arguments of R. Bauckham, *Jude* 1101–1102, with the conclusion: "The letter of Jude 'could very plausibly be dated in the 50s, and might be one of the earliest of the NT writings.'"

[6]  Clearly H. Paulsen, *Der zweite Petrusbrief* 79, against R. Bauckham, *Jude, 2 Peter* 103, who on the basis of ὑμῖν in v. 18 proceeds on the basis that the apostles had personally brought the Christian message to the church. But this content of the apostolic message named in v. 18 belongs to the basic information in the possession of all Christian communities (2 Pet 3:3; Matt 7:15; Acts 20:29–30; 1 Tim 4:1, and other such texts).

thor writes in the name of Judas the lord's brother, who was still known among the churches at the end of the first century C. E. (Hegesippus in Eusebius EH III 19.1–20.1; 32.5), with a supplementary reference to the authority of James the lord's brother. The tract thereby places itself in a specific Jewish Christian tradition but probably not only in order thereby to attain an adequate authority for its content, but rather because this tradition already was connected with opposition to the false teachers the author wants to oppose. There are also ecclesiological aspects that will have led to adoption of the pseudepigraphical form. This tradition was nourished by a broad Jewish tradition of which the Enoch literature is the most prominent example.[7]

*Second Peter* presents itself as a letter both by its own claim (2 Pet 3:1) and on the basis of its formal structure (prescript, proömium, concluding expressions). To be sure, this letter is interspersed with elements of the genre "testament" (reference to the soon death of the apostle received by revelation, 1:12–14; the binding character of his last words, 1:19; 3:2).[8] The apostle Peter who knows that the time of his departure is near, who is represented as the witness authorized in the time of Jesus' earthly life (1:18), writes his letter as a testament to "those who have received a faith as precious as ours" (1:1). As he says farewell he exhorts his readers to remember the beginnings (1:12–13; 3:1) but at the same time he appears as the bearer of a special revelation for the endtime (3:3). This is doubtless a pseudepigraphical writing in the name of the (long dead) apostle Peter.[9] His words of farewell, whose predictions are even now being fulfilled (3:3–4), are intended to bind the churches to the norm of the origin of the Christian faith.

The author of 2 Peter has adopted Jude as the basic source for his letter and incorporated it in essential parts of his composition.[10] In addition, the author seems to presuppose a collection of Pauline letters, the extent of which is not known (3:15–16), and possibly 1 Peter as well (cf. 2 Pet 3:1).

---

[7]   For details, cf. the data in R. Heiligenthal, *Zwischen Henoch und Paulus*.

[8]   G. Strecker, *History of New Testament Literature* 49, with Ph. Vielhauer, *Geschichte* 595: "testament in letter form."

[9]   No recent commentary has argued for the authenticity of 2 Peter. On the contrary, this document is overwhelmingly considered to be the latest document in the New Testament. Besides 1:1 and 3:1, especially the reference to Peter's participation in the transfiguration scene is supposed to support the fiction of Petrine authorship. To be sure, this fiction is not consistently maintained, since according to 3:4 the "fathers"—among whom Peter himself is numbered—have already fallen asleep. The choice of the pseudepigraphon "Peter" stands within the context of a broad stream of Petrine literature in the second century C. E. (Acts of Peter, Apocalypse of Peter, Gospel of Peter). The correlation with 1 Peter in 2 Peter 3:1 is formal; there is no substantial connection in content of the two writings.

[10]   Cf. the synopsis in H. Paulsen, *Der zweite Petrusbrief* 97–98; on the source critical issue see especially J. H. Elliott, "The Second Epistle of Peter," *ABD* 5:283–284.

The points of contact with Jewish-apocalyptic and early Christian writings of the second century also speak in favor of locating 2 Peter in this period.[11] The literary relation of 2 Peter to Jude requires an explanation that goes beyond the merely formal. It is to be supposed that Jude was a foundation for the author of 2 Peter in formulating his struggle against the false teachers, even though one can observe different emphases in the situations presupposed by the two writings. The author of 2 Peter could have wanted to replace Jude only if he had had the original copy of this tractate.[12]

## b)   The Faith Delivered Once for All

The theology of Jude moves in a "peculiar tension between memory of the past and opposition to heresy."[13] The author does not carry on an open debate with his opponents, whom he calls the ἀσεβεῖς (v. 4; cf. also vv. 15, 18) but binds the Christians loyal to him to the faith as it has been transmitted (vv. 3, 20). According to v. 12, there is table fellowship with the opposition at the eucharist, though it is not without tensions (ἑαυτοὺς ποιμαίνοντες). One must suppose that the separatist tendencies (vv. 19, 22–24) could not be countered in the long run by a simple recourse to the principle of tradition.

We must therefore attempt to determine the nature of the opposition as precisely as possible, in order to understand the theological orientation of the Letter of Jude.[14] According to v. 4, the opponents have invaded the churches from outside (cf. to the word παρεισέδυσαν, hapax for the New Testament, and Gal 2:4 and 1 Tim 3:6, which are related in terms of subject matter),[15] but now belong to it (v. 12). The accusation τὴν τοῦ θεοῦ

---

[11]   Cf. R. Bauckham, *2 Peter* 149–151; J. H. Elliott, "The Second Epistle of Peter" 283–284. Contra P. Dschulnigg, "Der theologische Ort," the allusions to the Synoptic tradition in 2 Peter cannot establish that the author's material is closely related to that of the Gospel of Matthew.

[12]   So H. Paulsen, *Der zweite Petrusbrief* 99: 2 Peter wanted to "replace" Jude, to make it "factually superfluous."

[13]   So H. Paulsen, *Der zweite Petrusbrief* 51; similarly F. Hahn, "Randbemerken" 211: "development and defense of the tradition are connected to the jeopardy of false teaching."

[14]   Cf. G. Sellin, "Heretiker;" R. Heiligenthal, *Zwischen Henoch und Paulus* 128–155; F. Wisse, "The Epistle of Jude in the History of Heresiology." *Essays on the Nag Hammadi Texts* (FS A. Böhlig) (NHS 3. Leiden: E. J. Brill, 1972) 133–143; R. Bauckham, "The Letter of Jude. An Account of Research," (ANRW II 25.5 Berlin—New York, 1988) 3791–3826.

[15]   Since the reproach that the enemies did not originally belong to the community is a traditional accusation (besides the examples named above, cf. 1 John 2:19), v. 4 alone cannot support the thesis that the text deals with wandering prophets (contra G. Sellin, "Häretiker" 222).

ἡμῶν χάριτα μετατιθέντες εἰς ἀσέλγειαν (v. 4b) does not belong to the usual heresiological inventory. It appears that here an accusation is made against the opponents that had already been made against Paul (Rom 3:8; 6:1, 15): the preaching of grace in connection with an antinomian attitude provides the basis for a licentious life. When this is combined with the allusions to immorality in vv. 7, 12, 16, 18, the opponents are often considered to represent a libertine element in the church. However, discrediting the opposition on the basis of their alleged morals is a standard element of anti-heretical polemic, and it may have been strengthened by the perspective of a Jewish Christian who was still anchored in Jewish tradition but who lived in a pagan environment. Alongside this is the central accusation, attained by applying the first Old Testament examples (vv. 5–7): the opponents "reject authority and slander the glorious ones" (v. 8), i.e. they disdain the angelic powers. This conduct is arrogant and presumptuous, since the opponents—at least according to the author's interpretation in v. 10)—take on God's own role as judge as their blasphemous statements place them on a higher level than even the archangel Michael. For the Letter of Jude in contrast, respect for the angels is central, as evidenced by his reception of the Old Testament-Jewish tradition on this matter (especially in vv. 6–7, 9, 14–15).[16] In comparison with this fundamental theological point of difference, the ethical-moral disqualification of the opponents recedes as an independent theme and becomes rather a secondary line of argument that reveals the unorthodox standpoint of the opponents.

It is to be supposed that this opposition had received its basic character in the context of Paulinism. This is already suggested by the possible allusion to the Pauline doctrine of grace in v. 4. Thus Jude 19 charges the opponents as being ψυχικοί, πνεῦμα μὴ ἔχοντες. This can hardly be understood in any other way than as a reflection of Paul's debate with the Corinthian enthusiasts, who distance themselves from the "psychical" on the basis of their claim to be the "pneumatic" Christians (1 Cor 2:14–15; 15:44). The claim of the enthusiasts of the Pauline tradition is turned upside down and used against them (as possibly also in James 3:15). Debates about the attitude of believers to angels belong in the context of Paulinism (one need only note 1 Cor 6:3; 13:1; Col 2:18). In the churches in which Jude and 2 Peter were read, according to 2 Peter 3:15–16 the problem of the right interpretation of the Pauline letters was a current issue. Thus if, with good reason, the opponents in the Letter of Jude are seen as standing in Pauline tradition, then the pseudepigraphical claim to authorship by "Jude ... brother of James" receives an important significance: here too those who stand in the Pauline tradition are opposed by a line of argument that comes from the Jacobite tradition.

---

16   Cf. the detailed evidence for each item of supposed Jewish tradition in G. Sellin, "Häretiker;" R. Heiligenthal, *Zwischen Henoch und Paulus* 95–127.

The theology of the Letter of Jude is characterized by its orientation to the beginnings. The church is called to remember (v. 17; cf. also v. 5), reference is made to the epoch of the apostolic word that lies in the past (v. 17), the church is pointed to the faith that was given once for all (ἅπαξ, v. 3), and the present circumstances of the church are to be explained with reference to the apostolic predictions made in the past (v. 18). We must be careful not to overburden such a brief tractate with theological expectations. All the same, certain emphases are undeniable.

In Jude 3 πίστις appears as a clearly outlined stock of doctrinal statements that were delivered by the apostles (v. 17) to "all the saints" (= believers) at a specific point in time. With this principle of tradition, "the faith" appears as *fides quae creditur*, even though Jude, differently than in 2 Peter 3:19–21, does not yet see the tradition as distilled in written documents.[17] By being incorporated within this "most holy faith" (v. 20), the church is set apart from these false teachers, just as the conduct of the false teachers is understood as splitting off from (v. 19) the structure built on this faith (v. 20). It is very probable that within these doctrinal statements that are the object and content of faith (πίστις) are included those Jewish traditions taken up in vv. 5–16 and interpreted with reference to the opponents. In this connection the Enoch literature receives a special prominence. The opponents appear to be unwilling to follow this tradition any longer.

The "marks of the church" (*signa ecclesiae*) according to Jude 20–21 are faith, prayer, love, and hope. Jude 14–15 quotes and comments on a form of the text of 1 Enoch 1:9,[18] in order to hold fast to an apocalyptic expectation—probably in contrast to the opponents, whose conduct is characteristic of the skeptical grumblers and malcontents with regard to godly behavior (v. 16). The word κύριος has been inserted into the Enoch text in order to transform its statements about the divine theophany into a christological text. The Christ of the parousia appears with his myriads of his holy ones, which is to be interpreted in terms of the angels that accompany the descending Lord,[19] in order to conduct the judgment of the godless. Here is the fulfillment of the promise already made in v. 4 of judgment on the ἀσεβεῖς, the false teachers within the church. This judgment cannot really be understood as "according to works." To be sure, on

---

[17]  F. Hahn, "Randbemerkungen" 209–211.

[18]  The question of text criticism, with regard to the version or versions of Enoch used by Jude, has not yet been satisfactorily answered. It is possible that Jude represents a unique form of the text (so H. Paulsen, *Der zweite Petrusbrief* 74–75).

[19]  Cf. alongside the Old Testament-Jewish statements (Zech 14:5; 1 Enoch 1:9) as early Christian documentation for this idea 1 Thessalonians 3:13. So also T. Holtz, *Der erste Brief an die Thessalonicher* (EKK 13) Neukirchen-Vluyn: Neukirchener, 1986) 146–147). In contrast, in Did 16.7 the reference is already to Christians as those who accompany the Lord.

the one hand the decision is based on sins of both word and deed, blasphemous speech against Christ, and deeds in which the heretical stance of the false teachers is revealed. On the other hand, at the judgment the believers encounter the mercy of Jesus Christ (v. 21; the prescript of v. 1 already declares the eschatological preservation of believers). Of course, Jude 24 also knows that the ethical purity required on the day of judgment calls for one's own striving for purity in the present (v. 23b) but it is not to be attained without God's gracious care for the believer (so already 1 Thess 5:23–24; Col 1:22; Eph 5:27).[20] Although the author sees his own time as the last time (v. 18), since the prophetic announcements of the false teachers to appear at the last time have already appeared in his own present (vv. 4, 18), he can speak of the end time that follows quite unapocalyptically as "eternal life" or "forever" (vv. 21, 25).

For the Letter of Jude, reverence for angels seems to be an integral part of Christian theology. This is seen not only from the positive adoption of this sort of Jewish tradition but especially from his retorts to the opponents' disdain for angels. This problem that was the subject of debate between the author and his opponents thematizes a substantial issue dealt with in several New Testament letters. Is the superiority of Jesus Christ to angels (Col 1:16; 1 Pet 3:22; 1 Tim 3:16; Heb 1:14) also something that belongs to believers, as suggested by Romans 8:38; 1 Corinthians 6:3 Hebrews 2:16, and 1 Peter 1:12? Can believers participate with angels when they pray? (1 Cor 13:1?).

Or even beyond that, are angelic beings themselves to receive adoration or worship (as in the heresy addressed in Col 2:16–18, where worship of angels is connected to food taboos and a festival calendar)? The positive stance toward angels is to be explained as an unmodified heritage of Judaism, as is also perceptible in the adoption of a judicial function for angels at Christ's parousia (v. 14).[21]

The christological statements of Jude appear to be consistently subordinated to statements about God (so in vv. 1, 4, 21, 25). There is no reference to the earthly Jesus, the perspective is focused exclusively on the

---

[20] According to R. Heiligenthal, *Zwischen Henoch und Paulus* 124, Jude advocates "an ancient exaltation Christology that was still without a conception of the atoning death of Christ and which could be inserted smoothly into the current angelology of Jewish apocalypticism." This judgment places a heavy burden on the argument from silence. After all, Jude also knows of the celebration of the agape-meal in his churches. Is it conceivable that in late New Testament times this meal was celebrated with no reference to the atoning death of Jesus?

[21] G. Sellin, "Häretiker" 222, offers more precise descriptions: "It thus appears to me that the heretics of the Letter of Jude stand in a Pauline tradition, whose oldest witness is the Letter to the Colossians." R. Heiligenthal, *Zwischen Henoch und Paulus* 157, places the circle of tradents from which Jude comes among Christian Pharisees, "who saw parts of the Enoch tradition as essential elements of their own tradition."

exalted (vv. 4, 25) and coming (vv. 1, 21) Lord, whose parousia is salvific because it gives eternal life (v. 21). The normative christological title of Jude is Ἰησοῦς Χριστός (vv. 1, 4, 17, 21, 25), except for the prescript always with the addition κύριος ἡμῶν. The christological use of the divine title δεσπότης is unusual (v. 4; copied as a christological title in 2 Pet 2:1); cf. also the transformation of the statement of the divine theophany in v. 14 into a christological term by inserting the title κύριος, which in vv. 5, 9 remains a predicate of God.

The charge[22] that in the Letter of Jude we have an early catholic document can be sustained only with qualifications. There is no indication of a developed hierarchical structure. The Letter of Jude is to be interpreted as an independent witness of Jewish Christian theology that was later adopted by the author of 2 Peter as the basic text for his own composition.

### c)   An Apology for Early Christian Eschatology

Second Peter responds several times to the appearance of false teachers (2:1 ψευδοδιδάσκαλοι; 3:3 ἐμπαῖκται), whose teaching must be seen as the real occasion of the letter.[23]

At the center of the opposing doctrine stands a critique of traditional eschatology that at the same time has consequences for Christology (2:1). Even though the author of 2 Peter does not cite quotations from the arguments of his opponents, it is still apparent according to 3:4 that questions were raised against (the fulfilling of) "the promise of his coming" and that according to 3:9 they spoke of "the delay of (the fulfillment of) the promise." Both statements stand within the argumentation of the opponents closely connected with the fact that the "fathers" have died.[24] To the mocking of the traditional eschatology, rejected by the opponents possibly by using the term μῦθος (1:16),[25] there corresponds an enlightened doctrine that expressed itself as skepticism with regard to the expectation of

---

[22]   Massively S. Schulz, *Die Mitte der Schrift. Der Frühkatholizismus im Neuen Testament als Herausforderung des Protestantismus* (Berlin: Evangelische Verlagsanstalt, 1976) 293. Critically reviewed by R. Bauckham, "The Letter of Jude," ANRW II 25.5, 3791–3826; 3804.

[23]   The appropriate approach is that suggested by H. Frankemölle, *1. und 2. Petrusbrief* (NEB 18. Würzburg: Echter, 1990²), which no longer regards the opponents as belonging to a Gnostic or libertine heresy but reads 2 Peter as a document responding to a crisis internal to the church.

[24]   From the point of view of the pseudepigraphical circumstance of the letter's composition, only one reference to the first Christian generation (= οἱ πατέρες) is significant. To this generation Peter himself belongs, who in the document before us—anachronistically—takes a position with regard to the fundamental issue of Christian eschatology in view of the death of the "fathers" and the unfulfilled promises.

[25]   So W. Grundmann, *Der Brief des Judas und der zweite Brief des Petrus* (ThHK 15. Berlin 1986³) 80–81.

the end of history as such (3:3–5). Along with the false teachers mentioned in Jude, this apparently also included a disdain of angels (2:10). Finally, it is worthy of special attention that these opponents—teachers within the church (2:1, ψευδοδιδάσκαλοι)—appealed especially to the Pauline letters (3:16), which from the perspective of the author they did not properly understand, while his own teaching was in agreement with "our beloved brother Paul" (3:15). The "message of freedom" promised by the false teachers (2:19) is also possibly in the view of the author connected with their (false) understanding of Paul (2:19).

Thus when particular early Christian presuppositions of the opponents come into view, it is nevertheless the case that their questions stand within the broad context of contemporary Jewish, pagan, and Christian debate about eschatology or the delay of the parousia, expressed as skepticism of the apocalyptic model as such.

Second Clement 11:2(-4) cites a Jewish apocalyptic writing that quotes the words of the doubter: "We heard this long ago, including already in the time of our fathers, but we have been waiting day after day, and haven't seen it happen yet." The Targum B on Genesis 4:8 (represented by Tosephta 90) has Cain say, "There is no judgment, and there is no judge, there is no other age, there is no reward for the righteous, and the evil will not be repaid for their evil." Alongside this Jewish background,[26] in which there was an intensive discussion about the fact of the 'delay of the parousia,' appeal is often made to a contemporary Epicureanism[27] and to the reception of and debate with Stoicism,[28] so that in this view it was "not particular exotic heresies that [stand] in the background, ... but merely widespread skepticism...".[29]

Over against this, prior to any apologetic for early Christian eschatology, in the section 1:12–21 that immediately follows the proömium and gives the theme of the letter, the author of 2 Peter points to the eyewitnesses and earwitnesses (1:16, 18)[30] of Jesus' transfiguration, on which the

---

[26]  Further documentation in H. Windisch—H. Preisker, *Die katholischen Briefe* 101; H. Paulsen, *Der zweite Petrusbrief* 151–158.

[27]  On the Epicurean background, cf. J. H. Neyrey, "The Form and Background of the Polemic in 2 Peter," JBL 99 (1980) 407–431; J. H. Elliott, "Peter, Second Epistle of" 285, 287.

[28]  K. Berger, "Streit um Gottes Vorsehung" 124–125, has pointed especially to Plutarch, *Moralia*, "On the Delays of the Divine Vengeance" 5–6, 9 (text translated in M. Eugene Boring, Klaus Berger, and Carsten Colpe, *Hellenistic Commentary to the New Testament* [Nashville: Abingdon, 1995] 538. Here Plutarch thematizes the charge of "God's patient delay" (cf. in 2 Pet 3:9, βραδύνω, βραδύτης in order to refute it in a positive sense: the patient delay of God provides time for repentance (cf. 2 Pet 3:9).

[29]  K. Berger, "Streit um Gottes Vorsehung" 135.

[30]  The term ἐπόπτης (hapax NT) in the language of the mystery cults designates the one who has been initiated to the highest level (cf. Bauer BAGD 305).

certainty of the future parousia is based. Thereby the past announcement of the δύναμις καὶ παρουσία (1:16) is not yet necessarily to be referred to the future parousia of Christ. In the vision of the μεγαλειότης the author has seen exclusively τὴν τοῦ κυρίου ἡμῶν Ἰησοῦ Χριστοῦ δύναμιν καὶ παρουσίαν, and it is for him a preliminary illustration of the second parousia that will be visible to all.[31] The proömium in 1:11 names the anthropological side of the eschatological expectation: entrance into the eternal kingdom (εἰς τὴν αἰώνιον βασιλείαν) of our Lord and Savior Jesus Christ.

The real apology for eschatology found in 3:5–13 makes exclusive use of traditional Jewish and Christian but also anti-Epicurean arguments: (a) the opponents' opposing thesis, that nothing has changed since the beginning of creation, is countered by referring to the end of the first creation by the flood (cf. already 2:5). Just as the first creation came to its end by means of water, so the present creation will be ended by fire (3:5–7).[32] (b) The human concept of time is not the same as that of the God who is Lord of history (3:8, reinterpreting Ps 90:4). (c) The apparent delay is in truth a pointer to the patience of God, who keeps open the time of repentance (3:9; cf. Hab 2:3 and the Jewish exegetical tradition attached to it; Rom 2:4). (d) The "Day of the Lord"[33] is coming "like a thief," i.e. the time factor cannot be calculated (3:10; cf. 1 Thess 5:2; Rev 3:3; 16:15). (e) The ethical conduct of believers can hasten the arrival of the end (3:11–12; cf. Sanh 97b/98a).

The parousia of Christ (3:4), the Day of the Lord (3:10), the "coming of the Day of God" (3:12), is painted on the pictorial level with only a few strokes, which resemble the familiar Jewish and Christian concepts, as the end of time and the judgment of creation (3:10). The real expectation focuses on a new creation that will be characterized by δικαιοσύνη (3:13). The event of the parousia itself is excluded from this picture, just as one misses any recourse to early Christian words about the parousia. It is rather the case that in 3:5–15 the author argues exclusively from God's own acts.[34]

---

[31] Παρουσία in 3:4, 12 is to be referred to the return of Christ. For an extensive argument on this point, cf. H. Paulsen, *Der zweite Petrusbrief* 118; further examples from the second century on the concept of the "two parousias of Christ" are found in W. Bauer—H. Paulsen, *Die Briefe des Ignatius von Antiochia und der Polykarpbrief* (HNT 18. Tübingen: J. C. B. Mohr [Paul Siebeck], 1985²) 87, commenting on Ign Phld 9.2.

[32] The concept of an eschatological "world conflagration" has penetrated Jewish literature from the Greek-Hellenistic tradition (Sib 4.172; 5.159, 211, 531; 1QH 3.29), which in turn mediated it to Christian apocalyptic and eschatology. Extensive discussion with documentation is found in H. Windisch—H. Preisker, *Die katholischen Briefe* 103; K. H. Schelkle, *Die Petrusbriefe* 226 note 1.

[33] The context indicates that by "Day of the Lord" the "Day of God" is intended.

[34] Evidence in A. Vögtle, "Christo-logie und Theo-logie" 392–393.

The number and extent of the arguments brought forth for holding fast to the eschatological expectation leaves no doubt that what lies before us is really an apology for early Christian eschatology. Since the author has made the basic decision to orient himself and his readers to the past, his method is quite consistent. To be sure, the fact of the multiplicity of arguments, which the author has drawn from a number of different contexts, suggests that he himself shares some of the problematic of finding a persuasive explanation for the nearness and certainty of the parousia as time has continued to lengthen. The appeal to the transfiguration scene and the knowledge gained from it implies that the Christian hope has a christological foundation, even if the particular connections between transfiguration and parousia are only suggested.[35] In addition, in the "word of prophecy"[36] (1:19) we have something we can depend on, something that refutes the objections of the false teachers and can strengthen the expectation of the parousia. The author claims for himself to know the right interpretation of Scripture. With regard to the Scripture, the Old Testament, the opponents are like those mockers for whom the analogous question of 3:4 is characteristic (ποῦ ἐστίν ...; cf. Mal 2:17 LXX; Jer 17:5 LXX, and elsewhere). But therein is found the self-deception (1:9; 2:10, 12, 14, 18) that does not recognize the extended time of the present as the gift of God's patience to allow for repentance. The extensive description of the moral deficit of the opponents in Chapter 2 illustrates this self-deception on another level, without it being necessary to connect every detail with something real in the background of the letter.

One does not do justice to the subject matter of 2 Peter by reducing its message to an apology for early Christian eschatology. This apology does make clear 2 Peter's orientation to the original situation of Christian faith but with this as a point of departure there are points at which the restructuring of the early Christian message is undeniable.

Within the christological statements of 2 Peter, we find in 1:1, 11; 2:20; 3:18 the title σωτὴρ Ἰησοῦς Χριστός, in 1:11; 2:20; 3:18 connected

---

[35] Contra E. Käsemann, "Apology" 178–179 who sees no christological orientation in the letter's eschatology.

[36] The προφητικὸς λόγος (1:19) refers to the Old Testament and to Christian writings. Within this comprehensive group, 1:20 then focuses on the group of Old Testament prophets and the problem of their right interpretation. The intention of the author, when he expresses himself on the subject of biblical interpretation in 1:20–21, is rightly described by A. Vögtle, "Christo-logie und Theo-logie 387–388: "In 1:20–21 he wants to ... make sure that he is himself guilty of no unauthorized, independent interpretation, when he ... argues in defense of faith in the parousia on the basis of the ancient biblical oral and written prophecy, because these ... come from God;" cf. also Vögtle, "'Keine Prophetie der Schrift ist Sache eigenwilliger Auslegung,' (2 Petr 1,20b)" in *Offenbarungsgeschehen und Wirkungsgeschichte* (Freiburg: Herder, 1985) 305–328.

with ὁ κύριος ἡμῶν. (ὁ κύριος ἡμῶν is also connected with Ἰησοῦς Χριστός in 1:8, 14, 16). From Jude 4 the term δεσπότης is taken over as a christological title. Except for the transfiguration scene (1:17–18) the earthly Jesus does not come in view. The combining of theological and christological statements we found in Jude is not maintained in 2 Peter (only 1:1–2) but in 1:3–4, 17; 3:18 the attributes of God are transferred to Christ.

The faith (πίστις) appears in 1:1, 5 as *fides quae creditur*, which has been distributed ("allotted," λαγχάνω). The existential dimension of faith seems to be expressed not with πίστις but by ἐπίγνωσις (1:2, 3, 8; 2:20; also γνῶσις in 1:5, 6; 3:18, and γινώσκω in 1:20; 3:8). The object of knowledge is mostly Jesus Christ (1:2, 8; 2:20; 3:18). In 1:5–7 knowledge (γνῶσις) is named as part of a chain composed primarily of commonplaces of Hellenistic ethics, which alongside faith (πίστις) lists goodness (ἀρετή), knowledge (γνῶσις), self-control (ἐγκράτεια), endurance (ὑπομονή), godliness (εὐσέβεια), mutual affection (φιλαδελφία), and love (ἀγάπη). This positive anchoring of knowledge within this list of pious virtues basically excludes the possibility that the theme of "knowledge" was taken over secondarily from the thought world of the false teachers.[37]

A description of salvation unique to the New Testament is presented in 1:3–4 which climaxes in the promise that believers "may become participants of the divine nature." This text—which as the grounding of the promise of salvation is still coordinated to the prescript by the keyword ἐπίγνωσις—is "permeated with the views and terminology of Hellenistic piety."[38]

If one attempts to straighten out the structure of the sentence, the following affirmations emerge: (a) The divine power (of Christ; cf. end of v. 2) has given us (probably all believers; not exclusively the apostles, v. 1) everything that facilitates life and piety (v. 3a). (b) ("Everything" is available) in the knowledge of God, who has called us into his own glory and power (v. 3b). (c) (δι᾽ ὧν = through his own glory and power) great and precious promises have been given (4a), (d) in order that you can become participants of the divine nature (διὰ τούτων = through these promises) (v. 4b) (e) and so escape the corruption of the cosmos, which is characterized by lust (ἐπιθυμία) (v. 4c).

Finally, vv. 3–4 ascribe the gift of salvation, which is perceived and appropriated by ἐπίγνωσις and contains the promises of God, to the divine

---

[37] So for example W. Hackenberg, EWNT II 64; the opposing view persuasively arguing the positive use of ἐπίγνωσις in 1 Timothy 2:4; 2 Timothy 2:25; 3:7; Titus 1:1; Hebrews 10:26; 1 Clement 59.2 and elsewhere (on which see K. H. Schelkle, *Die Petrusbriefe* 186) as well as the use of the term as presupposed in the tradition of the conversion literature (on which see H. Paulsen, *Der zweite Petrusbrief* 105).

[38] So H. Windisch—H. Preisker, *Die katholischen Briefe* 85 (Excursus: "Hellenistic Piety in 2 Peter").

power of Christ. What these promises give assurance of is stated in v. 11: entrance into the eternal kingdom of our Lord and Savior Jesus Christ.[39] The essential content of this kingdom is expressed in v. 4b: participation in the divine nature. "The escape from the world of corruption, the participation in the divine nature granted by God's power, living 'in' God, the knowledge of God and the incorruptible nature of the believer, expresses the epitome of Hellenistic piety...".[40] It is not to be overlooked, however, that this "divination" of the believer is not mediated by gnostic means or by the sacraments but remains a reality of the promised future (cf. also the future perspective of 1:11). The possible contrast to the apocalyptic statements of chapter 3 are thus somewhat relativized. Notwithstanding the massive apology for apocalyptic eschatology, the author appears in some passages to reflect more of an individualized, unapocalyptic eschatology (one need note only 1:14, 19),[41] without necessarily understanding these passages as the reception and reinterpretation of the theology of the opponents.[42] E. Käsemann[43] has explicitly argued for the necessity of a theological critique of such statements about divinization of the believer from the center of early Christian witness, because even within such an eschatology God remains the Lord of the new creation, which is not absorbed into his being.

---

[39]  V. 4c names the other side of the coin of this entrance into the eternal glory of Christ, namely separation from the cosmos.

[40]  H. Windisch—H. Preisker, *Die katholischen Briefe* 85. The basic structure of the statement in 2 Peter 1:3–4 is already found in Plato Theaet 176ab, probably reflected here as well as being mediated to Christianity by Philo Fug 62–64 and elsewhere.

[41]  The rising of the morning star "in your hearts" (1:19b) need not be seen as is the author's own allusion to the Messianic interpretation of Numbers 24:17, an interpretation also reflected in CD VII 19–20; 1QM XI 6–7; 4Qtest 12–13; Testament of Judah 24:1 but rather documents the fact that for the author of 2 Peter it was possible to incorporate apocalyptic traditions into the framework of individual-eschatological statements.

[42]  Though H. Koester, φύσις TDNT 9:275 understands it this way. Against this, one should take into consideration that the concept of divinization is alien to the New Testament except for 2 Peter 1:4 but became increasingly important in the apologetic literature of the second century (H. Paulsen, *Der zweite Petrusbrief* 108–109)—which is another argument for the late date of 2 Peter. Also to be kept in mind in this connection is that the often-mentioned adoption of Hellenistic terminology in 2 Peter may not be reduced merely to the linguistic level, since it always—possibly in an apologetic sense intended by the author—is also connected with specific content.

[43]  E. Käsemann, "Apology."

# IV. The Perfect Law of Freedom—The Letter of James

Cantinat, J. *Les Épîtres de Saint Jacques et de Saint Jude. Sbi.* Paris: Gabalda, 1973, 9–263.

Dibelius, M. and Greeven, H. *A Commentary on the Epistle of James.* Hermeneia. Philadelphia: Fortress Press, 1975.

Frankemölle, H. *Der Brief des Jakobus.* ÖTK 17/1+2. Gütersloh: Gerd Mohn, 1994.

Frankemölle, H." Gesetz im Jakobusbrief," in K. Kertelge (ed.), *Das Gesetz im Neuen Testament.* QD 108. Freiburg: Herder, 1986, 175–221.

Hauck, F. *Der Brief des Jakobus.* KNT 16. Leipzig: A. Deichert, 1926.

Hengel, M. "Jakobus der Herrenbruder—der erste ,Papst'?," in *Glaube und Eschatologie, FS W. G. Kümmel,* Tübingen: J. C. B. Mohr (Paul Siebeck), 1985, 71–104.

Hoppe, R. *Der theologische Hintergrund des Jakobusbriefes.* fzb 28. Würzburg: Echter, 1977.

Luck, U. "Die Theologie des Jakobusbriefes," *ZThK* 81 (1984) 1–30.

Meyer, A. *Das Rätsel des Jacobusbriefes.* BZNW 10. Giessen: A. Töpelmann, 1930.

Mussner, F. *Der Jakobusbrief.* HThK XIII/1. Freiburg: Herder, 1975³.

Popkes, W.*Adressaten, Situation und Form des Jakobusbriefes.* SBS 125/126. Stuttgart: Katholische Bibelwerk, 1986.

Pratscher, W. *Der Herrenbruder Jakobus und die Jakobustradition.* FRLANT 139. Göttingen: Vandenhoeck & Ruprecht, 1987.

Ropes, J. H. *A Critical and Exegetical Commentary on the Epistle of St. James.* ICC. Edinburgh: T & T Clark, 1916 (= 1954).

Schammberger H., *Die Einheitlichkeit des Jakobusbriefes im antignostischen Kampf.* Gotha: Klotz, 1936.

Schnider, F. *Der Jakobusbrief.* RNT. Regensburg: Pustet, 1987.

Schrage, W. and Balz, H. *Die Katholischen Briefe.* NTD 10. Göttingen: Vandenhoeck & Ruprecht, 1986.

Windisch, H. and Preisker, H. *Die Katholischen Briefe.* HNT 15. Tübingen: J. C. B. Mohr (Paul Siebeck), 1951.

Wuellner, W. H. "Der Jakobusbrief im Licht der Rhetorik und Textpragmatik," *LingBibl* 43 (1978) 5–66.

## a)    The Relation of Composition and Tradition History

The writing transmitted under the name of "James, slave of God and of the Lord Jesus Christ" (1:1), was composed by an unknown author, not by James the brother of the Lord. Among all those who bore the name of James in early Christianity, it was only the brother of Jesus who had such respect in later times that claiming his name as a pseudonym would have been understandable by the bare reference to "James." That such an attribution, which is paralleled in other pseudo-Jacobite writings,[1] does not

---

[1]    Examples: the Protevangelium of James (cf. O. Cullmann in Schneemelcher, *New Testament Apocrypha* 1:414–425; the apocryphal *Letter of James* (NHC I 2:1.1–16.30 = Apocryphon of James; cf. D. Kirchner, in: W. Schneemelcher, *New Testament Apocrypha* I 285–299; *Nag Hammadi Library* 29–37); two apocalypses of James

correspond to the historical facts, can here once again be briefly explained—since the traditional view has reemerged again in recent exegesis.[2] That the Letter of James was not composed by the brother of Jesus, who came from simple circumstances, is seen in the first place from the highly-cultivated Greek in which the document is written, which despite Semitic linguistic influence lives up to the standards of Greek rhetoric.[3] Even though in Jerusalem at the time of Jesus the Aramaic, Hebrew, Greek, and Latin languages were all used,[4] the vocabulary and style of James manifests much more than a superficial acquaintance with Greek as it was used in the everyday conversation of the cities of the empire.[5] Moreover,

---

(NHC V 3:24.10–44.10; 3:44.11–63.32 = *Nag Hammadi Library* 260–276). James the Lord's brother is treated in the Anabathmoi Jakobou (cf. PsClem Rec I 43ff, Epiph Haer XXX 16), *Passion* or *Martyrdom of James* (cf. R. A. Lipsius, *Die apokryphen Apostelgeschichten und Apostellegenden* [Braunschweig: C. A. Schwetschke, 1883–1884], I 145–146, 178, 180; II 2.250ff) and the reports about James in ancient Christian and non-Christian sources such as Jos Ant XX 9.1 and elsewhere (see below, note 6). As guarantor of the authentic tradition, he is named by Clement of Alexandria, *Hypotyposes* (in Eusebius HE II 1.3–4), by the Naassenes (Hippolytus, Ref V 7.1; cf. also Gospel of Thomas 12). Additional information and discussion in R. A. Lipsius, *Die apokryphen Apostelgeschichten* II 2:238ff; cf. also the extensive discussion of the ancient references in W. Pratscher, *Der Herrenbruder*.

2  Cf. F. Mussner, *Der Jakobusbrief* 8; the last influential Protestant scholars to advocate this position were A. Schlatter, *Der Brief des Jakobus*, reprinted with an accompanying essay by F. Mussner, Stuttgart, 1985[3] and G. Kittel, "Der geschichtliche Ort des Jakobusbriefes," ZNW 41 (1942) 71–105. This view has reappeared in M. Hengel, "Der Jakobusbrief als antipaulinische Polemik," in *Tradition and Interpretation in the New Testament*, (FS E. E. Ellis) (Tübingen/Grand Rapids: W. B. Eerdmans, 1987) 248–278. The extreme position of J. A. T. Robinson, *Redating the New Testament* (Philadelphia: Westminster, 1976), is consistent with his view as a whole in arguing that James is the oldest writing in the New Testament canon. In opposition to this view cf. K. Aland, "Der Herrenbruder Jakobus und der Jakobusbrief," in *Neutestamentliche Entwürfe* (TB 63. Munich: Kaiser, 1979) 233–245.

3  Detailed evidence in Martin Dibelius, *A Commentary on the Epistle of James*. Revised by Heinrich Greeven (Hermeneia. Philadelphia: Fortress Press, 1976) 33–37; F. Mussner, Der Jakobusbrief 26ff.

4  Cf. J. A. Fitzmyer, "The Languages of Palestine in the First Century A. D.", CBQ 32 (1970) 501–531.

5  Authorship by the brother of Jesus is excluded on linguistic grounds by A. Jülicher-E. Fascher, *Einleitung in das Neue Testament* (Tübingen: J. C. B. Mohr [Paul Siebeck], 1931) 205; J. H. Ropes, *Commentary* 49ff; A. H. McNeile, *Introduction to the New Testament* (Oxford 1927) 192; H. Windisch, *Die Katholischen Briefe* 35–36; Ph. Vielhauer, *Geschichte* 568–587.—So also the penetrating investigation of J. N. Sevenster, *Do You know Greek? How Much Greek could the First Jewish Christians have known?* (NT.S 19. Leiden: E. J. Brill, 1968), despite its tendency in the opposite direction, arrives only at this result: "Even though absolute certainty cannot be attained [on this point] ..., the possibility can no longer be precluded that a Palestine Jewish Christian of the first century A. D. wrote an epistle in good Greek" (191). The probability that this possibility ever actually occurred is—as the exceptional example drawn by Sevenster from Josephus (Ant XX 262–265) shows—extraordinarily small.

the witness of the New Testament indicates that James the Lord's brother was an adherent of the ritual law (Acts 15:13ff; 21:18ff), and as the later leader of the Jerusalem church attempted to influence the Hellenistic churches in the direction of Jewish observance (cf. Gal 2:12). Presumably this is the reason he was called ὁ δίκαιος ("the righteous one").[6] In contrast, the author of the Letter of James does not even hint that he is an advocate of the ceremonial law. In addition, we will see in the following that the tradition of Jesus' words reflected in James is not an adequate foundation for assuming that the author represents an early stage of the tradition of the Jesus material. We will also see that the relation to Paul is not that of a rival for leadership of the church but that there is no evidence of a direct acquaintance with Paul and the Pauline letters. Finally, the fact that the "authenticity" of the writing was still disputed in the time of Eusebius (Eus HE II 23.24–25) does not encourage us to think the document was written by Jesus' brother, especially since no concrete situation can be perceived that makes it any easier to locate the composition of the letter in the early Jerusalem church.

Except for the prescript, the document has none of the characteristics of a letter.[7] As indicated by the archaizing manner of expression referring to the addressees as "the twelve tribes of the Diaspora," the writing is directed to a universal Christian readership, not to a concrete situation.[8] Thus the time of its composition cannot be fixed very precisely; due to the similarity of some points of its content with other early Christian writings, it can be dated approximately within the last decades of the first century. According to its form and content, the Letter of James should be consid-

---

[6] Hegesippus in Jerome, VirInl 2; Gospel of Thomas 12; Hegesippus in Eusebius HE II 1.3; 23.4–6; on these texts cf. H. Kemler, *Der Herrenbruder Jakobus bei Hegesipp und in der frühchristlichen Literatur* (partial reprint of a dissertation, Göttingen 1966).

[7] James 1:1. Of course, there are elements in James analogous to the epistolary literature (cf. F. O. Francis, "The Form and Function of the Opening and Closing Paragraphs of James and I John," ZNW 61 [1970] 110–126). These, however, may be found not only in letters but also in other genres. The word μακάριος (1:12, 25), for example, is not a parallel to the εὐλογητός of 2 Corinthians 1:3, thus is not an element of the proem of a letter but has its closest parallel in the Psalms and especially in the wisdom literature: Psalms 1:1; 33:9; 40:1; 83:6; 93:12; 110:1; Proverbs 8:34; 28:14; Sirach 14:1, 20; Isaiah 56:2 LXX, and elsewhere.

[8] Compare James 1:1 with 1 Peter 1:1. The difficulty of determining the location both author and addressees is not only due to the intention of the author to speak to the church as a whole but also by the fact that this intention overlaps concrete experiences (as reflected for example in the theme "poor and rich" in 1:9ff and 2:1ff), as well as by the way in which the specific directions of the traditional material are now no longer appropriate to the context (cf. for example the prophetic-apocalyptic polemic against the rich, which contradicts the ethical style of James not only formally: 5:1–6).

ered a *parenetic tract*.[9] The "doctrine" it contains is concerned exclusively with theoretical problems of ethics, e.g. the relation of faith and works, and thus is directed to a practical-parenetic goal, as also indicated by the frequent direct address "my brothers and sisters,"[10] the pictures and metaphors, and the numerous imperatives.[11] The asyndetic compositional technique in terms of catchwords corresponds to a type of parenesis structured as lists of commands, and contributes to the impersonal character of the Letter of James. Nonetheless, we have here more than a mere "collection of aphorisms;"[12] the individual sayings are partially structured as chains that are connected by their content. Even though the context only rarely attains the stringency of the kind of argument found in a letter such as we find in the Pauline parenesis, it is still clear that there are particular subjects that are of concern to the author.[13]

From the point of view of the history of religions, the parenesis of James is influenced by a variety of influences, as indicated already by the different linguistic colorings: alongside elements of cultivated Greek that show a close connection to the Hellenistic philosophic diatribe (especially 2:14ff; 4:11) there are Semitisms, which in part may be recognized as Septuagint-

---

[9]  Cf. G. Strecker, *History of New Testament Literature* 49, and "Jakobusbrief" in EKL[3] 2 (1989) 794–795.

[10]  Ἀδελφοί μου ἀγαπητοί: 1:16, 19; 2:5; cf. ἀδελφοί μου: 1:2; 2:1, 14; 3:1, 10, 12; 5:10 (v.l.), 12, 19; ἀδελφοί 4:11; 5:7, 9.

[11]  Of 108 verses of James, 54 have an imperative structure; cf. G. Eichholz, *Jakobus und Paulus* (THE 39. Munich: Kaiser, 1953) 34. The imperative participles also belong here (1:3, 6; the interpretation of some aorist participles as imperatives is disputed: 1:21; 3:1; 5:14), which are not to be claimed as evidence for the presumed Semitic background of James. So also the lack of the genitive absolute, since this construction is found primarily in the narrative books of the New Testament.

[12]  As still regarded by Blass-Debrunner, §463.

[13]  On the outline: It is worthy of note but still artificial, that A. Meyer has attempted in *Das Rätsel des Jacobusbriefes* to divide James into twelve sections corresponding to the twelve tribes of Israel, from Rueben to Benjamin. The attempt of M. Dibelius has received a better response, *A Commentary on the Epistle of James*, according to whom the document is to be divided into three groups of proverbs arranged in a series (1:2–18, on temptations; 1:19–27, on hearing and doing; 5:7–20, on a variety of themes), two groups of sayings (3:13–4:12, against quarreling; 4:13–5:6: against worldly business leaders and rich people), and three brief essays (2:1–13, on respecting persons; 2:14–26, on faith and works; 3:1–12, on the tongue). From this arrangement which is based on grounds of both form and content we can discern that the composition of the Letter of James as a whole has been worked out more carefully than one would suppose on the basis of Dibelius' exegesis, which essentially deals with the sayings as isolated units. Cf. R. Walker, who points to the distinction between concrete (e.g. 1:2–4, 26–27; 3:1, 3–12; 4:11–12; 5:7ff) and general parenesis (1:22–25; 2:10–12; 14–26) ("Allein aus Werken. Zur Auslegung von Jakobus 2,14–26," ZThK 61 [1964] 155–156). To be sure, the boundaries between special and general parenesis remain fluid (cf. e.g. 2:8–9). For determining the theological profile of the document, one must begin with the general statements.

isms.[14] The intellectual sphere in and for which the author composes his message thus represents a broad spectrum. The content of the parenesis corresponds to this. In broad terms we may say that this content reflects the ethical tradition that belongs to the heritage of the cultural realm of the Old Testament and Hellenistic Judaism, and that this tradition has found an entré into early Christian tradition without any break in its continuity. No particular orientation or direction seems to provide the exclusive framework within which the author has sorted out and interpreted these traditions. There are certainly elements adopted from the wisdom tradition of Hellenistic Judaism. The pragmatic ethic of the Hellenistic Jewish wisdom teaching has parallels in James not only with regard to items of content.[15] Thus in two passages the divine sophia appears as an almost personal being but characteristically not within the framework of a developed wisdom myth but in delineating the ethical difference between right and wrong.[16] There is no literary dependence on the wisdom writings. The transition points to the traditions of the wider Hellenistic-Jewish traditions are fluid. That from the viewpoint of the history of religions, this wider Hellenistic-Jewish tradition is the ultimate background of the parenesis in James is seen from numerous items of tradition: the citation of Old Testament commands according to the Septuagint (2:11, the Decalogue), the way the relation of poor and rich is conceived, and in particular the biblical material that has developed independently beyond the text of the Old Testament without having a Christian origin.[17] So also the threats reminiscent of Old Testament prophecy (5:1ff, against the rich) and the apocalyptic ideas (1:12; 4:12; 5:3, 7–8) are ultimately based on this foundation. In this process Stoic traditions were also influential, especially in the metaphors that illumine the parenesis.[18] Finally, it was the early

---

[14]  For the specifics, cf. J. H. Ropes, *Commentary* 10–16; F. Mussner, *Der Jakobusbrief* 30–31.

[15]  The agreements are emphasized by U. Luck, "Weisheit und Leiden," ThLZ 92 (1967) 254–256. Compare especially James 1:2ff with WisSol 3:4–5; 6:12–21; Sir 4:17 (LXX); 1:4–5 with WisSol 9:1ff (cf. Matt 11:29); 1:10 with Sir 10:13–22; Koheleth 10:6; Isaiah 40:6–7; 1:12, 25 with Daniel 12:12 (Theod); WisSol 3:5–6 5:16; 1:19 with Sir 5:13; Koheleth 5:1; 7:9; Aboth I 15; James 3:15, 17 with Prov 2:6; WisSol 7:15ff; 9:13ff; 4:6 with Sir 3:20–21; Prov 3:24; 29:25 (LXX); 4:10 with Job 5:11.

[16]  James 3:15, 17 (the wisdom that comes from above in contrast to earthly, psychic wisdom); cf. 1 Enoch 42:1–3 (descent and return of Wisdom, and her opposition to "unrighteousness"). Cf. F. Christ, *Jesus Sophia. Die Sophia-Christologie bei den Synoptikern* (AThANT 57. Zürich: Zwingli, 1970) 48ff.

[17]  Thus the reference to the prayer of Elijah in 5:17 presupposes the legend that the drought lasted three and a half years (so also Luke 4:25; cf. also 5:17), while in 1 Kings 18:1 rain came in the third year.

[18]  Compare to 1:6 ("waves of the sea"): Dio Chrys Or 32:23; already Demosthenes Or 19.136; to 1:23 ("mirror"): Epictetus II 14.21; Seneca Nat I 17.4; to 3:3ff ("the

Christian ethical tradition that was the primary factor in shaping the parenesis in James. It was the final, decisive stage through which the other materials passed, even though a direct adoption of non-Christian ethical material may not be excluded.

The disparity among the various traditional elements of the ethical material becomes especially visible when the question is researched of whether or to what extent *the tradition of Jesus' words* has been used. After a critical screening of the passages listed by G. Kittel and the elimination of clearly secondary Synoptic material, 27 texts remain, most of which appear to be connected to the Sermon on the Mount.[19] Careful examination shows that the problems are of strikingly different kinds. The sayings material may be sorted into five categories:

1. To be excluded from the discussion are the texts for which neither a linguistic nor material parallel to the dominical sayings can be recognized. *2:6* That the rich people oppress their debtors has a material point of contact in the Jesus tradition at the most in Luke 18:3; one might more readily think of Amos 4:1; 8:4 as the background for this motif in the tradition. So also *5:9a* can hardly be compared with Matthew 5:22 and 7:1; while in James it is a matter of inner-congregational lament for the injustice that the community must endure (cf. also the "inner sighing" of Rom 8:23), the Matthean text is a warning not to do wrong to each other. Finally, the text in *1:17* is of Hellenistic Jewish origin ("Every generous act of giving, with every perfect gift, is from above, coming down from the Father of lights, with whom there is no variation or shadow due to change") and has only a weak parallel in Matthew 7:11; its structure and language point to independent Jewish tradition (on the expression "Father of lights," cf. especially Apoc Mos 36:38; Test Abr 7:6; Philo Ebr 81).

2. Not Jesus but *early Christian* tradition is reflected in the following texts: *1:6* (of faith that does not doubt); there is no close connection to Matthew 21:21, since James does not use the picture of the faith that moves mountains; on the other hand, διακρίνομαι is not found with the meaning "doubt" prior to New Testament usage, and is thus an element

---

tongue"): not only the "optimistic" but also the "pessimistic" tone characteristic of James is already found in the Greek-Stoic tradition: Dio Chrys Or 12.34; 36.50 (comparison with a ship or the tongue of a wagon); Lucretius rer nat IV 860ff (domination over the body): Epict I 12:26 (small cause; great effect); to 3:11–12 (that sweet and bitter water are not found in the same fountain; different fruits from one tree); Epictetus II 20.18; Plutarch Tranq 13; Seneca Ep 87.25; cf. H. Windisch, *Die Katholischen Briefe* 25 ("Stoic school tradition").

19  Cf. G. Kittel, "Der geschichtliche Ort des Jakobusbriefes," ZNW 41 (1942) 71–105 (esp. 84–94); M. H. Shepherd, "The Epistle of James and the Gospel of Matthew," JBL 75 (1956) 40–51; F. Mussner, *Der Jakobusbrief* 42–52 (esp. 48–50); W. D. Davies, *The Setting of the Sermon on the Mount* (Cambridge: Cambridge University Press, 1964) 401–404; J. Cantinat, *St. Jacques* 27–28.

of the language of early Christian faith (cf. James 2:4; Rom 4:20; 14:23; Acts 10:20; Jude 22). *2:14–16* (faith and works): There are Jewish parallels to this theme, also presupposed in Matthew 7:21; 25:35–36. James, however, reflects a specifically Christian discussion of justification already influenced by Paul (see below). *5:9b* ("See, the Judge is standing at the doors!"), documents early Christian apocalyptic tradition (cf. Mark 13:29; Rev 3:20); so also *5:7* ("Be patient, therefore, beloved, until the coming of the Lord"), although in each case it is a matter of secondary Christianizing of an originally Jewish-apocalyptic motif (cf. Mal 3:1; 1 Enoch 1:3ff; 92ff; Test Jud 22:2). *5:12* goes back to a pre-Synoptic piece of tradition that is still secondary in comparison to the original antithesis of Matthew 5:33–34a. *5:19–20* (admonition to restore the erring brother or sister) reflects the structure of the early Christian congregation, which has a parallel in Matthew 18:15ff; Jewish influence can be detected in each case.

3. The majority of passages are to be placed in neither group 1. or 2. above. But here too the "Jesus tradition" is not the only possible source. Thus in the following texts a *Hellenistic element* can be discerned such as is found in the other material in James: *1:5* ("... ask God, who gives to all generously and ungrudgingly, and it will be given you;" cf. 4:3): Differently than in Matthew 7:7, despite the passive construction the name of God is not avoided;[20] the content of the prayer refers to σοφία, as transmitted in the wisdom tradition of Hellenistic Judaism (e.g. WisSol 7:7; 9:4; for the Old Testament background cf. also 2 Chron 1:10 [prayer for wisdom]; Jer 29:12 [hearing of prayer]). *1:23* connects the juxtaposition of hearing and doing[21] with the image of the mirror, which was widespread in Hellenistic ethical instruction (e.g. Seneca Nat I 17.4; Epictetus II 14.21). *3:12* That the fig tree bears no olives, the grapevine bears no figs, is a picture found not only in Matthew 7:16par but generally in the Hellenistic world (e.g. Seneca Ep 87.25; Plutarch Tranq 13; Epictetus II 20.18; Philo Aet 66). *4:13–15* Making plans for the future is disapproved not only in Matthew 6:34, to which there are no linguistic bridges except for the little word αὔριον, but also in Proverbs 27:1; Sirach 11:19, and in several relevant texts of Hellenistic Judaism. *5:5* (condemnation of the luxury and indulgence of the rich) should not only be compared with Luke 16:19 and 21:34, which have a similar theme but no linguistic points of contact. It is rather the case that σπαταλάω ("live in self-indulgence") is found elsewhere in the New Testament only in the Pastorals, where as here Hellenistic material has been adopted (1 Tim 5:6; cf. also Sir 21:15 LXX); cf. also Barnabas 10:3 (the rich are compared to swine that live well but do not acknowledge their master; similarly Hermas Sim VI 1.6; 2.6 [well-fed sheep in the meadow];

---

20   Correspondingly, 4:10 vs. Matthew 23:12par.
21   See below on 1:22 (cf. Matt 7:24).

the verb τρυφάω ("live in luxury") is found only here in the New Testament; cf. also Hermas Sim VI 4.1–2, 4; 5.3–5 (about the rich); in a disdainful sense also Sirach 14:4 LXX.

4. A few texts represent the stream of tradition of *"piety of the poor,"* which apart from James is found elsewhere in the New Testament especially in the Lucan historical work but which goes back to the Old Testament and pre-Christian Judaism.[22] *2:5ff* A comparison with the blessing of the poor in Luke 6:20 (Matt 5:3) reveals that the two texts are not very close; in James there is no corresponding beatitude. One might rather think of Luke 12:16ff; 16:19ff and other New Testament pericopes that speak of Jesus' mission to the poor and disenfranchised, and beyond that to the pre-Christian tradition in the Old Testament and Judaism according to which the poor and oppressed are the special objects of God's mercy: Psalm 37; Isaiah 57:15; 61:1ff, and others (see below). *5:1* The threat against the rich has no verbal points of contact with the woe against the rich in Luke 6:24. To *5:2* (riches are temporary) there is a thematic parallel in Matthew 6:19–20 but no verbal parallels (on the picture of moth and rust, cf. also Isa 51:8). 5:5 also belongs in this context (cf. the preceding paragraph).

5. Finally, another category is represented by the following texts, which, while they have points of contact with the Synoptic tradition and are the most likely of the texts considered to go back to Jesus tradition but also have an Old Testament-Jewish background in terms of their content and to some extent in terms of their language. *1:22* (cf. 1:23, 25): The contrast between hearing and doing of the word is also found in Matthew 7:24, 26; the parable of the builders, however, is not found in James. This contrast itself is not only known to the early Christian ethical tradition (cf. Matt 7:21; Rom 2:13) but is already found in the Old Testament (e.g. Deut 30:8ff; Ezek 33:32), just as it is also present in later Jewish tradition (cf. M. Dibelius, *Commentary on the Epistle of James* 114). *2:13* The saying about compassion, that "mercy triumphs over judgment," not only has a parallel in Matthew 5:7 (though of course James has no corresponding beatitude) but elsewhere in early Christian parenesis as well (cf. James 3:17; Matt 9:13; 12:7; 18:21ff; 25:34ff; Luke 10:37; Rom 12:8, and elsewhere) but also in the Old Testament (e.g. Prov 17:5) and in later Jewish tradition (e.g. Sir 28:4; Tob 4:9–11; Ps.-Phocylides XI; Shab 151b). *3:1–12:* These admonitions are climaxed by the command to keep one's tongue under control. They not only are reminiscent of Matthew 12:36–37 but connect the wisdom tradition of Jewish ethics and the Greek diatribe (cf. Sir 5:13; 19:16; 25:8; 28:17 LXX; 1QS 10.21ff; Av 1.17). *3:18* That "peace" and "fruit of righteousness" belong together is not said in the Beatitude of

---

[22] Cf. below F. IV. d.

Matthew 5:9 but is closer to Isaiah 32:17 and Hebrews 12:11. *4:4* is not to be compared primarily with the saying about serving mammon or God in Matthew 6:24par but has Old Testament roots (cf. the figurative meaning of "adultery:" Isa 57:3–4; Ezek 16:15ff; also Matt 12:39par); the eschatological-ethical contrast "God/world" is already included in it, which is expressed in the second part and is parallel not only to Matthew 6:24 but also to Romans 8:1ff; 1 John 2:15ff; 2 Clement 6:3; Philo Her 243; Josephus Ant 9.14.1. *4:9* The transformation of laughter into sorrow is also found in the late layer of tradition represented by the woe of Luke 6:25. While in James the saying is an ethical admonition, in Luke it is a prophetic threat (similarly Amos 8:10). *4:10* That humbling oneself leads to exaltation is also said in Matthew 23:12par; a similar saying is found in 1 Peter 5:6; it derives from Old Testament tradition (cf. Job 22:29; Ezek 17:24; 21:31; Prov 3:34; 29:23). *4:17* ("Anyone, then, who knows the right thing to do and fails to do it, commits sin.") This saying has at the most a material parallel in Luke 12:47. There are numerous similar text in the tradition of the New Testament (John 9:41; 13:17; 2 Pet 2:21), the Old Testament (Job 31:16–18), Hellenistic Judaism (Philo Flacc 7), and the rabbinic literature (LevR 25). Thus the Synoptic tradition is only one of several possible parallels for its content. *5:17* The reference to Elijah's prayer for the drought has no parallel in Luke 4:25, except for the datum that the drought lasted three and a half years; the reference in 1 Kings 18:1 is to the "third year." It may be that the period specified in Daniel 7:25 and 12:7 has influenced both passages. It is possible that James and Luke independently drew the datum from a Jewish exegetical tradition.

*We may summarize the results as follows:* The investigation of the so-called tradition of Jesus' words in James actually represents the same streams of tradition we have found in the rest of James: ethical instructions derived primarily from the Old Testament and Judaism, in which Hellenistic-Jewish elements predominate but which also contain influences from the pagan Hellenistic world and from early Christian traditions. There is no evidence that the author used either the Gospel of Matthew, the other canonical Gospels, or the Q-source. The individual parallels to Synoptic speech material seem to go back to pre-Synoptic tradition (e.g. 1:22; 4:9–10; 5:12); of course, a clear distinction between non-Christian and early Christian materials cannot always be made. Thus the question of whether authentic words of Jesus have been reworked in these texts can only be posed but not definitively answered. Against an affirmative answer stands the fact that the form of a saying of Jesus never appears in James—it is an intelligent but somewhat daring conclusion, to infer from this as does F. Hauck that precisely this is a sign of the living oral tradition that stands especially close to the historical Jesus.[23] And

23    F. Hauck, *Der Brief des Jakobus* 12.

against the view that the "spirit of Jesus" can be detected in James[24] stands the decisive fact that the preaching of the historical Jesus presupposes a prophetic-apocalyptic orientation that belongs within the realm of Judaism, while the author of James represents an ethical-wisdom kind of thought that—despite his borrowing from the parenetic and apocalyptic tradition of Judaism—is molded by the medium of Christian tradition. His goal is, supported by the authority of James the brother of the Lord, to communicate binding ethical instruction to the Christian community of his time, which lives as the New Israel in the Diaspora (1:1), and thereby to provide them with a goal and support for their journey.

## b)   The Foundation for Ethics—The Perfect Law of Freedom

The fact that there are thus several layers and streams of tradition to be found in the Letter of James means that it is not to be explained merely from Jewish presuppositions; it is rather the case that we have here *an authentic Christian document*. The polished formula found in the prescript already presupposes the Kyrios Christology familiar from the beginnings of other New Testament letters.[25] Here also the Christ title has become a proper name (cf. already 1 Thess 1:1, 3; 5:9, 23, 28). Faith is oriented to the "Lord Jesus Christ," the exalted Kyrios, whose essential being is marked by eschatological glory.[26]

Even though nothing further is said about the content of the confession of Christ, it is still clear that the credo is not to be separated from the apocalyptic orientation of the ethic of James as a whole. These apocalyptic statements are a further indication of the non-Jewish, Christian character

---

[24]   F. Mussner, *Der Jakobusbrief* 31.

[25]   To James 1:1 compare 1 Thessalonians 1:1; Romans 1:1–4; 2 Peter 1:2. Thus κύριος in James 1:1, as elsewhere in James, designates the exalted Lord of the church. To be sure, the boundary between this usage and the word as a designation of God is fluid. In any case, the latter meaning is presupposed in 1:7; 3:9; 4:10, 15; 5:4, 10–11.

[26]   James 2:1. The exegetical difficulty consists not only in the fact that apart from 1:1 only here in James does the designation τοῦ κυρίου ἡμῶν Ἰησοῦ Χριστοῦ appear but especially in the grammatical connection with τῆς δόξης. The suggestion of F. Spitta and H. Windisch that ἡμῶν Ἰησοῦ Χριστοῦ be removed as a later interpolation is too violent. Likewise unsatisfactory is the attempt to understand τῆς δόξης as a second genitive dependent on τοῦ κυρίου (corresponding to the construction in 1 Cor 2:8); this would not adequately explain the doubling of the genitive and would postulate a repetition of the κύριος title. Placing τῆς δόξης at the beginning, directly connected to τὴν πίστιν (as found in the Syriac texts and elsewhere—obviously a secondary smoothing of the awkward expression) is too weakly attested to represent the original text. The most probable interpretation, suggested by the context, is to interpret the expression as a qualitative genitive modifying the preceding name Ἰησοῦ Χριστοῦ (cf. Heb 9:5).

of the document. Analogous to other contemporary Christian literature, an awareness of the delay of the parousia is presupposed (5:7; cf. also the admonitions to "patience," that reckon with a long time before the end comes (1:3–4; 5:11), which stands alongside the cry of early Christianity that is still preserved, "the parousia of the Lord is near.[27] That the apocalyptic expectation is an essential ethical motivation is seen in the explicit sharpening of the community's responsibility in view of the future judgment (2:12–13). The Judge stands before the door (5:9); he will save or condemn (4:12). It is emphasized that the group of Christian teachers must expect an especially strict judgment (3:1). The final judgment[28] will strictly punish transgressions (judging one's brother or sister, 5:9; taking oaths and falsehood, 5:12; cf. also the judgment on the rich, 5:1–6) but will also reward good conduct (the promise of the "crown of life," 1:12; the inheritance of the kingdom, 2:5).

Just as older Jewish elements have been woven into the apocalyptic statements and given a Christian horizon, this is also the case, though to a smaller degree, with allusions to *baptism*. Just as in the Old Testament perspective the name of God was invoked on Israel and the people thereby declared to be Yahweh's property,[29] so something similar has happened for the Christian community. At baptism "the good name," obviously the name of the Lord Jesus Christ, is pronounced over the baptismal candidates.[30] They know that henceforth they are bound to Christ and are considered his property. While further conclusions about a baptismal parenesis among James' traditions remain hypothetical, it is still clear that the event of baptism coincides with the event of the believer's being chosen to belong to the people of God.[31] As the transfer of the believer to the realm

---

[27]  James 5:8; cf. Philippians 4:5; 1 Peter 4:7; Revelation 1:1, 3; 22:20; Didache 10:6; 16:1–7; Ignatius Eph 11:1; Hermas Vis II 2.5ff; Barnabas 4:9; 2 Clement 12.1–6; 16.3.

[28]  On the terminology: κρίσις can be used in both a neutral sense (2:13) and a negative sense (5:12), just as the κριτής can bring both salvation and destruction (4:12; cf. 5:9). Despite its neutral use in 2:12, the verb κρίνω has a negative accent (5:9). Κρίμα means the destructive condemnation of the judge's decision (3:1). As to secular usage: 4:11–12 (κρίνω in the negative sense); 2:4 and 4:11 (κριτής); 2:6 (κριτήρια = courts).

[29]  Deuteronomy 28:10; Isaiah 43:7; Jeremiah 14:9; 2 Chronicles 7:14; 2 Maccabees 8:15.

[30]  James 2:7; cf. Acts 2:38; 8:16; 10:48; 19:5; cf. also Galatians 3:27; 1 Corinthians 1:15; Romans 6:3. So also anointing the sick with oil happens "in the name of the Lord" (5:14); κύριος here means the exalted Christ. Early Christian tradition, despite the Old Testament connection, mostly interpreted the expression "to call on the name of the Lord" christologically (Acts 2:21/Joel 3:5; Acts 15:17/Amos 9:12) and used it as a designation of Christian prayer (1 Cor 1:2; Acts 22:16).

[31]  James 2:5, 7; cf. G. Braumann, "Der theologische Hintergrund des Jakobusbriefes," ThZ 18 (1962) 401–410; esp. 409–410.

of Christ, baptism is the foundation of Christian existence; thus the persecutions suffered by members of the church are understood as directed against Christ himself (2:7 as exposition of 2:6b). A reflection of baptism is also found in the statement that "In fulfillment of his own purpose he gave us birth (ἀπεκύησεν) by the word of truth, so that we would become a kind of first fruits of his creatures" (1:18). The sacrament of baptism is accordingly not only interpreted soteriologically, as the regeneration of the person who becomes a Christian, but at the same time is placed in a cosmic perspective (similarly Rom 8:21): those who are baptized are placed in a new existence by the "word of truth," whose power is manifest through the sacrament, a new existence that not only means salvation for them but bears with it hope for the whole cosmos.[32]

The "word of truth" is not only bound to the sacrament; it is also mediated by preaching. By mediating "truth," this word separates the church from "error" (5:19). It is the "implanted word" that is spoken not only in baptismal instruction but is spoken by the proclamation of the church in general (1:21; cf. Barnabas 9:9). Such a word includes both eschatological promise and ethical instruction. It is not enough to learn the content of this word; it must be realized in action. Only in this way does it lead to the eschatological goal that is its purpose, "to save your souls" (1:21–23; cf. Barnabas 19:10), and only through such activity does the church correspond to the Spirit that God has given it.[33]

As a parenetic tractate, the Letter of James as a whole can be understood as a "word of address," or more precisely as an wisdom instruction, a concretion of "sophia." Just as this is given to the believer in response

---

[32] On the image of baptism as a (re-)birth, cf. 1 John 3:9; John 3:5; Romans 6:4; Titus 3:5; 1 Peter 1:23. Apart from James 1:15, 18 the word ἀποκυέω is not found in the New Testament; in extra-canonical literature it is used mostly of childbirth. It is referred to God also in Clement of Alexandria Paed I 6.45 (ἀποκυηθέντες ... ἀναγεννηθέντες); of cosmic "begetting:" Pseudo-Clementine Homilies VI 4.3; 5.1, 3; 12.1. The idea of begetting by God is found especially in Hellenistic Judaism (Philo); cf. H. Windisch, *Die Katholischen Briefe* 122–123, on 1 John 3:9.

On the cosmic "new creation" cf. also C.-M. Edsman, "Schöpferwille und Geburt. Jak 1,18. Eine Studie zur altchristlichen Kosmologie," ZNW 38 (1939) 11–44; G. Schneider, *Neuschöpfung oder Wiederkehr* (Düsseldorf: Patmos, 1961). According to H. Schammberger, 1:18 intentionally takes up "gnostic ideas" and Christianizes them (*Die Einheitlichkeit des Jakobusbriefes* 58–63)—an improbable assumption. G. Braumann ("Der theologische Hintergrund" 406) counts among the early Christian traditions reworked by James: 1:21; 2:14; 4:12; 5:15, 20). His basis is that each of these passages contains the verb σῴζω; but this word cannot be restricted to the act of baptism.

[33] James 4:5b; this is the only passage in James that speaks of the πνεῦμα [θεοῦ] (cf. 2:26, the human spirit), obviously a quotation (hexameter) from an unknown source. The original meaning remains obscure. Within this context it means that the Spirit given by God should cause people to struggle against worldly passions and to decide for God's claim upon them.

to prayer (1:5), it is a gift that "comes from above" (3:15, 17) and fulfills its function in ethical instruction: those who have wisdom also practice patient endurance (1:4–5) and know that they are obligated to embody "meekness" in their own lives.[34] Earthly and heavenly wisdom are just as mutually exclusive as vices and virtues. If the former include jealousy and quarreling, disorder and every evil deed,[35] the "wisdom from above" includes purity, then peaceableness, gentleness, willingness to yield, mercy, good fruits, without partiality or hypocrisy (3:17). The supposition that such a separation from the world reflects a confrontation with a Gnostic-libertine wisdom teaching has no basis either in its content or in its reference to earthly wisdom as "psychic" or "demonic."[36] It is rather the case that this catalogue of alternatives brings to expression that true wisdom, by teaching the way of right conduct, always stands over against false teaching. Those who follow right instruction will become a "perfect" (τέλειος) or "complete" (ὁλόκληρος) person, i.e. they will realize in their own lives the counsels of wisdom not only qualitatively but in a complete, full sense (1:4; on ὁλόκληρος cf. also 1 Thess 5:23: complete in the ethical sense). Since this wisdom excludes "impurity" and "sins," but is identical with the "healing of the hearts," such wholeness does away with the inner division of the believer (4:8 δίψυχοι; cf. 1:8).

If one by the leadership of wisdom becomes "simple" and thus "perfect," this corresponds to the "perfect law of liberty" (1:25 νόμος τέλειος ὁ τῆς ἐλευθερίας; cf. 2:12) that is, the "royal law" (2:8 νόμος βασιλικός), i.e. the law given by God as from a king,[37] but also itself possessing a royal rank, since it has a liberating effect and points to the future βασιλεία.[38] This understanding of the law is very different from the understanding current in the Gentile Christianity contemporary with the author, according to which the Jewish law was understood as an enslaving yoke that was taken

---

[34] James 3:13 ἐν πραΰτητι σοφίας; so also 1:21 (P, 1852).
[35] James 3:16; on the (uncertain) meaning of ἐριθεία ("quarrelsomeness;" "selfish ambition") cf. Bauer BAGD 309.
[36] Cf. ἐπίγειος, ψυχική, δαιμονιώδης (3:15); H. Schammberger, *Einheitlichkeit* 33ff; U. Wilckens, TDNT 7:525; this assumption presupposes that James combats the Gnostic teaching with its own weapons. The listed expressions, however, are not genuinely Gnostic; cf. F. Mussner, *Der Jakobusbrief* 171–172.
[37] Cf. K. L. Schmidt, TDNT 1:591.
[38] James 2:5; W. D. Davies, *Setting* 405, understands the "royal law" as "messianic Torah," the "Torah of the Messiah." The terminology used here occurs nowhere else in the New Testament, nor is it documented in the New Testament environment. The attempt of E. Stauffer to identify the expression "law of liberty" in the Qumran Manual of Discipline (Das "Gesetz der Freiheit" in der Ordensregel von Jericho, ThLZ 77 [1952] 527–532) has been thoroughly refuted by F. Nötscher, "'Gesetz der Freiheit' im Neuen Testament und in der Mönchsgemeinde am Toten Meer," *Bib* 34 (1953) 193–194; cf. H. Braun, *Qumran und das Neue Testament* I 279–280.

away by the preaching of Christ (Acts 15:10; Barnabas 2:6). Over against this James advocates an independent position, which does not disown the influence of Jewish tradition. After all, in Judaism one can also speak of the liberating effect of the Torah.[39] So also Stoic teaching is familiar with the idea that obedience to God leads to inner freedom.[40] Differently than in the Jewish tradition, however, in James there is no affirmation of the Old Testament-Jewish ceremonial law; but there is also no purely internal "ethic of principles/attitudes." It is rather the case that the "law of liberty" designates *the concrete ethical demand, as grounded in the Old Testament and interpreted by James' own wisdom instruction.* It thereby becomes clear that the freedom that James teaches does not bypass the law but takes place through fulfilling the law. In contrast to the core affirmation of Pauline theology, obedience to the law and consciousness of freedom stand in a positive relation to one another. The statement that Christ is the end of the law (Rom 10:4) could not be understood by James,[41] just as the "law of liberty" cannot be identified with the norm that Christ himself is (νόμος τοῦ Χριστοῦ Gal 6:2). Differently than the Pauline norm of faith (Rom 3:27), James "law of liberty" has no critique of the law inherent within it. It is rather the case that the law's ethical demand makes a total, unbroken claim. According to an ancient Jewish rule, the transgression of a single commandment makes one guilty of the whole law (cf. Aboth 3.9). James 2:10 says the same. In applying the "usus elenchticus legis" there is at first an agreement with the Pauline parallel,[42] but James does not draw the conclusion that the inference that the law is no way of salvation but rather places the traditional Jewish thesis in the context of parenetic admonition (2:8–13): salvation comes through the law. The law is identical with the "gospel!"

How is the "law of liberty" related to the "love commandment?" If the former is also identical with the "royal law," this suggests a further identification with the command to love the neighbor (2:8). However, this appears as only one requirement of the law alongside others; the author has not attempted to reflect in principle on the "real" requirement of the law as such. Although he knows that alongside the command to love the neighbor (according to Lev 19:18) Christians are obligated to love God (1:12; 2:5), the double commandment of love is not handled thematically

---

39 Aboth 3.6 ("He that takes upon himself the yoke of the Law, from him shall be taken away the yoke of the kingdom [the troubles suffered at the hands of those in power] and the yoke of worldly care"); 6:2 ("Only those are free who are occupied with the Torah.")

40 E.g. Seneca, Vita 15.

41 Contra J. Cantinat, *Saint Jacques* 111.

42 Galatians 3:10 (cf. Deut 27:26); Galatians 2:18; 5:3; Romans 2:25, 27; for the Jewish background cf. Philo All 3.241; Pseudo-Clementine Homilies XIII 14.3.

and—differently than Matthew 22:40—is not described as the sum of the law.[43] The "law of liberty" as the "royal law" means rather "the law of which the commandment in question is only a part."[44] That there are other individual commands alongside the command to love the neighbor is seen by the enumeration in 2:8ff, which commends impartiality and the keeping of the sixth and fifth commands as examples of the particular demands of "the whole law," which in this same way must be fulfilled in its totality (2:10–11). If the author had intentionally wanted to emphasize the love commandment as the comprehensive content of the "law of liberty," it would be expected that he would have said so at the conclusion of this section. The concluding appeal to practice "mercy," corresponding to the whole context (2:1ff), does mean substantially the same thing as the command to love the neighbor but does not use this terminology. This may have been caused by the use of traditional material here,[45] but at the same time it is an indication that in the Letter of James there is no intention to make the whole law subordinate to the love command as the chief command of the law. At the most one may say on the basis of the tendency of this section that the author is on the way to representing the command of love for the neighbor as the essential content of the demand of the law binding on Christians. His intention, of explaining the whole content of the Old Testament law, with the obvious exception of its ritual elements, as binding on Christians, inhibits his drawing the ultimate consequences of this tendency and declaring the love command as the standard for the binding character and the summary of the Old Testament.[46]

The question of whether the ethic of the Letter of James is grounded in its theology need no longer be explicitly posed. Even though the Letter of James is a Christian document and presupposes the confession of faith in the Christ kerygma, there is still no reflection on the relation of the christological indicative to the ethical imperative. The concentration on wisdom instruction, the establishment of the word of truth, i.e. the exposition of the law of liberty, seems to the author to make unnecessary any reflection on a motivation for ethics that is prior to his own practical-parenetic intention, a reflection that might in fact show its limitations. To

---

[43]   C. Spicq, *Agape in the New Testament* (3 vols. St. Louis & London: B. Herder Book Co., 1963) 2:1–2 points to the fact that the substantive ἀγάπη is not found in James and the verb ἀγαπάω only three times. This is not an argument for the early date of James but more correctly an indication how much James is indebted to Jewish or early Christian ethical tradition.

[44]   M. Dibelius, *Commentary on the Epistle of James* 142.

[45]   Cf. H. Windisch, *Die Katholischen Briefe* 16.

[46]   Contra R. Schnackenburg, *The Moral Teaching of the New Testament* (New York: Seabury, 1973); K.-G. Eckart, "Zur Terminologie des Jakobusbriefes," ThLZ 89 (1964) 521–526 (523).

the extent that a grounding of ethics is attempted at all, it is connected with the wisdom-apocalyptic horizon of the writing, with the expectation of judgment at the future appearance of the Kyrios. The lack of ethical grounding on the basis of the Christ event of the past fits a specific theological concern of the author's, namely his discussion of the relation of faith and works.

## c)   Faith and Works[47]

The section *2:14–26* deals with the problem of faith and works in an extensive debate with a Christian position that had already become traditional. The section is thematically independent; despite the unquestionable parenetic concern the connection to the context is not simply additive but consciously formed: the sharpening of responsibility before the judgment (2:13) is taken up with the admonition not to have faith without works (2:14). The command not to disdain the poor in the community (v. 2ff) and to practice mercy (v. 13) is continued in the example of "faith without works," as the lack of charity for fellow Christians in need is portrayed.[48] The key word "have faith" in v. 14 points back to v. 1. Moreover, the echoes of the Pauline thought world, which have already been heard in the preceding (v. 10), attain particular strength in this section. As this already makes clear that the passage is integrated into a more comprehensive compositional plan, it is also seen in the discussions that follow: the announcement of judgment (3:1) takes up 2:13, and the warning against misuse of the tongue (3:2ff) is prepared for in 1:19, 26. The author has thus intentionally inserted the theme "faith and works" into

---

[47]   Literature: M. Dibelius, *A Commentary on the Epistle of James* 174–180 (Excursus: "Faith and Works in Paul and James"); E. Lohse, "Glaube und Werke. Zur Theologie des Jakobusbriefes," ZNW 48 (1957) 1–22, = *Einheit des Neuen Testaments*, (Göttingen: Vandenhoeck & Ruprecht, 1976²) 285–306; G. Eichholz, *Glaube und Werke bei Paulus und Jakobus* (TEH 88. Munich: Kaiser, 1961); R. Walker, "Allein aus Glauben. Zur Auslegung von Jak 2,14–26," ZThK 61 (1964), 155–192; U. Luck, "Der Jakobusbrief und die Theologie des Paulus" ThGl 61 (1971) 161–179; F. Mussner, *Der Jakobusbrief* 146–150 (Excursus: "Die Rechtfertigung des Menschen nach Jakobus"); D. Lührmann, *Glaube im frühen Christentum* (Gütersloh: Gerd Mohn, 1976) 78–84; R. Heiligenthal, *Werke als Zeichen* (WUNT II/9. Tübingen: J. C. B. Mohr [Paul Siebeck], 1983) 26–52; Chr. Burchard, "Zu Jakobus 2,14–16" ZNW 71 (1980) 27–45; G. Lüdemann, *Opposition to Paul in Jewish Christianity* (Minneapolis: Fortress, 1989) 140–149.

[48]   James 2:15–16; the problem of whether we have here an "example" or a "comparison," is unimportant when one sees that the theme "faith without works" permeates the whole section and the question of whether the author has an actual case in mind to which he alludes is not even to be raised (cf. M. Dibelius, *A Commentary on the Epistle of James* 152–153).

this particular parenetic context and attempted to deepen it in the direction of a fundamental problem.

The basic *intention* is made clear by the introductory questions: "What good is it, my brothers and sisters, if you say you have faith but do not have works? Can faith (without works) save you?" The point of this question is not only to emphasize the necessity of good works but rather to demonstrate the theological impossibility of separating faith from works. The exposition proceeds in the form of a dialogical instruction that shows the influence of the Stoic lecturing style. The characteristic expression is "What good is it..." (2:14, 16);[49] so also the quoting of imaginary conversation partners, "If someone says..." (2:14); "You believe..." (2:19); "Do you want to be shown, you senseless person,...?" (2:20). The objection of an imaginary opponent, usually called a "second," is also an indication of rhetorical formulation. This objector—even when he takes his stand on the side of works—appears to recommend the separation of faith and works and thus contradicts the real intention of the author, which is to show that faith without works is useless.[50]

The reference to the faith of demons is characteristic of the *understanding of faith* that is presupposed throughout. The demons confess their "faith" that there is one God but still only "tremble" (v. 19). Although the author himself explicitly affirms the content of this confession, for him such a faith that is restricted to theoretical truth is of no value, because the obedience that is the necessary ingredient of true faith is missing. It is not that James is rejecting a purely theoretical faith—such an understanding is in fact characteristic of his own concept of πίστις—but what he does reject is the idea that salvation can come by faith alone (2:20; cf. v. 14). There is no denying the implicit anti-Pauline point of this thesis, even though there is no direct polemic against Paul. One is standing too much under the spell of Pauline-Reformation theology when it is affirmed that "according to James the only [justifying] faith is that which shows it is true faith by works of love."[51] This is also true when one would like to exclude this position and instead affirm that in James faith is to be understood as

---

[49] Compare to τί (τὸ) ὄφελος; Epictetus I 4.16; 6.3–4, 33; II 17.20; III 1.30; 7.31; 10.7; 24.51, and elsewhere; also Sirach 41:14; Philo Post 86.

[50] To the voice of this opponent there belongs not only the juxtaposition "You have faith—I have works," neither part of which represents the theological position of James (v. 18a) but apparently also the following antithetically constructed statement: "Show me your faith without works" — "I by my works will show you my faith" (18b). In any case, this statement does not express the real intention of the author, for whom it is not a matter of being able to recognize faith by works (as for instance in Matt 7:16, 20); the author's thesis is rather "There is no faith apart from works."

[51] So F. Mussner, *Der Jakobusbrief* 150.

"passive-nomistic, as Christian law-piety."[52] It is rather the case that for the author of James seeks to overcome this separation of faith and works but does not succeed in doing so terminologically without making such a distinction himself, and precisely thereby falls into a contradiction to the Pauline concept of faith, according to which faith and act are inseparably connected (cf. Gal 5:6).

The material antithesis to Paul is especially to be seen in their respective interpretations of the example of Abraham, since here James wants to prove a person is in fact justified by works, "not by faith alone" (2:24). This suggests that a "Pauline" position that has already become traditional is presupposed and challenged.[53]

The second part of this section (2:21–23) introduces the Scriptural texts Genesis 22:2, 9–10 (sacrifice of Isaac) and 15:6 (Abraham's faith). It is not so much this combination itself but rather the interpretation the author gives these passages, that distinguishes the author's treatment of them from both the Old Testament-Jewish tradition and Paul's interpretation.

1. In *Genesis 15:6* the distinction between faith and works is unknown. Faith as the "steadfast trust" of Abraham in Yahweh's promise is understood as "righteousness." This leads to a reading of a Pauline line of thought into the Old Testament text, when modern exegesis wants to see this as meaning "that belief alone has brought Abraham into a proper relationship to God."[54]

2. So also the tradition of *post-biblical Judaism* knows of no faith/works alternative. It is rather the case that Abraham is considered to be the representative of the proper religious attitude as such. He keeps the commandments of God and also remains "faithful" to God even under testing (connection of Gen 15:6 and 22:1–19 is made in 1 Macc 2:25; Sir 44:19–21 LXX; Jub 18:11 and 25; cf. Jub 23:10; 24:11). To the extent that Abraham's "faith" is spoken of in this connection, it is understood as "faithfulness," "loyalty," or understood as response to Yahweh's command (cf. Mekilta Exod 14:15 [35b]; 14:31 [40b]; Strack-Billerbeck 3:200.

3. The way in which the faith of Abraham is spoken of in Hebrews corresponds to a widespread stream of *early Christian thought*. Abraham's faith is interpreted as "obedience" and placed in parallel to "patient endurance," without the terminology or concepts of "works righteousness" coming in view (Heb 6:13–ff; 11:8ff, 17; cf. Barn 13.7; 1 Clem 10.6–7).

4. *Paul* was the first person to pose the alternative "faith or works" on the basis of Genesis 15:6 and the figure of Abraham. That Abraham's faith was reckoned to him as righteousness accordingly confirms Paul's thesis that God's justifying act is made effective for human beings without the mediation of the law and without human achievement. In Paul's exegesis Abraham became the prototype of justifying faith without works of the law (Gal 3:6; Rom 4:3).

5. The way Abraham is used as an example in the *Letter of James* by combining Genesis 22:1ff and 15:6, it reflects both Jewish and Christian traditional material (on the latter cf. especially Heb 11:17; 1 Clem 10:6–7); so also the designation of Abraham as "friend of God" (James 2:23) has parallels in both Jewish (CD 3.2; Jub

---

52   R. Walker, "Allein aus Glauben," *ZThK* 61 (1964) 189.
53   Cf. Galatians 2:16; Romans 3:28.
54   Cf. G. von Rad, *Genesis: A Commentary* (OTL. Philadelphia: Westminster, 1972) 185).

19.9; 30.20; cf. Strack-Billerbeck 3:755) and Christian tradition (e.g. 1 Clem 10.1; 17.2), both streams of tradition based on Genesis 18:17 and especially Isaiah 41:8 (cf. 2 Chron 20:7; Daniel 3:35 LXX). Analogous to these traditions, James takes over the idea that the example to be imitated is the pious conduct of Abraham who was obedient to God. Differently than in Jewish and early Christian references, James has a special interest in the contrast between righteousness-by-faith and righteousness-by-works. Abraham's works (ἔργα) are the basis of his "justification." His faith merely functions in conjunction with his works and was made "complete" by them (2:22–23). These formulations did not originate independently of Paul's doctrine of justification and intend to establish an independent position over against "Pauline' tradition.

The reference to the prostitute Rahab has the same goal. She received the Israelite scouts into her house before the capture of Jericho, and was spared by the grateful conquerors, along with her relatives (2:25; cf. Josh 2:1–24; 6:17, 22–23, 25). Jewish sources celebrate Rahab as an example of good works, to which she owed her deliverance (Midrash Ruth 2; Ber 4.1; Strack-Billerbeck 1:21–22). She is praised in early Christian literature as an example of faith (Heb 11:31; 1 Clem 12:1–8). Since James does not refer to the faith of Rahab but takes her story as an example of justification on the ground of works, he also here modifies the tradition that had come to him. It is not accidental that instead of ἐσώθη (Josh 6:25) James reads ἐδικαιώθη: James is the first to associate the issue of justification with the figure of Rahab (2:25).

Refrain-like, with only partial variations in the language with which it is expressed, the theses repeatedly recurs that "faith without works is dead" (2:17, 20, 24, 26). Faith must have added to it *human works*. It is not by faith alone but only in connection with works, that the believer is made complete (2:22). James accordingly teaches a synergistic understanding of salvation, in which faith and works are connected to each other in an additive sense. The decisive concern of the author is to set forth the idea that faith and works must work together. This thereby corresponds to the theoretical understanding of faith,[55] that there is no concern to show an inherent connection between the two, and to the parenetic interest that places the emphasis on "works." It is thus not good to dispute the idea that James, even though he has not thought the concepts through theologically and makes his statements in the situation of a debate, leaves room for the idea of human achievement.[56] It is true, however, that he does not affirm that human beings can "save themselves," but points to baptism and the "word of truth" at work in it as the foundation for the Christian life (1:18).

---

[55]  Differently F. Mussner, *Der Jakobusbrief* 146: "For James, works are the necessary result of a living faith." This understanding, however, can hardly be supported by appeal to 2:18b and 22, since 2:18 does not represent the position of the author himself (see above), and in 2:22 the use of the verbs συνεργέω and τελειόω confirms the additive relation of faith and works.

U. Luck, "Der Jakobusbrief und die Theologie des Paulus," 178, has advocated the formula "Faith becomes effective through wisdom," according to which in James' understanding faith as such is aimed at works as its goal. But this goes too far in the direction of a substantial connection between faith and works.

[56]  This and the following is against F. Mussner, *Der Jakobusbrief* 147–148.

He knows the sovereignty of God that grants the sinner forgiveness in response to prayer (5:15). But sin for him is not a radical power that could frustrate all human activity and bring it to ruinous condemnation. And God is not finally the judge (4:6, 12) who lays an unconditional obligation on human beings, namely to do what the law requires as the presupposition for the gift of the "crown of life" (1:12). Although James does not explicitly deny that faith has justifying power,[57] he also does not affirm this position. It is impossible for him, because it would contradict his understanding of faith and his emphasis on the necessity of good works. Differently than in the theology of Paul, the ethical imperative is not grounded in and limited by a preceding soteriological indicative, and justification is promised not to human faith but to human action. He states without reservation: "… be doers of the word, and not merely hearers who deceive themselves. … doers who act—they will be blessed in their doing" (1:22, 25).

To the extent that one regards the Letter of James as having been written prior to the time of the Pauline letters, one must separate the treatment of the theme "faith and works" from the Pauline doctrine of justification. However, if as in the above presentation James is understood to be evidence of a developed stage of early Christian literature and refined christological views, then the tractate cannot be placed prior to Paul. This then makes it likely that the Pauline doctrine of justification influenced James directly or—more probably—indirectly. Two considerations especially favor this conclusion: (1) Although traditional Jewish material has extensively influenced the parenesis of James, it is inconceivable that there was a theological separation of faith and works in contemporary Judaism. (2) The striking use of Abraham as an example can hardly be coincidental, even if it is cited by James and Paul to make opposite points.

That the problem before us has not yet been adequately investigated in the critical commentaries is due to the fact that James is either dated in the Pauline period[58] or is understood as a more or less random collection of parenetic sayings, so that the relation of James to Paul and the Pauline tradition is at the most discussed only in connection with the exegesis of 2:13ff (e.g. M. Dibelius, H. Windisch). The problem here discussed therefore deserves more attention, especially as an element in the issue of the place of James in early Christian tradition.

In this connection I offer the following observations on the terminological problem:

There are noticeable parallels to the Pauline style and language.

Κατακαυχάομαι: Apart from one instance in an inscription, the word is found only in the New Testament, namely only in Paul (Rom 11:18) and James (2:13; 3:14). The negative understanding (3:14) accords with the Pauline passage.

---

57 So F. Mussner, *Der Jakobusbrief* 147; but cf. 2:11: "Can faith save you?" the presupposed answer must be, "No!" [translator's note: as indicated by the grammar itself: question introduced by μή]. Faith as such, as it is to be understood in the present passage as a theoretical phenomenon (indicated by the absolute use of the term "faith") does not mediate justification in James' understanding of the issue.
58 So F. Mussner, *Der Jakobusbrief* 19: no knowledge of the Pauline letters.

Καυχάομαι appears in the New Testament only in Pauline and deutero-Pauline writings, and in the Letter of James—and here in the context of an eschatological paradox (1:9–10, "Let the believer who is lowly boast in being raised up, and the rich in being brought low, because the rich will disappear like a flower in the field." This is different from the use of the word in 4:16 in a negative ethical sense); cf. 2 Corinthians 2:19 (boasting in one's weaknesses).

Καύχησις is used in the New Testament only by Paul and James; compare 4:16 ("such boasting is evil") especially with Romans 3:27.

Δικαιοσύνη θεοῦ: in the ethical sense 1:20 (corresponding to Matt 6:33); this is different from Pauline usage (Rom 1:17; 3:5, 21ff, and elsewhere); the Pauline usage is possibly presupposed in a negative perspective.

Δικαιόω: the passages 2:21 and 24–25 read like an antithesis to Romans 4:2; cf. also Romans 3:20; Galatians 2:16; 3:11, 24 and the "deutero-Pauline" examples in Acts 13:38–39; Titus 3:7.

Ὅλον τὸν κόσμον: in 2:10 the expression means the absolute demand of the law as in Galatians 5:3 (cf. Gal 3:10). Despite the presence of parallels in Jewish tradition,[59] it is revealing that both Paul (cf. Gal 2:18; Rom 2:25, 27) and James (2:9–12) connect this with the *usus elenchticus legis* though in different ways: according to Paul the absolute demand of the law prepares for the grace of God in a negative way, while for James it is a strengthening of the command to practice mercy.

Ἀκροαταὶ καὶ ποιηταὶ λόγου (or νόμου): 1:22 (cf. 4:11) and Romans 2:13 (in each case the unconditioned obligation imposed by the law is emphasized).

Other agreements are less informative; they could in part go back to the common Jewish and/or early Christian background shared by Paul and James. Thus κληρονόμοι τῆς βασιλείας: 2:5 (in regard to the poor of the Christian community); cf. Galatians 5:21; 1 Corinthians 6:9–10; 15:50 (+ θεοῦ; in the negative context of ethical warning). Κύριος τῆς δόξης: 2:1 (?); cf. 1 Corinthians 2:8. Προσωπολημψίαι: 2:1; cf. Romans 2:11 (singular: Col 3:25; Eph 6:9). Ἡδοναί: 4:1; cf. Galatians 5:17; Romans 7:23. Ἐπιθυμία: 1:14–15; cf. Romans 1:24; 6:12; 7:7–8; 13:14. Τοῖς ἀγαπῶσιν αὐτόν: 1:12; 2:5; cf. 1 Corinthians 2:9. Στέφανος τῆς ζωῆς: 1:12; cf. 1 Corinthians 9:25 (also Rev 2:10). Καρπὸς δικαιοσύνης: 3:18 (+ ἐν εἰρήνῃ): cf. Galatians 5:21; Philippians 1:11 (esp. Heb 12:11). Cf. further on 1:2–5 (the effects of patient endurance): Romans 5:3–5; on 2:5 (the poor in the world as God's elect): 1 Corinthians 1:26–27.

These parallels of vocabulary and subject matter hardly demonstrate that James knew the Pauline letters; there is no direct quotation. The relationship is not so close that direct literary dependence must be assumed. The data are better explained by the hypothesis that James is aware of a stream of Pauline tradition dealing with the doctrine of justification, presumably derived from Pauline circles that had in fact misunderstood Paul's message of justification that faith justifies apart from human achievement. They abstract from the Pauline concept of faith, which had included Christian existence and activity within the realm of love, and had made it into a theoretical faith in the sense of "considering something to be true." Possibly they had inferred from this libertine or quietist consequences, because they felt themselves to be released from the problems of ethical actions. If the author was faced with such a position, then it is

---

[59]   Cf. M. Dibelius, *A Commentary on the Epistle of James* 144–146.

understandable why he repeatedly harps on the thesis that faith without works is dead and has no saving significance. James attempts to oppose the dangers that had arisen for Christian thought and life from a misunderstanding of the Pauline doctrine of justification.[60]

By attempting to straighten out a Paulinist theology, James did not himself become a Paulinist. It is rather the case that his super-sharp demand for works makes him as distant from Paul as those interpreters he opposes:

1. Although James knows of a "usus elenchticus legis" (2:9ff), he achieves what Paul did not: his theology does not call the law as such into question. It is rather the case that he sees an unbroken continuity between the law of the Old Testament understood in an ethical sense and the "law of liberty" that is foundational for his parenesis.

2. Since James accepts the unbroken demand of the law as binding, he directly emphasizes the necessity of good works. Analogous to the (Hellenistic) Jewish[61] and early Christian tradition,[62] "works" are the "conditio sine qua non" of salvation (2:24, 26). While James is different in this from the characteristic usage of Paul (where the term ἔργα has primarily a negative connotation; "works of the flesh," Gal 5:19; "works of the law," Gal 2:16; 3:2, 10; Rom 3:20, 28), he is like Paul in using the distinction between "faith" and "works" that was unknown in contemporary Judaism (James 2:21ff; Rom 4:2, 6); this confirms the observation that Paul and James were connected by the history of early Christian traditions.

3. Despite his struggle against the Pauline-solipsist understanding of faith, James takes over unchanged the post-Pauline theoretical concept of faith that came to him in the tradition (in that he argues works must be added to faith).[63] The statement of 2:20 ("faith apart from works is barren") cannot be conceptually reconciled with Galatians 5:6 ("... in Christ

---

[60] According to E. Trocmé, James reflects the contrast between Hellenistic and Pauline churches; James resists an intellectualization of the Pauline understanding of faith ("Les Églises pauliniennes vues du dehors: Jacques 2,1 à 3,13," in F. L. Cross [ed.], *StEv* II, Teil I [TU 87. Berlin: Evangelische Verlagsanstalt, 1964] 660–669). To what extent the position of the Paulinists can be reconstructed remains debatable, especially whether James wanted to show the problematic of the Paulinists' understanding of faith by pointing to the disorder of the worship services and the number of their false teachers ("Les Églises pauliniennes" 665–666).

[61] Cf. Psalm 15:2; 18:21; Jonah 3:10; 2 Baruch 14:12; 51:7; 69:4; 85:2; 1 Ezra 8:83 LXX; 4 Ezra 8:33; 9:7–8; Philo Sacr 78; Jos Ant 9.22.

[62] Cf. especially the Pastoral Epistles: 1 Timothy 5:10, 25; 6:18; Titus 2:7, 14; 3:8; also 2 Clement 6:9, and elsewhere.

[63] This is also seen in the fact that πίστις in other passages of the ethical tradition thus means "trust" (1:6; 5:15) or "loyalty," "faithfulness" (1:3); more in the technical sense, 2:1, 5. In contrast to this, the use of the verb πιστεύω is remarkable: only in 2:19, understood as "to consider something (theoretically) true."

... the only thing that counts is faith working through love). Characteristic for James is the terminological and thus also material separation of faith and works. Even if this goes against the real intention of the author but connecting up with the position of his opponents, with the Letter of James an un-Pauline, intellectualized concept of "faith" has found entrance into the New Testament canon.[64]

### d) Poor and Rich

Among the multiplicity of individual admonitions in the Letter of James which have numerous parallels in the ethical literature of the New Testament and early Christianity, the reference to the problem of "poor and rich" has a special place (1:9–11; 2:1–7; 5:1–6). It is obviously a theme that has current relevance for the author, although as will be shown below, traditional materials are reworked. This means that the statements taken as a whole cannot be related directly to his situation, and that the understanding of "poor and rich" by both author and readers can only be reconstructed with difficulty.

1. The point of departure must thus be the warning against partiality and favoritism (2:1ff) that is closely integrated into its context; it is bound to the preceding by the material connection with 1:27,[65] to the following through the material connection with the theme "faith and works," which of course to some extent is a separate section in terms of both form and content (2:14ff). To be sure, the section 2:1–13 is not a homogenized unit, since from 2:8 on the problem "poor and rich" is overtaken by a basic reflection on the obligatory nature of the law. Thus the command not to be partial is the real theme of only *2:1–7* as the representation of the responsibility that comes with a "religion that is pure and undefiled before God" (1:27). The meaning is explained by presenting only one individual case: when a rich person comes into the gathering[66] of the Christian community, he or she is given preferential treatment and receives a place of honor. This partiality (προσωπολημψία) gives the church a bad reputation, for the result is "bad judgments" (2:4). Perhaps this example was created

---

[64]   This is the reason the reformer Martin Luther described the Letter of James as an "epistle of straw" and changed the traditional order of New Testament books by placing it as next-to-last among the New Testament letters (WA DB 7.384–385; WA II 425.10ff; XII 268.17ff; WA TR 5.157).

[65]   Sirach 32:15–17 LXX also connects the motifs of James 1:27 (care for the widows and orphans) and 2:1 (impartiality).

[66]   Συναγωγή (v. 2) here probably does not mean "place of assembly" but "assembly" of the community itself. This corresponds to its etymological sense. So also Acts 13:43; Hermas Mandates XI 9.13; Ignatius Polycarp 4.2; to translate "synagogue" would fail to appreciate the historical location of James in time and space.

by the author in dependence on Stoic educational practice.[67] Of course this observation does not answer the further question, how the rich and poor in the congregations presupposed by the Letter of James actually related to each other.

That the author is dealing with a real problem, however, is shown by his threats against the rich (*5:1–6*). Here too the connection with the context was already given by the tradition.[68] Moreover, the motifs used in this section are for the most part traditional. Formally, we have here a series of individual threats of different types, whose common orientation is indicated by the announcement of apocalyptic judgment: moths and rust, which destroy stored-up treasures, are not only a sign of the passing nature of riches but also witnesses against the rich that will offer their testimony in the last judgment.[69] On the day of judgment the rich will be delivered over to destruction (5:3b), for they have stored up for themselves treasures "in the last days," i.e. despite the approaching end they have only thought of themselves.[70] Future witnesses for the prosecution are represented above all by the workers whose earned wages have been withheld.[71] Therefore the judgment will break in on the "murderers of the righteous" as "a day of slaughter."[72]

Doubtless the traditional apocalyptic structure prohibits the attempt to look behind such statements for a concrete situation on which they are based. This is also true of the problem of whether only the non-Christian rich are condemned, or the author is thinking of inner-church relationships. Nonetheless, the section is still basically informative for the rela-

---

[67] Cf. M. Dibelius, *A Commentary on the Epistle of James* 143–144 ; F. Mussner, *Der Jakobusbrief* 117.

[68] On the connection of 4:13–16 (business people making plans for the future) with 5:1 (the perishability of riches), cf. 1 Enoch 97.9–10 and Revelation 18:10ff.

[69] James 5:3a; the perfect in vv. 2–3a has a future meaning, in dependence on the usage of the Old Testament prophetic books ("prophetic perfect"); this is also suggested by the following future verb forms; cf. Blass-DeBrunner §344.

[70] James 5:3d: ἐν ἐσχάταις ἡμέραις (only here in James); in Isaiah 2:2; cf. Jeremiah 23:20; Ezekiel 38:16; Daniel 2:28; Acts 2:17 (cf. Joel 3:1–5); 2 Timothy 3:1; Didache 16:3; Barnabas 4:9; 6:13; 12:9; 16:5; Ignatius Eph 11:1.

[71] James 5:4; for the Old Testament background cf. especially Deuteronomy 24:15; Job 31:38–40; Tobit 4:14.

[72] James 5:5–6. ἡμέρα σφαγῆς. The aorist tense of ἐθρέψατε does not of course point to the future, and ἐν is likewise difficult to interpret in the sense of εἰς. Nonetheless, the interpretation by H. Windisch and M. Dibelius in the sense of "unlucky day," although apparently suggested by the immediate context, cannot be convincingly supported, especially since 1 Enoch 100.7 offers no real parallel. In the Old Testament the expression designates the judgment day of Yahweh (Jer 12:3b; cf. 32:34; Ps 35:13 LXX). This future-eschatological sense is the meaning intended in our context, as indicated by the orientation of the whole section. The meaning is that the extravagant, overindulgent life of the rich lasts not only "up to" but even "on" the (future) day of slaughter.

tion of the Christian community envisioned by James to the circles of the wealthy. There is an unbridgeable chasm between a church that knows it is obligated to engage social issues (cf. v. 6; also 1:27; 2:8ff, and elsewhere) and the self-seeking lifestyle of the propertied class. The slant of the text toward the future eschaton makes clear: there is no hope for the selfish striving of the rich for more!

The following admonition to the church to hold out until the parousia of the Lord (5:7–11) is no less grounded in a consistent apocalyptic. This church recognizes itself in the picture of the innocent sufferers, the righteous, who are not called to withstand the injustice they are suffering but to thereby express their attitude of "patience" and "steadfast endurance" in concrete reality.[73]

Likewise of fundamental importance is the section *1:9–11* derived from the Old Testament-Jewish wisdom tradition: "Let the believer who is lowly boast in being raised up, and the rich in being brought low, ...".[74] In both cases it is a matter of binding instruction. The poor are instructed not to be overcome by their depressing situation but to let the promised salvation become an object of boasting as it is realized in a life that manifests this salvation in devout thoughts and actions. The rich are instructed not to exalt themselves but to be aware of their actual lowliness. The latter admonition is not a matter of irony but the challenge to reflect on the frailty of human life and to draw the necessary consequences.

It thus becomes clear that this section is not concerned with apocalyptic instruction, nor is it interested only in ethical directions but wants to portray the paradox that is to be realized in human existence according to the understanding of the Letter of James.[75] Arguments from wisdom are used in the course of this argument.[76] Before the forum of divine wisdom as the sole norm of human life (1:5), the knowledge of the perishability of riches is occasion enough commend humility to the rich. On the other

---

[73]    On James 5:6, cf. Matthew 5:39; δίκαιος is also found in the Christian sense in James 5:16; the connection between oppression of the righteous by the rich with the threat of apocalyptic judgment is also found in Isaiah 3:13–14; 1 Enoch 96.4–8; 99.15; Wisdom of Solomon 2:19–20.

There is no reference in the text to the Messiah Jesus as the "Righteous One" (Acts 3:14; 7:52; cf. Isa 53:7 and elsewhere), since "the rich" can hardly be made responsible for the passion and execution of Jesus.

[74]    The ταπεινός are already identified in the LXX: Ps 73:21; 81:3; 101:18 (v. l.); 112:7 LXX; Amos 8:6; Isa 61:1 (v. l.); Jer 22:16; Proverbs 30:14; Sirach 13:21–22 LXX.

[75]    Similarly 2:5: the poor are "rich in faith" the inheritance is promised to them as "those who love God." The "reversal of values" intended here is thus connected to its ethical realization.

[76]    Vv. 10–11: an allusion to Isaiah 40:6–7, perhaps with a side reference to Job 15:29–30. With regard to the subject matter cf. especially Sirach 10:14–18 (judgment on the rich as the proud; acceptance of the poor).

hand, in the statement that the "poor brother" should boast in his being raised up the motif of "piety of the poor" is also at work.

2. The question of whether or to what extent the texts named above are related to a particular situation and reflect the relation of rich and poor in the Christian congregations may now be answered with more confidence. While it is clear that James has undisguised sympathy for the "poor," it is also clear that the term πτωχοί is not an ecclesiological self-description intended to characterize the Christian community as a whole. Contrary to a widespread view, it cannot be shown that this title was ever used for the early Jerusalem church but was only later adopted by Jewish Christianity for itself.[77] Neither is it to be presupposed for the church of James. It is rather the case that this document differentiates clearly between the poor who belong to the church (2:5), and the church itself (2:6). Nor is it to be assumed on the other side that the rich stand exclusively outside the church. To be sure, in distinction from the poor the wealthy are not called ἀδελφοί (1:9–10); this is not, however, an intentional differentiation but rather points to both sides of the paradoxical formulation that it is not only the poor but also the rich, who are to be led by the "word of truth" to an appropriate attitude. And since also in the "artificial case" (2:2ff) the possibility is reckoned with that a rich person might come into the Christian assembly, the supposition of an absolute separation of the church from the rich is too weakly supported. To be sure, it is not unlikely that the radical polemic of 5:1ff (cf. also 2:6–7), to the extent that it is not simply the repetition of traditional material, predominantly addresses relations outside the church. Still, they would hardly have been incorporated into a parenetic tractate such as James represents if the question of the relation to possessions had not been an issue that directly concerned the church, and that means an inner-church problem.[78] The author thus reckons with some wealthy people within the Christian community and does not oppose their admission. It is for precisely this reason, in fact, that he believes it depends on him to impress upon his readership that one's economic status must not become a dominant factor within the Christian community.[79] Such a position fits well into the period we are here presup-

---

[77] Cf. G. Strecker, "On the Problem of Jewish Christianity." Appendix 1 to W. Bauer, *Orthodoxy and Heresy in Earliest Christianity* (Philadelphia: Fortress Press, 1971) 271–273. On the problem cf. further: L. E. Keck, "The Poor among the Saints in the New Testament," ZNW 56 (1965) 100–129; "The Poor among the Saints in the Jewish Christianity and Qumran," ZNW 57 (1966) 54–78; F. W. Horn, *Glaube und Handeln in der Theologie des Lukas* (GTA 26. Göttingen: Vandenhoeck & Ruprecht, 1986²) 39–49.

[78] One can also ask whether 5:9 in the present context (the grumbling of Christian brothers and sisters among one another) includes the problem of poor and rich and points to this as an inner-church problem.

[79] Cf. also the example of merchants who are occupied with their own plans for carrying on business (4:13ff). They are admonished to live by the "condicio Jaco-

posing for the composition of the Letter of James. The question of the incorporation of wealthy circles into the church has become acute in Hermas (Vis III 9.4ff; Similitudes II 1ff; Visions II 3; Mandates III 3). While there the incorporation of the wealthy, among whom the author obviously numbers himself, has already been largely accomplished, in James this is still in the early stages.[80] The social problem generated by having rich and poor alongside each other in the one church is thus announced in James for the first time.

That James interprets the word πτωχός not only in the material but also in the eschatological sense (2:2ff), i.e. that he equates "poor" and "pious," makes him, along with Luke, one of the outstanding representatives of that early Christian stream whose roots are found in the Old Testament-Jewish "piety of the poor."

Cf. the *election of the poor* (1:9; 2:5): Isaiah 61:1; Jeremiah 20:13; Zephaniah 3:11–13; Psalm 40:18; 86:1–2; 109:22, 31; 132:15; 140:13; Sirach 35:16; Psalms of Solomon 10:6; 15:1; Luke 6:20.

*Social responsibility for the poor:* (1:27): Deuteronomy 24:14ff; Leviticus 19:13; Amos 4:1; 5:11; Malachi 3:5; Proverbs 14:21, 31; Mark 10:21parr; Matthew 6:1–4; Acts 2:44–45; 4:32ff; 6:1.

*Condemnation of the rich and riches:* (1:10ff; 2:6; 5:1ff): Jeremiah 5:26ff; Micah 6:11ff; Ecclesiastes 5:9ff; Proverbs 15:15–16; 23:45; Sirach 11:18–19; 1 Enoch 97:8–10; Psalms of Solomon 1:4–8; Mark 10:25parr; Luke 6:24; 12:16–21; 16:19–31; 1 Timothy 6:17ff.

As was shown above, these elements of a theologically-motivated pauperist conception do not place James so exclusively on the side of the poor that the rich are excluded from belonging to the Christian community. On the other hand, James of course does not make so many concessions to the rich that would prevent him from consciously allowing the feeling for the poor inherent in his tradition to shape his parenesis. It is obvious that the rich cannot enter the community without subjecting themselves to a radical revision of their relationship to material wealth (cf. 1:9ff). The beginnings of a socio-political stance of the church are here visible, for

---

baea," the "Jacobite conditional" (v. 15). They are obviously not merely to be identified with the rich but it is still clear from the use of this example that the author presupposes that there are some people with money and a striving after possessions within the church.

[80] The variety of ways in which James expresses himself about the rich may be traced back above all to the fact that—alongside his typical dependence on tradition—the problem has not yet arisen in an especially pressing form. That James sets himself against any further readiness on the part of the church to accept the rich (M. Dibelius, *A Commentary on the Epistle of James* 48), or wants "to keep the rich at a distance from the church" (M. Dibelius, *Der Hirt des Hermas* [HNT Supplementary Volume 4] Tübingen: J. C. B. Mohr [Paul Siebeck], 1923) 555) is an assumption that deals too freely with the text.

despite the apparent uncompromising distancing of the community from the rich (5:1ff) the contrast of poor and rich is incorporated within and subordinated to the all-encompassing ethical demand that is required of the Christian community as a whole.

The parenesis of James may be understood as an ecclesiological ethic that seeks to keep up with the practical concern of regulating the life of the Christian community. The judgement would be too severe, however, if one were to declare that the teaching of James represents a "conventicle ethic."[81] For although James' church consciously distances itself from the "world"[82] and is concerned with regulating its own affairs,[83] it is nonetheless the case that the formation of an introverted, conventicle-like self-understanding would be against the churchly, universal orientation of the tractate as a whole, whose author explicitly directs his writing to the whole church with its variety of sociological and theological graduations (1:1). Moreover, although there is no missionary impetus visible, it is clear that the claim of the divine sophia, i.e. the "law of liberty," to which James holds his readers responsible, does not end at the borders of the existing church. This corresponds to James' understanding that the eschatological judgment not to be a matter of "faith" or belonging to the church but that people will be asked about their "works" (2:12ff), and that the hope of the church at the same time includes within itself hope for the whole creation (1:18). Just as the boundaries of a conventicle-Christianity are here broken through, so this also happens in the matter-of-fact standardization of ethics. The numerous parallels to the parenesis of James, especially in the tradition of Hellenistic Judaism, make it clear that the conduct of the members of the Christian church is judged by essentially the same standard that applies to the non-Christian world. If this is due to the horizon for James' ethic established by the wisdom tradition, it is at the same time the basis for the fundamental solidarity of the church with the world.

Since W. Bousset evaluated the church of James as an example of a "liberated Diaspora Judaism,"[84] this easily-misunderstood label has been frequently repeated. In contrast, we have shown that James consciously intends to practice Christian theology, and that his own theological horizon also appears in those places where he has taken over traditional material from Hellenistic Judaism—for these passages are also have a Christian orientation. To be sure, if one measures how "Christian" James' document is by the number of specifically christological elements, then it

---

[81]  So M. Dibelius, *A Commentary on the Epistle of James* 49.
[82]  Cf. 1:27; 2:5; 4:4. On the basis of 3:15 this contrast may be called ethical dualism but it is kept within bounds.
[83]  Cf. the rules for church order (e.g. 5:19–20 and elsewhere).
[84]  W. Bousset, *Kyrios Christos: A History of the Belief in Christ from the Beginnings of Christianity to Irenaeus* (Nashville & New York: Abingdon Press, 1970) 367.

is not easy to reject R. Bultmann's judgment that what is "specifically Christian is surprisingly thin."[85] In order to dispute this thesis, it is not adequate to claim that the theology of James is especially close to the teaching of Jesus; as shown above, the direct adoption of authentic Jesus material by James is not probable. The term "Christian" for James is also to be used only in a limited sense if one is motivated by a comparison with Paul. Both the depth and the highly-charged, tensive nature of Paul's theology remained foreign to the author of James. The lack of a critical understanding of the law, of a radical concept of sin, an insight into the dialectic of human existence, the enclosing of the ethical imperative within the christological-soteriological indicative—all these let the unbridgeable distance between Paul and James clearly appear. We have seen, to be sure, that James' position is not conditioned by a conscious opposition to Paul but the results of his debate with an exaggerated Paulinism that had distorted Paul's thesis of the justification of the sinner "through faith alone" and had separated faith and ethics as mutually incompatible. In the face of such a contrast, the theological merit of James becomes apparent. It consists in the fact that by teaching an unqualified directness of the ethical demand, like the Gospel of Matthew he rejects any intellectualistic misunderstanding of the Christian faith, any neglect of ethical responsibility and—by affirming the validity and application of the pre-Christian Jewish and early Christian ethical tradition, he proclaims the importance for the Christian life of concrete acts in a way that cannot be missed.

---

[85]   R. Bultmann, *Theology of the New Testament* 2:143.

# General Bibliography

Balz, H. *Methodische Probleme der neutestamentlichen Christologie*, WMANT 25, Neukirchen-Vluyn: Neukirchener, 1967.

Barrett C. K. *The New Testament Background: Selected Documents*. San Francisco: Harper and Row, 1989[2].

Bauer, W. *A Greek-English Lexicon of the New Testament and Other Early Christian Literature*. Rev. and augmented by F. W. Gingrich and F. W. Danker. Chicago: University of Chicago Press, 1979.

Bauer, W. *Orthodoxy and Heresy in Earliest Christianity, with Additional Appendices by Georg Strecker*. Philadelphia: Fortress, 1971.

Becker, J. *Paul: Apostle to the Gentiles*. Louisville: Westminster/John Knox, 1993.

Boring, M. E., Berger, K. und Colpe, C., eds. *Hellenistic Commentary to the New Testament*. Nashville: Abingdon, 1994.

Braun, H. *Qumran und das Neue Testament* (2 Vols.). Tübingen: J. C. B. Mohr (Paul Siebeck), 1966.

Büchsel, F. *Theologie des Neuen Testaments*. Gütersloh: C. Bertelmann, 1937.

Bultmann, R. *The History of the Synoptic Tradition*. Peabody, Mass.: Hendrickson, 1994. Reprint of the translation of the third German edition.

Bultmann, R. *Exegetica. Aufsätze zur Erforschung des Neuen Testaments*, E. Dinkler, ed. Tübingen: J. C. B. Mohr (Paul Siebeck), 1967.

Bultmann, R. *Glauben und Verstehen. Gesammelte Aufsätze*. Tübingen: J. C. B. Mohr (Paul Siebeck), I 1980[8], II 1968[5], III 1965[3], IV 1975[3].

Bultmann, R. *Theology of the New Testament*. New York: Scribner, 1951–1955.

Conzelmann, H. *An Outline of the Theology of the New Testament*. New York: Harper & Row, 1969.

Conzelmann, H. and Lindemann, A. *Interpreting the New Testament*. Peabody, Mass.: Hendrickson, 1988.

Cullmann, O. *The Christology of the New Testament*. Philadelphia: Westminster, 1959.

Deissmann, A. *Light from the Ancient East; the New Testament Illustrated by Recently Discovered Texts of the Graeco-Roman World*. New York: Hodder and Stoughton, 1923.

Dibelius, M. *From Tradition to Gospel*. New York: Scribners, 1965.

Feine, P. *Theologie des Neuen Testaments*. Leipzig [3]1919 (= Reprinted, Berlin: Evangelische Verlagsanstalt, 1953[8]).

Gnilka, J. *Jesus of Nazareth: Message and History*. Peabody, Mass.: Hendrickson, 1997.

Gnilka, J. *Neutestamentliche Theologie. Ein Überblick*. NEB Ergänzungsband. Würzburg: Echter, 1989.

Gnilka, J. *Theologie des Neuen Testaments*. HThK.S V, Freiburg 1994.

Goppelt, L. *Theology of the New Testament*. Grand Rapids: Wm. B. Eerdmans Publishing Co., 1981.

Hahn, F. *The Titles of Jesus in Christology; their History in Early Christianity*. London: Lutterworth, 1969.

Hahn, F. "Methodenprobleme einer Christologie des Neuen Testaments," *VF* 15, 1970, 3–41.

Hengel, M. *Judaism and Hellenism: Studies in Their Encounter in Palestine during the Early Hellenistic Period.* Philadelphia: Fortress, 1974.

Horn, F. W., ed. *Bilanz und Perspektiven gegenwärtiger Auslegung des Neuen Testaments.* BZNW 75, Berlin—New York: W. de Gruyter, 1995.

Horn, F. W. *Das Angeld des Geistes. Studien zur paulinischen Pneumatologie.* FRLANT 152, Göttingen: Vandenhoeck & Ruprecht, 1992.

Hübner, H. *Biblische Theologie des Neuen Testaments.* Vols. 1 and 2. Göttingen: Vandenhoeck & Ruprecht, 1990.1993.

Jeremias, J. *New Testament Theology I: The Proclamation of Jesus.* New York: Scribners, 1971.

Kaftan, J. *Neutestamentliche Theologie. Im Abriss dargestellt.* Berlin: Warmeck, 1927.

Käsemann, E. *Exegetische Versuche und Besinnungen* I.II. Göttingen: Vandenhoeck & Ruprecht, 1970.

Koester, H. *History and Literature of Early Christianity.* Vol. I History, Culture, and Literature of the Hellenistic Age. Vol. II, Introduction to the New Testament. Berlin and New York: W. de Gruyter, 1982, 1985.

Kümmel, W. G. *The New Testament: the History of the Investigation of Its Problems.* Nashville: Abingdon, 1974.

Kümmel, W. G. *The Theology of the New Testament according to Its Major Witnesses.* Nashville: Abingdon, 1973.

Kümmel, W. G. *Introduction to the New Testament.* Nashville: Abingdon, 1975.

Leipoldt, J. und Grundmann, W. *Umwelt des Urchristentums.* Berlin: Evangelische Verlagsanstalt, I 1990, II 1986, III 1987.

Lietzmann, H. *A History of the Early Church.* 4 Vols. New York: Scribners, 1949–1952.

Lohse, E. *Grundriss der neutestamentlichen Theologie.* ThW 5, Stuttgart: Calwer, 1989.

Lührmann, D. *An Itinerary for New Testament Study.* London/Philadelphia: SCM Press/Trinity Press International, 1989.

Merk, O. "Biblische Theologie II. Neues Testament," *TRE* 6 (1980) 455–477.

Norden, E. *Agnostos Theos. Untersuchungen zur Formengeschichte religiöser Rede.* Darmstadt: Wissenschaftliche Buchgesellschaft, 1956.

Norden, E. *Die Geburt des Kindes. Geschichte einer religiösen Idee.* SBW 3. Leipzig—Berlin: Teubner, 1931.

Pohlenz, M. *Die Stoa. Geschichte einer geistigen Bewegung.* Göttingen: Vandenhoeck & Ruprecht, 1959.

Reicke, B. *The New Testament Era.* Philadelphia: Fortress, 1968.

Reitzenstein, R. *Hellenistic Mystery Religions: their Basic Ideas and Significance.* Pittsburgh: Pickwick, 1978.

Roloff, J. *Neues Testament.* Neukirchener Arbeitsbücher. Neukirchen-Vluyn: Neukirchener, 1985.

Schelkle, K. H. *Theologie des Neuen Testaments* I-IV/2. KBANT. Düsseldorf: Patmos, 1968–1976.

Schlatter, A. *Die Theologie des Neuen Testaments* I-II. Stuttgart: Calver, 1909, 1910.

Schmithals, W. *Einleitung in die drei ersten Evangelien.* Berlin—New York: W. de Gruyter, 1985.

Schnackenburg, R. *Jesus in the Gospels: a Biblical Christology.* Louisville: Westminster/John Knox, 1995.

Schnackenburg, R. *New Testament Theology Today.* New York: Herder and Herder, 1963.

Schneemelcher, W. ed. *New Testament Apocrypha* I, II. Louisville: Westminster/John Knox, 1989.

Schnelle, U. *Antidocetic Christology in the Gospel of John: An Investigation of the Place of the Fourth Gospel in the Johannine School.* Minneapolis: Fortress, 1992.
Schnelle, U. *The History and Theology of the New Testament Writings.* Minneapolis: Fortress, 1998.
Schulz, S. *Die Mitte der Schrift. Der Frühkatholizismus im Neuen Testament als Herausforderung an den Protestantismus.* Stuttgart: Kreuz Verlag, 1976.
Schürer, E. *The History of the Jewish People in the Age of Jesus Christ (175 B.C.-A.D. 135).* A New English Version Revised and Edited by G. Vermes and F. Millar, Vol. 1–3/2, Edinburgh: T. & T. Clark, 1973–1987.
Schweitzer, A. *The Mysticism of Paul the Apostle.* London: A. & C. Black, 1931.
Stauffer, E. *New Testament Theology.* London: SCM, 1955.
Strack, H. und Billerbeck, P. *Kommentar zum Neuen Testament aus Talmud und Midrasch,* 6 Vols., Munich: Beck, 1926–1961.
Strecker, G., ed. *Das Problem der Theologie des Neuen Testaments.* WdF 367. Darmstadt: Wissenschaftliche Buchgesellschaft, 1975.
Strecker, G. *Der Weg der Gerechtigkeit. Untersuchung zur Theologie des Matthäus.* FRLANT 82. Göttingen: Vandenhoeck & Ruprecht, 1971.
Strecker, G. *Eschaton und Historie. Aufsätze.* Göttingen: Vandenhoeck & Ruprecht, 1979.
Strecker, G. *History of New Testament Literature.* Harrisburg: Trinity Press International, 1997.
Strecker, G. and Maier, J. *Neues Testament—Antikes Judentum.* GKT 2. Stuttgart: Calver, 1989.
Stuhlmacher, P. *Biblische Theologie des Neuen Testaments,* Bd. 1. *Grundlegung. Von Jesus zu Paulus.* Göttingen: Vandenhoeck & Ruprecht, 1992.
Vielhauer, Ph. "Ein Weg zur neutestamentlichen Christologie," *Aufsätze zum Neuen Testament.* TB 31. Munich: Kaiser, 1965, 141–198.
Vielhauer, Ph. *Geschichte der urchristlichen Literatur.* Berlin—New York: W. de Gruyter, 1975.
Weinel, H. *Biblische Theologie des Neuen Testaments.* GThW 3.2. Tübingen: J. C. B. Mohr (Paul Siebeck), 1928.
Weiser, A. *Theologie des Neuen Testaments II. Die Theologie der Evangelien.* Studienbücher Theologie 8. Stuttgart: Kohlhammer, 1993.
Wrede, W. *Paul.* Boston: American Unitarian Association, 1908.
Wrede, W. *Über Aufgabe und Methode der Sogenannten Neutestamentlichen Theologie.* Göttingen: Vandenhoeck & Ruprecht, 1897.
Zahn, Th. *Grundriss der neutestamentlichen Theologie.* Leipzig: A. Deichert, 1928.

# Index

## Old Testament

# New Testament

# Apocryphal/Deuterocanonical

# Pseudepigraphical Works

## 1 Enoch

| | |
|---|---|
| 1:9 | 646 |
| 10:15 | 635 |
| 13:6 | 635 |
| 15:11 | 635 |
| 19:1 | 635 |
| 37:4 | 428, 498 |
| 40:9 | 428, 498 |
| 42:1-3 | 658 |
| 42:1ff | 479 |
| 45:3 | 86 |
| 45:3ff | 80 |
| 45:46 | 80 |
| 46:2-4 | 486 |
| 47:2 | 507 |
| 48:2 | 486 |
| 48:10 | 92 |
| 52:4 | 92 |
| 61:5 | 86 |
| 62:1 | 86 |
| 62:7 | 486 |
| 62:9 | 486 |
| 62:14 | 486 |
| 63:11 | 486 |
| 69:26-27 | 486 |
| 70:1 | 486 |
| 71:17 | 486 |
| 84:2 | 256 |
| 91:7 | 599 |
| 92:4 | 256 |
| 96.4-8 | 678 |
| 97.9-10 | 677 |
| 99.15 | 678 |
| 103:1, | 256 |
| 104:1 | 507 |
| 105:2 | 82 |

## 2 Enoch

| | |
|---|---|
| 31:6 | 61 |

## 2 Baruch

| | |
|---|---|
| 13:3 | 273 |
| 14:12 | 675 |
| 14:13 | 428 |
| 17:3 | 183 |
| 23:4 | 183 |
| 35-40 | 518 |
| 39:7 | 92 |
| 40:1 | 92 |

| | |
|---|---|
| 48:34-37 | 284 |
| 51:7 | 675 |
| 53-71 | 518 |
| 69:4 | 675 |
| 72:2 | 92 |
| 85:1ff | 284 |
| 85:2 | 675 |

## 4 Ezra

| | |
|---|---|
| 3:7 | 183 |
| 5:1-2 | 599 |
| 7:28ff | 80 |
| 7:28 | 82 |
| 7:118 | 183 |
| 8:33 | 675 |
| 9:7-8 | 675 |
| 12:32 | 80 |
| 13:3 | 86, 486 |
| 13:5 | 486 |
| 13:12 | 486 |
| 13:25 | 486 |
| 13:26 | 122 |
| 13:32 | 82, 486 |
| 13:37 | 82 |
| 13:51 | 486 |
| 13:52 | 82, 86 |
| 14:11-12 | 518 |
| 14:9 | 82 |
| 14:35 | 428 |

## Apocalypse of Abraham

| | |
|---|---|
| 13-14 | 449 |
| 27-30 | 518 |

## Assumption of Moses

| | |
|---|---|
| 2-10 | 518 |
| 5 | 599 |

## Joseph and Aseneth

| | |
|---|---|
| 21:4 | 82, 83 |

## Jubilees

| | |
|---|---|
| 15.26ff | 449 |
| 23:14-23 | 599 |

## Psalms of Solomon

| | |
|---|---|
| 3:12 | 428 |
| 9:5 | 428 |
| 13:9 | 556 |
| 13:11 | 428 |
| 17:21 | 68, 80 |

## Other Classical and Hellenistic Writings

# Subject Index

ness of God) 141, 148, 149, 150,
151, 152, 153, 157, 640, 674
Δικαιοσύνη 141, 143, 146, 147, 148,
149, 150, 151, 152, 157, 175, 379,
382, 383, 384, 386, 630, 640, 650,
674
Discipleship 257, 312, 314, 317,
360, 387, 407, 504, 512, 514, 626,
632
Divorce 99, 260, 379, 380, 381, 385
Docetism 94, 102, 251, 323, 424,
437, 438, 439, 440, 442, 451, 452,
481, 482, 483, 484, 510, 512, 521
Domitian 80, 520, 540, 626
Dragon 426, 519, 541, 542
Dualism 53, 55, 61, 63, 102, 126,
137, 432, 438, 449, 482, 489, 495,
519, 554

Earliest Christianity 10, 20, 80, 86,
168, 211, 216, 239, 275, 278, 280,
283, 285, 286, 288, 289, 290, 291,
292, 300, 305, 465, 521, 543
Early Catholic Church, Early Catholicism 18, 293, 424, 466, 508, 547
Ecclesiology 14, 281, 305, 361, 386,
388, 410, 449, 481, 501, 530, 545,
550, 557, 568, 575, 586, 616, 637
Ἐγώ εἰμι Sayings 487
Ἐκκλησία 181, 182, 188, 191, 297,
389, 550, 555, 558, 590
Elders, Presbyters 13, 193, 323, 370,
420, 421, 518, 532, 534, 587, 638
Elect, Ἐκλεκτός. 86, 206, 224, 280,
283, 284, 289, 306, 307, 318, 413,
433, 519, 585, 590, 592, 625, 637,
638, 674
Elijah 83, 220, 222, 273, 358, 397,
517, 534, 662
Emperor Cult 531
Empty Tomb 75, 77, 107, 109, 265,
266, 267, 269, 273, 462, 463, 465,
466
Enoch 39, 46, 61, 80, 82, 86, 92, 210,
244, 256, 257, 258, 273, 382, 517,
608, 633, 635, 636, 643, 646, 660,
680
Eschatological Reservation 53, 63,
127, 164, 562, 575

Eschatology 15, 79, 98, 122, 138, 211,
327, 387, 417, 422, 437, 444, 446,
457, 483, 496, 564, 573, 575, 576,
595, 598, 648, 649, 650, 651, 653
Eschaton 38, 58, 97, 98, 101, 103,
108, 120, 126, 134, 146, 157, 158,
161, 162, 172, 173, 176, 195, 211,
224, 225, 250, 255, 259, 285, 306,
326, 328, 331, 335, 336, 340, 363,
395, 396, 415, 483, 484, 497, 498,
499, 501, 512, 678
Eternal Life 386, 428, 436, 445, 452,
454, 487, 498, 499, 503, 552, 593,
619, 647, 648
Ethics 1, 19, 38, 46, 47, 48, 145, 150,
245, 261, 364, 381, 384, 512, 543,
564, 572, 582, 589, 590, 652, 657,
661, 663, 668, 681, 682
Εὐαγγέλιον 94, 140, 157, 337, 338,
339, 340, 341, 342, 363, 559, 570,
602

Faith and Works 17, 175, 289, 585,
657, 660, 669, 670, 671, 672, 673,
676
Farewell Discourses 500, 505, 506
Flesh and Spirit 67, 509, 581
Forgiveness of Sins 106, 147, 148,
172, 279, 281, 282, 286, 308, 391,
404, 555, 567, 617, 620
Form Criticism 237, 238, 320
Freedom, Liberty 12, 16, 34, 50, 56,
62, 106, 121, 128, 134, 142, 144,
145, 149, 155, 156, 162, 163, 177,
187, 188, 189, 193, 196, 199, 216,
292, 294, 296, 304, 406, 411, 412,
432, 445, 447, 486, 489, 515, 629,
649, 654, 663, 666, 667, 668, 675,
681

Galilee 76, 253, 254, 265, 266, 267,
268, 270, 297, 316, 350, 361, 366,
398, 400, 405, 457, 458, 459, 495
Gentile Christians 12, 179, 201, 206,
290, 295, 296, 412, 578
Gentile Mission 11, 24, 142, 262,
267, 290, 293, 368, 369, 400, 412
Gentiles 11, 21, 22, 23, 24, 34, 44,
46, 47, 49, 56, 57, 64, 65, 69, 84,

# Authors Index